BOOK OF THE BRITISH COUNTRYSIDE

Published by Drive Publications Limited
for the Automobile Association
Fanum House, Leicester Square, London WC2H 7LY

BOOK OF THE
BRITISH COUNTRYSIDE

was edited and designed by Drive Publications Limited
Berkeley Square House, London W1X 5PD
for the Automobile Association
Fanum House, Leicester Square, London WC2H 7LY

First edition Copyright © 1973 Drive Publications Limited

Printed in Holland

Cover photograph: *Ox-eye daisies in grass by Neville Fox-Davies*

Book of the British Countryside

BOOK OF THE BRITISH COUNTRYSIDE

The publishers express their gratitude for major contributions by the following people:

Heather Angel, M.SC., F.R.P.S.
A. Hugh F. Brown, B.SC.; *The Nature Conservancy*
Ian Campbell, LL.B., *Barrister at Law; Secretary of the Commons Preservation Society*
Professor T. J. Chandler, M.SC., PH.D.; *Professor of Geography, University College, London*
S. B. Chapman, B.SC., PH.D., M.I.BIOL.
Professor Keith Clayton, M.SC., PH.D.; *School of Environmental Sciences, University of East Anglia*
David Corke, B.SC.; *Department of Biological Sciences, North East London Polytechnic*
Herbert L. Edlin, B.SC., DIP. FORESTRY OXFORD; *Publications Officer, Forestry Commission*
Dr Clive A. Edwards, M.SC., M.S., F.I.BIOL.; *Principal Scientific Officer at Rothamsted Experimental Station*
The late Sir Arthur Elton, BT., B.A.
John Gooders
Christopher Hall, *Secretary of the Ramblers Association*
Alfred Leutscher, B.SC.; *British Museum (Natural History,*
Richard Mabey, M.A. (OXON.)
D. Macer Wright
G. R. Miller, B.SC., PH.D.; *Principal Scientific Officer at the Nature Conservancy at Banchory*
M. G. Morris, M.A., PH.D.; *Monks Wood Experimental Station of the Nature Conservancy*
Pamela North, B.PHARM., M.P.S.
John Oates, B.SC.
John Parslow, *Monks Wood Experimental Station of the Nature Conservancy*
Franklyn Perring, M.A., PH.D., F.L.S.; *Head of the Biological Records Centre, Monks Wood Experimental Station of the Nature Conservancy*
Margaret Perring, B.SC.
Ian Plant
Cedric Rogers
M. W. Shaw, B.SC.; *The Nature Conservancy*
Gordon E. Simmons, F.L.S., F.R.E.S.; *Senior Lecturer in Field Studies at the Worcester College of Education*
Keith R. Snow, PH.D.; *Lecturer in Biological Science at the North East London Polytechnic*
H. N. Southern, M.A., D.SC.
K. Southern, M.SC., D.PHIL.
T. C. E. Wells, B.SC.; *Monks Wood Experimental Station of the Nature Conservancy*
Alwyne Wheeler, *British Museum (Natural History)*
John Talbot White
Ralph Whitlock
Gerald Wilkinson
Derek Yalden, B.SC., PH.D.; *Lecturer in Zoology, Manchester University*

CONTENTS A guide to the

living world of the countryside

FEATURES

THE MAKING OF THE BRITISH ISLES

*The story of these islands began 3000 million years ago when
convulsive earth movements threw up a vast mountain range in north-west Scotland.
Drowned by the sea, crumbled by ice and wind, the bedrock of the land was
shaped and reshaped over the ages, and is still being changed today*

That part of the earth's crust called the British Isles seems eternal and unchanging in its shape. But this is only when it is viewed against the time-scale of human history, which measures time in hundreds or at the most thousands of years. Viewed against a geological time-scale, where the years are measured in their thousands of millions, the surface of Britain has been in continual movement: folding, twisting, collapsing, erupting and heaving itself above and below the sea under the stresses set up in the bowels of the earth.

These geological birth-pangs have produced the Britain of today, with her richly varied scenery, her fertile agricultural land, and her many wild plants and animals. The shape of the land, the type of rocks, the colour of the soil and the plants that grow in it are all clues with which to 'read' a landscape.

The story of the British countryside opens in the far north-west corner of Scotland, where folding of the earth's crust formed a mountain range 3000 million years ago. The main theme of the story is of a succession of thick layers of sediment settling on the ocean floor, hardening under compression and later being raised to the surface by subterranean upheavals. There is also a secondary theme; as Britain was formed it was gradually tilted towards the south-east so that the Thames Valley was among the last land to emerge above the waves.

The most ancient rocks in Britain are also the hardest, and in general the highest. For the mountains have resisted erosion far better than the soft lowland areas.

The Outer Hebrides are made almost entirely of rocks believed to be 3000 million years old. The rest of the Highlands of Scotland were formed during another great upheaval. In the process, molten rock was forced up through cracks in the crust to create huge granite outcrops, including the Cairngorm Mountains. The Scottish Highlands were once many times their present height; they have been eroded by centuries of weathering. The next-oldest section of the British Isles was formed when the area between the north of Scotland and what is now the Midlands of England subsided, leaving a great ocean trough. Mud and sand accumulated tens of thousands of feet deep, and became compressed by its own weight into layers of sandstone, limestone and shale. In North Wales and the Lake District, lava poured up through the layers. A violent upheaval in the earth's crust forced the rock layers out of the ocean into a great range of mountains called the Caledonian Range.

These mountains ran from north-east to south-west, and 350 million years ago they were closer in height to present-day Mount Everest (29,028 ft) than to Mount Snowdon (3560 ft). What is now the peak of Snowdon was once the bottom of a fold in the Caledonian Range. Climbers on Snowdon can see that the rock structure at the summit consists of layers curving upwards. Because the rock in the bottom of a great fold is more compressed, and so harder than

THE BRITISH ISLES DURING THE ICE AGE

About a quarter of a million years ago, during the Ice Age, the whole of Britain north of a line reaching from the Thames to the mouth of the Severn lay beneath a crushing weight of sheet ice.

The advancing ice had carved U-shaped valleys in the highlands, creating the typical scenery of North Wales, the Lake District and the Scottish Highlands. In the lowlands the ice lay 3000 ft thick in places. Beyond the ice, the glacial landscape was bleak and open and the frozen land supported only the hardiest of plants, with animals confined to a few Arctic species such as the mammoth, woolly rhinoceros, musk ox and reindeer.

When the ice finally retreated, about 10,000 years ago, the land, eased of its burden, began to 'spring back' into shape. In Scotland, this process is still going on, and the Highlands are rising at the rate of about 1 ft every 100 years

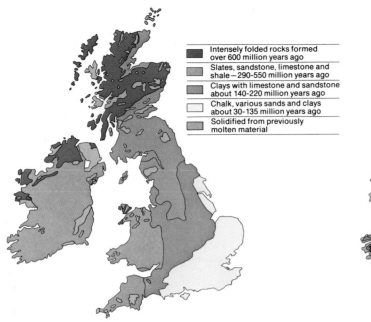

THE PATTERN OF THE ROCKS

The rocks of the British Isles range from ancient materials spewed from the earth's core 3000 million years ago, to sediments laid down in a now-vanished sea about 30 million years ago

Legend:
- Intensely folded rocks formed over 600 million years ago
- Slates, sandstone, limestone and shale – 290-550 million years ago
- Clays with limestone and sandstone about 140-220 million years ago
- Chalk, various sands and clays about 30-135 million years ago
- Solidified from previously molten material

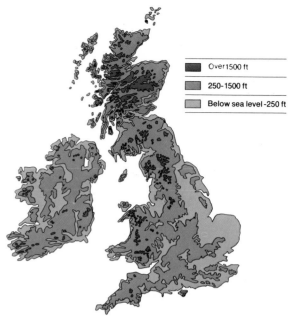

THE SHAPE OF THE LAND

The landscape of the British Isles slopes from the mountains of the north-west, formed of the oldest and hardest rocks, to the lowlands of the south-east, based on recent, soft sediments

Legend:
- Over 1500 ft
- 250-1500 ft
- Below sea level – 250 ft

the rock in the 'swell' of the fold, Snowdon has resisted the onslaughts of time, while the peaks that once towered above it on either side have worn away. This action was just part of a titanic eroding force that wore down the Caledonian Range, and turned much of Britain into a desert of red dust. The red sandstone that had largely formed the range was weathered into fine particles that were swirled by the wind into inland basins and lakes, where they solidified again into sandstone and shale. Exmoor, the Brecon Beacons and Central Scotland are formed from this rock, called Old Red Sandstone. The remains of the Caledonian Range form some of the most dramatic mountain scenery in Britain – the Southern Uplands of Scotland, the Lake District, and most of Wales.

At the end of the desert period the area that was to become England sank again and the sea flooded in, bringing thick layers of limestone. This in turn was covered by silt from the deltas of great rivers to the north. As the deltas rose above sea level, thick forests grew in the swampy land. The land sank again and the forests were later covered by more mud, and rotted trees were compressed into layers of coal. Some 220 million years ago, pressure in the earth's crust once more buckled the land, producing the Pennine Range down the centre of northern England and the mountains of South Wales. The coal layers at the tops of these ranges were later eroded away, but those lower down on the sides of the hills remained, to provide the source of Britain's power in the 19th century. The highest levels of the Pennines, like the other mountain areas, are largely barren moorland, covered by heather and peat bogs with rocky gorges in places such as the Peak District. Lower down, sheep graze on the hills. The upheaval that created the Pennines was the final act in the creation of the mountain and hill country of Britain.

The fertile lowlands of England, where most of the early settlement of Britain occurred, were created in three main earth movements. About 180 million years ago, most of

England subsided and the sea flowed in, bringing with it more deposits of limestone. These limestone rocks now form a long ridge, stretching from the North York Moors through the Cotswolds to Lyme Bay in Dorset.

About 135 million years ago, most of England again sank, and a thick layer of chalk was deposited, made up of countless billions of shells and the skeletons of tiny sea creatures. Flints also occurred in the chalk and were later used by man as tools and building materials. The chalk belt covers a wide strip running across the south of England from the North and South Downs to Dorset, and then swinging back north-east along the Chilterns to Norfolk, and on to the Lincoln Wolds and the East Riding of Yorkshire. Where the chalk is not covered by grass and soil, it stands out startlingly white. Where it reaches the coast it forms white cliffs, as at Dover, Beachy Head and the Needles in the Isle of Wight.

The third great earth movement in the creation of the British lowlands began 70 million years ago when the south-east corner of England again subsided and was covered by a layer of sand and clay. For 55 million years it lay beneath the sea; then in the earth storm that raised the Alps, the surface of south-east England was buckled into low folds. The sand and clay forming the top layer of the folds have been eroded in many places, but they are preserved in Hampshire and underneath London.

After the general shape of Britain had been established, today's landscape was sculpted by a great sheet of ice brought by the Ice Age about a quarter of a million years ago. As the ice melted, the sea rose and broke a land-bridge joining Britain to the Continent. Britain was now the British Isles.

The story has not ended yet. It may be difficult for a man, with his short time-scale, to relate himself to the birth of the land, but should he bend down and pick up a pebble on the Isle of Lewis in the Outer Hebrides, he will have spanned in an instant 3000 million years of time.

9

THE MOUNTAINS

Compared with what they were originally, Britain's mountains today are worn down to mere stumps. The last great mountain-building convulsion to affect these islands happened 270 million years ago, when the earth's crust buckled to throw up the rocks that underlie the Pennine range and the mountains of South Wales. Since then, the erosive forces of time and nature have produced today's mountain landscape.

The most ancient rocks in Britain are also the hardest, and in general the highest, for mountains have always resisted erosion far better than the soft lowland areas.

The highlands, which take in south-west England, and most of Ireland, Wales and Scotland, consist largely of rocky terrain between 1500 ft and 4000 ft above sea level. The winds which bring most of Britain's rain blow in from the Atlantic, and when they reach the highlands of the west coast, they drop most of their moisture. Constant heavy rainfall reaching 100 in. a year in some parts of the Scottish Highlands continually washes away the rock fragments that would form soil. The soil in the highlands is too poor and the climate too

The granite mountains of Inverness, in the Scottish Highlands, are among the oldest and highest in Britain

wet for trees to grow more than 1500 ft above sea level. This is a harsh landscape and climate, hostile to human settlement. But the highlands are a haven for the red deer and the roe deer, and for Britain's largest bird of prey, the golden eagle. As temperatures fluctuate between day and night the rocks expand at uneven rates and cracks appear. Rainwater seeps into the cracks and expands as it freezes, to split the rock further, and the broken fragments are washed down the steep slopes. Anybody who has ever seen a stone trickle down a rock face has seen a process of erosion that has been going on every day since mountains were created.

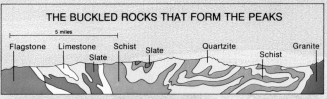

THE BUCKLED ROCKS THAT FORM THE PEAKS

5 miles

Flagstone   Limestone   Schist   Slate   Quartzite   Granite
Slate   Schist

The mountains are the survivors of the most violent of the earth movements which created the British Isles. Intense heat and pressure folded, buckled and interleaved the older rocks, while others, such as basalt, forced their way in molten form through cracks and joints

HILL COUNTRY

Scattered throughout the length of Britain, halfway between mountains and lowlands, and shading into each, the gently folding hill country offers rich grazing for sheep and cattle, and a sturdy way of life for men.

Typical of this kind of landscape are the hills formed by the long ridge of limestone and sandstone that stretches from the North York Moors through the Cotswolds to Lyme Bay in Dorset. These rocks contain most of Britain's iron ore, conveniently close to the coalfields along the edge of the Pennines. They also supply England's finest building stone – limestone – which is soft enough to be worked easily and weathers to rich browns and yellows. The showpiece villages of the Cotswolds are built of this stone, and almost the whole of Bath is built from a limestone known as Bath Stone.

Limestone can be seen in its rough state in walls that separate the fields in the Cotswolds, and sometimes a close look will reveal shells or coral in the rock, showing that it once lay beneath the sea. Britain's first farmers settled widely in the Cotswolds 4500 years ago, working the light soil with primitive

The smooth, grassy slopes of the Stiperstones Ridge on the Welsh border of Shropshire typify hill country

ploughs and leaving behind their long burial mounds, called barrows. Rain quickly soaks through the porous limestone, leaving the surface dry; so beeches, with their long, probing roots, are the most common trees of limestone country. Chalk country is easily recognised by its smooth grassy hills.

Beeches are typical, too, of the chalklands, where the clumps that grow on the summits of many of the hills are believed to be the remnants of forests which were cleared by early farmers. Rainwater soaks straight through the porous surface, so there are few rivers; water collects underground and eventually flows away in streams called bournes.

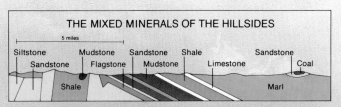

THE MIXED MINERALS OF THE HILLSIDES

5 miles

Siltstone   Mudstone   Sandstone   Shale   Sandstone
Sandstone   Flagstone   Mudstone   Limestone   Coal
Shale   Marl

Most hills in the British Isles once lay beneath the sea. The main rocks in hill country—limestone, chalk and sandstone—are made up of sediments which were deposited and compressed on the sea bed, then thrust above the waters by movements of the earth's crust about 220 million years ago

THE LOWLANDS

To the east and south of a diagonal line running from the mouth of the Tees in County Durham to the mouth of the Exe in Devon are the lowlands—flat in places, undulating in others, and only in a few places rising more than a few hundred feet above sea level.

The soft underlying rocks have weathered to produce fertile soils and good grazing land for cattle. The 'typical' English countryside, a patchwork quilt of fields separated by hedges and winding lanes, has developed in the lowlands. Three times in the past 180 million years, the lowlands of England have lain beneath the sea. And three times the sea has receded, leaving behind deposits of limestone, chalk, clay, sand and gravel. The last time the land 'won' this eternal struggle was 15 million years ago, when the surface of south-east England was buckled into gigantic folds, ripples of the convulsions that raised the Alps. The sand and clay at the top of the folds were eroded away, and remain only in the Hampshire Basin, the Thames Valley, Essex and the East Anglian coast. The clay in the London area is used in making the yellow

A patchwork of growing crops patterns the rich farmland of the fens near Peterborough in Huntingdonshire

stock bricks that are so typical of many of the city's houses.
   The ice that until 10,000 years ago lay over Britain as far
south as the Thames sculpted the mountains in the north and
west. In the lowlands, the slow-moving, irresistible ice sheet —
in places over 3000 ft thick — acted like a gigantic plane, shav-
ing the land almost flat. At the same time, it carried along
immense tonnages of earth and rock, spreading them as
hummocks of sand and gravel, and as sheets of lime-rich
clay that provide patches of fertile soil. Parts of East Anglia
would be below sea level if it were not for the 50-100 ft of
glacial clay and gravel.

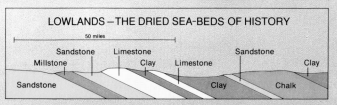

About 70 million years ago, long after the buckling of the earth's crust which
raised the hills, southern and eastern Britain sank beneath the sea again.
There, for 55 million years, deposits of sand and clay were laid down, until
new earth movements lifted them above the sea

Acacia *Robinia pseudoacacia*

The name acacia is commonly given to the false acacia or locust tree, a decorative species once so popular that 'Acacia Avenue' became a synonym for suburbia. True acacias, which include many African thorn trees, the gum arabic tree and Australian wattles, do not grow in Britain.

The false acacia's feathery foliage is carried on branches which divide regularly to form an open crown. Thorns grow in pairs at the junction of the leaf-stalks and the main stem. In June, the tree bears hanging chains of fragrant white flowers which look like those of the laburnum. In autumn, it has black, papery seed pods and bright gold leaves.

The false acacia was brought to Europe from North America in the 17th century. It became popular in the early 19th century when the writer William Cobbett praised its rapid timber-producing qualities. The wood was once used for tool handles instead of ash, but its grain is too irregular for modern use.

Nowadays, it tends to be planted chiefly for its picturesque value, or grows wild on waste ground, since it can survive on poor soil because of its ability to extract nitrogen from the atmosphere through bacteria on its roots. The false acacia grows 90 ft tall and may live for 100 years.

Aconite, Winter *Eranthis hyemalis*

The flowers of the winter aconite appear soon after Christmas along with the snowdrops, provided the temperature exceeds 10°C (50°F). Each flower grows on a separate stalk, 2-6 in. long. They open in sunshine and close in dull weather. The leaves, which do not appear until the flowers have faded, wither by June and the plant rests underground as a tuber until the following year.

Introduced from southern Europe, the winter aconite is now well established in parkland and copses in England and southern Scotland. It is closely related to monkshood and, like it, is highly poisonous.

Winter aconite flowers open surrounded by leaf-like bracts. The real leaves appear later

The ruins of Fountains Abbey, once the centre of a thriving estate of more than a million acres

Abbey

The ruins of a medieval abbey often mark an area that was once of great agricultural importance. An abbey was an independent monastery, ruled by an abbot, answerable only to the pope. But even in the Middle Ages, the term abbey was used loosely for any wealthy or influential monastery. The earliest abbeys were founded in Italy in the 6th century by St Benedict. By the next century they had spread to Britain. These early monks preserved Roman agricultural practices, such as growing fruit, vegetables and herbs. In addition, the Benedictines are credited with developing the growth of vineyards, the use of hops in brewing, bee-keeping and the earliest practice of artificial insemination—to breed carp for their fishponds.

All these practices were kept alive in small, self-supporting religious communities. But, over the centuries, gifts and legacies meant that many abbeys came to hold large estates. The abbots acted as ordinary feudal landlords, working the land with their tenants on the open field system of strip-farming. By the middle of the 12th century, however, towns and population began to grow, creating new markets for farm produce. To meet this demand some abbeys began to abandon strip-farming and to enclose their land and farm it on a large scale, using either the monks' own labour, or that of hired hands.

While these changes were taking place among the older communities the Cistercians arrived in Britain from Burgundy. They settled in the more remote regions of the country, such as Yorkshire and the Welsh borders, enclosing large estates from what was often wilderness, and starting sheep farming on a large scale. Sheep farming for wool was the great export industry of medieval Britain, so the Cistercians prospered and built splendid abbeys such as those at Fountains, Rievaulx and Tintern. Fountains at one time owned more than a million acres—equivalent to nearly one-third of Yorkshire—on which it grazed 20,000 sheep.

Other landowners were slow to imitate the abbeys by enclosing land and farming on a large scale, so the abbeys remained the pacesetters in British agriculture until their dissolution by Henry VIII when, in the four years 1536-40, almost all of them were destroyed and their lands confiscated and sold by the Crown.

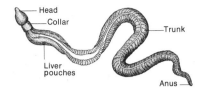

The acorn worm *Glossobalanus sarniensis* lives in muddy sand and shell gravel on the lower shore. Sand casts mark its burrows

Acorn worm

A worm which lives in sand and shell gravel on the shore and offshore. The 6 in. long body consists of a head, collar and long trunk. It is soft and breaks easily if picked up, but if the damage is not too severe the worm can grow a new part.

The hollow, muscular, water-filled head and collar are used for burrowing. The acorn worm swallows large quantities of sand, feeding on small fragments of organic material contained in it. Like the lugworm, it excretes the sand as worm casts.

The larvae, which hatch from eggs, live in the water before changing into worms. There are males and females. The common name is derived from the acorn-shaped head of one species, *Glossobalanus sarniensis*.

Acre

An acre is 4840 square yds—the area enclosed by a square whose sides are just under 70 yds long. The measure, originally a long, narrow strip, was fixed by Edward I in 1305. It was based on the amount of land which a man with two oxen could plough in a day—40 rods long, 4 rods wide. The rod, which was the pole used to drive the oxen, was 5½ yds long. An acre can produce 10 tons of potatoes, worth about £150 to the farmer, or 19 cwt of hops, worth £650. It can support four sheep for a year or one milk cow for six months. A football pitch is about 1¾ acres, and a square mile contains 640 acres. See also HECTARE

Adder or northern viper *Vipera berus*

The most common of Britain's three snakes, absent only from Ireland and some Scottish islands, and the only poisonous one. The other two British snakes are the grass snake and the smooth snake. Its most distinctive features are a dark zigzag along the back and a V or X mark behind the head. Males are silvery, pale yellow or brown and about 18 in. long. Females are duller, ranging from red-brown to yellow, and longer— about 2 ft. Both red and black specimens sometimes occur.

Adders live in almost any dry place but prefer sandy heathland and rough common. They are mainly encountered in early summer, especially pregnant females, which lie in the sun reluctant to move. With the first frosts, they hibernate by retiring into a ready-made hole underground. On rare occasions dens of adders entwined in winter sleep have been uncovered. In winter they

Snakes have no eyelids. The adder's vertical slit pupil closes to cut out strong sunlight

sometimes lie on the snow in the sun.

The males emerge from hibernation in February or March, before the females, and establish territories, which they sometimes contest. Two rivals will rear up, sway their bodies and try to push one another to the ground. There is no biting.

Mating takes place about May. The fertilised eggs develop into embryos inside the mother's oviducts. In September, 6-20 young are born live. They become independent of their mother immediately. The old story that a female facing danger will swallow her brood to protect them is untrue.

Adders feed chiefly on lizards, slow-worms, mice, voles and shrews. A large meal can last the snake for a week. Adders follow the scent trail of their prey with the tongue, which is an organ of smell, and kill it with a bite from the hollow venom fangs in the front of the upper jaw. Adder venom is a

THE ADDER'S POISON BITE

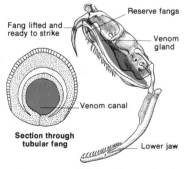

Fang lifted and ready to strike

Reserve fangs

Venom gland

Venom canal

Section through tubular fang

Lower jaw

Side view of adder skull

Adder fangs are hollow teeth through which venom is injected into prey. Fangs are shed with wear and replaced by reserves

powerful heart depressant, causing rapid death of natural prey. With human beings the symptoms are pain, swelling and discoloration in the area of the bite; these spread and are followed by prostration, diarrhoea and vomiting. Death has been known to occur in six hours. However, there have been fewer than 12 fatalities in Britain in the past 60 years, for the adder is not dangerous to man if left alone. A victim should be kept quiet, reassured and taken to the nearest doctor or hospital.

The adder population is slowly declining as heathland and common are being afforested or reclaimed for agriculture. The name adder is a corruption of Anglo-Saxon *noedre*. This changed to nadder and 'a nadder' became 'an adder'. See also SNAKE

Adit

A horizontal opening to a mine is known as a level or adit. Adits are found in hill areas, where seams of minerals reach the surface and can be mined directly from the hillside. Hundreds of adits survive in the Pennines, the Lake District, and the South-west—all areas associated with the early days of mining.

As easily reached deposits were exhausted, adits fell into disuse and deep-mining by way of shafts took their place. Fewer than ten working adits now remain in Britain, most of them exploiting coal seams in Scotland and South Wales.

Exploring old adits is dangerous and is best left to pot-holers with special equipment. Some, in the Pennines for example, lead to natural caverns in the limestone, which often extend for miles underground. Others are now flooded and water is an additional hazard to the explorer.

18

Adonis blue see Blue butterflies

Adze
A cutting tool whose blade is at an angle to the handle. It was the predecessor of the plane. It is among the earliest of tools and in Britain Stone Age adzes, dating to 3000 BC, are known. The carpenter's adze has a straight edge and is still used in canal workshops, for smoothing lock gates. The chairmaker's adze has a concave cutting edge and is used to hollow out chair seats. An adze gives timber a dimpled texture—one of the attractive features of half-timbered cottages.

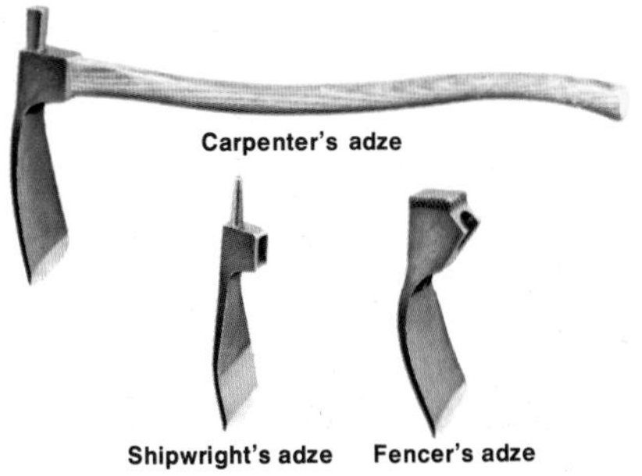

Adzes, tools for smoothing wood, are made in different shapes for different crafts

Agate
A semi-precious stone, a form of chalcedony. It is almost pure silica, the same material as sand. Agates are concentrically banded like an onion—some more distinctly than others—as a result of having been built up by layers in rock cavities. The bands are usually of black, white, brown, red, cream or grey, though yellow, green and blue are sometimes found. The colouring is produced by small quantities of iron and other minerals. Large, attractive agates are rare. Those used for decorative purposes have often been dyed; agate is slightly porous and absorbs artificial colouring. Agates break easily, with a smooth, rounded fracture like flint.

Agrimony *Agrimonia eupatoria*
The small starry flowers of agrimony bloom in spikes during summer and autumn on hedgebanks and roadsides throughout most of the British Isles.

Agrimony, also called lemmade or bunchflower, is a perennial and grows up to 2 ft high. Its apricot-scented foliage is used by herbalists to make herb tea and medicine to treat liver complaints. The whole plant contains tannin, which produces a yellow dye for textiles.

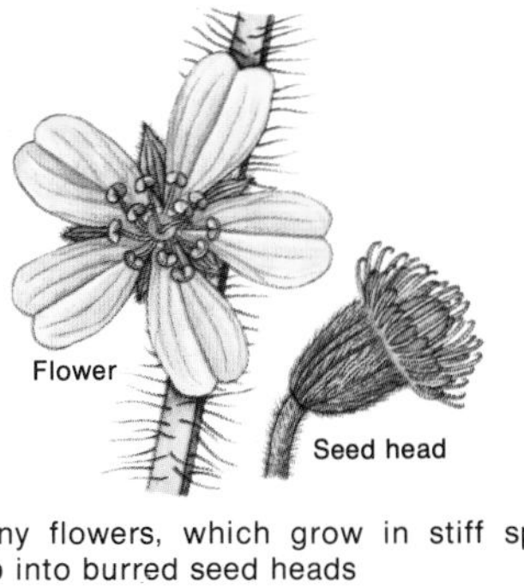

Agrimony flowers, which grow in stiff spikes, develop into burred seed heads

Air
The atmosphere consists of various gases, water droplets, ice crystals and solid particles—such as dust or pollen. The concentration of these elements varies from place to place but two gases, nitrogen and oxygen, form 99 per cent of the total and are always present in the proportions of 78 and 21 per cent respectively.

Photosynthesis, the result of sunlight acting on green plants and releasing oxygen in their cells, is thought to be responsible for all the gaseous oxygen in the atmosphere.

Other gases, present in minute quantities, are more important than their concentration would suggest. Less than 3 parts per thousand of air is carbon dioxide—yet it is a vital ingredient of plant food.

Ozone, which is present in less than 1 part per 100 million, is the gas which screens all life on earth from the sun's dangerous shortwave radiations.

Water vapour is always in the air but the amount varies with the temperature, air pressure and other meteorological controls.

Air also contains varying quantities of dust from the weathering of rocks; rock particles and gases from volcanoes; smoke from forest and bush fires, domestic and industrial chimneys; and salt from the sea.

The air extends upwards to a height of 600 miles above the earth's surface, behaving like the waters of the seas or oceans; drifting calmly in some places, and swirling violently in others.

The bottom of the air belt, like the bottom of the sea, is where the greatest air pressure is exerted. On the earth's surface this pressure is 14·7 lb. per square inch—equal to about 10 tons on a human being.

At 60 miles above the surface the air is almost a vacuum, having only one-millionth of the pressure it has at ground level.

Alder *Alnus glutinosa*
The most common waterside tree in the British Isles, the alder usually grows on the banks of rivers, lakes and marshes—from the lowlands of eastern England up to 1500 ft in the Scottish Highlands. But it seldom grows on drier ground.

The alder is able to thrive in marshy conditions because its roots are able to form an association with bacteria which are capable of utilising nitrogen from the atmosphere.

Nitrogen is essential to all plant growth—and most plants obtain their nitrogen from the soil. But there is little nitrogen in waterlogged soil and, without the ability to use atmospheric nitrogen, the alder could not grow. Alder trees put more nitrogen in the soil than they use, so they build up fertility and alder swamps, when cleared and drained, yield heavy crops. The fertile fens of East Anglia once supported many alder thickets.

An established alder also has a deep-probing tap root, about 5 ft long, which enables the tree to survive falling water levels during drought.

The name alder comes from the Anglo-Saxon *aler* and is a common element in place names: Aldershot, for example, means alder wood.

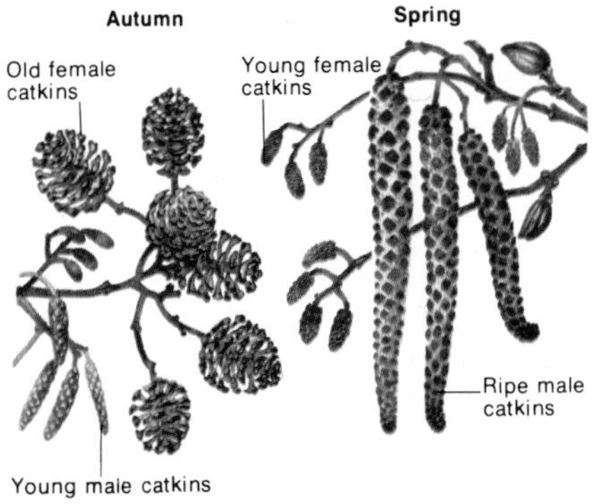

Ripe male catkins scatter their pollen on to the females, which develop into cones

A characteristic of the alder—growing in clumps along the waterside—is its broad, blunt leaves

The alder is easily identified by its black, fissured bark and broad, unpointed, dull green leaves. In winter, brownish-grey male catkins hang like lambs' tails from the tree.

Male and female catkins grow in separate clusters on the ends of the tree's leafless twigs—the males opening in March and scattering golden pollen to fertilise the bud-like females. These develop into green cone-like structures that turn brown in the autumn and shed buoyant seeds, which float on water until reaching muddy shores and germinating.

Alder is a hard but easily carved yellow timber that is still used occasionally as the traditional material for the soles of clogs or wooden shoes. After felling, it turns orange, then red. When it is dry it is water-resistant, and it does not split when nailed. It is also used for broom and tool handles.

Nowadays, the chief value of alder lies in the protection its roots give to the banks of streams against erosion, and the shelter its mass of foliage gives to cattle.

The charcoal derived from alder wood is excellent for making gunpowder, and at one time powder factories operated in the New Forest and the Lake District in the vicinity of alder coppices.

Alderfly

In early summer alderflies settle in fairly large numbers on waterside plants, including alder trees—hence their name. The adults are $\frac{3}{4}$ in. long, dull brown insects with heavily

Alderfly *Sialis fulginosa* × 1½

veined wings. There are two species: *Sialis lutaria* which is widespread and flies in May and June; and *S. fulginosa* which flies in June and July. Both species are poor flyers and live only for about three weeks. They do not feed but perform their only role as adults—mating. Batches of 500-600 brown, cigar-shaped eggs are laid on plants and stones near the water. After 10-14 days the brown larvae are hatched. They live under stones or in the mud at the bottom of the pond, preying on small pond creatures. In their turn, they are eaten by bass and trout. It can take two years for the larvae to reach full size—about 1 in. long. They then leave the water and spend their three-week pupa or resting stage in cells of mud and vegetable debris on land.

Ale-hoof see Ground ivy
Alevin see Salmon
Alexanders see Parsley
Alfalfa see Lucerne

Algae

The simplest of all plants, algae have neither flowers nor roots. They grow wherever there is moisture on land, in fresh water and in the sea. Algae may be green, blue-green, red or brown, but all contain green chlorophyll, the substance which, with the energy of sunlight, enables plants to make their own food from water and carbon dioxide. This process, called photosynthesis, produces as a by-product some of the oxygen used by animals and plants. Algae range in size from microscopic single-celled organisms less than $\frac{1}{1000}$ in. across, to one of the largest living plants, a giant Pacific seaweed that can grow to 600 ft.

In Britain, the single-celled *Pleurococcus* forms the powdery, bright green growth seen on damp, shaded tree trunks, walls and roofs. Other microscopic algae live in fresh water where they may drift in large numbers, forming a major element in the phytoplankton, the food on which all aquatic life depends. Sometimes a lake produces as much plant material in the form of phytoplankton as a meadow of the same size.

Other freshwater algae include the blanket-weeds: *Cladophora* is a dark green many-threaded plant which attaches itself to rocks in fast-moving streams; *Spirogyra*, seen as slimy green scum in ponds and ditches, is another thread-like alga. *Volvox*, which consists of thousands of individuals grouped in pinhead-sized spheres, is also common in ponds.

Some algae form remarkable associations with other living plants and animals. One grows inside the fronds of the water fern *Azolla*, another lives inside the hydra *Chlorohydra viridissima*, where it provides oxygen for the animal. Lichens are dual plants containing both algae and fungi.

The cell walls of two minute forms of alga —diatoms and desmids—are made of silica. Accumulations of their fossils are known as diatomite or kieselguhr, which is mined at Kentmere in Westmorland. Being resistant to heat and chemical action, it is used as insulating material and also as an absorbent in dynamite manufacture. See also SEAWEED

The green film on oak tree bark is made up of millions of individual *Pleurococcus* plants

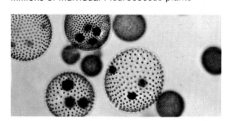

Volvox spheres, each comprising thousands of linked plants, often turn water green

Alkanet, Green *Pentaglottis sempervirens*

A hairy evergreen plant up to 3 ft tall, widespread on roadsides and woodland margins

The white centre of green alkanet is produced by scales on the petals

throughout Britain. Alkanet is particularly common in the South-west. It has bright blue flowers, which resemble those of a garden forget-me-not. They appear in small clusters from May to July. It was probably introduced from south-west Europe in medieval times for the red dye which its roots yield. Alkanet is derived from Spanish and Arabic words meaning little henna plant, a reference to the dye. Several other dye-yielding species also bear the name. *Pentaglottis* is Latin for five tongues—a reference to the five white scales inside its petals.

All-heal see Valerian
Allis see Shad
Alsike see Clover

Amber

A hard, pale yellow to deep orange material, which is fossilised resin from pine trees that lived about 50 million years ago. It was preserved in Ice Age glaciers and, when they melted, deposited in the seas of Europe—chiefly the Baltic. It is washed up on the beaches of Britain—especially those between Yorkshire and Essex. Some pieces have insects inside; these were trapped in the sticky resin as it oozed out of the trees. Amber found on British beaches is rarely larger than a small pebble, though a piece found in Suffolk in the 19th century weighed 13 lb. and was worth more than £4000. Amber burns with a pale flame and an aromatic odour. It is used to make jewellery and the mouthpieces of pipes. It has electrical properties; if rubbed, it builds up a negative electric charge and attracts paper.

The ancient Greek word for amber is *elektron*—the basis of our word electricity.

Ambrosia beetle

There are 55 species of ambrosia beetle in Britain of which the best known are the two elm bark beetles *Scolytus destructor* and *S. multistriatus*, which spread Dutch elm disease. This disease, which is caused by a fungus carried by the beetles, has reached epidemic proportions in Britain and is killing thousands of elms each year. Other ambrosia beetles, each of which is usually associated with a particular species of fungus, live on other trees and plants, including holly, oak, pine, plum and other fruit trees which also suffer from the spread of fungi. The name ambrosia refers to the fungus, which the beetles cultivate with their droppings.

Ambrosia beetles are brown, cylindrical insects, $\frac{1}{16}$-$\frac{1}{4}$ in. long, and are found throughout Britain. A typical ambrosia beetle, such as the elm bark beetle, colonises a tree some time between May and October by burrowing under the bark. There, mating takes place and the female lays her eggs in niches off the original tunnel. These eggs eventually hatch into white legless larvae. At first the beetles feed solely on the tree sap. Then gradually the spores of fungus carried on their bodies are spread through the

ELM TREE KILLER

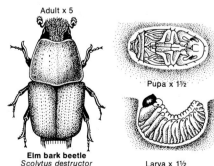

Adult × 5

Pupa × 1½

Elm bark beetle
Scolytus destructor

Larva × 1½

Both adult ambrosia beetles and their larvae spread the fungus which kills elms

tunnels and start to grow. Later the beetles and their larvae extend the tunnels, often into the living wood, feeding on both sap and fungus. The larvae grow to several times the size of the adult beetle before entering their pupa or resting stage in a chamber just below the surface. They emerge as adults the following summer.

Ambrosia beetles are an important food source for birds such as woodpeckers and nuthatches and insect predators, including wasps and carnivorous beetles. See also BARK BEETLE, ELM

Amethyst see Quartz

Amoeba *Amoeba proteus*

A minute, single-celled animal which is just visible to the naked eye. It lives in ponds and streams, where it feeds on tiny plants and small fragments of organic material. It has no mouth or stomach and engulfs food, digesting it with juices secreted in its tissue. An amoeba has no distinct outline and constantly changes shape as it moves, which it does by pushing out part of its body into a pseudopodium (false foot); the rest of the body flows into this, then further false feet are extended, and so on. Amoebas reproduce by splitting into two equal halves—a process which takes less than an hour.

Ancona see Chicken

Wood anemone flowers droop in damp weather and at night to protect the pollen

Anemone, Wood *Anemone nemorosa*

A plant 3-6 in. high, found in woods and hedgerows and flowering from March to May. It is abundant and widespread throughout Britain, and in spring white sheets of it cover the woodland floor before the trees come into leaf.

Wood anemone is also known as granny's nightcap and wind-flower. Anemone is derived from *anemos*, Greek for wind.

The feathery leaves persist for several weeks after the flowers have died, building food reserves for the following year, but by mid-summer they have yellowed and withered, and the plant rests underground in autumn and winter as a slender brown rhizome until the following spring.

Angelica, Wild see Parsley

Animal

This word is sometimes loosely applied to fur-bearing or hairy creatures which suckle their young. But these form only a small group—properly called mammals—within the animal kingdom which includes birds, fish, insects; in fact, everything from the amoeba to man.

All life on earth is divided between the animal and plant kingdom. Plants are basically those life forms which can manufacture their own food. Animals must get their nourishment from plants or from other animals. Consequently they need to move, either to search for things to eat or to avoid being eaten. They also need a mouth to take in their food and a digestive system to break it down.

More than a million different types or species of animals are known to exist in the world, and new ones are still being discovered. Animals can be classified according to the way they are built. There are 26 major groups called phyla. Of these groups, 25 are made up of invertebrates—animals without backbones. Insects are by far the most numerous invertebrates: there are about 800,000 species. Many of the more familiar animals belong to a sub-division of the remaining phylum and are known as vertebrates—animals with backbones. These are further sub-divided into fish, amphibians, reptiles, birds and mammals.

Fossilised remains of prehistoric creatures have helped to establish the evolutionary chain from which the present rich variety of animal life has developed over millions of years. Many fossil animals bear a strong resemblance to living species in the same area, demonstrating the continuity of life over millions of years.

In temperate regions such as Britain, the animal life is restricted due to the succession of seasons separating the year into growing and non-growing periods. This limits the amount of plant food available and so the number and variety of animals.

The native animal population of the British Isles is further reduced by the very fact that they are islands. The wild animals in Britain are mostly the descendants of creatures that were present when the sea finally cut off Britain from continental Europe about 5000 BC. In addition a number of animals, such as the rabbit and house mouse, have been introduced from abroad either deliberately or by accident. Consequently Britain has a comparatively small number of species as the following table shows:

	WORLD	BRITAIN
Mammals	4200	70
Birds	8600	300 (approx.)
Reptiles	5000	6
Amphibians	3000	8
Fish	13,000	34
Insects	800,000	20,000 (approx.)
Other invertebrates	200,000	30,000 (approx.)

See also EVOLUTION

Instinct and learning, keys to animal survival

The study of animal behaviour includes such topics as courtship, defence, group life and communication in which inborn natural instincts and the ability to learn through experience complement each other

Animals moving through the countryside—the gliding bird, the fluttering butterfly, the gambolling rabbit, or the fish that rises in the water—may appear to the casual observer to be behaving aimlessly. But scientists who study animal behaviour have discovered that all animal activity has some purpose—usually connected with survival, mating or establishing and maintaining a position within a group.

Every animal is born with a set of instincts that fit it for survival, help it to find and attract a mate or, in the case of social animals, equip it to live among others. Behaviourists make a special study of such instincts. However, instincts can sometimes be a trap, especially if there is a change in an animal's environment. A garden spider taken to a place where there is nothing to catch will expend its energy uselessly in spinning its intricate orb web, because web-spinning is something it does instinctively. The animals which, as individuals and as a species, have the best chance of surviving a drastic change of environment are those which, as well as acting instinctively, are able to learn from experience.

Courtship

The survival of a species is dependent, among other things, on successful mating. Courtship behaviour, whether bizarre and complicated or brief and sketchy, helps to ensure this success. Most animals become sexually active—'in season'—once a year when the courting drive is triggered off by hormones which stimulate the production of fertile eggs in the female and sperm in the male. Usually this occurs in the spring when the hours of daylight are increasing. This means that the future parents will have more time in which to find food for their young. The first stage of courtship is concerned with the mutual recognition of male and female—especially necessary where different species which look alike are crowded together. Recognition may be through scent as in many mammals, or song as in the birds. Birds also rely on colour in courting. The effect of colour is usually emphasised by ritual displays. Once recognition is accomplished the initial apprehension of the female and the aggressiveness of the male must be overcome. Finally the mating instincts of the pair must be synchronised. The communication of scent, sound or colour signals or a flamboyant display help to achieve the necessary synchronisation.

Defence

Displays and signals are important also in an animal's defence behaviour. Animals of the same kind, usually males, will fight each other over food, mates and living space. Each animal usually has a home or territory in which it feels secure enough to mate and rear young. Every male has his own special way of marking his property, warning others to stay away. The fox sprinkles urine on stones and trees round the frontier of his territory. Other male foxes are well aware of these 'keep out' signs, but should they trespass a form of ritualised combat is likely to take place. This involves much bluffing and threatening, rather than a real battle. All the same a definite result is achieved. Feeling safe within his home, the occupant threatens confidently and is nearly always victorious over the intruder, who admits defeat and remains unharmed.

Defence against a predator is a different matter, for the fight means life or death for one of the combatants. Weapons and physical skill are brought into play. Speed, alert senses, teeth, claws and poison mechanisms are used against the intended victim, which defends itself by running for its life, finding a safe hiding place, using counter-weapons or, in the case of the hedgehog, an armour of spines.

STICKLEBACK DISPUTE

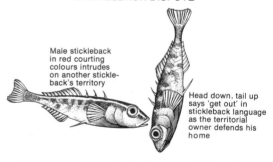

Male stickleback in red courting colours intrudes on another stickleback's territory

Head down, tail up says 'get out' in stickleback language as the territorial owner defends his home

Arguments between animals often occur in the mating season when one ventures into another's territory. Threat rather than violent action settles such disputes

Peck order

Animals that live in groups usually have a well-organised social or hierarchical system. It is vital when large numbers of animals are living together that they are led by one or more strong members, so that when danger threatens the group is kept together in a co-ordinated defence. The caste system also helps to keep order and discipline between its members. As each individual recognises his position disagreements are quickly settled.

Several animals—deer, seals, jackdaws and chickens for instance—live in orderly societies with the members arranged in ranks. With domestic chickens the position in the rank is worked out by pecking. This has led to the term 'peck order'

COURTSHIP DANCE OF THE CRESTED NEWT

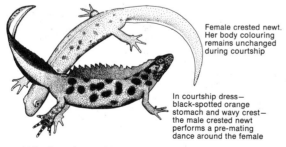

Female crested newt. Her body colouring remains unchanged during courtship

In courtship dress— black-spotted orange stomach and wavy crest— the male crested newt performs a pre-mating dance around the female

At the time of courtship the male crested newt develops a black-spotted orange stomach and wavy crest along his back especially to attract a female

when talking about an animal's caste system. The hen that is the most aggressive, pecks the others hardest and most persistently, reaches the top and becomes dominant in the society. She will be the one that has the first peck at any food. The other hens are arranged in descending peck order. The second in line is submissive to the top hen but will attack all the other birds. The third hen is submissive to the two birds above her but will attack all those below her and so on down the rank. Generally a male is the leader in a group. However, a female can reach a position of equal status with this leader through 'marriage'. If a 'boss' jackdaw mates with a low-caste female then she immediately rises to his level and is respected by the whole jackdaw colony.

For the majority of animals this social system is a temporary arrangement which functions in the breeding season only.

The well-organised colonies of ants, bees and wasps, on the other hand, are permanent societies each of which is governed by a rigid caste system. These insects are born into the position of queen, worker or drone—positions in which they spend the rest of their lives.

HEN HIERARCHY

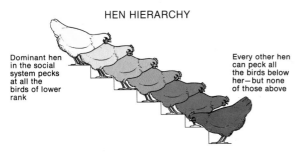

Dominant hen in the social system pecks at all the birds of lower rank

Every other hen can peck all the birds below her—but none of those above

The peck order can be thought of as a hierarchical staircase. Each hen occupies a step on the staircase, pecking aggressively at the bird below

Communication

In all forms of animal behaviour, whether courtship or defence, understanding between the animals concerned is vital, especially in the group-living species. Animals have their own language of sound, scent and display through which they can communicate with each other. The song of a bird contains an extensive range of notes and calls used to proclaim his home boundaries or to indicate his courting mood to a female. Such sound messages are employed by many animals—dogs bark, horses neigh, deer stags roar during the rutting season, frogs croak and bats have a vocabulary of high-pitched ultrasonic calls. Even the underwater world of fish echoes with their calls, keeping shoals together or scattering them when danger threatens. Fish can also communicate through vibrations in the water picked up by a line of sensitive cells along the sides of their body.

Other animals with an extremely efficient sense of smell rely on scent signals. The badger, like the fox, sprinkles its trail and sett with urine as a way of keeping in touch with the family and as a warning to any intruder to keep away. The feathery antennae of a moth are highly sensitive to the scent emitted by a female and this scent can be picked up more than a mile away by the male.

Just as a man will express his feelings of aggression or friendliness to a companion through facial expressions, so too do many animals. The domestic cat and dog use their ears and mouth to indicate feelings such as anger, contentedness or

THE GRASSHOPPER'S SONG

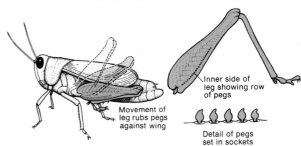

Inner side of leg showing row of pegs

Movement of leg rubs pegs against wing

Detail of pegs set in sockets

Grasshoppers have no voice. But the male can communicate his love overtures in 'song'—by rubbing his hind legs against his forewings

hunger. A silent mime involving body postures and colour signals can be equally expressive. The dog bares its teeth in a threat display, and cowers with its tail between its legs to show fear. A bee 'dances' to show other members of the hive where food is to be found. The peacock shimmers his magnificent coloured tail, informing the peahen of his amorous intentions.

Learning

Courtship and defence displays, scent and sound communications are all instinctive reactions of an animal. Many young animals learn a great deal by imitating their parents, especially in the antics of their play. They copy the hunting and killing actions of their parents, and in this way develop the strength and timing needed for successful hunting in adult life. Predators such as the fox play at crouching and ambushing when they are young, while prey animals such as the vole scamper from one hiding place to another in preparation for their hunted adult life.

The ability to learn is not restricted to young animals: adults can learn also through experience. It may be vital in fact for many animals to have this capacity of learning to be able to survive their ever-changing environment. This is perhaps most significant where town life is encroaching more and more on to the country. Blue tits and great tits, for instance, have discovered that by applying their natural feeding technique of hammering at nuts to get at the kernel they can pierce milk-bottle tops and drink the cream off the top of the milk. See also COLOUR AND CAMOUFLAGE and EVOLUTION

LEARNING TO CRACK A NUT

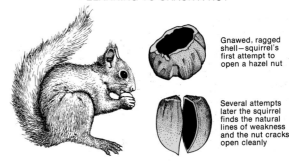

Gnawed, ragged shell—squirrel's first attempt to open a hazel nut

Several attempts later the squirrel finds the natural lines of weakness and the nut cracks open cleanly

A young squirrel will instinctively gnaw at a nut, but several tries are needed before it learns the secret of cracking the nut efficiently

Ant

The highly organised working and social life of ants tempts many people to draw comparisons with human society. However, the organisation of an ant colony is based on instinct and communication by body secretions called pheromones. These attract mates and help in locating food and the nest.

Ants are yellow, brown or red-black insects, $\frac{1}{12}$-$\frac{3}{8}$ in. long. There are 47 British species. They live in colonies, housed in networks of tunnels which they dig in soil or wood. These colonies, which number anything from a few dozen to 100,000 individuals, sometimes last more than 50 years. There is at least one queen in each colony. Queens, which are larger than other ants, do little more than lay eggs.

Each egg hatches into a larva, which in turn develops into a pupa—a motionless, resting stage of development. In some species the pupa is protected by a cocoon; these are the 'ant eggs' used for feeding fish. Most pupae hatch into workers—sterile, wingless females, who take on the nest-building, food-gathering and defence of the colony. The remainder develop into males or queens; both develop wings.

In the summer, winged ants from nests over a wide area—determined in extent by local weather—make their first and last flight, in which each queen is fertilised by a male. The fertilised queen either returns to her old nest or starts a new one. She loses, or bites off, her wings and lays a few eggs. These develop into small, sterile female workers which she feeds with salivary secretions. Continuing to lay eggs for up to 15 years, the queen never leaves her nest and never needs to mate again, using sperm stored from her mating flight to fertilise eggs as she lays them. Sometimes she withholds sperm from an egg and such unfertilised eggs develop into males.

Ants eat animal or vegetable food, but also

A wood ant adopts a threatening posture as it guards an aphid 'farm'. Wood ants feed on sugary honey-dew which they milk from the aphids by stroking them with their antennae

attack and kill other insects and scavenge generally. On finding food, a foraging worker leaves a scent trail which is followed by other ants.

Often found in gardens, the black ant *Lasius niger* feeds in part on the honeydew of aphids. The mound-building ant *L. flavus* keeps aphid eggs in its nest through winter and puts the newly hatched aphids out to graze in spring. The largest British

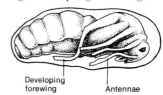

Developing forewing   Antennae

The so-called egg sold as fish food is really a cocoon containing the pupal stage of the ant

ant is the wood ant *Formica rufa* — $\frac{3}{8}$ in. long. These ants often attract attention in woodlands by the rustling they make as they move through the litter carrying leaves and twigs. Their nests resemble tidy swept-up heaps of pine needles, twigs and refuse 2-3 ft high. They defend themselves by biting or squirting formic acid, but the red ant *Myrmica ruginodis*, which nests under stones, can sting.

Birds sometimes apply ants to their feathers, in order, it is thought, to use the formic acid as pesticide to kill parasites.

Two British species exploit other ants. The queen of the parasitic ant *Anergates atratulus*, which lives in the New Forest, takes over the nest of another species by persuading the workers to kill their own queen. The more common slave-making ant *Formica sanguinea* 'kidnaps' pupae from other ant nests and hatches them as slaves.

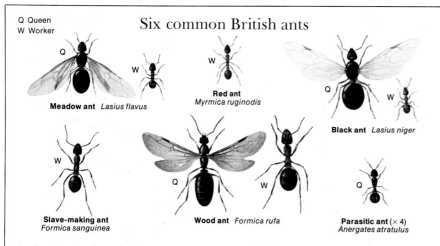

Q Queen
W Worker

Six common British ants

Meadow ant *Lasius flavus*

Red ant *Myrmica ruginodis*

Black ant *Lasius niger*

Slave-making ant *Formica sanguinea*

Wood ant *Formica rufa*

Parasitic ant (× 4) *Anergates atratulus*

A selection of common British ants. There are 47 British species leading highly successful social lives. All are shown twice life size excepting the parasitic ant

Exposed eggs from a disturbed nest are carried to safety by wood ant workers

Antennae see Insect
Anther see Flower

Anthrax

A disease, usually fatal, which attacks cattle, pigs, sheep and horses. It is caused by a germ *Bacillus anthracis* which enters the animal through minute cuts. Human beings can also become infected, with serious, sometimes fatal, results. Stringent regulations are applied during a suspected outbreak.

Antler

Only the male deer grows antlers. They are shed each year and rapidly regrown in time for the rutting season when the male uses them to compete for females. Antlers are solid and bony and grow from two knobs or pedicles on the skull. These are covered with a soft skin called velvet which is richly supplied with blood vessels and nerves. When the antlers are fully grown the blood supply is cut off and the dried velvet shed. The deer rubs his antlers against branches until they are clean. Each succeeding year more points or tines are added. See also DEER

Anvil

The traditional blacksmith's anvil is a solid block of iron weighing about 2 cwt capable of withstanding hammer blows. It is mounted on a rough-hewn base of hardwood, usually oak or elm, giving elasticity in the base, so minimising repercussions dangerous to the smith. It has a flat top, on which hot iron can be hammered into shape. The top has two tapering extensions. The square-nosed one—which is to the left as the smith faces his anvil—is the wedge and has sockets to take attachments for thickening, thinning, twisting and hollowing hot metal. The pointed extension is the beak and is used for shaping horseshoes.

Metal is first shaped on the anvil face. Curves, such as horseshoes, are formed on the beak

Aphid

In a year, one aphid's descendants would, if they all survived and multiplied, equal the weight of 600 million men. It is only this phenomenal reproduction rate which ensures the survival of the species since, apart from those protected by ants, aphids are defenceless against predators such as birds, ladybirds and their larvae and lace-wing larvae. Aphids are also vulnerable to cold weather.

There are about 500 species of aphids in the British Isles, many of which are known as blackfly or greenfly. They are soft-bodied bugs, up to $\frac{1}{8}$ in. long, which feed by sucking sap from the leaves or stems of plants. They excrete honeydew, a sweet, sticky substance which some ants feed on. These ants maintain herds of aphids to obtain the honeydew.

In autumn, females lay eggs on trees and shrubs where they pass the winter before hatching into wingless females in the spring. These wingless females—no males are hatched from the eggs—give birth to live females, some of which have wings. These fly to soft-stemmed plants, such as beans, where they give birth to another generation of wingless females. This process of virgin birth—called parthenogenesis from the Latin *parthenos,* virgin and *genesis,* origin—continues throughout the summer, winged and wingless generations alternating, with each female producing up to 50 daughters in her two or three weeks of life. After only eight or ten days the young may be sufficiently developed to reproduce in the same way, warmth being the vital factor in their reproduction rate. In October some males are born. These and the winged females fly to the winter host plant where they mate. Fertilised eggs are laid which can survive the winter and start the life-cycle again the following year.

Black bean aphids *Aphis fabae* are found on broad beans in summer, and winter on spindle trees; rosy aphids *Anuraphis roseus* overwinter on apple trees and stay on them until early summer when they migrate to other plants, the fertilised females returning to lay eggs in the autumn.

A distinctive feature of the aphids is the pair of tubes—called cornicles—at the rear of the abdomen which produce a waxy secretion. This takes the form of a protective white fluff in the woolly aphid species such as *Eriosoma lanigerum,* which attacks apple trees, and *Prosiphalus tesselatus,* which lives on alder and maple.

Aphids damage many crops, especially beans, cabbages, peas and mangolds, not only by draining the sap but also by carrying plant infections such as the yellow virus disease which attacks sugar beet.

The British populations of the black bean aphid and the aphid *Myzus persicae*—responsible for the spread of many virus diseases among potatoes—are often increased by migration from the Continent. Winged aphids are caught and dispersed by ascending air currents.

Young greenfly swarm over rose stems. Dense populations build up rapidly during the summer

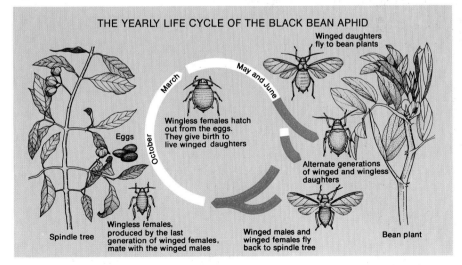

THE YEARLY LIFE CYCLE OF THE BLACK BEAN APHID

Winged daughters fly to bean plants

March

May and June

October

Wingless females hatch out from the eggs. They give birth to live winged daughters

Eggs

Alternate generations of winged and wingless daughters

Spindle tree

Wingless females, produced by the last generation of winged females, mate with the winged males

Winged males and winged females fly back to spindle tree

Bean plant

For most of the year the black bean aphid lives on the spindle tree. In the summer, winged females fly to bean plants where alternate generations of winged and wingless daughters are produced by virgin birth. Males are born in the autumn only. They mate with wingless females, offspring of the last generation of winged females that have flown back to a spindle tree, and eggs are laid again

Apple

Prehistoric man is known to have eaten wild apples and to have used them to make a primitive form of cider. Wild apples have a wide range of colour, shape, size and season. These qualities, with careful selection and cross-breeding, have produced the many modern apple varieties which are very different from Britain's native wild apple *Malus pumila*, a small, hard, sour fruit.

The Romans, who had developed distinct varieties of dessert apples, introduced them to Britain and it is possible that one of these was Court Pendu Plat, a variety still used in modern breeding programmes. Cato the Elder (234-149 BC) wrote a treatise on the art of grafting and by the time of the Elder Pliny (AD 23-79), more than 20 varieties of apple had been produced.

From the late 7th century until about 1100 apple cultivation in Britain was largely a monastic enterprise, and is known to have flourished before the Norman conquest at the Benedictine monasteries of Evesham and Pershore in Worcestershire.

Under the Normans the feudal system saw the spread of orchards on noblemen's estates. The first recorded mention of a named apple was in a deed of 1205, when 200 Pearmains were specified as part of the annual payment to the Crown made by Robert de Evermere for the lordship of Runham in Norfolk. The Pearmain—whose name derives from its pear-like shape—and the Costard cooking apple were Britain's most widely grown apples of the 13th century. Pearmains were esteemed 400 years later in the improved form of the Great Pearmain. The richly

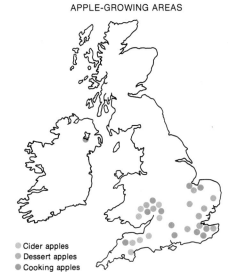

APPLE-GROWING AREAS

● Cider apples
● Dessert apples
● Cooking apples

Kent and Worcestershire are old established areas for growing dessert and cooking apples. Here the rainfall is low and sunshine high. Cider apples are grown mainly in the West Country

flavoured Adam's Pearmain is probably the nearest to its medieval ancestor, the Old Pearmain, which was exhibited at a Royal Horticultural Show in 1945. The Worcester Pearmain, a crisp, sweet and juicy apple, was introduced about 1873.

Costards were hawked by London costard-mongers—the forerunners of the expression coster-mongers—in the late 15th century at about 4d. a 100 for the top grade apple.

Pippins, which were seedlings—trees grown from pips either deliberately or accidentally sown—became widely acclaimed after 1500. Tudor and Elizabethan England knew pippins as Apple-johns, Queenings, Leathercoats and Russetings.

Apple-johns, or John-apples, were so named because they ripened about St John's Day, and were said to have the remarkable quality of keeping for two years and to be in perfect condition even when shrivelled and withered. Perhaps the most famous of these early varieties was the Golden Pippin.

Codlings, which were coddled or parboiled, were favourite cooking apples of the 16th century; these have come down to us minus the 'g', as codlins, such as the Early Victoria Codlin, discovered near Wisbech, Cambridgeshire, in the 1890's, and Keswick Codlin, first found growing among rubbish at Gleaston Castle, Ulverston, Lancashire.

The 18th and 19th centuries embraced the golden age of apples. Seedlings such as Bramley Seedling, Cox's Orange Pippin and Ribston Pippin became household names. Scores of people, from professional raisers and head gardeners to the humblest amateurs, introduced good seedlings. In 1830, Richard Cox, a retired brewer, reared Cox's Orange Pippin, which became the nation's premier dessert apple; Thomas

Apple blossom is always a welcome sign of spring.

Thorpe, a handloom weaver, raised the excellent cooker Lord Suffield, in 1831; and in the early 1800's 'white-haired Kempster, a plain, practical, labouring man', produced at Woodstock the Blenheim Orange, one of the most celebrated apples in history.

The story of the Blenheim Orange is typical of the way different varieties had appeared up to this stage. Kempster noticed that the apples on a particular tree were distinctly different from those on other trees. In 1818, there was just one tree producing these apples. By grafting and budding on to other tree stock, they were soon being grown on hundreds of trees. Today, the Blenheim Orange is grown throughout Britain, Europe, America and Australia.

Apple-growers classified as new varieties any which had distinctive, usually visible, characteristics which could be reproduced in any climate. For example, James Grieve apples are normally pale yellow with red streaks. A grower noticed that on one branch of one tree, all the apples were almost wholly red. This chance difference is known as a 'sport'. Graftings from this one branch continued to produce wholly red apples on other trees, wherever they were grown. The red apples were accepted as a new variety, called Rosamund.

Blenheim Orange, a late-ripening dessert apple, as painted in 1820 by William Hooker

But, too early, it may be killed off by frost; and too late, the crop may not bring the best price

The genius of the age was Thomas Andrew Knight, 1759-1838, perhaps the greatest horticulturist of his or any preceding time. He produced the first known deliberately created crosses ever recorded, thus inaugurating the technique of apple hybridising and true breeding, as distinct from merely propagating existing seedlings. In 1800 he produced Red Ingestrie and Bringewood Pippin; in 1801 Breinton Seedling; in 1802 Grange Apple, and seven more up to 1811.

Knight was followed by Thomas Laxton, 1830-90, and his sons, whose names are renowned for such apples as Laxton's Superb bred from Wyken Pippin × Cox's Orange, Lord Lambourne (James Grieve × Worcester Pearmain), Laxton's Epicure (Cox's Orange × Wealthy) and many others.

Varieties suitable for the production of cider were recognised and cultivated in the West Midlands and the South-west.

More than 80 such varieties are still grown, some with picturesque names such as slackma-girdle and cap of liberty.

Most of the apple-growing regions have local sayings. Some are about the timing of blossom which is crucial to the crop because of the danger of frost damage. In a West Somerset saying, May 21 — the date of Culmstock fair — is a vital date: 'Til Culmstock fair be come and gone, There mid be apples and mid be none.' A Herefordshire saw, and a similar one from East Sussex, take a less positive view: 'When the apple blooms in March, You need not for barrels search; But when the apple blooms in May, search for barrels every day.'

The value of apples which store well is noted in a Shropshire saying — 'When the snow is in the orchard, A crab is worth a costard.' Another Herefordshire saying concerns the life of an apple tree: 'Who sets an apple tree may live to see it end, Who sets a pear tree may set it for a friend.'

Cider is the fermented juice of apples. The skin of a ripe apple bears many yeast plants, invisible to the naked eye. These ferment and turn the sugar in the apples into alcohol when they are crushed. Cider usually contains 4-5 per cent of alcohol by volume. The art of cider-making is in the blending of the different varieties of apple. In the old days this was often done in circular stone troughs, round which a horse would be driven pulling a stone to crush the apples. Some of these troughs still survive in the cider-making areas.

Before the present century, cider was produced by farmers from their own apples and sold locally. A few home producers survive, but cider-making is now a substantial factory industry based on more than 20,000 acres of trees grown in the traditional cider counties of Devon, Somerset and Herefordshire.

The past half century or so has seen a revolution in apple growing, the majority of new apples arising from deliberate crossings of varieties known to have desirable features. The emphasis is on pest and disease resistance, using parents combining these attributes. World-famous research and experimental stations, like those at East Malling and Long Ashton, are devoted to every conceivable aspect of the science and practice of fruit culture. But even today new varieties arise from accidentally sown seeds. A new variety which was judged to be promising in 1971 is Florence Bennett. This appeared as a seedling in the garden of a Liverpool woman, Mrs Florence Bennett, after she had thrown away a baked apple.

Other lines of active research are biological control, or the control of pests by their natural enemies; the development of systemic chemicals that destroy or prevent pests and diseases from within the tree; the formulation of fruit thinning and anti-drop sprays and, perhaps closer to the fundamentals of nature, a more precise understanding of the habits and value of bees in orchards.

More than 6000 distinct varieties of apples, known by 22,000 different names, are registered with the National Fruit Trials Centre, but commercial apple growing in Britain is confined to the few varieties that meet the hard economic demands of fruit farming. These include attractive appearance, good cropping powers and keeping qualities. A much wider range of varieties is grown by gardeners and some of the older types can still be seen in cottage gardens. Efforts are being made to save certain apples from extinction, like the Irish Peach, Cornish Aromatic and Cornish Gillyflower — first discovered in a garden near Truro at the beginning of the 19th century. Apples with a special place in history are also still available, like the Pride of Kent — or Flower of Kent — which inspired Sir Isaac Newton to his study of gravity after he had watched apples falling from a tree.

HORSE-POWERED CIDER MILL

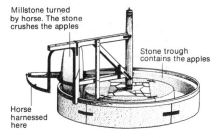

Millstone turned by horse. The stone crushes the apples

Stone trough contains the apples

Horse harnessed here

A typical farm cider mill in which the apples were crushed by a horse-drawn stone wheel. A few such mills survive in the West Country

A 19th-century view of the Dundas Aqueduct on the Kennet and Avon Canal near Bath

Aqueduct

A channel or structure—usually raised—for carrying water over long distances. The Romans built many aqueducts; there is fragmentary evidence of one north of Haltwhistle in Northumberland, built in the 2nd or 3rd century AD, which probably supplied the garrisons along Hadrian's Wall. The New River, a 38-mile artificial stream built between 1609 and 1613 to carry drinking water from springs in Hertfordshire to Islington in north London, was the first attempt to supply the capital with fresh water in this way. It still functions but has been shortened to 24 miles and now ends at Stoke Newington. The longest raised structure for carrying water in the United Kingdom is Thomas Telford's 1007 ft aqueduct over the valley of the River Dee at Pont-Cysyllte in Wales. Built between 1795 and 1805, the 19-arched aqueduct carries the Shropshire Union Canal 121 ft above the river. It is still used by pleasure craft.

Arable see Farming

Arboretum

A collection of living trees, maintained to show their variety of form and colour. Many arboreta were established in Victorian times to provide specimens for study. Some of the best arboreta, open at moderate charges, are those at Kew, Surrey; Wakehurst Place, near Ardingly, Sussex; Edinburgh; and Glasnevin, Dublin. The Forestry Commission maintains an arboretum at Westonbirt, south-west of Tetbury, Gloucestershire, magnificent conifers at Bedgebury, near Hawkhurst, Kent, and rare eucalyptus trees at Kilmun, near Dunoon, Argyll. The Royal Horticultural Society grows notable trees at Wisley, Surrey, and the National Trust and the National Trust for Scotland maintain fine collections of trees at many of their country mansions throughout England, Scotland and Wales. There are other good arboreta in public parks and private gardens.

Archangel, Yellow *Galeobdolon luteum*

A plant 1-2 ft high found on heavy soils in woods throughout England and Wales, but rare in Scotland and Ireland. Also known as weasel-snout, it flowers from April to June. *Galeobdolon* derives from two Greek words meaning weasel and stench—probably a reference to the unpleasant smell produced when the stems or leaves are rubbed between the fingers. This deters plant-eating animals and insects.

The mouth-shaped flowers of yellow archangel grow in whorls round the hairy stem

Arrowhead

Prehistoric man hardened the tips of his arrows by fire to give greater penetration on impact. To make them more lethal, stone, bone or metal arrowheads were fixed to the shaft.

Stone arrowheads, especially flint flakes, were used from Upper Paleolithic times, around 38,000 BC. They continued to be used throughout the Bronze Age, from about 2000 BC, since bronze was too precious.

Iron began to replace stone around 1000 BC. Bone was probably used extensively where suitable stone was scarce. Since it disintegrates fairly rapidly in acid soils, there are few surviving bone arrowheads.

Neolithic flint arrowheads dating from before 3000 BC, found at Windmill Hill, Wiltshire, are characteristically leaf shaped. Nearly all arrowheads have pointed ends, though the trailing edge may be cut to form barbs. Instead of points, some arrowheads have transversely shaped cutting edges called tranchets.

Arrowhead *Sagittaria sagittifolia*

A water plant which grows in the mud of slow-moving lowland rivers and canals. Its name comes from the arrow-shaped leaves, the two 'barbs' of which are almost as long as the end lobe. The leaves rise up to 3 ft above the water on three-sided stalks.

There are also ribbon-like submerged and floating leaves, which trail downstream from the plant. The three-petalled flowers, up to 1 in. across, are white with purple bases and are borne from June to August on branched, leafless stalks which rise up to 18 in. out of the water. Male and female flowers are separate. The males are larger and grow higher on the stem. A milky juice seeps from the stem when it is cut. The Chinese cultivate arrowhead in order to eat the tubers.

Arrowhead plants bear separate female and male flowers, the males having petals

Arrow worm

An almost transparent sea worm with a torpedo-shaped body, $\frac{1}{2}$-$1\frac{1}{2}$ in. long. It has a rounded head with tiny black eyes, two pairs of fins and a tail. There is a fold of the body wall which can be pulled forward to enclose the head. There are about 50 species but of the four or five British species the most likely to be seen is *Spadella cephaloptera*, which inhabits rock pools in south-west England. It hangs motionless in the water for most of the time, attaching itself to rocks with suckers on its tail, but from time to time darts suddenly at its prey—small crustaceans—which it seizes with the many small spines on its head. It manoeuvres the prey into its mouth with these spines and swallows it whole. Arrow worms are hermaphrodites—they have both male and female reproductive organs. They deposit masses of eggs and sperm in the water, which develop into larvae, then adults.

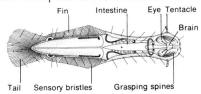

Its broad tail speeds the arrow worm *Spadella* after prey which it seizes with its spines

Artificial insemination

The process of breeding animals by artificial impregnation of the female was developed in Britain during the 1930's. It came into general use after the Second World War, and now millions of cattle are bred each year by this process. It is also used, to a lesser extent, with pigs, sheep and bees. The Milk Marketing Board has more than 1200 bulls —selected for their quality and covering all the major breeds—at studs in England and Wales. Each bull can theoretically sire 20,000-30,000 offspring a year, though the actual number is less than 2000. The farmer applies to a stud for semen, which is brought to the farm and implanted in the female cattle by a trained inseminator.

Semen is preserved in deep-freeze and may be used long after the sire is dead. The longest stored semen to produce a calf so far was that of a Buckinghamshire bull which died in 1955; the calf was born in 1971.

Ash *Fraxinus excelsior*

A tree easily recognised by its grey, olive-tinged bark and hard, velvety black buds, especially in winter. As the tree ages the bark gradually becomes pure grey and develops a network of shallow ridges. The buds grow in pairs, except at the ends of twigs where they are single. The twigs are slightly flattened at each bud joint. The leaves are a dull mid-green. They open in late April, turn to pale yellow in September and fall in early October. Each 8-12 in. long leaf consists of about nine oval, tooth-edged leaflets, 2-4 in. long and 1 in. wide.

Because ash comes into leaf late—seldom before May—and because it loses its leaves in October, earlier than most trees, it is a poor shelterbelt tree, though it is hardy and can thrive high up on exposed hills. It casts only light shade and in autumn its fallen leaves decompose rapidly, so that the soil beneath the ash is often rich in insects.

Ash is a valuable crop for foresters, but it must be fast-grown, as slow-grown ash has more pore space and so is soft, weak and brittle. Fast-grown ash is much harder, stronger and heavier because its wider annual rings have more structural fibres.

Tufts of green, catkin-like flowers appear in May. They may be male, female or of both sexes, with all types on the same tree. They are fertilised by wind-blown pollen.

The female flowers and those of both sexes have seeds that ripen into bunches of pale yellow-brown keys by September. They are so-called because they look like the keys used in medieval locks. Each consists of a seed with a thin, twisted wing attached, to aid its dispersal by winter winds. Ash seedlings spring up readily on bare ground.

Ash seeds are eaten by small mammals and birds and form the most important food for the bullfinch in winter. Fewer insects live on ash than most other British trees.

The timber is white, and sometimes pale brown at the centre. Each annual ring is marked by pores, which appear as shallow grooves in timber cut lengthwise. Ash wood is both tough and supple and resists shock

Ash can be recognised by its black buds, which are present from autumn to spring

without splintering. It is therefore ideal for the handles of picks, axes, hammers and garden implements. It makes good oars, skis, frames and shafts for carts and wooden wheel rims.

Ash is also used to make furniture. It bends easily after steaming to form the curved back of a Windsor chair and the crossbars in ladder-back chairs. Norse warriors also used it to make weapon handles and arrows, and the ash tree held an honoured place in their mythology. The Norse name for ash, *ask*, occurs in many place-names—for example, Askrigg (meaning ash ridge) in north Yorkshire.

Though it is a waste of good wood, ash burns sweetly even while green. As Walter de la Mare once wrote:

> *Of all the trees in England,*
> *Her sweet three corners in,*
> *Only the Ash, the bonnie Ash,*
> *Burns fierce while it is green.*

The ash—a member of the olive family—usually grows to a height of 60-70 ft but can reach over 140 ft. Its maximum age is about 120 years. It forms woods in limestone districts and is found singly, in mixed woods and along hedges, throughout the British Isles. There are fine stands in the dales of Derbyshire and on the Yorkshire Pennines, near the north Lancashire coast, and on the Mendips and Cotswold Hills. Columbine, celandine, wild garlic, dog's mercury and wild arum usually grow in the same area.

The large, spreading crown of the ash shows up best in winter after the leaves have fallen

Heath assassin
Coranus subapterus

Flying assassin
Reduvius personatus

Assassin bug

As their name suggests, assassin bugs are predators. There are six British species; the most common, the ½ in. heath assassin *Coranus subapterus,* is active on heaths and sand dunes from July to October. Most adult heath assassins have poorly developed wings and cannot fly, so are restricted to hunting on the ground. The bug grasps insects and spiders with its 'jack-knife' forelegs, then injects toxic digestive juices into the prey through its long, sharp beak. These juices break down the victim's body tissues which are subsequently sucked in. When the beak is not used for feeding it is curved under the head, resting against a ridged groove. If the bug is disturbed it scrapes the beak against these ridges, so producing a grating sound.

Heath assassins mate in the autumn. The female lays her dark brown eggs in moss and leaf litter where they overwinter, hatching in the following April or May. The young, predators from the start, take two months to mature, moulting several times.

A bug often found on walls in houses and outbuildings is the ⅔ in. flying assassin *Reduvius personatus.* Unlike the heath assassin it is a strong flyer and is often attracted to lights at night. It feeds on flies, silverfish and other household pests.

Aster, Sea *Aster tripolium*

A 1-3 ft high fleshy-leaved plant that can tolerate growing in salt-water surroundings, the sea aster adds colour to cliffs and salt marshes in late summer. It blooms between July and October, its blue-purple or whitish flowers being very similar to those of its

Petalled form   Petalless form

Sea aster grows in two distinct forms, one with petal-like rays, and one without

close relative the garden michaelmas daisy. Each flower is really a tight head of small flowers or florets. There are two kinds: purple ray florets at the edge and yellow disk florets in the centre. Some plants have both types, others are ray-less. Often the two kinds of sea aster grow together. However, north of Lincolnshire the ray-less variety is absent.

Auk

Steep, rugged cliffs on the north and west coasts of the British Isles provide the main nesting sites for our four resident species of auks: razorbills *Alca torda,* puffins *Fratercula arctica,* guillemots *Uria aalge,* and black guillemots *Cepphus grylle.* These species also occur on other coasts but in nothing like the same numbers—perhaps because of human pressures on their environment.

Auks are ideally adapted to an aquatic life: their short wings and webbed feet, set well back on their bodies, provide an excellent form of propulsion under water. But this adaptation to swimming makes them

seem ungainly or comical on land where they appear only for breeding or when driven by storms. Their short wings have to work hard on take-off and in flight.

All auks are mainly black or blackish above, and white below, but they are fairly easy to distinguish. The 10 in. puffin has a heavy triangular bill which is coloured red, yellow and grey in winter but develops a blue marking in the mating season. The 16 in. razorbill has a heavy dark bill with a white ring. Guillemots—about the same size as razorbills—have a stout straight bill. Black guillemots, as their name suggests, are all black but for a distinctive white wing patch.

Auks live in flocks all the year round and the various species often share the same nesting sites. Puffins occupy the cliff tops, digging their own burrows or nesting in rabbit burrows, guillemots nest on narrow rocky ledges, black guillemots in broken rocks at the foot of cliffs, where razorbills may also nest, as well as in rock clefts.

The pear shape of the guillemot's egg enables it to spin round on the narrow nest-

Guillemots crowd together in a cliff-top breeding colony. There are no nests—the guillemot lays a pear-shaped egg which it holds between its feet and body. Its shape means that it turns in a narrow circle, rather than rolling away, when the parents change places during incubation

ing ledges where hundreds of these birds roost, holding their eggs between their feet among their belly feathers during the four to five week incubation period – which in the other species varies from three to six weeks. Guillemots accompany their young from the nest when they are about five weeks old; young razorbills take to sea with one parent at two weeks and puffins set off alone when they are six weeks old.

Two other auks visit these islands in winter; the rare Brunnich's guillemot *Uria lomvia*, identified only by an inconspicuous mark on its bill, and the little auk *Plautus alle*, only 8 in. long and regularly seen as it moves south from its Arctic breeding islands, often being blown inland by Atlantic gales.

Auks live on fish, shellfish and plankton. One guillemot was timed to dive for 68 seconds and reached a depth of 28 ft in search of fish. As swimming birds auks are the most numerous casualties after oil spillage. However, scientists have discounted this as the main reason for auks diminishing in numbers and disappearing from their former southern haunts, and are still looking for the basic cause of the decline. Auks are long lived and, having few natural enemies, have increased in numbers until recent years in spite of the fact that all except the black guillemot lay only one egg a year. The black guillemot usually lays two. However, the biggest of the species – the great auk – was over-hunted and is the only British bird to have become extinct in historic times. The last one was killed in 1844.

Puffin in peril

Alarmed by a 'catastrophic' decline in the puffin population of the British Isles, ornithologists are trying urgently to find the cause. Expeditions to their main breeding ground – the St Kilda islands, in the Outer Hebrides – have reported a 90 per cent fall in population in less than 10 years. A breeding population of 3 million pairs in the early 1960's had fallen to about 300,000 by 1971.

Ornithologists think it unlikely that oil pollution, predation, food shortage, climate changes or disease are to blame. They are now considering chemical pollution at the puffin's winter feeding grounds, of which little is known, and are calling for intensive

A puffin in flight – its distinctive red bill in its winter colouring

ringing programmes to determine possible 'danger zones' to try to prevent the puffin following the great auk into extinction. See also POLLUTION

The great auk, 30 in. high, unable to fly, and prized for food and for its skin, was hunted mercilessly and was extinct by 1844

Aurora borealis

Northern Lights is another name for this magnificent display which occurs high in the sky of the Northern Hemisphere most often in spring and autumn, especially at times of sunspot activity. The aurora is present on about 150 nights of the year in northern Scotland and on about ten nights a year in southern England, though often it is not visible from the ground because of cloud. Sometimes it appears as a grey-white glow; on other occasions there are rapidly changing displays of light in vivid shades of red, yellow and green. The light is produced about 60 miles up in the atmosphere when electrically charged particles from the sun are caught in the earth's magnetic field and focused on to the magnetic pole.

Aurora borealis is seen in four basic forms: drapery, shown here, and arc, band or corona

Australian fungus beetle *Cis bilamellatus*

This insect, though a native of Australia, was first identified as a separate species in England in 1884. Recent 'detective' work by an Oxford scientist shows that it probably reached Britain in the 1870's in fungus sent from Australia to Kew Botanical Gardens. Since the 19th century it has spread considerably, and it is now common in many parts of southern England and lowland Wales.

A small, yellow-brown insect about $\frac{1}{16}$ in.

long, the Australian fungus beetle usually lives in a bracket fungus *Polyporus betulinus*, a shelf-like growth common on the trunks of birch trees. This fungus, which resembles the beetle's Australian host plant, is both home and food for the beetle throughout its life. In spring, adults colonise newly dead fungi, tunnelling inside them. There the female lays about 40 eggs at intervals throughout the year. Each egg hatches into a larva within a week. Six weeks later the larva pupates, emerging as an adult after another week.

Feeding and tunnelling as larvae and adults, the insects help to break down the fungus and return its essential elements to the soil. In its turn the Australian fungus beetle is preyed on by a number of carnivorous insects.

Avens

One of the most common plants of hedgerow and woodland throughout Britain is the wood avens or herb bennet *Geum urbanum*. About 1-2 ft tall, it has erect yellow flowers (June-August) and fruits with hooked prickles which easily catch on clothing and animal fur. The root has an aromatic clove-like smell and was once used to flavour ale. In the 15th and 16th centuries it was hung in houses to keep the Devil away.

Water avens *G. rivale* is common in the north of Britain but rare in the south. It grows in marshes, damp woods and beside streams, its dull orange-pink flowers (May-September) nodding in the breeze. Where wood and water avens grow together they hybridise freely, producing many different plants with intermediate features.

A third species, the mountain avens *Dryas octopetala*, is really an Arctic plant, occasionally found in northern England, Scotland and Ireland. It has white flowers (June-August) and glossy leaves with a silver felt of hairs on the underside. The feathery plumed fruits, like those of traveller's joy, are conspicuous in winter.

Water avens *Geum rivale*

Mountain avens *Dryas octopetala*

Wood avens *Geum urbanum*

Wood avens flowers June-August, water avens May-September, mountain avens June-August

Avenue

Tree-lined paths leading to 17th-century country houses derived their name avenue from the French *avenir,* 'to come to'. The word may have been introduced by John Evelyn, the diarist and tree-planting enthusiast. At the beginning of the 17th century the Duke of Montagu planted 72 miles of avenue, mostly elm and lime trees, on his Northamptonshire estate at Boughton.

The 18th-century landscape architects disliked these straight paths of lime, beech, horse-chestnut, elm and sycamore, claiming that their formality destroyed the unity of a view. But by the end of the century this attitude began to change and Humphry Repton—one of the country's leading landscape gardeners—wrote in 1795 that avenues were acceptable in hilly terrain where their sense of formality could be diminished. The introduction of new ornamental conifers such as wellingtonia and Lawson's cypress in the 19th century, accelerated the revival.

The cypress and yew, especially, are favourites in churchyards, often being planted to form an avenue from lych-gate to porch.

The longest avenue in England was planted in 1840, winding its way for 3 miles through Clumber Park, Nottinghamshire. It still flourishes, though the house has gone.

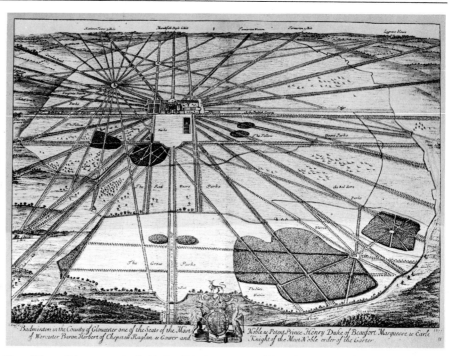

Plan of the radial avenues planted in the 17th century around Badminton House, Gloucestershire

The avocet's soft, grunting flight note contrasts with its shrill yelps as it protects its nest

Avocet *Recurvirostra avosetta*

This graceful black and white wader is the subject of the greatest success story of bird protection in Britain. Because of this, and its general attractiveness, it has been adopted as the symbol for the Royal Society for the Protection of Birds. Until the middle of the last century avocets were quite numerous from the Humber to Sussex, but marsh drainage, the theft of their eggs to make puddings and indiscriminate killing for their feathers wiped them out in Britain. After the Second World War a few pairs began nesting on Minsmere and Havergate Island in Suffolk. They probably came from Holland. Both breeding places are now RSPB reserves and the protected birds number more than 100 pairs each year. The avocet is also found on the Tamar estuary on the Cornwall-Devon border. About 50 or so birds spend each winter there.

About 17 in. long, the avocet has striking piebald plumage and long dusky-blue legs which project behind the tail in flight. Its fine upturned awl-shaped bill is perhaps its most distinctive feature, hence its old nickname: awl-bird. It sweeps the bill in a side-to-side action in shallow water, sifting out small shrimps, water insects and seeds of water plants.

The avocet nests in small colonies near the water's edge on sandbanks. The nest is just an unlined hollow in the sand or mud or a pile of dead vegetation. Its four buff-brown spotted eggs are incubated by both parents in turn for about 23 days. The chicks are capable of feeding themselves when only a few hours old but cannot fly until about six weeks. The helpless chicks are protected from predatory gulls by the swooping attacking flights and shrill yelping calls of their parents if an intruder approaches the nest too closely.

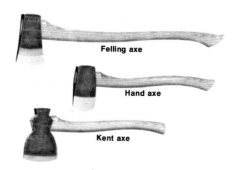

Three of the wide variety of modern axes, each of which is designed for a particular task

Axe

Man and his predecessors have used axes for more than 600,000 years. For most of this time axes were merely stones with sharp edges, held in the hand. Then, at the dawn of the New Stone Age, about 6000 years ago, man fitted handles of bone and wood to flints with cutting edges. Hand axes more than 200,000 years old have been found in the Thames Valley, and sites of particularly good hard stone, for example on the Langdale Pikes in the Lake District, have been identified as New Stone Age axe factories. In recent years the axe has been used as a weapon of war and for judicial beheadings. Today it is used for clearing, hewing and chopping timber. It usually has a square-shaped head made of steel with a cutting edge parallel to the haft or handle.

B

Backswimmer see Water boatman

Bacteria

The soil abounds with vast numbers of bacteria—plant organisms so small that a million of them would barely cover the head of a pin. Most bacteria multiply rapidly, often just by breaking in two. In this way a single bacterial cell can produce 16 million progeny in 24 hours, most of which do not survive.

Bacteria help break down the vast range of organic matter in the soil; without them the soil would become sterile and grow nothing. Different soil bacteria have different roles: one of the most important is *Bacillus radicicola* which turns nitrogen from the air into a form in which it can be used as plant food. Bacteria are also present in air and water, and in and on the bodies of plants and animals. Some have beneficial relationships with their animal hosts, for example breaking down waste products in the gut; many are responsible for disease.

Badger *Meles meles*

This handsome mammal, a relative of the stoat and weasel, is known by several names including brock, bawson, grey and badget. It has a 3 ft long, powerful, barrel-shaped body, short powerful legs with strong claws, and a short, blunt tail. Its coat is of rather stiff, coarse hairs which are whitish with a black band just behind the tip giving a silver-grey appearance. Its belly and legs are black. Perhaps the most distinctive feature of the

A cautious pair of badgers emerge from their underground sett at night to go foraging

badger is its white head which has a black stripe over each ear and eye. The male or boar has a broader head and thicker neck than the sow.

The badger lives throughout the British Isles. Being nocturnal it is rarely seen but is nevertheless quite numerous. It prefers woodland, especially where it borders pasture land, but will also live in quarries,

hedgerows or cliffs. Life centres on its underground home or sett. This is made of chambers and tunnels about 10-20 yds long and has several entrances. It is kept very clean by both boar and sow bringing in fresh bedding or bracken, dry leaves, grass and bluebells on fine nights. After such activity the badger cleans its front claws on a nearby tree trunk, its scratching post. Close by the sett small pits are dug and used regularly as latrines. The badger usually ambles from its sett just after sunset. It is very wary even though it has no enemies, except man. Excursions for food are made, always returning along the same well-defined pathways. It will eat anything from earthworms, mice, voles, frogs, snails and wasps to windfall apples, blackberries and grass. If it does wander on to unfamiliar ground the badger marks its whereabouts by squatting so that scent from the anal gland is left behind. It then uses this scent trail to find the way back to the sett. The badger also scents objects to mark the boundaries of its territory.

Mating may take place at any time from February to October but the fertilised egg does not start developing until December. From one to five cubs are born, usually in February. The cubs live with their parents at least until the autumn, and occasionally through the winter.

Baler see Farm machinery
Ballan see Wrasse

THE BADGER'S SETT

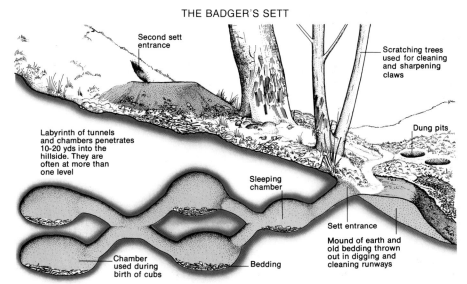

Second sett entrance

Scratching trees used for cleaning and sharpening claws

Dung pits

Labyrinth of tunnels and chambers penetrates 10-20 yds into the hillside. They are often at more than one level

Sleeping chamber

Sett entrance

Mound of earth and old bedding thrown out in digging and cleaning runways

Chamber used during birth of cubs

Bedding

The badger is an active nest digger and clean housekeeper. The sett is usually excavated in a woodland hillside where there is some cover from undergrowth, and accessible hunting ground

Balm *Melissa officinalis*

A herb which was formerly grown in gardens for its sweet lemon-scented leaves, but has since spread to roadsides. Bee keepers plant balm near hives, since its small white flowers produce an abundance of nectar during August and September—hence the name bee-balm.

The dried leaves of balm can be used as a substitute for lemon juice to flavour marrow jam and apple jelly. Balm tea—made by steeping the leaves in boiling water—is prescribed by herbalists as a 'nerve tonic'.

Balm, found chiefly in southern England and southern Ireland, was also used in the preparation of *Eau des carmes,* which was popular before the days of *Eau de cologne.*

Balm flower in close-up. The flowers grow in dense clusters on the plant stem

Balsam

Four species of this flower occur in Britain but only one is a native: the remainder are introductions from abroad. A feature common to all species is that when the seed pods are ripe the slightest touch will cause them

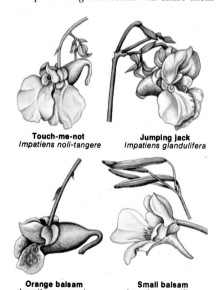

Touch-me-not
Impatiens noli-tangere

Jumping jack
Impatiens glandulifera

Orange balsam
Impatiens capensis

Small balsam
Impatiens parviflora

All balsam flowers have a broad-lipped lower petal with a prominent spur at its base

to burst, scattering seeds. This characteristic is responsible for their evocative names.

The native balsam is the rare yellow-flowered touch-me-not. It grows 2 ft high and is found by streams in the Lake District and North Wales.

Jumping jack is the most common species, first introduced early last century and now covering thousands of miles of river banks. It is also called policeman's helmet because of its hooded purplish-pink flowers and is easily recognised by its tall succulent stems, up to 6 ft high.

Orange balsam, another tall plant, came from eastern North America and is also naturalised on river banks, particularly in the London area.

Small balsam, a native of Siberia, is only 1-2 ft tall with yellow flowers; it is more often found in woods and other shady places. It often forms a carpet amongst bushes.

Barbastelle see Bat

Barbel *Barbus barbus*

Both the common and scientific names of this freshwater fish refer to the four long feelers—or barbels—around its mouth. These and its thick lips distinguish the barbel which is found in flowing water, over stony or sandy bottoms.

Barbels are usually found in the rough water at the foot of weirs, attracted either by the better oxygenated water or floating food debris. Originally, barbels were found only in the rivers of eastern England but they have since been introduced to the Severn and other rivers. Barbels are rarely seen for they are most active in the twilight hours and at night, when they are foraging for food. They also feed during daylight but usually remain in deep water.

Their natural food seems to be mainly bottom-living molluscs, crustaceans, worms and insect larvae, but large specimens—often more than 30 in. in length—feed on a wider range of organisms.

Anglers even find that sausage-meat is a successful bait for the large fish. For illustration, see FISH

Barberry *Berberis vulgaris*

This plant was a common hedgerow shrub in England and Wales until it was discovered to harbour the wheat disease, black rust fungus. Because of this, farmers destroy barberry on sight and it is now scarce nearly everywhere in the British Isles. It grows 6-7 ft tall with oval leaves sprouting in tufts along the stems, and three-forked spines pricking out from the base of each tuft. Barberry flowers have abundant nectar which attracts bees. When a bee enters a flower, the stamens close over it, covering it with pollen which the bee carries to the next flower it visits. The stamens can be made to move by touching them with a sharp twig or pencil.

The red, oblong fruits of barberry are edible but sour if eaten raw. However, they

can be cooked with sugar and made into jellies and jams. The wood is yellow and its inner bark yields a bright yellow dye. See also RUST FUNGUS

Bark

The protective tissue that grows on the outside of tree trunks and shrub stems. Bark retains moisture in the trunk; keeps out fungal spores that start decay; resists damage by insects and animals; and protects the tree from frost or excessive sunlight. Bark is so important that if a ring of it is cut away around the tree, growth will be checked or the tree will die.

On young trees the bark is smooth and thin, but as the tree grows and fresh layers of bark are formed they gradually expand, splitting the older, outer layer to form cambium bark. This creates a pattern of ribs or fissures which varies from tree to tree and—with colour differences—aids identification. Bark is rich in tannins—particularly that of the oak tree—and it is still in use for tanning hides to make leather.

Bark beetle

There are 66 species of bark beetle, known as Scolytidae, found in the British Isles. Some live in tunnels just beneath the bark, feeding on sap. Others—such as ambrosia beetles—burrow deeper into living wood, feeding not only on sap but on fungi that grow in the tunnels. Each male beetle lives with a number of females in a system of inter-communicating tunnels. The complexity of the system depends on the number of females—from one to 50—since each makes a separate tunnel.

The bark beetles' larvae are legless grubs,

Intricate trackways trace the damage inflicted on a tree by bark beetle larvae

each of which burrows at right angles away from its mother's tunnel. As the larva grows, it makes a longer and wider tunnel. Many bark beetles damage the trees they live in; one spreads Dutch elm disease. They are eaten by birds, particularly woodpeckers. See also AMBROSIA BEETLE and ELM

Barley

The most abundant cereal crop in the British Isles, barley is grown in most areas, but particularly in the south and east. United Kingdom production is about 8 million tons from 6 million acres, a yield of nearly 30 cwt an acre.

Barley is sometimes used for bread in parts of Europe and for a form of bread known as barley bannocks in Scotland. Some of the best quality is used to make malt for brewing beer. But it is grown mainly to feed livestock. The husk content of barley is much lower than that of oats, and it is an ideal cereal for pigs when crushed or soaked. Barley's protein matter turns into a solution when boiled. It is known as barley water and given to infants and invalids who require easily digested food rich in nitrogen.

The grain is encased in a hard, close-fitting shell, the tip of which is elongated and set with tiny hooks. It often has the shape of a cat's whiskers. There are two species. The most widely grown in Britain is *Hordeum distichum,* the grains of which are arranged in two rows, one on each side of the stem. The other species, *H. polystichum,* has six rows of grain, arranged in a seed-head similar to that of wheat. There are many cultivated varieties of each species which have developed from wild forms first cultivated more than 8000 years ago. Both species are believed to be derived from grasses native to northern Africa and western Asia.

Ripe barley is uncomfortable to handle, and the tips break into small pieces and cling to clothing. Barley is usually sown in spring, but there are winter varieties usually sown in October. Barley thrives on soils less fertile than those required for wheat. The straw makes good litter for livestock. See also CROPS

Barn

Although the word 'barn' is often used for any farm out-building, it is more precisely applied to one which stores grain or fodder. The word comes from the Old English *bern,* which meant 'barley house'. Barley was the main crop of the Anglo-Saxon farmers. The traditional barn is a long, rectangular building with large doors opposite each other in the central section. A wagon· loaded with corn would be brought through one of the doors, be unloaded on each side, and leave through the other door.

The middle section of the barn has a strong wooden floor, on which in winter the corn stored on either side was threshed by men with flails. The further parts of the barn

This 13th-century stone barn at Frocester, Gloucestershire is a typical tithe barn, once used to store tithes—one-tenth of the produce of farms in a parish, paid to support the church and clergy

were used to store the threshed straw, and also hay, rootcrops and sacks of grain. Lean-to sheds are often built along their sides to house farm machinery.

Many traditional barns survive. New barns are built mostly of concrete and steel and their designs reflect the changed needs of farmers. Many are fitted with drying machines to remove the moisture from cereals so that they can be stored without risk of deterioration. Others have air conditioning to provide a controlled environment in which poultry or pigs can be reared in batteries.

Open-sided barns, comprised simply of

The open-sided design of a Dutch barn permits adequate ventilation, and at the same time the roof provides adequate cover against rain and snow for crops such as hay

A modern barn in which the temperature is controlled automatically. Buildings such as this are used to store grain in an atmosphere that is free from excessive moisture

heavy pillars supporting a roof with the sides left open, are called Dutch barns. They are used to store hay, straw and silage. See also FARM, SILO

Barnacle

This sea creature encrusts rocks and the piles of piers. Barnacles are crustaceans, and although they look like limpets, which are molluscs, they are related to lobsters and shrimps. In some areas there may be as many as a thousand million along a mile stretch of shore.

Secretions from the antennae cement the barnacle's head to rock or timber. Its body has a wall of six outer plates with four smaller ones covering the top. Inside are six pairs of forked limbs. When the tide is in, these limbs, fringed with stiff hair, flick through a gap in the plates to sweep the water for food—minute plankton animals.

The most common barnacle is the acorn barnacle *Balanus balanoides* which grows to $\frac{1}{2}$ in. in diameter. The goose barnacle *Lepas anatifera* hangs from a tough stalk, like a miniature goose, formed from the front of the head. They were once thought to grow into barnacle geese by sprouting feathers. See also SEASHORE

How a barnacle looks when viewed from above and (right) with its limbs out searching for food

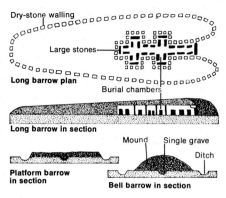

Dry-stone walling

Large stones

Long barrow plan

Burial chambers

Long barrow in section

Mound   Single grave

Ditch

**Platform barrow
in section**

Bell barrow in section

Long barrows were built from about 2300-1800
BC while round barrows, such as the bell and
platform types, were built during the Bronze
Age, from about 1800-550 BC

Barrow

There are more than 20,000 barrows, or
burial mounds, in the British Isles. They were
first raised over tombs in the late Stone Age,
more than 5000 years ago, and the practice
continued until the 7th century AD, well into
Saxon times. They are chiefly to be found in
areas of chalk and other limestone uplands
from Dorset to east Yorkshire.

The earliest were long barrows, up to 300
ft long and 100 ft wide with a height of about
12 ft, but there are many variations. In
contrast, the standard tomb of the Bronze
Age (*c.* 1800 BC to 550 BC) was the round
barrow, in which bodies were placed with
food and drink. The burial mounds of the
Iron Age, following the Bronze Age, were
smaller and round. The Romans also built
barrows, usually conical. Barrows were the
burial places of chiefs, their families and
other prominent people, and even the largest
rarely contain more than a dozen graves.

Bartsia, Red *Odontites verna*

This plant has almost square stems and
many branches which bear small flowers on
one side of the stem. It is prolific in arable
fields, roadsides and grassy places throughout the British Isles.

There are two forms of red bartsia, both
growing about 1 ft tall. In the north the
plants have branches which are straight and
upright, with flowers shorter than the bract
below. In the south the branches almost
make a right angle with the stem, but the
ends are upturned, and the flowers are

Northern red bartsia, left, with large leaf-like
bracts beneath the flowers

Dark, volcanic basalt rocks dominate the landscape in Co. Antrim, Northern Ireland

Basalt

This rock varies in colour from dark grey-
blue to pale blue, and from brown to black,
but it is mostly dark. It is an igneous rock
which was erupted in a molten state and
consists of a fine mass of crystals of minerals
(augite and feldspar and sometimes olivine)
formed by the rapid cooling of molten
material. Basalt is tough, and is sometimes
quarried for use as a road-making material.

The biggest areas of basalt in the British
Isles are in Antrim in Northern Ireland and
the Hebrides. In some places—at the Giant's
Causeway in Antrim and at Fingal's Cave on
the island of Staffa in the Hebrides—it can
be seen as six-sided columns. This structure
is the result of the molten material cooling
slowly.

longer than the bracts. *Odontites* was the name
given by the Romans to a plant supposed to
relieve toothache.

Basic slag

A common fertiliser used to provide soil
with phosphates and lime. Basic slag is a by-
product of the manufacture of steel, consisting largely of phosphorus and lime, and
occasionally traces of manganese. Slag is
supplied in the form of a fine, blackish powder which is insoluble in water.

Though to some extent superseded by
chemically balanced fertilisers, slag is still
used extensively on grassland. It is slow-
acting, and is usually applied in autumn.

Mixed with tar, basic slag forms the road-
surfacing material known as Tarmac.

Basil-thyme *Acinos arvensis*

The white mark on the lower lip of the basil-
thyme flower acts as a guide to bees which
visit the bloom to reach the nectar inside.
The plant grows to about 6 in. high and
has thyme-like leaves and spreading stems.
Its lilac-coloured flowers grow in whorls of
six round the stem.

Basil-thyme is common on bare ground on
dry chalk and limestone in south and east
England, but rare elsewhere.

The whole plant is aromatic, and the 16th-
century herbalist Gerard claimed that its
'seede cureth thee infirmities of the hart,
taketh away sorrowfulnesse which commeth
of melancholie, and maketh a man merrie
and glad'.

The white mark on the lower lip of the basil-
thyme flower guides bees to its nectar

Bass *Dicentrarchus labrax*

This is a prime sporting fish for the sea
angler, fighting well on light tackle and suspicious of all but the most natural baits.
The bass's slender, powerful body is brilliantly silver; and this, with its fighting
qualities, causes many anglers to call the fish
salmon-bass. It is found in the sea, in
estuaries and even in fresh water. It is most
abundant along the southern coasts. Bass
are predators. Adults feed on smaller fish,
such as sprats, sand-eels, and gobies, as well
as shrimps and crabs. Young bass prey on
smaller fry, especially small crustaceans.
They weigh up to 20 lb. and grow very
slowly.

Common British bats

There are over 900 different species of bats in the world, forming one of the largest orders of mammals. The majority live in the tropics and sub-tropics, 14 live in the British Isles. Of these the eight illustrated are the most common. These unmistakable, nocturnal creatures can be separated into two groups: the greater and lesser horseshoe bats belong to the family of leaf-nosed bats; the others to the family of simple-nosed bats. The only mammals that can fly, bats are able to exploit a source of food, flying insects, that their landbound insect-eating relatives are unable to catch. However, in winter when food is scarce, they must find a safe place to hibernate, such as in a cave or wood. The young, one per female, are born in the summer. They have an expected life span of at least 4½ years, much longer than other small mammals, but then bats sleep for most of their lives

Greater horseshoe bat
Rhinolophus ferrum-equinum
Length 4 in. Wingspan 14 in.

Natterer's bat
Myotis nattereri
Length 3½ in. Wingspan 10 in.

Lesser horseshoe bat
Rhinolophus hipposideros
Length 2¼ in. Wingspan 10 in.

Pipistrelle
Pipistrellus pipistrellus
Length 2 in. Wingspan 8 in.

Daubenton's bat
Myotis daubentoni
Length 3½ in. Wingspan 9½ in.

Noctule
Nyctalus noctula
Length 5 in. Wingspan 14-16 in.

Whiskered bat
Myotis mystacinus
Length 3½ in. Wingspan 9 in.

Long-eared bat
Plecotus auritus
Length 4 in. Wingspan 10 in.

Bat

This elusive nocturnal creature was once called flying mouse or flittermouse because of its fluttering flight; but it belongs to a distinct order of mammals, Chiroptera (meaning hand-winged), and is the only mammal that can fly.

The bat's greatly elongated finger joints form a framework across which the skin is stretched to make a wing. Flight, though not fast, is far more efficient than that of most birds and consists of rapid twists and turns. Bats have poor eyesight, but radar-like powers of echo-location enable them to catch their prey — mainly insects — in the air and to avoid obstacles.

Although bats can be heard squeaking, in flight they also make a high-pitched sound which humans cannot hear. This sound is reflected from any object — even an insect — in the bat's path. The bat hears the reflected sound and so locates the object. In Britain and other northern countries, bats hibernate. They hunt mostly at dusk and dawn, living mainly on insects.

British bats fall into two groups, the leaf-nosed or horseshoe bats and the typical bats. The first have curiously shaped noses, and the second a simple nose, also ear lobes.

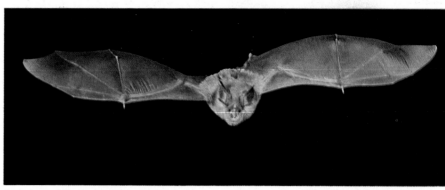

As darkness falls, the greater horseshoe bat — so named because of the shape of its nose — takes to the air to hunt for food. Its wings are 14 in. across, and it flies low — rarely above 10 ft

THE WING OF A BAT

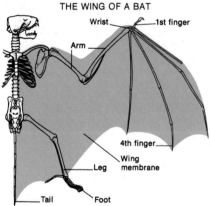

The wing of a bat is a double fold of skin supported by arm, hand, leg and tail bones

The greater horseshoe lives in colonies mostly in the hills of Wales and the West Country. Its smaller but more active relative, the lesser horseshoe, has similar habits, but is also found in North Wales and western Ireland.

Of the typical bats the pipistrelle is the smallest — weighing only $\frac{1}{2}$ oz. — and the most common in the British Isles. It is widespread and can be seen in woodlands and even town parks and squares. It is easily recognisable by its rather high and jerky flight. In summer it sleeps by day. It hibernates in hollow trees and buildings. Daubenton's bat, sometimes called the water bat, occurs throughout the British Isles. It usually lives near water and, unlike most bats, can be seen in daytime.

Natterer's bat is also widespread. Its flight is slow and it keeps to woodlands. The whiskered bat, which is largely confined to England, is solitary. The long-eared bat, found over most of Britain, sleeps and hibernates in cellars, caves and lofts. Britain's largest bat, with a wingspan of up to 16 in., is the noctule. It is a lowland bat which flies with steep dives.

At rest, bats hang upside-down because their limbs are so adapted for flying that their muscles cannot support their weight in a standing, sitting or lying position.

HUNTING IN THE DARK

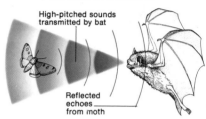

High-pitched sounds transmitted by bat

Reflected echoes from moth

To find food and avoid obstacles at night a bat emits high-pitched sounds. Echoes of the sound reflect from objects such as moths and are picked up by the bat which locates and catches its prey in flight

Bats mate in the autumn, but in some species the sperm is stored by the female until spring when she uses it to fertilise an egg. The young are born singly in June or July.

Young bats are blind and naked when born. They fall into a pouch which their mother makes by bending her tail forward as she hangs, for once head upwards. After cleaning the baby bat, the mother puts it to one of the two teats on her breast where it clings for about a fortnight. After this period, the mother hangs her offspring by its feet in a safe place while she flies in search of food. The young bat flies by autumn.

Battery cage see Chicken
Bay, Beach see Coast
Beagle see Dog

Bean

In the days before imported animal-feed protein — such as fish meal and soya-bean flour — beans were widely grown as a field crop to mix with cereals for livestock feeding. More recently they have been reintroduced as a break crop in soils exhausted by consecutive crops of cereals.

Beans have been cultivated in Britain since prehistoric times. Three types are now grown as market-garden crops. Broad beans, a summer vegetable with white flowers, are grown for their edible, fleshy seeds. They

are the hardiest of the three types and grow well on most soils. Both runner beans, with scarlet flowers, and French beans, which usually have white flowers, are grown for their long edible pods.

There are several varieties of field bean, which is the same species as the broad bean, only smaller. They have weak climbing or straggling stems. An especially small variety, the tic bean, is grown to feed racing and homing pigeons. Two other varieties are the winter bean and horse bean. The winter bean is hardy and slow-growing with short, cylindrical seeds. The horse bean is similar, but the seeds are flatter. The fragrant bean flowers are a valuable source of nectar for bees.

In spring the stately stems of the broad bean are covered in white flowers

Bearberry *Arctostaphylos uva-ursi*
This low-growing evergreen shrub has long, self-rooting branches, which form dense ground cover. The dark oval leaves have a conspicuous network of veins. The bell-like flowers appear in spring. The berries which the plant produces are an important food for grouse and other birds which live in the mountainous areas of northern Britain and western Ireland where bearberry flourishes.

Bearded tit see Thrush
Beck see Stream

Bedstraw
Bedstraws are easily recognised by their slender, often trailing, square stems with whorls of 4-12 leaves and clusters of tiny flowers. One or more of the dozen native British species occur all over the country.

The hedge bedstraw, which has white flowers, grows on roadside banks. Lady's bedstraw is one of the most common species of old grassland. It has narrow, needle-like, dark green leaves, 8-12 in a whorl, and yellow flowers.

The trailing heath bedstraw grows on heaths and moors where the soil is acid. The more upright marsh bedstraw grows in marshes and beside ponds. Both heath and marsh bedstraw bear white flowers during the summer.

Hedge bedstraw *Galium mollugo*   **Lady's bedstraw** *G. verum*

Heath bedstraw *G. saxatile*   **Marsh bedstraw** *G. palustre*

Bedstraws are a widespread group of small-flowered plants mostly with trailing stems

Bee
There are nearly 250 different types of bee in Britain, and fewer than 30 of them live and work together in colonies like the honey bee. Most bees are solitary insects which nest in holes in soil, sand, decaying stumps of wood, rock fissures or hollow stems, providing a store of food for their larvae but leaving them to hatch alone.

Social bees have developed a sophisticated system of group organisation, each colony

A bee collects pollen from a dandelion—brushing it from its hairy legs into sacs on its legs—to carry back to the nest. Pollen clinging to the bee's body pollinates other dandelions

feeding and caring for its larvae as they grow. A colony consists of three different types of bee: queen, worker and drone. The queen bee is the only fertilised female and her sole function is to lay eggs. The remainder of the females are the workers. They collect food, build the honeycomb—in which eggs are laid and honey and pollen stored—care for the eggs and do all the other work of the colony. The drones—males—help to maintain the hive temperature and provide the initial fertilisation of the queen. Towards the end of summer they are driven off by the workers to die.

A flourishing honey-bee colony may consist of up to 60,000 bees; a bumble-bee colony 20-150. In both cases it is the worker bees which form the majority.

All bees depend on flowers for food. The female bees of most species feed on nectar—a sweet juice secreted by many plants—collecting a surplus in a compartment of their stomachs; they return to the hive and regurgitate the surplus where, within a few days, it is converted by them into honey and stored in cells as food.

Some worker bees gather pollen, collecting it either on their furry bodies or in sacs on their hind legs. As the bees move from flower to flower, pollen—the male element in the reproduction of flowers—is transferred and the flowers are fertilised. Flowers depend on bees as much as bees depend on flowers.

Bees will sting only if provoked, and only the honey bee and a few other, larger species are capable of inflicting painful wounds.

Bumble and honey-bee workers exude thin scales of wax from the folds of skin on the undersides of their abdomens. The bees knead the wax into lumps with their jaws, using it to build nests or honeycombs.

THE BEE'S STING

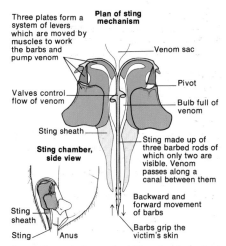

Three plates form a system of levers which are moved by muscles to work the barbs and pump venom

Plan of sting mechanism

Venom sac

Pivot

Valves control flow of venom

Bulb full of venom

Sting sheath

Sting chamber, side view

Sting made up of three barbed rods of which only two are visible. Venom passes along a canal between them

Backward and forward movement of barbs

Sting sheath

Sting   Anus

Barbs grip the victim's skin

Bees sting only if provoked. The sting is worked by a system of articulated plates which dig the barbs into the victim and pump in venom

Honey bee *Apis mellifera*

Most honey bees in Britain come from domestic hive colonies. Sometimes, however, a swarm which has left a hive will be found living in the hollow of a tree.

An average colony depends upon the efforts of nearly 60,000 workers (sterile females) for its food and care. Since workers as well as the queen live through the winter months, honey bees need to store large quantities of honey; in a good season the workers in a large hive may accumulate as much as 480 lb. of honey, using only a third for their own consumption.

A queen honey bee lives from four to five years; worker bees live a few weeks if hatched in summer, six or more months if hatched in autumn. A colony may outlive its queen or a new queen may take over, killing the old one. A new colony, however, can be formed only by a queen swarming with half of the hive's workers to a new site. Not until a young queen has been reared can a new colony be founded.

New colonies are formed to ensure the survival of the species, since their numbers

Drone male **Queen** fertile female **Worker** sterile female

A rigid caste system rules the life of the honey bee. Each bee—queen, drone and worker—has a specialist role in the hive

Queen honey bee and attendant workers and drones. The white cell contains a larva, the yellow ones pollen and the black ones honey. Cells sealed with wax contain pupating larvae

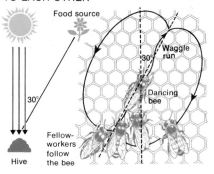

HOW BEES SPEAK TO EACH OTHER

If a honey bee finds a fresh source of food, she tells her fellow-workers where it is by dancing outside the hive or inside against the face of the comb. The round dance—quick, circular movements flown first in one direction, then the other—means food is within 100 yds or so. The waggle dance—a figure-of-eight with the loops separated by a straight run—means the food is further away. The bee wags her body on the straight run only. If she dances upwards on the comb the food is in the direction of the sun. Upward wagging runs 30 degrees to the right of the vertical means food is 30 degrees to the right of the sun

can be drastically reduced by bad summers, which cause famine, or disease.

The workers care for the larvae, feeding them honey, pollen and food juice—a milky substance rich in nutrition produced by glands in the workers' mouths. Eggs destined to become queens are given larger cells and larger quantities of the food juice. The queens eventually produce a similar but more concentrated substance, sometimes called royal jelly, that calms the workers in a hive—by inhibiting the growth of their ovaries—and preventing them from rearing new queens.

As the queen grooms herself, the royal jelly coats her body. The workers group around the queen, licking off the jelly. When she ages and the supply begins to fail the workers immediately begin rearing new queens; although only one is needed, several are reared in case a single queen should die.

About the end of May, when the young queens are ready to emerge from their cells, many of the workers grow restless and start to gather around the entrance to the hive. Suddenly, and by instinct, they rush into the hive and fill their honey-sacs from the honey cells in readiness for their departure. Half the workers then gather excitedly outside the hive until the queen emerges, when they cluster around her in a thick swarm, whirling and buzzing up into the air.

The swarm, led by the queen, settles on the branch of a nearby tree or fence and waits while a few of the workers go scouting to find a suitable nesting site for a permanent home.

About 7-14 days after the swarm has left the old hive, one of the virgin queens leaves to mate with a drone. Mating never occurs in the hive.

Once fertilised—she mates only once in her life and stores the sperm in her body—the new queen returns to the hive and the surplus queens are destroyed by the workers. The queen will only leave the hive again if her throne is threatened by a young queen. It is when this happens that swarming takes place and the young queen takes over the

remainder of the colony in the old hive.

The fertilised queen starts laying from early spring to late autumn at a maximum rate of 1500 eggs a day—approximately one every minute. By controlling the release of the sperm inside her, the queen can lay fertilised or unfertilised eggs. Unfertilised eggs—from which males develop—are laid in special cells which are larger than the average. Thus, although it is the queen who decides which eggs are to be fertilised, the worker-bees are able to influence her decision—according to the needs of the hive—by the type of cells they provide.

Why it is that a bee's sex is determined by fertilisation is not known.

Bumble bee

The 16 species of bumble bees include Britain's largest bee, the common bumble bee *Bombus terrestris*, and *B. lapidarius*, which both have queens about $\frac{7}{8}$ in. long. Bumble bees live in colonies of up to 150 individuals. Each colony lasts only one season, all the members, except new queens, dying off in the autumn. The new queens hibernate, waking in the spring to found new colonies. Each queen makes a nest between tufts of grass in a meadow, a deserted mouse-hole or a rock crevice.

She uses a mixture of pollen, resin and wax to build about a dozen small cells in which she lays eggs or stores honey. When the eggs hatch, the larvae develop into small, undernourished females having stunted ovaries. These sterile bees become the first generation of workers, foraging for food and increasing the size of the nest, while the queen lays more eggs. With more food and larger cells the next generation of larvae develop into bigger and healthier workers.

A bumble-bee's nest when complete is about the size of a man's fist. It may contain from 20 to 150 bees. Late in summer some of the eggs develop into queen bees and drones, which ultimately fly and mate. Shortly after mating the drones die, and the fertilised queens then seek a hibernation site. All the workers die too, and the nest finally disintegrates.

As a bumble bee sucks nectar, pollen rubs off on its legs which become involuntary pollinators

Bumble Queen
B. terrestris

Cuckoo Queen
P. vestalis

Parasites in disguise—cuckoo bees mimic the bumble bees on which they prey

Cuckoo bee

There are six species of cuckoo bee, each closely resembling one of the bumble-bee species; for example, *Psithyrus vestalis* is similar to the common bumble bee.

Like the bird after which it is named, the cuckoo bee is unable to feed and care for its young; it has less fur on its body than bumble bees and no pollen-collecting sacs on its legs, so each female occupies a bumble-bee nest in early summer. At first the cuckoo-bee female is attacked by the bumble-bee workers but she is eventually accepted by the colony as their queen. She then kills the bumble-bee queen and starts laying eggs which are cared for by the bumble-bee workers.

Cuckoo-bee eggs develop into queens and drones only, which eventually leave the nest to pair and mate. Once queens have been fertilised they hibernate until the following spring; the drones die after mating.

Cuckoo bees are found mainly in southern England.

SOLITARY BEES

female · male · female

Leaf-cutter bee
Megachile centuncularis

Wool carder bee
Anthidium manicatum

Mining bee
Andrena haemorrhoa

Most British bees do not live in organised communities but, like these three, live alone

Wool carder bee *Anthidium manicatum*

Sometimes called the hoop shaver, the wool carder bee resembles the honey bee in shape, but has only a fairly light covering of brown hairs over its back. Unlike other British bees the male, $\frac{2}{3}$ in. long, is bigger than the female, which grows to $\frac{1}{2}$ in. A solitary bee, the wool carder nests in holes in trees, often in those left by boring beetles or goat-moth caterpillars. The female strips the down from the stems and leaves of such plants as mullein and campion. She uses this down to upholster each hole and the flimsy cells she builds within them. The upper joints of the female's legs are shaped to help her carry a ball of down, which may be as large as herself.

The wool carder is found chiefly in the south of England.

Leaf-cutter bee

Neat oval pieces missing from the edges of rose and other leaves are a sign of the leaf-cutter bee. The pieces are cut out by the female bee, who holds on to the leaf with her legs while using her powerful scissor-like jaws. She rolls the pieces into cylinders and flies back with them to line her nest. This is a tunnel, up to a foot long, usually in rotten wood. Leaf-cutter bees often bore their own tunnels, though they will also use tunnels left by other insects or, on occasions, burrow into soil or sand. Sometimes they nest in keyholes.

One end of the tunnel is sealed with a piece of leaf and a store of honey and pollen is placed against it. An egg is laid on the food and the cell sealed with another piece of leaf. Additional cells, provided

Collecting nest material, an industrious leaf-cutter bee takes a neat slice out of a rose leaf

with food and eggs, are constructed along the length of the tunnel. Several tunnels, made by the same bee, may be made adjoining each other. When the last tunnel is full the bee flies away and dies.

The eggs hatch into larvae which feed on the honey and pollen until they enter the pupa, or resting stage. The new bees emerge from the tunnel the following spring—the occupant of the last cell emerging first. The first bees are always males; females, who form the majority of the nest, leave last.

The most common British species is *Megachile centuncularis*. There are eight other species, all of which look like honey bees but have larger heads and well-developed jaws. All live mainly in southern England and are rare elsewhere.

In some areas of the United States, farmers provide leaf-cutter bees with ready-made burrows to pollinate crops.

Mining bee

Similar to honey bees but solitary, smaller and less furry, mining bees nest in the ground. There are more than 100 species scattered throughout the British Isles, except in the Shetlands. *Andrena armata*—sometimes called the lawn bee—nests in lawns raising conical piles of soil; others, such as *Halictus xanthopus,* prefer sandy soil. All mining bees are important pollinators of fruit trees.

Each female makes her own burrow, sometimes 2 ft deep. She digs with her fore feet and brushes the earth behind her with her hind feet. The earth is left scattered around the entrance hole, helping to conceal it. Inside the burrow, the female makes three to six cells, provisioning each with nectar and pollen rolled into a ball. Every time she visits a flower she brings back half her own weight in pollen. She lays an egg on each ball and closes the cells. Afterwards, she returns to the surface and dies. In suitable areas many of these bees nest close to one another.

UNDERGROUND NEST

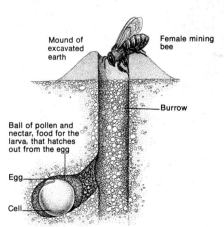

Mound of excavated earth

Female mining bee

Burrow

Ball of pollen and nectar, food for the larva, that hatches out from the egg

Egg

Cell

The female mining bee makes a nest underground and lays each egg on a ball of pollen and nectar

41

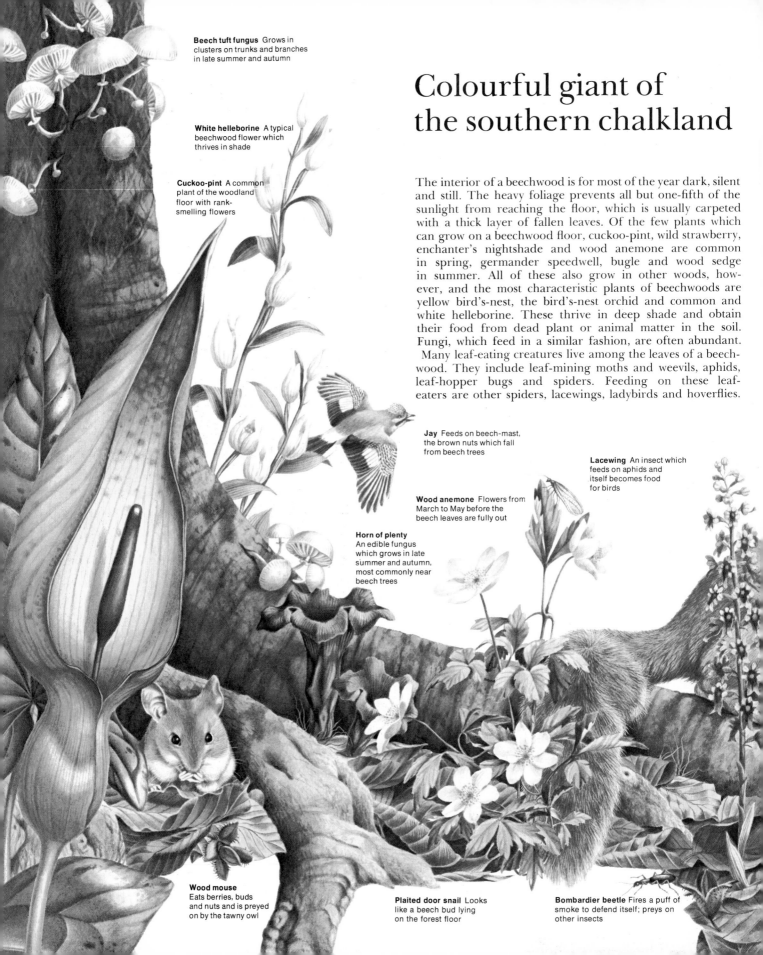

Beech tuft fungus Grows in clusters on trunks and branches in late summer and autumn

White helleborine A typical beechwood flower which thrives in shade

Cuckoo-pint A common plant of the woodland floor with rank-smelling flowers

Colourful giant of the southern chalkland

The interior of a beechwood is for most of the year dark, silent and still. The heavy foliage prevents all but one-fifth of the sunlight from reaching the floor, which is usually carpeted with a thick layer of fallen leaves. Of the few plants which can grow on a beechwood floor, cuckoo-pint, wild strawberry, enchanter's nightshade and wood anemone are common in spring, germander speedwell, bugle and wood sedge in summer. All of these also grow in other woods, however, and the most characteristic plants of beechwoods are yellow bird's-nest, the bird's-nest orchid and common and white helleborine. These thrive in deep shade and obtain their food from dead plant or animal matter in the soil. Fungi, which feed in a similar fashion, are often abundant.

Many leaf-eating creatures live among the leaves of a beechwood. They include leaf-mining moths and weevils, aphids, leaf-hopper bugs and spiders. Feeding on these leaf-eaters are other spiders, lacewings, ladybirds and hoverflies.

Jay Feeds on beech-mast, the brown nuts which fall from beech trees

Lacewing An insect which feeds on aphids and itself becomes food for birds

Wood anemone Flowers from March to May before the beech leaves are fully out

Horn of plenty An edible fungus which grows in late summer and autumn, most commonly near beech trees

Wood mouse Eats berries, buds and nuts and is preyed on by the tawny owl

Plaited door snail Looks like a beech bud lying on the forest floor

Bombardier beetle Fires a puff of smoke to defend itself; preys on other insects

These in turn form the prey of titmice and other small birds. The beechwood floor, like that of all woodland, is rich in animals. Among the most common are woodmice, bank voles, badgers, snails, spiders, beetles and earthworms. Dead and dying trees support a multitude of insects and other invertebrates — about one-fifth of the wood's animal life. Among the most common are centipedes, earwigs, woodlice, stag-beetles, crane-flies and wasps.

The finest beechwoods in Britain grow on the escarpment of the limestone Cotswolds near Cheltenham. Other beechwoods dominate the crests of chalk country — the North Downs in Kent and Surrey, the South Downs of Sussex, the Downs of Hampshire, Dorset and Wiltshire and the Chiltern Hills.

Beech *Fagus sylvatica* is a native tree. It does not reproduce naturally north of the Midlands and South Wales because it needs warm summers to ripen its seeds, but it has been planted throughout Britain and Ireland. It is easily recognised by its smooth, grey bark and slender, slightly zigzag twigs which bear at each angle a thin-pointed, brown-scaled bud. The oval leaves are pale green in spring, dark green in summer and golden-brown before they fall in autumn. These leaves are tough and do not rot easily. This is the chief reason why they form litter as much as 4 in. deep.

In May the short-lived male catkins appear in groups of two or three; each is a tassel of many stamens that sheds yellow pollen which is spread by the wind. Female catkins, which grow on the same tree, are small, green and bud-shaped and expand during summer to green husks bearing soft spines. They open to release triangular brown nuts — sometimes called beech-mast — which fall and are eaten by squirrels,

woodmice, jays, rooks, pheasants, wood pigeons, great tits, chaffinches and bramblings. Years ago the nuts were valued as food for pigs, and even today commoners drive their pigs into parts of the New Forest in Hampshire for this purpose. Seedlings, which sprout from some nuts, may grow into trees 140 ft tall that live for more than 200 years. The dense, even-textured timber of beech is much used for furniture, but is rarely used out of doors because it rots quickly.

The name beech comes from the Old English *bece*. Variations of the word survive in place-names such as Buckinghamshire, whose furniture industry was founded on the Chiltern beechwoods.

THE BEECHWOOD FLOOR

Thin shafts of light, that penetrate the dense beech foliage, make sunlit pools on the woodland floor where plants can grow. The remainder of the floor is shaded and lifeless

Leaf litter. The shade inhibits decay, so the leaves take a long time to decompose

Humus. The large animal population hidden beneath the litter eventually decomposes the leaves and fallen branches into humus

Soil and subsoil. Beech roots spread horizontally, growing well in a shallow layer of fertile loam

Beech thrives on a variety of soils especially loam, a mixture of clay, sand and humus. Its shallow roots allow few other trees to grow

Bird's-nest orchid Obtains its food from dead plant or animal matter

Grey squirrel Damages trees by gnawing at the sappy layers beneath the bark

Fungus (*Russula mairei*) Smells of honey, but if eaten can cause sickness

As much as 80 per cent of the sunlight is cut off by the heavy foliage in a beechwood. As a result, a thick carpet of fallen leaves and twigs is formed and few green plants grow

Beefly

There are 12 species of British beefly—two-winged flies with furry bodies. Not only do they look like bees, but they behave like them, feeding from flowers with their tubular mouth-parts. Unlike bees, however, their mouth-parts, long slender probosces, stick out straight in front of the head, even when not engaged in feeding.

The flies scatter their eggs in areas in which solitary bees are nesting and the larvae find their way into the bee cells and feed by sucking the bee larvae dry.

Beeflies are more common in the south of England than elsewhere. Despite their formidable appearance they are harmless to man.

Beef shorthorn see Cattle

Beefsteak fungus

This fungus appears in late summer and autumn on living broad-leaved trees—usually on oak and occasionally on sweet chestnut. It reaches full size—up to 12 in. across—in two weeks.

The upper surface of the tongue-shaped fruit body is reddish-brown. It is sticky and jelly-like and is also slightly rough to the touch owing to a mat of short, tufted hair. On the underside are small, pale yellow pores which become reddish when damaged. The inner flesh resembles red meat and yields a red juice when cut.

The rich brown timber produced by trees on which the fungus has grown is known as brown oak and is much valued by cabinet-makers. Beefsteak fungus is edible, but even when young, no amount of cooking will make it tasty. See also FUNGUS

Bee moth

Three moths have caterpillars that prey on bee-hives or nests. All members of the Pyralid family, these moths are green-brown with a wing-span of about 1 in.

The bee moth is common throughout the British Isles. It attacks the nests of wasps and bumble bees—not those of honey bees—and most often preys on nests made at or above ground level. The caterpillars make silken tunnels through the nest. At first they feed mainly on droppings or debris but later they attack the honeycomb and bee larvae. Fully grown by autumn, the caterpillar then spins a silken cocoon in which it rests—still in the nest—until it turns into a chrysalis in the spring. The moth emerges in June.

The honey moth is comparatively rare in

Honey moth
Achroia grisella

Honeycomb moth
Galleria mellonella

Bee moth
Aphoma sociella

Scotland but otherwise widespread. Its larvae are parasites of honey bees, feeding on the wax of the honeycomb, brood cells and dead insects. They prefer old wax and can destroy an old colony by driving the bees away. The moths fly around the hives from June to October. Another serious pest of the honey bee is the honeycomb moth. The caterpillars feed on the wax of the honeycomb, leaving a trail of food galleries, webs and excrement, and spoiling the honey. Their life cycle is like that of the bee moth.

Beet, Sea *Beta vulgaris*

This common seashore plant is the wild ancestor of beetroot, sugar beet and mangold. It is found on cliffs and rocky and muddy shores in most places, though it is rare in Scotland. Sea beet's base leaves are large, about 5 in. long and 3 in. wide. The leaves grow smaller along the stem, which can be 1-4 ft long. Clusters of small green flowers appear from July to September where the leaves join the stem. See also SUGAR BEET

Hardened forewings, common to all beetles, are raised to reveal the cockchafer's flying wings

Beetle

About 3700 species of beetles have been found in the British Isles. They come in an immense variety of shapes and sizes—from the 2½ in. long stag beetle to the flea beetle, which can measure less than $\frac{1}{30}$ in. A small suburban garden is likely to have at least 20 sorts of beetle, and any small wood will contain several hundred species.

Like most insects, beetles have two pairs of wings, but only the hind pair are used for flying. The forewings are hardened, often brightly coloured, wing cases which protect the body and cover the delicate hind wings when the beetle is not flying. Most species can fly, even water beetles, but a few, such as the ground beetles, have lost this ability.

The beetle's life history includes an egg, larva, pupa and adult stage. The larvae are as varied as the adults, ranging from the active predatory ground beetle larva to the legless weevil grub which lives surrounded by plant food and never needs to move. Like all larvae they are wingless and none has

more than six legs. The pupae are pale and soft and usually found on plants or in the soil.

All beetles have mouth-parts which can be used for biting and chewing. Many, such as tiger beetles, prey on other insects. Weevils are plant feeders, between their many species exploiting almost every part of a plant. Wood, either rotting or still growing, provides food for stag beetles and many others. There are also beetles, like the burying beetles, which scavenge dead animals, recycling their remains into the life of the countryside.

Most beetles pass their lives without attracting the attention of man; but wood-boring beetles damage growing trees, furniture and house timber, and plant-eaters, of course, attack crops. On the other hand, many predators help to keep insect pests in check, especially the aphid-eating ladybirds. No beetle is dangerous to man. But some bite if handled, and the blister beetle emits a substance which causes small blisters.

Common beetles of the British Isles

Beetles are the largest group of animals in the world. There are 250,000 species, of which 3700 live in the British Isles. Those shown in the chart are a representative selection of the common and spectacular British species. Each beetle named in the chart has a separate entry

Carnivores

Tiger beetle   **Glow-worm**
F   M
Snail beetle   **Ladybird**   **Soldier beetle**   **Devil's coach horse**

Wood-eating beetles

Longhorn beetle
Musk beetle
Bark beetle
Elm bark beetle
Cardinal beetle
Deathwatch beetle
Powder post beetle
Furniture beetle
Stag beetle

Plant feeders

Weevil
Large pine weevil
Flea beetle
Potato flea beetle
Australian fungus beetle
Rose beetle
Cockchafer
Bloody-nosed beetle
Colorado beetle
Click beetle
Redbrown skipjack
Blister beetle
Oil beetle

Scavengers

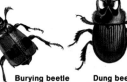

Ground beetle
Violet ground beetle
Bombardier beetle
Rove beetle
Churchyard beetle
Burying beetle
Sexton beetle
Dung beetle
Minotaur beetle
Scavenger beetle

Water beetles

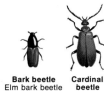
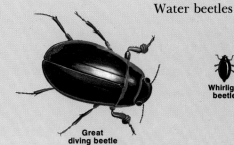

Screech beetle
Great diving beetle
Whirligig beetle
Great silver water beetle

45

Belladonna see Nightshade
Bellbine see Bindweed

Bellflower

The garden Canterbury bell is one of the bellflowers which grow wild, particularly on railway embankments in south-east England, where seed has blown from nearby gardens. It produces blue-purple and occasionally white flowers, 1-1½ in. long, in mid-summer. Its scientific name, *Campanula*, is derived from the Latin *campana*, a bell.

There are three other fairly common species which all produce similar blue-purple, bell-like flowers in summer.

The nettle-leaved bellflower, also called bats in the belfry, has nettle-shaped leaves. It reaches 3 ft and is found in woods on clay soil in southern England.

The stately giant bellflower grows in the woods of northern England and southern Scotland. It has flowers as big as the Canterbury bell.

The clustered bellflower is a small plant, rarely exceeding 12 in. in height, but with a cluster of intensely coloured flowers at the top of the stem. It can be found growing on chalk downs and limestone grasslands in England.

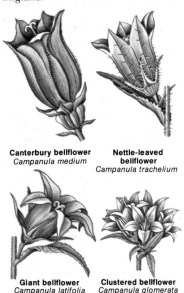

Canterbury bellflower
Campanula medium

Nettle-leaved bellflower
Campanula trachelium

Giant bellflower
Campanula latifolia

Clustered bellflower
Campanula glomerata

The four most common bellflowers growing in Britain. Several rare species also occur

Bell-wether see Sheep

Beltane fire

These are bonfires dating from pre-Christian times that were traditionally lit at the beginning of the summer, often on May 1. Beltane was an ancient Celtic festival, but the name also became linked with the mid-summer fires, still lit in many places such as Whalton in Northumberland. The name is still used for May Day in some Gaelic-speaking parts of Scotland.

There is a link between the Beltane fire and the moving of cattle to summer pastures in the hills. Often two fires were lit and livestock were driven between them as a safeguard against disease—a practice that continued in parts of Ireland and Scotland until the late 19th century. Beltane bannocks or oatcakes are still baked in parts of Scotland to mark the onset of summer.

Beltane has been traditionally linked with Baal, a Phoenician god, but it is more likely to be associated with the Celtic sun god Beal.

Belted Galloway see Cattle

Bench mark

An Ordnance Survey arrowhead sign found on walls, bridges, churches and specially erected concrete posts where the altitude above sea-level has been accurately measured by surveyors. The arrowhead points to a horizontal line above it which marks the exact altitude. At places below sea-level the arrowhead points down. The marks are mapped on the large-scale Ordnance Survey maps, such as the 6 in. and 25 in. to the mile.

When a surveyor takes other altitude measurements from the mark, an angle-iron is fixed at the level of the horizontal bar to form a temporary bracket or 'bench' which supports the levelling instrument.

Bent see Grass
Berry see p. 48

Betony *Stachys officinalis*

Herbalists have treasured betony since ancient times as a remedy for many ills, especially for reducing fevers. The Romans prescribed it for digestive troubles and liver complaints. The dried leaves can be used as a substitute for tea, or they can be powdered as a snuff.

It may be found in the ruins of abbeys, where it was planted as a charm—hence its other name, bishopwort.

Growing from 6 in. to 24 in., it is common in woods and poor grassland in England and Wales, but scarce in Scotland and Ireland.

Betony has square stems and bears bright maroon flowers from June to September. The leaves are stalked, and have rounded teeth with blunt tips.

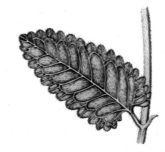

Betony leaves are heavily veined and coarsely toothed, and the stems are square

Bib *Trisopterus luscus*

The barbel or feeler under the chin of the bib marks it as a member of the cod family. It is common in shallow water all around the British coast and is frequently caught by trawlers, as well as anglers on rocky shores. Bibs living around rocks are a beautiful coppery tint with five darker broad crossbands, while those on sandy bottoms are dull fawn and rarely show these bands.

The bib, which grows to about 16 in., skims slowly over the sea-bed with its chin barbel projecting forwards and the rays of its pelvic fins extended. These rays and the barbel have taste organs with which the fish detects buried food. Not surprisingly, most of the bib's food is bottom-dwelling—worms, crabs and shrimps—although the larger specimens also eat fish. The bib is sometimes known as the pout or pouting. For illustration, see FISH

Biennial see Glossary

Bilberry *Vaccinium myrtillus*

A low, spreading shrub, up to 2 ft tall, bilberry is one of the most common plants of moorlands and mountains, growing among the heather nearly everywhere. The green-pink bell-shaped flowers appear from April to June and are followed in July by round blue-black berries covered with a grape-like bloom. The berries, which can be used to make jam, are an important part of

Bilberry blooms wherever there is peaty soil, even on mountains up to 3500 ft

the diet of grouse and other moorland birds.

Bilberry is known as whortleberry in some parts of England: this is a corruption of myrtleberry from its Latin name. Among its many other local names are whorts, bloomberry and blaeberry, from the old Scandinavian *blaa*, meaning dark blue.

Billhook

A short-handled chopping tool, with a double-edged blade about 9 in. long, used for general work on a farm including weed-cutting and making bean or hop poles. Bill-hooks are also used by skilled craftsmen for splitting hazel rods for hurdles, shaping fence stakes and palings, and for making and shaping hedges.

Most billhooks have a wide blade with a small hook at the end, but there are dif-ferent designs in different regions; there are said to be at least 40 different types in Britain.

The development of power-driven hedge-cutters has robbed the billhook of much work, but it is still an important tool on most farms.

Bindweed

Black bindweed flourishes in arable fields and gardens throughout lowland Britain. It has shiny stems which, unlike those of other bindweeds, twine in a clockwise direction. The leaves look like arrowheads and the small green flowers are not easily seen.

Black bindweed is a serious weed on farm-land, growing up to 4 ft tall. In summer its twining stems compete with the corn, re-ducing the yield. In autumn its shining, black, triangular fruits are poisonous to animals if eaten in large quantities.

A very persistent and troublesome weed reaching 2 ft, field bindweed has arrowhead leaves like those of black bindweed, but differs in its handsome pink or white bell-like flowers. Field bindweed has stout under-ground stems which often reach a depth of more than 6 ft, and any part of these stems can form a new plant if broken off.

It climbs by twining its stem anti-clockwise around other plants. The flowers have a strong perfume which attracts many pollin-ating insects. Field bindweed is found com-monly in lowland Britain in arable fields and gardens, on roadsides and railway banks, and among grass near the sea. It is also known as small bindweed, bellbine, cornbine or devil's-guts.

Hedge bindweed twines up to 10 ft high through hedges. Its scentless, bell-shaped flowers are up to 2 in. across. Some are pure white, while others are pink with alter-nating white bands. They remain open on fine nights, when they are pollinated by moths.

Farmers discourage the growth of bindweed by spraying with a herbicide when the weed is approaching the flowering stage.

Sea bindweed creeps over sand-dunes round most of the coast. Above ground it has fleshy, kidney-shaped leaves and funnel-shaped pink flowers up to 1½ in. across, which appear from June to September. Its stems are often half buried in the sand and below ground, its long white runners help to bind the dunes.

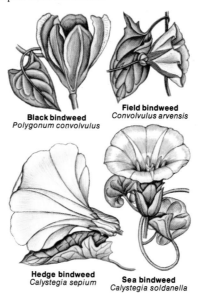

Black bindweed
Polygonum convolvulus

Field bindweed
Convolvulus arvensis

Hedge bindweed
Calystegia sepium

Sea bindweed
Calystegia soldanella

Except for sea bindweed, these flowers are all troublesome weeds of farm and garden

Bioluminescence see Night

Birch

It is easy to recognise birch by the white bark of its trunk and its long, whip-like twigs, which are purple-brown. In winter, these twigs bear minute alternate buds, which open in spring to display dainty oval or diamond-shaped pale green leaves, long-stalked with toothed edges. Birch leaves turn golden-brown in autumn.

Except in gardens and parks, birch is rarely planted. Foresters find that more than enough are seeded naturally, and they often cut it out as a weed. It is one of the hardiest trees in the world and grows further north and, with the mountain ash, higher up mountains than any other species. Birch will soon establish itself on bare land, and often spreads on to commons where animals no longer graze.

Common birch *Betula pendula* has warty swellings on smooth twigs; the less common hairy birch *B. pubescens* is named after its hairy twigs; shrubby dwarf birch *B. nana* grows in northern Scotland. Common birch is sometimes called silver birch because of its particularly bright bark, but the term is widely used for all the birches, which all have white bark. As they mature, the bark becomes covered with dark patches, which are diamond-shaped on the common birch.

In winter, male catkins hang from leafless twigs, like grey lambs' tails. In April, as the leaves expand, these catkins shed golden

The hairy birch has downy twigs with upright branches and bark that peels easily

pollen which the wind carries to female catkins, short, scaly green spikes, which open with the leaves, on the same tree. After fertilisation these female structures swell and, in their turn, droop in lamb's-tail fashion. In September they break up, scattering myriad wind-borne winged seeds all through the woods. The following spring tiny seedlings appear, each starting life with two minute, rounded seed-leaves.

Birch never becomes large or long-lived; 80 ft is a good height and 60 years a long life-span. Dwarf birch rarely exceeds 4 ft. Most old trees are invaded by wood-rotting fungi such as the birch bracket *Polyporus betulinus*. The fungi weaken the trees by inner decay, eventually killing them. The white-spotted scarlet caps of the fly agaric often grow under birch trees, feeding on their roots. But this fungus, though poisonous to man, does not harm the trees.

The timber is uniform pale brown, un-attractive, and not naturally durable out of doors. But it is hard and was once used for turned items like cotton reels, tool handles and spoons, and cottage furniture. Nowadays it is used for paper pulp or as firewood, since it burns well. Twigs are made into besoms, or garden brooms.

Birchwoods are valued mainly for their beauty and for the shelter they give in winter to sheep, cattle and deer, especially in the Scottish Highlands.

Birch or birk, from Old English *birce*, ap-pears in many place names. Birkenhead, Cheshire means 'headland overgrown with birch'; Birchanger, Essex is 'birch slope'.

Sloes, the fruits of the blackthorn, ripen in hedgerows throughout the British Isles in September. Though edible, sloes are acid-tasting, and are used only to make wine and to flavour gin

Berries and fruits

The familiar wild blackberry is just one of many of the berries seen ripening in the hedgerows which can be eaten by man; many others, however, are poisonous.

Every flowering plant produces a fruit, containing the seed which ensures the survival of the species. Some of these fruits swell and become attractive, usually to encourage animals to carry them away and eat the juicy portion but leave or excrete the pip or stone to germinate far from the parent plant.

These swollen or succulent fruits are of two main kinds: the true fruits and the false ones.

True succulent fruits develop solely from the ovary of a flower; and there are two types among wild plants, the drupe and the berry. The drupe has a single stone or pip in the centre as in cherries and plums. Many hedgerow plants, such as blackberries and raspberries, bear fruits formed from a collection of drupes. This type of fruit has many seeds, each of which is enclosed in a separate case of succulent pulp.

Berries also have many seeds, but they differ from drupes in that all the seeds are contained in a single case. Most wild fruits in the British Isles are berries, including bilberries, cranberries, gooseberries and blackcurrants.

The false succulent fruits are those which

HOW BERRIES ARE CONSTRUCTED

Drupe   Multi-drupe

Berry   False fruit   Composite

True fruits are drupes with one seed, or berries with many. False fruits develop from parts other than the ovary. The strawberry's true fruits are its surface pips

develop from parts of the flower other than the ovary. In the rose family the receptacle below the petals, which contains the ovaries, also swells to form the fruit, or rose hip. Apples and pears also have this structure, but among wild fruits the rose hip is the most familiar.

The strawberry is a curious kind of false fruit. Each pip is set in a fleshy pulp which develops from the receptacle on which these pips were arranged. The strawberry is therefore composed of many false fruits.

Edible berries

Cowberry The acid fruits are common on moors and in woods in northern Britain and Ireland

Wild strawberry This grows in woods and shady hedgerows, and bears fruits from June to October

Blackberry There are hundreds of species in the British Isles. Fruits ripen from August to October

Cloudberry A low-growing plant of boggy moorland. It fruits in June and July

Cranberry The fruits, which appear from June to August, are widespread on moorland

Bilberry The best fruits are found in sheltered places on mountains from July onwards

Elderberry The berries ripen from July to September in hedgerows and woods

Raspberry The fruits, which grow on tall canes, appear in all parts of the British Isles from June

Poisonous and inedible berries

Hawthorn, inedible Haws, the fruits of hawthorn —widespread in the British Isles—appear from July to December

Rowan, inedible These berries, which ripen from July to September, are unpleasant when raw, but make a tasty jelly

Rose hips, inedible Hips yield Vitamin C when processed. They appear from July to October, often remaining after leaves fall

Guelder rose, poisonous Found in hedges and woods throughout Britain, the guelder rose bears berries from July to October

Spindle tree, poisonous Growing in chalky areas, spindle trees bear their berries from July to November

Woody nightshade, poisonous Growing in damp, shady places in England and Wales, the berries start to appear in September

White bryony, poisonous The fruits of this hedge-climber appear from July to October, often remaining after the leaves fall

Holly, poisonous Holly trees grow throughout the British Isles. The berries remain on the trees until February

Black nightshade, poisonous A weed of cultivated land, found only in southern England. It fruits from August onwards

Black bryony, poisonous Found only in England and Wales, black bryony is a hedgerow climber, fruiting September onwards

Privet, poisonous The berries appear from July to November. Privet only grows wild on chalky soil in southern England

Deadly nightshade, poisonous Growing by roadsides and wood margins in England and Wales, its berries ripen in August

49

The precision of flight: a great tit bringing food to its nest shows how wing and tail feathers are spread out to increase air resistance and give the maximum braking effect when coming in to land

Bird

Birds are among the most numerous, widespread and noticeable of all creatures on earth. There are some 8600 living species in the world, of which about 470 have been recorded in Britain and Ireland. This 470 includes many birds from far off places, some of which appear in Britain year after year, while others are only occasional visitors. But to rank as truly British, a bird must breed in the British Isles. The rarest bird in this category is the snowy owl, a pair of which has bred on the island of Fetlar in the Shetlands since the late 1960's. On the other hand, the house sparrow, chaffinch, blackbird and starling, each with a population of about 10 million, are Britain's most numerous birds. There may be as many as 100 million birds in the British Isles.

Over an immense period of time, birds evolved from reptiles; the scales on their legs are evidence of this remote ancestry. Feathers, which enable birds to fly, probably evolved from scales as a temperature control device, about 200 million years ago. Feathers vary enormously, from the semi-fur of penguins to the huge, closely meshed wing feathers of eagles. Not all birds can fly, but there are no flightless species in Britain.

The number of feathers on a bird varies according to its size and species; for instance, a swan may have more than 25,000, while a thrush has about 2000. The majority of feathers are small, and can be fluffed-up in cold weather to provide insulation. Those concerned with flight are the most important. A bird flies by flapping its wings to create an airstream against which it can launch itself, and from which the aerodynamic curve of its spread wings can gain and maintain lift.

Only some 50 feathers are designed for flight. Those of the wing are divided into primaries—the large, strong feathers on the outer trailing edge which propel the bird and enable it to change direction—and secondaries along the inner trailing edge, which provide lift. The tail feathers act as a rudder, aiding changes of direction and braking.

The larger British birds—such as gulls, cranes, ducks, geese and swans—often fly together in V-shaped formation, each bird gaining some extra aerodynamic power from the slipstream of the bird in front. From time to time the leading bird drops back to allow another to take the lead and maintain the punishing pace.

Smaller birds also flock together but—since they create little useful slipstream—it is probably an instinctive means of defence against birds of prey.

The flight endurance of some species is remarkable. The Manx shearwater roams on the strong winds of the open sea, not coming to land except to breed. It is so specialised for an oceanic life that it is thoroughly awkward on land and only able to shuffle to and from its nesting site. Buzzards, too, are masters of the air, staying aloft for hours at a time with barely a flap of their great sail-plane wings as they soar on rising air currents. Swifts are probably the most aerial of all birds. They even sleep and mate on the wing. Moorhens, on the other hand, are poor flyers; they run, rather than fly when danger threatens.

The structure of birds is adapted to flight and, consequently, weight saving. They have hollow lightweight bones, and are very lightly muscled. Anyone who has carved a chicken knows that the largest amount of flesh is on the breast. This flesh forms the flight muscles — the heaviest part of a bird — and is attached to a deeply keeled breastbone. Chickens have large legs too, but this is simply because, having almost lost the power of flight, they run in the face of danger.

The mute swan, which weighs up to 40 lb., is arguably the world's heaviest flying bird and certainly the heaviest in Britain, while the goldcrest, at $3\frac{1}{2}$ in. and less than $\frac{1}{3}$ oz., is Britain's smallest bird.

Every bird is adapted in size, coloration and structure to take advantage of differing natural conditions. They are found everywhere from the open oceans, where the fulmars fly, to the highest mountain tops, where ptarmigan live.

Every corner of Britain has its birds. Some 200-odd species manage to find a place to breed, others come here for the winter to evade the harsh climates of north and east Europe, while still others use these islands as a staging post on their way to and from their breeding grounds. Spring and autumn are often thought of as the best times for bird-watching, simply because at these seasons all three categories of birds are present side by side.

Some birds enjoy a lengthy life-span — the fulmar, for example, does not begin to breed until it is seven years old. Others barely survive more than a year or two — the average life expectancy of a British robin is 17 months, though individuals can live considerably longer. If a pair of robins have ten young in a season, then including the original pair there will be 12 robins in the autumn. Ten of these must die before the following spring or there may be too many birds searching for unavailable territories. In fact, after a good breeding season and a mild winter, there will be more robins breeding the following year. But each pair will then rear fewer young, or more will die in the following winter, so that a balance is reached once more. Without such factors their numbers would soon reach plague proportions.

Britain's birds are among the most studied in the world. We know that there are about 220,000 gannets breeding around our coasts, that there are about 2000 pairs of great crested grebes, and 3000-5000 pairs of herons. The British Trust for Ornithology conducts a census of all birds occurring in Britain based on the work of observers at

HOW A BIRD FLIES

Gull's skeleton and flight feathers

The alula, three or four short feathers attached to the thumb, is extended at slow speeds to prevent stalling

Primary feathers propel the bird through the air

Coverts, small feathers covering the bases of larger feathers, make the flight surface smooth

Secondary feathers sustain the bird in the air giving it 'lift'

Upper arm bone is honeycombed

Ploughshare bone, fused vertebrae, supports the tail and is an anchor for its muscles

Wishbone, formed by fusion of the collarbones, helps to support the wings from the body in flight

Tail feathers steer and stabilise the bird in flight and are important in landing and braking

Breastbone to which the powerful flight muscles are attached

Structure of a flight feather

Quill

Vane

Barbule

Magnified

Hooks on upper barbule lock with ridges on lower barbule

Barb

Barbule

Action of wing feathers during flight

Air passes between vanes   Upstroke

Air resistance closes vanes   Downstroke

Honeycombed bone

Many bones of a bird, such as those of the upper arm, are hollow and criss-crossed with struts for strength and lightness

Muscle control of wings

Breastbone

Pectoralis minor muscle contracts and raises the wing

Body lifted

Air resistance gives upthrust on wing

Pectoralis major muscle contracts and lowers the wing

Upper arm

Wing pulled down

Birds can fly in two ways, either by gliding or soaring when the wings are outspread and used as aerofoils, or by flapping. In the downstroke of flapping flight, the power stroke, the feathers are closed flat to meet maximum air resistance and lift the bird. The wings move downwards and forwards and the primaries are bent up at their ends. In the upstroke, a rapid recovery stroke, the wings are raised in an arc and the primaries twist open, allowing air to pass between them

some 250 sites. The Trust is also compiling an atlas to show where each species is found. Birds that might otherwise not breed in Britain are encouraged by the creation of reserves, such as that run by the Royal Society for the Protection of Birds at Minsmere in Suffolk. There, avocets, little terns and others have been persuaded to breed on artificial islands. When unusual birds try to breed, the Society protects them rigorously, as in the case of the ospreys which have started to breed at Loch Garten on Speyside.

Birds are the most familiar wild animals in our countryside. They can be colourful like the kingfisher, or sombre like the hedge-sparrow. They can sing as purely as the nightingale, or drive a listener to distraction with the endless monotony of their calls, like the 'coo, coo-oo, cuk' of the collared dove.

Increasingly, this variety of forms and attributes is being affected by man changing the face of the landscape. The removal of hedges, filling in of ponds, drainage of marshes and the extension of industrial and housing areas are all on the debit side. On the other hand, new reservoirs and gravel pits create new living space for birds, bringing them to areas where they have never bred before. Some species decrease, others increase — the pattern is never stable. As birds, under protection, began to recover from the effects of the shooting mania in the 19th century, they had to face the more insidious 20th-century dangers of poisonous insecticides. Fortunately, the threat has now been reduced, since the use of the more dangerous of these substances has been brought under government control.

Birds of the British Isles

There are 8600 species of birds in the world, of which about 470 can be seen in the British Isles during the course of a year. Of these, 200 live here permanently. Others are visitors which come here to breed. Some, such as swallows, come north from Africa; while others, such as the brambling and the scaup, fly down from the Arctic and Scandinavia. Many other species use the British Isles as a staging post on long migrations south or north.

In Britain, the spring and autumn months are best for watching birds, times when all three categories—residents, visitors and passing migrants—can be seen, sometimes side by side.

The 235 birds shown here are mainly either all-the-year-round residents or birds that stay long enough to breed. A few of the more interesting passing migrants are also included.

The information with each of the illustrations indicates whether the bird is male or female, adult or juvenile and wearing summer or winter plumage. Where only one bird is shown, it is an adult male of the species in which the sexes are alike and there is little seasonal change in plumage. The size given for an adult bird is from the tip of the bill to the end of the tail. Birds are described in the book under entries corresponding to the names in large type.

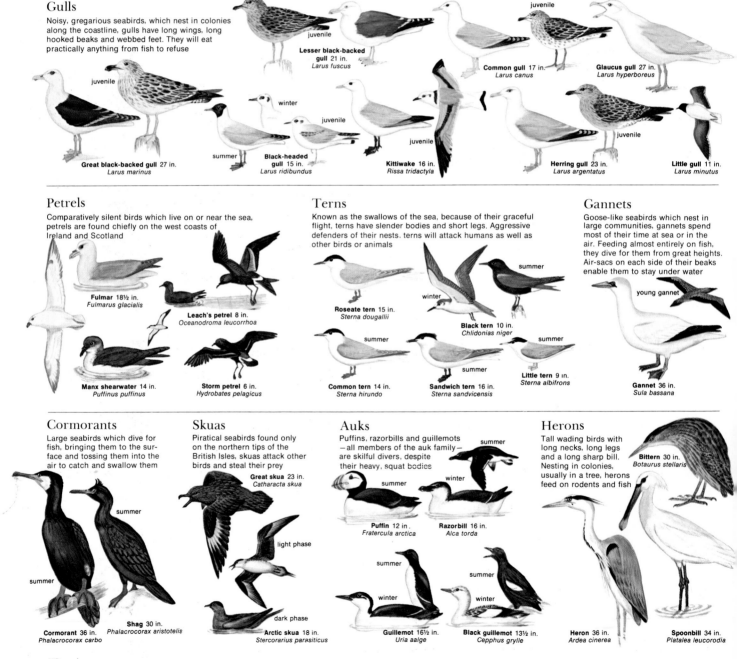

Swans

Solitary birds, swans are the largest members of the duck family, with an all-white plumage and long, graceful necks

Geese

Large web-footed birds belonging to the same family as swans
and ducks. They graze on grass,
crops and water weed, often
in large flocks, on marshes,
lakes and rivers

Whooper swan 60 in.
Cygnus cygnus

Bewick's swan 48 in.
Cygnus columbianus

Mute swan 60 in.*Cygnus olor*

Greenland race

Brent goose 22-24 in.
Branta bernicla

Pink-footed goose 24-30 in.
Anser brachyrhynchus

White-fronted goose 26-30 in.
Anser albifrons

Divers

Awkward on land but remarkably agile
on and beneath the water, divers eat
fish, crustaceans and insects. They can
be seen in the Scottish islands, the
Highlands and the west coast of Ireland

summer / winter

Red-throated diver 24 in.
Gavia stellata

winter

Black-throated diver 27 in.
Gavia arctica

winter

summer

Great northern diver M 33 in. F 30 in.
Gavia immer

Canada goose 38 in.
Branta canadensis

Egyptian goose 25 in.
Alopochen aegyptiacus

Bean goose 28-35 in.
Anser fabalis

Lesser white-fronted goose 21-25 in.
Anser erythropus

Barnacle goose 23-27 in.
Branta leucopsis

Greylag goose 30-35 in.
Anser anser

Ducks

Fresh or salt-water birds—as agile in the air as they are in the water—ducks have stout bodies and long powerful wings. Some feed on land, some on the surface of the water and others dive for fish. Drakes are usually more colourful and slightly larger than the ducks. All ducks have webbed feet.

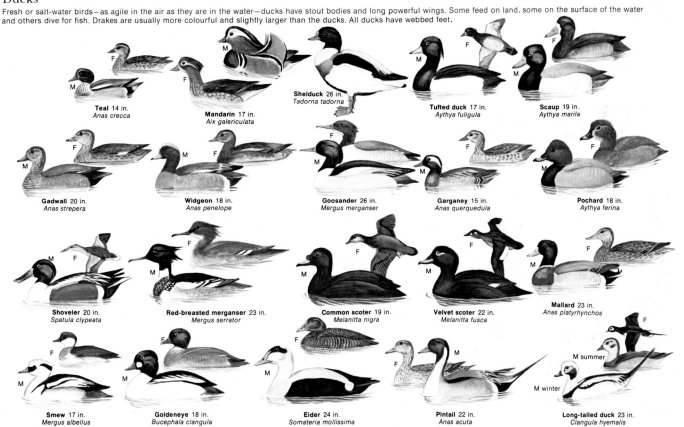

Teal 14 in.
Anas crecca

Mandarin 17 in.
Aix galericulata

Shelduck 26 in.
Tadorna tadorna

Tufted duck 17 in.
Aythya fuligula

Scaup 19 in.
Aythya marila

Gadwall 20 in.
Anas strepera

Widgeon 18 in.
Anas penelope

Goosander 26 in.
Mergus merganser

Garganey 15 in.
Anas querquedula

Pochard 18 in.
Aythya ferina

Shoveler 20 in.
Spatula clypeata

Red-breasted merganser 23 in.
Mergus serrator

Common scoter 19 in.
Melanitta nigra

Velvet scoter 22 in.
Melanitta fusca

Mallard 23 in.
Anas platyrhynchos

Smew 17 in.
Mergus albellus

Goldeneye 18 in.
Bucephala clangula

Eider 24 in.
Somateria mollissima

Pintail 22 in.
Anas acuta

M summer

M winter

Long-tailed duck 23 in.
Clangula hyemalis

BIRDS

Grebes

Clumsy on land, grebes are freshwater birds which often spend their winters at sea, coming inland only during hard weather

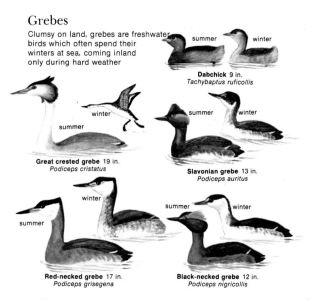

Dabchick 9 in.
Tachybaptus ruficollis

Great crested grebe 19 in.
Podiceps cristatus

Slavonian grebe 13 in.
Podiceps auritus

Red-necked grebe 17 in.
Podiceps grisegena

Black-necked grebe 12 in.
Podiceps nigricollis

Crakes and rails

Secretive, nervous birds which live in marshes, fens and swamps. The group includes moorhens, corncrakes, water and land rails and coots. Most are poor flyers but powerful swimmers

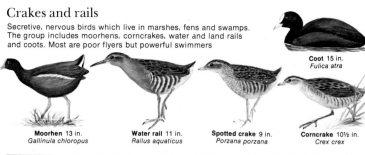

Coot 15 in.
Fulica atra

Moorhen 13 in.
Gallinula chloropus

Water rail 11 in.
Rallus aquaticus

Spotted crake 9 in.
Porzana porzana

Corncrake 10½ in.
Crex crex

Falcons

Birds of prey with long pointed wings and short curved beaks. Their speed and accuracy in the air enable them to catch birds on the wing

Hobby 13 in.
Falco subbuteo

Peregrine M 15 in. F 19 in.
Falco peregrinus

Merlin M 10½ in. F 13 in.
Falco columbarius

Kestrel 13½ in.
Falco tinnunculus

Buzzards

Deceptively slow-flying birds of prey which glide through the air in wide circles, plummeting down at high speed when rabbits are seen. Mostly carnivorous—although they occasionally eat berries—buzzards are common on the west coast of Britain

Honey buzzard 21½ in.
Pernis apivorus

Buzzard M 20 in. F 23 in.
Buteo buteo

Rough-legged buzzard 22 in.
Buteo lagopus

Kite

A rare bird of prey, confined to the hilly country of central Wales. Easily identified by its forked tail, effortless flight and diving ability

Kite M 22 in. F 24 in.
Milvus milvus

Osprey

Also known as the fish-hawk, the osprey has sharp-taloned claws which it uses to snatch fish near the surface of the water. Normally seen near lakes and estuaries

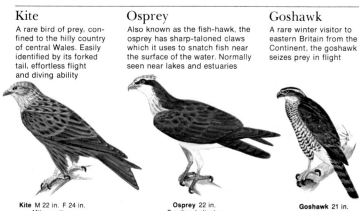

Osprey 22 in.
Pandion haliaetus

Goshawk

A rare winter visitor to eastern Britain from the Continent, the goshawk seizes prey in flight

Goshawk 21 in.
Accipiter gentilis

Harriers

Relatives of the buzzard, but rare summer visitors to this country—with the exception of small numbers of marsh harriers, which nest in Suffolk. Harriers glide low over the ground, systematically tracking lizards, field mice, frogs, birds or insects, dropping on to their prey and seizing it with their talons. The male does the killing, passing the prey in mid-air to the female harrier, who returns to the nest

Hen-harrier M 17 in. F 20 in.
Circus cyaneus

Marsh harrier 21 in.
Circus aeruginosus

Montagu's harrier M 15½ in. F. 17 in.
Circus pygargus

Sparrowhawk

Resident birds of prey which snatch small birds from hedgerows with surprise attacks and lightning speed

Sparrowhawk M 11 in. F 15 in.
Accipiter nisus

Grouse

Game birds with plump bodies, short wings and strong legs which, together with the toes, are feathered. They are fast runners and fast flyers with a low whirring flight. When flushed from cover they rise rapidly. All nest on the ground, where the dull plumage of the hen is a camouflage as she sits on a large clutch of eggs. The red grouse is unique to Britain, only occurring elsewhere as an introduction

Capercaillie M 33 in. F 25 in.
Tetrao urogallus

Black grouse
Blackcock M 21 in. Greyhen F 14 in.
Lyrurus tetrix

Ptarmigan 14 in.
Lagopus mutus

Red grouse
M 15 in. F 13½ in.
Lagopus lagopus

Pigeons

A group of vegetarian birds which includes doves. They have heavy, squat bodies and walk with a waddling gait. Their broad, pointed wings, angled in the middle, enable them to fly quickly and directly. Some species are now regarded as serious pests

Rock dove 13 in.
Columba livia

Collared dove 12½ in.
Streptopelia decaocto

Stock dove 13 in.
Columba oenas

Turtle dove 11 in.
Streptopelia turtur

Wood-pigeon 16 in.
Columba palumbus

Feral pigeon 13 in.
Columba livia

Eagle

Its broad wings, short broad tail and strong projecting head prevent the eagle being confused with the buzzard—the only other large bird of prey resident in Britain. The eagle glides low over mountain slopes when hunting, using its hooked talons to seize grouse, small mammals or carrion

Golden eagle M 30 in. F 35 in.
Aquila chrysaëtos

Pheasant

Game birds with chicken-like bodies and relatively long, unfeathered legs. The males have a variety of brightly coloured plumage and are aggressive fighters. They nest in hollows in the ground, lined with grass and leaves, and feed on weed seeds, grain and insects of all kinds

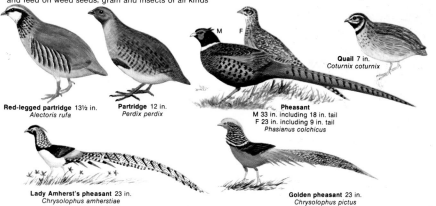

Red-legged partridge 13½ in.
Alectoris rufa

Partridge 12 in.
Perdix perdix

Pheasant
M 33 in. including 18 in. tail
F 23 in. including 9 in. tail
Phasianus colchicus

Quail 7 in.
Coturnix coturnix

Lady Amherst's pheasant 23 in.
Chrysolophus amherstiae

Golden pheasant 23 in.
Chrysolophus pictus

Cuckoo

The only British bird to rear its young by fostering them on other birds. It is the male's song which is heard in spring

Cuckoo 13 in.
Cuculus canorus

Kingfisher

The most brilliantly coloured of British birds, it lives by waterways, diving for small fish, tadpoles and water insects

Kingfisher 6½ in.
Alcedo atthis

Swift

A bird which rarely alights on the ground—because its legs are so weak and small—so feeds, mates and sleeps in the air

Swift 6½ in.
Apus apus

Nightjar

A night-flying bird that is almost invisible during the day as it sits on the ground, camouflaged by feathers which resemble dead leaves

Nightjar 10½ in.
Caprimulgus europaeus

Woodpeckers

Equipped with stout, pointed bills, woodpeckers probe the bark of trees for wood-boring beetles, grubs and moths, which they extract with long tongues. They also use their bills to produce sharp, drumming sounds on resonant dead wood

Lesser spotted woodpecker 5¾ in.
Dendrocopos minor

Green woodpecker 12½ in.
Picus viridis

Wryneck 8½ in.
Jynx torquilla

Great spotted woodpecker 9 in.
Dendrocopos major

Owls

Largely nocturnal birds of prey with sharp claws and hooked, flesh-tearing beaks. Although they have limited eye movement, their acute sense of hearing, coupled with an almost soundless flight, makes them deadly accurate killers in the dark

Short-eared owl
M 14 in. F 16½ in.
Asio flammeus

Snowy owl 24 in.
Nyctea scandiaca

Little owl 8½ in.
Athene noctua

Long-eared owl 14 in.
Asio otus

Barn owl 13½ in.
Tyto alba

Tawny owl 15 in.
Strix aluco

Plovers

Resident waders—except for the dotterel which is a summer visitor—plovers haunt sandy shores and mudflats in search of sea creatures and insects. The lapwing performs aerial acrobatics during courtship, and will feign a leg or wing injury to lure intruders away from its nest

 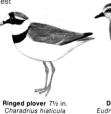  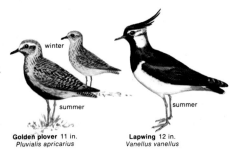

Little ringed plover 6 in.
Charadrius dubius

Ringed plover 7½ in.
Charadrius hiaticula

Dotterel 8½ in.
Eudromias morinellus

summer
winter

Grey plover 11 in.
Pluvialis squatarola

winter
summer

Golden plover 11 in.
Pluvialis apricarius

summer

Lapwing 12 in.
Vanellus vanellus

Woodcock

A resident wading bird that has taken to the land in recent years, invading marshes and copses. Its eyes are set high in its head, giving it all-round vision

Woodcock 13½ in.
Scolopax rusticola

Phalaropes

Among the smallest of swimming birds, the phalaropes are migrants from northern countries, breeding mainly in Orkney and Shetland. They feed on waterside plants and insects

M winter
F summer

summer
winter

Red-necked phalarope 7 in.
Phalaropus lobatus

Grey phalarope 8 in.
Phalaropus fulicarius

Turnstones

A winter visitor to coastlines throughout the British Isles, these noisy birds move stones as they hunt for food

Turnstone 9 in.
Arenaria interpres

Ruff

A summer migrant with exotic plumage, given to violent displays during courtship. Found on sewage farms, swamps and marshes, the ruff feeds on worms, shellfish and plant seeds

males in summer
M
F

Ruff M 11 in. F 9 in.
Philomachus pugnax

Stone curlew

A summer visitor to south-east Britain, the stone curlew is a rare bird, relying upon camouflage rather than flight when disturbed

Stone curlew 16 in.
Burhinus oedicnemus

Oystercatcher

A short-legged resident of rocky coasts and sandy shores. It does not feed on oysters but sandworms, and other shellfish

Oystercatcher 17 in.
Haematopus ostralegus

Snipe

A valued table bird, it flies in erratic zig-zag courses when disturbed. Common in Scotland and the north of England, it is active at night, feeding on worms and insects, and sleeping in marshes by day

Jack snipe 7½ in.
Lymnocryptes minimus

Snipe 10½ in.
Gallinago gallinago

Avocet

One of the rarest of British wading birds, encouraged to nest in Britain by the Royal Society for the Protection of Birds, whose emblem it now is

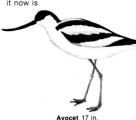

Avocet 17 in.
Recurvirostra avosetta

Shanks

Waders with long colourful legs, found on salt and freshwater marshes. Their flight is rather erratic. Both greenshank and redshank are residents; the spotted redshank is a spring and autumn visitor from Scandinavia

Greenshank 12 in.
Tringa nebularia

Spotted redshank 12 in.
Tringa erythropus

Redshank 11 in.
Tringa totanus

Curlews

Long-legged, long-billed wading birds, most often seen on estuaries, mudflats and freshwater marshes. Both species breed in northern Scotland

Curlew 22 in.
Numenius arquata

Whimbrel 16 in.
Numenius phaeopus

Godwits

Large birds with long legs and long straight bills, which they use to probe into marshes and mud-flats to obtain crustaceans, molluscs and worms. Both species form large flocks in spring and autumn

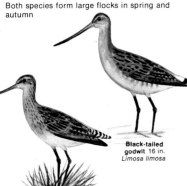

Black-tailed godwit 16 in.
Limosa limosa

Bar-tailed godwit 15 in.
Limosa lapponica

Sandpipers

A large group of small, graceful wading birds with long, slender bills. The dunlin is one of the most common and smallest of Britain's shore birds. The common sandpiper, a more widespread summer visitor, has a peculiar bobbing motion which makes it easy to identify

Common sandpiper 7¾ in.
Tringa hypoleucos

summer
winter

Dunlin 7 in.
Calidris alpina

Little stint 5¼ in.
Calidris minuta

Curlew sandpiper 7½ in.
Calidris ferruginea

Knot 10 in.
Calidris canutus

Wood sandpiper 8 in.
Tringa glareola

Temminck's stint 5¼ in.
Calidris temminckii

Green sandpiper 9 in.
Tringa ochropus

Purple sandpiper 8¼ in.
Calidris maritima

Sanderling 8 in.
Calidris alba

Thrushes

Plump, medium-sized perching birds that find most of their food on the ground. They include some of Britain's finest songsters. Thrushes feed on berries, worms, slugs and snails; the song thrush is the only species to drop snails to break their shells. With the exception of the fieldfare and redwing, which are visitors from Scandinavia, thrushes are residents

immature blackbird

Song thrush 9 in.
Turdus philomelos

Mistle thrush 10½ in.
Turdus viscivorus

Redwing 8¼ in.
Turdus iliacus

Fieldfare 10 in.
Turdus pilaris

Ring ouzel 9½ in.
Turdus torquatus

Blackbird 10 in.
Turdus merula

Pipits

Slim, dainty birds with short tails and thin, straight bills. They occupy a number of different habitats, but all build nests on the ground

Rock pipit 6¼ in.
Anthus spinoletta petrosus

Water pipit 6½ in.
Anthus spinoletta

Tree pipit 6 in.
Anthus trivialis

Flycatchers

Closely related to thrushes and warblers, these summer visitors to Britain catch insects on the wing. The spotted flycatcher is the better known and more widespread of the two

M winter or F

M summer

Pied flycatcher 5 in.
Ficedula hypoleuca

Spotted flycatcher 5½ in.
Muscicapa striata

Starling

A bird which swarms in tens of thousands and can thrive as well in city centres as in remote Highland crofts

Starling 8½ in.
Sturnus vulgaris

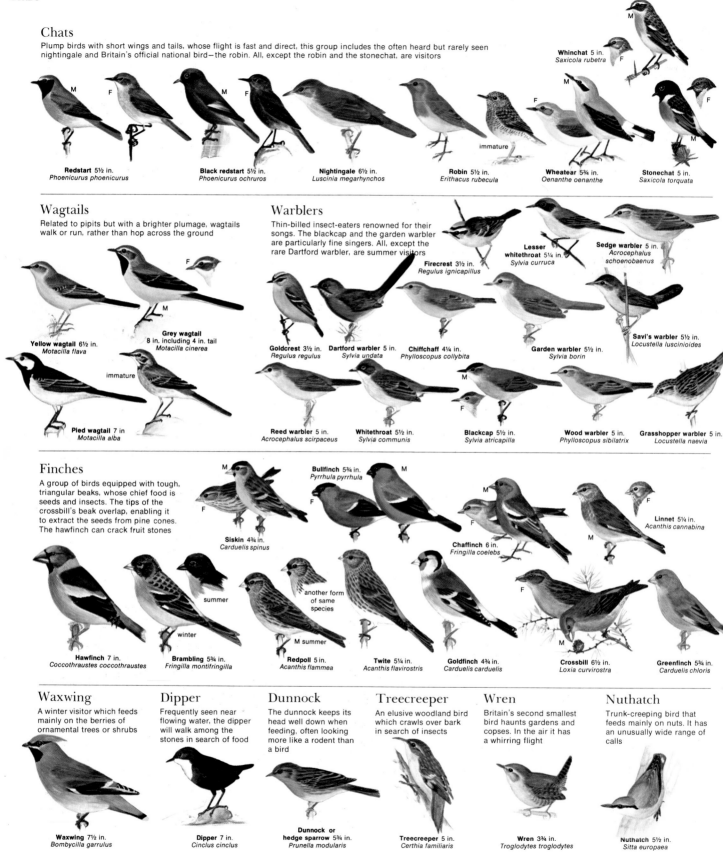

Chats

Plump birds with short wings and tails, whose flight is fast and direct, this group includes the often heard but rarely seen nightingale and Britain's official national bird—the robin. All, except the robin and the stonechat, are visitors

Whinchat 5 in.
Saxicola rubetra

Redstart 5½ in.
Phoenicurus phoenicurus

Black redstart 5½ in.
Phoenicurus ochruros

Nightingale 6½ in.
Luscinia megarhynchos

Robin 5½ in.
Erithacus rubecula

immature

Wheatear 5¾ in.
Oenanthe oenanthe

Stonechat 5 in.
Saxicola torquata

Wagtails

Related to pipits but with a brighter plumage, wagtails walk or run, rather than hop across the ground

Yellow wagtail 6½ in.
Motacilla flava

Grey wagtail
8 in. including 4 in. tail
Motacilla cinerea

immature

Pied wagtail 7 in
Motacilla alba

Warblers

Thin-billed insect-eaters renowned for their songs. The blackcap and the garden warbler are particularly fine singers. All, except the rare Dartford warbler, are summer visitors

Lesser whitethroat 5¼ in.
Sylvia curruca

Sedge warbler 5 in.
Acrocephalus schoenobaenus

Firecrest 3½ in.
Regulus ignicapillus

Goldcrest 3½ in.
Regulus regulus

Dartford warbler 5 in.
Sylvia undata

Chiffchaff 4¼ in.
Phylloscopus collybita

Garden warbler 5½ in.
Sylvia borin

Savi's warbler 5½ in.
Locustella luscinioides

Reed warbler 5 in.
Acrocephalus scirpaceus

Whitethroat 5½ in.
Sylvia communis

Blackcap 5½ in.
Sylvia atricapilla

Wood warbler 5 in.
Phylloscopus sibilatrix

Grasshopper warbler 5 in.
Locustella naevia

Finches

A group of birds equipped with tough, triangular beaks, whose chief food is seeds and insects. The tips of the crossbill's beak overlap, enabling it to extract the seeds from pine cones. The hawfinch can crack fruit stones

Bullfinch 5¾ in.
Pyrrhula pyrrhula

Siskin 4¾ in.
Carduelis spinus

Chaffinch 6 in.
Fringilla coelebs

Linnet 5¼ in.
Acanthis cannabina

summer

winter

Hawfinch 7 in.
Coccothraustes coccothraustes

Brambling 5¾ in.
Fringilla montifringilla

another form of same species

M summer

Redpoll 5 in.
Acanthis flammea

Twite 5¼ in.
Acanthis flavirostris

Goldfinch 4¾ in.
Carduelis carduelis

Crossbill 6½ in.
Loxia curvirostra

Greenfinch 5¾ in.
Carduelis chloris

Waxwing

A winter visitor which feeds mainly on the berries of ornamental trees or shrubs

Waxwing 7½ in.
Bombycilla garrulus

Dipper

Frequently seen near flowing water, the dipper will walk among the stones in search of food

Dipper 7 in.
Cinclus cinclus

Dunnock

The dunnock keeps its head well down when feeding, often looking more like a rodent than a bird

Dunnock or hedge sparrow 5¾ in.
Prunella modularis

Treecreeper

An elusive woodland bird which crawls over bark in search of insects

Treecreeper 5 in.
Certhia familiaris

Wren

Britain's second smallest bird haunts gardens and copses. In the air it has a whirring flight

Wren 3¾ in.
Troglodytes troglodytes

Nuthatch

Trunk-creeping bird that feeds mainly on nuts. It has an unusually wide range of calls

Nuthatch 5½ in.
Sitta europaea

Buntings

Like finches, these birds have short, tough bills for breaking open seeds. The yellowhammer is the most common bunting and is found in open country and hedgerows. The largest—the corn-bunting—is also common in open country

Larks

Small birds which live on the ground in the open countryside, they closely resemble pipits. Larks deliver their beautiful songs while hovering high in the sky

Shore lark 6½ in.
Eremophila alpestris

Corn bunting 7 in.
Emberiza calandra

Cirl bunting 6¼ in.
Emberiza cirlus

Reed bunting 6 in.
Emberiza schoeniclus

Yellowhammer 6½ in.
Emberiza citrinella

Lapland bunting 6 in.
Caicarius lapponicus

Snow bunting 6½ in.
Plectrophenax nivalis

Skylark 7 in.
Alauda arvensis

Woodlark 6 in.
Lullula arborea

Shrikes

Long-tailed birds of prey with hawk-like beaks. Also known as 'butcher birds', they impale their victims—mice or small birds—on thorn bushes

Tits

Small, thin-billed birds which feed mainly on insects. They have small plump bodies and brown wings. Tits mob a predator, such as a sparrowhawk or tawny owl, by darting at it with excited calls and flicking it with wings and tail

Red-backed shrike 6¾ in.
Lanius cristatus

Great grey shrike 9½ in.
Lanius excubitor

Blue tit 4½ in.
Parus caeruleus

Great tit 5½ in.
Parus major

Long-tailed tit 5½ in.
Aegithalos caudatus

Marsh tit 4½ in.
Parus palustris

Crested tit 4½ in.
Parus cristatus

Coal tit 4¼ in.
Parus ater

Sparrows

The two species feed chiefly on seeds and insects. They have similar chirruping calls and often flock together in winter

Bearded tit

Also known as the reedling, it has an easily recognisable wedge-shaped tail. Found only in eastern England, it breeds in reed and sedge beds, feeding on freshwater molluscs and insects

Martins and swallow

Streamlined birds with long wings and long forked tails. They catch insects on the wing and spend most of their time in the air, except when breeding and roosting

Tree sparrow 5½ in.
Passer montanus

House sparrow 5¾ in.
Passer domesticus

Bearded tit 6½ in. including 3 in. tail
Panurus biarmicus

House martin 5 in.
Delichon urbica

Swallow 7½ in.
Hirundo rustica

Sand martin 4¾ in.
Riparia riparia

Crows

Large birds which eat almost anything, including the eggs and young of other birds. Crows have large tough bills, and are considered to be among the most intelligent of birds

Magpie 18 in. including 8-10 in. tail
Pica pica

Raven 25 in.
Corvus corax

Jackdaw 13 in.
Corvus monedula

Rook 18 in.
Corvus frugilegus

Hooded crow 18½ in.
Corvus corone cornix

Carrion crow 18½ in.
Corvus corone corone

Jay 13½ in.
Garrulus glandarius

Chough 15 in.
Pyrrhocorax pyrrhocorax

Birdsfoot *Ornithopus perpusillus*
Curved, jointed seed pods, grouped at the ends of stems in claw-like bunches, give birdsfoot its name. It is a low-growing plant, widespread on dry sandy grassland or gravel throughout the British Isles, except in the extreme north. The pea-like flowers which appear in spring and summer are self-pollinating and contain no nectar. The leaves and stalks are slightly hairy.

Birdsfoot-trefoil
The common birdsfoot-trefoil *Lotus corniculatus*, also called bacon and eggs, is widespread throughout the British Isles, in meadows and on roadside banks. In early summer it has masses of pea-like flowers in groups of five. The greater birdsfoot-trefoil *L. uliginosus* is less common and occurs in damper, marshy places. Its dark green leaves are hairy and there are usually eight or more flowers in each head. In spite of their Latin name, *Lotus*, these plants have no connection with the sacred lotus of the East. Red streaks which often appear on the back petals guide bees to the nectar.

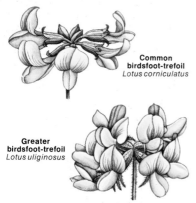

Common birdsfoot-trefoil
Lotus corniculatus

Greater birdsfoot-trefoil
Lotus uliginosus

Common birdsfoot-trefoil contributes sheets of colour to the countryside in early summer

Birdsnest fungus see Fungus
Birdsnest orchid see Orchid
Birks see Birch

Birthwort *Aristolochia clematitis*
This rare plant was formerly grown for its supposed medicinal value in easing the pains of childbirth. It is now found around the ruins of old buildings and occasionally in country lanes in south and east England.

Birthwort has slender, erect stems which reach over 2 ft. The leaves are heart-shaped, and clusters of greenish-yellow flowers appear from June to September. Each flower springs from a tubular base. The scientific name comes from the Greek for 'best birth'.

The flowers are insect traps. Each flower tube is lined with hairs directed downwards, which allow insects to enter but not to crawl out. After pollination, however, the flower droops, the hairs wither and the insects can escape to carry pollen to another flower. See also HERB

Bishop's mitre *Aelia acuminata*
This bug, less than ½ in. in length, lives in southern England among long grass, especially at the sides of roads and on sand dunes. It feeds by sucking sap from blades of grass and from its ripening seeds.

On the Continent where the bug is more common, it feeds on wheat, damaging the crop. The adult bug spends the winter among the grass roots. Eggs are laid in two rows on blades of grass in spring. These hatch into nymphs, miniature replicas of the adults, which mature after moulting.

The shape of the bug, rather pointed at each end, resembles a bishop's mitre. Ants and some beetles prey on it.

Bistort
The common bistort or snakeweed *Polygonum bistorta* often occurs in large circular patches in old meadows near villages, particularly in northern England, suggesting that it may once have been cultivated. It is still eaten in the Lake District where the young leaves are an important ingredient of a dish called Easter Ledger pudding.

The name of the plant, which has distorted underground stems, is derived from the Latin *bis*, twice, and *tortus*, twisted.

Clusters of the bright reddish-white flowers of the common bistort make a fine display from June to August.

The amphibious bistort *P. amphibium* gives a similar display in summer, usually on water. This plant has two forms: an aquatic one with hairless floating leaves, and a land-growing form which has hairy leaves and a more rounded base. Both forms sometimes occur on the same plant growing at the water's edge.

Close-up of leaf

Common bistort is also known as snakeweed on account of its twisted underground stems

Bittercress
There are three widespread species of bittercress. The flowers and leaves are agreeably bitter, rather like watercress, and sometimes used in salads.

Wavy or wood bittercress *Cardamine flexuosa* is a shade-loving species growing on banks and at the sides of streams where it flowers from April to August. Its name comes from the zigzag growth of the stem.

Hairy bittercress *C. hirsuta* occurs in much drier places on bare ground, walls and rocks. It is badly named as it is only slightly hairy.

This plant is sometimes confused with shepherd's purse, which is larger and has heart-shaped leaves. Hairy bittercress is a common garden weed. Large bittercress *C. amara* occurs in wet areas, outside south-west England, north-west Scotland and the whole of Ireland and Wales. Its flowers are ½ in. in diameter and bloom in May and June.

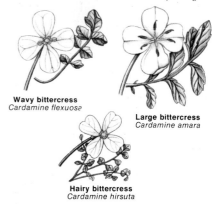

Wavy bittercress
Cardamine flexuosa

Large bittercress
Cardamine amara

Hairy bittercress
Cardamine hirsuta

The three common species of bittercress have edible leaves which taste like watercress

Bittern see Heron
Bittersweet see Nightshade
Black beetle see Cockroach

Blackberry *Rubus fruticosus*
Woods, hedges and heaths abound with blackberries in autumn, but some are not as good to eat as others. Throughout the British Isles, except the extreme north and west, there are several hundred species of blackberry, also called bramble, each with its own characteristic pattern of thorn, leaf shape, flower colour, fruit shape and taste. The white or pink flowers appear from May to September. The seeds are carried long distances by birds which eat the fruit and then pass the seeds unharmed in their droppings. Once established, blackberries spread vigorously as the stems arch over and root. In Gloucestershire, passing through a blackberry arch was said to be a cure for rupture. Bramble leaves were once placed on inflammations to reduce swelling. An orange dye was made from the roots. See also BRAMBLE

Blackbird see Thrush

Black bream *Spondyliosoma cantharus*
The black bream, or old wife, is one of several species of sea bream found in British coastal waters. None of them is related to the freshwater bream. Sea breams are perch-like with spiny fin rays and strong, sharply pointed, slightly curved teeth. The black bream grows to between 4 lb. and 6 lb. Colour varies according to age and sex but is generally dark above, with a silvery-white belly, and about six dark bars on its side. The fins are grey and a series of light lines mark the scale rows.

The black bream is the most common of the sea bream and is found in large numbers in the English Channel from early summer to October. This local concentration is probably because it migrates for spawning. It prefers rocky haunts and digs a shallow depression in the sea-bed for the eggs. The male guards them throughout their development.

Black bulgar fungus see Fungus
Blackcap see Warblers, Scrub

Blackcurrant *Ribes nigrum*
Throughout the British Isles, blackcurrant bushes up to 6 ft high can often be found in woods and hedgerows, but only rarely in Wales, Ireland and northern Scotland. Some may be of wild origin, but most have grown from seeds carried by birds from cultivated bushes.

The fruit, which is ready to eat in July, appears on the previous season's shoots. This distinguishes it from the redcurrant, in which the fruit forms on spurs of the old wood. The two can be identified even before the fruit appears, as the smell of blackcurrant can be detected in the crushed leaves which, when dried, give a pleasant additional flavour to tea.

Blackcurrants, which are rich in Vitamin C, were first cultivated to make jelly or wine as a cure for the quinsy. They are now grown commercially in Herefordshire and East Anglia, mainly for processing into jam or soft drinks.

Black fly
This small fly which swarms near streams and rivers should not be confused with the blackfly aphids which infest beans, dahlias and other garden plants.

There are 41 species of black fly. The females bite and suck the blood of birds and mammals, including humans, whereas the males feed only on nectar.

The females lay their eggs under water, sometimes by crawling down a plant stem. After the eggs are laid, the tired flies are often washed downstream, providing food for fish. Some anglers use live or imitation black flies as bait. The larvae attach themselves to stones or leaves by their suckers and with the help of silk webs which they spin. They feed among water plants, filtering small particles of food from the water. See also APHID

Black medick see Clover

Blacksmith
Metalwork of any kind is the blacksmith's province. Smiths specialising in shoeing horses are properly termed farriers. This craft dates back about 2000 years, although iron shoes were uncommon in Europe until AD 450, when the Romans started to use them on cavalry horses. They are thought to have arrived in Britain with William the Conqueror.

The farrier's art—increasingly required as riding becomes more popular each year

The farrier's traditional tools include tongs to heat iron bars in his bellows-blown fire; a steel hammer to shape the red-hot bar into a shoe on the anvil; a 'fuller' to make the groove in which nail-holes are punched and a quenching-trough to temper the shoe and cool the tools.

A modern smithy, usually serving a district rather than a single village, frequently provides a mobile service. Its equipment will often include power drills, electric welders and an oxy-acetylene plant, and the smith will not only shoe horses, but provide on-the-spot repairs to farm machinery. See also HORSES

Blackthorn *Prunus spinosa*
Sloe gin and the Irishman's shillelagh both come from the blackthorn, a shrubby tree, up to 12 ft high, often seen in hedgerows. Recognisable by its black bark and long sharp thorns, it has very small brown buds, oval leaves set alternately on red-tinged stalks and a bright display of white blossom early in April.

Blackthorn's Latin name means literally 'spiny plum'. An ancestor of our garden plums, it belongs to the rose family. Each flower has five white petals. After pollination a 'stone' fruit is formed, holding a single hard, woody seed in a mass of soft pulp. This fruit, or sloe, has a tough blue-black outer skin, covered with a white waxy bloom. Sloes mature in October and are intensely bitter. Ample sugar added to their pulp makes a tasty jelly. Sloe gin is made by steeping them in gin, to which they give a piquant flavour.

Blackthorn stems trimmed and polished to a handsome black surface are used for walking sticks; stouter and rougher ones for the shillelagh, a cudgel secured to the wrist by a leather strap.

Blackthorn is spread mainly by birds that eat the sloe's flesh and drop or swallow the hard, indigestible seed. A thicket persists indefinitely, spreading into adjoining pasture by means of sucker shoots from the roots.

In a late cold spring, the flowers break on leafless black branches, but in milder weather they open amid emerald green leaflets. Autumn leaf colours are gold, crimson and purple.

Bladderwort *Utricularia vulgaris*
An insect-eating water plant which has no roots and nourishes itself entirely through its leaves, the bladderwort is declining through improved drainage and pollution. The bladders of the finely divided leaves catch small aquatic animals and digest the decomposed remains. Its yellow flowers may still be seen rising above the surface of lakes and ponds in summer. The leaves, covering an area of up to 12 sq. in., are submerged. Bladderwort usually spreads by detached pieces floating away, and rarely by seed. In winter, the buds sink to the bottom until growth begins again in spring.

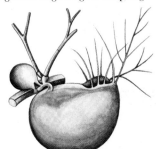
Close-up view of the air-filled bladders which grow on the leaves of bladderwort

Bladderwrack see Seaweed

Bleak *Alburnus alburnus*
A member of the carp family, the bleak is a lively, gregarious fish found at the surface of most English rivers—even moderately polluted ones as it inhabits the top few inches of well-oxygenated water.

Its brilliantly silvery sides make it conspicuous, and its scales were once used to line artificial pearls. But the bleak has only nuisance value for the serious angler, taking bait intended for bigger fish.

The bleak grows to 6 in. long. It feeds on insects at the surface—even leaping out of the water to catch them—and small crustaceans. As an abundant small fish, the bleak is significant in the diet of trout, perch, pike, kingfishers and grebes.

At spawning time—April to June—the male develops white lumps on its head and back and its lower fins become tinged with orange. Spawning takes place in gravel shallows.

Blenny

One of the blennies, the yellow or greenish coloured shanny *Blennius pholis,* is probably the most abundant and widespread fish on British shores. About 4 in. long, it is blotched with dark patches to blend with its normal background of rock and weed. Other blennies are less widespread. Montagu's blenny *Coryphoblennius galerita* lives only on south-west coasts from Dorset to Cornwall, South Wales and in Ireland from Co. Cork north-wards to Co. Mayo. It can be seen in the smallest and apparently barest shore pools, with a crosswise flap of skin above the eyes giving it a gnomish look.

The portly tompot blenny *Blennius gatto-rugine,* and the butterfly blenny *B. ocellaris,* occur at lower shore levels. The latter has a very high fin on the back with a conspicuous 'eye-spot' marking—a white ring round a black spot—similar to that of many butterflies; hence its name.

Blewits

These are edible fungi. The blewit or 'blue-leg' *Tricholoma saevum* was once sold at Covent Garden and at Midland markets. It has a bluish scaly stalk and a flat, pale clay-coloured cap, 2½-5 in. across. Its white gills turn flesh-coloured later. Blewits can be found from early autumn in pastures and on downs, often in large rings.

Wood blewits or 'amethyst' *T. nudum* are bluish-white all over, but the convex to flat cap may turn reddish-brown with age. They grow among dead leaves and sometimes on old compost heaps. The flesh has a pleasant fruity smell.

Blindhouse see Roundhouse

Blister beetle *Lytta vesicatoria*

Beware of handling this rather rare golden-green beetle—its body contains the chemical catharidin, which causes blisters. This substance used to be extracted for medical use as a counter-irritant.

Occasionally found on willow, ash and some other trees in south-east England, the blister beetle is between ½-¾ in. long. The female lays up to 10,000 eggs near the nest-entrance of a solitary bee, whose larvae are preyed on by the newly hatched beetle grubs.

Long-legged and active at first, the beetle grub becomes fatter and more sluggish on

Blister beetle
Lytta vesicatoria

The blister beetle earned its name because it secretes an irritant chemical in its body

a diet of bee larvae. It continues to live and develop in the bee cell, feeding on the store of pollen and nectar which should have nourished the bee larvae.

Blizzard

A blinding snowstorm, when a fierce, cold wind is accompanied by snow driven almost horizontally so that visibility is reduced to only a few yards. Deep snowdrifts are formed in sheltered places such as the lee of hedges and walls.

When, as often happens in upland Britain in winter, cloud and air temperatures fall well below freezing, minute but extremely hard ice crystals are formed. These can cause stinging discomfort to travellers as well as constituting a serious hazard, particularly to drivers.

Drifting is more common in upland rather than lowland areas, because of the stronger winds and lower temperatures at higher levels. These conditions give rise to greater quantities of tiny ice crystals, which are more easily drifted than large snowflakes. The latter, made up of interlocking, branching crystals, form at temperatures just below zero centigrade.

Blood-drop emlets see Monkey-flower

Bloodynose beetle

Its unusual name indicates this widespread beetle's method of defence, for if disturbed it emits a repellent bright red liquid from its mouth. Because of this means of protection, the fact that it is large (up to ¾ in.), fat and slow-moving is no disadvantage.

These black beetles are often seen on the ground or feeding on bedstraw plants in roadside hedgerows between April and June. Their soft-bodied, greenish-black larvae feed on the same plants.

The large bloodynose beetle *Timarcha tenebricosa* is widespread throughout Britain, but most common in western England. Its smaller relative, *T. goettingensis,* is usually found only in southern England.

Blowfly see Bluebottle

Bluebell *Endymion non-scriptus*

Flowering from late April until early June the spikes of nodding, bell-shaped blue flowers carpet the ground in shady woods, copses, hedge banks and sea-cliffs.

For most of the year the bluebell survives as a small, white, juice-filled bulb about 6 in. below the surface of the ground. In spring, a succulent stem rises from it to a height of about 12-18 in. surrounded at ground level by long, strap-like leaves.

Called the wild hyacinth in Scotland (the Scots bluebell is the English harebell) the individual flowers are very like those of the garden hyacinth and have a similar, though more subtle scent. Most of the bluebells found in gardens are not the wild species but the bigger and coarser *E. hispanicus*—a native of Spain and Portugal.

Bloodworms measure ½-2 in. long and can swim or move across a leaf rapidly by wriggling their bodies

Bloodworm

The bright red larvae of midges abundant in rainwater butts and the muddy bottoms of ponds, bloodworms get their colour from large amounts of the blood pigment, haemoglobin. This combines readily with oxygen, allowing bloodworms to live in highly polluted, oxygen-deficient water.

Some live in tubes of mud and silk, feeding off organic matter in the mud. They can swim rapidly by wriggling their bodies. After a red pupal stage, the bloodworm develops finally into a non-biting, mosquito-like fly or midge, which emerges from the water. Swarms of these perform their mating dances on warm evenings. See also MIDGE

chalk and limestone, because horseshoe vetch, the food plant of their caterpillars, grows in only such soils. Though both species are restricted to the south of England, they appear at different times of the year. There is only one generation of chalk-hill blue a year and it is the eggs that overwinter, that is, survive to hatch out the following year. The adonis blue has two generations a year, the first flying from May to June and the second generation in August and September. The caterpillars of this second generation hibernate, attaching themselves to the underside of a leaf on the food plant by a mass of silk threads. They turn into yellow-brown pupae the following spring.

The small blue and the silver-studded blue are common in some chalky areas but also live elsewhere in open country. The small blue is Britain's smallest butterfly with little blue colouring in either sex. The butterflies are on the wing in June but do not fly far, and so they tend to live in clearly defined colonies. These occur throughout the British Isles—but mostly in southern England. Small blues feed only on kidney vetch.

The silver-studded blues breed in England and Wales, flying from June to August. They feed on various plants of the vetch family and also heather.

Pests in the house, bluebottles are important as scavengers in the countryside

Bluebottle

There are two common species of bluebottle —also known as blowfly—which resemble each other closely. *Calliphora erythrocephala* is the more common and has reddish sides to the head, *C. vomitoria* has red hair over a black face: both have hairy, metallic-blue bodies.

It is usually the female bluebottle which enters houses during the summer, drawing attention to itself by its loud buzzing flight, in search of food on which to lay its eggs. It may lay up to 600 eggs, in small batches, on a piece of meat or on a dead animal.

The larvae, or maggots, hatch in a day and grow rapidly, often taking only a week to reach full size. They then burrow into the ground and pupate; in two weeks the pupa hatches. Fishermen breed bluebottle maggots for bait, calling them gentles. Male bluebottles spend much time feeding on nectar from flowers and visiting carrion to meet their mates.

During the winter months bluebottles often remain hidden in houses.

Blue butterfly

There are eight species of blue butterfly which breed in Britain, but in spite of their name not all are blue in colour. One species, the brown argus, has no blue in either sex. In most other species the males are blue and the females brown.

The majority of blue butterflies are found in open habitats and are especially common on chalk or limestone downlands. The adonis blue and the chalk-hill blue are found on

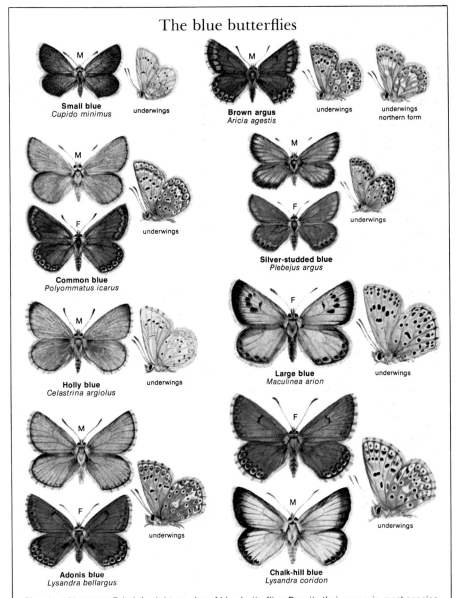

The blue butterflies

Small blue
Cupido minimus
underwings

Brown argus
Aricia agestis
underwings
underwings northern form

Common blue
Polyommatus icarus
underwings

Silver-studded blue
Plebejus argus
underwings

Holly blue
Celastrina argiolus
underwings

Large blue
Maculinea arion
underwings

Adonis blue
Lysandra bellargus
underwings

Chalk-hill blue
Lysandra coridon
underwings

The chart illustrates Britain's eight species of blue butterflies. Despite their name, in most species only the males are blue—the females are usually brown. Except for the common blue, they are most often seen flying in the chalk country of southern England from May to September

The chalk-hill blue butterfly is fond of basking in the sunlight with its wings half open

The common blue generally lays its eggs on birdsfoot-trefoil, the plant on which its caterpillars feed. It is more likely to be seen than any other blue. It lives in open grassy areas in all parts of the British Isles. It can be found throughout summer from May until September, two generations hatching during this period. As with the adonis blue, the second generation lives through the winter as a caterpillar.

The brown argus is almost as widely distributed as the common blue in Britain, but is not found in Ireland. Those in the northern areas of Britain, which often have a white spot on the forewings, are considered by some experts to belong to a continental species.

The caterpillars of all blue butterflies, except the holly blue, have a gland on their backs which produces a sugary fluid that ants collect. The caterpillars are not harmed by the ants.

Britain's rarest blue butterfly – the large blue – is totally dependent on ants. The young caterpillar feeds on wild thyme but later in its life crawls about until it is found by an ant, which collects the sticky fluid and carries the caterpillar back to the ants' nest.

Here the ants look after the caterpillar while it grows fat on a diet of ant larvae throughout the winter. The caterpillar pupates in the spring and the butterfly hatches in June or July. Both male and female are blue, but the female has larger black spots on the upper wings.

There are now only a few areas left in the south-west of England where the large blue still lives and it is likely to become extinct soon unless it is carefully protected.

The holly blue is fairly common in England, Wales and Ireland, though absent from Scotland. Unlike the other blues it is a woodland or garden species. Both sexes are blue. There are two generations a year: the first caterpillars hatch from eggs laid in the spring on holly and feed on holly flower buds, hatching as butterflies in the late summer.

These butterflies lay eggs on ivy and the second generation of caterpillars feed on ivy flower buds before pupating, in which form they pass the winter.

Blue haze

The lower atmosphere always contains smoke and dust particles that interfere with sunlight, which is made up of the combined colours of the rainbow. The smaller particles scatter the shorter blue wavelengths, tinting the whole scene blue and making the sun – the light source – seem red. Blue haze is common in deep valleys viewed from above, and on shores where salt particles thrown up by breaking waves serve to scatter the blue wavelengths.

Blue John

A variety of fluorspar rock mined in Derbyshire, Blue John is a beautiful translucent mineral which may be blue or purple. It is valued for making vases, ash-trays and similar objects. Blue John becomes phosphorescent and gives off a green light when gently heated.

Hydrofluoric acid, one of the few acids capable of dissolving glass and therefore useful for etching work, is derived from fluorspar, which is also used as a flux in steel manufacture.

Blue moon

A rare meteorological phenomenon – hence its use in everyday speech to signify a rare event.

A blue moon is caused by dust and smoke particles collecting in the air, during a protracted period of settled weather. These particles filter all colours, except blue, from sunlight. Since moonlight is reflected sunlight, this causes the moon to appear blue.

A blue moon was seen in Britain on September 26, 1950, when smoke particles hung in the air – between 30,000 and 40,000 ft high – following extensive forest fires which raged through Alberta in Canada.

Bluethroat see Chat
Blusher see Fungus
Bog see p. 66

Bog asphodel *Nathecium ossifragum*
Brilliant golden patches of bog asphodel colour wet upland heaths and moss in summer. It is more often seen in the west and north. The flowers form a stiff spike, rising about 12 in. high among the strap-like leaves. Sheep which graze boggy land are liable to develop foot rot; it was once thought that this was caused by the plants

The golden flowers of bog asphodel grow straight from the stem on short stalks

they ate, hence asphodel's Latin name *ossifragum* or bone breaker. Bog asphodel is also reputed to be poisonous to cows and goats whose milk may be affected if they eat it.

Young women in Lancashire at one time gathered the plant to make a golden dye for their hair.

Bogbean *Menyanthes trifoliata*
Spikes of pink and white flowers appear on the bogbean in May and June. For most of the year the plant is recognisable only by the large, clover-like leaves, up to 4 in. across, which rise above the surface of ponds or the wettest parts of bogs throughout Britain.

In northern England the leaves were once used instead of hops to give a bitter flavour to beer and an infusion of its leaves used to be prescribed by herbalists as a cure for fever. It is also known as the buckbean.

The rose-red buds of bogbean open into white flowers that are tinged with pink

Bog myrtle *Myrica gale*
On hot summer days in the bogs of the western regions the air will be filled with the fragrance of bog myrtle. It is a small, deciduous shrub, 2-6 ft high. Catkins, up to 1½ in. long, appear in spring before the grey-green leaves. Male and female catkins grow on separate plants, but plants may change sex from year to year. Wind disperses the winged seeds. Sweet gale, as it is called in northern England, has been used as a substitute for hops. It also provided a yellow dye.

Bombardier beetle *Brachinus crepitans*
At first glance, this small insect looks like a typical ground beetle of which there are several hundred species in Britain. But it

has an unusual defence mechanism: when disturbed, it fires a puff of caustic smoke from a vent at the rear of its body. This deters quite large predators, such as birds and toads, and is strong enough to stain human skin.

Hydrogen peroxide, a component of rocket fuels, is one of several chemical secretions which are brought together in a hardened chamber inside the beetle to produce both the caustic smoke and the audible explosion which expels it.

Bombardier beetles, which grow to about $\frac{1}{3}$ in. long, live under stones and among roots in many chalky areas of southern England, Wales and Ireland. They are mainly active at night, preying on other small creatures.

Bootlace worm *Lineus longissimus*
Growing up to 30 yds long, the bootlace worm is probably the longest animal in Britain. Five yards is not an uncommon length, and from this the worm can contract to just a few inches. Bootlace worms are dark brown, except for a pale head, and have an overall purple sheen. They live coiled under stones on muddy shingle beaches, and move slowly, gliding over a trail of slime to hunt small bristleworms and crustaceans which they catch and swallow whole.

The worms break easily but regenerate lost parts provided they contain part of the nerve cord. Fragmentation is one means of reproduction. They also reproduce sexually, the female laying thousands of eggs in long sticky ribbons.

Borage *Borago officinalis*
The brilliant blue, star-like flowers and greyish-green leaves of this hairy annual are seen during July on banks and in hedges. It is more often found in southern England.

The young leaves have a faint cucumber flavour and make an interesting addition to salads. The leaves can be infused to make a refreshing drink. Borage flowers will add flavour to a claret cup and can be candied to decorate confectionery.

John Gerard, the famous 16th-century herbalist, wrote of borage: 'Those of our time do use the flour in salads, to exhilerate and make the minde glad.'

The name may be derived from the Latin *burra*, a shaggy garment, on account of the rough, hairy leaves of the plant.

Bore
A tidal phenomenon of several rivers, including the Trent, Severn, Wye, Solway and Parrett. It occurs when flood-tides drive into the wide mouth of an estuary in greater volume than can flow up the main channel of the river. The incoming tide sweeps in as a wall of water, over-rides the slower river flow and rushes noisily upstream.

The height of the wall is governed by the width and depth of the river as well as the extent of the tide. The largest bores in Britain are those which flood up the River Severn. These may be 9 ft high in midstream. One measured in October 1966 was 9 ft 3 in. high and travelled at 13 mph from Awre, where the estuary narrows, to Gloucester, 21 miles upstream.

Botfly *Gasterophilus intestinalis*
Sometimes horses run about as if trying to avoid something which is irritating them. Often the disturbance is caused by a botfly laying its eggs on the horse's hair. The eggs hatch into larvae which the horse picks up on its tongue, from where they migrate to its stomach. There the larvae attach themselves by two hook-like teeth to the stomach wall. At this stage the larvae may cause indigestion. Nine months later, when the larvae are about 1 in. long, they pass out of the horse in its dung, burrow into the ground and pupate. They emerge as adults after about six weeks, usually in July or August. Botflies, which are slightly larger than common house flies, may also infest cattle. Related species attack deer and sheep.

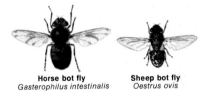

Horse bot fly
Gasterophilus intestinalis

Sheep bot fly
Oestrus ovis

Boundary mark
Boulders, trees and streams have all served to denote the limits of land ownership, and civil or ecclesiastical jurisdiction. From early times these natural features were supplemented by man-made marks, including banks, ditches, hedges and roads. Such early boundary marks include the 8th-century Offa's Dyke, defining the border between Mercia and Wales, and the stone crosses which marked the limits of sanctuary at Hexham Abbey, Northumberland.

The most common surviving boundary marks, often taking the form of carved stones, were put up during the 19th century when parish boundaries were re-drawn. Some have the initials of adjacent parishes carved on the appropriate sides. Others consist of metal posts or old cannon bought from the army and filled with cement; later versions were specially cast in the shape of cannon. See also DYKE, HEDGE, STANDING STONES

Boletus
Most of the 50 species of boletus toadstools grow in woodland during late summer and autumn. Many can be eaten, especially the cep or edible boletus *Boletus eduli*; but the devil's boletus *B. satanus* is poisonous. Spores are produced in long tubes under the cap. These tubes are easily separated from the cap, and there is a central stalk. In the devil's boletus the tube openings are red. The fleshy caps, which may be up to 8 in. across, are yellow, orange or brown, and soon decay. The spores are usually olive-brown. The flesh of several species turns green, blue or black when damaged.

On the Continent cep is considered the best of the edible fungi, eaten fried or used in soups and casseroles.

The cep – or edible boletus toadstool – is eaten widely on the Continent, where it is often dried for winter use. It is richer in protein than any other plant food except nuts

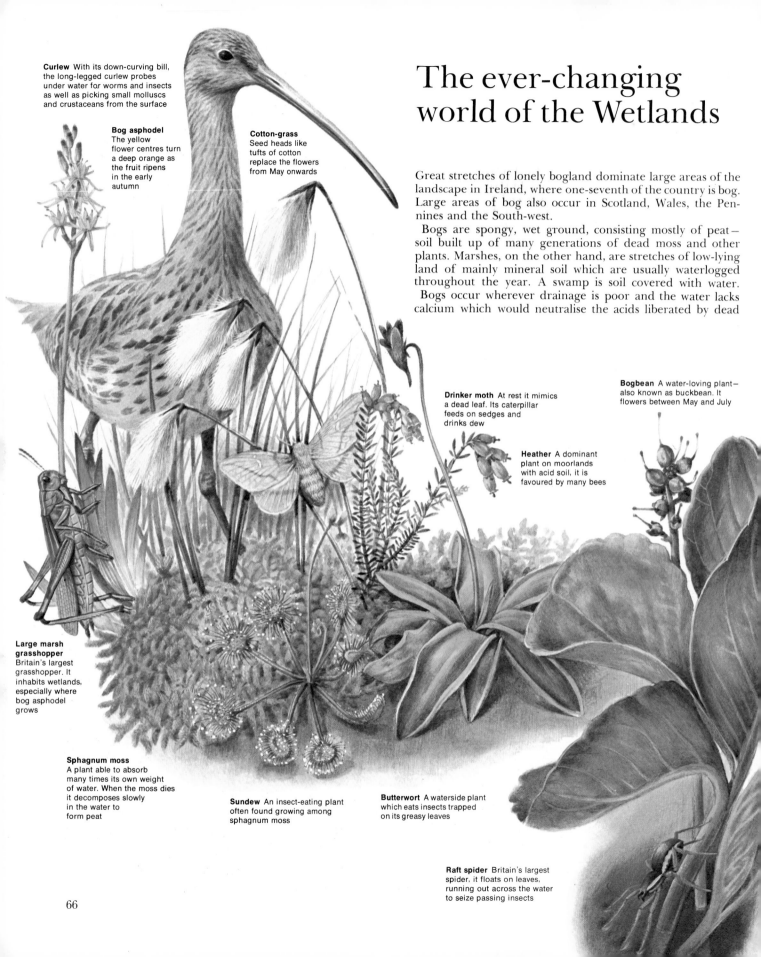

The ever-changing world of the Wetlands

Curlew With its down-curving bill, the long-legged curlew probes under water for worms and insects as well as picking small molluscs and crustaceans from the surface

Bog asphodel The yellow flower centres turn a deep orange as the fruit ripens in the early autumn

Cotton-grass Seed heads like tufts of cotton replace the flowers from May onwards

Great stretches of lonely bogland dominate large areas of the landscape in Ireland, where one-seventh of the country is bog. Large areas of bog also occur in Scotland, Wales, the Pennines and the South-west.

Bogs are spongy, wet ground, consisting mostly of peat — soil built up of many generations of dead moss and other plants. Marshes, on the other hand, are stretches of low-lying land of mainly mineral soil which are usually waterlogged throughout the year. A swamp is soil covered with water.

Bogs occur wherever drainage is poor and the water lacks calcium which would neutralise the acids liberated by dead

Drinker moth At rest it mimics a dead leaf. Its caterpillar feeds on sedges and drinks dew

Bogbean A water-loving plant — also known as buckbean. It flowers between May and July

Heather A dominant plant on moorlands with acid soil, it is favoured by many bees

Large marsh grasshopper Britain's largest grasshopper. It inhabits wetlands, especially where bog asphodel grows

Sphagnum moss A plant able to absorb many times its own weight of water. When the moss dies it decomposes slowly in the water to form peat

Sundew An insect-eating plant often found growing among sphagnum moss

Butterwort A waterside plant which eats insects trapped on its greasy leaves

Raft spider Britain's largest spider, it floats on leaves, running out across the water to seize passing insects

plants. Small bogs form in hollows below rocky uplands, and in areas of poor boulder-clay. Plants which grow in these waterlogged conditions do not decompose properly when they die, because lack of oxygen prevents bacteria from acting on them. Thus large quantities of dead plant material accumulate.

There are three basic types of bog—valley, raised and blanket. Valley bogs may be found even in the comparatively dry eastern part of England—in shallow depressions among wet heathland. Good examples in the New Forest and the west Surrey heaths are dominated by carpets of sphagnum— the generic name for mosses that grow in bogs. Other plants include cross-leaved heath, marsh cinquefoil, bog myrtle, the insect-eating sundews and, in standing water, sedges.

Raised bogs develop on the top of valley bogs through the continued growth of bog moss. This leads to an accumulation of moss peat, which may grow over a stream or small lake as a floating mat. This is how quaking bogs (or quagmires), such as Fox Tor Mires on Dartmoor, originated. They quake when walked upon and can swallow people and animals.

When the annual rainfall is very high, raised bogs can develop and engulf vegetation, as has happened extensively in central Ireland. Raised bogs which have not been dug for peat are domed, with progressively more acid and fewer species of plants towards the centre. The surface is broken into a series of pools and hummocks. A succession of other plants, including cotton grass, deer sedge, heather and lichens, become established on and around the hummocks. Eventually, the tops of the hummocks grow so high above the level of the water table—the surface below which the bog is saturated with water—that it becomes too dry for the bog moss to survive. The heather becomes leggy and dries; the hummock tops erode and a new cycle of growth begins.

Blanket bogs occur in places where the rainfall and humidity are high. A thick covering of bog moss develops everywhere, except in spots where the drainage is good. The best examples are in Connemara, Ireland, and in the Scottish Highlands at places such as Rannoch Moor. They are also found in Wales, the Pennines and Dartmoor, and even hillsides where, despite good drainage, the rainfall keeps ahead.

Plants found in raised bogs also occur in blanket bogs plus, in the drier parts, tormentil and bilberry. In and near water bogbean, bog pondweed, bladderworts and butterworts grow.

Boglands have few animals. Pools contain pondskaters, water boatmen, water beetles and dragonfly larvae. Crane flies and biting midges are abundant. There are spiders, lizards, short-tailed voles and—in drier areas—adders. A few birds—curlews, wheatears, skylarks and meadow pipits —are resident.

Man changes bogs in various ways, sometimes draining them. In spring and autumn, plants are burnt to encourage the fresh growths of heather and to improve grazing for sheep and grouse. Peat is used for fuel and mixed in light soils to improve their water-holding capacities.

PEAT LAYERS OF A RAISED BOG

Three different species of bog moss or sphagnum grow over the hummock surface

Continuously formed layers of peat raise the bog surface above the water table

Bog soil, a thick compressed layer of wet acid peat. It is formed from generations of partially decayed mosses and other plants

Bog wood, the preserved remains of forests destroyed thousands of years ago

Waterlogged hollows and sphagnum-covered hummocks are characteristic features of the raised bog that often grows over a valley bog

The many plants nourished by the waterlogged soil of a bog ultimately contribute to its growth with the products of their decay

Bourne

Small streams are known by many different names in the British Isles—for example, burn, gilt, beck and slack. Bourne is a variant of burn, and is the form commonly used in the south of England since the 14th century. It is most usually applied to streams on the chalk downs which are dry in summer. The heavier rain of winter causes springs to rise higher up the valley, and has given the name Winterbourne to a number of places in Berkshire, Gloucestershire, Dorset and Wiltshire, and the name Bourne End in Buckinghamshire.

Box *Buxus sempervirens*

As a wild tree, box grows only in a few small districts with chalk or limestone soil in southern England. One such place is Box Hill, Surrey, another is at Box in the Gloucestershire Cotswolds, and a third spot is on the downs near Dunstable in Bedfordshire. It has been successfully planted elsewhere.

Box is a neat, evergreen, mature tree rarely exceeding 15 ft in height. The trunk is rarely more than 6 in. thick. It has thick, oval leaves, dark green above and paler below. The leaves have a waxy surface which checks water loss, and enable the tree to thrive in dry conditions. It has dark grey bark, patterned with shallow squares, and greenish-yellow four-angled twigs.

The flowers, which open in May, form small, greenish-yellow clusters. Separate male and female flowers are borne on the same tree. The female flowers, which appear near the tips of the twigs, develop into round seed-pods, which ripen in autumn, bear six horns and hold black seeds which are spread by the wind. Box lends itself to shaping and clipping and has been used for many years for ornamental hedges and topiary. Garden box is a variety with extra-dense foliage which is propagated by cuttings. Box does not flower if it is clipped.

It has an orange-brown wood that is hard,

The thin, grey trunks of box trees produce the hardest and heaviest wood of any British tree

stable and even-grained, and was once used extensively for rulers and mathematical instruments, and wood-engraving blocks. Today it is used as a decorative timber, for fine wood carving, inlaid work, chessmen and similar small figures. Box is not harvested in Britain and the small amount used is imported from Turkey. The name comes from the Latin *buxus* meaning boxwood.

Bracken see Fern

Bracket fungus

This type of fungus forms distinctive fan-shaped shelves on stumps and trunks of living trees causing serious rot. Most persist for several years, often developing hard, woody brackets. They play an essential role in hastening the decomposition of dead wood. Different species of bracket fungi are adapted to life on a particular species of tree and only long-lived trees such as yew and the giant redwoods are immune from attack.

For instance, root fomes *Fomes annosus* attacks conifers, especially spruce, growing out at ground level as a brown, irregular crust with white pores underneath. The ganoderma *Ganoderma applanatum* produces woody brackets, strong enough to support a man. It grows mainly on old beech and in summer produces cocoa-brown spores which cover the surrounding vegetation. Dryad's saddle *Polyporus squamosa* lives mainly on elm where it causes a white stringy rot.

Bramble

The bare soil of newly cleared ground rarely stays bare for long. Seeds brought by wind or dropped by passing animals soon take root. Often one of the first plants to arrive in such a situation is a bramble.

There are several hundred species of bramble in Britain, adapted to living in conditions ranging from exposed mountainsides to densely shaded woods.

Bramble shrubs can be erect, sprawling or climbing. They are deciduous with prickly stems and compound leaves. These usually have three to five toothed oval leaflets. Once established on a site, a bramble soon spreads as its long trailing stems take root in the soil. Just as the bramble colonises the ground in this way, it is itself colonised by a wide range of insects and birds—a typical example of the interdependence of plant and animal life.

Most insect life is seen during the blossom and fruit seasons. Sap-sucking insects such as aphids and the foam-secreting larvae of frog-hoppers live on the young shoots, together with various species of shield bugs. The shield bug *Elasmucha grisea* is one of the few insects that cares for its young. In late July the female can sometimes be seen on a leaf with her 30-40 young. Then, at the least cause for alarm, she will herd them under the leaf while she stays exposed on the upper side as a decoy.

A bramble spreads swiftly, creating shelter for

Throughout the year, bramble leaves are scribbled with the white winding tunnels made by the larvae of the moth *Nepticula aurella*. The tunnel begins where the egg was laid, charts the larva's progress as it eats its way between the upper and lower skins of the leaf and ends at the opening where the moth emerged. In winter, the white of the mine shows up vividly against the brown of the dying leaf.

Most species are self-fertile, but some are pollinated by insects which visit the flowers to obtain nectar or pollen. One of these is the wasp-like hover-fly *Syrphus ribesii*. This insect's larvae, which look like small, transparent slugs, often live on bramble leaves, where they prey on the aphids. Each larvae eats up to 50 aphids a day. The grubs which are found in black-berries are those of the raspberry beetle *Byturus tomentosus* or the raspberry moth *Lampronia rubiella*.

The common wasp, which preys on flies early in the summer, starts to feed on sugars in late August. The wasp comes to the bramble to feed on the berries, biting through the skin of the individual fruitlets to reach the flesh inside. Once the wasp has pierced the skin other insects swarm to the fruit. The oozing juice attracts metallic greenbottle flies and grey-haired, red-eyed flesh flies. They dribble saliva on to the fruit, partly digesting the flesh which they then suck up in the form of juice.

As the blackberries become more mushy, they attract butterflies such as commas, speckled woods and red admirals. The tattered-looking commas suck up the juice through their long, hollow tongues while slowly beating their wings ready for a quick departure.

Spiders, whose webs shine among the bramble tangles in the early autumn mists, feed on the flies attracted to the berries. Long-legged hunting spiders lurk motion-less beneath leaves, pouncing out on their

other plants and providing food for many animals

unsuspecting prey. Birds also haunt brambles. In spring, the tangle of stems makes an ideal nesting site for many species, including thrushes, blackcaps, robins and woodcock. Later the insect life and berries are a major source of food for many birds. Blackbirds eat the berries, then wipe their bills on leaves to get rid of the seeds—an action called 'pip-spitting'.

Around decaying tree stumps, seeds voided by different birds may be seen together with young bramble shoots growing amidst moss and decaying humus. Other animals that feed on the berries include the badger, the yellow-coloured dusky slug and a number of snails, including the grey-bodied banded snail.

Some leaves are killed by a parasitic rust fungus before the first frosts arrive, but in others the green chlorophyll content breaks down to reveal yellow and orange pigments. Life slows almost to a standstill before the new year's sun restarts the cycle of growth, flowers and fruit formation.

The world of the bramble bush

Comma butterfly Through its long tongue it sucks up the juice of mushy blackberries

Red admiral Like the comma, this butterfly feeds on mushy fruits

Banded snail Hibernates until mid-summer, then emerges in damp weather

Flesh fly Dribbles saliva on pierced fruit, then sucks up juice

Shield bug Female hides young under bramble leaf while she stays in the open to decoy predators

Blackbird By spitting out the seeds of the blackberries it eats, it helps to spread the plant

Wasp Pierces the skin of the berries to reach their sugary flesh

Spider and crane fly Flies attracted to blackberries are often trapped in spiders' webs spun in the bush

Breakwater

Generally, a timber framework or low broad wall, also called a groyne, built to control sea encroachment by checking wave action on the foreshore. Shingle is swept away from one side of the groyne and piles up on the other, where it is moved up the beach at right angles to the waves.

Often the wave action round a groyne is too great to allow the growth of seaweeds or the settlement of animals. Where it is less strong, seaweeds, sea anemones, barnacles, winkles and dog whelks build up on the breakwater, while crabs, prawns and even fish take refuge in pools hollowed out around the end of it. Wooden groynes are good sites to look for the wood-boring gribble.

Sometimes a breakwater is a massive structure built of reinforced concrete or masonry and reaching far out to sea to form a harbour or improve a natural harbour. The longest breakwater in Britain protects the port of Holyhead, Anglesey, and is 9860 ft long. See also COAST

A wooden and reinforced concrete breakwater at Lyme Regis, Dorset

Bream

Of the two species found in fresh water in Britain, only the bronze bream *Abramis brama* is widespread. Deep-bodied and dull bronze or grey in colour, it grows to about 20 in. long, and specimens of up to 15 lb. have been recorded. It is abundant in the larger rivers, lowland lakes, reservoirs and gravel pits of England, southern Scotland and most of Ireland.

It is a bottom-living fish with a mouth which extends into a downward-pointing tube to suck up worms, insect larvae and molluscs. When young, the bronze bream lives more in mid-water, feeding on actively swimming prey. It is more silvery at this stage, and is often confused with the silver bream *Blicca bjoerkna*. This is silver all its life, and has larger eyes, but rarely grows more than 9 in. long or more than 1 lb. in weight. Native to the rivers of eastern England, it has been introduced elsewhere. See also BLACK BREAM

Breccia

Most rocks are made up of fragments bonded together. When the fragments are irregular, angular and about 4-6 in. across, the rock is called a breccia. Breccia is formed of rock fractured by volcanic action or the pressure of earth movements, and bonded together again with sediment or by further volcanic action.

Breccia can be seen in Britain among the sandstones of the Midlands and the south Devon coast.

Breck

Where the Norsemen once settled, and particularly in Yorkshire, Lancashire and the Lake District, breck in a place name signifies a hill or hillside. In modern usage, a breck is a stretch of open heathland with sandy soil and thin grass.

This derives from the Breckland in southwest Norfolk, once a vast area of heath formed of gravel and sand resting on chalk —the result of a glacial retreat. The Breckland's former reputation for dust storms is now fading, since much of it has been taken over by the Forestry Commission and planted with pines and firs.

The term breck is also used for the local recreation ground (originally wasteland) in Cheshire and Lancashire villages.

Breeding, Selective

Since man emerged from his Old Stone Age way of life as a nomadic hunter he has tried to domesticate various wild animals and to cultivate plants as food. By selecting animals and plants with desirable qualities, such as a higher milk yield, better wool, larger fruits or heavier crops, and breeding only from them, breeders have developed animal and plant varieties far removed from the wild ancestral stock.

The selection process was largely haphazard until the 18th century when Robert Bakewell of Dishley, Leicestershire, began the systematic breeding of cattle and sheep. Today the geneticist who studies heredity can determine from his records the kind of offspring likely to result from crossing selected parent animals or plants. See also FARMING

Briar see Rose

Brickfield

The musty smell of raw clay pervades all working brickfields, which resemble moonscapes with conical hills of waste material standing in the waterlogged excavations from which the clay has been removed. These excavations are often up to 100 ft deep and many acres in extent. There are many of them in Bedfordshire and near Peterborough. Tall chimneys rise above the kilns where the bricks are fired.

Until the late 19th century brickmaking was widespread on a small scale, each area producing distinctive coloured bricks from its local clay. Disused claypits, many of them now flooded, often with the remains of beehive-shaped kilns, mark the sites of abandoned brickworks in many parts of the British Isles.

A section of the nine-arched bridge which dates from

Bridge

While the canal, railway and motorway ages may have produced more dramatic structures, the older bridges of the British Isles often provide the key to the economic, social and architectural history of a region. Although some are no longer in general use, and others may have been by-passed by the development of modern roads, all have played a vital part at some stage of the growth of inland communication.

The earliest surviving bridges, dating from prehistoric times, were clam and clapperbridges—primitive affairs made of stone, chiefly granite and sandstone slabs. A clambridge consists of a large boulder placed between the banks of a narrow stream and is little more than a stepping stone. For a wider and perhaps deeper stream a clapperbridge was used. This was a succession of flat-topped boulders, placed at regular intervals apart, supporting large flat slabs up to 15 ft long and 6 ft wide. Sometimes, the central supports, or piers, consisted of piles of flat stones. Many examples survive in the West Country; a particularly good one can be seen at Tarr Steps, north Devon.

During the Roman occupation, the first London Bridge—made of timber—was built across the River Thames, not far from the site of the modern bridge. The Romans also built stone bridges, incorporating semicircular arches and cutwaters—boat-shaped piers that reduce the effects of water pressure. With the departure of the Romans in the 5th century, stone bridge building declined for the next 600 years until an order of monks, related to the Italian Brotherhood of Bridge-builders, revived the craft.

Medieval bridges, ranging from the small single spans to larger multi-span structures, with pointed as well as semi-circular arches —reflecting new architectural techniques

the 14th century at Bradford-on-Avon in Wiltshire

which gave larger spans—were built by the hundred. A fine surviving example is the medieval bridge at Bradford-on-Avon. Bridges of this period often incorporated unusual features, such as shrines, V-shaped spaces in the parapets for pedestrians to stand in when waggons passed by, chapels and, in some cases, houses. The Old London Bridge, demolished in 1834, was 900 ft long and carried up to five storeys of shops and houses on each side. Pulteney Bridge at Bath, designed by Robert Adam in 1769, still supports houses—now converted to shops. Renaissance bridges of the 18th century were often designed by eminent architects and included much ornamental detail.

From the 14th to the 18th century bridges with low parapets, or none at all, were built primarily for the passage of pack-horses, heavily laden with side-saddle packs.

In 1779, cast iron was used for the first time in a bridge at Coalbrookdale, Shropshire, marking the decline of stone for bridge building in favour of the new materials developed by the Industrial Revolution.

Cast iron, and later wrought iron, gave way to steel and reinforced concrete which were used to create the much larger bridges of the late 19th and 20th centuries.

Bristle-tail

Probably the most primitive insects alive to-day, bristle-tails, unlike most other insects, have no wings. But, like other insects, bristle-tails have six legs, though they also have several pairs of short knobs which may be vestiges of the legs possessed by the many-legged ancestors of the insects. Bristle-tail eggs hatch as small bristle-tails which do not change in appearance as they grow. Flat creatures, between $\frac{1}{4}$ in. and $\frac{3}{4}$ in. long, that squeeze into crevices and under stones, bristle-tails have very long antennae and

their bodies terminate in three long bristles.

Seven of the nine British species are found in the countryside. The largest and most common of the seven is *Petrobius maritimus,* which lives in the crevices of cliffs close to rocky seashores. The two other species of bristle-tail, the silverfish and the firebrat, are always found in association with man, living off food scraps. A coat of shining scales gives the $\frac{1}{2}$ in. long silverfish its name. It is often found in kitchens, where it lives in crevices, emerging at night to feed on crumbs. The firebrat is brown and lives in warm places, such as bakehouses.

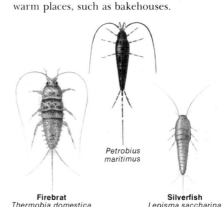

Petrobius
maritimus

Firebrat
Thermobia domestica

Silverfish
Lepisma saccharina

The scale-covered bristle-tails are among the few insects that have no wings

Bristleworm

These are shore-living relatives of the earthworm. Each segment of a bristleworm's body has a pair of paddles bearing bristles on each side. Some, like the paddle worm and ragworm, move and swim freely and burrow in the sand. Others live in permanent tubes from which only their heads emerge. Several fan worms and the honeycomb worm build tubes with sand; other species secrete a hard limy tube. The worms enlarge these tubes as they grow, and some can replace damaged ones. Some bristleworms catch small marine animals, while others filter food particles from sand, water or mud. Some species are luminous, which may serve to attract prey. See also CATWORM, LUGWORM and TUBEWORM

A bristleworm's mass of feeding tentacles extend from its burrow in search of prey

Brittle star

Many species of brittle star are found on British seashores. Some bury themselves in the sand, while others, like the common European brittle star *Ophiothrix fragilis,* hide under stones or cling to weed. In deep water, divers have reported huge concentrations of them on the sea bottom, and they form a major part of the cod's diet. They feed on small sea creatures.

Brittle stars resemble starfish in having five arms arranged symmetrically around a central body, but the arms are thin and clearly demarcated from the central disc which is usually less than an inch in diameter. As their name suggests, they lose their limbs easily but they can grow new ones. However, few brittle stars are seen with all their limbs intact. Most brittle stars discharge eggs or sperm into the water in the spring. The eggs then hatch into larvae which float in the plankton until they settle on the sea-bed.

Brittle stars: the shorter limbs are replacements for ones broken off earlier

Broad-leaved tree

Any tree whose leaves are basically flat, as distinct from being needle-shaped like those of conifers. A broad leaf is efficient in obtaining carbon dioxide from the air to build up the tree's tissues, but it also loses water rapidly; therefore, since a tree cannot obtain water from cold or frozen soil, most broad-leaved trees are deciduous—that is, they shed leaves when winter approaches. Without their leaves, broad-leaved trees remain dormant until the warmth of spring stimulates new growth. The exceptions in

Britain are the three evergreens, holly, box and strawberry tree: the waxy surface of their leaves checks water loss.

Most of Britain's broad-leaved trees are natives and form part of the great broad-leaved forest that once stretched over the whole of northern Europe. See also CONIFER, TREE

Broads

Extensive peat digging in the Middle Ages produced the Broads which lie on the middle courses of the rivers Bure, Yare and Waveney in Norfolk. There are 12 large and 24 small Broads. Each Broad lies in a different parish, and in the past provided its fuel and much of its prosperity. The large, rectangular pits, which lay alongside river courses, were flooded in the late Middle Ages when land subsided and river levels rose. The narrow banks and peninsulas which project into the Broad or marsh are the remains of boundary banks which separated medieval strips.

Today, the Broads are popular for sailing, fishing—for perch, bream, pike and rudd— and the surrounding marshes produce reed for use in thatching. Resembling the great areas of British fenland of 400 years ago, the Broads are now a haven for wild life.

Broccoli

Cauliflower, the best known type of broccoli, comes in two forms: cauliflower proper, which is a summer crop, and the more hardy winter cauliflower which is harvested up to November. Each produces a dense, white flower head or curd. Sprouting broccoli produces clusters of small purple, white or green curds. See also CABBAGE, HERB

Brook see River

Brooklime *Veronica beccabunga.*

Once used in salads, the brooklime's leaves have a taste which is not unpleasant and were said to cure scurvy. Brooklime has spikes of dark blue flowers and shining, rounded, fleshy leaves. It grows in muddy places by streams, in ditches and by the edges of ponds. Self-pollination occurs when the flowers half close in bad weather bringing the pollen-bearing anthers into contact with the stigmas; the plant also spreads by stems rooting whenever they touch the ground. See also SPEEDWELL

Brookweed *Samolus valerandi*

This white-flowered plant with glossy, round, fleshy leaves grows on most of the coasts of the British Isles, usually where a small stream trickles over the rocks, or in damp cracks on cliffs just above a beach. It also occurs in the Fens.

The minute five-petalled flowers are borne in loose spikes from June to August and are mainly self-pollinating. The plant is up to 12 in. high.

The fleshy, shiny leaves of brookweed grow in rosettes at the base of the stems

Broom *Sarothamnus scoparius*

One of the glories of spring, broom turns heaths golden in May and June. Favouring sandy, acid soils, it can be found throughout the British Isles, except for Orkney and Shetland, growing as high as 6 ft.

Broom produces no nectar to attract insects; instead it has a 'trigger' device in its yellow flowers which sprays pollen on to bees. The anthers release their pollen into a fold at the front of the flower petal. When a bee alights on the flower, its weight causes the loaded petal to flick upwards, dusting pollen on to the bee which flies off to pollinate another flower.

Under its former name *Planta genista* broom was the badge of Geoffrey, Duke of Anjou, father of England's Henry II, who adopted the name for his family, the Plantagenets.

Broomrape

A parasite growing on broom and gorse has given its name to ten similar plants living on different hosts. Broomrapes obtain their food by attaching their underground stems to the roots of other plants. They have dingy brown stems, 6-18 in. tall, which bear overlapping leaf-like scales and yellow flowers tinged with pink or purple. Common broomrape *Orobanche minor* grows in south-east England, usually among clover. It flowers from June to September. The other species are all rather rare.

The dingy brown stems of broomrape bear overlapping leaf-like scales

Dun Telve, near Glenelg, Inverness-shire—one of the best preserved brochs in Scotland

Broch

These Scottish strongholds, dating back about 2000 years, were built by the Picts as fortified homesteads. Centuries later they were named brochs from the Old Norse word *borg*—a place of defence. They were massive round stone towers standing above walled courtyards in which there were small huts.

Being 40-50 ft high they were good lookout points. They had an inside diameter of 40 ft or more and 15 ft thick walls containing stairways and rooms. They were therefore fireproof, too thick to batter down and too steep to climb. Brochs were surrounded by deep ditches forming outer courtyards in which remnants of circular huts have been found.

About 500 brochs have been noted in Scotland. The best surviving example is the Broch of Mousa on Shetland.

Brown butterfly

A family of butterflies, mostly brown or yellowish-brown, with black spots and white markings resembling eyes on their wings. The advantage of the eyespots is that they confuse enemies. Birds attacking a brown butterfly sometimes go for the false 'eyes' allowing the butterfly to escape with only a damaged wing. Brown butterflies vary in wingspan from 1¼ in. to 2 in. Most are slow and weak in flight and can be seen from June to August or September, although some species produce two broods, the first appearing in April or May. They do not hibernate completely, usually overwintering as caterpillars, which wake on warm days to feed on grass.

One of the most common and widespread butterflies in the British Isles is the meadow brown which usually lives in open grassland or at road-sides. The gatekeeper is known by two other names: the hedge brown, which indicates its favourite habitat, and the small meadow brown, as it is closely related to the meadow brown. It is common in most of lowland England and Wales, but rare in Ireland and unknown in Scotland.

The largest of the browns is the grayling with a wingspan of 2 in. or more. It lives in dry grassland, usually chalk downlands or sandy heathlands. Most grayling colonies are near the sea.

There are two species of heath butterfly in the British Isles. The small heath is very common. The large heath *C. tullia* is restricted to Ireland and the northern half of Britain from North Wales and Shropshire to the Orkneys. Large heaths vary greatly in colour; the Scottish, or Northern, forms are mostly light orange, but further south they are usually darker.

The marbled white, with its bold brown and

The brown butterflies

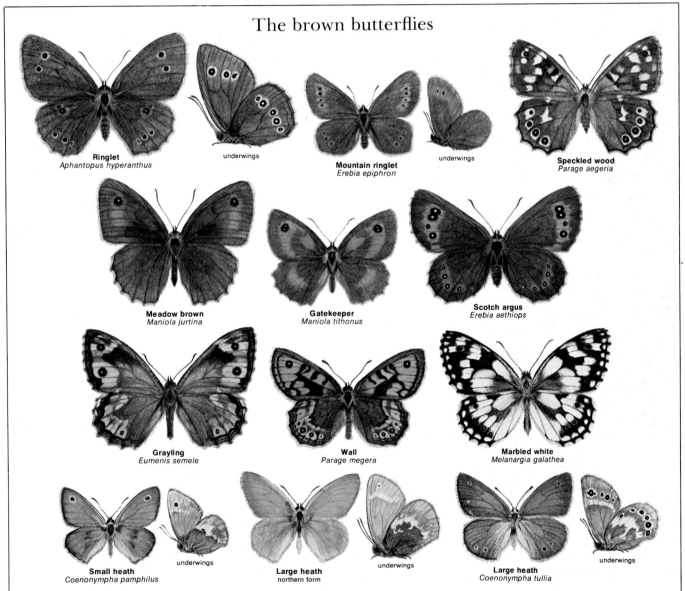

Ringlet
Aphantopus hyperanthus

underwings

Mountain ringlet
Erebia epiphron

underwings

Speckled wood
Parage aegeria

Meadow brown
Maniola jurtina

Gatekeeper
Maniola tithonus

Scotch argus
Erebia aethiops

Grayling
Eumenis semele

Wall
Parage megera

Marbled white
Melanargia galathea

Small heath
Coenonympha pamphilus

underwings

Large heath
northern form

underwings

Large heath
Coenonympha tullia

underwings

The 11 species of brown butterflies, all drawn life-size, are a family of butterflies with grass-eating caterpillars found in summer on open grassland, among hedgerows and on the edges of woodlands. In most species the female is larger and paler than the male. They are generally slow flyers—the wall and grayling are exceptions—relying on the camouflage of their brown wings to escape predators. They vary in wingspan from 1¼ in.-2 in. and have black spots and white markings on their wings resembling eyes. They can be seen from June to August or September

white markings, is unlike the other members of the brown butterfly family. It is mostly found south of a line from Swansea to The Wash, and sometimes in Yorkshire.

The female marbled white does not attach her eggs to a leaf, but scatters them as she flies over grass. The eggs hatch into caterpillars which hibernate until spring when they feed on grass.

The mountain ringlet is an alpine species which has survived in Britain since the last Ice Age, about 10,000 years ago. It is found only above 1800 ft in the Lake District and above 1500 ft in the Grampians. It flies in June and July but is active only when the sun shines because in the cold conditions of mountain tops it needs warmth before it can produce enough energy to fly. The Scotch argus is common only in Scotland. It is closely related to the mountain ringlet, but prefers lower ground, particularly damp grassland near woods. The caterpillars sometimes hibernate for two winters.

The ringlet looks dull in flight but when it settles on a flower and closes its wings the numerous black and white circles from which it gets its name can be seen on the undersides. It lives in woodland clearings or damp grassland in July and August throughout the British Isles except northern Scotland.

Brown and yellow mottled wings make the speckled wood butterfly difficult to see as it rests on sun-dappled leaves on the edges of woodland. It is common in the lowland parts of England, Wales and Ireland but rare in Scotland. The wall butterfly likes to fly in strong sunlight over rough grassland and to bask in the sun on warm stone walls. It is spread throughout the British Isles except the Scottish Highlands.

A brown ringlet butterfly busy extracting some nectar from a flower on a summer's day

Brucellosis see Cattle

Brussels sprout
Increasing demand from supermarkets, and its suitability for quick freezing, means that this market-garden crop is now being grown in general agricultural areas. Brussels sprouts have dense, compact buds like miniature cabbages, borne close together on a tall, single stem. The plant is a cultivated variety of the wild cabbage *Brassica oleracea*.

Bryony, Black *Tamus communis*
A high-climbing hedgerow plant found in England and Wales, black bryony climbs by twining its 6-12 ft long, unbranched stem up shrubs and trees. Its green flowers have six petals. These are of separate sexes, borne on different plants. The female flowers are followed in autumn by poisonous, scarlet berries. Though superficially like the white bryony, it is not related. It has a tuber from which fresh stems arise every spring.

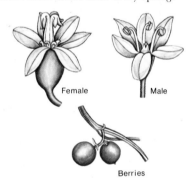

Female   Male

Berries

Close-up of the green flowers and heart-shaped leaves of the high-climbing black bryony

Bryony, White *Bryonia dioica*
The only native British plant belonging to the cucumber family, the stems of white bryony coil 10-20 ft up the hedgerows of England and Wales. It differs from black bryony in having dull, hairy, lobed leaves and by climbing with the aid of tendrils. The spiral coils of the tendrils which draw the plant to the hedge are unusual in that they coil then change direction in the middle.

Dark-veined, green-yellow flowers with five petals appear in June and July, the males and females being on separate plants. The female flowers develop into poisonous scarlet berries in September. The massive, yellowish rootstock is also poisonous and was formerly sold as a cheap substitute for the mandrake *Mandragora officinalis*, a herb much prized for its magical and allegedly aphrodisiac properties.

Buckthorn
Two scarce and usually small shrubs growing in quite different conditions bear the name buckthorn, although one has no thorns at all. Purging buckthorn *Rhamnus cathartica*, a small grey-barked tree resembling the blackthorn, grows on dry chalk downs and other lime-rich soils. Its oval, long-stalked

leaves are set in pairs, as are its twigs and branches. Spines on its twigs discourage animals from eating its leaves.

Inconspicuous green flowers, either male or female, are borne on separate plants on ridged spurs which resemble a roebuck's antlers, giving rise to the shrub's former name 'buck's horn tree'. The flowers which open in May are followed by black berries in September. The berries are strongly purgative and were once used in herbal medicine.

Alder buckthorn *Frangula alnus* grows near alders on marshy ground and belongs to the same botanical family as purging buckthorn. Quite thornless, it has black twigs, paired oval leaves and small, whitish flowers.

The berries, which ripen in autumn from green through red to black, contain two or three seeds, which are spread by birds. When unripe the berries yield a green dye, and this was once used extensively by calico printers. Charcoal made from alder buckthorn stems gives gunpowder an even rate of burning and is still used in slow fuses.

Caterpillars of the brimstone butterfly feed on the leaves of both British species. See also SEA BUCKTHORN

Buckwheat *Fagopyrum esculentum*
A quick-growing crop on the poorest land, this ruddy-stemmed plant has clusters of pink-white flowers from July to September and dark, triangular, sharp-edged seeds. Buckwheat stands about 12 in. high, and has broad, arrow-shaped leaves. In the 16th-19th centuries it was grown for cattle and hen food and was a 'poor man's flour'. Today it is seldom cultivated except to feed game birds, or to be ploughed in as a 'green manure' to improve the water-holding capacity of a light, hungry soil.

Detail of the flower head and leaf of buckwheat, which is in flower from July to September

Buddleia *Buddleja davidii*
In mid-summer, the scented lilac flowers of this shrub attract many butterflies, especially tortoiseshells, peacocks and red admirals; hence its other name, butterfly-bush. It has dull grey-green lance-shaped leaves, 4-6 in. long, with a thin felt of white hairs on the undersurface, and often exceeds 15 ft in height. Introduced from western China in the late 19th century, it soon spread by means of its tiny winged seeds. It spread further on Second World War bomb sites and is now common in southern England.

Two shield bugs of the species *Picromerus bidens* feed on a sawfly grub. These bugs eat many pests

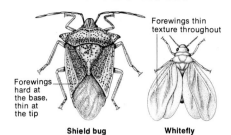

THE TWO TYPES OF BUG WING

Forewings thin texture throughout

Forewings hard at the base, thin at the tip

Shield bug **Whitefly**

There are two main types of bug: one has hard, beetle-like forewings with thin tips; the other has forewings that are of a uniform texture throughout their length

Bug

This word, loosely used to describe almost any non-flying insect, applies strictly to a distinct group known scientifically as Hemiptera. There are 55,000 species of bugs in the world of which more than 1600 live in Britain, including creatures as diverse as greenfly and the water boatmen. All bugs are distinguished by having beak-like mouths which are carried under the head when not in use and erected for feeding. Most bugs are vegetarian, using their beaks to pierce the skin of plants to suck sap. A few are carnivores, some of which suck the blood of man and other mammals.

Some species of bugs are a nuisance to man, by eating agricultural crops and by carrying viruses from one plant to another; but most species of bugs feed on weeds and are completely harmless to man. A few species are carriers of diseases, transmitting them among humans. The carnivorous bugs are welcomed by the farmers as they help to control pests by preying on them. Bugs, like all insects, form a valuable source of food for some birds and small mammals such as the hedgehog and badger.

Unlike most insects, such as butterflies or beetles, the life cycle of bugs involves only three stages. The eggs hatch as nymphs, not caterpillars. These resemble tiny, wingless adults. They grow and change their skins several times, but finally change directly into adults without a pupal, or resting, stage. Adult bugs usually have two pairs of wings and most can fly.

Most of the larger British bugs, including plant bugs and shield bugs, belong to a group of 500 species called the Heteroptera, or cross-winged bugs. These have forewings hardened near their base but transparent nearer the tip. These wings are held crossing over each other, unlike beetle forewings which are hardened along their length and meet edge to edge. This group includes water bugs, most of which are carnivorous.

The other 1100 or so species of British bugs, which include aphids such as greenfly, are called Homoptera. They have wings which are either entirely transparent, like those of greenfly, or forewings hardened along the whole of their length, like frog-hoppers.

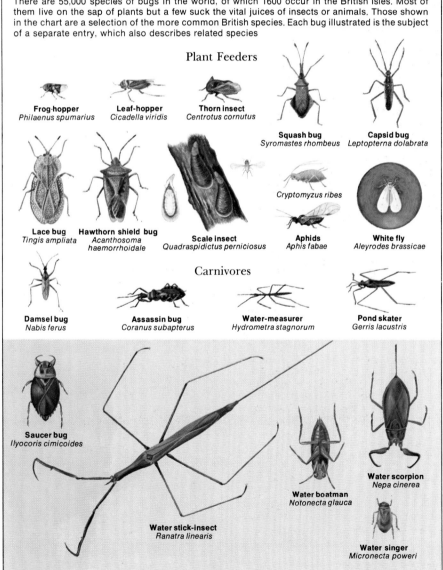

Common British bugs

There are 55,000 species of bugs in the world, of which 1600 occur in the British Isles. Most of them live on the sap of plants but a few suck the vital juices of insects or animals. Those shown in the chart are a selection of the more common British species. Each bug illustrated is the subject of a separate entry, which also describes related species

Plant Feeders

Frog-hopper
Philaenus spumarius

Leaf-hopper
Cicadella viridis

Thorn insect
Centrotus cornutus

Squash bug
Syromastes rhombeus

Capsid bug
Leptopterna dolabrata

Lace bug
Tingis ampliata

Hawthorn shield bug
Acanthosoma haemorrhoidale

Scale insect
Quadraspidictus perniciosus

Cryptomyzus ribes

Aphids
Aphis fabae

White fly
Aleyrodes brassicae

Carnivores

Damsel bug
Nabis ferus

Assassin bug
Coranus subapterus

Water-measurer
Hydrometra stagnorum

Pond skater
Gerris lacustris

Saucer bug
Ilyocoris cimicoides

Water stick-insect
Ranatra linearis

Water boatman
Notonecta glauca

Water scorpion
Nepa cinerea

Water singer
Micronecta poweri

Bugle *Ajuga reptans*

Throughout Britain in May and June, damp woods and meadows are coloured by small spikes of blue flowers set on short, stiff stems amid dark shining purple leaves. Bugle tolerates shade, and is often found deep in oakwoods.

It often grows in large patches, as it spreads easily with long overground runners, which can be troublesome to gardeners. It was an ingredient of the 17th-century 'Traumatick Decoction' or wound-healing drink, and was also made into an ointment for treating ulcers and bruises.

Bugloss *Anchusa arvensis*

The bright blue flowers of this bristly herb, which stands 1-2 ft high, can be seen in summer in sandy or chalky arable fields throughout Britain, and particularly near the sea in the west. The flowers resemble forget-me-nots, except that the tube to which the petals are attached has a kink in the middle. Bugloss gets its name from a Greek word meaning 'ox-tongued', referring to the shape and roughness of the leaves. Related species are often grown in gardens from which they sometimes spread to establish themselves in waste places.

The tube to which the petals of the bugloss flower are attached bends in the middle

Bull see Cattle

Bullhead *Cottus gobio*

A freshwater fish, up to 4 in. long. The bullhead is usually found in running water, mainly on stony beds, but also around lake shores and in muddy streams throughout England, Wales and southern Scotland. It skulks under large, hollow stones or in dense weed beds, rarely emerging into open water and then only at night. Its eggs are laid beneath the roof of a cavity hollowed out under a stone. The bullhead has a broad, heavy head with weak spines and is dark grey or brown with darker speckles. It feeds on insect larvae and crustaceans. Its flattened head gives rise to its other name 'miller's thumb', since millers traditionally developed broad thumbs through rubbing grain between thumb and forefinger.

Bulrush

Reedmace is the other common name for the bulrush, a water-loving plant with dark

brown spikes. These spikes are the developing seed heads. They appear in June and July, but do not shed their seeds until February. The bulrush also spreads by division of its thick underground stems. The common bulrush has leaves more than $\frac{1}{2}$ in. wide and grows 4-7 ft high. It is widespread in lakes, ponds and slow-moving rivers throughout the lowlands of the British Isles. The lesser bulrush, which is rare outside the English lowlands, has leaves less than $\frac{3}{4}$ in. wide and grows 3-9 ft high. Its spike has a gap up to 2 in. long in the middle.

Bunting

Five species of bunting breed in Britain. They form part of the large Passerine, or perching, order of birds, and measure 6-7 in. in length, having long tails about three-quarters the size of the body. Buntings are characterised by strong beaks, needed for breaking into seeds, their chief food. They tend to be polygamous. The cocks take no part in incubating the eggs, but they help to feed the young. Nests, containing two to five eggs, are made on or near the ground.

The most common bunting is the yellowhammer *Emberiza citrinella*, which lives among heaths, hedgerows and farmland throughout Britain and Ireland. The cock has a vivid yellow head and breast. The hen

A cock reed bunting in distinctive summer plumage sings his four-note phrase

is duller, and both have chestnut rumps. Cocks sing in spring and summer in quick, hard notes, ending in a long wheeze, to which the words 'Little bit of bread and no cheese' can be fitted. During courtship the cock flies after the hen in a twisting pursuit, at the end of which both birds fall to the ground and mate. Sometimes the cock parades around the hen with spread wings and tail and erect crest. In winter some yellowhammers fly into Britain from Europe.

Corn buntings *E. calandra* are scattered throughout England and Scotland and in a few places in Wales and Ireland. Both cocks and hens have streaked, dull brown plumage. Cocks sing a monotonous song which sounds like the jangling of keys. They do this from any song-perch that commands a view of their nest.

Reed buntings *E. schoeniclus* like to live in reed beds and marshy places, but they have recently moved into farmland and even suburban parks. Cocks have black heads and throats, and white collars. They have dark brown streaked backs and are grey-white below. Hens are streaked brown. Both birds decoy intruders from their nest by shuffling along as though their wings are broken.

Cirl buntings *E. cirlus* are rare, but can sometimes be seen on warm slopes in southern and western England. Cocks have black and yellow heads, black throats and grey-green bands across their yellow breasts. Hens have olive rumps. These are the only buntings that sometimes nest in gardens. The cirl bunting is a Mediterranean species that does not like the British winter and is rarely found nesting north of the Thames.

A few snow buntings *Plectrophenax nivalis* nest in Scotland. Scandinavian migrants are common along the east coast from autumn until spring. These winter migrants are sometimes seen in large flocks, fluttering up and down together in their search for food. In winter, both sexes are buff-brown above and white beneath, with more white on males. In summer cocks are pure white with black on back, wings and tail.

Bur see Seed

Burbot *Lota lota*

This is the only freshwater representative of the cod family and in Britain it is extremely rare. Few specimens have been caught since 1900 and it was thought to be extinct, but one was caught in the Old West River at Aldreth Bridge, Cambridgeshire, in 1969. Burbot are 12-24 in. long and olive-green, with brown blotches on their backs and creamy-yellow bellies. They have a barbel (feeler) on the lower jaw, and are difficult to see, being active only at dawn and dusk. By day they lie in crevices under banks or in holes in river beds. They feed mostly on small fish. Breeding takes place from December to March, and several spawnings take place within the period.

The bur-covered seed heads of great burdock cling to fur and feathers and are spread by animals

Burdock

Three species of this herb are common throughout the British Isles, except in the far north.

Great burdock *Arctium lappa* is profuse on river banks and roadsides. It is strong and grows up to 4 ft with rhubarb-like leaves which can be 15 in. long.

Lesser burdock *A. minus* is similar but smaller with almost unstalked flower heads. It grows in woods and hedgerows and on waste ground. Another species *A. nemorosum,* which is also small, has large, stalked flower heads. All three species flower in July and August, and the hooked bristles surrounding the flower heads form burs which stick to clothing when dry.

The stalks and roots used to be boiled or eaten raw and used as a general tonic and an aphrodisiac. An essence made from the plant is used in the soft drink dandelion and burdock, which is popular in the Midlands.

Buried forest

At several places along the English coast beds of peat with fossil tree trunks can be seen near the low-water mark when waves wash away the sand of the beach. The trees in these buried forests, usually pines, are often well preserved. The forests, about 8000 years old, flourished when the sea-level was lower. As the sea-level rose, peat was formed in the marshy conditions, and finally the forests were overwhelmed by the sea. Sandy beach material protected them from erosion. A good example can be seen at low tide at Little Galley Hill, Bexhill, Sussex, where the present sea-level is 20-30 ft higher than when the trees were growing. Other examples are at Tenby, Pembrokeshire, and Ingoldmells, Lincolnshire.

Bur-marigold

The purple stems and dingy yellow flowers of bur-marigolds can be seen in waterside places in summer, usually in sites which are under water in winter.

There are two species. Nodding bur-marigold has drooping flowers and long, toothed leaves. Three-lobed, or trifid, bur-marigold has leaves divided into three. Both grow up to 2 ft.

In the autumn the ripe flower heads open to expose the seeds. Each seed has a long bristle covered in barbs. The three-lobed bur-marigold has two bristles and the nodding type has three or four. They are dispersed on animals' fur.

Burnet moth

This brightly coloured moth, like the butterfly, flies during the day, but unlike the butterfly it has long, narrow wings. Seven species of burnet moth live in Britain. All are bronze-green, marked with bright red. The bronze-green colour varies with the direction of the light, as the colour is not a pigment. It is created by the layered structure of the scales covering the wings. This structure interferes with the light waves, in the same way that a thin layer of oil on a wet road does.

Burnet moths exude a yellow fluid when attacked. This contains hydrogen cyanide (prussic acid), but they are not harmful to humans—unless eaten. The poison is acquired in the caterpillar state from trefoil and vetch, on which they feed.

Once a bird has attacked a burnet moth and tasted it, it will not do so again; the moth's bright colours are ample warning.

The caterpillars depend mainly on camouflage for protection. They occur in shades of green which merge into the background of the food plant. Caterpillars of all seven species are very much alike. In early summer each caterpillar spins a cocoon on a grass stem. The cocoon is often found after the moth has hatched, from May to July, with the chrysalis case half-hanging out of the cocoon.

The six-spot burnet *Zygaena filipendulae* is the most common species, occurring throughout the British Isles. The innermost two spots on each forewing often merge into one, but six-spot burnets can be distinguished from the five-spot species because in these the fifth spot is always the odd one nearest the outer tip of the wing. Two of the five-spot species are widespread in England and Wales. One of these, the burnet companion *Ectypa glyphica*, is particularly common in the south. The five-spot *Zygaena trifolii* occurs in two forms: one flies over downland, the other is slightly larger and usually seen over marshland. The other four five-spot species are rare and confined to limited areas.

Burnet moths live in colonies, so that, even in the case of the rare species, if one is seen there are likely to be others around.

The bright colours of the burnet moth are a warning to predators that it is distasteful

Burnet-saxifrage see Parsley

Bur-reed *Sparganium erectum*

This erect water plant, which grows to 4 ft, is found throughout Britain on mud or in the shallow water of ponds, streams, ditches and lakes. Its yellow-green flowers cluster together in separate male and female heads along the stems. After flowering from June to August, the female heads produce seeds in a variety of shapes, ranging from spherical to boat-shaped. It used to be believed that a preparation made from the root was an antidote for snake bites.

Burying beetle

An excellent sense of smell will take a burying beetle to the corpse of a small animal. A male may then release a scent to attract a female, and together they will tunnel beneath the body until it sinks into the ground. Fur or feather is gnawed off, and the flesh is moulded into a ball. The female lays about 15 eggs in a short tunnel leading off the grave, and feeds from the ball. Eggs hatch in ten days, and the female feeds the larvae on regurgitated food until they can feed themselves.

Seven species of burying beetle are common in the British Isles, of which the largest, the black burying beetle *Necrophorus humator*, measures up to 1½ in. long. The small species are about ¾ in. and are black with orange bands on their wing cases.

This pygmy shrew carcass will soon be food for the larvae of the inspecting burying beetle

Bush cricket see Grasshopper

Bushel

For more than 1000 years the bushel was the measure for dry goods, from corn to coal. But it was imprecise, as bushel vessels were not identical. The capacity varied from place to place and according to the goods being measured. For example, a Durham corn bushel held 8-8½ gallons, while a Somer-set coal bushel contained 20 gallons. Efforts were made to standardise the measure, but it fell into disuse and in 1963 was made illegal for trade in the United Kingdom. It is legal in the Irish Republic, but not widely used. In 1878 Parliament defined a bushel as 56 lb. of flour, 60 lb. of wheat and 40 lb. of apples — weights still applicable in Ireland. International trade in wheat is transacted in bushels, one bushel equalling 60 lb.

Bustard

Now a rare visitor from eastern Europe, the great bustard *Otis tarda* bred in Norfolk until the middle of the last century. It is one of the largest flying birds: males are 40 in. long, and females 10 in. shorter. Males weigh 24-35 lb., but females only 11-13 lb. They are ostrich-like, nesting in natural depressions in the ground, and easy game to shoot. They are brown above and white below. A few brought from Portugal have been settled on Salisbury Plain in an effort to re-introduce the species. The little bustard *O. tetrax*, 12 in. long and mottled brown, is another rare visitor from the Continent.

Butcher's broom *Ruscus aculeatus*

This 2 ft high evergreen shrub bears tiny green-white flowers from January to April and red berries from October to May. Both appear to come from the centre of the spiny leaves. These 'leaves' are really flattened branches, the true leaves being reduced to small scales. Butcher's broom grows in dry woods in southern England and Wales. At one time it was made into brooms by butchers who found the prickly leaves ideal for cleaning chopping blocks.

Butterbur *Petasites hybridus*

Following the course of many lowland streams and growing in water meadows throughout the British Isles is the rhubarb-like butterbur. Its enormous leaves, often 3 ft across, form a dense shade under which few other plants will grow. The leaves appear after the reddish-violet flowers which bloom between March and May. They are frequently visited by bees. Male and female flower heads grow on separate plants in spikes up to 1 ft long. Butterbur is rarely found north of the Forth and Clyde.

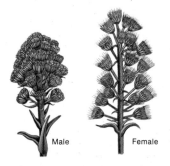

Male butterbur flowers grow in a cluster: the females are spread out along the stem

Buttercup meadows disappear as permanent pasture

Buttercup

Though they look attractive, buttercups are poisonous in varying degrees. Probably the most poisonous is the celery-leaved buttercup *Ranunculus sceleratus*. It has no connection with celery; the English name is a false translation of *sceleratus*, Latin for wicked or vicious. It grows on mud, in ditches or near the edge of lowland ponds and streams. A fleshy branched stem up to 2 ft high bears very small yellow flowers from May to September, and when the petals have fallen each flower produces nearly 100 tiny fruits. All parts of the plant may produce blistering and sores if they touch the skin.

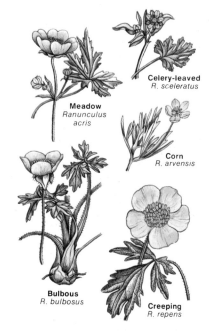

Celery-leaved
R. sceleratus

Meadow
Ranunculus acris

Corn
R. arvensis

Bulbous
R. bulbosus

Creeping
R. repens

Buttercups vary widely in size and habit of growth, but all have similar golden flowers

are ploughed and resown with grass and clover

Sheep have been killed by eating the corn buttercup *R. arvensis,* once a common weed in cornfields on lime-rich soils in England. It is becoming less frequent because of the widespread use of weedkillers. Corn buttercup differs from other native species in having heads of prickly fruits, which in Shropshire earned it the name of devil's currycomb.

The meadow buttercup *R. acris,* seen in damp meadows and even on Scottish mountain ledges, is the tallest of the three most common British buttercups, growing up to 3 ft on good soil. Its stalk beneath the flower is smooth, and its upright sepals encircle the petals. The bulbous buttercup *R. bulbosus* has ribbed flower stalks, and a swollen, bulb-like stem base. It is usually found on dry, lime-rich grassland, flowering in May and June. Creeping buttercup *R. repens* spreads rapidly by overground runners in many locations—even meadows which are flooded in winter.

Butterfish *Pholis gunnellus*
Like other inshore fish, the slippery-skinned butterfish or gunnel shelters under stones and seaweeds on rocky shores when the tide is out. It is about 10 in. long and reddish-brown with a row of dark spots along its back. Spawning is from December to March. The eggs are laid in a tight mass about 1 in. in diameter under a loose rock. After hatching, the young drift out to sea for several months before returning to swim in inshore waters.

Butterfly see p. 80

Butterwort *Pinguicula vulgaris*
This harmless-looking plant, with 1-3 in. leaves arranged in a flat rosette, traps and eats insects. The fleshy leaves are incurved at the edges and covered in a sticky secretion. When an insect lands on the sticky surface

The butterwort absorbs essential nutrients from insects trapped on its sticky leaves

the leaf curls to trap it. The leaf glands then produce a digestive fluid and the insect is absorbed. Pollen or heather leaves which fall on to butterworts are also 'eaten'. Nitrogen is the main element obtained in this way, enabling the butterwort to grow on acid peat which is normally short of nitrogen. It is rare outside mountainous areas of the north and west. Its violet flowers appear from May to July at the end of 4 in. leafless stalks. See also INSECT-EATING PLANTS

Buzzard
This is Britain's most common large bird of prey; it soars or flies in slow, wide circles over moors and woodland, searching for prey. The buzzard has keen eyes—up to eight times sharper than human eyes at picking out details. Though frequently seen in the air, it usually hunts from low perches such as gate posts and fences. It is sometimes mobbed by gulls or members of the crow family.

Britain has three species of buzzard, most easily distinguished by their seasonal distribution. The common buzzard *Buteo buteo* is a resident, mainly in hilly districts in the north and west of England, Wales and Scotland. After being driven out by game preservers, they have been breeding again on the north coast of Ireland since the 1950's. Although common buzzards sometimes take young game birds, they do more good than harm in killing rabbits, rodents and other small mammals, which, with birds, worms, insects and sheep carrion, make up their diet.

Buzzards were increasing in numbers and spreading eastwards until 1953 when myxomatosis decimated the rabbit population, reducing their food supply. Rabbits and common buzzards are now showing signs of recovery, and some of these birds have been seen in south-east England.

The rough-legged buzzard *B. lagopus,* which has never bred in Britain, is a winter visitor from Scandinavia to northern Scotland and eastern England as far south as Kent. Unlike the other two species, its legs are feathered—hence its name.

Rough-legged buzzards are rare in this country but their numbers increase in those years when there is an abundance of small mammals on their Arctic and sub-Arctic

breeding grounds. The population explosion of lemmings, which occurs every five or six years, is reflected by a ten-fold increase in the number of rough-legged buzzards visiting Britain.

The honey buzzard *Pernis apivorus*—so-called because of its habit of raiding wasp and bee nests for grubs—is even more rare. It is a summer visitor, and breeds regularly in a few localities in southern England, especially in the New Forest on its summer visits. Honey buzzards have long, thin necks, small heads and a narrow bill shaped for feeding on insects rather than tearing flesh. Their heads are protected from stings by densely packed short feathers.

The common buzzard has dark brown plumage, with bars and streaks on its paler underside. It has broad wings with slotted tips, a blunt, rounded tail, a stout body and varies in length from 20 to 24 in. The female is usually slightly larger than the male. The buzzard soars on wings held slightly forward in a shallow V. The rough-legged buzzard holds its wings flatter when soaring and has a white tail with a broad black band at the tip. It frequently hovers like a kestrel. The honey buzzard has long wings which droop in flight and are marked with two prominent bars, a motif repeated at the base of its longer tail.

Buzzards build their nests of sticks in trees, and sometimes on cliff ledges. Both parents incubate the eggs which hatch after about 30 days; the young fly six weeks later.

A buzzard tears at a rabbit—when rabbits are scarce the buzzard population falls

Byre see Cattle

Butterfly

The butterflies are some of the least destructive and most beautiful of insects. Together with moths they make up the order of Lepidoptera, from the Greek *lepis* meaning scale and *pteron* meaning wing. Butterflies and moths are distinguished from other insects by the scales on their wings.

To distinguish between butterflies and moths is fairly easy. Most butterflies fly by day and have brightly coloured wings, each with a distinct colouring according to the species. Moths are usually dull and fly by night. Most butterflies sit with the upper surfaces of their wings meeting over their back. Moths rest with their wings fanned out. However, there are exceptions to these guides and the only sure way of recognising a butterfly is to examine its antennae. Butterfly antennae are club-tipped, while those of a moth are feathery or finely pointed. Antennae are often referred to as feelers. In butterflies and moths they are not organs of touch but organs of smell.

The 70 different species of butterfly found regularly in Britain are grouped into seven families. The small or medium-sized browns, of the Satyridae family, have eye-like spots on their wings. The marbled white is included in this family. The fritillaries and vanessids belong to the Nymphalidae family. The brilliantly coloured blues, coppers and hairstreaks are included in the Lycaenidae family. The white and yellow butterflies are members of the Pieridae family and the moth-like skippers are the Hesperiidae family. The swallowtail, Papilionidae family, and the Duke of Burgundy fritillary, Riodinidae family, are the sole representatives of their families in Britain.

A number of factors may confuse identification. In most European butterflies, the males are markedly different from the females, but male and female coloration is sometimes seen in the same butterfly, known as a mosaic. In this fairly rare condition, wings may show male characteristics above and female below, be completely male on one

IDENTIFYING BUTTERFLIES

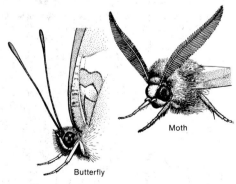

One way of distinguishing a moth from a butterfly is to look at the antennae. Generally, butterflies have club-tipped antennae and moths finely pointed or feathery structures

A key to all British butterflies

There are about 380 species of butterflies in Europe, 70 of which reside regularly in Britain. Those illustrated, two-thirds life size, are representative of the several groups, each of which has a separate entry elsewhere in the book. To identify a particular butterfly, first find the example on the chart which it most closely resembles, then look up the appropriate entry where all members of the group are shown and described together

side of the body and female on the other, or bear scattered patches of each.

All species have individual variations: the eyespots of the heaths and ringlets vary in size and number, and other spotted species may have streaks rather than spots. Especially in industrial areas, an excess of black pigment produces darker specimens. At the opposite end of the scale are albinos.

Scales

The dust that rubs off easily from a captured butterfly is, in fact, the scales from its wings. Each scale is a minute, flattened bag with a short stalk fitting into a socket in the wing membrane. Arranged like slates on a roof, the scales are responsible for the wing patterns. Some scales are filled with coloured pigments; others are grooved and surfaced to produce, by reflection, the effect of colour. The iridescence on the wings of the blues is formed in this way. The underside of the wing is often markedly different from the upper wing. When the butterfly rests, with wings held over its back, the dull under-colours blend well with their surroundings, and sometimes they resemble the petals or leaves of the plant on which they rest.

The metallic colour of the blues and coppers is accentuated by a thin film of oil on the scales.

Scent plays a large part in the mating of butterflies: males, attracted by the females' scent, in turn stimulate them by producing a scent from glandular areas at the base of the scales on their wings. The scent is diffused through tufts of very fine hairs at the tips of the scales, which the males sometimes brush over the females' antennae.

Life cycle

In the course of its brief life a butterfly undergoes dramatic changes in shape and appearance. As with many insects there are four stages in its life cycle: from egg to caterpillar or larva, to chrysalis or pupa and finally to butterfly or imago. One of these stages has to survive the rigours of winter, and which stage this is varies from species to species. Some butterflies have about six months in which to breed and leave offspring to survive to the following year. Other species may go through the complete life cycle two or even three times in a year.

The female lays 200 or so sticky eggs, depositing them on the leaves and flower stalks best suited to the food needs of the caterpillar. Some butterflies lay their eggs singly, others lay them in small batches or in masses. Each egg, varying in shape according to the species, is fluted, ribbed or pitted, rarely smooth. This ornamentation is best seen through a hand lens. Unless the egg is the overwintering stage in the life cycle the caterpillar usually hatches in a week. The caterpillar or larva phase is the feeding stage. The larva stores as much food as possible to sustain it through the non-eating pupal phase. Solitary caterpillars are well

camouflaged. Gregarious ones are often conspicuously coloured, relying on their unpleasant taste or armour of spines, which makes them difficult to swallow, as protection from birds, mice, lizards and other predators.

After about a month and several moults the caterpillar settles in a suitable spot to pupate. It may hang from a plant by a silken thread, or wind itself to a stem with a girdle of silk. Others pupate on the ground. After a few days the caterpillar's skin shrivels and is cast off, leaving the chrysalis or pupa. The outside of the chrysalis is marked with the rudimentary outlines of wings, eyes, tongue and legs of the developing butterfly. Inside the pupa a great reconstruction process is taking place. After two or three weeks a perfect adult insect is ready to emerge. The chrysalis splits, and a butterfly pulls itself free. Immediately, the butterfly climbs on to a twig or leaf where it rests while its wings dry and expand to their full size as blood starts to flow through the veins. An hour later it flies off in search of nectar to drink through its long, tube-like tongue or proboscis. The nectar merely provides enough energy for flight. The adult butterfly does not grow: its sole purpose is to reproduce. After an aerial courtship, fluttering and spiralling around each other, the butterflies settle on a plant to mate. Some days later the female lays her eggs and a new generation begins.

The life span of a butterfly varies from ten days to ten months according to its species.

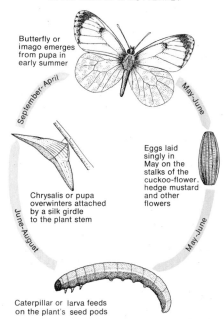

LIFE CYCLE OF A BUTTERFLY

Butterfly or imago emerges from pupa in early summer

September–April

May–June

Eggs laid singly in May on the stalks of the cuckoo-flower, hedge mustard and other flowers

May–June

June–August

Chrysalis or pupa overwinters attached by a silk girdle to the plant stem

Caterpillar or larva feeds on the plant's seed pods

The life cycle of the orange-tip is typical of many butterflies. In May the female—which has no orange markings—lays her eggs on plants such as the cuckoo-flower. The caterpillars that hatch out feed from June to August, then in September form the chrysalis in which they spend the winter

A butterfly is born: first the pupa case splits along a pre-formed line; then the head emerges, to be followed by the wings. Free of its case, the newly born butterfly hangs still for several minutes while its wings dry, until finally the full glory of a small tortoiseshell is revealed

C

Cabbage *Brassica oleracea*

Brussels sprouts, cauliflower, kale, kohl-rabi, sprouting broccoli and cabbage are all descended from wild cabbage, a plant which still grows on sea cliffs, particularly of chalk and limestone, from Kent along the south and west coasts to North Wales.

Wild cabbage is abundant on the cliffs beside Dover harbour. It used to be sold in Dover market, but the leaves are bitter and need a lot of boiling to make them palatable.

Sometimes called sea cabbage, it is very different from the cultivated varieties. It grows 2-3 ft high with a much branched woody stem, fleshy, wavy-edged leaves and no heart. Its yellow flowers appear from May to August and it spreads by seed.

Wild cabbage was an early food plant, and although it is not known exactly when it was brought into cultivation, some types were grown in Mediterranean areas more than 2000 years ago. Cabbage is known to have been cultivated in Britain since well before the Norman Conquest, and a mid-17th-century writer refers to its use as animal fodder. A century later, fodder cabbage was yielding 33 tons to the acre.

ALL BRED FROM CABBAGE

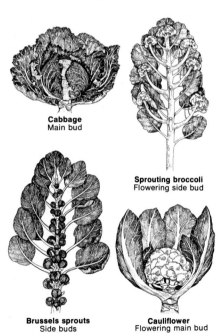

Cabbage
Main bud

Sprouting broccoli
Flowering side bud

Brussels sprouts
Side buds

Cauliflower
Flowering main bud

These four quite different vegetables have all been developed from the same wild plant—the wild cabbage. Each of the four exploits a different part of the wild plant

Kale is perhaps the nearest to the wild form of cabbage. Its young stems and leaves are the edible part. Large varieties are grown as winter fodder for livestock, and a number of other varieties, including cottager's kale, curly kale and Russian kale, are grown for human consumption.

Kohl-rabi has been known since at least the 16th century as a garden crop. Most of its root is really a swollen stem and grows above ground. Sometimes it is called turnip cabbage. In the second half of the 17th century its tops were fed to cattle and its stems to pigs.

Cauliflower was first cultivated in Britain in the early 17th century and sprouts were first recorded near Brussels, in Belgium, in the 13th century. See also CROPS

Cabbage moth *Mamestra brassicae*

The brown or greenish cabbage moth caterpillar can be a pest on garden cabbages, but it is not as harmful as that of the cabbage white butterfly. The cabbage moth caterpillar is one of the least fussy about its diet, and has been found on many species of low-growing plants and on some shrubs and trees.

The caterpillars hatch in July and are fully grown by October when they bury themselves in the soil. There, each makes a cell in which it pupates. The adult moth hatches from the pupa the following June.

The dull grey to brown moths have a 1¾ in. wingspan with a white kidney-shaped mark on their forewings. They fly at night during June and July, laying their eggs in one large batch on the leaf of a plant. They are widespread in the British Isles.

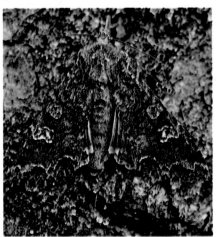

Like most night-flying moths, the cabbage moth is dull-coloured and well camouflaged

Cabbage root fly

A small fly, rather like a house fly, which lays its eggs on the stems of cabbages and related plants. The eggs hatch into small white maggots which eat into the stems of young plants, then move down to eat the roots. The pupae overwinter in the soil, and the fly hatches in early May. Overlapping generations produce many larvae in a few weeks.

Affected plants are easily recognised as their leaves droop and turn bluish. The maggots can cause extensive crop damage, but this is partly kept in check by black ground-beetles which feed on cabbage root fly pupae and eggs.

Market gardens throughout Britain, especially in Lincolnshire, are badly affected by this pest, and insecticides are used to control it. These insecticides are carefully selected and applied to avoid killing the predatory beetles as well.

Cabbage root fly
Erioischia brassicae

Cabbage white see White butterfly

Caddis fly

The adult flies are like brownish moths, but differ from moths in having a sparse covering of small hairs on the wings instead of scales. Like moths they cannot eat but can only drink nectar and similar plant fluids.

There are 188 British species of caddis fly which are mostly nocturnal and range in size from ¼ in. to 2½ in. across the outspread wings. Some species are popular bait for angling.

The largest species, the great red sedge *Phryganea grandis*, has a wingspan of 2½ in. and can be found from May to July near still or slow-running water. The silverhorns *Mystacides azurea* were so called because of their long black and white antennae. The male form swarms over slow sections of rivers during the day.

The Welshman's button *Sericostoma personatum* is another day-flying species, liked by fish and so used for angling.

Caddis eggs are usually laid in or near water and the larvae of most species make tubes from sand grains or bits of vegetation to protect their soft body and gills. The tubes are often camouflaged by being

Caddis fly eggs, embedded in a mass of protective jelly, are laid on waterside plants

decorated with pieces of shell and stone. It is this characteristic which gives the insect its name. It is named after the caddis man—an old word for pedlar—who wandered the countryside with his clothes decorated with samples of his wares. Most caddis larvae feed only on plant material, although the larvae of the great red sedge also attack small water animals. In their turn caddis fly larvae are eaten by trout and other fish.

HOW CADDIS FLY LARVAE HIDE

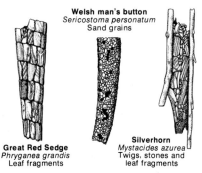

Welsh man's button
Sericostoma personatum
Sand grains

Great Red Sedge
Phryganea grandis
Leaf fragments

Silverhorn
Mystacides azurea
Twigs, stones and
leaf fragments

Characteristic cases are produced by each caddis larvae species. A variety of materials sticks to the silk tubes they spin. Twigs give some protection from predatory fish

Cage see Round house

Cairn

A heap of stones, often found on a peak or summit ridge. It is derived from the Gaelic *carn*, meaning a heap of stones, and occurs in place names especially of summits, such as Carnedd in North Wales. Many cairns date back to the Bronze and Iron Ages and mark ancient burial sites. They are also recorded in medieval documents as parish boundary markers. In more recent times waymarker cairns, usually much smaller than the ancient ones, indicate paths, especially over moorland routes with few natural landmarks. The Pennine Way, for example, is marked with cairns. See also BARROW

Calamint *Calamintha ascendens*

An aromatic herb with a mint-like odour, once used in making herb tea. It is a low-growing plant with pale, reddish-purple or lilac flowers in stalked tufts arising from the base of pairs of opposite leaves. It is found mostly on dry roadside banks in the southern half of England, but also grows on the Welsh coast and in southern Ireland.

The ½ in. long flowers of calamint spring from large calyx pouches in whorls of three or more

Camouflage see p. 110

Campion

Common in cornfields, roadside verges and other dry, grassy places, bladder campion *Silene vulgaris* has grey-green leaves and white flowers which have an inflated bladder-like calyx. The flowers can be male, female or bisexual. They are fragrant and attract bees and night-flying moths. The plant stands 1-2 ft high and flowers from June to September. Sea campion *S. maritima*, with smaller leaves, shorter stems and larger flowers, occurs on rocky shores.

Red and white campion are hedgerow plants, 1-3 ft high. Both have separate male and female flowers and are so closely related that pink hybrids occur naturally and are often found where the parents grow together. White campion *S. alba* is also a weed of arable land and tends to be much rarer in the north and west. Its flowers are fragrant, opening in the evening and attracting night-flying moths. Red campion *S. dioica* is more shade-loving and occurs in woods throughout the British Isles, though it is rare in southern Ireland.

Sea campion
Silene maritima

Bladder campion
S. vulgaris

White campion
S. alba

Red campion
S. dioica

Petal shape and size help to distinguish between these four varieties of campion

Canal see p. 84

Capsid bug

Britain has more than 200 species of this largest family of cross-winged bugs, varying widely in shape, structure and diet. Most live on plants of various kinds and have fairly narrow bodies, ⅙ to ⅓ in. long, and are either green or brown.

Like most capsids, the common meadow plant bug *Leptoterna dolabrata* lays its eggs in the lower parts of grass stems, especially timothy, couch grass and meadow foxtail. The young bugs hatch in May from over-wintered eggs, and feed by probing their mouthparts into the host plant, usually into the seeds, and injecting saliva. The partly digested food is then sucked in through the mouth.

The apple capsid *Plesiocoris rugicollis* feeds on apples in this way. The injected saliva causes brown spots which develop into rough, corky patches as the fruit grows.

The common green capsid *Lygocoris pabulinus* is numerous throughout the British Isles. It attacks potatoes, strawberries, apples, gooseberries, blackberries and pears.

The eggs are laid in young twigs on hawthorn, currant, cherry or limes in September. The young hatch in spring and after two moults move to herbaceous plants to feed and grow. They mature by June and lay eggs in June and July on the foodplants.

Potato capsid *Calocoris norvegicus* and European tarnished plant bug *Lygus rugulipennis* are among other capsid bugs which can be minor pests of crops.

Meadow plant bug
Leptoptwrna dolabrata

Apple capsid
Plesiocoris rugicoilis

Britain's canals, rich in history and wildlife

Lumbering, horse-drawn waggons, which for centuries had carried the inland commerce of Britain, proved inadequate to cope with the growth of trade brought about by the Industrial Revolution in the 18th century. The answer was found in canals, which not only provided swifter transport but also the enormous increase in capacity needed to carry the raw materials of industry and its finished products.

Britain's first canal, the Fossdyke, which is still in use, was built by the Romans in the 2nd century AD, or possibly earlier, to join Lincoln to the River Trent. Canal building was largely neglected until 1755, when a 12-mile waterway was cut to carry coal from St Helens in Lancashire to workshops near Winsford, Cheshire. Its success inspired the Bridgewater Canal, completed in 1761 by James Brindley to carry coal from the Duke of Bridgewater's mines $10\frac{1}{4}$ miles to Manchester.

In the next 80 years more than 4000 miles of navigable waterways were engineered by Brindley and his successors, men like Thomas Telford, John Rennie and John Smeaton. Towns like Manchester and Birmingham grew larger, and new canal ports like Stourport, in Worcestershire, were built.

Waterways in decline

The railways brought cheaper, faster transport and in a few years the waterways began to decline. Today (excluding Ireland) there are 1607 miles of navigable canals and 1645 miles of rivers made navigable by locks and short stretches of canal. A further 151 miles of canal, built for drainage purposes, can be used by boats. One can still travel from London to Liverpool and from Liverpool to Hull on canals.

Canals varied greatly in width, some being only 35 ft wide. The traditional narrow boat was the most practical for journeys involving several different canals, although wider craft were used where possible. Horse-drawn boats survived alongside steam-powered craft, whose large engines limited cargo space. The diesel engine, introduced just before the First World War, finally ousted the horse.

The bargee's family boat evolved when competition from the railways in the late 1840's forced rate-cutting for canal carriage and lower wages for boatmen, who brought their families on board to save rent. Decorated boats, on which it became the custom to paint patterns of roses and castles, date from the 1870's.

Engineering feats to overcome physical barriers impeding canal construction include the staircase of 30 locks at Tardebigge on the Worcester and Birmingham Canal, and the Blisworth Tunnel, 3506 yds long, on the Grand Union.

A canal's water supply comes mainly from adjacent rivers and streams supplemented by large reservoirs like Rudyard Lake, near Leek, Staffordshire, established in 1797 to supply the Trent and Mersey Canal. The flow of water into canals is only sufficient to maintain the water level. For this reason they take on the character of shallow lakes or ponds rather than that of rivers which they superficially resemble.

Many canals, especially along their disused stretches, are

Bingley Five Rise on the Leeds and Liverpool Canal lifts boats 59 ft up its

havens for wildlife. By being linked to river systems some canals have allowed freshwater fish—sticklebacks, pike, roach, perch, tench, carp, bream and chub, together with frogs, toads and newts—to spread. Rudd are common in canals where the water is brackish, and the Bridgwater and Taunton Canal is well known for its large eels, which enter the canal from the River Parrett.

If unattended, they become filled with black, foul-smelling sludge and reeds grow across the whole width of a canal. By dying down each year and impeding silt-bearing currents, reeds can gradually add to the quantity of organic matter, eventually allowing the invasion of bramble thickets and trees such as birch, hawthorn, willow and alder.

A network of nature trails

The water supports an abundance of insects and other small animals, such as the larvae of dragonflies and caddisflies, water boatmen and water stick beetles; also myriads of planktonic water fleas and copepods which feed on microscopic algae. Among the weeds live hydra, which look like miniature sea anemones, freshwater shrimps and water lice. Bivalves are common on the bottom and, around working locks where the water becomes stirred up, freshwater sponges and moss animals or bryozoans encrust the walls. Water worms abound in polluted water.

In the deeper water, many plants grow totally submerged. Others, such as the flowers of water milfoil, curled pondweed, hornwort and the very local water violet, can be seen above the surface. One of Britain's rarest aquatic plants, the water fern *Azolla filiculoides*, floats freely on the Basingstoke Canal. In shallower, muddy water, stalwort abounds. Along the edges grow grasses, rushes and many wild flowers.

Canal tunnels sometimes provide a home for nocturnal bats. Warblers, wagtails and flycatchers nest in the reeds, swallows and house martins find rich feeding on the wing, herons stalk fish and small mammals at the water's edge, and moorhens and mallards dabble for food.

Bulrush This 6 ft sentinel of the water's edge, which is also called reedmace, has been used for centuries to make baskets and the seats of chairs

Yellow flag This spectacular waterside flower is common throughout the British Isles

Dragonfly It lays its eggs in water, often inside the stems of plants. Its larvae live in the water, where many are eaten by fish

Arrowhead Two distinct types of leaf identify arrowhead: lance-shaped floating leaves and transparent, ribbon-like leaves that grow under water

Water vole A tunnel in the bank, often with an under-water entrance, marks the home of the water vole. It feeds largely on water snails and mussels

staircase of locks

Common reed The broad leaves and purple flower spikes of the common reed will soon choke a canal if left unchecked

Dabchick This bird nests in reeds or on floating vegetation and feeds mainly on insects, frogs and fish. Parents give the young chicks pick-a-back rides

Rudd The pink-finned rudd is happy in brackish water. In late spring or early summer it spawns on plants in shallow water

Yellow waterlily Bottle-shaped fruit give this plant its alternative name, brandy bottle

Great diving beetle A killer that preys on other insects and small fish

Waterboatman This insect swims on its boat-shaped back, hunting tadpoles and insect larvae

Common frog Its tadpoles, which hatch in the spring and leave the water by late summer, are one of the chief food sources for predators in the canal

The ½-⅔ in. long black-headed cardinal beetle, its red wing cases defiantly eye-catching

Cardinal beetle

From the Midlands southwards, these bright red beetles can be seen on flowers and nettles near woodlands in June. They crawl slowly and make no effort to hide, for as with many other conspicuous insects their colour exists to draw attention and warn off predators such as birds. A bird seeing a cardinal beetle is reminded that the last one it ate tasted unpleasant. Cardinal beetles have unusual antennae, rather like fretsaw blades, which are serrated along the inner edge. The black-headed cardinal beetle *Pyrochroa coccinea* is the larger of the two species and is a deep blood red. It is not found in Ireland. The cardinal beetle *P. serraticornis* has a red head. Both have yellowish, long, flattened larvae with two prongs at the tail end which live in dead wood and take three years to mature.

Carp *Cyprinus carpio*

Widely distributed, the carp is a good food fish which grows well in man-made waters. It was introduced, probably by monks, before the 16th century. Its original range was around the Black Sea and Eastern Mediterranean. Several varieties have been bred. The almost scaleless form is the leather carp; a similar fish with a row of large scales is the mirror carp; the fully scaled form, which is the most common in Britain, is the wild or king carp.

Carp usually live in still waters, ponds and small lakes, although some inhabit slow-flowing rivers. They prefer warm and densely weeded waters, and can often be seen basking near the surface in fine weather. They are often found in small shoals.

Carp have a mainly vegetable diet, but also eat worms and insects. Because they require a high temperature for successful spawning – which is only attained in occasional years – many carp populations in this country are maintained only by restocking. Eggs are laid on plants at the water's edge or on weeds in shallow water. Carp are long-lived, reaching up to 15 years in the wild, 40 years or more in captivity.

Carp can vary in colour from muddy slate to blue-green or brownish-green upper parts with blue-green, golden-yellow or straw-coloured sides. The average mature adult can grow to 20 in. in length, making carp popular with anglers, and specimens up to 36 in. long and 40 lb. in weight have been caught. See also CRUCIAN CARP

Carpet beetle

An indoor pest of increasing importance, the golden-brown larvae of the carpet beetle *Anthrenus verbasci* probably cause more damage than the clothes moth. The adult beetles, about ⅛ in. long and black, appear in April and June and feed on nectar and pollen. The females find their way into houses to lay 20-100 eggs on furs, wool, particularly carpets, and other dry materials of animal origin on which the larvae will feed. The larvae, sometimes called woolly-bears, not to be confused with the harmless woolly-bear caterpillars of tiger moths, are covered in a coat of hair-like scales. All the larvae of the Dermestidae family feed on the dried remains of animals, and the museum beetle *A. muscorum* is a pest in museum collections. In the wild, the beetles live in areas in which such dry remains accumulate, such as among spiders' webs and under loose bark.

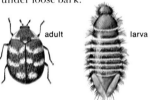

Carpet beetle *Anthranus verbasci*

Carpet moth

The wings of this group of night-flying moths have intricate, carpet-like patterns, and the shape of the wings, together with the thin body, gives each moth a resemblance to a butterfly. At rest, the forewings are spread out, sometimes exposing the hindwings; wingspans range from ¾ in. to 1½ in.

The garden carpet moth *Xanthoroe fluctuata* is one of the most common of the 20 or so British species. Its caterpillars feed on plants of the cabbage family between June and October. The brown pupae lie in the soil in a silken cocoon. There are two generations of moths in the year, in May-June and August-September, although some may be seen at other times. Garden carpet moths living in Scotland have a darker ground colour than those found in the south. Carpet moths belong to the huge Geometer family of moths, distinguished by the looping walk of their caterpillars.

Another common species is the red twin-spot carpet moth *X. spadiceara*, which has two black spots on each forewing.

Garden carpet moth
Xanthoroe fluctuata

Carr see Alder
Carragheen see Seaweed

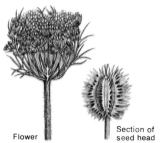

Flower   Section of seed head

The spreading flower head of the wild carrot develops into a mass of bristly seed pods

Carrot, Wild *Daucus carota*

The vertical root of this 1-3 ft high, native British herb is pale orange, and it has feathery leaves and white, flat-topped, saucer-shaped clusters of flowers, often with a single red or purple flower in the middle. It grows in grassy places and along roadsides, especially on lime-rich soils, or near the sea. After flowering, the outer stalks grow upwards and inwards to enclose the spiky seeds in a kind of nest—hence its Somerset name, bird's nest. These stalks may be roughly hairy, especially on the south and west coasts where a fleshy, shorter form occurs, sometimes called sea carrot.

Cultivated carrots are derived from the Mediterranean wild carrot *D. sativus.* Known to the Romans, they became popular here in the Tudor period. Their orange colour is due to the pigment carotene, a rich source of vitamin A. Carotene is extracted from the plant and used in medicine for its antiseptic properties. Modern weedkillers which do not damage the slow-growing seedlings have encouraged their large-scale cultivation on very deep sandy loams and particularly in the light peats of the Fens. Carrots belong to the Parsley family of plants. See also PARSLEY

Cat *Felis catus*

Ever since farmers realised its value as a vermin controller, possibly in Saxon times, the domestic cat has secured a place in the barn, if not at the hearthside.

Introduced by the Romans, the domestic cat is probably descended from races of the European wild cat *F. silvestris.* However, the cat remains independent of man and a range of breeds for special tasks is not developed as in dogs. Scotland has Britain's only true wild cat, the rare *F. s. grampia.* Today, the domestic cat is a vital farm animal. Since every rat is officially estimated to cause £1 worth of damage a year, the cat which catches 100 rats a year is of great value to its farmer. See also WILD CAT

Cataract see Waterfall

Catch-crop

This is a quick-growing crop planted between two major crops. For instance, after harvesting spring broccoli or a crop of rye for early grazing, a quick-growing fodder crop like maize or vetches may fill in time before the land is needed for sowing wheat in autumn. Or, after harvesting a cereal crop in August, ryegrass may be sown to provide autumn fodder for cattle or sheep. Towards the end of winter, the remainder of the crop can be ploughed in to provide a quick-decaying green manure and the land prepared for sowing a new crop of cereals in the spring. White turnips are a catch-crop which provides a useful green manure, as they decay rapidly and have a high nitrogen content.

Cart

Only a sledge among vehicles has a more ancient lineage than the two-wheeled cart, once a major feature of horse-drawn transport and now a fast-disappearing farm vehicle, superseded by the tractor and trailer. Less cumbersome and easier to turn than the four-wheeled wagon, it is thought to have been in use 3000 years ago. It was only in the middle of the last century that the horse finally replaced the ox as a means of drawing carts.

Cart designs and size varied according to their use. For example, low-bodied types were used to carry livestock, while corn and hay, being light but bulky, were carried on carts with high end frames, called ladders, to keep their loads in place. Design also varied from county to county, the width between the wheels usually governed by permanent cart-ruts on the roads until tarmac became common. Today, fixed-bodied carts are used alongside the tipping type, which can be up-ended to deposit its load by shooting a simple catch. This is useful when hauling dung, mangolds, straw and other farm produce.

Traditionally, the shafts are made of ash, as is the frame of the cart which is panelled with elm or deal. The wheel hubs are elm with oak spokes and ash rims bound with iron. The design and craftsmanship are such that each part interlocks together without the use of glue and can be removed and repaired or replaced easily.

The wheels of carts and wagons are 'dished', or concave, somewhat like saucers with the hollow side outwards. This serves two functions. First, by keeping the top half of the wheel well away from the body of the vehicle, it enables the sides of the body to slope outwards and a much larger load to be carried. Second, when a loaded horse-drawn cart is in motion, the body slides from side to side and batters into the centre of each wheel; 'dishing' counteracts this and prevents the wheels from breaking up.

Carts for farmers and tradesmen

A harvest cart. The ladders at front and back enabled hay to overhang the cart and a load of up to 30 cwt to be carried

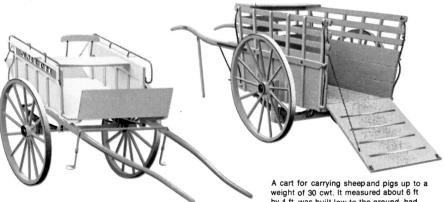

A light market cart fitted with springs to provide a comfortable ride; it was used to carry goods bought at market, and luggage

A cart for carrying sheep and pigs up to a weight of 30 cwt. It measured about 6 ft by 4 ft, was built low to the ground, had a tailboard for loading and was mounted on three springs

Castles — survivors of Britain's turbulent past

The medieval castle — stronghold of the feudal baron and symbol of his wealth and power — dominated important towns and strategic regions of the British countryside, during 500 years of political unrest and violence

Arundel Castle, begun in the reign of Edward the Confessor (1042-66), was strategically sited to guard one of the gaps in the South Downs, overlooking the River Arun. During the 12th century Henry II erected the existing stone

The castle was brought to Britain with the Normans and began to decline with the introduction of gunpowder. Although hundreds of defensive structures, including Iron Age fortifications, are called castles, the word applies strictly only to those fortified buildings erected by monarchs and the nobility from the time of the Norman Conquest.

Before the Norman invasion, Anglo-Saxons repulsed attacks from *burhs* — communal fortifications on hilltops, consisting of little more than ditches and timber stockades. In later years the sites of burhs were built over, leaving only the word as part of a place-name, as in Bamburgh and Canterbury.

The earliest form of true castle — a word derived from the Latin *castellum*, meaning a fortified place — was the motte and bailey. The motte was a steep-sided, flat-topped mound of earth surrounded by a ditch and surmounted by a square, two-storied wooden tower, and the bailey was a courtyard. Mottes varied from 50 ft to 120 ft high and 50 ft to 300 ft across. Ditches were filled with water or sharpened stakes, and crossed by wooden bridges. During an attack the castle's dependants, peasants and stock took refuge inside the baileys and the bridges were removed.

In time the word motte was transposed to describe the water-filled ditch surrounding the mound — hence, moat.

More than a hundred mottes were built between 1066 and 1100, and many more during the following century, some as far afield as Sutherlandshire and Ireland. Hundreds have survived in Britain, many little more than grassy mounds with ditches defining the limits of the baileys.

The next stage in castle development was stone-built towers or, as they were later called, keeps. The stockades or palisades were replaced with stone walls.

Castles occupying important strongpoints of the Norman Conquest had immense stone keeps, usually three or more storeys high, with walls thick enough to contain small rooms, fireplaces, latrines and even spiral staircases. The keep was the final defensive structure that could be held, even after the walls had been breached and the inner bailey invaded.

The strongpoints of a medieval castle

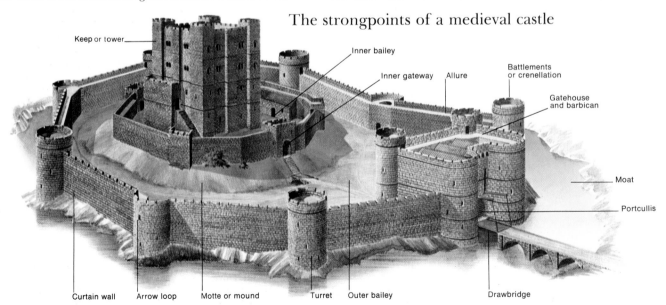

Keep or tower — Inner bailey — Inner gateway — Allure — Battlements or crenellation — Gatehouse and barbican — Moat — Portcullis — Curtain wall — Arrow loop — Motte or mound — Turret — Outer bailey — Drawbridge

The nerve-centre of the medieval castle was its massive keep. Protected from the enemy by a formidable series of obstacles — from which the defenders could launch attacks — the keep could still remain an inviolate stronghold, even if the inner and outer baileys had been breached

keep on the original motte, enclosing the two baileys with high curtain walls and towers. The castle was ruined by Cromwell's troops between 1643 and 1649 and restored with Gothic additions during the 19th century

STAGES IN CASTLE DEVELOPMENT

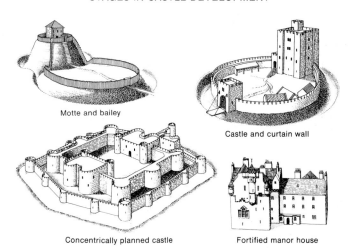

Motte and bailey

Castle and curtain wall

Concentrically planned castle

Fortified manor house

The Norman motte and bailey flourished for 100 years until stone-built castles and curtain walls appeared. By 1500, the lesser nobility were building fortified manor houses and many royal castles were almost impregnable

During the 13th century curtain walls were built higher with turrets—towers—projecting from the outer face at regular intervals. These increased the defenders' view of the walls and strengthened a castle's security.

The castle builders of the 13th century learnt much from the Crusaders who, to hold down a land that was often hostile and always dangerous, built great concentric castles with a sequence of strong walls within each other. The Tower of London and Beaumaris Castle in Anglesey are on this pattern. This feature reached its zenith in the castles built by the early Edwardian kings, especially Edward I, who set out to build a chain of invincible strongholds across North Wales.

Window openings were small, narrow and protected by an iron grille, giving the occupants limited light and ventilation. The later crucifix-shaped apertures—arrow-loops—provided maximum defence, with vertical slits for the use of longbow and horizontal slits for the crossbow. Circular holes at the ends—oilets—allowed greater manoeuvrability of weapons. During the 15th century when cannons were used in the defence of some castles, gun-loops were provided; the sides were angled to provide a larger opening on the inside.

The tops of walls, towers and turrets were fortified with battlements. These tooth-like indentations—the openings were called crenelles or embrasures, the raised portions merlons—provided bowmen with protection. On some castles the battlements projected outwards and machicolations—openings in the floor of the parapet—gave defenders a means of dropping missiles on attackers.

Since medieval warfare highlighted the weaknesses of square corners that were easy to undermine or fracture with battering rams and vulnerable to missiles, particularly cannon shot, round towers were introduced.

The weakest point of the defences was the gateway through the outer curtain wall. During the 13th century this was fortified with a portcullis and drawbridge. The portcullis was a massive iron-clad grille that could be lowered to the ground to seal the entry. The drawbridge, also controlled from inside the castle, could be lowered as a means of crossing the moat or raised to provide a further barrier.

The turbulence of the late medieval period, especially on the Anglo-Scottish border, led many of the lesser nobility to apply to the Crown for permission to crenellate, that is fortify, their manor houses; one of the first was Stokesay, built in Shropshire in 1291.

The border counties of England and Scotland have a great variety of castles. They vary from the royal castles, such as Berwick-upon-Tweed of which only Norman fragments remain, to the massive tower-houses—larger versions of pele towers—which were the homes of clan chieftains, such as Cessford in Roxburghshire, once home of the Kerrs.

Many of the greater Irish castles were built by invaders from Britain. The 13th-century keep at Trim, County Neath, is 75 ft high—strengthened by a gatehouse and moat—standing on a Norman motte and bailey raised in 1170. The castle at nearby Slane, also built on a motte and bailey, was incorporated into one of Ireland's finest Gothic Revival structures during the 19th century.

Britain's long coastline has always been vulnerable to attack and even in Roman times a series of forts, such as the ruins at Reculver and Lympne, were built to protect the coast against Saxon raiders. The Roman fortress, unlike the castle, was built for the occupation of a garrison rather than a feudal lord and his retainers. The castles built by the Crown along the coast span the whole period of castle building from Norman to Tudor times. Camber Castle in Sussex, and Deal and Walmer castles in Kent—erected during the 1540's against possible invasion by the French—were immense gun-emplacements rather than castles. The strong government of the Tudors and the later union of England and Scotland made all except coastal defence unnecessary. To curb possible rebellions private castle building was discouraged.

Many of the great mansions built during the 18th and 19th centuries adopted the word castle, decorating their façades with arrow-loops, turrets, crenellations and other features of their fortified predecessors.

Few castles that have survived in Britain are of any one period; each has been shaped by the effects of successive additions and centuries of decay.

Catchfly

Although most varieties have sticky stems which catch flies, straw and leaves, this plant does not eat insects. Of the eight species growing wild in Britain, only two are common. Both flower in cornfields from July to October. The larger, which reaches 2 ft, is the night-flowering catchfly most common in eastern England. Its dirty yellow flowers are tinged with rose and open in the evening. They are sweet-scented and attract moths, which assist in pollination.

The small-flowered or English catchfly, which grows up to 12 in. high, bears tiny, dingy white or pink flowers about ⅛ in. across. It is scattered throughout England and Wales especially in sandy or gravelly fields.

Night-flowering catchfly
Silene noctiflora

Small-flowered catchfly
S. gallica

Catchflies have sticky stems which trap insects, though the plants do not feed on them

Caterpillar

Like most other insects, butterflies and moths start their life cycle in an egg, hatch as a larva, spend a resting stage as a pupa in a cocoon or chrysalis, and finally emerge from this as an adult. Most female moths and butterflies lay several hundred eggs, but out of every hundred laid only two survive to adulthood. The larvae of butterflies and moths are called caterpillars. They generally hatch on the food plants where they will spend the whole caterpillar stage, and begin

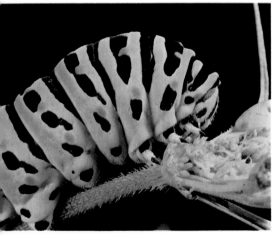

The caterpillar of the swallowtail butterfly feeds only on the leaves of milk parsley

---

Caterpillars of British butterflies and moths

More than 2000 species of butterflies and moths live in the British Isles, each of which has its own particular type of caterpillar. The caterpillars illustrated are a selection of the more common species. In each case the food plants on which they are likely to be found are indicated

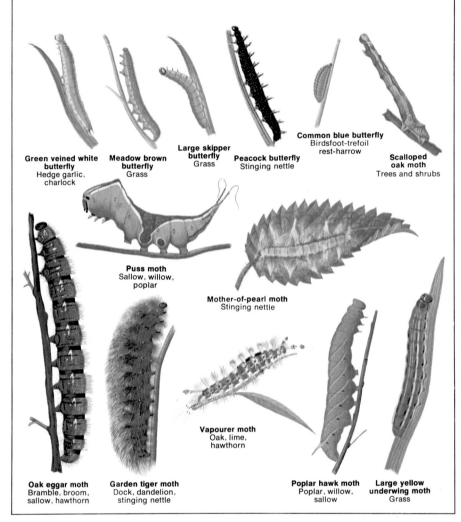

Green veined white butterfly
Hedge garlic, charlock

Meadow brown butterfly
Grass

Large skipper butterfly
Grass

Peacock butterfly
Stinging nettle

Common blue butterfly
Birdsfoot-trefoil rest-harrow

Scalloped oak moth
Trees and shrubs

Puss moth
Sallow, willow, poplar

Mother-of-pearl moth
Stinging nettle

Vapourer moth
Oak, lime, hawthorn

Oak eggar moth
Bramble, broom, sallow, hawthorn

Garden tiger moth
Dock, dandelion, stinging nettle

Poplar hawk moth
Poplar, willow, sallow

Large yellow underwing moth
Grass

---

to eat at once, taking the egg shell as their first meal. Caterpillars spend most of the time eating—they consume 10-15 times their own weight before pupating—and most moths and butterflies live out their brief lives on food stored in the caterpillar stage.

Most insect larvae have only six legs, but caterpillars have extra leg-like structures on their abdomens—usually five pairs. These enable them to cling tightly to wind-blown plants. The geometer family of moths have only two pairs of extra 'legs'. They are called loopers because their middle, legless, segments bend up in loops as they walk. All butterfly caterpillars are structurally much alike, consisting of a head and 13 segments. But there are wide differences in size, shape and colouring.

Caterpillars of the family of brown butterflies are green and russet—well camouflaged for their life among grass. Others, such as those of the peacock butterfly, are covered in spiny growths which make them indigestible for predators.

Moth caterpillars are more variable than those of butterflies, but many have similar growths on their bodies to deter predators. Some are hairy, like the woolly-bear tiger moth caterpillars and the brightly coloured tussock moth caterpillars whose hairs can irritate human skin. Hawk moth caterpillars have a spine at their rear end.

Glands in the bodies of caterpillars secrete the raw materials for silk, used to secure the caterpillar to a twig or leaf while it sheds a skin as it grows. The silk is also used to make the cocoon or support the chrysalis.

Caterpillar fungus *Cordyceps militaris*

A small fungus which appears in autumn as a waxy, reddish-orange club tapered at both ends, in damp, grassy places, including lawns and hedgerows. Usually it grows singly, but on rare occasions hundreds may appear together looking like toy soldiers.

The caterpillar fungus grows up to 1½ in. high from the body of a living caterpillar or chrysalis in the ground. A mass of root-like threads from the fungus spread throughout the insect's body and it eventually dies.

The orange clubs are covered with minute rough markings through which the spores are liberated. The spores germinate only if they land on moist caterpillar skin.

Catfish or wels *Siluris glanis*

Sinister stories are told in eastern Europe of giant catfish seizing and eating swimming children. As this fish, which is also called the wels, can grow to a length of 16 ft such a reputation is not surprising. British specimens, however, seldom exceed 4 ft.

The catfish, a native of central Europe, was introduced into lakes at Woburn Abbey, Bedfordshire, at the beginning of the century. Later, more were put into a number of lakes in other parts of the county and in Buckinghamshire. It is also found in the reservoirs at Tring in Hertfordshire. The catfish is mainly active at night, hiding in holes in the bank or under tree roots during the day. It has a broad head, a large mouth with long barbels, and a smooth, greeny-brown skin. It eats all kinds of fish, frogs, small water birds and mammals.

Catsear *Hypochoeris radicata*

One of the most common wild flowers in meadows and pastures and on roadside verges throughout the British Isles. Catsear has yellow, dandelion-like flowers which appear from June to September. It can be distinguished from the dandelion and other similar species by its 2 ft high, branched, flowering stems which are leafless except for some tiny scales. Its oblong, dull green leaves are 3-10 in. long with wavy margins and rather stiff unbranched hairs. The leaves usually form a flat rosette on the ground, smothering the grass beneath.

Aurochs in a German zoo. The wild aurochs, extinct since 1627, has been re-created by selective breeding

Cattle

There are more than 12 million cattle in the United Kingdom and another 6 million in the Irish Republic. All are descended from two species of wild cattle: the aurochs *Bos primigenius*, large oxen varying from black through brown-black to dun, which once roamed the forests of Europe; and smaller short-horned animals *B. longifrons* whose origins are uncertain. Prehistoric man first hunted these animals for their meat, then, about 9000 years ago, began to domesticate them. Cattle were kept not only for their meat, milk and hides, but as beasts of burden as well.

As the centuries passed, successive invaders brought their own breeds to Britain: for example, the Romans introduced improved dairy strains from the Mediterranean and the Anglo-Saxons brought large red cattle. Different types evolved in different parts of the country. With the growth of new markets in the growing towns of 17th-century England, sporadic and unsystematic attempts were made to produce better beef cattle by cross-breeding. Then, at the end of the 18th century, Robert Bakewell, a Leicestershire farmer, pioneered improvement by inbreeding. His experiments with longhorn cattle were bettered by brothers

Catkin

The flower spikes found in several species of trees such as willow and birch, so-called because those on the willow carry unusual hairs in a compact mass—hence the likeness to a little cat, or catkin.

Basically, each catkin is a cluster of small flowers, usually all male or all female. The pollen is spread by the wind, and so the individual flowers are insignificant, lacking bright petals and nectar to attract insects, though exceptions occur.

Many trees bear their catkins before their leaves, adding colour to the countryside in early spring. Some of the more spectacular have descriptive country names. Goat willow is called pussy willow on account of its bright yellow fluffy male catkins. These are the 'palms' still used to decorate many churches on Palm Sunday.

Hazel catkins also have pleasant associations—they are known as lambs' tails, because of the way they hang on the tree. But the long, red male catkins of the black poplar have earned the name devil's fingers, and it is considered unlucky to pick them up.

The golden male catkins of the grey-leaved willow grow on separate trees to the silver females

A wild bull from Chillingham, Northumberland, engraved by Thomas Bewick, 1753-1828

Robert and Charles Colling of County Durham, who aimed to produce better beef shorthorns by inbreeding.

Other breeds arrived at various times in the course of trade. They are still coming—the French Charolais made its first appearance in 1961, and the Swiss Simmental started arriving in large numbers in 1970.

Today there are more than 20 breeds in Britain which are divided into three types: beef, dairy and dual-purpose (see chart for the characteristics of the main breeds).

Although breeds are classified as beef, dairy or dual-purpose, this classification is not rigid. For instance, there are beef herds of Friesians, normally dairy cattle. There are also numerous crosses, as farmers try to produce higher-yielding stock.

An example is the Hereford cross. The pure-bred Hereford is always red with a white face, but Hereford bulls have been used with other breeds, particularly the Dairy Shorthorns. The result is a beef animal with the body colour of the mother and the white face of the Hereford.

Other popular crosses are Beef Shorthorn crosses and Blue-Greys. Beef Shorthorns are crossed with other breeds, particularly Ayrshire, which gives the bull's beef-producing qualities and the mother's longer legs. Blue-Greys are beef calves produced from a white Shorthorn bull and a black cow, usually a Galloway or Aberdeen Angus.

Beef and dairy cattle can usually be identified by their shape. As the beef breeds are intended for their meat production they are fleshy, stocky, rather small animals with a broad girth and short legs. This gives them a rectangular appearance. The dairy breeds are more wedge-shaped in outline, narrow in the forequarters and widening towards the rear. They vary in size from the large,

heavy Friesians to the rather small, dainty Jerseys. Dairy cows have capacious udders which extend well forward and back and though they hang lower than those of beef cattle, dairy cows have longer legs which keep their udders away from the ground.

The largest British breed is the South Devon, with mature bulls weighing a ton or more. The cows weigh an average of 650 lb., but produce high-quality milk. Not all Britain's beef comes from cattle bred exclusively for its meat. Dairy cows have to produce calves in order to supply milk, and most of these are not needed as replacements in the herd. Dairy cows are crossed with beef bulls to produce calves which can be reared for beef. Two-thirds of our home-produced beef comes in this way from dairy herds. The

other one-third comes from the offspring of the 1,300,000 cows in the beef herds.

Many dairy farms breed and rear their own replacement cattle, but more farmers are concentrating on milk production and sending their calves to specialist farms for rearing. Artificial insemination now accounts for about two-thirds of the calves born in the UK, as fewer farmers now keep a bull.

Most cows produce their first calf when two years old and then produce a calf once a year, the average gestation period being 280 days. Calves at birth usually weigh between 50 and 100 lb., according to breeding and feeding. Autumn is popular for calving in dairy herds, as the cow comes into milk when prices are at their highest.

Many beef calves are born in spring and are fed by their mothers all summer to be

EATING 33 LB. A DAY

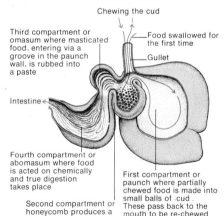

Chewing the cud

Food swallowed for the first time

Gullet

Third compartment or omasum where masticated food, entering via a groove in the paunch wall, is rubbed into a paste

Intestine

Fourth compartment or abomasum where food is acted on chemically and true digestion takes place

First compartment or paunch where partially chewed food is made into small balls of cud. These pass back to the mouth to be re-chewed

Second compartment or honeycomb produces a liquid which moistens the balls of cud

A Friesian cow weighing 1250 lb. needs about 33 lb. of food a day. To accommodate this vast quantity of matter and to process it thoroughly the cow's stomach is separated into four compartments. The first three store and prepare the food for digestion by the fourth

Beef cattle

Aberdeen Angus
A breed native in Scotland but now widespread throughout the British Isles. A quick-maturing and hardy animal producing a high-quality beef

Sussex
Developed from ancient working oxen in Sussex and Kent. Still found mostly in the south-east. Heavy, hardy breed, thriving on coarse feeding. Has a red, almost purple, coat

Beef Shorthorn
Once the most common breed in Britain, the pure-bred animal is now rare. The bulls are often crossed with other breeds to produce a high-quality beef

Charolais
Introduced from France in 1961, the bulls are used chiefly for crossing with dairy breeds to produce quick-maturing beef calves. The pure-bred Charolais is a creamy-white

Galloway
A heavily built and hornless breed with a thick coat—usually black, occasionally dun or silver dun. Numerous in Scotland where it originated, it is now common in the Home Counties

Hereford
Most abundant of all beef breeds, it originated in the Welsh Border counties but is now widespread. Pure-breds are always red and white; other colours with white faces are cross-breeds

Lincoln Red
Not common, except in Lincolnshire where it originated, and neighbouring counties. Becoming popular in Scotland. Hardy and quick-maturing

Highland
Found mostly in Scottish mountains, where it originated, this tough breed thrives in poor conditions. Excellent beef but slow to mature. Usually yellowish, sometimes black, red or brindled

Devon
Native of Devon and west Somerset, where it is long-established and numerous, this breed is rarely found elsewhere. Good grazing animal. Also known as the Red Devon.

ready for fattening at the beginning of winter. But there is no hard and fast rule; dairy cows may calve in spring and beef cows in autumn.

Dairy calves are usually taken from their mothers at birth or within a few days and are reared artificially. This is because the cow's milk is the prime product of the dairy farmer. Beef cows are not normally milked, so their calves stay with them as long as possible. The average milk yield from a dairy cow is 822 gallons a year. The little Dexter gives 400-600 gallons a year, while it is not uncommon for a Friesian to yield 2000 gallons or more.

Britain has about 3¼ million mature dairy cows which produce between 2500 million and 3000 million gallons a year, which is enough for our liquid consumption, but

provides only 45 per cent of our cheese and 14 per cent of our butter requirements. The manufacture of butter, cheese and cream serves as a safety valve, taking milk that cannot be immediately consumed in liquid form.

Home beef and veal production is between 900,000 and 1 million tons a year, which is about 80 per cent of our requirements.

In 1970, there were 109,600 dairy farms, with an average herd of 30 cows. The number of farms is steadily decreasing, while the size of herd is increasing. Many farms now have herds of several hundreds.

In the same year there were 102,000 farms devoted to beef cattle, with an average herd of 13. Many beef-breeding farms are found in north and west England, Wales and eastern Scotland. The calves spend the

summer on the moors, and then are sold and transported to lowland farms for fattening in sheltered yards. Cattle are also brought over from Ireland for fattening.

Dairy farming is concentrated in the lowland areas of western England, Wales, central and south-west Scotland and in the south and west of Ireland. All milk produced in Britain, except in Shetland and part of north-west Scotland, has to be sold through one of the five Milk Marketing Boards. These operate a pooling arrangement providing standard prices to dairy farmers, regardless of whether their milk is for liquid consumption or manufacture.

All herds in Britain are free from tuberculosis and a campaign is in progress to eradicate brucellosis, an udder infection which causes undulant fever in humans.

Dual-purpose cattle

Belted Galloway
Hardy, hornless breed which runs with sheep on hill pastures. Black, sometimes dun, this rare breed is kept more for its milk—rich in butterfat—than for its beef

Dexter
A rare dwarf breed, with short legs and a heavy head. Native of the mountains of western Ireland, it is the smallest breed in Britain. The average cow weighs only 650 lb.

South Devon
The largest British breed, with bulls weighing up to a ton. Found mainly in south Devon and east Cornwall. Many cows produce more than 1000 gallons of extra-rich milk a year

Simmental
The most numerous breed on the Continent, introduced into Britain in 1970. Widespread and increasing rapidly, it is comparable with the South Devon and is renowned for its docility and easy calving

Red Poll
A hornless breed that originated in East Anglia. Though not numerous they are fairly widespread. They are the longest-living milk cattle

Welsh Black
Developed from the native Welsh cattle, it is common in Wales but rare elsewhere. There are a variety of beef and dairy strains varying from district to district

Dairy cattle

Ayrshire
Second most numerous breed in Britain; originated in south-west Scotland. Hardy, healthy breed with milk rich in butterfat content. Brown patches range from near-red to almost black. Bulls massive

Dairy Shorthorn
Originated in Durham and Yorkshire, this breed is still the most numerous in the north-east, though it is gradually being superseded by Friesians

Friesian
Large, heavy breed that is the most numerous of any in Britain—dairy or beef. Introduced from the Netherlands after 1909. Primarily dairy

Guernsey
Small breed, which originated in Guernsey and is the only one permitted there. Now widespread on the mainland. Lean, healthy animal that produces a rich, creamy milk. Exclusively dairy

Kerry
Hardy and economical to feed, giving a milk yield comparable to that of larger breeds. Originated in south-west Ireland and rare in Britain

Jersey
Lean, dainty, fine-boned cattle which originated in Jersey and are the only breed permitted there. Widespread in Britain. Milk very rich with high level of butterfat content. Easy to rear

Cattle grid

A shallow pit covered with a grating of steel bars running the full width of a road to stop sheep or cattle crossing from one piece of land to another.

The bars are usually spaced at least 5 in. apart so that the animals can find no foothold. A narrower gap might allow a broad-hoofed animal to cross or might trap a narrow-hoofed animal. Flanking fences stop animals getting round the grid. Cattle grids make motoring easier because there are no gates to open and close.

Catworm   *Nephtys hombergi*

A pearly pink or white segmented bristle-worm, with a grey line down its back, up to 8 in. long, which lives in all forms of sediment except fine mud. Catworms are used as bait by fishermen, and when dug up will either actively burrow back into the sand or swim over the wet surface with a rapid wave-like motion running from the tail towards the head.

Each body segment is equipped with stiff bristles or setae which are used to 'row' the worm along through its burrow. Catworms feed on small worms and crustaceans.

HOW A CATWORM SEIZES PREY

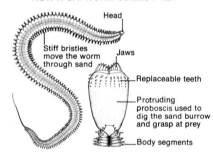

The iridescent catworm is a carnivorous animal, seizing prey with its jaws as it burrows in sand

Causeway

A raised track crossing marshes, fens and the flood plain of rivers. The word, often shortened to 'causey', occurs frequently in modern road names. Maud Heath's Causey, Wiltshire, 4½ miles long, was built and is maintained from the endowments of a 15th-century widow. Newington Causeway in London gives access to London Bridge.

Early causeways were made of stone slabs or timbers such as oak trunks. Some dating back to the Bronze Age have been found near Wicken, Cambridgeshire. Roman roads in the same area were built along old causeways. Several stone causeways have been found by probing the turf in the marshy areas of Kent, near Smarden. Prehistoric camps with causeways leading to them have been found in southern England, as at Windmill Hill, near Avebury, Wiltshire.

Cave   see Underground Britain

The blue-green, needle-like leaves of Atlas cedar enable it to withstand the hottest sun

Cedar

Many trees with fragrant wood or foliage are called 'cedar', but foresters reserve the name for conifers in the genus Cedrus, which belongs to the pine family. These true cedars have evergreen, tough needles set in clusters on short shoots along their twigs; long shoots near the tip carry solitary needles.

Cedars flower at an unusual time—about September. Male catkins, which have a distorted cone shape, and are about ½ in. long, shed abundant golden wind-borne pollen. Female flowers, even smaller, are soft green cones borne on the same tree. After pollination, they take two years to ripen into large, brown woody cones, up to 2 in. long and 2 in. across.

Cedar cones are identified by their squat barrel shape with hollow tips and broad flat scales. As they slowly break up they release triangular brown seeds, each attached to a triangular papery wing that carries it away on the wind. Saplings grow for 40 years before flowering, while mature trees last for 500 years.

Cedarwood is rich brown in colour, with an attractive grain due to the wavy outline of its annual rings. It holds a fragrant oil that makes it naturally durable. Where cedars grow plentifully in forests the wood is used for building. Elsewhere the rarity value of the wood makes it too expensive to use except in high-grade carvings or furniture, often as a decorative veneer over cheaper timbers. The oil is distilled for use in perfumes.

In prehistoric times cedars were widespread throughout the Old World, but climatic change has isolated the four kinds so that in the wild each now survives only in a particular mountain area of the sub-tropics.

Atlas cedar *Cedrus atlantica* comes from the Altas Mountains of Morocco, where it gets moisture from winter snowfall. Its bluish foliage, carried on branches rising to distinct tips, enables it to stand intense summer sun. The very blue variety *C. glauca* is often planted in British gardens.

The Indian cedar or deodar *C. deodara*, from the cool Himalayas, has also been widely planted for its pleasing green foliage.

Lebanon cedar *C. libani* grows on the mountains of Lebanon and Syria, and provided the timber used by King Solomon for building his temple. It has been planted in Britain for 350 years and fine old specimens, with enormous horizontal branches springing from massive trunks, can be seen in the gardens of many old houses. There is a 132 ft high cedar at Petworth Park, Sussex, and another with a 27 ft circumference in Blenheim Park at Woodstock, near Oxford. On Mount Lebanon there are trees 40 ft round and up to 2000 years old.

The fourth species, the Cyprus cedar *C. brevifolia*, is very like the Lebanon cedar. In the wild it grows only in Cyprus, where there are large forests of it, and is rarely planted in Britain.

The small yellow flowers of greater celandine soon give way to 2 in. long seed pods

Celandine, Greater *Chelidonium majus*
A perennial, 1-2½ ft high, with yellow, four-petalled flowers and much-divided hairless leaves. It is a member of the poppy family and is easily identified by the drop of poisonous, deep-orange latex which is exuded if a stem is broken. This was once used as a cure for warts, and was also believed to be a cure for sore eyes. Because it was grown for its herbal properties it survives plentifully around old gardens. Widespread except in the north and west.

Celandine, Lesser *Ranunculus ficaria*
One of the most widespread and attractive wild flowers, which turns hedgebanks yellow early in spring. It is related to the buttercup and has heart-shaped leaves, 8-12 petals and only three sepals. There are two common forms which can be identified after flowering. One has small white bulbs where the leaf stalk joins the stem and is abundant as a garden weed. The other has no stem bulbs and is usually found in old grassland and woodlands.

The lesser celandine appears early in spring, before the buttercups which it resembles

Celery see Parsley

Centaury, Common *Centaurium erythraea*
This plant varies in size from a single stem only 1 in. high to a much-branched plant up to 18 in. tall. The pink flowers have five small, pointed petals connected to a long tube. Common centaury is bitter to the taste. It survives the winter as a ground-hugging rosette of spoon-shaped leaves.

Common centaury occurs in dry grassland and on sandy banks throughout the lowlands of England, Wales and Ireland. In Scotland it is mainly a coastal plant.

Centipede
These are distantly related to insects and spiders. Although there are numerous species, centipedes are seen only occasionally, and usually when running for cover. The best known of the British species is *Lithobius forficatus* which may be discovered when stones and logs are disturbed.

The name centipede literally means 'a hundred legs' but the number of legs varies from species to species, ranging from 17 to 177 pairs. Each of the many segments of their bodies bears a pair of legs.

During the day centipedes hide in dark, damp places, emerging at night when it is cool. Since their body covering is not fully waterproof they soon die of desiccation in dry conditions.

They kill their prey—mostly worms, insects and spiders—by catching them in their sickle-shaped jaws and injecting a paralysing poison. Female centipedes lay their eggs in the soil and other humid places in spring and summer. *L. forficatus* takes about three years to mature and the adults may live for a further two or three years. Centipedes are efficient runners, moving their legs in rhythmical waves.

HOW CENTIPEDES MOVE

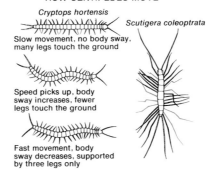

Cryptops hortensis

Scutigera coleoptrata

Slow movement, no body sway, many legs touch the ground

Speed picks up, body sway increases, fewer legs touch the ground

Fast movement, body sway decreases, supported by three legs only

A centipede moves by waves of limb movements travelling alternately along each side of its body. The longer the legs (right) the smaller these waves. Legs in blue are those in contact with the ground, propelling the centipede forwards

Chafer
This name is given to a number of beetles, with distinctive fan-like antennae, which emerge from the soil and fly in May or June, often tapping on lighted windows of houses at night as they fly into them.

The most familiar and largest is the cockchafer or May bug, but there are several common smaller species that resemble the cockchafer. These include the garden chafer, the summer chafer and the iridescent green rose beetle.

The larvae are large white grubs, sometimes called rookworms, with greatly swollen abdomens, and brownish heads bearing formidable curved jaws. They usually live in pasture soils, feeding voraciously on the grass roots, sometimes removing so many of them that the turf can be rolled up like

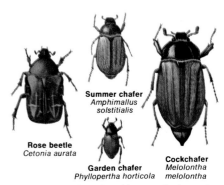

Summer chafer *Amphimallus solstitialis*

Rose beetle *Cetonia aurata*

Garden chafer *Phyllopertha horticola*

Cockchafer *Melolontha melolontha*

a carpet. Regular ploughing to eliminate the grubs is necessary when grassland gives way to corn; otherwise the grubs will damage the crop.

Chaffinch see Finch
Chalcedony see Quartz
Chalk see Down

Chamomile
The three native species of chamomile in the British Isles have strong aromatic scents, white flowers with yellow centres like a daisy, and very finely divided leaves.

Corn chamomile and stinking chamomile are both troublesome weeds of farmland. Corn chamomile has a sweet smell and is a hairy plant; stinking chamomile smells rank and is almost hairless.

Lawn chamomile is a low-growing perennial which is pleasantly fragrant in a lawn when it is walked on and the leaves are crushed. The flowers, which appear in July or August, can be used fresh or dried to make tea for digestive troubles. It grows wild in grassland and on sandy commons in southern England and south-west Ireland.

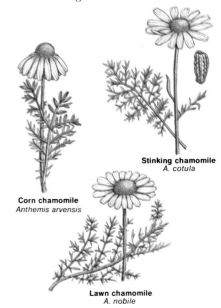

Stinking chamomile *A. cotula*

Corn chamomile *Anthemis arvensis*

Lawn chamomile *A. nobile*

Corn chamomile flowers May-July, lawn chamomile July-Aug., stinking chamomile July-Sept.

Chanterelle

A popular edible fungus which smells faintly of apricots. All parts, including the funnel-shaped cap, the gills and stalk, are apricot coloured. The gills on the underside of the cap continue down the top part of the stem. Chanterelle *Cantharellus cibarius* appears in deciduous woodlands, especially beech, in autumn. It is sometimes confused with the false chanterelle *Hygrophoropsis aurantiaca* which grows in pinewoods. This is orange coloured, does not smell of apricots and, though harmless, is not good to eat.

Charlock *Sinapis arvensis*

A cornfield weed, the charlock or wild mustard is considered a great nuisance by farmers. Its seeds may remain dormant in the soil for 50 years or more and will germinate when brought to the surface by ploughing. Between 1 and 2 ft high, the charlock has boldly toothed, lyre-shaped leaves. Its bright yellow, four-petalled flowers bloom between May and July. The fruit is an angular pod, the hairy valves containing one row of dark brown seeds.

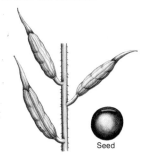

Seed

Long, hairy pods, with a single row of seeds, follow the bright yellow flowers of charlock

Charr *Salvelinus alpinus*

Since the last Ice Age the charr, a cold-water fish, has moved northwards, leaving isolated populations in deep lakes cool enough for their survival. Today the charr lives in the waters of the Lake District, several Irish loughs, Caernarvonshire lakes and numerous Scottish lochs. Local varieties include the haddy of Loch Killin, Scotland and the torgoch of Wales. The charr, a member of the salmon family, is about 16 in. long. It has a greenish-brown back with light spots grading to a silvery-orange belly. The white edges of its belly fins are noticeable even from a distance. The male is particularly colourful in the winter spawning season.

Chase

Norman and Plantagenet kings used forests for hunting, coursing and falconry, as a source of charcoal, and as pasture for pigs. An area where the hunting rights alone were ceded to a private person or monastery was designated a chase, from the Norman/French word, *chace*, meaning hunt. Cannock Chase, Staffordshire, still covers 26 square

miles, while Chevy Chase in the Cheviot Hills gave its name to a 15th-century ballad concerning a dispute over its hunting rights. The word survives in many other place names, including Enfield Chase in Middlesex.

The rise of fox hunting in the 18th century owed much to the practice of clearing and enclosing ancient chases to turn them into more profitable farmland. This meant there were fewer forests harbouring fewer deer for the hunters, while at the same time there were more farms to protect from foxes.

Chat

The robin, nightingale, whinchat, stonechat, wheatear, redstart and bluethroat can be grouped together under the collective name of chat. They are small birds, 5-7 in. long, and often boldly coloured. They spend much of their time on the ground looking for insects, worms, spiders and centipedes to eat, but when they fly they move swiftly and can be identified by their short wings and tails. Like thrushes, their close relatives, they perch motionless before suddenly pouncing on their prey. The female builds a substantial nest, often on the ground or in a hole in a tree or wall and lays between four and six eggs. The male does not help in nest-building or in the 13-day incubation. He does, however, help to feed the nestlings which leave the nest after about a fortnight.

A summer visitor, the whinchat *Saxicola rubetra* nests mainly in the west and north on open heathland and rough grassland. A creamy eyestripe distinguishes it from the stonechat *S. torquata*. This chat is found throughout the year living mainly along the west coast and in Ireland, on heaths and moorlands or open rough ground often near water. The wheatear *Oenanthe oenanthe* is an early summer visitor. It can be recognised by its black and white tail. It too nests mainly in the west and north on rough open wasteland in holes and rock crevices.

The red breast and tail, grey back, black face and bib make the redstart *Phoenicurus phoenicurus* a particularly attractive bird. It is a summer visitor, nesting throughout the British Isles mainly in wooded areas. The black redstart *P. ochruros* is a black bird with a red tail. A winter visitor, it often nests in towns. In the 1940's it started to breed in Britain using nest sites provided by bombed buildings. There are now about 12-20 nesting pairs in the south-east.

The robin *Erithacus rubecula* is a familiar garden dweller, but was originally a woodland species. Both male and female have red breasts which act as signals to warn off other robins that invade their territory.

The white-chested, rusty-tailed nightingale *Luscinia megarhynchos* is a summer visitor to the south-east. It nests hidden among ground vegetation, often under ivy, and is notoriously difficult to find. It sings by day as well as by night but is best heard on a quiet summer evening. The bluethroat *L. svecica*

is another skulker, a passage migrant mostly seen in the autumn on the east coast on its way south from Scandinavia.

A male whinchat after a successful foraging flight. Both parents feed the young

Cheese

Cows as milk producers were not fully exploited in Britain before the 13th century, and most early references concern goats' or ewes' milk cheese. Although large quantities of milk are necessary for cheese-making, its by-product, whey, is useful for fattening pigs and other farm animals.

To make cheese, rennet is added to milk at 30°C (86°F) to produce curds, which are then separated from the whey, heated to 38°C (100°F), salted and pressed into cakes. These are kept at 10°C (50°F) while ripening —sometimes for years. Variations on this method, together with the amount of fermentation during ripening, determines the final flavour and texture.

The principal British cheeses are Stilton, Cheddar, Cheshire, Double Gloucester, Wensleydale, Leicester, Caerphilly and Lancashire. Various 'blue' varieties such as Blue Stilton, are due to moulds growing in the cheese. Dairy farmers who still make their own cheese usually do so only in summer, when cheap milk can be produced by cows living entirely on grass. Most cheeses available today are factory made.

Cheese presses are devices for pressing the cheeses while they are maturing and consist of two flat plates manipulated by turning a screw.

Cherry

An outburst of white blossom transforms the bare branches of the wild cherry in late April, just before the pale green leaves appear. The flowers have five petals and are

The wild cherry's beauty is short-lived—its delicate white blossom falls within a week

grouped in clusters on separate stalks. By July, each flower has developed into a small, shiny black fruit with thin, sweet pulp and a large, pale brown stone. The abundance of the cherry crop was once held to be a guide to good fortune.

Cherry stones are swallowed or scattered by birds, resulting in small seedlings the following spring, each with two oval seed-leaves. Cherry bark is dull purplish-grey, with horizontal bands of pale brown, corky breathing pores. If the wood is damaged, it bleeds a light brown resin which seals the wound. The serrated, pointed oval leaves have long stalks and turn orange, crimson and purple in autumn. The trunk has a narrow zone of pale brown sapwood and a mid-brown heartwood with hints of green and gold. The wood is used for furniture, sometimes on its own, but usually as veneer, and for pipes and fine carving.

The common wild cherry or gean *Prunus avium* grows up to 100 ft high, and is a parent of garden cherries. It grows throughout the British Isles, especially in the south. The much smaller bird cherry *P. padus* of Scottish glens and Welsh valleys, bears many small white blossoms on dainty spikes with long central stems in June. Its small, bitter, black fruits attract birds in late summer.

Other varieties and hybrids, grown for their decorative blossom in May, came originally from Asia, Japan and America. Some, like the Japanese 'Kanzan', which has bright pink flowers, are sterile and fruitless. These are increased by grafting, often with wild cherry as the stock.

Chert
A hard, flint-like rock, and one of the many forms of silica, chert breaks on crushing into angular fragments. It is frequently found as layers within the Carboniferous or mountain limestone. Pinhole chert is an unusual variety with small holes, found in the gravels of rivers draining northwards from the Weald into the Thames.

Chervil see Parsley

Chestnut, Sweet *Castanea sativa*
A staple ration for the Roman legions was a nutritious flour called *pollenta*, made from chestnuts. This is why the Romans are credited with introducing the chestnut from Italy nearly 2000 years ago. It now grows

wild in England, and is common in Nottingham, Norfolk and Gloucester. It is rare in Scotland and Ireland. The nuts normally ripen only in the warm southern counties.

The chestnut, which belongs to the beech family Fagaceae, has stout, round buds which develop into large, broad, oval leaves edged with saw-toothed points. The smooth grey bark of young trees becomes brown, deeply ridged and often spiral with age. Chestnut catkins open about July. Each has a long green stem carrying many yellow male flowers. At the base of some catkins a few female flowers sit like buds. The catkins contain nectar to attract bees, but pollen is also wind-borne.

By October, the female flowers develop into plump, triangular, bright brown nuts set in husks that carry a tangle of soft yellow-green spines. Squirrels act as distributors, either dropping nuts or forgetting those they have buried. Chestnut stems have exceptionally thin white sapwood, enclosing a mid-brown heartwood.

Although a superb tree, up to 120 ft high with a 500-year life-span, chestnut is rarely planted for timber because natural cracks or 'shakes' make it hard to saw into large, sound planks. Most chestnut is grown as coppice—that is, the trunks are cut back close to ground level causing clusters of stout stems to spring up. These are cut after 12 years of growth, a process which can be repeated for 100 years or more. In Kent and neighbouring counties, coppice cutters buy a few acres of mature coppice annually, fell the poles and cleave them on the spot into triangular pales. Strung on wires, these make cleft-pale fencing, which is cheap, durable and hard to climb. It is also used for gateposts and hop poles.

Britain's most famous chestnut, at Tortworth, Gloucestershire, once thought to be the largest in the country, is in fact a natural fake—its 52 ft girth is made up of several trees incorporated together.

CHESTNUT LEAVES AND FRUIT

Long, sharply toothed leaves and spiny fruits characterise the sweet or Spanish chestnut

Chicken

All domestic chickens were developed largely from the jungle fowl *Gallus gallus*, which still lives wild in south-east Asia. Centuries of selective breeding have produced hundreds of distinct strains of domestic chickens, of which some 50 to 60 are standard in Britain. Despite the fact that chicken and egg production today depends on hybrids, it is these standard breeds which still provide stock for hybrid development, and for the small market in 'free range' eggs and meat.

Domesticated fowls were introduced to Britain before Roman times—mainly for cock-fighting and the table. The most significant strides in poultry-breeding have been concentrated in the last 100 years.

In the middle of the 19th century most British poultry were mongrels. Leghorns and Plymouth Rocks were introduced from America in the 1870's, followed by Wyandottes in the 1880's. At about the same time the Orpington was developed in Kent. The most popular breed of all, the Rhode Island Red, arrived in 1906. Several other popular breeds, such as the Dutch Barnevelder and the French Marans, did not appear until the 1920's. The standard breeds were moderately specialised for either egg or meat production, though many were dual-purpose. Cross-breeding produced more specialised birds. By the 1950's specialisation was virtually complete. The layers were bred for high egg output under intensive artificial conditions, while table poultry were likewise mass-produced, and given the name broilers.

A cockerel lords it over the hens in a chicken run. Once a common sight of the countryside, it is becoming rare as more and more poultry are reared in deep-litter or battery units

The natural season for a hen to start laying is towards the end of winter, when the days lengthen. In the late 1940's many farmers began keeping poultry for the winter in deep-litter houses—barns strewn with about 2 ft of straw. It was then realised that by increasing the length of day with electric light, hens could be induced to lay out of their normal season.

In modern windowless buildings, the poultryman can manipulate light, temperature, humidity, ventilation and food intake at will. Hybrid chicks bred for broilers are kept by the tens of thousands and slaugh-

---

Standard breeds of chicken in Britain

There are 50-60 standard breeds of chicken in Britain, some of which are shown here. The standard breeds are no longer used for commercial egg and meat production, but they are still important as the basic stock from which hybrids are produced for commercial purposes. Most of the chickens and eggs consumed in this country nowadays are produced in broiler houses and battery cages, with less than 5 per cent free ranging

Dual-purpose birds

| Marans | Buff Orpington | Plymouth Rock | Rhode Island Red | Sussex | Wyandotte |

Table birds

Laying birds

| Indian game | Dorking | Old English game | Ancona | Leghorn | Andalusian |

tered at about 11 weeks. Batteries of layers in stacked cages produce eggs by the million. The system is often criticised by animal lovers, yet has helped to make chicken and eggs cheap foods on a mass scale. Nearly 600,000 tons of broiler chickens and 1300 million dozen eggs are produced annually in Britain. The highest number of eggs laid by a bird in one year was 353, by a Rhode Island Red at Milford, Surrey in 1957. The normal laying period is 300 days, after which hens are usually killed for eating.

In the 25 years from 1946, the average number of eggs produced by each hen in a year rose from 108 to 215. Only 136,600 farms keep laying hens today compared with 202,200 in 1967, and the average flock size has increased from 257 to 404. In the broiler field, the number of farms is 2900 compared with 4700, and the average flock size has gone up from 7600 to 16,900.

Bantams are miniature strains of no commercial importance. Most of them are small versions of standard breeds, though some have no full-size equivalents. See also FARMING

Chickweed

This low-growing weed is found throughout the British Isles. It flowers even in the depth of winter, when the seeds provide food for small birds. The tiny, star-like flowers have five deeply divided petals and the stems have a line of water-absorbing hairs which changes sides at each pair of leaves. Common chickweed was once eaten as a spring salad or as a boiled vegetable and also made into ointment for treating rheumatism.

Water chickweed is often found straggling on river banks or in large patches at the edge of damp woods, except in Wales and Scotland where it is rare. It has hairless, fleshy leaves, up to $2\frac{1}{2}$ in. long, and drooping white flowers.

Common chickweed
Stellaria media

Water chickweed
Myosoton aquaticum

Fleshy, hairless leaves mark out water chickweed from the common species

Chicory *Cichorium intybus*

The large blue flowers of this herb cluster towards the top of tough stiff stems beside roads, meadows and railway lines throughout Britain, but it is common only in south and east England. It is still sometimes sown on shallow chalk soil both because cattle like it and because its deep tap-root helps break up the subsoil. Like other blue flowers, including bluebells, it turns red through the acid of ants if placed in an ant-hill. The chicory mixed with coffee is produced by roasting and grinding the dried roots. Its cultivated version, the endive, is used in salads after blanching.

If insects fail to pollinate chicory, the flowers are capable of self-pollination

Chiff chaff see Warbler

China-mark moth

Leaves of floating plants, such as duckweed, punctured by oval holes signal the presence of china-mark moth larvae in stagnant ponds and slow-flowing water in all parts of the British Isles. The eggs are laid beneath floating pondweeds or lily leaves and the young caterpillars burrow into the leaf, living in the air spaces inside.

Later, the caterpillar makes a watertight case of leaf fragments and silk in which it lives on the underside of the leaf. It remains inactive during winter, finishing its growth in spring. The pupa or resting stage occurs

THE AQUATIC CATERPILLAR

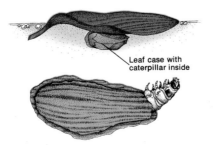

Leaf case with caterpillar inside

The brown china-mark moth caterpillar hatches out in July to start its unusual aquatic life. It makes a leaf case and attaches it to the underside of a floating pondweed leaf with silk. When hungry the caterpillar puts its head outside the case and nibbles the pondweed

in a cocoon just above the water level on a piece of vegetation, and the night-flying moths emerge in June and fly until August.

The name refers to the wing pattern, which resembles a potter's mark. The brown china-mark moth *Nymphula nympheata* is common everywhere, living mainly on leaves of bur-reed and pond-weeds; the larger *N. stratiotata* is more usual in southern England, where it lives on the leaves of the water-soldier. These moths have a wing-span of up to 1 in. across.

Chine

Narrow, steep-sided ravines cut into cliffs on the Isle of Wight and the Hampshire coast round Bournemouth are known locally as chines or bunnies. They have been cut by small streams and rivulets which swiftly eat into the soft material of the cliffs, which usually consist of sand and clay. Chines are subject to constant landslips because their sand and clay banks are unstable.

Chiton see Shell
Chough see Crow
Chrysalis see Insect

Chub *Leuciscus cephalus*
A river fish, common throughout England and southern Scotland, 12-20 in. long, the chub can weigh 10 lb. or more. In the spawning season (May to June) the male becomes covered with small, white, hard spots, particularly over the head. Otherwise the chub's colour varies between dark green to greyish-blue, with silvery sides.

Shoals of young chub are common in warmer months, but the large fish is a shy, solitary creature. It has a favoured pool and will chase other large chub away. The adult eats quantities of smaller fish, even frogs and small water-voles, as well as insects and insect larvae, freshwater shrimps and some plant material.

The chub is often confused with the dace, but has a bigger, heavier head and dark-edged scales. Its anal fin is rounded; the dace's concave.

Church see p. 100

Churchyard beetle

These large black beetles are quite common in scattered localities throughout the British Isles. There are three species, of which the most common is *Blaps mucronata*. The name churchyard beetle and their alternative name, cellar beetle, both refer to the sort of place where they are found. They feed at night on vegetable debris.

The larvae live in cracks in the floor and feed on scraps of food which accumulate there. The adult beetles have a rather unpleasant smell. They can run fast but cannot fly. As with most of their family—the night ground beetles—the wing-cases, which no longer have any wings to protect, are fused together and protect the body of the beetle.

Church

In many British villages and towns the church is often the oldest surviving building, its spire or tower dominating the skyline—a physical symbol of a community's unity.

Originally, the church was the centre of communal life and, in addition to giving spiritual comfort to lord and peasant alike, it provided the sick and needy with care; it acted as a meeting place for guildsmen to conduct business, and as a courtroom for receiving tithes, holding inquests and conducting other administrative matters. Dances and fairs were often held in the churchyard where ale was drunk.

In the 12th century most churches kept a parish chest, containing parishioners' wills, churchwardens' accounts, various documents and, from 1597, a register of all parish births, baptisms, marriages and deaths.

The chest, together with plaques, inscriptions and tombstones—as well as the size, architecture and furnishings of the church—provides a social history of the community.

Communities that had benefited from the woollen trade during the 15th and 16th centuries built new churches, or added towers, spires or battlements to existing ones, as an expression of local pride and wealth. Hundreds of these 'woollen' churches can be found throughout southern England and East Anglia, often in small villages which were once large and prosperous.

Churches found in isolated settings may reflect the desertion of a village through plague, war or repeated crop failure.

Churches, like cottages, often used local building materials. Exceptions were those churches attached to wealthy monasteries; these were often built of materials transported from other parts of the country. As communications and inland transportation improved, so church builders were no longer restricted to the use of local materials. Nomadic craftsmen also helped to spread different designs.

Saxon churches were often built of timber, the one material readily available throughout most of the country; the oldest survivor is the oak log nave of Greensted-Juxta-Ongar, Essex. As the importance of the church increased, more durable materials were used. Many Saxon stone towers survive, for example at Escomb, Monkwearmouth and Jarrow in County Durham.

More churches were built during the 13th century than any other, many suffered during the Dissolution of the Monasteries in 1536-9 and again during the Civil War of the 17th century, with the loss of priceless artistic treasures, such as font covers, frescoes, rood screens, images and carvings.

The simplicity of most non-Conformist chapels and Scottish kirks, built from the 17th century onwards, reflects the Puritan ideals of their congregations.

Many churches have yew trees in the churchyards, possibly because the site was once part of a pre-Christian sacred grove where Ancient Britons worshipped. Edward I is thought to have ordered yew trees to be planted near churches to help protect buildings from high winds and storms.

This church at Widecombe-in-the-Moor, Devon, has

Church architectural styles

There are more than 16,000 parish churches in Britain, spanning 900 years of architectural development. The dates assigned to the principal styles are arbitrary, since a line of demarcation between the closing of one style and the opening of another cannot be drawn with accuracy.

Each of the buildings below embodies the chief characteristics of a particular style and will help in identifying and dating an unfamiliar church

Saxon: before 1066
Thick walls. Windows and doors small; round or triangular arches. Corners alternating upright and horizontal stones

Norman: 1066-1180
Thick walls and massive columns. Windows and doors have round arches and splayed sides. Zigzag and chevron mouldings. Roofs flat or pitched. External buttressing

Early English: 1160-80
Light walls and large, pointed windows. Doors framed with deeply cut mouldings. Towers buttressed at corners and roofed with steeples—often octagonal and without parapets

Perpendicular: 1350-1550
Shallow arches over doors and windows, carving expressing verticality. Decorative tops to towers

been at the heart of a farming community for 600 years

Renaissance: 1550-1840
Revival of Ancient Greek and Roman styles. Round arches, domes, columns—used inside and out. Walls stuccoed. Elaborate carvings, mouldings and steeples. Symmetrical exteriors

Cinquefoil, Creeping *Potentilla reptans*

This creeping herb with long runners like those of the strawberry is well known to gardeners: once established in the rockery, it is difficult to remove. It is widespread on roadside verges, in chalk quarries and on other disturbed ground throughout lowland Britain and Ireland, but is rare in Scotland. Its yellow flowers appear from June to September.

In the Middle Ages it was hung over doors to repel witches and was sometimes represented in church carvings.. The ancient Greeks used cinquefoil as a medicine.

Above-ground runners give creeping cinquefoil its name, but it also spreads by seed

Clamp

Root crops are protected from winter weather in long, covered heaps called clamps. A clamp is made by piling up the crop until it forms a stable heap, then extending the heap lengthwise. The root crops, usually potatoes, mangolds, swedes or fodder beet, are protected from frost by a layer of straw which is often kept in place by an outer covering of soil. In some areas farmers roof clamps with straw thatch. Clamps vary from 3 ft to 5 ft in height, depending on the size of roots being stored.

Clapboarding

This is another name for weatherboarding, the protective timbers often found on buildings in south-eastern England. The boards are fixed to the framework of a building horizontally, overlapping from top to bottom to keep out rain. At first, local hardwood was used for this purpose, but owing to shortages—due to shipbuilding priorities —imported softwood began to be used as early as the 17th century.

Clapboarding is thought to have been devised from the boatbuilders' practice of cladding the outside of their houses in the same way as the framework of their boats.

Most surviving clapboard is softwood which has been painted or tarred.

Clary *Salvia horminoides*

This plant, which is related to garden sage, may be seen in dry grassland and on roadside banks in south and east England. The leaves, which are arranged in pairs, are crinkly and strongly veined. Clary begins to bloom in May, producing flowers of two

Two sizes of flower appear on clary—the smaller ones are self-pollinating

sizes: large, open violet-blue ones more than $\frac{1}{2}$ in. long, and some much smaller which never fully open. Seed placed in water swells like frogspawn and was once used to treat sore eyes.

Clay

Clay is a rock composed of minute particles of the mineral silica. Since the spaces between the particles are also small, clay holds water, and soils containing clay are hard to cultivate. However, such soils, if properly drained, can support most plants. The trees most commonly found on clay are ash, hazel, oak and hornbeam. Thick beds of clay in central and south-east England are usually left under grass.

Most clays can be burnt in kilns to make bricks and tiles, and that found in Cornwall is particularly suitable for making pottery. Boulder clay is material left behind by an ice-sheet millions of years ago. It usually contains rocks and stones.

Clearwing moth

All 15 species of this day-flying moth mimic various types of wasp for protection. Their striped bodies are similar to those of wasps, though not narrow-waisted. In addition, parts of the wings—which span from $\frac{3}{4}$ in. to $1\frac{1}{2}$ in. —are transparent. Most clearwing caterpillars burrow into the wood of trees, though a few species enter the stems and roots of smaller plants. Growth is slow; the caterpillars take two or three years to mature and reach the pupal, or resting, stage which takes place in the burrow near the surface. When the adult emerges it leaves its pupa case sticking out of the hole.

The hornet clearwing *Sesia apiformis* mimics a hornet very accurately. The caterpillars burrow low down on the trunks of large aspens and poplars. The moth emerges from its pupa in May and may be seen from then until July, most commonly in the eastern counties of England.

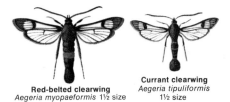

Red-belted clearwing
Aegeria myopaeformis 1½ size

Currant clearwing
Aegeria tipuliformis 1½ size

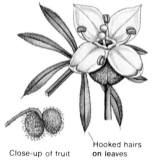

Close-up of fruit | Hooked hairs on leaves

The straggling stems of cleavers have bristles that help it cling to other plants for support

Cleavers *Galium aparine*
The stem, leaves and small round fruits of this plant have hooked hairs which catch in the clothing and cleave to the passer-by, hence its name. It grows 1-4 ft high, in hedges and on waste ground and woodland in all lowland areas of the British Isles. It is also called sticky billy, hug-me-close and goosegrass. It was formerly fed to newly hatched goslings.

Cleg
These dark brown, ½ in. long, blood-sucking insects are related to horse-flies. They are sometimes called thunder flies, as the females are more persistent in their blood-sucking in thundery weather. Only the females suck blood; males feed on nectar from flowers. It is thought that the females need the protein from blood for egg production. Clegs are common over damp meadows because the larvae require moist conditions for their development. The larvae attack worms in damp soil, sucking out the body contents. There are four British species. *Haematopota pulvialis* is common in the southeast and *H. crassicornis* is widespread in Scotland. The others are rare.

Click beetle
If these dull brown, oval beetles roll over on their backs when basking on grass, they recover by suddenly flexing their bodies

THE SOMERSAULTING BEETLE

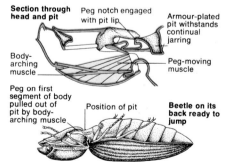

Section through head and pit | Peg notch engaged with pit lip | **Armour-plated pit withstands continual jarring**

Body-arching muscle | Peg-moving muscle

Peg on first segment of body pulled out of pit by body-arching muscle | Position of pit | **Beetle on its back ready to jump**

When the click beetle falls on its back It rights itself by somersaulting. It arches its back so that a notch on the peg locks with a lip on the edge of the pit. Under the tension of the peg-moving muscle the peg slams into the pit, throwing the beetle into the air, sometimes 12 in. high

with a clicking noise, hence their name. There are about 60 British species, ¼-¾ in. long. Many, such as the red-brown skipjack *Athous haemorrhoidalis* live in woodland. Others, such as *Agriotes lineatus*, have soil-living larvae called wireworms. These have yellow skins, three pairs of legs and brown heads. The natural home of wireworms is under grass, but when this is ploughed up, they can do considerable damage to the roots of crops which are planted later.

Cliff see Coast
Climate see Weather

Clingfish, Shore *Lepadogaster lepadogaster*
The most common of the four species of clingfish found on British coasts was once called the Cornish sucker and thought to be confined to Cornish shores. It is now known to live along the whole western coastline of the British Isles. It habitually clamps itself to the undersides of rocks by means of a suction disc on its belly. Like all clingfish, it has a flattened body, a head with a duck-like mouth and relatively small fins.

The sucker helps the clingfish to cope with life on the shore where wave action may be strong. It also means that the adults can guard their golden eggs, laid in patches on the undersides of boulders in summer.

Clint see Limestone

Clitter
These are collections of angular boulders found on the steeper slopes of areas such as Dartmoor or the Pennines. The boulders were detached from the solid rock at the top of the slope through the action of frost, and gradually slipped down. Most frosts are not now severe enough to fracture rock. Nearly all clitter is a relic of the Ice Age, which ended about 11,000 years ago.

Clothes moth
The damage caused to clothes and furnishing fabrics by these wool-digesting insects makes them a serious household pest. The caterpillars have very strong enzymes in their gut, enabling them to break down the tough molecules of hair and fur. The common clothes moth *Tineola bisselliella* may be present all year round in suitably heated houses. The creamy-white caterpillars have brown heads and make silk galleries in all materials of animal origin, such as fur and woollen garments, carpets and hair. They feed from October to June, storing up reserves of food to support the two to three week life span of the adult moth.

The brown house moth *Borkenhausia pseudopretella* is more common in many houses and attacks a wider range of materials. The tapestry moth *Trichophaga tapetzella* is more often seen in stables and outhouses, where coarser materials form its diet. The white shouldered house moth *Endrosis sarcitrella* has the distinctive marking its name suggests.

Lens-shaped clouds form on crests of air waves flowing over hills. The clouds appear stationary

Cloud
A cloud forms when invisible water vapour turns into visible water drops. All air contains water vapour. This is produced by the evaporation of moisture from seas, rivers, lakes, soil and plants. Each year 475 million tons of water pass between earth and the atmosphere. The warmer the air the greater its capacity for holding vapour. When air rises and cools it contracts and its capacity to hold vapour is reduced until it becomes saturated. Any further cooling results in a shedding of moisture as tiny water droplets, which form clouds. Clouds therefore indicate areas of rising, cooling air; clear skies indicate areas of sinking, warming air.

Air masses sometimes rise quickly and vertically. When this happens they form one of the two basic types of cloud—*cumulus*, or heap, cloud, sometimes known as cauliflower cloud because of its appearance. These clouds are brilliant white in those upper parts lit by the sun, dark grey in shaded areas. A *cumulus* cloud is constantly changing. From parts of it fresh towers of cloud rise, while other parts are caught in downdraughts of air and disappear by evaporation of their droplets. Sometimes the top of the cloud rises high enough for its droplets to freeze into tiny ice crystals. These show in the sky as a frothy, dazzling white mass, falling diagonally in the direction of the wind to form what is known as an anvil because of its shape. This type of cloud, known as a *cumulonimbus*, or thunder, cloud, can contain up to 50,000 tons of water and usually produces heavy rain or hail.

At other times air masses rise slowly and on a low gradient—often as low as 1 in 150. This is the case with a warm front, which is warm air gliding above a shallow wedge of colder air from more northern latitudes. As this warm air slowly rises and cools, it forms the second basic type of cloud—*stratus*, or sheet, cloud. Light rain often falls from the thickest parts of this bank of cloud and in winter it tends to reach ground level as fog.

A cloud composed of small droplets re-

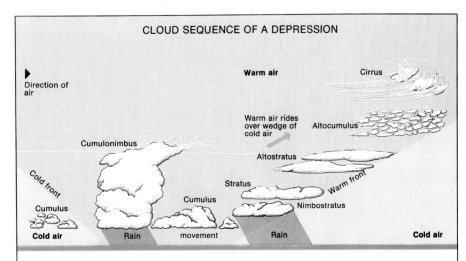

CLOUD SEQUENCE OF A DEPRESSION

Direction of air

Warm air

Cirrus

Warm air rides over wedge of cold air

Cumulonimbus

Altocumulus

Altostratus

Cold front

Stratus

Warm front

Cumulus

Nimbostratus

Cumulus

movement

Cold air

Rain

Rain

Cold air

but are continuously forming, dispersing and re-forming as the wind moves through them

flects sunlight more than one consisting of large droplets. A silver lining occurs when sunlight behind a cloud composed of large droplets filters through its edges. A layer of strato-cumulus reflects 55-80 per cent of the sun's energy. The amount reflected by other clouds depends on their density.

The highest clouds, known as noctilucent clouds, shine after dark on clear nights. They are found at heights about 50 miles above earth and consist of ice-coated dust particles from outer space. But nearly all water vapour is found in the 6-9 miles nearest earth. A slight amount of vapour is found at about 16 miles from earth where 'mother of pearl' clouds can be seen on rare occasions.

Cold front

Warm front

Much of Britain's weather is associated with depressions from the Atlantic, where cold air masses from the polar regions meet warm air masses from the sub-tropics. As the warm air rises over the cold air, water vapour in the warm air condenses into clouds, and the cloud droplets sometimes combine to form rain. Seen from the ground the sequence of clouds in a depression is as follows: high cirrus wisps, altocumulus, altostratus, stratus, nimbostratus, cumulus and cumulonimbus.

A depression can be plotted on a weather map. The thick lines indicate the edges or fronts of air masses. The spiked line is a cold front moving in the direction of the spikes, the line with semi-circles indicates a warm front and its direction of movement

Cirrus, or mare's-tail clouds, are the highest clouds formed of ice crystals

Altocumulus—mackerel sky—small, regularly arranged globular masses of cloud

Nimbostratus, low clouds with a ragged base that blanket the sky and give continuous rain

Stratus, a flat, grey, low sheet of cloud from which light rain may fall

Cumulus, the fair-weather clouds, are fluffy white masses separated by clear sky

Cumulonimbus, the towering thunder cloud, seen here from the crystalline 'anvil' end

Cloudberry *Rubus chamaemorus*

This low-growing shrub, a relation of the blackberry, grows in patches among moss and heather in wet mountain bogs in northern England and Scotland, usually above 2000 ft. Male and female flowers are borne on separate plants and appear among the kidney-shaped leaves at mid-summer. On the female plants they are followed in autumn by large, yellow, edible raspberry-like fruits. Cloudberries spread mainly by underground stems and rarely by seed, so that large areas of cloudberries may be of only one sex.

The edible fruit of the cloudberry resembles a large, hard, yellow raspberry

Clouded yellow see Yellow butterfly
Clough see Valley

Clover

One of the most valuable crops for feeding cattle and sheep, clover has leaves divided into three and is usually grown with grass. Occasionally one is found with four leaves, and the rarity of such a discovery has led to the belief that this brings luck to the finder. Clover grown as a crop is usually raised from specially bred strains of the wild species.

There are two common white-flowered clovers, white or dutch clover which has creeping stems, and the more upright alsike, with flowers which are at first white and erect but later turn rose red and curve down so that the flowers appear red with a white centre.

Alsike was introduced from Europe for fodder but is now firmly established on roadsides. The two most common purple-flowered clovers are red and zigzag. They are not easily told apart, but the latter has zigzag stems, narrower leaflets and flatter, redder heads of flowers. Red clover flowers make splendid wine and were once used, when dried, as a cough cure. A pretty clover is haresfoot, which is found on sandy soils and takes its name from the fluffy heads of flowers which look like the feet of a hare.

Red and white clover are important to bee-keepers. The nectar attracts the bees, which are essential for pollination, their weight operating a mechanism which brushes pollen on their undersides. Many flowers are robbed of their nectar by insects which bore a hole from the outside and take the nectar without touching the pollen sacs.

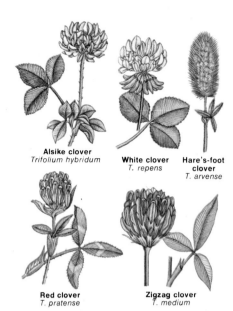

Alsike clover
Trifolium hybridum

White clover
T. repens

Hare's-foot clover
T. arvense

Red clover
T. pratense

Zigzag clover
T. medium

Clover, an important farm crop, also grows wild throughout the British Isles

Clover roots house bacteria which convert atmospheric nitrogen into a form which is usable by plants. See also CROP

Clubmoss, Fir *Huperzia selago*

A miniature, yellow-green fir tree found among rocks or on peat in a heather moor, the fir clubmoss is about 6 in. high and is neither a fir nor a moss, but a primitive plant related to ancestors of the ferns. Fir clubmoss was once common on acid soil throughout Britain, but it is now confined mainly to mountainous areas in northern England, Scotland, Wales and Ireland. It can be seen even near the summits of the highest mountains. Fir clubmoss produces spores that do not function, and reproduction is by leaf-like buds which separate from the mother plant and grow independently when they reach the ground.

Round spore cases grow on the base of the narrow, pointed leaves of fir clubmoss

Coal

Most of the coal in Britain began to form during the Carboniferous Age—about 280 million years ago—which lasted for 55 million years. The compressed remains of former swamp forests, which formed thick beds of peat, were buried beneath layers of sand as the channels of swampy deltas changed their course. Eventually, these peats were deeply buried, so that the weight of overlying rock compressed them into coal. Most coal is found in South Wales, in Yorkshire east of the Pennines, Nottinghamshire, Derbyshire and Durham. Mines have been sunk to more than half a mile in depth, and in some places galleries extend beneath the sea.

Though known to the Romans, coal was not mined extensively in Britain until the 16th century. See also MINE

Cockle

Edible cockles live close to the surface of the sand on tidal shores and are easy to gather by raking. As cockles draw in sand with the plant plankton they feed on, they must be kept for several hours in sea water before being cooked, to give them time to expel the sand.

Cockles reproduce by each cockle discharging both eggs and sperm into the sea where fertilisation takes place. The free-swimming larvae settle on the shore after about eight weeks.

The edible cockle *Cardium edule* can be found anywhere on the shore, but the biggest—up to 2 in. across—and the greatest numbers are low down on the shore where the tides keep the sand cleanest. Commercially, they are gathered in the large estuaries of the Thames, the Dee, The Wash, Morecambe Bay and at Llanrhidian Sands, South Wales. The prickly cockle *C. echinata* is less common.

Cockroach

Six of the nine species of cockroach living in Britain were introduced accidentally by man, most of them probably from North Africa. None of the six can survive the British winter outdoors and they are found in warm buildings where food is stored.

All the introduced species are much larger than the natives. They include the common cockroach *Blatta orientalis*. This insect is about 1 in. long and chocolate-brown. It is often called a black beetle, but cockroaches are not closely related to beetles. Another common introduction is the German cockroach *Blatella germanica*, about ⅜ in. long and yellow-brown. The largest species is the 1½ in. long American cockroach *Periplaneta americana*.

The three native species look like smaller versions of the German cockroach. They are found only in southern England and South Wales.

Most cockroaches have wings, though many, like the common cockroach, cannot fly. They are nocturnal scavengers, feeding mainly on vegetable matter, relying largely on their antennae, which are as long as their bodies, to find their way around. The female produces about 40 eggs which she carries around in a case beneath her body. These hatch after about five weeks into nymphs which look like small adults. The German cockroach matures in two to four months. In two of the native species, the tawny *Ectobius pallidus*, and the dusky *E. lapponicus*, the nymph takes a year to mature.

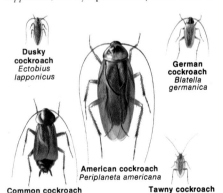

Dusky cockroach
Ectobius lapponicus

German cockroach
Blatella germanica

American cockroach
Periplaneta americana

Common cockroach
Blatta orientalis

Tawny cockroach
Ectobius pallidus

Cod *Gadus morhua*
From earliest times man has eaten cod. Their bones have been found in archaeological sites in east Scotland dating back 4000 years.

Cod are common in the seas around the northern part of the British Isles. In the winter they migrate south, appearing off East Anglia and the Channel coast. Young cod, or codling, move inshore and are often caught in shallow water in winter.

Adults are about 4 ft long and weigh up to 60 lb. Cod vary in colour, but are usually yellow-brown and white underneath. They have a chin barbel, or feeler, three separate fins on the back, and two underneath. They are predators, feeding on crustaceans, worms and small fish.

Codlins-and-cream see Willowherb
Coley see Saithe
Collared dove see Pigeon

Colorado beetle *Leptinotarsa decemlineata*
The larvae of this little black-and-yellow striped beetle are a serious pest of potato crops over much of Europe, but the English Channel and stringent regulations have kept Britain largely free of them. The beetle, only ½ in. long, slow moving and conspicuous, is a menace by sheer weight of numbers. If allowed to breed unchecked, a female lays 500-800 eggs which hatch in a few days. The larvae, which resemble those of ladybirds, are red with black spots and have black heads and legs. They feed voraciously on potato leaves and soon kill the plants. They grow quickly and, after pupation, emerge as adults in less than six weeks.

Originally the colorado beetle lived in semi-desert regions of the western USA. When potatoes began to be widely cultivated in the early 1800's it soon became a serious pest.

The first outbreak in Britain was in 1901, but the colorado beetle has never become established here because of control by a 'flying squad' of Ministry of Agriculture chemical operators, who act whenever a beetle is found. The law requires that findings must be reported immediately. There are about 30 such reports a year. Most of the beetles arrive from Europe in fruit, vegetables or flowers.

The last time a colony was found in England was in 1952, although precautionary spraying was carried out in 1955. Ladybirds, burying beetles and summer chafers have been mistaken for colorado beetles.

Colour and camouflage see p. 110

Coltsfoot *Tussilago farfara*
Waste land and roadsides everywhere are made gay in early spring by the 1 in. golden-yellow flower heads of this plant. After pollination the heads droop until the fruits are ripe, when they become upright again. The leaves are often 6-9 in. across, their shape giving the plant its English name. Its

Coltsfoot flowers appear on pink-scaled stems from February to April, before the leaves

Latin name, *Tussilago*, means cough plant—the Romans prized coltsfoot and allied herbs as cough cures. It can be used to brew a tonic or dried and smoked. Lowland Scots, who call the plant Tussilugi, also use it to relieve coughs.

Columbine *Aquilegia vulgaris*
The name of this plant comes from *columba*, a dove, referring to its bird-like flowers. Each drooping blue flower has five spurred petals arranged like doves round a food source, with the sepals resembling wings. It grows in England on lime-rich soils, in wet woodlands and fens. Elsewhere it may be found in hedgerows, but in such situations it has always spread from nearby gardens.

Combine harvester see Farm machinery

Comfrey *Symphytum officinale*
This plant occurs in a wide range of colours; its drooping, bell-like flowers vary from pale yellow to purple and violet. The stems are tough and difficult to pick. Large colonies of the plant cover long stretches of river banks and roadside ditches, brightening the countryside from May to September when they are in flower. Preparations from the roots and leaves were once used to treat sores, wounds and various ailments.

Comma *Polygonia c-album*
White, comma-shaped marks on the undersides of its wings give the comma butterfly its name. The comma is also identified by its tattered-looking wings which help it to remain undetected among dead leaves on the trees where it hibernates. Not all commas hibernate. Some which hatch in early summer die in the autumn. These need no winter camouflage and are lighter than those which hibernate.

Comma caterpillars are brown and white, and spiky. They feed on nettles and hops for about seven weeks before pupating. The stronghold of the comma is in Monmouthshire and the surrounding counties, though it also occurs in southern England and Wales. It is not found in Ireland and Scotland. See also VANESSID

Britain's coast–a buffer that defies the sea

The arithmetic of the sea governs the ever-changing shape of the British Isles. Every day the waves eat into the coast, but every day they add more land to these islands than they take away

The familiar shape of the British Isles is, in fact, constantly altering as the waves and currents of the surrounding seas break down the coast in some places and build it up in others. This process of constant change has been going on for millions of years. Some parts of the coast are carved away by the sea water, creating cliffs and bays; in other parts the sea sweeps together shingle, sand or mud to form beaches or marshes which can sometimes be reclaimed as farmland.

This basic distinction between coasts cut by erosion and coasts built out by deposition corresponds to a general division between high coasts and low coasts. High coasts have cliffs and are dominated by erosion; low coasts are those where sediment accumulates.

Whether high or low, most of the coastline has a beach. This is formed of shingle or sand, and is a belt of sediment which the waves move as the tide rises and falls and as storms build up and die away. The beach acts as a natural buffer between sea and land, absorbing most of the energy of the waves which pound on the shore.

During storms the beach is usually combed down, and much of the sand is carried out below low-water mark. At such times the underlying rock, or perhaps a buried forest, may be exposed. Such storms are most common during the winter, when there is often very little sand on the beach. In contrast, the smaller waves of summer wash the sand up the shore, often building up quite a wide sandy beach above high-water mark. Many people, who visit the coast only in summer, never see these seasonal changes and would not recognise a familiar sandy beach in its winter form with rock or shingle exposed.

The steepness of a beach is the combined result of the waves moving sand upwards and the scouring effect of the backwash which follows. Where swell rolls in from the open ocean, so much water covers the beach with each wave that only a small proportion of it can soak in and the scouring effect of the backwash is strong, pulling the sand out to sea. A gently sloping beach results. This, in turn, causes the waves

The ceaseless pounding of waves finds weak spots among the hardest rocks, so that even the most unyielding coast finally gives way to the sea. At Sandy-mouth, north Cornwall, material carved from the rock of jutting headlands is deposited as sand in the bays they protect. There is no end to this

to break a long way out and they are likely to be good for surfing. Such beaches occur on the west coast of Scotland and the north coast of Devon and Cornwall.

Coasts on more enclosed seas, such as the Irish Sea, face waves of smaller volume and, since a larger proportion of the water soaks into the sand, more sand is deposited and the beach becomes steeper. Where there is a lot of sand on the beach, ridges with steep faces on the seaward side are formed, together with runnels, which flood as the tide races in.

The Solway Firth and Morecambe Bay opening on to the Irish Sea are great funnel-shaped bays which have a large tidal range exposing extensive sand banks at low tide. The inner parts of the bays are protected from wave action and generally have broad strips of salt marshes. Much of the Lancashire coast is low and rather sandy, with sand dunes well developed between Southport and Formby.

Beach angle is also affected by the size of the material which makes up the beach, as this determines how much of each wave can soak away. For this reason shingle beaches are steep, and beaches of fine sand slope gently. Where fine sand accumulates and the beach grows, some of it will be lifted from the beach by the wind and deposited behind it as a line of sand dunes. Marram grass grows up through the dunes and helps to trap the sand.

On the east coast of Scotland are many sandy bays backed by dunes. At Culbin Sands, on the south coast of the Moray Firth, blown sand has been carried far inland, covering soil that was once good farmland with dunes up to 100 ft high. Buried buildings are sometimes uncovered as the sand shifts, but conifers have been planted to stabilise the dunes and to halt their advance inland.

When waves approach the beach at an angle or when there are tidal currents offshore, sand, silt and mud are moved parallel to the coast. This often leads to erosion where these forces have their source and to the building up of sediment further along the coast; in some places the beach is extended out to sea to form a spit, as at Spurn Head, Yorkshire. As the spit extends into deeper water, it is shaped by waves approaching from other directions and will often be curved round at the end.

Behind the spit, and in other places sheltered from waves, finer sediment builds up mudflats and marshes. As the mud builds up and is exposed for a longer period with each tide, grasses and other plants adapted to these special conditions grow and help to trap the mud, just as marram grass traps sand on a dune. Broad salt marshes, built up to high-tide level in this way, can be reclaimed by building dykes, as around The Wash, on the Norfolk-Lincoln border, or at Romney Marsh, in Kent. Breakwaters or groynes are often built to slow down erosion of beaches by waves moving parallel to the shore.

Although there is sometimes a beach at the foot of a cliff, often the sand is swept into the heads of bays, and at most headlands the cliffs descend straight into the sea at high water. At low water a broad platform cut in the cliff by waves can be seen; often this contains small rock pools, showing the partial success of erosion. During storms, waves sweep across this platform to attack the base of the cliffs, cutting a notch and eventually causing them to crumble and collapse. The sea acts like a saw, trimming back the land and gradually widening the rock platform.

sequence of erosion and deposition, for even if the sea straightens the coastline, new weak spots will emerge for the waves to attack

A COAST THAT RETREATS BEFORE THE SEA

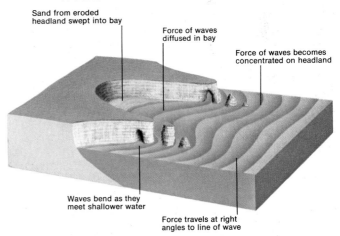

Sand from eroded headland swept into bay

Force of waves diffused in bay

Force of waves becomes concentrated on headland

Waves bend as they meet shallower water

Force travels at right angles to line of wave

A wave travelling towards a coast moves in a straight front, but when it approaches an uneven coast it bends around headlands as the water becomes shallower. The force of a wave travels at 90 degrees to its front and so, as the wave bends around the headland, the force is focused on the point, causing the greatest amount of erosion. In the bay, the waves bend in the opposite direction and the force is diffused. Material eroded from the headland is eventually carried into the bay. In this way the most jagged coast is gradually straightened

LAND BUILT UP FROM THE SEA

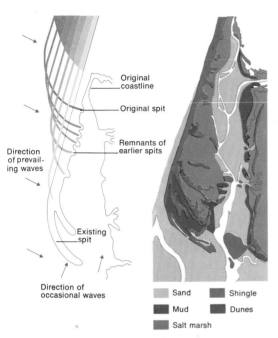

Waves approaching a coast at an angle move sediment parallel to the coast, sometimes extending the beach out to sea and forming a spit. Silt accumulates behind the spit, creating salt marshes where once there was sea. Plants, such as spartina grass and marsh samphire, grow on the marshes and help to stabilise the new land. At Blakeney Point the growing spit extended its outer curve, leaving the tips of the old curves as ridges running towards the shore

Land from the sea. Blakeney Point, Norfolk, a complex of salt marsh and dunes, has grown up on a skeleton of shingle brought in by waves moving along the coast

Along such coasts the success of the waves is very closely related to the strength of the rocks forming the land. Along soft beds, or where the rock is broken by joints and faults, bays and caves are excavated. Concentration of wave attack near high-tide level means that caves usually occur at the foot of cliffs. As the caves expand inwards, the air compressed within by the weight of the pounding waves may produce a blowhole at the surface, sometimes a considerable distance inland. There is a fine example of a blowhole at Holborn Head, Caithness. In the same way, arches may be cut through promontories and isolated stacks may be formed. The Old Man of Hoy, a 450 ft pillar of rock rising sheer from the sea in the Orkneys, is a spectacular example. The highest cliffs occur where powerful Atlantic breakers have bitten into hilly coastlines. The highest in the British Isles are along the west coast of Ireland, where the Cliffs of Moher rise well over 1000 ft above the sea. In England, the highest cliffs are on the north coast of Devon and Cornwall. Those at Countisbury, Devon, are 900 ft high.

All these features may be combined in different ways in different areas. The reclaimed marshes below Winchelsea in Sussex stretch out from the foot of a former sea cliff from which the sea has retreated. Changes in sea level over the ages also complicate the appearance of the coast; in some places fragments of shingle beach can be found well above high-tide level, as on the Gower Peninsula in Wales. In parts of the

western islands of Scotland, where the land has risen since the ice sheets melted, broad platforms backed by former cliffs stand as much as 100 ft above present beaches. These platforms, called raised beaches, often have new cliffs cut along the new shoreline.

On the mainland of north-west Scotland long sea lochs were scooped out by Ice Age glaciers. The ice left smooth, polished surfaces on the hard rocks which have been little altered by the waves. But even here, the sea has won ground: its level has risen, relative to the coast, and it has flooded up the lower arms of the lochs.

In south-west Ireland and south Cornwall, river valleys, such as those of the Fal and the Tamar, have been invaded by the sea, creating deep inlets. These often make sheltered deep-water anchorages as at Falmouth and Bantry Bay. In contrast, the ice-cut sea lochs of Scotland usually have a shallow rocky bar at the entrance formed by the debris which accumulated at the glacier face.

In most places, however, coastal forms are being fashioned by the same sort of waves and currents that were at work thousands of years ago.

Along many parts of the coast erosion is a serious problem. Waves and currents carry sand and clay away from the beach into deeper water, or carry them along the shore to build up marshes or lengthen a spit further along the coast. Where erosion occurs, waves are able to attack the land behind the beach and the coastline moves landwards. In some places on the Norfolk coast and in Holderness, Yorkshire, 1 yd of land is lost every year. This has been happening for thousands of years, so that not only farms and cottages but whole villages have vanished, and their sites lie out at sea. In some places 2-3 miles have been lost since Roman times. For example, Dunwich, on the Suffolk coast, originally a thriving Roman port big enough to contain 70 ships, was an important trading centre until the 14th century. Then, in 1326, the sea swept in, washing away several hundred houses. Over the centuries, erosion continued and the old town was finally destroyed by the sea in 1740. All that is left today are a few old houses and a graveyard, which is still under attack from the waves. At Selsey Bill, Sussex, about 200 yds of land have been swallowed up in the last 50 years.

To protect towns concrete walls are built but, such is the power of the sea, even these are sometimes damaged. Where the land along the coast is less valuable, cheaper defences, such as groynes, are used. These delay erosion for a few years, but are often unsuccessful in keeping a good beach, which remains the best defence against wave attack.

It has been calculated that about 500 million cu. ft of soil is eroded from the coastline of England and Wales each year.

In spite of these losses the amount of land gained from the sea each year is greater than that eroded away. This is because silt and sand are washed from high cliffs or brought down as sediment by rivers to form extensive marshes at or near sea level. By building dykes these marshes can be reclaimed. Large areas of farmland around The Wash and Humber have been gained from the sea in this way.

Loch Craignish, 6 miles long and 1-3 miles wide, on the west coast of Argyllshire, Scotland—a typical drowned coast. Since the end of the Ice Age the sea has risen, flooding river valleys and creating a succession of long, narrow inlets and headlands

Hide and seek in a world of colour

The life-and-death struggle to eat and yet avoid being eaten has seen the evolution of elaborate disguises in both predators and prey. But many inedible animals wear blatant advertisements of their unpleasant taste

Almost every animal, whether hunter or hunted, makes use of camouflage to escape its enemies or deceive its prey. The hermit crab, living in rock pools, covers its borrowed whelk shell with seaweed and sea anemones in an attempt to disguise itself. But for the majority of animals concealment depends on their body colours and patterning. Colour has another function, too — one which sometimes conflicts directly with the need for camouflage. For as well as concealing, it can also reveal. These contradictory roles of colour are well illustrated in birds, where the males are often boldly coloured to attract mates, while the females, which usually look after the eggs and chicks, are drab. Most mammals can see only in black and white, but those that have colour vision — birds, reptiles, fish and insects — are themselves often beautifully patterned and adorned. Colour helps them to recognise their own species and is used in displays between male and female during courtship.

Hunter and hunted use camouflage

The simplest way in which one animal can elude another is to be indistinguishable from its surroundings. The green grasshopper disappears among the grass and leaves, the streaked bittern among reeds, the banded adder among the undergrowth and the brown woodland snail on tree bark. Some animals are capable of changing their colours to suit the surroundings. The stoat and mountain hare moult their brown summer coats for white winter ones.

However well an animal merges with its surroundings, the 'solidness' of its body may still betray it. As light shines from above its back is highlighted, its belly put in shadow. To counteract this effect many animals have a dark-coloured back and a light-coloured belly. In most animals the demarcation between the two is gradual, as in the trout or rabbit.

A black-green crab lurks among seaweed and shows that a simple but effective way to evade a predator is to merge with the surroundings

In the water shrew, however, it is strongly marked. As this small mammal swims on the surface of a pond its slaty-black body merges with the water when seen from above. Looked at from below, from water into sunlight, its white belly is almost invisible.

The professionals in the camouflage act are the insects that pretend to be some inedible object. The angle shades moth has forewings patterned with angle shapes and the colour of dead leaves. When it rests by day among leaf litter it is practically impossible to tell moth from leaves. But, to be completely successful, it must not only look like a leaf, it must act like one — fluttering when there is a breeze, remaining still on a calm day.

Brilliant colours that say keep off

Some animals put on a terrifying act to frighten a predator away. If a bird penetrates the camouflage of the eyed hawk-moth, the moth suddenly lifts its blotched-brown forewings

Buff tip moth or freshly broken twig? An impenetrable disguise achieved by

FLASH COLOURS

Eyed hawk-moth at rest   Eye-spots displayed

As a last line of defence to frighten an enemy the eyed hawk-moth suddenly opens its forewings to flash the large eye-spots on its hind wings

to reveal two large eye-spots on its hind wings. The startling effect on the predator gives the moth time to escape. The moth is playing on the bird's fear of its own enemies, cats and owls, which it recognises by their eyes.

Using colours not to camouflage but to advertise is another way of scaring off enemies. Vivid patterns of black, white,

No creature will enjoy eating the foul-tasting kingfisher, and its brilliantly coloured plumage effectively advertises this fact. Predators discover through experience to leave this river-bank inhabitant well alone

red and yellow are displayed as 'warning colours' announcing the unpleasant taste or sting of the animal wearing them. A bird that has once eaten a cinnabar moth will avoid this evil-tasting insect for the rest of its life. It will associate the disagreeable taste with the distinctive crimson and black colours of the moth. The black-and-yellow body of the wasp says 'sting' to the whole animal kingdom, not just men. In the long run it pays for the species to be conspicuous. Some wasps will be eaten by young birds, but the population as a whole will survive.

Mimicry

Some harmless and edible animals have bright colours which mimic those of poisonous or distasteful creatures. In this way the mimic shares the protection of the animal with warning colours, and deceives its enemies. Many flies resemble wasps in shape and colour. Similarly the hornet moth looks like the hornet. To get full benefit from these disguises the mimics must live in the same areas as their models.

An unusual form of colour imitation has developed in the cuckoo, which lays eggs to match those of another bird, which then hatches them as if they were her own.

WASP IMITATORS

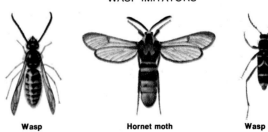

Wasp   **Hornet moth**   **Wasp beetle**

The wasp is a favourite model for the many insect mimics. The hornet moth and wasp beetle both copy its bright warning colours

combination of colour, wing patterning and resting position

Common land

The term common land, or common, may apply equally to a small village green, Epping Forest and vast tracts of Dartmoor. The commons of England and Wales (there is no common land in Scotland) total about 1½ million acres.

Many people believe that the public owns common land, that the heaths where campers set up their tents, the woods where families picnic and the commons where children fly kites are public property. This is only exceptionally the case. All common land is in the possession of what the law terms 'a legal person'. This was originally the lord of the manor concerned, but is now usually a local authority in towns and a private individual or commercial company in the country.

The public does not even have legal access to all common land—only access to commons within a borough or urban district, for air and exercise. This was laid down by the Law of Property Act 1925. However, in practice, country commons are being treated more and more like town ones—as places of recreation for everybody to use.

Common land has been handed down to us from the past. In the Middle Ages each manor had its share of arable land, pasture and waste land, all of which was owned by the lord of the manor. But the cottagers, or commoners as they came to be known, were given the right by medieval courts to take away, or allow their animals to take away, products of their lord's waste land.

There were, and are, six basic rights of common. Common of pasture is the most important. This enables commoners to graze their animals on the owner's common

Pigs forage for beech mast and acorns in the New Forest, exercising their owner's right of Mast

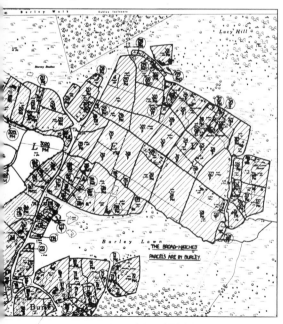

A page of the *Atlas of Rights* in which the common rights of the New Forest are recorded

land. Turbary is the right to extract peat or turf for use as fuel. Estovers entitles commoners to take small branches of wood and brushwood for fuel or for repairing fences and buildings. Piscary is the right to take fish from lakes or streams. Pannage—called Mast in the New Forest, one of the few places where it is still exercised—enables pig owners to graze their animals on fallen acorns and beech mast. Common in the soil is the right to take stones, minerals and even coal from common land.

These rights, called commons, still exist today. Without them, many hill farmers, for instance, would be unable to continue. Again, the commoners of Newcastle-upon-Tyne still exercise grazing rights on Town Moor—which, as an urban common, is also used by the other citizens for recreation.

In the 18th century, agriculturalists proved it was possible to cultivate waste land, and landlords began to enclose it. Enclosure had been going on sporadically and on a small scale since at least the 12th century. But from about 1750 the pace quickened and successive Acts of Parliament caused hundreds of thousands of acres of common land to be enclosed and transferred all rights of usage to the lords of the manor.

By 1850 all Britain's common land was in danger of disappearing. However, there was sufficient public concern, headed by the Commons, Open Spaces and Footpaths Preservation Society, to prevent this. Bills were passed in Parliament in the 1860's and

1870's restricting enclosures and maintaining common land.

The most recent development in the law concerning common land has been the Commons Registration Act of 1965. This provides for a register of common land and a legal record of who has what rights.

Conger *Conger conger*

This is a large and entirely marine eel, common around southern and western coasts, and found in small numbers on northern coasts. Specimens of 7-8 ft in length are often caught, while the largest recorded specimen weighed 143 lb. and was 15 ft long. Congers are found mainly in rocky areas where they lie concealed in crevices, under boulders or in caves. Another favourite haunt is in the artificial cover provided by sunken ships, and divers tell hair-raising tales of giant congers encountered lurking in the gloom of wrecks. Small specimens, often up to 4 ft long, can be found in rock pools near low-tide mark. Inshore congers are usually dull brown above, with pale bellies. They eat all kinds of fish and crustaceans, particularly bottom-living forms.

Congers spawn in mid-summer in an area between Gibraltar and the Azores. It has been estimated that the journey from the spawning grounds to the British Isles takes from one to two years. Congers grow swiftly. A 3 lb. specimen weighed 90 lb. after five years in captivity.

Conifer

The cone is the most distinctive feature of the great group of tall forest trees known as conifers—the cone-bearers. The group includes the largest living thing on earth, a 272 ft tall giant sequoia growing in California; and the tallest tree in Britain, a 180 ft tall Douglas fir, at Powis Castle, Montgomeryshire.

Conifers are of enormous value to industry. This fact and their fast growth rate on poor land account for the wide scale on which they are planted in the British Isles today—approaching 100,000 acres a year. Conifers are also called softwoods, since the wood of most, though not all, is soft compared with that of the broad-leaved trees, or hardwoods.

Botanists call them gymnosperms, meaning naked-seeded, because at first the ovule, which produces a seed, lies exposed on a cone scale. Later the cone closes and holds the seed firm until it ripens.

Before cones appear, conifers can be recognised by their narrow leaves, or needles. The size of the needle in relation to its surface area enables the tree to limit water loss, and to grow in cold or dry climates and on poor soil. It also means that with a few exceptions, for example larch and swamp cypress, conifers can retain green leaves through the winter. The usual name for the group in North America is evergreens.

Many conifers have remarkably regular patterns of growth and shape. Each spring they send up a straight shoot, and extend their side branches equally. A new whorl or cluster of branches is formed annually, so, by counting the whorls, it is possible to tell the age of most conifers. This even growth results in the symmetrical cone-shaped outlines, which are held for scores of years by trees grown in open situations, although gradually lost by those in forests due to competition from other trees.

Conifers bear catkin-like flowers, and the two sexes are always separate, though usually on the same tree. The flowers are wind-pollinated, and because of this they have neither bright petals to attract insects, nor nectar to reward them. In spring male flowers appear on most conifers in small clusters near the branch tips, shedding showers of golden pollen. Female flowers—the future cones—are bud-like structures that vary in colour from green to blue, white or red. After pollination they enlarge, turn green and eventually develop into cones.

When fully ripe the cones become brown and woody, their scales open, and the seeds fall out; the cone remaining on the tree. Most conifer seeds are small brown grains with papery wings that help the wind to carry them away from their parent tree. Exceptions are found in yew and juniper. These have nut-like seeds which are spread by birds. Cones do not, as is popularly supposed, forecast weather. They open and close as the weather changes from dry to wet—not in advance of the change. Cones open when it is dry and their seeds have a chance to scatter; they close in wet weather, when rain would carry the seeds straight to the ground. Opening and closing is controlled by moisture-sensitive cells at the base of each scale.

Most conifers produce resin—another aid to identifying the group. This is a fragrant white or yellow substance which oozes from the wood, cones, shoots and bark, especially if they become cut or bruised. Resin seals a wound against harmful insects and fungi. It is distilled to produce turpentine.

The bark of conifers is smooth on young twigs, but later develops patterns of plates, fibres or ridges, each species having its own distinctive patterns. Bark on trunks may become very thick and some are rich in tannin, a chemical used in treating hides to make leather.

The straight, regular trunks of conifers are valued for their timber, being easy to fell, handle and saw into straight planks. It is used as building or packaging timber, and in the manufacture of chipboard, hardboard and similar 'man-made' timbers.

It is the main raw material for the world's paper industry, with products ranging from newsprint to writing paper and food cartons. It is also the raw material for Cellophane, rayon fabrics, and the wood flour used in plastics. See also FOREST, TREE

A key to conifers

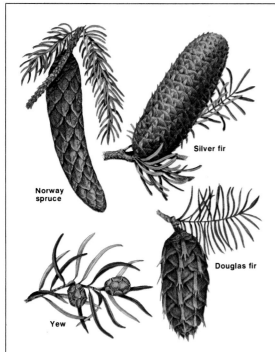

Norway spruce

Silver fir

Douglas fir

Yew

Spruces, yews, silver and Douglas firs have needles that stand singly. The needles of the spruces are on woody pegs. Silver firs have blunt buds, Douglas firs pointed ones, and those of yews are leafy

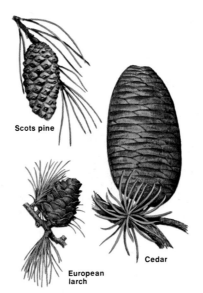

Scots pine

European larch

Cedar

Pines, cedars and larches have needles that stand free from the twigs in groups. Pines have groupings of two, three or five needles. Those of larches and cedars grow in numerous clusters. Larch needles fall in the autumn

Hemlock

Hemlocks have single needles that are extremely irregular in length. The long and short ones are intermixed along the twigs in random fashion

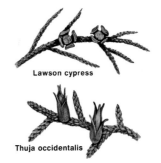

Lawson cypress

Thuja occidentalis

The needles of cypresses and thuja clasp and hide the twigs and buds, as do those found on the monkey puzzles and wellingtonias

Man-made forests where silence reigns

About half of Britain's woodland consists of conifers, but only three species are native to the country. These are Scots pine, yew and juniper. All the other types of conifers have been introduced, mainly from Europe and north-west America. At first these trees were grown for ornamental purposes, but many of them thrived so well in Britain's temperate climate that they began to be planted for timber production.

Today coniferous woodlands range from a few remnants of the native Caledonian pine forest of the Scottish Highlands to large forests of fast-growing spruce planted in the last 50 years. Sitka spruce is the most widely planted timber tree.

Man-made coniferous woodlands nearly always have fewer animals than the native deciduous forests, even though in their native countries conifer forests are rich in wildlife. The main reason is that, although we have imported foreign trees, we have left behind their associated wildlife, and most British animals and birds have not adapted themselves to the new conditions. Native deciduous trees, such as the oak, provide food directly to hundreds of animal species — mainly insects — but conifers support only a comparatively small number. Consequently our native animals and birds have not been encouraged to move into these barren coniferous plantations.

They are also discouraged by the shortage of plants growing on the forest floor, which would provide food in themselves and attract edible insects. In coniferous forests the growth of plants is inhibited because, with the exception of larches, conifers are evergreen and cast a heavy shadow all year round. Plants are therefore usually restricted to a few ferns, such as the broad buckler fern, common male fern and some inconspicuous mosses — although bracken, wood sorrel and wavy-hair grass grow where there are gaps in the trees.

In addition to the natural differences between coniferous and deciduous forests, wildlife is also deterred by the artificial nature of most conifer plantations. In intensively managed plantations the trees are usually uniform in species, age and spacing, and so lack variety. In a plantation, too, trees are

CONIFEROUS PLANTATION

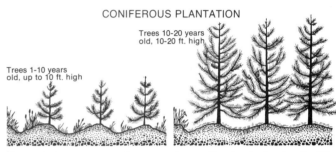

Trees 1-10 years old, up to 10 ft. high

Trees 10-20 years old, 10-20 ft. high

Green plants grow among the young pines on the ploughed, wet and acidic soil. After about ten years, however, the heavy shade and thick layer of fallen needles kill the plants, the soil becomes dry and the furrows fill in

Gwydyr Forest, a coniferous forest in Denbighshire. These unnatural man-made surroundings encourage few wild animals, and green plants are unable to grow among the fallen needles and branches

Wavy-hair grass This slender-stemmed grass has delicate branches and silvery spikelets

Pine-wood mushroom Grows among the needle litter in autumn. Its white stalk has a conspicuous ring around it

Pine weevil Eats into the bark of young conifer branches to feast on the more tender tissues beneath

cropped rather than being left to die, and so there is an absence of rotten wood, a material which provides food and living conditions for fungi, insects and birds. Moreover, coniferous trees are often planted on poor soil, such as that of exposed hillsides, to make economic use of it.

In these artificial conditions the process known as the food chain can never develop fully. The basis of the food chain is the trees and plants which provide the original sources of food for nearly all other organisms. Many animals depend directly on plants for their food; others feed on the plant-feeders, and still others feed on them. Then the dead material, both plant and animal, is broken down in the soil by invertebrates, bacteria and fungi, for re-use by the trees.

However, the average coniferous forest is not a uniform unbroken tract of trees. It contains stands of trees in different stages of growth, providing different conditions and habitats. A working forest in which timber is being regularly harvested is also broken up by a network of roads, rides and timber stacking places, creating biologically rich woodland-edge conditions for plants and animals. Disturbance of the soil by timber felling brings in a range of plants which colonise bare ground, such as willow herb and foxgloves.

Many coniferous plantations offer shelter for animals from the surrounding countryside, such as deer, hares and foxes, and for owls. Coniferous woodlands also provide a 'corridor' for shy or vulnerable animals, enabling them to travel long distances under cover. The rapid spread of deer results from the planting of new forests, and rarer mammals, such as pine martens and wild cats, have also benefited.

Long-eared owl Haunts the woodland at night making its low moaning hoot; its 'ears' are simply long head feathers and have no connection with hearing

Fallow deer The buck keeps watch while the doe feeds. The sheltered corridors of woodland are ideal cover for these shy creatures

Sweet vernal grass The compact, fragrantly scented head flowers in the middle of April

Red squirrel A destructive animal that eats the seeds from cones and strips bark off shoots

Broad buckler fern This common British fern has fronds 1-2 ft high

Wood sorrel Flowers in early spring. At night the leaflets close downwards

Goldcrest Britain's smallest bird builds a hanging nest from the branch of a conifer

Bramble Grows over the woodland floor where the trees have been felled and light penetrates

Coombe

A steep-sided, short valley cut into the steep face of an escarpment, usually by the action of spring water. Many are now dry. The word is often found in place-names, such as Salcombe in Devon, Batcombe in Somerset, and Langdale Coombe in the Lake District. The chalk downs of southern England have many coombes. One of the most dramatic is the Devil's Dyke, north of Brighton, Sussex; another is the Devil's Kneadingtrough, near Ashford, Kent.

Coot see Crake

Copper butterfly

In 1848, butterfly collectors finally exterminated the native large copper butterfly *Lycaena dispar*. It had become rare with the draining of the fens where it lived, its larvae feeding on the great water dock. In 1927 large coppers were introduced to Wood Walton Fen, Huntingdonshire from the Netherlands and became established. Today the Nature Conservancy maintains a supply of great water dock for them in the Fen and also rears them in captivity. The larvae secrete a sweet substance and are attended by ants. Like the small coppers *L. phlaeas*, the adults have iridescent copper-coloured wings.

Female small coppers lay their yellow eggs singly on the undersides of dock and sorrel—the food plants of the species—and the green caterpillars can be found wherever these plants grow in open grassy areas throughout the British Isles. Up to three generations of small coppers appear in a year, the last generation spending the winter as a pupa on the food plant. Adults fly from April to October.

Coppice

If a broad-leaved tree is cut back to a stump, or stool, it will send up fresh shoots from side-buds just above ground level. It is then called a coppiced tree—one without a single trunk. The shoots provide a crop of poles and, when these are felled, further shoots sprout and provide further crops. The poles are cut every 7-20 years, depending on the species of tree, and the process can continue for 100 years or more. The word coppice, often shortened to copse, comes from the Norman-French *couper*, meaning to cut. Trees that have been coppiced need to be fenced off from grazing cattle which would otherwise damage the new growth. See also POLLARD

Coral

Two species of this sea animal live on rocky shores round British coasts, but unlike tropical corals they are solitary and never form reefs. Related to the sea anemone, they have slender, petal-like tentacles and a flat-topped cup formed from a hard skeleton of carbonate of lime. The cup grows to $\frac{1}{2}$ in. high and $\frac{1}{2}$ in. across and is attached to rock by a short

Tentacles around this cup coral paralyse small animals and feed them into its mouth

stalk. They feed on tiny creatures which they extract from the sea with their tentacles.

The Devonshire cup coral *Caryophyllia smithii* has a white cup, sometimes tinged with pink, and about 50 tentacles with brown markings and white tips. The scarlet and gold star coral *Balanophyllia regia* is so called because of its scarlet body and yellow-spotted transparent tentacles.

When coral dies—either due to an accumulation of silt and debris or certain types of seaweed growing across it—the delicately coloured tissue deteriorates, leaving the familiar bleached and rock-hard skeleton.

Coral spot see Fungus
Corkwing see Wrasse

Cormorant

Many fishermen view the cormorant and its relative, the shag, as rivals for their catch, since the presence of cormorants and shags indicates that fish are plentiful. Both birds are common along the southern, western and northern coasts of Britain. The cormorant *Phalacrocorax carbo* also frequents inland lakes and reservoirs; the shag *P. aristotelis* appears inland only when driven there by storms.

The adult cormorant, which is about 36 in. long, has black and dark brown plumage, with a green and purple sheen and a white chin; in spring the thigh bears a white patch. Immature birds are dark brown above, off-white underneath. The shag is 6 in. shorter and has no white markings. The adult is glossy green, and in spring has an erect crest on its head. Immature birds are brown, lighter underneath, and difficult to distinguish from immature cormorants apart from size. In flight to their feeding grounds, cormorants fly in geese-like V formation; shags in line ahead.

Both birds can swim with only their heads and long, curved necks above water, giving

them a serpent-like appearance. They often sit on rocks and buoys with wings outspread to dry.

Their plumage is not as effectively waterproofed as that of most other water birds. It is not oiled and must be dried from time to time to prevent the birds from becoming waterlogged.

Cormorants and shags breed at the foot of sea cliffs and on isolated rock stacks and islands; the cormorant also nests occasionally in lakeside trees. The nests have a foul smell of decaying fish and seaweed. About three to five chalky white eggs, with pale blue undershells, are laid, usually in April or May. Shags' breeding colonies are remarkable for the birds' hissing and croaking in defence of their nests. The young of both species almost disappear inside the adults' gullets to reach the regurgitated fish on which they feed.

A shag, like its closest relative the cormorant, spreads its wings to dry on coming ashore

Corn

In Britain, cereals, including wheat, oats, barley and rye, are collectively known as corn. In America, corn applies only to maize, originally known as Indian corn.

Corncrake see Crake

Corn dolly

As it was considered unlucky to cut the last sheaf of the harvest, the growing stems were plaited into a corn dolly and felled by the reapers' thrown sickles. The dolly was then dressed and garlanded, carried home in procession and kept through the winter in farmhouse or church to ensure a good harvest next year. The custom was a survival of pagan rites originating in the Middle East 7000 years ago. These appeased the corn spirit or fertility goddess who took her final refuge in the last sheaf.

Variously called the kirn baby, the mare,

hag or maiden, the dolly was woven into many elaborate shapes. The Suffolk horse-shoe, Staffordshire knot and Northamptonshire horn-of-plenty are among typical good luck symbols. Modern dollies are often woven from artificial straw.

CORN DOLLY STYLES

Corn dollies are made in many traditional patterns which vary from village to village. Three typical examples are shown here

Cornflower *Centaurea cyanus*
Modern methods of cleaning grain of weed seed are so effective that they have eliminated the bright blue cornflower from mid-summer fields, along with the marigold and poppy. The 2-3 ft flowers, once scattered throughout the lowlands, are now rare. Today, corn-flowers are mainly garden flowers, and any growing wild in hedges and banks are usually from gardens. Their other name, hurt-sickle, arose because their tough stems blunted reapers' sickles.

Cornsalad *Valerianella locusta*
This low-growing weed appears before early lettuces and its long, narrow, grass-green leaves can be eaten in salad, although they are somewhat tasteless. Cornsalad, which is also called lamb's lettuce, has pale blue or lilac flowers which bloom from April to June. It grows throughout the British Isles in dry cornfields and on railway banks, rocks and dunes.

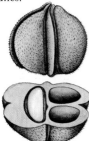

Cornsalad has a three-chambered seed pod in which two of the chambers are always empty

Looking south over Lake Managh, a corrie-lake in a corrie near Mangerton Mountain, Co. Kerry

Corrie
Known also as cwms or cirques, corries are steep-sided, horseshoe-shaped basins—sometimes with a small circular lake at the bottom. They were formed in mountainous regions during the Ice Age when most of Britain, including the highest mountains, was covered in ice.

Each corrie probably started with snow collecting in slight depressions near the tops of mountains and freezing. Snow penetrated cracks in the rock face so that later freezing and thawing caused the rock to split and break away. As the snow became ice it flowed out of the corrie and down the mountains, scouring the depressions and tearing away the loosened rock to create steep walls and a deep valley.

Cotoneaster
Mainly grown for the brilliant red and orange autumn berries, these shrubs have been introduced to Britain from all over the world. The berries are attractive to birds, which occasionally eat the seeds that are later spread by their droppings. Of the many species, only one is native to Britain, *Cotoneaster integerrimus.* This is one of the rarest British wild plants, growing only on cliffs in North Wales.

Three introduced species are common, however. *C. simonsii,* from India, has pointed deciduous leaves and pink flowers, and often reaches 12 ft. The low-growing *C. horizontalis,* from China, is similar in leaf and flower but has distinctive herringbone branches. Another, *C. microphyllus,* from the Himalayas, is also low-growing but has small, rounded, evergreen leaves and white flowers.

Cottage see p. 118

Cotton-grass
On the bogs of north and west Britain, expanses of cotton-grass can often be seen, in May and June, waving white downy heads. These consist of fine, brittle hairs which grow from the fruits and carry them long distances in the wind.

Common cotton-grass *Eriophorum angusti-folium* has five to seven nodding heads at the top of each stem, while hare's tail cotton-grass *E. vaginatum* has only a single upright head. *Eriophorum* is derived from the Greek and means wool-bearing.

Courtship see Animal behaviour

Covert
Woods with low undergrowth where game-birds, deer or foxes can hide are known as covers or coverts. Woods named on maps as Fox Covert may hold a fox's den.

Gamekeepers often maintain coverts where hen pheasants can nest and raise their chicks in shelter and comparative safety. Coppice, particularly hazel, is often retained for this purpose and sometimes low shrubs, preferably berry-bearing to provide winter food for pheasants, are deliberately planted. These include snowberry, cherry-laurel, rhododendron, cotoneaster and guelder rose.

Cowbane see Parsley

Traditional homes of the countryside

The wide variety of natural materials available in the British Isles is clearly reflected in many of its cottages. For centuries, local materials dictated local building methods, so that in any region cottages tended to be similar in style. The cottages shown below indicate some of the styles which developed throughout the British Isles

The name cottage originates from *cotage*, a medieval term used to describe a small one-roomed peasant dwelling, usually consisting of a tent-like structure, made of poles, covered with interlaced twigs and branches and daubed with mud.

Elizabethan cottages, the homes of yeomen and prosperous farmers and so made of more durable materials, are the earliest to have survived. At first, only local materials were used in building, and since medieval England had abundant sources of wood and stone, these materials were in common use. Many cottages built between the 11th and 16th centuries had two or more A-shaped cruck frames. Each cruck was made from a curved tree, cut in half lengthways with the two pieces reversed and joined at the top to form an arch. A strengthening beam across the arch completed the A-shape.

Elizabethan cottages were of box-frame construction, made of heavy, closely spaced timbers. Later, wood became dearer because of increasing demands from shipbuilding and iron-smelting industries, and builders were forced to use lighter timbers, spaced further apart. The spaces were filled with wattle and daub—interlaced hazel sticks daubed with a mixture of clay and chopped straw—or brickwork in varying patterns.

Bricks, introduced by the Romans but neglected after their departure for nearly 1000 years, were re-introduced from the Netherlands in the late 15th century. Brick subsequently became a commonplace material for chimney-stacks, walls and floor pavings, as well as the infilling on timber-framed structures. Oak-framed cottages were weatherproofed with clay tiles, slates, horizontal overlapping boards or plaster.

On restricted sites, upper storeys were cantilevered above each other by about a foot or so to give them greater stability and protect the ground-floor walls from rain. Ground floors consisted of rammed clay covered with dry rushes, later replaced with stone slabs and brick paving. Upper floors were made of wood and reached by ladders.

Window openings were at first covered with animal skins. Later, sheets of oiled parchment or diagonal lattice-works of twigs were used to let in light but keep out rain. By the late 16th century, the lattice-work was made of lead and the spaces filled with a crude glass that resembled the bottoms of bottles. Sheet glass, mass-produced in 1840, meant the humblest cottage could have simpler and larger windows.

Roofing materials consisted of thatch—usually of reed or straw in England, though in parts of Ireland and Scotland, broom, gorse or heather was used. Where stone slabs or slate was available, they were used instead of thatch. In other areas tiles, which like bricks were made from clay, were used.

The Industrial Revolution, beginning in the middle of the 18th century, saw the start of large-scale production of bricks, tiles and slates, followed by the development of canals and railways, which enabled them to be distributed throughout the country. The result was the spread of the Victorian brick cottage and the decline of regional styles.

Boulders and turf
Boulders gathered from the coastline or moorland were once used to make two-roomed cottages—often windowless and with a single door. The roofs were covered with turfs on branches and held in place with weighted ropes. Found in Wales, Ireland and the Scottish Highlands and islands. Generally in use nowadays as barns for storage

Cob and thatch
Cob walls, often 2-3 ft thick, consisted of earth and chopped straw, built up in layers and reinforced with cow-hair. The outside is usually whitewashed and the top of the wall protected by a thatched roof. Thatch—either reed, straw or heather—was once used throughout most of the British Isles, and over 50,000 thatched roofs survive in England alone. Cob and thatch cottages are found chiefly in Cornwall, Devon and Somerset

Timber-frame with infilling
The walls of many Elizabethan cottages had a box-framework transmitting the weight of the roof to the ground. This construction meant that non-structural materials could be used in the spaces between the framing—usually wattle and daub. During the late 17th century, this was often replaced with brickwork. The bricks did not need to be bonded and were laid in varying patterns—notably herringbone to create watertight joints

Decorated plasterwork

The external plasterwork on timber-framed cottages in the east of England was often pargetted, that is, decorated with raised or cut designs before it had dried. The fashion is thought to have been derived from the elaborate plaster ceilings of the Elizabethan mansion houses, and was commonly used on cottages in the towns and larger villages of Suffolk, Essex and Hertfordshire.

Pargetting was first used in England during the late 16th century and reached a peak of popularity during the second half of the 17th century; 50 years later it faded out

Brick and tiled walls

Clay tiles were used in the eastern counties during the 17th century for cladding the outside of timber-framed buildings, often replacing, on the top half only, the less durable wattle and daub. On cantilevered cottages a brick wall was sometimes built around the bottom storey, and the old timber wall removed to increase the floor space. Later, during the 18th century, brick walls on the ground floor with clay tiling above became a standard method of construction

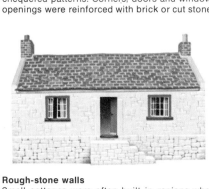

Flint walling

Cobble-shaped flints were used a great deal for cottage walls in south and east England, faced with whole or half-flints set at random or in chequered patterns. Corners, doors and window openings were reinforced with brick or cut stone

Stone and slate

In parts of Cornwall and south Devon, where slate is plentiful, the walls of coastal cottages were often built of brick or rough slate-stone, covered with a thin coat of lime plaster and whitewashed, or clad with slates. During the 17th century slate was also used for roofs, often covered with a weak mixture of cement

Corbie-gables and pantiles

Clay pantiles—S-shaped in section—came from the Netherlands during the 17th century. Originally manufactured in Essex by Daniel Defoe, author of *Robinson Crusoe,* they often replaced thatch. The corbie—or crow-stepped—gable, which also originated in the Low Countries, is most often seen in Scotland and the eastern counties of England. In some areas, specially moulded bricks were used

Rough-stone walls

Small cottages were often built in regions where rough stone that could be shaped was available. Walls were thick and openings small and narrow; roofs low-pitched and covered with slate

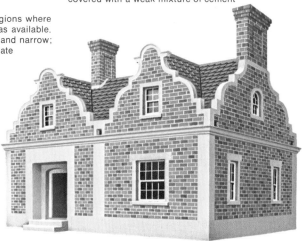

Clapboarding

Although 16th-century farm buildings often used clapboarding—oak, elm or deal boards fixed to a timber framework—it was not used on cottages until the end of the 18th century. Common in the south-eastern counties of England, the boards were painted white or cream, or—in some coastal districts—coated with tar as a protection against the salty air

Flemish brick and stone

The bricks brought to Britain as ballast in empty wool-ships returning from the Netherlands, during the 15th century, generated a revival in their use.

During the next 400 years bricklayers and masons came to Britain from the Low Countries bringing Flemish techniques and flamboyant designs, which characterised many of the small houses and cottages of East Anglia and Essex

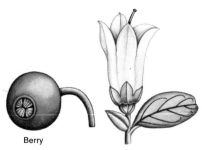

Berry

Cowberries are about the size of red currants, but much darker in colour

Cowberry *Vaccinium vitis-idaea*

This low-growing shrub is widespread in mountainous areas. Also called red whortle-berry, it differs from the closely related bilberry in having evergreen leaves and pink-ish-white flowers instead of green ones.

The small, dark red fruits, produced in late summer, are edible but bitter though they can be made into jelly. The leaves and stems yield a yellow dye. Although cowberry's botanical name means vine of Mount Ida, a mountain in Turkey, it is a native of northern Europe and unknown in that country

Cowslip *Primula veris*

A springtime flower of established grassland throughout the British Isles, the cowslip is becoming more rare as old meadows are ploughed up—it has always been scarce in

Cowslip, the yellow flower of cattle pastures on chalky, limestone and clay soils

northern Scotland. Its name is a polite form of cowslop or cowpat, referring to its occurrence in scattered clumps in pasture-land. Cowslip favours lime-rich soils and is found in meadows, pastures and on banks.

Flowers collected in May or June make a delicate wine, once recommended as a cure for insomnia. Ointment made from cowslips was claimed to remove spots and wrinkles.

Cow-wheat *Melampyrum pratense*

This slender herb frequently occurs in large colonies in dry woods and on moors through-out the British Isles, flowering from May to October. It grows attached to the roots of other plants, getting nourishment from them.

It grows up to 24 in. high, with pairs of narrow leaves and two-lipped yellow or white flowers. Both its botanical and common names refer to the resemblance of the seeds to blackened grains of wheat.

The prefix 'cow' usually means 'false', in that the plant resembles the one after which it is named, but is worthless. Cow-wheat is useless for cooking; cow-parsley is useless for sauces.

Coypu *Myocastor coypus*

A native of South America, the coypu is a rat-like animal as big as a dog, and formerly starred in fairground sideshows as the 'big-gest rat on earth'. It was first brought to Britain in the 1930's for fur-farming. Some escaped and established themselves in marsh-land areas of East Anglia, and now live wild in Norfolk and Suffolk. They soon earned a bad name by wandering on to farmland and digging up sugar beet and bulbs, and bur-rowing into river banks, causing flooding. In 1962 a campaign was planned to reduce their numbers, but the harsh winter of that year killed them off in large numbers.

Coypus prefer coarse foods with fibrous textures, such as the tissues around the base of plants, and the roots of reeds, rushes, sedges, water parsnips, pond weeds and brassicas. They also eat freshwater molluscs, such as mussels and snails, and are known to graze on grassy banksides.

The coypu, which grows to about 2 ft long, with an 18 in. long scaly tail, has a massive head and humped back. Its hind feet are webbed for swimming. Its body is covered with a thick, dark brown coat which overlays

waterproof under-fur. The belly is greyish and velvety and, once the long outer or guard hairs are removed, forms the 'nutria' used by furriers.

Coypus are solitary animals, living in marshy areas in reed beds, river banks in the Broads and along canals. They are active mainly at dusk, dawn and at night when their grunting and 'mooing' sounds can be heard. During a harsh winter they are likely to be seen on land in search of food, and may fall victims to frostbite, losing part of their tail or a limb. Their tracks are large and five-toed, and impressions of the hind webs show up in mud.

Breeding throughout most of the year the coypu is very prolific, usually producing two litters of four or five young each year. The

nest is built of marsh plants and grass above the water level. The young can see and move almost from birth, and swim in a couple of days. The female's teats are on the side of her body, above the surface of the water when she is swimming, allowing her to feed her young without going ashore. The young are weaned at two months and may breed at three months, before they are fully grown. The young coypu is sufficiently well develop-ed when born to be able to fend for itself when little more than a week old.

The weasel, otter, brown rat, owls and hawks take the young, but if a coypu reaches adult size it can live for at least five years. The coypu will attack man or dog if provoked, using its sharp, prominent teeth and claws to inflict injuries.

The 2 ft long coypu, Britain's largest rodent, lives wild in Norfolk and Suffolk

Easily mistaken for an oversized rat or an otter, the coypu spends much of its time swimming. Its webbed hind feet and waterproof coat make it well suited to its life in the water

Eyes on stalks, two pairs of antennae and raised claws on either side of a gaping mouth, give a formidable appearance to the shore crab as it scurries over the beach

NEW LEGS FOR OLD

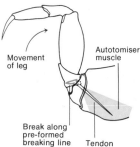

Crabs can shed damaged limbs and grow replacements. A special autotomiser muscle in the upper limb is attached to a point in the lower limb just above a pre-formed breaking line. If the limb is trapped or injured, the muscle automatically contracts, bending the lower limb so far back that it fractures along the breaking line. The exposed surface of the upper limb is covered by a membrane which seals off the upper limb when the damaged portion is shed. Soon afterwards the new limb starts to grow

Crab

Like most sea creatures, crabs do not care for their offspring and rely on producing large numbers of young to ensure the survival of the species. Females of some species lay a million or more eggs at a time. These eggs are carried beneath the small, flap-like tail which is held under the body between the legs, and in this condition the female is said to be 'in berry'. The eggs hatch as tiny free-swimming larvae, very unlike the adult. Eventually, after casting the skin several times and increasing in size, the larvae attain the typical crab form. They have hard, close-fitting shells and ten limbs—two pincers and four pairs of walking legs that can also be used for digging and swimming.

The crab most likely to be encountered on our shores is the green shore crab *Carcinus maenas*. One of the most handsome is the velvet swimming crab *Macropipus puber* with its last pair of legs flattened into swimming paddles. Many of the spider crabs, so named because of their long slender legs and small bodies, camouflage themselves by sticking pieces of seaweed or sponge on their spiny shells. The largest British crab is the edible crab *Cancer pagurus* which measures up to 10 in. across the shell and can weigh 12 lb. It usually lives some distance off shore, though small specimens are often found between the tidemarks.

The familiar hermit crabs, of which *Pagurus bernhardus* is the most common, are not true crabs at all. The hermit's soft, fleshy tail is not tucked beneath the body but twisted to fit the spiral of the empty winkle or whelk shell which the crustacean carries around for protection. The shell is often shared with marine worms and has anemones attached to the outside. The anemones help to camouflage the crab and in turn benefit from food scraps left over from the hermit's meal.

Crabs of British coasts

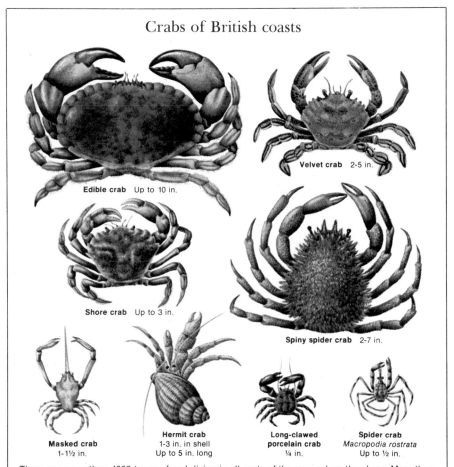

Edible crab Up to 10 in.

Velvet crab 2-5 in.

Shore crab Up to 3 in.

Spiny spider crab 2-7 in.

Masked crab 1-1½ in.

Hermit crab 1-3 in. in shell Up to 5 in. long

Long-clawed porcelain crab ¼ in.

Spider crab *Macropodia rostrata* Up to ½ in.

There are more than 4000 types of crab living in all parts of the sea and on the shore. More than 50 species live round the coasts of Britain, of which the eight shown here are those most likely to be seen. Some, such as the velvet crab and the edible crab, spend most of their time in the sea. Others, like the shore crab and the porcelain crabs, live mainly in shore pools

The crab-apple, which produces fruit too sour to eat, is the parent of all edible apples

Crab-apple *Malus pumila*

The pinkish-white blossom of this tree, the parent of all cultivated apples, enlivens hedgerows in spring; in autumn its leaves turn gold. Its apples, small and greenish-yellow, often flushed with red, have a hard, woody texture and a sour taste, but make excellent jelly.

Crab-apple derives its name from the Old Norse word *skrab*, meaning small rough tree. It seldom grows above 30 ft and lives for up to 50 years. The twigs bear spines, and the purple-brown bark becomes rough with age. Like garden apples, the crab-apple grows by putting out long shoots, but bears flowers only on short shoots or spurs. Its downy, red-brown winter buds expand in April to produce long-stalked, oval, mid-green leaves. The five-petalled, delicately perfumed flowers open late in April above the leaves. They are typical of the rose family, to which the crab-apple belongs. The flowers are pollinated by early bees. Birds scatter the black pips of the apples when eating them, and seedlings are often found in hedgerows where birds roost. White sapwood surrounds the trunk's tough, red-brown heartwood, once used for mallet heads.

Most ornamental crab-apples have been introduced from Asia or North America, or are gardeners' varieties. In autumn their fruits are richly coloured red, rose and gold. Two popular red crab-apples are the Dartmouth crab and 'John Downie'.

Crag

In northern Britain, crag is a common word for a rocky cliff. The word is also used to describe a series of shelly sand beds in East Anglia. These are fossil-rich deposits of the Ice Age and are of three types. Coraline Crag is the fossils of sea-mats, Red Crag has been stained red by iron oxides, and Norwich Crag is so called because it was once visible around the city, but is now built on.

Crakes and rails

Crakes and rails are medium-sized marsh birds that skulk in the shelter of thick vegetation. They are poor flyers and prefer to avoid danger by running or pattering away over the surface of water. The black coot and moorhen look quite unlike their relatives, the true crakes and rails, which spend so much time hidden in marsh vegetation that their exact population is unknown.

The 15 in. long coot is a large black water bird with a white blob on the forehead. It builds a substantial nest well hidden among river or lakeside vegetation and defends this territory aggressively. The six to nine eggs, which are laid from March to May, hatch in 21-24 days. In winter coots form huge flocks on gravel pits, lakes and reservoirs, feeding on roots, small animals and insects. When disturbed, the flock paddles fast over the water, flapping their wings and raising a cloud of spray to confuse enemies.

The moorhen is smaller than the coot and is distinguished by its red forehead and white under-tail flash, much used in courtship displays. It is not a moorland bird—its name is a form of mere-hen, bird of the lakes. Seldom seen in flocks, it spends its whole year on shallow water, near thick cover in which it can hide when danger threatens. It can sink when alarmed, leaving only its bill above water. Its nest is built near the water—often in a bush—and in defending it the moorhen is almost as aggressive as the coot. Between March and July it lays 5-11 eggs. These hatch after three weeks and the young leave the nest after two or three days. As the moorhen swims, it jerks its head like a domestic hen, picking worms, slugs, snails, insects, wild fruit, seeds, grain and waterweed from the water surface or bank. Both coot and moorhen live on the lakes of town parks and feed on scraps thrown into the water. Like other crakes and rails, they are poor flyers and avoid flight as much as possible.

The water rail is seldom seen as it hides in the reed beds and sedges of marshes, particularly in East Anglia and Ireland. It seeks its food among shallow waters and darts from one clump of dense cover to the next. It betrays its presence only by squealing, somewhat like a pig. The water rail has a long red bill, slate-grey breast, face and throat, barred flanks and brown upper parts streaked with black. It flies weakly, with its long legs dangling. During icy weather, water rails search out unfrozen spots in the open. If disturbed there, they stand motionless.

Spotted crakes probably breed in Britain every year, but are so secretive that years go by without any proof of their presence. They not only hide, but they do not call until after dark; then their 'quip-quip-quip' may be repeated endlessly.

About half a century ago the corncrake or landrail was widespread and numerous

FEET FOR WALKING AND SWIMMING

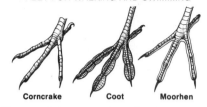

Corncrake   Coot   Moorhen

The water-living coot and moorhen have partially webbed toes to move them through water. The toes of the land-living corncrake are webless but widely spaced, so that the bird is able to walk over damp meadows where it often feeds

in Britain as a summer visitor. Its rasping 'creck-creck' was a familiar sound. The introduction of mechanical harvesting and quick-ripening strains of cereals has since led to a rapid decline in its numbers. This is because earlier and faster harvesting gives the corncrake less time to rear its young in the long grass, where it nests. Birds and nest can be destroyed by a mechanical harvester. It is now numerous only in the hay fields of Scotland and Ireland and their islands.

The corncrake is a brown bird, streaked darker above and with chestnut on the wings and dark bars on the flank. It stands $10\frac{1}{2}$ in. tall, and trails its legs behind its body in flight. Its diet consists of insects, small snails, earthworms and some vegetable food. Nests, made of dried grasses, are always well hidden, and the eight to ten pale cream eggs, heavily spotted with red-brown and grey, are laid from May to June.

Cranberry *Vaccinium oxycoccus*

The acid fruits of this low-growing shrub make a sauce to accompany venison and, through American influence, turkey. It grows mainly in bogs in north and west England and southern Scotland. It formerly grew in southern England, but has largely disappeared because of improved drainage.

The red berries, often speckled with brown, ripen in August and September. These are much easier to see than the rest of the plant, which has inconspicuous pink flowers, wiry stems and small, rounded, evergreen leaves.

Commercial cranberries are usually larger than the wild ones and come from a different North American species.

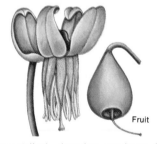

The long-stalked, drooping cranberry flower gives way to a red fruit in late summer

Common craneflies pair soon after emerging from their pupae. Eggs are laid from June onwards

Cranefly

Their long bodies and legs have given craneflies the common name of daddy-longlegs. Their legs break off easily (but cannot be regrown), which helps the insect to escape when caught by a predator. About 300 species of cranefly, ½-1½ in. long, can be seen in all parts of the British Isles. Most common craneflies, such as the widespread *Tipula paludosa*, are dull in colour; but a few, for example the black and yellow *Nephrotoma maculosa*, are brightly marked.

The females lay 50-150 eggs through an egg-laying tube at the end of their bodies, which they insert deep into the soil. The eggs hatch in the autumn. The larvae, known as leatherjackets, are serious destructive pests. They are grey cylindrical maggots about ¾ in. long and can be found in moist soil, usually attacking the roots of plants. In some years, particularly after warm, damp autumns, their activities are so great that bare patches appear in pastures.

After six to nine months the larvae enter the pupa, or resting, stage from which they emerge as adults the following summer. Some adult craneflies feed on nectar, others rely on the food reserves built up in the larval stage. They live for only one year.

Cranesbill

Among the most common of roadside plants, cranesbills have rounded leaves and flowers that vary from pink to violet-blue. The flowers are usually in pairs and have five petals narrowed at the base to a point, or

claw. Cranesbill's scientific name *Geranium* is derived from a Greek word meaning 'crane'. It refers to the resemblance of the plant's fruit to the beak of a crane.

There are three common annual cranesbills, which occur throughout the British Isles, except the high mountain regions. They are usually under 12 in. high, with leaves up to 1½ in. across, and small, pinkish flowers. The most abundant is probably cut-leaved cranesbill, which flowers from May to August. Shining cranesbill has bright green leaves and pink flowers. It is often seen on limestone walls and banks from May to August. Dove's foot cranesbill has rose-purple flowers which bloom from April to September on dry grassland, dunes and waste ground. It was once thought that if the plant, together with nine red slugs, were dried in an oven and powdered, it would cure rupture in old people.

The most widespread perennial species reach 2-3 ft in height, have leaves 3-6 in. across and large purple to violet-blue flowers. The most attractive is meadow cranesbill which has crimson-veined violet-blue petals and deeply divided leaves. It covers long stretches of roadside throughout the summer. Wood cranesbill flowers in June and July in Scotland and northern England. It has smaller, darker flowers and less divided leaves. Hedgerow cranesbill, a native of Spain and Portugal, is common on roadsides in south and east England, flowering from June to August.

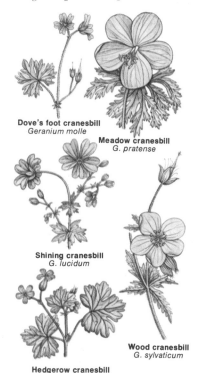

Dove's foot cranesbill
Geranium molle

Meadow cranesbill
G. pratense

Shining cranesbill
G. lucidum

Wood cranesbill
G. sylvaticum

Hedgerow cranesbill
G. pyrenaicum

The paired flowers of cranesbill each have petals narrowed to a point at the base

Crannog

The drainage of bogs, especially in Ireland and Scotland, has led to the discovery of ancient lake dwellings made of timber and in use from prehistoric times until the 17th century. Some were made by sinking a foundation of stones into shallow water; others by first enlarging islets in the lake. A platform about a foot above the water-level was created on which a homestead was built. Many of those in Ireland and Scotland were built mainly as strongholds against enemies. There are good examples in County Tyrone and Lough Gara, in Ireland, and at Glastonbury in Somerset. The Glastonbury crannog, built before the Roman conquest of 55 BC, originally had about 70 buildings within a stockaded area of 3½ acres.

Most crannogs date from a period beginning with the late Bronze Age and ending in the Middle Ages.

HOW CRANNOGS WERE MADE

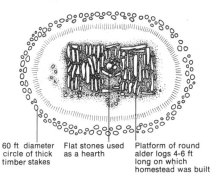

60 ft diameter circle of thick timber stakes

Flat stones used as a hearth

Platform of round alder logs 4-6 ft long on which homestead was built

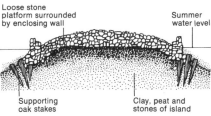

Loose stone platform surrounded by enclosing wall

Summer water level

Supporting oak stakes

Clay, peat and stones of island

Two types of Irish crannogs—one of timber construction, the other of stone. Ancient canoes were often found near these stockaded islands

Crawfish *Palinurus vulgaris*

Sometimes called spiny lobster or rock lobster, the crawfish can grow up to 2 ft in length—slightly longer than the true lobster. Unlike the lobster, it has only small pincers. These are used for feeding, but cannot crack tough shells. Crawfish are not fish, but are related to crabs. They have spiny shells, and are generally brown with plum-coloured markings. They have antennae as long as their bodies. Crawfish can be found on rocky ground, usually well below low-tide marks, on south and west coasts. Most of those caught in Britain are sold in France, where the crawfish is known as langouste, and regarded as a great delicacy.

Crayfish need lime to build their shells, and so are found only in lime-rich hard water

Crayfish *Astacus pallipes*

Looking like small lobsters, crayfish are the largest freshwater crustaceans in Britain. They grow to 4 in. long and are found in well-oxygenated hard-water rivers and canals. During the day they hide under stones or in burrows in the bank. At night they crawl over the bottom and feed on snails, worms and insect larvae.

If disturbed, a crayfish escapes by shooting backwards with a vigorous flick of its fan-like tail. After mating in the autumn, the female lays about 100 eggs which she carries under her abdomen until they hatch the following spring.

The native British crayfish has white claws. A larger red-clawed species *A. fluviatilis* has been introduced into the Thames in Oxfordshire from France in an attempt to breed them for eating, as the British species is of inferior taste.

Creeping jenny *Lysimachia nummularia*

Also known as moneywort or herb two-pence because the leaves lie like old pennies on each side of the stems, creeping jenny snakes through the grass of damp meadows or over the banks of ditches. It is common in England and Wales, but rare elsewhere.

Creeping jenny is also called herb twopence because its round leaves grow in pairs

From June to August it bears bright yellow flowers, $\frac{1}{2}$ in. across, rising singly from the junction between the leaves and the stem. Although it rarely produces ripe seeds in this country, it is often grown in rock gardens or hanging baskets for its beauty.

Cricket see Grasshopper

Crocus, Autumn *Colchicum autumnale*

This 6-12 in. high plant is poisonous. It is sometimes fatal to animals and its poison persists in cows' milk. But in controlled doses, an extract from its seeds is used to treat gout. The purple flowers emerge in August in damp meadows and woodlands in England and Wales. Pollination then occurs and the flower dies leaving the underdeveloped seeds to pass the winter within the corm. Fruits develop in spring and grow upwards to maturity in the centre of a bunch of leaves.

Because of its dangers, this plant, which is also known as meadow saffron and naked ladies, is destroyed when found and is, therefore, becoming rare.

Crop mark

Photographs taken from the air, especially during the dry season, often reveal differences in coloration of areas of similar vegetation. These differences, known as crop or vegetation marks, are most pronounced in grasses and crops such as cereals, which change colour and grow shorter in the shallower ground above hard features like buried road surfaces or the foundations of ruined buildings, and taller over covered pits or ditches which once existed in the subsoil.

Too subtle to be seen from the ground, except from very high points, these differ-

Croft and crofting

A medieval survival, crofting is a form of subsistence farming found in the Highlands and islands of Scotland. A croft is a smallholding of fewer than 50 acres, excluding grazing, or with an annual rent under £50. A typical crofter rents 2-10 acres of arable land and usually has hill grazing rights in addition. He may own four or five cattle and up to 100 sheep. Often communal grazing after harvest limits the crops grown: oats and potatoes predominate.

Many crofters in Scotland were expelled when sheep were introduced after the Jacobite risings. In 1886, the Crofters Act gave them security of tenure, the right to bequeath the tenancy and, on relinquishing it, the right to compensation for the value of the buildings and improvements.

Though eligible for loans and grants under a 1955 Act, crofters barely make a living from the land and many of them supplement their incomes with other occupations, such as fishing, weaving and tourism.

Crofts like this one on Taransay, Inverness-shire, were once common throughout the Highlands

ences reveal medieval farming patterns, old hedgerow positions and boundaries as well as disused roads and sites of archaeological interest. Woodhenge, a Neolithic earthwork near Stonehenge, in Wiltshire, was discovered in 1925 when the underlying structure showed up in an aerial photograph.

Cross

For centuries, crosses have served many purposes in British community life: as memorials; to denote the sites from which itinerant missionaries preached or to denote a place of sanctuary. Edward I built nine ornate crosses to mark the resting places on the route of the funeral procession of his wife, Eleanor, from Lincoln to London in 1290; the last one was in London, at the place now known as Charing Cross. Three of the original crosses survive—at Geddington and Hardingstone, Northants, and at Waltham Cross, Herts. Sometimes, crosses marked special boundaries such as the limits of sanctuary at Hexham Abbey, Northumberland, where their bases can be found under nearby hedgerows.

Market crosses were well-known focal points, sometimes used to calculate distances between towns. Varying from simple to elaborate styles, some market crosses were put on arched bases large enough to give shelter to traders. After the Reformation, the big plinths which bore mercats—market stones—were used in Scotland to deliver proclamations.

Some of the earliest crosses, found in Cornwall and Devon, were made of prehistoric stones. During the Anglo-Saxon period simple stones were embellished with elaborate narrative designs, notably in the Kingdom of Northumbria. Many carvings show Viking influences.

Crossbill see Finch

Crosswort *Cruciata chersonensis*

The petals and leaves of the crosswort are arranged in fours and this may be the origin of its name. It grows in clumps 1-2 ft high in woods and hedgerows on lime-rich soil throughout England, Wales and southern Scotland.

Flowering in May and June, the crosswort gives off a strong honey smell, attracting pollinating insects to its pale yellow flowers which grow in clusters on the stem.

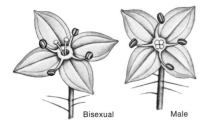

Bisexual   Male

Each cluster of crosswort flowers has males at the centre enclosed by bisexual blooms

Crow

The seven distinct but closely related members of the crow family that live in Britain are regarded as being among the most intelligent of birds. The 'thieving' of the magpie and the jackdaw's fondness for jewellery and other bright objects are two examples of traits on which their reputation is based. Yet their cunning has also earned them man's hatred—most crows can still be shot all the year round in Britain. Rooks and carrion crows are hunted by the farmer to protect his seed; jays, crows and magpies by the gamekeeper to preserve his young birds; and ravens by the sheep-farmer to save weakling lambs.

Paradoxically, crows tend to move closer to man to escape this persecution, infiltrating cities where they are safe from the guns of the countryside. The triple 'kaah' of the carrion crow is familiar to many city dwellers. Man is their only constant enemy, since all are large birds, from about 13 in. to 25 in. long, and capable of fighting off most predators. In addition, they usually nest high in trees, cliffs and buildings.

Carrion crows are often confused with rooks by non-countrymen. The traditional rule of thumb, that the solitary birds are crows and those in flocks are rooks, is not necessarily true, since crows gather at good feeding grounds and to roost. Rooks, however, are entirely gregarious, living in communities called rookeries. These consist of large, untidy nests of twigs in trees on open farmland, and vary in number from a few pairs to 9000 in one Scottish rookery. Pairs of birds renovate the same nests season after season, and some rookeries are thought to be centuries old. Rooks eat corn, supplemented by fruit and insects; they specialise in digging in soft ground for worms and other invertebrates, and hot summers which bake the ground are bad for them. Carrion crows eat anything from small mammals to young injured birds, eggs, corn and fruit.

In Scotland and northern England there is a distinct grey and black variety of carrion crow called the hooded crow, but it breeds freely with the normal crow and is regarded as belonging to the same species. It inhabits open moorland, where it is hunted by gamekeepers protecting grouse, and where it often nests on the ground among the heather.

The raven, largest of the crows and often over 2 ft from bill tip to tail, was once a common scavenger on the streets of London, where now only the tame guardians of the Tower remain. Apart from these birds it is confined to the west and north, nesting on cliffs or, occasionally, in trees, preying on sea-birds and flying over sheep country in search of carrion.

The distinctive black-and-white flash of the 18 in. long magpie in flight is seen increasingly in cities. It has spread to the middle of Dublin and the suburbs of other towns, though, unlike the jay, carrion crow

The parent jay continues to feed its young until well beyond the age at which it can fly

and jackdaw, it has not yet penetrated central London. It feeds on insects and seeds but also robs birds, including game birds, of their eggs and young; this has brought about stern retribution. The magpie's fondness for sparkling objects is the most striking example of the hoarding instinct found in all crows.

But not even the magpie is a bigger thief than the jackdaw, the smallest and perhaps most versatile of crows, which is at home anywhere from city streets to rugged cliffs. Its home is invariably high off the ground, and many cathedrals echo to the 'tchak-tchak' of a colony. It will feed in fields beside rooks and starlings, and in addition to nest-robbing will compulsively take and hide objects for which it has no use. It sometimes scavenges alongside gulls on city rubbish dumps.

The jay is the most colourful of the family, a pink-buff bird about 13 in. long, marked with white on wing and rump and with distinctive blue and black barring on the leading edges of its wings. An inhabitant of dense woodland, it preys on eggs and nestlings, and in autumn hoards acorns with squirrel-like fervour as a winter stand-by. The germination of its forgotten acorns helps in the spread of oak woods. Although a solitary bird it forms raucous flocks during the spring courtship.

The red-billed, red-footed chough nests on west-coast cliffs, in Wales, Scotland and Ireland, mixing with colonies of auks and kittiwakes. Only 700 pairs remain in Britain, mostly in Wales, where they often inhabit slate quarries. They are spectacular aerial acrobats. With a shrill 'kyaw' they sail or hang on updraughts along cliff tops. They build their bulky nests, which are lined with wool or hair, in the most inaccessible crevices and caves.

Crops

Britain is said to have the best climate in the world for growing crops and one of the worst for harvesting them. The crops grown in Britain can be roughly divided into six groups: cereals or grain, root crops, seed crops, peas and beans, leaf and fodder crops, and clover and vetch.

The largest cereal crop is barley, which is grown chiefly for animal feeding, but the best grain is used in brewing. Wheat is grown primarily for making flour but it also is added to made-up animal feeds. Oats, grown mainly as food for horses before the motor age, is still an important crop. It provides rolled oats and oatmeal for the table and on the farm has a double use. The grain is used for feeding livestock and the straw, which is superior in food value to all other cereal straws, is often used as a winter feed instead of hay.

Rye is grown in Britain today on a small scale, as there is a limited demand for its grain for rye crispbreads and as a fodder for cattle and sheep; and its straw is used for thatching. Maize, the popular sweet corn

A field of ripening wheat. Britain's farmers grow nearly half the nation's needs

or corn-on-the-cob of the table, is grown in Britain mainly as green fodder or silage, all parts of the plant including the cob being chopped up together. But new varieties, which overcome the problem of ripening in our northern climate, are becoming more popular and may change the pattern of maize growing in the British Isles.

Buckwheat is uncommon, but is occasionally grown as food for sheep and game birds, or to plough in as green manure.

One of the most useful of the root crops is the sugar beet. The tops are slashed off at harvest and fed to livestock; sugar is extracted from the roots in factories and the pulp is returned to the farm for feeding animals. Fodder beet, which is similar to sugar beet, is grown exclusively as animal food and often stored in clamps.

The turnip is grown chiefly as food for sheep and cattle, but it is not as winter-hardy as the swede which is grown exten-

A key to the identification of the

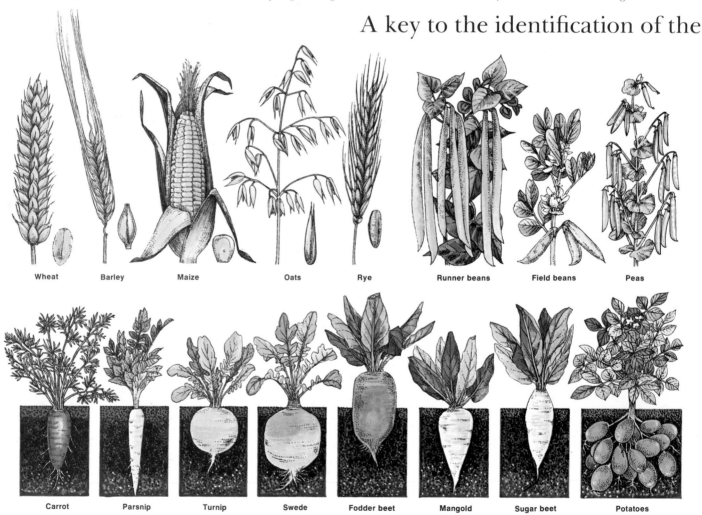

Wheat   Barley   Maize   Oats   Rye   Runner beans   Field beans   Peas

Carrot   Parsnip   Turnip   Swede   Fodder beet   Mangold   Sugar beet   Potatoes

sively in Scotland and northern England both for livestock and human consumption. The mangold, a large turnip-like root crop, was once used extensively in winter rations for cattle, but it has now been largely superseded by kale which is grown for its foliage and its stem.

Carrots are grown mainly for human consumption, but any surplus is fed to horses and cattle. Brussels sprouts and cabbages are grown on a large scale for human consumption, though one variety of cabbage, an enormous round-headed type, called flatpoll, is grown as food for livestock.

Several species of bean are cultivated in Britain: broad beans, runner beans and dwarf beans for human consumption; and the field bean, or tic bean, for livestock. Peas are grown for the table, for drying and for feeding livestock.

British farmers cultivate two species of mustard: black mustard for its seed to produce oil and table mustard, and white mustard for ploughing in as green manure.

Hop clover, also known as hop trefoil and black medick, is used in grazing mixtures.

Red clover is sown with rye grass for making hay, and white clover is often sown with grass seed mixtures for grazing.

Lucerne, or alfalfa, is useful as green feed, for hay or, more usually, for silage. A similar plant, sainfoin, is sown, particularly on limestone and chalk soils, for both grazing and hay. It has deep, drought-resistant roots.

The biggest crop of all is grass, which occupies about half the 34 million acres of farmland in Britain. The advantage of grass is that it thrives naturally and cattle and sheep can feed on it where it grows, without the trouble and hazards of harvesting, although much grass is harvested to make hay for winter fodder.

Since the late 1940's there has been a spectacular increase in crop yields. From 19·1 cwt per acre in 1946-7, the average wheat yield has climbed to 32·2 cwt; that of barley from 17·8 cwt to 28·5 cwt; that of oats from 16·3 cwt to 27·3 cwt; that of potatoes from 7·1 tons to 10 tons.

The record yield for British wheat is 71·4 cwt per acre from 9·5 acres near Doncaster in 1962. For barley it is 64·8 cwt per

Fodder beet in a clamp. Many root crops are stored this way: piled up and covered with earth and straw

acre on 20 acres also near Doncaster in the same year. While improved methods of farming and increased use of pesticides have contributed to this increase in agricultural productivity, the plant breeders have done most by developing heavier cropping varieties. See also separate entries and FARMING

main crops grown on British farms

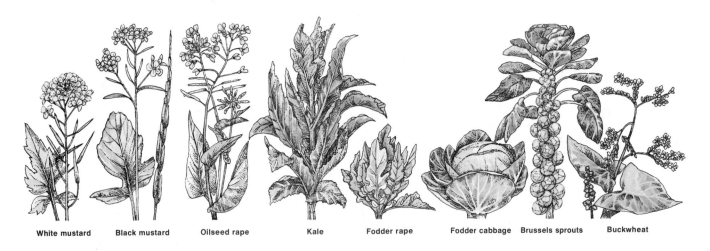

White mustard   Black mustard   Oilseed rape   Kale   Fodder rape   Fodder cabbage   Brussels sprouts   Buckwheat

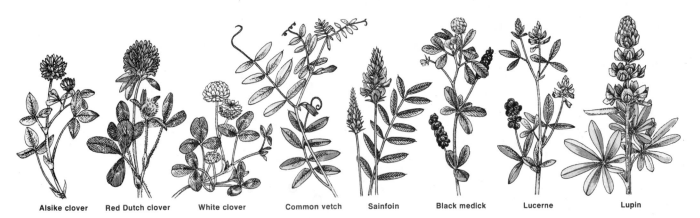

Alsike clover   Red Dutch clover   White clover   Common vetch   Sainfoin   Black medick   Lucerne   Lupin

Crowberry *Empetrum nigrum*

A small, trailing, much-branched shrub, 3-12 in. high, crowberry·has tiny, bright green, heather-like leaves whose edges roll under to hide their undersides, and form tubes.

Its pinkish-purple flowers appear in May and June in clusters near the ends of the stems. They are followed in August by brown-black berries which are edible, but almost tasteless.

Growing in mountainous areas throughout the north and west, they provide an important food for grouse and other moorland birds.

Crowberry flowers spring from the base of the leaves, which curl lengthways into tubes

Crowfoot, Water *Ranunculus aquatilis*

Widespread throughout lowlands in the British Isles, water crowfoot covers ponds and streams with its white flowers in May and June. It is a member of the buttercup family and its flowers are a similar size to those of buttercups. Most of the plant is submerged and has finely divided underwater leaves which can be up to 3 ft long. In swift-running water, the floating leaves and flowers do not develop and the submerged leaves wave in the current.

Growth in chalk streams in southern England is so prolific that they have to be weeded. Unlike most buttercups, which are poisonous to cattle, water crowfoot is palatable and nutritious.

Crucian carp *Carassius carassius*

A small relative of the carp, this is a hardy fish which can survive a high degree of oxygen shortage in the water of the small ponds it inhabits. It is widespread in southeast England in still waters. It is always fully scaled and usually a dull bronze to light orange colour on the back: the young fish have a dusky spot near the base of the tail. Its fins are golden or red. Unlike the carp, it has no barbels or feelers. The crucian carp has a hump-backed body, and varies in length from 5 in. to 18 in. It feeds on small animals and plants.

A close relative of the goldfish, the crucian carp will interbreed with it and also with carp. Breeding takes place in May and June and the female lays her eggs on the leaves of water plants. The young fish hatch in five to ten days. In eastern Europe the crucian carp is bred in fish farms.

Cuckoo *Cuculus canorus*

Signalling the arrival of spring in Britain, the familiar call of the male cuckoo in April and May makes this one of the best-known although least seen birds. The female's bubbling call and the angry coughing noises of both sexes are far less well known. Cuckoos are rarely heard or seen after the end of June, but they are still present throughout the British Isles in heaths, woods and moorland until the end of July and early August, when the adults return to Africa for the winter.

They are medium-sized birds, about 13 in. long, with pointed wings and long tails. Their bodies are blue-grey with white underparts boldly striped with grey—like a female sparrowhawk. Some females are barred brown all over.

Cuckoos do not build nests. Instead the hen lays her eggs in the nests of other birds. She finds a suitable nest, waits until the foster-parent starts laying, then adds her own egg as soon as the other hen leaves the nest. Sometimes cuckoos are attacked by prospective foster-parents as they approach to lay. The cuckoo lays about 12 eggs, but only one to a nest. Several cuckoo eggs in a nest mean that several hens have overlapping territories. Cuckoo eggs have been found in the nests of more than 50 species; most frequently in those of meadow pipits, dunnocks and reed warblers, followed by robins, pied wagtails and sedge warblers. Individual cuckoos tend to stick to one species of host, and cuckoo eggs, which are small for the size of the bird, often tend to resemble those of the foster-parents. But some birds, such as dunnocks and reed warblers, will accept a cuckoo's egg which is quite unlike their own in colouring and pattern.

Hen cuckoos are the only British birds to foster their young. By doing so, they are able to raise more young than they could feed by themselves.

Cuckoos eat insects, especially large caterpillars, and also spiders, worms and centipedes. They take hairy caterpillars which other birds find distasteful or even poisonous, with no apparent ill-effects.

The young cuckoo hatches out after $12\frac{1}{2}$ days and pushes the other eggs or fledglings from the nest. For its three weeks in their nest and two weeks after, the young cuckoo is fed by the foster-parents. It grows rapidly

Though it dwarfs its dunnock foster-parent, the young cuckoo still demands to be fed

from $\frac{1}{4}$ oz. to 50 times that weight in three weeks. It stays in Britain until September when it migrates alone to its winter quarters, using inborn navigational skill.

Cuckoo fish see Wrasse

Cuckoo flower *Cardamine pratensis*
Among the delights of early spring everywhere in the British Isles are wet meadows and marshes washed with the lilac colour of cuckoo flowers. They come into flower about the time the cuckoo arrives and disappear when it has finished singing in June.

The large patches of flowers, 6-24 in. tall, are occasionally white, resembling linen bleaching in the sun. This could be the origin of the other name, lady's smock. It is traditionally unlucky to pick cuckoo flowers and take them into the house. The leaves can be eaten in salads as a substitute for watercress, which they resemble in shape and taste.

The four-petalled blooms of the cuckoo flower cluster at the head of the stem

Cuckoo-pint *Arum maculatum*
One of the most common wild flowers, and one of the strangest, the cuckoo-pint appears in April as a cowl-like green and purple sheath enclosing a fleshy stem bearing separate male and female flowers. The colours, and the flower's smell of decomposing manure, attract small flies, which are trapped in the sheath by downward-pointing hairs until they have carried out pollination. When the sheath withers they escape, well dusted with pollen to deposit upon another flower. The red berries, appearing in July and August, are poisonous—fatally so to children. The strange form of the 9-18 in. flower has given rise to many local names, including lords-and-ladies, parson-in-the-pulpit and Adam and Eve. In Elizabethan days, a white starch was made from its roots. See also MOTH FLY and POISONOUS PLANTS

Cuckoo-spit
The blobs of white froth found on the leaves and stems of many plants in the spring are the hallmark of the frog-hopper. The young, or nymphs, of this insect expel air through a sticky secretion in their abdomens and surround themselves with the froth while they suck sap. It serves as a

Sluggish young frog-hoppers like this become active adults and stop making cuckoo-spit

protection against desiccation, and possibly also against enemies. Each blob marks a nymph. Cuckoo-spit is so named because its appearance coincides with that of the cuckoo, and the two have become associated in folklore. See also FROG-HOPPER

Cuckoo-spit is often found in the angle between a side shoot and the main stem of a plant

Cudweed *Filago germanica*
Ball-shaped heads of small yellow flowers sunk in woolly hairs appear in July and August on the short, leaf-covered stems of cudweed. Then, from the base of each head two or three new stems sprout and produce flower heads. The 16th-century herbalist Gerard called it 'wicked Cudweede', because the later flowers 'over-top those that came first as many wicked children do unto their parents'. One of its other names is son-before-the-father. It grows 2-12 in. tall on heaths and dry pasture throughout lowlands, especially where the soil has been disturbed.

Medieval farmers mistakenly believed that when cattle stopped ruminating they had 'lost their cud'. Cudweed was used, sometimes dipped in fat, to replace the 'lost' cud —hence the name.

Cudweed's yellow flowers are almost totally concealed by tufts of woolly hairs

Cultivator
After the plough has done the heavy work of turning the soil, cultivators are brought in to break up the furrows and produce a tilth for sowing seed. Harrowing may be necessary after cultivating to create the seed bed.

The most common type of cultivator has a frame which carries curved arms fitted with tines, or cutters, which rip the earth. Heavy cultivators have rigid tines, others have tines mounted on springs or chains which allow the blades to deflect from hard objects which might damage them. The latest cultivators have power-driven rotary blades which pulverise the soil. The biggest rotary cultivator can break up the soil to a depth of 18 in. and clear scrubland.

Curlew
Throughout the year, the long-legged, long-billed curlew *Numenius arquata*—at 22 in. long Britain's largest wader—can be seen on estuaries, mudflats and freshwater marshes. The smaller and scarcer whimbrel, which it resembles, is mainly seen on moorland and the western islands of Scotland between May and September, on its way from Africa to Scandinavia.

The curlew has extended its breeding range in the last century and nests everywhere in the British Isles, except for parts of the Outer Hebrides and south-eastern England; it is most abundant in the north and west. Its 5 in. long, downward-curving bill enables it to feed on creatures deep in the mud, although it also picks small molluscs and shellfish from the surface. It has grey-brown, speckled plumage, a white rump and a distinctive 'coorli' call from which its name arises. During its courtship display flight over moorland in spring, a trilling song is added to the basic call.

Three or four buff, brown or olive eggs are laid in grass or heather-lined hollows on the ground in late April or May. The young hatch out in just under a month, leaving the nest almost immediately. Before the end of July, the birds flock on estuaries,

Male curlew calls as it glides in wide circles marking out its breeding territory

and most then move south and west within Britain and Ireland.

The streaky-brown whimbrel *N. phaeopus*, which is 16 in. long, is distinguished from the curlew by broad, dark stripes on its crown and a shorter bill. Its call, uttered in flight, is a repeated high-pitched whistle—hence its colloquial name of seven-whistler. It flies in small flocks, often at night. Some 50-60 pairs regularly stay in Britain to nest and breed in the Shetland and Orkney Islands. Breeding and feeding habits resemble those of the curlew.

Cuttlefish *Sepia officinalis*
Vast numbers of cuttlefish live round the shores of the British Isles, particularly off the south coast. The white, boat-shaped bones of the dead ones—cuttlebones—are common on many beaches. Cuttlefish, which are related to octopuses, live in shallow waters. They have oval, shield-shaped bodies, 12-15 in. long, with a fin along each edge, eight short arms and two long tentacles. The tentacles, which are up to 20 in. long, are used to grab crabs and prawns.

A cuttlefish will also force water from the siphon when alarmed, and this propels it rapidly backwards—a natural form of jet propulsion. Pigment cells, which the cuttlefish can contract or expand at will, allow it

HOW A CUTTLEFISH SWIMS

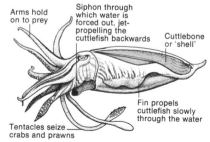

Arms hold on to prey

Siphon through which water is forced out, jet-propelling the cuttlefish backwards

Cuttlebone or 'shell'

Fin propels cuttlefish slowly through the water

Tentacles seize crabs and prawns

A swimming cuttlefish is kept afloat by its chalky, gas-filled cuttlebone or 'shell'

to change from its usual creamy-grey colour to mimic the background. If attacked it ejects an inky fluid producing a kind of smokescreen to distract the attacker's attention while the cuttlefish escapes. This is the basis of the sepia used by artists. The cuttlebone is a modified internal shell made up of fine bony plates enclosing gas-filled chambers. It acts as a buoyancy organ.

Cutworm see Noctuid moth
Cwm see Corrie

Cyclops
The most numerous planktonic animals in any type of fresh water, cyclops are sometimes so abundant that the water looks like soup. They have only one eye and are named after the one-eyed giants of Greek mythology. Their pear-shaped bodies are only a few millimetres long; most species are transparent, but some are coloured red, green or blue. Females are recognisable by the pair of egg sacs, one on each side of the abdomen. Cyclops belong to a group of animals called copepods, relations of the shrimps and crabs. They are important food for damsel fly larvae and other insects. The small cyclops eat minute algae; the larger are scavengers or predators on microscopic animals.

The female cyclops carries her eggs in two bags attached to her body until they hatch

Cypress
These trees are often associated with funerals and cemeteries, a link which goes back to the myth of the Greek youth Cyparissus, who pined away after killing Apollo's favourite stag until the god turned him into a cypress tree. The myth properly belongs to the Mediterranean cypress *Cupressus sempervirens*, rarely grown in Britain. The species

commonly seen in parks and gardens and occasionally as forest trees is Lawson's cypress *Chamaecyparis lawsoniana*, which comes from North America.

All cypresses have fern-like foliage, popular with florists, made up of tiny needles that clasp the twigs and completely hide the smaller branchlets and buds. The small, globe-shaped male catkins, seen in spring, release golden pollen. Female catkins, even smaller, look like blue-green buds. They ripen by autumn into round, brown, woody cones with squarish scales. The tiny brown seeds, each edged by a papery wing, are wind-borne. Seedlings bear two seed-leaves followed by sharp-pointed, free needles but, after the first year, all the new needles clasp and hide the stem. The bark on tree trunks is rather stringy. Cypress timber, which is tough, strong and durable, is rarely used in Britain.

Chests and cupboards made of Lawson cypress are mothproof, since the wood contains scented, insect-repellent oil. This tree is named after an Edinburgh nurseryman, Peter Lawson, who introduced it from Oregon in the 1850's. Many varieties are cultivated, being increased by cuttings. It can be distinguished by its flat foliage and pea-sized cones.

Monterey cypress *Cupressus macrocarpa*, grown here since 1838, comes from California and is really hardy only in Devon, Cornwall and on the south coast, where it is often planted as a windbreak. It can grow up to 120 ft and live for over 100 years. It has dark, plume-like foliage and large, woody cones with a knob on each scale.

Britain's fastest growing evergreen, Leyland cypress *Cupressocyparis leylandii* is a hybrid between this and the hardier Nootka cypress *Chamaecyparis nootkatensis* from Alaska. It is increased by cuttings, and grows 3 ft a year.

Cypress, Swamp
The swamp cypress *Taxodium distichum*, which was introduced to Britain from the marshes of Florida in 1640, is often planted on lake shores and beside streams in country parks. Each of its leafy branchlets is a fern-like frond, opening bright green in April and turning fiery orange before falling in October, leaving the thin brown twigs leafless throughout winter.

The swamp cypress can grow in waterlogged soil because it sends up breathing roots or 'knees', that carry air underground. It bears open male catkins and knobby, woody female cones, holding minute winged seeds, and can reach 100 ft.

Dawn redwood *Metasequoia glyptostroboides* closely resembles the swamp cypress but is unique in that its buds are set *below* its leaf fronds. This waterside tree, which can be raised from cuttings, was only known from fossil remains until 1944, when live trees were found in China. The tallest in Britain now scale 50 ft.

D

Dab *Limanda limanda*

A small fish found in abundance on all sandy shores, the dab's length rarely exceeds 15 in. Young dabs, about 1 in. long, are sometimes caught by shrimpers.

The dab eats most of the smaller organisms it encounters: bottom-living crustaceans, molluscs and worms. It is distinguished from other flatfish by the rough feel of its back.

Dabs are spawned in off-shore waters from February to May and carried landwards by tide and currents. Hatching takes place in 3-12 days depending on water temperature. Though like other fish when born, they begin to turn on their left side as they grow, and the eye on the underside migrates to the upper surface. See also FISH

DAB CHANGES SHAPE

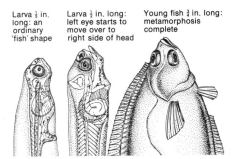

Larva ⅛ in. long: an ordinary 'fish' shape

Larva ½ in. long: left eye starts to move over to right side of head

Young fish ¾ in. long: metamorphosis complete

A month after hatching out the young dab, shaped like other fish, begins its metamorphosis into a flatfish. Within 2½ weeks its left eye has moved over to the right side of its head

Dabchick   see Grebe

Dace *Leuciscus leuciscus*

A typical fish of clear, swiftly flowing streams and rivers, the dace also lives in some lakes. It is a lively, surface-living fish often found in large shoals. It is common in England and has been introduced to some Welsh and Irish rivers.

Its back is a light blue-green, its sides brilliantly silvery with a golden sheen. Its name comes from the Old English for dart. The dace rarely grows longer than about 10 in. and feeds on insects, molluscs and crustaceans. It spawns in spring, in gravel shallows.

Daddy longlegs   see Cranefly

Daffodil, Wild *Narcissus pseudonarcissus*

Garden daffodils are derived by breeding and selection from the 60 or more wild species which have been found in the world. There are now more than 10,000 named cultivated varieties.

Wild daffodils, which grow in damp meadows and woods in England and Wales, have smaller flowers than most garden daffodils. They are becoming rare in many areas because of drainage and gardeners digging them up, though they are still abundant in some parts of the West country, such as on the banks of the M5 motorway where they are safe from pickers.

Narcissus, the genus of bulbous plants which includes daffodils, gets its name from a boy in Greek mythology. He was told he would be happy as long as he never saw his face, but one day he saw his reflection in a pool, fell in love with it, and pined away, leaving a yellow flower on the spot where he died.

Dairy   see Farm

Daisy *Bellis perennis*

The daisy is probably the best known of British plants. It can be found in short grassland everywhere, from low, coastal areas to the tops of mountains. Perhaps because it is so common and, in a lawn, regarded as a nuisance, the beauty of the daisy is often overlooked. It grows in patches with prostrate rosettes of leaves too close to the ground for animals to bite or mowers to cut. Daisies flower nearly all year round, but in

bad weather and after dark they close their petals — hence their name, which is a contraction of day's eye. See also OX-EYE DAISY

The daisy as a light meter: in full sunshine, the flower head is fully open. In hazy light, the petals begin to close. In cloudy weather, the petals fold to show their external pink tingeing. At night or in very dark weather, the flower head is completely closed

Dale

A local name for a valley, widely used in the northern hill country from Derbyshire to the Southern Uplands of Scotland. The word is Scandinavian and may mark the extent to which invading Norsemen and Danes penetrated the hills. Regional names such as Lauderdale and Teviotdale remained in use after the organisation of land into shires. In Yorkshire, people who inhabit the valleys are referred to as 'dalesmen'. See also VALLEY

Windy Gyle, Northumberland, typical of the dales with rolling hills, drystone walls and small farms

Dam

A barrier built across a river or lake to raise the water level and create a reservoir. The supply may be used for domestic purposes, for the production of electricity or to regulate the flow of water during flood conditions. A dam has sluice gates or spillways in it to enable the water level to be controlled and the reservoir emptied.

The major dams in Britain, developed from the end of the 19th century, were mostly earth dams, using clay at the core. Earth dams have long, gently sloping sides, which distribute the weight of the water down to the river bed.

A modern example of an earth dam, with a concrete facing, is the Derwent Reservoir, built across the River Derwent – partly in Durham and partly in Northumberland. Completed in 1966 at a cost of £5,250,000, it can supply 40 gallons of water a day per head to a million people in County Durham.

A gravity dam is the simplest structure: a substantial barrier which resists the pressure of water against it by its sheer weight. Lake Vyrnwy in Montgomeryshire is held behind a gravity dam, 1172 ft long and 161 ft high. It was built by Liverpool Corporation in 1892 and is also one of the earliest solid masonry dams. These are rare, however, the more usual construction nowadays being concrete. See also HYDRO-ELECTRICITY

Dame's violet *Hesperis matronalis*

Not a true violet, but smelling like one – especially on a humid evening – dame's violet was introduced into gardens from central Europe in the 16th century. It has since spread to meadows and hedgerows throughout Britain. It was named in error: the French *violette de Damas* – violet from Damascus – was misunderstood as *violette des dames*.

Dame's violet grows 3 ft high, and bears violet or white flowers from May to July

Damsel bug

The way these fierce predators earned their name is a mystery, since damsel bugs are neither elegant nor gentle. There are 13 British species, most of them found among grass. In some species the adults overwinter; other species survive the winter in the egg stage. The eggs are laid inside grass stems, and both young bugs and adults feed on a wide range of other insects.

The feathery white 'parachutes' of the dandelion 'clock' make it easy for the wind to disperse the seed

Dandelion

This plant's odd name is a corruption of the French *dent de lion*, meaning lion's tooth; but it is not known whether this refers to the long root, the toothed leaves or the bright yellow flowers. Another common name for the plant is schoolboy's clock. This arises from the traditional children's game of puffing away the feathery white seed heads, the number of puffs supposedly giving the hour.

The root contains a milky juice, once used in a medicine for liver complaints. The root was dried and ground as a substitute for chicory during the Second World War. The blanched leaves make a bitter addition to salads, and wine and beer are made from the flower heads.

The common dandelion *Taraxacum officinale* flowers from March to October, but most profusely in May. The flowers open in the morning and close at night. There are more than 100 species, adapted to differing conditions throughout the British Isles and varying widely in the size and shape of flowers and leaves. One common British type is the lesser dandelion *T. laevigatum*, which grows in dry places.

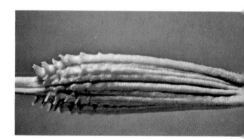

Short, sharp points at the upper end of the dandelion seed help it cling to the soil on landing

Many species produce mainly short-winged or wingless adults, but the field damsel bug *Nabis ferus* always has winged adults and so can easily invade grassy areas and cereal crops. Here they help reduce the populations of insect pests. The tree damsel bug *Himacerus apterus* is the only species not restricted to low-growing plants. It lives in both deciduous and coniferous trees in southern England and Wales.

Damselfly see Dragonfly
Danewort see Elder, Dwarf

Dawn chorus

The mystery of why more birds sing in the 20-40 minutes around dawn than at any other time has yet to be solved. One theory is that each bird proclaims its territorial rights by singing, and learns the positions of other birds by their individual songs.

The first to break into song in spring and summer is the lark, singing as it soars in the sky. It is soon joined by the blackbird, song thrush, robin, wood pigeon, turtle dove, mistle thrush, willow warbler, wren, chiffchaff and other birds – roughly in that order. In mid-summer this dawn chorus starts before 4 a.m., and is best heard at about 5 a.m., when most birds have joined in. Most birds sing from the same perch morning after morning.

Birds sing less in the cold, dark months of the year, so when there is a heavy, overcast sky at daybreak the dawn chorus starts later.

Dead-nettle

Although they have square stems and coarsely toothed leaves like stinging-nettles, dead-nettles have different flowers and do not sting. For most of the year they carry large, conspicuous flowers. White dead-nettle is found in hedgerows and waste places throughout lowland Britain, but is rare in the west. Its hooded white flowers are suffused with green and attract long-tongued bees. Red dead-nettle, a common weed of cultivated land, has smaller flowers.

White dead-nettle
Lamium album

Red dead-nettle
L. purpureum

Red dead-nettle flowers from April to August, white dead-nettle from April to June

Death cap *Amanita phalloides*

A deadly poisonous fungus, sometimes mistaken for a mushroom, which is responsible for more than 90 per cent of human deaths from fungus poisoning. The death cap grows in deciduous woods, particularly beech and oak, appearing in late summer and autumn with a pale olive-yellow cap and white gills and stalk. As with the related fly agaric *A. muscaria* the stalk rests in a cup-like base which may remain below the ground. Once it is eaten, intense stomach pains start a few hours later, followed by paralysis. There is no known antidote, although a serum produced from a rabbit's stomach and brains is said to relieve patients.

Death-watch beetle *Xestobium rufovillosum*

Heard in the stillness of the night, the tapping of the death-watch beetle is an eerie sound. The tapping is done by striking the head against the wood on which it is standing. It is probably a mating signal, and certainly indicates nothing more sinister than damp, rotting wood in an old house—for this is where these chocolate brown, yellow-mottled, $\frac{1}{4}$ in. long beetles now chiefly live. They were formerly most prevalent in dead tree stumps.

Larvae hatch two or three weeks after eggs are laid and take up to three years to mature. Like the adults they feed on wood. Adults hatch in autumn, but spend the winter in the remains of the pupal chamber. In April and May they become active and start tapping. The origin of the beetle's name is

unknown. One theory is that, as the tapping is most clear in the middle of the night, those most likely to hear it are sick people.

This beetle has rarely been known to fly, so it is usually found near the wood it is infesting, or where it has dropped when attacking timber in a roof.

Deceiver, The see Fungus
Deciduous tree see Broad-leaved tree
Deer see pp. 134-5

Dene hole

How these holes got their name, why they were dug and at what period, is uncertain. One theory is they may be Dane holes, or hiding places for property during the Danish invasions in the 7th and 8th centuries. They are found in the chalklands of southern England and chalk areas elsewhere, often in groups. Dene holes consist of a narrow shaft, up to 70 ft deep, ending in a bell-shaped chamber or a series of chambers and galleries. Sometimes the shafts are notched for climbing.

Dene holes were probably marl-pits or chalk workings. Medieval farmers, for instance, spread chalky clay over acid land. But some may be Stone Age flint workings, up to 5000 years old. Where no flint is present, dene holes may have been dug at any time from the Neolithic period as silos—pits into which fodder was compressed to make winter silage. *Dene* is an Anglo-Saxon word meaning a valley or cave.

Destroying angel see Fungus

Devil's coach horse *Ocypus olens*

Associated with the Devil since the Middle Ages, this large black beetle has a fierce appearance and a painful bite. It is also

The Devil's coach horse helps the farmer by preying mostly on young cabbage root flies

called cock-tail beetle, as it faces an attacker with wide open jaws and its tail arched forwards over its head, like a scorpion's sting. At $1\frac{1}{8}$ in. long, it is one of the biggest of the rove beetles. Like other rove beetles, it has short wing cases, though the wings are well developed.

The Devil's coach horse is quite common throughout the British Isles but is not likely to be seen unless disturbed from its daytime resting place among rubbish or under stones. It feeds at night, on small insects and decaying animal matter.

Dew

Unless there is a blanket of cloud acting as an insulator, the earth cools rapidly after sunset and may reach the temperature (known as the dew point) at which water vapour (an invisible gas) in the air and from the earth condenses on to cool surfaces as beads of water known as dew.

The heaviest dew formation is often found on grass because its leaves lose heat rather quickly. Although dew will form heavily on stones, grass and leaves, it will appear only lightly on earth, sand and gravel. Intense dew frequently occurs in autumn, when high humidity combines with long, clear, calm nights. Lawns and fields are then saturated, and glisten in the early morning sunshine.

Anyone who has been camping will have noticed that if there is dew in the morning, it is because there was little cloud and little wind during the night—this also usually means a fine day. There is an old saying about dew: 'With dew before midnight, the next day will sure be bright.'

Dewberry *Rubus caesius*

Similar to the blackberry, but with smaller fruits, the dewberry grows on lime-rich soil in England and Wales, but is rare in southern Scotland and Ireland. A dew-like bloom covers the fruits and a grey bloom covers the trailing stem. Dewberries have fewer but larger individual fruitlets, or drupes, than blackberries. The berries ripen earlier than blackberries and have more flavour. They follow white flowers, sometimes tinged pink. Dewberry leaves have three lobes, unlike blackberry leaves which have five.

Berry

Dewberries are smaller than blackberries, but are considered to have more flavour

133

WHERE BRITAIN'S DEER LIVE

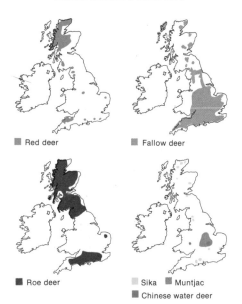

■ Red deer   ■ Fallow deer

■ Roe deer   ☐ Sika   ■ Muntjac
             ■ Chinese water deer

These distribution maps show six of the seven species of deer which live in Great Britain. The 100 or so head of reindeer live only in the Cairngorms, Scotland, and are not included. Only two species are native—the red deer, Britain's largest wild animal, and the roe deer. The others have been introduced

Deer

Royal beasts, the wild deer of Britain were for centuries preserved for hunting by the king and his court. William the Conqueror backed up his exclusive right to hunt deer with laws that provided the death penalty for killing a deer and maiming for attempting to kill a deer. These harsh penalties were abolished by Henry III, but deer were protected until the 19th century.

The royal beasts of the chase were Britain's two native deer—the red deer and the roe deer—and the fallow deer, which the Romans are believed to have introduced. Since the 17th century they have been joined by sika, muntjac and Chinese water deer, which have escaped from parks, and a herd of reindeer, which was established in Scotland in 1952.

Deer usually live socially in groups or herds. Like cattle they are ruminants, that is they chew the cud. They come out into the open at dawn and dusk to feed on leaves, grass, berries, shoots, ferns, root crops and cereals. Some even eat bark, so damaging the trees. During the day the deer settle down in some quiet place to regurgitate and digest their food. Leaves and other herbage are needed in large quantities to satisfy the deer's appetite. The process of chewing the cud allows this shy animal to swallow a large amount of food in a short time and to digest it at leisure. The most outstanding feature

Red deer stags do battle in the rutting season—the time for fighting over the possession of

of deer, the antlers, are usually possessed by the males only. The antlers are grown afresh each year in time for the rutting season, when fights take place for the possession of females. The males find their voices at this time, too, and a loud roar is a not uncommon sound in deer country. After rutting the antlers are shed.

Once hunted by the bear, wolf and lynx, the deer's only enemy today is man. Deer are woodland creatures, but farmlands and dwellings have taken the place of many

Deer in Britain

Reindeer 4 ft
Rangifer tarandus

Chinese water deer 18 in.
Hydropotes inermis

Fallow deer 3 ft
Dama dama

Red deer 4 ft
Cervus elaphus

Roe deer 2 ft
Capreolus capreolus

Sika 4 ft
Cervus nippon

Muntjac 16-25 in.
Muntiacus muntjak

Seven species of deer live wild in Britain, but only two of them, red deer and roe deer, are native. Fallow deer are believed to have been introduced by the Romans; sika, muntjac and Chinese water deer have spread after escaping from private parks and zoos. Reindeer were introduced to the Cairngorms by a Lapp farmer only 20 years ago. Deer are shy animals and during the day keep to woodlands and moorlands

females. Although one deer could kill another with its antlers, injuries are usually accidental

forests, so driving them into unnatural habitats. They turn to feeding on crops and so come to be regarded as pests by man. However, experiments in farming Scotland's red deer as a food source are in progress.

Britain's largest wild animal is the red deer, which is 4 ft high at the shoulder. It lives on the open mountains and moorlands in parts of Scotland, Cumberland, the West Country, and in Kerry, Ireland. For much of the year the stags and hinds live in separate groups. But in the rutting season, from mid-September to the end of October, the stags collect harems—challenging one another with their magnificent antlers and roaring to show their territorial ownership. Each hind bears one calf. Calves are born from the first week in May to the first week in June.

The other native British deer is the 2 ft high roe deer, found in Scotland, the Lake District, many parts of the southern counties and in East Anglia. It is easily overlooked as it slips quietly through the undergrowth, even crawling on its belly. Roe deer live in small family parties of buck, doe and her kids. Rutting occurs from mid-July to mid-August. Courtship often involves the buck chasing the doe in circles, usually around a tree or bush, so forming a 'roe ring' in the soil. The kids, frequently twins, are born from the end of April to mid-June.

It was probably the Romans who introduced the 3 ft high fallow deer into Britain from Asia Minor. It was brought as a decorative estate animal and beast of the chase. Now it lives wild in southern England and parts of Ireland. There are herds in Epping Forest, the New Forest and Cannock Chase. Fallow deer prefer living in dense woodlands but will enter gardens and fields to raid crops and vegetables. During the summer the bucks and does keep apart, but in the rutting season, from the middle to the end of October, and throughout the winter, they herd together. The doe gives birth to a single fawn during the first three weeks in June.

Resembling the red deer in body and

antler shape is the 4 ft high sika. It was introduced into parks from Japan during the 17th century. Today it lives wild in Dorset, Hampshire, Lancashire and eastern Ireland. The sika has a rutting season from mid-September to the end of November. The calves, one per hind, are born from the beginning of June to the end of July.

The humped-back appearance of the tiny 16-25 in. high muntjac makes it instantly recognisable. This deer has lived wild in Britain since it escaped from Woburn Park in about 1890. It has spread to the Home Counties, southern counties and East Anglia. Most are probably of the Chinese race. The upper canines of the buck form short tusks, and it has small antlers on hairy bases called pedicles.

The muntjac is not a herding deer, but often pairs up for company or moves around in family groups. There does not seem to be any particular rutting season, but antler growth nevertheless keeps to an annual cycle. The antlers reach full development in about September. The single fawns are usually born between March and September.

Often confused with the muntjac is the 18 in. high Chinese water deer, another escapee from Woburn and also Whipsnade Zoo. Neither male nor female water deer has antlers, but the buck has large upper canines which protrude as tusks. Since the 1940's this deer has spread from Bedfordshire to Huntingdonshire, Hertfordshire, the Chilterns and Oxfordshire. The rutting season lasts from the end of November to the end of January. The fawns, often as many as three or four per doe,

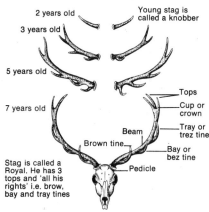

ANTLER GROWTH OF THE RED STAG

Each year the stag sheds and regrows his bony antlers, adding more branches as he gets older

are born from mid-May to the end of June.

Until the 12th century reindeer were hunted in Scotland. It was probably through over-killing and gradual deforestation, the trees being a refuge for the rather slow deer, that they disappeared from Britain. In 1952 a Lapp farmer brought some of his Swedish mountain reindeer to the Cairngorms as an experiment to see if they could live and breed there. At present the herd stands at about 100 head. The 4 ft high reindeer is unusual in that both bull and cow carry antlers. The rutting season is in October and the one or two unspotted calves are born from May to June.

During the autumn rut the red stag rounds up as many hinds as he can find. He watches over his 'harem' jealously, using his head or antlers to drive off any young intruders

Dewpond

More dependent on rainwater than dew, these scooped-out hollows, 20-30 yds across, are still built in chalk and limestone areas where there is a poor supply of surface water, to provide drinking water for livestock. The oldest are probably 17th century, although Iron Age people living in hill forts may have used similar devices.

Traditionally, dewponds are lined with puddled clay and flints, but modern ones are usually lined with plastic sheeting. They are seen mostly in the hilly sheep country of Sussex, Hampshire, Wiltshire, Dorset and Derbyshire.

Dipper *Cinclus cinclus*

The short-tailed, chunky dipper or water ouzel has a shape which allows it to walk under water, searching for food. As it walks upstream on the river bed with its head down, the force of a fast current against its slanting back is sufficient to hold it on the bottom. It turns over pebbles in search of water beetles, insect larvae, small crustaceans and molluscs.

The dipper is found mainly in the fast streams of hilly districts in north and west Britain. It is 7 in. long, its black plumage broken only by a large white bib that extends from the throat over the chest. Each dipper has a narrow territory, up to 2 miles long beside a watercourse over which it flies before wading for food.

The three to six eggs are laid in cup-shaped nests in holes in banks, bridges, buildings and ivy-covered trees overlooking streams. They are incubated by the female alone, although the male helps with the feeding. Two, sometimes three, broods are reared. In winter, continental birds of a black-bellied sub-species appear on some east-coast streams where dippers are otherwise seldom seen.

An unorthodox way of catching food—the dipper walks upstream along the river bottom

Ditch

Ditches on farms serve two purposes: to drain the land and to act as boundaries. In the flat, wet countryside of the Fens and Romney Marshes, deep water-filled ditches merge into the landscape, often remaining invisible to the casual observer. Large open ditches in the south-west are sometimes called rhines. In drier areas, many ditches run alongside hedges which mark their course. Once these ditches were there to keep animals from reaching the hedge, and so helped to make it stock-proof.

Cleaning ditches is a laborious task, for which several types of machines have been devised. Trench-cutting ploughs cut U or V-shaped ditches, and diggers excavate surplus earth and carry it away in a scoop with an endless chain of buckets. A powerful and effective ditch-cleaner has a rotating disc with sharp blades mounted on a flexible arm and powered by a tractor. See also DRAINAGE, DYKES

Diver

Perfectly adapted water birds, the divers spend most of their lives at sea. Their legs, which are set back, are well designed for swimming and diving but make them clumsy on land. During the May-June breeding season, they nest on remote lochs and lakes, a few yards from the water's edge.

Of the four species known to Britain, two breed regularly, one is a rare breeder and the other is a rare visitor. All are dark-coloured birds and visit offshore fishing banks in winter. They can dive to more than 30 ft in their search for fish and stay submerged for up to a minute and a half. Quite large flocks may be seen, though groups of less than six are more usual. They spend most of their time sitting low in the water, but also fly strongly over the sea with a characteristic hunched-back appearance.

In summer, divers move northwards to breed, and sport the distinguishing plumage that serves to name the two common British breeders: the red-throated diver and the black-throated diver.

Divers breed on the banks of small lochs or on islets. The female normally lays two dark brown eggs on the ground or a heap of weed, and creates a slipway from the eggs to the water which she scuttles down at the first sign of danger.

At 21 in., the red-throated is the smallest diver; it is also the most common. It has a grey head with an inverted rust-red triangle on the neck.

The up-tilted appearance of the red-throated diver's bill, and its greyish-brown colour, help to distinguish it from the black-throated diver. When nesting it flies out to sea to feed. The black-throated diver is slightly larger and has a black neck patch with flecked white ovals on its back. It feeds in the lake where it breeds.

The great northern diver, at 27-32 in., is considerably larger. In summer, the black neck may show an iridescent green and is broken by two collars of black and white, while its back is speckled with white squares. It has a comparatively big bill. A frequent visitor to the north and west in winter, this bird bred in Scotland for the first time in 1970.

The white-billed diver is the Arctic equivalent of the great northern diver and on rare occasions reaches the British Isles in winter. Its massive light-coloured bill is the best identification mark.

When disturbed, divers slip quietly into the water and dive for a considerable distance before surfacing. Their cries vary from a barking noise to a melancholy wail.

Diving beetle, Great *Dytiscus marginalis*

Both adults and larvae of the ferocious great diving beetle can give painful bites. The larvae grow to 2 in. long, with huge jaws, and, like the adults, attack and eat anything they can catch—newts, fish, tadpoles and aquatic insects, including their own kind. The oval adults grow to 1½ in. long and are black with an edging of yellow. They may live three years and are quite common in ponds throughout the British Isles. They fly after dusk and spread to other ponds, where they swim with their elongated, flattened hind limbs.

Adults and larvae feed by injecting digestive juices into their prey and sucking in its body fluids. To breathe they float to the surface tail first, protrude their tails out of the water, and draw in air to store in their breathing tubes. Adults can also store air under their wing covers. Females have grooved wing covers, the males smooth.

The larva of the great diving beetle has jaws large enough to tackle a tadpole

Dock

The leaves often used as a remedy for nettle stings belong to the broad-leaved dock. They are over 4 in. wide with blunt tips and were formerly used to wrap butter to keep it fresh. Curled dock has long narrow leaves with wavy margins. The two types are so closely related that hybrids are often found. Docks are troublesome weeds of grassland and cultivated fields throughout the British Isles, but curled dock also occurs in dunes and on shingle beaches. Both grow up to 3 ft tall and flower from June to October. The flowers consist of two whorls of three segments, the inner ones surrounding the single triangular nut as it ripens, developing a swelling or tubercle in the centre.

Broad-leaved dock
Rumex obtusifolius

Curled dock
R. crispus

Broad-leaved and curled dock are distinctive, but hybrids show features of both species

Dodder

A leafless parasite, dodder grows by twining its red, wiry stem counter-clockwise round other plants and sending suckers into them. Through these roots, dodder absorbs from the host plant all the materials needed for its own growth and in doing so may completely kill its host.

Common dodder grows on gorse, heather, clover and several other plants. It is common in southern England, but scarce everywhere else in the British Isles. Greater dodder, which grows on stinging-nettles, is quite rare.

Greater dodder
Cuscuta europaea

Common dodder
C. epithymum

Dodders are parasites, feeding on their hosts through roots put out from wiry stems

Working dogs of the countryside

Dogs in the country have to earn their living. Many types are bred for different jobs, and illustrated below are some of the main British breeds of working farm dogs and sporting dogs. Missing from this chart, because it can be any shape, colour or size, is the mongrel, which on many farms fills an all-purpose role as rat-catcher, rabbiter and guard dog

Sporting dogs

Clumber spaniel

Fox terrier

Labrador retriever

Beagle

Gordon setter

Foxhound

Farm dogs

Rough collie

Corgi

Welsh sheepdog

Dog *Canis familiaris*

One of the first animals to become domesticated, the dog has been man's companion for about 10,000 years. There is some disagreement over the domestic dog's ancestry but it is believed to be a descendant of the smaller southern races of wolf such as the Indian wolf *Canis lupus pallipes*. In the wild, the dog is one of a pack, subordinate to a pack leader; domesticated, it has transferred this subordination to man and is now wholly dependent on him.

There are more than 90 different pure breeds, ranging from the 200 lb. St Bernard to the 2 lb. chihuahua. Few resemble their ancestor, although a dog may mate with a wolf and produce fertile cubs. Similarly pure breeds may interbreed producing cross-breeds, and cross-breeds mate to produce mongrels.

Country dogs can be divided into two groups: farm dogs—the sheepdog, collie, corgi and terrier; and sporting dogs—the foxhound, beagle, retriever, setter and spaniel.

The Welsh sheepdog and collie, both sheep herders, are renowned for their intelligence and initiative. They are indispensable to the hill and moorland farmer for rounding up and guiding sheep, often on unfenced land.

They also put on spectacular displays at sheepdog trials. The Old English sheepdog is rarely used today as a working dog.

The corgi has been bred for centuries as a working dog in Wales. Its role is to follow behind a herd of cattle, nipping at the heels of stragglers. Being a short dog it avoids any flying kicks. The tough, untiring and aggressive terrier is used by farmers for the destruction of rats and other vermin.

In the case of the fox terrier, this was bred to go down the earths of foxes to rout them out, and often accompanies packs of foxhounds for this purpose.

The two chase-dogs, the foxhound and beagle, are trained to use their good sense of smell for hunting. Foxhounds hunt foxes, beagles hunt hares. They are not particularly fast dogs but have the stamina to spend a day running over rough country. The muscular, long-legged setter and retriever are gun dogs trained to find shot birds and to retrieve them, rather than to hunt. They, too, must be able to cover many miles in a day. Although the spaniel will retrieve, it also instinctively looks for hidden pheasants and rabbits, flushing them into the open. It revels in working in thick undergrowth and, like the retriever, readily goes into water after game.

Dog's mercury *Mercurialis perennis*

One of Britain's most common woodland herbs which, though poisonous, is so unattractive that it is unlikely to be eaten. It forms a carpet of oval-shaped light-green leaves about 12 in. high. There are separate male and female plants which usually grow in large patches entirely of one sex.

Long spikes with yellow-green stamens make the male flowers conspicuous in early spring. The female flowers are less easy to see as they are hidden among the upper leaves. Dog's mercury is abundant except in north Scotland and Ireland.

Dogwhelk see Whelk

Dogwood *Cornus sanguinea*

A shrub which grows in thickets on dry downs or over limestone rocks, particularly in southern England. The first part of its botanical name, *Cornus,* means horny, and refers to the hard, firm texture of its wood which was once used for small, strong objects such as meat skewers. *Sanguinea,* meaning bloody, comes from the blood-red colour of the dogwood's twigs and leaves. *C. alba,* an Asian species introduced as a garden plant, often grows wild on waste land.

In May, the dogwood opens small, white flowers each having four petals united in a tube. The flower develops by October to a soft, round, black berry holding two hard seeds. Birds gather these berries, swallow them and later deposit the seeds; in this way dogwood is constantly being spread to fresh sites. Occasionally, it grows into a small tree up to 10 ft tall, with grey wrinkled bark.

Dogwood poses a serious problem to the Nature Conservancy and other bodies which seek to preserve open downland, since it is a vigorous grower and when cut back sends up both coppice shoots and sucker shoots from its roots. Grazing animals, such as sheep, will check it completely, but if left alone, dogwood scrub is invaded by seedlings of oak, ash, beech and other trees which eventually suppress it.

Dolmen see Standing stones

Donkey

Though common in Ireland, donkeys have never been used extensively in Britain for farm work. Nowadays they are popular as children's pets. They are members of the horse family, with which they cross breed, producing mules, and are descended from the wild asses of northern Africa, *Equus asinus,* and central Asia, *E. hemionus.*

They stand between 3 ft and 4½ ft high and have a grey or brownish coat, long ears and a loose mane without forelock. They eat grass, sedge and herbs. Foals are born 11 or 12 months after a spring or summer mating. Asses' milk was once prescribed for tuberculosis patients, and magical properties were ascribed to the hair from the black cross on their shoulders.

One suggestion for the origin of the name dormouse is the French word *dormir,* to sleep

Dormouse *Muscardinus avellanarius*

Victorian children often kept dormice as pets, just as modern children keep hamsters. But from being a common creature of southern Britain, it has become quite rare. It hibernates from September to April, and is usually active by night during the rest of the year.

The dormouse looks more like a small squirrel than a mouse. It can be recognised by its plump 3 in. long chestnut body, blunt snout, small ears, large eyes and 2½ in. long bushy tail. It is agile and lively and climbs well, but spends a lot of time in thick undergrowth among hazel bushes, beech and sweet chestnut, for it likes to eat the nuts. It usually builds its winter nest below ground or inside a hollow tree stump. There, it curls up into a tight ball, chin resting on belly and tail curved over head.

The summer nest is a loose ball of grass, leaves and shredded honeysuckle bark, usually wedged in a forked branch. From this the dormouse emerges at dusk to look for berries, nuts and insects. The female produces one or two litters a year of between three and five young. The dormouse has a relatively long life span of about four years; this may be because it spends so much time asleep, out of the reach of enemies.

At the turn of the century, Lord Rothschild introduced the edible or fat dormouse *Glis glis* from Europe to his estate at Tring, Hertfordshire. This soft, squirrel-like, 6 in. long, silvery-grey animal, locally known as the little chinchilla, now inhabits a triangular area bounded by Beaconsfield, Aylesbury and Luton. It is normally a woodland species but has taken to living in outhouses, barns and lofts of large country houses, especially where fruit is stored. It was a delicacy in Roman times and was fattened up on walnuts for banquets.

Dory *Zeus faber*

Probably the oddest-looking fish in the seas around Britain with its deep body, big mouth, spiny outline and long fins, the dory is uncommon except on the southern and western coasts. The dory is not a strong swimmer, yet it is a predator on fish. It drifts passively under ships, or lies close to weeds or rocks. When other fish approach, its jaws swing open, creating a rush of water which carries the prey into its mouth.

The round, dark marks on the dory's sides are said to be the thumbprints left by the Apostle Peter when he took money from a fish's mouth.

Dotterel see Plover
Dove see Pigeon

Dovecot

A building erected for housing doves and pigeons. Some are so impressive that they can be mistaken for the base of a windmill or a small defensive tower. Many were erected during the improvement of estates in the 17th and 18th centuries, and achieved sufficient architectural and historical merit to be safeguarded as scheduled buildings.

Some dovecots are attached to farmsteads or let into the gable end of a barn or granary —much to the annoyance of tenant farmers as doves damage crops. Dovecots and pigeon lofts were not just ornamental; the birds provided a source of fresh meat in winter.

A fine 16th-century example at Willington, in Bedfordshire, is estimated to have housed 1200 doves. The dovecot built in the 17th century among the monastic buildings of Penmon, in Anglesey, housed 1000 nests.

A 15th-century dovecot at Basing House, Hants. The birds provided a winter meat supply

Dowsing see Water divining

Dragonet *Callionymus lyra*

The male dragonet is an inshore fish which has high fins on its back. Its body and fins are striped with yellow and green-blue and are brightest in the February to March breeding season. The female is brown.

The dragonet is ideally adapted to life on sandy bottoms and it spends much of its time partially buried in sand. It feeds mainly on sand-burrowing crustaceans and worms. It is found on all sandy coasts around Britain.

Dragonfly and damselfly

Colourful dragonflies are among the fastest-flying and oldest insects in the world: estimates of their speed vary from 35 mph to 60 mph, and fossilised remains show that they existed 300 million years ago.

Four large wings, ranging in span from 2 in. to 4 in., and enormous eyes which cover the top and sides of the head help to make dragonflies efficient hunters. They prey on flying insects up to the size of butterflies. Damselflies are small relatives of dragonflies and feed on smaller insects. Their eyes do not cover their heads, and they rest with their wings above their bodies, rather like butterflies, while dragonflies rest with their wings straight out beside the body. Dragonflies and damselflies are on the wing during late spring and summer, usually near water, though some can be seen hunting in woodlands or fields a long way from water.

Hawker dragonflies, such as the common aeshna and the emperor, spend a lot of time patrolling a particular stretch of water, while darter dragonflies, such as the common sympetrum, choose a perch from which they dart out to catch prey.

Sometimes two damsel or dragonflies may be seen flying 'in tandem'. This is part of their mating procedure. Before he flies in pursuit of a female, the male transfers his sperm to a special organ on the underside of his body. He grasps a female by the neck using claspers at the tip of his body. The female then twists her body forwards below him to receive the sperm.

Some damselflies, including the banded agrion, crawl below the surface of the water to lay their eggs, male and female making the plunge together. Female hawkers insert their eggs in a plant stem, a floating piece of vegetation or in mud. The

The large red damselfly *Pyrrhosoma nymphula* seen by lakes and rivers in summer months

darters wash the eggs from the end of the body directly into the water as they fly along. The male keeps hold of the female to lift her into the air again.

The adult life span of the dragonfly is about a month, but the aquatic nymphs take at least a year to mature; some species take up to five years. Damselfly nymphs are slender and live among pondweeds. Dragonfly nymphs are stouter, more sluggish creatures and live in mud at the bottom of ponds, lakes or slow-flowing streams. Like adults, they are carnivorous, eating any-thing from tiny insect larvae to large tadpoles, depending on the size of the nymph. They capture the prey with an extension of the lower lip which is called the 'mask'. This has two hooks on the end like a lobster's claw and is shot out to capture passing prey. The nymph then draws the victim to its jaws, pumps in digestive fluids and sucks out its vital juices. There is no pupal stage; when nearly mature the nymphs climb up plant stems, out of the water, and shed their skins. After expanding and drying their wings they fly away as perfect adults.

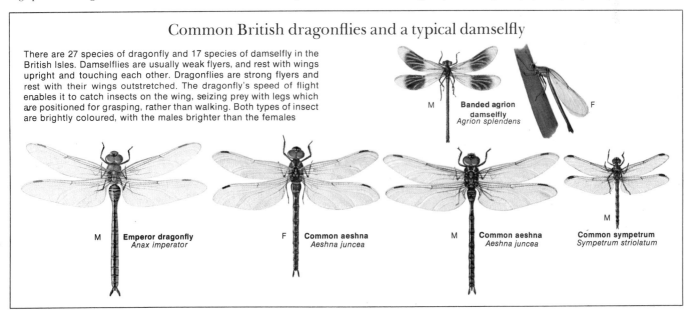

Common British dragonflies and a typical damselfly

There are 27 species of dragonfly and 17 species of damselfly in the British Isles. Damselflies are usually weak flyers, and rest with wings upright and touching each other. Dragonflies are strong flyers and rest with their wings outstretched. The dragonfly's speed of flight enables it to catch insects on the wing, seizing prey with legs which are positioned for grasping, rather than walking. Both types of insect are brightly coloured, with the males brighter than the females

M · **Banded agrion damselfly** *Agrion splendens* · F

M · **Emperor dragonfly** *Anax imperator*

F · **Common aeshna** *Aeshna juncea*

M · **Common aeshna** *Aeshna juncea*

Common sympetrum *Sympetrum striolatum* · M

The gentle downs where man first farmed

Smooth, rounded slopes covered with springy turf, deep valleys without streams, the white gleam of a chalk pit, a beech copse on a summit—these are the unmistakable signs of downland.

Downs are chalk uplands. They are widespread in southern England, where they provide fine vantage points for viewing the flat clay plains from which they invariably rise. They were formed during the Cretaceous period roughly 120-75 million years ago. Neolithic man (3000-1850 BC) discovered flints for tool and weapon-making in the chalk of the downs and made them his home, as did Bronze Age man after him. The burial mounds and other earthworks of prehistoric man, his figures cut out of chalk, his track-ways, and traces of his field systems still exist on the downs. It is thought that the downs were once covered with beechwoods and that these early settlers cleared them for cultivation.

Downland soils are shallow; they drain easily—rain soaks into the chalk and flows away beneath the surface to emerge elsewhere as springs; and they warm up quickly after rain. For these reasons grassland, which is the most widespread form of vegetation on downland, supports a wide range of flowering plants and a wealth of insects.

Some plants are found on every down. These include the sheep's fescue and red fescue grasses, crested hair-grass, quaking grass, clover, cowslip, cocksfoot, the aromatic wild thyme, the edible salad burnet, chalk milkwort, glaucous sedge and vetches, of which the horseshoe vetch, with its plumes of yellow flowers and horseshoe-shaped pods, is the most attractive. Other plants are less widespread—for example, the pasque flower grows only north of the Thames, the round-headed rampion only south. Orchids, which have drought-resisting tuberous roots, grow more plentifully on downs than anywhere else in Britain. They include the fragrant orchid and the pyramidal orchid, which both occur in their thousands on some areas of downland, and the rare and beautiful bee orchid, monkey orchid and military orchid.

Many downland plants—the stemless thistle, for example—grow flat on the ground, forming a mat of leaves.

The best-known downland insects are butterflies, of which the chalk-hill blue, adonis blue and silver-spotted skipper live almost exclusively on the downs. Other characteristic down-

CHALK GRASSLAND

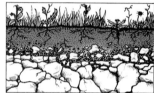

Humus and topsoil in which grasses and colourful plants grow

Subsoil—a shallow layer formed from the bedrock partly by weathering

Bedrock—chalk, a fine, soft rock from which water drains rapidly

Chalk soil is very porous and consequently dry, warm and well aerated. It is often used as sheep pastureland, being too shallow for the plough

The South Downs from Truleigh Hill, Sussex. These smooth grassy hills are believed to have been covered with beechwoods until Stone Age man felled them to start farming

Skylark Renowned for its warbling song which continues uninterrupted for at least three minutes

Stemless thistle The large flower grows stemless in the middle of the rosette of prickly leaves

land butterflies are the marbled white, dark green fritillary and small blue. Moths include many day-flying species, such as burnets. The caterpillars of these butterflies and moths eat the leaves of downland plants. For instance, the caterpillar of the chalk carpet moth feeds on clovers. Other common inhabitants of the downs are the purse spider, which catches its prey in a web at the entrance to its subterranean home, and the yellow meadow ant, which builds oval ant-hills. Grasshoppers, bushcrickets, glow-worms, beetles, millipedes, centipedes, woodlice, bumble bees and saw flies are also plentiful.

More snails—including the large, edible Roman snail—are found on downland than in any other type of district. This is because snails, by means of special glands, form their shells from chalk.

Birdlife on the downs is limited by the general lack of surface water. Among the common woodland species are song thrush, blackbird, chaffinch, green woodpecker, wood pigeon, robin, wren, blue tit and willow warbler. Scrub species include linnet, magpie, whitethroat (which often frequents hedges) and lesser whitethroat, bullfinch, pheasant and turtle dove. On grassland, which supports fewer species, are found wheatear, skylark and meadow pipit. The kestrel also ranges over the downs, preying on small mammals and insects.

Common mammals are moles (except in yew and beechwoods), hedgehogs, voles, hares and shrews. Moles are prevalent because the light downland soil is ideal for tunnelling operations and because it is rich in earthworms, the mole's staple diet. Two reptiles, the slow-worm and the common lizard, are abundant, especially on sunny banks.

The two dominant forms of woodland on downs are beech and yew. The evergreen yew, which is sometimes mixed with ash and whitebeam, is an important winter home for many small animals.

Scrub, which may be formed of mixed shrubs or of a single species such as juniper, has increased on the downs as sheep-grazing has gradually declined and also since the fall in the rabbit population caused by the 1953 outbreak of myxomatosis.

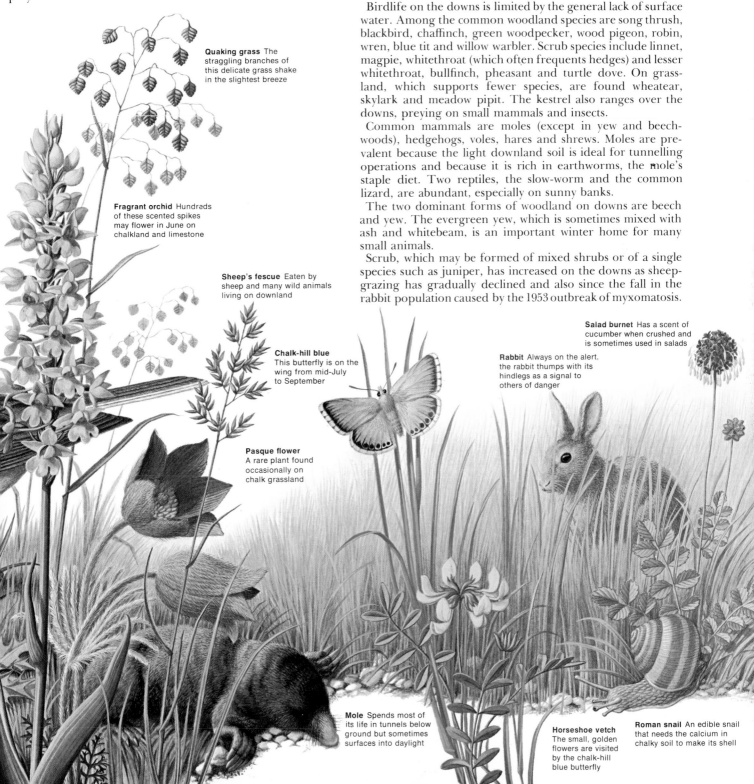

Quaking grass The straggling branches of this delicate grass shake in the slightest breeze

Fragrant orchid Hundreds of these scented spikes may flower in June on chalkland and limestone

Sheep's fescue Eaten by sheep and many wild animals living on downland

Chalk-hill blue This butterfly is on the wing from mid-July to September

Pasque flower A rare plant found occasionally on chalk grassland

Salad burnet Has a scent of cucumber when crushed and is sometimes used in salads

Rabbit Always on the alert, the rabbit thumps with its hindlegs as a signal to others of danger

Mole Spends most of its life in tunnels below ground but sometimes surfaces into daylight

Horseshoe vetch The small, golden flowers are visited by the chalk-hill blue butterfly

Roman snail An edible snail that needs the calcium in chalky soil to make its shell

Drain

An artificial channel cut to carry away surplus water from the land. Surplus water in or on the soil is a problem, usually arising either from an impervious soil or because the terrain is so flat that the water will not flow away in natural channels. Rainfall in Britain is spread fairly evenly throughout the year, but winter's lower rate of evaporation and transpiration means that good drainage is essential, especially on arable land, and drainage work can qualify for government grants.

Waterlogged impervious soil is drained either by digging open ditches or by inserting drains beneath the surface. Sometimes, underground drains are made by digging a trench, laying pipes, then filling in the trench.

On heavy ground a channel may be cut below the surface by a mole-plough. The main part of this is the mole, a steel cylinder about 2½ in. across, attached to the bottom of a rigid vertical blade. Dragged by a tractor, the mole carves a tunnel about 15 in. underground which may last eight years. Experimental machines which line mole drains with plastic pipes or concrete to prolong their life promise to reduce the cost of drain-laying.

The problems of surface drainage are seen most clearly in the Fens, where the fields are often below the level of the rivers or main drainage channels, and these channels in their turn are below sea level. The solution is to pump the water up from one level to the next.

One of the many dikes that drain Romney Marsh. Most of the land has been reclaimed from the sea over the centuries, the first drainage work having been started by the Romans at Dymchurch. Local freeholders still pay for the maintenance of these ditches and dikes

Drey see Squirrel

Drill

Jethro Tull, a Berkshire farmer, is usually credited with inventing the seed drill in 1701. But the principle was apparently known in China 5000 years ago. A drill consists of a box on wheels, with tubes running at intervals from the bottom of the box to channel seed into the soil. Many modern drills have a second box, with separate tubes, to deposit fertiliser near the seed. See also FARMING

Drizzle

The meteorological definition of drizzle is rain composed of small droplets—each less than 0·02 in. in diameter. Such small droplets are generally formed by the collision and merging of hundreds of tiny cloud droplets inside layers of cloud known as stratus.

The updraughts in such clouds are usually fairly weak, and drizzle droplets soon grow big enough to overcome these internal currents and fall out of the cloud.

The air below the cloud must be humid enough to prevent the droplets from evaporating before reaching the ground. Such overcast, humid conditions are particularly common during the winter and in western Britain when the winds are from the east or south-west.

Dropwort *Filipendula vulgaris*

A similar plant to meadowsweet, but its creamy-white flowers are not fragrant and the leaves are more jagged and deeply divided. It is common on dry chalk and limestone grassland in England, but rarely found elsewhere in the British Isles. Both the common and botanical names refer to the roots which are swollen in places into oblong,

Dropwort roots with their characteristic tubers, in which starch and protein are stored

pea-sized tubers—the drops. *Filipendula* comes from the Latin: *filium*, a thread and *pendulus,* hanging.

The plant is a perennial which bears its flowers from July to September.

Drought

This can be 'absolute' or 'partial', depending on the number of days which have elapsed since certain amounts of rainfall were recorded. An absolute drought is a period of at least 15 consecutive days during which the total rainfall is less than 0·01 in.; a partial drought is a period of 29 days in which the rainfall does not exceed 0·01 in. on any single day. In the driest parts of England—Essex and the Thames estuary—droughts occur two or three times a year, but in the wet areas of north-west Scotland, they occur only about once every five years. In south-east England droughts have lasted for 60 days. See also IRRIGATION

Drove road

A broad, grassy track along which cattle and sheep were driven to fairs and markets. Drove roads were extensively used in the 17th and 18th centuries for driving large herds of Scottish and Welsh cattle to the growing towns and cities of England. Drove roads declined in the early 19th century with the spread of the railways. The tracks follow well-marked routes, and inns with such names as The Drovers' Arms and The Kentish Drover sprang up beside them. Sewstern Lane on the Leicestershire border, and the Welsh Road, south-east from Kenilworth, were famous drove roads.

Drumlin

Small, oval-shaped, low hills usually found in groups, mainly in lowland areas and valley floors. They are formed of glacial sediment—boulder clay—produced under an ice sheet. Drumlins are streamlined and lie with the long axis of their oval shape in line with the direction of movement of the ice.

They can be 100 ft high, half a mile long and a quarter of a mile wide. They are common in Northern Ireland, the Vale of Eden and other areas around the Lake District and the Craven lowlands of west Yorkshire.

Drystone walls criss-cross the valleys of Wensleydale, near Hawes, giving emphasis to the contours of the landscape and clearly defining the enclosure patterns of the 19th century

Drystone wall

One of the most impressive features of the hill country of Britain is the drystone wall, which marches for mile after mile across fell country, often in dramatic straight lines up the sides of steep hills, dividing rough grazing into large fields.

Drystone walls are built without mortar, and their stability—they can stand for 200 years—is due to the skill of the craftsmen who place rough boulders and angular stones together.

Many drystone walls were constructed in the last century as part of the enclosure of open grazing. They were especially useful in areas too exposed for hedgerows to survive and where stones were readily available.

Most drystone walls are wider at the base than at the crown, and are often capped with coping stones. A typical wall has two outer layers of large, flattish stones enclosing an inner 'heart' of smaller, rounder stones. Often it is reinforced with 'through bands' of even larger, flat stones which can also be used as stiles.

The very dryness of a wall makes it more likely to endure wind and frost and to act as shelter for livestock as well as a boundary. Unusual walls are found in Caithness and the Orkney Islands, composed of large slabs of stone standing on end.

Drystone walling is common throughout north and west Britain including parts of Ireland, but is rare in most of eastern and southern England. Many old stone walls in Devon and Cornwall have been obscured by grass and shrubs. In recent years damage has been done to walls lining the lanes in the Pennines, particularly in Derbyshire. Much of it may be caused by lorries using the lanes to avoid traffic, and possibly brushing the walls, causing them to collapse later.

Drystone walling—an ancient craft—is found in Stone Age dwellings at Skara Brae in the Orkneys and was widely used throughout the Iron Age.

Duck, Domestic

Nearly all farmyard ducks in Britain are descended from the wild mallard which still thrives throughout the country. Though certain breeds are specialist egg-producers, ducks are generally kept for the table. There are about a million of them in the British Isles, mainly reared in small units on mixed farms. There are some large-scale specialist enterprises, however, notably in Lincolnshire.

Although hardy and easy to look after, the domestic duck does not take well to intensive-breeding methods. It likes to forage for itself, eating grass and other vegetation and digging up worms. A duck depends on the farmer for additional food such as mash or cereals. It is a messy creature, but cheap to house. Preferably it should have a water trough, pond or river within its home range and should be kept in an enclosure overnight as it lays eggs in the early morning and is apt to drop them anywhere.

The laying breeds, the Indian runner and Khaki Campbell, lay up to 300 eggs in a year, a number that equals and often exceeds that of the hen. The Khaki Campbell is a cross between an Indian runner, wild mallard and a Rouen. Other breeds, the Aylesbury, Muscovy, Pekin and Rouen are farmed for their meat and lay only 30-60 eggs a year.

Duck eggs take 28 days to hatch and the ducklings can run and pick up food within a few hours. But they depend on their mother for warmth until they are three or four weeks old. They grow quickly, reaching a weight of 6 lb. at ten weeks, though table birds are usually killed at eight weeks, a prime stage of development.

The six common breeds of British ducks

Muscovy Duck   **Khaki Campbell** Drake   **Aylesbury** Drake   **Pekin** Drake   **Indian runner** Drake   **Rouen** Drake

Heavy breeds like Aylesbury, Pekin and Rouen are table birds. The lighter Indian runners were introduced in 1835 from Malaya for egg production. Khaki Campbells are dual-purpose breeds but with the emphasis on egg production. Muscovy ducks—descendants of a wild species from South and Central America—are good table birds, also popular for their ornamental value on ponds. Drakes are more colourful than ducks

Duck, Wild

Fifteen species of wild duck breed regularly in Britain and five others are winter visitors. With so many species occupying the same area each has adapted to its own particular niche. Nevertheless, all ducks have many common characteristics. They are water-birds, between 14 in. and 26 in. long, and spend much of their time swimming.

Ducks have stout bodies, long, pointed wings and powerful breast muscles. They fly swiftly with their long necks stretched out and their wings flapping rapidly, gliding only as they land. They often fly in groups and are gregarious in winter, frequently forming flocks on the bleak February marshes.

Some ducks breed in loose colonies. The drakes—males—are usually brighter than the ducks and take no part in nesting and the rearing of the ducklings. Most ducks undergo a complete moult in the late summer which makes them temporarily flightless. However, they develop a camouflaged plumage at this time, called 'eclipse', which helps to protect them from attack. The shelducks migrate in July to a special moulting-ground, the Heligoland Bight off northwest Germany, returning in the autumn.

Courtship among ducks is a highly ritualised affair. Each species has its own display sequence in which the male exposes bright parts of his plumage to the female.

Ducks can be divided into four well-defined groups: the surface-feeding or dabbling ducks, which feed on or near the surface of fresh water; the freshwater ducks which dive for their food; the sea ducks; and the sawbills, a group distinguished by the structure of their bills.

Each of these groups consists of similar birds that share various characteristics, yet

The red-breasted merganser is recognised by his double crest. Mergansers feed on fish which they seize under water with their saw-toothed bills, from which the fish, however slippery, cannot escape

The mandarin drake courts the female by flicking his head back and softly burping

are sufficiently distinct not to compete totally. For where two related species are direct competitors, one will be less successful and will be gradually eliminated.

Thus, among the sawbills, the serrated bill enables the goosander, red-breasted merganser and smew to grasp slippery fish under water. Because of this they are the only true fishing ducks. But although the goosander and the red-breasted merganser are so closely related, the former hunts for freshwater fish, while the latter spends most of the year hunting sea fish. The smew is a winter visitor from northern Scandinavia and Siberia, and is regularly seen on reservoirs in and around London.

Sea ducks include the eider, scoter, scaup, long-tailed duck, goldeneye and shelduck. As species they have little in common except their habitat, the sea. Most dive for their food, except the shelduck, which is more like a small goose in that it finds its food in the mud of large estuaries. Several species apparently feed on the same food, usually mussels, congregating in large flocks.

Both the common scoter and the velvet scoter live on mussels, but the velvet scoter dives longer and deeper than the common scoter and often feeds further out to sea. The common scoter forms large flocks round Britain's shores between April and September, when large numbers fly in from their breeding grounds in northern Europe and the Arctic. Some non-breeders stay after September, and a few breeders nest in Scotland and Ireland. The drake is black, with an orange mark on the bill, and the female is dark brown with pale buff cheeks. The velvet scoter is about 3 in. longer than the common scoter, with which it is seen mainly in winter. A few can be found in Scotland during the summer, but they do not breed in Britain. The drake has a white spot near the eye and the female has two white face patches.

Other sea ducks that feed on the shellfish banks in shallow waters are the long-tailed duck, goldeneye, scaup and eider. The long-tailed duck and goldeneye are both winter visitors: the first is found only in small flocks in a few favoured areas, mostly in Scotland, whereas the second is common in many coastal waters, as well as freshwater reservoirs and gravel pits. Scaup are among the most numerous of sea ducks, forming flocks of many thousands on several Scottish firths, especially the Firth of Forth. They are primarily diving birds. Their webbed feet, set on legs well to the rear of the body, enable them to drive down to mussel beds on the sea floor. Except in the breeding season few venture on to land. When they do, they waddle even more than other ducks because their centre of gravity

Mergansers breed on lakes and rivers in Scotland and Ireland, spending the winter on estuaries

is set so far back. Scaup breed in the Arctic.

The eider, the largest and most robust of sea ducks, eats crabs as well as molluscs. It breeds in large colonies and lines its nest with down plucked from its own breast. This down, taken from the nests, was the basis of the eiderdown industry in Iceland, one of the eider duck's main breeding areas. The breeding range of the eider in Britain extends from Coquet Island off Northumberland in the east to Walney Island off Lancashire in the west, and to parts of Ireland. When ducks are seen bobbing up and down among big waves in a storm they are almost certainly eiders. The drake is white above and black below, and the female is brown, except for white on the wing.

The freshwater diving ducks, the tufted duck and pochard, often form composite flocks of several thousands on inland reservoirs. Both prefer to dive in shallow water, but the tufted duck takes mainly animal food, whereas the pochard is mostly vegetarian. In the winter pochards can be seen on the lakes of many town parks, for they are among the most common of Britain's freshwater ducks; but most of them fly to eastern Europe for the breeding season.

The surface-feeders, or dabblers, form the largest and most familiar group. They include mallard, pintail, teal, shoveler, wigeon, garganey, gadwall and the ornamental

mandarin duck. The drakes are boldly marked, while the ducks are almost identical to one another in their brown-speckled camouflaging plumage. The mallard is the most numerous and widespread of all our ducks. It is the prime target of the wildfowler who has increased the population in some areas by releasing birds reared in captivity. Like other surface-feeders, the mallard dabbles for its food, which consists largely of water plants and their seeds. It is, therefore, restricted to shallow water up to the maximum depth that it can reach by up-ending. The pintail up-ends also, but breeds further north than the mallard and is mainly a winter visitor to our marshes.

The teal is the smallest of the British ducks and feeds almost entirely at the surface. Teal often form dense flocks that wheel high in the sky in tight formation before flying down to their favoured marsh. The shoveler has a unique feeding system built into its large spatulate bill which it uses to sieve tiny food particles from shallow water and mud. The size of the bill helps to identify the bird in flight.

Wigeon are surface-feeders that have forsaken the marsh to graze on damp meadows in the same way as geese. As their feeding is so goose-like, they tend to occupy the same areas as their larger cousins. Like geese they often form huge flocks and need a safe roosting place within range of a plentiful food supply. Such roosts are often on the coast or by the banks of rivers and lakes.

Garganey are small, graceful ducks with discreetly coloured plumage. They leave Britain and Ireland during the winter, and thus compete with other ducks only during the breeding season in southern England.

The gadwall was introduced into Britain following the capture of a pair of vagrants in 1850. It has since spread but is not numerous, except at Minsmere in Suffolk. The dull

Eider eggs are laid in a nest of grass and seaweed lined with down plucked from the duck's own breast. The ducklings usually emerge within 30 days and are led to the sea by their mother

plumage of the male is quite varied when seen at close quarters. The mandarin duck is also an import that has spread to breed in Surrey and Berkshire. It is restricted to lakes and ponds in wooded country and is not likely to become very widespread.

Several species of duck occur as migrants, vagrants or as escapers from captivity. These include a regular number of wild redcrested pochard in East Anglia; ruddy shelduck which breed in Gloucestershire, following their escape from the Wildfowl Trust's collection at Slimbridge; blue-winged teal, American wigeon, black duck, ring-necked duck, bufflehead and hooded merganser that are vagrants in variable numbers from across the Atlantic; and the ferruginous duck which is an irregular winter visitor from the Mediterranean.

HOW A DUCK LANDS AND TAKES OFF

Going down! The pochard, like other ducks, comes in low over the water, then splashes down, using its webbed feet as brakes and its wings to 'back-pedal' and reduce speed

Going up! The object is to get air moving over the wings to produce 'lift'. This is achieved by pattering over the water and flapping the wings until the duck gains sufficient momentum to fly into the on-coming airstream or be thrown up by a collision with a wave

Duckweed *Lemna minor*

Thousands of individual duckweed plants form green carpets on pond surfaces, and are eaten by ducks and fish. Each plant consists of a tiny flat, round, leaf-like structure called a thallus with a single hanging, root on the underside. It spreads by each thallus producing buds which break off, increase in size and produce buds in their turn. A pond or ditch is rapidly covered.

It rarely flowers, and then only in shallow water or on drying mud fully exposed to the sun. The flowers are minute, borne in a pocket on the margin of the thallus.

Duke of Burgundy fritillary

Hamearis lucina

Despite its name, this butterfly is not related to the other butterflies called fritillaries. It is the only European representative of a family of tropical butterflies. It lives in woods where primroses and cowslips grow. The slug-like caterpillars feed on these plants and grow quickly, being ready to enter their pupa or resting stage in two months. This lasts for ten months, the newly hatched butterflies appearing in May and June. These are small with a 1 in. wingspan and fly for about a month. Males are dark brown with tawny spots; females slightly paler.

It is a butterfly widespread in the south of England but rare elsewhere.

Duke of Burgundy fritillaries fly to any flower but lay eggs only on cowslips and primroses

Dulse see Seaweed
Dun see Mayfly

Dune

The action of wind, sand and vegetation combine to form dunes or small hills of sand behind broad beaches. Dunes may be more than 50 ft high, with a gentle incline towards the prevailing wind and a steep slope away from the wind. They are built up by dry sand being blown by the wind until it is checked by vegetation, principally marram grass, which has a web of creeping roots that trap the sand. In some places, when the vegetation dies, the wind scoops out hollows. A dune can be formed from a very small nucleus, as fresh grains are blown from the windward side and accumulate in the lee.

There are extensive dunes on many parts of the British coast. Among the most spectacular are the Culbin Sands on the Moray Firth in Scotland, which reach 100 ft in height. A few old dunes are found inland on sandy heaths such as those of the Norfolk and Suffolk Brecklands. But these are now covered in vegetation and the sand can no longer move. See also GRASS

Dung beetle

A cow produces 7 tons of dung a year and this is a rich source of food for many plants and animals, including a number of species of beetle. A typical dung beetle is the common dor beetle which gets its name 'dor' from an Old English word meaning drone, as it has a loud humming flight when it takes to the air on summer evenings. It is black with very broad legs with which the female digs numerous short galleries in the soil beneath a cowpat. Each gallery is provided with a large sausage of dung on which an egg is laid. The dung provides food for the larvae when they hatch. Dor beetles are important in breaking down dung and incorporating it in the soil. The common dor beetle is also called the lousy watchman, as it is often infested with large numbers of parasitic mites.

Other dung beetles have similar habits. The minotaur beetle uses rabbit droppings. Beetles belonging to a genus called Aphodius, of which there are over 40 species, lay eggs in the dung itself, although the larvae enter their pupa or resting stage in the ground. Two of the most common are *A. fimetarius* and *A. rufipes,* which use the dung of horses, cattle and sheep.

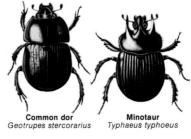

Common dor
Geotrupes stercorarius

Minotaur
Typhaeus typhoeus

Red-legged aphodius
Aphodius rufipes

Dung aphodius
Aphodius fimetarius

Dung beetles are well equipped for digging, with robust bodies and tough spiny legs

Mating dung flies: their larvae help to re-cycle dung back into the soil

Dung fly *Scatophaga stercoraria*

Large numbers of these bright yellow, rather furry flies gather round cowpats in spring and summer. The females are smaller and grey-green, and there is usually a flurry of activity when one joins the males. After mating, she lays her eggs in the cowpat. These hatch into grubs which feed on the dung until they enter their pupa or resting stage in the soil beneath. The grubs thus play an important part in aiding the rapid breakdown of the cowpat, and its incorporation into the soil. The adults feed on nectar and insects, including other dung flies.

Dunlin see Sandpiper

Dunnock *Prunella modularis*

This bird often looks more like a rodent as it feeds on the ground with its head well down and only its dull brown upper plumage showing. Although it is known as the hedge sparrow, the dunnock is not a sparrow at all. It has the typical sharp, thin bill of an insect eater as distinct from the stout bill of the seed-eating house sparrow. However, it survives the winter largely on small seeds, when the insects it picks from leaf litter and bushes in summer are not available.

No one knows why the dunnock is so often the victim of cuckoos. Its four or five blue eggs are rarely matched by the eggs laid by the cuckoo. Two clutches are laid each season in a grass cup, usually low down in the bush. Numerous and tame in gardens and parks everywhere, dunnocks are also common in open woodland and hedgerows. A recent census by the British Trust for Ornithology estimated that there are two dunnocks to the acre on farmland in England.

The high, piping song of the dunnock can be heard throughout most of the year. Sometimes it can even be heard at night, for the dunnock sings if woken.

Dust

Particles of dust from a variety of sources such as volcanoes, forest fires, domestic and industrial smoke, or picked up from the earth's surface by wind, are always present in the air. Dust may be carried for thousands of miles, high in the atmosphere, before being brought down by descending currents of air and by rain: sometimes the dust-laden rain leaves a red stain and is called 'blood rain'. A famous dust fall of this type occurred on July 1, 1968, when about a million tons of fine sand, probably from North Africa, was deposited over many parts of England and Wales, having been carried northwards for more than 2000 miles.

Dust whirls, revolving cones of dust, often with a dust-free centre and on rare occasions rising to 10 ft high or more, move across flat land such as the fens on very hot, dry summer days. Dust whirls also occur on a smaller scale over hot city pavements. In both cases the dust or dry soil is lifted by strong rotating currents of hot air.

Dusty miller *Cerastium tomentosum*

The starry white flowers and grey leaves of this low-growing plant have earned it the alternative name of snow-in-summer. It roots where its branches touch the earth and spreads rapidly, swamping other smaller plants. Often planted in rock gardens, it has spread to hedgerows here and there in the British Isles.

Dusty miller also grows wild on limestone rocks in parts of Italy and Sicily.

Dense patches of white flowers explain dusty miller's alternative name, snow-in-summer

Dutch elm disease see Elm

Dwarf cornel *Cornus suecica*

Clusters of small red berries, said to stimulate the appetite, give dwarf cornel its Gaelic name *lus-a-chraois,* plant of gluttony. It carpets the ground under heather and bilberry for large areas with tiny black-purple flowers and white petal-like leaflets, but is found only in mountainous areas in Scotland and a few places in northern England. It flowers during July and August.

Dwarf cornel has stalkless, egg-shaped leaves and creeping underground roots which produce new stems, 2-8 in. high, every year.

Dyer's greenweed *Genista tinctoria*

Flemish immigrants first used this once important dye plant in the 14th century. It was used to obtain Kendal Green, a colour developed in Kendal, Westmorland. Dyer's greenweed, or woadwax, dyes cloth a bright yellow which changes to green when dipped in a solution of blue woad. Today, this small shrub, rarely growing more than 2 ft high, with stiff angular branches and sprays of yellow flowers, grows wild on rough grassland throughout England, Wales and southern Scotland.

Dyer's greenweed was once cultivated to make a dye called Kendal Green

Devil's Dyke, Cambridgeshire, 7½ miles long. It was probably built in late Roman or early Saxon times

Dyke

There are two types of dyke: one natural, the other man-made. Natural dykes were formed when molten rock was forced vertically through faults in layers of older rocks. They can be seen along the coast of north-west Scotland and on the North Yorkshire moors where the Cleveland dyke can be traced for many miles.

Offa's Dyke is an example of a man-made dyke. It consists of an earthwork or wall with a ditch, and was built in the 8th century by command of the Saxon King Offa of Mercia as a frontier between his kingdom and Wales. Not all dykes were built as protective frontiers—the pre-Roman Grim's Dyke in Dorset appears to have been used simply to confine grazing animals.

HOW DYKES ARE FORMED

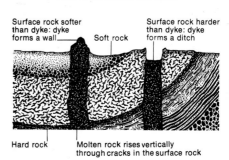

Surface rock softer than dyke: dyke forms a wall

Soft rock

Surface rock harder than dyke: dyke forms a ditch

Hard rock

Molten rock rises vertically through cracks in the surface rock

Natural dykes are cooled molten rock, forming a wall or ditch, depending on whether they are harder or softer than the surrounding rocks

E

Predator and carrion-eater – a golden eagle tears at the fox's carcass with its strong hooked bill

Eagle, Golden *Aquila chrysaetos*

With a wingspan of 7 ft, the golden eagle is a magnificent sight as it soars across the Highland skies, gliding swiftly, with wings angled back, over a crag to its eyrie, or nest. It can be seen all year in the Scottish Highlands, where less than 200 pairs breed. Apart from one pair which have nested in the English Lake District since 1970, and a pair based in Northern Ireland but which hunt 18 miles away, in Scotland, golden eagles are rarely seen outside Scotland.

The birds are identified by their sheer size and by their broad wings, short broad tails and strong, projecting heads, which prevent confusion with buzzards, the only other large British birds of prey. Males grow to 30 in. long, and females are about 5 in. longer. Both sexes are almost uniformly dark brown with a golden-tinged head and heavy bill. They feed on grouse, blue hares and ptarmigan, which they hunt by gliding alertly over the mountain slopes; they also eat carrion, including dead sheep and lambs.

Golden eagles pair for life. They usually have two or three eyries, used in rotation, built on high mountain ledges or in pine trees growing at high altitudes. The same eyries are used year after year and consist of ever-increasing masses of branches which are decorated with fresh greenery. Both sexes make or repair the eyries in November or December, and two white eggs are laid in March or April. The incubation period is about 40 days. Usually only one eaglet is reared. The weaker of the pair is ousted by the stronger, which is fed by both parents until leaving the nest after 12 weeks.

The golden eagle has been the only eagle to breed in Britain since the white-tailed sea-eagle was finally exterminated in Scotland during the First World War. The greatest danger to the golden eagle is not shooting but its own eating of sheep that have been dipped in pesticides.

Early brown see Stonefly
Earthnut see Pignut

Earth star

A fungus which resembles a puff ball when it first breaks through the soil. Within a day or two the outer skin splits at the top and folds back into star-like rays, to expose the central spore sac. The rays close when dry and unfurl when wet.

Of the seven British species, the two most common, both found in woods, are *Geastrum rufescens*, which appears between July and November, and *G. triplex,* which grows between August and October. Both are pale brown on the outside, but the rays of *G. rufescens* are yellow-brown inside, those of *G. triplex* flesh-coloured. See also FUNGUS

Earthwork

A bank or mound, often used for fortification, and usually consisting of soil and stones which have become grassed over. Examples are the circular embankments around the sites of early settlements, and the straight embankments marking territorial boundaries.

Earthworks date back 3000 years, to the time of Neolithic man, and have been produced by every age since. Some mine workings closed at the beginning of this century have become covered with grass and resemble ancient earthworks.

The 130 ft high Silbury Hill in Wiltshire, which occupies 5 acres, is the largest earthwork in Europe. Excavations have shown it to be pre-Roman, but its purpose is unknown.

Earthworm

Up to 3 million earthworms are estimated to live in every acre of grassland. Deciduous woodland may contain even more.

The 8-in. common earthworm *Lumbricus terrestris* is the best known species but there are 24 others, of which ten are common. Earthworms have segmented bodies and no legs or distinct head. The common earthworm lives in a deep, permanent burrow 3-4 ft deep, but other species have shallow, temporary ones. All earthworms move through soil in the same way. They anchor the rear of the body with hooked hairs that grow on each segment, force the pointed front of the body through soil crevices, then anchor it and draw the rear after it. When soil is compact, they eat their way through, swallowing the soil as they go.

The soil and organic matter eaten by worms are eventually deposited as casts, either in the burrows or on the surface. The earthworms act as ploughs, continually churning the soil over, mixing, sifting and aerating it, all of which is beneficial to the land. Charles Darwin estimated that earthworms brought 8-18 tons of soil annually to the surface of an acre of land.

Earthworms are sensitive to vibration, and stamping will often bring them out of their burrows. On damp nights some species leave their burrows to search for leaves or decaying matter which they pull back to their burrows to eat. Large numbers of worms are seen on soil and roads after heavy rain at night—hence the old tale that worms fall with rain. In extreme heat or cold, the earthworm will coil up in a tight knot in a chamber at the end of its burrow.

Each worm has male and female organs. Sexually mature worms have a saddle-shaped unsegmented bulge called a clitellum. Earthworms mate at night or in the early morning, usually in damp weather, on the soil surface or in their burrows. They lie head to tail with their sexual organs close together, clasping each other with hooked hairs which line the undersides of their bodies. After separation the clitellum of each worm slides along its body, collecting the eggs and sperm from the appropriate sexual openings,

and finally slipping over the head of the worm. Then the ends of the clitellum seal themselves to form a cocoon containing up to 20 fertilised eggs. Small worms hatch from the eggs one to five months later. They mature at 8-18 months and can live for ten years.

The popular notion that if an earthworm is cut in half it will grow into two worms is false. But if only a short length is severed, a new head or tail can be grown. Moles collect worms, bite their heads off and store their bodies to eat when hungry. Other earthworm enemies, besides birds, are badgers, hedgehogs, beetles, centipedes and slugs.

Earwig

The only basis for the belief that the common earwig *Forficula auricularia* likes to crawl into human ears is that it is always hiding in small crevices.

Earwigs are sinuous, brown, winged insects about ½ in. long, easily recognized by a pair of forceps at the end of the body; these are curved on males, straight on females. They are opened and raised when the earwig is alarmed but it is not known whether they inflict damage upon enemies. Common earwigs rarely fly, but some of the nine

smaller species such as the lesser earwig *Labia minor* do fly.

Earwigs mate in the autumn, and the females lay their 20-80 eggs under a stone or in a hollow in the soil; they guard them and lick them during the winter to stop mould growing. The eggs hatch in the spring, and the young disperse in June.

Earwigs feed on carrion, leaves and roots and are found throughout the British Isles.

Eel-grass

The once-extensive meadows of these sea-flowering plants were markedly reduced in the early 1930's by a disease thought to have originated in America. This caused a large reduction in the flocks of ducks, geese and swans dependent on eel-grass, and the collapse of an industry which used its dried, grass-like leaves to stuff mattresses and furniture. There are three British species; *Zostera marina* is the most important. Eel-grasses occur in estuaries and are the only flowering plants that grow in the sea, on sandy-muddy shores from about neap-tide level downwards. The tiny, single-sexed flowers appear between June and September. Pioneer plants for salt-marsh formation, eel-grasses or grass wracks accelerate the trapping of silt and the stabilisation of the mud.

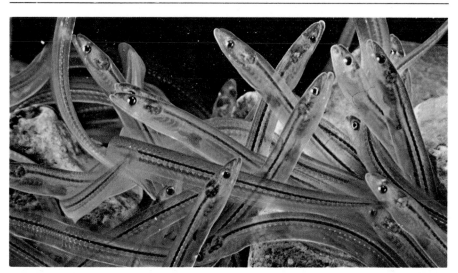

Transparent leptocephalus larvae hatch from the eel egg and drift with the ocean currents

Eel *Anguilla anguilla*
The spawning ground of the eel is believed to be near the Sargasso Sea. It is known that sexually mature adults set off across the Atlantic, apparently to spawn and die, but none has been caught in the ocean. Their transparent, leaf-like larvae are carried by currents to coastal waters, where they change into 3-in. elvers and eventually find their way into virtually all British rivers and most still waters. Many rivers too polluted for other fish contain eels, and they are also plentiful in estuaries and around the sea

coast. Eels can live out of water and they may travel overland for short distances in the autumn when the ground is wet, breathing aerated water carried in their gills.

Females may be about 36 in. long, with a maximum of 60 in., while males normally reach 12 in., often growing to 20 in. Their normal dark grey or green-brown colour with yellow undersides turns to silvery-grey when they reach sexual maturity and are ready to migrate. Their diet consists of insects, snails, worms, crayfish, frogs, fish and small rodents.

HOW THE EARTHWORM MOVES

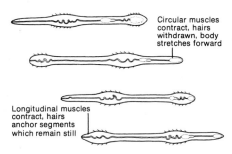

Circular muscles contract, hairs withdrawn, body stretches forward

Longitudinal muscles contract, hairs anchor segments which remain still

The earthworm moves its body a bit at a time, swelling some parts to anchor them and thinning the others to stretch or pull them forward

Eelpout *Zoarces viviparus*

One of the few British fish to give birth to live young, the eelpout or viviparous blenny is seldom seen because of its habit of hiding under stones or burying itself in mud. An eel-like fish, about 18 in. long, it is usually coloured olive-brown with a yellowish belly. Its eggs are fertilised internally and develop within the mother's body; she eventually gives birth to young about 1½ in. long and perfect miniatures of the parents. However, there is no placenta or cord connecting the mother with the young, as is found in mammals. The eelpout can be found in shore pools and under rocks along the east coasts of England and Scotland, and sometimes on the Scottish west coast, particularly towards the north. See also BURBOT

Eelworm see Roundworm
Egret see Heron
Eider see Duck

Eggar moth

Adult eggar moths have no proper mouths —they are unnecessary since the moths do not feed during their one to three weeks of active life. There are ten British species, named for the egg-shaped marks which some, such as the oak eggar *Lasiocampa quercus*, carry on their forewings.

In summer, the large, hairy caterpillars of the oak eggar feed on shrubs, fruit trees, bramble and heather, but their life cycle varies in different parts of the country. In the south, the grey eggs are laid in summer, hatch, and the young caterpillars hibernate, completing their growth the following year and reaching the moth stage in July or August. In the north, where the caterpillars are common on heather moors, the pupa, or resting stage, survives the winter before hatching in May or June. The young caterpillars also hibernate, so the life cycle lasts two years. The male moths are a darker brown and smaller than the females.

The caterpillars of the drinker moth *Philudoria potatoria* feed on long grass in damp surroundings. They like to drink dew and raindrops. The moths fly by night in July, and are attracted to artificial light. By day they rest, their colour aiding their disguise as dead leaves. This camouflage is even more effectively adopted by the lappet moth *Gastropacha quercifolia* whose wing outline and habit of resting with the hindwings forward adds to the resemblance. The caterpillar has lappets of skin hiding its legs, and resembles a bulge on the twig of its food plant, usually the blackthorn.

Of the smaller species, the lackey moth *Malacosoma neustria* is the most common. It flies by night in July and August throughout England and Wales, as far north as Lancashire and Yorkshire. On rare occasions it also occurs in Scotland and Northern Ireland. The name refers to the red, white and blue striped 'livery' of the caterpillar, also called the coronation caterpillar since 1953, when it was common in parts of London. The caterpillars hatch from overwintered eggs and live as a group on fruit trees, hawthorn and blackthorn bushes.

The colouring and configuration of the lappet moth at rest enable it to merge with a background of dead leaves in the daytime. During June, July and August they may be seen flying rapidly at night, especially near the edge of woods or alongside hedgerows in open country

Elder *Sambucus nigra*

The only tree which rabbits find distasteful, elder thrives on rabbit warrens and any soil rich in nitrogen from the dung of beasts or bird droppings. It can be found around badger setts or forming shrubberies below tall trees used as roosts by starlings, pigeons and other birds. Elder is mainly spread by birds, which scatter its berries or swallow them whole, later voiding the tough seeds.

The leaves, set in pairs, are composed of five or more tooth-edged leaflets. They grow on stout twigs; these hold a thick, white pith. This pith is easily hollowed out to make peashooters or whistles. Elder gets it name from an Anglo-Saxon word meaning 'hollow tree'. Older stems develop hard, white wood, used by watchmakers to make fine prickers for cleaning mechanical parts, and also for carving combs and chessmen.

In June, the elder has showy clusters of creamy-white flowers with a heavy, fruity fragrance. The flowers are used to make elder tea, and add a musky flavour to pies. By September the branches become heavy with bunches of lustrous black juicy fruits. Insipid when raw, they make a distinctively flavoured wine and are also used in pies and jellies.

Elder rarely exceeds 20 ft in height or 1 ft in diameter. Its yellowish-grey bark, thick and soft, is used by badgers to scratch their claws clean. Elder shoots are short-lived, but the tree produces a continuous succession of new shoots.

Elder, Dwarf *Sambucus ebulus*

Wherever the blood of Danes has been spilt, there grows danewort, runs an old legend. Danewort is another name for dwarf elder, which is usually found in hedgerows, churchyards and near old ruins, and was probably introduced from the Continent and cultivated to make a black dye.

Dwarf elder is a luxuriant herb with a creeping underground system which produces new pithy stems up to 5 ft high every year. In midsummer, a little later than common elder, it produces large flat clusters of white or pink flowers with purple, vanilla-scented anthers. The black berries which appear in autumn have a strong purgative effect and are slightly poisonous. In spite of its size, it is closely related to the elder tree.

Elecampane *Inula helenium*

A rare plant, scattered through the British Isles in hedgerows and copses and near old gardens where it was once cultivated, elecampane was formerly prized for medicinal purposes. It grows up to 5 ft high and has fairly large yellow 'sunflowers' with finely toothed leaves, the upper ones clasping the stem. The aromatic rootstock was used as a tonic, and to treat coughs and snake bites. In Elizabethan times the roots were candied as sweetmeats.

It was probably introduced from the Continent by the Anglo-Saxons.

Elm trees in a Hertfordshire landscape, with their complement of sucker shoots at the base

Elm

The elm trees that beautify the lowland hedgerows of the Midlands and southern England are there due to the foresight and enthusiasm of 18th-century landowners. When the open fields were enclosed with hawthorn hedges, the landowners insisted that their tenant farmers planted elms at intervals, to provide timber and to improve the landscape.

The timber belonged to the landlords and, as the trees were felled, they replaced them with elm saplings raised from cuttings on the estate or in a nursery. The result was that all the elms on a particular estate or district looked much alike, but differed from those on a neighbouring estate.

These varied forms of English elm *Ulmus procera* are grouped as field elms, because they are usually growing in hedgerows between fields. Botanists have been puzzled by the origins of these various forms, which are all probably derived from the native Wych elm or Scots elm *U. glabra,* and certain continental elms which spread to Britain before the land bridge with Europe was breached about 8000 years ago.

Other elms found in Britain are the smooth-leaved elm *U. carpinifolia,* which has several narrow-crowned varieties (the Cornish Wheatley and Jersey elms) and the Dutch elm *U. × hollandica* (a hybrid between the Scots elm and smooth-leaved elm).

The Scots elm is more common in the north and in Scotland. It sprouts readily from seed and forms woods on valley sides. It has larger leaves than other elms, often 4 in. long, and its short trunk has wide, spreading branches. All elms bear oval leaves with toothed edges and pointed tips, and in most forms the surface is rough to the touch. The leaves are lop-sided, with one side always larger than the other. In winter, the rounded buds develop on alternate sides of the twigs.

Elms flower in February or March before their leaves open. Massed clusters of flowers show as a reddish purple haze on bare twigs. They have neither petals nor nectar to attract insects, and pollination is by the wind. The fruits ripen quickly and in May fruit clusters —which many people mistake for flowers— appear, showing above the foliage. Each small, pale brown seed is surrounded by a thin oval wing to ensure wind dispersal.

Field elms are rarely found growing wild, as few seeds are fertile. They reproduce mainly by sucker shoots that spring up vigorously from their roots—especially after a tall parent tree is cut down. In hedges, these shoots are protected and form trees. Those that come up in the fields are destroyed by ploughing or bitten back by sheep or cows, which relish elm foliage.

Elms grow rapidly and can reach a height of 120 ft in 100 years. They produce a distinctive timber, with deep brown heartwood and a thin, pale brown sapwood zone.

The wood is strong and tough but durable only if kept continually dry or continually wet. A peculiar feature is the irregular arrangement of pores and fibres through each annual ring, which results in a beautiful dappled 'partridge breast' figure on skilfully sawn surfaces. It also makes the wood almost impossible to split. These pro-perties, together with the availability of large planks from tall trees, have led to the development of a wide range of uses for elm timber.

Broad planks, often with an irregular, wavy edge, are used for sides of barns and outdoor rustic furniture. Selected timber is used for coffins and for high-quality furniture. Chair seats are often of elm, as it does not split when the legs are driven home; the hubs of wooden wheels are also elm, as it holds together when spokes are forced in.

In early water engineering, elm was used for pipes, whole trunks being bored out and driven together, with the ends suitably tapered, to make water mains. Village pumps were also of elm, right down to moving parts and valves. It is also a fine carver's wood.

Elm has a bad name as a dangerous tree, prone to disease. This is partly because it grows to large sizes in situations, like roadsides, where a fallen tree can cause serious damage. Even sound trees are apt to shed large branches in summer, or to collapse through root-hold failure during a gale.

Dutch elm disease, which is carried from tree to tree by two species of ambrosia beetle, *Scolytus destructor* and *S. multistriatus,* first appeared in Britain in 1930, and there were major outbreaks in 1970, 1971 and 1972.

The beetle burrows into the tree, spreading a fungus which destroys the veining in the layer of wood immediately underneath the

TYPICAL ELM LEAVES

English
Lower surface hairy

Smooth-leaved
Small, smooth and oval

Wych
Both surfaces rough

Leaf texture is a guide to the identification of these three typical elms

Elms were planted in hedgerows by landowners to provide timber and improve the landscape

bark on which the tree relies for the circulation of its sap.

A survey of 23 million trees in southern England and South Wales at the end of 1972 showed that nearly 1½ million of them were dead or dying as a result of the disease. Another 1½ million had a slight to moderate infection. English elm seems to have been affected more than the other species, and trees in the open countryside were more badly affected than those in woodland.

Little groups of dead branches and twigs are usually an indication that an elm is suffering from the disease. Often a tree will survive a small attack, but in cases where half the crown or more is dead it is likely that the whole tree will eventually die. It is easiest to spot diseased trees when the leaves are out. From June to September, newly infected trees can be identified by the dying foliage. The leaves on infected branches turn yellow, then brown, and wither as if the season were autumn while the rest of the foliage remains green. Twigs of infected young shoots show a 'shepherd's crook' bend in their tips, and channels can be seen where the beetles have eaten the bark in the angles between twigs. A twig cut across the grain will show a brown stain in the current—that is, the outer—annual ring.

Dutch botanists are hoping to produce varieties of elm resistant to the disease, and at Basildon, in Essex, horticulturists are experimenting with a gnat-like wasp which feeds on the beetle.

All elms provide feeding grounds for a large number of insects, including the larvae of the whiteletter hairstreak, comma and large tortoiseshell butterflies. Birds such as stock doves, kestrels and jackdaws are attracted to old elms in the nesting season. See also AMBROSIA BEETLE, BARK BEETLE

Elver see Eel

Common emerald moth
Hemithea aestivaria
1½ size

Emerald moth

Green is a common colour for caterpillars, but few butterflies or moths produce a green pigment in the scales covering their wings. Several butterflies, such as the green-veined white, fake green with black dots on a yellow background as part of their camouflage. Emerald moths, however, produce a true green pigment. The newly emerged moth is a beautiful green shade, but this fades fairly rapidly to a greyish-green colour. The long green caterpillar, which walks in a looping manner, has a wide gap between its six legs and the pair of claspers at the end of its body.

Common emerald, one of seven related species, is found in all parts of the British Isles except Scotland. The caterpillar feeds on low-growing plants in autumn and on various tree and shrub leaves after hibernation. It pupates in May or June, the moth hatching in late June or July.

Enchanter's nightshade
Circaea lutetiana

Its Latin name refers to the witch Circe who turned Ulysses' crew into pigs, and its English name has a similar magical connotation, but enchanter's nightshade has no dark properties attributed to it in English folklore. It grows in dark, shady places such as glades in woods—a tall, slender plant with pairs of long-stalked, pointed oval leaves and spikes of small pink or white flowers, each with only two deeply notched petals from June to August. It has little

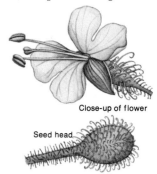

Close-up of flower

Seed head

Enchanter's nightshade is not related to deadly nightshade and is not poisonous

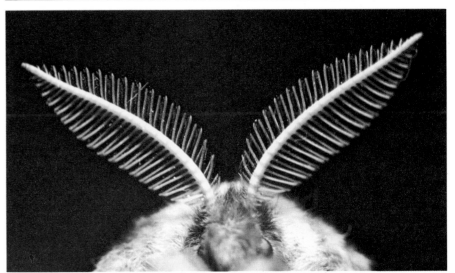

The male emperor moth uses its feathery antennae to detect the scent emitted by the female

Emperor moth *Saturnia pavonia*

The feathery antennae of the male emperor moth can detect the scent of a virgin female half a mile away. It flies by day in April and May over heather and bramble, its grey colouring and tawny hindwings made distinctive by prominent eye-spots. The female, a lighter grey all over, also has eye-spots on her wings and is slightly larger, with a 3 in. wingspan. After mating, she flies by night to lay olive-brown eggs on heather and bramble. The fat green caterpillars

ringed with black and yellow spots feed in summer. In spite of their size and colour, they are not easy to spot on heather.

The emperors are the only British species of the silk-yielding Saturnidae family, but their silk is of no commercial value. The caterpillar spins its coarse brown silk cocoon in August, and develops inside it. The cocoon's exit is like a lobster pot in reverse: a ring of spines allows the moth to escape, but prevents anything entering to eat it during its resting stage.

egg-shaped seeds covered with hooked, stiff bristles which cling to clothes and to the fur of animals, and creeping underground roots which make it difficult to eradicate from a shrubbery if it gets established. It grows throughout the British Isles, although it is rare in northern Scotland.

Enclosure roads

One of the side-effects of the 18th and 19th-century enclosure movement was that, together with the enclosure of fields, went the cutting off of many tracks and paths which had run between them and connected village to village.

But in making the enclosures, parliament provided for new roads and these are the enclosure roads. Laid out among the neat pattern of newly enclosed fields, they often ran straight for mile upon mile. They are quite wide—a minimum width of 40 ft was usually stipulated—because they were usually unsurfaced and room was needed to detour round bad patches.

Enclosure roads became the feeders to the main turnpike system, which was introduced in the second half of the 18th century, but most of them remained unsurfaced until late in the 19th century. See also FARMING, FIELD

Ergot

A disease of cereals and grasses produced by the fungus *Claviceps purpurea*. Rye is the most susceptible cereal, oats the least.

Ergots are purple-black bodies, up to 2 in. long, which develop on the seed-heads in summer. These fall to the ground in autumn and germinate into drumstick-shaped, spore-producing bodies in spring. The spores infect the cereal or grass flowers, causing them to exude a sticky honeydew and then form new ergots.

Ergots are poisonous, and infected rye flour caused many deaths in the Middle Ages. Today grain is thoroughly cleaned before it is milled. However, ergot still causes dry gangrene in cattle.

Ermine see Stoat

Ermine moth

These close relatives of the tiger moth have light-coloured wings speckled with black, hence their name. The two most common species are the white *Spilosoma lubricipeda* and buff ermine *S. lutea*. Both emerge in June from chrysalids which have spent the winter in a cocoon, sown up among vegetation or leaf litter. The white ermine caterpillar has almost black fur with an orange line running down its back, while the furry buff ermine caterpillar is greyish-brown. They are full grown in late summer. Just before they spin their cocoons, they feel the urge to migrate away from the dock and dandelion leaves on which they have been feeding. Caterpillars on the march across a road are a common sight in September.

White wings speckled with black that resemble ermine give the white ermine moth its name

Water ermine *S. urticae* is similar to white ermine, but is restricted to marshy surroundings in the south. All three moths fly at night during May to July.

Erosion

The slow but relentless attack of frost, rain and rivers on the landscape is called erosion. This attack, unnoticed from day to day but of great effect over long periods of geological time, has shaped the scenery of the British Isles. In general, more resistant rocks form hills and uplands, while the more easily eroded and weaker rocks form the lowlands. Along sea coasts erosion works at a faster rate. The constant tendency is for material to be removed from higher ground and transported towards, and eventually into, the sea, thus lowering the land level.

Material can be removed as solid grains suspended in water, ice or wind, rolled along a river bed, or dissolved and carried away in solution. An average of rather more than 1 in. is removed every 1000 years, but in steep mountains the rate of erosion may be 20 times higher.

Erratics

During the Ice Age glaciers moved across most of the British Isles, reaching as far south as the Bristol Channel and the Thames. These glaciers carried large amounts of rock, which was left behind when they melted. As a result, rocks from Scandinavia and Scotland can be found in England. These are known as erratics. They are usually small stones, although a few are larger and better known. Masses of chalk several hundred feet long found in the Norfolk cliffs at West Runton are erratics. Some erratics are very distinctive and trace

the route of the ice very accurately, such as the blue-flecked rock from Ailsa Craig in the Firth of Clyde, which is found in many parts of Lancashire and Cheshire.

Escarpment see Scarp
Estuary see p. 154

Evening primrose *Oenothera biennis*

The yellow flowers of the evening primrose are often more than 2 in. in diameter. Introduced as a garden flower from North America, it has spread widely in England, Wales and southern Scotland, especially on sand dunes and waste places.

Evening primrose is more closely related to the willowherb than to the primrose family. It grows 2-3 ft tall and has fragrant flowers which open on summer evenings and are pollinated by night-flying moths.

Evening primrose flowers open on summer evenings when they are pollinated by moths

Evolution see p. 156

Eyebright *Euphrasia officinalis*

A powder for brightening the eyes was prepared by herbalists in the Middle Ages from this plant—hence its name. Its Latin name *Euphrasia* is derived from the Greek words meaning 'to see well'.

More than 20 species occur throughout the British Isles in heath and grassland, especially near the sea, varying in height from 1 in. to 12 in. The flowers are white or violet, streaked with purple, and appear from May to September in clusters near the ends of stems. Eyebright is a semi-parasite, growing successfully only when its roots attach themselves to plants such as clovers and plantains.

Close-up of flower

Eyebright's tiny, lipped flowers grow in clusters. They bloom from May to September.

Estuaries — where two worlds of water meet

An estuary is a meeting place, where the fresh water of a river joins the salt water of the sea. There, sediment carried in the river water builds mudbanks which are alternately covered and uncovered by the tides. Living in the mudbanks are great concentrations of lugworms, ragworms, crustaceans, molluscs and other animals. Many of these feed on minute particles of organic matter that are brought down by the river. These animals are in turn eaten by birds, which feed in great flocks on the mudbanks, especially those of the Dee, Camel, Solway, Tay and Severn estuaries. Waders, such as godwits and knots, which have long legs and long beaks, are especially fitted for feeding on mudbanks. Black-headed gulls often breed in large colonies on saltings; common terns nest on shingle and assemble in flocks in the autumn; and oystercatchers are usually present, as are geese.

In the estuary itself the water is layered; fresh water at the surface, flowing seawards, heavier salt water at the bottom, which flows upstream with the tides, and between them brackish water — a mixture of river water and sea water — moving in either direction according to the ebb and flow of the tide. Thus freshwater creatures live at the surface of an estuary and sea creatures at the bottom. Few species can withstand the continual changes in salt content of brackish water, as the tides ebb and flow twice daily. Those that can include shore crabs, lugworms, ragworms, grey mullet, three-spined sticklebacks, flounders, gobies, bass, spire shells and some sea anemones, prawns and shrimps.

Some animals are migrants, moving up or down estuaries. Salmon, sea lampreys and sea trout swim up-river to spawn, and the young fish move down to the sea to feed. Eels move in the opposite direction: young eels, or elvers, swim up-river to feed and mature in fresh water, then return to the sea to spawn. In the Severn estuary, elvers are caught in large numbers and exported live to stock continental lakes.

Near the sea the estuary shores consist of saltings or salt marshes. Here, in the shallows, sea and river water are mixed rather than layered. The plants which grow there have long roots or underground stems, which not only anchor them

The deep estuary of the River Fal, Cornwall, where the ebb and flow of the tide

but help to stabilise the shifting sand and mud. The plants also help to build up the level of the land: their stems trap pieces of seaweed and other debris, which in turn trap mud and silt. Among the most common salt-marsh plants are seablite, sea poa grass, sea aster, cord-grass and sea purslane. These provide excellent grazing for cattle and sheep. In many parts of East Anglia the sites of estuaries from which the sea has retreated and the salt has been washed away by the rain have been claimed for farming.

Fennel pondweed and horned pondweed grow in the brackish water of the salt marsh, together with common reed, yellow flag, sea club-rush, hastate orache, broad-leaved willow-herb and large bindweed.

All Britain's major ports are situated on estuaries, and many of the older industries were similarly sited to take advantage of sea transport. Consequently estuaries are often heavily polluted. New threats to estuaries include the proposed third London airport at Foulness in Essex and atomic power stations, such as those at Hinckley Point on the Severn, and at Chapelcron on the Solway Firth, which discharge huge volumes of hot water.

Suggestions have been made that barrages should be built across a number of estuaries to turn them into reservoirs for the supply of water to towns. The water would be treated in desalination plants to make it fit for drinking. The four sites most favoured for such schemes are the Solway Firth, Morecambe Bay, the Dee estuary, and The Wash. There is criticism of the proposals by some naturalists who see in them a threat to wildlife. The most important factor affecting the life of an estuary is the ebb and flow of the tide, and a barrage would eliminate this. Moreover, if the mudbanks were always under water many birds would not be able to find their food in estuaries.

LIFE IN THE CHANGING WATERS

River water flows seawards

Roach

Bream

3-spined stickleback

Brackish prawn

Ragworm   Shore crab

Flounder

Brackish water flows in either direction

Grey mullet

Shrimp

Mussel

Limpet

Sea water flows upstream

Mudbank formed mainly of river sediment

Where a river enters the sea is a region of mixed fresh and salt water. Animals living in this brackish estuarine water must be able to survive the constantly changing salinity brought about by the movement of the tides

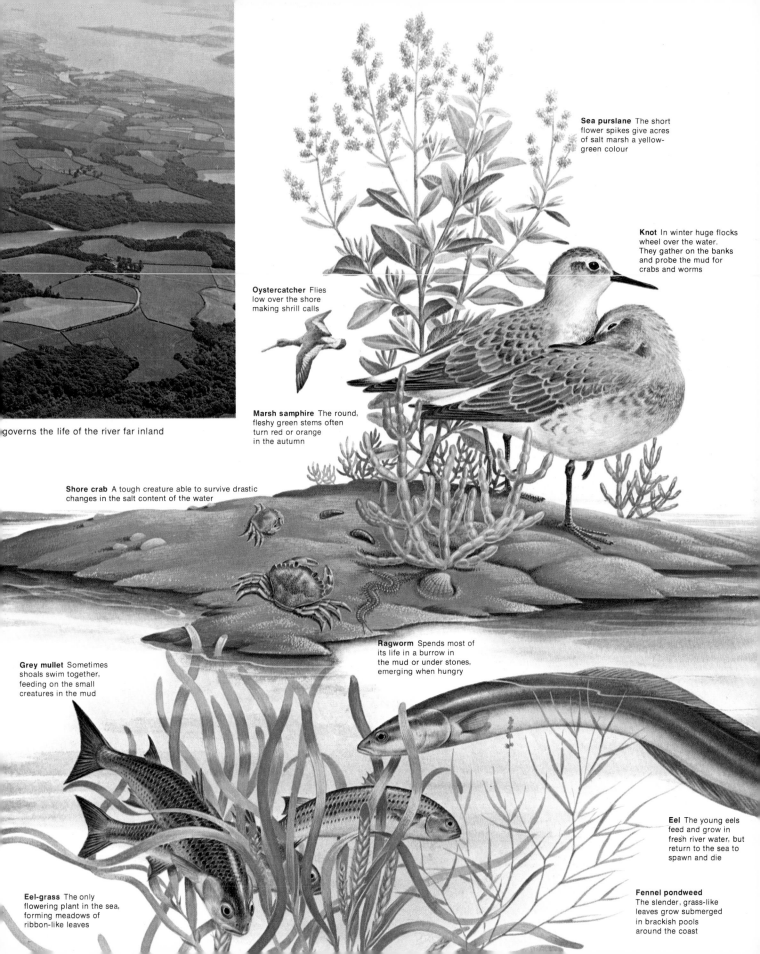

Sea purslane The short flower spikes give acres of salt marsh a yellow-green colour

Knot In winter huge flocks wheel over the water. They gather on the banks and probe the mud for crabs and worms

Oystercatcher Flies low over the shore making shrill calls

Marsh samphire The round, fleshy green stems often turn red or orange in the autumn

governs the life of the river far inland

Shore crab A tough creature able to survive drastic changes in the salt content of the water

Ragworm Spends most of its life in a burrow in the mud or under stones, emerging when hungry

Grey mullet Sometimes shoals swim together, feeding on the small creatures in the mud

Eel The young eels feed and grow in fresh river water, but return to the sea to spawn and die

Eel-grass The only flowering plant in the sea, forming meadows of ribbon-like leaves

Fennel pondweed The slender, grass-like leaves grow submerged in brackish pools around the coast

Evolution in action in a changing world

Charles Darwin turned 19th-century man's beliefs upside-down with his theory of ever-changing and evolving life. Today his theory is generally accepted—and the process of evolution can be observed in the countryside

In 1858 the British naturalist Charles Darwin revolutionised the world's thinking with his theory of evolution. He put forward the idea that all animals and plants are descended from a few original forms of life. Before this concept of the succession of life it was generally believed that the earth had acquired all its creatures and plants at the Creation and that they had remained unchanged ever since. This belief is understandable, for the process of evolution is a very slow one, making it difficult in man's short lifetime to witness significant change in a species.

Through careful observation, Darwin was able to piece together his theory of evolving life. He noted that in any species many more individuals were born than survived, and reasoned that there must therefore be a struggle for existence. He noticed, too, that every individual is different from all other individuals, and reasoned that some of these differences must confer an advantage, however slight, in the struggle to survive. An animal or plant species which was best fitted or adapted to its environment was most likely to survive—the survival of the fittest. Since the environment was constantly changing it followed that living things must continually re-adapt in order to survive, and the study of fossils told a story of constant change in living organisms. These changes and variations were passed on from one generation to the next; that is, they were inherited. By selection of variations best suited to meet a new situation, evolution worked on animals and plants to produce new species equipped to live successfully.

Since Darwin's time the discoveries of geologists, zoologists and botanists have elevated the theory to a generally accepted truth. The story of evolution has been plotted, with surprisingly few gaps, from when the first primitive form of life appeared, about 2000 million years ago, to the present day when the world is inhabited by millions of different species.

Evolution is a continuing process, and even within the past 100 years has been observed in progress as wildlife adapts to changes in the environment. In towns many woodland birds such as the robin, thrush and chaffinch have taken over the parks and gardens as a substitute for their disappearing woodlands. Rock and cliff-dwelling birds such as the house martin and kestrel use buildings on which to roost and nest. At one time the shy great crested grebe lived on remote lakes, but is now a common sight on reservoirs and inland lakes. The adaptable house mouse, man's constant companion, seems to be able to survive in cold stores. These 'refrigerated' mice grow thick woolly coats, make good use of the pipe lagging as nest material and eat the unlimited food supply.

Herring gulls are the most common gulls in Britain, probably because they can eat almost anything from fish offal to rubbish

FLOWERS THAT FILL A NICHE

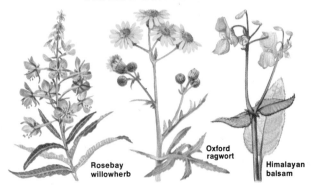

Rosebay willowherb

Oxford ragwort

Himalayan balsam

Empty food niches, such as river and railway banks or the many recently formed waste areas in the countryside, are quickly invaded by the Oxford ragwort, Himalayan balsam and rosebay willowherb

These are examples of animals which readily adapt to new surroundings. Others apparently cannot do this. Badgers keep to their diminishing woods while foxes move into towns. Puffins remain faithful to their declining cliff-top burrows while gulls come inland.

As long as there is available space somewhere in the countryside an animal or plant will occupy it sooner or later. Animals fit into community life by occupying certain zones or niches associated with food supply. Three closely related woodpecker species may share the same tree but are not in direct competition with each other. The lesser spotted woodpecker feeds mainly among the topmost branches, the drumming great spotted woodpecker lives among the lower branches, while the green woodpecker feeds mainly on the ground under the tree.

Thousands of species of plants and animals have been living in Britain since the beginning of time, each on its own 'patch', but even today species new to this country can still find empty niches where they can move in. The Australian fungus beetle, introduced from Australia in the 19th century, is now widespread in birch bracket fungus where it found a living space unoccupied by a native species.

The Oxford ragwort, introduced to Oxford from southern Italy in 1794, is now a common plant of railway lines, streets, walls and waste places. It is thought to have spread along the Great Western Railway. In the last half century it has been found in the London area and other parts of the south, and in the Midlands. It has not necessarily ousted the other ragworts, but propagates rapidly in any empty niche. Similarly the rosebay willowherb, once rare, has in the last 100 years become very common, especially on waste land. The Himalayan balsam, introduced in the last century, now covers thousands of miles of river banks and is still spreading.

Where there is an empty food niche, 'take-over' moves are often possible. The grey squirrel from North America began

NATURAL SELECTION

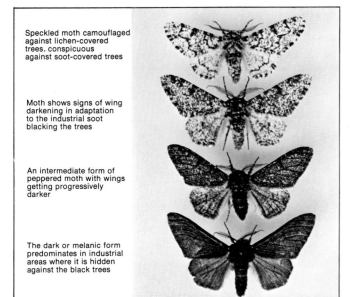

Speckled moth camouflaged against lichen-covered trees, conspicuous against soot-covered trees

Moth shows signs of wing darkening in adaptation to the industrial soot blacking the trees

An intermediate form of peppered moth with wings getting progressively darker

The dark or melanic form predominates in industrial areas where it is hidden against the black trees

Evolution of the peppered moth from a light, speckled form to a dark form as an adaptation to its black, soot-covered surroundings

ARTIFICIAL SELECTION

Hampshire Down   Soay sheep

Selective breeding—evolution through artificial selection—can produce sheep such as the Hampshire Down, bred for its good-quality meat. This breed is quite distinct from the wild, goat-like Soay sheep that roams on the Isle of Soay in the St Kilda group

living wild in the countryside at the turn of the century, having been set free, accidentally or deliberately, from London Zoo and Woburn Park. It did not drive out the native red squirrel, but merely took over at a time when the reds were dying off from disease. After myxomatosis in the early 1950's, hares occupied wooded areas once the domain of rabbits. Normally, these two do not mix.

A classic case of evolution happening today concerns the peppered moth, a speckled woodland insect which matches perfectly the lichen on woodland trees where it settles. About 100 years ago a dark, or melanic, specimen was discovered near Manchester. At this time black peppered moths were rare because sharp-eyed birds quickly spotted them against the mottled lichen. Since then, factory and chimney smoke, a by-product of the Industrial Revolution, has killed off the lichens and darkened the bare tree trunks. As a result the dark moth, now inconspicuous against the blackened trees, is dominant in the Midlands and eastern England. In non-industrial areas such as the West Country and parts of Wales, the normal coloured peppered moth still predominates.

This particular example of a dark colour variation being selected naturally and adapting to the surroundings is called industrial melanism. It has affected up to 70 different species of insects. Many ladybirds, for example, are coloured black with red spots rather than the normal red with black spots. It is true that the black colouring is a more effective camouflage in dark surroundings, but ladybirds are distasteful to most birds anyway and so do not need camouflage. It is thought, however, that the black varieties may be more resistant to pollution than the red.

Dark or melanic colouring is common in animals living in isolation on off-shore islands, although the reason for this is not clear. Changes in physical build are more noticeable in these isolated animals, too, for example the larger-sized races of the St Kilda wren and the Orkney vole.

Not all evolutionary changes occur naturally. In artificial selection man takes a hand and speeds up the process by selective breeding. Domestic animals—dogs, cats, rabbits, pigeons and farm animals—and cultivated plants—cereals and fruits—are now a very far cry from their wild ancestors. A rye grass produced artificially by crossing two different grasses has recently been produced in Wales. This new grass, the first fully fertile plant ever created in this way, combines the best features of two distinct plants in a single breed. Qualities of faster growth, greater disease resistance and higher yield could help in the fight against world starvation.

F

Fairy ring fungus *Marasmius oreades*
Even when it is not fruiting, this fungus, which is common in lawns and pastures, makes circles of dark, lush grass through the fertilising effects of the nitrates it produces. In addition to various magical explanations advanced for the formation of these circles, they were attributed to stallions running in circles, tethered goats and lightning.

The underground threads, mycelium, of this fungus spread outwards at a rate of 6-12 in. a year, so the size of the ring is a guide to its age. On the South Downs, rings are sometimes several yards across and centuries old.

The fruiting bodies, which appear from late summer onwards, have convex buff-coloured caps up to 2½ in. across; the stems are the same colour. The flesh is white and good to eat. If dried, the fungus can be used as a flavouring for soups and stews.

Fairy shrimp *Chirocephalus diaphanus*
A freshwater crustacean living in pools that dry out in summer, the fairy shrimp lays drought-resistant eggs which hatch out into larvae when rain refills the pools. These shrimps, 1-1¼ in. long, are transparent, tinted brown, and have 11 pairs of limbs and a forked tail. Because they are transparent, food can be seen in their gut.

The paired limbs move incessantly, creating currents which bring food and oxygen to the shrimp. They swim on their backs and the eggs are carried by the female in a brood pouch. Fairy shrimps have triangular second antennae which are longer in the male and used for clasping the female during mating. Mostly seen in southern England, these shrimps often die before the pond dries up.

The kestrel is the most numerous and widespread of the four British species of falcon

Fairy shrimps live in pools, but lay eggs that can survive when the water dries up

Falcon

These long-winged, sometimes long-tailed, predators with hooked beaks and sharp talons kill their prey in the air, and breed on cliffs and in trees. The female or falcon is usually larger than the male or tiercel. Of the four species breeding in Britain, the kestrel is the most numerous and widespread, often nesting on ledges of tall buildings, including a tower in the House of Lords, as well as the most remote and desolate moorland. It is a hovering bird, feeding on mice and voles in its rural habitat and on sparrows in cities.

The kestrel has pointed wings and a long tail; the male is coloured blue-grey, with a black band at the end of its tail. The female's tail is similar but barred. Along with other birds of prey, the kestrel suffered a serious decline in the 1960's which a recent ban on certain agricultural chemicals has relieved.

The merlin, a small falcon of the north-

FALCONS IN FLIGHT

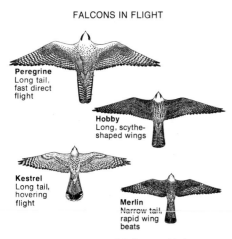

Peregrine
Long tail,
fast direct
flight

Hobby
Long, scythe-
shaped wings

Kestrel
Long tail,
hovering
flight

Merlin
Narrow tail,
rapid wing
beats

Falcons are all powerful flyers, chasing prey on the wing and diving to kill

ern and western heather moorlands, frequently breeds on the ground, though it will use an old crow's nest. The male has a slate-blue back and tail, the female is larger with a brown back and banded tail. Both have heavily streaked underparts. They swoop low over the moors, spiralling and banking in pursuit of meadow pipits, twite and ring ouzels—their chief prey. In winter, merlins come down to lower levels to coastal marshes and estuaries, where their numbers are boosted by continental immigrants. They also feed on small mammals, birds and insects.

The hobby is a summer visitor to the downs and copses of southern England, where it catches flying insects on the wing. It has a slate-grey back, black moustaches, white breast and underparts streaked with black, and rust-red 'trousers'. Hobbys have scythe-shaped wings and go in for aerobatics. Later in the summer when their young need feeding they frequently turn their attention from insects to catching young swallows, martins and occasionally even swifts on the wing—a formidable feat. Only 75-100 pairs now breed in England, usually in old crows' nests and mostly in Hampshire, Sussex and Dorset. Their numbers have been kept down by egg-collectors systematically robbing known nests.

A peregrine can dive at speeds estimated at up to 180 mph, striking its prey with instant death and swirling upwards again on sickle-shaped wings. Pigeons and rock doves form the bulk of its food. In the mid-1950's a strong and healthy population of peregrines was re-established, but by 1962 only 68 pairs were left in England, Scotland and Wales. The rest had been killed off by agricultural chemicals used on seeds eaten by the peregrine's prey. It is now confined to northern and western coasts. It nests in a bare scrape on a rock ledge or another bird's abandoned nest, laying three or four brown eggs in April.

The large, white or speckled gyr falcon

is an exceptionally rare visitor from Greenland, Iceland or Norway that occasionally winters in the extreme north of Britain. The red-footed falcon is a summer visitor to eastern Europe which is occasionally seen in eastern England. The male is a uniform slate-black with red feet and leg feathers and a red ring round each eye. The female is a sandy rust colour. They hover like kestrels, but are gregarious birds, usually appearing in small groups.

Before effective firearms were invented falcons were trained to hunt game birds. It is thought that falconry was introduced to Britain by French nobles about AD 860. Today it is carried on by a few enthusiasts. Falcons are used on US Air Force bases in Britain and the naval air station at Lossiemouth to keep them free of birds.

Fallow

A method of resting the ground and cleaning soil of weeds by leaving a field unused, which is effective during a long spell of dry weather. The soil is kept in large clods throughout most of the summer, and turned at intervals to dry out thoroughly. This exposure to the air kills off couch grass, water grass and other weeds.

Bastard fallow starts later—in June—after clover or a similar crop has been mown. The same process is carried out, but within a shorter period. Most land is cleaned today by the use of selective herbicides.

Fallowing is an ancient practice, and there is some evidence that it aerates the soil, whose nitrogen content is improved by the decaying weeds, giving rise to heavier crops. However, it is an expensive and uncertain process.

False scorpion

In general appearance false scorpions resemble true scorpions, to which they are related, although they have no sting and the rear part of their bodies does not form a tail. There are about 20 British species, none more than $\frac{1}{8}$ in. long, living mostly under bark, stones and in vegetable debris. They run backwards and forwards with equal rapidity but remain stationary when disturbed.

False scorpions pounce on insects and small spiders from their hiding places, injecting fluids into and over the victim's body to pre-digest it before eating. Like spiders, false scorpions produce silk, although in their case it comes from glands in the front of the body. It is used in the construction of nests in which egg-laying and moulting take place.

Each female lays 5-50 eggs before dying. They are retained beneath her body in a transparent membrane. Here the eggs hatch to give larvae which feed on secretions derived from the female's degenerating ovaries. The larvae moult to nymphs and leave the sac, moulting a further three times before the adult stage is reached, one or

two years later. The average life span of a false scorpion is not known, but in captivity one lived for three-and-a-half years.

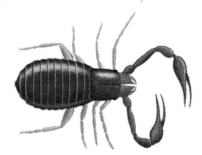

False scorpion *Neoeisium muscorum* ×22
In spite of its name and appearance, the false scorpion is harmless to man

Fan worm

The peacock worm *Sabella penicillus* is the most widespread of the four common species of fan worms found near low-water mark on British shores. It builds a smooth round tube of $\frac{1}{4}$ in. diameter with fine mud particles. This projects about 2 in. above muddy flats at low tide, extending some 18 in. below the surface. When the tube is covered by sea water, a crown of delicate tentacles expands from the top to filter tiny food particles from the water. The crown also acts like a fish's gill, extracting oxygen from the water.

On gravelly sands in south-west England, *Megalomma vesiculosum* builds a tougher tube with pieces of shell attached to it; this closes when the tide is out.

A less common inhabitant of muddy shores is *Myxicola infundibulum,* which lives in a thick slimy tube made from translucent layers of mucus. The fourth species *Bispira volutacornis* has two spiral lobes of white tentacles and lives in rock cracks in pools, under shady overhangs and also offshore.

The fan, which gives this worm its name, is quickly retracted if danger threatens

The changing face of the farmer's landscape

Farmers occupy most of the land in the British Isles. The way in which they work the soil moulds the landscape, and the farming methods of the second half of the 20th century have drastically changed the look of the countryside

At first sight, most of the farms in the United Kingdom would still look familiar to the last two generations that occupied them. The farmhouse is still at the hub of the operation. About it are ranged the farm buildings, many of them dating back to the halcyon days of Victorian agriculture.

Britain's hill farms are perhaps the most changeless. Round the farmhouse there is a small amount of arable land where grass crops are rotated with roots and cereals. On the hills are large fields of permanent pasture enclosed by drystone walls. This style of farming goes back generations in the north of England and Scotland.

Elsewhere the farm's main productive fields are bigger than in the past and allow the most efficient use of the farm's machines. Their boundaries are still traditional. On clay soils, where there is no local stone but plenty of timber, the fields will be divided by wooden post-and-rail fences or thick hawthorn hedges, skilfully 'laid' in the winter with their branches woven between the upright stems. In Devon and Somerset there are sandstone banks, grassed and perhaps with a hedge on top, while in marshy country the boundaries are formed by ditches—dykes in Lincolnshire, rhines on Sedgemoor.

This landscape of neatly patterned fields, which is accepted as 'natural' today, is man-made. It is a landscape created by enclosures made largely in the 100 years between 1750 and

The traditional English landscape, near Melmerby in Cumberland. On the higher ground, drystone walls enclose sheep pasture while, lower down, hedges keep grazing cattle from the arable land

1850 to exploit new methods of farming, and already it is giving way to a new pattern, based on the farming methods of the second half of the 20th century.

Man the farmer wrought his first changes on the British landscape about 5000 years ago, when he began to clear the forest which then covered most of the country. He created small rectangular fields bounded by earth banks in which he grew wheat and barley. He also kept sheep, cattle and pigs. Stone Age man was a nomad; as he exhausted the land he simply moved on. Permanent farmsteads began to be established around 1000 BC, and by the time of the Roman invasion farming had become static.

Agriculture advanced rapidly under the Romans. During their 350 year occupation there were probably as many as 4 million acres under cultivation. After the Romans' departure, at the beginning of the 5th century, the land reverted to its former state of wilderness. When the Saxons started to settle 100 years later they had to set about clearing the still heavily forested river valleys.

The landscape which vanished with the enclosure movement is the one that the Saxons began to shape. They worked on the land with heavy ploughs drawn by teams of oxen. Large, open fields were divided into unfenced strips about 200 yds long and 10-20 yds wide. It was a communal system. Each farmer had several strips which were intermingled with those of his neighbours, so that the fertile and infertile land alike was fairly shared out. The villagers shared implements, and common land was set aside for grazing. All land was owned by the lord of the manor.

Open field farming has left its mark on the landscape in many places—in fields whose surface appears to be folded in gigantic corrugations. The 'troughs' between the bumps were once drainage ditches or footpaths between strips.

A 17th-century map of Laxton, Nottinghamshire, showing the huge open fields, divided into strips. Laxton is still farmed on the open field system

Open field farming lasted while agriculture was a community effort and produced only enough for subsistence. It survived the Norman Conquest—in places until the end of the 19th century—and even today the land in the village of Laxton in Nottinghamshire is farmed on the open field system.

But in general, as soon as farming began to show a profit, landowners started to consolidate their holdings to work the land more efficiently. To do this they took over the open fields, dispossessing the villagers, and dividing the land into smaller fields, enclosed by hedges or drystone walls.

Enclosure was a long process. It started on a small scale in the 15th century, and continued spasmodically until the 18th century. Then, with the start of the Industrial Revolution, towns expanded providing huge new markets. New farming methods were also developed, more landlords saw profit in the land and the enclosure movement became a flood.

In 1815 most Englishmen worked on the land: within a generation most were employed in industry. An ancient agriculture had to be modernised to cater for the vast populations of the new manufacturing towns and a country block-

aded during the Napoleonic Wars. Farm landscape was by then taking on the appearance familiar today.

For about 100 years the pattern held good, then once again new techniques began to impose change. First the tractor replaced the horse, to be followed by larger machines, such as the combine harvester which can only operate really efficiently in large fields. In eastern Britain, particularly the fen country, many farms already have huge prairie-like fields in which the new machines can operate, and this open-look farming is spreading to the Midlands and the West.

Farms are growing in size and declining in numbers. When tenancies fall vacant, estate owners are taking over the land and farming it for themselves. The large estates can boost production because they are well equipped with capital and machinery.

There are still many small farms—65 acres or less—particularly in Wales, Northern Ireland and the Irish Republic. Those of around 130 acres are mostly dairy farms or produce livestock. Most of the big farms—42,000 averaging 310 acres and mostly arable land—are in England and Scotland.

Ploughing on the Downs near Avebury, Wiltshire: modern farm machinery needs large, prairie-like fields in order to operate efficiently

Machines that work the land for man

About 120 years ago, one person in 12 worked on the land in Britain. Today, the figure is one in 165. Mechanisation of farming, giving enormously increased efficiency, has been a major factor in this exodus from the land

Virtually every job on a farm can now be performed by machines, but since man learnt to prepare the soil and plant seeds there have always been 'machines' of a kind.

One of the earliest, its origins lost in pre-history, was the plough. At first it was made of wood and simply 'scratched' the soil without turning it over. The heavier, iron-shod, furrow-turning plough was brought to Britain by the Celts in the 1st century BC from Europe.

Other early farm implements were the hoe, scythe and sickle. The sickle had a tooth-edged blade; reapers would grasp the ears of corn with one hand and sever the stalks with the sickle held in the other.

Today, British agriculture is highly mechanised. Its basic power unit is the tractor, costing up to £3000 or more.

A modern tractor has power steering, disc brakes, snug driving cab and an adjustable steering column. The diesel engine has a 12-speed gear box and a powerful hydraulic system capable of lifting nearly 2½ tons.

Few implements are towed by tractors now. Instead they are mounted on the hydraulic arms at the back of the tractor, thus becoming an integral part of a single machine. Implements such as mowers are driven by the tractor's engine.

Even the plough, the basic design of which has hardly changed in two centuries, has become increasingly sophisticated. Its job is still to perform the vital early stage of cultivation—breaking up the soil.

The traditional type is the fixed plough, which may cut as many as six furrows at a time. The soil is sliced vertically by the coulter—a knife-edged disc—and horizontally by the share, before being turned over by the mouldboard.

There are adjustments that the ploughman can make. In autumn the furrow is turned to expose the maximum surface to the frosts which crumble and assist aeration of the soil. In spring the furrow is turned over completely, to bury previous crop debris.

With a fixed plough the field has to be divided into sections, or lands, which are ploughed alternately to avoid having to make a sharp turn at the end of each furrow. With a reversible plough this procedure is unnecessary. The reversible plough is really two ploughs mounted on opposite sides of a beam attached to the tractor. At the end of a furrow the plough is lifted from the soil, and the beam rotated, so that the second plough will turn the furrow in the same direction as the first when the outfit is turned round.

The latest type of plough, the chisel plough, has 5-16 stout prongs. It is used by farmers who believe in keeping stubble undisturbed and stirring the soil rather than turning it.

Before sowing, the furrows are broken up by cultivators or harrows. One type is the disc harrow, which has sharp, dished blades to cut through earth clods.

The sower proceeded wastefully until the 18th century, scattering the seed by hand, much of it to be eaten by birds or to fall on stony ground. Jethro Tull, born at Basildon, Berkshire, in 1674, invented a seed drill inspired by the pipes of the church organ he played on Sundays. Seed, he realised, could be accurately sown through a series of pipes.

Modern drills sow up to 20 rows or more at a time; they can also be used for spreading chemical fertiliser. The seeds are dropped through a pipe into a shallow furrow made by a blade and covered with soil by a harrow. Root crops are sown by precision drills that plant one seed at a time.

The first crop to be harvested is grass. A forage harvester shaped like a giant chimney cowl is used to take off the lush young growth for silage. It both cuts and chops grass, kale or maize with flailing rotary blades. The pulverised crop is blown through a tall chute into a trailer.

When haymaking starts the grass is cut by a mower mounted on the back of a tractor. Machines seldom do a job better than the man or the horse they have replaced. They do it quicker. Haymaking, where the weather is critical, can be completed while the sun shines—or at least before rain sets in.

Combine harvesters lumber into the fields at corn harvest

Farming through the ages

Penned in A medieval peasant and his wife tend their sheep. The woman is milking a ewe to make cheese. From the earliest times, sheep were kept mainly for their milk and wool—in the Middle Ages England prospered by selling wool to the Continent. It was only in the 18th century that sheep began to be bred for meat

Soil-breaker The modern plough is basically of the same design as this 18th-century version

Ox-power The ox was the farmer's main working animal until the 19th century. Ox-drawn ploughs, like this 14th-century example, were used until the 1920's

Harvesting An early 19th-century reaper at work. He grasped the ears of corn in one hand and cut the stalks with a sickle held in the other. This laborious method of reaping, dating from prehistoric times, lasted into the 20th century in parts of Britain

In harness Horses were used to pull ploughs, harrows and other farm implements for only a brief part of their long association with man. The 18th and 19th centuries were the heyday of the farm horse, and even in this period they never entirely replaced the ox. Today they have reverted to their original role, that of riding animals

Harvest in the age of steam: portable threshing machines, powered by traction engines, were used until the development of the combine harvester

time. A big, self-propelled combine has a 6-cylinder, 120 hp diesel engine, 16 ft cutters, costs around £6000 and weighs almost 7 tons. It cuts and threshes grain in one operation. In the days of the reaper-binder, harvesting and threshing took about 20 man-hours per acre. A modern combine, operated by one man, can harvest more than 4 acres an hour in good conditions. Combine harvesters, developed in the United States early this century, only became common in Britain after the Second World War. Combines have also led

to further investment in machinery. Because freshly harvested grain has a high moisture content, it needs drying.

In the old days it would dry in the field in stooks waiting to be carted; now elaborate grain driers are needed. Stooks can still be seen in places: 10-12 bound sheaves, leaning against one another in two rows, the rows set north and south so that each side gets the benefit of the sun.

The straw is either burnt or collected by a pick-up baler, compressed and tied up in rectangular bales 4 ft long.

How a modern combine harvester works

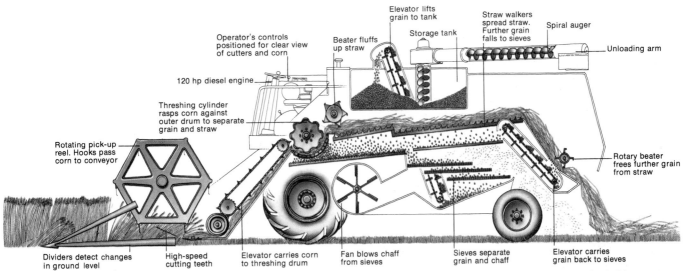

The modern combine harvests corn at a rate of more than 4 acres an hour enabling the farmer to cut a crop quickly when the weather is fine. The threshed grain is collected in a storage tank and unloaded into carts or trailers; the straw and chaff are collected by a pick-up baler

The smooth routine of a modern dairy farm

Fifty years ago it took eight men to do the work now done by one on a dairy farm. In that time, scientific breeding and the use of specialised equipment have made milk production one of Britain's biggest industries

The average Briton consumes 30 gallons of milk a year, apart from butter and cheese. More than 30 million pints are delivered to British doorsteps every day.

To meet this demand there are 3¼ million cows on the 95,000 dairy farms in the United Kingdom. Most dairy farms are in the west where high rainfall makes for a good growth of grass for grazing, and in the Midlands where the heavy clay soil also grows good grass. The milk is carried to the cities in bulk tankers, taking two days from cow to doorstep.

The Republic of Ireland has just over a million cows on its 90,000 dairy farms. Its average herd is 12. In Northern Ireland the average is 15, England and Wales 35 and Scotland 60. At a typical dairy farm in England, Wales and Ireland the cattle are likely to be Friesians; in Scotland the Ayrshire predominates. Both breeds have high milk yields.

The specialist farm has large fodder stores—a Dutch barn for hay and straw, a covered silage pit for winter feeding and a granary and mill where barley grown on the farm is mixed with concentrated protein for winter food. The farm also has housing for cows in winter and calf boxes where young calves are hand-reared. There is a milking parlour with stalls arranged herringbone pattern. Machinery for conserving grass as hay includes grass-turning equipment and a baler; for silage, the forage harvester both cuts and chops grass.

The dairy cow's life falls into a daily routine for the lactation period of about 305 days—the time she is producing milk after calving. She will have a calf a year for five or six years, starting at the age of two.

The cows are milked twice a day, arriving in relays at the milking parlour. But on the largest and most modern farms the cows come in for milking in round-the-clock relays. A cow produces a daily average of 3 gallons; at her peak, soon after calving, it will be 6 gallons. In a year she will average 900 gallons, but many produce 1000-2000 gallons.

The cows are machine-milked and the milk flows through pipes to a tank for cooling to 4°C (40°F) and storing until a tanker arrives to take it away.

Milk Marketing Boards buy and sell the milk. England and Wales have one board, Northern Ireland one and Scotland three. The boards decide whether the milk should be bottled or become butter or cheese. Higher prices are paid to encourage winter milk production.

Few farms have their own bulls, relying instead on artificial insemination; about two-thirds of Britain's cattle are bred in this way. The bulls are kept at cattle-breeding centres. About four-fifths of Britain's home-produced beef comes from male calves born to dairy cows after mating with beef bulls. See also ARTIFICIAL INSEMINATION

This dairy farm is run by two men who look after 75 cows on 70 acres of land. During the summer the cows are put out to graze, when each of them eats about 150 lb. of grass a day. In winter, they are kept in the dairy complex where they are fed each day on 20 lb. of hay or silage, plus 12 lb. of concentrated food, such as grain. Milked morning and evening, each cow yields about 3 gallons of milk a day

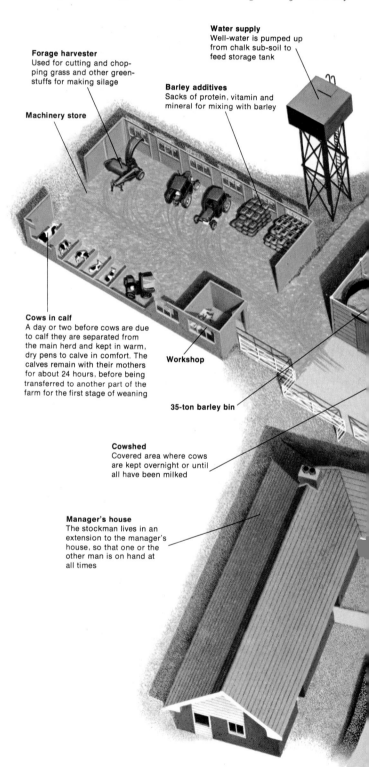

Water supply
Well-water is pumped up from chalk sub-soil to feed storage tank

Forage harvester
Used for cutting and chopping grass and other greenstuffs for making silage

Barley additives
Sacks of protein, vitamin and mineral for mixing with barley

Machinery store

Cows in calf
A day or two before cows are due to calf they are separated from the main herd and kept in warm, dry pens to calve in comfort. The calves remain with their mothers for about 24 hours, before being transferred to another part of the farm for the first stage of weaning

Workshop

35-ton barley bin

Cowshed
Covered area where cows are kept overnight or until all have been milked

Manager's house
The stockman lives in an extension to the manager's house, so that one or the other man is on hand at all times

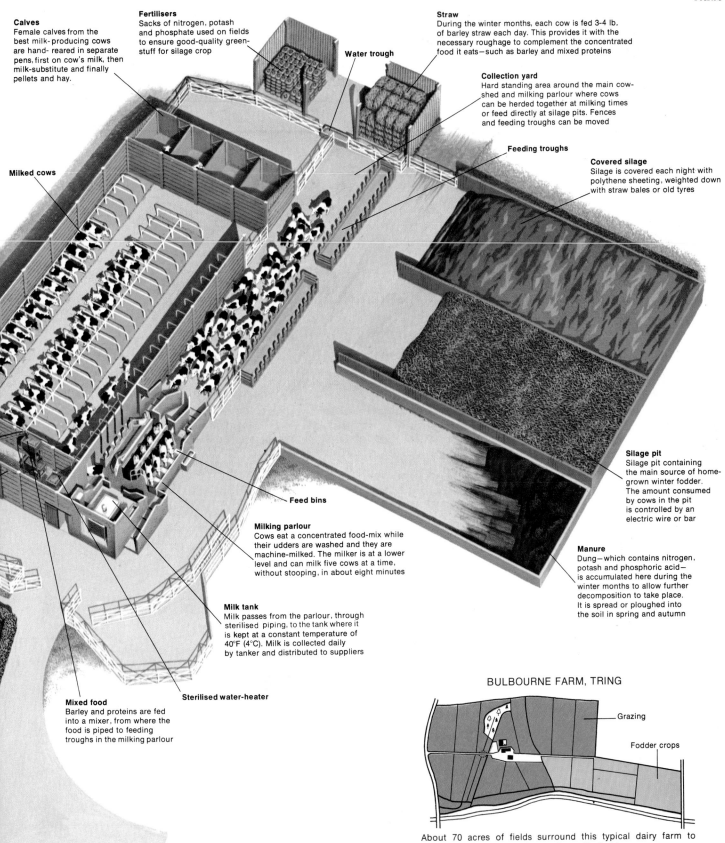

Calves
Female calves from the best milk-producing cows are hand-reared in separate pens, first on cow's milk, then milk-substitute and finally pellets and hay.

Fertilisers
Sacks of nitrogen, potash and phosphate used on fields to ensure good-quality green-stuff for silage crop

Water trough

Straw
During the winter months, each cow is fed 3-4 lb. of barley straw each day. This provides it with the necessary roughage to complement the concentrated food it eats—such as barley and mixed proteins

Collection yard
Hard standing area around the main cow-shed and milking parlour where cows can be herded together at milking times or feed directly at silage pits. Fences and feeding troughs can be moved

Feeding troughs

Covered silage
Silage is covered each night with polythene sheeting, weighted down with straw bales or old tyres

Milked cows

Silage pit
Silage pit containing the main source of home-grown winter fodder. The amount consumed by cows in the pit is controlled by an electric wire or bar

Manure
Dung—which contains nitrogen, potash and phosphoric acid—is accumulated here during the winter months to allow further decomposition to take place. It is spread or ploughed into the soil in spring and autumn

Feed bins

Milking parlour
Cows eat a concentrated food-mix while their udders are washed and they are machine-milked. The milker is at a lower level and can milk five cows at a time, without stooping, in about eight minutes

Milk tank
Milk passes from the parlour, through sterilised piping, to the tank where it is kept at a constant temperature of 40°F (4°C). Milk is collected daily by tanker and distributed to suppliers

Sterilised water-heater

Mixed food
Barley and proteins are fed into a mixer, from where the food is piped to feeding troughs in the milking parlour

BULBOURNE FARM, TRING

Grazing

Fodder crops

About 70 acres of fields surround this typical dairy farm to provide grazing land and crops for cattle fodder

165

Farmers – producers of half the nation's food

The farmers of Britain produce more than half the nation's food, and the proportion is increasing each year in spite of the fact that every year they lose 70,000 acres of land to industry, housing and roads

The changing face of the English farmland: a combine harvester works its way

Farming is one of Britain's biggest industries. In 1971 agricultural output for the United Kingdom was valued at more than £2600 million – nearly 3 per cent of the nation's total earnings.

In the Irish Republic, agriculture is even more significant – 12 million of the country's 17 million acres are farmed, mostly for stock-rearing. One-fifth of the national income is provided by farmers and one-third of the work force earn their living from the land. Ninety per cent of the food eaten in Ireland is home produced.

Since prehistory, cereals have been the staple food of most of the world's population: their importance has not diminished today. Of more than 12 million acres devoted to crops in the United Kingdom, 9 million grow cereals. More than 13 million tons of grain are produced each year and 7 million tons of straw.

Barley is the biggest of the cereal crops. In the United Kingdom there are nearly 6 million acres of barley, producing 8½ million tons. In the Irish Republic, where arable farming is relatively insignificant, there are another 415,000 acres. Of the barley consumed in Britain 86 per cent is home-grown.

The bulk of the barley crop – about 7 million tons – goes into animal foodstuffs. Most of the remaining 1½ million tons is top quality grain used for brewing. The best barley-growing areas are the eastern and southern counties of England.

Wheat, oats and rye

Wheat, grown mainly in the east of England, is the next most important grain. While 2 million acres are sown each year, producing 3·3 million tons, more than half of the nation's wheat supply is imported. Between one-third and a half of the crop goes for flour milling, the rest mainly for animal food. Most wheat in the British Isles is winter wheat, sown in October and November and harvested in late summer or early autumn. Winter wheat usually has a 15-20 per cent higher yield than the best spring varieties.

More oats than wheat is grown in Scotland; 1·2 million tons are harvested in the United Kingdom from 943,000 acres. Almost 90 per cent of the crop is used as animal food. Oat straw has a higher nutritional value than any other, and is sometimes fed to livestock.

Rye is not a popular crop in Britain, chiefly because the population has never acquired a taste for rye bread. About 11,000 tons are grown a year on 9000 acres. About half goes into making rye biscuits and half is fed to stock.

Mixed corn – generally an equal mixture of barley and oats – produces a crop of about 200,000 tons a year and is retained on the farms for stockfeeding.

Grass and clover are included in crop rotation with a number of advantages. A clover crop introduces nitrogen to the soil; pasture brings animals on to the land to manure it; the turf adds humus to the soil when it is ploughed; and temporary grassland usually yields a richer crop than permanent pasture.

The grass crop may be cut early, when it is rich in protein, to make silage. Compressed into a pit or tall silo tower, often with a solution of molasses or a chemical such as sulphur dioxide to preserve it, the crop is left to ferment. The grass and other greenstuff in the silage retain around 80 per cent of their original nutritional value.

The rotation methods that made possible an adequate supply of winter feeding stuffs and that still provide the framework for modern arable farming, are based on the work of the 2nd Viscount Townshend in the 18th century. He established the Norfolk four-course crop rotation, sowing a field in successive years with wheat, turnips, barley or oats and clover and rye-grass. The advantage of this system was that before each cereal crop was sown, sheep were introduced to the field to manure it. Sheep grazed on the clover and rye-grass after it had been cut for hay in June and before it was ploughed under for wheat. In the year following the wheat crop, sheep ate the turnips. It was the introduction of turnips into the rotation which earned its founder the nickname 'Turnip' Townshend.

Cattle are the most valuable product of farms in the British Isles. In the United Kingdom and Ireland, the annual production of beef and milk is worth £963 million – as much as

across a vast prairie-like cornfield in the fen country

is spent in a year buying both new and used cars. Meat of all kinds is a staple part of the British diet. In 1971 the average Briton ate 132·5 lb. of meat.

Large numbers of breeding cattle, mostly beef, live on hill farms in the north and west of the country. They spend their first summer grazing on the hills and then in autumn are sold to lowland farms in the east for fattening. Many lowland farms have a surplus of fodder crops and are therefore able to support more livestock in winter than in summer. Besides stock from hill farms, store cattle—beasts about one year old—may be bought for fattening.

Traditionally, beef cattle, fed outdoors the year round, took three or four years to prepare for market. Now, store cattle are sent to the butcher at 12-14 months. They are fattened in yards on hay, roots, sugar beet pulp and coarse grains, as well as proprietary brands of concentrated foodstuffs—starch and protein equivalents.

Britain's famous breeds of beef cattle, like the Aberdeen Angus and Hereford, have stocked some of the greatest beef-producing countries in the world, the United States, South Africa, Australia, Argentina and Brazil among them.

The father of British stock-breeding

Milk accounts for one-fifth of the annual agricultural output of the United Kingdom and Ireland and is worth more than £500 million a year. More than 2700 million gallons leave the farms each year, 1600 million for liquid consumption and the rest for processing.

Robert Bakewell, born in 1725, the son of a Leicestershire farmer, is generally acclaimed as the father of British stock-breeding. To improve his livestock he concentrated on developing a few sound principles already proved in the breeding of racehorses.

He decided on the qualities he wished to develop and selected his breeding stock from animals that displayed as many of those qualities as possible. By in-breeding and eliminating any beasts that did not meet his requirements, he gradually developed a breed to match his ideal.

Bakewell's basic stock was the existing Longhorn cattle, Leicester sheep and Large White pigs. While the Longhorn did not produce the quick-maturing, light-boned animal that Bakewell had in mind, his sheep and pigs did.

The new Leicester sheep, which advanced the species from a scrawny, goat-like creature to the animal we know today, were superb meat-producing animals. They have been used to improve most British and many overseas breeds.

Sheep farming on the hills

Sheep are the chief product of Britain's hill farms, which have changed less than most other farms. Round the farmhouse there is a small amount of arable land where grass crops are rotated with roots and cereals. The practice is called 'ley farming', and goes back generations throughout the north of England and Scotland.

The sheep are fed from these fields round the house in winter. The flock may be systematically moved in pens, or folds, across a crop of roots or field cabbage such as kale. This practice of 'folding' is dying out because of the labour cost of moving the flock each day.

Egg and poultry production is worth more than £318 million a year. It is an industry now almost wholly controlled by the most advanced methods of management. About 80 per cent of the country's laying birds are in flocks of 1000 or more; there are now some 60 flocks of more than 100,000 birds each.

Both laying and table birds—broilers—are kept in windowless, controlled-environment houses where temperature, light, ventilation and the automated food and water supplies can be manipulated. With this method labour costs are low and production is high.

Ninety-nine per cent of broilers are kept in conditions like these; 80 per cent of laying birds live in the wire cages of battery houses. Only 5 per cent of hens are able to range outdoors, the remainder are kept in intensive systems.

The modern laying bird is bred to begin laying young, to continue laying for most of the year, to lay more eggs than its predecessors, seldom to go broody or sick, and to eat economically. The average hen lays around 300 eggs a year—five or six times her own weight—compared with 90 in 1946.

But there are places where free-range eggs and birds can be had—where poultry farming is still only a sideline of general farming. It is a sideline encouraged by the readiness of many British motorists to stop and buy at the farm.

Pigs, calves and sometimes even fattening cattle and lambs are kept in controlled-environment houses. But the most controversial factory farming methods, like keeping calves in cramped and darkened cubicles for the production of white veal, are rare in Britain. In 1971, the feeding of most antibiotics, which had been used to make young stock grow faster, was prohibited unless the farmer had a prescription from a veterinary surgeon.

Autumn—the start of the farmer's year

The farmer is engaged in an endless battle with the weather. Intensive 'factory farm' units for poultry and pig production do provide control over the environment in which the animals live, but these are the exception in farming

Autumn

If the farmer's year can be said to begin at any fixed point, it is at the time when one crop is harvested and preparations for the next one begin.

Harvest usually begins in southern England towards the end of July, generally with winter barley or winter oats. The farmer then sets about preparing a seed-bed in the stubble of the harvested crop.

He may use chisel ploughs rather than take the longer time needed to plough the soil and break the furrows by harrowing. In the shallowly worked fields he sows grass or rye as autumn grazing for sheep or cows. If sown in August or even early September, such a crop—called a catch crop—can provide fodder in November. With an application of nitrogenous fertiliser, rye and rye-grass will survive the winter and supply grazing the following spring.

August is the main harvest month in the south; this is a time to bring in wheat, barley, oats and many vegetables. September is the month in the north (and in the south in a wet summer). The combine harvesters take charge in many fields; in other fields the potato crop is lifted. The sowing of catch crops intensifies.

As the later cereal crops are harvested, the plough is set to turning the soil, burying the debris of the old crop. If the weather is favourable, the farmer sows as much autumn grain as possible.

In October, winter wheat, barley and oats are sown. If the weather is fine, it is better to sow winter wheat than wait for the main barley sowing time the next March, for that month may be wet. The comparative acreages of wheat and barley grown in Britain in any year therefore fluctuate according to the dryness of the autumn.

The sugar-beet harvest can last almost to Christmas. However, farmers like to get all their crops harvested and all their arable land ploughed before Christmas so that the winter frosts can crumble the soil and do much of their cultural work for them.

On farms where livestock are kept, the winter routine is introduced in the late autumn. At great sales and fairs, sheep and cattle, particularly those born during the year, are dispersed to farms better stocked with winter fodder.

For dairy cows some grazing is still available, especially of kale and fodder beet. This often has to be carted to them because the soil is too wet to provide access for grazing. Sheep in their folds are also fed on fodder roots. October and early November is the mating season for sheep—the lambs are born early in the following spring.

Winter

This is the season for farm maintenance work, which includes hedging, ditching and fence repairs. Hedge-cutting is done by large machines equipped with a circular saw at the end of a flexible arm or by hedge-clippers which have cutter-bars like those on a lawnmower. Hedges are also laid while the bushes are dormant: the bushes are cut above ground level, bent over and woven between stakes.

After the cereals have been harvested, the farmer, to save time in preparing a seed-bed in the stubble, may decide to make furrows with a chisel plough instead of ploughing and turning over the soil

The farmer sometimes burns a field to clear it of weeds and pests before sowing. Liquefied petroleum gas is often used as fuel

Sheep on a hill farm withstand the rigours of winter by feeding on silage, cut grass whose moisture and nutritional value have been conserved

Ditching machines clean and excavate ditches with a scoop, a rotating disc or an Archimedean screw, which draws up the earth and litter.

Repairs are made to buildings and machinery. Snow and frost can keep the farmer busy thawing water supplies and attending to the needs of his animals.

With livestock, the farm follows a routine of feeding, watering, cleaning out and, where dairy cows are concerned, milking. Fatstock are prepared for the Christmas markets, though the modern demand is for a steady supply of meat all the year round. Most of the kale and roots have now been eaten. The winter rations tend to be based on silage and hay.

Farmyard manure is hauled to the fields ready for ploughing-in later. Where it has not been possible to finish the ploughing by Christmas, the ploughs may be out when the weather is favourable.

In January orders for seed corn and fertiliser for the coming spring are completed. On farms that can provide winter food for the ewes the first lambs may be born about Christmas. Indoor quarters have to be made for the many sheep flocks which lamb in early February, and whose lambs feed on the early spring grass.

Fruit trees are sprayed to kill pests and fungi and are pruned before their sap begins to rise.

Depending on the weather, February can be a month of great progress with a start made on spring work — or it can be a standstill month, a prolonging of winter.

As the days gradually lengthen, free-range hens increase their production of eggs. In the last week of February cows can sometimes be put out to graze early on a fodder crop, such as rye or Italian rye-grass; this helps to increase the milk yield.

Other early pastures receive a dressing of nitrogenous fertiliser to promote healthy stem and leaf growth.

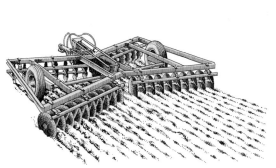

The disc harrow breaks down the heavy earth of a ploughed field to prepare it for sowing. The sharp-edged discs slice up the furrows

The reversible plough, unlike the fixed plough, can work backwards and forwards, thus turning all the furrows in one direction

The plough shares slice through the stubble of an old crop, turning the soil as the first stage in preparing for a new crop

Spring and summer
—the vital seasons

Harvest time completes the cycle of the farming year; it is then that the farmer sees the result of all his work. But the harvest depends on what and how he sows. So perhaps spring is the most important season of his year

Sheep-shearing by machine is now normal practice. The sheep are usually washed a week before clipping, washed wool being in greater demand

Spring

In the south, wide-awake farmers are ready to start sowing at any time after the middle of February, although they may have to wait until April in some years. April is the main planting season in the north.

Soil rough-ploughed in autumn has to be first worked down with cultivators and harrows to form a fine seed-bed. Barley and oats are the chief cereal crops for spring sowing, though there are now spring varieties of wheat. Potatoes are planted, and all kinds of vegetables sown.

Grassland and autumn-sown crops receive a top-dressing of fertiliser. Fields are harrowed to break up the surface of the soil, which has been compacted by winter rains, so that the soil is aerated and fertiliser can penetrate to the plant roots. New grass is also sown, often in the same fields as barley and oats; the grass will grow under the cereals and be ready for grazing after harvest.

The spring cereals are usually given an application of 2-3 cwt an acre of fertiliser at the time of sowing, and a top-dressing when the crop is growing.

Potatoes and some vegetable crops are treated with a herbicide at the time of sowing or planting. This controls weed growth for two or three important months. Cereal crops have to be sprayed with a selective weedkiller, which destroys the weeds without harming the cereals.

From March onwards grazing livestock go out to pasture. The earliest grass, rich in protein, is usually reserved for dairy cows and for ewes and lambs. Young cattle move out of their winter quarters towards the end of April or in early May.

Silage-making—cutting young grass, lucerne or other plants and conserving their moisture by compressing them to expel air—starts in April.

Summer

Grass is harvested in the middle of its growth period. Apart from harvesting by grazing, silage-making gets into full swing during May. Successive cuts are made until the farmer has enough for winter needs. By early June, grasses are cut for hay. In the south, hay-making begins about mid-June, for fields of sown grass; July for permanent meadows.

Early potatoes and some other vegetables are harvested in June. This is the month when the sheep are shorn in the south. In the north it may be a month later.

Hoeing of root and vegetable crops goes on, and in June vegetables, notably brussels sprouts, are transplanted from seed beds to the fields where they will grow whenever rain makes this possible. Thundery weather in early July may herald an attack of potato blight, and farmers spray the crop.

Cattle and sheep graze all summer, but the year's lambs become fat and are sent off to market from early June onwards. At August markets or fairs, lambs from hill flocks are dispersed for fattening on lowland farms.

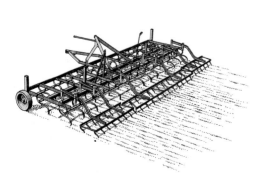

A cultivator breaks up the land with spring-mounted tines or prongs. These are fitted on a sturdy frame which is towed by a tractor

In a seed drill, iron coulter blades cut grooves in the soil. The seeds are mechanically fed and planted from the storage hopper above

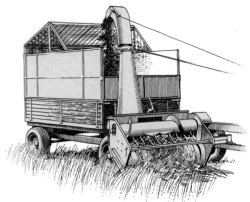

Mowers are used to cut grass to make hay. This mower has fast-moving knives powered by a hydraulic link to the tractor's engine

Stooks of corn mark the last stage of the traditional harvest prior to carting. The rows run from north to south to allow even exposure to the sun

A forage harvester gathers green crops for use as silage. The machine chops the crop and blows the pieces into a waiting trailer

A combine harvester and a baler can be used either separately or in tandem. The combine cuts and threshes the corn, leaving the straw to be picked up by the baler, where it is tightly moulded and bound with wire or string. The bales are dropped for collection later

171

Farrier see Blacksmith

Fat hen *Chenopodium album*
Now regarded only as a weed, fat hen was used as a food from prehistoric times until the 19th century. The seeds, black and shining, have a high fat content, and were eaten with other grain. The leaves were also boiled and mixed with butter. It fell out of favour following the introduction of spinach from Asia.

Fat hen is a widespread weed of waste-tips, waste-land and arable fields. The plant, whose leaves are sometimes covered with a white mealy substance, stands 1-3 ft high with triangular leaves. Clusters of small green flowers bloom from July to October. It is also known as goosefoot, muckweed, wild pottage and wild spinach.

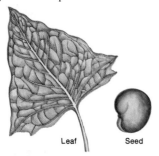

Leaf   Seed

Fat hen's distinctive spikes bear clusters of inconspicuous flowers from July onwards

Fault
The layers of rock at the surface of the earth have been subjected to immense forces from within, becoming folded. In some places the stress causes fractures in entire layers of rock. Where these fractures occur, one section moves vertically or horizontally in relation to the other; movement may be a few centimetres or many kilometres. Such a break is a fault, which shows at the surface as a straight line with different types of rock on each side of the line.

Faults are best seen in rocky cliffs where they are often emphasised by erosion opening out the break to reveal layers of rock which do not match across the gap. Sometimes faults bring hard rocks against softer rocks, which are eroded to form inland escarpments. One of the best examples in the British Isles is Giggleswick Scar, between Settle and Ingleton, Yorkshire. Here, hard mountain limestone has been faulted against softer shales which have eroded away, and the limestone remains as an abrupt scarp, or steep cliff.

Sometimes adjacent faults develop in roughly parallel lines, and in these situations rock between the faults may be squeezed upwards, bringing subterranean rocks to the surface, or it may subside to produce a rift valley. The central lowlands of Scotland lie in such a valley between two faults, one running from Stonehaven to Greenock, the other from Dunbar to Girvan.

The cliff face at Hartland Point, Devon, reveals contorted strata and an almost vertical fault

Further north, the Great Glen divides the Western Highlands from the Grampian Mountains in a 100 mile trench eroded along the line of a fault.

Faulting is still going on and movement

HOW FAULTS AFFECT THE LANDSCAPE

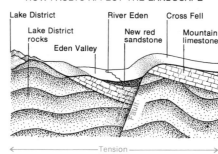

Cross Fell fault—tension on the rocks caused them to crack, then the two sides of the crack slipped against one another. The higher side of the crack stands up as the scarp of Cross Fell

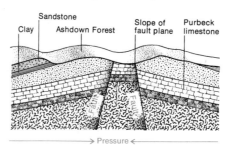

When two faults occur side by side the rocks between may be squeezed upwards, as in this case on the Kentish Weald, where underlying Purbeck limestone has been forced to the surface

along the line of faults is one cause of earthquakes. In Britain, slight movement takes place from time to time, giving rise to earth tremors and noise. Distinct bangs heard in Manchester have been attributed to movements of the Irwell Valley fault and others in the area.

Sometimes the folding of the earth's surface has resulted in rock strata coming to rest on a layer of clay. This is the situation on the south coast of the Isle of Wight. Here the clay has been made slippery by springs, causing the rock above to break away and slide downwards. This is known as slip faulting.

Fawn see Deer
Feather see Bird

Feather-star *Antedon bifida*
The rosy feather-star is the only British member of a group of animals which are primitive relatives of the starfish. Although it is often red, the rosy feather-star can also be yellow, deep purple or orange. Because it is so fragile and can easily be smashed by the waves, the feather-star normally lives on muddy sea bottoms, pier-piles or wrecks below the low-tide line, but may occasionally be found closer inshore in sheltered spots all round the coast. They are often found attached to freshly lifted lobster pots.

It is an elegant animal with ten arms, each 3-6 in. long, growing up from a central disc. Each arm has a row of short stalks down each side, giving a feathery appearance. The rosy feather-star feeds and moves by slowly waving its arms. These have grooves lined with fine hairs which waft tiny particles of food into the mouth at the centre of the disc. On the underside of the disc there are about 25 short stalks which are equipped with small claws; these enable the animal to temporarily anchor itself to the sea-bed.

SWIMMING FEATHER-STAR

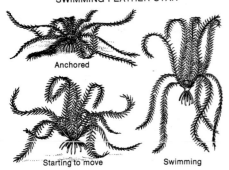

Anchored

Starting to move   Swimming

The feather-star remains anchored to the sea-bed most of the time but can swim gracefully, beating five arms upwards and five downwards alternately

Fell

A word used for 'mountain' in the south of Scotland, the Isle of Man and the north-western counties of England. These were areas colonised by the Norsemen, and the word is from the Old Norse *fiall*; in modern Norwegian *fjell*. Originally the word meant rocky, but it came to be applied to any mountain. It occurs in proper names, such as Bowfell and Scafell in the Lake District, and Culter Fell, Lanarkshire.

The plural, fells, has become a synonym for high moorlands.

Fen see p. 174

Fence

The word is related to 'defence' because the first fences were used to enclose land and bar intruders, or to keep livestock in check. Landowners used the nearest and cheapest materials, hence the variety of drystone walls, hedges, hurdles and palings in different parts of the country. Then, at the turn of the century, barbed wire and wire netting became available and were used extensively.

Electric fences are a recent development. They consist of strands of wire or wire mesh —carried on insulated supports—through which a low-voltage current is passed. Electric fences which are used to control grazing in large fields are moved regularly to pen the stock—cattle, sheep or pigs—into an area of fresh grazing. The animals soon learn that the fence will give them a small shock and keep away from it.

Fennel see Parsley
Fern see p. 176

Ferret *Mustela putorius*

A member of the weasel family, the ferret is a semi-domesticated form of polecat, which has been used certainly since Roman times for hunting rabbits and destroying rats and other vermin. When put into burrows to drive out rabbits, ferrets are muzzled to prevent their killing and eating them. The fleeing rabbits are trapped in a net placed over the exit of the burrow.

With white fur and pink eyes, the ferret is normally 14 in. long with a 5 in. tail. It is a prolific breeder, producing more than a dozen young in two broods.

Escaped ferrets often cross-breed with polecats. Their bite is strong, but they can be made to release their prey by applying pressure just above their eyes. Underground, ferrets hunt by scent and sound. See also POLECAT

Though the ferret has a ferocious bite, it is delicate and cannot stand cold

Ferry

Although they have been largely replaced by bridges and tunnels, a few ferries still operate throughout the country. Among the most important are those over the tidal creeks of East Anglia, and across the deep inlets of the west coast of Scotland, where ferries form essential links in the main coastal route. Chain ferries, where the vessel is winched across the water on chains, still operate at Renfrew on the Clyde and at Poole Harbour in Dorset among other places. Small ferries, where a man pulls a dinghy across a narrow river on a fixed rope for a small toll, have almost died out, though a few survive, such as the one across the Avon at Offenham, Worcestershire.

Fertiliser

Plants cannot grow without adequate amounts of carbon, hydrogen, oxygen, nitrogen, phosphorus and potassium. The first three elements are supplied by air and water. When the soil lacks the others, fertilisers must be applied.

For centuries, natural fertilisers such as compost or manure have been applied to the soil. Other natural fertilisers include bone meal, dried blood, seaweed, wood ashes and peat. Clover, beans and other leguminous plants enrich a soil with nitrogen: they have on their roots nodules of bacteria which gather nitrogen from the air and, when the plants die, it is absorbed into the soil.

Chemical fertilisers have largely replaced natural ones on farms. Until the 1930's they were applied, like manure, by shovel; but since then machines have been used. One of these, the combine-drill, inserts the fertiliser into the soil, with the seed, at the time of sowing; another, the spinner, is mounted behind a tractor and spreads the fertiliser evenly over the surface of the field.

When sown, autumn cereal crops usually receive 2 or 3 cwt per acre of compound fertiliser—one in which the important elements are mixed, according to the condition of the soil and the needs of the crop. Plants need nitrogen for leaf growth and phosphorus and potassium for root development. Potassium also helps in the manufacture of carbohydrates. During the spring an application of 1 or 2 cwt per acre of fertiliser is given to provide nitrogen.

In addition to the elements already mentioned, plants sometimes require smaller quantities of calcium, magnesium, sulphur, copper, iron, boron, molybdenum, manganese, cobalt and zinc. Without them poor crops may result, showing stunted growth, curling leaves and faded colour. To correct this, fertilisers containing the missing elements are sprayed on to the crops. Mineral fertilisers are used on some soils solely to ensure the health of grazing stock.

Lime, though not basically a fertiliser, does supply calcium to plants. Its main functions, however, are to lighten the texture of heavy soils; to free nutrients locked in acid soils and to counteract the excessive acid produced by other fertilisers. It is usually applied in the form of ground limestone.

Fescue see Grass

Feverfew *Chrysanthemum parthenium*

The name feverfew is a corruption of fibrifuge—a substance which puts fever to flight. The plant was probably introduced from Europe in the Middle Ages and cultivated for the sake of a drug it contains which was once used to reduce high temperatures and cure headaches.

Feverfew now grows wild throughout the British Isles, at roadsides, on walls and in old churchyards. It grows to about 18 in. and bears yellow-centred white flowers between July and September. Its leaves have a strong smell which some people find unpleasant.

Feverfew is a European plant first brought to Britain by medieval herbalists

The fens – a wilderness tamed by man

The little original fenland that survives illustrates what great areas of England in the eastern lowlands looked like 1000 years ago. Although the region inland of The Wash is generally regarded as fenland, the drainage which began in earnest in the 17th century to make the richly fertile peat available for agriculture has resulted in true fen conditions being preserved today in only a few isolated areas such as the Nature Reserves of Wicken, Holme and Woodwalton Fens. Other places with fen conditions are on the shores of Lough Neagh, Ireland, the head of Esthwaite Water in the Lake District, and round the Norfolk Broads.

A fen is basically a waterlogged place with reeds and other plants growing in the patches of standing water. The bulk of fenland consists of peats on the landward side of East Anglia and marine silts on the seaward side immediately around The Wash. In fen country the peat is saturated with lime and develops an entirely different type of vegetation from the lime-deficient peat of bogland or the non-peaty marshland. The flat landscape of fenland is interrupted only by villages and towns—such as the Isle of Ely which was an island before the fens were drained—situated on isolated outcrops of Jurassic boulder clay, more than 136 million years old. This clay underlies the fens, often at a great depth and rarely reaching the surface.

The first attempt to drain the fens came with the Romans, who dug open channels to divert the water. But the agricultural use of the fenland remained a dream until 1629 when the 4th Earl of Bedford and a group of like-minded specu-

Common reed A tall grass that grows in thick masses along the water's edge. The leaves and stems are used for thatching

Bulrush The rigid stem carries a large velvety brown cylinder of tiny male and female flowers

Heron Flies with heavy flapping of its long grey wings, its legs trailing behind and head drawn in

Reed canary-grass The branched flower heads open out as the seeds ripen

Swallowtail The largest butterfly in Britain, now found only in the Norfolk Broads

Otter A shy creature that spends the day in its holt. Its thick waterproof fur keeps it dry when it swims

Water violet Rooted in the peat with leaves submerged. The delicate flowers appear in May and June

Spiked water milfoil The floating stems bear whorls of submerged slender leaves. The upper red flowers are male, the lower ones female

Duckweed Floats on the water surface, sometimes forming a dense mat

Fen pondweed The tiny flower spike is inconspicuous among the veined, oval leaves

lators hired the Dutch engineer Cornelius Vermuyden to begin a wholesale programme of drainage and reclamation. Vermuyden cut the Old Bedford River, 70 ft wide and 21 miles long, between Earith and Denver, and then the New Bedford River, 100 ft wide and parallel to his first cut.

Flax, hemp, oats and wheat were grown and the newly won pastures were used for grazing, fattening up cattle from the north on their way to London markets. However, an effect of draining that nobody had foreseen was land shrinkage as the peat dried out. The silt lands around The Wash were not seriously affected, but the level of the fenland was soon lower than that of the channels that were supposed to drain it. By 1700 there were fens again where there had been farms. Windmills were installed to pump water from the land into drainage channels. These were replaced early in the 19th century by steam pumps, and from 1913 the steam pumps were replaced first by diesel pumps and subsequently by modern electrical apparatus.

The problems of maintaining the fenland are demonstrated by the Holme Fen post. In the mid-19th century an iron post was driven through the peat at Holme into the clay beneath, until its top was level with the ground. Today the top of the post is 12½ ft above the peat.

The fenland is now some of Britain's richest farming land, producing wheat and corn, potatoes, sugar beet, celery, peas, carrots, fruit, daffodils and other bulbs. It is also a naturalist's paradise. In the dykes and waterways grow pondweeds, mil-foils, duckweeds, great yellow cress, water violets and water lilies. The open water is invaded by a reed swamp community with bulrushes, sedges and reed grasses; cut reeds are still used for thatching and basketry. The vegetation can vary according to the amount of reed cutting, and clumps of trees and shrubs often develop. Along the verges of drainage channels are willows, alders and green-winged orchids. Some 267 different plants have been recorded from Wicken Fen.

This in turn results in an abundant variety of animals. From Wicken Fen alone 72 species of molluscs and 212 different kinds of spiders have been recorded. Coypus and otters may occasionally be seen. Roach, bream, rudd, perch, tench, pike and carp swim in the rivers and channels.

In 1927 a Dutch race of the large copper butterfly was successfully re-introduced to Woodwalton Fen where it had become extinct in 1851. Conservationists are also attempting to re-establish Britain's largest butterfly, the swallowtail, on Wicken Fen, where it was re-introduced in 1955 from the Norfolk Broads.

The excellent agricultural land offers, above all, a rich feeding ground for birds, among them geese, swans and other wildfowl. Lapwings, redshanks, snipe, reed and sedge warblers, reed buntings and many kinds of duck nest on the Ouse Washes together with ruffs, black terns and black-tailed godwits. The winter floods bring thousands of waders and ducks and the largest herd of Bewick's swans in Britain.

Black-tailed godwit A few pairs nest in damp, grassy places

Saw sedge Stems carry small tufts of reddish-brown flowers.

Reed warbler It weaves its cup nest among reed stems

Wicken Fen, a Nature Reserve. This undrained, original peatland is higher than the surrounding shrunken fens. Reeds and marsh plants thrive here supporting a large variety of wild animals

Ferns reproduce by spores, seen here bursting from their sacs on a bracken leaf

Fern

In fossil form, ferns date back more than 300 million years; today's ferns are among the most primitive plants on earth. Prehistoric ferns were generally much larger than those of today; tree ferns reaching 100 ft high formed the world's first forests and the wood of those trees is the basis of present-day coal deposits. A few tree ferns survive in the tropics, but the largest British fern, bracken, only occasionally grows to more than 6 ft.

Over 50 species are now found in Britain although several have become rare through atmospheric pollution and uprooting by over-enthusiastic collectors.

Ferns are flowerless plants, reproducing by means of spores, not seeds. They are perennials and the leaves first appear as coils which unroll. On the undersides of the leaves, spores are born in minute, club-shaped sacs, called sporangia, which are usually covered with a flap. The spores, which appear from August to November, are dispersed by wind or animals. Each grows into a green, scale-like disc, called a prothallus, often less than ½ in. long, which has male and female organs. Sperms are produced and travel in a film of rainwater to the female organ to fertilise egg cells from which new plants develop.

The higher humidity of western Britain ensures the moisture necessary for fertilisation, and it is here that ferns are most numerous. The polypody, rare or absent from eastern England, grows on trees, walls and rock-faces. Four other wall ferns are found most frequently in the west. Rustyback has very hairy undersides to its wavy-margined leaves. Wall-rue looks like small bunches of dark green parsley. Maidenhair spleenwort has a black leaf-stalk and many opposite pairs of oval lobes. And black spleenwort, the largest and one

Common ferns of the British Isles

More than 50 species of fern, ranging in height from 1 in. to 6 ft, grow in Britain. Twelve typical examples are shown here. Because most ferns need damp conditions for fertilisation to take place, they are more abundant in the high-rainfall areas of the west. All British ferns, except hartstongue and rustyback, have fretted leaves and are distinguished from other plants by clumps of spores on the undersides of the leaves

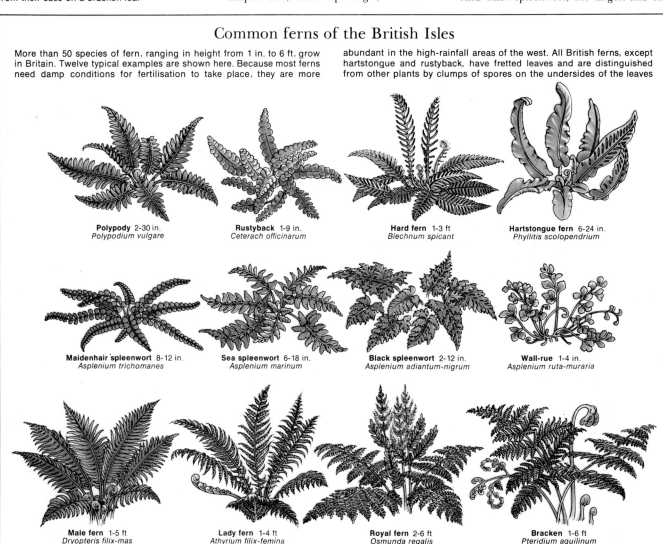

Polypody 2-30 in.
Polypodium vulgare

Rustyback 1-9 in.
Ceterach officinarum

Hard fern 1-3 ft
Blechnum spicant

Hartstongue fern 6-24 in.
Phyllitis scolopendrium

Maidenhair spleenwort 8-12 in.
Asplenium trichomanes

Sea spleenwort 6-18 in.
Asplenium marinum

Black spleenwort 2-12 in.
Asplenium adiantum-nigrum

Wall-rue 1-4 in.
Asplenium ruta-muraria

Male fern 1-5 ft
Dryopteris filix-mas

Lady fern 1-4 ft
Athyrium filix-femina

Royal fern 2-6 ft
Osmunda regalis

Bracken 1-6 ft
Pteridium aquilinum

LIFE CYCLE OF A FERN

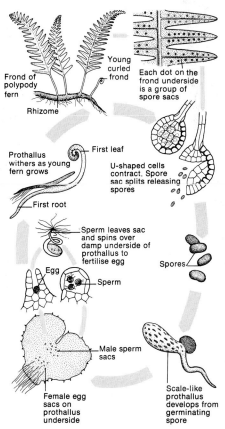

Frond of polypody fern

Rhizome

Young curled frond

Each dot on the frond underside is a group of spore sacs

U-shaped cells contract. Spore sac splits releasing spores

Prothallus withers as young fern grows

First leaf

First root

Sperm leaves sac and spins over damp underside of prothallus to fertilise egg

Spores

Egg

Sperm

Male sperm sacs

Female egg sacs on prothallus underside

Scale-like prothallus develops from germinating spore

The fern is a flowerless plant that reproduces by spores rather than seeds. Each year released spores germinate into prothalli, scale-like structures that contain male and female cells. These cells unite and grow into young ferns

of the last to unfold new fronds, also has a black leaf-stalk but with much-divided leaves.

Sea spleenwort occurs only in the mouths of caves or on sheltered sea cliffs. It is killed by the slightest frost.

Hartstongue with its long, narrow, parallel-sided leaves occurs on walls, but is abundant in woods, particularly on lime-rich soils, where it will be found with male fern and lady fern; both have divided leaves but the divisions are deeper and more delicate in lady fern.

In the wet moorlands of the north and west, two species tolerant of acid soils are common. Most ditch banks contain the yellow-green leaves of hard fern; in deeper ditches and loch margins royal fern is common where sheep do not graze. Both species have fertile and infertile fronds which differ in shape.

Perhaps the best-known fern, bracken, spreads as much by its rhizomes as its spores, especially on open heathland. Bracken is basically a woodland species, and on mountains it never grows above the timber line — the altitude above which trees will not grow.

In Scotland it can be found at up to 2000 ft, but only in sheltered places.

Unique among British ferns is Jersey fern, 3-6 in. high and limited to the Channel Islands, where it is not uncommon. It is an annual and goes through its complete life cycle, from spore to mature spore-bearing plant, in less than a year.

Field

A piece of land used for pasture or for growing crops. The sizes and shapes of fields can reveal a great deal about the history, farming methods and underlying geological structure of a region. The patchwork pattern of fields which has come to be regarded as typical of Britain's countryside has not always been with us; nor will it stay for ever. It is the work of man, and like many such works is constantly changing. Modern farming equipment and techniques require fields to be bigger than those which emerged from the Enclosures of the late 18th and early 19th centuries.

Traces of New Stone Age fields of more than 3500 years ago can be seen around Dartmoor, on White Ridge and Standon Down. The fields are small circular clearances about an acre in size which were cleared of stones and scrub, then hoed with sticks or antlers to plant corn.

Early ox-drawn ploughs, such as those used by the Celts, were light, and fields tended to be small and rectangular to allow cross-ploughing. They farmed mainly on chalk uplands of southern England, where traces of their fields still remain, including the lynchets which abound along the ridge behind Brighton as far as the Salisbury Plain. These small banks, which show up when the sun is low enough to cast a shadow, were formed by the downhill movement of soil as these ancient fields were ploughed.

The Saxon invaders brought heavier ploughs, resulting in longer furrows being ploughed on open fields which were communally farmed in strips, separated by baulks of stones or turf. Each strip was approximately a furlong (220 yds) long and a chain (22 yds) wide, giving an area of the acre — 4840 sq. yds — as a land unit. The corrugations produced by this system of farming can be seen in the ridges and furrows of old meadows, especially in the Midlands, where names like Yatesbury Field and Sutton Coldfield survive to mark land once owned by villages of that name.

This type of farming continued, imposing its pattern on the landscape, until the middle of the 18th century. However, as early as the 12th century, landowners had seen the economic advantage of enclosing land and farming in large units. Enclosures increased with the growth of sheep-farming in Tudor times, reaching a peak with the Parliamentary Enclosures between 1760 and 1820 as landowners sought greater efficiency in farming and set the pattern of fields which largely exists today. Typical enclosure fields

are rectangular with regular hedgerows, although peculiarities of land tenure occasionally produced the odd-shaped field.

In the poorer farming country of the west coast, and in the hill country, fields are smaller. This is because good arable land was scarce and each member of the community had less land. On some hillsides, evidence of fields which once existed can be seen in the different coloured vegetation growing over old boundaries. Some of this marginal land may have fallen into disuse after 14th-century plagues, including the Black Death, had severely reduced the population.

The small fields of the south-west, especially Cornwall, owe their odd shapes to the ground configuration and probably the efforts of the Celtic farmers.

The best field sizes are determined by the type and system of farming. Livestock farmers are far less limited by small fields with odd shapes than are farmers growing crops. The ideal arable field is now considered to be 50 acres, or about 500 yds square, which enables modern machines to be used most efficiently. Because of this, many farmers are removing hedges, which is changing the landscape and depriving many birds and other animals of places to live and breed. See also ACRE, DRYSTONE WALLS, ENCLOSURE ROADS and FARMING

Fieldfare see Thrush
Fieldmouse, Long-tailed see Mouse

Figwort

Either of two square-stemmed herbs with pairs of opposite stalked leaves and green-and-brown flowers which appear in June and July and are pollinated by wasps. Common figwort, which is up to 2 ft 6 in. high, grows in woods and on hedge banks. Its knobbed roots were used by ancient herbalists as a remedy for piles. It is found throughout lowland Britain.

Water figwort grows in wet woods and damp meadows and on stream banks. It is distinguished from common figwort by its rounded, as opposed to pointed, leaf tips. It grows throughout Britain, but is rare in most of Scotland.

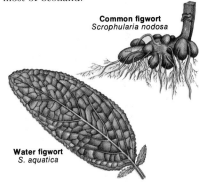

Common figwort
Scrophularia nodosa

Water figwort
S. aquatica

Tuberous roots identify common figwort while water figwort has round leaf tips

Display of temper by a siskin—a Scottish and Irish resident and a winter visitor elsewhere

Finch

All finches have the short, stout bills of seed-eating birds, but there are marked variations between the bills of different members of this family, corresponding to differences in diet. The hawfinch, which at 7 in. including the tail is the largest of the 12 British finches, also has the most powerful bill—it is capable of cracking open a cherry stone. The smallest British finch is the 4¾ in. goldfinch which feeds on thistle seeds; and the most specialised is the crossbill, the only British bird with crossed bill-tips used to extract seeds from pine cones. The rarest is the serin, which has only just begun to breed in Britain.

Outside the breeding season, finches roam the countryside in flocks by day to search for food and return at night to their roosts in hedgerows or trees. In mixed flocks, separate species can be distinguished by characteristic rump patterns and wing bars.

Flocks are usually small, but over 1000 linnets or redpolls often join together, and mixed flocks of chaffinches, bramblings, greenfinches and goldfinches may number 5000 or more at feeding sites.

Finches have a courting ritual in which male and female touch bills in a 'kiss'. During nest-building, the bullfinch regurgitates food into its mate's bill.

The chaffinch and brambling are related and often flock together at winter feeding sites, where the brambling can often be identified by its greater mobility and its habit of forming larger flocks than the chaffinch. It is a migrant from the forests of Scandinavia, and only rarely breeds in Britain. In a mixed flock, it is distinguished from the chaffinch by its white rump. The chaffinch is one of Britain's most numerous birds and breeds wherever there are trees and bushes. It scavenges around hayricks and farmyards and visits gardens where food is available. Chaffinches and bramblings feed their young on caterpillars; other finches feed their young on a mixture of pre-digested caterpillars and seeds.

The greenfinch is a farmland and garden bird. It likes peanuts and may depend for survival on food from bird tables in hard weather. Yellow wing-bars and tail sides brighten its olive-green plumage.

The elusive hawfinch has a large head and bill and buff plumage, but is difficult to spot, as it perches stock-still, high in the

One of the characteristics of finches is that they search the countryside for food in flocks, often of

branches of a deciduous tree. It constantly changes the area where it lives. It is widespread, but local in southern Britain; rare in Wales and Scotland; and has only once bred in Ireland. The hawfinch breeds in deciduous forests, orchards, large gardens and bushy places with scattered trees. Haws, hips and holly berries form part of its diet, but the stones of sloes, damsons and particularly cherries are its basic food.

Only the bullfinch can approach the hawfinch in bill size. Bullfinches feed on tree seeds, particularly ash, but since the seed crop of this tree fails about every second year, bullfinches take to orchards, where they can ruin a crop by stripping the early buds of fruit trees with their rounded beaks. Though originally birds of woodland, bullfinches are increasingly living in parks, woodlands and hedgerows, and have even bred in central London. The male has a rose-pink breast with black face, crown, wings and tail and square white rump. The female is duller, with a pink-brown breast.

The linnet, redpoll and twite form a closely related group. All are about 5 in. long and dull brown in colour, with varying amounts of pink in the plumage. All are dependent on seeds. Of the three, the linnet is the most widespread. It feeds on weed seeds on agricultural land, frequently forming large flocks where such food is plentiful. In hard frosts it often gathers on unfrozen coastal marshes where it feeds alongside flocks of twite that have moved down from the northern hills. Though the brown wings and crimson breast and crown of the cock linnet are sure identification marks, the hen resembles both the male and female twite.

The twite breeds on heather-covered moorland, high country with bracken and grass, and other rough open ground in Ireland, the western Highlands, the Pennines and sometimes North Wales. It is a dull brown

BRITAIN'S FINCHES AND THEIR VARIABLE BEAKS

Hawfinch
Coccothraustes coccothraustes
Buds, elm and hornbeam seeds

Goldfinch
Carduelis carduelis
Thistle and groundsel seeds

Chaffinch
Fringilla coelebs
Weed seeds, beechmast

Crossbill
Loxia curvirostra
Conifer seeds

Serin
Serinus serinus
Small weed seeds

Bullfinch
Pyrrhula pyrrhula
Buds, ash and weed seeds

Greenfinch
Carduelis chloris
Weed and elm seeds, corn

Brambling
Fringilla montifringilla
Weed seeds, beechmast

Linnet
Acanthis cannabina
Chickweed and dandelion seeds

Siskin
Carduelis spinus
Conifer, alder and birch seeds

Twite
Acanthis flavirostris
Seeds of coastal plants

Redpoll
Acanthis flammea
Buds, birch and weed seeds

Variations in the bills of the 12 finches can readily be spotted. With their powerful bills the hawfinches can smash cherry stones. Goldfinches have delicate bills, for eating thistle seeds

mixed species, and return in the evening to roost in trees or, as here, in a hedgerow

bird with a pink rump. In winter it often feeds in vast flocks on coastal marshes. Redpolls, also gregarious, feed mainly in trees, particularly birches. They have adopted the new conifer plantations, but also feed on weed seeds in the surrounding countryside. They often rise in a mass from the tree tops with a characteristic 'buzzing' call, wheeling in the air a few times before settling again.

The liquid, twittering song of the goldfinch made it a favourite cagebird in Victorian times. Charms—small groups or family parties—of goldfinches displaying broad golden wing-bars as they flit from one thistle head to another are a common sight in late summer and early autumn. The goldfinch clings to the head of thistles, groundsel or burdock as it extracts the seeds.

Conifer seeds are almost the only food of crossbills and the occasional failure of Scandinavia to produce spruce cones probably triggers off the mass invasions to Britain that occur every few years. Crossbills nest in January and February, so that the young leave the nest just as the cones are opening to release their seeds. They bred only in Scotland and the brecks of East Anglia for many years, but the early 1960's saw them colonising mature Forestry Commission plantations which have encouraged the siskin to breed in areas outside northern Scotland. A widespread winter visitor, it now breeds in East Anglia, Wales, Northumberland, Devon and the New Forest. The male's yellow-green plumage is enlivened by a black bib and crown; the female is more drab.

Fir

Although fir loosely describes any conifer, experts reserve the word for Douglas and silver firs. These evergreens are closely related members of the pine family. They are not native to Britain but grow profusely here.

Their timber can be used for almost anything from flagpoles to furniture.

Both have their needles set singly on the twigs. On vertical shoots the needles project all round, but on horizontal ones they form flat surfaces; in this way they catch the maximum amount of light. Each needle emerges from a flat base, which is easily noticed if the needle is pulled gently away. It does not leave behind a wooden peg, and this distinguishes firs from other members of the pine family. The needles of the Douglas fir emit a lemon-like scent if rubbed. Both firs have triangular brown seeds with pale brown triangular papery wings which assist their dispersal by the wind.

Douglas and silver firs can be told apart by their buds and cones. The buds of the Douglas fir are slender, oval and sharply pointed. Those of the silver fir are blunt, plump and often coated with white resin. The cones of the Douglas fir are egg-shaped and hang downwards. In contrast, the silver fir produces upright cylindrical cones. Male flowers on both are clusters of yellow stamens that open in May, scatter pollen and then wither. The female flowers are small and bud-shaped.

The Douglas fir is named after David Douglas (1799-1834), a Scottish plant collector who sent seed to Britain from Canada in 1827. The tree had been discovered on Vancouver Island in 1791 by another Scot, Archibald Menzies, and he is commemorated in its scientific name, *Pseudotsuga menziesii*. Its pyramidal outline, with the lower branches bending gracefully towards the ground, made it a favourite for ornamental purposes shortly after its introduction into Britain, and its rapid growth—it can reach up to 75 ft in 25 years—induced foresters to plant it commercially. Its timber is resinous and knotty. To grow well it needs fertile and well-drained soil.

There are three species of silver fir—the European *Abies alba*, the grand *A. grandis*, and the noble *A. procera*.

The natural home of the European silver is the mountains of southern and central

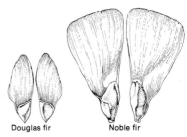

Douglas fir   Noble fir

Although they are different in size, the seeds of the Douglas fir and the noble fir trees both have papery wings

Europe. It was first planted here in the 17th century. It is no longer grown in Britain for timber, as it is attacked by the aphid *Adelges nordmannianae*, but it may be seen in old plantations.

In its place foresters grow the grand fir (discovered by Douglas in Canada in 1825), which can resist the insect. The grand fir is distinguished from the European by its resinous buds. It is a tall tree and grows quickly, especially in the wetter, western areas. Its yellowish timber is used for box-making.

The noble fir was also discovered in Canada by Douglas in 1825. It is planted in many places as an ornamental tree, and commercially in the mountains of Wales and Scotland. It is identifiable by its metallic blue-green upswept needles and its large upright cones. The noble fir grows well in damp, cold places. In the United States lumbermen called the tree 'Oregon larch' for marketing reasons.

The two tallest trees in Britain—each about 181 ft—are Douglas firs. One is in the park of Powis Castle, near Welshpool, Montgomeryshire, and the other is beside the Hermitage forest trail, a mile west of Dunkeld in Perthshire. There is a European silver fir of 180 ft at Inveraray, Argyllshire, a grand fir of 170 ft at Leighton Park, Montgomeryshire, and a noble fir of 150 ft at Duncraig Castle, Ross-shire. All are still growing. Douglas firs live for about 250 years, 50 years longer than silver firs. See also CONE

The bark of a Douglas fir becomes reddish-brown, deeply ridged, thick and corky

Noble firs have greyish-brown bark broken by grooves. Young trees have resin blisters

Heathland fire—here the plants will grow again, but in forests the destruction is total

Fire

The living, moist tissues of trees, shrubs and grasses turn each winter to dead, dry leaves, branches and stems that make good fuel for a spreading fire. In a dry spring, cold east winds draw all the moisture from them and, if they catch alight, spread the blaze rapidly. Many plants, including most grasses, mosses and heather, survive these fires, because their roots persist in the cooler soil below. But other plants, particularly conifers, are killed outright. If the fire rises into the crowns of resinous conifer trees, whole plantations can be destroyed in an hour or less.

To reduce losses, foresters divide their woods into plantations of less than 25 acres, separated by 30 ft wide fire breaks. In large forests watchmen look out for smoke from hilltop towers and report sightings by telephone or short-wave radio. At prominent points in woods and on heaths fire-beating brooms are set in stands; these are for campers or walkers to use on small fires.

On heaths and moorlands, fires are started deliberately by farmers and gamekeepers in spring, to obtain early fresh growth of short grass and heather, valued as grazing for cattle, sheep, deer and grouse. This centuries-old custom is called muirburn in Scotland and swaling in northern England.

Firebrat see Bristle-tail
Firecrest see Goldcrest

Fish

The fish is the ancestor of all vertebrates—animals with backbones. Frogs, snakes, birds, even man, are descended from fish-like ancestors. A fish can be defined scientifically as a cold-blooded creature that breathes by using its gills to obtain oxygen from the water. Such a definition automatically excludes many animals which include 'fish' in their names, such as shellfish, cuttlefish and starfish, none of which has backbones. Whales and dolphins do have backbones but they are mammals and must surface to breathe oxygen from the air through their lungs.

Many fish have a useful organ in the middle of their body—a swim-bladder. It is a silvery gas-filled bag that functions like the buoyancy tank in a submarine. It allows the fish to float and swim at any depth without rising or sinking. Fish that lack such an organ have to spend their lives on the move.

Fish eyes have a wide range of vision, while the lateral line, a series of highly sensitive cells ranged along each side of the fish's body, records pressure waves to indicate distances and warn of hazards.

There are three groups or classes of fish, all as distinct from each other as reptiles are from mammals. The first class, the agnathan fish, includes the lamprey, a jawless creature with a skeleton of cartilage or gristle. The second class, the elasmobranchs, are fish that have a cartilage skeleton and jaws, for example the ray. The elasmobranchs living in British waters are all marine and none has a swim-bladder. The teleosts, or bony fish, the third group, have jaws and a skeleton of bone. Many possess a swim-bladder. Most British fish, marine or freshwater, belong to this group.

Our shallow seas are very rich in fish. Archaeologists have discovered that sea fish were an important part of the diet of Stone Age man, more than 10,000 years ago. Britain has, however, comparatively few freshwater species, due to the isolation of these islands soon after the last Ice Age. Compared with the colourful fish of the tropics, the inhabitants of Britain's temperate rivers and seas seem dull and uniform. Many, however, become remarkably handsome in the spawning season. Male stickle-backs, salmon and char all sport brilliant red and orange courtship colours.

At one time the distribution of the fresh-water fish followed a definite pattern. The eastern rivers had the greatest variety, with the number of species decreasing to the west until in Ireland the only native fish were the salmon family, stickleback and eel, all of which originated in the sea. However, this distribution has been obscured because so many fish have been deliberately introduced into rivers. Ireland now has more introduced species than natives.

It is not only in this way that the fish distribution has been tampered with. Weirs and dams have been built preventing migrating fish from passing freely along a waterway. Canals have been cut between rivers, allowing fish to move into waters where they would not naturally occur. Factories, mills, paper works and distilleries have been built, all using water and discharging it back into the river in a polluted state, destroying fish.

Despite these man-made changes, fish are still of major economic importance in the British Isles. The seas still provide abundant food and other fish products, and angling is now a major sport in the British Isles. An increase in the number of fish farms, where trout are raised to stock lakes and reservoirs, illustrates a new trend.

Marine fish farming on a large scale might also become increasingly important as natural supplies diminish through over-fishing. At Ardtoe, Argyllshire, fish are reared offshore in cages away from predators and dirty water. Plaice and sole can be grown to marketable size in two years, or 18 months in the warm-water outflow from a nuclear power plant at Hunterston, near Glasgow. This is half the normal growing time of these fish. When just under 2 in. long they are put in steel mesh cages anchored

A TYPICAL FISH

Dorsal fin with rigid spiny rays

Dorsal fin with soft branched rays

Nostril: organ of smell, not used for breathing

Caudal or tail fin

Gill cover protects the gills

Pelvic fin: one each side of body

Anal fin

Lateral line sensitive to movements in the water

Pectoral fin

A fish swims by wriggling movements of its body
The fins control stability and direction

HOW A FISH BREATHES

Valve in mouth prevents exit of water

Part of curved gill arch

Direction of water flow

Gill filaments

Gill cover

Gullet

Gill filament: long, fine, blood-rich tubes

Skin fold functions as a valve

Gill rakers on inner side of gill arch sieve out food particles in the water

Enlarged gill lamella: tightly packed series of small thin plates

Blood vessel

Blood flow

Gill lamella

Fine network of blood capillaries absorb oxygen in the water

Water flow

The fish breathes with its gills—thin-skinned, blood-filled filaments supported by rigid gill arches. The blood absorbs oxygen dissolved in the water that is forced past the gills

to the sea bottom. They are fed five times a week and, like trout kept in freshwater farms, eat pellets made mainly from fishmeal. Fish farming is still in its infancy, but as techniques improve it could be a major food source for the future.

Fish louse

A common external parasite of a wide variety of freshwater fish. Fish lice are transparent, saucer-shaped, and grow as big as $\frac{1}{4}$ in. long. They have two large compound eyes, two short antennae ending in suction cups and five pairs of feathery legs. The underside of the body is covered with backward-pointing spines which, together with the antennae and streamlined body shape, help the fish louse to cling on while it pierces the fish with its sucking mouthparts to feed on blood. The most common species are *Argulus foliaceus* and *A. coregoni*.

Mating occurs on the fish. The female swims off to lay her eggs in gravel, and when the young hatch after eight weeks they seek out a host fish. Fish lice survive attacks from the stickleback by clinging temporarily to the inside of the fish's mouth.

In the sea, the name fish louse is given to 1 in. long parasitic relatives of woodlice.

Flax

Two varieties of flax are cultivated. They differ in appearance according to their purpose. Flax grown for its fibre, and used to make linen, the oldest known textile, reaches 40 in. and has few, short branches. Flax grown for linseed, to be used as cattle food or to make linseed oil, is much shorter, with many branches, and yields a heavier seed crop. Both varieties have blue flowers, and

produce seed in globular fruits. Some linen flax is grown in Northern Ireland. Linseed is occasionally grown in other parts of Britain to rest soils exhausted by cereal crops. It sometimes spreads to roadsides.

Fairy flax, also called purging flax, is a slender, white-flowered plant, common on grassland, especially downland, and on moors and sand dunes throughout the country. It has a thin, wiry stem with many pairs of leaves, and was once used as a laxative, the bruised stems being cooked in white wine. Peppermint was sometimes added to hide the bitter taste.

Fairy flax
Linum catharticum

Flax
L. usitatissimum

Fairy flax is a small delicate plant, unlike the sturdy species used to make linen

Flea

These small wingless insects are flattened from side to side, enabling them to run easily between the fur or feathers of the animals on which they live. The majority of the 47 British species are parasites of mammals, although a few live on birds. All feed by sucking the blood of their host. Most are very small: the largest is the mole flea *Hystrichopsylla talpae* which is $\frac{1}{4}$ in. long.

A hedgehog flea, like most fleas, is parasitic on only one type of animal

Fleas are parasites only during the adult stage. They are most successful on mammals and birds that live in the same dens or nests for a long time. The eggs fall out of the host's coat and the larvae live on nest debris.

Rabbit fleas *Spilopsyllus cuniculi* are a particularly successful species. They are remarkably efficient at getting back on to a rabbit if they fall off. When a rabbit approaches a displaced flea, the flea jumps at the host, spinning in the air as it does so. The spinning motion helps the flea to gain a grip on the host's fur instead of just bouncing off. Rabbit fleas do not breed while they are on an adult rabbit. A flea which finds itself on a pregnant rabbit (it knows by substances in the rabbit's blood) stays with its host until the young are born. Then the fleas jump on to the nestling rabbits, feed rapidly and start breeding. All the eggs are laid in the rabbit's nest and the flea larvae will have plenty of food. After egg laying the adult fleas jump back to the adult rabbit.

Fleabane

The yellow daisy-like flower-heads of common fleabane appear from August to September and consist of up to 600 separate flowers. Each is slightly darker at the centre. Common fleabane has wrinkled, woolly leaves and grows in marshes and in wet meadows in England, Wales and Ireland. When burnt, its smoke supposedly drives away fleas.

Blue fleabane is found in sunny spots on gravel pits, dunes and chalk downs. Its erect 18 in. stems branch in July and August. Each branch ends in a head containing three kinds of flowers. The 40 or so outer flowers are crimson with long, pale purple tongues; inside these are white flowers without tongues; at the centre are 6-12 yellow flowers.

Pinkish-white Canadian fleabane is particularly common in towns, growing in pavement cracks and on building sites. Thought to have arrived in London in 1690, it is now found throughout south-eastern England.

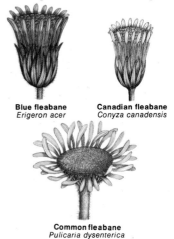

Blue fleabane
Erigeron acer

Canadian fleabane
Conyza canadensis

Common fleabane
Pulicaria dysenterica

Fleabane earned its name because of its supposed power to drive away fleas

Freshwater fish of the British Isles

About 5000 of the 20,000 known species of fish live in fresh waters. Of these, 38 occur in British waters, and 35 are shown here. This small number of British species dates back to the Ice Age, which made most British rivers uninhabitable by fish. Even so, the total would be smaller still if it were

not for species such as the carp and rainbow trout, introduced by man for sport or food. The size of each fish is given—measured from the tip of the snout to the beginning of the tail fin— together with a key to the type of water in which it is found

1 Fast-flowing rivers
2 Slow-flowing rivers
3 Streams
4 Natural deep lakes
5 Reservoirs. gravel pits, ponds, canals

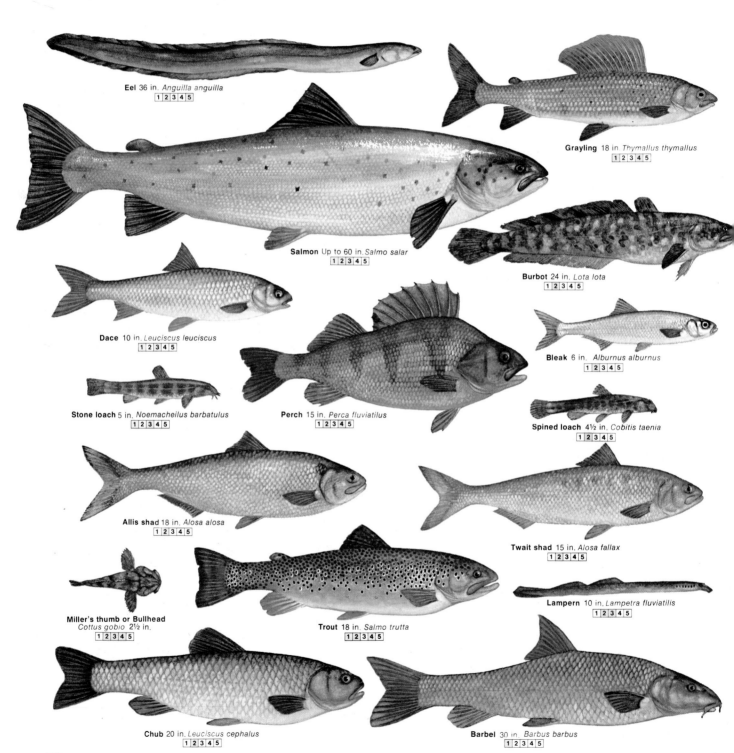

Eel 36 in. *Anguilla anguilla*
1 2 3 4 5

Grayling 18 in *Thymallus thymallus*
1 2 3 4 5

Salmon Up to 60 in. *Salmo salar*
1 2 3 4 5

Burbot 24 in. *Lota lota*
1 2 3 4 5

Dace 10 in. *Leuciscus leuciscus*
1 2 3 4 5

Bleak 6 in. *Alburnus alburnus*
1 2 3 4 5

Stone loach 5 in. *Noemacheilus barbatulus*
1 2 3 4 5

Perch 15 in. *Perca fluviatilus*
1 2 3 4 5

Spined loach 4½ in. *Cobitis taenia*
1 2 3 4 5

Allis shad 18 in. *Alosa alosa*
1 2 3 4 5

Twait shad 15 in. *Alosa fallax*
1 2 3 4 5

Miller's thumb or Bullhead
Cottus gobio 2½ in.
1 2 3 4 5

Trout 18 in. *Salmo trutta*
1 2 3 4 5

Lampern 10 in. *Lampetra fluviatilis*
1 2 3 4 5

Chub 20 in. *Leuciscus cephalus*
1 2 3 4 5

Barbel 30 in *Barbus barbus*
1 2 3 4 5

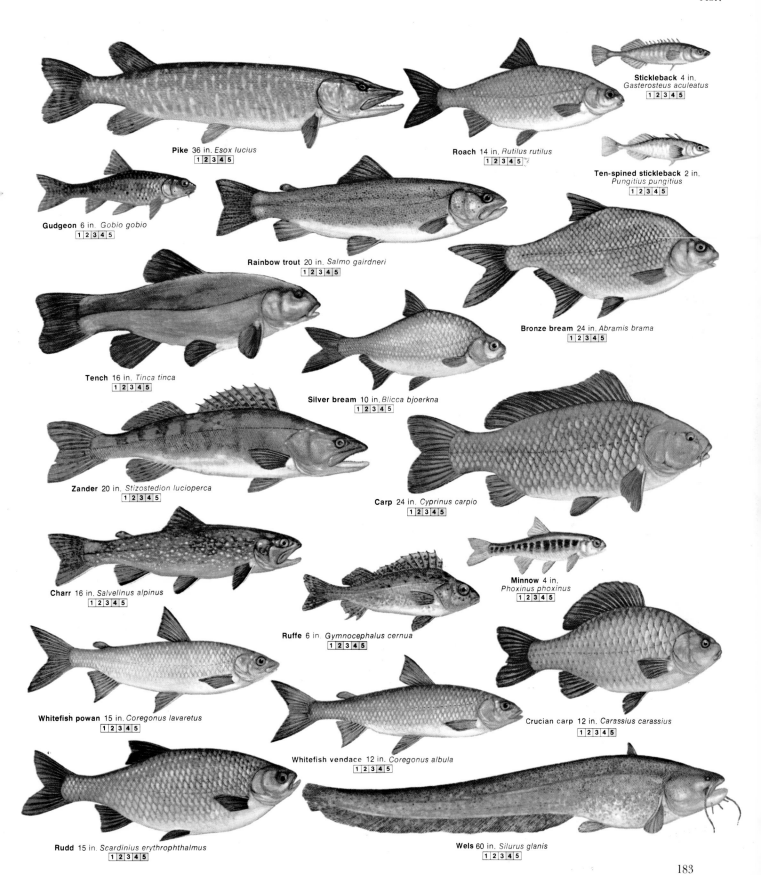

Pike 36 in. *Esox lucius*
1 2 3 4 5

Roach 14 in. *Rutilus rutilus*
1 2 3 4 5

Stickleback 4 in.
Gasterosteus aculeatus
1 2 3 4 5

Ten-spined stickleback 2 in.
Pungitius pungitius
1 2 3 4 5

Gudgeon 6 in. *Gobio gobio*
1 2 3 4 5

Rainbow trout 20 in. *Salmo gairdneri*
1 2 3 4 5

Bronze bream 24 in. *Abramis brama*
1 2 3 4 5

Tench 16 in. *Tinca tinca*
1 2 3 4 5

Silver bream 10 in. *Blicca bjoerkna*
1 2 3 4 5

Zander 20 in. *Stizostedion lucioperca*
1 2 3 4 5

Carp 24 in. *Cyprinus carpio*
1 2 3 4 5

Charr 16 in. *Salvelinus alpinus*
1 2 3 4 5

Ruffe 6 in. *Gymnocephalus cernua*
1 2 3 4 5

Minnow 4 in.
Phoxinus phoxinus
1 2 3 4 5

Whitefish powan 15 in. *Coregonus lavaretus*
1 2 3 4 5

Whitefish vendace 12 in. *Coregonus albula*
1 2 3 4 5

Crucian carp 12 in. *Carassius carassius*
1 2 3 4 5

Rudd 15 in. *Scardinius erythrophthalmus*
1 2 3 4 5

Wels 60 in. *Silurus glanis*
1 2 3 4 5

183

Inshore fish of the British Isles

About 15,000 species of fish live in the oceans of the world, of which about 400 inhabit the seas of north-west Europe. Many of these live far out at sea, or at considerable depths. But the 48 shown here all occur in inshore waters round the British Isles. Some species, such as the shanny, are common on all shores and at all seasons. Others, such as the sturgeon, are rare visitors to British waters. Because of the enormous range in size—from the 2 in. long gobies to the 35 ft basking shark—the illustrations are not all to the same scale, but the size of each fish is indicated. The measurement given is the length of the body from the tip of the snout to the beginning of the tail fin

Bass 30 in. *Dicentrarchus labrax*

Bib 14 in. *Trisopterus luscus*

Black bream 12 in. *Spondyliosoma cantharus*

Butterfish 6 in. *Pholis gunnellus*

Tompot blenny 5 in. *Blennius gattorugine*

Butterfly blenny 5 in. *Blennius ocellaris*

Clingfish 2 in. *Lepadogaster lepadogaster*

Montagu's blenny 3 in. *Coryphoblennius galerita*

Cod 30 in. *Gadus morhua*

Eelpout 10 in. *Zoarces vivaparus*

Conger 60 in. *Conger conger*

Dragonet 5 in. *Callionymus lyra*

Dab 7 in. *Limanda limanda*

Painted goby 2 in. *Pomatoschistus pictus*

Common goby 3 in. *Pomatoschistus microps*

Flounder 12 in. *Platichthys flesus*

Rock goby 5 in. *Gobius paganellus*

Lumpsucker 15 in. *Cyclopterus lumpus*

Montagu's sea snail 2 in. *Liparis montagui*

Dory 15 in. *Zeus faber*

Shore rockling 5 in. *Gaidropsarus mediterraneus*

Tub gurnard 22 in. *Trigla lucerna*

Great pipefish 18 in. *Syngnathus acus*

Lamprey 30 in. *Petromyzon marinus*

Worm pipefish 5 in. *Nerophis lumbriciformis*

Garfish 30 in. *Belone belone*

Pollack 30 in. *Pollachius pollachius*

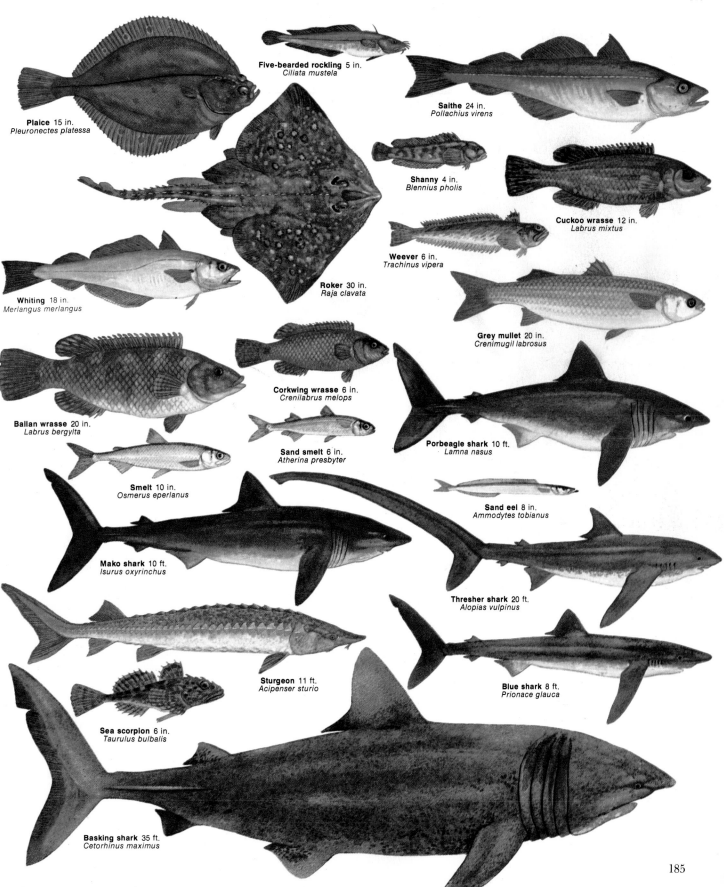

Plaice 15 in.
Pleuronectes platessa

Five-bearded rockling 5 in.
Ciliata mustela

Saithe 24 in.
Pollachius virens

Shanny 4 in.
Blennius pholis

Cuckoo wrasse 12 in.
Labrus mixtus

Weever 6 in.
Trachinus vipera

Roker 30 in.
Raja clavata

Whiting 18 in.
Merlangus merlangus

Grey mullet 20 in.
Crenimugil labrosus

Ballan wrasse 20 in.
Labrus bergylta

Corkwing wrasse 6 in.
Crenilabrus melops

Sand smelt 6 in.
Atherina presbyter

Porbeagle shark 10 ft.
Lamna nasus

Smelt 10 in.
Osmerus eperlanus

Sand eel 8 in.
Ammodytes tobianus

Mako shark 10 ft.
Isurus oxyrinchus

Thresher shark 20 ft.
Alopias vulpinus

Sturgeon 11 ft.
Acipenser sturio

Blue shark 8 ft.
Prionace glauca

Sea scorpion 6 in.
Taurulus bulbalis

Basking shark 35 ft.
Cetorhinus maximus

Flea beetle

This small, round relative of the leaf beetle jumps with its hind legs, like a true flea, and has extra large leg muscles. Most of the 130 British species are no longer than ⅛ in. and live on wild plants, although some have become pests of farm crops.

The potato flea beetle is very common on woody nightshade, although it also attacks potatoes. It has black hind legs that contrast with its general yellow-green colour.

The turnip flea beetle, which is striped black and yellow, attacks not only turnips, but the leaves of all members of the cabbage family. It does most damage to the tender leaves of seedlings, retarding growth. The larvae of most flea beetles feed by mining into the leaves of plants, rather than eating from outside in the manner of the adults.

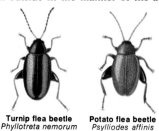

Turnip flea beetle
Phyllotreta nemorum

Potato flea beetle
Psylliodes affinis

As their names suggest, these beetles feed on farm crops, attacking the leaves of seedlings

Fleece see Sheep

Flint

Man's most essential raw material in prehistoric times. Flint is hard and durable, can be chipped into a cutting edge, and produces sparks when struck by ironstone or another piece of flint. It is found throughout the British Isles in layers a few inches thick and in scattered lumps among limestone and chalk; and it is the most common stone in the gravels of southern England.

Flint consists of crystalline silica. It is extremely hard, and is black, dark grey or brown, except when dug straight from chalk, when it is often a dull white. But many flints have a porous layer of minute particles of silica on the surface which scatter the light, thus appearing to be white. Broken bits often weather into shades of blue, and thin pieces are translucent. Sometimes the stone becomes stained, for instance by absorbing iron when being carried along by streams and rivers, which also wear the stone into smooth pebbles or shingle. Most flints have a glossy patina.

Crudely shaped pieces of flint used as simple tools 400,000 years ago have been found at Swanscombe in the Thames Valley. They were used by the earliest people to inhabit the British Isles in a temperate period during the second Ice Age. These and others like them found at Grays in Essex, Northfleet and Crayford in Kent, and along the coasts of Norfolk and Suffolk are called eoliths—a combination of Greek words indicating stone implements from the dawn of time. Most owe their shape to the forces of nature rather than to man.

It is difficult even for experts to distinguish between those flints which early man used as tools because they had been fashioned into useful forms by the weather and those which man himself hammered into shape. The earliest flint implements made by man were rough axes manufactured by striking flakes from the central core of a stone, leaving one end thick and easy to grasp and the other pointed. Examples have been found at Mildenhall in Suffolk. More sophisticated versions—sometimes mounted in wood or antlers or other bone—came to be used for hunting, skinning, cutting up animals for the pot, digging up roots and carving wood.

Flint was the first mineral to be mined. In the Neolithic Age, 3750-2000 BC, men sank mines to obtain the stone, the most important areas for this being in Suffolk, Norfolk and Surrey.

FLINT TOOLS

Cutting edge

Cutting edge

Eolith formed by natural forces

Eolith possibly made by man

Cutting edge

Cutting edge

Hand axe

Hand axe

Scraping edge

Cutting edge

Cutting edges

Scraper

Burin

Microliths

Microlith arrowhead mounted on wood and secured with sinew

Piercing edge

Piercing edge

Piercing edge

Leaf-shaped arrowhead

Barbed arrowhead

The first implements used by Stone Age man were usually made of flint. This tough, fine-grained material can be hammered to form strong cutting edges and sharp points

In 1612, the flintlock gun was invented in France, a spark struck from the stone being used to ignite the gunpowder. Flints for flintlock guns are still shaped at Thetford, Norfolk. The 'flints' used in modern cigarette lighters are an alloy of iron and cerium.

Many cottages and churches in East Anglia are built of flint cobbles. See also COTTAGES

Flixweed *Descurainia sophia*

This delicate-looking plant has much divided, fern-like leaves and narrow wiry stems up to 3 ft high. The tiny yellow flowers develop into 1 in. long slightly curved pods in July and August. Flixweed belongs to the wallflower family. Though probably not native to Britain, it is abundant in some parts of East Anglia and thinly scattered elsewhere in the lowlands in arable fields and waste places.

Flood

Many towns have been built close to river banks on land naturally flooded every few years. The channel (or bed) of a river can accommodate the average-sized flood that occurs once a year, but anything larger causes the river to overflow its banks, covering the lowest part of its valley, which is known as the flood plain. Once the river has covered the flood plain, much larger floods can be discharged with only a small increase in depth. Unfortunately man has obstructed the flood plains of rivers in many ways, building raised embankments leading to bridges and using the level flood-plain land for factories or housing.

But embankments will not stop floods; indeed, by confining the flow of water on the flood plain they may make them more severe. This happens because the embankments force the flow into a narrow channel, bringing the water above its natural level. The embankments cope with average conditions, including occasional heavy flows of water brought about by prolonged rain; but from time to time exceptional amounts of water will pour into the river and overtop the embankments, causing catastrophic damage.

Floods can also occur along the coast during exceptionally high tides.

In 1099 the sea flooded the coast of southeast England and Holland, and this is believed to have been when the Goodwin Sands were formed. The heaviest loss of life through flooding in Britain occurred in 1606 when about 2000 people were drowned after the Severn estuary overflowed. In August, 1952, intense rain caused the East and West Lyn rivers to overflow and overwhelm the Devon holiday town of Lynmouth. The day's rainfall was 9 in.—equivalent to more than 5000 million gallons of water being dumped on the 39 square miles of Exmoor, from which rainwater pours into the rivers. The flood killed 34 people—nine men, 16 women and nine children. See also WARPLAND, WATER MEADOW

A head-on view of a flounder shows how the mouth and eyes of a flatfish are positioned

Flounder *Platichthys flesus*

The only flatfish to live in British fresh waters, the flounder is often found in river estuaries and is common all round the coast of the British Isles. The flounder is distinguished from other flatfish by a series of small spines—easier felt than seen—at the bases of the two long fins which fringe its body, and on the top of its head.

Its underside is a dead creamy white, while the eyed upper side is usually olive-brown or dark brown, to blend with its surroundings. This dark colour, compared to the colours of other flatfish, gives the flounder its Welsh name *Lleden ddu* or black flatfish. The flounder usually grows to about 12-14 in. long, and breeds in the sea between January and April when about three years old. When in the sea, its diet consists of marine worms and cockles; in fresh water it eats insect larvae, snails, crustaceans and worms.

Flowering rush *Butomus umbellatus*

Not really a rush, this water plant was probably named after its long, narrow, rush-like leaves, which rise above the surface of the margins of canals and slow-running rivers. From July to September it bears 20-30 pink flowers, in clusters on a long, smooth stem standing 2-4 ft above the water. Flowering rush is more often seen from mid-stream than the bank.

Flowering rush, in bloom from July, is common only in central and southern England

Fluellen

Two low-growing, creeping weeds with small snapdragon-like flowers are both called fluellen. They are so alike that they have

Fluellen *Kickxia spuria*

Sharp-leaved fluellen *K. elatine*

The two types of fluellen can be told apart by their different leaf shapes

never been given separate English names. They can, however, be told apart by their leaf shape.

Round-leaved fluellen has all its leaves circular or oval, while sharp-leaved fluellen has pointed upper leaves. The purple-lipped yellow flowers bloom in stubble and ripen into capsules from which the seeds escape through pores with little lids, which drop off.

Fluke

Two distinct groups of parasitic flatworms are called flukes. All flukes are hermaphrodites—that is, each individual is both male and female—and they cross-fertilise one another. The eggs must reach water in order to develop. The members of one group attach themselves to the outside of fish and other water animals, while species of the other group live inside the bodies of animals with backbones. Both types have suckers to attach themselves to their hosts.

The most harmful of the internal parasites is the liver fluke *Fasciola hepatica* which attacks the livers of sheep and cattle, inflicting severe damage or death and making the livers inedible for humans. Liver flukes enter the bodies of sheep and cattle in the form of larvae, attached to vegetation which is eaten. They hatch in the intestines, then make their way to the liver, where they attack the tissue. A single fluke lays about 40,000 eggs at the rate of 3000-4000 a day, which pass out of the animal in its droppings. The eggs can survive for a year in dry conditions, but after rain they hatch and the larvae 'swim' through the damp grass until they reach a pond or ditch where water snails live. There they penetrate the soft tissues of a snail and multiply, developing into a further stage before escaping and swimming to the water's edge. Here they crawl on to the vegetation, where they proceed to secrete a resistant coat about themselves while waiting for the plant to be eaten by grazing sheep or cattle and for the strange life cycle to begin again.

LIFE CYCLE OF THE LIVER FLUKE

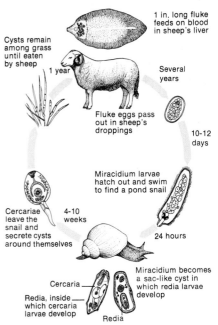

The life cycle of the liver fluke *Fasciola hepatica* involves two hosts—sheep and snail

187

Fly

Although the word fly is used to describe most flying insects, true flies have only one pair of wings, instead of the two which most other insects have. What originally was a second pair of wings evolved into a pair of knobbed organs, which work like a gyroscope and help a fly to keep its balance. Because they fly fast, this sophisticated control is essential. The characteristic buzz or hum is produced by the rapid wing beat.

Flies, like most insects, have four main stages in their life cycle: egg, larva, pupa and adult.

A feature common to all flies is that their larvae are legless, irrespective of habitat. Many flies have maggot-like larvae which are virtually headless, but those with aquatic larvae – larvae which exist in water – have well-developed heads. Most fly larvae live in decaying matter and help to break down organic refuse. Adult flies have tubular mouths, adapted for sucking, and in the case of bloodsuckers the tube is strengthened for piercing skin.

More than 5000 species of flies live in the British Isles. They range in size from midges no bigger than a pin-head to craneflies with a 2½ in. wingspan. There are three main sub-

Like most flies, the horse fly *Tabanus distugendus* has a compound, iridescent eye; the colours of this will fade after death

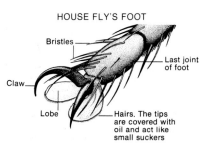

HOUSE FLY'S FOOT

Bristles
Claw
Lobe
Last joint of foot
Hairs. The tips are covered with oil and act like small suckers

The house fly is able to walk on smooth surfaces, such as glass, and upside-down on ceilings, with the help of the 'suckers' on its feet

groups. One consists of craneflies, gnats and midges, all of which have long bodies and long legs.

The second sub-group consists of several families of flies with short, stout bodies. They include horse flies, which feed on blood; robber flies, which pounce on other flying insects; and bee flies, which resemble bumble bees.

Most of the third sub-group are flies that look like bluebottles; the brightly coloured hover fly, however, resembles a bee or wasp. Included in this group are house flies, bot and warble flies, and the curious keds.

Common flies of the British Isles

Many different flying insects are called flies but, scientifically, the name applies to a particular group, which are distinguished by having only one pair of wings, instead of the two pairs which most other insects possess. In the fly, the second pair of wings has been replaced with two knobbed organs which help the fly to keep its balance in flight. Flies cannot chew food, they take nourishment in liquid form through tube-like

mouths constructed for sucking. There are about 90,000 species of flies in the world, of which more than 5000 live in Britain. They range in size from midges, less than $\frac{1}{10}$ in. long, to craneflies with a 2½ in. wingspan. Those shown here are representative of the more common groups. Each one illustrated is the subject of a separate entry, under which related species are also described

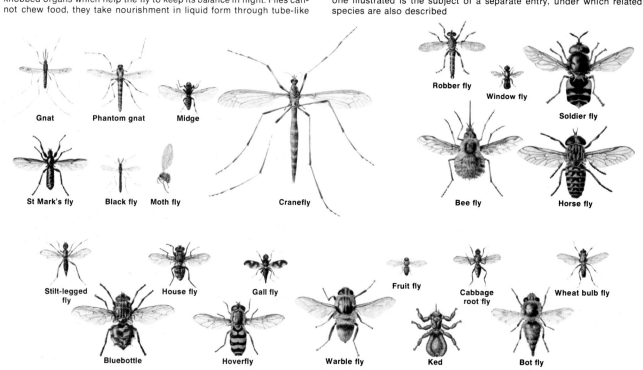

Gnat   Phantom gnat   Midge

Robber fly   Window fly   Soldier fly

St Mark's fly   Black fly   Moth fly   Cranefly   Bee fly   Horse fly

Stilt-legged fly   House fly   Gall fly   Fruit fly   Cabbage root fly   Wheat bulb fly

Bluebottle   Hoverfly   Warble fly   Ked   Bot fly

Fly agaric *Amanita muscaria*

This poisonous, red-and-white capped fungus causes violent intoxication and sickness if eaten, though it is seldom fatal to man. Laplanders make an intoxicating drink from it and Vikings are believed to have eaten small amounts before going into battle. An infusion of fly agaric was once used as a fly poison – hence its name.

Fly agaric appears from August to November beneath birches and pines. From a small white button, the mushroom-shaped fungi grow 8-9 in. high, with a diameter of 6-8 in., in a day or two. For illustration see FUNGUS

Flycatcher

There are two species of British flycatcher; they are summer visitors that migrate south across the Mediterranean and Sahara in search of the insects that form their diet. Both flycatchers sit upright on prominent perches before flying in search of food, but while the spotted flycatcher returns to the same perch, the pied flycatcher usually finds another.

The spotted flycatcher *Muscicapa striata* is the better known and the more widespread, being a bird of open parkland and gardens where it shows little fear of man, building its nest in crevices or creepers on walls or tree trunks. It arrives in the British Isles in early May – about the same time as the swifts. Both sexes are brown above and – except for juveniles – streaked, not spotted, below.

The cock pied flycatcher *Ficedula hypoleuca* has black upper parts, broken only by a bold patch of white on the wing and two white spots above the bill. The underparts are pure white. The hen is brown and cream.

The pied flycatcher arrives in April. It nests in holes in trees and is confined mainly to the hillside oak woods characteristic of Wales, the Lake District and moorland areas of northern England. Its distribution coincides with areas having a yearly rainfall of more than 40 in. It is scarce in Scotland and southern England, though the erection of large numbers of nesting boxes in the Forest of Dean has encouraged the build-up of a substantial population.

The pied flycatcher nests from April to July and lays five to eight pale greenish-blue eggs which hatch in about 13 days. Both parents feed the young, which fly at about 16 days.

Spotted flycatchers lay four or five eggs, usually pale blue with reddish markings, but spotless eggs are known. Both sexes share the 12-13 days of incubation and feed the young, which fly in just less than a fortnight. In early seasons both species sometimes produce second broods.

In autumn, pied flycatchers are common migrants from Scandinavia, especially on the east coast, but they may also be seen in town parks, gardens and even in the middle of cities.

Fly orchid see Orchid

Only the suspension towers show where the Severn road bridge lies submerged in a sea of fog

Fog

By an international standard, mist is defined as a fog when visibility is less than 1 km. Fog may be composed of water droplets or dust particles in the air. In order to form, each water droplet needs a condensation nucleus – such as the microscopic pieces of carbon contained in smoke. Such particles sometimes stain the droplets which appear yellow; and the mixtures can be so dense that they cut visibility to only a few yards and may be heavily charged with a variety of chemicals. Because they are composed of smoke and fog, such mixtures are called smogs. In London they sometimes lasted for days on end and were known as pea-soupers. Most industrial cities in Britain suffered from smogs each winter until the passing of the Clean Air Act in 1956.

In country areas, the droplets forming the fog are generally larger and fewer in number than in cities; consequently rural fogs are not only cleaner but give better visibility.

In Great Britain, fogs are most common in autumn and winter inland and in spring near the coast. They occur when the air cools below saturation or 'dew' point and water droplets form. This can happen in several ways.

Radiation fogs occur when the ground and moist air immediately above it are cooled by radiation losses of heat on clear, still nights. Because cold air accumulates in low-lying parts, this type is common in valley bottoms where light winds and moist soils are also conducive to their formation. In the early morning, such fogs often form a dense blanket close to the ground out of which trees and houses protrude into clear air.

Advection fogs are caused when moist air passes over a cooling surface. They are common on British coasts, especially when there is a warm, moist, south-westerly airstream in spring when coastal waters are cool. On north-east coasts such fogs have local names: 'haar' in east Scotland, 'roke' in Yorkshire and 'sea fret' in Lincolnshire. To escape such fogs, it is often necessary to move only a few hundred yards inland or to climb nearby hills.

Evaporation or steam fog, sometimes known as Arctic sea smoke, rises as wisps over relatively warm lakes or rivers, often warmed by discharges from power stations or industrial plants, when air, cooled by radiation, passes over them. It usually happens on calm, cloudless nights and early mornings.

Hill fog forms when a moist airstream cools as it passes up the hill.

Fog drip is moisture deposited on trees as droplets which join together until they are big enough to fall. Fogbow is a white bow seen in fog when facing away from the sun. The outer margin is faintly red and the inner margin tinged with blue, but the colours are far less bright than in a rainbow, although a fogbow is formed in a similar way. Because the droplets are smaller than raindrops, they fail to completely separate the colours in sunlight.

An early morning fog, which disperses as the day progresses, is popularly supposed to herald a fine day. There is some truth in this, for the clear skies which bring about condensation at night enable the sun's rays to evaporate the fog and produce a sunny day with blue sky. See also MIST and RAINBOW

Fogou

The Cornish name for an artificial cave built to conceal and protect people and property. Other names are weem and souterrain.

The making of fogous spread about 2000 years ago from the Atlantic coast of France to Cornwall, then to Ireland and Scotland. One Cornish example is to be found at Brane, primarily associated with an Iron Age settlement. Souterrains are a feature of Irish ditch and rampart defences like those at Ballintemple, near Garvargh. Weems, dating back to the Pictish Iron Age, are found near old fortified hamlets in the Scottish Highlands and islands. Fogous were used for storage by smugglers.

Fool's gold

The common name for a mineral called pyrites. It is a crystalline form of iron sulphide, is shiny gold in colour and is of little value—hence fool's gold. It can be found, in the shape of cubes, in coal and on the tips of lead mines. When heated in a flame it gives off a sulphurous smell like that of a rotten egg. Real gold usually occurs as small flecks in rock. See also STONE CHART

Fool's watercress see Parsley

Foot-and-mouth disease

This is the most serious disease that faces cloven-hoofed animals—cattle, sheep, pigs, goats, deer—in Britain. It is controlled by law, which requires the slaughter not only of any infected animal, but of the whole herd or flock to which it belongs. This is because the disease is highly contagious and the authorities are determined not to allow it to become established in Britain.

The slaughter system keeps Britain free from the disease most of the time, but occasional outbreaks occur. There was an epidemic in the winter of 1967-8, when more than 400,000 animals were slaughtered. This outbreak is believed to have been started from infected imported meat.

Foot-and-mouth disease is caused by a virus often carried by birds. Its main symptoms are blisters on the feet and mouth. These are painful, and the afflicted animals produce excessive saliva and develop high fevers, but the disease is not usually fatal.

Footman moth

This moth rests with its wings pressed tightly against its body, giving the buttoned-up appearance of a liveried footman, hence the name. The caterpillars resemble small versions of the tiger moth 'woolly-bears', but do not normally feed on leaves. They live on the lichens and green algae which grow on trees. They survive the winter, but do not often go into a deep hibernation. They awaken and nibble food on a warm winter day.

The 16 species of footman moth are relatives of the tiger moth, but are much less brightly coloured. Most are yellowish or brown, and some have a speckling of black.

The common footman *Lithosia lurideola* is one of the most widely distributed species. It is common in the southern half of Britain and flies by night during July and August.

Common footman *Lithosia lurideola*

The footman moth rests on branches and leaves by day and often falls off when disturbed

Footpaths

There are more than 103,000 miles of public footpaths and bridleways in England and Wales—2 miles for every square mile of land. Most of them have been literally walked into existence over the centuries by country people on their way to church, pub, farm or market. The walker is entitled to use all of them, together with roads used as public footpaths. They will take him into the heart of the countryside—through a busy farmyard or across a field of corn—and are the finest way of getting to know it well. Many paths are now looked after by teams of volunteers from footpath societies and rambling groups all over the country. These keep the paths clear of vegetation, mark them with arrows when their direction is obscure, and hack out lost routes.

Since 1968 Parliament has required county councils to signpost all public footpaths and bridleways where they leave a metalled road. The growing number of signposts has helped walkers considerably, but it still remains difficult to find some paths well away from

![The 'Rousham eyecatcher'—a sham castle gateway at Oxford, designed by William Kent in 1740]

The 'Rousham eyecatcher'—a sham castle gateway at Oxford, designed by William Kent in 1740

Folly

A name generally given to any extravagant building whose utility is not apparent. It is usually applied to the flourishings of artificiality in the 18th and 19th centuries by landowners inspired by classical education and sights seen during travels in Europe.

Thus the landscape became dotted with Greek and Roman temples, Roman arches, as at Mereworth, Kent, Druids' temples at Ilton in the North Riding of Yorkshire, and even pyramids, at Castle Howard, Yorkshire. Many fake castles were built, and genuine ones on the Scottish border were embellished with spires and turrets which obscured the authentic defensive architecture. Mock portcullises were built, as at Ford, Northumberland.

Although the building of follies reached a peak in the 18th and 19th centuries, there are examples from earlier periods. For instance, in 1601 the house of Lyveden New Bield in Northamptonshire was designed in the shape of a cross to illustrate Christ's Passion; but it was not completed. Indeed, the use of the word folly in this connection goes back to 1228, when Hubert de Burgh began to build a castle near the Welsh border. When laying the foundations he described the proposed structure as 'Hubert's Folie', doubtless with the French meaning of 'a favourite abode', or 'a delight'. However, the English made a treaty with the Welsh which required the elimination of border fortresses, and Hubert's castle was pulled down before he could live in it. The local people then cruelly applied the English meaning to the word 'folie'.

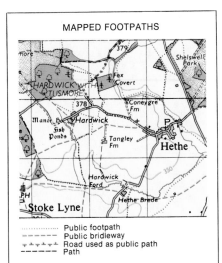

MAPPED FOOTPATHS

.... Public footpath
- - - - - Public bridleway
⊥⊥⊥⊥ Road used as public path
- - - - Path

A 1 in. to 1 mile Ordnance Survey map of part of Buckinghamshire showing four footpaths. The first three are public rights of way. The fourth may be public or private

roads. The best guide is the Ordnance Survey 1 in. map, which usually shows in red all the paths recorded by county councils. Doubts about the precise route of a path can be resolved by reference to the Ordnance Survey 2½ in. map or the definitive county map, which can be consulted at the county council, or district council, offices.

Footpaths take the traveller back in time. After the Romans left Britain there was very little road-building. Paths were simply worn into being by the feet of men and animals. When road-building started again in Tudor times some of the paths were turned into roads, but many remained in their old state. When modern man walks along these he treads the same paths used by medieval or earlier travellers.

If the hiker follows the wide green track of the Icknield Way south-west over the Chiltern Hills through Buckinghamshire and Oxfordshire and then across the Thames until it meets the Berkshire Ridge Way, he is taking the route travelled by the Iceni, Queen Boadicea's tribe, when they marched in revolt against the Romans in AD 61. It is also the track used by Midland cattle-drovers who, before the coming of the railway, took meat 'on the hoof' to towns in the south. In the Pennines ancient salt ways still exist; these were paths taken by pack-horses carrying salt — vital, in the days before refrigeration, for preserving meat during long winters. And the paths in Snowdonia and some other mountain areas were first trodden centuries ago by slate, tin and lead miners on their way to and from work.

The varying density of paths in different parts of the country reflects the varying nature of the land. Lincolnshire has barely 1 mile of path to each square mile of countryside, as opposed to the 4½ miles per square

mile of Worcestershire, richer in paths than any other county, mainly because Lincolnshire is an exceptionally fertile county so intensively farmed that a mass of public footpaths would be regarded as a waste of good land. In the same way, as farmers all over lowland Britain are rooting out hedges to create bigger fields and make more efficient use of powerful combine harvesters, so they are ploughing up and planting over the paths that run beside them. Even so, the walker still has a legal right to cross the field on the line that has been officially designated a public footpath.

Not all footpaths are old. The 250 mile long Pennine Way, which links scores of ancient tracks, was opened by the Countryside Commission in 1965. It runs along the spine of Britain, from Edale in Derbyshire to Kirk Yetholm in Scotland. Other long-distance paths now open are the 95 mile long Cleveland Way, which describes a horseshoe along the northern edge of the North Yorkshire Moors National Park and down the coast from Saltburn to Filey; the 167 mile long Pembrokeshire Coast Path; the 80 mile long South Downs Way; and the 168 mile long Offa's Dyke Path from Chepstow, on the Bristol Channel, to Prestatyn, on the North Wales coast. This path — much of which hugs the dyke built in the 8th century by Offa, King of Mercia, to mark the border with Wales — commands views of perhaps a greater variety of scenery than any other long-distance path.

A long-distance path nearing completion is the North Downs Way, from Farnham in Surrey to Dover in Kent, following the Pilgrims' Way to Canterbury. The longest route in preparation is the 500 mile long South-West Peninsula Coast Path, which will link Minehead in Somerset with Poole in Dorset.

To enjoy these paths it is not necessary to tramp their whole length in mountain boots and rucksack. It is easy to drive a car up to some point along their route and, after parking, to enjoy a casual day's walking. Some of the long-distance paths are especially suited to family walking. For example, much of the Dales Way, between Ilkley in Yorkshire and the Lake District, is easy walking along the valleys of gently flowing rivers. The Wolds Way in the East Riding of Yorkshire, which links the Cleveland Way at Filey to the Humber west of Hull, is also easy. There are plans to extend this path south through Lincolnshire and East Anglia to provide a through walking route from the Tees to the Thames; it will be known as the Viking Way.

In Scotland, county councils have not been required to record their paths, so they are not on the Ordnance Survey maps; nor are they signposted. However, fear of trespass should not deter the walker from using footpaths; the trespass law is so imprecise in Scotland that it is rarely enforced. The only time it is necessary to ask permission for

walking over hills and mountains is during the deer-stalking season — mid-August to mid-October.

Although legally there is no public right of way to most canal towpaths, in practice they are available to everybody. They take the walker deep into the heart of both rural and industrial scenery.

Some local authorities have turned disused branch railway lines into walking and riding routes. A fine example of this is the Tissington Trail in Derbyshire, owned by the Peak National Park Planning Board. The trail provides 11 miles of well-surfaced walking on gentle gradients, and there are frequent car parks.

Ford

A shallow place at which a river may be crossed. They are usually found in the upper reaches near a bend. This is because the slowing of the water caused by the bend results in sand and other deposits building up in these places.

The growth of motorised transport and the building of metalled roads caused a decline in the usefulness of fords, but many can still be found on country roads. In the Scottish borders fords were often the sites of battles between English and Scottish raiders, and on the Scottish side ceremonial rides across fords still commemorate ancient victories.

The previous importance of fords is demonstrated by the many place names which terminate in 'ford' — Oxford, Stamford and Wallingford, for example. In many cases a ford was replaced by a bridge, and sometimes a ford can still be seen by a bridge, as at Eynsford, Kent. The Romans were great developers of fords, and the stone slabs of one of their paved fords may be seen at Iden Green, Kent.

Foreshore see Law
Forest see p. 194

Forester moth, Common *Procris statices*

This day-flying moth has the bronze-green ground colour of its relations, the burnet moths, without their bright warning colours. The common forester is the largest of the three British species and usually lives in damp meadows, where it feeds on the flowers of ragged robin in June. Its pale yellow eggs are laid on sorrel in June and July, hatching about a month later. At first the caterpillars are leaf-miners, feeding

Common forester *Procris statices*

The forester moth lives in damp meadows, where it feeds on the flowers of ragged robin

inside the sorrel leaf. Later, they eat the leaf's underside. By April they are full-grown and spin strong, oval, white silken cocoons beneath the leaf. In these they spend their pupa, or resting, stage.

Common foresters are found mainly in southern England. The two other species, which are uncommon, are similar in appearance, but feed on different plants.

Forge see Blacksmith

Forget-me-not

Ten different species of this pretty blue-flowering plant grow in Britain, but the true forget-me-not is the widespread and common water forget-me-not *Myosotis scorpioides* which flowers from May to September in wet, shady places throughout the British Isles. Its stem often grows along the ground, sending out runners.

Myosotis is derived from two Greek words meaning mouse-ear, referring to the shape and hairiness of the leaves.

The familiar garden border plant which often becomes a weed is the wood forget-me-not. This is found growing wild in damp woods, most commonly in the north. It flowers in May and June.

Common forget-me-not is also called field scorpion grass because its stem is at first curled like a scorpion's tail, gradually uncurling as the flowers open. It is widespread, establishing itself in arable fields, roadsides and sand dunes. Its tiny flowers, which grow in forked spikes, appear from April to September.

Changing forget-me-not, which also grows in arable fields and by roadsides, was given its name because its tiny flowers are yellow or white when they first open but later change to bright blue.

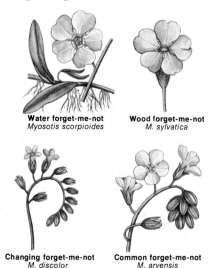

Water forget-me-not
Myosotis scorpioides

Wood forget-me-not
M. sylvatica

Changing forget-me-not
M. discolor

Common forget-me-not
M. arvensis

Forget-me-nots were worn as symbols of love by young people in the Middle Ages

Form see Hare

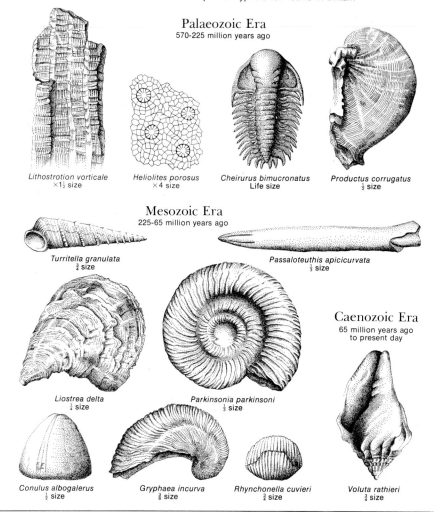

Common British fossils

Thousands of different fossils have been found in Britain, ranging from the skeleton of a 60 ft long reptile unearthed near Peterborough, to microscopic shellfish which occur everywhere in chalk. Fossils can often be found in cliffs and on beaches, where the action of the sea has freed them from the rock. The 12 shown are examples of types often found in Britain

Palaeozoic Era
570-225 million years ago

Lithostrotion vorticale
×1½ size

Heliolites porosus
×4 size

Cheirurus bimucronatus
Life size

Productus corrugatus
½ size

Mesozoic Era
225-65 million years ago

Turritella granulata
¾ size

Passaloteuthis apicicurvata
⅓ size

Liostrea delta
¼ size

Parkinsonia parkinsoni
⅓ size

Caenozoic Era
65 million years ago
to present day

Conulus albogalerus
½ size

Gryphaea incurva
¾ size

Rhynchonella cuvieri
¾ size

Voluta rathieri
¾ size

Fossil

The petrified traces or remains of a plant or animal which, millions of years ago, sank into the mud beneath the sea or was quickly buried following an earthquake, volcanic eruption, avalanche or sandstorm. The remains are turned to stone as silica filters into the space occupied by the decaying organism to leave a hard, mineralised replica in its place.

Fossils may also be the petrified impressions, or casts, of plants and boneless animals—such as algae or jellyfish—whose tissues have decomposed.

In some cases, coral reefs or shell banks consist largely of the skeletons of myriads of animals, creating highly fossilised limestones. The hard structures of plants—such as tree trunks and roots—have also produced

fossils which are clearly recognisable as such.

Fossils survive for millions of years and provide valuable information to geologists about past life forms and the earth's evolution, for different strata of rock contain the remains of animals and plants from different periods of geological time.

Thousands of fossils have been unearthed in Britain, not least of which are the dinosaurs, giant reptiles that lived about 195 million years ago. Mary Anning, a carpenter's daughter, found one of the first dinosaur skeletons, an ichthyosaurus, in 1811 near Lyme Regis, on the Dorset coast. In fact, the richest places for fossils are along the coastline where continuous erosion, caused by waves, frequently exposes new fossils on the beaches and cliffs. Few quarries or roadside cuttings are likely to be as rich in fossils.

Chalk cliffs are full of minute fossils which are invisible to the naked eye. Many larger shells are also found, including sharp, cigar-shaped fossils, such as the belemnite *Passaloteuthis*, which was the ancestor of today's squid and cuttlefish.

The sand and clay cliffs of Christchurch Bay, Hampshire, yield many perfect shells, such as the tall spiral *Turritella*, or the flatter, almost snail-shaped *Voluta*. Fish teeth may also be found in this region.

Further west, the cliffs of Lyme Bay are famous for ammonites—spirally coiled fossils of marine animals which are now extinct, for example *Parkinsonia*. They vary from a few millimetres to several feet in diameter; if unrolled, some of the largest would be 40 ft long. Ammonites can also be found on the beaches of the North Yorkshire coast, especially near Whitby where they are known as St Hilda's serpents. They were given this name in the Middle Ages, because their shape resembles a headless coiled snake, and they were thought to have been petrified by St Hilda, who was at that time the abbess of Whitby. Besides ammonites, oyster *Liostrea* and many deeply grooved shells—such as *Rhynchonella*—are found in this region. In south Devon, near Torquay, limestone beds often contain the beautifully patterned shells of *Heliolites*.

Cliffs of carboniferous limestone—such as those at Great Orme in North Wales and those near Clevedon, Somerset—contain an abundance of coral: the curious pentagonal forms of *Lithostrotion*, grouped together in stalk-like clusters, and *Productus* shells. The chalky boulder clay of the East Anglian cliffs may yield *Gryphaea incurva*—a shell often known as 'The Devil's Toenail'.

Trilobites, such as *Cheirurus* which had a three-lobed body, were the forerunners of today's lobsters, crayfish and shrimps, and are fairly common throughout the country. So, too, are aechinoderm fossils, for example *Conulus*. The strongly developed skeletons of starfish, sea-urchins, sea-lilies and sea-cucumbers preserve well.

Fowl pest

A respiratory disease which attacks poultry. It first occurred in Britain in 1926. The symptoms are partial paralysis, rapid, troubled breathing, diarrhoea, drowsiness, ruffled feathers and loss of appetite. The death rate is high.

Until 1940 outbreaks were sporadic but by 1950 fowl pest was crippling the poultry industry. Vaccination was introduced in the early 1960's on a voluntary basis, with great success. However, it is an expensive and difficult procedure and many farmers discontinued it when the epidemics were brought under control. Despite annual financial losses of £20 million arising from fowl pest, in 1971 the Government ruled out compulsory vaccination as unenforceable.

Poultry workers sometimes catch conjunctivitis from handling infected birds.

Fox *Vulpes vulpes*

The long, pointed muzzle, erect ears and glinting eyes give the red fox an astute appearance. It is acutely aware of its surroundings, and its highly developed sense of smell makes it difficult to approach other than upwind. When hunted it will double back on its tracks, climb trees, take to water or mingle with sheep to conceal its strong, musty smell. The red fox thrives well in the British Isles. It lives in woods and copses but often visits large towns to scavenge from dustbins and catch rats and mice.

The red fox is the only wild relative of the dog in Britain. It is a slender animal, about 2 ft long and 14 in. high at the shoulders, and has a bushy tail, or brush, about 16 in. long and tipped with white. Its coat is red-brown above and white or grey below. There are black patches behind its ears and on the front of its legs. The hill fox of Scotland, an introduction from Scandinavia, is slightly larger than the native type and usually has greyer fur.

For most of the year the dog-fox and vixen lead solitary lives but in mid-winter the dog seeks out a female. Often several dog foxes will fight over a vixen. During mating the sharp barks of the dog and eerie screams of the vixen are likely to be heard. They usually make their den, or earth, in a quiet spot—the hollow under a tree root, among rocks in hilly country, in a rabbit warren, which they enlarge, or in part of a badger's hole, or sett. They may also breed in cemeteries or along railway cuttings. There is no evidence for the widespread belief that a fox will cross with a dog. A fox's earth, which has a tell-tale musty smell, is untidy, with food remains and excrement left about. Several earths may be made before one for breeding is decided on.

Three to six cubs are born in April. The dog-fox sometimes plays with his offspring,

In profile, the panting fox displays its long muzzle, erect ears and sharp-pointed teeth

and the vixen takes them hunting with her when they are about a month old. They quickly learn how to hunt and defend themselves and a month later are ready to leave the earth. After the breeding season the dog-fox also leaves.

The fox hunts at night, and is as stealthy as a cat. It eats rabbits, rats, mice, voles, squirrels, hedgehogs, frogs and ground birds such as partridge, pheasant and poultry. When times are hard it will eat beetles. Cleanly severed feathers indicate that a fox has killed a bird; a bird of prey tears out the feathers of its victim. A hedgehog skin also reveals the recent presence of a fox. The badger, which is the only other hedgehog killer in Britain, does not leave the skin behind.

The fox plays a large part in folk-lore—one story tells how it rids itself of fleas. Taking a twig or some sheep's wool in its mouth, the fox backs slowly into water, driving the fleas towards its head and on to the twig or wool, which it then drops. See also TRACKS

Night skulker: the fox is becoming increasingly common in towns, scavenging from dustbins

New forests replace royal hunting grounds

Britain's forests were a little-known wilderness until the Norman kings turned them into playgrounds for hunting. Later the trees were felled for farming and industry. Today new forests are being planted for industry and recreation

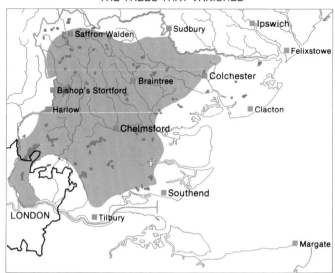

THE TREES THAT VANISHED

The Domesday Book, 1086, showed Essex to be heavily wooded—typical of Britain at that time. Today, Essex is still typical—a county of open farmland with scattered patches of woodland

In the Middle Ages, forest dominated the lives of the British common people. It surrounded them, occupying more than one-third of the land; it provided them with their livelihood; and its myths and legends haunted their imaginations. By the early 19th century these expanses of forest had been reduced to a mere 5 per cent of Britain's land area. The dangers were obvious. A country without trees would be dependent on others for all its timber. It would be much poorer in wildlife. Its upland farms, without trees to shelter crops and stock, would become unprofitable. Its landscape would become bleak. And many outdoor activities, such as walking and nature study, would lose much of their interest and enjoyment. Since that time determined efforts, private and national, have raised the amount of afforested land to 8 per cent, and more is being added each year.

The word forest derives from *forestem silvam,* a medieval Latin phrase introduced by the Normans, meaning the wood outside; this referred to the wood outside the fenced-in estates of the castles, manors and churches of the period. Forest was mainly land covered with trees but included treeless heath and moorland. Much of it was reserved as royal forests. The most famous of these, and the largest surviving medieval forest today, is the New Forest in Hampshire,

A 14th-century manuscript shows King John in the New Forest. Once a royal hunting ground, it is the largest surviving medieval forest

decreed as a royal forest by William the Conqueror in 1079.

In the royal forests the king's right to hunt took precedence over all other activities, and poachers could be punished with death. Timber was also royal property, but the common people, or commoners, were allowed to graze their animals and to gather small branches and rushes for building, turf and brushwood for fuel, bracken for bedding and hay for fodder. Few seedlings could survive this treatment and, as the old trees died, the gradual decline in forest began. It was hastened by successive kings selling forests to wealthy landowners to obtain income in times of need. The buyers felled the trees and turned the land over to farming.

A plantation movement started in the 17th century under the lead of John Evelyn, who was alarmed by the threats of the timber shortage to shipbuilding, and ironmaking which used charcoal in its forges. And until the beginning of the Industrial Revolution in the late 18th century the production of these forests kept pace with demand. Nineteenth-century industry, however, needed vast amounts of timber for, among other uses, building, pulp, pit props and telegraph poles. The demand was chiefly for softwoods from coniferous trees, and large-scale planting of these was started in the 19th century by private landowners. Even so, by the beginning of the 20th century the state had recognised the urgent need for its intervention, and in 1919 the Forestry Commission was established. It began immediately to plant conifers on a large scale. Today it controls 3 million acres of land and advises the private owners of another million acres. In addition, it has formed seven regions of Britain into National Forest Parks for recreation. These are, in England, the Forest of Dean in Gloucestershire and the Border Forest Park on the border with Scotland; in Wales, Snowdonia; and in Scotland, Glen Trool in Galloway, the Argyll Forest Park, Glen More amid the high Cairngorms, and the Queen Elizabeth Forest Park between Loch Lomond and the Trossachs. Tree planting usually takes place either in woodland in which timber has recently been felled or on hillsides, heaths and moors

Man-made forest in the Duddon Valley, Lancashire. The dark green trees are spruce and the light ones larch. They cover barren hillsides where little else will grow. Like most land planted by the Forestry Commission, the valley sides make poor farmland

which have proved to be no longer agriculturally profitable.

Britain's only native timber-producing conifer is the Scots pine. This is slower-growing than many introduced species which were therefore preferred by commercial growers. Trees such as the Norway spruce, European larch and Corsican pine were established in Britain by the middle of the 18th century. These were followed in the next 100 years by North American trees, such as Douglas fir, western hemlock and sitka spruce, a native of Alaska, which yields more timber in a given time than any other tree. It is now the most widely planted timber tree in Britain. Nowadays timber trees are selectively bred, in the same way as other plants, to produce the best crop. Scientific tree-breeding starts with the selection of suitable parent trees in a well-grown plantation. These will have grown fast, shown disease resistance, maintained straight trunks with light branches and have been found—on microscopic examination—to have good timber characteristics.

Foresters raise most young trees from seeds sown in spring in forest nurseries. The seeds will have been obtained by collecting cones just as they ripen, drying them in gentle heat to make their scales expand, then tumbling them in a wire mesh drum so that the seeds fall out and drop through the meshwork. Another machine rubs off the seed-wings. The seeds are kept in sealed tins in a refrigerated store. The fer-tilised beds of soil are raised to ensure drainage and, after sowing, the seeds are covered with sand and rolled firm to ensure sufficient moisture. After one or two seasons of growth the tiny trees are transplanted to another nursery bed to provide more growing space. A season later, when they are up to 2 ft high, they are packed in polythene bags to check water loss and sent to the forest for permanent planting.

During the first few summers the new plantation is weeded thoroughly, to prevent fast-growing plants from overtopping the small trees. Once firmly established, the crop is left to form a thicket and, eventually, a stand of sturdy poles. When the trees are about 20 years old and 25 ft high, foresters begin thinning them out. They fell the poorer trees with a power saw, haul them out with a tractor or winch and sell them to make fences or to be pulped. The remaining trees then have more growing space. Thinning is repeated every five years or so until the trees are between 60 and 120 years old and about 100 ft high. These fine specimens are cut down as the final, most valuable crop. The land is then cleared and replanted.

The forester tries to ensure that he always has some men planting, some raising young trees, some thinning and some felling. In this way there is continuous employment and, where the forester is managing a private forest, a regular income for the owner. See also COMMON LAND and WOODLAND

A cluster of foxgloves in the New Forest. Each unbranched stem bears between 20 and 80 flowers

Foxglove *Digitalis purpurea*

All parts of this plant are poisonous, but at the same time the drug digitalis, prepared from its dried leaves, is used in small doses to treat certain heart ailments. Foxgloves grow 3-6 ft tall in open woods, hedgebanks and waste ground throughout the British Isles. Their pink-purple, drooping flowers first open in May low on the stem. New flowers appear higher and higher up the stem until September. Each flower is shaped like a glove finger with dark spots inside. Its many local names include goblin's thimble and fairy fingers. Foxgloves spread by creeping stems and seeds. The seeds are very small and are easily scattered by the swaying of the stems in autumn winds.

Freshwater mussel

Pearl fisheries, dependent on freshwater mussels, flourished in Britain in Roman times; and the River Tay, in Perthshire, is still a source of pearls. The pearl mussel is kidney-shaped, with dark yellow-brown or almost black paired shells, $4\frac{1}{2}$ in. long; it prefers swift, soft-water rivers but produces its best pearls in neutral or slightly hard waters. The pearls are made from nacre, a smooth, shining, iridescent substance produced by the mussel to surround a foreign body such as an encysted parasitic worm. The shells of another hard-water species, the painter's mussel, were once used by artists to hold their paints.

The most common freshwater mussels in Britain are the swan mussels. Their 9 in. long shells are oval and yellow-green. They lie half buried in the mud of hard-water streams and lakes. Like salt-water mussels, they filter fine particles of algal food and minute animals through their large gills. Young swan mussels are hermaphrodites, but develop into males or females. The female lays her many thousands of eggs in the summer, keeping them in brood pouches on the gills, where they are fertilised. The

duck mussel, which is slightly smaller, is found in similar waters.

The larvae are released in spring and become parasitic on the tails or fins of fish such as the three-spined stickleback until they can drop off and live independently.

In turn, another fish, the bitterling, lays its eggs inside a swan mussel, where the larval bitterlings spend three to four weeks until their yolk sacs are exhausted. They then leave the mussel, which is unharmed by their intrusion.

Canals aided the spread of the zebra mussel. This mollusc appeared in Surrey Commercial Docks in 1824, having probably been carried on the bottoms of ships arriving from the Baltic. Within 20 years it had spread throughout the inland waterways. Today, its 2 in. long yellow shells with brown zigzags are found even in water pipes. It prefers brackish water.

The swollen river mussel and compressed

FRESHWATER MUSSELS

Swan mussel 9 in.
Anodonta cygnaea

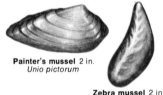

Painter's mussel 2 in.
Unio pictorum

Zebra mussel 2 in.
Dreissena polymorpha

Pearl mussel $4\frac{1}{2}$ in.
Margaritifera margaritifera

Duck mussel 4 in.
Anodonta anatina

Seven species of large freshwater mussels live on the beds of Britain's rivers, lakes, ponds and canals. The five most common are illustrated. The sizes are for fully grown specimens, but size and shape of shells varies, depending on the hardness of the water and its rate of flow. There are also 20 species of tiny pea mussels

river mussel can be found in slow-moving rivers and sometimes in canal waters.

The tiny pea mussels live in all types of fresh waters. The 20 species look very similar but each has a clearly defined habitat preference. The common $\frac{1}{2}$ in. horny orb mussel climbs among water plants in clean moving water in rivers and large drainage ditches. The $\frac{2}{5}$ in. river or giant pea mussel favours the fine sand or mud in clean, hard, flowing water in rivers, streams and lakes. Some, such as the pygmy pea mussel, which is less than 1/10 in. long, are small enough to steal 'lifts' on the legs of water beetles and ducks, travelling long distances in this way. Pea mussels, however, are a favourite food of birds and fish, which will swallow them whole.

Freshwater shrimp *Gammarus pulex*

The name shrimp is misleading, as this tiny crustacean is related to sandhoppers rather than salt-water shrimps. Large numbers of freshwater shrimps live under stones and among weeds in most rivers and well-oxygenated ponds where the water is not too acid. Freshwater shrimps swim on their side; the male often carries the female under his body. The female, in her turn, carries the eggs and newly hatched young in a brood pouch. Occasionally the whole family swims about together. A fully grown male is $\frac{3}{4}$ in. long, and the female is slightly smaller. They feed on decaying matter, and are themselves eaten by many freshwater fish.

Another species of freshwater shrimp *Crangonyx pseudogracilis* which swims in an upright position was accidentally introduced into Britain from America in 1930. It can live with little oxygen and is widespread, even in polluted water.

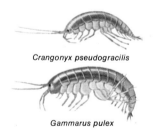

Crangonyx pseudogracilis

Gammarus pulex

Freshwater shrimps, in spite of their name and appearance, are not related to sea shrimps

Fritillary *Fritillaria meleagris*

The shape of fritillary's nodding purple and white mottled bells have earned it the name snake's head. *Meleagris* is Latin for guinea fowl and the mottled pattern of this bird's plumage resembles that on the flowers. Fritillary is 9-18 in. high, blooms in April and May and is much visited by bumble bees. It grows chiefly in the damp meadows of the south-east, particularly the Thames Valley, but is becoming rarer as these meadows are drained and ploughed. The bulbs of the fritillary are poisonous.

Fritillary butterfly

A group of orange-brown butterflies with dark spots, named for their resemblance to the spotted flower. Nine species are found in Britain, although the Queen of Spain fritillary is a rare migrant from the Continent. Five resident species have silver markings on the undersides of their hind wings. Their caterpillars feed on the leaves of dog violet and related plants.

The largest of these fritillaries, with a wingspan of $2\frac{1}{2}$ in., is the Silver-washed, a woodland species. Found south of the Lake District, it flies from July to September, feeding from bramble flowers. Its eggs are laid on tree bark, not on the caterpillar's foodplant. The spiny caterpillars hatch out in two weeks. They hibernate after eating their eggshells and in the spring seek out dog violets on which to feed.

The High brown fritillary lives in similar woodland areas. It is the only fritillary that winters as an egg; the others overwinter in the caterpillar stage. The Dark green fritillary, which has a green tinge to the underside of its hind wings, is found in more open places. Two smaller species are very similar. The Pearl bordered fritillary flies in May and June, mainly in woods. Appearing a month later, the Small pearl bordered favours marshy places. Of these five, neither the Small pearl bordered nor the High brown are found in Ireland.

The other fritillaries have a higher proportion of dark colouring and no silver on their undersides. Found in Ireland, Wales and western England, the Marsh fritillary lives in damp places and flies in May and June. Its caterpillars feed on scabious and spin a web in which a large group feed and spend the winter. The Heath fritillary is found only in Kent and parts of the West Country. Its spiny caterpillars feed on cow-wheat in woodland clearings and are eaten in turn by pheasants and wood ants. The Glanville fritillary is found only on the Isle of Wight, where its caterpillars feed on the leaves of ribwort plantain. It is named after an 18th-century collector, Lady Glanville. Attempts to introduce it elsewhere have so far failed. See also DUKE OF BURGUNDY FRITILLARY

After mating, the female Glanville fritillary lays her yellowish eggs in large batches on sea or ribwort plantain on which the larvae feed

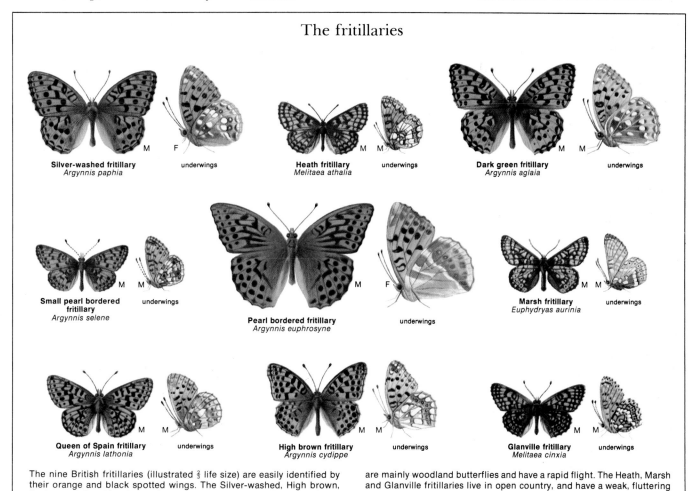

The fritillaries

Silver-washed fritillary
Argynnis paphia
M   F   underwings

Heath fritillary
Melitaea athalia
M   M   underwings

Dark green fritillary
Argynnis aglaia
M   M   underwings

Small pearl bordered fritillary
Argynnis selene
M   M   underwings

Pearl bordered fritillary
Argynnis euphrosyne
M   F   underwings

Marsh fritillary
Euphydryas aurinia
M   M   underwings

Queen of Spain fritillary
Argynnis lathonia
M   M   underwings

High brown fritillary
Argynnis cydippe
M   M   underwings

Glanville fritillary
Melitaea cinxia
M   M   underwings

The nine British fritillaries (illustrated $\frac{2}{3}$ life size) are easily identified by their orange and black spotted wings. The Silver-washed, High brown, Dark green, Pearl bordered, Small pearl bordered and Queen of Spain are mainly woodland butterflies and have a rapid flight. The Heath, Marsh and Glanville fritillaries live in open country, and have a weak, fluttering flight and frequently rest with their wings open like moths

Large eyes at the top of the head give the frog good all-round vision. Under water, the eyes are protected by transparent lids

Frog

Newts, toads and frogs are collectively known as amphibians. This name refers to their double lives, their ability to live on land and in fresh water. Toads and frogs are tailless amphibians whereas the newts are tailed. The frog has soft, smooth, moist skin; the toad's is warty, relatively dry, thick and tough. Of the three frogs that live in the British Isles only one, the common frog, is native. The others, the marsh and edible frogs, are introductions.

The common frog varies greatly in colour. Its back may be grey, yellow, brown, orange, red, speckled or marbled with black, brown or red. Markings are the dark cross-bars on the limbs and a dark patch which covers the region of the eardrum. The frog is capable of changing its ground colour slowly to match its surroundings, but the basic pattern always remains the same. The $2\frac{3}{4}$ in. long male differs from the $3\frac{1}{4}$ in. long female in having swollen pads on his thumbs. In the breeding season these pads are covered with a coat of black thorny spines used to grasp the female's body during spawning.

The common frog lives almost everywhere in the British Isles, usually near water, in damp grass and undergrowth. In mid-October it creeps into a ready-made hole in the soft mud at the bottom of a ditch or pond to hibernate under water. Frogs have lungs, and when on land draw in air through the nostrils. But they also absorb oxygen through the skin, and during hibernation this is their sole means of respiration. Immature frogs usually hibernate away from water in any convenient hole. In February the frogs wake and congregate in ponds, possibly guided to these by the smell of algae; exactly how they find the water is uncertain.

Spawning occurs in March and April and it is at this time the males find their voice. They swell their throats and croak loudly and the females chirp and grunt. The males do not croak amorously at any particular female; there is no courtship ritual. Each male clasps the nearest female

HOW A FROG LEAPS

Long hind legs give frogs immense leverage when jumping. The $3\frac{1}{4}$ in. long common frog can clear up to 20 in. in a standing jump

around the body in an embrace called amplexus. While the male lies on her back she sheds her eggs, often as many as 2000-3000, and the male fertilises them. After spawning, the frogs disperse into the countryside.

At first, the eggs sink to the bottom of the pond, but float to the surface as their protective coat of jelly swells to form frogspawn. At the end of May the tadpoles hatch. They breathe through outer gills; legs develop; gills and tail are lost; and then a final transformation into a miniature adult with lungs and legs takes place. In mid-July tiny $\frac{1}{2}$ in. frogs jump on to the bank. In three years they are completely mature.

One common frog lived for 12 years in captivity but very few tadpoles survive to the frog stage, as they form the main food supply for other pond creatures. Fish, newts, water insects and water birds all feed freely on them. Adult frogs are also preyed on by many creatures including grass-snakes, rats, hedgehogs, pike, otters and herons. Only the frog's phenomenal rate of reproduction ensures the survival of the species. The frog in its turn preys upon insects, slugs, snails—eating the shell as well—and earthworms. It catches insects with a rapid flick of the tongue. As a worm

---

British frogs and toads

There are three species of frogs and two species of toads in the British Isles, of which the edible and marsh frogs are introductions from Europe. Frogs and toads are amphibians, able to live on land and in water. At first sight they look very much alike, but there are some distinguishing features between the two. Frogs have soft, smooth, moist skin. Toads have warty, relatively dry, thick, tough skin and are more squat in appearance with shorter limbs than frogs. Toads lay their eggs in long strings, unlike the mass of spawn of frogs

Common frog 3 in.
Rana temporaria

Edible frog 3 in.
Rana esculenta

Marsh frog $4\frac{1}{2}$ in.
Rana ridibunda

Common toad $3\frac{1}{2}$ in.
Bufo bufo

Natterjack $2\frac{1}{2}$ in.
Bufo calamita

is swallowed the frog scrapes the dirt off with its fingers. Slippery food is held in the mouth by minute teeth.

The edible frog is a native of western and central Europe, introduced in 1837 to Morton and Hockering in Norfolk and to the fens at Foulden near Stoke Ferry. Today, the main breeding colonies are around London, in Middlesex, Kent and Surrey. The 3 in. long edible frog spends much more time in the water than the common frog. Individuals vary in colour but in spring and summer usually have green backs, and sides with large, often squarish, black spots. Along the centre of the back is a light green, yellow or golden stripe. The frog emerges from hibernation at the end of March. Spawning occurs between mid-May and mid-June when the male's loud croak is amplified by sacs like little balloons at the sides of the mouth. Froglets leave the water at the end of October and hibernate in November.

In 1935 a second European frog, the marsh frog, was brought to Britain. Some were put in a garden pond at Stone-in-Oxney on the edge of Romney Marsh, Kent. They soon escaped and in a few years were spawning in ditches and canals. Now they live in the area of the Grand Military Canal, Romney, and Walland Marshes. Most marsh frogs are light or dark brown to greyish-brown often suffused with light green on the back with irregular black spots. When kept in captivity away from the sun the edible and marsh frogs lose their beautiful colours and become brown or black. A full-grown female is about 5 in. long, a male about 3½ in. It can catch prey under water as well as on land and is capable of swallowing small mice, nestlings, common frogs, newts and fish up to 3 in. long. It emerges from hibernation in early April and spawns at the end of May or early June. See also TOAD

Paired common frogs and frogspawn. After separating, the males may find another mate

Frogbit *Hydrocharis morsus-ranae*

In autumn, this floating plant develops underwater shoots called turions or winter buds. These sink to the bottom and remain buried in mud all winter. In spring warmth the buds grow, using their stored food. The subsequent loss of weight causes them to rise to the surface again, where they develop into new frogbit plants. These have kidney-shaped leaves and three-petalled white flowers which appear in July and August. Frogbit spreads by putting out long runners, and is found in ditches, ponds and canals throughout lowland England, parts of Wales and central Ireland.

Froghopper

These jumping, frog-like bugs are responsible for cuckoo spit, the froth found on grass and hedgerows in spring. Ten British species are found, usually in rough grassland in summer. Generally either green or brown, they are ¼-½ in. long. Like the common frog-hopper *Philaenus spumarius*, most lay eggs in plant stem crevices in November, hatching as underdeveloped adults in spring. The young feed on sap from leaves or stems. They screen themselves from the sun and deter predators with a sticky fluid which they froth by blowing into it. The adults emerge from June to November.

The largest British froghopper differs from the others in colour and habits. It is the red and black *Cercopsis vulnerata*, which is most often found in southern England. The nymphs live underground and feed from roots. They do not make cuckoo spit, and the adults emerge earlier—from April onwards. See also CUCKOO SPIT

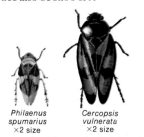

Philaenus   *Cercopsis*
spumarius   *vulnerata*
×2 size   ×2 size

Froghoppers are best known in their larval stage when they form cuckoo spit on plants

Frost

Frost occurs whenever the temperature falls to the freezing point of water, 0°C (32°F). There are two basic types of frost, ground frost and air frost. Ground frost occurs when the surface of the earth and air immediately above it cools to freezing point. Moisture in the air is then deposited on vegetation or other surfaces as crystals of ice. Sometimes ground frost is accompanied by air frost, which occurs when the air temperature 4 ft above ground level falls below freezing point.

Winter frosts are linked at times with a cold easterly airstream and at other seasons with a cold northerly airstream. Tem-

Crystals of hoar frost appear when moisture in the air freezes upon cold surfaces

peratures may also drop below freezing when nights are calm and clear, causing the ground to cool rapidly by radiation heat losses. Frost occurs most often in the open countryside, especially on hilltops and valley bottoms. In south-east England, frost can occur at any time between early October and early May. In the central Highlands of Scotland, only the period from mid-June to mid-August can be relied upon to be frost free.

Ice crystals in the form of scales, needles, feathers or fans, known as hoar frost, is the type usually seen. It is a deposit formed directly from water vapour, usually during the night.

Low cloud and fog act as natural blankets to the earth, checking the radiation heat loss from natural surfaces and preventing a heavy deposit of hoar frost. If a fog at temperatures below freezing drifts against solid objects, an ice deposit known as rime frost will build up. It forms long streamers of loose ice facing upwind. Rime frost is uncommon at low altitudes in Britain, but is fairly frequent on mountain tops during the winter.

Glazed frost or black ice is the coating of ice formed when raindrops fall on surfaces which have been cooled below freezing point. Sometimes its weight brings down electricity cables and telegraph wires. Black ice on roads is extremely dangerous and can halt electric trains when it coats conductor lines.

A black frost occurs without ice deposits when the air is particularly dry and temperature does not fall low enough to condense the water vapour in the air.

All forms of frost are a hazard to farmers. It kills off young shoots and leaves, freezing the moisture inside them.

Frost hollow

In some low-lying areas of the countryside, ground frost can occur in any month of the year, and air frost on as many as two nights in five. It is important for farmers to identify these pockets or frost hollows, to avoid the expense of frost-damaged crops. Valleys and dells, and pockets formed by railway embankments and thick hedges, are all susceptible.

Frost hollows can best be discovered in autumn, when the first frosts occur. Cold air drains downhill during calm, clear autumn and winter nights to collect in hollows below. By morning, patches of hoar frost form in the pockets, where night-time minimum temperatures may be as much as 6°C (12°F) below those of more protected areas or higher ground.

Fruit farming

Differences of climate and soil determine where different fruits are grown. For example, Kent and the Wisbech district of Cambridgeshire specialise in growing eating apples, Somerset and Herefordshire in cider apples, the Vale of Evesham in plums, the Tamar valley and the coast of Hampshire in early strawberries, the countryside around Perth in raspberries, and Norfolk and Herefordshire in blackcurrants.

Many fruit crops, notably raspberries, plums, gooseberries and strawberries, are grown largely for jam-making. Blackcurrant growing has increased in recent years through the demand for blackcurrant drinks. In southern England grapes are now grown for the market and many vineyards have been established. Peaches, quinces, apricots and medlars are also grown commercially on a small scale, and cob nuts are produced in a few plantations in Kent.

The life of the fruit farmer is one of endless battle against pests and frost. He is constantly spraying to destroy the apple-eating larvae of moths and the aphids which infest trees with American blight. In May, when the trees are in bloom, he has to be prepared for the arrival of frost at night, and if it comes he has to light fires in his orchards to warm the air and keep it circulating and so prevent damage. See also APPLE, PEAR, VINEYARD

Fruit flies

Most species of fruit flies are about $\frac{1}{8}$ in. long and look like small house flies. The best known species are those which live in association with man, the most common being the fruit and vinegar fly *Drosophila melanogaster*, attracted to the smell of beer, wine and fruit juices.

Fruit flies and their larvae feed on rotting fruit and, because they are dependent on yeast, are particularly common in breweries and cider factories.

A generation of fruit flies lives for only a fortnight and their fairly simple diet makes it easy to rear them in captivity. This has made them important in the study of genetics and evolution, and many mutant strains with unusual coloured eyes or bodies – or shortened wings – have been bred.

Fuchsia *Fuchsia magellanica*

This plant was introduced to the British Isles from South America in the early 19th century. It is best known in its many cultivated forms as an indoor or summer plant, but the wild plant thrives out of doors in western areas and is used as a hedge plant in the west of Ireland and the Isle of Man. It is mixed with montbretia to produce the crimson and orange hedges which are one of the sights of Cork, Kerry and Connemara.

The hanging flowers which are borne from June to September have four violet petals drooping from a funnel-shaped crimson calyx. More than 1000 garden varieties of fuchsia have been produced by hybridisation.

Fuchsia bushes vary in height from 2 ft to 10 ft.

Fuller's earth

A stiff, highly absorbent clay, often blue-grey, that occurs in isolated pockets. Because of its absorbency, fuller's earth was used in the early woollen industry to remove grease from wool fibre – a process known as fulling, which gave the clay its name. It was so important that its export was forbidden until the early 18th century. It is used today in oil-bleaching and pesticide production.

There are deposits in the rocks around Maidstone, Kent, and in those around Bala in Wales. The clay is obtained from pits, up to 70 ft deep. Names such as Follingpits Wood, near Maidstone, point to the whereabouts of workings. Fuller's earth is also found in Surrey and near Bath.

Fulmar *Fulmarus glacialis*

The effortless gliding of this seabird is a familiar sight along the clifftops of Britain. It is the most widespread of British petrels, although 90 years ago fulmars bred only on St Kilda, in the Outer Hebrides. There are now 500 colonies, totalling about 10,000 birds, occupying almost every cliff and

GLIDING FULMAR

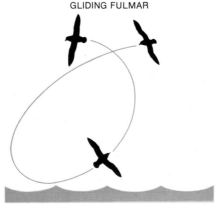

A fulmar soars on its long, narrow wings, making use of the varying wind speeds over the sea

Except for the breeding season the fulmar spends its life at sea, endlessly searching for food

stack round the coast, except in the southeast. The reason for this population explosion is not clear, but it is believed to be due to intensive North Atlantic whaling in the last century and deep-sea trawling since then, which have produced abundant fish offal for the birds to feed on.

Fulmars are easily recognised by their stiff-winged flight, interspersed with an occasional quick flapping, their white, somewhat owl-like heads and underparts, and their pale grey backs, wings and tails. The plumage is impregnated with oil which has a strong musky smell. The average length is 18½ in.

The fulmar's gracefulness disappears when it reaches land. It often needs several attempts to settle on a cliff and, once there, shuffles about clumsily.

Outside the breeding season, the fulmar wanders over the open sea, ranging as far as Newfoundland and Greenland, feeding on fish and crustaceans. In April and May birds of seven years old and more arrive at their nesting places – usually crevices or ledges on cliffs, but sometimes the grassy top of a stack or a disused building inland. The single white egg is laid in May on bare rock or in a hollow scraped out of turf by the hen. Incubation, by both parents, lasts seven or eight weeks. The young bird is fed with fish regurgitated by the parents. It leaves the nest after about 53 days.

In the middle of the breeding season, immature birds prospect the cliffs for their future nesting sites. Fulmars react to intruders by ejecting a stream of foul-smelling oily vomit from the beak.

Fumitory *Fumaria officinalis*

A common weed, 3-12 in. high, fumitory has slender spikes of pink flowers, which are often tipped with purple, and grows throughout the summer. It is widespread in Britain, although rare in the west. Nectar is produced in a pouch on the upper petals but the flower is self-pollinating.

The smoky grey, feathery leaves are the origin of its medieval name *Fumus terrae*, meaning smoke of the earth. When the plant is pulled up it smells of smoke, and its juice makes the eyes smart. It once had a reputation as a cure for all ills.

Fumitory flowers have four petals: an outer pair enclosing an inner pair

Fungus

A non-flowering plant which lacks chlorophyll—the green matter which helps other plants to produce food from sunlight—and so relies for sustenance and growth on organic matter. Those which feed on dead plants and animals are saprophytes; those which feed on living ones are called parasites.

It is sometimes assumed that all club-shaped fungi can be divided into two groups, edible mushrooms and poisonous toadstools, but there are hundreds of fungi which fall into neither category. In the British Isles, the common mushroom is the only one generally eaten but other species are edible

and the remainder are not all poisonous.

Fungi are divided into three main groups: the familiar club-shaped ascomycetes and basidiomycetes, and the tiny, thread-like phycomycetes.

The first group includes truffles, which develop underground, and morels, both edible fungi; and the blue-green moulds that grow on damp clothing and leather and which are used to colour Stilton, Gorgonzola and Roquefort cheese. It is from one of these blue-green moulds that penicillin is obtained. The group also includes yeasts, powdery mildews, such as the one that attacks oak seedlings in late summer and autumn, and ergot, the growth which infects rye and caused many deaths from gangrene in the Middle Ages. Ergot can also produce paralysis in cattle and was once used as a drug in childbirth to speed up the contraction of the uterine muscles during labour.

The second group includes mushrooms, toadstools, puff-balls, earth stars, bracket fungi and the rusts which attack wheat and vegetables. The two groups are different in that the first produces spores inside a sac, the second outside.

The most familiar members of the third group are the white and grey moulds which grow on bread, jam and other foods; and the fungi which produce 'fluff' on aquarium fish and athlete's foot on humans.

Related to fungi are slime moulds, which consist of jelly-like protoplasm not threads, and move about and feed on rotting vege-

THE STRUCTURE OF A FUNGUS

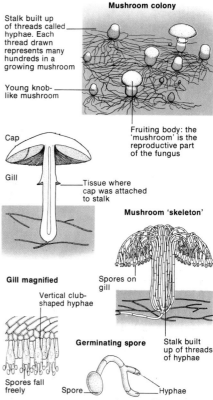

A mushroom is a typical fungus. The umbrella-shaped part is the fruiting body. The rest of the plant is a mass of interwoven threads that spread over or into the soil. Other fungi grow in a similar way on plants and animals

table matter, such as decaying tree trunks. The protoplasm eventually turns into spore cases. Some slime moulds are individual, others are joined together.

Fungi grow from spores, not seeds. Fine threads, called hyphae, emerge from the spore then branch and intertwine. In this mesh of threads small knobs appear which enlarge, push their way to the surface and eventually form the fruiting bodies. In ascomycetes and basidiomycetes these consist of a stalk and cap, on the underside of which are either pores, as in the edible boletus, or radiating gills, as in the edible mushroom and the poisonous fly agaric.

The fruiting bodies, in turn, produce more spores—millions of them. A mushroom with a 4 in. wide cap, for example, produces about 16,000 million spores. However, only a minute proportion of these settle on suitable ground and germinate. Most fungi which grow from the ground produce fruiting bodies in autumn, mainly September, but only when the soil is damp. Growth normally ceases with the onset of the first frosts, but a few fungi, such as the edible winter fungus, appear after this. Morels, some cup fungi and St George's mushroom fruit in spring.

Crumble cap *Coprinus disseminatus* is found in mixed woodland, often on rotten stumps

Common fungi of the British Isles

There are about 100,000 species of fungi in the world, of which more than 10,000 grow in the British Isles. Fungi grow either on the dead remains of plants and animals, or as parasites on living organisms. They range in size from pinhead moulds, which grow on bread and other food, to the giant puffball, which can be as big as a football. The part of a fungus seen above ground—the mushroom or toadstool—is the fruit. The main structure of a fungus consists of a mass of threads running through the soil. The fungi shown here include all the more poisonous species, together with a selection of edible and inedible species. No fungus should be eaten unless it has been positively identified as edible

Edible

Saffron milk-cap
Lactarius deliciosus
Coniferous woods
July-October

Morel
Morchella esculenta
Deciduous woods, grassland
Spring

Beefsteak fungus
Fistulina hepatica
On deciduous trees
Late summer and autumn

Honey fungus
Armillaria mellea
At the bases of trees
Autumn

Cep
Boletus edulis
Woods, especially beech
September-November

Oyster fungus
Pleurotus ostreatus
On trees, especially beech
Late autumn, winter

Wood mushroom
Agaricus silvicola
Woods
August-November

Winter fungus
Flammulina velutipes
Deciduous woods
September-March

Truffle
Tuber aestivum
Chalky soil,
beechwoods
Late summer

Common puff-ball
Lycoperdon pereatum
Mixed woodlands
July-December

Chanterelle
Cantharellus cibarius
Woods, especially beech
July-December

Grisette
Amanita vaginata
Deciduous woods, heaths
Summer and autumn

Field mushroom
Agaricus campestris
Meadows
Late summer and autumn

Fairy ring champignon
Marasmius oreades
Commons, heathland
July-November

Wood blewitt
Trioholoma nudum
Woods, especially beechwoods
October-November

Shaggy ink cap
Coprinus comatus
Rich soil
Late spring until autumn

Horn of plenty
Craterellus cornucopioides
Near beech trees
Late summer and autumn

Deceiver
Laccaria laccata
Woodlands, boggy places
Summer to winter

Jew's ear fungus
Auricularia auricula
On elder trees
All year, but especially autumn

St George's mushroom
Tricholoma gambosum
In undergrowth and light scrub
Spring

Parasol mushroom
Lepiota procera
Edges of woodland
Summer and autumn

Inedible

Earth star
Geastrum triplex
Beech woods
Summer and autumn

Black bulgar
Bulgaria inquinans
Oak and beech trees
Autumn

Sickener
Russula emetica
Under conifers
and mixed woods
July-October

Elf cup
Peziza coccinea
On rotting wood
December-February

Witches' butter
Exidia glandulosa
Dead branches, especially oak
Usually winter

Razor strop
Piptoporus betulinus
Birch trees
All year round

Stinkhorn
Phallus impudicus
Rich soil in woods
Mid-summer to autumn

Tinder
Fomes fomentarius
Birch trees
All year round

Bracket fungus
Grifola gigantea
Oak and beech trees
July-January

Funnel cap
Clitocybe infundibuliformis
Woods, heaths
July-November

Dead men's fingers
Xylosphaera polymorpha
Stumps of trees
All times

Wood woolly foot
Collybia peronata
Woodlands
Late summer and autumn

Beech tuft
Oudemansiella mucida
Beech trees
Late summer and autumn

Blusher
Amanita rubescens
Woodland
Summer and autumn

Poisonous

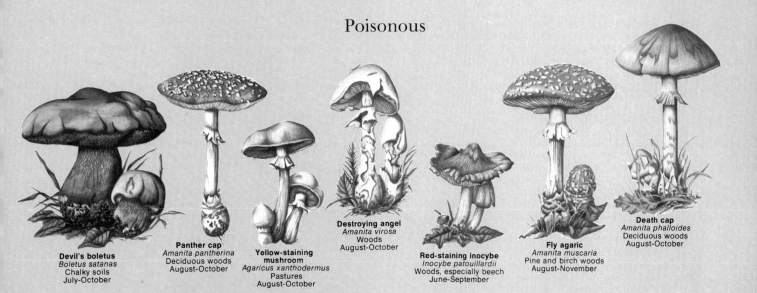

Devil's boletus
Boletus satanas
Chalky soils
July-October

Panther cap
Amanita pantherina
Deciduous woods
August-October

**Yellow-staining
mushroom**
Agaricus xanthodermus
Pastures
August-October

Destroying angel
Amanita virosa
Woods
August-October

Red-staining inocybe
Inocybe patouillardii
Woods, especially beech
June-September

Fly agaric
Amanita muscaria
Pine and birch woods
August-November

Death cap
Amanita phalloides
Deciduous woods
August-October

G

Gabbro

This dark, coarse, granite-like rock was formed by the cooling of a mass of molten material more than 400 million years ago. Gabbro differs from granite in the minerals it contains. It has a little quartz, some feldspar and a large amount of darker minerals, such as hornblende. Sometimes it also contains pale green olivine. Gabbro is found in Cornwall near the Lizard, near St David's, Pembrokeshire, in the Lake District and parts of Scotland. One of the most famous outcrops forms the Cuillin ridge in Skye.

Gadfly

Cattle can sometimes be seen dashing about in a frenzy with their tails erect. They are gadding, behaviour which it used to be believed was caused by attacks of biting flies such as horse flies and clegs—collectively called gadflies. More recent observations have shown that cattle tolerate biting flies with remarkable patience, and that they only start gadding at the approach of certain non-biting flies. These are the bot and warble flies which lay their eggs on the cattle. The eggs hatch into larvae which eat their way through the hide to become internal parasites. See also BOT FLY, WARBLE FLY

Gadwall see Duck

Gale

Strong winds can tear down trees, rip off roofs, destroy bridges and other structures and whip the sea into mountainous waves which pound the coast and flood low-lying land. Such winds are called gales, though strictly speaking the term applies only to winds of 34-40 knots (39-46 mph). Sometimes the high-speed wind lasts only a few seconds, followed by an equally dramatic lull; at other times the speed is maintained fairly constantly for minutes or hours.

Gales are most common along western and northern coasts exposed to winds moving in from the Atlantic. This is because winds build up speed more easily over the smooth surface of the sea than over the uneven surface of the land. In such coastal areas trees often lean away from the direction of strong prevailing winds. Gales are expected on 20-30 days a year in western Scotland, compared with five days a year in central eastern Scotland.

Winds are also much stronger on hill tops, partly because friction with the ground is less and partly because the flow of the wind is concentrated and so accelerated by any broad obstruction lying in its path, such as a range of hills. See also WIND

Gall

Any abnormal plant growth or swelling which results from a parasitic organism within the plant is called a gall. Many are caused by insects, such as gall flies, gall wasps, bugs and midges, together with a few beetles and moth caterpillars. Mites, eel worms, fungi and bacteria also cause galls. Some galls are formed by the parasite physically interfering with the plant's growth, others by substances secreted by the parasite.

Oaks are likely to have several different types of galls. One stage in the life cycle of the gall wasp *Biorhiza pallida* causes the familiar oak apple gall, which turns yellowish-brown with age. It has an irregular, globular shape. The gall formed on Norway and sitka spruce by the aphid *Adelges abietis* swells into a false cone.

Galls on the underside of an oak leaf. Each houses the larva of a gall wasp

Gall fly

Gooseberry-sized swellings on the stems of thistles indicate the presence of thistle gall fly larvae—one of the most common of the 74 British species of gall fly. Thistle gall flies *Urophora cardui* are up to ⅜ in. long, with a mottled pattern on their wings, and resemble house flies. In May, the females lay their eggs inside the thistle stems. These

hatch into larvae which cause the gall to swell. The galls are easily noticeable on the dead thistle stems in winter. Between one and seven larvae live in each gall, from which they emerge the following spring.

The name fruit fly is given to some of the species whose larvae feed inside fruits rather than galls. The ¾ in. long *Rhagoletis alternata* feeds on wild rose hips and a few species attack cultivated fruits, but these are not a serious pest in Britain. The flies have lightly banded wings.

The celery fly *Philophylla heraclei*, which also has banded wings, attacks celery, parsnips and plants of the parsley family, such as angelica and hogweed.

HOW A GALL IS FORMED

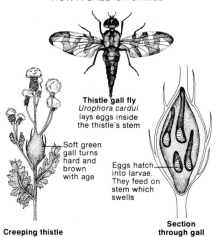

Thistle gall fly
Urophora cardui
lays eggs inside
the thistle's stem

Soft green
gall turns
hard and
brown
with age

Eggs hatch
into larvae.
They feed on
stem which
swells

Creeping thistle

Section through gall

A gall forms on a creeping thistle stem as tunnelling fly larvae make plant cells swell

Gannet *Sula bassana*

Two-thirds of the world's gannets or solan geese, as they were once called, live on the cliff-ledges of Britain's 13 noisy gannetries. Their largest colony is on the remote island of St Kilda in the Outer Hebrides, where about 17,000 nests can be found. The nests are made of seaweed in tufts of grass. In all, about 100,000 gannets breed in Britain. These large seabirds are 3 ft long, with a wingspan of up to 6 ft. Their huge webbed feet are used to incubate the single white egg, laid between March and June. The incubation period is about 44 days. The nestling, which is fed by both parents, flies and makes its own way to the sea after 90 days. Adult gannets have white plumage with black wingtips and a yellow cast over the head and neck. The bill is pale blue. Immature birds are dark brown with white cheeks and resemble

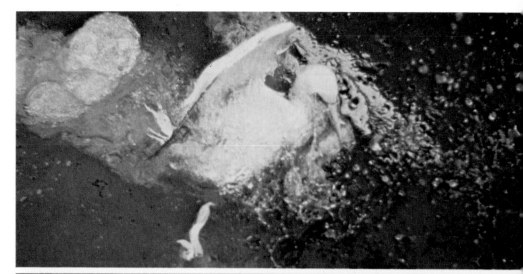

adults by their fourth year. On the gannetries, separate areas of territory are established by the stabbing distance of each bird's dagger-like bill. An incoming bird which misjudges its landing point has to run the gauntlet of its neighbours as it scuttles through their territories, and young gannets wandering from their nests are mercilessly stabbed to death.

In flight, gannets resemble huge winged torpedoes. They dive down on fish from up to 100 ft above the sea, plunging into the water in a fountain of spray. An increase in mackerel in the Irish Sea has probably assisted the rapid growth of the Welsh gannetry on Grassholm, now about 15,500 pairs. Other colonies are on Alderney and the Scottish islands of Ailsa Craig, Scar Rocks, Sula Sgeir, Sule Stack, Noss, Hermaness and the Bass Rock. In Ireland they breed on Bull Rock and Little Skellig. They nest at only one place on the mainland, Bempton in Yorkshire.

Gannets are now on the increase, because of the 1954 Bird Protection Act, after suffering a serious decline in numbers during the 19th century, when they were hunted for food. Today only the men from the Ness district of the Isle of Lewis hunt them. They take a proportion of the young gannets of Sula Sgeir, in the Outer Hebrides, each year under a special provision of the Act.

Gannets have an elaborate courtship display, with fencing between male and female, and the biting of the female's neck. Older, experienced males will reclaim old nesting sites, fighting for possession if necessary, before 'advertising' for a female with repeated bowing.

Gannets are silent for most of the year, but emit short, harsh, screeching cries throughout the breeding season.

WHERE GANNETS LIVE

There are 13 gannet colonies in the British Isles of which only one, at Bempton, is on the mainland. The largest flock is on St Kilda

The spectacular dive-bombing technique of the gannet. The bird drops like a stone from up to 100 ft with its wings, which can span 6 ft, folded back to form a living arrowhead, plunging into the sea and emerging triumphant with a fish, which it swallows whole

THE JAWS OF THE GARFISH

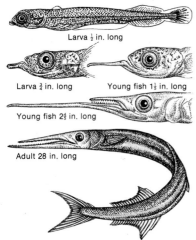

Larva ½ in. long

Larva ¾ in. long   Young fish 1¼ in. long

Young fish 2⅜ in. long

Adult 28 in. long

The young garfish starts life with an ordinary shaped mouth like any other fish, but as it grows the jaws develop unevenly

Garfish *Belone belone*
The bright green bones of a large, 20-30 in. long garfish make it look unappetising, but its dry flesh is not unpleasant. It swims in the surface layers of the sea feeding on the larger planktonic animals, particularly young fish and crustacean larvae. It has long, beak-like jaws with many teeth, and a head more than a quarter the length of its body.

The garfish, or garpike, is found off the southern and western coasts of Britain in early summer when it moves into shallow, warm water to breed. The eggs have long, sticky threads which tangle in seaweed and flotsam, keeping them afloat until they hatch. In late summer the garfish is more common off the northern coasts.

Garganey see Duck
Garlic, Crow see Onion
Garpike see Garfish

Garth
A small plot of enclosed land, usually by a house or cottage. The word, similar to the Scandinavian *gaard,* meaning farm, comes from Old Norse. Garth is still used in the north of England and appears in place names such as Hogarth and Aysgarth. The common words 'garden' and 'yard' are related to 'garth' linguistically, and have a similar meaning.

Gate
The word gate comes from the Old English *geat,* an opening, and in the north it is often corrupted to 'yet' as in Kirk Yetholm, the gate town, just across the Northumbrian border in Scotland.

Gate is applied to the simplest of wooden structures opening into a field or garden and equally to the impressive stone and brick entrances to medieval towns. Many fine medieval examples survive in Britain, such as the 15th-century Hotspur Tower in Alnwick, Northumberland, and West Gate, the sole surviving city gate in Canterbury.

Roman gates survive in Lincoln, Cirencester and Colchester. The word as it occurs in many street names does not necessarily imply an entrance, but may mean 'way' or 'path' as in Cowgate, Newcastle-upon-Tyne, and Gallowgate, Glasgow.

Oak is the best wood for gates. An oak gate will last for up to a century, if it is fastened together with oak pegs, not iron.

The most common pattern is the five-barred gate, although there are six-barred gates and, rarely, gates with four bars. Five-barred gates are usually hung on strap hinges and are heavier at the hinge end. The bars are reinforced by diagonal braces, the pattern of which varies from district to district.

Farm gates are generally 9-10 ft wide by 3-4 ft high; the rails are closer together at the bottom to prevent lambs getting through. As farm machines, particularly combine harvesters, have become larger, the problem of getting them through gates of the old type has become serious. Many farms have dispensed with wooden gates, barring field entrances with electric fences or with roughly made gates of wire.

Gatehouse
The apartments over town gates or over the entry to the enclosed property of a monastic house. A fine example of such a gatehouse survives over the entry to Jedburgh Abbey in Roxburghshire.

Gatehouses are also the houses built for servants at the entrance to estates. Many built in the 18th and 19th centuries were designed as miniature castles or as highly ornate cottages, almost deserving the description of folly.

The hamlet of Gatehouse, near Bellingham, Northumberland, is notable for two bastle houses (stronghouses) built in the 16th century for defence against the Scots.

Gatekeeper butterfly see Brown butterfly
Gean see Cherry

Gentian
Purple and blue gentians colour many sunny slopes in short grassland throughout the country in late summer. Two species are commonly found in Britain.

Field gentian is found mainly in the north on acid or neutral soils. It can be recognised by its purplish flowers which grow in sprays and each of which has four petals, two large and two small.

Autumn gentian flowers later. It is widespread in the south, particularly on lime-rich soils, and has five petals, each more or less equal in size.

The name honours Gentius, a pirate king of Illyria (Hungary), who lived *c.* 170 BC and is considered to be the discoverer of the medicinal uses of plants. The roots of gen-

Field gentian
Gentianella campestris

Autumn gentian
G. amarella

Common gentian has four petals and flowers earlier than the five-petalled autumn gentian

tians have been used since ancient times to produce a substance, brownish and bitter, which is added to medicines designed to act as general tonics.

Ghost moth see Swift moth

Gibbet
An upright post with a projecting arm, similar to a gallows, from which criminals were strung up after execution, near the scene of the crime, as an awesome lesson on the consequences of crime.

Gibbets were in use up to the 18th century for this purpose and some still survive in lonely places, such as near the remains of the Steng Cross, south-east of Elsdon, Northumberland.

The 'jib' crane, still a feature of many warehouses, is so called because of its resemblance to the gibbet.

Gill see Valley

Ginkgo *Ginkgo biloba*
This charming tree, found only in parks and gardens, puzzles people by its unique foliage. It bears wedge-shaped leaves, or fronds, like those of a maidenhair fern, though larger; so it is often called the maidenhair tree.

It is bright green in spring, then the leaves mellow to golden-yellow in autumn and fall leaving odd, knobbly twigs. Ginkgo stands in a botanical order of its own, *Ginkgoaceae,* older than all other living trees. Its fossils can be found in British coal measures 250

Fossilised leaves of a ginkgo, millions of years old, found in a British coal measure

million years old, but it survives in the wild only in Chekiang, China.

It has long been cultivated in Chinese and Japanese gardens and was brought to Europe in the 1730's. Each tree is either male or female and bears catkin-like flowers. The fruit, rarely seen, looks like a plum with foul-smelling green pulp round a brown thin-shelled nut, which in China is washed, roasted and eaten. The record height is 90 ft at Linton Park, Kent. The ginkgo lives for 300 years.

The ornamental ginkgo or maidenhair tree survives in the wild only in Chekiang, China

Gipsy

A member of a wandering race, probably of Indian origin. Their language, Romany, is a corrupted dialect of Hindi. On their arrival in Britain, probably in the late 15th century, they were wrongly thought to have come from Egypt: hence the name.

The Faa Gipsies of the Scottish border counties supplied the last crowned Queen of the Gipsies, Esther Faa Blythe, late in the 19th century. The Gipsy 'palace', a cottage where she held court, still stands in the Roxburghshire village of Kirk Yetholm.

It was as metal-workers that most Gipsies made a living. Their activities broadened to include basket and peg-making, horse-dealing, flower and herb-selling and fortune-telling. They were also entertainers and considered to be splendid fiddlers and pipers.

The traditional, gaily decorated Gipsy caravan can still be seen in parts of Ireland and occasionally in southern England during the hop and fruit-picking seasons. But the decline of the county fair at which the Gipsies used to trade has led to many abandoning the traditional nomadic life.

Section of flower

The small, white flowers of gipsywort grow in dense clusters close to the leaves

Gipsywort *Lycopus europaeus*

A flower which looks like mint with white flowers and jagged, yellowish-green leaves. Gipsywort can easily be seen in flower in marshes and at the sides of streams and ditches throughout the lowlands from June to September.

It is a slightly hairy plant, growing up to 3 ft. The flowers have only two stamens but the vestiges of two others can be seen between them. Occasionally there are some smaller, female flowers which have no stamens.

The plant produces a strong black dye, formerly used by Gipsies to make them darker-skinned. It is a fast or permanent dye, and has also been used for linen.

Gladdon see Iris

Glasshouse

The biggest concentration of glasshouses in the British Isles is in the Lea Valley, on the western borders of Essex, where some 1500 acres are under glass. Influenced by the close proximity of the valley to the London market, large-scale expansion of hothouse horticulture began there in the 1880's and 1890's. It was a natural development of the popular 19th-century hobby of growing ferns, orchids and vines.

The basic function of a glasshouse is to protect plants against adverse weather conditions, at the same time allowing just as much light to reach them as if they were growing in the open. The glasshouse also acts as a heat trap. The short sun rays pass through the glass and are absorbed by the plants. They are then re-radiated as long heat rays which cannot go through the glass.

The modern glasshouse industry concentrates on growing tomatoes, lettuces, cucumbers, flowers and pot plants. In 1970-1 £15,250,000 worth of tomatoes were grown in Britain's heated glasshouses and £4,050,000 worth in cold glasshouses. Today, much of the tomato-growing Channel Island of Guernsey is under glass, and important glasshouse centres in England include the Worthing district, southern Hampshire, north-west Kent, the outskirts of Blackpool and the Clyde Valley in Lanarkshire.

Glasswort see Samphire
Gleaning see Stubble

Glebe

In the days when the Anglican clergy, like their parishioners, grew their own food, a glebe (or glebeland), was an important part of a churchman's 'living', or benefice. From the Latin *glaeba*, meaning clod or soil, a glebe is an area of cultivated land usually, but not necessarily, attached to the parsonage. Distant glebes were often the result of deals or exchanges between the clergymen and other landowners.

The word manse may apply to the glebe and the minister's house together. Many old parsonages still have buildings such as barns, cowsheds and pigsties attached to them; these are other relics of the days when the vicar and his family were self-supporting.

Glen see Valley

Globeflower *Trollius europaeus*

Its northern name, locker gowlan, accurately describes the globeflower, since 'locker' means locked or closed in and 'gowlan' is a yellow flower.

Globeflowers grow in gullies and pastures in mountain areas in north and west Britain and Ireland, though penetrating as far south as Derbyshire and South Wales. They resemble large buttercups, but are taller, paler yellow and have palm-like leaves. The flowers are globe-shaped before they are fully open, and appear between June and August.

Globeflower is a poisonous plant. Its visible 'petals' are in fact sepals (the outer parts of the flower), the small narrow true petals being hidden inside.

Growing in small clumps, the 6-24 in. globeflower looks superficially like a buttercup

Glow-worm *Lampyris noctiluca*

In 1891, a tiny but recognisable photograph was taken with the eye of a male glow-worm used as the camera lens during a series of experiments to discover how insects can see. The male glow-worm's eyes are particularly suitable for this purpose, since they are very large so that the insect can detect the bright glow emitted at night by the female during the mating season in July. This pale yellow-green light comes from luminous organs on the underside of her tail segments, and she climbs on to a low plant and twists her body round to display it. Males and larvae can also produce light.

The female, like an overgrown beetle larva, has no trace of wings or wing cases, while the male is more beetle-like and can fly. By day they hide under stones and rubbish in grassy banks, especially on chalk and limestone. Glow-worm larvae eat slugs and snails, reaching the adult stage in three years. The adult beetle lives for only eight or nine days and does not feed.

The glow-worm larva injects a digestive juice into the snail and sucks up the fluid remains

Gnat

There are 50 British species of insects which are variously called gnats or mosquitoes. Two common species found in stagnant water are the common gnat *Culex pipiens,* the females of which suck mainly birds' blood, and the spotted gnat *Anopheles maculipennis.* A form of the spotted gnat carries the British strain of malaria, called ague. This once occurred regularly in Britain. Male gnats have hairy antennae with which they can hear the humming sound made by the dusk-flying females.

After mating in autumn, the female flies off to take at least one meal of blood before she lays her eggs. This meal may be essential for the growth of the fertile eggs, but this is not the case for all gnats. The eggs are laid on any still water, from water-filled tin cans to rocky coastal pools; the common gnat's in rafts and the spotted gnat's singly. The eggs of both species float until they hatch, when the larvae swim by wriggling actively and feed by filtering the water for planktonic plant life. A common gnat larva breathes with only its tail in contact with the surface, while the spotted gnat larva has its whole side touching the surface layer. The pupae are comma-shaped.

HOW A GNAT FEEDS

Mouthparts spread apart

Maxilla Mandible
Piercing stylets
Sheath
Mandible
Maxilla
Labrum Hypopharynx

Female gnat feeding

Eye
Antenna
Palp
Sheath bends back and supports the stylet bundle
Stylet bundle pierces the host's skin and blood is pumped up

Section through mouthparts
Labrum or upper lip with food channel
Mandible or upper jaw
Hypopharynx, a projection from the lower lip
Maxilla or lower jaw
Sheath

Only female gnats have mouthparts sharp enough to pierce skin and suck blood; males feed on nectar

Goat *Capra hirens*

Few goats are kept on British farms, but many smallholders keep them to produce milk and cheese for home use. There are four main breeds in Britain: the Anglo-Nubian, British Alpine, Saanen and Toggenburg. They are voracious eaters, and damage trees and hedges. They are therefore often tethered. A good nanny will give 6-8 pints of milk a day at the peak of her lactation, and some will produce 400 to 500 gallons a year.

Goats breed readily only in autumn and winter. The gestation period is five months. Twins are born as often as single kids, and triplets are not uncommon. The useful life of a goat is eight to ten years.

Goats are particularly hardy, and flourish in conditions under which cows or sheep would find difficulty in surviving. They can stay healthy on the poorest of herbage. Billy goats usually have beards, bad tempers and nasty smells. Both sexes have horns.

Gneiss see Stone

Goat moth *Cossus cossus*

The caterpillars of the goat moth spend three or four years burrowing into the living wood of a tree, particularly ash, poplar or willow. When the caterpillars are fully grown they often leave their burrow and wander about before burying themselves and making cocoons.

It is in this wandering period that the caterpillars can be seen. They smell like he-goats—hence the name of the moth. They are found in all parts of Britain in the autumn, but are most common in the south.

The chrysalis stage survives the winter and the moths emerge in June or July. Although the mouthparts are not well developed and the moth cannot feed, the females are attracted to the sap which exudes from damaged trees. This enables them to find suitable places in which to lay eggs.

Goatsbeard *Tragopogon pratensis*

The long narrow leaves and dandelion-like flowers of goatsbeard may be seen in summer along roadsides or in rough grassland throughout the lowlands, except in the west.

Breeds of goat

British Toggenburg—a cross between British goats and Swiss Toggenburgs

British Saanen—a cross between British goats and Swiss Saanen

Anglo-Nubian—a cross between British goats and goats of oriental or Nubian type

British Alpine—a cross between British and Swiss stock

The goat, which still roams wild in the mountains of Persia and Iraq, was one of the first animals to be domesticated. Remains nearly 10,000 years old are known from the Middle East. Today there are many domestic breeds, of which the four illustrated are those most commonly bred in Britain. They are kept for their milk, which is easier to digest than that of cows

But the flowers will be seen only in the morning as they close around midday: hence another popular name, Jack-go-to-bed-at-noon.

The plant's name refers to the long, silky 'parachute' hairs which appear when the flower re-opens and help to distribute the seed in the wind.

The similar purple-flowered salsify *T. porrifolius* is sometimes grown as a root vegetable, and may be found as a wayside weed.

Goatsucker see Nightjar
Goatweed see Parsley

Goby, Common

A small fish usually found in sandy and muddy shore pools. It is rarely more than 2 in. long and is usually a freckled brown, matching its background. The common goby *Pomatoschistus microps* remains in the security of the bottom of the pool, where it rests on its single pelvic fin.

It breeds under an empty half-shell of a cockle or other deep-shelled bivalve, the male guarding the eggs which are stuck on to the roof of the cavity. It can thrive in conditions of low salinity and is often found in estuaries in almost fresh water.

The painted goby *P. pictus* lives mainly below the low-tide mark on rocky shores.

A male rock goby guards its clutch of eggs until they hatch, aerating them with its fins

Goby, Rock

On south-western and western coasts the rock goby *Gobius paganellus* is found mostly in rock pools, but some can be spotted sheltering under rocks in the sea at low tide.

They grow to about 5 in. long and are usually dark in colour, the exact shade varying with that of the rocks among which they live. The males have a bright orange edge to the first fin on the back and large protuberant eyes and lips. A related species, the giant goby *G. cobitis* grows to 8 in. long.

Both these gobies are found in the Mediterranean and northwards to the British Isles, but the giant goby's range extends only to Cornwall and south Devon. The rock goby is found as far north as the Inner Hebrides

Godwit

Two species of godwit, long-legged wading birds, appear in Britain on migration, and can be seen on mudflats and marshes around the coast. They are large birds, 15-16 in. long, with long, straight bills. They use their bills to probe deeply for invertebrates, such as snails and small shellfish, below the surface.

The bar-tailed godwit *Limosa lapponica* nests in the Arctic and comes to Britain as a winter visitor. The black-tailed godwit *L. limosa* lives on the marshes of northern Europe and Asia. During the past 20 years it has returned to Britain to breed after an absence of more than 100 years, having been driven from its breeding grounds by the draining of the fens, and because it was netted as game. It winters in Britain—in East Anglia and occasionally in Somerset, south-east Scotland and Orkney.

The bar-tailed godwit is essentially a bird of the estuaries, feeding in flocks on mudflats. While the black-tailed godwit can also be found on mudflats, it is more often on freshwater marshes and flooded grassland.

In summer the bar-tailed is rust-red, but for most of the time that it spends in Britain it is speckled brown. It has a slightly up-curved bill and a barred tail. The black-tailed is also rust-red in breeding plumage, but there is black and white barring on the belly. It has longer legs and a longer, straight bill. The tail has a broad, black band at the tip and the wings show a prominent white bar in flight.

In Britain it breeds only on the Ouse 'washes' of the Cambridgeshire fens. There

and eastwards up the English Channel. The giant is seen most often in pools near the upper levels of the tide.

Gold

Little gold is found in the British Isles, and although it has been mined in Wales since Roman times, there are no mines in commercial operation today. The centre of Welsh gold mining was Dolgellau, Merionethshire. Gold has also been mined in Scotland in the Lowther Hills of Lanarkshire and in Sutherland. In Ireland, the Wicklow Hills were yielding gold nearly 4000 years ago.

The Queen's wedding ring was made from a block of Welsh gold, which also provided Princess Margaret's wedding ring.

All gold in Britain is the property of the Crown, except for gold in Sutherland, the rights there being vested in the Duke of Sutherland. This is in an area known as the Kildonan-Kinbrace gold field, north of Helmsdale. All the streams serving the River Helmsdale are a source of gold and, during the 19th century, there was a minor gold rush there. But gold mining in the area is now discouraged, as it would pollute the salmon-rich Helmsdale.

The nest of the black-tailed godwit is just a scrape in the ground hidden among thick grass

is some evidence that it breeds on wet grazing meadows elsewhere, but there are few suitable areas of grassland which are flooded in winter.

The black-tailed godwit lays a clutch of four eggs in a well-hidden scrape on the ground in May though they are often smashed, accidentally, by cattle.

Goldcrest

The $3\frac{1}{2}$ in. long goldcrest is Britain's smallest bird with an aggressive nature that belies its size. It hangs its basket-like nest hammock-style from the branches of a tree, often a conifer, and usually lays two broods of seven to ten eggs in a season. Seven eggs equal the weight of the bird itself. Since many goldcrests are killed off by a hard winter, this

The goldcrest builds a hanging nest of moss and spiders' webs, attaching it to twigs on the underside of a conifer branch

209

double brood helps to keep up numbers.

The firecrest, also 3½ in. long, is similar to the goldcrest in appearance and habits. It is mainly an autumn visitor from Europe, though in recent years it has begun to breed in the New Forest and other southern areas. Like the goldcrest, it suspends its nest from a branch—up to 50 ft above ground.

Both birds construct their intricate, basket-like nests from shreds of wool, spiders' webs and moss, lined with feathers.

Both birds are green with lighter underparts, double wing bars and prominent black, yellow and flame crests. The firecrest is distinguished mainly by a white streak over the eyes, underlined by a black stripe. The cocks raise their crests in courtship and to threaten other males.

Both birds eat flies and other small insects, often in the company of tits and creepers.

The main difference between the birds is in their habitats. The goldcrest has always been found in northern coniferous forests and has become more widespread due to the planting of coniferous trees in other areas. It sometimes flies south in winter. Visiting firecrests are seen only in the south and west in a more varied habitat marked by bushes and scrub.

Goldeneye see Duck

Native golden rod bears flowers in clusters; garden species have sprays

Golden rod *Solidago virgaurea*
In Tudor times golden rod was prized for treating wounds. It could be infused and drunk, or applied in an ointment. The Elizabethans imported golden rod and it sold at a great price in London until it was discovered growing wild at nearby Hampstead, when it became worthless.

Golden rod is common throughout Britain in dry woods, on rock ledges and in sand dunes, growing to a height of 2½ ft with a cluster of yellow flowers and broad, basal leaves. It also grows at altitudes higher than 3000 ft in the Scottish and Welsh mountains, where it is often small, producing only a few flower heads.

Many North American species have been introduced into cultivation, and some of these have spread to railway banks and other waste places. These species, such as *S. canadensis,* are taller with pyramid-shaped clusters of flowers.

Golden saxifrage grows in large patches in damp places on mountains up to 3000 ft

Golden saxifrage
Chrysosplenium oppositifolium
In hilly areas a line of bright green often indicates the presence of both golden saxifrage and the source of a mountain spring. Extensive patches of this low-growing herb are found in wet, shady woods and marshy ground throughout the British Isles except in eastern England. The roots are matted together, producing numerous succulent stems 3-4 in. high, with rounded leaves in opposite pairs.

The flowers, which appear in April and May, have no petals but have bright yellow-green bracts and sepals.

The plant's botanical name *Chrysosplenium* is derived from Greek words meaning gold and spleen, the latter referring to its supposed value in treating diseases of the spleen.

Goldfish see Crucian carp

Goldilocks *Ranunculus auricomus*
The only British buttercup that grows in woodlands, goldilocks differs from other buttercups in having deeply divided, hairless fan-shaped leaves and flowers with a variable number of petals. The maximum is five, but some have none, others one or two. Where petals are missing, the sepals are often coloured yellow in their place.

Goldilocks flowers in April and May and occurs throughout the British Isles in woods and shady hedge bottoms, but it is rare in the north and west.

Its English and botanical names have the same meaning, since *auricomus* means golden-haired.

Goldilocks may have any number of petals up to five, or none at all

Good King Henry
Chenopodium bonushenricus
Originally introduced, in Roman times, from central Europe as a vegetable, Good King Henry is found by roadsides and round old buildings throughout lowland Britain. It is a spinach-like plant with broad spear-shaped leaves and spikes of tiny green-yellow flowers. The flower clusters are mostly at the end of the stem, and leafless. The young shoots and flowering tops can be boiled and eaten with butter.

The name Good Henry or Good King Henry distinguishes it from Bad Henry, another name for the poisonous plant dog's mercury. The name came from Germany where Henry, or Heinrich, is an elf-name for a woodland creature.

Goosander see Duck

Goose, Domestic
In the middle of the 16th century, geese played a vital role at the Nottingham Goose Fair but by the middle of the 18th century they were no longer an important commodity; horses, cattle and cheese were the main attractions. Today it is almost impossible to buy these large well-fleshed birds for the table except at Christmas. Only about 296,000 geese are kept in the British Isles, mostly in small numbers on mixed farms. About half of the total number are in the Irish Republic. No way has yet been found of keeping geese intensively.

According to country lore, the presence of geese on a farm signifies that the farmer's wife wears the trousers. Although clean in appearance, geese pass large quantities of droppings and soon foul pasture. No farmer would want them on his pastures, but a dominant wife would insist on having them, since she would profit from the sale of geese

Chinese geese (above) derive from the Siberian swan goose. The other types of domestic goose were bred from the greylag

A gaggle of geese, from a 12th-century English bestiary, or animal book. Geese were probably first domesticated by New Stone Age man

for the table. It was the custom that money from such a sale went to the wife.

The goose was probably domesticated before any other type of fowl, and was bred in Egypt at least 4000 years ago. There are nine British types of goose—eight of which are descendants of the wild greylag. The main commercial breeds today are the Toulouse, Embden and Chinese. A Toulouse/Embden cross is common.

Goose, Wild

Sportsmen, farmers and a natural disaster which destroyed a major food source, have all combined to reduce drastically the number of geese in the British Isles. However, human intervention to re-establish old breeding grounds and new food supplies, together with laws regulating shooting, are helping to reverse this situation.

Geese are large, long-necked, web-footed birds, essentially gregarious and frequently gathering in large numbers, though seldom seen outside their established localities. Although they swim easily, they spend most of their time feeding on land, mainly resorting to the water when alarmed.

They are widespread in Scotland and Ireland, where many birds from Iceland and Greenland winter. Those in Wales and England come mainly from northern Scandinavia and northern Russia. Often hard frosts in Germany and Holland are responsible for driving them to Britain.

The species commonly found in Britain can be divided into two types, black or grey. The black geese are the brent, barnacle and Canada geese; the grey types are the greylag, white-fronted, pink-footed and bean geese. Other species, such as the red-breasted, lesser white-fronted and snow geese usually occur in company with flocks of other geese. Only the greylag and Canada geese breed in the British Isles.

The native greylags, the ancestors of farmyard geese, are being helped to re-establish themselves. Once widespread and numerous, they now breed naturally only in South Uist and other parts of the Outer Hebrides, and in the extreme north of Scotland. However, greylags have been successfully re-introduced to Norfolk, the Lake District and other parts of the country. Greylags wintering in Britain from Iceland outnumber the native breeders, chiefly in Scotland.

When disturbed, white-fronted geese are able to rise almost vertically from the ground, flocks often splitting up into family parties. Their name comes from the white area round the bill and forehead

Canada geese, introduced as ornamental birds in the 17th and 18th centuries, came originally from North America. They have now spread to most parts of England, but are rare in Scotland and Wales. As with the greylag, this spread has been assisted. They eat crops as well as grass and aquatic vegetation.

The other geese are all winter visitors in varying numbers. Pink-feet are most numerous with a mid-winter population of more than 50,000. However, they are confined to Scotland except for flocks round The Wash, the Fens, the Humber and in Lancashire. Huge flocks form on both banks of the Firth of Forth. Since pink-footed geese habitually fly up to 25 miles from their roost, they are a familiar sight in eastern Scotland. They are recognisable by their pink feet, small size and small dark heads and necks. They are also the only grey geese which have both pink legs and a pink bill.

Pink-feet are often regarded as a sub-species of bean geese which breed throughout Europe and Asia. Bean geese are larger, have bigger heads and orange feet, their bills orange or yellow and black. Once widespread and common, they are now Britain's rarest regular winter geese with flocks only on the Solway Firth in south-west Scotland, and in Northumberland and Norfolk. Like pink-feet, they roost in marshes and estuaries, moving inland to feed on grain, potatoes and other crops as well as grass, wild shoots and roots.

White-fronted geese are more widespread in England than any other species, and are also numerous in Ireland. Large flocks are found at Slimbridge on the Severn Estuary, the Isle of Islay in the Inner Hebrides, and the marshes round Wexford Harbour in Ireland. The Scottish and Irish birds come from Greenland. The English and Welsh birds originate in the Siberian tundra and Arctic islands, belonging to a population·which winters in Germany and Holland. They arrive in Britain in large numbers after Christmas.

Although grassland birds, white-fronted geese favour marshy areas where they do no harm to agriculture, feeding mainly on grass, clover and plant shoots. The lesser white-front is rare, although in most winters a solitary bird can be seen among white-fronts or bean geese. It is smaller, with a large amount of white on the forehead and a yellow eye ring.

Barnacle geese are small grey geese marked with a black neck and white face. Most barnacles arrive from Greenland to spend the winter grazing along the uninhabited western isles of Scotland and the west coast of Ireland. A separate population from Spitsbergen winters at Caerlaverock on the Solway Firth, where it is protected from disturbance in Nature Conservancy and Wildfowl Trust reserves. The barnacle has also increased and prospered from a total ban on shooting in Britain. As it spends most of its time grazing in poor sea meadows, it causes no harm to farmers.

Two distinct populations of brent geese winter in Britain and Ireland. Between 10,000 and 20,000 of the dark-bellied race from Siberia winter mainly in Essex, notably the Foulness area and its adjacent estuaries. Some have recently moved to the River Medway, in Kent, the Wells area of Norfolk, and Langstone Harbour in Hampshire. The light-bellied race goes to Ireland, where its numbers are around 12,000. They are found in large concentrations at several points around the coast including Strangford Lough in Co. Down and Tralee Bay in Co. Kerry.

Only a ban on shooting has saved brent geese from extinction. They were also hit by disease which killed off the sea-flowering eel-grass, their main food, in the 1930's. This is now growing again in many estuaries.

Red-breasted geese from the Siberian tundra have been seen in Britain only 20 times in the last 200 years; snow geese from Arctic America are occasionally seen in Ireland. One other species of goose can be seen in Britain. This is the Hawaiian goose, which has been saved from probable extinction by being bred by the Wildfowl Trust at Slimbridge, Gloucestershire. At one time fewer than 50 birds remained in their native Hawaii. Breeding started at Slimbridge in 1949 where hundreds have since been raised.

Gooseberry *Ribes uva-crispa*
Gooseberry bushes not only grow in the garden, but also in wild places in woods and hedges. They are less common in the north and rare in Ireland. Most have been spread by birds who have stolen the fruits from a garden and left the seeds in their droppings some distance away; but the bush is regarded as native in some woods.

The name means what it says—a berry eaten by geese. It is also popular with humans, of course, in tarts, pies, jams and sauces, especially with roast goose.

The first greenish flowers appear on the 2-3 ft high bushes in March and the fruits can be eaten in June, although they may need a lot of sugar if picked early.

Goosefoot, Red *Chenopodium rubrum*
About 15 species of goosefoot, all similar in appearance, may be found on waste land, in arable fields, round the muddy margins of ponds and in other places where there is plenty of nitrogen in the soil, such as sewage farms. Most are rare, but red goosefoot, which grows about 2 ft high, is fairly common in the south and east of England.

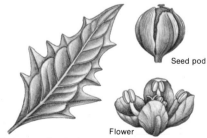

Seed pod

Flower

Red goosefoot is the most common of 15 closely related plants. It is known by its red tinge

The whole plant has a reddish tinge; otherwise it is almost identical to the prolific fat hen. Its broad, triangular leaf with a coarsely toothed margin is supposed to resemble the webbed foot of a goose.

Goosegrass see Cleavers

Gorge
A narrow, steep-sided valley that usually gives passage to a stream or river. Often the water has eroded the rock to form a channel. Gorges are common in limestone regions.

The Cheddar Gorge in Somerset (Britain's nearest approach to a canyon), the Avon Gorge in Bristol and Gordale Scar in the northern Pennines are good examples.

In limestone areas water sometimes percolates through harder stone on the surface, and dissolves softer stone underneath to form tunnels, the roofs of which eventually collapse leaving a gorge. This process may then be repeated on lower limestone layers. In other cases, especially in sandstone areas, the force of the water has washed out loose stones in a valley of rocks to form a gorge.

The limestone gorge at Gordale, Yorkshire, was an underground cavern until its roof collapsed

The flowers of common gorse are among the first to colour the countryside at the end of winter

Gorse *Ulex europaeus*
Heaths and hills are turned to a glorious yellow by the flowers of gorse in March—or even earlier after a mild winter. A member of the pea family, it is also known as furze and, in Scotland, as whin.

The 2-6 ft bushes are useful as well as beautiful, being planted for hedges in Ireland. In Scotland the young shoots used to be crushed in whinmills and fed to cattle. Whinbark is still used for a yellow dye in the manufacture of tartan cloth.

An old country saying is that when gorse is out of bloom kissing is out of fashion. Common gorse ceases to flower in June, but lovers are safe because there are two rarer species which ensure that there are some flowers throughout the year.

The sight of gorse in flower on Putney Heath so affected the Swedish botanist Linnaeus, father of modern systems of classifying plants and animals, that on coming to England in 1736, he fell on his knees and thanked God for its loveliness.

Gossamer see Spider

Granary
As the name implies, a granary is a building for storing grain. Nowadays, most grain is kept in great bins in multi-purpose drying, cleaning and storing units; but

An unusual-looking brick granary built at Little-hampton, Sussex, about 1731

A MODERN GRAIN STORAGE BIN

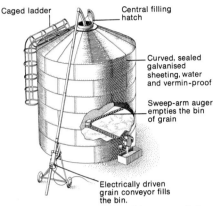
The modern granary is a multi-purpose drying, cleaning and storing unit for grain

until this century buildings were erected on most farms for the storage of grain.

There was not a standard size or type of roof, but the structure had to meet the essential requirements of being dry and vermin-proof. Granaries were usually square, wooden buildings set on pillars capped with mushroom-shaped stones. The overlap of the stones prevented mice and rats from entering, and the air circulating beneath the stones helped to keep the grain dry. A few of these old granaries still exist. The mushroom-shaped stones—called staddle stones—are treasured by collectors. In the late 18th century, cart shed and granary were often combined into one building. Carts and farm machinery were protected from bad weather at ground level, while the floor above was used to store threshed grain: there was less likelihood of rats at this level, and filling a cart with grain was made simpler.

Granite
Volcanic larva cooling beneath the earth's surface millions of years ago formed, among other rocks, granite. The extreme slowness with which the molten material cooled is shown in the size and perfection of the crystals of which granite is composed. The word granite is often used loosely to describe any coarsely grained crystalline rock, but geologists apply the word only to rocks which contain a considerable quantity of quartz.

Granites are made up, in addition to quartz, with crystals of feldspar and, sometimes, hornblende and mica which gives the 'sparkle' in granite. Thus the rock has a multi-coloured appearance. In some, pink or red dominate; others are mainly grey or black and white.

It is one of the hardest building materials, and is used for kerbstones and cobbles as well as for large buildings—usually applied nowadays as a facing material only. Aberdeen, known as the Granite City, is built mainly of local pink granite. The Embankment

along the Thames in London is made of Cornish granite. China clay, mined in Cornwall, comes from the feldspar in granite.

Erosion of softer rocks often reveals granite below, producing rugged scenery.

Haytor granite tramway, Devon, opened in 1820 to link the granite quarries there to a canal. Horse teams pulled the large waggons until 1858

Grape hyacinth *Muscari atlanticum*
Clumps of these bright blue flowers are familiar to gardeners throughout the country. Sometimes the plant spreads to roadsides, and in Breckland, East Anglia, it grows as a wild flower, adorning sandy fields and chalk banks in April and May.

It is an abundant weed of arable fields in southern Europe and may have been brought to Britain by prehistoric man as seed in the corn he carried. The wild flowers are sometimes called starch flowers, as their scent resembles the smell of wet starch. Garden varieties have other scents.

Graphite
This is the mineral from which 'lead' pencils are made. It is a form of carbon and has no connection with the metal lead, except that lead makes a black mark when drawn over paper.

Graphite used to be mined extensively in the northern part of the Lake District, and this led to the founding of the pencil industry in Keswick, Cumberland. The mines are now almost exhausted, and most pencils are made there from graphite imported from Ceylon, Mexico, Madagascar and Korea.

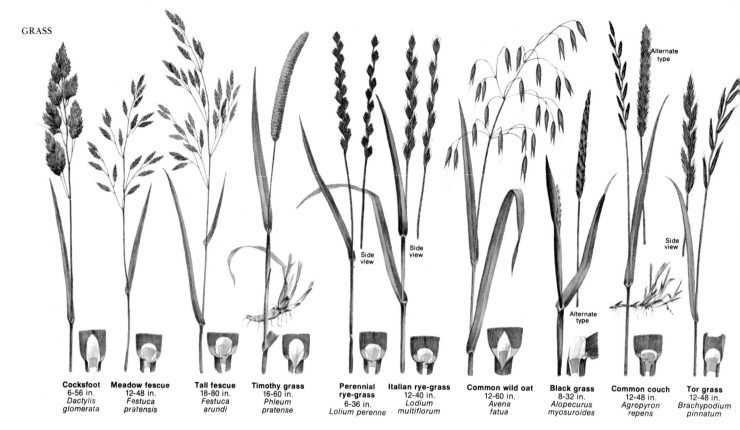

Cocksfoot
6-56 in.
Dactylis glomerata

Meadow fescue
12-48 in.
Festuca pratensis

Tall fescue
18-80 in.
Festuca arundi

Timothy grass
16-60 in.
Phleum pratense

Perennial rye-grass
6-36 in.
Lolium perenne

Italian rye-grass
12-40 in.
Lodium multiflorum

Common wild oat
12-60 in.
Avena fatua

Black grass
8-32 in.
Alopecurus myosuroides

Common couch
12-48 in.
Agropyron repens

Tor grass
12-48 in.
Brachypodium pinnatum

Grass

Grass is the most abundant and economically important crop in the British Isles. Of the islands' 195 million acres, approximately 45 million are grassland—this does not include the acreage under cereal crops, which are botanically classed as grasses.

The grass family is the largest and most important family of flowering plants in the British Isles. It comprises the cereals wheat, barley and oats, grasses grown for hay, silage and grazing, and more than 150 wild species.

Grass is extremely important to the farmer because it feeds his livestock all year round —as grazing for at least seven months, and hay or silage (young grass from which air is excluded to keep it green) for the rest of the year. It is also sometimes cut when tender, dried in a furnace, powdered and sold as a vitamin-rich meal for pigs, poultry, cattle and sheep.

Any untended field will eventually become overgrown with grass and weeds, but usually with the less nutritious species, such as annual meadow-grass on grazing land and black grass in stubble-fields. For this reason farmers sow their fields with grasses bred for a particular purpose: for early grazing, late grazing, hay-making or silage-making. Some fields are sown with only one variety, others are sown with four or five, together with some clovers.

The British farmer favours six grasses: timothy grass, a perennial that produces a luxuriant, soft-leaved crop for both grazing and cutting in all but the driest summers;

perennial rye-grass, which produces an abundance of leafy grass; Italian rye-grass, similar but taller, which lasts for only two years and is also used for hay and silage; cocksfoot, which is coarse, with stiff, hard stems and hairy, sharp-edged leaves, but is nutritious and drought-resistant (it was formerly used chiefly for hay, but grazing varieties are now available); and meadow fescue and tall fescue, which provide both grazing and cutting varieties.

Besides these grasses, pastures may include white clovers and such herbs as yarrow, chicory, ribwort plantain and dandelion which, by tapping minerals deep in the soil, provide a valuable supplement to the nutrition contained in the grass. Grazing may be controlled by movable electric fences, in which case the animals are provided with a fresh strip each day.

Permanent pastures occupy soils too heavy, waterlogged, inaccessible or stony to be ploughed and cultivated with other crops. There may also be one or two permanent pastures on good ground conveniently near the farmyard, for grazing newly born calves, lame sheep and children's ponies. These are known as paddocks or meadows.

Sometimes grasses are grown as a break crop, or ley—a crop that replenishes the richness of a field after it has been exhausted by successive crops of cereals. A short-term ley lasts from one to three years and usually consists of one grass only—usually a rye-grass—although it may also include red clover and sainfoin. A long-term ley lasts from four to six years and often contains

about five grass species with three or four strains of clover. During their final year, long-term leys are grazed intensively; the dung left by the livestock is ploughed in to increase the fertility of the soil.

Silage is generally cut from the surplus grass of permanent pastures in May, before the flowering season.

On mountains and moorland, cattle and sheep feed on the coarse grasses that grow there naturally, together with rushes, bracken and weeds.

The fodder grasses are wild species which have been bred to produce better crops or to grow for a longer season. Cocksfoot is deep-rooted and grows in drier conditions than other fodder species. Perennial rye-grass grows vigorously. Italian rye-grass is equally vigorous but only short-lived. It differs from perennial rye-grass in having long hairs, or awns, which protrude from each flower in the head. Timothy grass grows best on damp, clayish soils, as do meadow fescue, and the taller kinds of tall fescue; the shorter types grow on drier chalky and sandy soils.

Wild strains of these grasses grow alongside the cultivated ones in meadows and pastures, together with less nutritious species, such as the needle-leaved fescue; the soft hairy Yorkshire fog, pink-striped at the base of the stem; and sweet vernal-grass which produces the scent of new-mown hay.

Some species of grass grow better in marshland that is flooded each winter. Such land is dominated by the common reed and the rough-leaved, feathery-flowered, tufted hair-

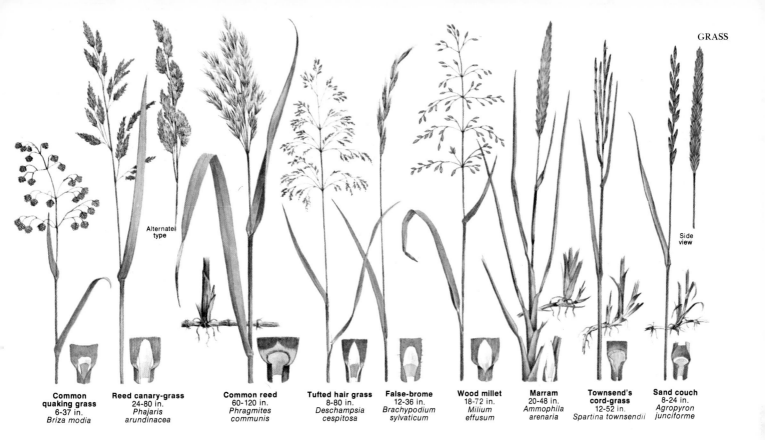

Common quaking grass
6-37 in.
Briza modia

Reed canary-grass
24-80 in.
Phajaris arundinacea

Common reed
60-120 in.
Phragmites communis

Tufted hair grass
8-80 in.
Deschampsia cespitosa

False-brome
12-36 in.
Brachypodium sylvaticum

Wood millet
18-72 in.
Milium effusum

Marram
20-48 in.
Ammophila arenaria

Townsend's cord-grass
12-52 in.
Spartina townsendii

Sand couch
8-24 in.
Agropyron junciforme

grass. A grass more than 6 ft high with flowers like those of cocksfoot sometimes fills ditches in lowland England. This is the reed canary-grass, distinguished from the common reed by having a membrane, instead of hairs, where the leaf joins the stem.

Several species have adapted themselves to the inhospitable seashore. In salt-marshes Townsend's cord-grass survives periodic inundations by the sea and stabilises banks of mud. Marram grass and sand couch prevent the erosion of sand dunes. Both have rolled leaves to reduce water loss and long rooting stems which bind the sand.

Common couch develops the same underground system in arable fields and spreads rapidly; it is one of the farmer's worst enemies. In the last 20 years two other grasses have also become widespread weeds: in some cornfields there seems to be more common wild oat than the crop which it infests; and dark heads of black grass are increasing rapidly, especially among crops of winter cereals and winter beans, in south and east England.

Chalk and limestone grassland have several characteristic species. Two of these are easily recognised: common quaking-grass, whose purplish-green flowers dance in the breeze; and tor grass, which forms large, yellow-green, circular patches and is so coarse it is eaten by only the hungriest bullock. Its relative, wood false-brome, has much softer leaves and longer awns on its flowers. It often grows with the much taller wood millet, which has dark green leaves and branches of flowering heads bent downwards.

Sheep grazing in the Cheviot Hills—grassland like this supports 22 million sheep in Britain

215

The armoured head of the great green grasshopper, which lives among tall grass

Grasshoppers and crickets

Insects with enlarged hind legs for jumping. The males 'sing' by rasping their wings or legs—a process called stridulating. Short-horned grasshoppers do this by rubbing a thick vein on the front wing with the roughened inside edge of the large hind leg; long-horned grasshoppers and crickets by rubbing their forewings together.

There are 29 species of grasshoppers, crickets and groundhoppers in the British Isles. They can be found from July to September on grassland, heaths or marshes. The largest is the 1¼ in. large marsh grasshopper. One of the most numerous is the common green grasshopper.

Some species are green, although there are great variations in colour, nearly as much between individuals as between species. Different species can be distinguished by their signature tunes—each has a different song pattern. Males sing most often, but females will also sing when they are ready to mate.

After mating, the females lay eggs in the summer. The eggs, surrounded by a solidified froth, are laid deep in the soil under grass tufts and hatch as larvae in April.

The larvae moult into adult-like nymphs and reach maturity in July after further moults.

Groundhoppers are similar insects, about ½ in. long and dark brown, but they have no song or hearing organs. Britain has only three species.

Grasshoppers may have long or short antennae. Long-horned grasshoppers are sometimes called bush crickets and have rather more spindly jumping legs than short-horned grasshoppers; the females have long, curved egg-laying organs which look like stings but are quite harmless. The eggs are laid in the ground or inserted into plants, but in other ways the life cycle is similar to that of short-horned grasshoppers. Most bush crickets are restricted to the southern parts of England and Wales. The mute bush cricket is common locally in England and Wales and has been found in one place in Ireland. It feeds on caterpillars and aphids.

The mole cricket is rare. As its name implies, it lives below ground in long burrows, which it digs with specially enlarged forelegs. These are equipped with shears for cutting through small roots. Mole crickets spend most of their time in their burrows feeding on insect larvae, earthworms and roots, but on warm nights they fly with a buzzing noise. Up to 2½ in. long, the red-brown mole cricket is the largest British cricket.

Females lay up to 640 eggs under ground and guard them for the two to four weeks they take to hatch. The nymphs hibernate under ground, emerging as adults the following autumn.

The house cricket is now misnamed in Britain, since modern hygiene has driven it outdoors in most places. Today, it is more likely to be found on rubbish tips where food is plentiful and decomposition produces warmth. Eggs, which are laid in crevices, take about ten weeks to hatch. Nymphs mature in six months and like their parents resemble small cockroaches.

Britain has three species of house crickets, from ⅜ to ¾ in. long; all are restricted to southern parts of the country.

THE MOLE CRICKET'S LOUDSPEAKER

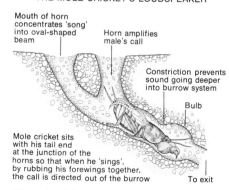

Mouth of horn concentrates 'song' into oval-shaped beam

Horn amplifies male's call

Constriction prevents sound going deeper into burrow system

Bulb

Mole cricket sits with his tail end at the junction of the horns so that when he 'sings', by rubbing his forewings together, the call is directed out of the burrow

To exit

The mole cricket digs a burrow with a two-horned 'loudspeaker' at the entrance. This both. amplifies and beams his song so that it is heard by as many passing females as possible

Grasshoppers, crickets and groundhoppers

There are 29 species of grasshoppers, crickets and groundhoppers in the British Isles. Some of the more common and more spectacular species are shown here. Their large rear legs, adapted for jumping, make these insects easily identifiable

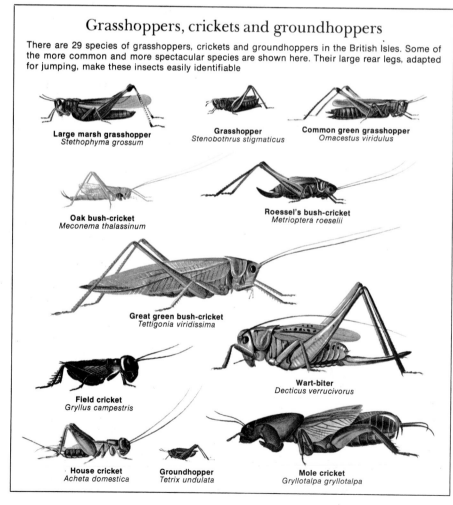

Large marsh grasshopper
Stethophyma grossum

Grasshopper
Stenobothrus stigmaticus

Common green grasshopper
Omacestus viridulus

Oak bush-cricket
Meconema thalassinum

Roessel's bush-cricket
Metrioptera roeselii

Great green bush-cricket
Tettigonia viridissima

Wart-biter
Decticus verrucivorus

Field cricket
Gryllus campestris

House cricket
Acheta domestica

Groundhopper
Tetrix undulata

Mole cricket
Gryllotalpa gryllotalpa

Grass moth

This moth is coloured in the buff shades of the dry grass stems on which it usually rests head downwards by day. The forewings tightly enclose the body and hide the broader hindwings. Expanded, the wings are ¾-1 in. across, the females usually being slightly larger than the males. The sharp-eyed may spot the snout-like projection in front of the head; it is a pair of palps (sense organs) for touch and taste, held closely together.

There are about 30 British species of grass moth; several are common and can be found in almost any grassy area from June to August.

The caterpillars appear from September to June and live at the base of the stems, on which they feed. In June the caterpillar makes a cocoon and camouflages it with its own droppings before changing into a chrysalis.

Grass-of-Parnassus *Parnassia palustris*

An attractive plant which is neither grass nor grass-like. White flowers, the size of daisies and smelling of honey, emerge from a cluster of heart-shaped leaves. Each flower is veined with green and faces the sky at the tip of a ribbed stem up to 12 in. high. The plant grows in marshes in northern Britain and central Ireland and occasionally in wet places among sand dunes elsewhere. Its old haunts in southern and central England have disappeared because of drainage and ploughing. It owes its name to the popular belief that such a beautiful flower could only have come from Mt Parnassus, the home of the god Apollo in ancient Greek legend.

Flower

Seed pod

Grass-of-Parnassus is not a grass, but a marsh plant which flowers from July to September

Grass snake *Natrix natrix*

The British grass snake, or barred grass snake, belongs to a sub-species, *Natrix natrix helvetica*, found throughout western Europe. It inhabits Britain as far north as the Scottish border counties, but not Ireland—suggesting that its ancestors arrived during the period, about 10,000 years ago, when Britain was still joined to the Continent by a land bridge, but after the formation of the Irish Sea. The range of this non-poisonous snake is governed by the climate: an incubation period which varies from six to ten weeks at a minimum temperature of 21°C (70°F)

Shamming dead: one way in which a grass snake protects itself from its enemies

is necessary for the snake's eggs to hatch.

Female grass snakes grow to an average of 3 ft, while males average 2 ft. Colouring is similar in both sexes. The upper side is generally olive-brown with vertical black bars along each flank. There are two yellow or orange crescent-shaped patches on the nape of the neck, with two black triangles behind. These give the snake its alternative name of ringed snake. The ring is sometimes missing in elderly females. The upper lip is white, edged in black, and the belly has a chequered pattern of black and white. The eye has a rounded pupil, unlike that of the adder which has a slit-shaped one.

Grass snakes are usually seen alongside ponds, ditches, streams, field borders and hedgerows. They often bask in the sun near undergrowth into which they can retreat if disturbed. They will usually seek cover when approached, as they are sensitive to

The female grass snake lays its eggs, usually 30-40 at a time, in June and July

earth vibrations. They have little means of defence, save putting up a show of aggression by darting the head about and hissing. They are expert swimmers and hunt fish, frogs, toads and newts, which are swallowed alive. Young birds and birds' eggs are also taken.

Hibernation, from October to March, takes place under logs or in leaf-litter, ditches or holes in the ground. Grass snakes have been known to live for up to nine years in captivity.

Gravel

Technically, gravel is rock that has disintegrated and been worn smooth by water into fragments about 1 in. long (finer deposits are sand, coarser ones shingle). Most gravel deposits date from the Ice Age, when they were carried down by rivers or glaciers. Gravel pits tend to be found near rivers, old river beds or beaches.

As a constituent of concrete, gravel is in great demand by the building and construction industry. Pits are therefore usually located near big cities—in the Lea Valley and Middlesex near London, in the Avon Valley near Birmingham, and the Trent Valley near Nottingham. Suitable sites are becoming scarce and an increasing amount of gravel is being taken from the sea. Thousands of worked-out gravel pits have become ponds which attract a wide variety of bird life, notably waders and wildfowl. The larger ponds have been used increasingly for sailing and water-skiing.

Grayling *Thymallus thymallus*

This fish, which lives in swift rivers and some mountain lakes, is related to the salmon and the trout. The grayling looks like a small salmon, but can easily be distinguished by the long, high fin on its back. It is silvery, shading to purple above and white below with grey-green sides on which dark lines mark the rows of scales.

Grayling join together in loose shoals for most of the year, except in the spring when the fish pair off for spawning. This takes place from March to May in gravelly shallows about 6 in. deep.

The grayling, which has a soft mouth and small teeth, eats insect larvae, snails and shrimps. It grows to about 18 in. and a weight of about 5 lb. When freshly killed, its flesh appears to be scented with thyme — hence its Latin name.

Grayling butterfly see Brown butterfly
Grazing see Grass

Great silver water beetle

A rare species in Britain, being found only in a few weedy ponds and ditches in southern England. The great silver water beetle *Hydrophilus piceus* is the biggest beetle found in Britain, being up to 2 in. long with a bulky body.

The shape of this beetle is similar to the more common diving beetle *Dyliscus marginalis*, but the habits of the two species are different. The adult great silver water beetle is a vegetarian and does not have the large jaws of the diving beetle.

In order to breathe, the great silver water beetle traps a bubble of air beneath its body. It rises to the surface head first, then turns on one side, and pierces the surface with one of its funnel-shaped antennae to replenish this store of air. The beetle gets its name from the fine hairs which trap the air and make it appear to be bright silver when it dives.

The larva is large and fairly slow moving. It feeds on pond snails.

Grebe

The courtship ceremony of the great crested grebe was studied intensively by Sir Julian Huxley early this century and his description of its elaborate rituals is regarded as a classic on the subject.

The 19 in. long great crested grebe is the largest and most numerous of the five species of European grebe found in Britain.

Its courtship begins in mid-winter when the birds form pairs and take up territories. They perform an extravagant ritual of postures and gestures which include head shaking, a penguin dance with weed in their bills, and fish offering.

In summer, the great crested grebe is resplendent in its nuptial plumage with tufts of feathers about the head, which play an important part in the ritual dance. In the 19th century this grebe nearly be-

came extinct owing to the demand for plumes to adorn women's hats.

All grebes live on inland stretches of fresh water, and can stay under water for long periods searching for fish, which form the bulk of their food.

Four species nest in Britain; the fifth is a regular winter visitor. They build floating nests anchored to reeds and cover their eggs with weed when they leave the nest.

The little grebe or dabchick is numerous but seen much less often, owing to its submerging at the slightest sign of danger and heading under water for the nearest patch of aquatic vegetation, in which it hides. Like the other grebes it can swim with its back awash, only the head and neck breaking the surface. At 9 in. it is the smallest grebe and its blunt rear end is a sure means of identification.

The slavonian grebe and black-necked grebe are so alike they are difficult to identify outside the breeding season. Both are about 12 in. long, but the slavonian has white cheeks and a white neck, while the black-necked is dusky with a light comma-shaped mark behind the eye.

At breeding time the plumage of both birds has golden head adornments. The slavonian grebe has prominent horns over the crown, and the black-necked has a delicate fan of feathers behind the eye. The only breeding sites are in central Scotland where some 20 pairs breed each year.

The slavonian grebe is similarly confined to Scotland, but further north on Highland lochs. One particular colony in Inverness has 15 pairs, but there are possibly 35 pairs on various other lochs in the extreme north.

A winter visitor to the eastern counties from north-eastern Europe is the red-necked grebe. It is 17 in. long and can be confused with the great crested grebe.

HEAD-SHAKING COURTSHIP CEREMONY

Two birds meet warily

Head shaking establishes recognition

Habit preening signals acceptance

Two birds approach with heads lowered threateningly. They straighten up and waggle and shake their heads. Then they start habit-preening — dipping back to peck at a wing feather

The great crested grebe feeds feathers to its young; this is believed to help in regurgitating fish bones

Green

A feature of many English villages is the green. Around it are often grouped the main buildings and on it may be a market cross, the lock-up, monument, pond or well. Many greens were once the centre of the community's social life and today some are still used for cricket matches and May Day dancing.

A green is a form of common land open to all for 'lawful exercise', and may owe its origin partly to the need to keep the community's livestock in a safe, central place. Greens vary in shape and size from small triangles of neglected grassland in front of the village inn to large commons, such as the 40 acres at Shipbourne in Kent.

Many impressive square and rectangular greens survive in Co. Durham, and by their regular shape suggest a planned origin. Some villages, such as Kirkheaton in Northumberland, still appoint a 'Guardian of the Green'.

Some greens have been encroached upon by squatters' cottages and gardens, which have established the right to be there by 'squatting' without objection from the other villagers. See also COMMON LAND

Green bottle

A fly which can be seen in large numbers on sunny days, buzzing around rotting vegetable matter and dung. Green-bottle eggs—up to 600 from one female—are laid on animal carcasses or dung, usually in parts shielded from the sun as the larvae need moist conditions.

The eggs hatch in a day and the maggots burrow into the food, causing it to liquefy. The maggots swallow this liquid food and, in warm weather, will reach their full size of $\frac{1}{2}$ in. after only two or three days. The maggots then burrow into the soil to pupate. In 7-14 days the pupa hatches.

The common green bottle *Lucilia caesar* and the sheep maggot fly *L. sericata* are attracted by the smell of festering wounds and lay their eggs there. The maggots feed on the animal's flesh.

Sheep are often affected in this way, and sometimes humans. But this is not always so harmful as it may appear: surgeons in the First World War discovered that soldiers' wounds cleaned by maggots healed more quickly.

Greenfly see Aphid

Green lane

A country road which has been left without a metalled surface. Many green lanes mark routes through the fields up to moorland grazing areas.

In the Pennines such lanes are called 'thrufts' or 'through ways'. Many of them were used by stock drovers until the 19th century.

There are splendid green lanes running over the Wiltshire Downs which may have

A green lane in Cornwall leads through enclosed farm fields to open moorland

been in use since the New Stone Age— 4000 years ago. The Icknield Way, which runs from Norfolk to Land's End, is one of these ancient tracks, parts of which still survive as green lanes. The Roman Dere Street, which linked Corbridge on the Tyne with garrisons in Scotland, is a good example of a green lane. It cuts a broad, grassy route through Roxburghshire. See also DROVE ROAD

Greensand

The sandstone which forms the yellow, sandy hills of Hindhead and Dorking in Surrey, and Woburn, Bedfordshire, is known as greensand. It owes its name to glauconite, a green compound of iron, which it contains in small amounts. This can be seen in freshly broken rock with a hand lens. When rainwater trickles through greensand the glauconite quickly alters to an orange or yellow form of iron, giving the colour of greensand at the surface.

Greensand lies below chalk in the rock sequence, so it occurs at the surface in places where chalk has eroded, such as the south of the North Downs, and to the northwest of the Chilterns, continuing to Sandringham in Norfolk. It is also found in the Haldon Hills of Devon.

Glauconite is used as a colouring agent in green paint and as a water softening mineral.

Greenshank see Shank

Green staining fungus
Chlorosplenium aeruginascens

Green, rotting branches found lying on woodland floors are infected with the green staining fungus. It attacks most deciduous

trees, particularly oak, ash, birch and hazel. This green wood, usually known as 'green oak', can be found throughout the year. In autumn, and occasionally in spring, small stalked blue-green cups, $\frac{1}{4}$-$\frac{1}{3}$ in. in diameter, may also appear on the surface of the branch.

Until the end of the last century green oak was inlaid with other coloured woods to make patterns on table tops, jewel boxes and snuff boxes. They were made at Tonbridge in Kent and were known as 'Tunbridge Ware'.

Green-winged orchid see Orchid
Greyhen see Grouse

Gribble *Limnoria lignorum*

Wooden pier piles are often eaten away at low-water mark by a tiny isopod (*iso* meaning the same, because its legs are of equal size), only $\frac{1}{8}$-$\frac{1}{6}$ in. long, called a gribble. It is related to the woodlouse and has rasp-like mandibles which it uses to tunnel below the surface of the wood.

Within each tunnel are a male and female gribble, the female doing most of the burrowing. The female produces 20-30 eggs three times a year, which she incubates in a pouch until they are about one-fifth of the size of the adult. When the miniature gribbles are released they immediately start making their own burrows, usually about 1 in. long. In winter and spring some adults swim off in search of new timber to infest.

Although they eat the wood, gribbles feed mainly on fungi contained in it. There may be as many as 400 gribbles to a cubic inch.

Protection against these wood borers is difficult, but certain woods, particularly the South American greenheart *Ocotea rodiaei*, contain a poison which resists attacks for a long period. The only sure protection against the gribble is to cover wood with a copper sheathing, a material that is often used for cladding that part of a boat's hull that is below the waterline.

Grilse see Salmon
Grisette fungus see Fungus

Gromwell

The name of this plant is of uncertain origin; its variations, grummel or grey myle, indicate that it may have been derived from a combination of the grey appearance of the hairy stems and leaves, and the seeds being like grains of *mil* or millet. The hard seeds are the origin of the botanical name *lithospermum*, which means stone seed.

Common gromwell *Lithospermum officinale* is an upright plant, 12-30 in. high, with narrow leaves and yellow-white 'forget-me-not' flowers, which produce shining seeds, and occurs in long grass in bushy places or along woodland margins. Corn gromwell *L. arvense* is an annual arable field weed, rarely exceeding 18 in. high, with blue-white

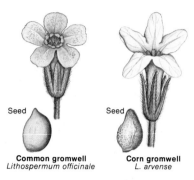

Common gromwell
Lithospermum officinale

Corn gromwell
L. arvense

Seed

Seed

Gromwell has a spike of tiny yellow-white flowers, each enclosed in a hairy cup

flowers and warty, grey-brown seeds. Both species are widespread in south and east England, but rare elsewhere.

Ground beetle

Kick over any stone or decaying log in summer, and the chances are that a ground beetle or two will scurry away to seek a new hiding place. Several hundred species of ground beetles live in the British Isles. The most common is the violet ground beetle *Carabus violaceus*, deriving its name from the violet sheen of its wing cases. Most ground beetles are black, but green and copper sheens are common. Few ground beetles can fly, and the wing cases are fused together, though one species, *C. granulatus,* has 'studded' wing cases which are not fused.

All are predators and both as larvae and adults hide in crevices by day, coming out at night to feed. They rely on powerful jaws and their long legs to prey on worms, caterpillars and small invertebrates. The larva has no wings or wing cases, and all its body segments are visible. Besides the larger ground beetles, which grow to about an inch long, there are many smaller related beetles in the sub-family Carabinae.

Ground-ivy *Glechoma hederacea*

The common name is misleading as ground-ivy is neither related to ivy, nor looks like it. It is an attractive creeping plant, 3-12 in. high, with square stems and heart-shaped leaves arranged in pairs. Clusters of blue flowers, which might be mistaken for violets, grow in the junctions between leaf and stem.

Ground-ivy, once used to flavour beer, flowers from March to May in damp places

Ground-ivy grows everywhere in the British Isles, though it is rare in the far north and west. It flowers from March until May, in damp woodlands, meadows and hedgebanks.

It was an important herb before the introduction of hops as it was then used in brewing to clear beer and give it a better flavour: hence its other name, alehoof.

Groundsel, Common *Senecio vulgaris*

An annual weed, 3-18 in. high, which is a nuisance to gardeners, but is useful in winter as fresh food for pet rabbits and cage birds. The yellow heads of the flowers are usually inconspicuous, lacking petals, although forms with petals do occur, particularly in the west of England.

A head develops many seeds, each with its own parachute of fine white hairs which helps it to be carried on the wind. The name *Senecio* is derived from the Latin *senex*, old man, because of this head of white hairs. Seeds germinate throughout the year, whenever temperature permits.

Seed head

The yellow flowers of groundsel produce many seeds with parachutes to carry them on the wind

Grouse

The 'Glorious Twelfth' marks the opening every August of one of the great British countryside rituals, when hundreds of marksmen take to the moors to seek the plump red grouse. There are four species of grouse in Britain, but only in Scotland are all present.

Each fills a different natural niche—the red grouse inhabits the heather-clad moorlands,

The ptarmigan's grey autumn plumage blends with

the black grouse is found in grassy woodland clearings, the capercaillie in coniferous woodland, and the ptarmigan only on the highest bare mountains. All are short-winged birds, with a low, whirring flight. All nest on the ground, where the dull plumage of the hen camouflages her. The chicks—up to a dozen —are able to walk and feed themselves soon after hatching.

The red grouse, which grows to about 15 in., is the prime target of sporting guns. Yet research shows that shooting does not permanently threaten its numbers, since there is usually a surplus population doomed to starve through being unable to obtain

COMMUNAL DANCES OF THE MALE GROUSE

Courtship display of the black grouse involves wing-flapping, mincing runs and crowing sounds

its rocky surroundings. It is the only British bird whose plumage turns white for winter camouflage

individual territories. The red grouse feeds on young heather.

The larger black grouse (males reach 21 in.) is noted for its leks—communal mating grounds—where the polygamous males, known as blackcocks, gather to joust in combat for the mottled females, called greyhens. Once his tiny territory is established, the blackcock defends it against all-comers during spring and summer, resplendent in his black plumage and spread lyre-shaped tail. The most successful at a jousting win territories in the middle of the lek, where they secure more matings than do the birds on the fringes. They feed on birch buds and other vegetation. Apart from a few pairs in the West Country, black grouse are confined to Scotland, Wales and northern England.

The name capercaillie, pronounced 'capper-kail-yee', is probably derived from Gaelic words meaning 'horse of the woods'. It was extinct in Britain by 1800, victim of hunters and dwindling pine forests, but was re-introduced to Perthshire in 1837, and is now established in eastern Scotland. Like the red and black grouse, it indulges in flamboyant spring courtship. The male, at 34 in., is the largest of our game-birds, and as it beats noisily away among pines with its tail spread it can easily be mistaken for a turkey. It can be very aggressive, and there is at least one recorded instance of a capercaillie

attacking people on a track crossing its territory. It feeds on the shoots of young pines, and is a menace to foresters as it often strips the bark.

The ptarmigan, about the same size as the red grouse, is an Arctic tundra bird found only on a few of the highest Scottish mountain tops. In summer, the cock is speckled grey, with pure white wings that stand out boldly as it flies. In winter both cock and hen are pure white with black tail tips. Like other mountain-top birds, they show little fear and rely on their camouflage to escape from predators.

The turkey-like capercaillie, hunted to extinction in Britain, was re-introduced in 1837

Groyne see Breakwater
Grub see Larva

Gudgeon *Gobio gobio*

A slim fish with a pair of fleshy barbels on its lips, the gudgeon is a member of the carp family. It rarely grows longer than 8 in., and is grey-green to blackish-grey with silvery, dark-spotted undersides. The gudgeon is found in rivers and lakes throughout England, and in Ireland, where it has been introduced. It prefers a gravelly or sandy bottom, feeding on snails, worms and small insects.

In May and June, the females lay up to 3000 eggs on the gravel, mostly at night. These cling to the stones and nearby vegetation. They hatch in two to four weeks, and the young fish can be found hiding in the loose gravel.

Because they are easy to keep alive in fresh water, gudgeon were formerly very popular as food, but are now rarely eaten.

Guelder rose *Viburnum opulus*

The showy white flower heads of the guelder rose which appear in June are fakes. In each umbrella-shaped cluster the larger white blooms on the outside are sterile, serving only as flags to attract insects to the fertile flowers further in. The leaves of this small shrub, sometimes called the snowball tree, are like those of the maple. They have three to five lobes and are set in pairs along the stems. Bright green in spring, they mellow to rich orange and russet in autumn, setting off the translucent scarlet berries. These, for all their ripe beauty, are bitter, but birds eat them.

Though rare, the guelder rose grows in all parts of the British Isles. It is a plant of moist hedgerows and the edges of woodland, and grows to between 6 ft and 15 ft tall.

Guelder rose, a shrub named after the ancient province of Guelderland in the Low Countries

Guillemot see Auk

Gull

In spite of their common name, seagull, most gulls are shorebirds, seldom venturing far out to sea, but often penetrating inland to scavenge on tips, parks and reservoirs. Gulls follow ploughs as readily as they follow steamers. Six species breed regularly in the British Isles, and many have increased their numbers so much that they are now a nuisance, polluting water and attacking other seabirds at nesting sites. Herring gulls, for instance, first bred on the Isle of Walney, off Barrow-in-Furness, in 1904. By 1934, 35 pairs were breeding; by 1964, 10,000-20,000 pairs.

Gulls are long-winged, buoyant flyers 11-27 in. long. They have white underparts, distinctive coloured legs and bills and their upper parts vary from black to light grey. Many species have a black-and-white pattern on the wing tips and several have a black or brown hood in the breeding season. Although most gulls find cliffs, stacks and uninhabited islands ideal for breeding, colonies of herring, common and black-headed gulls often nest in coastal dunes or on bogs and marshes far inland. Almost all create a nest of some sort, though few build as well as the kittiwake which constructs a cupped structure on the tiniest of cliff ledges. The three or four pear-shaped eggs are cream to brown, speckled with darker markings, often with an olive cast, and the chicks are well camouflaged as a defence against predators such as foxes, stoats, skuas and other gulls.

Juveniles soon leave the colonies and all species show a distinctive immature plumage during the first year of life. The largest birds take three or four years to mature during which they pass through a highly confusing set of plumages, making identification difficult.

The largest gulls at 27 in., including the tail, are the great black-backs. Their huge size and black backs, powerful heads and bills make them easy to distinguish even from the similarly marked lesser black-backed gulls.

Great black-backs may be found well out to sea as well as around the coasts. They breed on remote headlands and islands in the north and west, where they are increasing, following near-extinction from shooting at the end of the last century. Island populations have increased considerably since the 1930's, and these ferocious killers present a serious hazard to shearwaters and other birds.

As with other gulls, great black-backs owe their increase in numbers to greater quantities of fish offal, rubbish and sewage being available, allowing more birds to survive the winter.

Lesser black-backed gulls are true migrants. Although a few hundred birds winter here, the vast majority move south into Africa. At 21 in. the lessers are the same size as herring gulls, with which they sometimes share breeding colonies. Their legs are yellow, but like the herring and great black-back gulls, the yellow bill has a red spot. Two distinct races occur in Britain. The light grey mantled birds breed here, while the black-backed race is a passage migrant and winter visitor from Scandinavia.

Lesser black-backs form large colonies, usually on the flat tops of islands. The colony of more than 10,000 pairs on Walney Island is still increasing. Outside the breeding season lessers often haunt playing fields in large flocks during migration periods.

Herring gulls are the large grey-backed birds with black-and-white wing tips, familiar to steamer passengers and from postcards of south-western fishing harbours. They are widespread, and have increased enormously this century. Though often found around cliffs where they hang gracefully on updraughts of air, they also form large colonies among dunes and on islands, and have taken to breeding on the roofs of factories and houses. One pair has even bred in central London alongside captive birds in Regent's Park Zoo.

Studies of the behaviour of herring gulls have yielded an explanation of the red spot on their yellow bills. Chicks instinctively peck at the spot to encourage their parents to feed them, and experiments have shown that this colour combination provokes more pecks than any other.

Often confused with herring gulls, common gulls are however smaller, but with the same grey-and-white pattern with black-and-white wing tips. They have smaller heads and shorter yellow-green bills. They breed on many Scottish moors and in north-

The hungry chick asks to be fed by pecking at the red spot on its parent's yellow bill. The parent then regurgitates food for the chick to eat

ern and western islands. In England, they are confined to Dungeness, and in Wales, to Anglesey. In winter, they are more widespread and numerous and are found inland and on coastal marshes. They search for worms and grubs and follow the plough, and are also common in London.

Kittiwakes resemble common gulls but have pure black wing tips. They are numerous and widespread, forming dense colonies in the north and west, and have recently started to spread to the east coast. This spread is probably due to a decline in persecution. Kittiwakes wander the open seas outside the breeding season and are seldom seen inland or on the shore, though a colony on a warehouse at Gateshead, Northumberland, is more than 9 miles from the sea. Young kittiwakes have an inverted black W on the mantle.

The black-headed gulls are the most numerous British gulls, but do not have black heads. In summer they sport chocolate-brown hoods which disappear in autumn, leaving only a dark smudge behind the eye. Otherwise they are light grey birds with red legs and bills, showing a white fore-wing in flight.

Black-headed gulls moved up the Thames Estuary during hard winters at the end of the 19th century, finding food sources around docks, parks and embankments. They are now familiar scavengers in almost every city. They breed on marshes and moorlands and are found along the shoreline only in spring, autumn and winter. Even then they often glean their living inland, resorting to the coast only to roost.

The breeding population of some 50,000 pairs is augmented in autumn by the mass arrival of continental birds, with more than 200,000 in London alone. Ringing—the placing of identification tags on the birds' legs —has shown that many come from the north and east, and that some migrate from Czechoslovakia. Ringing has also established that once in winter quarters the birds feed in the same place every day. The birds of London Embankment seldom mix with the birds of St James's Park, while even within

The herring gull in flight. It has pink legs and a yellow bill. When mature its back is grey

Ivory gulls are rare winter vagrants from the Arctic, visiting Orkney and Shetland and other northern islands. They are almost pigeon-like in appearance, with long wings and white plumage, often speckled black. Among the rarest gulls, only the Sabine's gulls are regular visitors. They breed in North America and pass across the Atlantic to winter off West Africa. Sometimes they are blown northwards to Britain's western shores. Their black primaries form a distinctive pattern, particularly on immature birds.

Recent observations have added three gulls to the British list: the slender-billed gull and two from North America, the laughing gull and Franklin's gull—popularly known as the 'prairie dove'.

Gully see Valley
Gunnel see Butterfish

Gurnard

There are several species of this fish around the coast. All gurnards have the lowest three rays of the pectoral fins separate from the rest of the fin. These rays are mobile and covered with taste organs. They are used to search the sea-bed for the creatures on which the gurnard feeds—sand-burrowing crabs, shrimps, small molluscs and fish. The rays also serve to raise the fish off the sea bottom, thus increasing its field of vision.

The most common and the largest is the tub or yellow gurnard *Trigla lucerna*, sometimes called the latchet. It grows to 24 in. and varies considerably in colour, although there is always a red tinge. The large fins behind and below the head are brightly coloured with red and blue. In profile it has a sharply pointed snout with small spines at the front.

Other gurnards regularly seen are the grey gurnard *Eutrigla gurnardus* which is a sharp-headed, spiny-sided species, 11-15 in. long, and the red gurnard *Aspitrigla cuculus* which is smaller.

Gurnards can make a great deal of noise by muscle contractions of the body which are amplified by their swim bladders. They grunt, groan and click to communicate with each other as they swim in loose shoals over the sea-bed. They sometimes make these noises when landed by anglers.

Black-headed gulls fight above a nest. Their characteristic dark heads turn white in autumn

the park each gull remains within the limits of its own feeding area.

Black-headed gulls have increased because of their ability to live near man. They haunt rubbish tips and roost on reservoirs; they follow the plough and even breed inland on gravel pits and sewage works.

Mediterranean gulls, often called Mediterranean black-headed gulls, have recently settled to breed at a private reserve at Needs Oar Point, Hampshire. In the breeding season they have black hoods extending to the neck, with grey backs and no black on the wings. In winter the hood disappears, making Mediterranean gulls easy to overlook among the slightly smaller and more numerous black-headed gulls, with whom they have paired, rearing hybrid young.

Little gulls also have black hoods in summer, but do not breed in Britain. They are birds of passage and autumn visitors, and their favourite haunt in southern England is Radpole Lake in Weymouth, Dorset. Large numbers occur in Northumberland and south-east Scotland. They are the smallest British gulls, with smoky black underwings and small stubby bills. Young birds have a pronounced inverted W on the back and wings, which shows well in flight.

Both Iceland gulls and glaucous gulls are found around British shores in winter, especially in the north. They are similar to large herring gulls, but the wings are without the dark areas on the flight feathers The Iceland gulls—which do not breed in Iceland—have smaller heads and bills. Glaucous gulls breed in Iceland, and have yellow rings round their eyes.

FINS USED AS LEGS

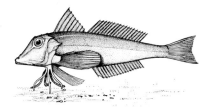

The gurnard uses its finger-like pectoral rays to move over the sea floor and search for food

Gwyniad see Whitefish

H

Haddy see Charr

Ha-ha

A concealed ditch round parkland which does not interrupt the view, but stops livestock from roaming. The name is believed to be derived from the exclamation ha! prompted by the shock of finding a hidden ditch. Ha-ha's were popular in the 18th century, when it was fashionable to have a view of the countryside from big houses. The side of the ditch nearest the house is usually perpendicular and lined with stone. Ha-ha's now provide a permanent alternative to fencing to keep cars from open land.

Hail

There are two sorts of hail—true and soft. True hail may fall from May to October. Soft hail, or graupel, falls mainly in winter. Hailstones are usually about the size of a pea, and rarely larger than a marble. Occasionally they can be the size of a golf ball. During a storm in the Horsham area of Sussex in 1958 some were the size and shape of half a grapefruit. Since hailstones hit the ground at speeds of between 50 and 100 miles per hour, such storms can cause enormous damage, especially to crops.

True hailstones are formed when warm, moist air rises on a hot day and condenses into huge cumulo-nimbus (or thunder) clouds within which moisture drops freeze and are carried upwards in a series of loops by strong currents. Layer upon layer of ice is added to the frozen drops as they rise until they become so heavy that they fall out of the updraught to the ground, often accompanied by thunder and lightning.

Soft hail consists of tiny frozen droplets which do not bounce on striking the ground. Each piece of soft hail consists of nothing more than minute particles of frozen cloud, loosely attached to one another.

Hairstreak

This butterfly is so named because it has a thin white line running across the underside of each wing, similar to a line formed by drawing a hair across wet paint. There are five British species all with a wingspan of $1\frac{1}{8}$ in. to $1\frac{1}{2}$ in. They are the woodland relations of the blue butterflies.

The most common is the green hairstreak, so called because the undersides of the wings are bright green. It is widespread throughout Britain and parts of southern Ireland in May and June, and is less restricted to woodland than the other species. Its caterpillars feed on gorse, broom and other shrubs

---

Hairstreak butterflies

There are five British species of hairstreak butterflies, all of which live in woodland. Their colours vary, but all have a fine white line streaking across the pattern of the underwing. The sexes are very similar. All the species have a wingspan of $1\frac{1}{8}$-$1\frac{1}{2}$ in.

Black hairstreak
Strymonidia pruni
M   F   underwings

Purple hairstreak
Thecla quercus
M   F   underwings

Brown hairstreak
Thecla betulae
M   F   underwings

White-letter hairstreak
Strymonidia w-album
M   F   underwings

Green hairstreak
Callophrys rubi
M   F   underwings

---

which can be found well away from woodland.

The purple hairstreak is found in oak woods mainly in England and Wales; there are no recent records of it in Scotland or Ireland. The butterflies appear in August and tend to keep to the tops of tall trees, so that even in places where they are common they are not often seen. Sometimes the upper sides of the wings appear dull brown or black, as the iridescent purple colour depends on the angle of light.

The brown hairstreak is found mainly in southern England, although it can be seen occasionally in Wales and Ireland. The caterpillars feed on blackthorn leaves and the butterflies live in woods where there is a good undergrowth of blackthorn.

Brown hairstreaks appear in August and September but, like the purple hairstreak, they tend to stay well hidden.

The black hairstreak is rare. It also feeds on blackthorn but is restricted to a few woods across the country from Oxford to southern Lincolnshire. One of the most important locations for the black hairstreak is Monks Wood

National Nature Reserve in Huntingdonshire, the place where it was first discovered in the 1850's.

Black hairstreaks fly in June and July and are easier to see than the secretive brown hairstreak. The chrysalis is attached to a blackthorn leaf and is camouflaged by its close resemblance to a bird dropping.

The white-letter hairstreak has its hairstreak in the form of a W—hence its unusual scientific name. The caterpillars feed on elm trees, and the butterflies can be seen in July and August in many areas of England, although their numbers seem to be declining. It is unusual for these butterflies to fly far from the tree on which they were born. They often flutter about the lower branches, settling with closed wings.

Hammer-pond

These ponds, some almost large enough to be called lakes, are a feature of the weald, the countryside of the Kent-Sussex border. They were formed by damming rivers and provided power to drive mill wheels which operated heavy hammers in local iron works.

Haloes such as this are formed by the refraction of light through masses of ice crystals

Halo

In the British Isles, haloes can be seen round the sun and moon on about one day in three, but because it is difficult and dangerous to look at a bright sun with the naked eye, the haloes most commonly noticed are those round the moon. On many clear nights the moon appears to have a luminous ring. Sometimes the ring appears to be white, but when it is clearly defined the inner edge is seen to be deep red, shading to yellow on the outside.

Haloes are formed by refraction of light through ice crystals at heights of from 16,000 to 45,000 ft. They often precede a storm, and one piece of country lore predicts that 'a ring round the moon means rain before morning'.

The iron trade flourished in the densely wooded weald as long as charcoal was needed to smelt the ore, but when coal replaced charcoal in the 18th century the iron industry moved nearer the coalfields.

In the valleys downstream from the dams and sluice gates the masonry of old furnaces may be found. The slag often includes large lumps of imperfectly fused ore called 'bears', full of shiny, metal flakes. Fine examples of hammer-ponds are at Cowden and Brenchley, Kent. See also MILL, WEIR

Hare

The mad hares of March are the males, which bound, kick and stand on their hind legs to box with each other in a ritual that impresses the females before mating. At such times they seem oblivious of danger and can easily be approached. The does, which are up to 2 ft long and slightly larger than the males, bear up to four litters of two to four leverets each year. The young are born above ground with a full coat of fur.

Hares are distinguished from their relatives the rabbits by their larger size, longer ears and longer hind legs. Normally the two animals do not mix. Hare tracks, especially in snow, can be identified by the longer stride and the absence of toe or pad marks due to their hairy soles. Hares live in well-defined territories, spending the day lying in shallow depressions under cover, known as forms. The leverets are sometimes distributed in separate 'milking' forms, visited at intervals by the does. Hares feed mainly at twilight on grass, roots, bark and the produce of fields and gardens. When disturbed, they will remain still up to the last moment, then dash away at high speed, twisting and doubling back to escape capture. They scream when in fear or agony and are said to grind their teeth as a warning sound.

Brown hares live on open downland and farmland, even on airfields, in the lowlands

Mountain hare
Lepus timidus

Brown hare
Lepus capensis

of the British Isles. They are tawny coloured with the upper parts a mixture of brown and grey hairs and the flanks and undersides paler. The ears have black tips. Hares are unaffected by myxomatosis, and since rabbits were killed off in large numbers by the disease, hares have spread into woodland.

Mountain or blue hares are slightly smaller than brown hares and have shorter ears. They live mainly on rocks in the Scottish mountains, choosing a terrain with enough cover to avoid their enemies, such as eagles and buzzards. During winter their coats turn white, camouflaging them against the snow. They are called blue hares because their fur has a bluish appearance in spring and autumn when the white hairs of their winter coats are mingled with the brown hairs of their summer coats. The ear tips always remain black.

To impress females in the mating season, hares stand on their hind legs and box with each other

The harebell, 6-15 in. high, blooms from July to September throughout the British Isles

Harebell *Campanula rotundifolia*

Throughout Britain, on high, acid moorland and low, chalky grasslands, the bright blue flowers of the harebell dance in the light summer and autumn breezes. Harebells are the bluebells of Scotland, where the woodland plant of spring, known as the bluebell elsewhere, is called wild hyacinth. They are not common in Ireland, where they are known as fairy bells, or goblin's thimbles.

The stems from which the flowers hang are very fine. Occasionally, the flowers are white.

The leaves on the stems are long and narrow, but a few at the base, usually hidden by other plants, are round. Hence *rotundifolia*, meaning round leaves.

Harness

The harness of a draught horse consists of the collar, the pads which take the weight of the shafts, and the strapwork. Around the front of the leather collar, which is packed with flock, are fastened wooden reinforcements called hames, to which are attached the chains by which the horse pulls its load. A second padded leather band behind the horse's shoulders is surmounted by a wooden frame, through which runs a chain that takes the weight of the shafts.

The horse collar-maker is a specialist. No two horses' necks are the same, and each collar has to be individually measured and fitted.

Cart horses in glossy black harness are still a feature of agricultural shows. The harness is adorned with sparkling horse brasses, which have become collectors' pieces. But, with the increase in farm mechanisation, harness making has become something of a luxury trade, catering for horse riders.

Harrier

Long-winged, long-tailed birds of prey that fly close to the ground, beating and gliding this way and that in search of prey—small birds, frogs and grass snakes. Three harriers

appear in Britain, hen-harriers, marsh harriers and Montagu's harriers. All are rare and migratory. Montagu's harrier is only present from April to September, though a few marsh harriers and hen-harriers are present all year round.

Harriers appear to be leisurely flyers, quartering the ground systematically and searching for prey. They fly low to increase the chances of a surprise encounter; and they seize the prey with their long legs. During the breeding season the male does most of the hunting and brings food to within a short distance of the nest. The female then rises and takes the food from her mate in the air, foot to foot, flying upside-down to do so.

Harriers build well-hidden nests on the ground and lay four to five eggs between April and June.

The marsh harrier is the largest, measuring 19-23 in. from bill to tail tip with a wing-span of 4 ft. The male is brown and has grey patches on the wings when mature. The female is chocolate-coloured with a creamy head and forewings. Once widespread in East Anglia, marsh harriers now breed only at Minsmere Reserve in Suffolk, where a single male often has two nesting mates.

The hen-harrier seldom breeds outside the Orkney Islands and northern Scotland, but a few have become established in North Wales. They breed on open moorland, but come southwards in winter to haunt coastal marshes and estuaries. Males are grey with a white rump patch, the females are brown with streaked underparts.

Spectacular display of aerobatics as the male hen-harrier passes food to the upside-down female

Hen-harriers are the only birds of prey to have significantly increased their numbers in recent years. There are now more than 100 breeding pairs.

Montagu's harriers are named after a 19th-century naturalist, Colonel George Montagu. These birds are more numerous and widespread than other harriers, breeding mainly in southern England on lowland heaths and in young conifer plantations which they desert as the trees grow. Males are grey with a black wing bar. Females closely resemble hen-harriers, but the two species are never in the same place at the same time. So, away from the main breeding ground of the hen-harrier in northern Scotland, a small harrier is almost certain to be a Montagu's harrier in summer and a hen-harrier in winter.

A female hen-harrier uses her wings to shield her chick from the sun. The female constructs her well-hidden nest on moorland, often in heather, and usually lays four eggs, which are white or pale blue

Harrow

An agricultural implement used to work down soil into a fine tilth. After a field has been ploughed and its clods of soil broken up, the harrow is dragged over the ground to prepare it for sowing. Immediately after sowing the harrow is used again to cover the seed.

Most harrows have rigid teeth mounted on an iron frame, although the frames of early harrows were of wood. Often the frame is fashioned in a zigzag pattern, to ensure efficient coverage of the ground. Spring-tine harrows, in which the curved teeth are really springs, can be used safely behind tractors travelling at relatively high speeds, as they can bounce over dangerous obstacles.

Disc harrows, which consist of a series of saucer-shaped discs mounted on an axle and rotating as the implement is pulled along, are a type of cultivator and can do heavier work. A chain harrow does not have a rigid frame and is simply a net of steel links, sometimes spiked. They are used mainly for rolling up couch grass and other rubbish when soil is being worked during a fallow.

Harrows of various types are also used in aerating grassland by pulling out dead grasses and other debris at the end of winter.

Hartstongue see Fern

Harvest

This can mean the gathering of crops, the crops themselves, or the season at which they are gathered. The word usually refers to the ripe grain or corn crops which are reaped between July and October.

A successful harvest is a time for rejoicing and until the turn of the century a feast known as the harvest home was held, when a Lord of the Harvest or a Harvest Queen was appointed. Today, almost all churches hold harvest festivals.

Harvestman

An eight-legged animal with a $\frac{1}{4}$-$\frac{1}{2}$ in. long body. It is a member of the same family as spiders, but differs from them in having longer legs and two glands in the head which produce an evil-smelling fluid.

Harvestmen feed on living or recently dead insects, which they seize in their pincer-like jaws, and on fungi or other vegetation. Females lay several batches of eggs under logs and stones. The eggs are injected deep into the ground through a long ovipositor, or egg-laying tube. They hatch as miniature adults but do not mature for a further nine months.

Harvestmen are found in forests, grasslands and short vegetation, under flower-pots, and in compost heaps and garden sheds. They are most often seen after rain, but in periods of drought they forage only at dawn or twilight. They are conspicuous in autumn—hence their name. Local names include harvest spider and daddy-longlegs—which leads to confusion with the crane fly.

To escape from enemies such as large spiders or centipedes, harvestmen sometimes sacrifice a leg which continues to wriggle and holds the attention of the predator. Severed legs are not replaced, but several can be lost before the animal's movements are affected.

Haw see Hawthorn

Hawk

Two hawks breed in Britain, but only the sparrowhawk does so regularly. The other, the goshawk, is rare and only a few pairs nest in southern England. Several birds of prey are commonly called hawks, but only sparrowhawks and goshawks among British birds merit the name.

They are short-winged, long-tailed birds of prey which live and hunt among the trees of woodlands and forests. Their structure is suited to the sharp turns required for flying fast through the trees in pursuit of small birds which are their main prey; but they also venture into open ground to dive among the finches and winter thrushes of the fields and hedgerows.

The sparrowhawk is 12-15 in. long, the hen being considerably larger than the cock. The hen is a dull brown bird, with barred brown underparts. The cock is slate grey and rust red below.

It is found throughout Britain and Ireland, except for the northern islands, but in 1963 nearly became extinct in eastern England owing to the use of a pesticide as a seed dressing. Seed-eating birds poisoned by the dressing were eaten by sparrowhawks which died as a result. The use of pesticide was controlled in 1964, and since then the number of sparrowhawks has increased.

Goshawks, which are 19-24 in. long, have always been rare in Britain. They need larger areas of woodland in which to search for slightly larger prey than that which satisfies the sparrowhawk. They bred in Sussex until 1951, when they were driven off or killed by gamekeepers. A few pairs are believed to have returned.

Both hawks are migratory, and sparrowhawks become more numerous in winter with the annual influx of Scandinavian birds, particularly on the east coast. They glide on stiff wings.

Hawkbit

Autumn hawkbit is a common perennial which colours the roadsides, meadows and rough grassland of Britain a golden-yellow in August and September, except during rainy weather when the flower heads close. Its leaves are dandelion-like, much divided, forming a basal rosette; but the flowering stems are branched with tiny scales. The plant stands 2-3 ft high.

Rough hawkbit, which is less common and absent from most of Scotland and the northern half of Ireland, thrives on lime. It can be distinguished from autumn hawkbit by the solitary heads of flowers on hairy,

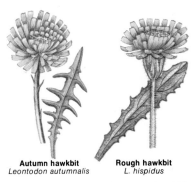

Autumn hawkbit
Leontodon autumnalis

Rough hawkbit
L. hispidus

The hairs on the leaves of autumn hawkbit are straight, those on rough hawkbit forked

scaleless stems up to 2 ft tall, and by the toothed, but never deeply divided, leaves covered in forked hairs.

Hawkmoth

Some of the most spectacular British moths are hawkmoths. All have stout bodies tapered at the rear and fairly narrow wings with a span of 2-4$\frac{1}{2}$ in. A few of the smaller species fly by day, but the others are nocturnal. Seven of the larger species live in Britain and there are a number of species which regularly migrate here, but are unable to survive the winter.

The life histories of the resident species follow a similar pattern. The pupae winter in the soil below food plants. The moths hatch in May, June or July, and the females lay large, green eggs on the underside of the leaves of the food plant. Each species concentrates on certain plants.

The lime hawk *Mimas tiliae* feeds on the leaves of lime and elm, the poplar hawk *Laothoe populi* on those of poplars and willows, and the eyed hawk *Smerinthus ocellata* on those of apples and sallows.

These three species are all common and the moths at rest on tree trunks sit in such a way that they resemble dead leaves. This disguise does not always fool predatory birds, but the eyed hawk has a second line of defence. If it is disturbed it brings its forewings forwards and displays the large eye markings on its hind wings. This gives the moth the appearance of an owl's face, which is believed to frighten small birds.

The elephant hawk *Deilephila elpenor* uses the same deterrent, and its caterpillar extends its head and neck rather like an elephant's trunk if disturbed. Then it draws back the head and swells up the thorax, which is marked with eye-spots. This gives the caterpillar a frightening appearance.

Elephant hawks feed on bedstraws and willow-herbs. The small elephant hawk *D. porcellus* is rare and more restricted to bedstraws.

The dull-coloured pine hawk *Hyloicus pinastri* was once a rarity, but is now widespread in England, feeding solely on pine needles.

The largest of the native species is the privet

227

hawk *Sphinx ligustri* which feeds on lilac and is rare outside southern England.

Hawkmoth caterpillars have a single spike at the end of their bodies. Those that feed on broad-leaved trees are green with diagonal stripes on the sides. This gives them a remarkably flat and leaf-like appearance.

The pine hawk caterpillar's stripes blend with surrounding pine needles. The caterpillars are fully grown in late summer when they burrow in the soil to pupate. Sometimes the poplar hawk manages to breed twice a year, but other hawkmoths have only one generation a year.

The most spectacular of the migrant species is the death's head hawk *Acherontia atropos,* named after the skull-like marking on its thorax. It also has the curious ability to produce a squeaking sound when confronted by enemies—forcing air through its short proboscis.

Occasionally it arrives in Britain in large numbers from the Continent, but is unable to survive the winter here. See also HUMMING-BIRD HAWKMOTH

Hawksbeard

These plants resemble both dandelions and hawkweeds. Smooth hawksbeard grows throughout the British Isles, except in high mountain areas, bearing heads of small flowers in summer and autumn.

Marsh hawksbeard is often confused with hawkweeds, but grows in wet places where hawkweeds scarcely ever occur, and the flower heads are covered with black, spreading hairs. It does not grow in southern or eastern England but is confined to the mountains. In contrast, beaked hawksbeard is common only in the lowlands of the south and east, developing much earlier than the other hawksbeards, and often found flowering during May.

It grows primarily in waste places, especially in lime-rich soils.

Smooth hawksbeard
Crepis capillaris

Beaked hawksbeard
C. vesicaria

Two common hawksbeards; each has a branching stem and numerous dandelion-like flowers

Hawkweed

There are more than 250 hawkweeds in the British Isles. They grow from 1 ft to 4 ft high, and all bear dandelion-like flowers, usually yellow, between June and August.

Hawkweeds are very difficult to identify, due to their peculiar type of reproduction.

They are capable of producing ripe seed without fertilisation, a process called apomixis. This leads to the perpetuation of minor differences which arise by mutation. The offspring of an isolated hawkweed, on a cliff for example, soon diverge from the parent form and become a new species.

Hawkweeds are most common on ungrazed cliffs and rocks, and are particularly abundant on limestone in the uplands of Derbyshire, Staffordshire, Yorkshire and the Lake District, Wales, central and northern Scotland and Ireland.

Mouse-ear hawkweed, one of the most common of the hundreds of hawkweeds growing in Britain

Hawthorn

The hawthorn hedges which divide the fields over mile upon mile of the English lowlands were planted mainly in the 18th century during the great land enclosure movement. Though threatened today by clearance, or replacement by wire fencing, they have proved long-lasting and cheap barriers to keep livestock from straying.

Hawthorn thrives on most soils. Individual trees, which develop from berries carried by birds, eventually spread to form thickets

To form a hedge, hawthorn berries, or 'haws', are gathered in autumn and stored in damp sand for 18 months before they will sprout. They are then sown and the seedlings transplanted to another bed. The small, thorny trees are finally planted out 9 in. apart. For a few years they need protection against animals by temporary fences.

Away from the hedges, hawthorn springs up frequently as a bird-sown bush. It colonises waste land everywhere and its thorns give protection against bad weather and grazing animals to the seedlings of larger trees like oak and ash that grow beneath it and eventually supplant it.

It is never a large tree, reaching about 15 ft tall. The trunk bears dark grey bark split into a pattern of squares. Each stem holds pale sapwood around tough, red-

The ½ in. flowers of the common hawthorn have five petals which are sometimes tinged with pink

brown heartwood. Hawthorn timber is sometimes used for hedge stakes, or as cudgels for driving them in. On the thin dark twigs, with small pinkish buds, many shoots take the form of sharp thorns. The leaves, bright green in spring, duller later, are deeply lobed. Flowers are borne in May, hence the name May blossom. They grow in clusters on unclipped trees, but never appear on close-clipped hedges.

Each flower has five white petals, many stamens and a central ovary. This ripens by October to a red berry which attracts birds, especially members of the thrush family, finches and tits. The haws are also an important food for the woodmouse and other small mammals.

The common hawthorn *Crataegus monogyna* has only one hard seed in each haw; the Midland hawthorn *C. oxyacanthoides* bears two or three. Beautiful red and pink-flowered varieties, some with double petals, are grown as ornamental shrubs. See also HEDGE

Hay

This is the form in which grass is dried and stored for feeding livestock in winter. Seed hay, usually a mixture of Italian rye-grass and red clover, is specially sown for cutting. Meadow hay is cut from permanent pasture and contains many species of grass and other plants.

Grass for hay is ready for mowing in June and July when it is 1-3 ft high, depending on species. Because there are often storms at this time of year, getting hay cut, dried and into storage is usually a race against the elements. Farmers try to hurry the drying process by turning the grass to expose the maximum area to air and sunlight. Hay always used to be built into stacks or ricks, but is now more likely to be baled and stored in barns.

Hay provides much of the winter feed for cattle, sheep and horses, especially in the western, high-rainfall, areas of the British Isles where grass grows best, but it has to be supplemented with root crops and concentrated foods that supply protein. Formerly, all but breeding cattle were slaughtered and salted down at the onset of winter. See also GRASS

Haze

This is a suspension of very small solid particles such as smoke and dust which obscure the view near the ground and give a milky appearance to the sky. Haze is particularly common in and around industrial areas such as the west Midlands, south Wales and the coalfields of northern England and Scotland, though conditions in these areas are improving with the conversion from coal to smokeless fuel. Even so, there will always be some dust in the atmosphere, both from the burning of fuels and from natural sources such as forest fires. See also DUST, POLLUTION

Hazel *Corylus avellana*

Though never more than a spreading bush, hazel was formerly of great economic importance in England, and thousands of acres of hazel coppice were tended in southern counties. If cut back every seven years, hazel sends up a dense mass of shoots, and the resulting branchy wood has many uses. It is good for pea sticks, bean rods, small stakes or clothes props, and small straight 'spars' and curved broaches or pegs used to secure thatch to the roofs of cottages or corn ricks. The long shoots can be split into thin wands and woven between stakes to form hurdles, useful as portable sheep fences. Hazel makes first-rate kindling, traditionally popular for bakers' ovens, and the rods used by water diviners are usually hazel.

Modern developments in fencing, roofing and fuel have made most hazel coppices redundant. They are being replaced by other, taller trees, but hazel will long survive along woodland rides and hedgerows. Rarely more than 10 ft tall, bushes endure for centuries. In some places coppices are still maintained to provide cover for game birds.

In winter, hazel can be identified by the small grey male catkins carried near the tips of twigs. In February they expand to become hanging pinkish-brown lambs' tails —carrying clusters of flowers that shed copious pollen. At the same time the bush puts out tiny female catkins, looking like large leaf buds that end in crimson tassels. By late spring, the broad, rounded-oval leaves with toothed edges have opened from their round, greenish winter buds, which are alternately set on brown twigs. In autumn the female flowers ripen to groups of two or three large round brown nuts, each set between conspicuous leaflets. Hazel nuts, which are also known as cob nuts, are good to eat, but most are taken by birds or squirrels, who help to spread the trees by dropping the nuts or burying them and forgetting them. Cultivated varieties, producing larger nuts, are grown in gardens and orchards, especially in Kent.

Heartsease see Pansy

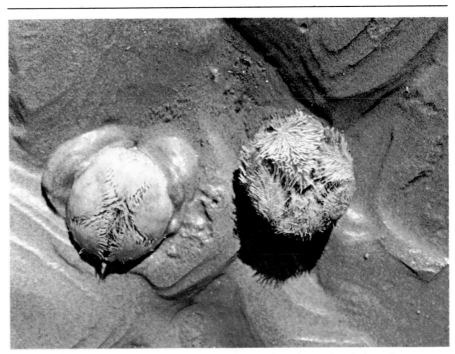

As one heart urchin begins to burrow, another reveals its undersurface and central mouth

Heart urchin *Echinocardium cordatum*

A heart-shaped sea animal about 2 in. long and 1½ in. across, covered with fine, soft, yellow spines. These wear off after the urchin dies, to reveal an off-white shell, known as the sea potato, which is often washed up on the shore.

The heart urchin is common on the lower shore of clean, sandy beaches around Britain. It uses flat spines near its mouth to dig an 8 in. deep burrow. To feed, it extends its long tube-feet from the burrow to search the surface of the sand for dead plant and animal remains. These the heart urchin passes down to its slit-like mouth on the underside of its body.

The animal moves continually under the sand. It digs a fresh tube to the surface every 15-20 minutes, and down this a current of water flows for respiration.

Heathland—where life depends on the heather

Heather, gorse and bracken cover the slopes of Hampton Ridge on the north-

Vast tracts of lowland, bleak in winter, but carpeted with purple heather in late summer and autumn, stretch over the sandy, gravelly areas of southern England. These are heaths, as distinct from moors, which are heather-clad uplands. They were cleared centuries ago of their natural woodland, usually by farmers to create more grazing land. But, apart from areas near the coastline where wind and salt-water spray are hostile to trees and woodland plants, most would have reverted gradually to forest, had they not been grazed by deer, cattle, sheep and goats and been periodically burnt to encourage the growth of new plants which are sweeter and more tender and acceptable to grazing animals. Many heaths in southern Britain are no longer used for grazing, and controlled burning has ceased. But accidental fires still devastate large areas.

The main areas of heath in Britain are found in the Hampshire and London basins, and on the Lower Greensand and Hastings beds of the south-east, the Breckland of East Anglia, the east Suffolk sandlings, the east Devon commons and the Lizard peninsula in Cornwall. Parts of Dartmoor, Exmoor and the Shropshire hills have vegetation midway between that of heath and that of upland.

Heathland soil is poor and acid. Heather, or ling, dominates the scene and, despite its small leaves, casts a deep shade in which soil temperatures remain low. Litter from vegetation accumulates and provides living space for small animals, although after a life of 25-30 years the heather plants die and vegetation becomes more open.

Where heathland is well drained, the most common plants are the red-purple bell heather, gorse, tormentil and common milkwort. On wet heathland the characteristic plants are cross-leaved heath, purple moor-grass, deer sedge, heath rush and bog moss. In very wet conditions and when peat accumulates, some rare species of bog plants may also be found—marsh gentian, marsh clubmoss and brown beak-sedge. These plants, which depend to a considerable extent upon constant moisture and low levels of nutrient, are vulnerable to changes of drainage and to the effects of fertilisers

THE HEATHLAND SOIL

Upper layers of soil dark with dead plant and animal matter

Whitish-grey layer produced by washing out of soluble materials

Pan—compact barrier of washed-down humus and iron compounds

Sandy soil—parent soil material

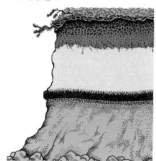

Roots are unable to penetrate the hard-pan layer of the poor, sandy heathland soil. Only heather and other shallow-rooted plants can grow

which are washed in from neighbouring agricultural land.

There are various local heathers. Cornish heather is confined to the Lizard peninsula, where the soils are rich in magnesium. Dorset heather grows in Cornwall and Devon but is more abundant on the Isle of Purbeck in Dorset.

A common heathland plant in certain areas is dwarf gorse. Western dwarf gorse is found mainly to the west of Poole harbour in Dorset; the less robust eastern dwarf gorse is restricted to areas in the south and south-east of England. A flowering parasite called dodder is often attached to the stems of gorse or heather.

Widespread heathland grasses are sheep's fescue, wavy hair-grass and soft grass. Bristle bent, a fine-leaved grass, is more common on drier heaths in the south-west.

A bird widely associated with Britain's heathland is the nightjar, although it is nowhere really common. The other characteristic heathland bird, the Dartford warbler, inhabits only a few areas of heathland in the south. However, kestrels can sometimes be seen above open heathland, and other birds such as Montagu's harrier occasionally nest on dry heaths.

Large colonies of ants are common in the light soil, feeding on heathland plants and insects. All six British reptiles can be found on heathland. The slow-worm and common lizard are widespread; the grass-snake sometimes lives on wet heaths, the adder on dry ones; the smooth snake, Britain's rarest reptile, and the sand lizard are almost entirely restricted to a few heathland areas in the south.

Few small mammals live on heaths. They are usually found on the outskirts, beside tracks or the banks of a stream.

Characteristic heathland butterflies are the grayling, silver-studded blue and the green hairstreak. Moths that may be seen include the emperor and the true lover's knot. Bees include the heath bumble bee and the mining bee. Other animals include dragonflies, spiders and crickets.

Nightjar Arrives from Africa in mid-May to nest on heaths. It feeds on the wing at night, catching moths in its gaping bill

Bracken Britain's commonest fern. The young green fronds, which appear in early spring, turn brown or yellow by late autumn

Marsh gentian Grows on damp heaths where the trumpet-shaped flowers open fully only in sunshine

west borders of the New Forest

Dartford warbler One of Britain's rarest breeding birds. It nests among the spiny branches of a gorse bush

Dorset heath Confined to small areas of Dorset heathland. The large flowers blossom throughout summer

Gorse A hardy bush that flowers in late summer and autumn, turning the heath a rich golden yellow

Silver-studded blue Flutters from gorse flower to flower, frequently settling, with wings half open, to feed

Tormentil A trailing herb that grows well on heathland, producing tiny bright flowers in June

Smooth snake Sometimes mistaken for the adder, this snake is not poisonous

Heather Covers large areas of heath. The flowers are full of nectar and attract many bees

Heath butterfly see Brown butterfly

Heather

An evergreen wild flower. There are seven
species in Britain, and the most common is
true heather, or ling; this grows in all
areas other than a few parts of central
and eastern England. It has pale purple,
bell-shaped flowers, which appear from
July to September, tiny triangular leaves
and a wiry stem, and is anything from
3 in. to 30 in. high. Some white heather is
also found on most moors. Heather's nectar-
filled flowers attract bees, and in August
hives are often taken on to the moors. Its
tender shoots, which spring up profusely
after controlled moor burning, are the main
food of grouse. The plant is still used in
some areas for thatching, and for weaving
into fences. Decayed heather is a constituent of peat.

Two other species commonly grow alongside true heather. Bell heather is found
in the drier parts of heaths and moors. It
has crimson-purple, bell-like flowers, larger
than those of true heather. Cross-leaved
heath grows in the wetter areas, especially
bogs. It has rose-pink flowers and leaves
arranged around the stem in fours, like
crosses.

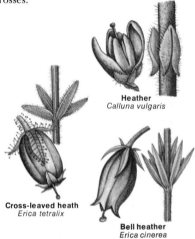

Heather
Calluna vulgaris

Cross-leaved heath
Erica tetralix

Bell heather
Erica cinerea

Bees are attracted to heather's nectar-filled
flowers, while grouse eat its tender shoots

Hectare

A metric unit of square measure, equal to
about 2½ acres. Hectare means literally 100
ares; an are is 100 sq. metres, or 119·6 sq.
yds. As Britain gradually adopts the metric
system, land buyers and users are measuring
land in hectares rather than acres. The
correct abbreviation, singular and plural,
is ha. See also ACRE

Hedge see p. 234

Hedgehog *Erinaceus europaeus*

A grey-brown animal which has yellow-
tipped spines on its back and sides and
coarse hair on its head and underside. The

The hedgehog comes out at night to hunt for food, which includes snails, slugs and worms

tough, ¾ in. long spines lie flat, but are erected
when the animal rolls up into a ball for protection. Because they are angled just above
their roots, they are not driven into the
body if the hedgehog falls from a height.
The spines are not as sharp as the porcu-
pine's, and a human can pick up a hedgehog comfortably. The legs and tail are very
short in relation to the body, the eyes and
ears small. Adult males are about 9 in. long.

The hedgehog lives in fields, open woods
(but not dense ones), hedgerows and gardens
throughout Britain. It lies hidden by day
and comes out at night to hunt for food,
which it finds through its keen senses of
smell and hearing. It is most active at dusk
and dawn. It feeds mainly on insects and
their larvae, snails, slugs, worms and fallen
fruit. It will overturn stones to find sleeping
lizards, take the eggs and young of ground-
nesting birds and occasionally attack mice,
rats, frogs and snakes. It provokes the adder,
to whose poison it is immune, by biting it.
The snake attacks the rolled-up hedgehog
repeatedly until its venom is exhausted.
Then the hedgehog kills the adder.

A traditional story is that hedgehogs suck
milk from the teats of resting cows. In fact,
they have been known to lick up the milk
oozing out of a cow left too long before
milking; and they are sometimes seen on
grazing land where they go to catch the
flies and insects which inhabit dried dung.

Hedgehogs mate between March and July.
One or two litters of between three and
seven young are born in nests of grass or
leaves from May to September. A nest may
be built in a hedge, under a tree root or in a
disused rabbit hole. The young are pale,
blind and covered in soft hair which, after
about 18 days, begins to turn into spines.
The mother suckles the young for a month,
after which they start hunting for food.

Hedgehogs hibernate between October and
early April in nests bigger than those in
which they nurse their young and spend
their summer days. They use leaves and
pieces of moss to keep the rain out and to
maintain an even temperature inside. Their
own temperature at this time sinks from
35°C (95°F) to just over 4°C (40°F). Like
dormice, they occasionally leave the nest—
even in extreme cold—in the hope of finding
food. Hedgehogs are generally flea-ridden.

Their natural enemies are foxes and
badgers. Foxes kill them by manoeuvring
them into water, where they are forced to
uncurl in order to swim; the fox then attacks
the head. Badgers somehow find a gap in
the spines and aim for the unprotected belly.
When a hedgehog hears a car approaching
it curls into a protective ball and remains
motionless—hence the prevalence of hedgehog corpses on roads. If they can survive
these perils, hedgehogs live for up to six
years.

Hedge parsley see Parsley
Hedge sparrow see Dunnock
Heifer see Cattle

Hellebore

There are two British species of hellebore.
Stinking hellebore has yellow-green, bell-
shaped or globular flowers edged with purple, and reaches a height of 30 in. Green

hellebore, up to 24 in. tall, has flat, wide open, yellow-green flowers. Both are confined to England and Wales, where they flower in March and April on lime-rich soils in woods and copses. Plants seen in Scotland and Ireland have spread from private gardens. Both plants are poisonous and there are recorded cases of cattle and children dying through eating them.

White-flowered hellebore, their close relative, is the Christmas rose that is often seen growing in gardens.

Green hellebore
Helleborus viridis

Stinking hellebore
H. foetidus

Both species of hellebore are poisonous, and have caused the deaths of children and cattle

Helm wind

A strong, at times violent, wind which blows, in special airflow conditions, down the slopes of hills or mountains, such as the cold northeast wind which sweeps down the steep western slope of Cross Fell in Cumberland, especially in late winter and early spring.

On reaching the sheltered lowlands, the wind rises like a wave. The air beneath the crest of this wave sometimes has a strong rotary movement, so that, near the ground, it moves against the prevailing wind. The helm wind—named after the helm or cloud cap which forms over the mountain's summit—sometimes causes extensive damage to trees and buildings.

Hemlock *Tsuga heterophylla*

This conifer, now widely planted in Britain as a timber tree, is no relation to the hemlock with which the Greeks are supposed to have poisoned condemned prisoners, including Socrates. The poison is derived from *Conium maculatum,* a tall, white-flowered plant with feathery foliage which grows beside streams.

The hemlock tree, introduced to Britain in 1851, is a native of British Columbia. Early settlers in North America named it because the odour of its crushed foliage resembled the smell of the poison plant they had known in Britain.

Hemlock is recognisable by its irregular evergreen needles, small, flat and blunt, and from the way its topmost shoot always droops, though the tree grows taller.

In spring, hemlock bears small male flowers with yellow pollen, and green female flowers that ripen by autumn to small, bright brown oval cones, holding tiny seeds with

triangular wings. Each seedling has three seed-leaves. Hemlock plantations yield large volumes of strong, pale brown timber, used for building, fencing, joinery and paper pulp. The record height in Britain is 157 ft in Benmore Botanic Gardens, Dunoon. See also PARSLEY

Hemp agrimony *Eupatorium cannabinum*

A wild flower that grows in damp places. Between July and September it bears clusters of red-mauve and white flowers at the top of its hairy stems, which may reach 4 ft in height. In Dorset it is known as 'raspberries and cream'. The downy leaves each consist of three or five leaflets with saw-tooth edges. The plant is common in fens, marshes and damp woods. It often colours the length of a ditch, or festoons a clifftop. It is widespread in Britain except inland Scotland.

Hemp-nettle, Common *Galeopsis tetrahit*

One of Britain's most common and widespread weeds, growing on cultivated ground and occasionally in wet woods and fens. A more suitable name for it would be hemp-dead-nettle, because, while its coarsely toothed, opposite leaves resemble those of hemp, its flowers are like those of the dead-nettle. They are pink, purple or white and appear from July to September. The plant, which can reach a height of 3 ft, is easily recognised by its square stems, covered in stiff, downward-pointing hairs and swollen where the leaves are attached.

Henbane *Hyoscyamus niger*

A highly poisonous wild flower, with an unpleasant smell. The stout stems, up to 3 ft high, have hairy, sticky, light green leaves

and bear yellow and purple flowers from June to August. The whole plant is poisonous and has proved fatal to animals. The leaves and flowers are too bitter to tempt children to eat them, but children have been poisoned by eating the nut-like seeds. Pain-killing drugs are produced from the seeds and leaves.

Henbane is not common, but because it was once extensively grown for medicinal use (it was considered to be a cure for toothache) it crops up all over Britain—by roadsides, around farms and in gardens.

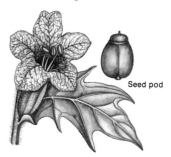

Seed pod

Pain-killing drugs are produced from henbane, which is highly poisonous in the natural state

Henbit *Lamium amplexicaule*

A weed, up to 12 in. high, which often grows alongside red dead-nettle, henbit is identified by its stalkless, opposite leaves which encircle the thin, square stem. Deep purple-pink flowers appear from April to August. Henbit grows on cultivated ground throughout Britain, but is especially prevalent in lowland south and east England. The name is derived from the story that nibbling hens originally produced the wavy leaf margins.

The layout of Stonehenge in relation to the sun suggests that it was used as a calendar

Henge

A ring of standing stones or timbers dating from the early Bronze Age. Encircling the stone or wood monuments is a ditch, then a bank containing one or two entrances. The most famous British examples are Stonehenge, Woodhenge and Avebury, which

are all in Wiltshire. The positioning of the ditch inside the embankment shows that henges were not defensive structures. They were almost certainly places of worship. The layout of the stones in relation to positions of the sun suggests that they were also used as calendars.

The hedge—Britain's biggest nature reserve

The familiar landscape of much of England—a chequered pattern of fields divided by hedges—dates largely from the 18th century. Before the enclosures, clearances and hedge planting of that period, the landscape was one of open tracts of land, some used for agriculture but much left wild as rough grazing or woodland. Hedges were used as dividers because it was cheaper to grow them than to build walls or fences. Moreover, they were self-renewing.

Where cattle had to be enclosed, hawthorn was the bush most usually planted, because of its dense growth and tough,

thorny branches. Other bushes were planted locally: elm in parts of East Anglia, beech on Exmoor. In many areas a mixture of hawthorn, blackthorn and hazel was popular. But, whatever the species planted, others grew in time—often from bird-carried seeds—and a mixed hedge would develop.

There is more to growing a farmland hedge than simply planting it. Hedges are made by bending over the saplings of the growing bush at an angle of 45 degrees. The bent saplings are woven around stakes driven into the ground at intervals of 1-2 yds. The crest is crowned by a tightly woven layer of severed rods, known as hethers, which prevent the growing wood from springing erect. Unwanted twigs and branches are removed.

To prevent it from running wild, a hedge needs this treatment every five to ten years. Because hedge-laying is a skilled, expensive and time-consuming task, many hedges have been neglected. These begin to take up too much land and are consequently rooted out. Other hedges have disappeared

Hartstongue fern The only British fern with undivided fronds. The young fronds are curled

Hawthorn Usually planted to make a hedge. It grows quickly into a thick, thorny barrier

Hedgehog Moves around noisily looking for food, frequently stopping to sniff the air

Wren A cover-loving bird that flies for the shelter of the hedge when alarmed, then 'freezes'

Bluebell The nodding fragrant flowers blossom from April to June. The bottom bells open first

Chaffinch One of the most common birds in Britain. It builds a cup-nest of moss among the hedge branches

Dog rose A prickly bush that clambers among hedges. The red hips form from the tops of the flower stalks

Common violet The delicate flowers of this abundant hedgerow plant appear from April to June

Yellow-necked mouse The largest of the four British mice. It lives mainly in the south

Lesser celandine The glossy stars open in March while other plants are still dormant

because a large arable field is easier to cultivate and harvest than a collection of small ones. However, some studies have shown that hedges can slow wind speeds for up to 100 yds, which decreases soil erosion and increases crop yields; and for this reason some hedges have been spared. Even so, it is estimated that between 1946 and 1970, 4500 miles of hedge were removed each year, leaving a total today of about 600,000 miles. However, the ending in 1972 of a government grant to farmers for removing hedgerows may slow this rate.

When a hedge is lost, a sanctuary for wildlife is lost. A managed hawthorn hedge contains more animal and plant species than a natural hawthorn thicket where little light penetrates. Under a hedge, grasses and herbaceous plants flourish, such as rye-grass and red campion, and climbers, such as brambles and briars, grow up through it; these support many animals, particularly insects.

Hawthorn leaves provide food for many moth caterpillars, chiefly small species such as the winter moth; other species

ANIMAL LIFE IN A HAWTHORN HEDGEROW

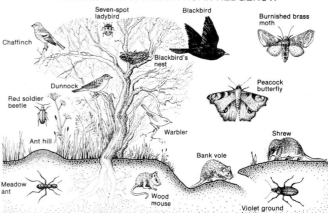

Hedges planted by man to shelter his crops and livestock also give shelter to many animals, each of which exploits a particular niche. For example, the wood mouse tunnels in the soil under the hedge, the peacock butterfly lays eggs on nettles and the blackbird nests among the hawthorn branches

include the brightly coloured vapourer and the well-camouflaged green-brindled crescent. Only one species of butterfly caterpillar feeds on a hedgerow bush; this is the brimstone, which eats buckthorn leaves. However, many butterfly caterpillars feed on the plants beneath hedges: the gatekeeper, wall and other brown butterflies eat grasses, the small tortoiseshell and peacock eat nettles, and the orange-tip and green-veined white eat garlic mustard. Butterflies, bumble bees, hoverflies and other insects fly in the sheltered air beside hedges, whose plants nearly all rely on insects for pollination.

Aphids and other plant-eating insects in hedges provide food for many predators—for example, ladybirds, lacewing larvae and birds. Many seed-eating birds catch insects to supplement the diet of their rapidly growing young. Among birds which weave their nests among the dense, tangled branches or the thick ground vegetation of a hedgerow are long-tailed tits, wrens, hedge sparrows, blackbirds and chaffinches. In winter, hedgerow berries sustain many birds, including two winter migrants, the redwing and fieldfare, which both eat haws, the fruits of hawthorn. Bank voles and wood mice also feed on haws, climbing branches to obtain them; voles usually eat only the flesh, while mice eat only the kernels. Both animals often use old birds' nests as feeding tables, and the wood mice use them as stores for surplus haws.

Many species of field insect hibernate in hedges. Some, such as black bean aphids, spend one stage of their life cycle on crops and another on a hedgerow plant—in the case of black bean aphids, the spindle tree. These insects, and the hedgerow weeds which spread into crop fields, cause some farmers to regard hedgerows as a nuisance—niches of plant and animal pests. However, hedges also contain insect-eaters such as the hedgehog, which moves out, chiefly at night, into the fields to feed on insect pests.

In the early 1960's it was estimated that the acreage of hedgerows in Britain—nearly half a million—was twice that of the country's nature reserves.

Today most woods are small and separated from each other by open fields. Were it not for the hedgerows which connect these woods like highways, those animals which shun the open —such as bank voles—would live in isolated woodland.

Garlic mustard Grows in colonies in the shade of hedges. It smells of garlic when crushed

Orange-tip butterfly Only the male has orange wings. The female lays her eggs on garlic mustard flowers

235

Wild herbs—a source of food, drugs and magic

The most valuable and versatile of the countryside's plants, herbs have been used as food and medicine since ancient times. They continue to provide important drugs and indispensable flavouring in the chef's kitchen

The general meaning of herb is any non-woody flowering plant; more particularly, it means a plant used as food or medicine. Over the centuries, hundreds of British flowering plants have been used in this way; and the names given to them have often described their uses. For example, what we now call sun spurge was once wartwort in the Midlands and whitlow-grass in East Anglia and was used to treat skin diseases.

Early knowledge of the culinary and medicinal value of plants emerged only after much trial and error. Neolithic men must have eaten many lethal dishes of black nightshade before they distinguished it from the similar but wholesome fat hen, which became one of their important foods (it has been used this century as a substitute for spinach). Again, many unpleasant and possibly harmful fumes from burning leaves must have been inhaled before it was found that those from coltsfoot leaves relieved coughs and asthma.

The Romans introduced many herbs to Britain. Like the Greeks, they valued the supposed supernatural powers of the plants, as well as their culinary and medicinal uses. Among their introductions were many that now grow profusely in the wild. They include fennel, whose feathery, aniseed-scented leaves adorn banks near the sea; and alexanders, which in the 17th century was ousted as a vegetable by celery and whose shiny green leaves now run wild alongside those of fennel. Wild fennel has more flavour than the cultivated form, and the boiled young stems of alexanders are as tender as asparagus.

By the Middle Ages the use of herbs for supernatural purposes had reached its height. Every village had its witch, every witch her herbs for potions and every villager his or her herbs, such as garlic, hyssop and wormwood, for combating the witch's powers. The Christian Church also used herbs in rites

and ceremonies. Herbs were so important in daily life that when people moved to a different part of the country they took with them specimens of those they valued most. Superstitions were rife. Houseleek was thought to protect a house from fire, lightning and witches. Yarrow was tied to a cradle to protect the baby from evil spirits. Chicory could open locked boxes. Picking scabious could bring a bedside visit from the Devil.

The medicinal properties of herbs were just as important. Herbal remedies were the stock-in-trade of all physicians until the 18th century, and even today certain drugs are produced from natural sources—for example, the pain-killing morphine from poppies and the heart stimulant digitalis from foxgloves.

The medieval housewife was an expert in the identification and use of wild herbs. From the countryside near her cottage

THE GOOD AND BAD IN HERBS

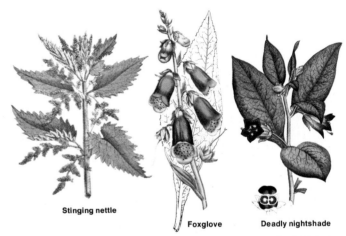

Stinging nettle **Foxglove** **Deadly nightshade**

The nettle stings but has many uses, and the foxglove and deadly nightshade are poisonous but produce two valuable drugs, digitalis and atropine

she would gather lamb's lettuce and salad burnet for salads, jack-by-the-hedge for a sauce with spring mutton, and sweet woodruff for scenting linen. The fern-like leaves and golden flowers of the spicy-scented tansy had many uses—from flavouring omelettes to hopefully procuring abortions. Its relative, feverfew, was pulped and applied externally to relieve pain.

Stinging nettles were especially versatile. Leaves boiled like spinach and served with butter provided an acceptable green vegetable; the remaining liquid was used as a basis for soup or as a long-lasting green dye. The roots, boiled with salt, provided a yellow dye. Fibres from the stalks of old nettles were used for sewing and were spun to make rope, fishing nets, lace and a form of linen. Nettles were also supposed to relieve a variety of illnesses, including pleurisy and sciatica.

The medieval housewife also took herbs into her garden—as did the monks—and gave us many of our modern vegetables. The forerunners of these still grow wild in the countryside. Wild celery thrives in brackish marshes on the English coast; too pungent to nibble raw, it is still suitable for soups. The yellow-flowered wild parsnip, so abundant on waste ground in late summer, was, until the 16th century, boiled, baked and even used to sweeten puddings. Modern palates would prob-

The medical use of herbs, as illustrated by a late 12th-century English manuscript: drugs are being mixed and medicines made up

Fang-like flowers and creamy, tooth-like scales on the roots gave toothwort its name. They also secured it a role as a remedy for toothache among early herbalists, who believed that the colour and shape of a plant were infallible pointers to its medicinal properties

A STRANGE BELIEF

Many herbal remedies once relied more on magic than on medicine. In the 16th century remedies were often prepared according to the doctrine of signatures. This stated that a plant's colour or shape governed its use, and that like must be administered to like. So infusions of yellow-flowered plants, such as broom and agrimony, were prescribed for 'yellow' illnesses, such as jaundice; and lung diseases were treated with concoctions made from lungwort, which has white-spotted leaves that resemble lungs. The walnut, with its skull-like shell and convoluted, brain-like nut, was supposed to be good for head wounds and brain diseases. Toothache gave rise to a wide range of remedies. One required sufferers to hunch over bowls of burning henbane seeds, because of a vague likeness between the seed and a jawbone. Other 'cures' for toothache were prepared from pine cones and toothwort, both of which have parts that resemble teeth. They are shown together, above, in a drawing by the 16th-century Italian Giambattista Porta, a leading advocate of the doctrine of signatures. Porta took his beliefs to such lengths that he maintained that a diet of long-lived plants would prolong life and that eating short-lived plants could be dangerous to health. The doctrine was originally worked out by a 16th-century German doctor, Theophrastus Bombast von Hohenheim, known as Paracelsus, who also believed that a plant's worth depended on the chemicals in it

ably find it bitter and woody compared to the cultivated parsnip; but specimens almost identical to cultivated parsnips have been obtained by no more than ten seasons' selective growing of seeds from the largest-rooted plants.

Not every vegetable has been improved by cultivation. Sea beet—which grows on shingle and from which beetroot, sugar beet and chards derive—still provides a more richly flavoured and smooth-textured spinach than any of its cultivated descendants. Wild horseradish, watercress and chives are as edible as their commercial forms, and wild marjoram, thyme, sweet cicely and mint have flavours subtly different from, but not inferior to, those of cultivated plants.

Housewife and monk also cultivated many herbs we now regard as weeds because they still persist where they were once grown. Ground elder—which, if boiled, makes a spicy vegetable—is a good example. Introduced into Britain in the Middle Ages as a remedy for gout (another of its common names is goutweed), it fell out of favour when gardeners realised how extensively it spread.

Herbs have uses other than culinary and medicinal. A sprig of sweet gale keeps midges away as effectively as any modern repellent. Pungent-smelling bitter herbs, such as mugwort and wormwood, if dried and sprinkled around seedlings, protect them from slugs and birds. Crushed soapwort leaves, boiled with a little water, provide a natural detergent. Deadly nightshade's Latin name, *Belladonna,* means beautiful lady, and refers to its former use as a cosmetic. Though the whole plant is deadly poisonous, women used it to blanch their skins and to dilate the pupils of their eyes. The dilation is caused by the drug atropine.

237

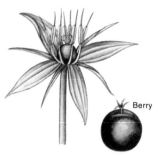

The distinctive pale green flower of herb paris develops into a poisonous purple berry

Berry

Herb paris *Paris quadrifolia*

A perennial plant which grows on lime-rich soils in the shade of damp woods. The smooth stem, 6-18 in. high, bears a single, unpleasant-smelling, pale green flower from May to August, followed by a dark purple berry. The juice of the berry is poisonous to humans and poultry, but under medical supervision is sometimes used to treat inflammation of the eyes. Most of the plant's parts are in four, including the leaves. This symmetry was regarded as magical in the Middle Ages, and the herb was used as a protection against witchcraft. Its name derives from the medieval Latin *herba paris*, meaning herb of a pair, referring to the resemblance of its four leaves to a love-knot, hence its other common name, herb true-love. It is scattered throughout England, Scotland and eastern Wales, but is not found in Ireland.

Herb Robert *Geranium robertianum*

The medieval Latin name of this herb, *Herba Sancti Ruperti*, may refer to Robert, Duke of Normandy, a celebrated medieval scholar. In Britain it is connected with Robin Good-fellow and other 'Robin' names which have links with goblins and evil.

Herb Robert is the most common of our native species of the genus Geranium, growing up to 18 in. tall in a great variety of places, including damp woods, hedgebanks, among rocks and on seashore shingle. It is easily recognised by its much divided leaves, often tinged with red, and by its strong, unpleasant smell. It flowers throughout the summer, the pink blossoms drooping downwards at night or in bad weather.

Herb Robert, which flowers all summer, is identifiable by deeply divided red-tinged leaves

Heron

All herons are long-legged, wading birds which live in wetlands, particularly in fens and marshes. There are two species in the British Isles—the grey heron and the bittern. A distant relative, the spoonbill, is a spring and autumn visitor to east-coast estuaries from Holland.

The grey heron, which is 36 in. long, often stands among the reeds on one leg, with its eyes half closed and its head hunched between its shoulders. Then, suddenly, it will pounce on a fish, eel, mouse or a frog with its pick-axe of a bill. It flies with its head drawn back and its legs trailing, an awkward flight which makes it vulnerable in the air to the attacks of terns and rooks. About 4000 pairs live in the British Isles and they usually build their nests in tall trees in colonies, returning to the same heronry year after year. Others nest on sea cliffs or in reed beds. A dance ceremony precedes courtship, the male stretching its long neck up and then lowering it over its back with the yellow bill pointing upwards. About four eggs are laid between February and May. Incubation lasts 25 days and the young leave the nest after two months. Both parents feed the young.

Bitterns are rare birds. They had ceased to breed in Britain by 1850 owing to the drainage of the marshes and the toll taken by hunters with shotguns, but by the turn of the century they had become re-established in the Norfolk Broads, and have since

Herons usually build nests in tall oak or elm trees in colonies, to which they return each year

spread to most large reed beds in East Anglia. The bird also breeds in several other counties, as far north as a reserve maintained by the Royal Society for the Protection of Birds at Leighton Moss in Lancashire. It is 30 in. long and has brown-streaked buff plumage, green feet and legs, and emits a booming sound which resembles something between a distant foghorn and a lowing cow. The bird stalks among the reeds in a hunch-backed manner, seldom venturing into the open or taking to the air, except in the courtship season. If disturbed on the ground it will 'freeze' with the neck extended and the bill pointing skywards, merging into the surrounding reeds. It eats frogs, small fish, insects and small birds, and nests on untidy piles of sedges in water or water vegetation. About five olive eggs are laid in

A startled bittern 'freezes'. With its neck extended, the brown and yellow streaks of its plumage merge with the vertical lines of the reeds among which it lives

April or May and incubation takes 25 days.

The 34 in. long spoonbill is all white, except for a buff patch at the base of the neck in summer. It may be seen from April to September. Its food includes water plants, small fish and tadpoles.

Hibernation

Animals which are unable to find suitable food during the winter, or cannot stand the cold, either migrate to warmer climates or retire to a safe hiding place to spend the cold months in a deep sleep.

During this hibernation an animal's body temperature falls almost to that of its surroundings, and body functions of respiration, heartbeat and digestion slow down so that minimum energy is used up. This state of complete inactivity is set off by several influences including the fall in temperature, lack of food and length of day.

The hedgehog, dormouse and bats are the only British mammals to spend winter asleep. Before hibernating they put on weight, accumulating fat to be drawn on during the long months of rest. The dormouse may lose nearly half of its weight during hibernation. Frogs, lizards and snakes bury themselves away from the effect of the winter frost, and garden snails huddle together under stones. Butterflies overwinter during their life cycle either as egg, caterpillar, chrysalis or adult.

Hide

A shelter, often camouflaged with foliage, erected to conceal deer-stalkers or wildlife observers. Butts or grouse-shooters' stands screened by low turf or a stone wall are a form of hide. Hides are being constructed by the Forestry Commission in Grizedale, North Lancashire, and elsewhere, for tourists to observe wildlife.

From pre-Norman times, a hide was a measure of land, in theory enough to support one free man and his dependants. The amount varied, according to locality, between 60 and 120 acres. The word 'hide' survives in place names such as Piddletrenthide, Dorset.

Hill fort

About 2500 years ago Celtic Iron Age people began to enclose their settlements with ditches and ramparts, sometimes with the additional protection of a fringe of sharp, upright stones. The custom continued for about 1000 years into the post-Roman era, and the remains of hundreds of such defensive forts are scattered throughout the British Isles. They vary from small, isolated enclosures of less than an acre to the 700 acres of Stanwick in Yorkshire.

Many hill forts contain hut circles, circular depressions or rings of boulders showing where a hut, either of wood or stone, once stood. Traces of fireplaces and cattle enclosures can sometimes be distinguished.

Some of the great forts, such as Maiden Castle in Dorset, were tribal administration centres. Maiden Castle was heavily fortified with four concentric ramparts—probably as a protection against sling shots—and encloses 45 acres. Excavation has shown that it was a permanent settlement with stone and wooden huts linked by surfaced trackways. One of the largest hill forts in Britain, it fell to an assault by the Romans under Vespasian in AD 43.

The Picts of eastern Scotland often interlaced their inner walls of stone rubble with timber. When this was fired by attackers (or by accident) such great heat was generated that the walls fused into a slaggy or glassy mass. Their remains today are known as vitrified forts.

Hill giant

These huge figures, cut out of turf to show the underlying white chalk on the South Downs of England, can be seen for miles. The earliest are thought to be the White Horse of Uffington, Berkshire, and the Giant of Cerne Abbas, Dorset, both cut about 2000 years ago. The Long Man of Wilmington, Sussex, is probably Saxon. All these early hill figures were tribal emblems or primitive gods.

In the 18th and 19th centuries more figures were carved—the Osmington horse in Dorset, showing George III in the saddle, was cut in 1815. The more recent figures are usually commemorative or ornamental.

Hind see Deer

Hirsel

A flock of sheep under the care of one shepherd, or the entire stock of sheep on one farm, is known as a hirsel, particularly in northern England and Scotland. When a hirsel consists of 400-600 lambing ewes, the shepherd usually has an assistant. Hirsel is of Old Norse origin, and is also sometimes applied to a sheep farm or an estate such as Hirsel, at Coldstream on the Scottish border, the home of a former Prime Minister, Sir Alec Douglas-Home.

Hoary-cress *Cardaria draba*

This troublesome weed is believed to have been introduced accidentally into Kent in fodder brought back by the British Army

Seed pod

In May and June hoary-cress forms large, dense, white patches of small flowers

from Walcheren, in the Netherlands, in 1809. Since then it has spread throughout south and east England.

It reproduces not only by seed but also by root buds which develop separate plants when broken from the parents. This accounts for the way it soon covers long stretches of roadside or causes problems for the farmer in arable fields.

In May and June, hoary-cress forms large, low-growing, dense white patches made up of thousands of small flowers. These produce heart-shaped pods, from which it gets the name *Cardaria* from the Greek *cardia*, a heart. It is also known as hoary-pepperwort, as the seeds were once ground as a substitute for pepper.

Hobby see Falcon

Hodge

A corruption of Roger. Hodge was a colloquial name for a rustic years ago. To a townsman, it conjured up the image of a broad-shouldered, sun-burnt yokel in a smock, slow in movement, speech and wits.

Hoe

An implement for breaking up the surface of the soil before sowing seed, for cutting down weeds and thinning crops. The first primitive hoes were probably antlers or branches, used simply for preparing the soil for seed sowing.

In the early 18th century, Jethro Tull adapted the idea of hoeing garden crops to a field scale. He believed, correctly, that stirring the soil would benefit the crop, besides destroying weeds, but hoeing was virtually impossible in broadcast-sown crops. So he invented the seed-drill, enabling seeds to be sown in straight lines. Then he set a number of hoe blades in an iron frame, fitted a few balancing wheels and set a horse to pull it between the rows of plants.

Modern tractor-drawn hoes operate on the same principle and, with refinements, have superseded the horse hoes. A hand hoe is still used between close rows of crops where tractors cannot go.

Hogweed see Parsley

Hollow way

Many of the sunken lanes crossing hill ridges have been trading routes and cattle tracks since the new Stone Age, 4000 years ago. Others may be older still, though a few are very recent. Hollow ways are roads and trackways worn down by constant use to a level well below the point of the surrounding ground.

Studies of a hollow way in the hard limestone at Willersley Hill, Gloucestershire, have indicated a wearing down of 2 in. a century, giving it a probable age of about 6000 years. The sunken tracks of Devon, Hampshire and the Weald of Kent are unlikely to be as old.

Holly seedlings emerge among a litter of dead leaves on a woodland floor

Holly *Ilex aquifolium*

One of Britain's few native evergreen trees, the holly is adapted in curious ways to live as an undershrub in woods throughout the British Isles. Its leaves are thick, with waxy surfaces, to enable them to resist water loss when the soil is frozen in winter. This explains why holly does not wither when it

Holly trees are either male or female, and only the females bear the bright red berries

is hung on walls as a Christmas decoration. Even so, it likes a mild winter climate, and grows best in western districts.

These leaves are pale green below but dark green above, a colour which results from the dim light in the shade of taller trees; but in winter, when broad-leaved trees are leafless, the evergreen holly gets more light and nourishment. The leaves last for up to four years on the tree.

As it is the only broad-leaved tree with foliage available in winter, holly could suffer severe harm from browsing deer. But it is protected by sharp spines on the lower foliage, although higher up, where the deer cannot reach, the leaves are spineless.

Holly trees are either male or female; both bear pretty, white, waxy flowers in May. These have four petals and nectar to attract bees. The female flowers develop into berries containing four seeds, which ripen by October, although in some years no berries appear.

As winter grows harder, birds, especially thrushes, wood pigeons and starlings, strip the trees, swallowing the fruit. The small hard seeds are passed in the birds' droppings, so spreading the tree. The seedling starts life with two soft deciduous seed leaves, which are followed by the normal evergreen foliage.

In cultivation the berries have to be stored for 18 months before seeds will sprout. There are many garden strains with varie-gated foliage, yellow or white berries, and smooth or prickly leaves. These are propagated by grafting on to common holly.

Large trees up to 40 ft tall live for 80 years. Their bark is smooth and grey, and the hard white wood—sometimes used for carving—burns brightly even when freshly felled.

The green foliage is also inflammable. Legends link holly's blood-red berries and spiky leaves with Christ's crucifixion and crown of thorns, which reinforces its use in church decoration. But it is probable that holly was used as a form of decoration in pre-Christian times. Even without religious associations, holly would naturally have been used to brighten people's houses in the leafless and flowerless depths of winter.

Holt see Otter

Honesty *Lunaria annua*

Chiefly valued for its decorative silver 'moons', honesty or moonwort has been grown in cottage gardens for more than 400 years, since being introduced from south-eastern Europe. These moons are the central translucent portions of the large, flat pods which follow the flowers. When the seeds are ripe the pods burst, scattering the seeds. The outer valves of the pod then drop away, leaving the 'moons'—hence the scientific name for the plant from the Latin *luna*, the moon.

Honesty seed often becomes established in hedgerows and waste places. The plant stands 1-3 ft tall and has bright purple (occasionally white) flowers in spring. A widespread superstition formerly credited people who grew honesty in their gardens with being trustworthy.

Honesty's silver 'moons' are portions of the large, flat seed pods which follow the flowers

Honey see Bee
Honeycomb moth see Bee moth

Honeycomb worm *Sabellaria alveolata*

These worms build themselves tubes for homes on rocks on the seashore from fragments of shell and grains of sand cemented together with water. The tubes often become fused into masses like honeycombs, several feet across, with up to 1700 worms to the square yard.

The worms are $1\frac{1}{2}$ in. long, coloured red with a collar of golden hairs round the head, and short, fine tentacles. They catch food particles and sand grains in the tentacles for tube building when the tide is in. Colonies usually survive for three or four years, the record being nine years. The older the worm, the larger the tube opening; a five-year-old worm has an opening $\frac{1}{5}$ in. across. At low tide worms draw in their heads and block the tubes with their bodies.

Battering by waves or severe frosts lead to the destruction of colonies. New colonies frequently arise on the ruins of the old, since the settling planktonic larvae are attracted to the old cement.

Honeydew

Plant sap is rich in sugar, and aphids feed so greedily on it that much is excreted in the form of honeydew. This is the sticky, sweet fluid which covers the leaves of some trees and plants in summer. The Roman naturalist Pliny poetically described it as the sweat of the heavens. For bees and ants honeydew is a great delicacy. Many species of ants collect honeydew from the leaves or direct from the aphids. So great is the passion of ants for honeydew that they will tend flocks of aphids like cattle. Sometimes they will collect and deposit the aphids on leaves, and 'milk' them of their honeydew by stroking them with their antennae, even going so far as to protect them by building shelters of earth over low plants. Sometimes the ant farmers tend the aphids in special chambers in the ant nest itself. Here the aphids live on the roots of plants that penetrate the nest. Most remarkable of all are the yellow ants which tend aphid eggs in the nest all winter until they are ready to hatch out. In the spring the ants carry the young aphids from the nest and deposit them on the leaves of the food plants.

Honey fungus *Armillaria mellea*

Clumps of 20 or more yellow toadstools, between 1 in. and 4 in. across and with brown, hairy scales, may be seen in autumn growing at the base of trees. Honey fungus is a destructive parasite and causes extensive rot to both deciduous and coniferous trees, as well as to garden shrubs. It can cause severe damage to young plantations and orchards. The rot is spread both by spores and by distinctive black strands, or rhizomorphs, which look like long black bootlaces. The fungus is sometimes known as bootlace fungus. The black rhizomorphs can spread under the ground for up to 30 ft to attack a tree. They force their way up beneath the bark and eventually bring about a soft, flaky white rot in the wood. Sometimes, honey fungus grows in conjunction with the orchid Gastrodia, as a result of which the orchid flowers more prolifically. Wood infected by the living spores of the fungus is luminous and can quite clearly be

seen in the dark. Country people once used infected wood to mark paths at night. Honey fungus is edible, the young plants especially being good to eat, although older specimens have a somewhat bitter flavour.

Honey moth see Bee moth

Honeysuckle *Lonicera periclymenum*

Woodbine, or honeysuckle, one of Britain's few woody climbers, has a remarkable way of raising its stem from the soil where the seedling sprouts. It twines spirally clockwise round any woody stem in reach. The firm grip of its wiry main shoot, which may grow up to 20 ft long, constricts the soft outer tissues of the supporting plant, and in plantations foresters have to cut the honeysuckle back before it distorts and ruins young trees.

Its lovely pink-yellow flowers have a strong fragrance. They appear in clusters throughout the summer, but with two particular flowering peaks, in early June and in September. Each flower-cluster is made up of from six to 12 or more separate blossoms. The flowers are one-sided tubes, made up of two lobes of united petals, reflexed, from which protrude the five stamens and the pale green pistil. The famous honeysuckle scent becomes perceptibly stronger towards dusk, which may account for the plant's special attraction for hawkmoths.

The base of each flower holds nectar. There is enough of this to be tasted, as most children know—hence the name 'honey-

The tough, twining stem of honeysuckle will soon deform the trunk of this young beech tree

Honeysuckle scent becomes stronger at dusk, attracting moths which pollinate the flowers

suckle'. Many insects, including the larvae of the white admiral butterfly, feed on the nectar, forcing their way down the tube past the pollen-bearing stamens. Honey bees, however, do not visit the flower, as the tube is too long for their tongues to reach the nectar. In the autumn, the flower-clusters ripen into bunches of red berries, and the insects are joined by birds, which spread the hard seeds. The berries, however, are unpalatable to human beings and should not be eaten.

Hook-tip moth

These thin-bodied, large-winged moths cannot eat or drink and so do not live more than a week or ten days. There are five species in Britain, and they are so named because at the tip of each fore-wing is a hook which helps to increase the resting moth's resemblance to a dead leaf. One species, the scarce hook-tip *Drepana harpagula* is rare and found only near Bristol.

The brown or green caterpillars feed on trees—two species on birch, one on oak, one on beech and the scarce hook-tip on small-leaved lime.

They are oddly shaped and, unlike most other caterpillars, have no claspers or gripping legs. Instead they rest by holding on to a stalk with four of their false legs, keeping their heads and tails raised.

The oak hook-tip *D. binaria* is typical of the group. Its caterpillars are found on oaks in many parts of Britain, although rarely in the north. The pebble hook-tip *D. falcataria*, also typical of the group, is common in areas where there are birch trees. In Ireland, although rare, it is widespread.

Pebble hook-tip moth
Drepana falcataria

Hop *Humulus lupulus*

This strong climbing plant grows in hedge-rows throughout Britain, where it has spread from cultivated fields and gardens.

The hop was growing in Britain long before it was taken into cultivation in the early 16th century for flavouring beer. Originally, it was probably a native of wet woods in southern England.

But hops, with their masses of greenery, are more commonly seen twining their way up 12-14 ft poles or strings in the hop fields of Kent, Hampshire, Worcestershire and Herefordshire. A few hops are also grown commercially in Surrey and east Sussex.

In spring the plant sends up several thin, twining stems which grow rapidly and have a rough surface, as do the leaves. There are male and female plants, and it is the female flowers which develop into the green-yellow cones covered in resinous glands which are used in brewing.

These are collected in the autumn and used by the brewers to clarify beer, help it to keep longer and give it a bitter flavour.

Hop cones ripen in late summer. The scales add flavour to beer and act as a preservative

Horehound *Ballota nigra*

A common flower of roadside verges and waste places throughout England and Wales. It is occasionally found in Scotland and Ireland.

It has an offensive smell, noticed as soon as the leaves are crushed between the fingers. This smell protects the plant from being eaten by cattle, hence its botanical name which comes from the Greek *ballo*, to reject. It can be recognised by its square, purple stems, clusters of dull, purple flowers and wrinkled leaves.

Horehound, White *Marrubium vulgare*

An erect, square-stemmed plant which is densely covered in cottony white hairs. The leaves are round, wrinkled, and soft to the touch; the flowers, which first appear in June, are white and crowded among the leaves. It grows 1-2 ft high.

White horehound occurs wild only on cliff-tops in a few places on the south and west coasts of England and Wales, but may be found elsewhere, having spread from gardens. It used to be grown as a cure for coughs: lozenges containing a preparation from the leaves are still sold.

Pollarded hornbeams in Epping Forest, Essex; the result of lopping which took place until the 1870's

Hornbeam *Carpinus betulus*

This tree is a member of the birch family although it is often mistaken for a beech, having similar smooth grey bark, narrow brown buds and oval leaves. A closer look shows that the trunk is always irregular, with wayward projections called 'flutes' that carry narrow bands of bright metallic sheen. The leaves carry bolder veins and are definitely toothed.

The catkin pattern differs, too, for hornbeam bears, each April, long hanging male catkins, like strings of pale yellow beads. The female catkins, at first erect like green buds, hang downwards later, in showy bunches.

Each separate fruit has a large, pale green,

Single fruit

Hornbeam catkins appear amongst the leaves in April or May, growing up to 5 in. long

papery bract, with three blunt points—a distinctive feature. This serves to carry away the single, small, green, nut-like seed on the wind. Seeds must lie on damp soil for 18 months before they will germinate.

Hornbeam grows wild only in southern England. It was once widely planted in Kent and the Thames Valley to yield firewood. Sometimes it was grown as coppice and sometimes as a pollard tree. Epping Forest still has many pollards, which were once lopped by commoners for fuel.

Hornbeam is a Saxon word meaning 'horny wooded tree'. It is exceptionally hard and was used traditionally for ox yokes, mallets, and gears in wooden windmill or watermill machinery. Today it is used for butchers' chopping blocks, the moving parts of a piano or for chessmen.

It can grow to 80 ft tall and live for more than 100 years. In gardens it is often grown as hedges, as it stands close clipping and holds faded pale-brown leaves all through the winter, providing attractive shelter. The hawfinch is particularly associated with hornbeam, as it lives in hornbeam woods in northern Europe, but relatively few insects feed on it. See also COPPICE, POLLARD

Horned poppy, Yellow *Glaucium flavum*

This is one of the most beautiful of British seashore plants. It grows on shingle banks all round the coast, although it is rare in the north and declining elsewhere. The large, yellow, poppy-like flower has four petals which last for only a day before falling. They may be seen from June to late September. However, as the flowers appear in turn, the lowest are seen first, and have formed into ripening fruits by the time the uppermost flowers have blossomed.

The fruits are in the form of long narrow curved pods – the 'horns'. These are unlike the short, round capsules of most members of the poppy family. The 6-12 in. pods are the longest of any British plant. It is easily recognised, even in winter, by the much divided, grey-green leaves.

Flowers of yellow horned poppy grow to 3 in. across, and appear amongst coastal shingle

Hornet *Vespa crabro*

The hornet is the largest British wasp – even the smallest workers are bigger than the queens of most other species, and hornet queens are more than 1 in. long. Apart from their size, they can be identified by their brown and orange markings instead of the black and yellow of other wasps. In the British Isles they are rare, living mainly in well-wooded areas of southern England. Like the common wasp, hornets build paper

The hornets' nest is built of paper combs, formed from chewed wood or plant fibres

nests in hollow trees, holes in banks or in outhouses. They make the paper by chewing hard wood to a paste and mixing it with sand or soil. The adults feed on nectar and juices from rotting fruit; the larvae are fed on flies and insect larvae. As a result of their size, hornets make a louder hum than other wasps. But, in spite of their reputation, they are relatively docile and will rarely sting. See also WASP

Hornet moth see Clearwing moth
Horse see p. 244

Horse chestnut

A wealth of lore – some true, some false – surrounds this handsome tree with its unmistakable fan-shaped, palmate, compound leaf, made up of five to seven spreading leaflets on a sturdy stalk. It won its name when Europeans found the Turks feeding its nuts – the familiar conkers – to sick horses in Constantinople in the 16th century, although normally animals do not touch them.

However, hungry horses do gnaw the tree's bark and an extract from it is used in veterinary medicine. The horseshoe-nail scars left on the twigs after the leaves have fallen are traces of main veins, one for each leaflet.

The large brown buds on stout twigs are always set in pairs – except for the terminal ones. They are covered in a sticky resin which checks invading insects. The twigs can be gathered in spring and put in water indoors; the leaves then gradually unfold. The underside of new leaves is covered with down, which soon goes. Its purpose is to check water loss.

The horse chestnut is widely planted as a park tree, and gives brilliant displays of candles of white blossom in May. Each separate flower has an irregular shape which ensures that a bee seeking nectar must brush past the stamens, the male organs of the flower, picking up pollen and transmitting it to the pistil, the female organ, where it fertilises the seeds.

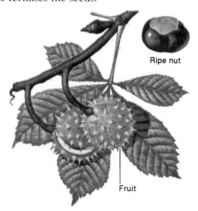

Ripe nut

Fruit

The fruit of the horse chestnut ripens in early autumn to yield the familiar conker

The patches of colour on horse chestnut flowers turn from yellow to red with age

Large brown nuts, each with a round grey patch, ripen by October within spiky green husks. Children thread them on strings and batter one against another in the game of conkers – originally conquerors. Nuts that fall on damp soil sprout readily in the following spring.

The horse chestnut's soft, white timber has no commercial use, except in wood carving. The common species is *Aesculus hippocastanum* which can grow to 125 ft tall and lives for up to 120 years.

Red horse chestnut, a less vigorous kind which is propagated by grafting, is the variety *A. × carnea*. It arose as a hybrid with the American species *A. pavia*.

Horse-power—for 200 years, until the advent of the tractor, plough horses worked the land, and even today some farmers still use them

Horse

Mechanisation reduced the number of horses on British farms from more than a million in 1918 to 54,000 in 1960, after which the Government ceased to include horses in the agricultural census.

But a decade later the decline in the number of horses had been arrested on the grounds of usefulness and cost. There was also an increase in the number of horses used by brewers to pull drays. At 1971 prices a London brewer found that a lorry cost twice as much to run as two shire horses. The number of horses being used for riding is also increasing, and there are nearly 10,000 thoroughbred racehorses in training

in Britain, in addition to a large breeding stock. There are about 18,000 thoroughbreds in Ireland.

The preference for farm horses still continues in some areas and is particularly noticeable in the fens, where farmers use them to cart away sugar beet from wet fields in which tractors get bogged. Other farmers in areas of heavy soil prefer them to tractors, which can damage the texture of the soil. Foresters still find horses invaluable for pulling tree trunks from places inaccessible to vehicles.

This renewed interest in the horse has caused a revival of ploughing contests, usually held in the autumn, and member-

ship of heavy horse (carthorse and drayhorse) societies, and an increase in the prices paid at horse sales.

Horses are native to Britain, and Stone Age men 4000 years ago hunted them for their meat and probably their milk. Many breeds have been introduced from abroad over the centuries, starting with those of the Roman cavalry, in whose warhorses were mingled the blood of breeds from the lands of their previous conquests. The British horses were admired by Julius Caesar, who can be said to have started Britain's flourishing export trade in bloodstock. The introduction of the stirrup to western Europe in the 10th century made it possible for heavy cavalry to deliver a devastating charge and stay on their mounts at the end of it. In the Middle Ages stallions were brought from the Continent to breed the substantial horses necessary to carry knights in full armour into battle. Arab horses were brought back by returning Crusaders.

For most of their history horses have not been farm animals. They were first hunted for food; later they were domesticated and ridden to war. They also pulled chariots, then carts, and were beasts of burden before farmers started using them for ploughing

HORSE BRASSES—CHARMS AGAINST EVIL

Favourite designs for horse brasses are representations of the sun, the moon and the stars. Others include crops, such as a wheatsheaf, and a bell to make a noise to frighten away evil spirits. The brass on the extreme right is a fly terret, worn on head harness in place of plumes

and harrowing. It was not until the early 18th century that horses replaced the oxen for farming purposes.

Whatever its role, the horse was valuable and had to be carefully looked after. This meant not only feeding and housing it, but protecting it from sickness and evil. To do this, charms were fixed to the harness. The

COLLAR HARNESS OF A DRAUGHT HORSE

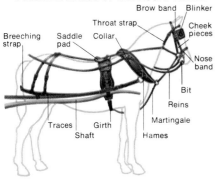

MODERN SADDLE AND DOUBLE BRIDLE

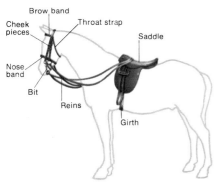

Harness and saddlery of a driven and ridden horse. The collar, made to measure to fit the animal's neck, carries only one pair of reins, while the riding bridle has two pairs

Dawn exercise on Newmarket Heath—the head-quarters of British racing

brasses, which are still used to decorate harness, are the modern descendants of these primitive charms.

There are about 60 breeds of horse, but the four main ones seen on British farms are Shire, Clydesdale, Percheron and Suffolk, some of which are descendants of medieval warhorses. Another fairly common breed is the Cleveland Bay, a light-heavyweight.

Cobs and hacks are not breeds: both terms refer to a good riding horse, up to a height of 15·3 hands. A horse's height is measured in hands and inches—a hand being equal to 4 in. A horse described as 14·2 hands is 14 hands and 2 in. high. The height is measured from the withers, just behind the shoulders, to the ground.

Horses often live 20 years or more, and ages of 30 to 40 are not uncommon. One is known to have died at 62. The young, which are produced about 11 months after mating, are called foals for their first year. Females are fillies until they produce young, when they become mares. Males are colts until they are four when they become stallions, except those which are castrated when a year old to make them easier to manage for work purposes. These are called geldings.

Horses of the British Isles

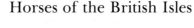

Arab
Small horse, but with great staying power. Head tapers to very small muzzle. Neck arched; strong, level back, and broad, deep chest. Stands 14·2 to 15 hands

Thoroughbred
Built for speed with deep body and generous quarters. All thoroughbreds trace their ancestry to three Arab stallions imported into England in the 18th century

Hunter
Varies according to type of country hunted over. Show hunters are grouped into three classes, based on the weight they are expected to carry

Percheron
Deep, compact body, powerful quarters and short legs with no feathers, or long, fluffed-out hairs. Originated in northern France. Stands from 16 hands

Cleveland Bay
Large head on slender neck, powerful limbs and quarters, short legs. White star on forehead. Used for producing heavy hunters. Stands 15 to 16 hands

Shire
Strong but not speedy, legs feathered. Usually has white blaze and white feet. Descendant of 'Great Horse of England'. Stands 16·3 to 17·3 hands

Irish draught
Type rather than a breed. A strong workhorse; mares are crossed with thoroughbred stallions to produce sturdy hunters. Stands 15·3 to 16 hands

Suffolk
Broad, deep body with short, unfeathered legs and short mane. Colour: always chestnut. The heavy horse of East Anglia. Stands about 16 hands

Clydesdale
Rather short in the back with powerful quarters and strong legs; feet well feathered. Usually has white blaze; hind legs often white. Stands from 16 hands

Horse-fly

The female horse-fly lives by biting and sucking the blood of animals, mostly horses and cattle, but it often bites humans. The bite can be painful and sometimes causes a swelling which lasts for several days. The male horse-fly is harmless, feeding on nectar.

Horse-flies lay their eggs on the leaves and stems of water plants and bog plants. The larvae live in wet soil and feed by slicing a hole in the side of their prey, usually earthworms, and sucking out the body contents. The larvae hibernate in the soil and pupate in late spring or early summer. About ten days later the adult emerges.

Most of the 28 species of British horse-flies are dull brown, but many have beautiful, iridescent eyes. They belong to the genus Tabanus and all grow up to 1 in. long, except *T. sudeticus,* the largest British species, which has a body length of 1¼ in. It is mainly confined to the New Forest where it is called a stout.

Four of the species are more brightly marked, with black and yellow bands on the abdomen. These are the Chrysops flies, sometimes called deer flies.

HOW A HORSE-FLY BITES

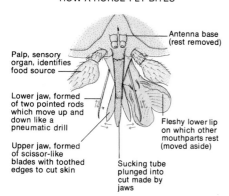

Antenna base (rest removed)

Palp, sensory organ, identifies food source

Lower jaw, formed of two pointed rods which move up and down like a pneumatic drill

Upper jaw, formed of scissor-like blades with toothed edges to cut skin

Fleshy lower lip on which other mouthparts rest (moved aside)

Sucking tube plunged into cut made by jaws

The female horse-fly bites and sucks blood from horses and cattle. She cuts through her victim's skin with scissor-like jaws, probes the wound open, then inserts a sucking tube to draw off blood. The male feeds on flower nectar

Horse-radish *Armoracia rusticana*

First introduced into this country from the Middle East in the 15th century as an alternative to mustard, horse-radish is now inseparable from roast beef. It has spread from gardens to hedges, roadside verges, and river banks and is well established in lowland England and Wales, though it is rare in Ireland. However, its small, four-petalled white flowers, produced in summer, rarely set seed in our climate, and its spread is almost entirely by the roots or underground stems. It is the roots that are used for making horse-radish sauce.

The plant can be identified by its leaves alone. The lower leaves are often deeply divided like the teeth of a comb, whilst the upper ones are small and undivided.

Seed pod

Horseshoe vetch is named after its curved seed pods, which follow the pea-like yellow flowers

Horseshoe vetch *Hippocrepis comosa*

The bright yellow flowers of horseshoe vetch are one of the great delights of England's dry chalk and limestone grassland. It also grows in a few places in Wales. Growing 3-15 in. tall, horseshoe vetch blooms in early summer. The characteristic from which it takes its name can only be seen later in the summer when it develops long, jointed seed pods, each joint shaped like a horseshoe. *Hippocrepis* is derived from the Greek for horseshoe.

Hottentot fig *Carpobrotus edulis*

This native of South Africa thrives in the frost-free area along the coasts of Devon and Cornwall and in the Channel Isles. Its fleshy leaves form great mats which lie in festoons over the cliffs and rocks. The handsome magenta or yellow flowers are about 2 in. across and appear between May and July. The fruits of this succulent are edible and have a pleasant acid flavour when ripe.

Carpobrotus is from the Greek, meaning edible fruit. It was previously called mesembryanthemum, a name which became converted in everyday Cornish speech to Sally-my-handsome.

Hound see Dog

Horsetail

The horsetails belong to a very primitive and once abundant group of plants. But they were gradually displaced and there are now only 23 species left in the world, and 11 of them occur in Britain. Horsetail stems are hollow and distinctly jointed. At each joint a whorl of branches arises so that the whole plant resembles a miniature Christmas tree. Five of the British species are widespread. The common horsetail *Equisetum arvense* occurs everywhere and can be a troublesome weed. Great horsetail, which reaches 6 ft in height, is found in shady woods and damp hedgebanks. It is very rare in Scotland. Wood horsetail also occurs in woods but is very rare in the south. Marsh horsetail and water horsetail are found growing throughout the British Isles, but usually in wetter places.

Water horsetail, survivor of a group of plants that flourished 200 million years ago

Hound's tongue *Cynoglossum officinale*

This may be recognised by its dirty purple flowers and soft, hairy grey leaves which are said to resemble the shape and colour of a hound's tongue. When the leaves are crushed another mammal comes to mind: they give off a strong smell of mice.

Each flower produces four nutlets which are about ¼ in. across and covered with short barbed spines. It used to be thought that hound's tongue could cure many ills, including dog bites, baldness and stuttering. It occurs throughout the lowlands of Britain and eastern Ireland, usually in bare places on dry soils such as sand dunes or lime quarries.

Housefly *Musca domestica*

This fly is known to spread diseases such as dysentery and typhoid. Adult flies feed on excrement, decaying vegetable matter and dead animals, as well as on exposed human food; they can often be seen rubbing their legs together to remove particles clinging to them. Contamination of food results not only from bacteria on the fly's feet, but also because houseflies regurgitate part of a previous meal while feeding.

The white eggs, about 1/25 in. long, are laid in masses on the materials that the adults feed on. Hatching can take place within eight hours in warm conditions and the larva or maggot may be fully grown in two days. Its skin then turns brown and hard while inside the delicate pupa is formed. The adult fly emerges in a few days. The housefly's life cycle can be completed in nine days in warm weather. During winter, both adults and pupae hibernate, generally in crannies in buildings.

House martin see Swallow

Hoverfly

The most common hoverflies, seen in gardens and fields, are the black and yellow flies which make up the genus Syrphus. They look remarkably like wasps but have only two wings, no 'wasp waist' and do not sting. They hover, apparently motionless, for several minutes. Their wasp-like appearance is an example of protective coloration — in this case known as mimicry; it prevents them from being devoured by birds which avoid eating wasps.

Some hoverflies, notably *Volucella bombylans,* resemble bumble bees. The advantage to the fly seems to be that its appearance deceives bees not birds, since it lays its eggs in bumble-bee nests. The fly's camouflage probably helps it to enter the bee's nest without being killed. It is common in open woodlands.

The larvae of other hoverflies live in a variety of situations. The Syrphus larvae creep around on leaves and suck aphids dry. The dronefly *Eristalis tenax,* which resembles a honey bee, has a larva that thrives in stagnant water. About 1 in. long,

it has a 6 in. telescopic tail which reaches the surface of the water like a snorkel to draw in air — hence its name, rat-tailed maggot. It moves to drier earth to pupate.

Swarms of this hoverfly *Syrphus balteatus* can be seen in the Thames Estuary in summer

Hummingbird hawkmoth

Macroglossum stellatarum

Many people who have watched this insect hovering in front of a flower as it feeds on nectar, mistakenly believe that they have seen a hummingbird in Britain. The moth unrolls a long tongue which it uses, as a hummingbird uses its beak, to suck nectar from flowers.

Hummingbird hawkmoths, which are about 1½ in. long and brown and orange in colour, migrate from southern Europe, often flying as far as 100 miles a day, and arriving from June onwards. Some arrive every year in the south of England, but rarely survive the winter. In good years they spread throughout the British Isles and sometimes they breed here, in which case the caterpillars feed on bedstraw. The

Hovering above a flower, a hummingbird hawkmoth sucks in nectar through its long tongue

new generation of moths either migrates back to Europe or dies in the winter. Eggs are laid on lady's bedstraw and similar plants in July and August. Hummingbird hawkmoths frequent parks and gardens well-stocked with flowers. In some years they are plentiful; in others rare.

There are two other day-flying British hawkmoths, neither of which is common. These are the broad-bordered bee hawk *Hemaris fuciformis*, whose caterpillars feed on honeysuckle, and the narrow-bordered bee hawk *H. tityus*, whose caterpillars feed on devil's-bit scabious. Both of these moths resemble bumble bees. See also HAWKMOTH

Humus

The end product of a long decomposition process, humus is the final form of soil organic matter. A gardener often assumes that the final material in his compost heap is humus, but this is not strictly true, for the organic matter, made up from plant and animal debris, can still break down further.

In appearance, humus is a black material composed of tiny remains of dead plants and soil organisms that have completely lost their structure. It is all-important in maintaining soil structure, as a nutrient reservoir for plants and soil organisms, and in enabling soil to hold moisture.

Hundred

A sub-division of a shire, dating from Anglo-Saxon times and continuing sporadically to the 19th century. A hundred indicated a land area of 100 hides, a hide being about 120 acres, the amount of land needed to support a free family and dependants. Originally, each hundred had its own court. In the Midlands the Danish unit of wapentake was used instead of hundred, and in the north the division was called a ward. A dip in a tilled field at Bingham, Nottinghamshire, on the Foss Way, still shows the rectangular form of the wapentake court site there. Each month the freemen assembled in the open air to deal with crime, lawsuits and taxes.

Hurdle

Standard hurdles, which are 6 or 7 ft long by 3 ft 6 in. high, are used to make temporary fences, particularly for penning sheep. There are two types: wattle hurdles and gate hurdles.

Wattle hurdles are made of woven hazel rods. They were once turned out in great numbers by woodland craftsmen, but demand has slackened with the introduction of meshed wire fences.

Gate hurdles resemble a six-barred gate. Made of split wood, usually ash, they are lighter than wattle hurdles but do not provide a wind-break. Gate-hurdle making survives chiefly in the Weald of Kent and Sussex. Wattle hurdles are made on the chalk downs of the south where hazel is abundant. Hurdles are fastened to stakes called 'shores'.

Hut circle

A shallow depression in the ground, or a wall or ring of boulders 20-25 ft in diameter and about 5 ft high, are the remains of a circular hut. Hut circles belong to any period from the New Stone Age to the Middle Ages but most are of the Iron Age, about 500 BC-AD 100. They are very common in stony districts throughout the British Isles and range from isolated circles to settlements, such as on Dartmoor and at Chysauster, Cornwall. The stone walls are all that is left of tent-like dwellings which probably had a cone-shaped roof of thatch or turf supported on wooden branches and forked uprights. The depressions mark the sites of grain storage huts. See also HILL FORT

Hydra

Tiny freshwater creatures related to sea anemones and jellyfish, hydras often emerge from duckweed, pondweeds or dead leaves collected from a stream bed or pond. When left undisturbed in a jar each tiny blob attached to the weed expands into a slender, tubular body with a crown of 5-13 tentacles. The tentacles are armed with batteries of stinging cells which paralyse prey. When a water flea or other small animal swims against them each stinging cell discharges a thread which traps and paralyses the flea. The tentacles then push the victim into the hydra's mouth, at the top of its body.

When food is abundant hydras may reproduce simply by budding off new individuals. At other times white swellings, testes and ovaries, develop on the body for the purpose of sexual reproduction.

There are five species of hydras. All are brown excepting the $\frac{1}{4}$-$\frac{3}{4}$ in. green hydra *Chlorohydra viridissima* which has green algae living inside its body.

STRUCTURE OF THE GREEN HYDRA

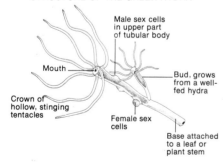

Male sex cells in upper part of tubular body

Mouth

Bud, grows from a well-fed hydra

Crown of hollow, stinging tentacles

Female sex cells

Base attached to a leaf or plant stem

In autumn the hydra may produce sex cells, either male or female or both. These reproductive cells are shed into the water, where fertilisation takes place. At other times, when there is plenty of food, little hydras will bud off from the main body

Hydro-electricity

The technique of harnessing water power for the generation of electricity is mostly confined to the hilly parts of Ireland and the Scottish Highlands, areas which have heavy rainfall and natural reservoirs of long narrow lakes in deep valleys. In 1971 the output of north Scotland's hydro installations was 3000 million units—enough electricity for the power needs of several towns. The total capacity was nearly 1½ million kilowatts, from 54 main power stations.

Hydro-electricity development on any scale is comparatively recent, water-power resources being relatively small and in remote areas. The North of Scotland Hydro-Electric Board was established in 1943 as a public corporation to develop the water-power resources of the Highlands.

At the Tummel Valley hydro-electric scheme, north-west of Pitlochry, nine generating stations are powered by the water of ten lochs, which have dams as their dominant landscape features. Water from behind the dams is led through tunnels and along aqueducts to the power stations. These house turbines which drive generators and produce electric current. At off-peak times the power generated is used to pump water back uphill to the catchment areas or reservoirs. In this way a constant head of water to feed the turbines is maintained. At Pitlochry, and other stations, observation chambers have been built so that salmon can be seen ascending the specially constructed steps back to their breeding grounds in the upper waters. There are 35 pools in the 900 ft long fish-pass at Pitlochry with a rise of 18 in. between each step.

At Loch Awe, Argyll, a massive dam, 1037 ft long and 153 ft high, spans a corrie 1200 ft up on Ben Cruachan, to create a water supply for a power station in the heart of the mountain. At night and at weekends, off-peak electricity from steam generating stations pumps water up to the reservoir. Because the surface area of Loch Awe is 15 sq. miles, the operation at Cruachan has little effect on the water level. The power of the pumping installations is such that if all machines were operated continuously for 24 hours to fill the upper reservoir— something which does not happen in practice—the level of Loch Awe would be lowered by only 9 in. The deepest part of the loch is 307 ft. See also DAM

A reservoir on Ben Cruachan, Argyll, supplies water by day to power the hydro-electric station 1200 ft below. At night, off-peak electricity is used to pump water up to the reservoir

HELPING FISH OVER A DAM

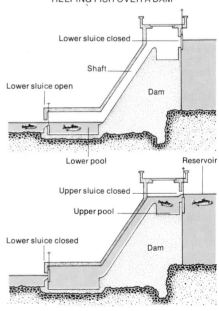

Lower sluice closed

Shaft

Lower sluice open

Dam

Lower pool

Reservoir

Upper sluice closed

Upper pool

Lower sluice closed

Dam

The Borland fish lift enables fish to surmount dams. The fish are attracted by a flow of water to enter a pool at the foot of a sloping shaft. The pool is closed but water continues to pour in so that the fish rise with it to the upper pool and the reservoir

I

Ice

The basic pattern of the landscape owes much to the Ice Age. About a million years ago great sheets of ice spread southwards from the mountains of Scandinavia and covered the British Isles as far south as the Severn and the Thames, disappearing about 10,000 years ago.

The ice lifted great rocks from Norway and carried them to England; it cut great ridges in mountains; formed deep, U-shaped valleys; and diverted the flow of rivers. The Severn, for instance, flowed into the Irish Sea until movements of ice forced it to run into the Bristol Channel. Parts of East Anglia would lie below sea level if it were not for the 50-100 ft layer of boulder clay and gravel deposited there during the Ice Age. Most natural lakes were scooped out by ice, and in some cases these descend below sea-level. The deepest (1017 ft) is Loch Morar, in Inverness-shire.

Lakes were also formed by ice blocking estuaries and causing rivers to spread inland – Lake Humber is an example.

In northern England and Scotland deposits of rock left by the ice gave irregular features to the valleys, and in more level areas blocks of ice melted away to leave small hollows which became lakes or 'kettle-holes'. The cause of the Ice Age is not certain, but one popular theory is that atmospheric conditions reduced the amount of heat received from the sun.

Water solidifies into ice at temperatures below 0°C (32°F) and, as it does so, expands (it is the only substance to react to cold in this way). Any ice which forms in cracks and fissures in rocks helps to widen and deepen those cracks. So, over aeons of time, ice has played a major part in the formation of the earth's soil by helping to break down rocks.

It is possible to skate on ice because pressure melts ice under the skates to a lubricant film of water. See also CORRIE, CWM

Ice house

Outdoor cold stores became popular with rich families in the 18th and 19th centuries, and disused ones can sometimes be seen in the grounds of country mansions.

Although they vary a lot in shape, many have a conical roof of brick and a doorway leading down to a small round room. Often the roof would be covered with a mound of earth to keep the inside cool.

Ice was laid on the floor between layers of straw. It would keep for up to two years if pounded and mixed with salt.

The idea was probably brought to Britain by travellers who had seen similar arrangements in Italy, where peasants stored food in caves with ice gathered from mountains.

Igneous rock

The word igneous comes from the Latin *ignis*, meaning fire, and signifies that such rock has been formed from molten substances forced towards the surface from the earth's core. In some places the molten material reached the surface and exploded into volcanic activity or flowed out as lava; but most cooled and solidified in the earth. The heat required for melting was almost certainly generated by radio-activity.

Rock such as basalt, which cooled at or near the surface, formed exceedingly small crystals because it cooled quickly. When rock cooled at a greater depth, larger crystals formed which can be seen with the naked eye. An example is dolerite. Very slow cooling at great depths allowed crystals up to 1 in. to form, as in granite. Sometimes, after large crystals (called phenocrysts) were made, the rock moved to a place where it cooled more quickly, and phenocrysts were then found in a background of smaller crystals. An example is syenite.

While many fine-grained igneous rocks, such as basalt, are rather dark in colour, the coarser-grained granites and related rocks can be brightly coloured – black and white or red and white are common combinations.

Igneous rocks are limited in Britain to the uplands of south-west and northern England, Wales and Scotland, but some isolated examples are found elsewhere. The most striking example is Charnwood Forest, near Leicester, where a series of small hills is formed of a number of igneous rocks.

HOW ICE AGE GLACIERS CARVED THE LANDSCAPE

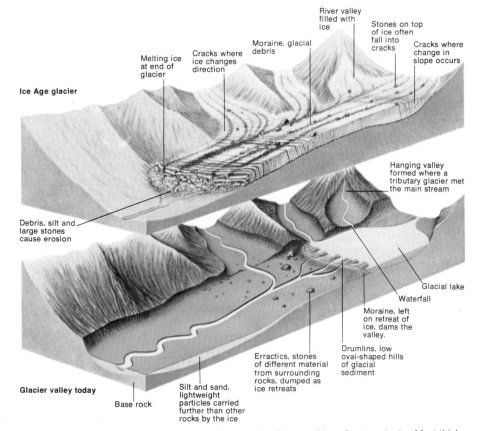

About a million years ago glaciers, massive rivers made of layers of ice often hundreds of feet thick, carved steep, U-shaped valleys out of the land. As the ice melted and the glaciers retreated they left lakes behind them, such as those in the Lake District, Wales, Scotland and Ireland

In-by

In northern England and Scotland this word is still used for the small enclosed fields near a farmhouse. 'By' is derived from the Scandinavian word for a settlement. The in-by were formerly the fields which received all the manure from the farms livestock, making them suitable for constant cultivation. In contrast, other fields known as the 'out-by' were brought into cultivation only occasionally.

Indian summer

In autumn there is often a short spell of extremely fine weather which is popularly termed 'Indian summer'. The description was introduced in the 19th century from North America, since during spells of fine autumn weather Indians used to store crops and prepare for the winter. Indian summers are usually caused in Britain by a temporary dominance of the North Atlantic anticyclone spreading to the north-east. Such conditions often occur during October and the first part of November. A warm spell on or about October 18 — St Luke's Day — is known as St Luke's Summer.

Industrial melanism see Evolution

Ink cap

In Britain there are about 60 species of ink caps—a group of fungi which make up the genus Coprinus. They have conical or bell-shaped caps, and most are edible when young, although they break down to a black, inky fluid when ripe. The fluid contains spores, which spread over the ground as the cap liquefies. At one time, the fluids from common ink cap and shaggy cap were used as cheap substitutes for Indian ink.

Common ink cap *Coprinus atramentarius* is bell-shaped, brown-grey and about 2 in. long. It is usually found along woodland paths, ditches or at the base of deciduous trees. Although edible when young, it will cause severe nausea if eaten with alcohol.

Shaggy cap *C. comatus* is another conspicuous species, often found on grassy roadsides or in fields. It has a hollow stem which grows 5-6 in. high. The fruit is torpedo-shaped, 2-4 in. high and white with shaggy, white scales. This appearance gives the fungus its other name of lawyer's wig. It is tasty when young, but should be eaten on the day it is collected.

Other species in the group include glistening ink cap *C. micaceus* and magpie ink cap *C. picaceus*. Glistening ink cap grows in tight clusters on tree stumps. The caps, about 2 in. high, are bell-shaped and yellowish-brown. When young, the fungus is covered with mica-like particles. Magpie ink cap has a brownish-black cap with white patches resembling the colouring of the magpie. It is found in deciduous woods during the autumn.

Insect see p. 252

Trapped in the sticky embrace of the sundew, this stone fly is doomed

Insect-eating plants

Three kinds of insect-eating plants grow in the British Isles—bladderworts, butterworts and sundews. They obtain part of their nitrogen—essential to all plant growth—by capturing, digesting and absorbing insects. This enables them to grow in places where they would otherwise be unable to acquire the essential nitrogen.

The bladderwort, which grows in water, has no roots; all the foods for growth are absorbed through its finely divided leaves. On these leaves are pear-shaped bladders with a 'door at the narrow end. When an insect touches a bladder the door opens under the pressure. The in-rushing water carries the insect inside and the door shuts behind it.

The land-living butterwort and sundew ensnare insects in sticky secretions. A small insect alighting on the tacky butterwort leaf is caught and later washed by rain to the edge of the leaf. This then curls over and covers the insect, which is slowly digested.

The long glandular hairs on the upper surfaces of sundew leaves are like pins in a pincushion. The tip of each hair secretes a drop of sticky fluid which attracts insects. As soon as one settles, the longer marginal hairs bend over and imprison it. The hairs produce a digestive fluid and the insects body is broken down for absorption. See also BLADDERWORT, BUTTERWORT and SUNDEW

Insecticide see Farming and Pollution

Iris

Two species of wild iris are native to Britain, and each flowers from May until late July. The most common is the yellow iris or flag, which flourishes in wet woods, damp meadows, and at the side of ponds. It grows up to 2 ft high and has sharp-edged, grey-green leaves with raised midribs. The stout, much-branched stems bear two or three bright yellow flowers which appear one at a time. They develop flat, oblong, pale brown seeds.

Stinking iris or gladdon is found only in southern England and on the Welsh coast. It grows in woods and scrub and on clifftops. The purple-violet, darkly veined flowers are short-lived and develop into bright green, oblong fruits, which split open to reveal bright red, round, fleshy seeds. The leaves produce an unpleasant, sweet smell when crushed. In the past, the iris was used medicinally, although the leaves and roots are poisonous to livestock.

Yellow iris
Iris pseudacorus

Stinking iris
I. foetidissima

Although one is yellow and the other purple, these wild irises are closely related

Iron

Many of the colours seen in rocks and soil are caused by the presence of iron compounds. Iron ore itself is dark in colour, but weathered pieces in soil tend to be red or buff. For the ore to be worth working, it must contain at least 20 per cent iron, and the best has more than 60 per cent.

Britain produces considerable quantities. The traditional source was in the limestone area of west Cumberland around Millom, where a rich, red ore called haematite is found; but this is now virtually worked out.

The Coal Measures ironstone, on which the Industrial Revolution was based, occurs in thin seams or beds of nodules. It is no longer worked, except as a by-product of coal mining in north Staffordshire and Scotland.

Some sedimentary ores have been worked in coalfields, and since 1930 the ores of Lincolnshire and Northamptonshire have become important for steel works at Corby and Scunthorpe. These ores are calcareous (lime-rich) sandstones with 25-30 per cent iron content. They are dug out of the ground directly from the surface, not by mining. Drag-line excavators or power-operated shovels capable of lifting about 15 tons at a time are used. After the ore has been removed the topsoil is replaced. See also MINE

Irrigation

Plants need water to grow and to absorb nutrients such as nitrogen, potash and phosphate in solution. Although Britain has a more than adequate annual rainfall, with many showers during hot periods, the driest parts of the country need some irrigation in nine summers out of ten. Moreover, rain is often absent at key periods. Farmers irrigate their fields at such times with sprays. The water is pumped through pipes, generally portable, and sprayed over the crops through revolving sprinklers.

The needs of various crops depend on the season, and the farmer or market gardener has to work out his irrigation plans from day to day. The key period for early potatoes, for instance, is April, May and June; for maincrop potatoes, June, July and August. Cereals benefit from irrigation in April and May, a period in which droughts often occur. With grass, a succession of cuts or heavy grazing occurs throughout the spring, summer and autumn, and fertiliser is usually applied after each period of use. Irrigation is then beneficial if rain does not fall within a few days to wash the fertiliser into the soil.

Water supplies are insufficient to permit all farmers to irrigate their land as they would wish. An inch of water spread over an acre of land amounts to 22,500 gallons, and there are about 29 million acres of farmland in Britain.

Some farmers make their own reservoir by lining a shallow depression in the ground with sheets of plastic to prevent the rain from draining into the soil.

Ivy reverses the normal plant seasons by flowering in autumn and bearing berries in spring

Ivy *Hedera helix*

Ivy uses tree trunks solely for support. Its climbing roots draw no nourishment through tree bark, nor does it strangle the tree. Its underground roots, however, do compete with tree roots for soil nutrients; only in that way is it harmful, and then to a trivial degree.

There are two distinct life phases of the ivy growing wild in most broad-leaved woodlands and hedgerows. In the juvenile stage its fleshy stem, bearing lobed leaves, grows along the forest or hedgerow floor until it reaches a tree trunk, rock face or wall, then climbs upwards, attaching itself to these surfaces with a cement-like substance.

Once it gains the upper branches, possibly 50 ft up, this juvenile form changes to the adult one. Ivy now bears an upright stem,

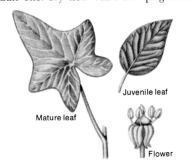

Juvenile leaf

Mature leaf

Flower

Climbing ivy clasps a tree trunk with roots on the inner side, leaves on the outer

with oval unlobed leaves all round it, flowers and fruits. All ivy leaves are evergreen, with glossy surfaces to resist water loss. Their dark green often turns to purple in winter. They provide cover and hibernation sites for many insects, which in turn attract birds.

Ivy bears greenish-yellow flowers in October. Each has five sepals, five petals, five stamens and a five-celled ovary. Purplish-black berries ripen in early spring, and are taken by birds that, after eating the fruit, scatter the small hard seeds. Insects, attracted by nectar in the greenish-yellow disc, cause cross-pollination by crawling among the flowers.

Ivy, like holly, was held to have magical powers, and at Christmas kept houses safe from demons. Shropshire people believed milk drunk from an ivy-wood cup cured whooping cough.

In winter, ivy profits from sunlight filtering through the leafless boughs overhead. The main stems become tough, up to 3 in. diameter, and may last a century.

Ivy-leaved toadflax *Cymbalaria muralis*

Introduced into Britain from southern Europe early in the 17th century, ivy-leaved toadflax soon spread from rock gardens, and can now be seen on old walls throughout the British Isles except northern Scotland, where it is found only rarely. It has ivy-shaped leaves, and from May to September has two-lipped, spurred lilac and white flowers similar to those of snapdragons. The seed capsules are carried on long stalks which curve away from light and deposit them in dark crevices, where the light, flat seeds are shed. Once established, the plant spreads by long-rooting runners, with delicately trailing stems extending up to 30 in. It is particularly resistant to drought.

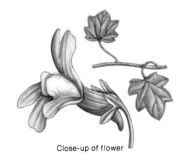

Close-up of flower

Ivy-leaved toadflax blooms from May to September, with small flowers similar to those of snapdragons

One insect eats another. The predatory field damsel bug keeps a firm hold on its fly victim

Insect

More than three-quarters of the known living species of animals are insects. Nearly a million species have been named throughout the world, the largest being the Goliath beetle of West Africa, which is nearly 6 in. long, and more are discovered every year. In Britain there are more than 20,000 species. The largest British insect is the privet hawk-moth which has a wingspan of more than 4 in. The 2½ in. long stag beetle is the longest ground-living insect.

The name insect means 'in sections', the body being in three parts: the head, thorax and abdomen. On the thorax are three pairs of jointed legs. Some relatives of insects, which are not true insects but often confused with them, are the spiders, centipedes and woodlice. They have similar jointed legs but usually more than three pairs.

Most insects have two pairs of wings attached to the thorax. They possess them in the adult stage only, which means there is a sharp transition between the young wing-less insect and the winged adult. A few primitive, mostly soil-living, insects have never evolved wings. The bristle-tails and spring-tails are common examples.

Insect skins cannot stretch much and so growth occurs when an insect sheds or moults its old skin, to reveal a new skin underneath which stretches while it is still soft. In this way growth is not uniform, but takes place in distinct steps. At the final moult a winged adult will appear. Thus insects have a life cycle which involves several stages.

Most insects have a complete four-stage life cycle. This consists of egg, larva in which no wing buds are visible, a resting or pupa stage and then the winged adult. The pupae of some butterflies are beautifully marked with gold spots and were given the name chrysalis from the Greek word for gold. The name is now applied to the pupae of most butterflies and moths and sometimes to the pupae of other insects.

Butterflies and moths have wings covered with coloured scales. Their larvae are called caterpillars and have extra, fleshy legs on the abdomen. Flies have only two wings and legless larvae. The bees, wasps, ants and sawflies have four wings. Many species live in large insect societies.

Beetles have the first pair of wings hardened into wing cases which protect the membranous second pair. The moth-like caddis flies and gauzy-winged alderflies have aquatic larval stages. Lacewings, snake-flies and scorpion flies are similar in appearance to alderflies, but have terrestrial larvae.

Fleas, like lice, have lost the wings that their ancestors once had and are parasites. They are flattened from side to side, enabling them to move more easily through the fur or feathers of their host animals, and they can jump well.

Many other insects have three stages: egg, followed by a nymph which moults several times and has traces of wing buds, and then the adult. This type of life cycle is called gradual metamorphosis. Some insects, which undergo gradual metamorphosis, have aquatic nymphs which spend their lives in water before developing into adults. Examples are dragonflies and damselflies whose adults have all four wings of equal size. The may-flies have large forewings and small hind-wings and two or three long tails at the end of the body. Stoneflies have two tails and rest with their wings either folded flat over their backs or rolled round their bodies.

Most of the other insects with gradual metamorphosis have land-living young stages. The grasshoppers and their relatives have hind legs enlarged for jumping. Cock-roaches are rather like non-jumping grass-hoppers. Earwigs have pincers which are for attack and defence, but also help in folding the wings. The bugs have mouthparts adapted for piercing and sucking, either for drinking blood from an animal or, more usually, sap from a plant. Several bugs are pond or river dwellers. The tiny thrips have feathery wings and the lice, which are flattened and wingless, are parasites on birds and mammals.

AN INSECT'S SUIT OF ARMOUR

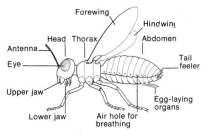

Forewing
Hindwing
Head Thorax
Abdomen
Antenna
Eye
Tail feeler
Upper jaw
Egg-laying organs
Lower jaw
Air hole for breathing

The insect's body is made up of sections covered by a hard outer skeleton, like a suit of armour

HOW AN INSECT SEES

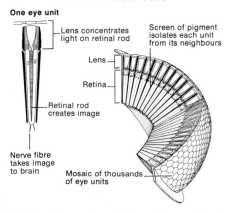

One eye unit
Lens concentrates light on retinal rod
Screen of pigment isolates each unit from its neighbours
Lens
Retina
Retinal rod creates image
Nerve fibre takes image to brain
Mosaic of thousands of eye units

The insect's eye is made up of thousands of lenses, each of which picks up part of a scene. The image registered on the insect's brain is a coarse-grained one made up of dots

Insects of the British Isles

More than 20,000 species of insects live in the British Isles. This chart shows examples from each of the main groups into which this enormous number is divided, together with examples of other small animals which are often mistaken for insects. To identify an insect-like creature, find the chart example which it most closely resembles, then look up the appropriate entry where further illustrations will help narrow the field of search. The true insect has a body in three parts: head, thorax and abdomen. On the thorax are three pairs of jointed legs

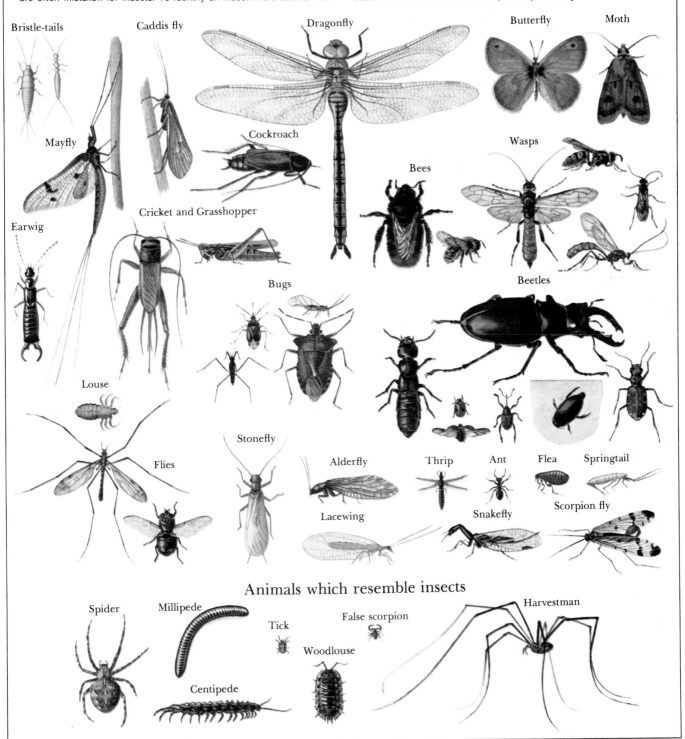

Animals which resemble insects

J K

Jack by the hedge see Mustard
Jackdaw see Crow
Jack go to bed at noon see Goatsbeard
Jay see Crow

Jellyfish

These creatures are not fish, but primitive animals consisting of two bell-shaped layers of cells, one inside the other, separated by a thick layer of jelly. Inside their fringe of stinging tentacles there are usually four longer ones, which surround the mouth and convey plankton, fish or shrimps to it after they have been stunned by the stings.

Jellyfish are unisexual and shed eggs or sperm into the sea where fertilisation takes place. Each fertilised egg develops into a larva which settles on weeds or stones and becomes a polyp; this then buds off small jellyfish, called ephyra larvae, which grow into adult jellyfish.

The coloured parts of jellyfish may either be light-sensitive pigment spots—which keep their upper side to the surface—or indicate the reproductive organs. The largest part of the animal is jelly made up almost entirely of water, so that jellyfish soon dry out and disintegrate if stranded on beaches in the sun.

Most jellyfish found in British waters are between $\frac{1}{4}$ in. and 8 in. in diameter though there are exceptions. The largest likely to be encountered is lion's mane, which can be up to 3 ft across the bell with 30-40 ft tentacles; brick red, it is most often seen in northern waters and has a powerful sting. The smallest are stalked jellyfish, $\frac{1}{4}$ in. across, which live attached to seaweed on the shore.

The most common British species is the moon jellyfish, 3-8 in. across and marked by four pale purple crescents. Though its young feed on fish, it eats plankton in the adult stage.

Another large species sometimes found in British waters is the compass jellyfish with 24 brown points on its white bell which may be 18 in. in diameter. Toadstool-shaped pearl jellyfish is strongly phosphorescent and glows if disturbed at night. *Cyanea lamareki*, a smaller relative of lion's mane, has an equally powerful sting. The Portuguese man

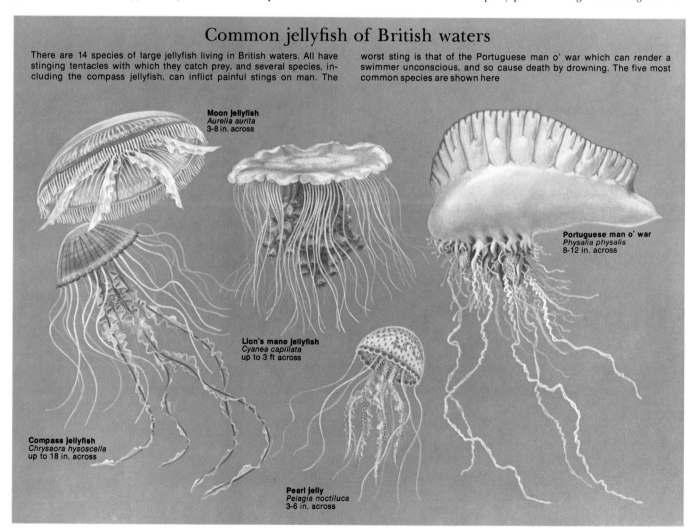

Common jellyfish of British waters

There are 14 species of large jellyfish living in British waters. All have stinging tentacles with which they catch prey, and several species, including the compass jellyfish, can inflict painful stings on man. The worst sting is that of the Portuguese man o' war which can render a swimmer unconscious, and so cause death by drowning. The five most common species are shown here

Moon jellyfish
Aurelia aurita
3-8 in. across

Portuguese man o' war
Physalia physalis
8-12 in. across

Lion's mane jellyfish
Cyanea capillata
up to 3 ft across

Compass jellyfish
Chrysaora hysoscella
up to 18 in. across

Pearl jelly
Pelagia noctiluca
3-6 in. across

o' war, Physalia, is a tropical relation of the jellyfish, occasionally found off the south-west coast. Its powerful sting can cause burning pain, nausea and even muscular paralysis. In 1955 a boy drowned at Camber, Sussex, after being stung by one.

A ¾ in. freshwater jellyfish *Craspedacusta sowerbii,* first discovered in Regent's Park, London, in 1880, has since been found in canals and reservoirs, mainly throughout southern England.

HOW THE STINGING CELL STINGS

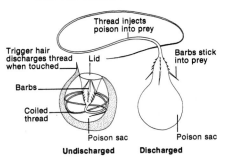

When the stinging cells along the jellyfish's tentacles are detonated, the coiled threads carrying poison turn inside out as they are discharged, and ensnare and paralyse the prey

Jet
Large quantities of this hard stone, a form of coal or anthracite, were once found in the rocks which form the cliffs along the north Yorkshire coast. Small pieces of jet may still be found on the beach at spots where the cliffs are being eroded by the sea.

It is black and shines well when polished. In Queen Victoria's time jet was a fashionable material for jewellery especially for people in mourning. During the 19th century, mines were dug in Yorkshire to obtain the stone, and Whitby became the manufacturing centre for jet jewellery and ornaments. In 1873 the industry had a turnover of £90,000 but it declined rapidly soon afterwards, and the manufacture of jet jewellery is now a rare craft in England. Most jet now comes from Spain.

Jew's ear *Auricularia auricula*
A brown, ear-shaped fungus usually found only on the dead branches of elder trees. It is 1-3 in. across and resembles a human ear in texture as well as appearance. There are fine, grey hairs on the surface. Judas Iscariot, the betrayer of Jesus Christ, is believed to have hanged himself on an elder tree, and 'Jew's ear' is thought to be a corruption of 'Judas's ear'. Dried remains of the fungus can be found throughout the year and new fruiting bodies are formed in October and November. These are edible and especially good for soup. Jew's ear is one of the *Tremellales* group of fungi, all of which have a jelly-like consistency. See also FUNGUS

John Dory see Dory

Juniper *Juniperus communis*
An evergreen tree of the pine family. Juniper resembles gorse, but is distinguished by its spiky needles set along the twigs in groups of three; these are blue-green, with a white waxy covering. The trees smell of gin—the spirit is flavoured with an oil distilled from their berries.

Although juniper is native to Britain and once grew throughout the land, it is common today in only two districts—the Central Highlands of Scotland and the chalk hills of southern England. Easily consumed by fire and choked by hardwood scrub, it is gradually disappearing.

The shape of junipers varies with the location and climate. In the south they are sometimes small, shapely trees; on the lower slopes of the Highlands, small shrubs; and at greater altitudes, shapeless, prostrate shrubs. Junipers rarely grow taller than 10 ft, and they live for more than 70 years.

In the spring the trees bear clusters of small, yellow male flowers and tiny, bud-like female ones. The female flowers ripen by late autumn to round berries—at first green, then dark blue. Birds appear to help germination: they swallow the berries and drop the hard, black seed from them. These often sprout where they fall, but seeds taken straight from the tree must be kept for 18 months in moist sand before they will germinate. Each seedling bears two seed-leaves.

The wood burns well because of its resinous oil, and because of its scent it is used for smoking hams and cheeses. It is of little use for furniture or building; but the trunk, with its reddish bark, pinkish-brown heart-wood and white sapwood, is attractive for ornamental carving.

As a shrub in some Scottish pine and birch woods, juniper provides nesting cover for many birds, including the thrush and gold-

After several months the green berries of the juniper turn blue with a waxy, grey sheen

crest. It is also popular with browsing deer.

Junipers may be seen in abundance in Rothiemurchus Forest, Inverness-shire, Tynron Juniper Wood, Thornhill, Dumfriesshire, and on the Wiltshire Downs.

Kale
A plant of the cabbage species. Several varieties are widely grown as food for cattle and sheep, others are grown for human consumption. There are two main types of fodder kale: marrowstem kale and thousand-headed kale.

Marrowstem has a tall thick stem, which contains nutritious pith, and large leaves. It is vulnerable to hard frost and generally has to be used before the New Year. Thousand-headed kale is smaller and bushier and can withstand most winter conditions. Cattle and sheep are often allowed to graze kale in the fields, but most is cut and taken to the animals in winter yards or made into silage.

Scotch curled kale and cottagers' kale are the varieties grown for human consumption, but kale originally intended for cattle is sometimes put on the market in hard winters. See also CROPS

Kale, Sea *Crambe maritima*
A plant which once grew widely on sand, shingle, rocks and cliffs around the coast of Britain, but is now rare. It has blue-green, cabbage-like leaves and can reach a height of up to 2 ft. White-petalled, honey-scented flowers, after pollination by insects, develop into pods that are blown into, and dispersed by, the sea.

A member of the cabbage family, the plant is rare as a result of over-picking by people who found that, boiled and served with butter, it was an excellent vegetable.

Kaolin
Peculiar chemical conditions caused by hot gases from within the earth have turned granite in some parts of Cornwall and Devon into an intensely white clay, in which silica and aluminium are important elements. This is kaolin or china clay, which melts when fired at high temperatures. It is used to make a glaze on pottery and is mixed with bones and ground-up flints to make fine china. Some is found on Bodmin Moor, but the largest quantities are produced around St Austell.

Chinese potters were the first to make use of this mineral—hence both its names; kaolin as a corruption of Kaoling, a hill in Shansi province where large deposits were found. The Cornish kaolin was first discovered in 1755.

Ked
A wingless fly which lives in the fleece of sheep. The absence of wings and its flattened body and backward-pointing hairs enable the sheep ked to move through the sheep's wool and make it difficult for the animal to

remove it. The sheep ked *Melophagus ovinus* is also known confusingly as the sheep tick. It is $\frac{3}{16}$ in. long and has a rigid, syringe-like set of mouthparts which it uses to suck the sheep's blood. Females live about four months and produce fully grown larvae which develop one at a time inside the mother. When born they are large enough to pupate immediately in the sheep's wool and hatch in a few days.

A similar parasitic fly, the deer ked *Lipoptena cervi,* which lives on wild deer, pupates on the ground and has wings which it sheds after settling on a suitable host.

Kelt see Salmon
Kestrel see Falcon

Kidney-vetch *Anthyllis vulneraria*

A plant which carpets the clifftops of British coasts with close-packed heads of pea-like flowers between June and September. It is also abundant on limestone grassland away from the sea. Sometimes known as lady's fingers, kidney-vetch is 6-24 in. high. The flowers vary in colour. Inland, they are normally yellow, but on the coast, particularly in the south-west, yellow, cream, white and crimson blossoms may grow together. The leaves consist of blue-green leaflets, often hairy underneath. The end leaflet is the largest.

Like other downy-leaved plants, it was once used to staunch bleeding.

Kiln

A building used for burning, baking or drying. Kilns have generally been superseded today by larger, more economic structures.

In the 18th and 19th centuries, when lime was extensively used on acid clay soil to improve cultivation, lime kilns were widespread. Beehive-shaped, with a hole in the top, kilns were usually built on the sides of steep hills and against cliff faces, to make the loading of limestone and coal easier. Alternating layers of limestone and coal were burnt to produce the lime.

Disused lime kilns exist throughout the Pennines, from the Peak District to the Cheviots, but the finest examples are in Wales, on the coast of Pembrokeshire and Cardigan Bay, and on the Northumberland coast, at Seahouses, Holy Island and Beadnell Bay.

Beehive-shaped brick kilns may still be found near the shallow pits from which clay was extracted.

The bottle-shaped, coal-fired pottery kilns of the Midlands are now being displaced by modern gas-fired kilns.

In areas of high rainfall, kilns for drying grain were often built into farm buildings— rounded kiln ends can be seen in the structure of many old Orkney farmhouses. See also OAST-HOUSE

Kingcup see Marsh marigold

A kingfisher with its catch—a bullhead. After killing the fish by banging its head the bird will swallow it head first, to avoid choking on the scales

Kingfisher *Alcedo atthis*

Usually seen as a flash of iridescent blue as it flies a few feet above a stream, the kingfisher's exotic colours warn predators that its flesh has a foul taste. The bird nests along rivers and streams in England, Wales and Ireland, but is now seen only rarely in southern Scotland and is unknown further north.

The kingfisher is green-blue above with rust-red underparts and has a pattern of red, white and blue on the cheeks. The huge, dagger-shaped bill, set on a strong head, is used for grabbing fish—not spearing them —when the bird makes headlong plunges beneath the surface of fresh water in search of food.

In 1963 the kingfisher population was decimated by a hard spell of frost that froze almost every stretch of fresh water throughout the country, and it has only recently recovered. The pollution of many rivers has driven kingfishers away from some areas.

Between April and August, the kingfishers excavate a 2-3 ft long burrow in a river bank. There, in a nest at the end of the tunnel, the female lays six or seven round white eggs. The young kingfishers are fed almost entirely on a diet of minnows and sticklebacks, with a few water beetles, dragonflies and other insects. The nest is soon fouled with fish bones.

A perch overlooking the stream or pond is habitually chosen as a fishing point. Once captured, the fish is carried back to the perch and turned round by careful manipulation of the bill until its head faces outwards. The kingfisher bangs the fish's head against the perch several times until it is dead or stunned, reverses it, and swallows it head first. In fishing grounds which lack perches, the kingfisher hovers with fast-beating wings to keep its head and eyes steady before diving.

Kite *Milvus milvus*

As scavengers in the refuse-strewn streets of medieval London, kites thrived on a diet of carrion, rats and mice. The red species was widespread in Britain until the 18th century, when the gradual cleaning up of towns, the introduction of refuse disposal systems and underground sewage pipes started a decline in their numbers. This was assisted by relentless persecution by gamekeepers and farmers protecting their chickens.

Today, though they are confined to a few remote Welsh valleys, red kites are on the increase due to the efforts of dedicated ornithologists and some understanding farmers. They nest in hanging oak woods on the steep sides of the valleys. There are over 20 pairs now, but egg collectors, motorised tourists and bird-watchers all combine to disturb them. It is feared that the felling of old woods and afforestation of the open moors may put them into serious danger once more.

Britain's red kite is a hawk-like bird with long, angled wings and a long tail, prominently forked and translucent when seen against the sun. Though it kills small mammals, which it takes with a sudden plunge to the ground, the kite is largely dependent on carrion. It feeds freely from dead lambs, sheep and rabbits, but in hard weather will eat almost anything.

The kites which children fly get their name from these birds, as they often hover on spread wings, apparently motionless, when searching for prey.

The rusty-brown plumage of the mature red kite is streaked with white about the head

Kitten moth see Puss moth
Kittiwake see Gulls

Knapweed usually has a dense, thistle-like head of flowers, but some specimens have extra petals round the outside of the head

Knapweed, Common *Centaurea nigra*

Resembling thistles without prickles, knapweed is widespread in grassland and on roadsides. It has hard, knob-like heads, and in consequence is sometimes called hardheads. These heads are brown-black and made up of many rows of closely overlapping scales, inside which are red-purple fertile florets.

The stems, which are usually swollen and hollow beneath the heads, are extremely wiry, difficult to pick, and unattractive to cattle. This has made the plant a serious weed of grassland in some areas.

In the West Country, and occasionally elsewhere, specimens of knapweed may be found with a row of large, sterile florets round the outside of the head; these provide an additional attraction to pollinating insects such as bees.

Knawel

All through the summer, knawel flowers in sandy or gravelly arable fields and waste places. It has many-branched stems, narrow leaves, grows from 1-9 in., and has greenish flowers. The flowers are unusual as they do not have petals, but the pointed sepals, modified leaves which surround the flower, have a narrow white border which gives it a variegated appearance. When the single seed ripens the sepals do not wither but become rigid.

The knawel is an annual plant that can be found growing throughout the British Isles; there is a perennial knawel but this is a rare species seen only in a few places in Norfolk and Suffolk. It has also been found on one hill in Radnorshire.

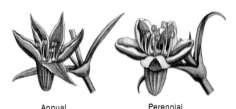

Annual   Perennial
Both the annual and perennial knawels are in flower during June and August

Knot see Sandpiper

Knotgrass, Common
Polygonum aviculare

Although this weed has a superficial resemblance to grass when seen growing among corn, it is a member of the dock family.

Knotgrass is variable in appearance. When found among corn it has upright stems and small, thin leaves; but on waste places and sea shores its stems are long and straggly, its leaves broader and closer together, and it lies flat on the ground.

Knotgrass, one of the most common weeds in the British Isles, can be between 6-36 in. long (erect or trailing), and bears small, pink or white flowers from May to October. These develop into three-angled nutlets and are an important food for birds in the autumn.

Knotweed

Japanese knotweed *Reynoutria japonica* grows to 6 ft tall with a cane-like stem. It has big, heart-shaped leaves, almost 6 in. across, and develops sprays of tiny, white flowers in late summer. Introduced from Japan as a garden plant after the First World War it is so vigorous and has such extensive underground stems that it soon became a weed and spread to roadside verges, railway lines and waste places. It now grows throughout the British Isles.

Great knotweed *R. sachalinensis*, which also comes from Asia, is seen much less often. It grows up to 12 ft tall, has leaves more than 1 ft long, and green flowers.

The abundant blossom of Japanese knotweed appears from July to October

Kyle

A term used in Scotland for a narrow sea channel between two islands or between an island and the mainland. It comes from the Gaelic word *caol*, narrow.

Perhaps the best known are the Kyles of Bute, two channels separating the northern end of the island of Bute from the mainland. Also well known to tourists is the Kyle of Lochalsh, which lies between Skye and the mainland, cutting across the narrow end of Loch Alsh.

L

In autumn the thin, grey pods of laburnum open to reveal hard, brown poisonous seeds

Laburnum

The golden-flowered laburnum tree seen in parks and gardens, along streets and in woodland fringes, was introduced to Britain from central Europe in the 16th century.

The tree belongs to the sweet pea family and has flowers typical of that family with two side petals, two folded lower petals, and one large upright petal. The flower attracts pollinating insects, which must force their way past the pollen-bearing stamens and the stigma to gain nectar.

Flowers are numerous, arranged in hanging clusters, which have gained this lovely tree the names of golden chain and golden rain. The flowers open in May; by autumn the ovary of each flower has ripened to a thin grey pod, holding several small hard black seeds. These are poisonous. If chil-

dren eat them, consult a doctor immediately.

The seeds need 18 months on moist soil to germinate. Each seedling bears two seed-leaves, then a few lobed ones, and finally adult ones, each consisting of three leaflets. The twigs are olive-green, the same colour as the smooth-barked trunk.

The trunk can reach 1 ft in diameter, but laburnums rarely exceed 30 ft in height or live for more than 50 years.

There are two common species, *Laburnum anagyroides* and *L. alpinus*, but gardeners have bred several hybrids which produce more blossom.

The tree has chocolate-brown heartwood, surrounded by cream-coloured sapwood Timber is available only in small sizes, and is used for turnery, decorative wood carving and inlay. Musical instruments, including the chanters of bagpipes, are made from seasoned wood, which is strong and firm, and can be bored with accuracy.

Lacebug

A white or green bug, flat in shape, with transparent front wings which have a lace-like network of veins. The largest of the 23 British species is only $\frac{1}{5}$ in. long.

Lacebugs feed on plants, many of them living among moss. Some of these moss-living lacebugs do not have wings, but the winged *Acalypta parvula* is common in autumn.

The creeping thistle lacebug *Tingis ampliata* spends the winter as an adult among moss. In the spring it moves to creeping thistle plants to mate. Females lay their eggs partially embedded in the thistle stems. The eggs hatch in late June, after most of the adults have died, and the young bugs reach full size by September.

Other species of lacebug are associated with certain plants: *Dictyonota strichnocera* is common on gorse, and *Stephanitis rhododendri* causes mottling or spotting of rhododendron leaves.

Lacewing

Slender insects with large wings covered with a lacework of veins. They are slow, clumsy flyers and are usually found in woods and hedgerows. Most lacewings fly at night. They vary in length from $\frac{1}{4}$ in. to $1\frac{3}{4}$ in.

Green lacewings such as *Chrysopa septempunctata* help the gardener by eating greenfly and other insect pests. Females lay green eggs, each on the end of a short stalk, on leaves where aphids are found.

The larvae have powerful jaws and feed on aphids by sucking out their body fluids. When fully grown, the larva spins a cocoon

The delicate-looking lacewing is a friend of the farmer, eating hundreds of aphids a day

and pupates inside it. The cocoons are usually attached to leaves or bark. The adults, which hatch in the summer, also feed on aphids; but they chew and eat them instead of sucking them dry.

After eating the aphids the lacewing uses the skins for camouflage against insect-eating birds. It presses each aphid skin on to its back where it is held by hooked hairs. After a while, the larva is covered with shrivelled aphid skins which make it look like a piece of dried rubbish.

The insect is a beautiful pale green colour with golden eyes. The adults hibernate, often entering houses to do so. During the winter lacewings turn red, becoming green again in the spring. Green lacewings are common in Britain and Ireland; they have many similar relatives, some of which are not as widespread.

The giant lacewing *Osmylus fulvicephalus* is Britain's largest species, with a 2 in. wingspan. It can be found near woodland streams from May to July, but not in Scotland. The larvae are aquatic, the eggs being laid on streamside plants, they live among wet moss where they also hibernate.

Another group of lacewings are also aquatic as larvae. These are the sponge flies. There are three species, but only one, *Sisyra fuscata*, is found throughout the British Isles, usually near fresh water from May to late autumn. The larvae feed on freshwater sponges.

Lackey moth see Eggar moth

Ladybird

The small, brightly coloured ladybird is the most familiar of beetles and is probably the only one most people will handle.

There are 44 species in Britain, many of which are small—$\frac{1}{12}$ in. long—and dull coloured, such as the marsh ladybird *Coccidula rufa*; but the more common species are larger, $\frac{1}{8}$-$\frac{1}{3}$ in. long, and coloured red or yellow with black spots.

Most of them are extremely helpful to gardeners as they have a voracious appetite for aphids, scale insects, mealy bugs, thrips and mites. The adult beetles and their grubs feed mostly on aphids and are important in keeping these pests in check. A fully grown grub can eat about 50 aphids a day. One exception is *Subcoccinella 24-punctata*, which feeds on leguminous plants and is sometimes a minor pest. Ladybirds are shunned by birds because of a nasty-tasting fluid which they exude when attacked. Adult ladybirds hibernate throughout the winter, often in groups of a few hundred, under loose bark or in a crevice. In spring they fly to plants infested with aphids and lay their eggs there. The eggs hatch in about a week as active, long-legged grubs. Three to six weeks after hatching, the ladybird grub turns into a pupa which attaches itself to a leaf like a small butterfly chrysalis. This hatches as a beetle in about a week.

Aphids often fight back when attacked. When a ladybird larva seizes a black-bean aphid, other members of the colony kick the larva to shake the aphid free. Small aphids are unable to resist being dragged away, but larger ones will often kick off their attacker

Flying ladybird. The first pair of wings, the spotted hard covering, are not moved in flight

Nettle aphids sometimes escape by dropping from the plant. If seized they daub their attacker's head with a waxy secretion which temporarily paralyses the ladybird larva. One species of aphid copiously waxes attacking ladybirds to such an extent that some of them die.

The best known species is the seven-spot ladybird *Coccinella 7-punctata*, which is bright red with seven black spots—three on each wing case and one where the wing cases meet. The yellow markings at the front are not eyes—the head is very small and almost hidden by the thorax on which are the eye-like spots.

The yellow and black 22-spot ladybird *Thea 22-punctata* is often found on nettles. The largest species is the eyed ladybird *Anatis ocellata*, which is red with black spots outlined in yellow. This ladybird is found on pine trees.

The common two-spot ladybird *Adalia bipunctata* is found almost everywhere. It is variable in colour, ranging from red with two black spots to black with two red spots. Intermediate forms have extra spots and there is a yellow and black form.

Lady's mantle *Alchemilla vulgaris*

A plant which grows near the summits of Britain's highest mountains, lady's mantle is also found in wet grassland and on the borders of woods throughout the British Isles, though it is rare in south-east England.

Lady's mantle is easily recognised by its clusters of small, golden-green flowers and the large, round leaves which have 7-11 lobes with toothed margins. If the leaves are held downward by the stalks they look like a cloak, hence its English name. When the leaves are young they are folded like a fan.

The plant grows between 3 in. and 18 in. high and is often found in gardens where it is valued for its pleasant green foliage rather than its flowers. The roots taste like parsnips, and are eaten by pigs. Lady's mantle was prized in the 16th and 17th centuries as a healer of wounds; a decoction was drunk to stem intestinal bleeding, and bandages were dipped in it to treat wounds.

Lady's slipper see Orchid
Lady's smock see Cuckoo flower
Lady's tresses see Orchid

Greenflies huddle under a leaf as an advancing seven-spot ladybird seizes one of their number

Lagoon

A stretch of water or lake which changes level, usually with the tide, and which is separated from the sea by a natural barrier. Most lagoons are formed between the straight or gently curved line of a beach and the irregular edge of the land behind.

The best examples in Britain are behind Looe Bar in Cornwall and The Fleet, behind Chesil Beach. Smaller lagoons may form along shingle ridges or sand dunes. They are usually only partly salty, particularly where a stream or river enters them.

Laird

The Scottish name for any landowner. The name was originally applied only to those who held their land direct from the Crown. The word is a variant of 'lord' and appeared in 15th-century documents in the form of 'lard'. It has a meaning similar to 'lord of the manor', but the Scottish clan system gave the word an additional implication of clan chieftain, head of the family in the widest sense of the word.

Lake see p. 262
Lambs' lettuce see Corn salad
Lambs' tails see Hazel
Lammas leaves see Oak

Lampern

A common fish in many streams and rivers of the British Isles, although it is rarely seen. It is a close relative of the lamprey and belongs to the class of jawless fish. It is a uniform leaden grey, creamy coloured on the belly and grows to about 20 in. long when fully developed.

As an adult, the lampern *Lampetra fluviatilis* lives in the sea, but migrates up-river to spawn on pebble-bottom shallows in a nest excavated by the male, who uses his sucker mouth to clear stones from the bed.

Young lamperns are blind and their mouths have fringed lips. They live buried in mud, feeding on minute organisms for four or five years. After this long larval life they migrate to the sea where they become parasites on many kinds of bony fish.

One form of lampern, the brook or planer's lamprey *L. planeri,* does not migrate to the sea but spawns soon after it changes from the larval state. Larval lamperns are known as prides.

Lamperns make a tasty dish, particularly as they have no bones. By custom the City of Gloucester sent lamperns from the Severn to the Court from Henry I's time until 1835. In 1893 the Mayor of Gloucester revived the custom, sending a lampern pie to Queen Victoria. The custom ceased during the First World War, and was not revived until 1953 when a lampern pie was sent to the Queen on her coronation.

Lamprey *Petromyzon marinus*

This is not strictly a fish, although it lives in water, has an eel-like shape and is popularly regarded as a fish. The lamprey is placed in the class of jawless fish for four reasons: the series of seven gill-openings along the sides of the body are not protected by a gill cover, the fins are not supported by bony rays, both pectoral and pelvic fins are lacking, and it has an open disc-like sucker mouth.

The lamprey is quite distinctive because of its blotchy yellow-brown colour and heavily toothed sucker. It can measure 36 in. in length when fully developed.

It spawns in fresh water and the young can be found in rivers and streams, but they eventually migrate to the sea, from which the adults later return to spawn. The adult lampreys are entirely parasitic on fish, fastening themselves to their temporary host with sharp teeth and producing a saliva which liquefies the host's body muscles.

Fish attacked by a lamprey are always greatly weakened and often killed, and where lampreys are in great numbers a tremendous amount of damage can be done to a fishery. A large number of fish are attacked by them, including salmon, trout, cod, haddock and shad.

In the sea, lampreys are often found attached to basking sharks, and scars from their suckers have been found on sperm whales, although there is no evidence that they were feeding on their hosts.

Landslide

Just as a wall will give way if strategically situated bricks are removed, so will rock and soil standing on a steep slope collapse in a landslip or landslide if their mutual bonding is weakened.

The weakening is brought about most commonly in Britain by heavy rain washing away soil, but the contraction caused by severe frost, or a slight earth-tremor shock, can also trigger a slide. Depending on the angle of the slope, enough momentum can be built up to damage and engulf roads and even buildings. Many of the major British landslips are on coastal cliffs, such as at St Catherine's Head in the Isle of Wight, and Folkestone Warren. Smaller examples are often seen in motorway cuttings, especially in clay, whose water content makes its slippery surface unstable on slopes.

Popularly, the term landslide is extended to include many other types of soil movement, including mud-flows, where saturated soil liquefies and cascades. An example is the Aberfan tragedy of 1966, in which 144 people, mostly children, died when water caused a tip heap to slide down into a Welsh valley.

Lappet moth see Eggar moth
Lapwing see Plover

Larch

Unlike other common conifers, larch, a member of the pine family, loses its leaves in winter. It can then easily be recognised by the knobs on its straw-coloured twigs.

Autumn sunshine filters through the branches of a

In the spring each knob bears a tuft of needles, bright green at first, darker later, which turn to bright yellow before they fall in autumn. The latest-formed twigs carry single needles. In April, just before the needles open, the tree bears clusters of yellow male flowers. The female flowers are rose-pink or white and, because of their rose-like shape, are often called 'larch roses'. They ripen quickly during the summer, forming barrel-shaped brown cones with

LARCH FLOWERS AND CONES

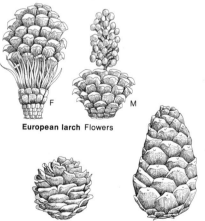

European larch Flowers

Japanese larch Cone   **European larch** Cone

Larch cones develop from fertile female flowers. European larch cones have straight scales; the scales of the Japanese cones curve outwards

larch wood to brighten the bracken-covered floor

autumn. The cone scales are bent back, so that each looks like a little rosette.

A cross between the European and the Japanese, the hybrid larch *L. eurolepis* grows faster than either and will tolerate poorer conditions. It shows many of the characteristics found in each of the others, and is being developed by the Forestry Commission.

This cross was produced by the chance cross-pollination of female flowers of the Japanese larch and male flowers of the European kind, on the Duke of Atholl's estate at Dunkeld in Perthshire, early this century.

Lark

Leaders of the dawn chorus, skylarks sing as they soar into the air, sustain their song as they hover and also sing as they descend. The skylark's song is frequently heard between January and July. It is less common at other times, and is rare during August and September. Skylarks often gather in flocks, and may be seen over most kinds of open countryside. Migrants from Scandinavia join the resident population during winter.

Woodlarks also sing in the air, as well as from the ground and from song-posts in trees. Their song is sweeter but less spirited than that of skylarks, and they are more often heard than seen. They sing for two reasons: to defend their territory, which they soar above, and to attract females.

Both breed in Britain, but while skylarks are numerous and widespread, the number of woodlarks is decreasing. Hit hard by a series of severe winters in the 1950's, they have also suffered from the disappearance of heaths. Woodlarks need areas providing short, sparse turf, some thicker ground cover and scattered trees and saplings to provide song-posts. They are now confined to East Anglia, the south coast and Wales.

Two other species of larks are found in Britain: shore larks are regular winter visitors to eastern England and crested larks have recently begun to breed in Kent, but are still very rare.

Larks are brownish ground-living birds of open countryside. They nest on the ground in a well-hidden cup of grass and moss, beneath a tuft of grass. The young are well camouflaged and remain motionless when danger threatens. They can be passed within a yard without being noticed.

Larks feed on seeds, usually of common weeds, and the leaves of clover and other plants.

Both skylarks and woodlarks are brown streaked with black above and buff streaked with brown below. Skylarks show prominent white outer tail feathers as they fly. Woodlarks lack the crests of skylarks and have light-coloured eye stripes that meet on the nape to give a capped effect. They also lack the white in the tail.

Shore larks are tubby buff birds marked with a bold yellow and black face pattern. Found only on the shores and marshes of

The skylark's streaked brown back provides good camouflage during nesting or foraging

the east coast of England, they are winter visitors from Scandinavia. In summer, the males have two tufts of feathers on their heads, giving rise to their North American name, horned lark.

Crested larks, rare visitors from Europe, are best distinguished by their crests, which are more prominent than those of the skylark.

Larkspur *Delphinium ajacis*

The mid-summer display of the larkspur is not made by its petals but by the sepals—modified leaves which protect the bud, and which in most flowers fold down into insignificance when the flower opens. Each flower has five sepals which, like petals in other flowers, attract pollinators, such as bumble bees. There are two petals which join in a spur enclosed within an outer spur formed by the sepals. Each flower develops into a pod containing several wrinkled seeds.

Larkspur grows 12-30 in. tall with spikes of blue, pink or white blossom. A native of the Mediterranean, it is grown in gardens from which it has spread to roadsides throughout the lowlands. Its botanical name is from the Latin *delphin*, a dolphin, which its upper sepal resembles.

Larkspur flowers appear by roadsides and on cultivated ground in June and July

flat tops. They are tough and break up slowly, releasing small brown seeds with triangular wings. These sprout the following spring and grow rapidly; seedlings are 18 in. high after two years. They then usually grow 3 ft a year, reaching about 145 ft, and live for 200 years.

The grey bark becomes thicker and more deeply fissured with age. The pinkish-brown durable heartwood is surrounded by paler sapwood. It is widely used on farms for building and fencing; and the outer planking of fishing boats on the east coast of Scotland is made of a superior grade of 'boatskin larch'. The trees can be used for timber when only 40 years old.

Larches grow quickly in youth, but each tree needs ample light and space, so the total timber crop is small.

The European larch *Larix decidua* was introduced into Britain from central Europe and the Alps before the 17th century, and at first was used for ornamental purposes. Then its value as a timber tree was recognised, especially by the Dukes of Atholl, who planted larches on a vast scale in Scotland.

The European larches, although by far the most widely planted, are no longer the most widely planted. Japanese larches *L. kaempferi* are now most favoured by foresters because they grow faster and are better adapted to the British climate. They can be distinguished from European larches by their rust-coloured twigs, blue-green needles and reflexed cone scales. Their needles are blue-green in summer, fading to orange in

Lakes — worlds doomed from their creation

Lakes are destined to disappear from the moment they are created, as their feeder streams fill them with silt and their outlets cut ever deeper channels. For plants and animals, lakes form isolated, ever-changing worlds

The richness and variety of animal and plant life supported by a lake depend mainly on how it was formed. There are basically two types of lakes, called primitive and evolved. Primitive lakes, such as many Scottish lochs, were formed mainly in mountainous areas by ice gouging deep hollows in solid rock. The water in them is soft and poor in minerals, supporting few plants and animals. Evolved lakes were formed in lowland areas either by subsidence, as with the Cheshire meres, by melting blocks of ice, as with Loch Leven, or by the kind of general sinking of the land which produced the East Anglian fens. These contain hard water and many plants and animals. Other lakes are man-made, usually by the construction of dams, as in the Scottish Highlands, where they are used to supply water for hydro-electric power stations.

Each type of lake is a virtually closed system — an independent world with its own shifting balance of plants and animals. In late spring, the water in the top layer of an evolved lake becomes warm and less dense. A wealth of minute plants grow in it and support such microscopic animals as protozoa. The bottom layer remains cold and dense and the two layers of water are prevented from mixing by a narrow intermediate layer in which the temperature drops rapidly throughout its depth. As summer progresses, the small plants and animals feeding on the nutrients in the top layer die and sink to the bottom. But because of the intermediate layer the nutrient salts produced by their decomposition cannot circulate into the upper layer. By autumn, therefore, this top layer has become unable to support vegetation. In autumn, when strong winds may stir up the lake, small plants grow again; but

they will disappear with the onset of short, cold winter days.

Within the shallow fringe of a lake, where light penetrates to the bottom — at depths of up to 13 ft — rooted plants can grow. In the deeper parts of this region, stonewort grows on clayey muds, and willow moss, Canadian pondweed, grassy pondweed, small bur-reed and white water lilies on more nutritious muds. In shallower water, long-leaved plants thrive on fine clays and the fern-like quillwort on stony bottoms. In still shallower water, shorewood and water lobelia grow on rocky or peat-covered gravel. In lakes fed by streams carrying silt, great reedmace is the most dominant lakeside plant.

Animals vary from lake to lake. Lake Windermere, which has been extensively studied, contains among its primitive forms of life water fleas; tiny, pear-shaped, one-eyed copepods; minute, cylindrical rotifers; and microscopic protozoa. Some of these, such as the $\frac{1}{2}$ in. long, transparent phantom midge larvae and the copepod *Cyclops strenuus*, swim up to the

HOW THE SUN LAYERS STILL WATER

0 ft

Warm layer (Epilimnion)

20 ft

Intermediate layer (Thermocline)

30 ft

Cold layer (Hypolimnion)

50 ft

Mud

Life in a lake depends on oxygen, which enters at the surface, either from the atmosphere or as a by-product of plant respiration. In summer, the sun heats the still surface water, forming a layer called the epilimnion. This floats on the denser cold water — the hypolimnion. As the surface water gets warmer, an intermediate layer — the thermocline — is formed, through which the temperature drops rapidly. The three layers do not mix, so the bottom layer receives no oxygen, though it does receive a constant rain of organic debris from above. Then, in winter, the surface cools and the water circulates until it is thoroughly mixed, with oxygen evenly distributed throughout, and dissolved nutrients from the bottom debris are returned to the upper layers

surface for food at dusk and down to the bottom at dawn. Phantom midge larvae, which have two gas bladders to maintain their equilibrium in the water so that they remain motionless for long periods, sometimes become sexually mature in very deep water and never hatch into adult midges. Apart from midge larvae, animals living on the lake bed include pea mussels and the oligochaete worms; in shallower water, alderfly larvae, freshwater shrimps, water lice, snails and water boatmen. The reed animals provide food for dragonfly and damselfly larvae, beetles and saucer-bugs. The fish in Windermere, which feed on the smaller creatures and plants, include brown trout, pike, perch, charr, minnows, miller's thumbs and eels.

An unexplained phenomenon is that each lake or group of lakes has its own sub-species of whitefish — for example, the powan of Loch Lomond, the schelly of Haweswater, Ullswater and Red Tarn in the Lake District, the gwyniad of Llyn Tegid in Wales, the vendace of Lochmaben in Scotland, Derwentwater and Bassenthwaite and the pollan of Loughs Neagh, Erne and Derg in Ireland. This could be because these groups of lakes were once connected, probably during the last glacial period.

Lakes attract a variety of water birds. Insect feeders among

LAKES FORMED BY GLACIERS

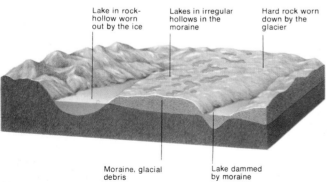

Lake in rock-hollow worn out by the ice

Lakes in irregular hollows in the moraine

Hard rock worn down by the glacier

Moraine, glacial debris

Lake dammed by moraine

Most natural lakes in the British Isles were formed by the action of Ice Age glaciers. Some fill basins eroded by the ice; others fill trenches cut by glaciers and then dammed by glacial debris; a third type occupy hollows left in larger areas of glacial debris when the ice melted

the reeds include warblers, mallard, moorhen, wigeon and teal. Long-billed herons stalk fish and frogs in the shallows, and mute swans use their long necks to probe for weeds and detritus on the bottom. Diving birds predominate over deep water—coot, grebe, tufted duck, scaup, pochard, golden-eye and merganser. Rarer diving birds, such as the Slavonian grebe and the black-throated diver, breed on the most northern Scottish lochs. Black-headed gulls and terns spend the winter on many lakes, and greylag and pink-footed geese do so on some Scottish lochs, such as Loch Leven. Whooper swans are winter visitors to the lakes of Snowdonia in Wales.

In recent years pollution has become a major problem. Watercourses feeding some lakes have brought in chemicals from fertilisers and sewage effluent, killing fish and over-producing algae, which make the water murky and shut out light. Sometimes de-oxygenation is not the result of man's activities. Parts of the Cheshire meres suffer from over-enrich-ment caused by the droppings from flocks of wintering birds. It is in Cheshire that the phenomenon of the Breaking of the Meres may be seen. On very calm days, usually in autumn, blooms of blue-green algae form a thick film on the water surface, making it appear opaque. The film breaks as soon as a breeze develops.

Further problems in lakes used for drinking water stem from rapidly fluctuating levels, which destroy the shore vegetation upon which so much animal life depends.

THE WEB OF LIFE IN A LAKE

Most of the life of a lake is in the shallows. Plants which flower above water, such as reeds and water lilies, grow on soft bottoms in sheltered spots. Submerged plants grow where light can penetrate, as do stoneworts—large, weedlike algae—which can form meadows at depths up to 3 ft. Other algae, tiny, free-floating diatoms, live in all the surface waters of the lake. The living plants supply food and shelter for crustaceans, insects and worms, while debris from both plants and animals feeds other worms and crus-taceans which scavenge in the mud on the lake bottom. Fish range through all the waters of the lake, feeding on plants, animals and debris, and are in turn preyed on by diving birds

Loch Sionascaig, Wester Ross, now prized for its trout, was scooped out by an Ice Age glacier. The ice forced its way into cracks in the surface rock, making them wider and deeper. When the ice retreated, a hollow was left into which water flowed from the surrounding hills

Larva

The description applied to an insect from the time it leaves the egg until it is transformed into a pupa, the inactive pre-adult form. The caterpillars of moths and butterflies are the most familiar larvae. Sawfly larvae resemble caterpillars, but can easily be told apart because they have six or more pairs of legs, whereas caterpillars have five pairs or less.

Most other insects, for instance beetles and lacewings, have six-legged larvae.

Those insects which provide a store of food for their young or feed them as they grow, such as bees and wasps, have legless, headless, maggot-type larvae. This is also the case among flies whose larvae live surrounded by food in the form of a decaying corpse or plant.

Some insects do not have a pupal stage. In these, the egg hatches as a young insect which grows and changes its skin several times until it becomes a winged adult. Unlike true larvae, they develop wing buds. Young stages of such 'no-pupa' insects are called nymphs.

The larva of the stag beetle lives in and feeds on the roots of rotting tree stumps

Larvae and nymphs of some common British insects

These larvae and nymphs represent early stages in the lives of some common insects. Land-living nymphs, such as those of the bugs, are very similar in shape to the adult insects, but water-living nymphs, such as those of dragonflies and damselflies, and most larvae, such as the maggots of flies, are utterly different from their adult forms. The drastic change from larva to adult involves an intermediate pupal stage

Ground-living larvae

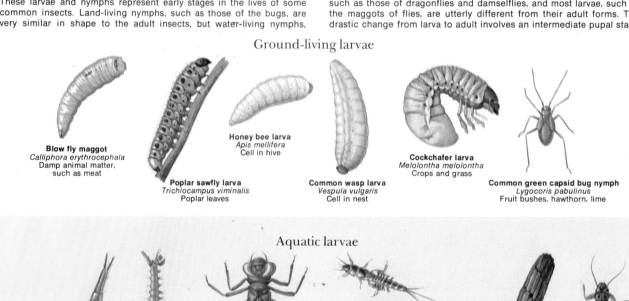

Blow fly maggot
Calliphora erythrocephala
Damp animal matter,
such as meat

Poplar sawfly larva
Trichiocampus viminalis
Poplar leaves

Honey bee larva
Apis mellifera
Cell in hive

Common wasp larva
Vespula vulgaris
Cell in nest

Cockchafer larva
Melolontha melolontha
Crops and grass

Common green capsid bug nymph
Lygocoris pabulinus
Fruit bushes, hawthorn, lime

Aquatic larvae

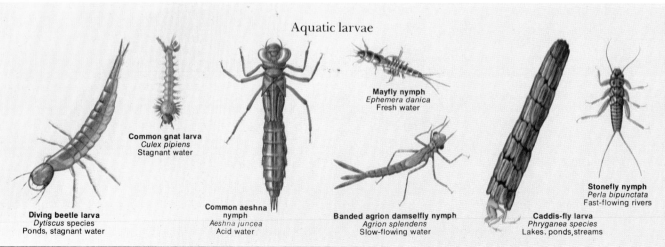

Common gnat larva
Culex pipiens
Stagnant water

Diving beetle larva
Dytiscus species
Ponds, stagnant water

Common aeshna
nymph
Aeshna juncea
Acid water

Mayfly nymph
Ephemera danica
Fresh water

Banded agrion damselfly nymph
Agrion splendens
Slow-flowing water

Caddis-fly larva
Phryganea species
Lakes, ponds, streams

Stonefly nymph
Perla bipunctata
Fast-flowing rivers

Lasher see Weir

Laurel

The true laurel or sweet bay tree *Laurus nobilis* grows only in southern gardens of Britain, sheltered by walls or planted in tubs. It is a shrubby evergreen with slender, dark green, oval leaves, identified by the aroma when crushed. This is the leaf used in cooking; it keeps well when dried.

Each laurel is either male or female; both produce clusters of small, greenish-yellow flowers in leaf joints in May. Female flowers develop into dark purple berries bearing single hard seeds in autumn.

Laurel is native to Mediterranean countries and features in classical literature and art. It provided the bay-leaf crown for victors of Olympic games and song contests. It was introduced to Britain in the 16th century. Two other evergreens bear the name laurel because of their similar foliage and habit. Both are related to plum trees, and they are widely planted for garden shelter.

Cherry laurel *Prunus laurocerasus* has black bark, long pale green leaves and an open growth. It may grow to 15 ft tall. If left unclipped it produces, in June, upright spikes of white flowers smelling of marzipan. In autumn a spike of black berries, each holding one hard seed, ripens and attracts birds. The seeds and leaves contain a poison allied to prussic acid, and when a leaf is crushed it releases the smell of bitter almonds which is typical of prussic acid. Entomologists use the leaves to kill butterflies enclosed in a glass bottle, without damaging them.

Portugal laurel *P. lusitanica* bears darker leaves, with crimson twigs and bitter berries that ripen through red to black.

Cherry laurel berries hold seeds which contain a poison related to prussic acid

Laver see Seaweed
Lawyer's wig fungus see Ink cap

Lazy beds

One way of growing potatoes in thin soils has traditionally been to lay them in beds about 6 ft across, and cover them with topsoil dug from shallow trenches about 3 ft wide on either side. Known as lazy beds because they were easy to prepare and look after, these plots were once common on the harsh terrain of the western coasts of Ireland and Scotland, but they are fast disappearing. Lazy-bed ridges can also be traced in hill areas such as the moorlands beside Hadrian's Wall.

Lead

This soft metal has been worked in Britain since at least Roman times. Pigs — or ingots — of lead bearing Roman lettering have been discovered in excavations, and lead pipes have been found in Roman villas at Bath. The word plumber derives from the Latin word for lead, *plumbum.*

Lead is extracted from a shiny black ore called galena, which is mined from the mountain limestone of Derbyshire and the northern Pennines in particular. It often contains quantities of silver.

In the 19th century Britain produced half the world's lead, but most of the mines are now completely worked out.

Leaf beetle

There are 16 different leaf beetles in the British Isles, each of which eats the foliage of a particular type of plant. The most common, *Chrysolina polita,* with its red wing cases and bronze-green head and thorax, feeds on the mint family. The most beautiful, the rare, multi-striped *C. cerealis,* eats thyme and is found in parts of Wales. The largest species, *C. banksi,* is ½ in. long and lives in many parts of the British Isles, feeding on black horehound. The specialised feeding of leaf beetles has been turned to use in other regions of the world by experimenting with types of beetle which can defoliate otherwise uncontrollable weeds.

In addition to the 16 beetles of the genus Chrysolina there are many related beetles

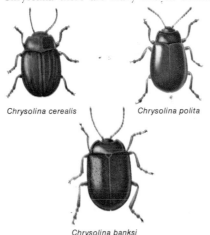

Chrysolina cerealis   Chrysolina polita

Chrysolina banksi

with similar habits, including the bloody-nosed beetle, the flea beetles and the Colorado beetle.

Leaf-hopper

More than 250 species of leaf-hoppers are known in Britain. They are flat-looking bugs between ¼ in. and ¾ in. long which live by sucking the sap of a wide range of plants. Most leaf-hoppers, like the common grass-eating green leaf-hopper *Cicadella viridis,* are agile leapers and flyers. The eared leaf-hopper *Ledra aurita* is ¾ in. long and lives on oaks.

It has been discovered that leaf-hoppers sing like cicadas, warm-country insects to which they are related. Leaf-hopper songs are important in courtship, but they are too soft and high-pitched to be heard easily by humans.

Leaf miner

The larvae of some moths and flies live in the tissue between the outer layers of leaves, and are called leaf miners. The larvae eat the tissue, leaving white or brown markings on the skin of the leaf.

Some larvae eat patches of tissue, which show up as blotches on the surface of the leaf; others mine a continuous winding tunnel, which shows up as an ever-widening line, marking the growth of the larva.

A typical blotch miner is the caterpillar of the moth *Lithocolletis coryli,* which feeds on hazel; while the scribblings on blackberry leaves are left by caterpillars of the moth *Nepticula aurella.*

A mine made in a bramble leaf by the caterpillar of the moth *Nepticula aurella*

Leatherjacket see Cranefly

Lee wave
Air moving across the earth s surface behaves rather like water flowing over the bed of a stream—the speed increases away from the frictional drag of the ground and obstructions disrupt the flow into waves. Even low lines of hills such as the Cotswolds or Chilterns can disturb the airflow to a height of several thousand feet, throwing it into a series of waves, known as lee waves,

HOW LEE WAVES FORM

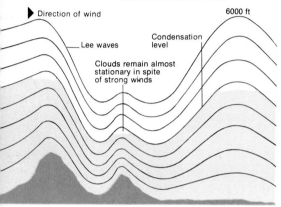

Direction of wind

6000 ft

Lee waves

Condensation level

Clouds remain almost stationary in spite of strong winds

Hills disturb the flow of air, shaping it into waves. Then on the lee side of the hills the down-flowing wind accelerates

Leech
Widely used by medieval doctors, themselves commonly called leeches, the medicinal leech *Hirudo medicinalis* is the only British species to feed on human blood. Leeches were applied to the patient's body to draw off blood thought to contain the 'evil humours' causing illness. They secrete the substance hirudin, which prevents blood from clotting, so that bleeding continued even after the sated leeches dropped off. Salt was then applied to the leeches to make them disgorge the blood, so that they could be used again.

The medicinal leech is a black worm with red markings, growing up to $3\frac{1}{2}$ in. long. It lives in fresh water where cattle, its main food source, drink. Today it is found only in the Lake District and the New Forest.

Other freshwater leeches feed by sucking animals' blood or swallowing whole worms and insect larvae, as does the misnamed horse leech *Haemopis sanguisuga*. This grows up to 6 in. long and is dark grey-green with black specks.

Some leeches prey on fish—including the inch-long fish leech *Piscicola geometra* whose yellow-green body is banded with paler dashes. The most common marine species is *Pontobdella muricata* which attacks skates and rays. It grows 2-5 in. long, with a flattened body and well-developed suckers.

downwind of the obstruction. The crests of these waves often have distinctive clouds which hover almost stationary for hours as water vapour condenses in the updraught and vaporises in the downdraught on opposite sides of the wave crest. Winds in the descending limb of a wave over Sheffield in February 1962 did widespread damage.

Lengthman
The man responsible for the maintenance of a given length of roadway, railway or canal. The name is no longer used for men working on railways, but still survives on roads and canal systems. The canal lengthman may live in a lock cottage and is responsible for the upkeep of the locks, banks and adjacent navigable waters.

A road lengthman looks after the roadside verges in one particular parish. Using traditional tools, such as scythe and hook, he follows up the work of the rotary cutter, doing jobs that the machine cannot do.

Leopard moth *Zeuzera pyrina*
This large white moth with grey speckles on its long, narrow wings, is related to the goat moth, and the caterpillars of both species have similar habits—spending two to three years burrowing into living wood and feeding on it. They live on a great range of deciduous trees. However, they rarely cause serious damage.

When fully grown, the greyish-speckled

One blood meal may have to last a leech several months, since its opportunities to feed generally depend on chance. As blood is taken in, the leech's excretory organs dispose of water, concentrating the meal for maximum nourishment.

If no suitable victim passes to provide a second meal, the leech may eventually draw on material in its own body, shrinking in the process.

THE BLOOD-SUCKING LEECH

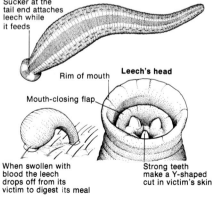

Sucker at the tail end attaches leech while it feeds

Rim of mouth

Leech's head

Mouth-closing flap

When swollen with blood the leech drops off from its victim to digest its meal

Strong teeth make a Y-shaped cut in victim's skin

As the leech cannot always depend on a readily available meal, it stores blood in the side pouches of its 'gut', often for several months

The leopard moth rests on tree trunks by day, and flies by night from June to August

caterpillars pupate just under the bark. The moths emerge from June to August, fly by night and rest by day on tree trunks.

The females, with a wingspan of $2\frac{1}{2}$ in., are much larger than the males and have pointed tips to their bodies; this probably helps them tuck their eggs into crevices in the bark. Leopard moths are rare outside south-east England.

Leopard's bane *Doronicum pardalianches*
A robust plant with large, round leaves and conspicuous yellow daisy-like flowers, leopard's bane grows up to 3 ft tall. It was introduced to Britain from southern Europe as a garden plant, later spreading to become established in woods and copses in England, Wales and especially southern Scotland. Several other species are commonly grown in herbaceous borders, providing a splendid splash of colour from April to June.

The 16th-century English herbalist, Gerard, said that 'it killeth panthers, swine, wolves and all kinds of wild beasts, being given them with flesh'. It appears that leopards and other 'fower footed beasts' were poisoned with one of the aconites called pardalianches.

Lettuce, Prickly *Lactuca serriola*
Widespread on dry banks, sand dunes, stony places, roadsides and waste land in south and east England, prickly lettuce grows up to 6 ft tall and blooms from July to September. It may have been introduced from eastern Europe for its medicinal value: the drug 'lactucarium', made from the milky juice which seeps from the broken stem and leaves, was a favourite sleep-inducer in the Middle Ages. Prickly lettuce is a 'compass

plant'; when fully exposed to the sun, its saw-edged leaves lie in a north-south plane. Its flavour is bitter and very different from that of the related garden lettuce.

The saw-edged leaves of the prickly lettuce lie north-south when exposed to sunlight

Lettuce, Wall *Mycelis muralis*

As its name suggests, this plant occurs frequently on walls. A shade-lover, it flowers from July to September on rocks and in woods, especially beechwoods. Its distribution is uneven: it is common in most of England and Wales, rare in East Anglia, Devon and Cornwall, and found only very occasionally in Scotland and Ireland. Wall lettuce grows from 1-3 ft tall, with a much-branched arrangement of flowers with many small heads. There are only four or five florets in each flower-head. The stems have a milky juice. The leaves are deeply lobed and often tinged with crimson.

Wall lettuce flowers, which are about ¾ in. across, are borne in sparse heads

Ley see Grass
Lichen see p. 268

Lightning

Contrary to the old adage, lightning usually does strike in the same place twice—first with a 'leader stroke' either from cloud to ground or, in the case of very high clouds, from ground to cloud. Then a fraction of a second later a vivid 'return stroke' runs along the path established by the 'leader'. This process can also take place within a cloud or between the cloud and the surrounding air.

It is the return stroke which carries the main current of the discharge—a giant spark commonly of the order of 10,000 amps, although more than 100,000 amps

Passing storm—three successive lightning flashes recorded on a single plate in an open camera

have been recorded. And there may be further leader and return strokes, draining electricity from different parts of the cloud. High-speed photography has shown that a 'single' flash really consists of a number of very rapid upward and downward strokes.

Lightning is associated with cumulo-nimbus clouds. Various theories, based on rising warm, moist air and falling ice particles, have been put forward to explain how the air within a cloud develops positive charged particles mainly at the top and negative ones below. The flash links the areas of positive and negative static electricity and the current, travelling at 186,000 miles per second, heats the surrounding air to 15,000°C (27,000°F). This brings about the sudden expansion of air which causes the thunderclap at the ground; it also causes the 'thunderbolt' effect by converting moisture into steam, producing instant expansion and setting fire to trees and buildings.

In the British Isles, two-thirds of lightning discharges occur within clouds. Such discharges illuminate the whole interior of the cloud—a phenomenon known popularly as sheet lightning; this name is also given to the reflection of forked lightning hidden by a cloud. Forked lightning is a flash which has branches from its main channel.

As the sound of thunder travels at about one-fifth of a mile a second, whereas lightning is almost instantly visible, an observer can calculate roughly how many miles he is from the centre of the storm by counting

the seconds between the lightning flash and the thunderclap, and dividing by five.

The chance of any individual being struck by lightning is one in 5 million in a year—about 12 people a year are struck in Britain. In a thunderstorm, it is safer indoors than out. If caught out in a storm, avoid flat open spaces like river valleys, beaches or golf courses. Do not stand under trees or near metal fences. Umbrellas and golf clubs may also attract lightning, which usually earths through the tallest object in the vicinity. Tall buildings thus offer some protection to surrounding property, but conductor research is continuing. See also THUNDER

HOW LIGHTNING STRIKES

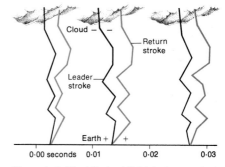

The main brilliant flash of lightning moves from the ground to the cloud. The stroke is repeated several times in less than one-tenth of a second but appears as a single flash to an observer

This lichen, *Cladonia floerkeana*, is common on peaty soil, usually forming a grey crust

Lichens of the genus *Usnea* are found on trees, where they branch out into hair-like tangles

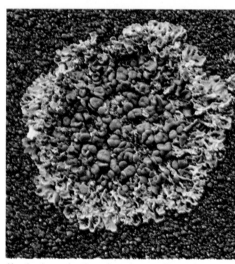

Xanthoria parientina—found on walls and tree trunks, especially where the air has mineral salts

Lichen

A dual plant formed by a fungus and a plant of the alga group. The algal cells contain green chlorophyll and manufacture sugars and other compounds to sustain the plant. The fungus provides shelter for the algal cells and prevents them from drying out. The various shapes of lichen depend on the fungus.

There are 1355 British species, of which 500 grow on shrubs and trees. The rest grow on walls, roofs, gravestones, rocks, chalk grasslands, heathlands and sand dunes.

Lichens do not have roots, but absorb water and gases through their upper surface, and are therefore sensitive to atmospheric pollution. For this reason they are rarely found around cities and grow best on the wetter, west side of the British Isles. Those on trees thrive best on the sunny, south-west aspects of trunks and branches. Disappearance of lichen species can be used to detect rising levels of air pollution.

There are three main types. The encrusting forms, including the bright orange *Xanthoria*, grow on roofs, walls, gravestones and tree trunks. Leaf-like species develop flat lobes spreading over bark or stones, and shrubby forms which grow vertically from the ground or hang like tassels from trees. Few have common names.

A leaf-like lichen seen in damp woods in the west is tree lungwort *Lobaria pulmonaria*, once used to treat coughs and asthma. Dog lichen *Peltigera canina* grows directly from the ground and has large, brown-green lobes, often with brown tips. Reindeer moss *Cladonia rangiferina* is a grey, branched lichen which grows on moors in Scotland and Wales and is eaten by the small, domesticated herd of reindeer in the Cairngorms of

Scotland. Related to reindeer moss are the cup lichens *C. chlorophaea* and *C. pyxidata*, which have conspicuous grey-green cups.

Seashore lichens include the grey-green tufts of sea ivory *Ramalina reliquosa*, common on rocks above high-tide level, and *Verricaria maura*, which resemble patches of tar.

Reproduction in lichens is complex. In a few British lichens, both the fungus and alga reproduce sexually. In others, the algal cells divide and multiply by simple fissions and the fungus reproduces spores sexually. Both the cells and spores are dispersed separately and have to come into contact before a new lichen plant is formed.

Lichens also reproduce vegetatively by means of a granule which contains a few algal cells surrounded by fungal threads and is dispersed by the wind.

HOW LICHENS REPRODUCE

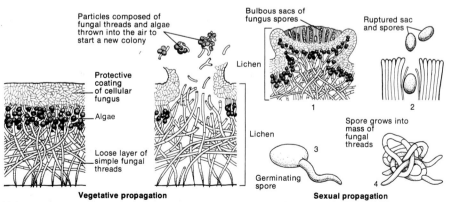

Lichens can reproduce in two ways. The most successful is vegetative propagation, whereby fragments of fungal threads and algae break off and germinate together. In sexual propagation, fungal spores germinate alone and a lichen is formed only when the normal algal partner is also present

Lilac *Syringa vulgaris*

A member of the olive family, this shrub was introduced from eastern Europe, probably in the late 16th century. Each growing shoot ends in two hard, green buds of equal size. In spring, each bud sprouts with equal vigour, and so the shoots fork repeatedly. Lilac, which grows to 20 ft, never forms a straight central stem, and is a long-lived bush rather than a tree. The thin grey bark has a rough surface and the hard, pale cream wood is tinged with purple. The heart-shaped leaves, borne in pairs, are pale green, becoming dark brown in autumn. Mauve flowers open in May in showy clusters. White, red and purple blossoms are natural freaks which are reproduced by grafting. The shrubs flourish particularly in sunny positions on rich, loamy soils, and are generally fragrant when in bloom. By October, lilac flowers have each produced two hard, brown, two-winged seeds in a leathery pod.

Lily, Martagon *Lilium martagon*

Introduced into Britain more than 500 years ago from the mountains of central Europe as a garden plant, this tall, purple-flowered lily with whorls of up to 15 leaves may be found occasionally growing wild in woods. Its large, showy flowers appear on 2-3 ft tall stems in August and September. Each flower has six distinct petals which turn back to expose six stamens and the stigma. Pollinated by moths, each flower develops a three-angled capsule containing numerous winged seeds. Once established, it spreads by the division of its scaly bulbs. Martagon comes from the Turkish name for a form of turban which the flower resembles, hence the plant's other name: Turk's-cap lily.

The large, showy, Turk's-cap lily gets its name from the turban-like shape of its purple flowers

Lily-of-the-valley *Convallaria majalis*

This familiar garden flower with its broad oval leaves and spikes of sweet-scented flowers also grows wild. Although 'convallaria' derives from the Latin for valley, the plant is not confined to valleys. It is sometimes abundant in dry woods on sand or limestone throughout England and, more rarely, in Scotland and Wales. It spreads by underground stems as well as seeds. Sometimes called the May lily because of its flowering time, it is also known as 'Muguet de Mai' in France, where it is worn as a buttonhole on May Day. Distilled in strong wine, lily-of-the-valley flowers were once used to treat apoplexy, poor memory and gout.

Lime

The stately lime tree is common in avenues and large estates, and in town and city streets. The lime's attractions include its ability to grow quickly to a great height, a pleasing mid-green foliage, and a tolerance of repeated clipping. Its faults are a tendency to hide its lower trunk in a mass of side shoots and burrs, and to become infested by foliage-feeding aphids. In July these aphids secrete honeydew—partly digested leaf sap, rich in sugar. If this or nectar from the tree's flowers falls on objects below, the blotches become unsightly, because a mould fungus turns them black.

Planters now overcome these faults by using the weeping, silver-leaved lime *Tilia petiolaris*, a garden variety of eastern European ancestry, which is immune from aphid attack.

Limes have heart-shaped leaves. Their slender twigs, which have alternate buds, are often crimson; the buds showing only two outer scales, one small and one large. Yellowish-green flowers appear in July; rich in nectar, they attract hive bees. Dried flowers make a pleasantly flavoured tea. Hard, grey, single-seeded fruits are produced in September. Lime is easily pruned and trained and is ideal for pleached, or interwoven, hedges, arbours and shady walks. Its bark is smooth, grey and stringy, and birds sometimes strip the bark as a nesting material. The strong bark fibres were once used by gardeners for tying bundles. The creamy-white timber is firm, easily carved and very stable. The English sculptor and carver Grinling Gibbons (1648-1720) used it extensively. It is also used for hat blocks, shoe trees and piano keys.

Britain has two rare native wild limes, the broad-leaved lime *T. platyphyllos* and the small-leaved lime *T. cordata*. Both arise from seedlings with strange, hand-shaped seed leaves. The stems of *T. cordata* are particu-

The broad-leaved lime has large, heart-shaped leaves and the fruit is conspicuously ridged

larly attractive to woodpeckers, which suck the sap through rows of holes they punch in the bark.

The common lime *T. europaea* is the hybrid between the broad-leaved and small-leaved limes. It is rarely fertile and is raised from layered shoots.

In Duncombe Park, Helmsley, Yorkshire; is a 154 ft high lime—Britain's tallest broad-leaved tree. The normal life span of the lime is 150 years.

Common lime—the name is a corruption of 'lind' and has no connection with the citrus fruit

Lesser horseshoe bat
Has a fluttering flight. It lives in colonies in caves

Lapwing Often seen in large flocks, feeding over farmland on insects and earthworms

Meadow oat
Grows in tufts among the rocks on limestone grassland. It flowers in June and July

Limestone country, remains of ancient seas

The bold escarpments of the Cotswolds, the rugged Mendip Hills and the gently rolling chalk downs of Sussex, though so different in appearance, are all composed of limestone—a sedimentary rock consisting mainly of calcium carbonate. The plants that grow on them are also more varied and colourful than those which grow elsewhere.

There are various types of limestone, which differ in composition, texture and colour. They were originally formed millions of years ago, most of them from the lime shells of primitive organisms which lived in the sea; the empty shells, broken and powdered, gradually accumulated to great depths.

Three main types of limestone occur widely in Britain, each

Mountain avens A small creeping alpine plant with toothed leaves that are downy white beneath

Crested hair-grass
A compact grass with spikelets clustered into oblong flower heads

Rock-rose The bright, conspicuous flowers of this plant, which is not a rose, close at night

Blue moor-grass
Grows in the northern limestone hills, flowering from April to June

Zebra spider The spider's striped body is a familiar sight on bare, warm, limestone rocks

Purple milk vetch
The rich violet flowers grow in upright crowded heads on leafless stalks

Round-mouthed snail
It can close the circular opening to its shell with a large, limey 'door'

Mountain pansy
A common flower in hilly districts which blossoms in June

PLANTS THAT GROW OVER LIMESTONE

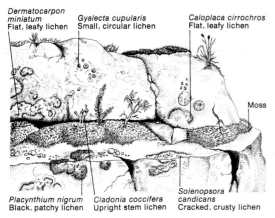

Dermatocarpon miniatum
Flat, leafy lichen

Gyalecta cupularis
Small, circular lichen

Caloplaca cirrochros
Flat, leafy lichen

Moss

Placynthium nigrum
Black, patchy lichen

Cladonia coccifera
Upright stem lichen

Solenopsora candicans
Cracked, crusty lichen

Limestone is quickly colonised by lichens that cling to the bare rock surface. Humus from dead lichens collects in rock crevices, and mosses start to grow. Then small herbs shoot up in the deeper moss humus

producing a characteristic land form. The chalk of south and east England is the most recent, softest and purest—some chalks being more than 90 per cent calcium carbonate.

The oldest limestones are the crystalline rocks—much harder and less pure than chalk—of north and west England, Wales, central Scotland and Ireland. These are known as Carboniferous limestones and tend to form steep cliffs and outcrops of bare rock. The third type, the Jurassic limestones, stretch from north Yorkshire to Dorset. These are softer than Carboniferous limestones but harder than chalk. There are also small areas of magnesian limestone and Cambrian limestone in Britain.

Limestone differs from most other common rocks in being soluble in weak acids. Even rainwater, acidified by the absorption of carbon dioxide from the atmosphere, dissolves it. Cracks are formed in surface limestone and these gradually widen. Sometimes they result in spacious underground caverns, such as Gaping Gill in Yorkshire, connected by watercourses and linked to the surface by pipes with funnel-shaped openings, known as swallow holes. Streams often disappear into these holes, reappearing from similar holes some distance away.

Limestone soils are usually thin, and because of this and the porous rock beneath, they are dry and well drained. They are also rich in calcium salts, and these determine the plants which will grow in them.

The two chief types of natural woodland on calcium soils are beech and ash. Beech is most prevalent on chalk downs but is also found extensively on Jurassic limestone in the Cotswolds. Ash is the most frequent type of woodland on Carboniferous limestone. Great stands of it grow in the Derbyshire dales, west Yorkshire and the Mendip Hills.

The limestone uplands of the north and west support large areas of sheep-grazed grassland, composed mainly of closely cropped sheep's fescue, with meadow oat, crested hair-grass, quaking grass and blue moor-grass. Flowers include several members of the pea family: lady's fingers, horseshoe vetch, purple milk vetch and birdsfoot-trefoil. These, together with clover, enrich the soil with nitrogen. Rock-roses are also prevalent. Some plants of the northern limestones, such as mountain pansy and several forms of lady's mantle, are rare

or absent on southern chalkland. Conversely, southern flowers such as stemless thistle extend to the Derbyshire area but no further north.

On the limestone of Derbyshire and Yorkshire are marshes containing rich vegetation, including globe-flower, great burnet, lesser valerian, sedges and rushes. Rugged limestone regions support some of Britain's rarest flowers, such as the Cheddar pink which grows on the rock ledges of Cheddar Gorge in Somerset, spiked speedwell, rock pepperwort and round-headed garlic in the Avon Gorge, and Jacob's ladder on the precipitous cliffs of Malham Cove. Rare flowers, such as mountain avens, also grow on limestone pavement—slabs of fissured rock found in the uplands of northern Britain.

Owing to the action of the weather in wearing away rocks, the landscape is more gentle in areas of softer chalk than it is in places where the chalk is harder.

A typical limestone animal is the black ant, which nests under broken slabs of limestone. Snails, which need lime to make their shells, are common. Palmate newts, capsid bugs, zebra spiders and horseshoe bats are also plentiful. Among the most common birds are the dipper, which catches insects from fast-flowing limestone streams, the jackdaw, which breeds in holes in limestone cliffs, and the lapwing, which nests on open limestone country. See also ASH, BEECH, DOWNS

The Burren, a limestone area in County Clare, is almost a botanical museum where Mediterranean ferns and a variety of woodland field-layer plants flourish in the cracks of the rock pavement

Limpet

These rock-clinging snails with conical shells are found both on the shore and in fresh water. Common limpets *Patella vulgata* grow their shells to fit a fixed spot on hard rock or grind out an oval scar in soft rock. They cling to the surface with a sucker-like organ, but make forays of up to 3 ft when the tide is in to scrape algae off shore rocks. At ebb tide, they return to their home rocks. They have few natural enemies, although oystercatchers sometimes eat them.

Limpets breed in September and October by shedding eggs into the sea. The larvae hatch after 24 hours, and ten days later a shell forms.

Two species liable to dry out are the keyhole limpet *Diodora apertura* and the slit limpet *Emarginula reticulata*. Tiny blue-rayed limpets *Patina pellucida* live on brown oarweeds. When young, they have translucent shells.

Slipper limpets *Crepidula fornicata* were introduced from America at the end of the 19th century. They gather, one on top of the other, and change sex as they age. The smaller and younger on top are males, the older and larger at the bottom are females. Slipper limpets are pests around oyster beds.

The lake limpet *Acroloxus lacustris* is found under lily pads in hard water or at the edges of slow-moving rivers. Like the river limpet *Ancylus fluviatilis* its conical shell is bent over at the top. The river limpet is found on hard surfaces in soft water.

HOW THE LIMPET FEEDS

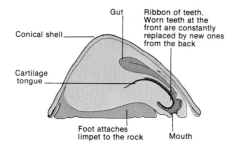

The limpet feeds when covered by water. It protrudes a cartilage tongue from its mouth so that the front teeth on the ribbon can rasp algae from the rock. Fine hairs in the roof of the mouth convey the food to the gut

Linden see Lime
Ling see Heather
Linnet see Finch

Liquorice, Wild

Also known as milk vetch, this plant was so named because of the initial sweet taste of its roots and leaves; this soon goes, however, leaving a bitter unpleasant flavour in the mouth.

Wild liquorice grows 2-3 ft tall in large patches on rough, roadside grassland, particularly on lime-rich soils in southern and central England, but it is not a common plant. Its greenish-white, pea-like flowers appear in July and August and its stout seed pods, which may reach a length of 1½ in., have two sections.

The liquorice used in sweets and cough mixtures, and which used to grow around Pontefract, Yorkshire, is a Mediterranean plant, *Glycyrrhiza glabra*.

Wild liquorice, or milk vetch, tastes pleasant at first, but has a bitter after-taste

Liverworts

Small plants similar in structure to mosses. There are more than 200 species in the British Isles, growing chiefly in places where the delicate leaves will not dry up: damp rocks, near the spray of waterfalls or mountain streams, in bogs and on old tree stumps and rotting timber.

The main difference between liverworts and mosses is that a moss spore-capsule releases spores through its lid, but a liverwort spore-capsule splits.

Many liverworts, unlike mosses, have no distinct stem and leaves, but consist of a prostrate flat frond with slender rootlets. Even leafy liverworts differ from mosses in having rounded, not pointed, leaves, which lack a central nerve. Liverworts were named because the fronds of some prostrate species looked like the lobes of the liver.

Like mosses, liverworts reproduce by means of alternate sexual and asexual generations. In the sexual generation, male and female organs are produced and fertilisation takes place. The fertile egg gives rise to the asexual generation, in which a spore-producing capsule develops on the end of a stalk. When the capsule ripens, it splits, releasing the spores which develop into new plants. Some species also reproduce vegetatively by means of small bud-like growths called gemmae. These develop in special cups on the surface of the plant, then break away and grow into new plants.

Lizard

More than 100 million years ago, lizards ruled the earth. (The name dinosaur comes from two Greek words meaning 'terrible lizard'.) Today, there are 2500 species of lizards in the world, most of them living in the tropics. Britain has only three native species: the common lizard, the sand lizard and the slow worm.

The most widespread is the common lizard. It is one of the hardiest reptiles, ranging further north—to the edge of the Arctic Circle—and living at greater heights—up to 10,000 ft in the Alps—than any other lizard. It is the only reptile found in Ireland.

The common lizard feeds on insects and other small animals, especially grasshoppers and spiders, and lives on commons, heaths, woodlands, cliffs and mountainsides, and can be found in hedgerows and quarries. It lives in loose colonies and enjoys basking on warm surfaces of stone, moss or bark. When disturbed it will dart into hiding, but once quiet returns it is quick to reappear.

Tiny buds, which develop into new plants, grow in cups on the liverwort *Lunularia cruciata*

A good adult size is 6 in., half of which consists of the tail. The colour can vary but is generally grey to brown, with rows of paler spots along the back. The underside is yellow to orange, brighter in the male, and spotted with black. Another name for the common lizard is the viviparous lizard, meaning one that bears live young. Most reptiles lay eggs, but the young of the common lizard are born in a transparent membrane which they break out of almost immediately. The litters—which range in number between five and ten—are born in mid-summer.

The sand lizard is now a comparative rarity in Britain. It is found mainly in dry woodlands, heaths and dunes, in Lancashire, Dorset, Kent, Norfolk and Surrey.

Usually, the sand lizard is grey to brown in colour with rows of conspicuous 'eye-spots' of dark brown rings with white centres, but during the May and June mating season, the male turns bright green on its flanks and underparts.

The sand lizard is 7-8 in. long and stockily built. The female lays up to 12 eggs in a hole in the soil and leaves them to hatch.

BRITISH LIZARDS

Sand lizard
Lacerta agilis

M   F

M   F

M   F

Common lizard
Lacerta vivipara

Slow worm
Anguis fragilis

There are 2500 species of lizards in the world, of which only these three live in Britain

The female common lizard—one of the world's hardiest reptiles and the only one found in Ireland

The slow worm or blind worm, which is neither blind nor a worm, is often mistaken for a snake but, although legless, it is a lizard. It grows to about 18 in. Its head is lizard-like and, unlike the snake which has no eyelids, its eyes have movable lids. It also has a fleshy tongue, ear openings and vertebrae of the lizard type. The body is covered in small tight-fitting scales, usually grey to deep bronze in colour, which give it a smooth appearance. The females may have a dark stripe along the back. Occasionally blue-spotted slow worms occur.

The slow worm lives in dampish places along woodland borders and hedgerows where it can burrow in leaf-mould. It also inhabits quiet spots such as churchyards, railway cuttings, quarries and rubbish dumps. It feeds mainly on earthworms, slugs and snails. When not basking, slow worms hide under logs and stones. Up to 20 young are born live in late summer; they are silver with a dark line on their backs.

Slow worms—like snakes, but unlike other lizards—shed their skins in one piece.

Like the other lizards, slow worms have

THE LIZARD'S ESCAPE DEVICE

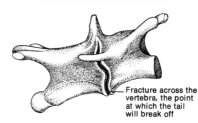

Fracture across the vertebra, the point at which the tail will break off

The lizard's tail has a pre-formed breaking point across each of its vertebrae, so that the tail can be broken off if it is trapped. Afterwards a new tail grows round a core of cartilage

the protective device of autotomy—the ability, if seized by the tail, to break it off by contraction of the muscles, and escape. The fracture takes place across vertebrae, not between them. At intervals along the tail the vertebrae have hairline cracks and it is at these points that lizards can choose to break them off. Lizards have the ability to grow new tails. Regrown tails can be recognised by their stumpy appearance.

273

The common lobster moves inshore in summer, often appearing in pools at low-tide level

Loach

Two kinds of this fish are found in Britain: the stone loach *Noemacheilus barbatulus* and the spined loach *Cobitis taenia*. The stone loach is abundant in running water – particularly shallow, stony streams – everywhere except the Scottish Highlands. Its back is dark olive or blue-black; its sides are buff, and there are brown spots over the whole body. It grows to a length of 5 in.

Although it is mainly active at night, it can often be seen in daylight darting through shallow water if the stones under which it hides are turned over. The fish feeds mainly on insect larvae, worms and algae, and is preyed upon by trout, eels and sometimes birds. It is sensitive to pollution, and its presence in streams is considered to be a sign that the water is in good condition.

The spined loach is found only in the eastern English rivers, usually in slow-flowing, deeper water with a sandy or muddy bottom where it hides itself in blankets of algae. It is about an inch shorter than the stone loach, lighter in colour, and has a spine below each eye. Spined loaches use atmospheric oxygen when that in the water becomes depleted. They swallow bubbles of air at the water s surface and absorb the oxygen through the gut.

Neither species is of any economic value; both spawn from April to June, laying their eggs among weeds and gravel.

Loam

A blend of different kinds of soil particles, mainly sand and clay, ideal for good plant growth. The sand content permits drainage and aeration, and the clay particles help to retain adequate moisture. Loam is easily penetrated by roots, yet gives them a firm hold. Varying proportions of the main ingredients can produce anything from a heavy, clay loam to a coarse, sandy one.

Lobelia, Water *Lobelia dortmanna*

The still, black waters of upland lakes in north or west Britain are often broken at their margins by the slender stems of water lobelia. The plant, which thrives only in shallow water, is immediately recognisable by its two-lipped, pale lilac flowers, the upper lip with two lobes, the lower with three; these appear in July and August. The rosette of flattened leaves lies 6-24 in. below the surface of the water, rooted in the stony bottom of the lake.

The plant is named after de Lobel, a 17th-century Flemish botanist at James I's court.

Lobster moth *Stauropus fagi*

The furry-bodied lobster moth can sometimes be seen resting on beeches, but its brownish colours make it easy to miss in spite of a wingspan of 2-2½ in.

Its larva is remarkable. Two pairs of its true legs are longer than those of any other caterpillar – hence the name lobster. The tail-end is enlarged and held forward over

Lobster, Common *Homarus vulgaris*

Britain's largest crustacean is the common lobster, which lives offshore along rocky coasts. A specimen caught off Pembrokeshire in 1967 weighed 14½ lb., but the average weight is 2-3 lb. The common lobster normally grows 8-20 in. long. It is blue with brown markings when alive, but turns red when cooked.

Lobsters feed mainly by night, using powerful claws to hold and crush crabs, molluscs and other invertebrates. They move forwards by walking along the sea-bed, or rapidly

the body, scorpion-fashion. If disturbed, the caterpillar waves its legs, rears up, and behaves aggressively. It can squirt formic acid from a gland between the legs – an action which protects it from attacks by wasps and flies. The acid can disable a small bird.

The larvae live on beech leaves, usually in southern and eastern England, from July to September. In September the caterpillars pupate in cocoons woven between leaves, emerging as moths in May.

The aggressive-looking larva of the lobster moth grows over 2 in. long. If alarmed it throws back its head and extends its forelegs

Loch

The Gaelic word used in Scotland for a lake becomes lough in Northumberland and Ireland. Most lochs are long, deep and narrow, filling the U-shaped valleys carved by glaciers along depressions caused by rivers or faults. The great depth of some lochs is usually due to a fault which underlies the trench cut by a glacier. This is the case with

backwards by flapping their tails beneath their abdomens. Like crabs, lobsters can shed legs and grow new ones. As lobsters grow, they moult their old shells, growing new and larger ones. They may live 30 years but diet, not age, determines their size.

The females carry up to 160,000 dark green eggs at a time on the underside of their abdomens, when they are said to be in berry. It is illegal to collect them at this period. They breed every two years, carrying the eggs 10-11 months. The larvae are ⅓ in. long when hatched. See also SQUAT LOBSTER

Loch Morar, Scotland's deepest loch, which plunges to 1015 ft, although its surface is only 30 ft above sea level.

Sea lochs, where glaciers reached the coast, often have deep water surrounded by hills and offer safe anchorages, such as those at Loch Ewe, in Ross and Cromarty, and Belfast Lough.

Small lochs are called lochans. There are thousands in Scotland, many in the wild, north-western highlands above the Great Glen. They are often circular and near the tops of mountains.

Lock

A portion of a river or canal, enclosed by gates, which enables craft to move from one level of the waterway to another. To pass to a higher level, the lower gates of the lock are opened and the craft enters; the gates are shut behind it. Sluices, known as paddles, in the higher gates are then opened and water pours in from the higher level and raises the craft. The higher gates are then opened and the craft passes through. To move to a lower level, water is let out of the lock. This, the pound-lock (so-called because water was impounded in it), is the main type of lock still in use. It was introduced to Britain in Elizabethan times, on the original Exeter ship canal.

To overcome a steep gradient, a flight or staircase of several consecutive locks is

Built in 1808, the Foxton flight in Leicestershire has ten lock chambers which lift boats 75 ft

needed. The largest flight of British locks is one of 30 at Tardebigge, near Bromsgrove, Worcestershire, on the Worcester and Birmingham Canal; these raise the canal 217 ft in 2½ miles.

Many locks are dated on the brickwork. Lock gates, which are made of well-seasoned oak and elm, are still fashioned with an adze, the old carpenter's tool.

SLUICES CONTROL A LOCK

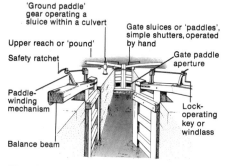

'Ground paddle' gear operating a sluice within a culvert

Gate sluices or 'paddles', simple shutters, operated by hand

Upper reach or 'pound'

Safety ratchet

Gate paddle aperture

Paddle-winding mechanism

Lock-operating key or windlass

Balance beam

Water is channelled into or out of a lock through culverts or openings in the gates. Sluices or 'paddles' control the flow, to empty or fill the lock as required

CANAL LOCK SECTION

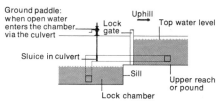

Ground paddle: when open water enters the chamber via the culvert

Uphill

Lock gate

Top water level

Sluice in culvert

Sill

Upper reach or pound

Lock chamber

The canal lock is a watertight chamber that links two lengths of canal of different levels

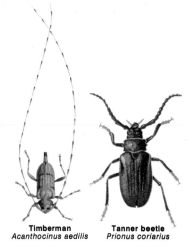

Timberman
Acanthocinus aedilis

Tanner beetle
Prionus coriarius

Two distinctive longhorn beetles. Some 70 species have been recorded in the British Isles

Longhorn beetle

The long antennae of these beetles—up to four times their body length of from ¼ in. to 1½ in.—earn them the name of longhorn or longicorn.

The larvae usually live in rotting wood, but they sometimes attack living trees. The whitish grubs grow slowly, and most take several years to reach their full size. Several of the 70 recorded British species arrived in this country in imported wood.

The species with the longest antennae is the timberman, which breeds only in Scottish pine forests. The male's body is about ¾ in. long and its antennae may be as much as 3 in. long.

Many adult longhorns do not feed and are short-lived. The adults of some smaller species take nectar, and spend a lot of time on flowers—for instance the common wasp beetle, whose colour pattern mimics the wasp and deters predators such as birds.

The largest British longhorn is the tanner beetle, which produces females more than 1½ in. long.

The musk beetle, which lives on or near willow trees, occurs in various metallic colourings, has a coppery sheen and exudes a musk-like scent. See also COLOUR AND CAMOUFLAGE

Longhorn moth

In May and June swarms of tiny metallic-looking moths are often seen flying around trees or hawthorn bushes. Each appears to be suspended at the end of two threads of fine silk. The swarms consist of male longhorn moths trying to attract mates, and the threads are their spectacularly long antennae—up to three times the length of the ¼-½ in. moth.

The females spend most of the time in hiding and have antennae which, although long compared with those of most other moths, are only about half as long as those of male longhorns.

The most common species is the bronze-green *Adela viridella,* found in all parts of England near oak or hawthorn, on the leaves of which its caterpillars feed. The cater-

pillars make portable protective cases from leaf fragments.

Another common longhorn moth *Nemotois degeerella* has prominent yellow markings on its wings.

Looper see Caterpillar
Lords-and-ladies see Cuckoo-pint

Lost village

Lumps of masonry embedded in meadows, unexplained—sometimes regular—humps in the ground, windmill stumps, ridges and furrows in old meadows or even prolific nettles, which flourish on the nitrogen of man's organic rubbish, are all vital clues to anyone searching for lost villages. The masonry may be from a medieval church and the humps may be the remains of cottage walls revealing the layout of old village streets. The open field system of farming was carried out on a communal basis and, especially in the Midlands, the pattern of ridges remains on the fields even though pastures displaced arable farming centuries ago.

There are more than 1300 deserted villages in England, mostly in the Midlands and the eastern half of England. About 100 are in the East Riding of Yorkshire, 150 in Lincolnshire, 130 in Norfolk and 250 in the counties of Warwickshire, Leicestershire and Northamptonshire. Ireland, Scotland and Wales also have quite a number, although the farmsteads and hamlets are often smaller and, especially in northern Britain, more difficult to find.

The oldest village remains are most often found in those parts of the country where poor soil or an inhospitable climate have deterred agriculture and settlements. The layout of a 2000-year-old Iron Age village can be seen at Chysauster in Cornwall, and other equally ancient settlements are discernible on Dartmoor and in Ireland, Wales and Scotland.

At Sumburgh Head, on Mainland, the largest island in the Shetlands, there is evidence of settlements dating back 4000 years to the Stone Age, together with items of Pictish, Viking and 16th-century origin.

Coastal erosion has led to the disappearance

MARKS THAT REVEAL THE PAST

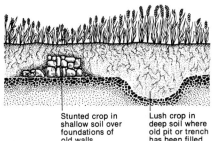

Stunted crop in shallow soil over foundations of old walls

Lush crop in deep soil where old pit or trench has been filled

Lost villages and other archaeological remains are often revealed by an uneven pattern of growth among crops which can be seen from the air

of some villages. Shipden, near Cromer in Norfolk, disappeared in this way some time before 1483 and there are other examples in Suffolk and Essex. Blown sand has covered some coastal villages. At Perranporth two churches can be seen half-buried. At Skara Brae in the Orkneys a late Stone Age settlement of about 2000 BC was found in the mid-19th century when a storm removed sand which had buried the village.

Aerial observation is a great aid to finding the sites of former villages. At Lower Ditchford, between Moreton-in-the-Marsh and Shipston-on-Stour in Gloucestershire, the irregular street pattern and ridges and furrows of the open fields can be seen clearly from the air, though the village disappeared some time in the mid-15th century.

The course of British history is reflected in the reasons why villages were abandoned. In coastal regions, some villages were destroyed or abandoned as a result of Viking raiding parties; others through conflicts on the Scottish and Welsh borders. Originally built in out of the way places for defence in troubled times, villages were abandoned and their inhabitants moved to more accessible places as law and order was established. The communities at Greatnam, near Lyndhurst, and Hartford, near Beaulieu, in Hampshire, were displaced in the reign of William I in 1079 when the king turned the New Forest into a hunting area.

In the 12th century the Cistercian monks came to Britain and displaced villages in order to establish 'solitudes' and sheep-walks around their abbeys and granges. Three Lincolnshire villages were destroyed when Revesby Abbey was built; Margam Abbey led to the disappearance of Llanhewydd village in Glamorgan.

Agriculture prospered in England from the mid-13th to the 14th century and villages expanded. Corn was exported in large quantities. The Domesday population of 1¼ million rose to 4 million and more arable land was cut out of forests.

But then the Black Death almost halved Britain's population between 1348 and 1350 and many villages were abandoned, especially those on the outer limits of cultivation on the dry chalk wolds, the sandy heaths of Breckland in Norfolk and Suffolk, and the high hillsides of western Britain.

With the sudden reduction in population many landowners could no longer find the labour for arable farming and so cleared villages to make sheep walks. Almost one-sixth of Britain's villages and hamlets disappeared between 1450 and 1600 and others shrank in size so that they could no longer support the churches which the former community had built. Around Breckland there are 28 deserted villages and in Norfolk there are four ruined churches within 4 miles of Colkirk. Lincolnshire has many church ruins with lost villages sited near by. A single farm may survive, bearing the name of the missing village.

Later enclosures destroyed more villages and as landlords began to establish parks around their houses, especially in the 18th century, the process was accelerated.

Often, landowners built new churches within their estate walls and, in some cases, in addition to destroying the old village, rehoused the inhabitants in model villages beyond the wall. Among the places where this was done were Ickwell in Bedfordshire, Wimpole in Cambridgeshire and, perhaps the best-preserved example of all, Milton Abbas in Dorset.

In more sparsely populated Highland Scotland homesteads, hamlets and crofts were deserted after the 1745 rebellion when landowners turned to sheep grazing, which was more profitable than the rents paid by crofters. In some places, such as Sutherland, whole glens were cleared. But others were deserted as a result of the drift to the coalfields or emigration in search of an easier living.

The failure of the crop in 1840 forced many Scottish and Irish farmers dependent on potatoes to leave the land.

Just as changes in agricultural methods caused population movements, so did the Industrial Revolution. Rows of deserted cottages may be seen near ruined waterwheels which powered cotton or woollen mills in Scotland, Yorkshire and Lancashire, before steam engines took over.

Mining villages were abandoned as seams ran out or ore could be obtained more cheaply elsewhere. Camborne in Cornwall was once the centre of a thriving tin-mining industry. But cheaper Malayan tin forced the 300 mines to close, and the ruins of settlements deserted in the 19th century can still be seen. Today mining villages are declining where coal pits have closed, especially in County Durham.

The growth of tourism, and the demands of holidaymakers and city dwellers who buy weekend cottages, have ensured the survival of many villages in coast and country by providing a living where otherwise none would exist. The tiny fishing village of Port Quinn in Cornwall was deserted in 1697 after 32 fishermen, most of the breadwinners of the village, were lost in a storm at sea. Today the fishermen's cottages are attractive holiday accommodation.

With the pressure of population and improved communications it is likely that the only lost villages of modern times will be those in valleys drowned to make reservoirs.

Louse

A parasitic insect which passes the whole of its life cycle on its host. Lice are wingless, rather flattened and rarely more than ⅛ in. long. There are two main types: biting lice and sucking lice.

Biting lice are found mainly on birds, though some live on mammals. They have mouthparts with which they feed on bits of feather and flakes of skin. Some take

This biting, or feather, louse *Goniodes pavonis* is found only on peacocks

blood by biting into the base of feathers. Mammals are the hosts of sucking lice which bury their piercing mouthparts in the skin and suck blood, causing irritation. The human louse *Pediculus humanus* is still common, mainly in children's hair.

There are about 300 species of louse in the British Isles, each of which lives on a particular species of bird or mammal.

Lousewort

There are two louseworts, so named because it was once thought they produced the lice which infested sheep; but the only link is that louseworts and lice both thrive in wet meadows and marshes unfavourable for sheep grazing. Both louseworts grow throughout the British Isles, but are comparatively scarce in central England. Points of recognition are the much-divided leaves and the inflated calyx.

Marsh lousewort is the more rare and favours wetter places, including shallow water. Known also as red rattle, it grows up to 18 in. high and flowers from May to September. Common lousewort occurs on damp heaths and grassland, grows up to 12 in. high and flowers from April to July.

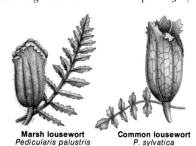

Marsh lousewort
Pedicularis palustris

Common lousewort
P. sylvatica

Lucerne *Medicago sativa*

Americans call this herb alfalfa. It has no connection with the Swiss canton of Lucerne and was brought to Britain in the 17th century from Mediterranean countries to provide forage for cattle and sheep.

Lucerne reaches a height of 3 ft and produces purple flowers in June and July. It has deep roots which enable it to resist drought and make it a particularly useful crop on light soils. It is being increasingly grown in south and east England where four or five cuts a year are obtainable. It often spreads to roadside verges or waste ground. Elsewhere it is rare. See also CROP

Lugworm

In the muddy sand along the shores of the British Isles, lugworms betray their presence by casts and depressions. At low tide, fishermen dig them up for bait. Lugworms, also called lobworms, are the most common bristle worms on British shores. They live at the bottom of U-shaped burrows and feed by swallowing sand and mud.

There are three species. *Arenicola marina* is the most common; large specimens are 9 in. long and as thick as a man's little finger. They vary in colour from dark brown to green-black and have 13 pairs of red gills. There are two other species, *A. ecaudata* and *A. brachialis*, both comparatively rare on British shores. During October the worms spawn, the incoming tide ensuring fertilisation of the eggs. See also BRISTLE WORM

THE LUGWORM'S BURROW

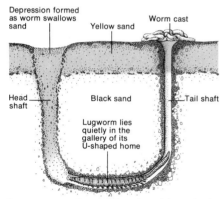

Lugworms swallow sand and mud in order to feed on the organic matter which they contain. Then, at precise 40-minute intervals, they pass out the debris which forms their casts

Lumpsucker *Cyclopterus lumpus*

Its behaviour and appearance make this shore fish unmistakable. It has a deep, rounded body, a broad mouth, rows of bony studs along its back and sides and, under its belly, a powerful sucker disc which it uses to anchor itself. Lumpsuckers feed on small crustaceans, worms and fish. When fully grown, the lumpsucker can be 2 ft long and weigh 10 lb. It lives all round the British Isles, but is most common in the north and north-east. It spawns from February to April, laying clumps of eggs on the tide-covered shore or in rock crevices in shallow water. Here the male mounts guard over the eggs during the six or seven weeks they take to develop. This habit gives the fish its other names of sea hen and hen fish.

The male aerates the eggs at low tide by fanning them with its pectoral fins or blowing a current of water on them with its mouth. In the northern spawning grounds, many male lumpsuckers are killed at low tide by gulls and crows.

Lungwort *Pulmonaria officinalis*

The white-spotted leaves of this perennial looked so much like lungs to our forefathers that they took its appearance as a sign that it could cure lung diseases.

Lungwort was introduced from central Europe. It grows 6-12 in. high and can be found occasionally in woods and hedgebanks throughout England, Wales and southern Scotland. The flowers which appear from March to May are pinkish at first but turn blue. This change accounts for the plant's alternative double names—Adam and Eve, Joseph and Mary. See also HERB

Lupin

Three species of lupins grow wild in Britain, all of them originating from North America. The most familiar is the garden lupin *Lupinus polyphyllus* which has spread from gardens to grow wild on railway banks in the London area. It grows up to 5 ft tall, and is recognised by its many-fingered leaves and handsome blue, white or pink spikes of pea-like flowers which bloom from June to August before developing into hairy seed pods.

The tree lupin *L. arboreus* is rare and almost confined to a few waste places on the coast. It is well named, for it often grows to 8 ft high, developing a trunk as thick as a man's arm. It produces bright yellow flowers from June to September and lives for four or five years. The third species *L. nootkatensis* is called wild lupin. Introduced from north-west America, it now grows wild on river shingle in north-east Scotland, producing showy blue and white flowers from May to July. Blue lupins are sometimes grown by farmers to plough into the soil as manure.

Lych gate

Many churches have a lych gate built over the main entrance to the enclosed area round the church. The name, also spelt lich or lytch, is from the Anglo Saxon *lich* meaning corpse. The gate marks the division between consecrated and unconsecrated ground, where the bearers sheltered with the coffin, waiting for the clergyman to lead the procession before the burial. Normally there is only one lych gate in a churchyard wall, although Troutbeck in Westmorland has three. The original lych gates had seats, a lych cross and a lych stone—a slab on which the coffin rested.

There are many surviving medieval lych gates, although no perfect example remains. Many such gates were destroyed or damaged

The lych gate at Chalfont St Giles, Bucks, which dates from the 17th or 18th century

after the Reformation, but most were rebuilt during the Gothic revival of Victorian times.

One of the oldest surviving is at St George's Church, Beckenham, Kent, a 13th-century gate restored early this century. The 15th-century structure at Boughton Monchelsea in the same county is composed of three Gothic arches.

Lynchet

A man-made step or terrace on a hill slope, carved out to make land fit for cultivation by the plough. Lynchets can be seen on hills from the South Downs to the lower slopes of the Scottish Highlands.

Some lynchets were deliberately created with stone facing on the 'riser' of the step supporting the level 'tread' above. Such lynchets often occur as a 'flight' ascending a slope, creating a series of 'strip lynchets' looking rather like a natural amphitheatre. Other lynchets were the result of ploughing on a slope, causing the soil to move downhill to produce artificial banks, such as in the early Celtic fields of Wiltshire.

Their dating is doubtful, although some are known to have been worked in Wiltshire and Northumberland as recently as the Napoleonic Wars (1789-1816), possibly when the price of corn made the use of difficult land profitable. Historians generally agree that most lynchets were made between early Anglo-Saxon times and the 16th century. Many lynchets show old ridges on their level surfaces and their construction suggests a shortage of good arable land on the plains, or periods of comparative land hunger.

Lynchets can be shown up with startling clarity in certain conditions of light and strong shadow. See also RIGG AND FURROW

M

Mackerel sky see Clouds

Madder, Field *Sherardia arvensis*

This small, trailing, blue-flowered plant with 1 ft long stems and whorls of six leaves grows in arable fields, pastures and waste places throughout lowland Britain. It is sometimes also found growing in garden beds and lawns.

The flowers, which appear from May to October, are of two kinds: bisexual ones, which often pollinate themselves, and females, which are fertilised by pollen from the bisexual flowers.

Madder, Wild *Rubia peregrina*

An evergreen trailing plant with whorls of four to six dark green, leathery leaves, green-yellow flowers, which appear from June to August, and prickled stems up to 4 ft long. Wild madder scrambles through hedges and scrub and over stony ground, in south and west Britain and the southern half of Ireland. It is particularly abundant near rocky coasts where it laces together plants on cliff faces. Mainly a Mediterranean species, wild madder reaches its northern limit in Britain.

The bright red dye, madder, was made from the roots of another Mediterranean species *R. tinctorum*, which was once grown in Britain. Wild madder yields a less intensely hued dye.

The flowers of wild madder are about $\frac{1}{8}$ in. across and grow in sprays from the stem

Maggot see Larva
Magpie see Crow

Magpie moth *Abraxas grossulariata*

This night-flying moth is patterned in the same way as its caterpillar: orange stripes and black spots on a white ground. These bright, distinctive markings warn away birds, who find the moths distasteful.

Butterfly-shaped and with a $1\frac{1}{2}$ in. wingspan, they are found throughout the British Isles. The caterpillar feeds on gooseberries and currants in gardens, on blackthorn in woods and hedgerows and on heather on Scottish moors. It is also found on elm and apple trees. The moth emerges in July from the chrysalis, which has an opaque black and orange skin, visible through its cocoon. It is on the wing until the end of August.

It was a study of the magpie moth which proved that it is the egg which determines sex in moths; in human beings, the sperm determines sex.

Magpie moth caterpillars belong to a group called 'loopers'—from the way they crawl

Maize *Zea mays*

In the past, maize was grown in Britain mainly as animal fodder, although sweetcorn varieties have been grown on a small scale in south-east England for the table. But new varieties which will ripen in our climate are now being introduced.

In Victorian times maize for silage was cut green and fed to cattle in June and July. Today it is left to become as ripe as possible and harvested with a special machine which chops stalk, leaf and head together; it is then stored in silos. One acre yields 15-30 tons of silage.

The plant produces a single stout stem with large leaves and broad blades. Male flowers grow in the terminal spike; female in the axils of the middle leaves, where the corn cob appears after windborne pollination. For illustration see CROP

Mallard see Duck

Mallow

Mallows are herbs with hairy stems and leaves, and large, showy, five-petalled flowers. After these have been fertilised, discs of fruits resembling small cakes develop; they are edible and taste like peanuts. From their resemblance to cheeses come many of their local names, such as bread and cheese, cheese cake flowers, fairy cheeses or lady's cheese.

Common mallow is an upright plant $1\frac{1}{2}$ ft-3 ft high, which bears blue or purple flowers up to 2 in. across between June and October. It is common on roadsides and in waste places throughout lowland Britain, but is rare in the north.

The leaves of common mallow were once used in salads and for poultices. Its roots were made into a soothing ointment.

Dwarf mallow is also a plant of waste places, common only in south and east England. The tough downy stems, up to 2 ft long, trail on the ground. The white, lilac-veined flowers, about 1 in. across, bloom between June and September. It was once used as a herb.

Musk mallow, *Malva moschata,* which is 12-30 in. high, is one of Britain's most handsome wild plants. The rose-pink or white flowers, borne in July and August, are over 2 in. across and the leaves are deeply divided. It is a plant of hedges, meadows and woodland margins. Like the other mallows, it is rare in the north and west. It is named after the musky smell it gives off in a warm confined space.

Because they are colourful and easily grown on poor soils, some species are cultivated as border perennials. See also MARSH-MALLOW

Dwarf mallow
Malva neglecta

Common mallow
M. sylvestris

The leaves of dwarf mallow are shallowly lobed, those of common mallow deeply lobed

Mandrake *Mandragora officinarum*
A native of Mediterranean countries and rarely found in Britain, the mandrake, nevertheless, is deeply embedded in British folklore, and the efforts of scientists over more than five centuries have failed to destroy belief in its mystical properties.

The superstitions arose from the twisted, many-forked roots in which the ancients saw a resemblance to the human body. Preparations from the plant were said to prevent sterility in man and to improve a woman's chance of conceiving. The plant does contain narcotic substances, used in Roman times in pain-killers or sleeping draughts.

Mandrake plants have tufts of large leaves which rise directly from the roots and bear purple, bell-shaped flowers on short stalks in May. In the autumn, the plant bears yellow or orange berries which are sometimes called Satan's apples. The plant is almost unknown in the wild in Britain, but is sometimes grown in gardens.

Mangold
A large, golden-red or crimson, turnip-like vegetable. Unlike other root vegetables, most of the root grows above ground. Once used extensively as winter food for cattle, it has been superseded by kale, silage and the extension of the grazing season by new varieties of grass. This is because, although a favourable season produces many mangolds per acre, their food value is low.

Manor
The basic unit of territory in the feudal system. It varied in size; most contained a single village, though some encompassed several villages. The lord of the manor owned a large tract of land, known as the demesne, around his house, and local people were obliged to work on this land for a certain number of days in the year. Beyond the demesne was arable land, divided into several, often three, large fields and cultivated on a strip system; the lord's strips usually alternated with those of the peasants or commoners. Beyond these was common land—forest and heath used by the commoners for grazing their animals and gathering wood. The heyday of the manorial system in Britain was from AD 1000 to 1300, and by AD 1500 it had practically disappeared, the people formerly required to work on the lord's land having commuted this service for cash payments.

Most manor houses have been rebuilt over the centuries, particularly during the Tudor period when the original medieval single hall—a large room where lord, family, servants and even livestock lived side by side—was divided into a series of rooms, new wings were added, minstrel galleries included and glass installed. Some were fortified, such as Stokesay Castle, a 13th-century manor house at Church Stretton, Shropshire.

Manure see Fertiliser

The broad wings of maple seeds catch the wind, which disperses them through the countryside

Maple
A family of trees, whose largest and most common member is the sycamore. The leaves and buds of maples are set in pairs, except for the terminal buds. The leaves of most species are five-lobed and shaped like the maple leaf on Canada's flag. They turn in autumn to magnificent reds, oranges and golds. All species are long-lived.

Maple flowers are borne in clusters, but are rarely all fully developed. They bear nectar and are pollinated by bees. Bunches of paired round seeds, each carrying a characteristic broad wing, develop in autumn. As a seed falls to the ground it twirls round like the blades of a helicopter.

Maple wood is pale brown, hard, strong, smooth and firm. It is used for furniture, dance floors and cotton reels, and for interior shipbuilding work.

In spring, when the leaves break, the ascending root sap of maples is rich in sugar. In Canada and the north-eastern United States, the sugar maple *Acer saccharum* is regularly tapped each year to collect this sap, which is concentrated into maple syrup and maple sugar.

Field maple *A. campestre,* Britain's only native species, is often just a hedgerow bush, but on lime-rich soils in the south-east it makes a tall, long-lived tree which provides good timber. It is easily recognised by its ribbed bark, corky twigs and deeply cut leaves with round lobes. The flowers, which appear in May, form small hanging clusters. The record height for a field maple is 78 ft attained by one in Mote Park, Maidstone, Kent.

Norway maple *A. platanoides*, which has sharp-pointed leaf-lobes, is widely planted for ornament. Groups of open, upright, bright yellow flowers which look like leaves, appear on leafless branches in March. In autumn these display brilliant golden-orange tints. The small maples with brilliant orange, scarlet or purple foliage that are seen growing in many gardens are usually grafted strains of two Japanese maples *A. palmatum* and *A. japonicum.*

Marbled White see Brown butterfly
March Brown see Mayfly

Marestail *Hippuris vulgaris*
A herb which grows in ponds, lakes or slow-moving rivers and canals—sometimes completely under water. The roots creep over the mud and send up many erect, un-branched, yellow-green stems, up to 30 in. high, bearing at intervals whorls of match-stick-like leaves. In June and July, tiny green flowers grow above water level at the joint of leaf and stem. The flowers are extremely simple, containing a single stamen, no petals and an ovary with one seed. Marestail grows throughout the British Isles, but rarely in the south-west. It resembles horsetail, and early botanists seeing the two plants growing together thought that horsetail was the male and marestail was the female of the same species.

Spikes of common marestail emerge through the weed-covered surface of a pond

Marigold, Corn *Chrysanthemum segetum*

This troublesome weed once grew in corn-fields on sandy soils throughout the country, but has been rare since the introduction of herbicides. It is 6-18 in. tall and the golden-yellow flowers appear from June to August.

Corn marigold was such a feature of the landscape that it influenced place names, supplying the gold of Goldhanger in Essex, and Golding in Shropshire. As a weed, not only did it starve and choke the corn but before the use of combine harvesters its fleshy leaves impeded harvesting. Undisturbed, the seeds may remain dormant for years before growing.

If it survives the harvest, the corn marigold will continue to flower late into autumn

Marjoram *Origanum vulgare*

This aromatic herb grows in dry, usually lime-rich grassland, scrub and hedgebanks throughout the British Isles other than north and west Scotland. From July to September rose-purple flowers bloom at the top of the 1-2½ ft tall stem, in oblong spikes similar to those of mint. It is the small downy leaves which exude the scent. Marjoram contains an oil sold in shops as oil of thyme; this was once used as a pain-killer. The flowering tops yield a dye which was once used for dyeing woollen cloth purple, and the leaves make a herb tea.

The marjoram used as a pleasantly pungent

herb in the kitchen is a Mediterranean species *O. onites*.

An ornamental variety *O. aureum*, which has golden-green foliage and pink flowers, is often seen in country gardens.

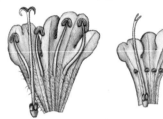

The bisexual flowers of the aromatic herb marjoram are always larger than the female

Markets and fairs

A market is held at least weekly, a fair only once or twice a year.

Country markets trade in everything from ferrets and fowl-houses to antique furniture and ornamental shrubs, but livestock predominates.

Although similarly commercial in origin, fairs survive chiefly as gatherings for entertainment—although large sheep and cattle fairs are still held in western England. Most medieval fairs were held on saints' days in late summer and autumn. At this time of the year the harvest was finished and farm-hands had an opportunity to look around for new jobs; at hiring fairs they could meet prospective employers. This was also the time—before the onset of winter—when surplus lambs and cattle could be sold at livestock fairs. In most markets livestock is sold by auction. This is a relatively modern innovation, dating in most instances only from the beginning of the present century.

The right to hold a market or fair could be granted to a medieval town corporation or lord of the manor only by royal charter, and armed patrols ensured that goods were not sold at unauthorised gatherings.

Great medieval fairs included those of St Giles at Winchester and of St Bartholomew at Smithfield, London. At the Falkirk Tryst in Scotland up to 40,000 cattle and 25,000 sheep would be traded.

Many towns in Britain have elaborate market crosses. One of the finest is in Chichester.

Marl

A chalky clay which until the development of modern fertilisers was spread over sandy, acid soils to improve their texture and fertility. Marl was mined throughout the country, particularly in the Midlands and south-east England. Rows of disused marl-pits, up to 50 ft across, may still be seen—now often water-filled; Wiltshire has miles of downland marl-pits. Cricket pitches are sometimes treated with marl to bind the soil.

Marram see Grass

Part of Minsmere Marsh, Suffolk, one of the largest

Marsh

A waterlogged area in which the soil is composed mainly of inorganic material, often at the edge of a pond or a lake. The water in a marsh is often seasonal, caused by flooding in winter, and this affects the nature of the vegetation.

Marshy areas usually contain many clumps of rushes, sedges and reeds, and wherever marshes are not heavily grazed there are lush growths of flowers. The first flowers to appear in the spring are yellow kingcups, soon followed by marsh violets. In May come brooklime, water forget-me-not and yellow flag iris. June sees the flowering of hemlock, water dropwort, marsh orchids and the tiny marsh pennywort. In July and August come the marsh thistle, water mint, large bindweed, fool's watercress and marsh ragwort.

Trees—usually alder, sallow and willow—grow only in places where there are long periods during which the area is not water-logged. Conditions which favour them also favour the growth of angelica, hemp agrimony, codlins and cream, and blinks.

This assortment of plants results in a rich insect life, with hordes of craneflies and flies. Big tussocks of purple moor grass provide shelter both for insects and the animals that eat them—including springtails, woodlice, spiders, amber snails, lizards, short-tailed voles, mice and shrews.

Other creatures breed in water and then spend much of their adult life in the marsh-land—caddis flies, mayflies, dragonflies and various amphibians. Predators such as hawker dragonflies and frogs are attracted by the abundance of flies. There are also grass snakes, which feed on amphibians, and adders which eat small mammals.

The insects also attract birds—sedge, reed and marsh warblers, meadow pipits, pied

areas of natural marshland in the United Kingdom

wagtails, water rails, and some of the small waders such as redshanks. In early summer the trilling call of the curlew and the drumming flight of the snipe can be heard. The rare marsh harrier, which now breeds only in Suffolk, can occasionally be spotted as it hunts its prey of water voles, frogs, snakes, moorhens and coots, by quartering the ground in marshy areas.

Many marshes are now being drained to provide more farm land.

Marsh-mallow *Althaea hirsuta*

A plant up to 4 ft high, related to mallow. It flowers in late summer on salt-marshes, and the sides of ditches near the sea in the southern half of England, Wales and Ireland. The flowers are large and pale pink, and the down on the leaves and stems gives them a grey appearance.

Marsh-mallow confectionery was once made from its dried, powdered roots, which were dug up in the salt-marshes of the Thames Estuary and sold in London markets. These sweets were believed to cure a wide range of diseases. Today's marsh-mallows, however, are pure gelatine and sugar.

The plant is becoming rare, as more and more marshes are being drained.

The down-covered leaves and stems of marsh-mallow have a grey appearance

Marsh marigold *Caltha palustris*

A plant which in spring and early summer brightens marshes, the banks of ditches and streams and wet woods throughout the British Isles. Masses of golden-yellow, buttercup-like flowers rise on 6-18 in. high stalks, from the deep green, glossy, toothed, heart-shaped leaves. The flowers are unusual: they lack petals and have five to eight petal-like sepals. Their buds were once gathered as a substitute for capers, the flower buds of a Mediterranean plant used for pickling. It is called kingcup in some areas and water gowan or water gowland in Scotland.

Marshwort, Lesser see Parsley

Martello tower

A circular defensive tower of which 74 were built along the south-east coast of England at the beginning of the 19th century, between Folkestone, in Kent, and Seaford, in Sussex, as a precaution against invasion by Napoleon Bonaparte. Others were built along the Suffolk coast as far north as Aldeburgh. Several still stand. They were 30-40 ft high, with 6 ft thick walls, a gun platform on top and a powder room below. The only entrance was a door 20 ft above ground.

The towers were styled after a fort on Cape Mortella in Corsica (of which Martello is a corruption), which in 1794 strongly resisted a British attacking force.

INSIDE A MARTELLO TOWER

Cannon on revolving platform

Chimney from fire in living quarters

Troop's living quarters, entered by ladder from outside

Store-room for ammunition and supplies, entered through hatch in ceiling

Defensive towers of this type, which survived the Napoleonic wars, were used in both world wars as observation posts

Martin see Swallow

Mayfly

It is popularly supposed that mayflies live for only a day. In fact, they can live for up to four days, but many are eaten by fish or birds in the first few hours of their existence. The most common and widespread of Britain's 46 species is the pond olive *Cloëon dipterum*.

Before its short winged life a mayfly has spent between four months and three years in the water as a nymph. The nymphs of many species are active swimmers, but those that live in fast-flowing streams settle under stones. Those of the largest British species *Ephemera danica*, known to fishermen as green drake, bury themselves in mud. All

Ephemera danica, the largest of the British mayflies, is called green drake by anglers

mayfly nymphs have feathery gills and most feed by scraping minute vegetable matter, such as algae, from stones or pondweed.

In late spring or early summer the fully grown nymphs float to the surface of the water and cast off their nymphal skin. Unlike other insects, they moult as young larvae or nymphs and once more after they become able to fly. The newly emerged mayflies are called duns because they are duller than the final adult stage. Fish immediately snap them up, but a few escape to the shelter of waterside plants. After a few hours they moult again to become glistening, longer-tailed, fully adult mayflies, or spinners.

The mayflies' bodies are between ½ in. and 1 in. long. Many species have three tails; a few have two.

Spinners do not need to eat. They obtain enough nutrition in the nymphal stage to last them their short life. Mating takes place in swarms over the water—usually in the afternoon or early evening. After sunset the female lays her eggs in the water.

Not all mayflies emerge in May. Some, like the March Brown, whose flat nymphs are adapted to live in fast-flowing rivers, first appear in March, others emerge in summer.

Maypole

A stripped tree erected on a village green as the focal point of May Day dancing and celebrations. The pole is often painted with stripes and decorated with foliage.

The maypole is pagan in origin. Early man worshipped trees as fertility symbols and, during his celebration of spring, selected one around which he could dance in homage. The practice fell into disuse as Christianity spread, but was revived in Victorian times by the writer John Ruskin. It still persists as a quaint custom in such places as Temple Sowerby, Westmorland, Barwick in Elmet, Yorkshire, and Knutsford, Cheshire.

Mayweed

Mayweeds trouble the farmer because they are abundant on farmland and resistant to modern weedkillers. There are several species, confusingly similar in appearance.

The easiest to identify is the pineapple mayweed or rayless mayweed, *Matricaria matricarioides*, which grows to 1 ft high: the green-yellow flowers, which bloom in June and July, exude a smell of pineapple when crushed between the fingers and lack the white ray florets of other mayweeds. Introduced accidentally from South America in 1871, it has spread throughout the British Isles and is now one of the most common weeds; it grows on farmland, waste places, roadsides and pathways.

Scentless mayweed *M. inodora* is the most common mayweed of arable fields and has the largest flowers—up to 1½ in. across. These are scentless and bloom between July and September, on top of stems up to 2 ft high. A seaside form, which is perhaps a separate species, has larger flowers and fleshier leaves. Scented mayweed or wild chamomile, *M. recutita*, produces a pleasant smell of chamomile when its flowers, which appear in June and July, are crushed. This weed, which can reach a height of 2 ft, is common throughout southern England.

Pineapple mayweed is named after the scent given off when its flowers are crushed

Meadow see Grass
Meadow brown see Brown butterfly
Meadow fescue see Grass

Long, pollen-bearing stamens take the place of petals in the flowers of common meadow-rue

Meadow-rue

The petal-less flowers of the meadow-rue are made up of coloured stamens. These are yellow in common meadow-rue *Thalictrum flavum* and purple-green in lesser meadow-rue *T. minus*.

Common meadow-rue is found throughout the British Isles but is rare in Scotland. It grows as high as 3 ft in marshes and fens and by the banks of streams and rivers, and flowers in July and August. Lesser meadow-rue blooms from June to August in dry areas such as chalk and limestone grassland or sand dunes. It has a strongly developed system of underground stems and often forms extensive patches in sand dunes, growing up to 18 in. high.

Meadowsweet *Filipendula ulmaria*

The scent of meadowsweet, or queen of the meadows, was appreciated by medieval householders who strewed it among the rushes which covered their floors. In the field it stands 2-4 ft high with branched, leafy flowering stems.

From June to September, meadows and wet woodlands are coloured creamy-white by the meadowsweet's feathery flowers. Found along the banks of streams and roadside ditches it is a prolific flower in the fen country; it also grows sparsely on mountain ledges up to 3000 ft above sea level.

The sweet-scented, fine-petalled flowers of meadowsweet appear in dense clusters in June

Meander

The River Meander in Turkey, which has smooth, swinging curves, has given its name to this common river feature. A river will pick up sediment in its upper and middle courses. By the time it reaches lowlands near its mouth, it will be travelling more slowly and carrying all the sediment it can hold. Some of this will be deposited wherever an obstruction occurs, and the river will curve as its flow is diverted from one bank to the other.

The stream washes away the bank on the outside of the curve, where the current is swiftest, and deposits it on the inner. The curve becomes gradually more pronounced, turning in on itself until only a thin strip of land prevents it from being a full circle. Both ends of the curve may then become choked with sediment, and the stream will break through the strip. Thus the river is temporarily straightened and the abandoned meander left as a horseshoe-shaped ox-bow lake. The land inside the curve of these lakes often remains as an isolated rounded hill, known as a meander core.

With the continuing process of erosion and silting, the position of each meander gradually moves downstream. The extent to which this has happened can sometimes be judged by comparing the county boundary (which often follows the old course of the river) with the new course.

Sometimes meandering rivers cut into the landscape, producing deeply entrenched meandering valleys. A good example of this is Symonds Yat, Herefordshire.

Meanders in their exaggerated form, as the River

THE STAGES OF A MEANDER

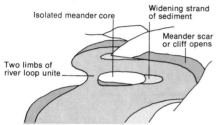

Swift water current washes away bank

Sediment deposited on inner curve

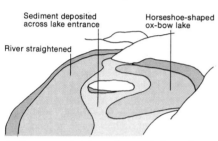

Isolated meander core

Widening strand of sediment

Meander scar or cliff opens

Two limbs of river loop unite

Sediment deposited across lake entrance

Horseshoe-shaped ox-bow lake

River straightened

Sediment, carried by a river as it flows downstream, may alter the shape of the banks and create small islands through the process of silting and erosion

Cuckmere nears the sea in Sussex

Medick

Sold on St Patrick's Day as shamrock, black medick *Medicago lupulina* is often called hop trefoil by farmers and closely resembles the yellow trefoils. The rarer spotted medick *M. arabica* is called cogweed in Somerset because its spirally coiled, prickly pods resemble cogwheels.

Both species have yellow flowers and three-lobed leaves resembling clover. Black medick has curly, one-seeded black pods and leaves whose veins protrude beyond the leaf edges. It is sown mixed with grasses and clover as a fodder crop.

Medlar *Mespilus germanica*

A small, long-lived tree with gnarled grey bark and a crooked trunk, found in old cottage orchards or running wild in hedgerows. Its large, pale green, oblong leaves are almost stalkless, with downy surfaces. The solitary white flowers, which have five frilled petals, open in May. After pollination by bees, the flower develops into a pear-shaped, yellowish-brown fruit with a cup-shaped base. Five seed vessels are visible through the 'cup rim'. The small, flat brown seeds are spread by birds.

Hard sour medlar fruits are gathered in October and stored until they become soft, when they are either made into jelly or eaten as a dessert.

Melanism see Evolution

Melilot

The three species of melilot which are commonly found growing wild in Britain were introduced from Europe as medicinal herbs and fodder plants. They were the main ingredient of melilot plasters and poultices. They grow 2-4 ft high and their clover-like leaves comprise three leaflets. They have long spikes of small yellow or white flowers and produce thick short pods. When dried, melilots give off the scent of newly mown hay because of the presence of the aromatic substance coumarin in their leaves.

The two yellow-flowered plants can be distinguished by their pods. Tall melilot

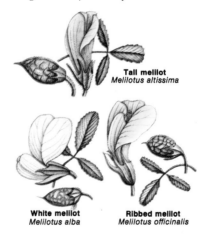

Tall melilot
Melilotus altissima

White melilot
Melilotus alba

Ribbed melilot
Melilotus officinalis

has hairy pods which are black when ripe. Ribbed melilot has brown, strongly wrinkled hairless pods. White melilot is attractive to bees.

Menhir see Standing stone
Mere see Lake
Merganser see Duck
Merlin see Falcon

Mermaid's purse

The egg-case of dogfish, skate and ray, from 1-4 in. long. The cases of skate and ray have each corner drawn into a short horn, and the dogfish case has corners which extend into long tendrils. In each of these species fertilisation is internal—before the protective, horny case is formed round the eggs.

Skate and ray 'purses' are laid in sand offshore, so only the empty, black cases are found along the tide line. But the dogfish winds the long tendrils of its cases around seaweed so that they are securely anchored. Sometimes several dozen intact cases can be found attached to one clump of seaweed low down on the shore. Each embryo takes several months to hatch.

Dogfish egg-cases, 2½ in. by 1 in., may be attached to seaweed above low-tide mark

Mesembryanthemum see Hottentot fig
Metasequoia see Cypress, Swamp

Mezereon *Daphne mezereum*

The small red fruits of mezereon are poisonous to humans but not to birds. It has highly scented purple flowers which appear in early spring before the leaves, making it a popular garden shrub.

Mezereon is a rare wild plant, growing only in a few chalk and limestone woods in England and Wales, where it forms a dwarf bush 2-3 ft high. It has a bitter bark, once used in medicine to induce sweating.

Mica

This mineral appears as black glistening specks in granite, and as dark bands in schist and gneiss. The largest pieces are found in the Scottish Highlands and on the beds of mountain streams.

Mica forms six-sided crystals, which split readily into thin, flat plates. These layers are sometimes called 'books' of mica. They are translucent, and were once used instead of glass in lanterns, although they are soft and can easily be scratched. They do not conduct electricity and have therefore been used in insulators and for the manufacture of radio condensers.

Michaelmas daisy

These tall flowers are so named because they start to bloom around Michaelmas – September 29 – continuing until the end of October or even longer.

They belong to the genus Aster, and grow vigorously from the smallest piece of root. Surplus plants discarded by gardeners have rooted on railway banks and beside streams and rivers throughout the lowlands.

None of the dozen or so species found in Britain is native. They have been introduced mainly from North America.

The species are difficult to tell apart, but the two most common are *Aster novi-belgii*, with smooth stems and bluish flowers, and *A. novi-angliae*, with hairy stems, reddish-purple flowers, and a smell like that of the garden marigold. The annual garden asters belong to another genus, Callistephus.

Microlith

The smallest tool associated with the Mesolithic peoples – from 12,000 to 3000 BC. It was usually made from a flint flake, hafted or set in rows in wood or bone to form a saw. Microliths were often less than 1 in. long and were worked into geometric shapes, especially a triangle, by flaking down a long blade of flint and then snapping it. They are found from Cornwall to the Pennines, especially on heathlands.

EARLY MAN'S USE OF FLINT FLAKES

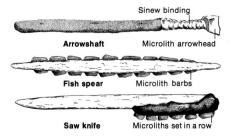

Sinew binding
Arrowshaft — Microlith arrowhead
Fish spear — Microlith barbs
Saw knife — Microliths set in a row

Microliths, tiny pieces of flint, were used singly as arrowheads or combined, mounted in rows, to form sawing edges or spears

Midge

There are two families of midge found in Britain, those that bite and those that do not. The non-biting midges are often mis-taken for gnats, but they have no mouthparts. Since the adults cannot feed they do not live long – from a week to two months at the most. They are ⅛-½ in. long, and are found near water or in woodlands. One of the largest, *Chironomus plumosus*, can be seen from April to September.

The male flies, which have feathery antennae, form swarms sometimes comprising thousands, which appear as dark clouds around rooftops. The females lay several hundred eggs in water in a mass of jelly which fixes them to something solid.

The newly hatched larvae swim freely, but later settle down in the mud at the bottom. In some species the blood of the larvae contains the oxygen-carrying pigment haemoglobin, like human blood. This gives the larvae a red colour, and in *C. plumosus* is responsible for the name 'blood worm'. The larvae feed on decaying plant material.

Biting midges live by sucking the blood of animals, birds and insects. They inject saliva into the bite to thin the blood before they suck it. This causes irritation, but the saliva itself is not poisonous. Not many bite humans, but those that do can make life a misery for holidaymakers in coastal areas and parts of Scotland. About 150 species live in the British Isles.

Members of the genus Culicoides are only ⅛ in. long but they attack humans, during warm, still weather, especially in the evening, causing painful bites. The larvae of many biting midges live in water, even a very small amount, such as the moisture from rotting plants. Midges are eaten by birds and fish.

Mignonette, Wild *Reseda lutea*

An upright herb with greenish-yellow flowers which appear in mid-summer. It is closely related to weld, but is easily distinguished by its divided leaves and its flowers which have six petals. Wild mignonette grows on roadsides and other disturbed ground and is common in the chalk and limestone areas of England, but is rare in Wales, Scotland and Ireland.

The word 'mignonette' is from the French and means 'little darling', a name originally applied to the fragrant mignonette of gardens, *R. odorata*.

Migration

There are two main reasons why animals migrate: to feed and to breed. But these instincts, powerful though they are, do not explain all the mysteries of migration. There appears to be no physical reason why, for example, the Arctic tern should fly 11,000 miles from Britain every year to winter in the Antarctic; or why painted lady butterflies should leave Africa and cross the Mediterranean, Europe and the Channel, to come to England, where neither they nor their offspring can survive the winter.

Not all migrations are long-distance affairs. Frogs migrate short distances to ponds in

Late April in England, and a flock of swallows crowd

spring in order to mate and lay the eggs that will eventually become swarms of tadpoles in April. Red deer that live on the tops of mountains in summer will move down into the milder valleys in winter.

Extensive ringing of birds, radar tracking, and a greater interest in the environment are all producing data which eventually may give the full explanation of why some species of animals follow an ages-old pattern of regularly moving from one part of the world to another.

Meanwhile, man has his theories, and references to the migratory habits of animals abound in literature and folklore. Until the 18th century, for instance, it was thought that swallows spent the winter hibernating at the bottom of ponds.

Birds are the most spectacular migrants of all, and their migrations can be observed all the year round in the British Isles. Birds which have come from north and east Europe leave in March or April. African visitors arrive in April or May. Summer visitors leave in August and September. Winter visitors arrive in October and November, and from December to February birds arrive and leave with each cold spell.

Most migratory birds are aquatic or insect-eating species, which depend for their food on creatures which hibernate, migrate or lie beneath an ice covering in winter. Areas that are cold and inhospitable, if not actually frozen in winter, have a wealth of life in summer – just at the time when birds are raising their young.

Many migrating birds move in large flocks – often of mixed species. Others, such as the cuckoo, fly separately.

on a budding tree to rest at the end of their long migration from Africa

The urge to migrate begins with chemical changes in the body which are triggered by the length of day. As the time nears for flight, the birds feed more actively and store fat, sometimes actually doubling their body weight. Day flyers steer their journeys by the sun; night flyers by the stars. Most of our rarer visitors are probably birds which have been blown off course by storms, or lost their way for some other reason. Various experiments have been made to test the navigational skill of birds. A Manx shearwater was taken to Boston, USA, and found its way back over 3050 miles of featureless ocean to its nest on Skokholm Island, off Pembrokeshire.

Regular winter visitors to the British Isles include the fieldfares and redwings from Scandinavia, barnacle geese from Spitzbergen, white-fronted geese from Siberia and pink-footed geese from Iceland. A number of species, such as waxwings and crossbills, are not true migrants, but are irregular visitors to our shores. In 1965 10,000 waxwings appeared, but in some years there are none. The cause seems to be a population build-up on their breeding grounds in northern Europe, which results in a bumper breeding season producing more birds than the land can support. The surplus birds then move to western Europe and the British Isles.

Less obvious migrants include butterflies, which arrive from the Continent in spring. Among them are large and small whites, red admirals and painted ladies. Migrant moths include the death's head, the silver Y and the hummingbird hawkmoth, all of which make one-way journeys. The insect with the longest range is probably the monarch butterfly, which normally migrates down the east coast of the USA, but in irruptive years it has been known to cross the Atlantic to this country.

Salmon are well-known migrants, which return each year from the sea to breed in the rivers where they were born. The reverse is true of eels, which live in freshwater rivers and set off for the Sargasso Sea in the Western Atlantic to breed.

Much remains to be learnt about migration and it may be that research programmes will confirm one of the most interesting theories: this states that at the end of the last Ice Age, as the ice retreated, animals from the Tropics pushed their range northwards in summer, returning to the warmth of the south in winter.

Milestone

The Romans were the first to use milestones in Britain and several of the tall, elegant stone columns they erected remain in their original positions. The Roman mile was a thousand paces (*mille* is the Latin for thousand) and equalled about 1600 yds. There are good examples of Roman milestones at Stinsford, Dorset, and near the Roman camp of Chesterholm by the Roman wall in Northumberland.

Milestones did not come into general use again until the Turnpike Act of 1766 made them compulsory on turnpike roads. These roads were built by private enterprise under licence from the Government and maintained by tolls on those who used them. Before this Act milestones were put up occasionally, often as charitable acts and commemorations. Surviving examples include the White Stone at Hereford and the Pelham Buckle at East Hoathley in Sussex. Many Turnpike Act stones still exist. They are usually 2-3 ft high, with the initial letter or abbreviation of the nearest market town shown on two faces, and the distance from it.

Although the 1760 yard mile was fixed by Elizabeth I in 1593, much longer customary miles remained in use in various parts of the country until the 19th century. Several milestones measuring distances in customary miles survive in Yorkshire. These miles measure anything from 2200 yds to 3300 yds. See also ROAD

Milk see Farm
Milkcap see Fungus

Milk vetch, Purple *Astragalus danicus*
This creeping perennial herb is inconspicuous until it comes into flower in May and produces heads of pea-like flowers on long stems. It forms purple patches in old grassland on the chalk and limestone of England, but becomes a seashore plant further north, colonising the coastal golf links of eastern Scotland. It was called milk vetch because of a belief that it increased the milk yield of goats which ate it.

Milkwort *Polygala vulgaris*
Patches of bright blue are formed by milkwort in dry grassland and sand dunes throughout the British Isles between May and September. With numerous spreading branches up to 1 ft long and shiny, pointed leaves, milkwort has flowers with five sepals. Two inner ones, called wings, are much larger than the rest and the same colour as the petals. The true petals are hidden inside the wings, and fused together to form a tube.

The flowers, which can also be pink or white, are similar to the rare chalk milkwort or heath milkwort whose lower leaves are arranged opposite each other, rather than alternately. It was given its name because it was supposed to increase the milk production of animals which fed on it.

Milkwort got its name because animals which fed on it were thought to produce extra milk

Mill see p. 286
Miller's thumb see Bullhead

Mills—machines driven by the power of nature

For 1000 years watermills and windmills were man's largest and most complex machines. With the development of steam in the 18th century, their use declined, but many remain as reminders of an age of silent power

The earliest form of mill used for grinding corn was a quern—a small primitive handmill. It had two circular stones—one fixed and one rotating—and was the forerunner of the grinding method used in watermills and windmills.

Watermills were known to the Greeks during the 1st century BC and are thought to have been introduced into Britain by the Romans. But it was the Saxons, 500 years after the Romans had left, who developed the use of watermills on a large scale. The Domesday Book records that between AD 1080 and 1086 there were 5264 watermills.

The five kinds of mill

Smock mill

Post mill

Water mill undershot

Water mill overshot

Tower mill

The post-mill is the only type of mill that revolves to face the wind; on smock and tower-mills only the top portion revolves. Water passes through the bottom of an undershot mill-wheel and the top of an overshot mill-wheel

Windmills—invented by the Arabs in the 7th century—are thought to have been introduced into Britain during the 12th century by returning Crusaders. Windmills were used where water power was unavailable or unsuitable for grinding corn or pumping water from the marshy land of the Fens and Broads. Sited on high ground to catch the wind, windmills were once conspicuous landmarks throughout the eastern half of England—from the Tweed to the Channel. In 1919 there were 350 windmills still working, but today the number has dwindled to 24.

Early mills were often owned by the lord of the manor, to whom everyone had to pay a toll for grinding his corn. Later, with the end of feudalism, mills were owned or rented privately, the miller exacting the toll. By custom, he was entitled to one-sixteenth of the flour he ground, but not all millers could resist the temptation to take more and many were prosecuted for dishonesty. An epitaph in an Essex graveyard to a miller named Strange notes: 'Here lies an honest miller, and that was Strange.'

The various types of watermills can be identified by the position at which the water strikes the paddle-wheel. An undershot mill is turned by water flowing through the vanes at the bottom of the wheel first; on an overshot wheel the water strikes the top first. An overshot wheel—usually placed on a man-made or natural weir—is the more expensive but more efficient of the two, needing only a quarter of the volume of water to produce the same amount of power.

Some watermills were sited on tidal rivers so that the ebb and flow of the tides could provide the motive power; a tidal mill at Woodbridge in Suffolk was in use until 1952.

From the middle of the 16th century, the iron industry depended upon water power to turn machinery—the average small mill generating the same power as a small car. The machinery in a hammer-mill operated huge tilt hammers, which crushed metal ore before it was finally shaped in a furnace; the bellows also worked by water power. Reserves of water were kept in vast hammer-ponds, formed by damming rivers. Another form of hammer-mill was used by the textile industry for fulling—a process of cleaning and thickening the weave of newly woven cloth by beating it under water. The Wellbrook Beetling Mill in County Tyrone, built in 1765 for hammering linen to produce a sheen on the cloth, is still in working order.

The largest watermill in the world is the Lady Isabella Wheel at Laxey, on the Isle of Man. Built to pump water from the lead mines, the wheel is $72\frac{1}{2}$ ft in diameter and capable of raising 250 gallons of water a minute to a height of 1000 ft.

During the era of the Industrial Revolution until 1784—when steam was introduced as a source of power—watermills were also used for making paper, gunpowder, tobacco, snuff, oil and leather.

Towards the end of the 18th century, popular taste changed from the flour ground between millstones to that ground between iron rollers; it was whiter and considered to be better since millstones tended to rasp the wheat, producing a dark discoloured flour.

From their external appearance windmills can be identified as one of three types: the post-mill, tower-mill and smock-mill. The oldest of these is the post-mill. Built on four brick piers, a massive cross of oak beams supported a large central oak post—sometimes a complete tree trunk. The remainder of the mill house could be rotated about this post, enabling the miller

The windmill at Cley next the Sea, Norfolk. A brick-built tower-mill, dating from the early 18th century, it was used to grind corn until 1908. It has since been restored, but is no longer working

HOW A WINDMILL WORKS

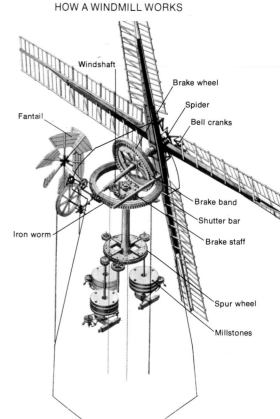

Windshaft
Brake wheel
Spider
Bell cranks
Fantail
Brake band
Shutter bar
Iron worm
Brake staff
Spur wheel
Millstones

Once the brake is released, wind power turns the cloth-covered sails, wheels and gears transferring the same movement to the grinding stones

to turn his sails to catch the wind from any direction. Projecting from below the superstructure at the back of the mill was a tiller beam, which could be pushed round by hand, winched by a capstan or harnessed to a horse. From about 1750, fantails—small wind vanes—were fixed at right angles to the main sails to turn them into the wind automatically.

The oldest working post-mill in England, built in 1665, is at Outwood, Surrey; men are said to have watched the Great Fire of London from the top.

The tower-mill, developed during the 18th century, consisted of a round or octagonal brick or stone tower—similar to a lighthouse—containing all the milling machinery. The domed top of the tower, to which the sails were attached, was the only part that revolved; the movement from the sails was transmitted to the millstones through a series of gear wheels. The tower-mill at Billingford, Norfolk, built in 1860, is a fine example still in working order.

Smock-mills, sometimes called frock-mills, were either octagonal or twelve-sided and built of wooden frames covered with clapboarding. They were similar to post-mills since only the top portion of the mill revolved. Smock-mills—so-called because their sloping sides gave them the appearance of a 19th-century countryman's smock—often had a painted or tarred brick base and a white-painted superstructure.

The Union Mill, at Cranbrook in Kent, is probably the finest

and certainly one of the tallest smock-mills in the country. It was built in 1814 and is more than 70 ft high, and was in use until 1950. The oldest smock-mill in Britain is at Lacey Green, Buckinghamshire. It was built at Chesham in 1650, and moved to its present site in 1821. Windmills were often moved from one area to another—from several yards to a quarter of a mile —to get the benefit of higher or unobstructed ground.

The first windmill sails were made of canvas or sailcloth laced over wooden latticeworks and arranged so that they could be furled. Each sail was curved along its length to catch the wind. From about 1780 hinged shutters, operated by a spring which yielded in high winds, were used instead of sailcloth.

A modern form of windmill is the wind pump. It has a small wheel like a fantail on a metal pylon and is primarily used for drainage and raising sub-soil water for livestock.

Millstones—whether for wind or water-driven mills—varied in size; but the average single stone was about 4 ft in diameter, 15 in. thick at the rim and weighed about 35 cwt. The stones turned at 150 revolutions a minute. The bedstone—the lower of the two—was stationary and slightly lower at the rim than the centre. This allowed the ground corn or grain to fall from the stone, where it passed through a chute and was collected in a bin. Millstones were made of millstone grit, German lava or freshwater quartz; these stones had different grinding qualities and were therefore used for different cereals.

287

Millipede

Although there are at least 44 species of millipedes in Britain, many are rare. They differ from centipedes in having two pairs of legs—rather than one pair—on most of their body segments, giving a total of about 150 legs in the largest British species. Scientifically, they are separated into hard and soft-bodied types, but the British species are all hard-bodied and can be divided into snake, flat and pill millipedes.

Snake millipedes are long and cylindrical and live in the soil. Flat millipedes, as their name suggests, have a series of flattened shields on their backs. Pill millipedes, like woodlice, roll into a ball when disturbed and, like the flat species, are found under logs or stones.

Female millipedes lay 10-300 eggs, depending on the species. Some protect their eggs with a hard casing of earth and excrement; others, using the same materials, make spherical nests. Some snake millipedes lay their eggs in a cell which they make from silk produced by special glands; their young make silk cells in which to moult. Most species go through about seven moults after hatching and reach maturity after 6-12 weeks. They live for several years, avoid the light and need a moist environment, soon dying if their surroundings dry out. They vary in colour from almost white, pink or brown to black, and measure from $\frac{3}{8}$ in. to 2 in. long.

Millipedes have fairly weak jaws and tend to feed on soft plants, decomposing vegetation and plants damaged by mechanical means or other pests. In Belgium and France they are serious pests of sugar beet and seem to be becoming so in England, where they are more often pests of the garden or allotment. Flat and snake millipedes are the most harmful types.

Even so, millipedes do some good by breaking down soil humus and making valuable salts available to growing plants.

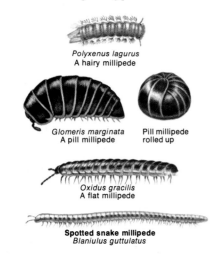

Polyxenus lagurus
A hairy millipede

Glomeris marginata
A pill millipede

Pill millipede
rolled up

Oxidus gracilis
A flat millipede

Spotted snake millipede
Blaniulus guttulatus

Millipedes occur in many shapes, but all have two pairs of legs on most body segments

Common species in the British Isles are: *Glomeris marginata*, a pill millipede found in woodlands and grassland; *Oxidus gracilis*, one of the flat species, which lives in greenhouses; *Blaniulus guttulatus*, a spotted snake millipede living in arable soil; *Polyxenus lagurus*, a hairy species found under stones and bark; and *Polydesmus augustus*, the common field flat-back species.

Millstone grit

This coarse sandstone is found in the Pennines and parts of South Wales. It is quarried for building purposes, and was formerly in demand for millstones.

The rock is often found in steep crags—such as Stanage Edge, near Sheffield, and Black Rocks. south of Matlock—and is attractive to climbers. The layers of grit are separated by weaker shales giving a stepped or layered landscape.

In South Wales rocks of the same age as millstone grit contain more shale and have many fossils, including the earlier types of ammonite.

Mind-your-own-business   see Mother-of-thousands

Mine

The earliest type of mine, dating back to the Stone Age, was a bell-pit—a hole cut through top layers of earth and widening out when it reached the minerals the miners were seeking. More than 700 of these were sunk in the Breckland of Norfolk and Suffolk 4000 years ago to obtain flints from the chalk beds 20 ft down. The most famous are Grime's Graves, named after Grim, a destroyer-figure in Norse mythology. The bell-pits on Town Moor, Newcastle upon Tyne, were medieval coal mines.

The less valuable minerals, such as sand, gravel, chalk, slate and ironstone, are quarried near the surface; the more valuable ones, such as copper, tin, lead and coal, are mined deep below the ground.

It was Britain's wealth of metals that lured the Romans to the island in the 1st century BC. Copper and tin had been discovered 2000 years before. They were blended to make bronze. Iron was found in about 400 BC and later lead was mined. The Romans exploited all these metals, using them to make weapons, coins, tools, plumbing systems and ornaments.

There is an abundance of evidence of past mining operations. On the bleak moors of the north Pennines, around Alston in Cumberland, horizontal mine entrances, or adits, lead into the hillsides—the work of 18th and 19th-century lead and silver miners.

Also in the 18th and 19th centuries the area around Rookhope in Durham produced thousands of tons of lead, zinc, fluorspar, barytes and witherite. The derelict buildings with their gaunt chimneys still stand. In them the mined rock, known as bowse, was crushed and rolled, and the ore extracted

The moon-like landscape of a brickfield where clay

from it and stored. Near them are the old water mills, which supplied power, and the smithies where tools were made. There are similar ruins, together with great spoil heaps of unwanted rock and gaping holes hundreds of feet deep, in the Lake District—especially above Coniston, where copper was once worked in the 19th century—at Parys, on Anglesey, and at Alderley Edge, south of Manchester.

Tin has been worked in Cornwall since pre-Roman times, and trade in it led to the development of some of the ancient routes of southern England. The chimneys of engine houses—buildings which contained the giant pumps that drained the mines—dating from 1730, are scattered throughout the landscape. At the industry's peak about 300 mines were worked. Typical was the Botallack mine, the remains of which still stand near St Just overlooking the Atlantic, and whose shafts followed lodes of tin and copper far out to sea. However, imports of cheap, newly found tin from Malaya in the 1870's eventually forced all but two of the mines—Geevor Tin and South Crofty, which are still working—to close.

Coal pits have left a distinctive mark on the landscape. Around Bishop Auckland in Durham, for example, disused pit-head gear,

has been extracted by opencast mining

empty cottages and spoil heaps strike a sombre note on the edge of the moors. Some cottages still bear a slate by the front door; on this the miner chalked for the village knocker-up what time he was to be called for his next shift.

A monument to early coal-mining days is Causey Arch, a 105 ft long stone bridge spanning Beamish Burn in Durham, built in 1727 to take coal wagons from nearby Tanfield. Relics of the last century include staithes—enormous wooden overhead structures which carried coal between the sea-end of wagon ways and waiting colliers. There are examples at Dunston, on the south bank of the Tyne, Amble in Northumberland and Seaham Harbour in Durham.

The search for minerals goes on—for copper, lead and zinc in the Welsh hills and the Lake District, and for nickel, uranium, copper and other metals in the Scottish Highlands. Iron ore has been found in Ireland, and in the Shetland Isles survey teams are looking for copper, nickel and chromium. Old lead mines are being reopened in the Pennines, and in 1971 the Wheal Jane tin mine near Truro in Cornwall, which closed down in 1913, was re-opened to work the remaining deposits of tin, copper and zinc.

Only a few mineral-tolerant species of plants grow on abandoned mineral workings. These are of two kinds: species which have adapted to these exacting soil conditions, such as common bent grass and plantain, and rare species restricted to these soils—for example, spring sandwort and alpine penny-cress, both of which grow around old lead mines in northern England. Two extremely rare species are confined to serpentine rocks, which contain copper, zinc, nickel and chromium. These are Shetland mouse-ear, on Unst, the most northerly island in Britain; and alpine catchfly, on a few mountains in Scotland and the Lake District.

Mining has disfigured the landscape in many places. The most serious ravager has been coal mining, which has thrown up towering black spoil heaps of waste materials, such as that which caused the Aberfan disaster of 1966. It has also left behind deep depressions filled with stagnant water and disused shafts, machinery and colliery buildings. The sand and gravel industries have caused nearly as much dereliction as coal mining. They have gouged out vast pits, as has the business of quarrying for limestone, chalk, sandstone, slate and other rocks.

The law now stipulates that the opencast mining and iron-stone industries must restore ravaged land. See also GOLD, OIL

Mineral spring

Rainwater soaks through the ground and passes slowly through rocks, eventually emerging at springs. When the water contains dissolved salts from the rocks it has passed through, it is known as a mineral spring. Medical treatment with it was fashionable in the late 18th and 19th centuries, and led to the development of spa towns, among them Bath, Buxton, Cheltenham, Droitwich, Harrogate, Leamington, Llandrindod and Strathpeffer. Many are still centres for the treatment of sufferers from poliomyelitis and rheumatic disorders.

Mink *Lutreola vison*

A relative of the weasel, the mink was introduced into England from the United States in 1929 to be bred for its fur. But numbers escaped and they have become a threat to game birds, fish and poultry. The mink grows to about 18 in. long and has a 6 in. tail. Wild males weigh 3-4 lb.—about twice as much as females. Ranch-bred males weigh up to 7 lb.

In 1956, the first wild mink were reported along the River Teign in Devon. Since then they have become established in many places in southern England, parts of East Anglia, the north Midlands, Pembrokeshire and southern and eastern Scotland.

The mink's rich, glossy coat is brown in the natural state, but ranch-bred mink can range in colour from white to almost black, and this is reflected in British wild mink.

They nest in tree roots or tunnel into steep banks, usually near water, in the spring, and produce five or six kittens. Breeding sites have been reported on Dartmoor, on the Avon and other Hampshire rivers, the Stour in Dorset, the Wyre in Lancashire, the Teifi in Wales, and on several Scottish rivers.

Wild mink are now posing serious problems. In nature there is normally a balance achieved through animals preying on each other. But the birds of prey and large carnivores which control the mink population in the United States have been severely reduced in Britain through hunting, the use of pesticides and the reduction in the amount of waste land. Consequently the number of wild mink is increasing rapidly. The Ministry of Agriculture classify mink as dangerous pests.

Because they can swim well, mink are able to raid islands which are sanctuaries for rare wild life. Moreover, unlike most wild animals, they will kill even when they are not hungry. Though normally silent, they scream when cornered.

The skins of wild mink are valueless. See also POLECAT

Mink nest in tree roots or tunnel into steep banks, usually near water

Minnow *Phoxinus phoxinus*

Anglers despise minnows except as bait, because they are small—rarely more than 4 in. long. However, they make a tasty dish when prepared in the same way as sprats. Izaak Walton, who wrote *The Compleat Angler*, suggested the dish of minnow-tansy—minnows fried, after being dipped in egg yolk, cowslip, primrose and tansy batter.

The minnow is one of the most common fish in small rivers, streams and large lakes throughout England, Scotland and Wales, although it is not widespread in Ireland. They are eaten in large numbers by pike, chub and trout, and provide food for kingfishers, herons and other birds. Females spawn 200-1000 eggs in batches. They are left in clumps between stones in running water and hatch after 5-10 days.

Minnows are often seen in compact, swiftly moving shoals in clear water. In summer, the breeding colours of the males make them conspicuous—an intense white flash on the pectoral fin, golden sides, scarlet belly, and a dark bar across the throat.

At other times of the year both males and females are olive-green on the back with a line of dark bars along the sides. Minnows feed on small crustaceans and aquatic insects.

Peppermint
Mentha × piperita

Water mint
Mentha aquatica

Corn mint
Mentha arvensis

Spearmint
Mentha spicata

There are several varieties of mint to be found by the roadside and on farms, as well as the type grown in kitchen gardens

Mint

The plant known as mint, and regarded by cooks as an essential accompaniment to lamb and new potatoes, is in fact spearmint. It was introduced from central Europe as a kitchen herb, and has established itself on roadsides and other waste places. It has unstalked, shiny leaves, smooth, branched stems and grows to 2 ft. During August and September it has lilac flowers.

There are several other kinds of mint, some grown commercially, others wild. Two wild mints—corn mint, common in fields, and water mint, found in damp places—occur throughout the country. Corn mint reproduces by seeds and lacks a normal minty smell, and the whorls of its lilac flowers are all hidden among the leaves. Water mint has showy flowers and a strong scent.

Commercial growers have cultivated a number of hybrids. The most important of these is peppermint. Oil obtained from its leaves is used in flavouring sweets and medicines. In its wild state peppermint can be found growing in damp places. Its lilac-red flowers appear between July and October.

Mirage

On hot, calm days when there is little cloud, motorists frequently see what appears to be a pool of water on the road ahead. Trees and hills a short distance away may appear as detached floating objects.

These mirages occur when the air near the road surface gets very hot. Light rays entering this layer of air are bent upwards. The image of the disembodied trees is projected upwards and the supposed pool is the refracted brightness of the sky.

HOW A MIRAGE IS FORMED

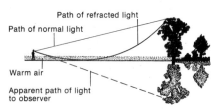

Path of refracted light

Path of normal light

Warm air

Apparent path of light to observer

Light reaches the eye by a second course as it refracts above a hot surface. Images of distant objects then appear, as if reflected

Mist

Moisture is constantly evaporating from the soil and being given off by the leaves of plants, especially on warm days. Some of this moisture is absorbed into the atmosphere, particularly if the air is warm, when its capacity to hold water is greater. When the air cools again its capacity lessens and any surplus moisture will condense out in the form of tiny suspended water droplets; these reduce visibility. When it is possible to see 1000 yds or more the phenomenon is termed mist; below this figure it is known as fog.

The cooling process happens after sunset—particularly during long, clear autumn and winter nights—when the ground and the air immediately above it cool quickly.

Mist frequently occurs over damp fields or inland waters; it will also lie longer in such regions, which are sheltered from both sun and wind.

The March sun has gone down, and as the evening air begins to cool, a mist forms over a sheltered pond in Alice Holt Forest, Hampshire

Mistletoe *Viscum album*

This evergreen lives as a semi-parasite high in the branches of broad-leaved trees in the southern half of Britain. It draws root-sap from its host tree, causing no real harm, and gets carbon dioxide from the air through its own leaves.

Its soft, white, sticky berries are often rubbed on bark and into crevices by birds. The single, round seed sprouts, invading the tree for nourishment. A green shoot develops, puts out a pair of slender, pale green leaves and eventually becomes woody. Branches divide repeatedly, making bushes that can grow 3 ft across, with life-spans of many years. Each mistletoe plant is either male or female. The tiny, yellow-green, wind-pollinated flowers, which open on joints in March, have four sepals, four petals and either four minute anthers or a hidden ovary. The juicy white berries ripen in the following winter, attracting mistle thrushes and other birds.

Mistletoe growing on oak denoted a sacred tree to the Druids, and the mistletoe was carefully cut down with a golden knife in a magic ritual. The custom of kissing under the mistletoe may be linked with a fertility rite, although it may be connected with the old custom of hanging mistletoe in a porch to denote peace and hospitality. A sprig in a cradle warded off fairies, and a sprig worn under a hat gave protection against witch-craft.

Mite

Flour, sugar, cheese and other stored foods may become so badly infested by these tiny creatures that the food will appear to be moving. Large numbers of mites may strip trees of their leaves. Other small mites are the cause of the red, pimple-like galls on lime and sycamore leaves and similar swellings on the leaves of other plants and trees. Many live in the soil, feeding on decomposing materials and fungi and are particularly numerous in leaf litter in woodland.

Mites are relatives of spiders and scorpions and differ greatly in size; the smallest are invisible to the naked eye, while some predatory species are about ⅜ in. across. Mite larvae have six legs and moult three or four times before the adult stage is reached. Those which prey upon insects and other invertebrates and their eggs usually have well-developed mouthparts. Others are parasites, living on or inside the bodies of other animals.

The harvest mite *Trombicula autumnalis* often bites people in late summer. Red spider mites of the Tetranychidae family attack fruit trees and other plants. They feed on sap, and are serious pests.

The parasitic itch mite of the genus Sarcoptes causes scabies, the skin disease which affects animals, including humans.

Moat see Castle

Mole *Talpa europaea*

Moles live almost entirely under ground in tunnels which they dig with a breast-stroke action of their short, shovel-shaped, out-turned front limbs. The tunnel system consists of main tunnels with subsidiary branches. Some tunnels are immediately below the surface; in these, the mole displaces the soil upwards into ridges. Other are 2-8 in. below ground. To make these, the mole excavates the soil and pushes it ahead; from time to time it thrusts the soil up, forming molehills. Moles, which are 6 in. long and weigh about 3½ oz., can excavate 10 lb. of earth in 20 minutes. Weight for weight, this is 12 times more material than a coalface miner can move with a pick and shovel.

Tunnelling is carried out from a base, or fortress—a cavity beneath a larger than normal molehill; this is also used for sleeping and breeding. Moles tunnel to find food—earthworms, insect larvae and slugs—and they occasionally store dead earthworms. Male moles sometimes make long surface tunnels in spring when searching for a mate.

The mole is a barrel-shaped animal covered in soft, shiny fur that lies well in any direction and appears black or slate-grey according to how the light strikes it. Its vision is very poor and the minute eyes are hidden beneath fur; the pink snout is pointed and heavily whiskered; the ears are flapless holes. The senses of touch and hearing are well developed, those of sight and smell much less so. The short tail is always held erect to gauge the size of the tunnel.

A solitary animal, the mole makes contact with its own kind only when it mates during its short breeding season, from March to May. The litter of two to six pink, furless, blind young is born between April and June in the underground fortress, in a nest of grass, dried leaves or moss. The young moles, which are suckled, grow hair during the first three weeks and leave the nest two weeks later. A mole's lifespan in the wild is about three years.

Moles live in loose, easily diggable soil throughout Britain, from sea level to about 3000 ft, but there are no moles in Ireland. They do not colonise poor mountain soil or acid, sandy soil because these contain few earthworms. The mole population has been estimated at about four per acre. Moles belong to the order of mammals called insectivores, and are related to hedgehogs.

Molehills spoil lawns and sports grounds and reduce the value of pasture. They may also damage the blades of cutting machines. In addition, moles rob the soil of earthworms and can seriously disturb the roots of crops. Farmers and gardeners are therefore their chief enemies. Other enemies include owls, foxes, dogs and cats.

The mole's name is possibly a shortened form of mouldiwarp, a name still used in northern England, which is derived from Old English *molde*, meaning earth, and *werpen*, meaning to throw.

The mole has powerful forelimbs for digging, but tiny eyes, usually hidden by fur

THE MOLE'S FORTRESS

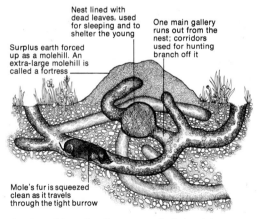

Nest lined with dead leaves, used for sleeping and to shelter the young

One main gallery runs out from the nest; corridors used for hunting branch off it

Surplus earth forced up as a molehill. An extra-large molehill is called a fortress

Mole's fur is squeezed clean as it travels through the tight burrow

A maze of tunnels often surrounds the mole's nest, with the characteristic hill above

Mole cricket see Grasshopper

ITCH MITE

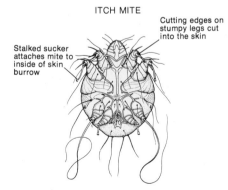

Cutting edges on stumpy legs cut into the skin

Stalked sucker attaches mite to inside of skin burrow

The itch mite *Sarcoptes scabiei* causes the skin disease scabies in humans and domestic animals. It burrows just into the skin, usually on the hand or wrist, and produces severe itching and a rash

Monkey-flower *Mimulus guttatus*

This plant was introduced to gardens from the Aleutian Islands off Alaska in 1812, but has since become naturalised. It is a perennial, 9-18 in. high, which forms ribbons of gold along streams through meadows in the north and west of Britain. The yellow flowers have two lips, the lower often marked with small red spots. They are pollinated by bees.

Blood drop emlets *M. luteus* is similar, but the flowers have large red spots on their lower lips. It is abundant in southern Scotland.

POLLINATION OF THE MONKEY-FLOWER

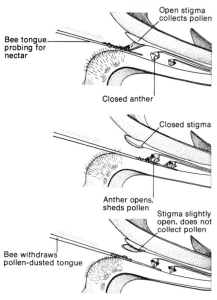

Monkey-flowers are pollinated by bees when they visit the flowers for nectar. Pollen, on a bee's tongue, is collected by the open stigma. The anthers then shed more pollen which the bee takes to another flower in its search for food

Monkey puzzle *Araucaria araucana*

The Chile pine, named after its country of origin, owes its popular English name to a joker who said: 'It would puzzle a monkey to climb that tree.' Its geometrical growth, with long side branches bearing regular offshoots, is emphasised by its thick, triangular, dark green leaves. These persist for ten years or more before fading and falling, leaving ragged twigs. Leaf traces can be seen low on the main trunk, which bears ribbed, dark grey bark.

Each monkey puzzle is either male or female, but they rarely flower in Britain. Males carry clusters of pollen-bearing flowers which open in October. The female flowers, opening at the same time, take 18 months to ripen into large round fruit-clusters, like small pineapples. Green at first, they become brown as they mature in autumn, and then break up to release large woody scales and edible winged seeds. When a seed sprouts, the two large seed-leaves remain in the husk, which is unusual for a conifer.

A joker said 'It would puzzle a monkey to climb that tree'—and gave it a name

Monkey puzzle was introduced to Europe in 1795 by the Scots botanist Archibald Menzies. He pocketed seeds served to him at a banquet and planted them on board his ship, *Discovery*.

Monkey puzzle yields a pale brown softwood timber with a pinkish tinge, but little is used. In Britain, its planting has been confined to parks and gardens, with a few formal avenues. It may live, growing slowly, for 100 years.

Monkshood *Aconitum napellus*

The powerful poison extracted from the roots of this plant was once used to tip arrows for shooting wild animals. This gave it the alternative name wolfsbane, while monkshood arises from the cowl-like shape of its mauve flowers.

Monkshood grows 2-3 ft tall, with glossy, deeply divided, fan-shaped leaves. Familiar as a garden plant, it grows wild by shady streams in south-west England and South Wales.

Tragedies have occurred in the past when its roots were confused with horseradish. The two plants are not alike, but the roots are similar.

Montbretia *Crocosmia crocosmiflora*

This is the hybrid of two species of Crocosmia introduced from South Africa and raised in Nancy, France, where it flowered for the first time in 1880. It was brought to Britain as a garden plant, and has spread by means of seed and the division of its underground corms to hedgebanks and streams. Montbretia is a common sight in Devon and Cornwall in July and August, when its deep orange, crocus-like flowers appear. It is also common throughout the south and west of Ireland.

Montbretia has narrow, sword-shaped leaves and grows 1-3 ft tall.

Moorhen see Crakes and Rails
Moorland see p. 294
Moraine see Ice

Morel

A fungus which fruits in the spring. The four species found in hedgerows, banks and grassland in Britain all grow on rich soil and are edible. They grow best on chalk or limestone and are often found on burnt ground in woods. It is unusual to find them on sandy or acid soil.

Morels are members of the sac fungi family, and all have a brittle stalk with an irregularly honeycombed cap. The largest, *Morchella esculenta,* has a 1-2 in. yellow ochre cap on top of a 2-4 in. white, mealy stem and is especially good to eat. It grows near trees, such as ash, elm and poplar, and thrives on the sites of old fires or where ground has been disturbed—particularly in the region of ruined buildings. There are several other similar species.

False morels of the Helvella genus which appear later in the year are edible but sometimes cause indigestion.

The honeycombed cap of the morel fungus, which grows best on chalk or limestone

Moschatel *Adoxa moschatellina*

Heads of five green flowers have earned moschatel its other name of townhall clock. Four of the flowers are arranged like the faces of a clock, the fifth points to the sky. In damp weather, the flowers give off a faint smell of musk in woods and hedge-banks throughout the British Isles. They appear in April and May, growing about 6 in. high.

Each flower should produce a berry, but rarely does so in this country; instead moschatel spreads mostly by its extensive underground stems.

Mosquito see Gnat

Moss

A small green plant, rarely more than a few inches high, which grows anywhere not overshadowed by taller vegetation or perpetually dry. There are more than 600 species in the British Isles, growing on rocks and walls, in woodlands and on tree trunks and branches. They are important pioneers of rock surfaces, holding moisture in their leaves and building up humus in which the seeds of flowering plants can germinate.

The Sphagna or bog mosses are easily recognised as a group, but are very difficult to distinguish from one another. They grow in large raised cushions with dense clusters of tiny leaves, varying in colour from green to dark red. Sphagnum moss makes the bogs of the north and west, its stems and leaves holding water like a sponge. The old, dead stems and leaves persist and accumulate in wet places to form peat. Nurserymen use sphagnum to make an absorbent bandage to keep plants moist in transit.

An easily recognised moss on clayey banks is *Fissidens taxifolius*. It has flattened leaves arranged on opposite sides of the stem and resembles a tiny fern. On soils that are drier and rich in lime, *Encalypta vulgaris* often grows. It forms small tufts and has leaves which twist when dry.

The silky, dark green leaves of *Dicranella heteromalla* are often found on sandy soils. Its leaves are bent to one side and it has bright orange capsules on pale stalks.

Atrichum undulatum grows in shady woods and hedgerows and looks like a miniature tree. It has long, toothed leaves, the margins of which become wavy in dry weather.

One of the few aquatic mosses growing in fresh water is *Fontinalis antipyretica*, recognised by its long green fronds trailing in fast-flowing streams. It anchors itself to stones or tree roots. The name *antipyretica*, Latin for 'against fire', arises from an old Swedish habit of packing the moss between the chimneys and walls of their wooden houses as a fire precaution.

Mosses that grow on trees include *Hypnum cupressiforme*, probably the most common British moss. It also grows on heaths, grassland and rocks. *Funaria hygrometrica* is unique among mosses: it grows in yellow-green patches on the site of old bonfires. Its stalks curl up in dry weather and straighten out when the weather is damp.

Mosses always have a stem and leaves, and produce capsules on stalks from the side or tip of a leafy stem, usually in spring. The capsules contain spores and are covered by a little hood, the calyptra.

There are two alternating generations in the life cycle of moss. The plant itself carries male and female organs. After fertilisation, these produce a capsule. Stalk and capsule together form an asexual, spore-bearing generation. The spores produced are capable of germinating into a new plant. Mosses also reproduce vegetatively, by small pieces breaking off and growing into a new plant.

Common mosses of the British Isles

Mosses are small, primitive plants which thrive almost anywhere provided moisture is present, often forming dense cushions. They have leaves and stems, but no flowers, and rarely grow more than a few inches high. There are about 14,000 species in the world, of which about 600 occur in the British Isles. Those shown here are a selection of the more common species

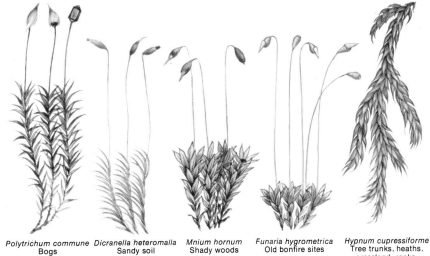

Polytrichum commune
Bogs

Dicranella heteromalla
Sandy soil

Mnium hornum
Shady woods
and hedgerows

Funaria hygrometrica
Old bonfire sites

Hypnum cupressiforme
Tree trunks, heaths,
grassland, rocks

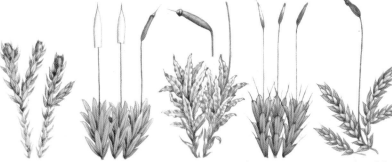

Grimmia apocarpa
Old walls

Encalypta vulgaris
Lime-rich soil

Atrichum undulatum
Shady woods
and hedgerows

Tortula muralis
Old walls

Fissidens taxifolius
Clayey banks

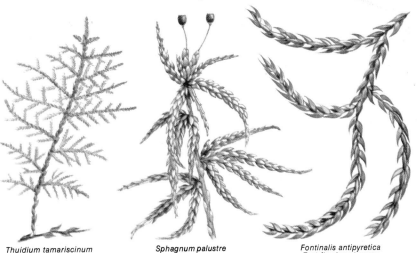

Thuidium tamariscinum
Woodland floor

Sphagnum palustre
Bogs

Fontinalis antipyretica
Fast-flowing streams

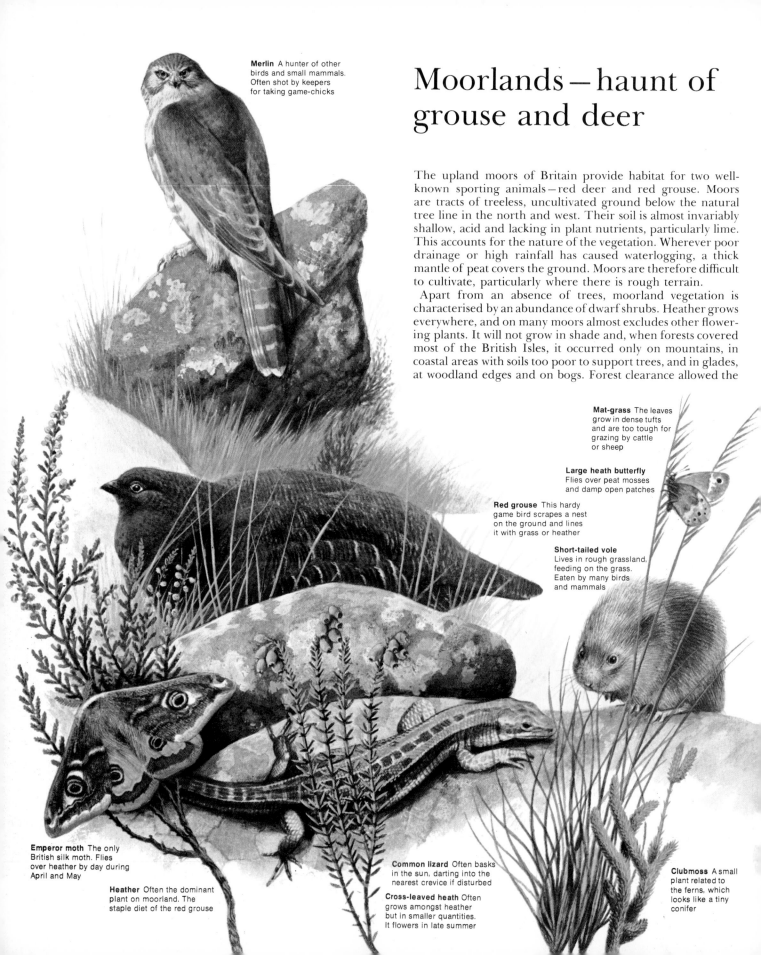

Moorlands—haunt of grouse and deer

The upland moors of Britain provide habitat for two well-known sporting animals—red deer and red grouse. Moors are tracts of treeless, uncultivated ground below the natural tree line in the north and west. Their soil is almost invariably shallow, acid and lacking in plant nutrients, particularly lime. This accounts for the nature of the vegetation. Wherever poor drainage or high rainfall has caused waterlogging, a thick mantle of peat covers the ground. Moors are therefore difficult to cultivate, particularly where there is rough terrain.

Apart from an absence of trees, moorland vegetation is characterised by an abundance of dwarf shrubs. Heather grows everywhere, and on many moors almost excludes other flowering plants. It will not grow in shade and, when forests covered most of the British Isles, it occurred only on mountains, in coastal areas with soils too poor to support trees, and in glades, at woodland edges and on bogs. Forest clearance allowed the

Merlin A hunter of other birds and small mammals. Often shot by keepers for taking game-chicks

Mat-grass The leaves grow in dense tufts and are too tough for grazing by cattle or sheep

Large heath butterfly Flies over peat mosses and damp open patches

Red grouse This hardy game bird scrapes a nest on the ground and lines it with grass or heather

Short-tailed vole Lives in rough grassland, feeding on the grass. Eaten by many birds and mammals

Emperor moth The only British silk moth. Flies over heather by day during April and May

Heather Often the dominant plant on moorland. The staple diet of the red grouse

Common lizard Often basks in the sun, darting into the nearest crevice if disturbed

Cross-leaved heath Often grows amongst heather but in smaller quantities. It flowers in late summer

Clubmoss A small plant related to the ferns, which looks like a tiny conifer

plant to spread and it covered vast areas, particularly on the eastern flanks of the Pennines and in the Scottish Highlands.

Sportsmen and farmers value heather highly. Red grouse and mountain hares depend on it for food and it is also grazed by red deer, sheep and cattle. It is evergreen and when young is useful as a winter feed for livestock. As it grows older and woodier, it becomes less valuable and needs rejuvenating. This is done by burning patches in rotation so that each patch is burnt every 7-20 years. The fire destroys the old, woody growth and stimulates the production of succulent young shoots.

Apart from burning, it is the acidity, fertility and water content of the soil and the thickness of the surface peat that determine which plants grow on moors. On wet, peaty ground the pink flowers of cross-leaved heath accompany heather in summer. As peat grows thicker and wetter, heather gives way to sedges and grasses which, in their turn, yield to bog. In contrast to cross-leaved heath, the purple-flowered bell heather flourishes on well-drained slopes with only a thin layer of peat. The purple-fruited bilberry is widespread on damp, acid peat and on the edges of moors. It sometimes grows with cowberry and crowberry. Bearberry is most abundant on the more fertile, less peaty soils of the east-central Scottish Highlands—where it often grows with such herbs as intermediate wintergreen, bitter vetch and birdsfoot-trefoil.

Where grazing and burning have destroyed heather, grasses may predominate. On dry, fertile soils bent and fescue grasses thrive (sometimes accompanied by bracken). Wavy hair-grass grows on dry, poor soils, while on wet, acid peats deer-sedge, mat-grass, purple moor-grass or heath-rush flourish.

The red deer, Britain's largest wild mammal, formerly inhabited woodland in the lowlands as well as in the hills. Tree destruction has forced it into a completely open habitat, and today the highest, most remote and poorest moors are managed as deer forests. Red deer are found in south-west England, the Lake District and southern Scotland, but are most widespread and abundant in the Scottish Highlands. They roam on to the tops of the highest hills until severe winter weather drives them down to the shelter of the glens. In recent years these traditional wintering grounds have been diminished by afforestation or hydro-electric schemes. The displaced deer have become pests by marauding on to agricultural land and into forestry plantations.

Mountain hares are abundant on the grouse moors of eastern Scotland. On rich soils the mole is active, and on grassy moors the short-tailed vole flourishes. The fox, though relentlessly hunted, occurs everywhere in moorland, preying on small mammals, birds and, occasionally, lambs and red deer calves. In the Scottish Highlands lives Britain's most savage animal, the wild cat. Other predators include stoats, weasels and pine martens. Common lizards and adders are both widespread on moors, except in Wales and north-west England. Frogs breed in many moorland pools.

From the landowner's point of view red grouse are the most important of the many birds which live on moorland. The rent from grouse shooting pays for the upkeep of many moorland estates; and the bird indirectly influences the fate of other animals and of plants. It depends on heather for food and cover, and often moors are burnt solely for its benefit. Any animals or birds that are likely to prey on it or its eggs are trapped, shot or poisoned. However, some predatory birds that were in danger of extinction, such as golden eagles, peregrines, merlins, buzzards, ravens and hen harriers, are now beginning to increase slightly.

Non-predatory moorland birds include golden plovers, curlews, dunlins, meadow pipits and ring ouzels. Lapwings and skylarks are common on grassy moorland, and snipe and redshank are characteristic of wet, peaty places.

Bilberry bumble bee Feeds on bilberry, having an extra-long tongue which probes deep into the flower for nectar

Bilberry Its flowers are rich in nectar and the berries succulent. Often grows with heather

A bleak expanse of moorland just north of Chapel-en-le-Frith in the Derbyshire Peak District

Moss animals

These minute creatures which mass together in colonies are often confused with seaweed, algae or the eggs of pond snails. The individuals (zooids) are seldom more than $\frac{1}{64}$ in. long, and live only a few weeks. They have two scientific names: bryozoa, Latin for moss animal, and polyzoa, meaning many animals—a reference to the fact that they always live in colonies.

Marine species, sometimes called 'sea mats', often form crusts on rocks and seaweed. Each animal lives in a separate protective case of horny material, into which it retreats for protection. At rest, it puts out a set of tentacles covered with tiny hairs which produce a current to propel micro-organisms, on which it feeds, into its mouth.

What is often taken for seaweed on the shore is the strap-like colony of the hornwrack moss animal, which is brown when alive and growing, attached to rocks or other solid objects, but off-white when washed on to the beach.

The orange-red rose 'coral' is found offshore attached to rocks and boulders. Large colonies resemble a coral reef and shelter marine animals such as crabs.

Moss animals of the Crisia group may be seen in rock pools, growing as dense white tufts attached to stones or algae and looking like miniature underwater shrubs. Those of the Bugula group form festoons on rocks at low tide on the lower and middle shore. Their branches are divided regularly.

Bugula is one of the many forms which produce modified individuals with pincer-like structures which protrude in place of the usual tentacles. These pincers fend off organisms which might impede the normal life of the other members of the colony. Because the defenders resemble a bird's head they are called avicularia; they can be seen through a hand lens.

Freshwater moss animals are widespread. Most species are found on stones and weeds. Those of the Plumatella group may live under canal bridges and landing stages; they sometimes encrust pipes in waterworks and restrict the flow. Colonies of Cristatella are often mistaken for snails' eggs. They develop under waterlily leaves or on stones. A colony of this form may move from $\frac{1}{2}$ to 1 in. a day, and can divide into two or more sections, each of which may continue as a separate colony.

Usually, new colonies are formed by sexual reproduction, eggs being released into the sea, or into a brooding chamber, where they develop. The free-swimming planktonic larvae swim away, settle, turn into adults and start to 'bud off' other individuals to form a colony.

Freshwater species also reproduce by forming special resistant bodies which contain a mass of cells from which new adults develop. These containers, called statoblasts, can withstand extremes of temperature and desiccation. They sometimes have a set of hooks which catch on rocks and vegetation. Statoblasts resemble two saucers clamped together with the mass of cells between them. The two halves fall apart in the spring, allowing the cells to resume growth. The statoblasts are dispersed by wind and current, and sometimes on the feet of animals or birds. Statoblasts in pond debris are a sign that adult colonies inhabit the area.

Moth see p. 298
Mother Carey's chicken see Petrel

Mother of pearl moth *Pleuroptya ruralis*

This moth takes its name from the inside of oyster shells, which their pale wing patterns resemble. It is found wherever nettles grow, its green caterpillars being hatched within a few weeks of laying. The caterpillars hibernate when small, but continue growing in spring while living inside rolled nettle leaves, where they also spend their three-week pupa or resting stage. The narrow-bodied moths emerge in July and fly by night, hiding in nettle patches in daytime.

Another moth with similar habits is the small magpie which appears a month earlier than the mother of pearl. Such moths are white with black spots. Their caterpillars hibernate in silken cocoons during the winter and pupate in spring. See also MOTH

Small magpie
Eurrhypara hortulata

Mother-of-thousands *Helxine soleirolii*

A tiny, creeping plant with bright green leaves introduced to this country from Corsica. It has spread and become naturalised on old walls and banks in sheltered spots in south and west England, particularly near the coast in areas which are moist and free from frost. The speed with which it produces cushions of many small leaves gives its name, mother-of-thousands. It is also known as baby's tears and mind-your-own-business.

Its inconspicuous green flowers, which appear from May to October, are like those of the stinging nettle to which it is closely related.

Mother Shipton see Noctuid moth

Moth fly

All the 73 British species of moth fly are harmless. Also known as owl midges, they fly by day and night in spring and summer and are often seen in large numbers on windows or tree trunks, especially near water. The adults have black bodies and hairy wings, frequently grey. They feed on nectar and are especially common in humid conditions. Moth flies are $\frac{1}{8}$ in. long or less and are found throughout the British Isles.

The larvae live in wet conditions and are useful in breaking down the decaying matter on which they feed; some species live in water, others live in cow-dung or dead animal matter.

Also found on sewage farms are larvae of *Psychoda phalaenoides*. The adult female of this species is responsible for the

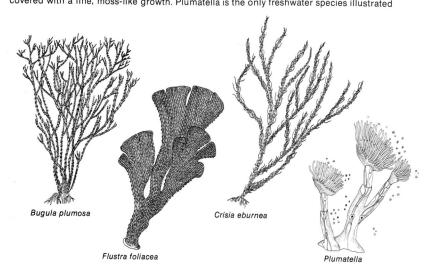

Common British moss animals

There are about 4000 different kinds of moss animals in the world. Most live in the sea, and many in British waters. They are often mistaken for small seaweeds, but are in fact colonies of microscopic animals. When all the tentacles of the animals are extended the colony appears to be covered with a fine, moss-like growth. Plumatella is the only freshwater species illustrated

Bugula plumosa

Flustra foliacea

Crisia eburnea

Plumatella

pollination of cuckoo-pint, or lords and ladies. The flower spike of cuckoo-pint contains hairs which trap the moth fly, often covered with pollen from another flower. While trapped, the fly pollinates the flower and receives a fresh dusting of pollen. It escapes with this to fertilise another flower.

THE MOTH FLY AND THE CUCKOO-PINT

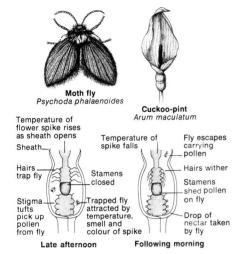

Moth fly
Psychoda phalaenoides

Cuckoo-pint
Arum maculatum

Temperature of flower spike rises as sheath opens
Sheath
Hairs trap fly
Stamens closed
Stigma tufts pick up pollen from fly
Trapped fly attracted by temperature, smell and colour of spike
Late afternoon

Temperature of spike falls
Fly escapes carrying pollen
Hairs wither
Stamens shed pollen on fly
Drop of nectar taken by fly
Following morning

Moth flies, enticed and trapped by the cuckoo-pint, are later released, carrying pollen to another flower. In this way cross-pollination occurs

Mottled umber see Winter moth

Mould
Velvety growths of small fungi which appear on plants, food, vegetables and damp clothing. Spores of these small plants are always present in the air and germinate when they find a suitable site.

White moulds are algal fungi. They include pin moulds such as *Mucor mucedo* which grows on bread. Other species appear on stale, moist jam or other foods and develop into a dense mass of whitish threads called hyphae. After a few days, vertical hyphae develop, each with a terminal black swelling, like a small pin head, which bears the spores.

Moulds of the Pythium family are responsible for the 'damping off' of seedlings, and *Phytophthora infestans* blights potatoes. Damp weather enables these moulds to cause serious damage to crops. *Saprolegnia ferox* causes cotton-wool disease in fish kept in aquaria.

Blue-green moulds of the sac fungi family grow on food and leather. Some provide the blue colour in Stilton and other blue cheeses. Others are also of service to man: penicillin, which has saved countless lives by countering bacterial infections, is obtained from the sac fungus *Penicillium*, and the mould *Aspergillus niger* converts sugar to citric acid, which is found naturally in lemons. Blue-green moulds flourish in warm, humid conditions.

Mountain see p. 300

Mountain ash, which can grow at altitudes of 3000 ft, is crowned with blossom in May

Mountain ash *Sorbus aucuparia*
The mountain ash is botanically related to the whitebeam and wild service tree and is so-called because its feather-shaped, compound leaves bear a close resemblance to those of the ash, though the edges of each leaflet are toothed. It is a very hardy tree and can be found, with the birch, higher up the British mountains than any other species. Mountain ash often springs up in crevices where birds that eat its berries have dropped its seeds.

The mountain ash is called rowan in Scotland, the name coming from the Gaelic *rudha-an*, the red one, referring to its berries. Another alternative name is fowlers' service tree, which refers to the use of its berries as bait for trapping birds.

Mountain ash is a small tree, growing to about 30 ft, with a smooth, grey-brown bark bearing well-marked breathing pores. Its winter buds are exceptionally large, purple in colour and oval in outline, with a long point. Unlike those of the ash, they are set singly on the twigs, not paired.

The pale green, feathery foliage opens in April and is followed in May by clusters of white blossoms spread evenly over the crown. Each flower has five green sepals, five white petals, many golden stamens and a central ovary.

By September, the flower heads have ripened into bunches of scarlet berries which soon attract the birds. Though too sour for man when eaten raw, rowan berries with sugar added make a tasty jelly used for seasoning venison and game.

The dark red-brown heartwood, which lies within a pale brown sapwood, is very tough, and was once widely used for tool handles and small turned or carved objects where larger timber was scarce.

Nowadays, mountain ash is planted to decorate streets and small gardens. In the Scottish Highlands crofters planted these trees by their farm buildings as a safeguard against witchcraft, but the reason for this superstition is unknown. In mythology, the tree is associated with the god Thor.

Remains of a Norman motte and bailey on a commanding hill near Powerstock, Dorset

Motte
A large mound on which a castle, usually wooden, was built, a practice introduced by the Normans. A motte was surrounded by one or more baileys, or oval forecourts, which were in turn surrounded by a moat and earthen rampart.

The mound provided a good lookout post, particularly in flat country such as East Anglia. Invaders who penetrated the bailey had to struggle up the slope under a barrage of missiles and arrows. Mottes remained in use throughout the Middle Ages, particularly where the original wooden keeps were

replaced by stone castles. Many were built during the troubled reign of King Stephen, 1135-54.

Today, mottes which have lost their keeps are recognisable as grass-grown mounds, varying from 50 to 120 ft high, with flat tops. Along the Welsh borders they are known as tumps, and in many other localities are still called mote or moot.

The Bayeux Tapestry illustrates this type of fortification. Most of the mottes on the Welsh borders were built between 1066 and 1100. During the next 100 years, the design spread to Ireland. See also CASTLE

The large elephant hawkmoth can often be spotted at dusk near patches of willow-herb

Moth

There are more than 2000 species of moths in Britain. They range in size from the death's head hawkmoth which, with a span of 5½ in., is Britain's largest insect, to species with a wingspan of only ⅛ in. Moths make up 97 per cent of the insect order Lepidoptera, the remaining 3 per cent being butterflies. Most moths are drab, night-flying creatures,

THE FLIGHT SPIRAL OF A MOTH

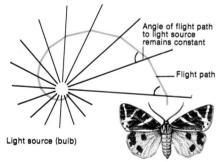

Angle of flight path to light source remains constant

Flight path

Light source (bulb)

A moth flies at a constant angle to light. It takes a straight course when steering by the moon, but will spiral inwards around a central light source such as a bulb

but there are some attractive day-flying species, whose life cycles and scaly wings are similar to those of butterflies.

A moth begins life as an egg. This hatches into a caterpillar, or larva, which in the larger species feeds on plants. After a period of rapid growth and a succession of moults, the caterpillar changes into a chrysalis, or pupa, sometimes within a silken cocoon. Finally the adult moth, or imago form, emerges, spreads and dries its wings and flies away to mate and repeat the cycle. Few live for more than a few weeks.

Most moths have feathery antennae, whereas butterflies have fine knob-ended antennae. And unlike butterflies, which can rest with their wings closed, most moths rest with them open. Another feature that many moths have is an interlocking device between the fore and hindwings, but this is absent in butterflies. At the base of the hindwings is a long bristle or group of bristles which fit under a hook-like catch on the underside of the forewing, effectively anchoring hind and forewings together during flight.

Most moths are tiny, with a wingspan of ¼-1 in.; they are called, collectively, micromoths. There are 1200 types in the British

Isles. They include the clothes moths and plume moths; the longhorns with antennae several times the length of the body; and the pigmy moths whose larvae tunnel between the upper and lower surfaces of leaves.

At the other extreme in size are the fast-flying hawkmoths whose fat caterpillars have a horn at the end of the body. The powerful convolvulus hawkmoth is 5 in. long and, like other moths, has a long hollow tongue or proboscis. While hovering in flight it probes into tubular flowers, such as petunias, for nectar. When the moth is not feeding, the proboscis is coiled up like a watch spring under the head. The day-flying emperor moth, the sole British member of the silkmoth family, has no functional tongue and does not feed as an adult.

The swift night-flying moths called prominents are so named from a tuft of scales which project prominently from the centre of the inner margin of their forewings. Hook-tip moths, a small group, have a curved hooked tip on their forewings.

The tussocks are covered in hairs, both in the caterpillar and in the adult stage, and can cause an irritating skin rash on anyone handling them. Other species with hairy caterpillars or 'woolly-bears' are the stout-bodied eggars and colourful tiger moths.

The most familiar of British moths is the large family of dull-coloured noctuas or owlets. During the day they rest camouflaged on tree-trunks and walls or hide.

The geometers, meaning 'earth measurers', is another large family easily distinguished by the caterpillars. These are sometimes called inch worms, stick caterpillars or loopers, as they loop their bodies up when moving. Geometer moths are small and butterfly-like, their wings large in proportion to their bodies. The brilliantly metallic burnets and foresters are also often mistaken for butterflies.

Two families with plant-boring caterpillars are the large goat moths and transparent-winged clearwings. The caterpillars of the narrowly winged swiftmoth tunnel below ground to feed on the roots of plants.

Moths are preyed on by a wide range of birds, including barn owls, swifts and gulls. See also BUTTERFLY

THE MOTH'S INTERLOCKED WINGS

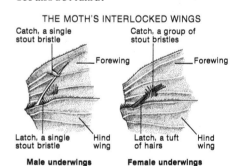

Catch, a single stout bristle

Catch, a group of stout bristles

Forewing

Forewing

Latch, a single stout bristle

Hind wing

Latch, a tuft of hairs

Hind wing

Male underwings

Female underwings

Simple latch and catch mechanisms lock the hind and forewings of moths, so that they move as a single unit in flight

Moths of the British Isles

Some of the more spectacular of the common moths which live in the British Isles are illustrated below. Each of the moths pictured has been chosen because it represents a number of similar ones. Most of these are described elsewhere in the book under their own names. Although moths usually fly by night and butterflies by day it is not always easy to tell one group from the other; but some tips are given in the text. The main distinguishing marks used to classify moths are the patterns formed by the veins on the wings

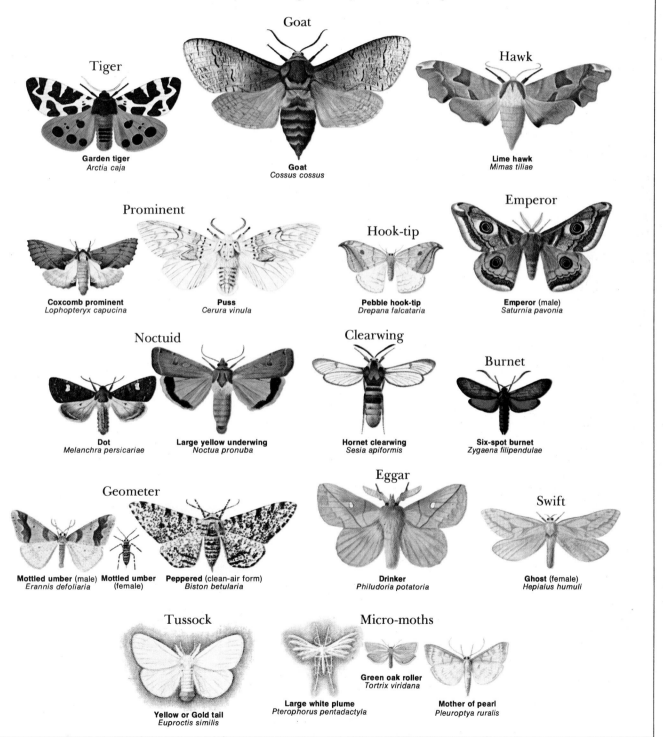

Tiger
Garden tiger
Arctia caja

Goat
Goat
Cossus cossus

Hawk
Lime hawk
Mimas tiliae

Prominent
Coxcomb prominent
Lophopteryx capucina

Puss
Cerura vinula

Hook-tip
Pebble hook-tip
Drepana falcataria

Emperor
Emperor (male)
Saturnia pavonia

Noctuid
Dot
Melanchra persicariae

Large yellow underwing
Noctua pronuba

Clearwing
Hornet clearwing
Sesia apiformis

Burnet
Six-spot burnet
Zygaena filipendulae

Geometer
Mottled umber (male)
Erannis defoliaria

Mottled umber (female)

Peppered (clean-air form)
Biston betularia

Eggar
Drinker
Philudoria potatoria

Swift
Ghost (female)
Hepialus humuli

Tussock
Yellow or Gold tail
Euproctis similis

Micro-moths
Large white plume
Pterophorus pentadactyla

Green oak roller
Tortrix viridana

Mother of pearl
Pleuroptya ruralis

Mountains—last of the lands still free of man

There is not a precise definition of a mountain, but in the British Isles it is usually regarded as a piece of the earth's surface which rises to a height of 2000 ft or more. Most of Britain's highest mountains—those over 3000 ft—are in the Scottish Highlands. They are composed mainly of hard rocks, such as quartzite and granite, which weather slowly to give shallow, infertile soils that are deficient in lime and phosphate. The wet mountain climate further impoverishes well-drained soils by washing out plant nutrients. In poorly drained areas deep, acid peat forms.

The higher mountains have a montane zone where trees cannot grow, and the only plants and animals to survive are those able to withstand low temperatures, strong winds and prolonged snow. This zone begins at about 2000 ft on most peaks, but is lower in exposed parts of the north-west Highlands. The inaccessibility, harsh climate and poor soil of the montane zone have protected it from the human interference that has transformed the greater part of the countryside. The absence of cultivation and settlement means that the plant and animal life there is more or less in the natural state.

Mountain pastures provide summer grazing for sheep and, in Scotland, red deer. The vegetation mostly resembles that of the moorlands, grasslands and bogs of lower ground—heaths, grasses and sedges predominate and herbaceous plants are scarce. Thus the landscape looks drab and uniform in contrast to the colourful slopes of European mountain ranges such as the Alps and Pyrenees.

Two types of plants grow in the montane zone: common ones, for example heather, mat grass and cotton sedge, and the true mountain plants which thrive in a harsh climate and are seldom found below the tree-line on mountains. These include dwarf shrubs such as crowberry and least willow, small herbs such as purple saxifrage and alpine lady's mantle; and grasses, sedges and rushes such as viviparous fescue, stiff sedge and three-leaved rush. Many montane plants are localised or rare; for example, spiderwort is confined to Wales and alpine milkvetch is known on only three Scottish mountains.

Most montane plants cannot tolerate much competition and usually grow in areas where the vegetation is sparse because of bare rocks, prolonged snow or continual soil disturbance. Also, they cannot withstand grazing, and so generally grow on steep cliffs and exposed summits free of sheep and deer. Most of them need lime-rich soils and these occur only on outcrops of limestone or near lime-rich springs. Combinations of these three conditions are rare in the British Isles. They are most extensive in the Highlands—on the mountains stretching from Breadalbane, Perthshire to Glen Doll, Angus. One of these mountains, Ben Lawers, is particularly rich in montane flowers, including such rarities as drooping saxifrage, alpine gentian, boreal fleabane and alpine forget-me-not.

There are few truly montane animals in the British Isles. The only mammal is the mountain hare, which is native to the Highlands and Ireland but has been introduced to southern Scotland, England and Wales. Its chief food is heather.

The Cumbrian Mountains seen from the 2960 ft summit of Bow Fell. Bleak and empty under a covering of winter snow, they will come to life again with the warmth of spring

Three-leaved rush
Grows on rocky ground at high altitudes. Flowers from June to August

Mountain ringlet
The only alpine butterfly found in Britain. Seen here on mat grass

Alpine gentian
A slender annual standing 1-4 in. high, found only in the Highlands of Scotland

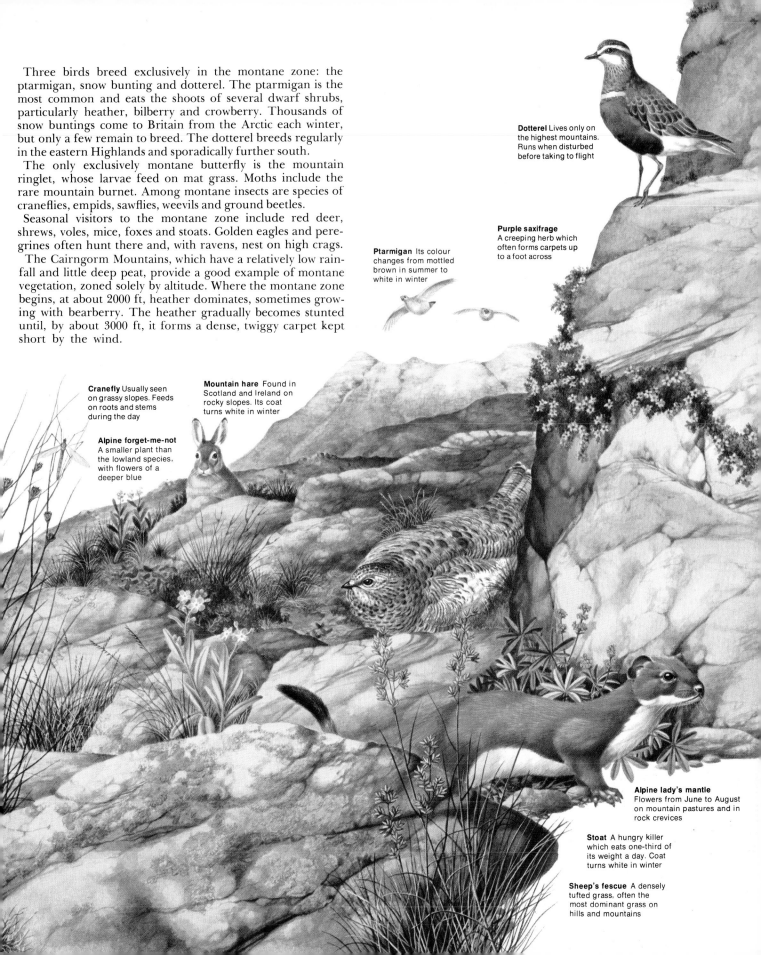

Three birds breed exclusively in the montane zone: the ptarmigan, snow bunting and dotterel. The ptarmigan is the most common and eats the shoots of several dwarf shrubs, particularly heather, bilberry and crowberry. Thousands of snow buntings come to Britain from the Arctic each winter, but only a few remain to breed. The dotterel breeds regularly in the eastern Highlands and sporadically further south.

The only exclusively montane butterfly is the mountain ringlet, whose larvae feed on mat grass. Moths include the rare mountain burnet. Among montane insects are species of craneflies, empids, sawflies, weevils and ground beetles.

Seasonal visitors to the montane zone include red deer, shrews, voles, mice, foxes and stoats. Golden eagles and peregrines often hunt there and, with ravens, nest on high crags.

The Cairngorm Mountains, which have a relatively low rainfall and little deep peat, provide a good example of montane vegetation, zoned solely by altitude. Where the montane zone begins, at about 2000 ft, heather dominates, sometimes growing with bearberry. The heather gradually becomes stunted until, by about 3000 ft, it forms a dense, twiggy carpet kept short by the wind.

Dotterel Lives only on the highest mountains. Runs when disturbed before taking to flight

Purple saxifrage A creeping herb which often forms carpets up to a foot across

Ptarmigan Its colour changes from mottled brown in summer to white in winter

Cranefly Usually seen on grassy slopes. Feeds on roots and stems during the day

Mountain hare Found in Scotland and Ireland on rocky slopes. Its coat turns white in winter

Alpine forget-me-not A smaller plant than the lowland species, with flowers of a deeper blue

Alpine lady's mantle Flowers from June to August on mountain pastures and in rock crevices

Stoat A hungry killer which eats one-third of its weight a day. Coat turns white in winter

Sheep's fescue A densely tufted grass, often the most dominant grass on hills and mountains

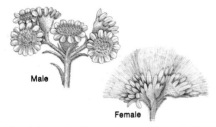

Male

Female

Mountain everlasting produces white male flowers and pink female flowers on separate plants

Mountain everlasting *Antennaria dioica*

Common in Scotland, Ireland and northern England, but scattered and rare elsewhere, mountain everlasting produces white male and rose-pink female flowers in June and July. Narrow, spoon-shaped leaves form small rosettes at the base of the slender 2-8 in. high stems; other, lance-shaped leaves hug the stem. The plant grows on heaths, dry grassland and among rocks in mountainous areas, spreading by overground stems as well as seed. It is also known as catsfoot and immortella, and has been used, dried, for floral decoration in winter.

Mountain ringlet see Brown butterfly

Mounting block

Blocks of masonry or brick, which enabled riders to mount their horses. They date from any period between the Middle Ages and the end of the horse-transport era in the 19th century. Mounting blocks are often seen in stableyards and at the entrances to country houses. They were also built in public places such as market squares and outside churches. Some survive in Yorkshire at the top of lanes where a rider would re-mount after leading his horse up the hill. Some mounting blocks were built as memorials and bear inscriptions. They usually have three or four steps, sometimes carved out of single blocks of stone. A good example survives by the churchyard gate at Chollerton, Northumberland.

The deeply worn steps of a mounting block by the side of a road in Nantwich, Cheshire

The summer nest of the harvest mouse is a ball of grass or corn blades in fields or hedgerows

Mouse

The paths of man and mouse did not cross until about 8000 BC when man first began to cultivate the wild grasses on which they both fed. Bright beady eyes, large rounded ears, pointed snout and scaly, sparsely haired tail as long as the body, characterise this small, secretive, nocturnal rodent. The mouse belongs to the same family, Muridae, as the rat. There are four British species, all of which live in close association with man whether in the town house, garden or among the hayricks and corn fields. They are all prolific breeders and can be very destructive, damaging crops and food.

Taking most advantage of man is the house mouse, a grey-brown creature with a 3 in. long body. The house mouse's original home is probably the Asiatic steppes but it quickly spread through the Middle East to Europe, travelling in man's baggage. Its adaptability enables it to survive everywhere, even in Antarctica, and long-haired, glossy-coated mice can be found living in refrigerated cold stores. In country districts the house mouse lives in walls, hedgerows and corn ricks during the summer but after the harvest invades barns and warehouses or any other place where food is stored. It eats grain and scraps of food left lying around. In its turn it is eaten by predators, especially the barn owl and domestic cat. The house mouse can breed throughout the year, producing at least five litters in urban areas with five to seven young in each and as many as ten litters in the country. It makes its nest of chewed-up wool, paper or straw in a wall near food stores. The 'mousy' smell so much associated with this animal is caused by its marking its home boundaries with urine. The more this boundary scent is eradicated the more strongly and persistently will the mouse scent his territory.

Also living in houses and buildings throughout Britain, especially where there are no house mice, is the timid wood mouse or long-tailed field mouse. It is slightly larger than

Wood mice, like many other small rodents, hide stockpiles of berries for winter use

Mice, rats, shrews and voles

Dormouse 3 in.
Muscardinus avellanarius

Harvest mouse 2½ in.
Micromys minutus

Yellow-necked mouse 4 in.
Apodemus flavicollis

Wood mouse or long-tailed field mouse 3½ in.
Apodemus sylvaticus

House mouse 3 in.
Mus musculus

Black rat 7 in
Rattus rattus

Water shrew 3½ in.
Neomys fodiens

White-toothed shrew Up to 3½ in.
Crocidura suaveolens

Brown rat 8-9 in.
Rattus norvegicus

Common vole 4-5 in.
Microtus arvalis

Pigmy shrew 2 in.
Sorex minutus

Bank vole 4 in.
Clethrionomys glareolus

Short-tailed vole 4 in.
Microtus agrestis

Common shrew Up to 3 in.
Sorex araneus

This chart provides a means of identifying 14 mouse-like mammals of the British countryside, which are sometimes confused by the inexpert. They range in size from the 2 in. long pygmy shrew to the brown rat, which can reach a length of 9 in. The shrews are insect-eaters. Rats, mice, dormice and voles are rodents, which are gnawing, chiefly vegetarian animals. The sizes given are for body length, excluding tail

the house mouse with a body length of about 3½ in. It has a reddish-brown back with a greyish-white belly. Many wood mice have a long yellow chest patch. The wood mouse lives in woodland, hedgerows, fields, gardens and nurseries eating grain, seedlings, berries, buds, fruits, nuts, snails and insects. Its enemies are other mammals and birds, particularly the tawny owl. It nests in a tunnel below ground and breeds from March to October and throughout the winter if mild. It will produce as many as five litters in a year with up to six young in each.

The yellow chest spot of the yellow-necked mouse forms a bright collar between its forelegs. The coat of this 4 in. long mouse is redder than that of the wood mouse and its belly is whiter. It lives in scattered colonies mainly in the southern part of England and in Wales in woods, hedges, shrubberies, gardens, houses and even churches and bee-hives. It is not present in Scotland or Ireland, and its habits are thought to be much the same as those of the wood mouse.

One of Britain's smallest mammals is the 2½ in. long harvest mouse. It has a bright chestnut coat and white belly and a blunter nose than the other three mice. It lives mainly in the south and east of Britain in corn-fields, surrounding hedgerows, dykes, reed-beds, long grass and allotments near towns and villages. It moves gracefully from stalk to stalk aided by its tail which can coil around anything, giving extra support to the mouse and acting as a fifth limb. It breeds from April to September, producing several litters of between five and nine young in each. These are born in a nest built a few inches above the ground, in corn or grain. In the winter it tunnels into hay and corn ricks or burrows just below ground level. Little is known about its diet in the wild. Lacking the mousy smell and requiring little attention, the harvest mouse makes a good pet. It has been known to live for five years in captivity but its life expectancy in the wild is about 1½ years. Mice are generally considered a nuisance, but are nevertheless clean-living little animals.

White and black mice are bred to be kept as pets. Mice are also specially bred for use by scientists in various experiments. Some have been sent into Space to see how they react to conditions there. See also RAT and VOLE.

303

Mouse-ear

Closely related to the stitchworts and chickweeds, mouse-ears are small white-flowered plants with rounded leaves. Twelve species grow in the British Isles; most are annuals covered in long, often sticky, hairs, but several are trailing perennials. They have five petals, usually deeply divided, and produce distinctive seed capsules.

The most abundant species is common mouse-ear which flowers in grassland everywhere from April to September. It often forms extensive patches, unlike the annual sticky mouse-ear with its simple erect stems. This is covered in glandular hairs, is sticky to touch and has flowers clustered at the top of the stem. It is found everywhere in arable fields, waste places and grassland.

Field mouse-ear, with handsome $\frac{3}{4}$ in. flowers and narrow leaves, is frequent only in the eastern parts of England and Scotland on lime-rich soils.

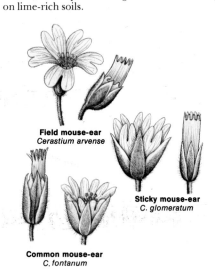

Field mouse-ear
Cerastium arvense

Sticky mouse-ear
C. glomeratum

Common mouse-ear
C. fontanum

Mouse-ear hawkweed *Hieracium pilosella*
This dwarf plant has creeping stems and oval leaves which lie flat on the ground. The leaves are white and woolly on the underside with a few long stiff hairs on top. Flower heads, which are borne from May to August on leafless stalks about 6 in. high, are lemon-yellow streaked with crimson below.

It is one of the daisy family and is found throughout the country on dry banks, among rocks and on walls. The name hawkweed refers to an old belief that hawks strengthened their vision with the plant's juice.

Mow see Stack

Mugwort *Artemisia vulgaris*
Common throughout lowlands in the British Isles, mugwort has divided leaves with tiny red-brown flowers which appear in July and August. Their pollen is spread by the wind and can bring on hay fever. Clumps of mugwort 3-4 ft high grow by roadsides and in hedge bottoms.

Various magical qualities were once attributed to mugwort: it was believed to be a protection against thunder and witchcraft and to offset the traveller's fatigue. In Europe it was known as the herb of St John the Baptist. A garland hung over the door on St John's Eve was supposed to keep away all the powers of evil.

Mulberry

A short, squat tree with a broad, round crown. It has rough, pink-brown bark and heart-shaped leaves with toothed edges. Mulberry trees were probably introduced into Britain by the Romans and are commonly found in the gardens of old country houses and rectories, often as the centrepiece of a lawn. Nearly all are of the black species *Morus nigra*.

Male and female flowers are borne on separate trees, but male trees are rare in Britain. The female trees carry open, oval catkins composed of crowded green flowers. During the summer these catkins, whether pollinated or not, swell and turn crimson, forming berries with a single hard seed and juicy pulp. They become purple or black when ripe and make excellent jam. Male trees bear green, hanging catkins in May. Each catkin holds many tiny four-petalled flowers.

The related white mulberry *M. alba* came originally from China and its leaves are the staple food of silkworms. In 1609, James I became alarmed at the money being spent by his courtiers on silks imported from France, and he caused the tree to be widely planted to encourage silk farming. However the species did not thrive.

Mulberries are propagated by cuttings, but tiny seedlings with two oblong seed-leaves are sometimes seen sprouting up in unweeded gardens.

Both species are slow growing, rarely exceed 30 ft in height, and may live for 150 years. The golden-brown heartwood is surrounded by a paler brown sapwood.

Catkin

Fruit

Black mulberry fruit and the catkin of a female tree, which is more common than the male

Mule

This is the infertile cross between a male donkey and a mare. Although sure-footed and not fastidious feeders, mules have never been extensively used on British farms. As pack animals, they served the British Army during the 1914-18 war. Up to the Elizabethan era, they were the approved mount for church dignitaries.

Mull and mor

A mull layer is what gardeners call leaf mould. It usually occurs on the floor of deciduous or mixed forests on moderately well-drained soils with a good supply of lime or calcium carbonate. The leaf litter is rapidly mixed with the mineral soil particles, a process aided by worms and other burrowing animals and micro-organisms. Decomposition consequently occurs in the upper layers of soil and not on its surface. The organic layer is crumbly and mixed with a high proportion of soil particles.

Mor is the thick, brown mat of leaf litter—and the humus produced by its partial decomposition—typical of coniferous forests and heaths. It accumulates on well-drained acid soils with a low calcium content. Such soils are devoid of earthworms and other creatures, with few micro-organisms. Consequently the leaf litter is not broken down, but remains matted.

Mullein

Tall, erect plants, covered with dense hairs, mulleins produce a rosette of large leaves from the centre of which the flowering stem arises the following summer—a spike which soon becomes covered in yellow or white flowers.

Six species occur in Britain but the great mullein is the most common. It grows throughout the lowlands on dry banks, waste places and on walls, where its dense spikes of yellow flowers attain heights of over 6 ft. In the West Country it is known as Aaron's rod.

Dark mullein or black mullein is a smaller plant—up to 4 ft high—found only on roadsides and banks on lime-rich soils in south and east England. It flowers from June to October, rather later than the great mullein which finishes by September. Dark mullein is so-called because the stamens in the centre of the flowers are purple.

Great mullein
Verbascum thapsus

Dark mullein
Verbascum nigrum

Mullet, Grey *Grenimugil labrosus*
The stomach contents of this thick-lipped fish appear to be mainly mud. The grey mullet feeds on fine green algae on rocks

and other solid surfaces such as piers and harbour walls, and also on microscopic organisms in the mud and soft sand of the sea-bed. These the mullet obtains by skimming the bottom with its lips, puffing out the coarser particles, but retaining a quantity of mud and the animals it contains. The lips have a fine, comb-like fringe—mullet have no teeth. Grey mullets have a thick-walled stomach and a very long gut.

This thick-lipped species is the most common of the three found around British coasts. Large numbers are found in southern estuaries and shallow water, and often penetrate several miles inland, almost to fresh water.

They have green-grey backs and white bellies, with silvery sides streaked with faint grey lines. There are two fins on the back, and the heads are blunt.

Muntjac see Deer

Mushroom

Although mushrooms have little nutrient value they constitute a £10 million a year industry. The field mushroom *Agaricus campestris,* with its white cap and dark, purple-brown gills, is cultivated in caves, old railway tunnels and purpose-built, light-proof buildings.

While field mushrooms are most prolific in autumn, when rain falls on a warm soil, commercial mushrooms grow all the year round in controlled conditions. A mushroom bed starts to produce within two months of spawning, continuing for several months. When production ceases, the compost is cleared out, the house disinfected, and a new crop started on fresh compost. During its brief life, a mature mushroom disperses 16,000 million spores.

Field mushrooms still grow in pastures, but are not as plentiful as in the days when horses were kept, as they flourish where horse manure has been dropped. It is never wise to pick field mushrooms without permission. If they are growing wild, anyone can pick them, but it is illegal to sell them; if they have been cultivated, picking them is theft.

Musk *Mimubus moschatus*

A creeping plant introduced to the British Isles from western North America for the beauty of its flowers and its musky scent. Musk made botanical history early this century by losing its smell. Today all plants are scentless and the only explanation for this loss advanced by botanists so far is that it may be an evolutionary change.

Musk is scattered throughout the British Isles, but is rare in Ireland. It has handsome yellow tubular flowers and is normally found in wet places in marshes or beside rivers, growing 3-18 in. high and bearing flowers in July and August.

Musk beetle see Longhorn beetle

Densely packed beds of mussels often form on sheltered, rocky shores

Mussel

Commercial exploitation of the common mussel is concentrated in estuaries like The Wash, Conway Bay and Morecambe Bay, where the water is full of organic matter carried down by rivers. The mussel beds occur below the low-tide mark, where the mussels are continually covered by water and can feed constantly.

Common mussels are found all round the British coasts, wherever there are suitable rocks and piers to which they can attach themselves. Those which live high up the shore remain small, since they can feed only

THREE BRITISH MUSSELS

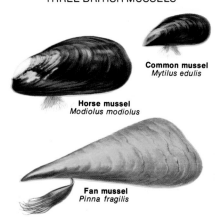

Common mussel *Mytilus edulis*

Horse mussel *Modiolus modiolus*

Fan mussel *Pinna fragilis*

The edible common mussel lives on all levels of the shore, the horse mussel on the lower shore or offshore, the fan mussel offshore

THE MUSSEL'S GUY ROPES

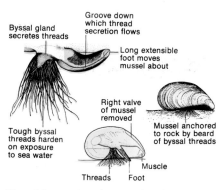

Byssal gland secretes threads

Groove down which thread secretion flows

Long extensible foot moves mussel about

Tough byssal threads harden on exposure to sea water

Right valve of mussel removed

Mussel anchored to rock by beard of byssal threads

Threads Foot Muscle

The adult mussel rarely moves but sits anchored by byssal threads to a rock. These threads, secreted by a gland in the foot, harden into strong guy ropes when covered by sea water

when covered by water. Mussels usually grow to 2 in. long, but in good conditions can reach 4-6 in. They are edible except when the sea is contaminated by sewage and they absorb bacteria harmful to man. On rocky shores sheltered from heavy seas, they form densely packed beds.

The female pea crab, the smallest British crab, lives within the common mussel's shell, feeding on food sucked in by the mussel; it scoops this off the mussel's lattice-like feeding organs.

Mussels are hermaphrodites, shedding their eggs and sperm into the water in spring. The fertilised eggs develop into tiny planktonic larvae which after several weeks of free life, settle on shore and develop into adults. These have curved, blue-black to dark brown shells, and live from three to five years.

Horse mussels grow up to 9 in. long with dark blue to purple shells. They live in rock pools on the lower shore, or offshore in large concentrations on coarse gravel bottoms, as off the Isle of Man.

The fan mussel produces the largest British shell. Up to 12 in. long, it is triangular and light to dark brown. Fan mussels live offshore with the pointed ends of the shells buried in mud.

Mustard

There are two kinds of cultivated mustard— black and white. Both are annuals which grow up to 3 ft high, produce yellow four-petalled flowers from June to August and have bristly leaves with large lobes at the tips. They are difficult to tell apart until their seed pods are ripe. Mustard is best known as a condiment and a salad plant, but it is also grown as a fodder crop and to enrich the soil with humus when ploughed in as a green manure.

Black mustard has erect, four-sided pods clinging to the stem which contain reddish-brown seeds. White mustard has flattened pods with a sabre-like appendage and yellow seeds; these pods, unlike those of black mustard, have whitish hairs on them. Both species are cultivated for the condiment contained in their seeds, although much commercial 'mustard' is actually rape, which keeps better in warm weather. The white variety is also sown with cress to produce the familiar mustard and cress.

White mustard has spread from cultivated areas to persist as a weed on arable land, especially on lime-rich soils in eastern England. In fields it is allowed to attain full height before being ploughed in. Sheep, especially ewes, just before mating, are penned on it in the autumn. Black mustard is also found in waste places but appears to be a native on cliffs and river banks in England and Wales.

Although related to the mustards, hedge mustard is of no culinary or commercial value. As its name suggests, it grows in hedge-

Fields of black mustard, grown commercially for seed, add colour to the Hampshire countryside

rows, on roadsides and waste places throughout the lowlands. It produces tiny yellow flowers in June and July and has jagged leaves with points turned towards the stem. Its rough pods are about ½ in. long.

A similar plant, treacle mustard, also grows in cultivated ground and waste places. Growing only 2½ ft high, it bears pale yellow flowers followed by smooth ¾ in. pods.

Garlic mustard, also known as Jack-by-the-hedge, is often seen in April and June when its white flowers stand out against hedges and woodland margins throughout the lowlands, though rarely in western Ireland.

Growing up to 4 ft high, it has heart-shaped leaves with very distinct veins. When the leaves are crushed they give off a strong smell of garlic. The flower was once valued in making a sauce for salt fish, and in Somerset was known by the popular name of 'sauce alone'.

Myxomatosis

A virus infection fatal to rabbits which was first reported in Uruguay, South America, in 1898. Attempts to use it as a means of controlling wild rabbits have resulted in epidemics. It can be transmitted by any biting or blood-sucking insect, such as a flea or mosquito.

The symptoms of myxomatosis include a watery discharge from the eyes and swelling of the eyelids and nose. Death follows in about two weeks. Since 1952, it has been illegal to spread the disease in Britain by using infected animals. Nevertheless, an epidemic broke out in Britain in 1953. It has been estimated that 99 per cent of the rabbit population of over 60 million died in this epidemic.

Apart from killing off large numbers of the rabbit population, myxomatosis had an indirect effect on the rabbit's predators. The buzzard population in particular suffered a serious setback. Grass on downlands quickly became long since there were fewer rabbits, and attacks by foxes on hen roosts and game became more frequent.

The disease is still liable to flare up in some areas, although there are indications that many rabbits are now immune.

Black mustard
Brassica nigra

White mustard
Sinapis alba

Hedge mustard
Sisymbrium officinale

Treacle mustard
Erysimum cheiranthoides

Garlic mustard
Alliaria petiolata

All mustards are named for the condiment prepared from the seeds of black and white mustard

N

Natterjack see Toad
Naturalists see p. 310

Navelwort *Umbilicus rupestris*
Also known as wall pennywort, this shade-loving plant grows on, or in the cracks of, damp rocks and walls. It can immediately be recognised during winter and spring by its round, shining leaves, which are about the size of an old penny. In mid-summer it produces many drooping, green-white flowers on a stem which may be 15 in. high. After the seeds have ripened, the stems and leaves wither and turn brown-red, and the plant rests until winter as a tuberous underground stem.

Navelwort is common in south and west England, Wales, south-west Scotland, and Ireland, except central areas.

Penny-sized leaves with navel-like dimples give rise to the names pennywort and navelwort

Needle fly see Stonefly

Ness
A small promontory, headland or cape, especially in East Anglia. A ness is not usually very high, having been built up gradually as the beach has moved seaward.

Nesses increase and decrease in size over the years, and a study of old maps shows that in many cases there has been a rate of movement of more than 6 ft each year in the last 100 years. This is probably due to the shifting of offshore sandbanks.

Nest see p. 312

Nettle
The stinging nettle, cursed by gardeners with ungloved hands and walkers with bare legs, was once regarded as valuable. Nettle beer was made from the young tops, which can also be boiled and eaten as a vegetable which tastes like spinach. The dried leaves can still be bought for making nettle tea. Before cotton was imported, the fibres in the stem were spun and made into cloth used for sheets and tablecloths. Cattle browse on stinging nettles; they are immune to the stinging hairs.

The plant, which can reach a height of 5 ft, grows throughout the British Isles in woods and waste places, by hedges and on grassland. It bears tiny green-white flowers from June onwards.

Annual nettle is a weed of arable fields and waste places, common in all but western areas of the British Isles. Smaller than the stinging nettle, 3-24 in. tall, it is just as painful to touch. Its inconspicuous flowers are borne from June to September.

The stinging hairs have a pointed single cell above a bulbous base holding a poisonous liquid. The hairs are brittle and, after piercing the skin, break off, allowing the poison to enter the wound and cause irritation.

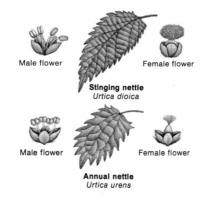

Male flower   Female flower
Stinging nettle
Urtica dioica

Male flower   Female flower
Annual nettle
Urtica urens

New Forest cicada *Cicadetta montana*
Only one species of cicada lives in the British Isles, although there are 1500 species in warmer parts of the world. Since 1812, when the presence of the cicada was first recorded, it has been seen only rarely, mostly in the New Forest and on a few occasions in the woodlands around Haslemere in Surrey.

The insect is about 1 in. long and when at rest it resembles a large aphid with transparent wings folded back and longer than its body. It whirrs into flight when disturbed with a buzz similar to that of a dragonfly but does not fly far. The male has an unusually high-pitched song which sounds like the hiss of a high-pressure air leak.

The cicada spends several years of its life as a grub-like underground nymph. When adult, it lives only about six weeks and rarely emerges from the vegetation on which it feeds, except on sunny days between mid-May and early June.

The rare New Forest species is Britain's only representative of the tropical cicadas

Newt
Three closely related species of newts (or salamanders) are found in the British Isles. They are amphibious, spending part of their lives in water and part on land. When on land they can be mistaken for lizards, except that lizards, being reptiles, have scaly skins. Newts have smooth skins but they are sometimes covered with lumps or warts.

In early spring newts enter the water to breed, and the differences between sexes can then be seen. The males are more brightly coloured than the females and develop a crest along the back and round the tail. The females lay 200-300 eggs singly on water plants, each enclosed in a protective coat of jelly. Like those of frogs and toads, the eggs hatch into a larval stage, similar to a tadpole, which has gills. In ten weeks lungs and legs have grown, the gills are lost, and the young newt, an eft, leaves the water. It may not return to water until mature, two or three years later. Adults also leave the water at the end of the breeding season and spend the rest of the year on land, hidden in damp places. They emerge at night to feed. Newts feed in water as well as on land, and catch food such as tadpoles, small fish, slugs and earthworms.

The smooth newt is the most common and is widespread, except on mountains and moorlands. It grows up to 4 in. long and has a spotted throat. The male has a wavy crest and is brown to olive-brown, marked with deeper spots. On the underside its colour is yellow to rose, and there is a middle area coloured red with black spots. Females do not have a crest and are a paler yellow-brown.

The palmate newt grows to 3 in. and favours mountains and acid soils. It varies from brown to olive-brown with small, dark spots, and is white to pale orange beneath. The male has a low, straight-edged crest on its back, and black webs between its hind toes.

The great crested or warty newt can grow up to 7 in., and some females can be even larger. It tends to prefer deeper water than the other species, and some stay in the water all the year round. The male has a high, serrated crest. Great crested newts are olive-brown, covered in black spots, and have a silvery band along each side of the tail. The underparts are yellow to orange and dotted in black. Females are similar but lack a crest.

The skin of the great crested newt is covered in wart-like glands which produce a sticky, white fluid that would-be predators, such as snakes, water birds, hedgehogs and rats, find distasteful. All newts can regenerate limbs amputated by predators or accidents.

British newts

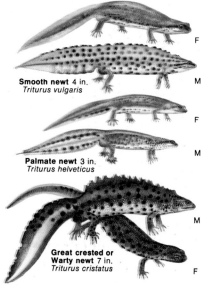

Smooth newt 4 in.
Triturus vulgaris

Palmate newt 3 in.
Triturus helveticus

Great crested or Warty newt 7 in.
Triturus cristatus

The three British newts spend most of their lives on land, returning to the water to breed

Night see p. 314
Nightingale see Chat

During the day the nightjar crouches on the ground, concealed among fallen leaves and twigs

Nightjar

One of the myths attached to this night-flying bird gives it the name goat-sucker. It was once widely believed that nightjars milked goats with their huge mouths, after which the goats went blind. The sound of their continuous churring, broken only by shrill squawks and bouts of noisy wing flapping, always performed after dark, was once familiar on any patch of rough heath or common. Now that many of these areas are being planted with trees, nightjars are becoming rare.

Arriving from Africa in May, nightjars spend their days on the ground, camouflaged by their mottled brown plumage which has delicate markings difficult to distinguish from dead leaves or wood. Within half an hour of sunset, the male flies up to a branch or stump and begins to chur, turning its head this way and that. It may continue for 15 minutes or more before calling up its mate and flying off to hunt for the large moths that form the major part of its diet.

The nightjar catches food on the wing. Its bill opens into a huge gape and is fringed with bristles which apparently help to funnel the moths inside.

Nightjars are inquisitive birds and will inspect animal or bird visitors to their territory, circling and hovering and then disappearing into the gloom with a call and wing clap. The male has white patches on wings and tail.

The hen lays two white eggs among dead bracken between May and July. The young are looked after by both parents, with the male finishing the task while the hen begins a second brood.

Nightshade

Deadly nightshade is one of Britain's most poisonous plants. Children have died after eating only three of its black, cherry-like berries. All parts of this bushy plant are poisonous. It reaches 4 ft high, with large, egg-shaped, dull green leaves, which exude a heavy smell, and dull purple flowers, which are borne from June to August. It grows in woodland, scrub and hedges on lime-rich soils throughout England, but is rare elsewhere. The plant sometimes grows on the ruins of old buildings, where it may attract children. It yields a drug called belladonna that is used by eye specialists to dilate the pupils.

Black nightshade is also poisonous, but the small, tomato-like, green or black berries are less likely to tempt children. It is a weed of arable fields, waste places and gardens, common in the lowlands of England and Wales but rare elsewhere. Its branching stems, which grow to 2 ft, bear white flowers between July and September.

Woody nightshade, or bittersweet, belongs to the same family as the potato and tomato; the flowers of all three plants are similar in

Deadly nightshade
Atropa belladonna

Black nightshade
Solanum nigrum

The berries of both deadly nightshade and black nightshade are highly poisonous

shape but those of the bittersweet are the most striking—five blue petals with a central core of bright yellow anthers. The flowers, which appear from June to September, develop into small, oval, red berries which, although they are not as poisonous as those of deadly nightshade, can still cause sickness if eaten.

The young stems of bittersweet used to be collected in autumn and dried for medicinal purposes; at first they taste bitter but later this changes to an agreeable sweetness. A decoction used to be recommended for rheumatism and skin complaints.

In Lincolnshire, garlands of bittersweet were once hung on pigs to protect them from witchcraft.

Bittersweet grows in hedges and damp woodlands throughout the lowlands, where it sometimes reaches well over 6 ft. It also spreads over pebbles on the seashore.

Nipplewort *Lapsana communis*

A weed that grows by roadsides, in woodlands, on walls and in waste places throughout the British Isles, except mountainous districts. The small heads of about 20 yellow flowers, which are borne on the 1-3 ft high stems between July and September, open early in the morning and close again in early afternoon; in dull weather they remain closed all day.

The plant is so-called because the buds resemble nipples. It was once used as a cure for sore nipples—an example of sympathetic magic. See also HERB

Noctuid moth

The 400 or so members of this family are what most people mean by the word 'moth' —a dull-coloured insect with a large body, which usually flies at night, and is most often seen when it comes to a lighted window.

There is considerable variation between the species, but the square-spot rustic is a typical noctuid. Its caterpillars feed on grasses and other low-growing plants and hibernate among grass roots.

The herald is a species which hibernates in the adult state. It resembles a dead leaf because of the jagged outline on its wings and its red-brown markings. Its first call on awaking is to pussy-willow catkins, which provide a good supply of nectar.

The snout has an unusual shape for a noctuid, being slim and having long palps protruding from its head to form a 'snout'. It is common in June and July on nettles, which are eaten by its caterpillars.

The Mother Shipton is more brightly marked than most noctuids. The name refers to a fancied portrait on its wings of a prophetess of that name. It flies over grassy fields by day in May and June.

The old lady moth has a dull, grey-brown pattern on its wings and often hides behind curtains. It flies by night in July and August and is common in most parts of the British Isles except the extreme north. The cater-

pillars bury themselves before changing to chrysalids in May.

Bats prey on night-flying noctuids, which they detect by means of their 'radar'-type location mechanism. But moths have good ears, at the base of their wings, and many species can escape by closing their wings and dropping to the ground or by going into a rapid zigzag flight. A few species can squeak ultrasonically themselves, and so confuse bats.

The caterpillars of some noctuid moths are known collectively as cutworms. They are dull in colour and get their name from their habit of gnawing at the base of many kinds of plants, including potato, turnip, lettuce and beet, and eventually cutting them off completely. They may work along a row of plants, severing them one after another.

They are mostly active at night and can be found curled up during the day under clods of soil or in turf.

SOME COMMON NOCTUID MOTHS

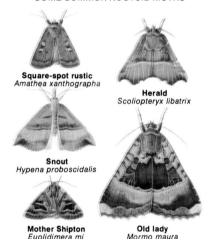

Square-spot rustic *Amathea xanthographa*

Herald *Scoliopteryx libatrix*

Snout *Hypena proboscidalis*

Mother Shipton *Euolidimera mi*

Old lady *Mormo maura*

Noctuid moths usually fly at night and are most commonly seen at lighted windows

Nut

A large, hard seed, usually the product of a single flower. Nuts are borne only by trees or sturdy shrubs, because large food reserves are needed to create them. But in turn each fallen nut provides enough nourishment for a large and vigorous seedling that can outgrow most weeds during its critical early stages.

Nuthatch

The habit of hacking at nuts—hazel, beech, acorns—to break them open has given the nuthatch its name. It is often heard banging vigorously with its bill on a nut wedged intentionally in a bark crevice. The nuthatch also feeds on beetles, earwigs and small caterpillars, and is a regular visitor to garden bird-tables.

The nuthatch is up to 5½ in. long, has a pastel-blue back with pale, rusty-pink underparts, and a black eye-stripe. It is the only

THE NUTHATCH'S NESTING CHAMBER

The nuthatch makes a nest of bark flakes or dead leaves, often in a woodpecker's old nest hole. It plasters the entrance to the chamber with mud to keep out larger birds

British bird which regularly climbs down trees head first.

In late April or May the female lays six to ten white, red-spotted eggs in a nest of bark flakes or dead leaves in a hole in a tree, usually more than 6 ft up, and plasters the entrance with mud to keep out intruders. Occasionally it builds the nest in a wall or nest-box.

The nuthatch is unknown in the Isle of Man and in Ireland, and is a rare visitor to Scotland and northern England. Elsewhere it is common, even in central London. Hard winters hit the nuthatch population, particularly when a heavy snowfall is followed by freezing weather which prevents the bird from finding nuts on woodland floors.

The nead-first approach down a tree is a habit peculiar to the nut-splitting nuthatch

Four men who found keys to nature's secrets

Britain's rich plant and animal life has always encouraged the study of natural history. Its finest flowering came in the 18th and 19th centuries when these four great men all contributed significantly to knowledge of the environment

John Ray

John Ray has been called the father of English natural history. His influence on naturalists was profound, but because he was a scholar who wrote in Latin, and perhaps because he did not seek popular acclaim, he is less well known than he deserves.

Ray — or Wray as he wrote his name until 1670 — was born in November 1628, the son of the blacksmith at Black Notley, near Braintree, Essex. He was educated at Braintree School and became a Fellow of Trinity College, Cambridge, in 1649. There he exerted a considerable influence on scientific studies, particularly botany. One of his students, Francis Willughby, became famous as a naturalist and also sponsored and assisted Ray in his later work.

Ray's first book, a catalogue of plants growing in the vicinity of Cambridge, was published in 1660. It is a model of what such a book should be; localities are described so exactly that it is possible to identify them today, and even find some of the plants still growing there. Ten years later he published a catalogue of English plants. Both books were arranged alphabetically, but Ray was working on a system of natural classification which he later published in his history of plants and in the *Methodus Plantarum Nova* of 1682. This was the foundation on which later scientists were to build, culminating in the work of the Swedish naturalist Carolus Linnaeus (1707-78) who, in 1753, introduced the system of naming every living thing with two Latin words — the system which is still used today.

Ray and Willughby travelled widely through the British Isles and Europe, meeting other naturalists and collecting specimens. Even in Ray's later years, when sickness kept him at home, his interest in local plants and insects was active and continuous. Nor was he simply a botanist — his zoological works have been described as the basis of all modern zoology.

Ray published a collection of English proverbs in 1670 and a book of 'out-of-the-way' English words in 1674. Both were instrumental in recording and keeping alive aspects of the English countryside which otherwise would have been lost.

Gilbert White

Like an explorer venturing into new lands, Gilbert White was one of the first to bring a trained and inquiring mind to bear on the simple but profound events of his native countryside. Generations of countrymen before him had noted the arrival of the cuckoo, and were aware that the bird did not hatch its own eggs. White wanted to know why. He even dissected cuckoos to see if anything in their anatomy prevented them from incubating eggs. Others had observed the annual arrival and disappearance of swallows, but White set down the dates

Gilbert White, who wrote *The Natural History and Antiquities of Selborne*, made more discoveries in the woods and fields of his beloved Selborne than many of his contemporaries did on voyages to the far side of the world

and speculated about whether they migrated or hibernated.

White noted the different ways in which a squirrel, a field-mouse and a nuthatch extracted the kernel from a nut. He first described the harvest mouse and its tiny spherical nest. He distinguished the wood-warbler from the more common willow-warbler and chiffchaff; and the lesser whitethroat from the common whitethroat. Why, he asked, does a young chicken snap up flies from a window, but show alarm when confronted with a bee or a wasp? Always he was trying to supply the answers, although sometimes he arrived at the wrong conclusions.

Gilbert White was born in Selborne, Hampshire, in 1720 and was educated at Basingstoke and Oxford. After graduating, he returned to Selborne as rector and settled there, unmarried, for the rest of his life. From all his observations he produced one book, *The Natural History and Antiquities of Selborne,* which was published in 1789 and has gone through innumerable editions. Written in the form of letters over a period of about 20 years, this book has given pleasure to millions of amateur naturalists and set the pattern of regard for accuracy and attention to detail on which modern science is built.

MONTAGU'S BIRDS AND FISH

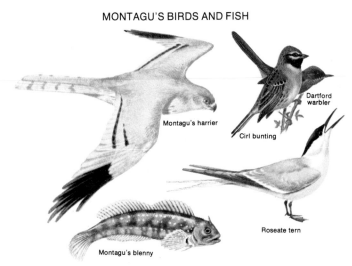

George Montagu identified many birds and sea creatures previously unknown in Britain, including the cirl bunting and the roseate tern. As a tribute to his discoveries, later naturalists named several species after him

George Montagu

George Montagu was one of the most capable and wide-ranging naturalists of the 18th and 19th centuries. He was the author of a famous *Ornithological Dictionary* (1802), of a classic textbook on British molluscs, *Testacea Britannica* (1803-8) and of numerous papers in learned journals.

Montagu is said to have taken an interest in birds from an early age, an interest confirmed when at 19 he served in North America as an officer in the 15th Regiment of Foot and started to prepare the skins of birds he had shot. After his return to England he settled on an estate in Wiltshire, leading the life of a country gentleman. Later he moved to a house at Kingsbridge, south Devon, where some of his best work—on marine animals—was undertaken.

Montagu corresponded with Gilbert White, but his letters lack the charm of the scholar of Selborne. He had a vigorous and direct style, and in plain, descriptive writing he was at his best. He was an acute observer who preferred to verify facts for himself where possible. In his *Ornithological Dictionary*, for instance, it is obvious that he did not share White's view that swallows hibernated rather than migrated.

His work on the notoriously difficult marine sponges—he called it an 'occult science'—was a great advance on earlier publications in that field. His studies of British molluscs added over a hundred species which were either new to science or which he had recognised for the first time in British seas.

But it is as an ornithologist that Montagu is best remembered. Because of his rational approach and deep knowledge of the subject, he exerted a considerable influence on the development of bird study. He encouraged birds to live in the grounds of his house at Kingsbridge. In 1800 he distinguished the cirl bunting from the yellowhammer for the first time in Britain. He was the first to describe the beautiful roseate tern; he also gave the first adequate account of the natural history of the Dartford warbler.

Today his name is commemorated in various animals, among them the bird Montagu's harrier and the fish Montagu's blenny and Montagu's sea snail.

Charles Darwin

Charles Robert Darwin is possibly the best known of British naturalists. His most famous work, *The Origin of Species by Means of Natural Selection,* was published in 1859 and gave an impetus to the systematic study of natural history and resulted in a re-evaluation of many of the social and religious tenets of his time. Because of the impact of Darwin's views on the philosophy of science, he is often regarded as an international figure, a thinker rather than an observer; but he was a countryman at heart.

Darwin was born at Shrewsbury, where he was educated, later going to Edinburgh University and then Christ's College, Cambridge. His grandfather, Erasmus Darwin, was an early evolutionist and his mother was a daughter of Josiah Wedgwood, the potter. At Cambridge, where his study of biology began in earnest, he met Professor J. S. Henslow, the botanist. In 1831 he took his B.A., and through Henslow he received an invitation to join HMS *Beagle* as expedition naturalist. For the next five years the *Beagle* sailed on a scientific survey of South American and Pacific waters, and Darwin conducted the field studies which formed the basis of his revolutionary theory of evolution.

In 1842, Darwin bought Downe House, near Bromley in Kent, where he passed the remainder of his life. There he worked on a succession of natural history topics, and eventually summarised his theories of natural selection. In 1871 he published *The Descent of Man,* which related the human race to the ancestors of the great apes and caused almost as much controversy as his *Origin of Species.*

At Downe he also studied the many strange forms developed by orchids, and proved that, far from being random creations, the flowers of each species were specially adapted to ensure cross-fertilisation by a particular type of insect. Another absorbing interest was the insect-eating plants. He also studied the role of earthworms in the production of vegetable mould and established that male bumble bees had regular flight paths which did not vary greatly from year to year. See also EVOLUTION

DARWIN'S ORCHIDS

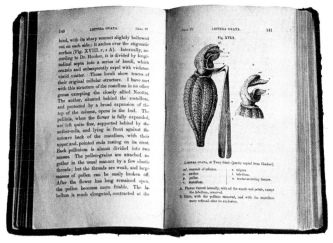

Charles Darwin expanded his theories on natural selection in a book on the cross-fertilisation of orchids by insects. These pages are from the finely illustrated first edition of 1862, describing the twayblade

The infinite variety of animals' nests

Birds are the most obvious nest-builders — evidence of their skill can be seen in every hedgerow. But a wide variety of other animals, including fish, insects and mammals, also build nests for shelter and to rear their young

Warm-blooded animals make nests to protect themselves and their offspring, chiefly against cold. Most cold-blooded animals do not make nests. Small mammals such as shrews, mice and voles make nests of shredded grass. These are often hidden in burrows, but field voles make theirs at the base of grass tussocks and harvest mice weave their breeding nests in the spring from reeds or corn leaves. The nests are ball-shaped and attached to the stalks of grass or weeds. When winter comes the harvest mice retreat to burrows just under the surface of the ground. Many mammals which do not need elaborate nests for themselves make them for their young before they are born. The female rabbit, for example, constructs for her naked litter a nest of grass and fur pulled from her belly.

Mammals such as the hare, deer and pony, whose young are born covered in hair, open-eyed and active, do not need nests. The young are already protected against the cold and they are soon able to move around and fend for themselves.

Mammals which hibernate need winter nests to prevent their temperature dropping to freezing point. Dormice build winter nests of grass and strips of bark in hollow trees or below ground. The hedgehog accumulates a heap of dried leaves under a bramble bush or woodpile, then twirls round inside it to make its nest.

All birds need some form of nest in which to lay and incubate their eggs. (The exception is the cuckoo, which leaves nest-building and incubation to other birds.) In its simplest form the nest is found, not built: the guillemot uses a cliff ledge, the little tern a hollow on a pebble beach. Plainest of all nests is the nightjar's — a mere scrape in a patch of clear ground.

Nest-building is instinctive, and each species of bird makes its own characteristic kind. The whole reproductive cycle — courtship, mating, nest-building, incubation of the eggs and rearing of the young — is triggered off when the lengthening daylight of spring causes the glands to secrete hormones which control the bird's behaviour. Birds can be made to build nests out of season by being injected with hormones.

The first birds probably copied their reptile ancestors by laying their eggs in holes in the ground and covering them with earth or leaves. As they gradually spread into open country they laid eggs in patches of firm ground sheltered by grass, which tended to be moulded into cup-like shapes as the birds turned on, the eggs. Over thousands of generations, these associations imprinted on the birds' nervous systems began to make them re-create these grass platforms, or nests.

Birds which nest among the branches of trees and bushes usually build cup-shaped nests. The tiny goldcrest uses moss, lichens and spiders' webs. The song thrush cements grass stems and small twigs together with a lining of mud. The

A key to some typical nests

Magpie covers its nest with a dome of twigs which conceal its bright colours from predators

Reed warbler weaves a neat cup nest of dried grasses attached to stiff reed stems alongside ponds and rivers

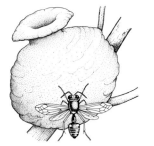

Potter wasp constructs a delicate vase-shaped nest of moulded clay, attaching it to a heather twig

Dormouse builds a summer breeding nest of leaves and moss close to the ground in a bush

Lapwing lays her four spotted eggs in a scraped hollow in the ground lined with dried grasses

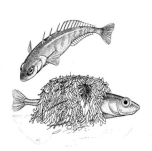

Stickleback lays her eggs in a nest of weeds bound together with sticky threads. It is made by the male

Crab-spider guards her egg-sac, a silk bag containing her eggs, which she has secured among twigs of heather

Grey squirrel constructs a domed drey of twigs lined with grass and leaves in a tree fork high above the ground

A young sand martin waits at the entrance of its nest to be fed with insects by its parents. The nest is a 2-3 ft long tunnel in the sand

larger the bird, the stronger the building materials must be. Rooks build substantial platforms of sticks, which they use for several years, repairing them when necessary.

Because a bird must be inconspicuous while it is incubating its eggs, most species which build cup-shaped nests are dull coloured; those that do bear bright colours have them on the underside, where they are hidden when the bird is on the nest, or they are restricted to the male. Most birds with overall bright plumage either nest in holes, as the kingfisher and blue tit do, or build a roofed nest, as the magpie does.

The Manx shearwater excavates a 3 ft long nesting burrow, sometimes taking over a rabbit burrow. Puffins dig tunnels up to 10 ft long, using their powerful bills and large feet. A colony may number thousands of pairs and the ground can become so honeycombed that it will collapse.

Bird nestlings, like the young of other animals, may be naked, blind nest-dwellers or fluffy, active nest-fleers. The nest-dwellers stay in the nest for days or weeks, being fed by the parents until they are big enough to fly. For this reason the number of eggs laid by such species is restricted to the number of young which it is possible to feed: if too many eggs were laid the nestlings would starve. Nest-fleeing species, which include many ground-nesting birds, lay much larger numbers of eggs. For example, the partridge lays up to 20. The chicks leave the nest immediately and, guarded by the parents, search for their own food. In these species the number of eggs laid is limited only by the egg-laying capacity of the female; the more she lays, the greater the number of her vulnerable chicks which are likely to survive.

A mammal's or bird's nest is thought of as a bed or nursery, but a bees', wasps' or ants' nest is more like a city. The nests, in which most of the members are the offspring of one or a few reproductive queen females, include food stores, rearing areas for the larval stages and a large force of sterile worker females who collect the food, defend and clean the nest and tend the young.

The homes of some other insects, such as the clay pot of the solitary potter wasp, are also known as nests; in these the insect makes cells in which it stores provisions, lays eggs and rears young. The tents of silk and leaves constructed by small tortoise-shell butterfly caterpillars are collectively known as a nest, as is the protective cocoon which a spider weaves around its eggs.

Some fish make nests in which to lay their eggs. The male stickleback scrapes a hollow in the sand in which he builds a nest of pieces of grass and water weed, which are glued together with a secretion produced by the kidneys. He attracts, or drives, up to five passing females into the nest, where they lay their eggs and swim away. The male then fertilises the eggs and guards them until they hatch, aerating them by waving his fins to create a current of water. When the eggs hatch, the male stickleback guards the young.

ANIMALS WHICH NEST IN HOLES

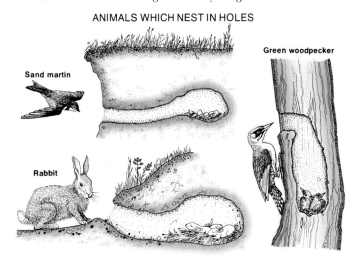

Among the birds and other animals that make nests in holes are the sand martin, which drives a tunnel into sandy soil; the female rabbit, which digs a nesting burrow; and the green woodpecker, which bores a hole in a tree

313

Animals that come out to feed as night falls

Animals which feed by night can exploit sources of food – plants and plant-eaters – that are also taken by day animals, but without coming into direct competition with them. A night shift of feeders, so to speak, takes over from the day shift so that a rhythm of activity goes on all round the clock. There are few animals that continue their search for food right through the night; many become active at dusk and dawn – for example, the badger, rabbit, toad, frog and deer – and in this way form a link between the truly day and night hunters. A few animals, such as the common shrew, are busy every hour of the day, pausing only for short rest periods.

Every animal is a link in the vast food chain of a community. At the bottom of this chain, however, is plant material – flowers, leaves, bark, nuts, fruits, fungi, moss, lichens and leaf-litter – which is eaten by earthworms, millipedes, snails, slugs, woodlice, moths, beetles, woodmice, dormice and rabbits at some time during the night. Frogs, toads, shrews, hedgehogs, bats, owls, nightjars and, if the night is warm, adders, hunt the plant-feeders and are, in turn, taken by weasels, stoats, badgers and foxes. It becomes evident from this hunter/hunted sequence that although many animals seek refuge in the dark, concealing themselves during the day, many of their predators have become twilight or nocturnal feeders also.

Bats catch the large-bodied moths and beetles that fly at night. They locate prey by transmitting high-pitched sounds, the reflected echoes of which are interpreted so accurately that even in complete darkness the insects are captured. The nightjar also takes these succulent insects at night, collecting them in its gaping mouth. During the day this bird crouches on its ground nest, its delicately mottled and streaked plumage making it invisible among the leaf-litter.

Owls are particularly fond of small secretive mammals such as woodmice. To exploit this food source they fly at night, finding their prey mainly by sounds, although their large forward-facing eyes are very sensitive to the dim light. The owls, nightjars and petrels are noted among British birds for their night activity.

The reasons for the nocturnal habits of some animals are not always apparent, because they were formed in the distant past before man had eliminated many of the carnivores which preyed on these animals. The badger, for example, whose only enemy today is man, may, in the past, have had deadly foes which could only be avoided by remaining hidden in the sett during the daylight hours. The roe deer, which browses on leaves and berries at dusk and dawn, has no predators today, but probably had them in the past when it was a woodland creature. However, the young kids are easy food for eagles and other large birds of prey, and it may be for this reason that deer are still so secretive during the day.

It is equally difficult to give a concrete explanation for the moths' preference for night-time activity. Two reasons may be that by feeding from flowers at this time they do not compete with the butterflies and that they also avoid many predators, for there are fewer bats and nightjars than day-flying birds. Moths are well adapted to their nocturnal existence. They are able to find scented flowers in the dark with their smell-sensitive feathery antennae, and when resting during the day their wing patterns and colouring camouflage them

Pine and larch silhouetted as dusk begins in the New Forest. This is the time when the predatory animals of the forest begin to stir

Old lady moth Often found hiding behind curtains, it is on the wing during summer evenings and is a favourite prey of bats

Honey fungus A blue-green glow is seen on decaying tree trunks on which it grows. Once used to light the way along dark paths

Rounded snail During the day it hides under moss and dead leaves, coming out at night to feed on fungi and decaying matter

against foliage, lichen-covered rocks or stones, or tree trunks.

Plants are also affected by the hours of darkness. At night photosynthesis stops, as energy from sunlight is vital for this chemical process. Respiration goes on all the time, although the production of carbon dioxide is only apparent at night when it is not being used in photosynthesis. Some flowers close at night, the daisy for example, while wood anemone flowers droop over to protect the pollen, and the three clover-like leaflets of the wood sorrel also droop. These plant movements may be triggered off by the change in temperature during the night. Some flowers do not open until dusk, and at this time emit a strong scent which attracts pollinating moths. The first honeysuckle blooms open at about 7 p.m. They are visited by hawkmoths, which hover in front of them, probing for nectar at the base of the long flower tubes.

Another feature of the countryside that becomes apparent only in the dark is the steady blue-green glow often seen on decaying tree trunks on which the honey fungus grows. At one time pieces of wood covered with the luminous threads of this fungus were put along dark paths to light the way. The wingless female glow-worm also produces such a light to attract her flying mate. To make the glow, luciferin, secreted by the moth's glands, is broken down by oxygen in the presence of the enzyme luciferase. The beetle's light goes out when the oxygen, supplied from blood vessels, is cut off. This chemically produced light, or bioluminescence, is cold and wastes little energy, unlike the light from an electric bulb. Many marine organisms can also make their own light. Some bristle worms and bristle stars glow brightly when disturbed.

Barn owl Using its keen ears and forward-facing eyes, the barn owl hunts small, secretive mammals like dormice and shrews

Long-eared bat A common woodland species. It picks moths and beetles off the tree foliage

Glow-worm Females give off a light to attract a mate. The cold, chemical light uses little energy

Badger After passing the day in its underground sett it comes out to feed on anything from beetles to berries and mice

Horseshoe bat Moths are caught by the bat giving out high-pitched sounds and homing in on echoes reflected from its prey

Small elephant hawk A night-flying moth frequently seen on honeysuckle, which it probes for nectar

Dormouse A night feeder on berries, seeds, insects and leaves, it is in turn eaten by owls and other predators

Stag beetle The huge antler-like jaws are not very powerful. The male can be up to 3 in. long

Honeysuckle A beautiful and fragrant plant which opens at dusk and attracts moths. These fly from one flower to another and pollinate them

Hedgehog By day it rests in thick undergrowth, roaming at night in search of worms, slugs and sometimes snakes

O

Oak apple galls are swellings caused by gall wasp larvae burrowing into leaf buds

Oak

England's traditional tree is also its most numerous. There are two native species. The common, or pedunculate, oak has stalked acorns and short-stalked leaves; the sessile, or durmast, oak has stalkless acorns and long-stalked leaves. The rounded lobed leaves of both types are familiar in decorative painting and carving. Many oaks are hybrids between the two species.

There are three introduced species. The American red oak is grown as a decorative tree in parks and gardens. It has more sharply lobed leaves, which turn vivid red in autumn. The Mediterranean holm, or evergreen, oak resembles a giant holly. It has dark green, glossy, spineless leaves, black bark, very hard wood, and acorns that take two years to ripen. Resistant to salt winds, it is planted for seaside shelter. It also provides winter shelter for shrubs planted round it. The Turkey oak grows wild in woods and parks. The leaves are zigzag-lobed and the acorn cups have bristles. It grows rapidly but the timber is of little value to craftsmen because it warps so easily.

All these oaks have many features in common. Most buds are set alternately along the twigs and form a cluster at the tip. This produces the irregular branching pattern that enables oaks to be recognised at a distance, particularly in winter.

Male flowers open in hanging catkins during April. After shedding their pollen, which is carried by the wind, they wither and disappear. Female flowers open with the first leaves as less conspicuous, bud-shaped catkins. During the summer the leafy bracts at the base of each female flower turn woody and fuse to form a hard green acorn cup. A single seed develops in this to become an oval brown acorn, so-named from the Scandinavian *ek korn,* meaning oak corn-seed. Acorns are also known as mast, from another Scandinavian word, *mat,* meaning food; this is because they once served extensively as winter fodder for herds of pigs allowed to roam the woods—a custom which continues in the New Forest. Oak produces seeds irregularly and provides abundant

The leaves, fruits and flowers of five oaks

Common and sessile oaks both have round-lobed leaves, while those of the Turkey oak and the red oak have pointed lobes. Holm oak leaves have no lobes. Oak flowers are catkins, opening in April. Male catkins have long stalks and the females, which are carried on the same tree, are shorter. The female flower develops the fruit—the acorn. All the oaks shown here are deciduous, except the holm oak. In autumn the leaves of the red oak turn red rather than yellow

Fruit

Female flowers × 4

Male flowers × 4

Common or pedunculate oak
Quercus robur

Fruit

Female flowers × 6

Male flowers × 6

Sessile oak
Quercus petraea

Male flowers × 6

Female flowers × 6

Holm oak
Quercus ilex

Fruit

Male flowers × 8

Female flowers × 8

Fruit

Red oak
Quercus borealis

Male flowers × 3

Female flowers × 3

Turkey oak
Quercus cerris

Fruit

mast only once in every three or four years.

Oak colonises cleared woodland, neglected commons and pastures, hedgerows and waysides. The sturdy seedling tolerates a wide range of soils and competes vigorously with grass, herbaceous plants and thorn bushes. Growth is slow and steady, but is influenced by soil and climate. The oakwoods of the western coast of Britain, and those of Ireland, usually grow in rock-strewn dells containing little fertile soil and swept by salt-laden winds. For this reason their trees are generally stunted and distorted and their trunks are hosts to lichens, mosses, ferns and ivy that cannot shelter elsewhere. By contrast, the oaks of the Midlands and southeast, where the soil is deep and fertile, attain their full height of 100 ft and may support only green algae.

Britain's tallest oak is a 135 ft high sessile oak that grows in the grounds of Whitfield House, Hereford, and the biggest-girthed oak—43½ ft round—is a common oak at Cilcochynyn Farm, Pontfadog, Wales. This, like many veteran trees, is a pollarded tree—that is, one lopped repeatedly. Because it is hollow, it is impossible to date it exactly, but it may be 800 years old, whereas the average life-span is 250 years.

As oak trunks expand, their bark becomes thicker and rougher and breaks up into a pattern of irregular squares. Oak bark was harvested from felled trees for centuries to extract tannin from it; this was used to tan hides. Below the bark is a layer of pale brown sapwood, which is not durable unless treated with preservative. Beyond the sapwood is the stout core of dark brown heartwood which, in its natural state, withstands centuries of hard use. This has clearly marked annual rings, and rays, radiating from the centre, across the rings.

Oak makes long-lasting fence posts and rails. Most oak timbers in half-timbered buildings are pegged together, because oak is difficult to nail; numbers scratched on a beam at each joint show how the builders planned where it should fit. Old oak floorboards are recognisable by the wavy surface left on them by the adzes with which they were smoothed.

The keel, frame and ribs of every great wooden sailing ship, from the time of the Vikings onwards, were made of oak. It took the timber from 3000 mature oak trees to build a man o' war, and the destruction of oak forests dates from the wholesale felling of trees for shipbuilding in the 17th and 18th centuries. Today the timber is used for the hulls of fishing craft built along the east coast of Scotland.

Oak has long been the best native timber for such furnishings as church pews and pulpits, and staircases and panelling in mansions and public buildings. Because of its strength, it is used for ladder rungs and cartwheel spokes and, because it is impervious to alcohol, beer barrels and wine casks are made of it.

Bog oak is oak that has lain for centuries in an acid peat bog, which has prevented its decay; such oaks are unearthed when fens are drained. The dark timber is used for gate posts or ornamental woodwork. Brown oak and green oak are timbers stained those colours by fungi.

Freshly felled oak often displays blue-black stains caused by a reaction between the iron of the axe and the tannin of the wood to produce a substance identical to old-fashioned writing ink; brass screws are often used to secure newly seasoned timber, because the acid in the oak will badly corrode steel screws. See also p. 318.

DRYING HOPS FOR BEER

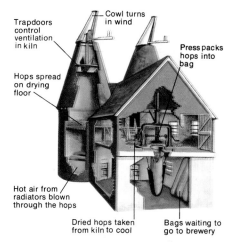

Hops, picked from late August, are dried in the circular kilns of an oast-house. They are then cooled and packed ready to be used in brewing

Oast-house

A stone or brick building containing a kiln for drying hops. Oast-houses, originally called oasts, are a familiar sight in Kent and Sussex, which produce more than half Britain's hops. Many were built in the mid-19th century and are circular (the most efficient shape for retaining heat) with a conical roof and a wooden ventilation cowl, driven round by a wind vane, often elaborately carved; a fine group of such vanes can be seen near Paddock Wood, Kent.

Oast-houses built in the late 1800's were often square. The furnace is usually in the lower part of the oast-house, and the drying room and cooling floor in the roof.

Hops are now dried with electric heaters, and many oast-houses are being used for storage or have been converted into houses. See also HOPS

Oat

Unlike wheat and barley, oats are probably native to Britain. They are immediately distinguishable from the other cereals: their grains do not point upwards in clusters at the top of the stem but hang individually at the side, forming an open, pyramidal seedhead called a panicle. The grains are encased in close-fitting husks like those of barley, but with light, loosely attached chaff. Oat straw has a high feeding value for livestock.

Oats were formerly a basic food for horses, and the decline in the number of these animals has led to smaller crops. Relatively more are produced in Scotland, as oats are the best cereal for growing on poor soil and ripen with the minimum of sunshine. Scots use oats extensively in cookery, especially for porridge and oat-cakes. The two most popular strains are grey oats for sowing in autumn and black oats for spring sowing. See also CROPS

Oaks in barren, windswept areas often become stunted hosts to ferns, lichens and mosses

The teeming world of the oak tree

The spreading crown of a giant New Forest oak, which even in winter supports a

Like man, the oak is subject to many diseases and is a host to many parasites; but, also like man, it does not suffer them all simultaneously. It is, in any case, so well-adjusted to British soils and climate that it can survive mass attacks by fungi, insects and parasites. During its life-span of about 250 years it may be inhabited by more than 200 different types of organisms. As a seedling it is sometimes attacked by one of the short-snouted weevils. The adults eat the soft bark of the oak's main shoot, mate and lay eggs that hatch into soil-dwelling larvae. These feed on the young oak's roots but have other foods, so that seedlings survive.

During wet summers, the oak's leaves may be infested by the oak mildew fungus, which spreads by wind-borne spores. When a spore alights on an oak leaf it develops thin threads known as hyphae, which invade the tissues. The growth of the hyphae and of the plant's sporophores, or spore-producing parts, eventually give the leaf a flour-dusted appearance.

The most conspicuous results of insect attack on oak are the various forms of protuberance known as galls, such as the hard, green marble galls and spongy, light brown oak apples on shoots, the button-like spangles on the undersides of leaves and the deformations of flowers and roots. All are caused by gall wasps. A typical gall wasp is *Biorhiza pallida*, which causes oak apples.

Oak leaves are the staple food of several insect larvae. One is the green oak-roller moth. After mating, the female moth lays many eggs during the summer on the rough bark of the oak's upper branches, where they remain dormant until the following May, when they hatch into caterpillars which feed on the developing oak leaves. They lower themselves from branch to branch on a silken thread that they spin.

As the tree grows taller, older and stouter it may be invaded by ivy and mistletoe and, in wetter districts, by mosses, algae, lichens and ferns. One of these is the common polypody fern, which spreads by means of wind-borne spores. Enough vegetable debris collects in the forks and on the side branches of an ageing oak to nourish this fern. Where rainfall is adequate and mists frequent, it grows as readily on bark as on the soil.

Acorns on the tree provide both a home and a food supply for the acorn weevil. The female bores a small hole in the soft shell of a developing acorn; in this she lays a single egg. The soft white larva develops between mid-summer and autumn, eating the acorn's flesh. In the autumn, when the acorn ripens and falls, the larva crawls out to pupate in the soil, emerging the following spring as an adult weevil.

Eventually an oak will be invaded by one of the many fungi that cause the decay of its heartwood and its eventual downfall. The sulphur bracket fungus, for example, develops from an air-borne spore that alights on an open wound, such as that left after the wind has broken off a branch. The fungal threads then penetrate deeply into the oak's heartwood, feeding on the cells and forming zones of rot. Decay then continues in the tree's heartwood until at last it causes the trunk to break under the weight of its crown or through the force of the wind.

The many insects that live on the oak attract birds. Woodpeckers, for example, which excavate nesting holes in the stems that have been decayed by the sulphur bracket fungus, also peck into rotting branches to find the grubs of boring beetles or the insects that feed on them.

High in the oak's crown a grey squirrel may build its nest, or drey, of leafy oak twigs. It feeds on acorns throughout autumn and winter, and in summer it may also strip bark from young branches and eat it. Squirrels also take eggs and young birds.

Because the oak casts only a light shade, a wide range of plants can flourish beneath it. Grasses, bracken and brambles may completely cover more open oakwood. These attract grazing and browsing animals—from field voles, shrews and rabbits to deer. The smaller animals are attacked by tawny owls, which nest in the holes in the trunks of rotting oaks, or by foxes, which dig earths beneath the roots of large oaks.

Common shrew For its size the most aggressive of mammals, it burrows in dead leaves and litter, preying on insects

Bracket fungus Airborne spores alight on gashes in the tree. As the plant develops it sends threads deep into the heartwood

Silk-button spangle gall Colonies of golden-brown discs grow on the under-side of oak leaves. Hairs give the impression of a silk-covered button

Oak- apple A female gall wasp inserts eggs in an oak shoot and a brown, spongy gall then develops

Woodpecker The great spotted woodpecker feeds on insect larvae, drilling into the tree to get at the wood-boring species

wealth of life beneath its bark

Acorn weevil The female lays a single egg in an acorn where it hatches into a grub which eats the flesh

Oak-roller A colony of these moths may strip an oak bare. It can recover by growing fresh leaves

Bluebell As trees break into leaf, this flower provides a sea of colour in the woodland glades

Ivy Insects find cover in its leaves as the plant climbs the trunk, and in turn birds are attracted

Polypody Winds carry the spores on to tree bark, where moisture helps them grow into mature ferns

Ramsons Abundant in the woods and shady spots, it is nourished by the rich litter of decayed leaves

Primrose Scented flowers bloom in spring, before the oak's summer leaf canopy cuts off the light

Oat, Wild *Avena fatua*

A stubborn weed in arable land. It is similar in appearance to the cultivated oat, but can be distinguished, when the head has emerged, by rings of hair surrounding the base of the seed. It was formerly confined to a few arable farming areas, particularly East Anglia, but is now abundant in most parts of the country.

The seed of the wild oat does not germinate regularly, and because of this the weed is a persistent nuisance, as once the seeds are in the soil they germinate at intervals over a period of years. Selective weed-killers are not an effective control for wild oats, because the plant is closely related to the crops among which it grows.

Obelisk

A column, square or rectangular in section and tapering to a point at the top. The most famous example in Britain is Cleopatra's Needle on London's Embankment. Obelisks became popular in Britain during the 18th and 19th centuries. They were often placed on the summit of a hill to honour a person or event. An outstanding example, 120 ft tall and built of millstone grit, stands on Stoodley Pike, Yorkshire, dominating the Upper Calder Valley. It was erected in 1814 to mark the abdication of Napoleon. At Great Ayton in Yorkshire's Cleveland Hills there is an obelisk in memory of Captain Cook, the discoverer of Australia, who went to school in the village.

Obelisk at Compton Wynyates, Warwickshire — a beacon built to warn of the Spanish Armada

Obsidian

An almost black, glassy rock which cooled too quickly from its molten state to crystallise into basalt. Outcrops occur in North Wales and in the western Highlands of Scotland. Obsidian stones, resembling bottle-glass, can occasionally be found on the beaches of eastern England, to which they were transported by glaciers. Early man used the rock to make cutting tools.

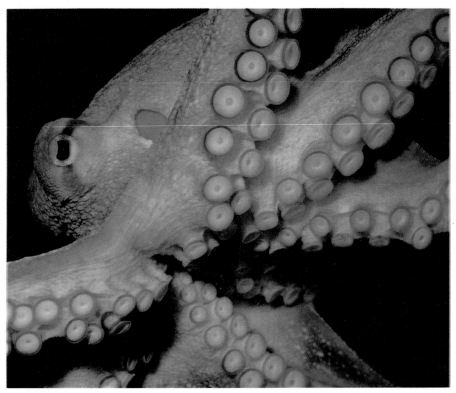

The common octopus, which in British waters can grow up to 6 ft across the tentacles

Octopus

These eight-armed molluscs are among the most intelligent creatures in the sea. In proportion to their size, octopuses have the largest brains of any invertebrate, or spineless, animal. They can distinguish between shapes, enabling them to learn by experience the best way to attack their prey, such as crabs with dangerous claws. Octopuses have been known to raid crab pots.

Like squid and cuttlefish, they belong to a group called cephalopods — 'head-foot'. They have vertebrate-like eyes with a lens capable of being focused by muscles. Behind the head with its horny beak is a muscular bag containing gills and a funnel for directing a jet of water to enable them to progress jerkily backwards with tentacles trailing. They can also crawl over the ocean bottom with tentacles outstretched.

The lesser octopus *Eledone cirrhosa*, with a single row of suckers on each arm, is common in more northern waters. The common octopus *Octopus vulgaris* has a double row of suckers and is restricted to the southwest and English Channel. While the maximum radial spread of the lesser octopus is less than 2 ft, the largest common octopus caught in Britain was taken at Brighton in 1960 and had a spread of 6 ft.

Both are bottom dwellers on rock or sand, sometimes in 'townships', with each animal marking its own territory with a stone or shell-strewn lair in the centre. They feed mainly on crabs, lobsters and fish, which are killed by venom produced by the salivary glands and then eaten by the horny beak in the centre of the eight arms. Digestion is a lengthy process — the common octopus may take 12-14 hours to digest a meal.

Octopuses have two defence mechanisms which confuse predators. They can change colour dramatically to merge with their surroundings by contracting or expanding pigment cells in their skins. They can also produce a smoke screen of inky fluid while jetting backwards to escape from the big fish which are their enemies.

The male mates with the female by extending the tip of his third right arm into her mantle cavity where sperm packets or spermatophores are deposited. Each octopus egg resembles a grain of rice. The eggs are laid in strings attached beneath rocky overhangs. The female continues to brood over them for several weeks until they hatch, after which she often dies of starvation.

Oil beetle

These beetles are the one exception to the rule that beetles' wing cases do not overlap. Oil beetles are wingless and have short overlapping wing cases which expose most of the abdomen.

Like their close relative, the blister beetle, oil beetles have blood which contains an oily irritant. This exudes from their leg joints when they are disturbed, making them unpalatable to predators.

The seven British species of oil beetle,

which all belong to the genus Meloë, are restricted to England and Wales and are rare, except for *Meloë proscarabaèus*. In most species the adult hatches in spring and lives for a maximum of two months. It has a complex life cycle. Females, which can lay up to 10,000 eggs in a lifetime, lay batches of up to 4000 in shallow pits in the ground. However, a newly hatched larva has only about a one in 5000 chance of becoming an adult.

After hatching, the larva climbs a flower stalk and waits among the petals for a furry insect to visit the flower. The larva grips the insect's fur. Only if it has attached itself to a female bee of a particular kind—one belonging to the genus Anthophora—can it survive. Upon reaching the bee's nest, it finds a cell containing a bee larva, which it eats. It spends the summer feeding on the nectar and pollen stored in the cell. After resting through the winter, the larva pupates in the spring.

Oilfield
Britain's oilfields are few and small. The biggest are in Nottinghamshire, Lincolnshire, Lancashire and Dorset. Their total production of crude oil in 1970 was 47,000 tons—half the annual production of one average Middle Eastern oil well.

The existence of oil in Britain was recorded by the Romans, but it was not until 1847 that the first crude oil was processed, from a Derbyshire coal mine. At the beginning of the century the first intensive search for petroleum deposits in Britain began. The first oil-producing well was sunk during the First World War at Hardstoft in Derbyshire; but most of the oilfields now in production were not discovered until the 1950's.

THE MAKING OF OIL

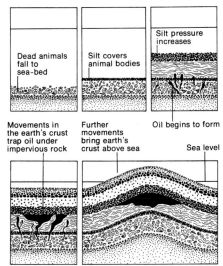

Dead animals fall to sea-bed

Silt covers animal bodies

Silt pressure increases

Movements in the earth's crust trap oil under impervious rock

Further movements bring earth's crust above sea

Oil begins to form

Sea level

Over millions of years pressure, heat and chemical reaction turned dead marine animals into oil, which was trapped as the earth's crust folded and rose above the sea level

---

In 1963, off Lulworth Cove, Dorset, the first British offshore drilling for oil took place. Since then several substantial oilfields have been discovered in the North Sea, and it is estimated that by the late 1970's they will be yielding 25 million tons of crude oil a year, a quarter of the amount that Britain currently imports.

Old lady moth see Noctuid
Old man's beard see Traveller's joy
Old wife see Bream, Black

Onion, Wild *Allium vineale*
Crow garlic, or wild onion, was once common in meadows. Eaten by cattle, it gave milk and butter an unpleasant flavour. Intensive methods of cultivation have largely eliminated it from farmland, and now it is usually found on roadsides, flowering in mid-summer throughout England, Wales and southern Scotland. In the east of England the pink or green-white flowers are replaced by little bulbs. Each of these, when it falls to the ground, can grow into a new plant.

Oolite see Limestone
Opencast mining see Mining

Open field
Under the early English system of arable farming, the ploughland of each parish was divided into open fields—as opposed to the enclosed ones which were to appear in the 18th century. The fields were sub-divided into long, narrow strips a few yards wide. Each farmer was allocated a number of strips, which were seldom together, on the principle that no one should have all the best or all the worst land. No choice of crop was allowed: when it was the turn of an open field to grow wheat, every farmer who owned a strip in that field had to sow it with wheat.

Crops were sown in rotation; usually this meant one year of wheat, one year of barley or oats, then one year in which the land lay fallow—although weeds and couchgrass were sometimes grown to be grazed by cattle and sheep or to be cut for a sparse crop of hay.

The strip system began to die out in the late Middle Ages as the fields fell into the possession of single owners. However, a few fields are still managed in the old way in north-west Lincolnshire and north-east Nottinghamshire. The corrugations left by the strip system can still be seen in some fields, particularly in the Midlands. See also RIGG AND FURROW

Opposum shrimp
Swarms of these shrimp-like animals, often less than 1 in. long, occur in rock pools among seaweed, in estuaries and around sandy shores. They often hang almost vertically in the water, and many species are transparent with only their black stalked eyes visible. Several species of opposum shrimps

---

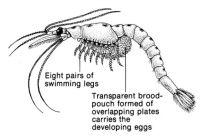

Eight pairs of swimming legs

Transparent brood-pouch formed of overlapping plates carries the developing eggs

The opposum shrimp became stranded in a few lakes as the Ice Age glaciers retreated

can change colour, including the chameleon shrimp *Praunus flexuosus*, which varies from black to green.

Opposum shrimps get their name from the way of carrying their eggs in a pouch beneath the carapace or upper body shell which covers the thorax or middle section. They are distinguished from true shrimps in having eight instead of five pairs of legs, none of which is developed into pincers. The body of the chameleon shrimp is markedly bent in the middle.

There is only one freshwater species in the British Isles, *Mysis relicta*. This is a relic of the last Ice Age, which occurred about 10,000 years ago. It became stranded in a few lakes, including Lough Neagh, Ireland, and Ennerdale Water, Cumberland, as the glaciers retreated.

Orache
The frosted appearance of some species of orache is due to a mealy coating on their leaves and stems. The fruits are enclosed in two leaflets which enlarge after flowering and develop large warts. They have green flowers which are borne from July until September.

Common orache grows throughout the lowlands in waste places and arable fields and near the sea on sand, shingle or mud. Its upper leaves are oblong, tapering into the stalk, unlike those of the rarer spear-leaved orache, which is common in south-east England, growing mainly near the sea, on salt marshes. Its leaves are mealy only on their undersides.

Common orache
Atriplex patula

Spear-leaved orache
A. hastata

Both species of orache grow 1-3 ft high, and their leaves have a mealy coating

Orchid

The plant that often springs to mind when orchid is mentioned has magnificently coloured large flowers and an exotic appearance. This is the orchid of the tropics, where the plant often grows on trees, and of the greenhouse. Native British orchids are small-flowered and much less spectacular plants.

There are about 7500 species of orchids, of which 54 grow in Britain. The roots of the plants are often fleshy or tuber-like and the flowers range widely in shape and colour. The leaves are flat, with parallel veins, and broadly spear-shaped. Many of the British species grow only on chalk or lime-rich soil, others flourish in woods and meadows on varying soils and a few grow on acid heaths and in swamps.

Each flower consists of three petals alternating with three sepals. It is the shape of one of these petals, called the lip, or labellum, which gives each species its own distinctive appearance. In lady's slipper the lip is shaped like a pouch; in the lizard orchid like a long tongue; and in the bee and fly orchids like those insects. Often the base of the lip is extended into a tube, or spur—short and broad like the finger of a glove in the marsh orchids, long and narrow in the fragrant orchid (which, like many other species, is pleasantly perfumed).

The inside of the orchid flower is unusual. The stamens (the male parts), and the stigmas (the female parts), are not separate, as in other flowers, but are fused in a central column, the stamens above the stigmas. Also, the pollen grains are not free and dust-like but, in their thousands, form pollen masses, or pollinia. Part of each pollen mass is sticky and attaches itself to the head of a visiting insect, such as a bumble bee. As the insect flies away the pollen mass swings from a vertical to a horizontal position, so that when the insect visits another flower of the same species the pollen mass comes in contact with the stigmas, below the stamens, and pollination takes place. It is possible to obtain a pollen mass by mimicking an insect with the tip of a pencil and then to watch its change of position.

The purple to dark brown flower of the bee orchid so much resembles the velvety body of the female bumble bee that the male bee tries to mate with it, and during this activity pollen masses attach themselves to the bee's head. In the same way, male burrowing wasps mistake the flowers of the fly orchid for females.

The numbers of the bee orchid in any one place vary from year to year, from a mere two or three to tens of thousands, depending on the effective pollination and distribution of the seeds.

Some orchids are saprophytes—they have no green chlorophyll with which to build energy from sunlight; instead they extract energy from the dead remains of other organisms. These orchids, which are leafless, can grow in deeply shaded woods. Bird's

The lady orchid, which grows on the Kent chalk, looks uncannily like a woman in a poke-bonnet

nest orchid is an example. Its dense spike of pale brown flowers is sometimes difficult to distinguish from its background of dead beech leaves. Its name derives from the untidy mass of roots that is reminiscent of a rook's or pigeon's nest.

The two butterfly orchids, the lesser and greater, attract night-flying moths, which pollinate the flowers in the process of feeding on the nectar in the flower's long, slender tubes.

The lesser butterfly orchid rarely exceeds 12 in. It is recognised by the two halves of the stamen, which are parallel and close together. In the greater butterfly orchid the two halves are further apart and converge towards the top. Both species grow in woods and grassland throughout the British Isles.

The fragrant orchid, which smells of clove carnation, also attracts moths, as does the pyramidal orchid, which has a foxy odour.

Twayblade, one of the most common orchids in the British Isles, is pollinated by flies and small beetles which, when they touch the centre of a flower, trigger off a mechanism which sticks the pollen mass to the insect's back; the frightened insect then

flies off to another flower. The inconspicuous green flowers are forked like the legs of a human body.

The man orchid flower is even more man-like in shape, possessing 'arms' as well as 'legs'; this is the only British orchid which does not have a spur—a hollow, usually cone-shaped, petal-like growth. It is a rare and declining species.

So, too, is the green-winged orchid, which 20 years ago was widespread in England, Wales and central Ireland but is now rare because most of the damp, lime-rich meadows in which it flourished have been drained and ploughed. Pollination by hive bees is partially halting the decline.

Autumn ladies' tresses is so-called because the stem entwined with a row of white flowers resembles a braid of hair similarly decorated. This species, rarely higher than 6 in., is among the smallest of British orchids, and is difficult to see unless the grass is short. It sometimes surprises gardeners by appearing on old lawns which have remained uncut for a few weeks in dry summers.

The roots of the early purple orchid, which flowers from April to June, were once supposed to have aphrodisiac powers.

The wild orchids of Britain

More than 50 species of orchids grow wild in Britain. Many are rare but the seeds are so light that the wind can carry them hundreds of miles, and for this reason orchids sometimes spring up in unexpected places. The seeds are also small, and development is slow; it can take years for seedlings to grow and many years after that for flowers to appear. The common twayblade, for example, takes 15 years to develop from seed to flower. British orchids range in size from the lizard orchid, which may be 5 ft tall, to the 6 in. high autumn ladies' tresses

Bee orchid 6-18 in.
Ophrys apifera
Grassland, banks, copses

Fly orchid 1-2 ft
Ophrys insectifera
Woods, copses, grassland

Man orchid 6-18 in.
Aceras anthropophorum
Grassland, quarries

Frog orchid 2-9 in.
Coeloglossum viride
Grassland

Fragrant orchid 6-24 in.
Gymnadenia conopsea
Grassland, fens, marshes

Autumn ladies' tresses
3-9 in. *Spiranthes spiralis*
Short grassland

Green-winged orchid
3-12 in. *Orchis morio*
Grassland

Heath spotted orchid 6-18 in.
Dactylorhiza ericetorum
Moist, acid heaths, grassland

Early marsh orchid 6-18 in.
Dactylorhiza incarnata
Marshes, fens, sand dunes

Pyramidal orchid 6-18 in.
Anacamptis pyramidalis
Pastures, sand dunes

Bird's nest orchid
1-2 ft. *Neottia nidus-avis*
Woods, mainly beech

Early purple orchid
6-18 in. *Orchis mascula*
Woods, copses, grassland

Greater butterfly orchid
9-18 in. *Platanthera chlorantha*
Woods, grassland

Lesser butterfly orchid
6-12 in. *Platanthera bifolia*
Open woods, grassland

Lizard orchid Up to 5 ft
Himantoglossum hircinum
Bushy places, tall grass

Twayblade Up to 2 ft
Listera ovata
Woods, hedges, damp pastures

Marsh helleborine
Up to 18 in. *Epipactis palustris*
Fens, marshes, sand dunes

Ormer see Shell

Orpine *Sedum telephium*
The fleshy leaves of orpine contain a large store of water so that the plant survives well when uprooted; hence its other name, livelong. Made into mid-summer garlands it will last for months if sprinkled with water once a week.

Orpine, which bears purple flowers from July to September, grows in shaded hedgerows and woodlands throughout lowland Britain. It has large, flat leaves, a carrot-like underground root tuber, and is 1-2 ft high.

Fleshy leaves and a tuberous root allow orpine to survive for some time without water

Osier see Willow

Osprey *Pandion haliaetus*
The return of the osprey to Britain as a breeding bird is a triumph for the bird experts who encouraged it to nest in the 1950's.

Ospreys had been reduced by hunting to only two pairs in 1900. One pair continued to breed until 1916, but for almost 40 years afterwards none was known to breed in Britain. Then, in 1954, a pair bred on

The osprey circles over water, waiting to pounce on a fish. The spiny scales on the bird's footpads give a firm grasp on the slippery prey

Speyside in Scotland; later they regularly used a nest at Loch Garten, Inverness-shire. Now three or four pairs breed in the area.

Ospreys—also known as fish hawks—are migrants that leave their northern European breeding grounds in winter. They are sometimes seen in southern England on passage south, and in the autumn they will stay at a good fishing ground for several weeks.

Fish form almost their entire diet. An osprey sails on big arched wings—it has a wingspan of $4\frac{1}{2}$ ft—over the water, hovers when it spots prey, and drops, talons first, into the water to seize a fish, often submerging completely. Large fish are taken in this way, and the osprey was hunted out of Scotland partly because fishermen feared for their trout.

The upper parts of the osprey, which grows to a length of 22 in., are dark brown, contrasting with white underparts speckled with brown, and there is a dark brown band on the side of the head. The bird, which looks very much like a small eagle, builds a large eyrie of twigs in the top of a tree, usually a pine, and in it the female lays three white, red-blotched eggs in April or May.

A streamlined body, waterproof fur and webbed feet

Otter *Lutra lutra*
This large carnivore of the weasel family is rarely seen today. Several factors contribute to its scarcity, including river pollution and hunting or trapping by water bailiffs along trout and salmon reaches. Otters have retreated from many lowland rivers into the hills and moorlands, and to deserted coastal areas and even offshore islands. They can also be found near lakes and reservoirs stocked with fish, and are most common in western Britain.

The otter grows to about $2\frac{1}{2}$ ft with a tail 20 in. long. The male, or dog, is larger than the bitch. Its beautifully streamlined body and thick tapering tail or 'rudder' betray its aquatic habit. The short, close-fitting chocolate-brown coat is waterproof, and the ears are small and just visible above the dense fur. Its five toes are webbed but they usually leave lopsided, four-toed tracks in the mud and sand. It can shut its ears and nostrils when diving for fish.

The otter is a solitary, secretive animal and lies up by day on the river bank, in a resting place called a hover. At night, when it wanders, it keeps to a regular beat, working up and down a river—often travelling great distances overland. However, the otter enjoys playing and will often slide down troughs of mud or snow into the water. It runs, swims and dives with great skill, swimming mainly with its tail and hind legs. The forelegs are used to steer and balance.

The otter's favourite foods are eels, salmon and trout, and it often does serious damage to fish hatcheries at spawning time. It also catches frogs and crayfish, water fowl, small mammals, crabs and other sea creatures.

There is no definite breeding season and

Once nearly extinct in Britain—an osprey feeds its young on a fish just seized from the water

make the otter a formidable aquatic hunter

the two to four blind cubs may be born in any month of the year, in the breeding nest or holt. The holt is merely a tunnel among tree roots, a hole in the river bank or in a hollow fallen tree. There is probably one litter a year and the bitch stays with her young until the next mating time.

Otters are good parents and enjoy playing with their cubs. However, the partnership between dog and bitch is temporary and as soon as the young can look after themselves the dog goes off to live on his own.

Tracks and droppings are the best indications that an otter is around. The animal itself is unlikely to be encountered. Droppings (spraints) are deposited at carefully selected places where they will be found by other otters. They act as 'keep out' territorial warnings, even though an otter's home boundaries are flexible. Spraints are usually left on boulders in sheltered places so as not to be destroyed by rain or sun. They may be left under a bridge or stone ledge, under an overhanging bank, at the entrance to the holt, on a sandcastle scraped up by the otter or on a grassy mound by the water. See also TRACKS

Out-by

In the Lake District, the Pennines and Scotland, the land at a distance from the farm buildings is called the out-by, in contrast to the in-by—the land near the farm house. The out-by receives little or no manure and only occasionally is sown to produce a crop, usually oats. The land is then left as pasture for several years to regain its fertility. In some areas it is also known as the out-field. See also IN-BY

Owl see p. 326

Ox see Cattle
Ox-bow lake see Meander

Ox-eye daisy
Chrysanthemum leucanthemum
Pulling petals off an ox-eye or moon daisy while reciting 'he loves me, he loves me not' is still a common charm. These daisies are found everywhere, forming white sheets on railway banks and old meadows. They can reach 2 ft high, but in exposed places such as cliff tops the wiry stems may be only a few inches tall, and the flowers no bigger than those of a common daisy.

Ox-eye daisies have small leaves similar to the garden chrysanthemum. The white-petalled flowers have yellow centres and appear from June to August.

Oxlip *Primula elatior*
True oxlips grow only in certain areas of Essex, Hertfordshire, Suffolk, east Norfolk, Cambridgeshire, Bedfordshire and Huntingdonshire in which primroses are rare or never appear. Oxlips grow 4-12 in. high in damp woods and hedge-banks, flowering in April and May. False oxlips arise wherever primroses and cowslips grow together, and are a hybrid of the two. True oxlips have cowslip-sized flowers, but of a paler yellow; false oxlip flowers are more like those of the primrose.

Ox-tongue
With dandelion-like flowers, bristly ox-tongue is common in England and Wales. It grows up to 3 ft high, flowering from June to October in hedgebanks and at roadsides on heavy lime-rich clays. Its oblong leaves are covered in bristles with anchor-like hooked tips which cling to fur and clothes.

Hawkweed ox-tongue is similar but has narrower leaves. It is common only in grassland and on dry banks on the chalk of south-east England.

Bristly ox-tongue
Picris echioides
Hawkweed ox-tongue
P. hieracioides

Ox-tongue has large leaves, covered with bristles which cling to clothing and fur

Oyster
The best-known species of this shellfish is the edible common oyster, found off-shore in shallow water. The richest beds are near Conway, in the Essex estuaries, and in the Helford River in Cornwall. Oysters were a

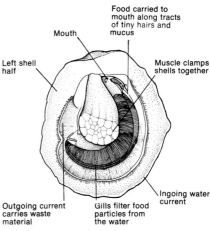

HOW THE OYSTER FEEDS

The oyster sieves food particles from water drawn in between its shells. At intervals it suddenly claps the shells together to expel any waste

favourite food of the Romans, and the shells are also common in prehistoric refuse heaps. The oyster is a bivalve, a soft-bodied animal that lives inside two hinged shells.

The common or native oyster *Ostrea edulis* has had a high mortality rate in recent years, owing to exceptionally cold winters. It is also attacked or eaten by sting winkles and the introduced American drill. Another serious pest on oyster beds is the slipper limpet. This does not attack the oysters but competes for the same food, sometimes in such numbers that the oysters are smothered.

The fully grown shells are up to 4 in. across, roughly round in shape, and usually grey or brown. The lower valve is concave and larger than the upper flat one. The large, single muscle which clamps the valves together is surrounded by reddish gills, with which the oyster filters food particles from the water. Each animal is bisexual, alternating from male to female many times a year.

Oysters spawn when the water temperature is about 12-14°C (54-57°F). Eggs are fertilised in the mantle cavity; the larvae float in the sea for 7-20 days. On falling to the sea-bed, those spats, or young oysters, which settle on rocks or pebbles will survive; those settling on sand or mud will die. The fortunate ones take only a few hours to change to the adult form and to cement down the lower shell. They become marketable in four or five years. Oysters are in season from September to April.

The Portuguese oyster *Crassostrea angulata* grows to 7 in. across. It is more oval and rougher than the native oyster, and rarely breeds here. It lives just below low water level on firm muddy bottoms; it is not considered such a delicacy as the native oyster.

The pearl oyster belongs to a different family of shellfish which lives in tropical seas. See also PEARL

The ghostly shape and the weird, moaning cry of the barn owl have inspired many eerie stories

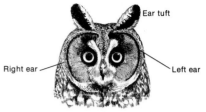

Ear tuft

Right ear

Left ear

The ear tufts of the long-eared owl have nothing to do with hearing but are used in courtship displays. Its true ears are lop-sided on its head, so creating a time-lag between the arrival at each ear of the same sound wave. This helps the bird to pinpoint the sound source

Owl

Most owls are large birds, well equipped for a life of stealthy, nocturnal hunting. Unlike most large-winged birds they are silent in flight, because their wing feathers have soft tips which break up the air flow over them. Their eyes face forwards, giving them binocular vision which enables them to judge distances with precision. The disadvantage of forward-looking eyes is overcome by the ability which owls have of being able to turn their heads through 180 degrees and look directly behind them. The retina of the eye is extremely sensitive to light and enables

Like all owls, this newly fledged little owl has excellent binocular vision

some species to see clearly in what would be pitch blackness for a human.

Most owls spend the day roosting, flying out only at dawn and dusk in search of their prey—mostly small mammals such as mice, voles and shrews. The prey is seized in powerful talons and usually swallowed whole. Undigestible parts such as fur and bones are later regurgitated in pellets.

Six species of owls breed in the British Isles. The most numerous is the 15 in. long tawny owl, often called the brown owl. The tawny owl is heard most often in late autumn when territories are being established. A familiar sound throughout southern and eastern England, its call has been described as 'to-whit-to-woo' but this sound is made by two

BARN OWL PELLETS

Compact mass of undigested fur and bones

Dry pellet broken open shows the bone remains of the owl's prey

The barn owl disgorges the indigestible parts of insects and the bones, fur and feathers of the animals on which it feeds as blackish pellets, 1-2 in. long. At breeding time the female lays her eggs on a pile of these pellets

birds. One owl hoots and the shrill 'kwick-kwick' is the answering call of the mate. Both sexes hoot and both call 'kwick-kwick' but the two calls are not uttered together by the same bird. They usually breed in hollow trees but often take to barrels placed as nest boxes. They can be fearsome in defence of their nests, attacking any intruders, and have been known to injure people who have disturbed them.

On farmland owls feed on small mammals, such as mice and voles; but those that live in the centre of cities feed mainly on sparrows. The two to four round, white eggs are laid as early as March and the young fly two months later. There are no tawny owls in Ireland and the northern and western islands of Scotland.

The slightly smaller barn owl is more widespread than the tawny owl—breeding in almost every county in Britain and Ireland —but is less numerous. Its white breast and patterned fawn back are unmistakable as it patrols over open fields and heathland in the dying evening light. In some parts of the country the barn owl has declined because of the modernisation of the barns where it nested, the covering of belfries with wire netting and the use of pesticides. These poisons accumulate in the bodies of small animals, and owls, feeding exclusively on these, soon amass lethal amounts within themselves.

Barn owls lay their eggs, usually in man-made structures or hollow trees, in April or May, and the young fly four months later. Two broods are often reared in a season.

The little owl is a dark grey and white streaked bird only 9 in. long, with a prominent facial disc and bright yellow eyes. It was introduced into Kent and Northamptonshire from the Continent in the late 19th century and spread rapidly over England and Wales into the southern counties of Scotland.

It can be seen by day and, if disturbed, flies away with an undulating flight. It feeds mainly on insects, and nests in tree holes as well as in walls and old buildings. The three to five white eggs are laid in late April or early May. The eggs hatch after 28 days and the young fly about five weeks later.

The short-eared owl and long-eared owl are similar in size and colour. Both are almost 15 in. long, and have buff plumage streaked with brown. But these long-winged birds lead totally different lives. The long-eared owl is a strictly nocturnal bird of coniferous woods; the short-eared owl hunts by day and nests on grassy upland moors and lowland marshes. Both are more numerous and widespread in the northern half of Britain.

The long-eared owl has prominent ear tufts that are held erect when the bird is nervous. The tufts, like those of the short-eared owl, play no part in hearing. It breeds in the old nests of crows in the tops of pines and hides itself by day by sitting still against the trunk of a tree. With their weak, sighing call, long-eared owls are frequently overlooked.

The range and breeding success of the short-eared owl are determined almost entirely by the number of field voles available on the moors. Concentrations of voles, even in southern England, will attract large numbers of these birds; in one winter over 100 were counted roosting in an old barn in Suffolk. The short-eared owl lays four to eight white eggs in a simple depression in the ground in April. They hatch after 26 days and the young fly about three weeks later.

As with short-eared owls, the number of snowy owls is dependent on the number of small mammals available. Snowy owls are Arctic birds which seldom fly far enough south from their breeding grounds to reach Britain. But in 1967 a pair bred on the island of Fetlar in the Shetlands, and young have since been reared there every year. These unmistakable large white birds can be seen at their protected nest by visitors to the island. The female is larger than the male and barred with black.

All owls are protected birds, for, although they take the occasional game chick, they also keep down the number of small animals such as mice, rats and voles which cause damage to crops.

Although the most common day-flying owl, the little owl hunts mainly at dusk and dawn

In courtship or territorial encounters, excited oystercatchers in small groups run up and down the beach uttering piping calls which stimulate other birds to call and parade

Oystercatcher *Haemotopus ostralegus*

The most distinctive and noisiest of shore birds, the oystercatcher is a large, round-bodied wader, 17 in. long, boldly patterned in black and white, with brilliant orange-red legs and a stout red bill. With its shrill, piping whistle, it is always one of the first shore birds to raise the alarm at any sign of intruders. Other oystercatchers in the same area respond to the 'klee-ee' alarm call by rising to mob predators such as gulls or crows. At the nesting sites, young birds 'freeze' and their mottled down acts as camouflage. When oystercatchers are not sure how to react to a situation, they put their bills in their plumage as if going to sleep. This could be a sign of submission or an attempt to hide their bright bills.

The bird is misnamed, for it does not eat oysters; these live below the low-tide mark, and oystercatchers feed between the tides or on land. But the birds do consume large quantities of shellfish and are particularly adept at breaking into mussels.

The oystercatcher has two ways of eating shellfish. When the shellfish is covered in water and the shell is open, the oystercatcher stabs it with its beak, severing the muscle which closes the two sides of the shell; these fall open, and the bird pecks out the flesh. When the shell is closed, the oystercatcher smashes it with its beak, aiming for the weakest part of the shell, the bottom end of the lower valve. The oystercatcher is also fond of other molluscs.

Oystercatchers are found all round the coast of Britain, but are more numerous in the west where rocky pools are most plentiful. In spring there seems to be a pair of the birds in almost every cove and a colony on every dune and island. In Morecambe Bay, Lancashire, and the Burry Inlet, South Wales, there are frequently tens of thousands, and local fishermen persistently demand control of their numbers. In Scotland and northern England they have spread inland to nest on the gravel banks of rivers, moorland and even in arable fields. Inland nesting birds feed their young on larvae, earthworms and moth caterpillars.

The two or three well-camouflaged eggs are laid in a scrape in the ground which the female lines with shells or pebbles. The eggs hatch after 27 days and the young leave the nest about a month later. The 20,000 pairs of oystercatchers that breed in the British Isles are joined each year by large numbers from Europe and Iceland during the winter. Some British birds migrate south along the Atlantic coast to Spain and Portugal.

Oyster drill see Shell

Ozone

A gas found mostly between 5 and 30 miles up in the atmosphere. Nitrogen and oxygen make up 99 per cent of the atmosphere. Ozone is one of a number of other gases which make up the remaining 1 per cent. Fortunately, there are only slight traces of ozone in the lower atmosphere, for it is poisonous — not a tonic as the Victorians supposed.

People living in industrial areas in the last century were urged to go to the coast to breathe 'refreshing ozone'. But the amount in the air is far too small to be detected by the human nose. The seaside smell extolled by the Victorians was probably that of iodine released by rotting seaweed.

P

Paddleworm

The body of this sea worm is made up of many segments, each segment having two paddle-shaped extensions which are used for swimming.

The large green paddleworm *Phyllodoce lamelliger* is found under stones on muddy shores. It is blue, with green paddles, and grows to 18 in. The 4 in. long brown paddleworm *P. maculata* has brown spots on its yellow-green body. It lives low down the shore on sandy beaches. The dark green paddleworm *Eulalia viridis* often occurs in large numbers on rocky shores.

The 3 in. long dark green paddleworm lives among rocks on the lower shore, preying on barnacles

Painted lady *Vanessa cardui*

A butterfly which migrates to the British Isles from the Mediterranean in May and June. The number of immigrants varies considerably from year to year; most are in a faded, tattered condition after their long journey.

After arrival, the painted lady, which has a 2½ in. wingspan, lays its eggs singly on thistles or nettles. During summer the caterpillars that hatch from these live in silky webs that they weave among the leaves. Striking black, orange and white butterflies emerge from the pupal, or resting, stage in late summer. Most of these migrate southwards in autumn. Those that stay behind usually do not survive the winter.

Painters see p. 332

Pansy

The flowers of this relation of the violet are blue-violet, yellow, creamy white or a combination of these colours. The leaves have rounded lobes. Pansies grow throughout the lowlands of the British Isles and flower from April to September.

Wild pansy or heartsease *Viola tricolor*, which is a cornfield weed 1½-18 in. high, has blue-violet flowers; a yellow-flowered form grows in sand dunes and grassland near the sea. Field pansy *V. arvensis* has much smaller flowers and grows in arable fields and waste places.

Panther cap see Fungus

Parasite

When an ancient Greek went to dinner uninvited he was termed a parasite — meaning someone who appeared 'beside food'. This practice of obtaining nourishment at somebody's or something else's expense is a life style for a wide variety of animals and plants that live in or on the bodies of other animals or plants, at least for some part of their existence.

Parasitism is a one-sided dependence of the parasite on its host. The parasite harms its host, but usually a balance is struck in which it does not multiply in numbers sufficient to kill or endanger the host, as this would result in the parasite losing its source of food. This balance is a natural example of not killing the goose that lays the golden egg.

Certain body structures are characteristic of most parasites — for example, hooks, claws, suckers and spines which are used to hold on to the skin or internal tissues of the host. The tapeworm is well equipped with these. Like many parasites it has no organs of locomotion, as it does not need actively to search for food. Similarly lice and fleas have lost their wings. Although well adapted to its way of life, the parasite must also be able to withstand the defence mechanisms of the host, which reacts with inflammation and cyst formation around any foreign body, or produces anti-toxins.

Some animals have a life history that is entirely parasitic — for example, the tapeworm. Others, such as the warble fly, are parasites during infancy only; the flea is a parasite only as an adult. Generally bloodsucking insects are nomadic parasites. They have a meal of blood and fly off to another host.

Common plant parasites include dodder, which twines round the stems of gorse and heather, from which it gets nourishment through suckers. Toothwort grows on the roots of beech, poplar, hazel and other plants, its thin roots penetrating the roots of the host. The mistletoe is only a partial parasite. It makes glucose from water and carbon dioxide and stores this as starch, but it does obtain water and salts through sucking organs which grow into the host tree. Many parasitic fungi are responsible for plant diseases such as wheat rust, potato blight and the various mildews.

Two unusual forms of parasitism occur among birds. The cuckoo, called a brood parasite, lays her eggs in the nest of another bird, which acts as a foster-parent. Then there are birds which harry smaller species, forcing them to drop their food, which the larger bird eats. The skua is one of the more persistent of these bullies, and this brand of thievery is called clepto-parasitism.

The relationship between two animals which live together is not always that of parasite and host. Both may derive benefit from the association, in which case it is called either commensalism or symbiosis.

Commensalism means literally 'together at the table' and an example of this is the relationship of the sea anemone *Calliactis parasitica* and the hermit crab *Eupagurus bernhardus*. The anemone lives on the crab's adopted shell, camouflages it, and provides protection with its tentacles and stinging cells. In return, the anemone picks up stray pieces of food left by the crab. Neither animal is dependent on the other, for each can and does live independently, but each gains by the partnership.

The situation where each organism is completely dependent on the other is called symbiosis, meaning 'living together'. Cattle and other ruminants which chew the cud are unable to digest most of the plant material, cellulose, on which they feed. The work of digestion is done for them by bacteria, tiny organisms that can be seen only through a microscope. The bacteria, which live in the stomachs of cattle, feed on the cellulose, breaking it into material which the cattle can absorb after chewing the cud.

Parasol mushroom

The common parasol is one of the largest British fungi, growing up to 12 in. or more high, with a cap 7-8 in. across. It does not tolerate shade, and so grows in woodland clearings and grassy places in the open — often in groups. The greyish-brown cap with dark brown scales is at first conical, but it soon splits away from the stalk and expands into a parasol. The point where the cap joins on to the stem is marked by a double ring of tissue.

The shaggy parasol is smaller and has shaggier brown scales on the 4-5 in. cap. Its white stalk has no scales. It prefers rich ground, and may appear in woods, gardens and parks. When the flesh is damaged it turns pink and then brown.

Both species appear in the autumn. Their caps are good to eat, especially when young, but the stalks are rather tough.

Parish

There are two sorts of parishes—ecclesiastical and civil. The word is derived from the Greek, meaning 'district around', and its early use signified the district around a church, in which the church looked after the spiritual needs of the people.

The parish in Britain dates from Saxon times. In those days bishops held sway over vast areas, often identical with kingdoms, and their dioceses were divided into parishes of considerable size. Even in the last century there were some enormous parishes. Whalley in Lancashire was 30 miles in length and 15 miles wide, and the parish of Halifax, in Yorkshire, extended over more than 100 square miles.

Sometimes the boundaries of a medieval township and a parish might coincide, as they often did in the south of England. Many of the old parish boundaries have been preserved, and it is occasionally possible to find the outline of an Anglo-Saxon estate by examining the map of a parish in a charter of the early Middle Ages.

Parish boundaries were usually drawn along streams and Roman roads and marked in addition by stones, dykes or trees. On the Herefordshire hills there is a splendid example—three yew trees, known as the Three Shepherds, which mark the boundaries of three parishes on Offa's Dyke.

Often there was an annual ceremony of beating the bounds—a procession round the boundary of the parish by boys who struck it with willow rods to ensure that no territory, especially common land, was lost. The custom still survives in some parishes.

The number of parishes gradually increased, largely by dividing the existing ones as populations grew and men of wealth built and endowed new churches. At the end of the 17th century there were about 9000 parishes in England and Wales, and there are now more than 16,000.

In the Middle Ages, the parish priest was often the only educated man in the neighbourhood and one of his important functions was to keep parish records, especially of births, deaths and marriages. The amount of taxes paid in the form of tithes to the clergy provided a fair guide to the wealth of a neighbourhood. All these factors were valuable to the temporal rulers as the basis for the civil administration of the country.

From Tudor times civil duties began to be imposed on the parish, which became responsible for the maintenance of the roads, the care of the poor and similar duties. This is the origin of the expression 'Going on the parish', which meant that a poor parishioner was receiving money from parish funds.

In the early 19th century these duties became considerable and were gradually removed to new units of local government; but later in the century the parish was re-established in rural areas of England and Wales as a civil authority, distinct and not necessarily identical in area with the ecclesiastical parish. The civil parish in these areas still has limited powers over such matters as lighting, allotments, burial and recreation grounds, bridleways, footpaths and other rights of way.

In Scotland and Ireland the ecclesiastical parish corresponds only roughly with the system in England and Wales, and there are no civil parishes.

Parish churches, especially those of some antiquity, are a happy hunting ground for genealogists and historians. The parish chest, where records of the district were kept, is a valuable guide to local history, often the only reliable one. Though boundaries may have changed, the pattern of parishes today still reflects the basic evolution of the landscape from the Anglo-Saxon period. See also CHURCH

Park see p. 334
Parr see Salmon
Parrot toadstool see Fungus

Parsley family

The botanical name of this family of plants is Umbelliferae, because the flowers of most of the 70 or so British species are arranged, umbrella-like, on ribs that spread from a central stem. Each flower head, or umbel, consists of hundreds of tiny, individual, five-petalled flowers, which appear in spring and summer; in some cases the flowers round the edge have larger petals than the rest. The flowers are usually white, but there are some which are tinged with pink or yellow.

The plants have ribbed stems, usually hollow, sometimes pithy, and many have much-divided fern-like leaves. Some have large tap-roots which, in the cultivated forms, are common vegetables—for example, carrots and parsnips.

Some species have been introduced. An example is alexanders, a Mediterranean plant which now grows abundantly around the coasts of Britain. Other species, such as the common weeds ground elder and fool's parsley, have spread from gardens and established themselves in waste ground.

Many species grow in wet or damp soil. Among them are wild celery, a seaside plant which, despite its name, is unpalatable; cowbane, a highly poisonous, but rare, plant of wet ditches, marshes and lakesides; and the seven species of water-dropwort, many of which are poisonous, especially hemlock water-dropwort, a 6 ft tall plant of ditches and streams in south and west Britain.

The most common of these water plants is fool's watercress, which is often mistaken for true watercress.

The smell of the different species varies considerably. For example, sweet cicely and giant hogweed have a sweet aroma, stone parsley has a peculiar smell of nutmeg and petrol, hemlock smells foetid and hemlock water-dropwort has a parsley-like scent.

Cow parsley, also known as Queen Anne's lace and hedge parsley, grows along roadsides and hedgerows throughout the British Isles. It also occurs on the edges of woods and in coppices. Children make pea shooters and whistles from its stout stems.

The narrow fleshy leaves of rock samphire are edible and can be pickled.

The red crescents in the centre of the hogweed's seed head are glands containing aromatic oils

The umbrella-flowered parsley family

With their characteristic neads of small white flowers and ribbed stems, the members of the parsley family are among the easiest of plants to recognise. But because of their similarity they are sometimes difficult to distinguish from one another. This chart provides identification pictures of 37 of the more common members. The parsley grown for flavouring and garnishing dishes, with its deep green, densely curled leaves, is a variety of wild parsley, introduced from the Mediterranean. Although many other species are edible, the family contains some of Britain's most poisonous plants, including hemlock and cowbane. The family is remarkable for the immense range in the size of its species: from fool's parsley, only 3 in. high, to giant hogweed, which may grow up to 12 ft in a single summer. When the petals of a flower in this family fall they leave behind a fruit which develops into two ribbed seed pods. The only certain method that botanists have of identifying a species is studying the number of ribs on its seed pod and the arrangement of the oil glands between them.

Alexanders Up to 3 ft.
Smyrnium olusatrum
Roadsides and waste
ground near the sea

Angelica, Wild Up to 5 ft.
Angelica sylvestris
Fens, damp woods
and grass, cliffs

Burnet saxifrage Up to 2 ft.
Pimpinella saxifraga
Pastures, banks, roadsides

Carrot, Wild Up to 3 ft.
Daucus carota
Fields, waste places

Celery, Wild 1-2 ft.
Apium graveolens
Damp places,
usually near the sea

Fool's watercress 1-3 ft.
Apium nodiflorum
Ditches, shallow ponds

Marshwort, Lesser 3-12 in.
Apium inundatum
Lakes, ponds, ditches

Cowbane
Cicuta virosa
3-4 ft. Wet ditches,
marshes, lake margins

Chervil, Rough 2-3 ft.
Chaerophyllum temulentum
Hedgerows, grassland

Cow parsley 2-3 ft.
Anthriscus sylvestris
Everywhere

Bur chervil 1-2 ft.
Anthriscus caucalis
Hedges and waste places,
especially near the sea

Hedge parsley, Upright
Up to 3 ft. *Torilis japonica*
Roadsides, grassy places

Hedge parsley, Spreading
Up to 18 in. *Torilis arvensis*
Arable fields

Hedge parsley, Knotted
Up to 15 in. *Torilis nodosa*
Dry banks, arable fields

Fool's parsley Up to 2 ft.
Aethusa cynapium
Cultivated ground, river banks

Hemlock 3-6 ft.
Conium maculatum
Riversides, damp
roadsides, open woods

Parsley, Wild 12-30 in.
Petroselinum crispum
Waste places, wells,
old quarries

Hogweed, Giant 6-12 ft.
Heracleum mantegazzianum
Waste places,
especially by rivers

Hogweed 2-6 ft.
Heracleum sphondylium
Roadsides, hedgerows,
woodland, mountain ledges

Parsnip, Wild Up to 6 ft.
Pastinaca sativa
Roadsides, dry banks

Ground elder 1-3 ft.
Aegopodium podagraria
Hegerows, wet woods
waste places

Fennel 2-4 ft.
Foeniculum vulgare
Sea cliffs, waste places

Samphire, Rock
Crithmum maritimum
6-12 in. Cliffs,
rocks by the sea

Sea holly
Eryngium maritimum
Up to 2 ft.
Sandy shores

Sanicle
Sanicula europaea
Up to 2 ft.
Beech and oak woods

Pignut 1-2 ft.
Conopodium majus
Woods, well-drained meadows

Pepper saxifrage 1-3 ft.
Silaum silaus
Damp meadows, grassy banks

Stone parsley
Sison amomum
Up to 2½ ft.
Hedgebanks, roadsides

Shepherd's needle
Scandix pecten-veneris
6-18 in. in arable fields
in south-east England

Sweet cicely
Myrrhis odorata
Up to 3 ft. In pastures and
near buildings

Water drop-wort, Tubular
Oenanthe fistulosa
1-2 ft. Marshes,
shallow water

Water drop-wort, Hemlock
Oenanthe crocata
2-6 ft. Rivers,
streams, ditches

Water drop-wort, Parsley
Oenanthe lachenalii
1-3 ft. Brackish and
freshwater marshes

Water drop-wort, Fine-leaved
Oenanthe aquatica
2-6 ft. Shallow,
stagnant water

Water parsnip, Greater
Sium latifolium
3-6 ft. Fens,
ditches, pond margins

Water parsnip, Lesser
Berula erecta
1-3 ft. Ditches,
canals, ponds, marshes

Thorow-wax 6-12 in.
Bupleurum rotundifolium
Arable fields

331

Artists who loved the countryside

Many artists turn to nature for inspiration. Some capture the mood of a broad sweep of landscape. Others portray the beauty of a single plant or animal. But each, in his own way, reveals new facets of nature to all who see his works

J. M. W. Turner (1775-1851): Walton Reach. The Thames was a favourite subject

Medieval artists decorated religious manuscripts with delicate drawings of the beasts and flowers they knew and loved, while hunting scenes, full of detail, were a favourite subject for tapestries. But it was not until the 17th century, in Holland, that the countryside became recognised as a proper subject for painting, instead of merely a background to an event or a portrait. At the same period two French artists, Claude Lorrain and Nicolas Poussin, were treating landscape in the classical style, painting it as they thought it had appeared in Roman times.

These two influences, the Dutch and the classical, worked strongly on one of the greatest of British landscape painters, J. M. W. Turner. Turner was a Londoner, but his real and constant inspiration was the British countryside. He loved to fish, and the combination of fishing and sketching produced some of his happiest and most original work. Turner, a master of oil painting, was also, with his friend Thomas Girtin, the creator of a direct style of watercolour painting that was to inspire a school of artists that included John Sell Cotman and Peter de Wint.

John Constable, though only a year younger than Turner, did little that was original until the second decade of the 19th century. He then proved himself to be a 'natural' painter in a class of his own. For his subjects Constable did not look far beyond his native Suffolk, Hampstead, Salisbury or Brighton beach.

From Samuel Palmer in the early 19th century, through the Pre-Raphaelites, to the surrealist Paul Nash, many excellent British artists have attempted to distil the peculiar magic which lurks in our woods and fields.

Other artists, just as sensitive, belong to a tradition of natural history illustration, which dates back to the pioneer botanists and zoologists of the 18th century. Thomas Bewick, working around 1800, was a countryman and an illustrator with a dedicated respect for the facts of natural history. He founded a style of wood-block engraving which has continued to influence engravers to the present day. His greatest work was the two-volume *History of British Birds*.

Many Victorian and Edwardian artists contributed to the great expansion of knowledge in botany, zoology and horticulture — none as well known as Beatrix Potter, who published her first animal stories in 1902. Her endearing mice, rabbits and hedgehogs are set in a closely studied landscape. She also did some beautifully drawn British fungi.

These standards are still maintained today, for example by the Rev. Keble Martin's *Concise British Flora*, the product of a lifetime's devotion to wild flowers, which is curiously reminiscent of the illustrations of early monks.

John Constable (1776-1837): Near Stoke-by-Nayland. The Suffolk country

for one of our greatest artists

Thomas Girtin (1775-1802): Kirkstall Abbey, Yorkshire. Girtin was one of our great watercolourists

Samuel Palmer (1805-81): A hilly scene

Paul Nash (1889-1946): Wood on the downs

side was Constable's chief inspiration

Thomas Bewick (1753-1828): Bass

Beatrix Potter (1866-1943): The day's news

W. Keble Martin (1877-1969): Poppies

Sunlight filters through the ancient groves of Richmond Park, outlining a watchful herd of deer. This 2500 acre expanse in Surrey still offers an illusion of the days when London was surrounded by primeval forests teeming with game. Nature here has been helped rather than remodelled.

Henry VIII preserved the park as a chase: the highest spot, the Henry VIII Mound, was his vantage point during hunting drives. Deer are culled twice a year, and haunches of venison are distributed to the two Archbishops, Cabinet Ministers, and the Mayors of Richmond and Kingston

Parks — havens where the hunter once ruled

As more of the countryside disappears under a tide of new houses, factories and roads, parks play an increasingly important role both as pleasure grounds for the public and havens for many species of wildlife and plants

Originally, the word park described an enclosed area used for hunting by the king and his nobles. The wealth of barons was calculated by the number of parks licensed to them by the king. One of the earliest was Woodstock in Oxfordshire, which certainly dates from 1113 and may even date back to the Saxon kings. In 1705 it was given by the state to the Duke of Marlborough as a reward for his services as a soldier.

Other early parks of this sort which survive are Overstones in Northamptonshire, which was enclosed in 1255, and Chillingham in Northumberland, which was established at about the same time. Roaming the park at Chillingham is the only surviving herd of wild white cattle in Britain — descendants of prehistoric oxen which lived in the ancient forests.

Over the centuries hunting was abandoned and some parks were built upon. Among those which escaped the builders and to which the public now has access are the 2500 acre Richmond Park in Surrey, 3650 acre Windsor Park in Berkshire and the 1000 acres of Knole in Kent, a National Trust property.

During the 18th century the word park began to mean the land which people laid out around their country homes. At this time the aristocracy began building themselves palatial homes, and decided they needed large areas of land to set them off. This created the occupation of landscape gardener. His object was to produce a compromise between the wildness of nature and the stiffness of art, with water-courses, lakes, gardens and ornamental trees.

One of the most famous landscape gardeners was Lancelot Brown, known as Capability Brown because of his habit of saying, when looking at grounds he was asked to landscape, 'this has great capabilities'. Capability Brown transformed the appearance of Woodstock with formal gardens and by damming the River Glyme to create a magnificent lake.

Brown's clients were great landowners and he was contracted to change their land into a new countryside.

The typical Brown landscape can still be seen at Moor Park in Hertfordshire, on which he worked during the late 1750's for Admiral Lord Anson. He moved enormous amounts of soil to create gently rolling hills. At Ragley in Warwickshire can be seen a typical Brown feature — a solitary clump of trees on top of a hill devoid of trees on its sides.

But in creating his landscapes Brown, like other landscape gardeners, destroyed many fine old woods and avenues and had whole villages moved if they interfered with the 'natural view' of the countryside. Sir Gilbert Heathcote demolished the medieval church and village at Normanton, Rutland, when he created Normanton Park in 1764.

In some parks 'ruined' cottages were built to give the park a 'natural look'. Toward the end of the 19th century, land-owners began to feel the effects of the agricultural depression and parks ceased to be laid out on the same grand scale. However, a large number of the great parks survive and still support game and other wildlife. Some remain in private hands, others belong to the National Trust or are publicly owned. There is public access to many of them.

In the 19th century the word park was also used for recreation grounds in urban areas. The 1848 Public Health Act empowered local authorities to provide these as 'a means of exercise or amusement for the middle or humbler classes', and towns vied with each other to create superior facilities. Many of these parks became centres of education in botany, which flourished in Victorian times, such as Kew Gardens. Some of the Royal Parks in London have a different history. Hyde Park originally belonged to Westminster Abbey and was taken over by Henry VIII at the Dissolution of the Monasteries between 1536 and 1539.

In 1949 Parliament established the National Parks Commission and gave it power to designate national parks in areas of exceptional beauty, to which the public has been given access. Ownership of the land is unaltered, but it is administered by county councils or special joint planning boards. The Commission — renamed the Countryside Commission in 1968 — is an advisory body.

In 1972 there were ten National Parks in the British Isles, covering 5254 square miles. All are in England and Wales — in the Peak District, the Lake District, the North Yorkshire Moors, the Yorkshire Dales, Northumberland, Exmoor, Dartmoor, Snowdonia, the Pembrokeshire coast and the Brecon Beacons. An eleventh — the Cambrian Mountains — is being considered. Local authorities have the power to set up 'countryside parks' on a smaller scale than the National Parks as areas of quiet recreation for visitors in cars.

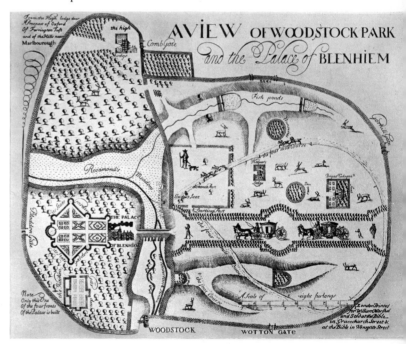

This sketch-plan of Woodstock Park and the Palace of Blenheim, drawn in about 1710, shows a horse-race in progress round the grounds. The Manor of Woodstock was given to the Duke of Marlborough by the state, and over a century and a half later was the birthplace of another hero, Winston Churchill

Parsley piert *Aphanes arvensis*

This inconspicuous plant carpets arable fields and bare patches in grassland throughout the lowlands. The delicate, fan-shaped leaves, which are deeply divided, less than ⅓ in. long and resemble those of parsley, hide clusters of tiny, green flowers, which consist of sepals, not petals, and which are borne between April and October.

The plant is a member of the rose family and is closely related to lady's mantle. Piert is a contraction of the French name for the plant, *perce-pierre*, meaning 'break stone' and signifying a plant which pushes its way through stony ground.

Close-up
of flower

The small green flowers of parsley piert, which have no petals, are concealed among the leaves

Partridge

A medium-sized, rather corpulent game bird, which seems well-suited to the British landscape of bare fields broken by hedgerows and copses. In winter, partridges gather in coveys and, when flushed, fly strongly away low over the ground, gliding for a considerable distance before alighting. They are no more than 12 in. long, and were once extensively shot for food.

In this century, partridge stocks, especially the native grey partridge, have suffered a serious decline. This is due to bad weather in breeding seasons and possibly the use of

Grey partridges form breeding pairs at the beginning of the year; the male is on the right

A victim of over-picking, the pasque-flower is now one of Britain's rarest wild flowers

Pasque-flower *Pulsatilla vulgaris*

This is one of Britain's most beautiful wild plants. It has delicately divided leaves and large, purple, bell-shaped flowers, which open in March, April and May to expose dozens of bright yellow stamens. When flowering is over, a head of hairy fruits develops; when ripe, these are dispersed by the wind. The plant is 4-12 in. high.

The flower takes its name from *Paques*, the

French word for Easter, because it is at its best as this time. It is also known as Danes' blood or Danes' flower. It is a rare and declining species, growing in only a few areas of dry chalk and limestone grassland in central and eastern England—perhaps because it is dug up too often by people who want to cultivate it in their gardens. Many nurserymen stock the plant and those who wish to grow it should obtain it from them.

toxic pesticides or shortage of adequate food at hatching time.

The grey partridge *Perdix perdix* is widespread and absent only from the south-west of Ireland and the western Highlands and islands of Scotland. From a distance, it looks a dull grey lump, but close approach shows the bird's beautiful mottled markings, with chestnut bars on the flanks, brown-streaked wings and delicate orange head. Its most noticeable mark is an inverted horseshoe of deep chestnut on the lower breast that is more pronounced in the male. The grey partridge's most frequent call note is a loud, high-pitched, creaking 'keev-it', often becoming a rapid cackle when it is disturbed.

The other species found in the British Isles is the red-legged partridge *Alectoris rufa*. It is a native of south-western Europe, and was first introduced into England in 1770. It is now established as a wild bird across the southern half of England, west to Somerset. Its country name of French partridge indicates the origin of some of these birds.

It is finely marked with delicate shades of grey and brown, broken by a prominent cream and black face pattern, a series of bold bars on the flanks and distinctive red legs and bill.

The red-legged partridge often perches to make its distinctive, loud, challenging call, 'chuck chuck-or'. Though preferring drier landscapes, the red-legged partridge is often found on agricultural land, sometimes alongside the grey partridge which it outnumbers in some areas, particularly in eastern England.

In courtship the red-legged partridge cock raises its head and holds it to one side; it erects the feathers of its white face and throat and of its barred flanks. Pairs of grey partridges often spring into the air and chase one another. Both species lay large clutches of eggs on the ground, well hidden under bracken or other thick cover, after pairing off at the end of the shooting season—September 1 to February 1. The 10-18 eggs are incubated for 24-25 days. Young chicks leave the nest after a few hours and are vulnerable to predators such as foxes and weasels until they fly two weeks later.

Partridges roost together, facing outwards to watch for predators.

Pea

Wild peas are related to the garden pea *Pisum sativum*. One of them, the sea pea *Lathyrus japonicus*, grows in patches on seashore

Sea pea
Lathyrus japonicus

Marsh pea
Lathyrus palustris

The sea pea is confined to shingle beaches, the rare marsh pea to nature reserves in England

shingle in south and east England. During a famine in 1555 the inhabitants of Aldeburgh and Orford in Suffolk kept themselves alive by eating its bitter, unpalatable peas. A creeping plant, 1-3 ft across, it bears purple to blue flowers from June to August.

Another wild pea, the marsh pea *L. palustris,* is now rare because of the drainage of many fens and damp bushy places where it was once common. It survives in nature reserves in eastern England. It is 2-4 ft high and puts out pale purplish-blue flowers between May and July.

The dry climate of the eastern counties is most suited to the cultivation of the sprawling, damp-susceptible garden pea plant. For this reason it is concentrated as a field crop on Lincolnshire, East Anglia and the Fens.

Grown as a field crop, peas are used for stock feed and — picked green or dried — for human consumption. Peas for stock feed are usually the small, hard, dry varieties.

Peacock butterfly *Nymphalis io*
The reason for this butterfly's name is obvious: the brightly coloured, eye-like markings on the wings — which have a 2½-in. span — are like the spots on a peacock's tail. The butterfly uses these eye-spots to protect itself from birds. When it is at rest the eye-spots are hidden, but when it is disturbed by a predatory bird it opens its wings to display them. Most birds fly off without waiting to decide whether the eyes belong to a large predator or are a bluff.

Like the small tortoiseshell butterflies, to which they are related, peacock butterflies are common throughout the British Isles. They breed once a year, laying their eggs on nettles in April or May. The caterpillars, which are jet black and finely speckled with white, feed on these. They enter the pupal, or resting, stage in July or August and the butterflies emerge to brighten the countryside until September or October, when hibernation begins.

A peacock butterfly displaying its eye-like markings on a spray of buddleia

Pear *Pyrus communis*
The wild pear is a small tree or shrub occasionally found on woodland edges in southern counties. It is a member of the rose family and can be recognised by its upright growth, grey bark divided into distinct squares, and brown twigs that carry, here and there, long sharp spines which are never found on garden pears.

The oval, pointed leaves are carried alternately on the twigs and have much longer stalks than the otherwise similar leaves of the crab apple. Wild pear flowers, completely white and borne in clusters in early April just before the leaves open, make the tree look as though it is covered in snow. The flower bases swell and ripen by October into greenish-brown fruits. The bases are never hollow, and this distinguishes pears from apples.

Wild pears are hard and sour at first, but as winter approaches they soften and become sweeter. Birds then peck the flesh, scattering the hard brown pips within. Wild pears are rarely planted and are usually bird-sown. They can grow to 40 ft and live for 60 years.

Pear-tree trunks have a pale brown outer sapwood around their crimson-brown

The peacock, which was probably introduced by the Romans, was eaten by medieval royalty

Peacock
Completely dependent on human protection in the British Isles, the peacock is often kept in gardens, parks and the grounds of stately homes.

It is correctly called peafowl and the most common blue species *Pavo cristatus* is a native of India or Ceylon, probably introduced to Britain by the Romans. The male has a colourful train with eye-like spots which makes up two-thirds of the bird's 7½ ft length. The train is formed by the particularly well-developed outer feathers of the tail. Light in weight, it seems not to impede flight. In captivity, a wide range of colour variations has been achieved by selective breeding and crosses with the Burmese green peacock *P. muticus.*

Peacocks roost in trees and often perch on walls. Each male has a harem of dull brown peahens which lay four to six creamy eggs in bare scrapes in the ground from January to March. The peacock has a loud, piercing cry, most often heard at roosting time.

Wild pear flowers, borne in spring, make the tree look as though it is snow-covered

heartwood, or 'fruit wood'. It is favoured by sculptors because of its warm colour, firm texture, and freedom from warping; for similar reasons it was once used for mathematical drawing instruments.

Wild pear is the ancestral stock of the many cultivated dessert pears, cooking pears and hard, bitter pears used to make perry. All these are propagated by grafting on to a vigorous stock, which may be a wild pear grown from seed or some closely related tree.

Cultivated dessert pears, many of which were introduced into Britain from France, need warmer sites than apples, as they flower earlier. They grow best on fertile, moisture-retaining loams. The chief growing areas are east and south-east England, particularly Kent.

'William's Bon Chrétien', a large, golden-yellow fruit dotted with russet, which has a slightly musky flavour, was first grown in England about 1770. It is widely used for canning. 'Doyenné du Comice', introduced to England in 1858, is a red-flushed, pale yellow fruit, with juicy, slightly cinnamon-flavoured flesh. 'Conference' is a tapering pear, the skin of which is green at first, becoming yellow at maturity. It is a sweet juicy fruit and stores well until late November. 'Bristol Cross' is similar but is clear bright yellow.

John Lawrence, rector of Yelvertoft, Northamptonshire, in the reign of Queen Anne, has a good claim to the title of father of garden pear culture. He wrote a fascinating account of his enterprise in *The Clergyman's Recreation*, published in 1714.

Perry—a cider-like drink probably introduced to Britain by the Normans—is made from the fermented juice of certain pears. Old names for it, such as merrylegs or devil-drink, give some idea of its potency. Today, perry pear trees are found mainly in the counties of Gloucestershire, Worcestershire and Herefordshire.

Pearl

While pearls are usually associated with the warm waters of the South Seas, some British shellfish produce tiny ones, though usually of little or no commercial value. Pearls result from the depositing of layers of mother of pearl round sand grains or parasites inside the shells. Mother-of-pearl layers are added by the mantle—the animal's soft outer layer—which usually re-lines the shell in the growing season. Foreign bodies are also coated and the thin layers build up to produce lustrous pearls. The size of British pearls is limited by the short growing season.

Britain's marine oysters from the Helford river in Cornwall and the Blackwater in Essex hold very few pearls, but a freshwater mussel *Margaritifera margaritifera* is another source. This species is found in clean, fast-flowing rivers with gravel or sandy stretches, and is therefore restricted to the north and west of the British Isles.

Freshwater mussels produce the best commercial pearls in neutral or slightly hard water. In the Tay and, to a lesser extent, the Spey rivers of Scotland about one in 100 mussels contains some sort of pearl, in varying colours: white, pink, green or brown. Britain's river pearls were known to the Romans, and today the number of pearls found in Britain each year varies from 1000 to 5000. A single pearl may sell for 10p while a cluster in an attractive setting may fetch from £200 to £300. The best British pearl—about ½ in. in diameter—was taken from the Tay in 1967 above the village of Stanley, Perthshire. Its value has been estimated at £5000 or £6000, but so far it has not been sold.

Pearlwort

Procumbent pearlwort *Sagina procumbens* is a widespread weed of gardens but also grows in grassland throughout the British Isles, usually in damp places. It has creeping stems 1-8 in. long and narrow, bristle-like leaves. It blooms from May to September. Some have tiny flower petals, others none.

Common pearlwort *S. apetala* grows in dry, bare places, such as gravel drives and disused railway platforms. It is an upright plant, 1-6 in. high, with flowers like those of procumbent pearlwort. Knotted pearlwort *S. nodosa*, which is confined to marshes and sand dunes, has white flowers, which appear on the 2-6 in. high stems from July to

Peat, the traditional fuel of Ireland, is now cut on a large scale to fire power stations

Peat

A surface layer of decaying organic matter, varying in colour from black to dark brown, and containing up to 50 per cent organic material in a partly decomposed state. It is usually formed in waterlogged districts where the water supply came from granite or sandstone areas with little limestone to neutralise the acid formed by decomposing vegetation. Peat has a sponge-like quality, and normally squelches underfoot. In Ireland, particularly, it is cut and dried for fuel.

Most of the more acid peats occur on high ground in the wetter areas of the British Isles, including Lancashire and Cheshire. These support few plants other than sphagnum moss, Molinia grass and heather, with occasional larger shrubs or trees.

In south-eastern England, where rainfall is much lighter, less acid lowland peats have been turned into extremely fertile farmland. The Fenland area round The Wash has been extensively drained and treated with lime to neutralise the acidity of the peat.

Raised peat bogs, dotted with rounded hillocks, are found in parts of Ireland and in the Cors Tregaron nature reserve near Aberystwyth. The hillocks are built up of successive layers of sphagnum moss and heather.

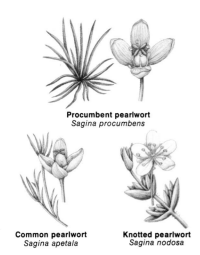

Procumbent pearlwort
Sagina procumbens

Common pearlwort
Sagina apetala

Knotted pearlwort
Sagina nodosa

Procumbent, common and knotted pearlwort flourish in very different localities

September. The plant derives its name from the knots of small leaves that grow on the upper part of the stem.

Pebble

Rock fragments smoothed and rounded by the action of water or glacial ice. Pebbles are not restricted to beaches, but are also found in lakes and rivers, on hillsides and even on the top of mountains where they have been deposited by melting glaciers. Changes in sea level account for inland shingle banks.

The water or ice which smooths the stones also carries them away from their mother rock; for example, volcanic-rock pebbles in Norfolk come from Norway. Less dramatic seaborne journeys often produce pebbles of stone different from the rocks in the area where they are found. Semi-precious stones such as rock crystal or onyx are sometimes found on British shores. See also STONE

Even ordinary pebbles from the beach can be attractive when polished or varnished

Peck order see Animal behaviour
Peewit see Plover

Pele tower

A defensive tower-house, also known as a bastle or fortelett. The pele tower derives its name from the pale (enclosure) which surrounded the tower and fenced in livestock. The towers were built by squires, lairds, landowners and clergymen on both sides of the border between England and Scotland from the late 13th to the late 16th century, as protection during the border wars and raids of the period.

They are usually rectangular with three storeys, and stone walls up to 8 ft thick. The entrance room gave access to the first-floor hall by a spiral staircase cut into the walls or by a ladder and trapdoor. If the family were attacked they retreated upstairs to the hall. The top floor in most towers was usually the bedroom.

Many pele towers survive, some in ruins and some incorporated into modern buildings. A ruined pele tower, built in the 15th century of stone from the nearby Roman wall, is attached to a 17th-century house at Welton Hall, 8 miles north-east of Hexham, Northumberland. Two parsons' peles survive at Elsdon and Embleton in the same county. Some Irish towers have a murder or peep hole in the hall floor above the entrance, as at Audley's Castle and Walshetown Castle, beside Strangford Lough, Co. Down.

Pellitory-of-the-wall *Parietaria diffusa*

This 1-3 ft spreading perennial grows on or beside old walls and hedgebanks throughout Britain, except in the north of Scotland. The rounded hairy stems have a reddish-brown tint. The plant flowers from June to October but the blossoms, like those of other members of the nettle family, are green and unattractive. However, their structure is remarkable; the young stamens are curved inwards but if touched when ripe, spring outwards, scattering pollen in a small cloud.

Pellitory is a corruption of *parietaria* from the Latin *paries*, a wall. So, curiously, the English name really means wall-of-the-wall.

Penny-cress, Field *Thlaspi arvense*

An unmistakable weed of arable fields and waste places. The field or common penny-cress grows throughout the lowlands of Britain but is rare in the north and west. It

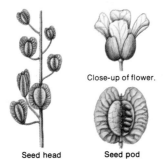

Close-up of flower.

Seed head

Seed pod

The tiny flowers of the penny-cress are followed by the distinctive winged pods

has a stout hairless stem up to 18 in. high and long, slightly toothed, hairless leaves. The lower leaves on the stem soon wither. The tiny, white, four-petalled flowers bloom from May to July. They are succeeded by rounded, flattened, winged fruits or pods ½-¾ in. across—about the size of a 10p piece. These pods form a conspicuous spike and have an unpleasant smell when crushed. Each pod has a deep notch at the top and consists of two parts attached to a thin central partition. This partition is at right angles to the pod and little remains when the seeds have fallen.

Pennyroyal *Mentha pulegium*

A small creeping mint with 3-12 in. reddish stems, oval leaves and whorls of lilac-coloured flowers that bloom from July to October. It used to be widespread in England and Wales but many of the damp pastures in which it grew have been drained and ploughed and now it is a rare plant of damp heaths mostly in the south.

In Tudor times pennyroyal was grown as a remedy for coughs, jaundice and dropsy. A spoonful of juice given to children was supposed to cure whooping cough. Its earliest use was to keep away fleas, hence the name *pulegium*, flea plant, from the Latin *pulex*, a flea. In the north of England it was used to flavour black puddings. It is from this that it gets its other name of pudding-grass.

Pennyroyal has been used as a cough cure and for flavouring black puddings

Pennywort, Marsh *Hydrocotyle vulgaris*

Often marshy or boggy land is covered with the circular leaves of the marsh pennywort. It is a creeping plant that grows throughout the British Isles in the wet mud of bogs and marshes or floating in the water. The leaves are conspicuous, being up to 2 in. across and growing on long, upright stalks. But the flowers, which bloom all summer, are difficult to see. Tiny and greenish-white, they are arranged in irregular clusters on short stalks.

Marsh pennywort, butterwort and sundew were once thought to be the cause of liver rot in sheep. However, the real culprit is the liver fluke that lives in the same damp habitat favoured by these plants.

Pennywort, Wall see Navelwort
Peppered moth see Thorn moth
Peppermint see Mint

Pepper saxifrage see Parsley

Pepperwort, Field *Lepidium campestre*
The dried powdered leaves of pepperwort were once used as pepper. This annual or biennial 1-2 ft herb has bitter-tasting roots and leaves, and branched, often woody, stems. The lower untoothed leaves form a loose rosette that soon withers; the upper leaves are toothed.

Clusters of small, white flowers blossom throughout the summer and develop egg-shaped fruits or pods. Each pod has a notch at the top, and its stalk looks like an old-fashioned ladle. Field pepperwort is common in south and east England but is rare elsewhere in Britain.

Perch *Perca fluviatilis*
A fish familiar to anglers throughout the British Isles, except in northernmost Scotland. It is often seen at the edge of lakes and rivers, or beneath bridges and overhanging trees. It has a large head and a large spiny fin on the back. Its back and sides are dark olive green, with five or six vertical, broad black bars; the belly is yellow and the lower fins red.

When young, the perch feeds on minute crustaceans, but later progresses to larger food, such as insect larvae. Once it grows longer than 10 in. it eats mainly small fish, or the fry of large species.

Perch spawn in April and May, twining their jelly-like strings of eggs around submerged plants or drooping tree branches in shallow water. One perch may produce hundreds of thousands of eggs in a spawning season, and some lakes may become over-populated with the fish. If there is a high survival rate in one year's perch, these can eat all the subsequent years' fish, so that in such years the whole population is the same age and size.

Peregrine see Falcon
Periwinkle see Winkle, Rock pool, Shell

Periwinkle
A seashore snail and a perennial garden plant share the name periwinkle. However, two kinds of periwinkle flower in the wild. The lesser periwinkle, which has flowers up

Lesser periwinkle
Vinca minor

Greater periwinkle
Vinca major

The flowers of lesser periwinkles are up to 1 in. across, those of greater up to 2 in.

to 1 in. across, grows throughout the lowlands. The greater periwinkle is common only in the south of England and has flowers up to 2 in. across. In both, the flowers are bluish-purple or white and the petals are twisted to the left in the bud. They appear early in the year on short stalks among the trailing stems of the leathery evergreen leaves. Periwinkles rarely produce ripe seeds in the British Isles but their stems root wherever they touch the ground. In this way the plants spread rapidly.

Periwinkles were originally introduced from Europe for their medicinal properties, and have spread into hedgebanks and copses.

Perry see Pear

Persicaria, Pale *Polygonum lapathifolium*
This annual weed is closely related to redshank *Polygonum persicaria*, and is usually found growing with it. However, pale persicaria can be distinguished by its greenish-white flowers, green stems and the absence of a black blotch on the leaves which is a characteristic of redshank. The leaves resemble those of a peach tree and give it its common name from the Latin *persicaria* meaning 'peach-leaved'.

Pale persicaria grows throughout the lowlands in waste places, arable fields and on manure heaps where it sets seed freely in the autumn and is subsequently distributed throughout the farm by the muck-spreader. See also REDSHANK

Pale persicaria
Polygonum lapathifolium

The leaves of pale persicaria, a widespread lowland weed, resemble those of the peach tree

Pest
Any living creature, such as an insect, mammal or bird, which attacks crops, domestic animals or fruit trees. There is a large variety of pests, ranging from potato-root eelworms, whose eggs can remain in the soil for up to 20 years before hatching and attacking potato roots, to rabbits and wild deer. Many birds, from wood pigeons to eagles, are also serious pests.

Rats and mice are particular enemies of the farmer. Each rat can cause £1 worth of damage a year. Cats, traps and poison have never succeeded in eliminating—or even completely controlling—rodents, which are capable of developing strains immune to the latest poisons.

Rabbits ceased to be a serious pest after the virus disease myxomatosis killed large numbers in 1953-5. But a strain of rabbits, immune to the disease, has grown in numbers, and once again they are causing much damage to crops, although not on the scale they did in the past.

Deer, like the eagles which prey on newborn lambs in Scotland, are a local problem. Their size increases their nuisance value. A comparatively small herd can cause much damage to fields of root crops; and in southern England they will eat rose bushes and other plants in private gardens.

Wood-pigeons, which breed everywhere, including town centres, are a year-round menace to farmers. In spring they eat fodder crops such as clover, and peck at seedling cabbage crops. In summer they descend in hordes on fields of ripening grain, spoiling more than they eat. In winter, they feed on anything they can find, including fields of kale and roots.

Starlings feed on most crops in season. However, they also eat large quantities of insect pests. Rooks do much damage to ripening grain and to newly sprouted crops in spring, often incidentally, as they search for insects feeding on the crops. Sparrows and some other finches feed on ripening grain. The damage which such small birds are capable of inflicting sometimes prevents farmers from growing the earliest varieties of barley and oats. Instead, farmers have to grow varieties that ripen when other food is available for the birds.

Bullfinches destroy fruit buds in winter and can ruin whole orchards. Blackbirds and thrushes also raid fruit plantations and orchards.

Although pheasants are often provided with specially sown cotoneasters and other berry-bearing shrubs, they sometimes scratch up newly sown grain and other crops.

Like other game birds, pheasants have become increasingly vulnerable to foxes, stoats, weasels and sparrow-hawks, since factory farming has made poultry inaccessible. Crows, magpies and jays—all egg thieves—have also been foiled by factory farms. In mountain areas, foxes still take a serious toll of lambs, as do the heavy-beaked larger members of the gull family and crows, ravens and magpies, which often peck at the eyes.

Moles feed mainly on earthworms, although they also eat harmful insects such as leatherjackets, wireworms and cutworms. But in spring they damage crops by creating networks of tunnels just below the surface of the soil in cornfields. This suspends the crop roots in the air, and the plants wither.

Insect pests which attack crops and animals are numerous and varied. Among the most damaging to crops are leather-jackets—the larvae of craneflies—which attack the roots and stems of cereals, flax, peas, beans and most vegetable crops. Spraying or laying poisoned bait controls them, but such methods, together with treating seed to make it poisonous or unpalatable to insects or birds, may have dangerous side-effects on humans.

Other serious crop pests include the mangold fly, which attacks mangolds, sugar beet and spinach, and the cabbage root fly, whose maggots attack the roots of cauliflowers, brussels sprouts, cabbages, turnips and radishes.

Free-ranging animals are subject to disease-bearing parasites. In Scotland and Northern Ireland particularly, mountain-grazing sheep are often infested with the sheep tick, which is common on coarse, dense-bottomed grass with a high humidity. The ticks carry two diseases which result in abscesses and blood-poisoning. They can be controlled by frequent sheep-dipping, draining the land, using cattle to eat the coarse grass or burning the vegetation.

Every method of pest control has its disadvantages. Sparrow-hawks and owls, which prey on pheasants, also help to control rodents and rabbits. Destroying starlings on a large scale is a boon to the crop-attacking insects they eat. Pesticides kill beneficial as well as harmful pests. Although grain crops grown from treated seed or sprayed with insecticide may not be eaten directly by man, they may be used to feed poultry, whose flesh and eggs can consequently be tainted. Similarly treated crops can affect cattle meat and milk. An Agricultural Chemicals Approved Scheme, however, does evaluate proprietary brands of agricultural chemicals before they are used.

Petrel

A seabird which spends most of its life on the open ocean, returning to an island colony only to breed. While breeding, petrels are completely nocturnal, coming to land after dark and uttering eerie calls as they flit around in the failing light.

Two species breed in Britain. Storm petrels, known to sailors as Mother Carey's chickens, breed on a string of islands along the western seaboard from the Isles of Scilly to the Shetlands and are seldom seen from land. The rarer Leach's petrels breed in about half-a-dozen well-established colonies in the outermost Scottish islands, including St Kilda, the Flannan Isles, North Rona and Sula Sgeir, and off the western coast of Ireland.

The two species can be distinguished by their tails. Leach's petrel has a noticeably longer forked tail; the tail of the storm petrel is square-ended. The black plumage of both is broken only by white rump patches where their tails join their bodies.

Both are buoyant swimmers, and their flight is marked by much wing-flapping. They feed on the larger planktonic animals and smaller fish, and gather at rich fishing banks. They frequently use their large webbed feet to patter over the surface as they pick food from the water with their bills. On these occasions they appear to be walking on the water, as St Peter did in a biblical episode, and their name is said to be derived from his.

The storm petrel also follows ships and feeds on refuse thrown from them.

Both petrels lay a single white egg in a crevice or in a hole taken over from rabbits or excavated by themselves. Storm petrels incubate their eggs for about 45 days; Leach's petrels for 50 days. The sitting bird is relieved by its mate every two or three days, and the young leave the nest after seven to eight weeks.

On rare occasions in autumn, western gales have driven storm petrels inland off their passage south to the open Atlantic.

Petty whin *Genista anglica*

A tiny shrub up to 1 ft high with thin, wiry, creeping stems, small, pointed, oval leaves and branches armed with long, slightly curved, sharp spines. It is from these that petty whin gets its other name of needle furze. Its gay yellow flowers blossom in spring and early summer, sometimes again in the autumn. There is no nectar secreted in the flowers, which discharge their pollen on to bees by an explosive mechanism.

Petty whin grows with other furzes, whins and gorse on poor acid soils on dry heaths and moors. It is strangely absent from Ireland but is scattered elsewhere throughout the British Isles.

The rare red-necked phalarope lays its four eggs in a grass cup in early summer

Phalarope

The cock performs all the duties of nest-making and rearing the young, and the hen phalarope, which is more brightly coloured, takes the dominant part in courtship and mating. The hen moves first into the breeding area, establishes a territory and leads the male to the nesting site. The phalarope is a small bird, 6-7 in. long, with a thin pointed bill. It spends the winter in the tropical Atlantic, returning to land to breed. Although it is a wader, the phalarope has semi-webbed feet well adapted to swimming. It finds most of its food on the surface, where in shallow water it often spins round rapidly to create currents which raise minute animals from the bottom.

Two species are seen in Britain. The red-necked phalarope *Phalaropus lobatus* breeds in northern Scotland and its islands, while the grey phalarope *P. fulicarius* is a regular autumn visitor to the coasts of southern and western England from its breeding grounds in Iceland and Greenland.

In summer, the red-necked phalarope has brown-grey plumage with white underparts and a prominent red neck patch. In winter it becomes dark grey above, with a dark smudge behind the eye. Its usual breeding grounds are Shetland, Orkney, Tiree and the Outer Hebrides, and one place in Co. Mayo, Ireland, but it may now also nest on the Scottish mainland. The four eggs are laid in a grass cup in late May or June and are incubated for 20 days. The chicks leave the nest within a few hours of being hatched and fly after 17 days.

After breeding, the red-necked phalarope moves back into the Atlantic but is liable to be blown onshore by autumn gales. At this time it may turn up on even the smallest ponds. During autumn and winter it may be confused with the grey phalarope which, though larger, also has grey winter plumage.

THE BUOYANT PHANTOM LARVA

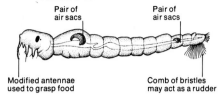

Pair of air sacs
Pair of air sacs
Modified antennae used to grasp food
Comb of bristles may act as a rudder

By adjusting its air sacs the phantom gnat larva can rise, sink or float in water at a constant level

Phantom gnat *Chaoborus crystallinus*

Transparent larvae, whose internal organs can clearly be seen, give the phantom gnat its name. They hatch from eggs laid in a jelly-like mass on the surface of a pond. Each larva resembles a pair of kidney-shaped bubbles. The bubbles are air sacs inside the larva. It can adjust the volume of air to maintain its position in the water or to rise or sink.

The larva feeds on water fleas and other small pond creatures, remaining motionless until its prey approaches close enough to be seized with a quick wriggle by means of its specially adapted antennae. It remains in the pond throughout winter, and also spends its pupal stage swimming near the surface of the water.

The mosquito-like adult gnat can be found near fresh water throughout summer. The male has feathery antennae and wings shorter than its ¼ in. long body. Neither sex has well-developed mouthparts and neither can suck blood. They feed on nectar.

Pheasant

Among the most savoury of game birds, pheasants provide sport by flying strongly and directly when driven over guns. When otherwise disturbed, they tend to run away rather than fly. Rearing and protecting them, and organising pheasant shoots after the shooting season begins on October 1, has become a major rural industry.

Pheasants, first recorded in England in 1059, are now widespread throughout Britain and Ireland. One theory is that they were introduced by the Romans from Asia. The common pheasant derives from the Chinese ring-necked, black-necked and Mongolian breeds, and accordingly varies in plumage. This has produced two forms—those with a white neck-ring and those without. The ring-necked, which is more common, is 33 in. long including its tail and has a mottled chestnut and black back. A white collar marks the iridescent blue-green head, which has red wattles. The hen is dull and buff coloured with a shorter tail.

Two other pheasants, introduced from east Asia, probably in the 18th century, are now recognised as self-supporting wild British birds. These are the golden pheasant and Lady Amherst's pheasant. The 23 in. long golden pheasant, established in the East Anglian brecks, or heathland, and in Kirkcudbrightshire, has rich red plumage. It is easily recognised by the golden tresses which fall over its crown, and by its long tail. Lady Amherst's pheasant, also 23 in. long, established itself in the south-eastern Midlands after escapes from the collection at Woburn, Bedfordshire. It has boldly patterned black and white plumage on the head and neck, which it erects during display. The male is dark green and white, the hen brown.

Pheasants are ground-dwelling birds, vulnerable to foxes, stoats, weasels and other predators. Due to the efforts of gamekeepers, who also supply winter feeding, pheasants survive in larger numbers than would be possible if they were left to fend for themselves. Their 10-15 olive-green eggs are laid from April to June in a well-hidden cup of grass and hatch out after 23-27 days.

The mottled colouring of the common pheasant's plumage helps to hide it from its predators

All snouts together. Large Whites—Britain's most

Pig

Proverbially pigs are 'either muck or money', with pig prices fluctuating between extremes. Pigs are prolific breeders; a sow can produce more than two litters a year with up to 15 pigs in a litter. A young sow can start breeding at the age of five to six months and the gestation period is only 16 weeks. Consequently, any especially heavy demand for pork or bacon is met without much difficulty; but often too many breeders try to cash in on the demand, the market becomes oversupplied and prices slump.

Pigs vary in size according to their use. A pig bred for pork weighs about 160 lb.; a bacon pig 220-230 lb. and pigs for use as processed meat—in foods such as sausages—weigh 250-500 lb. Some exceptionally fat pigs weigh up to 1000 lb.

A pig has a smaller digestive tract than other animals, such as sheep and horses, but in relation to its size it eats much more. Its food includes white-fish meal, bean meal, barley, maize, flaked maize, potatoes and fodder beet.

Pigs for breeding are sometimes kept on free range—this makes them use more energy and keeps them healthy; pigs for consumption are usually confined to sties, so they will use little energy and become fat. However, because of their thin coat of bristles, pigs are not as hardy as other animals and even free-range pigs need some protection from British weather. They suffer from cold and draughts, and in hot weather can get sunburn. Many farmers consider pigs to be more intelligent animals than horses or cattle.

Pigs have always been popular because they are such versatile providers of food—pork, bacon and ham. In the Middle Ages they were used to clean the streets by eating the refuse. But they became such a nuisance that in 1292 four men were appointed as 'killers of swine', with licence to slaughter any pig found wandering along the king's highway. As a result there were fewer pigs in towns and countrymen found an increased market. Wild pigs have not been seen in the countryside since the end of the 17th cen-

numerous breed—basking in the sunshine

tury. Those kept in the country in medieval times were half-wild and sometimes dangerous. During the 19th century these were crossed with more docile varieties introduced from south-east Asia, which produced to-day's breeds.

About 70 per cent of United Kingdom-produced pig meat is marketed as pork or used for processing. The remainder—about 256,000 tons—is used for ham and bacon. While virtually all pork is home produced, nearly 60 per cent of Britain's bacon and ham is imported. The Irish Republic is self-sufficient in all pig products. Country folk say that all parts of the pig can be utilised except the squeak. Apart from the flesh being used for food, the bristles are made into brushes, and the skin is used for hides.

The pig industry is highly organised, with artificial insemination services available in most districts. Scientists are aiming to produce a 'super-pig', the product of cross-breeding. It will be fast-growing and heavier than present breeds and provide leaner meat.

Although pigs keep themselves cleaner than do other farm animals, the eating of pork, particularly badly cooked pork, is potentially dangerous, as the animals are hosts of many parasites. Jews and Moslems are forbidden to eat pig meat by their religions.

Pigeon

Plump, soft-plumaged birds that feed almost entirely on plants and grain. The five distinct species that breed in the British Isles have all adapted themselves to the encroachment of town upon country. Each usually lays two white eggs.

The wood-pigeon is the largest species—16 in. long—and is the farmer's greatest enemy. It feeds on newly sown grain and clover, peas, ripe corn and other crops. Year-round shooting has failed to reduce its numbers; indeed, autumn shooting, by reducing the population to a level able to survive on the limited winter food supply, may help to keep the numbers up. The bird has adapted itself to town parks and gardens where its five-note cry 'cooooo-coo, coo-coo, coo' is now familiar.

It breeds throughout the British Isles, laying its eggs on a flat nest of twigs in a tree or bush and, very exceptionally, on a building ledge or on the ground. The young hatch after 17 days, when they are fed by both parents with 'milk'. Pigeons are the only birds to produce a milk similar to that of mammals. It is rich in protein and appears as a cheesy substance in the birds' crop.

The true rock dove, which is 13 in. long, is now found only on the rocky cliffs of north and west Scotland and Ireland. Doves seen on inland cliffs and in caves are domestic pigeons which have become wild. The rock dove feeds mainly on seeds and grain, and also on seaweed and shellfish. It makes an untidy nest on a cliff or in a cave and lays eggs at intervals throughout the year. The hatching period is 18 days. The bird's major enemy, the peregrine, is now rare.

Rock doves were kept for food in the Middle Ages, but many escaped from dove-cots and their descendants are the feral pigeons common in city squares, streets and railway stations. They also nest on sea-cliffs and often interbreed with rock doves. All have a low cooing call.

The stock dove, 13 in. long, is distinguished from the rock dove by having no white rump. It breeds in holes in trees, buildings, cliffs and sand dunes, where it lays eggs between March and September; these hatch after 17 days. Also a bird of farmland, the stock dove is less of a pest than the wood-pigeon, because it feeds chiefly on the seeds of weeds, such as fat hen, knot-grass, chickweed,

PIGEON IN FLIGHT

At the end of a down-stroke in flight the pigeon's wings sweep forward, the primary feathers curling upwards and backwards

Nine main breeds of British pigs

Large White
The most numerous and the most prolific British breed. It is derived from an early north-country type. Primarily a bacon producer, the Large White is the basis of many crosses

Landrace
Introduced through Sweden from Danish stock in the 1950's, the Landrace is a bacon-producing breed which is now much used for crossing as well as pure breeding throughout Britain

Berkshire
Developed in the Thames Valley early in the 19th century, the Berkshire is now rare. It is a small, pork-producing pig, also used for crossing with the Large White to produce bacon pigs

Middle White
A small pig, derived from the Large White and the extinct Small Yorkshire breed. Now rare, it was developed for pork production. It has a thicker coat than most breeds

Tamworth
An all-purpose breed found in the Midlands, particularly around Birmingham. Pure-breeds are rare, as the Tamworth is a good crossing breed. It produces high quality bacon

Welsh
An increasingly popular all-purpose breed founded on the traditional hardy pigs of Wales. The Welsh is much used for cross-breeding, and closely resembles the Landrace

Gloucester Old Spots
An all-purpose breed, which evolved from a hardy, foraging type native to the lower Severn Valley. The Gloucester Old Spots is white, marked with black spots in variable patterns

Saddleback
An all-purpose breed established recently by the amalgamation of the Wessex Saddleback and the Essex Saddleback strains, which differed chiefly in the width of the white band on the shoulder

Large Black
The original stock of the all-purpose Large Black came partly from Devon and Cornwall, partly from Suffolk and Essex. It is widely distributed and is often crossed with the Large White

343

A young wood-pigeon – this species has adapted itself to parks and gardens in towns.

and charlock. Its call is a double grunt. Confined to southern and eastern England in the early 18th century, it has spread over the British Isles.

The collared dove was unknown in Britain until 1952, and in 1955 a pair from the Continent nested in Norfolk. Now it breeds throughout Britain and in most of Ireland, and its 'coo, coo-o, cuk' call, accented on the second syllable, is a familiar sound. It feeds chiefly on grain, in fields and hen-runs, but also eats weed-seeds and berries. Collared doves build flat nests of twigs in trees and on building ledges. Eggs are laid between March and September and hatch in 14 days.

The deep, purring 'tur-tur' of the turtle dove can be heard from April to September, when it visits Britain from tropical Africa. At 11 in. long it is the smallest of Britain's pigeons and doves, and breeds commonly in the south and Midlands, rarely in Scotland and Ireland. It lives in woods, parks and gardens, building its flimsy nest of twigs in trees or shrubs. The eggs are laid between May and July, and hatch after 14 days. The turtle dove feeds on the seeds of weeds such as common fumitory, chickweed, charlock and grass.

Pig-nut see Parsley

Pike *Esox lucius*
The largest purely freshwater fish native to the British Isles. Pike grow to an average length of 16-40 in. and a weight of 30 lb. or more. A 53 lb. specimen was caught at Lough Conn in Ireland in 1920 and one weighing 47 lb. 11 oz. was taken from Loch Lomond in 1945.

Pike are recognisable by their elongated

heads and bodies, pointed duck-bill shaped snouts and rearward-placed fins. They vary in colour but are usually greeny-brown with the sides spotted and barred with light gold. The females grow faster and live longer than the males. Giant pike in Endrick Water, by Loch Lomond and Loch Ken, in Scotland, have been recorded at between 70 and 72 lb. Previously thought to be 25-50 years old, they are now believed to be 13-15 years.

Pike spawn in the shallows in early spring, often when the melted winter snowfall has raised the levels of rivers and lakes. Large females swim along the flooded banks accompanied by two or even three smaller males. The eggs are shed freely over the vegetation. In their first year young pike, known as jacks, live in shallow, densely weeded water often no more than 6 in. deep. They move into deeper water as they grow.

Pike of all ages like to lie close to vegetation where their barred and freckled bodies merge with the background cover. From here they will ambush and attack almost any smaller creature, using their powerful tail to overtake victims. The fiercest predatory fish in fresh waters, the pike has a large mouth, bristling with backward sloping teeth

THE JAWS OF THE PREDATORY PIKE

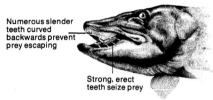

Numerous slender teeth curved backwards prevent prey escaping

Strong, erect teeth seize prey

The pike's jaws can open wide enough for it to swallow a fish almost as big as itself

which prevent a victim escaping once seized.

Young pike will eat insect larvae and the fry of other fish, but as they grow they become entirely fish eaters; perch is a favourite food. Pike have to be kept down in the trout waters of the north and west to give the more valued fish a chance to survive. A pike of 4½ lb. is estimated to have an annual food intake of 47 lb. of fish.

Water voles, moorhens and ducklings have been found in the stomachs of large pike, and the Lough Conn pike contained a 24 in. long salmon. Since most pike caught have empty stomachs, these large meals probably have to last the fish a long time.

Bright clusters of the pretty bog pimpernel smother bogs and areas of damp grassland

Pimpernel
Creeping plants bearing pairs of small opposite leaves. They are members of the primrose family and the most familiar is the annual scarlet pimpernel *Anagallis arvensis* with its bright red, sometimes blue, flowers. It is a lowland plant of arable fields, waste places and sand dunes. It is also known as poor-man's weather-glass because the flowers close before and during rain. When the petals fall, a globe-shaped capsule develops which splits around the middle; the lid with a tiny stalk on top looks like a little cap.

A creeping perennial, the bog pimpernel

A. tenella has tiny delicate funnel-shaped pink flowers. It grows over the surface of bogs and among other herbs in short damp grassland. It is rare in central and southern England, but is found quite often in the south-west, Wales, western Scotland and Ireland.

The yellow pimpernel *Lysimachia nemorum* is a perennial of damp woods and shaded hedgebanks, common except in the driest parts of eastern England. It is very similar to creeping jenny but its leaves are more pointed and it flowers on longer, more slender stalks. See also CREEPING JENNY

Pine

The general name for about 100 species of evergreen trees. Pines are distinguished from other conifers by the arrangement of their needles in twos, threes or fives.

Five-needled pines are rare and are usually found only in botanical gardens. In the south-west the Californian three-needled Monterey pine can be found growing as a sea-side shelter tree. All pines common in the British Isles have needles in pairs.

Scots pine is native throughout the British Isles, and was once widespread. Natural forests survive in the Scottish Highlands, notably at Rothiemurchus, near Aviemore, and in Glen Affric, west of Inverness. This tree is widely planted for timber production and has helped spread the crossbill, a finch whose chief food is conifer seeds.

Scots pine is distinguished by its short, blue-green needles and pinkish-brown upper bark. It produces clusters of male flowers which shed golden pollen in May, and little red female flowers which open at the tips of newly expanded shoots. Two types of cones can be seen in winter: one-year-old, immature, pea-sized, brown cones at branch tips; and much larger, tapering, green, two-year-old cones. These mature in spring when their scales turn brown and open, releasing winged, wind-borne seeds.

Corsican pine has long, grey-green twisted needles, sharp pointed buds and grey bark. It is a rapid timber producer in the English lowlands.

Austrian pine has straighter needles and coarser branches. It is planted for shelter along the coast and on limestone hills.

Lodgepole pine, which was brought to Britain from British Columbia, has mid-green, straight needles, a little prickle on

The stately, straight, leafless trunks of Corsican pines majestically set off a woodland scene

each cone-scale, and thin, black bark. It is planted for quick timber production in Scotland and Ireland.

The record heights for these trees in Britain are: Corsican pine, 144 ft; Scots pine, 120 ft; Austrian, 115 ft; lodgepole, 92 ft.

Pine timber, often called redwood, has red-brown heartwood and paler sapwood. It is strong and resinous, and is used for building, fencing and paper pulp. See also CONIFER

Pineapple weed see Mayweed

Pine marten *Martes martes*

This member of the weasel family, sometimes called the tree weasel, is Britain's rarest mammal. It lives only in mountainous or wooded country—though, despite its name, not necessarily pine forests—in the central and western Highlands of Scotland, North Wales, the Lake District and parts of Ireland. Its rarity is the result of centuries of trapping for its fur. This has now almost stopped, and its numbers are increasing.

The body is slender and up to 20 in. long, with a tail half that length. The legs are short but the five-toed, sharply clawed feet, whose soles are covered in hair, are large, for climbing. Colouring is grey-brown, with the face, legs, tail and underparts usually darker. The throat has a cream-coloured bib, sometimes tinged orange or pink in autumn.

Both lair and breeding den are a hollow tree, rock fissure or a large, disused bird's nest, such as a magpie's or buzzard's; they are lined with soft material, such as grass. By day the pine marten rests in its lair. Hunting begins at dusk and the animal may cover 5 miles in a night. It is agile and strong-limbed, and pursues squirrels, which are its chief diet, through trees, racing along branches, balancing on high, slender shoots and making leaps of up to 12 ft. It usually falls to the ground with the exhausted squirrel and kills it there. Apart from squirrels, it preys on other small mammals, such as voles, rabbits and rats, small birds, insects, slugs and frogs. It occasionally raids farms for poultry and can strike down wasps and bees with a paw and eat them. It also takes birds' eggs and feeds on berries.

Mating occurs in July or August and, because implantation of the fertilised eggs in the womb is delayed, the litter of two to five white-coated, thin-tailed cubs is not born until the following April. Cubs first leave the den after two months. They are afraid of heights at first and stay with the mother until autumn, by which time they have acquired their bushy winter coat. They are ready to mate the following summer.

SCATTERED HAUNTS OF THE PINE MARTEN

Mountainous regions
• Pine marten

The pine marten, a rare animal in Britain, lives only in remote mountainous areas and woodland

---

Five common pines

Details of the foliage and cones of the five major pines found in the British Isles. The cones of the Scots and lodgepole grow singly; the others in pairs. The needles of the Scots, Corsican, lodgepole and Austrian pines appear in pairs; those of the Monterey grow in threes

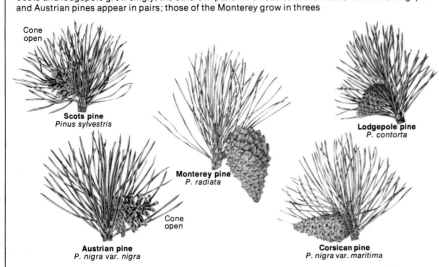

Cone open

Scots pine
Pinus sylvestris

Lodgepole pine
P. contorta

Monterey pine
P. radiata

Cone open

Austrian pine
P. nigra var. *nigra*

Corsican pine
P. nigra var. *maritima*

The pine marten, Britain's rarest mammal, hunts squirrels through the tree tops

Pine martens leave scent trails by rubbing the rear of the body against a branch, stone or other object. There is a musk gland under the tail, which produces a powerful scent. The scent trails mark out territory and establish contact with the opposite sex.

Tell-tale signs of marten country are dark, cylindrical droppings left in the open.

Pink

Rare summer flowers, pinks are related to the garden carnations and sweet williams, both of which sometimes become naturalised on old walls or in hedgebanks.

Deptford pink is an annual with a branched 1-2 ft stem, stiff, narrow dark green leaves and clusters of small, bright pink flowers. It grows in hedgerows and open grassland, in the south of England. Gerard, the herbalist, gave an early account of this flower, describing it as growing in a 'great field next to Detford, by the path side . . .'

Supposedly the colour of blushing maidens, the maiden pink grows as far north as the Moray Firth in eastern Scotland on limestone and other dry grassland. It is a perennial with 6-18 in. creeping stems. Its leaves

Deptford pink
Dianthus armeria

Maiden pink
Dianthus deltoides

The wild pinks are both rare summer flowers, related to garden pinks and carnations

are smaller and greyer than those of the Deptford pink. Its flowers are pink or white, with white spots and a dark ring in the centre. They are borne singly or in pairs, and are not easy to see during overcast weather as their petals close up.

Pintail see Duck

Pipefish

Shaped as their name suggests, pipefish have bony external skeletons. They feed on small crustaceans.

Of the three species that live in Britain's inshore waters, the greater pipefish *Syngnathus acus* is the most common and, at 18 in., the longest. Grey-brown or green, with darker bands, it lives in sea grass and seaweed on most British coasts and often in river estuaries. Almost identical in appearance, but with a shorter snout, is the 6 in. long Nilsson's pipefish *S. rostellatus*, most common on sandy shores. The males of both these species have a pouch on the underside of the body, into which the female deposits her eggs. The males carry the eggs and larvae until they hatch.

The almost black, 6 in. long worm pipefish *Nerophis lumbriciformis*, also known as the sea adder, has less prominent bony plates and lives in shallower water. It is most common on rocky coasts, where it can be found under boulders and among the seaweed of tidal pools. The male carries eggs in a shallow groove on its belly.

Pipistrelle see Bat

Pipit

A brown, rather nondescript ground bird. There are three species which are both common and widespread. They resemble larks but are slimmer and have longer tails.

The meadow pipit breeds around the coasts of Britain and is numerous on moors and mountains. It is olive-brown, streaked dark brown above and white below, with white outer tail feathers. Its call is a shrill 'pheet-pheet-pheet', and in summer it performs a territorial song-flight that ends with a parachute-like descent. It lays its three to five dull brown-grey, mottled eggs in a nest well hidden under a tuft of grass. Meadow pipits' nests are often chosen by cuckoos as host nests for their eggs. Meadow pipits gather at favoured feeding grounds, where they eat insects, spiders and seeds.

The tree pipit is a summer visitor only. It arrives in Britain in April and May from wintering grounds in northern tropical Africa. Similar in appearance to the meadow pipit, it is slightly larger and lighter-coloured. The tree pipit prefers heathland, with scattered trees, where it performs its song-flight, but will breed on any rough country that has trees or telegraph poles for song posts. The bird is widespread but has never bred in Ireland and is absent from the extreme north of Scotland. It feeds on

insects and spiders. It lays four to six red-brown or grey eggs in May or June in a nest of dried grass built on the ground.

The rock pipit and the water pipit are both sub-species of *Anthus spinoletta*. The first is found along the shores of Britain all year round, whereas the second is a bird of high moors and streams which descends to coasts and marshes only in winter.

In winter the two sub-species look similar —dark above, light and heavily streaked below. But in summer the water pipit is grey above and buff-pink below. Both birds nest in rock crevices and lay four or five off-white, speckled eggs in a nest of dried grass.

Meadow pipit and insect victim. In its turn the pipit is preyed upon by merlins

Pitchfork

Strictly speaking, a pitchfork has two long, curved prongs and a third, shorter prong set at an angle between them. This type of fork, long obsolete, had a short, wooden handle with a cross-grip. With it a man could carry enormous quantities of hay or straw. A pitchfork is also known in parts of the Midlands and western counties as a pykle or poikel.

The two-pronged lifting fork is a modern version of the more traditional pitchfork designs

Place names

The names of most of Britain's cities, towns and villages originated in Celtic, Anglo-Saxon, Scandinavian and Norman names. The place names of the original inhabitants of Britain, the Celts, survive chiefly down the west coast, especially in the hills of Scotland, Wales and Cornwall. An old jingle commemorates some of the Celtic elements in Cornish names:

By Tre, Ros, Pol, Lan, Caer, and Pen
You may known the most Cornishmen.

These mean, respectively, settlement, moor, inlet, sacred enclosure, camp and headland or hill. Penzance, for example, means holy headland.

The Anglo-Saxons began colonising Britain in the 5th century AD. Landing on the east coast, they moved inland, following river valleys, Roman roads and ancient tracks. Their earliest settlements are indicated by the ending *-ing*, meaning of, as in Reading, Spalding and Hastings. The first part of such names was often the name of a person or tribe. Hastings, for example, was the settlement of the Haesta tribe. The ending *-ham* meant estate, village or manor and some settlements so named may have been offshoots of earlier ones.

The most common Anglo-Saxon place name ending was *-ton*, meaning enclosure. It is the root of *town* and survives in hundreds of place names today. Some *-ton* settlements were again probably offshoots of existing ones. Ovington in Northumberland, for example, was probably settled by people from Ovingham. Another Anglo-Saxon ending meaning enclosure was *-worth*. Isleworth in London was already recorded by the 7th century.

An early Anglo-Saxon name given to fortified sites was *-bury* or *-burgh*, as in Bamburgh in Northumberland, established in AD 547. Existing Roman or British camps were given the ending *-chester*, a corruption of Latin *castrum*, a camp.

As the Anglo-Saxons moved from their original settlements into the forests in search of new pastures, new place names emerged, ending in *-hurst*, *-den* and *-ley*, all meaning forest pasture. There are hundreds of examples in the Weald of Kent and Sussex. Tenterden in Kent was the forest pasture of the people of Thanet.

The Viking invaders of the 8th century onwards also left their mark in place names. Occurring chiefly in north and north-west Britain, these Norse and Danish names usually have short, harsh-sounding elements —for example, *-dal*, meaning valley, *-thwaite*, meaning forest clearance, and *-scale*, meaning a hut for summer pastures. The Norse *vik*, meaning creek (Viking was Anglo-Saxon for 'of the creek') was corrupted into *wick*, as in Lerwick in the Shetlands. In Yorkshire there are more than 200 settlements ending in *-by*, meaning village or farm, such as Whitby. Another Scandinavian ending is *-holm*, meaning island—as in the Isle of Axholme in Lincolnshire.

The Norman conquerors introduced such elements as *beau*, meaning beautiful, and *bois*, meaning wood. Beaulieu, in Hampshire, means 'beautiful place'.

Plaice *Pleuronectes platessa*

Britain's most common and commercially important flatfish is distinguishable from others by its orange-spotted back and white underside. Large specimens, 14-18 in. long, live in deep waters, but 3-5 in. long plaice are plentiful in inshore waters and, with the rising tide, move into estuaries or on to sandy shores to join young, even smaller fish.

Plaice spawn in winter. The floating eggs gradually sink to the bottom and hatch after three weeks. The $\frac{1}{8}$ in. long larva has an eye on each side of the head, but as it drifts inshore and grows, the left eye moves up and over the head to join the other; this side of the body acquires orange markings and becomes the back. By the time the young plaice has reached shallow water it is fitted to live flat on the sea-bottom.

Plain

Plains are wide expanses of level land and are formed by long-continued erosion or wearing away of rocks, which lowers an area towards sea level. This can occur most easily where the rocks are weak, and the most extensive plains occur on clays and shales. In Britain, the Midland Plain extends across Warwickshire and part of Leicestershire, and the Cheshire Plain includes most of the county of Cheshire. Other level areas that could qualify for the term include the Fens, the lowlands of Lancashire and the area round the head of the Humber, notably the Vale of York. While these were in part created by erosion, they were also in part built up and extended by the deposition of silt by rivers and the sea. The central lowlands of Ireland, bounded by the Wicklow Mountains, the uplands of Tipperary, Connaught, Sligo and Leitrim and the Mourne Mountains, form a plain which is more than 8000 sq. miles in extent.

Plaistow

An open space for recreation. Plaistow is Anglo-Saxon in origin and once described what is now known as the village green. It survives in such place names as Plastow Green in Hampshire and Plaistow in London, Kent, Sussex, Herefordshire and Derbyshire. See also GREEN

Plane

The dappled bark of a plane tree—yellow patches mixed with olive-brown—makes it easily recognisable. Unlike other trees, plane sheds ageing bark in irregular patches. This helps it to thrive in smoky towns, for all trees breathe in oxygen through their trunks as well as through their leaves.

Each plane leaf is pale green, five-lobed and solitary, not paired. At the base of its long stalk is a curious hollow, shaped to hold next year's bud. In winter, the dunce's-cap form of this bud provides one way of identifying the tree.

Plane flowers, which open in May, are

The new wood exposed when a plane tree sheds patches of bark helps it survive in grimy towns

grouped in separate male and female catkins on the same tree; each catkin is a green globe on a long hanging stalk. Pollination is by wind. The following winter the female catkins turn brown and break up into hundreds of tiny seeds, each carrying a tuft of fine hairs to aid dispersal by the wind. Most seed is infertile, but sometimes a grain does produce sickle-shaped seed-leaves in the spring. Planes are usually propagated by means of cuttings.

London plane *Platanus × acerifolia* is the only kind commonly grown. A hardy, vigorous hybrid between Oriental plane *P. orientalis* and American plane *P. occidentalis*, it grows throughout the British Isles.

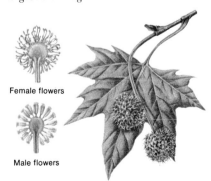

Female flowers

Male flowers

Plane tree flowers, which grow in ball-like clusters, rarely produce viable seeds

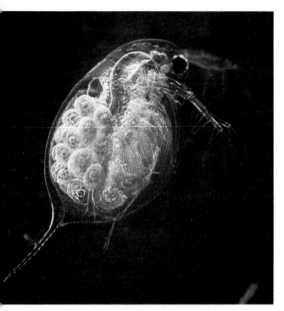

A water flea – one of 25 species that make up the greater part of Britain's freshwater plankton

Plankton

Derived from a Greek word meaning 'that which wanders or drifts', the term plankton applies to the plants, phytoplankton, and animals, zooplankton, which are carried along by the currents in the sea and fresh waters. It also includes small insects of the air, such as aphids and minute spiders which ride on gossamer threads at altitudes of up to 20,000 ft.

Phytoplankton, which consists of microscopic algae, provide the major source of food in the sea. They form the pasture on which many of the zooplankton graze. These in turn are eaten by carnivorous zooplankton which are food for larger sea creatures, including the biggest creature on earth, the massive blue whale, which lives entirely on a diet of plankton, strained from sea water. Plants need the energy of sunlight to manufacture food, and for this reason the phytoplankton live in the light-penetrated surface waters. In spring, when the hours of daylight increase, the phytoplankton multiply and, in response to the more abundant food supply, the zooplankton population also increases.

Zooplankton range from minute protozoans to tentacled jellyfish 2-3 ft across. They cannot swim but can migrate vertically, moving towards the surface at dusk and down again at dawn.

Many zooplankton are permanent members of this community, but some, such as the larval stages of many crabs, molluscs and fish, are only temporary members and as adults adopt a different way of life. By spending their early life as zooplankton, these animals have a plentiful food supply during an important period of growth and are carried to new areas by currents.

Ribwort plantain
Plantago lanceolata

Greater plantain
Plantago major

Buckshorn plantain
Plantago coronopus

Hoary plantain
Plantago media

Sea plantain
Plantago maritima

The five species of plantain which grow in the British Isles. Because they are so tough, thriving in spite of being trodden on along paths, people in early times thought they had magical powers

Plantain

A herb with a rosette of leaves, from the centre of which several cylindrical leafless stalks, up to 12 in. high, rise in summer. At the tip these bear long spikes of green or brown petals, which are succeeded by many-seeded capsules, once collected as food for cage birds.

Five species grow in the British Isles, of which the most common is greater plantain. This grows 4-6 in. high wherever man disturbs the ground on paths, tracks and roadsides. So resistant is it to treading and crushing that it was once believed to contain a remedy for bruises. The leaves are broad, strongly ribbed and tapered at both ends, and lie flat to the ground. Those of the hoary plantain, which is 3-12 in. high, are similar. This plant is common only on lime-rich soils in England. It bears a spike of lilac and purple stamens from May to August.

Ribwort plantain also has strongly ribbed leaves, but they are longer and narrower

Ribwort, like all the other flowers in the plantain family, is pollinated by the wind

than those of greater and hoary plantain. It grows in grassland throughout the British Isles and varies in size from 1 to 18 in. The smallest forms occur in dry grassland and the largest in lush meadows, where the plant is sometimes sown to enrich the mineral content of the grazing.

The two other species are most abundant near the sea, but occasionally grow inland. Buck's-horn plantain, 1-4 in. high, grows in sandy places and rock crevices. Its toothed leaves radiate in a star-shaped rosette – hence its other common name, star of the earth. Sea plantain is found in salt marshes, on cliff-tops exposed to salt-laden winds, and on limestone rocks and by mountain streams a long way from the sea. It is 3-9 in. high and has narrow fleshy leaves.

In some parts of the world plantain is known as white man's foot, since it is said to grow wherever an Englishman treads.

Plateau

A high tract of comparatively level land. Its flatness and height distinguishes it from both mountain and plain. Some mountain ranges were originally plateaux which became greatly dissected by erosion. Good examples are in the Pennines and the Cairngorms. If viewed from Aviemore the Cairngorm range of peaks is seen as a nearly level land mass.

Plough

The earliest form of cultivation consisted simply of scratching the soil with a branch or antler to enable a seed to be buried. Early ploughs did no more than this. Later models were designed to bury the remains of the previous crop and surface debris.

The Romans designed a plough with stout iron teeth mounted on a wooden sole which turned the soil. Celts and Romans, using light ploughs, adopted the practice of cross-ploughing, so that their fields tended to be almost square. The Saxons, using a heavy, eight-oxen plough, made their fields long, to reduce the number of turns. The old English furlong, one-eighth of a mile, is derived from 'Furrow long'.

The earliest mould-board plough, similar to that used today, dates from Saxon times.

But the really modern mould-board dates from the 18th century with the introduction of iron. Double-furrow ploughs, pulled by two horses, were common until tractors were introduced. Today, powerful tractors pull banks of ploughs which cut many furrows at the same time.

Experiments in crop cultivation without the necessity of ploughing are being carried out. See also FARM.

Ploughman's spikenard *Inula conyza*

Spikenard is a costly, perfumed ointment made from the roots of an Indian plant. Ploughman's spikenard also has sweet-smelling roots and may once have been used for the same purpose. Its leaves, too, give off a pleasant aroma when crushed. The lower ones are similar in shape to those of the foxglove but are distinguishable by their smell and roughness.

The plant bears yellow flowers from July to September and reaches a height of 3 ft. It grows in hedges, open woods and old quarries, and on roadsides, especially on dry, lime-rich soil, throughout England and Wales.

Plover

A plump short-billed wading bird. The most widespread and familiar of the six British species is the lapwing, or peewit. It is 12 in. long and derives its common names from its song of 'peewit-peewit' and the 'lap-wing' manner of its flight. The lapwing is a crested black and white bird with large wings; the back has a metallic green sheen and the tail is bright chestnut underneath. It is equally at home on marshes, moorland and dry arable fields. In winter it resorts to grassland and the open mudflats of estuaries. In all these places it often forms large flocks.

Like the other plovers and the blackbird, the lapwing stands motionless until a movement in the earth reveals the presence of a worm or insect, which the bird then pounces on. Its four buff-olive, heavily black-speckled eggs are laid in a nest of dried grass on the ground.

The ringed plover and little ringed plover are two closely related species that look alike. Both have a brown back, with a black-collared white throat and breast. They may be distinguished by the absence in the little ringed plover of a wing bar in flight, and by the ringed plover having orange, as opposed to yellow, legs.

The ringed plover — at 7½ in. long, the larger of the two — is a common sight along the coasts of the British Isles all year round, but in winter many leave and move south along the west coast of Europe.

The ringed plover breeds on shingle beaches, where it is being increasingly disturbed by holiday-makers. A few pairs breed on dry places inland, such as the Breckland of East Anglia. The little ringed plover is a summer visitor, confined to pebbly inland sites; it first colonised England in

The lapwing can be distinguished from other members of the plover family by its broad rounded wings

1938, when a single pair bred at Tring in Hertfordshire, but has since spread throughout the country. It is fond of nesting in gravel pits — even those loud with the clatter of machinery — where it will tolerate men and equipment within a few yards of its nest. Both birds lay four drab-coloured, mottled eggs, which merge with the shingle background. They feed on worms and insects. The ringed plover also eats shellfish.

The colouring of the ringed plover, with black markings on its face and breast, help it to melt into the background when nesting on an open beach. Light coloured underparts also help to camouflage the bird, when it stands, by blurring its outline. If danger is present the bird remains motionless.

If foxes, dogs or hedgehogs come within the vicinity of the ringed plover's eggs or chicks, the bird moves away from its nest and feigns injury by squatting on the ground and flapping a wing, as if broken. The hunting animal moves in for an easy kill and is gradually lured away from the nest. Once the parent bird is satisfied the danger is over it takes to the air.

The golden plover and the grey plover are another closely related pair of species. Both are 11 in. long and are coloured in the way their names indicate. In summer both acquire a black face and belly. In addition, the grey plover has a black 'arm-pit' at the base of the underwing at all seasons. The golden plover nests on moorland and resorts to arable and grassland in winter, whereas the grey plover, which breeds in Siberia, is only a winter visitor to Britain's tidal estuaries and mudbanks. Both lay four buff-coloured eggs marked with dark brown blotches in hollows scraped in the ground and lined with lichen. Both feed on insects, worms and small shellfish.

The Kentish plover, which nested in southeast England until the 1950's, is now only a rare spring and autumn visitor. It is a smaller version of the ringed plover.

The dotterel, a rare member of the plover family, breeds on the Cairngorms, nesting on mossy ground at heights above 2000 ft. Once numerous, the bird's tameness and reputation as a table delicacy led to its decline and fewer than 80 pairs now nest in Britain. Dotterels sometimes visit England.

Plum

The orchard plum *Prunus domestica* belongs to the rose family. It occasionally springs up in hedgerows or copses where people or birds have scattered plum stones. Unlike the allied blackthorn, the plum has spineless twigs. Its black-barked stems bear green twigs tinged with crimson, carrying dull-green oval leaves with toothed edges and irregular side veins.

The pretty white flowers, opening late in April, are single; each ripens, by September, into a juicy plum. Fruit colour varies from green or gold to red or purple. The hard stone germinates a year later, sending up two plump oval seed-leaves.

The bullace *P. insititia* found in southern hedgerows, resembles a blackthorn but has larger white flowers and golden-green plum fruits, just sweet enough to be eaten raw.

Wild plums rarely exceed 20 ft in height, but thickets may endure for a century because they readily send up suckers from their roots.

Plum wood has pale brown sapwood and a crimson-brown heart. It is used occasionally by wood carvers or turners, but most goes for firewood.

Plume moth

There are 35 British species of plume moths, the only moths with really featherlike wings of from ¾ in. to 1¼ in. span. Most of them have the forewings almost divided in two and the hindwings split into three main parts; each part of the wing looks like a single feather.

Many of the species are brown, but one of the most common and easily seen is the white plume *Alucita pentadactyla*.

During June and July, white plume moths may be disturbed from hedgerows in most parts, except Scotland.

The eggs are laid on bindweed and the tiny caterpillars hibernate. During April and May they complete their growth and these green hairy caterpillars are easy to find on bindweed leaves.

Plusia moth

These are among the most beautiful of the noctuids, a large family of small and medium-sized moths. Many of the 17 species migrate from Europe but eight of them are only occasional visitors. A distinctive characteristic is given to their resting outline by the tufts of scales on the thorax; each is marked by a bright or metallic-coloured spot on its forewings. The adults feed on nectar.

A day-flying species common all over the British Isles is the Silver Y *Plusia gamma*. Its caterpillars eat almost any type of low-growing plant. A similar, but mainly resident species is the Beautiful Golden Y *P. pulchrina*. Their names are derived from their Y-shaped wing markings. The caterpillars,

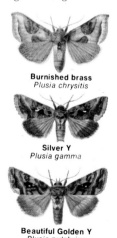

Burnished brass
Plusia chrysitis

Silver Y
Plusia gamma

Beautiful Golden Y
Plusia pulchrina

Three common plusia moths, all of which have a metallic-coloured spot on their forewings

which hibernate, feed mainly on dead nettles. The moths are common in June and July over most of the country. One of several species whose wings have a metallic sheen, the burnished brass *P. chrysitis* is found in most parts of the British Isles.

Poa see Grass

Poaching

Once land and the wild animals on it ceased to be common property and hunting became a sport rather than a means of subsistence, poaching began—especially if the rights of ownership were claimed by conquering overlords such as the Danes, Saxons or Normans. Under their rule, areas of suitable countryside, once common land, were set aside for the sport of venerie, the hunting of deer, boar and other 'roiall beastes'. Penalties were severe—even death—for anyone taking game illegally.

During the 18th and 19th centuries, deer stalking, salmon fishing, grouse and pheasant shooting, and hare coursing took place on enclosed private land, and gamekeepers and water bailiffs were hired to protect the game. The poacher not only had to catch his game, he had to avoid being caught himself—man-traps and spring guns lay in wait.

Today, some poaching is carried out on a commercial scale. Fish are stunned with explosives and electricity, and deer shot with automatic firearms. Meanwhile, the country amateur poaches for his own use or for the price of a drink, using well-tried methods of snaring pheasants, tickling for trout and ferreting for rabbits.

Pochard see Duck
Podweed see Seaweed

Poisonous plants

Deaths from plant poisoning are extremely rare in the British Isles, although many of the plants and fungi found here are poisonous and some of them are potentially lethal. The acid or pungent taste of some plants containing potent poisons stops people from eating them; so while plant poisoning may cause pain and sickness, it is rarely fatal.

Children are the most vulnerable: they are particularly attracted to colourful berries or to seeds in pods which resemble peas or beans. When adults are affected, it is usually through mistaking a poisonous plant for an edible one: for example, the corm of meadow saffron looks like an onion; deadly nightshade berries resemble cherries, and death has been caused by mistaking monkshood roots for horse radish. Most cases of plant poisoning occur in July and August when laburnum pods fall to the ground; the majority of other cases of poisoning occur between September and January, when many berries are ripe and Christmas decorations bring holly and mistletoe within the reach of children.

Dangerous plants most frequently involved

in poisoning cases are laburnum, nightshade and lupins. The incidence of poisoning from fungi is less common in this country than on the Continent, where mushroom picking is much more popular.

The severity of poisoning depends on many factors. The amount of poison in plants varies according to where they grow, the climate and the season when they are picked. The quantity and distribution of poison also varies from plant to plant. In some species only one part, for example the berry or root, is toxic; in others, the whole plant is poisonous.

Plant poisons are complex chemical substances, some of which are innocuous in small doses; and many, in minute amounts, have a medicinal action. They become dangerous when consumed in larger amounts. Poisons in this class include atropine from deadly nightshade and digitalis from foxgloves.

There are many gaps in our knowledge of plant poisons and their effects. As there is generally no known antidote, treatment for poisoning cases usually consists of washing out the stomach and dealing with symptoms if they arise. In all cases of suspected poisoning medical help should be sought as soon as possible and a sample of the plant, or part of it, should be taken to assist in identifying the poison. Prevention is better than cure, however, and children should be taught at an early age not to sample plants or fungi.

Animals and livestock are also affected by poisonous plants, which are usually eaten accidentally with grass or hay. The young are more likely to eat them deliberately, although some adult animals, having recovered from one poisoning, immediately return to the same type of plant as if they had become addicted. Ragwort probably causes more animal loss to the livestock industry than all other poisonous plants put together.

The following table lists the most important poisonous plants growing wild in the British Isles

POISONOUS FUNGI

Death cap	Red staining inocybe
Destroying angel	Sulphur tuft
Devil's boletus	Yellow staining
Fly agaric	mushroom
Panther cap	

POISONOUS FLOWERING PLANTS

Black bryony	Lily of the valley
Black nightshade	Lupin
Caper spurge	Meadow saffron
Cherry laurel	Mezereon
Cuckoo pint	Mistletoe
Deadly nightshade	Monkshood
Foxglove	Privet
Hemlock	Spindle tree
Hemlock water	Thorn apple
dropwort	White bryony
Henbane	Woody nightshade
Holly	Yew
Laburnum	

See also BERRY, FUNGUS, WILD FLOWER and separate entries on the individual plants

A polecat emerges from its burrow at the bottom of a tree to begin a night's hunting

Polecat *Putorius putorius*

One hundred years ago, polecats were to be found all over Britain. Today they are confined mainly to Wales, but there are signs that they may be returning over the borders to England. Their habit of killing for the sake of killing led to their extinction early this century in England and Scotland to protect game and poultry.

The principal means of eradicating polecats by about 1910 was the gin-trap, and its banning may lead to an increase in the polecat population which will need more territory to survive. The development of forestry is providing ideal habitats.

The polecat, which is a member of the weasel family, grows to about 16 in. long with a 6 in. long bushy tail. The rather coarse fur has a brownish undercoat with black outer hairs, giving an overall black-brown colour. A distinct feature is the 'mask' over the face, a dark band passing over the eyes. In front, the muzzle, chin and lips and, behind, the sides of the head and ear borders, are creamy white.

The polecat is mainly nocturnal and inhabits woodland, especially on farmland, and ranges from coastal dunes to hill valleys. It is mainly a ground dweller and good swimmer but a poor climber. Its prey—small mammals, rabbits, game, poultry, frogs, snakes and eggs—is located by sound and scent. Eels also form part of their diet. They are known to have made stores of frogs for winter food; the polecat bites them at the base of the skull so that they are paralysed, not killed, and remain fresh for long periods. Hoards of 40-120 frogs have been found preserved in polecats' burrows—usually old rabbit burrows between tree roots or rocks. Polecats can dig their own burrows and these usually have more than one entrance and contain a side chamber where they sleep and a larder.

Polecats mate in March or April. During the six-week gestation period, the female converts her bedding of grass and leaves into a spherical nest with a single small opening. The female—a jill—has five or six kittens and sometimes produces a second litter.

The ferret is a domesticated form of polecat whose exact origin is obscure but possibly derives from the East European form, *P. eversmanni*.

Polecats moult in May and June when they assume a much darker shorter coat. See also FERRET, STOAT

Policeman's helmet see Balsam

Pollack *Pollachius pollachius*

Principally an inshore fish, the pollack is a member of the cod family and is especially common on the southern and western coasts of the British Isles.

Like other cod, it has three fins on the back and two beneath the tail, the first of which is longer than the second. The pollack has no chin barbel or feeler and its lower jaw is longer than the upper. It may be found in small shoals over rocky grounds but the larger fish, which may reach 50 in. long, are more solitary and are found in deeper waters.

It breeds in spring in relatively deep off-shore water and the eggs and fry float near the surface into shallower water.

During their first year, many pollack live close inshore and may be seen in small shoals under piers or the keels of moored boats. At this size they feed on small crustaceans, but the larger fish are fish eaters.

Pollan see Whitefish

Pollard

If a young, broad-leaved tree is cut across about 6 ft from the ground, it will send out fresh shoots and form a bushy crown. This practice, called pollarding from the Norman-French word *poll*, meaning head, was once widespread. Because the young shoots started growth well clear of the ground, they were safe from grazing cattle and deer.

Repeated pollarding gave successive crops of small poles suitable for fencing, basketry or firewood. Old pollards of oak, beech, hornbeam and willow are frequent in southern woods and along lanes and stream sides.

Old pollards of wych elms. They once produced crops of poles from the tops of their stumps

Pollution — the menace to Britain's countryside

As industry and more sophisticated methods of farming grow, so pesticides destroy more of Britain's wildlife, factory effluents more of her fish, oil more of her seabirds, and mining and quarrying more of her landscape

As Britain's population increases, agriculture grows more intensive to provide the extra food needed. One of agriculture's main aids in raising production is the pesticide, a chemical which kills insects, weeds or fungi. The drawback of the pesticide is that it may kill, harm or seriously interfere with the habits of living things other than the pests at which it is aimed.

Few weed-killers directly poison animals, because after doing the work for which they are intended they quickly break down to a harmless state and because, unlike insecticides which are sprayed into the air, they are not carried and spread. They can, however, harm animals indirectly. For example, the diminishing supply of the insects upon which partridge chicks are dependent during their early days has been caused not by insecticides but by weed-killers destroying the plants upon which these insects live. The survival rate of the chicks is consequently poor and accounts for the marked decline in the partridge, once a common farmland bird, over the past 20 years.

It is the pesticides that spread and whose effects persist — such as the group of insecticides that includes DDT — which are most harmful to animals and man. These can be carried by wind, rain, rivers and ocean currents to places far removed from where they were applied; the polar bears of the Arctic, the penguins of the Antarctic and the fish of the mid-Pacific have all been found to contain DDT. In addition, because of their chemical structure, these insecticides accumulate in fatty tissue and are passed in increasing amounts along the animal food chain; in Britain almost every vertebrate animal, including man, contains minute amounts of DDT, and many animals also contain dieldrin, a more poisonous insecticide.

Dieldrin, first applied to seeds in the mid-1950's, has killed thousands of seed-eating birds, such as pheasants, woodpigeons and finches. Because these are numerous and reproduce at a high rate, their population has not declined seriously; but scarce and low-breeding birds of prey, such as peregrines and sparrowhawks, have declined seriously — especially as they feed not on seed but on small birds and mammals containing accumulated amounts of dieldrin. A 1962 survey showed that

CHAIN OF POISON

Pigeons in a farmer's field feed on seeds coated with dieldrin, a poisonous insecticide introduced in the mid-1950's. The dieldrin accumulates in the bodies of the pigeons, which are in turn eaten by peregrines. Each time a peregrine eats a contaminated bird it adds to an intake of poison that will eventually either kill it or make it infertile. Britain's peregrine population declined until 1964 when the use of dieldrin was finally brought under control

Although overgrown, waste from a medieval colliery still pollutes the soil near Amroth, Pembrokeshire. In this infra-red photograph, healthy vegetation is red, unhealthy is blue or mauve

WATERWAY POLLUTION

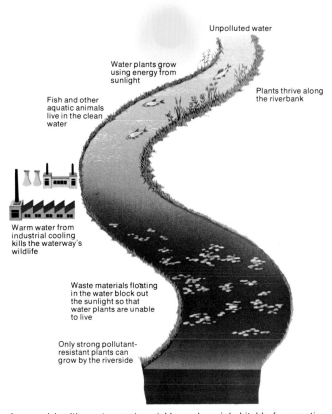

Unpolluted water

Water plants grow using energy from sunlight

Plants thrive along the riverbank

Fish and other aquatic animals live in the clean water

Warm water from industrial cooling kills the waterway's wildlife

Waste materials floating in the water block out the sunlight so that water plants are unable to live

Only strong pollutant-resistant plants can grow by the riverside

A clean and healthy waterway is quickly made uninhabitable for aquatic animals and plants by the waste materials pumped into it

down very slowly and accumulate readily in plant tissue it will be many years before traces of them finally disappear from the environment.

In some countries many birds of prey have been found dead from mercury poisoning. Although there are few recorded cases of this in Britain, ecologists are concerned about the prevalence of mercury in industrial effluent and its use as a coating on seeds to protect them from fungi.

Poisons can be released into waterways from many industrial processes—chromium salts from electro-plating, zinc from galvanising, mercury from paper-making, phenols and cyanides from chemical manufacture and DDT from agriculture. Apart from sometimes making the water foul in appearance and smell, they may kill off all the fish.

Mining also pollutes rivers. The unwanted material from

Lancashire's River Mersey—a victim of factory effluents. Oil, chemicals and lack of oxygen produce scum and a foul smell, and also kill fish

peregrines had decreased to almost half their pre-war population of 650 pairs. Since 1964 the use of dieldrin as an insecticide has been controlled and the population of some birds of prey has consequently increased.

During the peregrine survey, broken eggs were found in the nests, and it was noticed that the adult birds were deliberately breaking them. From 1946 onwards the eggshells of peregrines and other birds of prey suddenly became markedly thinner. The chemical processes which cause the changes in the parent birds' behaviour and in the eggshells are complex and not yet fully understood.

Two new insecticides, called pyrethrins, that are highly effective in killing insects but which quickly break down to a harmless state, have recently been produced. These are synthetic versions of pyrethrum, a natural insecticide produced from chrysanthemum flowers and in use since the early 19th century. Pyrethrins still have two drawbacks: they are highly poisonous to fish (although water helps to break them down) and their cost may be too high for widespread application by farmers.

Industry has also polluted the countryside with factory effluents containing PCBs (polychlorinated biphenyls). Some of the highest concentrations of these are found in fish-eating birds. Some of the 12,000 guillemots which died in the Irish Sea in the autumn of 1969 were found to contain high levels of PCBs. Following this incident, PCBs were voluntarily withdrawn from most industrial usage, but because they break

Doomed seal. Oil spilt at sea covers the fur of a grey seal which will die from swallowing the oil as it tries to lick itself clean

china-clay digging and coal mining often finds its way into rivers where, suspended in the water, it blocks out the light. Robbed of light, water plants cannot grow and, without these, insect larvae cannot survive. When it settles, the material also smothers the spawning grounds of many fish, especially salmon and trout. Solids present in treated sewage may also have the same effect, but the worst pollution by sewage is caused by the large amounts of dissolved oxygen which its minute organisms extract from the water, thus making it uninhabitable by animals and unpleasant in appearance – fouled with black mud, surface scum and sewage fungus on the bed.

Effluents from slaughter-houses, milk-processing plants, fish-meal factories, breweries and paper mills also contain organisms which take oxygen from the water.

Many industries use river water for cooling, and discharge the warm water back into the river. This can have several harmful effects. Fish may be killed by a high rise in the water temperature. Migratory fish such as salmon and sea trout may be prevented by the warm water from entering the river where they spawn. And a river whose temperature has been raised can carry less oxygen, which hastens the decay of organic matter – heated water discharged into an already polluted river can have disastrous results.

AIR POLLUTION

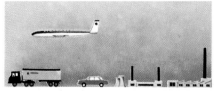

Exhaust gases from vehicles and sulphur dioxide from industrial chimneys drift for hundreds of miles before being brought to earth by rain

In England and Wales pollution control is mainly the responsibility of river authorities, and in Scotland of river purification boards and county councils. Many heavily polluted rivers have been restored to a purer state by the combined efforts of such control bodies, local authorities and the industries causing the pollution. As a result of such measures on the Thames fish have returned in large quantities and many species of birds have come back. Thousands of wading birds, such as dunlins, lapwings and redshanks, now feed on the large supply of invertebrates which are always uncovered at low tide.

Money is the biggest obstacle to keeping waterways clean. It is estimated that £500,000 extra is needed each year to keep pace with the increase in river pollution.

Oil pollution kills thousands of seabirds every year. The worst sufferers are those that spend most of their life on or just under the surface of the sea and are unable to escape the effects of the oil on their plumage: diving ducks, such as scoters and scaup, guillemots and razorbills. More than 10,000 seabirds were killed by oil following the wreck of the *Torrey Canyon* in the spring of 1967, and since then oil has killed at least as many seabirds each year.

Pollution of the atmosphere is not now as serious as that of waterways since the introduction of smokeless zones in many parts of Britain. But not all of Britain's towns have improved as much as London, where winter sunshine amounts have increased by more than 50 per cent in the last ten years and where the 'pea souper' smog of Victorian days and the 1950's has probably gone for ever.

Although the amount of smoke emitted annually into the atmosphere above Britain fell from nearly 3 million tons in the 1930's to less than 1 million tons by the late 1960's, the amount of sulphur dioxide emitted annually in the same period increased from more than 4 million tons to over 6 million tons. Much of this gas may drift for hundreds of miles before being brought to earth by air currents or rain, where it can cause leaf blotch on plants and reduce their yield.

Exhaust gases from vehicles include carbon monoxide and lead, and over the years these could accumulate along roadsides to the level where they could interfere harmfully with food chains.

Another form of pollution – pollution of the landscape – is derelict land, of which there are well over 150,000 acres in England, Wales and Scotland. Scattered over Britain's landscape, sometimes in areas otherwise green and pleasant, are thousands of heaps, holes and other disfigurements. Most of these are industrial relics, scars which have been produced by mineral extraction.

The most serious ravager of the landscape, coal mining, has thrown up towering black spoil heaps, such as that which caused the Aberfan disaster of 1966; or left behind deep depressions filled with stagnant water, disused shafts, machinery and colliery buildings.

The sand and gravel industry, which has caused nearly as much dereliction as the coal industry, has gouged out vast pits, as has quarrying for limestone, chalk, sandstone, slate and other rocks. The excavations of the china-clay industry in Cornwall and of the brick-clay industry in Bedfordshire and Peterborough have produced, with their gigantic conical spoil heaps and yawning chasms, landscapes which are more lunar than earthly.

In addition to these thousands of heaps and holes of industry there are hundreds of disused railway tracks, derelict airfields, abandoned wartime installations such as gun emplacements, and unused canals.

Cornwall, Northumberland, Lancashire, Staffordshire, Durham and the West Riding of Yorkshire contain the greater part of this dereliction in England; Glamorgan and Monmouthshire in Wales.

The chief objection to derelict land is that it is an eyesore. But it can also be dangerous—derelict canals, mines and quarries claim many victims every year. And it can be unhealthy—stagnant waterways and refuse-filled pits are breeding grounds for rats and flies.

Many conservationists claim that derelict land is economically wasteful to a degree that overcrowded Britain cannot afford—particularly as, with the increase of industry, the total acreage will probably be almost doubled by the year 2000. If reclaimed, however, it can provide sites for housing, new industry and playing fields, or be used for farming.

Both the open-cast mining and the iron-stone industry are required by law to restore land. After extraction of the valuable ore, surplus rock and soil are bulldozed back into the excavations in their correct order, and the ground levelled and returned to agriculture.

The responsibility of reclaiming the derelict land produced by other industries rests with local authorities, aided by government grants. Although reclamation is expensive, some counties have achieved miracles of transformation. Lancashire has turned one area of mining subsidence, with a disused canal and a rubbish dump—Whalley's Basin, near Wigan—into a large sports field.

Elsewhere tips have been flattened and planted with grass and trees to blend with the green landscape around them. Gravel pits filled with water are now used by sailing clubs. But some derelict land, such as the moonscapes of Cornwall, appears beyond redemption. This may even have a value left as it is—as a record of the landscape upheavals man can wreak.

The remedies for all forms of pollution are available and public awareness has been awakened to the dangers involved. All that is needed to ensure a healthy environment is determination and money.

Industrial blight: these oaks on a hillside above Swansea, in South Wales, have been killed by fumes from local industry

Life in the changing world of the pond

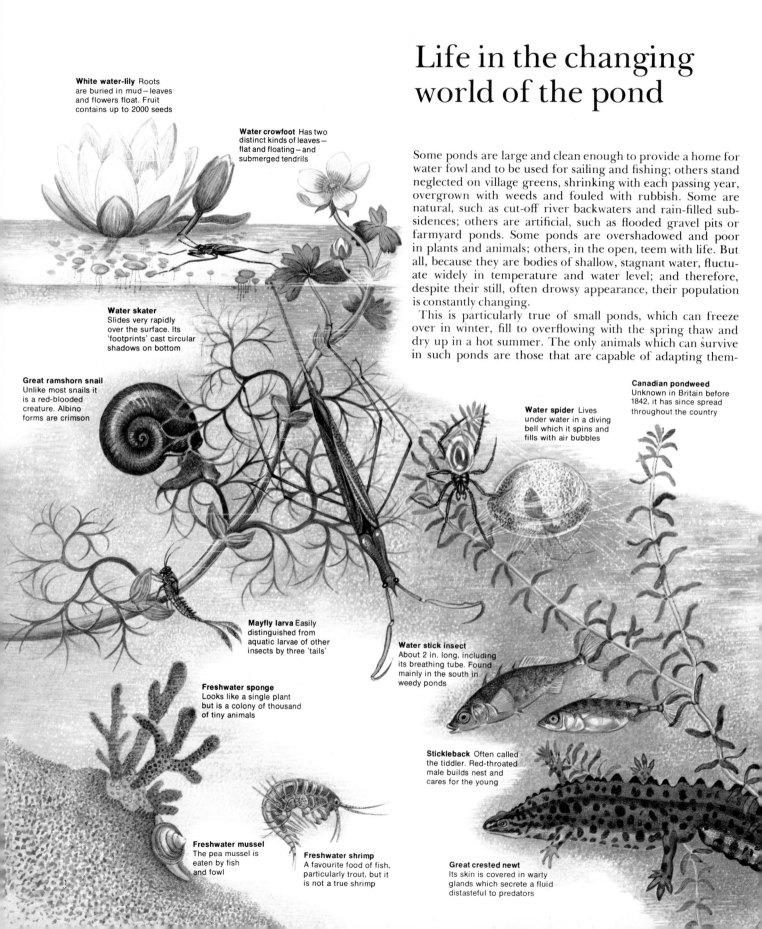

White water-lily Roots are buried in mud—leaves and flowers float. Fruit contains up to 2000 seeds

Water crowfoot Has two distinct kinds of leaves—flat and floating—and submerged tendrils

Water skater Slides very rapidly over the surface. Its 'footprints' cast circular shadows on bottom

Great ramshorn snail Unlike most snails it is a red-blooded creature. Albino forms are crimson

Water spider Lives under water in a diving bell which it spins and fills with air bubbles

Canadian pondweed Unknown in Britain before 1842, it has since spread throughout the country

Mayfly larva Easily distinguished from aquatic larvae of other insects by three 'tails'

Water stick insect About 2 in. long, including its breathing tube. Found mainly in the south in weedy ponds

Freshwater sponge Looks like a single plant but is a colony of thousand of tiny animals

Stickleback Often called the tiddler. Red-throated male builds nest and cares for the young

Freshwater mussel The pea mussel is eaten by fish and fowl

Freshwater shrimp A favourite food of fish, particularly trout, but it is not a true shrimp

Great crested newt Its skin is covered in warty glands which secrete a fluid distasteful to predators

Some ponds are large and clean enough to provide a home for water fowl and to be used for sailing and fishing; others stand neglected on village greens, shrinking with each passing year, overgrown with weeds and fouled with rubbish. Some are natural, such as cut-off river backwaters and rain-filled subsidences; others are artificial, such as flooded gravel pits or farmyard ponds. Some ponds are overshadowed and poor in plants and animals; others, in the open, teem with life. But all, because they are bodies of shallow, stagnant water, fluctuate widely in temperature and water level; and therefore, despite their still, often drowsy appearance, their population is constantly changing.

This is particularly true of small ponds, which can freeze over in winter, fill to overflowing with the spring thaw and dry up in a hot summer. The only animals which can survive in such ponds are those that are capable of adapting themselves to the unstable and extreme conditions: water fleas, water bears and fairy shrimps, which all produce drought-resistant eggs; mosquitoes, midges, horseflies, newts and frogs, which all spend the early part of their lives beneath water before moving into the air or on to land; and lesser water boatmen and water beetles, which migrate to other water once a pond dries.

Woodland ponds are usually too overshadowed to support much plant or animal life. Vegetation is normally restricted to algae and a few clumps of starwort. The bottom is choked with dead leaves, often covered with the rust-red or purple scum produced by iron or sulphur bacteria. Stirring up the leaves releases clouds of black mud and foul-smelling gas. Few types of animal can survive the lack of oxygen and of plant food in such ponds. The few include water lice, which feed on algae and decaying matter; tubifex worms and the red larvae of chironomid midges, sometimes called blood worms, both of which feed on bacteria and can, because their blood contains haemoglobin, live in oxygen-scarce water; mosquito larvae and rat-tailed maggots, which take in air from above the surface with breathing tubes; and pond skaters, water crickets and water beetles, which prey on other insects.

Open ponds receiving plenty of sunlight contain a rich plant and animal life. Microscopic algae are abundant and cover underwater plants with a green film; sometimes they appear as a green or red scum on the water surface. In ponds contaminated with manure the gently spinning, tiny green balls of the alga *Volvox* are common. Water weeds are also abundant. Some, such as duckweed, aquatic fern and aquatic liverwort, float on the surface. The others are rooted in the bottom of the pond. Canadian pondweed is totally submerged, water crowfoot and arrowhead have some leaves submerged and others on the surface, and amphibious persicaria and pond lilies have only surface leaves. Open ponds are usually fringed with a rich variety of plants: rushes, bulrushes, spike-rushes, reeds, reed poas, bur-reeds, sedges, water-dropworts, meadowsweet, purple loosestrife, yellow flags, water forget-me-nots, water plantains, codlins-and-cream, kingcups and water parsnips. Willow and alder are the most common trees found near such ponds.

The animal life of open ponds is just as varied: microscopic protozoa, hairy backs and rotifers, which all feed on bacteria, algae and detritus (dead animal matter); water fleas and cope-pods, which filter algae from the water, as do such bottom-living animals as the freshwater sponge and pea mussels; water boatmen, mayfly larvae, pond snails and ramshorn snails, which feed on plants, as do frog and toad tadpoles before moving on to insects; freshwater shrimps, pot-worms, caddis fly larvae and rat-tailed maggots, which feed on detritus and themselves form the diet of predators such as water stick insects, water beetles, water spiders, alderfly, dragonfly and damselfly larvae, pond skaters, whirligig beetles and water crickets.

Most ponds contain mites—red, brown, green or blue, globular, eight-legged animals which look like minute spiders. When young, they attach themselves to, and feed on, water beetles or water bugs; later they swim free and prey on other minute creatures.

Sticklebacks are often introduced into ponds to reduce the numbers of mosquitoes and midges; and carp, tench, roach and other fish are introduced to provide sport for anglers. These may attract kingfishers, even to small ponds.

Water birds such as moorhens and reed warblers are common, and swallows and martins often gather mud from ponds to build their nests. Water voles and water shrews are the most common animals.

Whirligig beetle
Legs serve as paddles and spin it over the water in a dizzy manner

Great pond snail
Common in larger ponds, feeding on plants and small animals. Shell may reach 2 in. long

Under the placid surface of a woodland pond such as this near Ashby Parva, Leicestershire, lies an aquatic 'jungle' with a wide range of bacteria, insects, animals and plants

357

Pondweed

There is scarcely a pond, lake, stream, river or canal that does not contain one or more of the 21 British species of pondweed. In some canals pondweed is so dense it makes rowing difficult and fouls the propellers of motor boats.

Those species which are partly or wholly submerged have cellular stems, translucent leaves and spikes of small, petal-less green flowers. Like many other floating plants, they reproduce mainly by fragmentation — winter buds develop on the roots or stems during summer and drop off when the plants die down in autumn, to grow into new plants in spring. However, some species do pollinate in water, and the spikes emerge to be wind-pollinated.

Three typical main species are represented by broadleaved pondweed *Potamogeton natans* which has large, elliptical surface leaves and long, narrow submerged leaves; curled pondweed *P. crispus* which has only wavy-edged submerged leaves; and small pondweed *P. berchtoldii* which has only grass-like submerged leaves.

Many species of fish and insects feed on pondweed.

Pony

Nine breeds of pony live on the mountains and moorlands of the British Isles, where they have roamed for centuries. Archaeologists have uncovered the remains of ponies which lived in Britain long before the Roman invasion in AD 43, the same type as those

seen today in the New Forest and on Exmoor.

The pony is a small horse not more than 14½ hands tall — a hand equals 4 in. — measured from the top of the front shoulder to ground level. It is thought to be the oldest type of domesticated horse, and is generally more intelligent, hard-working and sure-footed. Ponies were once in danger of being neglected, but various pony societies — in particular, the Pony Club, founded in 1929 — have for many years ensured that the

various breeds are kept pure. Britain's rich grasslands provide nutrients which develop strong bones in ponies.

The British breeds are the Fell and the Dale, of northern England; the Welsh Mountain; the Exmoor, the Dartmoor and the New Forest, of southern England; the Shetland and the Highland, of Scotland; and the Connemara, of Ireland.

The Dale and the Fell, once identical in type, are both capable of carrying heavy

Freedom of the hills. For most of the year, Welsh mountain ponies roam free on their native hills, watched

Britain's nine breeds of pony

Fell
A hardy pony found on the western side of the Pennines. At 13·2 hands it is smaller and lighter than the Dale, which lives on the eastern side

Dale
The native pony of the eastern slopes of the Pennines. Tough and stocky, it was once used as a pack-horse. It stands 14·2 hands

Connemara
This pony comes from an area in western Ireland roughly centred on Connemara. Hardy, it has short legs, and stands 13-14 hands

Highland
An all-purpose beast of burden for crofters and estate-owners in the Scottish Highlands. It is strong and muscular and stands 14·2 hands

New Forest
A large breed — 12-14 hands — but rather slightly built. It has roamed free in the New Forest for at least 1000 years

Welsh Mountain
This pony is a favourite with children. Although small — up to 12 hands — it is strong and was once used in pits

Shetland
A tough breed which can survive on seaweed. Because it is so small, it is measured in inches; average height: 39½ in.

Exmoor
An all-purpose breed native to Exmoor. Its head is longer and larger than the Dartmoor's. It stands 12·2 hands

Dartmoor
This compact, good-looking pony has lived on Dartmoor for centuries. Once popular as a packhorse, it stands 12·2 hands

over by mounted stewards

weights. On Tyneside, both breeds used to take lead—2 cwt at a time—from the mines to the docks—about 240 miles a week.

In addition to the pure breeds, there are many ponies of mixed breed, and sometimes the word is used indiscriminately for small horses. Many show ponies are not ponies at all but simply small versions of thorough-bred horses. Polo ponies are a type, not one particular breed, and often have Indian or Argentine origins. They are bred simply for their performance and most would never win a prize in a show ring. A polo pony has to be able to gallop at full speed, stop quickly, swerve, swing round and immediately gallop in the opposite direction.

Before farming became mechanical, when animals were more extensively used for ploughing and for pulling small vans and carts, farmers in hilly and wild regions preferred the pony to the horse. It is smaller and lighter, and more suited to such terrains. Ponies are still used as work animals in areas of Scotland, Ireland and Wales

Until the earlier part of the 20th century it was fashionable—as well as often being essential—to have a pony and trap. The number of ponies then declined until a revival of interest in the 1950's. Ponies are now popular for riding, especially in the suburbs of cities; and in many parts of the country, particularly Wales, southern Ireland, northern England and Scotland, pony-trekking—a touring holiday in the saddle—has become a tourist attraction.

Ponies are gregarious and in the wild are seldom encountered alone. On Dartmoor, Exmoor and in the New Forest they live in an almost wild state.

Poorman's beefsteak see Beefsteak fungus
Poorman's weatherglass see Pimpernel
Pope see Ruffe

Poplar

Tall trees belonging to the willow family. Their large leaves—oval, diamond-shaped, triangular or lobed—are borne singly on long stalks and flutter in the slightest breeze. This, and the fact that poplar branches, buds and leaf veins are randomly arranged, make identification easy.

Every poplar tree is either male or female. Males bear drooping yellow lamb's tail catkins, often tinged pink. These scatter golden pollen just before the leaves expand in early April.

Females have hanging green catkins like strings of tiny beads, which ripen by mid-summer to fruit catkins. Each pod then bursts, releasing minute seeds carrying white cottony hairs, which bear the seeds away on the wind. To germinate successfully, a seed must land on damp earth within a few days. The seed puts forth two fleshy green seed-leaves. Most seeds fail, and in practice poplars are raised from cuttings, which retain the sex of the parent tree.

The most conspicuous and easily recognised poplar is the Lombardy poplar, brought into Britain from northern Italy about 1758. It is usually a male tree which forms a slender, plume-shaped crown because its branches all follow the trend of the main trunk, instead of spreading outwards. Like all poplars, it grows quickly and is often planted as a screen or windbreak. Its knotty stem is useless for timber.

The related black poplar grows wild in marshy places in the English lowlands. It has a spreading crown and characteristic swellings on its rough-barked trunk.

Most poplars planted today are hybrids between this tree and American black poplars such as *Populus deltoides*, which are chosen for good form, fast growth and freedom from disease. The late-leafing variety 'Serotina' is the most common.

White poplar is so called because of its greenish-white bark and the pale undersides to its leaves, which may be lobed. It is rare, and mainly confined to southern fenland woods.

Grey poplar, similar to the white poplar but less pale, is a hybrid between it and the aspen poplar—a fairly common small tree growing in wet spots throughout Britain. Aspen poplar forms dense thickets because it continually sends up sucker shoots from a network of underground roots. It can be recognised by its long flattened leaf stalks which let the leaves quiver in the slightest breeze—hence its Welsh folk name *coed tafod merched*, the tree of the woman's tongue.

The balsam poplar is fragrant in spring; the bursting buds bear a sticky, aromatic gum—possibly a protection against insects. The tree comes from America and decorates parks with its bright yellow-green early foliage.

Poplars are unsafe near buildings—their large crowns of quivering foliage lose water rapidly, and the tree draws moisture from the soil, often drying it out and disturbing foundations, especially on clays.

Poplar timber is generally pale, light, and woolly and useless for firewood. However, it is excellent for making matches: when seasoned, it holds paraffin wax, which keeps the burning match alight and it splits into match sticks without breaking, withstands

Poplars are quick-growing, hardy trees, and are often planted to form a windbreak or screen

the pressure of striking and does not drop ash. Other uses are for everyday joinery and chip baskets.

Britain's tallest poplar, which has reached 140 ft at Fairlawne, Kent, is a 'Serotina'; black poplar is the next highest, at 126 ft; Lombardy poplar, which always looks tall, has reached only 115 ft. Although poplars often grow to 20 ft in diameter, few live long; 100 years is a ripe old age.

Eight common poplars

Balsam
Populus trichocarpa

White
Populus alba

Grey
Populus canescens

Aspen
Populus tremula

American black
Populus deltoides

Lombardy
Populus nigra var. italica

Italian black
Populus serotina

Black
Populus nigra

The many varieties of poplar are best distinguished from one another by differences in the size and shape of their leaves. This chart makes identification easy

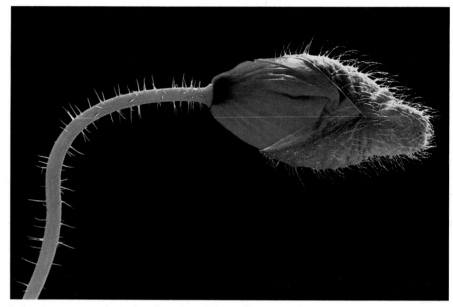

As the common poppy bursts into flower the two sepals covering the bud drop off

Poppy

Weedkillers have eradicated poppies from most cornfields, but the flowers still cover railway banks and waste places with a blaze of crimson from June to August. They also spring up in many places where the ground has been disturbed, as they did in Flanders after the battle had passed in the First World War. It is for this reason that artificial poppies are sold for war charities on Remembrance Day each November.

The common poppy, 1-2 ft high, has smooth, globular fruits and bristles on the stem. The petals were once used to make a syrup, and the seeds yield two grades of oil:

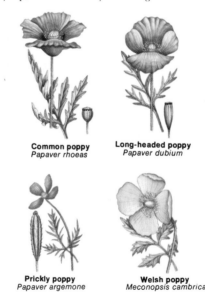

Common poppy
Papaver rhoeas

Long-headed poppy
Papaver dubium

Prickly poppy
Papaver argemone

Welsh poppy
Meconopsis cambrica

Poppies flower from June to August in waste places and disturbed ground

an edible cooking oil, and a coarser type used by artists in mixing paints.

The long-headed poppy, which grows to about 18 in., has fruits which are twice as long as they are broad, and bristles flattened against the stem. The 12 in. high prickly poppy also has long fruits, but they are covered in short, upward-turned hairs.

The Welsh poppy grows 1-2 ft high in deeply shaded rocky places in the Welsh mountains, south-west England and Ireland. It is also grown in gardens for its brilliant green leaves and large, sulphur-yellow flowers, up to 3 in. across; each flower is at the end of a slender stem, drooping while in bud but turning upwards to open. The petals soon fall. This species grows widely in western Europe as far south as the Pyrenees, but the first specimen described by Linnaeus, the 18th-century botanist, came from Wales and he gave it the Latin name *Cambrica*—of Wales.

Portland stone

A stone used in the construction of many famous buildings, including St Paul's Cathedral. It is an oolitic limestone quarried on the Isle of Portland—which is not an island but a promontory, 4 miles long and 1½ miles wide, attached to the coast of Dorset by a shingle ridge.

It is a hard stone, easily worked, but suffers damage from the chemical action of rain water laden with soot and sulphuric acid. Many buildings in London and other cities were damaged in this way before smoke pollution laws were enacted.

Portland cement is so called because of its supposed resemblance to Portland stone when hardened.

Portuguese man o' war see Jellyfish

Potato *Solanum tuberosum*

Although the potato was introduced into the British Isles from South America in the 16th century, it was not until the 18th that it was widely cultivated. It was grown first in Ireland, where there were large crops in the 17th century. The Industrial Revolution led to large quantities being grown in England near big towns to feed factory workers, and by the middle of the 18th century it rivalled bread as their main food. Today, it is one of the country's most important crops. Each year it is grown on more than 500,000 acres, and the average yield in 1971 was 11 tons an acre.

The plant grows 1-3 ft high and is a relative of the tomato and tobacco plants. Potatoes are tubers or short, thick parts of the plant's underground stem. The eyes on a potato correspond to the buds on an ordinary stem, and from them new shoots arise. The crop is usually grown from small tubers —seed potatoes.

As a general crop, potatoes are planted in March and April, although there are earlier and later plantings. September and October are the main harvest months.

Pothole

A hole drilled into the rocky foundation of a river bed or rocky shore by water swirling around stones within the hole. The hole can be seen when the water is low and usually contains the pebbles which have worn away the rock. Potholes are best observed on steep, rocky stretches of rivers. See also UNDERGROUND BRITAIN

Pottery

Fragments of pottery many centuries old are often found in the countryside, and it is the most common material found on archaeological digs. This is because although it breaks easily, pottery is extremely durable. Experts can tell the date of pottery by studying its fabric, shape and design. In this way it is an important clue to the dating of other objects with which it is found. Finds of pottery away from their known source of origin have also helped to identify old trading routes.

Old Stone Age man probably discovered how to make pottery more than 15,000 years ago. The earliest British pottery comes from New Stone Age sites in Berkshire and Devon and is about 4500 years old. It consists of bag-shaped pots probably used for cooking and storage, and is usually buff or grey. Pottery dating from this period was shaped by hand and any decoration was added by making marks with the fingernails, sticks or bones, or by painting.

The potter's wheel, which helps the potter to form clay into regular shapes, appeared in the Middle East in about 3500 BC. It was brought to Britain by Iron Age Celts in the 1st century BC, after which the variety in pottery shapes and patterns multiplied enormously.

Pound

An enclosure for impounding stray or trespassing farm animals. In former times pounds were often built by a parish and the animals were kept there until their owners had paid for any damage caused by them. Parish pounds are no longer maintained, but the word is still used to describe an enclosure built to hold cattle or sheep.

Pounds are usually round and of drystone walling. However, a square brick one may be seen at Newnham, Gloucestershire. A good example of a round one is at Elsdon, Northumberland.

A shepherd's pound at Grisedale, Westmorland, used as a fold for sheep from the hills

Pouting see Bib
Powan see Whitefish

Powder-post beetle

Four of the six British species of powder-post beetles have been introduced in imported wood. All of the six are listed loosely as wood-worms with other beetles whose larvae have the similar habit of boring into wood. They are brown, rather elongated, cylindrical insects up to ¼ in. long and can be found in timber or furniture indoors or in dead and dying trees or palings.

The native, fairly common species, *Lyctus fuscus*, lays its eggs on oak and some other trees, either on freshly cut surfaces or in the living tree. Its larvae feed only on the sapwood, but they can damage dead wood, which is in store or has been made into furniture, by boring holes. The other native species, *L. linearis*, is fairly uncommon in this country.

By far the most common beetle of this genus is *L. brunneaus*, whose wing-cases are covered with fine, short hair.

The fine powder which falls out of the burrows of powder-post beetles, and has the texture of flour, distinguishes them from other wood-boring beetles, which produce a much coarser, grittier textured sawdust. Powder-post beetles appear to attack only the wood of broad-leaved trees.

Prawn

The common prawn is often abundant, especially during autumn, among seaweed in rock pools on the south and west coasts of Britain. Its 1-4 in. long transparent body is dotted with purple pigment cells. Like all prawns and similar crustaceans it only turns pink when it is boiled. Its shape is similar to that of the shrimp but the number of spines on the 'snout' between the eyes is a distinguishing characteristic. The first two of the five pairs of legs end in nippers which are used to manipulate food.

Prawns move by walking slowly forwards on their last three pairs of legs, by swimming with the small flaps under the abdomen or by using their large tail flaps to shoot backwards.

The 1-2½ in. species *Palaemon squilla* is more widely distributed. The 1 in. species *Palaemonetes varians* is common in brackish water in estuaries. The chameleon prawn is common in pools on the lower shore. By day its colour merges with weeds, varying from green to reddish-brown.

Most prawns sold in this country are *Pandalus borealis,* a deep-water species fished mainly off Greenland. The much larger Dublin Bay prawn, or scampi, *Nephrops norvegicus* is not a true prawn but a close relative of the common lobster.

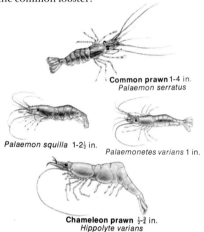

Common prawn 1-4 in.
Palaemon serratus

Palaemon squilla 1-2½ in.

Palaemonetes varians 1 in.

Chameleon prawn ½-¾ in.
Hippolyte varians

Of these four prawns *Palaemonetes* lives in brackish pools, the others in marine rock pools

Primrose

In the west of the British Isles the common primrose begins to flower soon after Christmas, and by the spring it can be seen in woods, hedgebanks and old grassland throughout the country. However, it is often scarce near towns, because of the number of people who have transferred the plants to their own gardens.

The plant grows 2-8 in. high and has a rosette of bright green, corrugated leaves. Its pale yellow flowers, 1 in. across, have deep yellow centres. In some woods in South Wales there is a form with pink flowers.

Two other species are seen occasionally. Both have leaves which are white above, mealy coloured beneath. Bird's eye primrose, up to 6 in. high, is found in the north of England in the spring. It has lilac flowers with a yellow spot in the centre resembling the eye of a bird. Rarer and only found on the windswept clifftops of the extreme north

Scottish primrose
Primula scotica

Common primrose
Primula vulgaris

Bird's eye primrose
Primula farinosa

of Scotland and Orkney, is the Scottish primrose. It has purple flowers and is usually only 2-3 in. high.

During medieval times an ointment, made from primrose leaves boiled with lard, was used by woodmen in the New Forest to treat cuts. On May Day, bunches of primroses were laid on the floor of cowsheds to protect cattle from witches at a time when they were considered to be most active.

Privet

Wild privet *Ligustrum vulgara* is a shrub that grows sparsely along hedgerows or over waste ground in southern England. It is not fully evergreen, and its dull green leaves, which are set in pairs along the twigs, usually fall by spring. They are larger than those of garden privet *L. ovalifolium,* more widely spaced and tinged with red. The shrub, a member of the olive family, is closely related to the garden privet which comes from Japan.

Both the wild and garden privets are easy to grow and produce a dense foliage ideal for border hedges.

The flowers, which open in May, are set in little spikes near branch ends. They are white and have a sickly scent, attractive to insects. The fruit, which ripens by October, is a black berry holding two hard seeds.

Birds take privet berries readily, void the

seeds later, and so spread the bushes. Under cultivation, seeds must be stored in damp sand for 18 months before they will germinate.

Privet wood is white, hard and horny. Wild privet lives for many years but rarely grows higher than 10 ft.

Prominent moth

Halfway along the hind edge of each forewing of this family of moths is a tuft of scales which makes a 'prominence' when the insect is at rest. There are 25 British species, mainly brown with complex and delicate wing patterns; all are fast, night-flying moths. They are widespread in the British Isles, but most common in the south.

The caterpillars of most prominents are green and hairless and feed on tree leaves. Often they rest with the hind claspers raised off the plant.

The larvae of the pale prominent *Pterostoma palpina* feed on poplar trees in summer and pupate for the winter at the foot of the trees. The moths emerge in May or June, with a second generation in July and August.

The buff-tip *Phalera bucephala* is a common prominent. Its caterpillars are yellow, downy and live in groups. The larvae pupate in cocoons below ground in September, and the moths emerge during the following

Profile

A sectional view of layers of soil or rock. The profile of land can be seen clearly by looking at a cliff, the side of a quarry, a newly cut embankment, or a hole dug to a depth of

several feet. In most soils distinct layers can be distinguished from the topsoil downwards. Usually each layer is of a different colour, showing a gradual transition to the next layer.

A profile of land in Hertfordshire, showing a layer of boulder clay on top of river-deposited gravels

Pale prominent moth resting on grass. It lays its eggs under the leaves of poplar trees

May. The buff-tip moth has an unpleasant smell that acts as a defence, warning enemies it is distasteful.

Prospect tower

A tower built on a hill to give a panoramic view. Most were constructed during the 18th and 19th centuries when landscape gardening was popular. They often commemorate a historic site, such as the one at Edgehill, Warwickshire, scene of a famous battle, where a tower has been raised to the memory of Charles II. On Kingsettle Hill, near Stourbridge, Worcestershire, a 160 ft tower was built to mark King Alfred's victory over the Danes.

Others were built for different reasons — for deer watching, observing the stars and simply as 'look outs'. In the grounds of Alton Towers, near Stoke-on-Trent, the prospect tower is only one of many follies. On 965 ft Leith Hill, Surrey, a tower was built in 1764 to the precise height of 1000 ft above sea-level. Battlements were added 100 years later raising the height. See also FOLLY

Ptarmigan see Grouse

Puck

A figure of English folklore corresponding to the Irish puca and the Cornish, pixie. Shakespeare used him in *A Midsummer Night's Dream*. With the variant 'Pook' he often appears in place names, such as Pook's Hill.

Alternative names include Robin Goodfellow, Lob and Hobgoblin, and he is usually included in rural festivals, especially in the celebration of May Day. Puck can assume the form of an animal or mislead travellers in the manner of a will o' the wisp.

Pudding-stone

Pebbles which have become stuck together with a natural cement that has washed between them and hardened into solid rock. Pudding-stone is usually found near an old river bed or shore.

Puffball

Ripe specimens of puffballs were once put on wounds, used for kindling fires and also for smoking bees when opening the hive. Most puffballs are edible. Young giant puffballs *Lycoperdon giganteum,* the largest species, are especially good when cut into slices and fried. They grow in pastures and beside roads.

The large, round fruiting body can sometimes be about the same size as a football.

Common puffball *L. perlatum* grows in woods, is 1-2 in. across and 3-4 in. high. It is white when young, turning yellow and then brown with age. The white mosaic puffball *L. caelatum* is 3-4 in. across and grows on chalk downland. When mature its surface becomes cracked.

Several puffballs of the genus Bovista which do not have common English names grow in grassland. They are white when young and from a distance resemble a golf ball. See also FUNGUS

Puffin see Auk

Pug moth

These small, thin moths tend to rest on flat surfaces, such as palings, with their wings spread out to their full, 1 in. span. In this resting position the hindwings and the forewings are visible.

There are 46 species regularly found in Britain. They are close relatives of the carpet moths and, like them, have caterpillars which walk in a looping manner. But, unlike the carpet moths, many pug caterpillars do not eat the usual diet of leaves, and live inside flowers or seed heads.

Most of the species' larvae pupate in the ground, overwintering in cocoons made from silk and pieces of earth.

Several of the species concentrate on a particular sort of flower. For instance the caterpillar of the foxglove pug live only inside foxglove flowers, where they feed on the stamens and seeds, after sewing up the entrance to the flower. The moths can be found in May and June around foxgloves.

The ling pug is a moorland species whose caterpillars feed in the small flowers of ling and heath plants during August and September. The moths of this species fly in June and July.

The green pug, on the wing during June and July, may also be brown, grey or black; the result of adaptation to industrial areas where the black form is particularly widespread. The green pug lays its eggs on wild or cultivated pears, apples and hawthorn; the larvae hatch during the spring and feed on the flowers.

Foxglove pug
Eupithecia pulchellata

Ling pug
Eupithecia goossensiata

Purple emperor *Apatura iris*

One of the rarest British butterflies, the purple emperor occurs only in a few woods inside a triangle formed by Oxford, Lyme Regis and Eastbourne. Even in these woods it is not often seen, since it spends most of its time high among oak trees when it is flying in July and August.

Females move down to lay their eggs on the leaves of the low-growing goat willow, which is also known as sallow, and the males sometimes descend to suck the juices from a rotting carcass.

Only the male really merits the name 'purple' as his wings are iridescent but appear purple when viewed from a particular angle. The female, which is slightly larger than the male, having a 3 in. wingspan, has a duller ground colour to her wings. The caterpillars are green with two horns on the head.

Female purple emperor feeding on honeydew. The species' name comes from the male moth, whose upper wings have a purple sheen

Purple loosestrife *Lythrum salicaria*

A tall, handsome plant which often grows 3-4 ft high beside lakes, sluggish rivers and canals, and also covers large areas of marshland. It flowers in mid-summer in the lowlands of England, Wales and Ireland, but is rare in Scotland, except near the southwest coast.

Charles Darwin discovered that there are three forms, with flowers differing in the length of stamens and styles, and that pollination takes place only when styles receive pollen from stamens of the same length. Pollination is effected by a bee.

Puss moth

This large furry moth depends on deception for its existence. The eggs, which are laid in June on leaves of the willow family, are reddish and resemble disease spots.

The caterpillar has two tails and when newly hatched is black, like a piece of withered bud. When the caterpillar gets too big for this disguise it turns green, blending with waving leaves. If attacked, it flourishes its tail and ejects formic acid from a gland. It also raises its brightly coloured head to make its appearance more terrifying. It is fully grown by September and becomes a purplish colour to match the bark before descending halfway down the tree. It then finds a crevice and spins a cocoon indistinguishable from a lump in the bark, and so strong that the moth has difficulty in emerging the following May or June. It produces caustic potash to soften the cocoon and uses the edge of its pupa case to cut its way out.

The puss moth *Cerura vinula* has a wingspan of 2½-2¾ in. and is white, patterned with darker lines.

There are three smaller relatives, named after their favourite food trees: the alder kitten *Harpyia bicuspis*: the poplar kitten *H. bifida* and the sallow kitten *H. furcula*.

A puss moth larva displays its false eye markings and red flush to scare off attackers

Pykle see Pitchfork

Pylons—part of the national grid—march through a gap in the mountains of Snowdonia

Pylon

Most people want electricity but few want pylons, a feature of the countryside since the national grid was started in 1927. The Central Electricity Generating Board virtually completed its super-grid in 1972. It is designed to meet demand until the 1980's, and because of the increased capacity of the transmission lines, the required mileage has been greatly reduced.

To carry the increased loads with safety, it was necessary to increase the size of pylons from the original 86 ft to 136 ft, and then to 165 ft on the super-grid. The tallest pylons in Britain are 630 ft high and carry lines across the Thames at Thurrock in Essex.

The Board is required to consider wildlife and the beauty of the countryside in planning its routes, which have to be approved by the Secretary for Trade and Industry. It also has to obtain rights of way from landowners and occupiers. A 400-kilovolt overhead line costs £97,000 a mile, an underground line £1,300,000 a mile. To disperse heat generated in underground cables, cooling equipment is necessary in the form of a bungalow-sized building constructed every 2 miles or concrete troughs which are filled with heat-dispersing material. Whichever method is used, no trees or buildings can be placed above the route.

In certain beauty spots, such as Boar's Hill near Oxford and the Heathfield and Ashburnham area of east Sussex, the electricity boards have laid cables underground; a half-mile stretch is also planned where a hydro-electric link passes along the shore of Loch Ness in Scotland.

Pyralid moth

A tiny moth with a wingspan of ½-1 in. There are more than 170 British species and they are usually grouped with the other smaller varieties of moths which are known as 'micro-moths'. They are night-flyers but also fly by day if disturbed while resting. Their flight is weak and clumsy.

Pyralid caterpillars always live inside a silk net of some kind, either in sown-up leaves like the mother of pearl moth, or in silken tubes among vegetable debris.

The tabby moth *Aglossa pinguinalis* is one of the larger types which lives in vegetable debris. It is usually found in outhouses and stables during June or July. It is a brownish colour and runs, rather than flies, for cover when disturbed during the day.

Tabby moth × 1½″
Aglossa pinguinalis

Its grey caterpillar feeds on pieces of hay and other rubbish, among which it makes a silken tube. The caterpillar grows slowly and sometimes takes almost two years before pupating.

The larvae of the Mediterranean flour moth *Ephestia kühniella* is a pest of bakeries and flour mills.

Q

Quail *Coturnix coturnix*
On the ground the quail looks a dumpy little bird, rather like a miniature partridge: In the air it is a strong flyer, migrating to England in May after wintering south of the Sahara.

The quail population has steadily declined in the last 100 years, and numbers have dropped abruptly since 1964. Changes in farming methods, such as the introduction of quick-growing crops, are partly to blame, because quails often nest among crops and the quick-growing types are harvested before the young birds are fully fledged. Continuous shooting has also taken its toll. Quail is considered a delicacy, particularly in southern Europe. They were netted and exported live from Britain until the practice was halted by law in 1937.

Quails' eggs are also prized by epicures and a Japanese species of quail is bred in increasing numbers. Wild quails' eggs are protected by law.

Quails are now confined to about eight counties in England, roughly south of a line between the Severn and Thames.

They lay from seven to twelve eggs in a scrape in the ground, and the well-camouflaged chicks leave the nest soon after hatching. A shy bird, the quail is usually first detected by its call, a repeated 'whic whic-ic'.

Quarry
Since the Stone Age, essential materials such as sand, clay and gravel have been excavated at surface workings or quarries throughout Britain. Today, stone is quarried for building and road surfacing; limestone for lime and cement, clay for bricks and tiles, chalk for lime and cement and sandstone for building, paving and roadstone. Marble—a form of limestone valued for its attractive veining and colours—is quarried in Britain chiefly for use as facing slabs to brickwork or concrete on building façades; the larger, structural blocks are usually imported.

Since the best material in a quarry is usually well below the surface, overburden—the material at the top—is too inferior for most commercial purposes.

Quarrying therefore results in large dry holes or lakes, flanked with tips of waste material. Sometimes these can be camouflaged with trees, used for boating or as local rubbish dumps which are covered and reclaimed at a later date. When this is impossible or too expensive, the countryside is disfigured for many years.

Slate quarries are particularly difficult to disguise. Up to 95 per cent of waste material is normal with slate quarrying, and the debris

A water jet washes out the kaolin from a vast china-clay quarry near St Austell, Cornwall

has a slow breakdown rate into the soil. This means years before any vegetation can establish itself. Slate quarries are often extensive—the largest in North Wales covers 700 acres, including its waste heaps. Slate has been quarried at Penrhyn, North Wales, since Tudor times.

The danger of modern quarrying lies in its efficiency. Modern machinery has led to larger and deeper quarries, which eat up land rapidly and are more difficult to fill in. Some quarrying attracts other industry, so that once-rural areas are transformed into industrial sites at the expense of wildlife and scenery.

Cement manufacture is usually concentrated in areas where limestone and clay are found together. A by-product of this industry is the fine dust which coats everything near by and turns to cement after rain.

When quarries are abandoned for many years, wild life and vegetation take over. Plants which can establish themselves on the bare rock face, such as moss and lichen, begin the process. Thickets of bramble and thorn grow in the soil and disintegrated shale at the base of the quarry. Steep faces, impossible to cultivate, are eventually softened by bushes and trees, providing homes

and food for insects, birds and animals. The age of a quarry can roughly be gauged from the size of the trees growing in it.

Freshwater life soon accumulates in flooded quarries. In chalk and limestone areas, the inaccessibility of the quarry face leads to the spread of chalk and lime-loving plants.

Until railways made the transport of stone over long distances practicable, local buildings usually reflected local geology, and small quarries were numerous. With rail transport came the enormous quarries of Aberdeen granite, millstone grit from the Pennines and the flagstone paving quarries of Caithness.

Old parish churches may provide a guide to local stone. Those in south Devon and west Somerset are often built of red sandstone, while other parts of Devon have slate or granite churches. Kentish rag, which could be ferried across the Thames, accounts for many south Essex churches as well as those in Kent itself. Ironstone churches in the Midlands show local variations in colour from dull brown to yellowish-gold.

The demand for modern materials, including cement, together with the comparatively high cost of worked stone, largely ended the centuries-old practice of poaching material from existing or ruined buildings. The Roman builders quarried extensively for suitable construction material like Bath oolite, Purbeck marble and Aldborough stone near York, and the Normans followed their example. Many 18th-century buildings included in their construction stone that was taken from ruined castles and villas.

The Roman Wall in northern England was poached by many 18th-century builders. Monasteries, which flourished between the Norman and Tudor eras, often included old stone and were themselves a valuable source of material after the Reformation, when they were closed.

Much of the craftsmanship once associated with quarries has now been lost with the advent of walking grabs, crushing plants and mechanical saws. A few quarries, particularly those used for 'facing' new buildings to bring them in keeping with local architecture, keep up the old traditions. Here craftsmen laboriously drill rows of holes in the rock face, insert wooden plugs and pour on water to cause the wood to swell. Alternatively, two conical-shaped, semi-circular steel plugs are hammered into each hole.

This enables the stone to break cleanly with no surface discoloration or fractures that occur when explosives are used.

Quartzite

Sand or quartz grains which have become cemented together with silica form the tough and durable sandstone rock called quartzite. A form of quartzite can be made by exposing a bed of sand to intense heat, so that the grains are melted and re-crystallised. The very hard rock so formed will break in all directions, showing smooth, greasy-looking surfaces.

Quartzite pebbles will emit an orange flash when struck together in darkness or under water. Many, including those found on the beaches of the south coast, are smooth and rounded. This is due to the action of water over the centuries in torrential rivers.

The best known quartzite pebbles are the rather large cobbles from the Bunter sandstone pebble beds in the West Midlands. These occur in the rock outcrops of Cannock Chase, Staffordshire, Sherwood Forest, Nottinghamshire, and other areas. Nottingham was founded on Bunter sandstone.

Because of its toughness quartzite is sometimes used for road making and in the manufacture of silica bricks.

Quern

A portable handmill used for grinding corn, spices, herbs or similar substances, thought to have been invented by the ancient Greeks 2500 years ago and brought to Britain by Celtic refugees from the Roman invasion of Gaul (France) in the 1st century BC.

The simplest quern consists of two stone discs—the upper of which is rotated by a small wooden handle. On some querns the grinding surfaces fit into each other, the upper stone slightly concave, the lower one convex.

In parts of the western islands of Ireland and in the Scottish Highlands querns are still in occasional use.

The stones were generally made from millstone grit and some places bear the name where many querns were quarried, such as Quernmore Crag near Lancaster. See also MILL, MILLSTONE GRIT

Quicksand

An area of wet, moving sand unable to bear the weight of a man. Quicksands are not usually extensive, often occur in estuaries, and are generally of a temporary nature in the British Isles.

Although scientists have not established exactly how quicksands are formed in all cases they are known to occur in places where an abnormal amount of water is trapped in the ground by a layer of clay or some other material which blocks drainage.

A beach may have quicksands one year and not the next. Occasionally they are caused by springs, on beaches with steep sides.

Quicksands often occur in the areas of the Bristol Channel and the Solway Firth.

Quince *Cydonia oblonga*

This is an apple-like tree occasionally seen in cottage gardens or naturalised along hedgerows. It has grey bark and oval leaves, which are dull green above and greyish and hairy beneath.

Beautiful, large-petalled pink or white flowers open in April, followed in September or October by large yellow soft fruits. Quince can be recognised by the fruit, with its woolly skin, its irregular shape—something between an apple and a pear—its hard, gritty seeds and its strong scent and taste.

Quinces are too strongly flavoured to be eaten raw and are used to make jelly, flavour apple pies, and in preserves. Since the seeds are rarely fertile in the British climate, quinces are increased by sucker shoots from their roots. These are also used by fruit growers as stocks on which to graft pear, a closely related tree, on which they have a useful dwarfing effect.

The quince is a native of the Mediterranean and Caucasus areas and has been cultivated in most of Europe since Roman times.

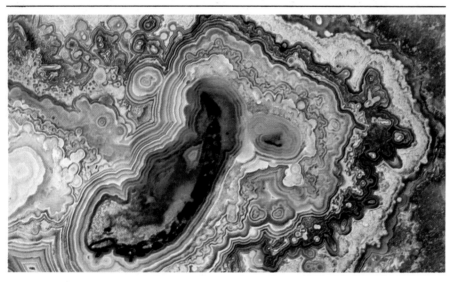

A polished section of chalcedony—shown half size—a variety of quartz, and a semi-precious stone

Quartz

Silicon is the most abundant element in rocks. Crystallised as quartz, it provides the material for sand grains, flints and man-made glass, and helps to build granite and other massive rocks. In rocks, it is mixed with other minerals, but also occurs as veins. It is one of the essential constituent minerals of granites.

Quartz is a hard and durable material, resistant to chemical erosion and weathering. Its crystals have six faces and a six-sided, pointed end. Because of its durability, quartz survives from one deposit to another—sand grains are fragments of older rocks that are

worn down to a small size in river beds or on the seashore.

Quartz crystals may be highly transparent, white or tinted by various impurities, as in the red and yellow stain imparted by iron to sand and sandstone. The clear rock crystal is used in electronic equipment, for instance in oscillators controlling radio frequency. Coloured varieties are valued as gems and include violet amethysts, dark red jasper and the rare rose quartz. White quartz veins are a guide to gold in some regions, such as Wales. A translucent form of quartz with small crystals is chalcedony—a semi-precious stone.

R

Rabbit *Oryctolagus cuniculus*

Introduced from France in the 12th century, the rabbit was for hundreds of years protected by landowners who valued it for its meat. Poaching was severely punished. It became the most familiar wild animal of the British countryside and one of the most destructive agricultural pests. Under the 1954 Pests Act, all occupiers of land in England and Wales are required to eliminate wild rabbits and 50 per cent grants may be paid towards the cost of clearance.

The rabbit measures about 16 in. and weighs 3-4 lb. When bred for meat, it can reach 15 lb. It has a black-buff coat, white belly and a short, upturned tail. The female or doe is smaller and has a narrower head than the buck.

A social animal, the rabbit lives in colonies in warrens. It can live almost anywhere, from sea level to the mountains, digging burrows on farmland, sand dunes, salt marshes, moorland, embankments and cliffs. Empty cliff burrows are often taken over by nesting puffins and shearwaters. The warren is dug in a haphazard way with interconnecting tunnels, bolt runs and emergency exits. The burrows damage field boundaries and hedges, and disturb the surrounding soil, encouraging the growth of weeds such as nettles and ragwort. At breeding time the doe digs a separate burrow called a stop, which she lines with hay or straw, and fur from her own body. The stop may either be a 2-3 ft long extension of the main warren or a completely separate excavation which may eventually be the starting point of a new community.

Breeding may occur sporadically throughout the year but mainly between January and June. A buck will mate with several does, but takes no part in rearing the young and may even kill them. Each doe keeps within her own territory in the warren. The popular notion of the rabbit's breeding capacity is not exaggerated, for it is possible for a doe to produce a litter of three to six young every month. However, this rarely happens, as over half of the young conceived die before they are born, and are reabsorbed back into the mother's body. On average a doe will produce about ten live young a year.

The young rabbits are born below ground, deaf, blind and without fur. The doe visits her stop once a day to suckle them and on leaving blocks the entrance to conserve heat and as a safeguard against enemies. Within a month the young are capable of looking after themselves. They reach adult size after about nine months but can breed after three or four months. A rabbit rarely lives

A young wild rabbit. The name originally applied only to the young, an adult being called a cony

more than a year and the mortality rate of the young is high. Among their enemies, apart from man, are cats, dogs, stoats, foxes, badgers, weasels, owls and buzzards.

At dawn and dusk rabbits emerge from the warren to feed. They establish clearly defined runways and communal latrines which are often on a mole-hill. A rabbit will eat a pound or more of fresh green food a day. It does extensive damage to young trees by nibbling at the bark and eating the shoots, and also to cereals, roots and pasture land. The short turf on downland is the result of centuries of grazing by rabbits and sheep.

Feeding is by refection, a similar method to chewing the cud. Food is eaten then excreted in semi-digested form as soft moist pellets. These are eaten again and passed through the intestines to be fully digested. It is the second, dry pellets that are seen lying on the ground.

The myxomatosis epidemic which began in 1954 in Britain almost wiped out the rabbit population of over 60 million, more than the human population. The effects were noticeable on crops and vegetation, and predators, such as buzzards, declined. But the disease is no longer so lethal and the rabbit population is increasing again. Today, rabbits are controlled by gassing them in their warrens, ferreting, shooting and snaring. Tame rabbits also continue to flourish and in recent years the number of rabbit farms has increased. See also MYXOMATOSIS

Radish

The cultivated garden radish *Raphanus sativus* is rarely allowed to flower, but when it does it produces large, jointed seed pods similar to those of radishes growing wild in the countryside.

Wild radish is a widespread and troublesome annual weed of arable fields and waste places. It is sometimes known as white charlock but this name is appropriate only in south-eastern England, where the white flowers bloom from May to September. Plants with yellow flowers are more abundant in the north and west, and lilac forms with dark veins on the petals are also seen in these areas. It grows from 6-24 in.

The sea radish is a taller and more handsome plant, reaching 12-30 in. It forms extensive colonies along the drift line of

THE SHARP TEETH OF THE RABBIT

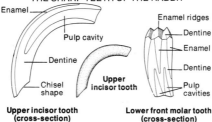

Upper incisor tooth (cross-section)

Lower front molar tooth (cross-section)

A rabbit's incisors are as sharp as chisels and used for cutting. Molars are ridged for grinding. They keep their shapes because dentine wears away more quickly than enamel

sandy and rocky shores, especially on the south and west coasts. It flowers throughout the summer and is normally yellow, but white-flowered plants have been recorded in the Channel Isles.

Wild radish
Raphanus raphanistrum

Sea radish
Raphanus maritimus

Sea radish, which is 12-30 in. high, is a taller, more handsome plant than wild radish

Ragged robin *Lychnis flos-cuculi*

The ragged and jagged rose-red petals of this perennial can be seen waving in the breezes of early summer in marshes, damp meadows and wet woods throughout the British Isles. The whole of this slightly hairy plant is reddish in colour and it grows from 12-30 in. It is in flower from May to June when the cuckoo is calling and this co-incidence has given the plant the Latin name *flos-cuculi* meaning cuckoo-flower. Plants with 'robin' in their names are often linked in folklore with goblins and evil. It is considered unlucky to pick the flowers and take them indoors.

Ragworm

Fishermen often dig up ragworms, which live in mucus-lined burrows and use them as bait. The largest species, the green and pink *Nereis virens,* has paddles on each of its segments and lives under rocks on muddy northern shores.

Specimens from North Wales grow more than 18 in. long and may be as thick as a finger. They sometimes bite.

Before mating, some species of ragworms develop extra large paddles which enable the adults to swarm to the surface of the sea where they discharge their eggs or sperm. Fertilised eggs develop into larvae and the

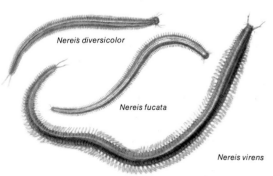

Nereis diversicolor

Nereis fucata

Nereis virens

Nereis virens lives in mud, *N. diversicolor* in estuaries and *N. fucata* in shells

The paddles of the ragworm enable it to swim at speed through the sea

adult ragworms die. Other species, such as the 3-4 in. *N. diversicolor*, found in estuaries, swarm in burrows in the mud to reproduce. A conspicuous red blood vessel down the centre of the upper surface of this worm accounts for its popularity as bait. It is often dug for on brackish estuaries. Another species *N. fucata* lives in the spirals of shells inhabited by hermit crabs and steals food as the crab eats.

Ragwort

A handsome herb with ragged leaves (hence ragwort) and much-branched heads of yellow, daisy-like flowers. Common ragwort,

Hoary ragwort
Senecio erucifolius

Marsh ragwort
Senecio aquaticus

Common ragwort
Senecio jacobaea

Oxford ragwort
Senecio squalidus

Ragworts, members of the daisy family, are so-called because of their ragged leaves

which grows 1-4 ft and occurs throughout the British Isles, is mildly poisonous and is usually avoided by cattle. Sheep tend to eat it, but appear to be unharmed by the experience. It is also a favourite food of the cinnabar moth, whose black-and-yellow striped caterpillars often leave nothing but the stem uneaten.

In damp pastures beside rivers, especially on peaty soils, common ragwort is replaced by marsh ragwort, a shorter plant with lower leaves which are scarcely divided, and larger flowers which have fewer ray petals. On lime-rich soils, particularly clay, in lowland England and Wales hoary ragwort is often seen. It can be identified by its hairy stems and leaves. The leaves have extremely narrow lobes at the tips, and the plant grows 1-4 ft.

Oxford ragwort is rapidly becoming the most common ragwort, especially around towns. It grows 9-15 in., and its flowers often brighten the corner of a building plot. It was introduced to Oxford from southern Italy and was first noticed spreading elsewhere in 1794.

Ragworts generally flower in late summer, but Oxford ragwort begins to bloom in May.

Rail see Crake
Railway see p. 372

Rain

In most parts of the British Isles the average rainfall is adequate without being excessive, and no month is either too wet or too dry. In general the west is wetter than the east, for the winds bring air which has sucked up moisture from the Atlantic; and as the air rises to clear the hills it cools and the moisture condenses, falling as rain.

Only in the western uplands is there too much rain for agriculture or comfort. In these areas more than 50 in. of rain fall each year, compared with between 30-40 in. over most of the country and less than 25 in. over parts of eastern England. The extreme range is from nearly 200 in. a year in a few of the higher parts of Scotland, the Lake District and Wales to less than 20 in. along a small part of the Thames Estuary.

Ireland has similar variations in the amount of rainfall, parts of the extreme west being the wettest with 60-100 in. of rain a year, but nowhere is it as wet as the Scottish Highlands.

Equally as important to the land as the total rainfall is how often it rains. This varies from fewer than 175 days a year in the Thames Estuary to more than 250 days in the Western Highlands and islands of Scotland. In terms of hours this amounts to one hour in 17 in south-eastern England and to one hour in seven in the wetter parts of western Britain.

Drizzle is associated with south-westerly winds and a blanket of low cloud. Heavy showers are common on days of calm or light north-westerly winds and broken clouds.

In western districts of the British Isles the months from October to January are usually wetter than the others, although August also receives more than average. In central England there is less variation between months, but July and August are rather wet owing to thunderstorms. September is a comparatively dry month in all districts except the Scottish Highlands.

There is, of course, no truth in the legend that if it rains on St Swithin's Day, July 15, it will rain for 40 days. See also WEATHER

THE WATER CYCLE

Rainfall is part of a continual water cycle. Water evaporates from the sea, lakes, soil and plants with the help of the sun and wind. The vapour is cooled and condenses into clouds, the droplets of which may combine into raindrops

Rainbow

This phenomenon is the result of sunlight from behind an observer being both reflected and refracted as it passes through raindrops falling ahead.

Reflection occurs at the far side of each raindrop and the light is directed back towards the observer. Refraction involves the separation of sunlight into its component colours. Each is of a slightly different wavelength of radiation (which the eye recognises as colours).

The width of the rainbow and the pre-

Rainbow trout *Salmo gairdneri*

This native of north-west America was introduced into the British Isles in the 1880's, but it has established breeding populations in only a few places. For this reason most of the reservoirs, rivers and lakes which contain rainbow trout have to be repeatedly stocked with hatchery-reared fish. British rainbow trout do not migrate to the sea as do the native sea trout.

It grows rapidly in comparison with the brown trout from which it can be distinguished by the rainbow-hued strip on the sides and spotting on the body and fins.

Rainbows tolerate higher temperatures and lower oxygen concentrations than brown trout.

Rampion, Round-headed
Phyteuma tenerum

This is a rare perennial, growing on the chalk downs of southern England. It has slender smooth stems ranging in height from 2 in. to 18 in. and narrowly heart-shaped hairless leaves. Deep violet flowers bloom from July to August. The round-headed rampion is related to the clustered bellflower, another downland plant.

dominant colour depends upon the size of the raindrops. Large drops produce wide bows in which red predominates, and small drops result in a narrow bow in which white predominates. The colours are arranged through the bow from top to bottom in the order red, orange, yellow, green, blue, indigo and violet—the colours of the spectrum.

Sometimes there is a second bow outside the first, and in this the order of the colours is reversed. This happens when the sunlight is reflected twice instead of once.

The starry white flowers of ramsons appear from April to June in damp woodlands

Ramsons *Allium ursinum*
A strong smell of garlic in a damp woodland in early summer means that ramsons are growing there. Often, thousands of plants, from 6 in. to 15 in. high, are grouped together.

They have long-stalked shiny leaves that resemble those of lily-of-the-valley and heads of starry white flowers that appear from April to June. These often grow together with bluebells and red campions to form a gay carpet on the woodland floor.

Ramsons is the only British plant whose leaf-stalk is twisted through 180 degrees.

It was once called buckram's and bear's garlic and is referred to in the ancient proverb:

> *Eat leckes in lide (March) and*
> *ramsins in May*
> *And all the year after physitians*
> *may play*

Rape *Brassica napus*
A leafy plant of the cabbage family grown chiefly as autumn and winter forage for cattle and sheep. It is a similar plant to the swede. There are several varieties varying in flowering time from April until August.

Rape has spiked, yellow flowers like mustard, and is grown as a substitute for mustard *Sinapsis alba*, as it has a superior flavour. Greengrocers sell it with cress as mustard.

Oilseed rape is a variety grown for its seeds, which develop in long narrow pods and are crushed to extract the oil they contain. This can be used for oiling woollens, lubrication or, when refined, for cooking. It is a relatively new crop in Britain.

A few plants may often be seen by the roadside or in waste places to which seed has blown or been carried by birds. Rape can be seen throughout the British Isles, but is rare in Ireland.

The raindrops which form a rainbow are usually no more than 1½ miles away from the observer

The railway makers who reshaped the land

Gouging out cuttings, throwing up lofty embankments, stalking across valleys with viaducts and leaping over rivers and roads with bridges, railways revolutionised the face of the British countryside

The introduction of the railways brought great changes to the British landscape. A railway had to be relatively level, rising or falling only a few feet in a mile; it had to be as straight as possible and have its own lines, segregated from existing roads and tracks. Consequently, vast areas of the countryside needed to be reshaped. Even the early horse-drawn railways often meant manipulating the landscape in a way unparalleled since the building of the Roman aqueducts.

One of the most spectacular early achievements was the Tanfield Arch built in 1726. With a single span of over 100 ft it carried a horse-drawn railway over the Beckley Burn valley, a few miles south-west of Newcastle upon Tyne. On the Cumberland coast, the 18th-century industrial town of Whitehaven could not have been established without horse-drawn railways cutting across fields and farmsteads from the pits inland to the coal jetties in the harbour.

At the turn of the 19th century, the proliferation of mills and factories created an enormous demand for coal and greatly increased the problems of its transportation. Engineers looked for a mechanical substitute for the horse and in 1804 Richard Trevithick sent the world's first practical locomotive trundling down a track at a colliery in South Wales. It was not until 1825, however, when George Stephenson opened the Stockton and Darlington Railway, that the first service in the world to carry goods and passengers was started. Its success inspired commercial interests in Liverpool to commission Stephenson to build the Liverpool and Manchester, the first inter-urban line in the world. Opened in September 1830, and wholly powered by steam, it was one of the engineering wonders of the age. From Edge Hill Station, in the heart of Liverpool, the line cut a narrow trench, more than a mile long and 90 ft deep, through the red sandstone of Olive Mount into the flowing agricultural landscape of the north Mersey. The ground was undulating most of the way into Manchester and to cross it the railway had to be carried through deep cuttings and over lofty embankments — one 3 miles long and over 45 ft high. The Sankey valley was crossed by a nine-arch viaduct. Stephenson floated the lines across the Chat Moss, a stretch of marsh outside Manchester, by supporting them on a road made of sand, earth and gravel,

Spanning a gap in the Downs on the outskirts of Brighton, this giant railway viaduct was opened in 1846. The line from Brighton to Lewes still goes across it

topped with cinders, and resting on a foundation woven from branches, heather and brushwood. The lines were carried across the River Irwell into Manchester on a causeway.

The Liverpool and Manchester line was followed by railways all over Britain, until the boom ended 20 years later. Engineers and architects constructed vast embankments, cuttings, viaducts and tunnels and, aware they were transforming the landscape, embellished them with brick and stone, timber and iron. Navvies—the men who built the railways—and their horses together shifted a daily average of 20 tons of earth.

The labour expended on constructing the London and Birmingham Railway was said to have equalled raising 25,000,000,000 cu. ft of earth by one foot. It included the enormous cutting at Tring in Hertfordshire—2½ miles long and passing through chalk subsoil at a depth of 42 ft—and the mile long Wolverton embankment, 50 ft high and carrying four railway lines across the Great Ouse valley.

During the construction of the South Eastern Railway, one engineer, Sir William Cubitt (1785-1861), flattened the 375 ft high Round Down Cliff on the Kent coast with one gigantic explosion. The cliff was in the path of the proposed track between Folkestone and Dover and digging or tunnelling were considered too costly. Cubitt and a selected audience watched as 19,000 lb. of gunpowder eliminated the cliff in two minutes.

Isambard Kingdom Brunel's Great Western Railway cut an almost level swathe, 30 ft wide, from London to Bristol. Little can equal his broad-gauge railway, striking up the Thames valley, through Reading to Didcot, skirting the Berkshire Downs by Wantage, plunging into the cavern of the Box Tunnel, crossing Bath on a castellated rampart and down into the Avon valley and Temple Meads Station at Bristol.

Brunel spanned the Thames at Maidenhead with a brick bridge having two of the largest and flattest arches that have ever been constructed, each spanning 128 ft and yet rising no more than 24 ft 3 in. His monumental stone viaduct over the Avon near Chippenham has a simplicity the Romans might have envied, and some of his elegant timber-framed viaducts —crossing the valleys of Devonshire and Cornwall and over 100 ft high—seemed incapable of supporting a railway.

Robert Stephenson—son of George—spanned the Tweed in 1850 with the Royal Border Bridge. The largest masonry viaduct ever constructed, it is 2000 ft long, and has 28 arches carrying the railway 126 ft above the water.

Between such masterpieces of engineering and architecture, countless smaller viaducts, bridges, causeways and tunnel-mouths were built that were as elegant as they were functional.

By the 1850's almost all the main routes of the British railways had been established—either under construction or being planned—and much of the earlier exuberance had faded. Nevertheless, some of the most spectacular and beautiful works had yet to come. These were the great iron bridges that closed the final gaps of the railway networks. They included the pair of oval wrought-iron tubes of Brunel's Royal Albert Bridge, in which the road-bed of the Cornwall Railway is suspended above the River Tamar; Robert Stephenson's tubular Britannia Bridge, carrying the London and North Western Railway across the Menai Straits on its last stage from North Wales to Anglesey; and last, and perhaps greatest of them all, Sir John Fowler's and Benjamin Baker's cantilever bridge towering above the Firth of Forth.

In less than 60 years the landscape of Britain had been

This disused railway line at Sturminster Newton, Dorset, is typical of the 2300 miles of track that have been taken out of service since the early 1960's and that now create a network of green ways throughout the country; many, like this one, make fine walks

reshaped; the lines and curves of the railway network, along which the commerce of the whole country flowed, had imposed a completely new feature on the countryside.

As well as creating vast suburbs outside major cities and ports, the growth of the railways brought fingers of the countryside into built-up areas, with wildlife returning on grass-lined cuttings and embankments. Existing towns in the proximity of main routes grew and in some cases, such as Swindon, new ones were established.

To sustain the new mobility of people and goods, new kinds of buildings had to be constructed. The trains needed sheds, sometimes with roofs of unparalleled spans—first of wood, then of iron—to bring platforms and lines under a single, unobstructed cover. Round-houses, like colossal stables, were required so that locomotives could be turned round. In the cities, stations were built on a grand scale to accommodate waiting rooms, booking halls, left-luggage offices and parcel offices. In the wake of these stations came railway hotels, often dominating the places they served. In small towns and villages, stations were usually constructed in the architectural style of local buildings.

Today, embankments and cuttings, bridges and viaducts, stations and hotels are accepted as naturally as the towers and spires of the great cathedrals were during the medieval era. All are equally part of Britain's landscape, but it was the railways that changed the face of the countryside as nothing else had done before.

Rare flowers in need of protection

About 1300 different flowers grow wild in the British Isles. There used to be another 20, but they have become extinct, either because they were wantonly picked or dug up, or because their habitats were destroyed through building work, the construction of reservoirs, or other types of development. About 100 other species are in danger of extinction, and botanists and conservationists have joined together to prepare a draft Bill for consideration by Parliament to give legal protection to these species. The plants shown here are the 20 most threatened species.

Lady's slipper orchid once grew in more than 30 places in northern England, but only one plant now remains. A guard is mounted over it in the flowering season. Another flower in peril is the military orchid, which lives up to its name by being defended by a strong barricade.

Mountain plants such as the Snowdon lily were once protected by their remoteness, but they are now in danger owing to the increasing number of people who tramp across their wild haunts and are unaware of the need to preserve them.

There has also been a sharp decline in the frequency of many other species which are rare though not facing imminent extinction. The fritillary, once found in more than 100 locations, now grows in only 23 well-guarded places; and the pasque flower, which flourished in at least 78 places, is now seen in only 30.

These, and the other plants illustrated here, are some of Britain's most beautiful wild flowers, but they will not exist for much longer if people continue to pick them or dig them up. Spotting rare plants is exhilarating, but they should be left for others—and oneself—to enjoy on future occasions.

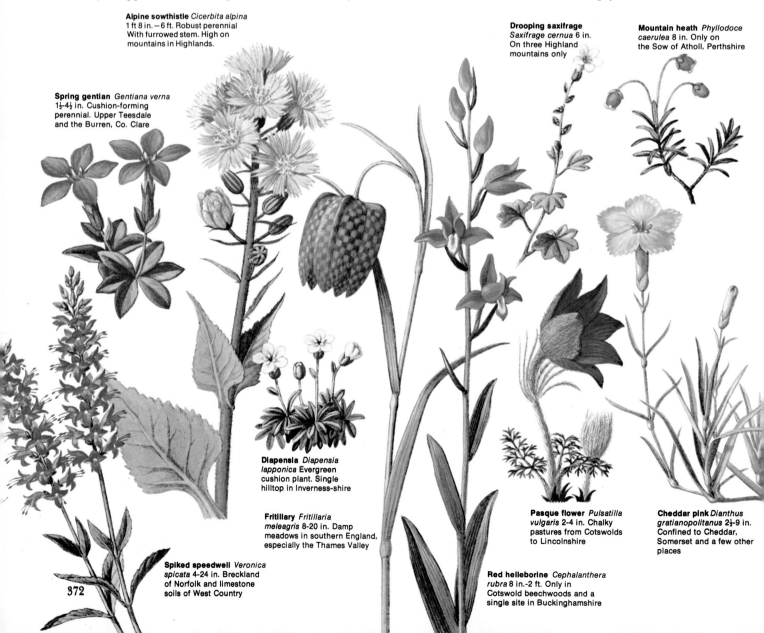

Alpine sowthistle *Cicerbita alpina* 1 ft 8 in. – 6 ft. Robust perennial With furrowed stem. High on mountains in Highlands.

Spring gentian *Gentiana verna* 1½-4½ in. Cushion-forming perennial. Upper Teesdale and the Burren, Co. Clare

Drooping saxifrage *Saxifrage cernua* 6 in. On three Highland mountains only

Mountain heath *Phyllodoce caerulea* 8 in. Only on the Sow of Atholl, Perthshire

Diapensia *Diapensia lapponica* Evergreen cushion plant. Single hilltop in Inverness-shire

Fritillary *Fritillaria meleagris* 8-20 in. Damp meadows in southern England, especially the Thames Valley

Spiked speedwell *Veronica spicata* 4-24 in. Breckland of Norfolk and limestone soils of West Country

Pasque flower *Pulsatilla vulgaris* 2-4 in. Chalky pastures from Cotswolds to Lincolnshire

Cheddar pink *Dianthus gratianopolitanus* 2½-9 in. Confined to Cheddar, Somerset and a few other places

Red helleborine *Cephalanthera rubra* 8 in.-2 ft. Only in Cotswold beechwoods and a single site in Buckinghamshire

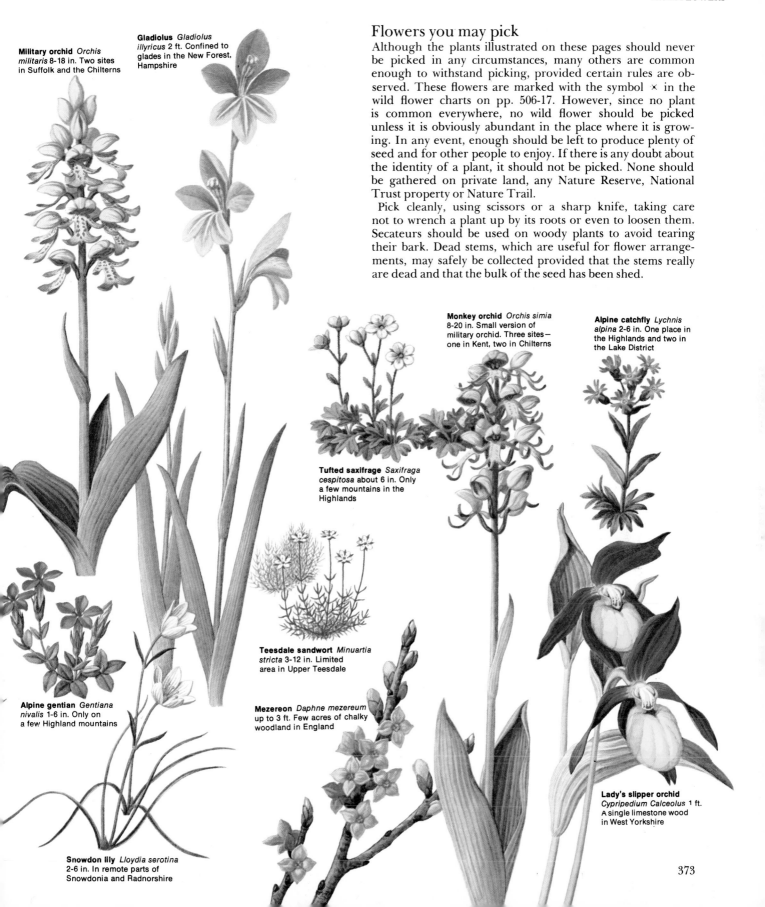

Military orchid *Orchis militaris* 8-18 in. Two sites in Suffolk and the Chilterns

Gladiolus *Gladiolus illyricus* 2 ft. Confined to glades in the New Forest, Hampshire

Flowers you may pick

Although the plants illustrated on these pages should never be picked in any circumstances, many others are common enough to withstand picking, provided certain rules are observed. These flowers are marked with the symbol ✕ in the wild flower charts on pp. 506-17. However, since no plant is common everywhere, no wild flower should be picked unless it is obviously abundant in the place where it is growing. In any event, enough should be left to produce plenty of seed and for other people to enjoy. If there is any doubt about the identity of a plant, it should not be picked. None should be gathered on private land, any Nature Reserve, National Trust property or Nature Trail.

Pick cleanly, using scissors or a sharp knife, taking care not to wrench a plant up by its roots or even to loosen them. Secateurs should be used on woody plants to avoid tearing their bark. Dead stems, which are useful for flower arrangements, may safely be collected provided that the stems really are dead and that the bulk of the seed has been shed.

Monkey orchid *Orchis simia* 8-20 in. Small version of military orchid. Three sites— one in Kent, two in Chilterns

Alpine catchfly *Lychnis alpina* 2-6 in. One place in the Highlands and two in the Lake District

Tufted saxifrage *Saxifraga cespitosa* about 6 in. Only a few mountains in the Highlands

Teesdale sandwort *Minuartia stricta* 3-12 in. Limited area in Upper Teesdale

Alpine gentian *Gentiana nivalis* 1-6 in. Only on a few Highland mountains

Mezereon *Daphne mezereum* up to 3 ft. Few acres of chalky woodland in England

Lady's slipper orchid *Cypripedium Calceolus* 1 ft. A single limestone wood in West Yorkshire

Snowdon lily *Lloydia serotina* 2-6 in. In remote parts of Snowdonia and Radnorshire

Raspberry *Rubus idaeus*

Wild raspberries grow in woods and hedges throughout the British Isles, but they grow more vigorously and the fruits are sweeter in the hilly areas of the north and west. In these areas they taste at least as good as the garden varieties, which are all derived from wild plants taken into cultivation centuries ago.

The stems, called canes, reach 5 ft and are round, downy and prickly. White, drooping flowers appear from June onwards. The origin of the name is obscure. It may come from a French wine, raspeit or raspei, which was the same deep red as the crushed berries, which are sometimes used to make raspberry wine; but in Scotland the plants are called 'rasps', so the name may simply be a reference to the roughness of the stems. An infusion of the leaves drunk during pregnancy is said to ease the pangs of childbirth and is still taken by expectant mothers in some country districts. See also BERRY

Raspberry beetle *Byturus tomentosus*

Both as an adult and as a larva, the raspberry beetle causes serious damage to commercial raspberry crops by damaging the flowers and spoiling the ripening fruit. It is ⅛ in. long and golden-yellow when it first appears in April or May to feed in the flowers of apple or hawthorn bushes. As the beetle ages, it becomes greyer in colour. It moves at the first opportunity to the flowers of raspberry and later on to brambles. Here it mates, and the female lays her shiny white eggs in the centre of the flowers just at the time they set fruit.

The brown-headed, yellow larva hatches in about ten days and feeds on the developing fruit, at first on the outside, then burrowing into the centre. Sometimes the first fruit attacked is abandoned and another fruit entered.

When the larva is about ⅓ in. long it leaves the fruit and burrows 1-2 in. into the soil. Here it builds a small cell and enters its pupal, or resting, stage, hatching into an adult in the autumn. The adult hibernates in the cell until spring.

Raspberry beetle
Byturus tomentosus

The raspberry beetle feeds on raspberry flowers, while its larvae eat the ripening fruit. The adult's colour fades from yellow to grey with age.

Raspberry moth *Lampronia rubiella*

A brown moth with yellow spots on its forewings and a wingspan of less than ½ in., the raspberry moth is a serious pest of

Raspberry moth
Lampronia rubiella

The adult raspberry moth is harmless, but its burrowing caterpillars damage raspberry plants

cultivated raspberry crops. Its eggs are laid in raspberry and bramble flowers in May or June and hatch in a week. The young white caterpillars immediately begin to feed on the developing fruit. They do not do much damage at this stage, as they leave the fruit when it begins to ripen.

Each caterpillar makes a tiny silk cocoon among the dead leaves below the bush and spends the winter inside. It reappears in April and makes its way up the canes or brambles to burrow into a new bud. The caterpillar feeds within the bud, turning red with a black head when nearly full grown. It is at this stage that the most serious damage is done, as the spoilt buds fail to develop into shoots. After about five weeks, the caterpillar enters its pupal, or resting, stage and emerges as an adult three or four weeks later.

Rat

A rodent which damages and contaminates crops and food stores and carries disease. The two species in Britain, the brown and black rats, belong to the same family as the mouse. They are shy, nocturnal animals which eat anything from cereals and fruits to animal food, soap and plaster. They can breed throughout the year with peak periods in summer and autumn. There are usually seven young in a litter and three to five litters in a year. The young can breed after three to four months. Although prolific, there is a high mortality rate of about 95 per cent, and the rat's life-span rarely exceeds 18 months. Even so, it has been estimated that there are 50-60 million rats in Britain—a number that equals the country's human population.

The black or ship rat *Rattus rattus*, the carrier of the bubonic plague, is a native of south-east Asia. It arrived in Britain during the early Middle Ages, possibly in the baggage of returning Crusaders. It is a slender animal about 7 in. long with an 8 in. long tail and large ears. The ship rat lives in the top storeys and roofs of buildings. It nests in rafters or behind pipes, being able to climb well along wires and beams. As it passes under cross-beams it leaves behind an oily smear from its fur.

The brown or common rat *R. norvegicus* of central Asia first arrived in Britain in the 18th century as a result of increased shipping activities. Through competition for food and living space this large, tough, aggressive rat slowly drove the ship rat back to the port towns such as London, Bristol and Liverpool. The common rat has a heavy

A nest of young brown or common rats; they remain in the nest until three weeks after birth

body, 8-9 in. long with a 7 in. tail. Its coat is long and shaggy, greyish-brown above, off-white below. It is a burrowing animal living in cellars, stables, sewers — wherever there is undisturbed shelter or stored food. The common rat is numerous in the sugar-beet areas of East Anglia and is a scavenger along the seashore. In the spring it moves into fields and hedgerows, haystacks and corn ricks, and to canal and river banks. It swims well and is often mistaken for the coypu, sometimes called the giant rat, or for the water vole.

Raven see Crow
Ray, Thornback see Roker
Razorbill see Auk

Razor strop fungus *Piptoporus betulinus*
As its name suggests, this fungus was once used for stropping razors. It was also used to make corn plasters, corks and tinder for kindling fires. Dried strips are still used by entomologists for setting and mounting insects for display.

The razor strop is a common bracket fungus on birch trees — the only plant on which it grows. When the fruiting body first bursts through the bark, it appears as a white knob, but soon expands into a bracket which is pale brown above and white beneath. The undersides of mature brackets, which grow 2-12 in. across, become perforated with fine pores, through which the spores are liberated. The timber of trees on which this fungus grows is gradually reduced to a brown, crumbling rot. Sometimes tiers of brackets grow out from a single dead or dying birch tree.

Reap-hook
A short-handled cutting tool with a curved blade, also called a sickle. It was originally used for cutting grain, probably by taking off just the ears with a short length of straw attached, but was largely superseded by the scythe, which severs the corn-stalks near the ground.

Reap-hooks are used today for chopping weeds, trimming hedges and by thatchers for trimming reeds. They are used with a chopping motion. The operation of a scythe requires a much more graceful pulling motion involving the whole body.

Red admiral *Vanessa atalanta*
Although this butterfly is fairly common over most of the British Isles, it is a migrant from Mediterranean countries. It has a wingspan of 2½ in. and its colours are a mixture of dark brown, black, red, white and blue, with a red transverse band.

The red admiral usually arrives in May or June, and eggs are laid on nettles. The caterpillars live a solitary life; like other caterpillars that live on nettles, each is sewn in a folded nettle leaf, the outer part being formed by the underside of the leaf. Then the fully grown caterpillar makes a tent of several

leaves. There are two types of caterpillars. Both are spiny, but some are black with yellow spots and others are greyish.

In late summer the butterflies feed from rotting fruit, sap from cuts in trees and from garden flowers such as buddleia. Each year there are reports of red admirals surviving hibernation in Britain. See also VANESSID

Red-breasted merganser see Duck

Redcurrant *Ribes sylvestre*
No one knows whether redcurrant is a native shrub, but it grows widely in the wild and may be found in woods and hedges anywhere in Britain, although it is rare in Ireland. Most, if not all, redcurrant shrubs in the wild have sprouted there through birds scattering the pips in their droppings.

Cultivation of the redcurrant began in north-west Europe, but the name originated in Greece owing to the similarity of the fruit to the raisins of Corinth. Until the fruit ripens in July the shrub is similar to the blackcurrant — up to 6 ft tall, many-branched and with lobed leaves — but it can be distinguished from it by the absence of smell when the leaves are crushed. The leaves give a yellow dye and the fruit a black dye.

Redpoll see Finch
Red rattle see Lousewort

Redshank *Polygonum persicaria*
A troublesome annual weed, growing 12-30 in. high, with red stalks or shanks. The redshank or persicaria is closely related to pale persicaria but can be distinguished by its pink — not greenish-yellow — flowers and by the large black blotch on the leaves. One explanation for this blotch is that the Devil pinched the leaves and made them useless as they lack the fiery flavour of the waterpepper, another related plant. However, Shetlanders found redshank useful because it contains a yellow dye.

Redshank flowers from June to October throughout the British Isles, especially in well-manured fields, waste places around farms and, occasionally, along the margins of ponds and lakes. See also PERSICARIA, PALE and WATER-PEPPER

Redshank is named for its red stalks. It bears pink flowers from June to October

Redshank see Shank
Redstart see Chat

A red underwing moth at rest on the bark of a tree (top); and displaying its red hindwings before taking-off (below)

Red underwing *Catocala nupta*
The beautiful colours of this moth are not seen except in flight. Its forewings are a dull grey-brown and cover the bright red and black hindwings which are only seen when the moth is in flight.

With a wingspan of 3 in., the red underwing is one of the largest British noctuid moths. It is fairly common in south-eastern England but is rare elsewhere. It flies in August and September and, like the other noctuid moths, normally only at night, when it is attracted to artificial light.

During the day it rests on tree trunks or walls, camouflaged by its muted colours. If disturbed by a predator it flies off, revealing its hindwings, which the predator follows. Suddenly, after a short flight, the moth settles and closes its wings. The sudden disappearance of the bright red makes it appear to its enemy that the whole moth has vanished.

Tree bark is important for the moth. The eggs are laid in crevices of poplar and willow bark and do not hatch until the following spring.

The caterpillars hide by day in bark crevices, climbing the tree at night to feed on the leaves. The fully grown caterpillar makes a leaf-covered cocoon and pupates in July. The adult moth emerges after four to six weeks. See also NOCTUID MOTH

Redwing see Thrush

Redwood, Californian *Sequoia sempervirens*

This magnificent conifer, which was introduced from California about 1843, grows in parks and arboreta throughout Britain. Two distinguishing features are the thick, soft, fibrous red bark which explains its name, and the fronds of mid-green evergreen foliage with flat needles that taper evenly in length between joints.

Male and female flowers, opening in spring, are small and catkin-like. The grey, oval cones, which ripen in autumn, have knobbly scales holding tiny brown seeds, each surrounded by a thin papery wing. Seedlings have only two leaves, followed by spirally set needles before the adult foliage appears.

A 384 ft high redwood in California is the world's tallest living tree. Veterans, 70 ft in circumference, live for 2000 years. Britain's tallest specimen, only 135 ft high, stands at Cuffnells in the New Forest.

Reed, Common *Phragmites communis*

Often growing to 10 ft, the common reed is the tallest native grass in the British Isles. It spreads by powerful underground stems, covering large areas of marsh and swamp, and also grows strongly in the shallow waters of lowland ponds, lakes and rivers. It is often planted on river banks where the stems bind the soil and prevent erosion.

The stem and leaves, purplish-brown or green, are tough and persist throughout the winter. The plant flowers from late summer until October. Reed beds are cultivated in the East Anglian fens and the crop is sold for thatching as Norfolk Reed. The stems are also gathered for decorative purposes. Some country folk refer to reed as windle-straw, and in Cornwall it is known as gos.

Reedmace see Bulrush
Reindeer see Deer
Reindeer moss see Lichen

Reservoir

A natural or constructed store for water. In addition to reservoirs built to supply towns with drinking water, several were constructed in the 19th century to provide water for canals. Some of these are now used for boating, as at Aldenham in Hertfordshire and the Welsh Harp in north-west London.

Many large towns obtain their water supplies from reservoirs built in hilly areas of high rainfall and low population. Such areas include the Lake District, Wales, the Pennines and Scotland.

In some cases, as at Haweswater in the Lake District, a dam is used to raise the level of an existing lake. Elsewhere, a dam across a valley traps the water draining into it. Making reservoirs often destroys valley pastures, and sometimes villages are submerged as in 1957 at Llyn Celyn, in the Tryweryn Valley, Merionethshire. In low-lying areas, where there are no valleys to dam, the whole perimeter of a reservoir has to be man-made. This is the case with the Queen Mary

Reservoir at Staines, Middlesex, which is contained by an embankment 4 miles long and which can store more than 8 million gallons of water.

Natural underground reservoirs occur where porous rock, such as chalk or limestone, overlies impermeable rock. The porous rock holds the water like a sponge, releasing it naturally through springs or through man-made wells.

Restharrow

The underground stems of common restharrow are so tough that they used to delay the passage of horse-drawn ploughs or harrows. That is how the plant, which is found throughout the British Isles, got its name. In many parts of southern England it is also called cammock. Cattle which eat the leaves give milk tainted with an unpleasant, goat-like smell. This becomes particularly pronounced when milk is made into cheese, and in such cases the cheese is termed 'cammocky'. The leaves give off this smell if they are crushed between the fingers. Common restharrow rarely grows to more than 2 ft, and has handsome, pink flowers between June and September.

Spiny restharrow is similar, but lacks underground stems. It is seen mostly on clay soils in south and south-east England.

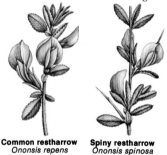

Common restharrow
Ononis repens

Spiny restharrow
Ononis spinosa

In fruit, the spiny restharrow has large pods, with a smaller outer covering

Rhododendron

About 200 varieties of rhododendron are grown in gardens and parks in the British Isles. They were introduced from Europe in the mid-17th century and later from western China, Tibet, north-west India and Burma. Only one species grows wild, *Rhododendron ponticum*, a native of the Caucasus.

The tall, evergreen shrub with its oblong, glossy leaves, 4-8 in. long, often grows to 20 ft, and makes a magnificent display in May and June when its purple, funnel-shaped flowers of about 2 in. diameter are fully open. Like nearly all rhododendrons, it grows vigorously on sandy and peaty soil, and in some woods in south-west Ireland it is so vigorous that plants die in its shade.

Rhubarb *Rheum rhaponicum*

Well known to gardeners and allotment-holders, rhubarb is grown commercially, on just over 3500 acres, mainly in the West

Riding of Yorkshire. The English crop is worth about £1½ million. In Scotland, about 550 acres are devoted to rhubarb.

The crop, which is harvested from February to mid-summer, consists of the plant's red edible stems. The large green leaves contain oxalic acid, a poison. Crowns, or roots, which are set just above soil level bear the stems. They are grown outdoors at the rate of 6000 per acre for two or three years. The crowns are then lifted and put in warm, dark sheds where they quickly produce light-coloured stems.

Forced rhubarb is in demand from January to early April, when fresh fruits are scarce. Crowns used for forcing produce only weak growth in the following year, so they are discarded.

Rick see Stack

Ride

A treeless break in forested areas, giving horse-riders a suitable track. The word comes from the Scandinavian *rud* — a forest clearing. Rides were important years ago for the hunting of deer. Today they offer good spots from which to observe wildlife and they are often rich in plants and birds.

In new forests they are constructed as tracks for foresters and their vehicles, and as firebreaks. They usually split plantations into blocks of 25 acres and are from 10-30 ft wide. There are good examples in the New Forest, Hampshire, on Drummond Hill, Perthshire, and in Kielder Forest, Northumberland.

Riding

The word was originally 'triding', meaning a third part. Then the letter 't' became absorbed in the preceding word, usually 'west', 'east' or 'north'. In the 13th century the word began to be applied to the three divisions of Yorkshire, and was similarly used elsewhere.

The Scottish border ridings — events in which people ride out from the towns to outlying places connected with local history — may have had their origin in ceremonies similar to the beating of the bounds of a parish. But after the battles with the English in the 16th century they became festivals for celebrating resistance.

Rigg and furrow

A corrugated effect seen in pastures and parkland, but especially on heavy clay soil in the Midlands and coastal lowlands. The earliest riggs and furrows were caused by teams of oxen constantly turning the soil in the same direction. Modern ploughing has destroyed them on arable land, but they are revealed by aerial photography.

They vary in width from 5-7 yds, but distances of 10 yds are not uncommon. Groups of riggs are known variously as furlongs and butts, and such names still appear in the names of fields.

Ringed snake see Grass snake
Ringlet see Brown butterfly
Ring ouzel see Thrush
River see p. 378

Roach *Rutilus rutilus*
A silvery fish with a dark, bluish back; the fins under the belly are coloured orange to red, and the iris of the eye is red. Specimens of 3 lb. have been caught.

Roach is found in abundance in lowland rivers and lakes throughout England, Wales and southern Scotland, and has recently been introduced into Ireland. It can tolerate moderately polluted water and is therefore important to anglers near industrial towns.

There is often difficulty in identifying roach because it interbreeds with the rudd and the bream, and the resulting progeny sometimes resemble the roach. The true roach has a less upturned mouth than the rudd, and its dorsal fin is further forward, but identification is certain only by expert examination of the pharyngeal bones.

It spawns in April and May among the dense vegetation at the water's edge, forming large shoals and causing considerable splashing. Like other members of the carp family, the males have distinct white tubercles on their heads and fins at this time of the year.

The young feed on small crustaceans, and the larger fish eat insect larvae, larger crustaceans and snails.

Road see p. 382

Robber fly
A fly of this family rests on a piece of vegetation or on open ground until another fly passes by. Then it darts forward, capturing the other with its bristle-covered legs, inserts its piercing mouthparts and sucks out the victim's juices. It may leap up to 20 in., sometimes attacking insects as they land, sometimes in the air.

There are 27 species of robber (or assassin) flies in Britain. A common one is *Epitriptus cingulatus*, which can be found from June to September in heathery or bracken-covered areas and on the outskirts of woods. Although about ½ in. long, it is one of the smaller robber flies.

The largest is the spectacular, 1¾ in. *Asilus crabroniformis*. Unlike most other species, it is brightly coloured, with a yellow abdomen, and is found only in southern England. It is on the wing in late summer.

Robber fly
Asilus crabroniformis

Nearly all the others are greyish-black. Robber fly eggs are laid in the soil, and the larvae feed on decaying plant material.

Robin see Chat

Robin's pin-cushion
A gall on wild rose bushes caused by a gall wasp *Diplolepis rosae*. In May the female wasp lays eggs in the unopened leaf buds of a rose bush. The presence of the larvae causes the buds to develop not into normal leaves, but as a bright red moss-like structure, an inch or more across. The larvae remain within the gall throughout winter, pupate in spring and hatch in May. There are always many more females than males.

After a gall wasp causes the pin-cushion to form, other insects exploit it, and another gall wasp *Periclistus brandtii* often colonises the gall. Larvae of the original wasp may be attacked by a parasite wasp, and this in turn is similarly preyed on by a still smaller species of wasp.

Robin's pin-cushion looks like a ball of bright moss and is at its best in September

Rock-cress, Hairy *Arabis hirsuta*
This stiff, erect herb is seen throughout the British Isles in lime-rich soils on dry banks, in sand dunes, on rocky slopes and walls. It rarely grows to more than 12 in. and has a basal rosette of stalked leaves. The upper leaves clasp the stem and the whole plant is thickly covered with forked hairs. A cluster of tiny white flowers appears in mid-summer, which develops into narrow, upright pods.

The name *Arabis* was probably given to the plant because many species of the herb grow best in the stony or sandy soils of Arabia.

Rocket, Sea *Cakile maritima*
A bushy plant found on sand and shingle, the sea rocket occurs on the strand line all around the British coast. It is 6-18 in. high and has smooth, fleshy leaves and lilac or white flowers from June to August. These develop into succulent seed capsules, which are divided into two. The upper part is twice as long as the lower, which is infertile. The capsules are dispersed by sea water, but this does not affect the germination of the seeds.

Rocking stone see Standing stone

Rockling
The long body and brown colour of rocklings and their habit of lurking furtively in crevices have earned them the name of weasel fish. They are common on most shores of the British Isles.

The shore rockling *Gaidropsarus mediterraneus* is usually dark brown, grows to 10 in. long, and is most common along the south and west coast on rocky shores, in tide pools and under stones.

The five-bearded rockling *Ciliata mustela*, which has a yellowish belly and grows to 8 in., is common on the North Sea coast and in northern Scotland.

Both have a fringe of hair-like rays along the back in front of the main back fin. In front of this fringe is a longer, thin ray. The fringe has a sensory function. So do the long barbels or feelers round the mouth, which are covered with taste organs. Rocklings feed mainly on small crustaceans.

The shore rockling has three of these barbels, one on each nostril and one on the chin. The five-bearded rockling has an additional pair of barbels on the front of the upper lip.

Rock pool see p. 384

Rockrose, Common
Helianthemum chamaecistus
In spite of its name, this is not a rose at all. A 2-12 in. trailing perennial that grows on chalk and limestone grassland, it is scattered throughout Great Britain but is rare in the west and found in only one place in Ireland—County Donegal.

The common rockrose has yellow, five-petalled flowers that blossom from June to September. The flowers produce no nectar, but they have many stamens producing a large quantity of pollen which attracts pollinating insects. If for some reason cross-pollination by insects fails, self-pollination may occur when the flowers close at night or in wet weather.

Many varieties with a wide colour range have been cultivated for rockeries.

Rockrose is not a rose, but a small trailing plant of chalk and limestone country

Rock samphire see Parsley
Roke see Fog

377

The river — a living road carved to the sea

From its tumbling source to its sluggish estuary, a river is constantly reshaping the landscape. In its upper reaches the river eats away at the land; but in its lower reaches it uses the material from the hills to create new land

Rain is the raw material of rivers. But only about 30 per cent of the rain that falls on the land finds its way into rivers. Of the rest, some seeps through the soil to form underground lakes or to be soaked up by porous rocks, some is evaporated by the sun ultimately to fall again as rain, and some is taken up by plants and returned to the atmosphere as they transpire, or breathe.

Rivers are among the main agents which have shaped the landscape in the past, and are continuing to shape it today. At the same time they provide a constantly changing medium of life for many plants and animals. For man, they have served in the past both as highways and as barriers. Early settlements often grew up alongside rivers, which afforded both a link with the outside world and a defence against marauders. Still today, rivers act as boundaries between nations — the River Tweed forms part of the border between England and Scotland. They also provide water for the home, agriculture and industry; and they are a source of hydro-electric power.

Most rivers have their sources in mountains and hills, which are areas of high rainfall. Although heavy rain can flow off a steep slope as a sheet of water, it is usually channelled by irregularities in the ground, which in time become well-defined watercourses. These join together, forming streams. High in the mountains, these streams are downward-rushing torrents carving through any soil and deep into the rock. Each fragment of rock removed by the water, whether a grain of sand or a boulder, adds to the cutting power of the torrent, helping to gouge the bed and banks of the stream as it is swept downwards. This mountain stage of a river's course, known as the torrent stage, cuts narrow, steep-sided, V-shaped valleys. The bed is strewn with boulders, and is frequently broken by rapids and occasionally by waterfalls. Waterfalls occur where a river which has been flowing over hard rock reaches an area of soft rock. The soft rock is worn away more quickly than the hard, and a vertical fall in the river bed is eroded; a fall which over immense periods of time can become hundreds of feet deep.

Eventually, the hills are left behind and the water moves more smoothly. But tributaries join the main stream, adding to the volume of water. The river grows wider, and so does its valley with the land sloping gently towards the watercourse. Although the current can no longer sweep along boulders, the water carries particles of mud and sand and still moves fast enough to eat into the river banks. There are occasional rapids. This part of the river's course is called the valley stage.

As the downward slope of the land decreases, the river channel curves from side to side, creating a flat valley floor.

Further levelling of the land slows the current still more; the curves in the river channel develop into broad loops called meanders, and the valley widens into a broad plain. The river continues to eat away at its banks, though it deposits material as well. Silt is deposited on the inside of meander bends, creating gently sloping banks, while the current cuts into the outer side of each bend, forming sheer banks.

On its final, slow approach to the sea, the river is carrying immense quantities of material eroded from its upper reaches — the River Thames is estimated to carry 300,000 tons of sediment a year — much of which goes to build up mud-flats and sand banks at the estuary. The river also carries large quantities of dissolved minerals to the sea.

The lower and middle reaches of rivers have been used for transport and have provided sites for settlement from the earliest times. In prehistoric times, when forest and marsh covered most of the country, rivers provided a path into the interior. Remains from all periods back to the Old Stone Age, 250,000 years ago, have been found alongside the Thames and other rivers. The people who lived on these sites travelled in dug-out canoes or light, skin-covered coracles which could be carried past obstacles such as rapids. Bulky items were probably carried on rafts.

THE THREE STAGES OF A RIVER

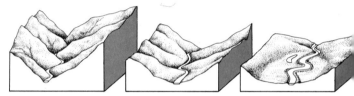

The fast-flowing torrent reach of a river cuts a steep-sided, V-shaped valley. In the mid or valley stage the V starts to open out, until in the final stage the river takes a constantly changing course across flat country

CARVING A PATH TO THE SEA

The young river Fast-flowing water wears away mountain rock

Gorge Cut through solid rock by young river

Its waters swollen by melting snow, the River Wharfe cascades down from its source high in the Yorkshire Pennines. Below this point, the river carves

the valley of Wharfedale, before slowing down on the Yorkshire Plain where it joins the River Ouse

When the Romans came, they too relied on the rivers, siting many of their settlements on them—London, on the Thames; York, on the Ouse; and Chester, on the Dee. They also made use of rivers when building their roads—often routing them along valleys, as with the London-Bath road.

Rivers continued to play a significant part in the siting of towns long after the Romans had gone. Ports such as Plymouth, Falmouth and Yarmouth grew up at the mouths of rivers; inland towns centred on river crossings—places such as Oxford, Nottingham and Perth.

The upper reaches of rivers were of little importance to man until the 18th century, when water power was harnessed to drive the machines of the textile mills; these were the first real factories, established beside fast-flowing streams, and

so the first phase of the Industrial Revolution got under way —in the heart of the countryside. Some of these early mills still exist. A well-preserved example is the Quarry Bank Mill in the Bollin Valley, at Styal, Cheshire. Others fell into decay, and their remains can be seen beside the rivers that once turned their wheels.

The longest river in the British Isles is the 240 mile long Shannon in Ireland: the longest in Great Britain is the Severn, which flows 220 miles through Montgomeryshire, Shropshire, Worcestershire and Gloucestershire. The Thames, 215 miles long, is the longest river wholly in England, and the Tay, 117 miles, is the longest in Scotland. The longest river wholly in Wales is the Towy, which is 64 miles long. See also BRIDGE, ESTUARY, ICE, MEANDER

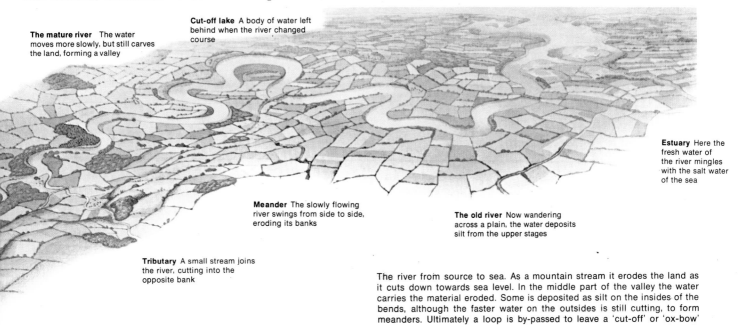

The mature river The water moves more slowly, but still carves the land, forming a valley

Cut-off lake A body of water left behind when the river changed course

Estuary Here the fresh water of the river mingles with the salt water of the sea

Meander The slowly flowing river swings from side to side, eroding its banks

The old river Now wandering across a plain, the water deposits silt from the upper stages

Tributary A small stream joins the river, cutting into the opposite bank

The river from source to sea. As a mountain stream it erodes the land as it cuts down towards sea level. In the middle part of the valley the water carries the material eroded. Some is deposited as silt on the insides of the bends, although the faster water on the outsides is still cutting, to form meanders. Ultimately a loop is by-passed to leave a 'cut-off' or 'ox-bow' lake. Near the estuary the river travels more slowly, still depositing silt but no longer eroding the land

The struggle for life in the moving waters

The character of life in a river varies from stage to stage of its course from the mountains to the sea. At each stage plants and animals live together in well-defined groups determined largely by the rate at which the water flows. A group which can tolerate the slow-moving, silt-laden water of the lower reaches would find life impossible in the fast-flowing upper reaches.

High in the mountains, torrent streams rush down steep, rocky slopes, often in the form of waterfalls. Here the current moves too fast for any flowering plants to take root, and only a few mosses and liverworts grow under water. However, the numerous waterfalls give the water plenty of oxygen, which supports animal life. The most common animals are insect larvae, including those of mayflies, stoneflies and caddis flies, which are well adapted with their flattened bodies and clawed feet for clinging beneath stones and between the gravel. Many of the caddis fly larvae are web spinners, weaving tiny silken nets across the current to catch their food. Other common insects are the translucent dumb-bell shaped larvae of the tiny, biting black flies and, when the water is hard, horned flatworms and snails, with their predators, leeches.

As the stream widens, brown trout, which feed on the insect larvae, and eels are among the first fish to appear. It is to this well-oxygenated stretch, often called the trout beck, that salmon come to spawn. Here dippers may dive into the water to grab an insect larva, or grey wagtails may catch an emerging mayfly. Willow moss, encrusting lichens and algae are among the few plants able to grow in the water.

Further downstream there are deep pools and quiet bays, interspersed with rapids. Trout, eel and salmon live here, together with grayling, dace, chub, minnows, bullheads and water shrimps. In spring, spawning masses of brook lampreys writhe in shallow water that has a fine gravel bottom. Mayfly and stonefly larvae and adult mayflies are still the predominant source of food for fish.

The river then flows on into the lowlands, where trees appear along the banks, among them alders and willows, which are often planted to stabilise the banks. Suspended algae make the water less clear here. It is inhabited by coarse fish, such as stone loach, pike, perch and roach. Soft waters contain river limpets, bladder snails, valve snails and tiny Jenkins' spire shells. Hard waters contain, in addition to these, river snails, Lister's river snails, lake limpets, nerites, whirlpool vortex, great pond snails, snail-eating leeches and fish leeches. Flowering plants grow in the water: watercress, fool's watercress, water crowfoot, curled pondweed and fennel-leaved pondweed. Reed grass, blinks, bog stitchwort and water speedwell grow on the muddy banks.

As the current slows down still more, other water plants appear: perfoliate pondweed, opposite-leaved pondweed, starwort, Canadian pondweed, spiked water milfoil, amphibious bistort, narrow-leaved water parsnip and bulrush. Where plants are regularly cut, to prevent floods or fouling of fishing lines, arrowhead and unbranched bur-reed become

Salmon A large adult can leap 11 ft to reach the spawning grounds up-river

Grey wagtail Hill streams are its home. It moves to the lowlands in winter

Dipper Usually confined to swift streams, where it walks under water seeking the insects it feeds on

Mayfly Before its winged life of only four days, a mayfly may spend up to three years as a nymph

Willow moss It grows in dense bunches on wood and stones in streams

Brown trout A non-migratory fish that is often found in the fast-flowing middle reaches of a river

Caddis fly larva Sand and debris are formed into a sheath by the larva to protect its soft body

Eel This fish spawns at sea, then the young swim up rivers where they grow to maturity before returning to the sea

the dominant species. On muddy bottoms grow the yellow water lily or brandy bottle, fringed water lily, shining water weed, marestail and water dropwort. The sides of the river are often rich with water mint, monkey flower, water forget-me-not, marsh yellow cress, yellow flag, water dock, meadow sweet, purple loosestrife, yellow loosestrife and flowering rush, together with reeds, reedmace and bur-reed. Animals living in the reeds include the amber snail, shiny glass snail, water shrew and water vole. The reed beds attract a host of water fowl, such as buntings, coots, moorhens and little grebes. Herons stalk their food among the reeds, and grass snakes occasionally swim across the water to new hunting grounds.

On the water surface of this stretch of the river pond skaters and whirligig beetles are common, while under water the many animals include lesser water boatmen, backswimmers, water lice, tubifex worms and pea mussels. Fish include tench, gudgeon, bleak, bream, carp and three-spined and ten-spined sticklebacks. Trout are fewer here, as there is less oxygen in the water, especially at night when the water plants continue to use it but no longer release it as in the day. Oxygen shortage is aggravated by sewage pollution and by warmed water—the effluent from industrial cooling processes. Downstream of such pollutants, life reappears; it includes stringy green algae, midge larvae and tubifex worms.

As the river flows on, it becomes more oxygenated and wandering snails, river limpets, water lice and snail-eating leeches can survive in large numbers. Water plants reappear and, if there is no further pollution, river life recovers. As the river nears the sea, it broadens and flows even more slowly. When it becomes an estuary its flow takes on a complex pattern and the water becomes progressively more brackish.

Flowering rush In late summer its pink flowers cluster on river margins

Kingfisher Water beetles and small fish form the diet of this most brightly coloured of British birds

Monkey-flower Introduced from islands off Alaska, it now forms ribbons of gold along our rivers

Water mint Very common in damp places. It has spikes of showy flowers and a strong minty scent

Moorhen A poor flyer, it nests near the river bank, often in a bush

Water speedwell These blue or pink flowers grow alongside the lowland reaches of many rivers

Water forget-me-not The pretty blue flowers are seen in wet, shady spots from May to September

Roach A common fish in slow-moving rivers, where it lives in shoals

River snail Eggs are kept in the parent's egg duct until the shells develop

Water vole Its home is a burrow. The entrance is often under the water

one loach The presence this fish, which is nsitive to pollution, a sign of clean water

Watercress Found in all parts of Britain in fast streams or around springs

BRITAIN'S ROADS IN AD 400

The vital links between town and country

From tracks trodden by prehistoric man to sophisticated 20th-century motorways, roads have been the foundation of Britain's growth, assisting in the spread of ideas and materials and linking town with country

Before Britain adopted the motorway system in the 1950's there were nearly 200,000 miles of classified roads in Great Britain, linking hamlet to village, village to market town and town to port—a complex network whose origins stretched back into the Stone Age.

Trade in stone and flint weapons was already developed in the New Stone Age (3750-2000 BC) and in this period there developed a web of long-distance trade routes, whose centre was Salisbury Plain and which spread along the Downs and the Chilterns and to the south-west. Whereas the main arteries of road transport today are in the lowlands these great highways of antiquity, known as ridgeways, followed hills and ridges in order to avoid the fens and forests of the plains. Sections of the ridgeways can still be followed, such as the Berkshire Ridge Way from the Thames Gap between Goring and Streatley to Old Sarum in Wiltshire. More easily traversed are the more direct and level routes, which followed the foot of the escarpments, such as the Pilgrims' Way and the Icknield Way. Other early roads are the hollow ways, deep, sunken

Aberdeen

Antonine wall
Edinburgh

Hadrian's wall
Carlisle   Newcastle

EBVRACVM
York

Liverpool   Manchester

DEVA
Chester

LINDVM
Lincoln

Birmingham

RATAE
CORITANORVM
Leicester

VIROCONIVM
CORNOVIORVM
Wroxeter

GLEVVM
Gloucester

CAMVLODVNVM
Colchester

CORINIVM
DOBVNNORVM
Cirencester

VERVLAMIVM
St Albans

DVRNOVARIA
Dorchester

LONDINIVM
London

ISCA
Caerleon

Cardiff

AQVAE SVLIS
Bath

CALLEVA ATREBATVM
Silchester

LINDINIS
Ilchester

VENTA BELGARVM
Winchester

Southampton

NOVIOMAGVS
Chichester

——— Known roadways
·········· Probable roadways
∿∿ Stone Age trackways

THE FIRST ENGINEERED ROADS

Limy gravel
Large gravel
Stiff clay

Limestone slabs

Hard gravel

Roman roads were built in several layers, creating a raised causeway. They were so finely engineered that, 2000 years later, they still form the foundations of many modern highways

Part of the M62, where a dual carriageway snakes over Moss Moor, from Rochdale, crossing some

tracks which cut across hill ridges and have been used for centuries by carts, packhorses and cattle.

Where ancient routes have not been superseded by modern surfaced roads, they are known as green lanes. In Somerset in about 2500 BC wooden trackways about 3 ft wide were laid across the swamps which stretched between the Polden Hills and the Mendips. They were built on the drier areas and were often held in position with birch pegs.

The Romans were the first to develop a true road system in Britain. They built three main types of road: the *iter*, which was about 5 ft wide—enough for a column of infantry to march along; the *actus*, about 7 ft wide—enough for a horse-drawn vehicle; and the *via*, about 14 ft wide, allowing for two-way carriage traffic. All were laid out in straight lines. The road was built in several layers—a foundation of stone laid in a shallow trench topped by rubble and mortar and paved with cut stone. The paving was cambered to shed water, and drainage ditches ran alongside the causeway. At Holtye Common, Sussex, a section of Roman road has been uncovered which is partly built with iron slag from the early Wealden furnaces.

Whenever possible, the Roman engineers built straight roads, as the quickest, most economic method of moving troops and stores. Their routes linked the great legionary camps, such as Chester, Lincoln, York and Carlisle, with bases in the south-east and the Channel ports. Cross-country routes, such as the Exeter-Lincoln road, tied the radiating strands of the web together. The northernmost extension of Watling Street, known as Dere Street, left Corbridge on the Tyne and went on over the Cheviot Hills, the Tweed and the Lammermuirs to Inveresk on the Forth. Some of it was used to form the present A68, but most of it is a green lane that can be followed only on foot; it has recently been signposted by local authorities, especially in Roxburghshire.

For 250 years turnpike companies raised money for the maintenance of roads by levying tolls on those who used them. Soon after this mid-19th-century sketch of a county toll gate was made, turnpikes began to decline; the last one was abolished in North Wales in 1895

Roman roads were neglected after the legions left Britain in the 5th century, but many were still used as main thoroughfares in the Middle Ages and were given new names; for example, Dere Street became Gamel's Path. The Anglo-Saxons often indicated the presence of a Roman road by inserting the word for street in a place name, as in Stratford.

The maintenance of most roads in the Middle Ages was the responsibility first of the manor and then of the parish. Local people saw no pressing reason to spend money on the upkeep of roads that were used by outsiders, so many roads degenerated into muddy passages; and the increasing trade in the Tudor period made them even more intolerable. It was not until the Turnpike Act of 1663 that roads began to be improved with money exacted from road-users at toll gates.

It was two Scottish engineers, Telford and Macadam, who in the early 19th century brought British roads back to Roman standards. They used broken stones, the largest at the bottom, the smallest on top, which constant traffic knitted into a compact, hard-wearing surface. Tarmac—short for Tarmacadam—a mixture of tar and stones, was first used as a road surface in the 1830's, as was asphalt, a mixture of bitumen and stones; both surfaces provided a degree of resilience to combat cracking. In the 1850's the first concrete roads appeared.

The introduction of the motor car in the early 20th century led to the establishment of the Ministry of Transport in 1919, the Road Fund in 1920, and to the classification of main roads into first-class A roads and second-class B roads.

The increase in traffic led to the development of dual carriageways and by-passes in the 1930's. Britain was one of the last industrial countries to embark on a motorway programme, partly because it already had a comprehensive network of well-maintained roads. Legislation permitting the building of motorways was passed in 1949 and in the mid-1950's five motorways were started. The first to be opened was the Preston motorway on December 5, 1958.

In the spring of 1973 there were three complete motorways, the M1, M4 and M6, and several sections of new ones had been completed, a total of 1000 motorway miles. It is planned to complete a further 1000 by the early 1980's. In addition, there were 8332 miles of all-purpose trunk roads, 20,323 miles of principal roads and more than 170,000 miles of secondary roads. Northern Ireland had 50 miles of motorway and 14,000 miles of public roads; and the Irish Republic had 54,185 miles of roads.

of the most rugged parts of the Pennines. When finished the motorway, reaching a maximum height of 1200 ft, will link Liverpool with Hull

A world in miniature ruled by the tide

Rock pools are natural aquariums, small bodies of sea water left behind on the shore when the tide goes out. They range from large weed-choked pools containing many hundreds of gallons of water providing fairly stable surroundings, to shallow depressions in which extreme changes in conditions occur.

Few animals and plants are restricted to the pools, and many can be found elsewhere on the shore. Indeed, a glance will show several animals on the surrounding dry rock.

For creatures that live in small rock pools, life is a series of massive and fairly abrupt changes of temperature. At low tide on a hot day the temperature in a pool can rise several degrees above that of the sea only to drop suddenly when the tide comes in. At night the pool temperature may drop well below that of the sea. A cold-blooded inhabitant of a rock pool, such as a limpet, has no built-in system of temperature control and its body temperature is that of the water it lives in.

The condition of the water in a rock pool also fluctuates. On a hot day, evaporation will make a pool saltier, but rain will dilute the brine. During the day, too, the water is well oxygenated, as seaweeds use the energy of sunlight to manufacture food and release oxygen in the process known as photosynthesis.

At night, when photosynthesis cannot take place, plants and animals in the pool use up dissolved oxygen and release carbon dioxide. This accumulates to levels which would kill many organisms, but the creatures of rock pools are adapted to withstand it.

One of the most adaptable animals of the rock pool is the common limpet, which is equally at home in or out of pools. A limpet appears to be fixed to a single spot, but in fact it is mobile. It has a home base which its shell fits exactly. If the limpet is on soft rock it will shuffle its shell until a groove is cut to match the shell; on hard rock, it is the limpet shell that wears until a perfect fit is made. The limpet clings so firmly to its base that the force needed to move it would break the shell first. When the tide is in the limpet leaves base to graze on tiny algae, or seaweed, on the rock. It can move up to a yard on a single broad foot rather like that of a snail.

The number of animal species in a pool depends on the number of hiding places it offers: a bare pool can offer little shelter and will be sparsely populated, whereas a pool with

A pool of water, trapped by rocks high on a Devon beach, provides a refuge for many sea plants and animals between the tides

Serrated wrack
The branching leathery fronds of this common brown seaweed have jagged edges

Snakelocks anemone
It waves its long snake-like tentacles constantly to trap unsuspecting prawns

Common periwinkle
The largest British winkle, it nestles in groups in cracks and crevices

Coral weed Pink tufts of stiff lime-encrusted branches grow just below the water's surface

many stones and plenty of seaweeds will support a wide variety of animals.

On the west coast, many pools are lined with a pale pink encrusting alga. Around the margins another pink seaweed, the coral weed, forms miniature forests which are refuges for a host of tiny organisms. The long trailing green strands of *Enteromorpha* provide additional food and shelter for browsing animals.

The larger brown seaweeds, such as bladder wrack, never grow well in pools, although plants growing around the edges can float out across the water. The serrated wrack that curtains the rocks covers numerous animals from sponges to starfish. Its fronds often have the tiny white spiral tubes of the worm *Spirorbis* attached to them.

Some of the animals are permanent inhabitants, such as the prawns which change colour during the day to merge with the weeds. Sponges, sea firs and mussels remain firmly anchored to weed or rock and live by filtering plankton—tiny free-floating plants and animals—from the water which is carried into the pool by each fresh tide.

The colourful red beadlet sea anemones and the green snakelocks anemones, despite the name and their plant-like appearance, are animals—killers which anchor themselves to the bottom of a pool, ready to paralyse and digest any small creature that blunders into their innocently swaying tentacles.

Snails, winkles and topshells, like limpets, scrape a seaweed film off the rock. Unlike the limpets that can withstand any amount of battering from the waves the periwinkles, huddling together in rock crevices, are more easily dislodged. Other animals, including prawns and hermit crabs, are scavengers. The hermit crab even scavenges its home—living in the empty shell of a whelk or other mollusc into which it retreats at the slightest disturbance.

Some inhabitants are migrants—moving from pool to pool at high tide. Others get stranded by the ebbing tide and then can only survive in rock pools. This is the case with many of the predators. The green shore crab will eat anything its pincers can crack, while starfish, such as the spiny starfish which feed mainly on bivalves like mussels, and grey sea slugs which feed only on beadlet anemones, are much more selective. Several fish, including blennies, gobies and rocklings, are predators which also regularly inhabit pools.

Mussel Usually lives in large groups permanently anchored to the rock by their strong 'guy ropes'

Pink encrusting seaweed It grows as a hard compact layer over any rock or stone

Grey sea slug It feeds on beadlet anemones, apparently unharmed by their stinging cells

Shanny This common blenny uses the rock pool as a home base, making excursions at high tide

Hermit crab Scuttles around the pool, its soft body tucked securely inside an empty whelk shell

Spiny starfish Has rows of large spines along its arms. It clings to rocks with its many tube-feet

Barnacle Lives firmly clamped to the rock, often in vast numbers forming a dense crusty covering

Limpet The hefty conical shell provides perfect protection against crashing waves

Beadlet anemone A common rock pool 'flower' that becomes a small blob of jelly when it contracts its tentacles

Roker *Raja clavata*

The regularity with which 'mermaids' purses'—the empty egg cases of this fish—are found in shore debris confirms it as one of the most common rays around the British coast—providing much of the 'skate' sold in fried-fish shops. The egg is enclosed in a 3 in. long, dark-coloured case which is oblong with a pointed horn at each corner and hard and leathery to touch. After the young ray has escaped, the case is washed ashore.

Roker is an East Anglian name, derived from the Danish 'rokke'. It is also known as the thornback ray because of the large spines down the mid-line of back and tail and on the underside and tail of adults. It is a flattened fish with large pectoral fins or 'wings' and a long tail. It has a pair of rounded spiracles near the eyes on its mottled fawn or grey back, and gill slits and mouth on the light underside. Adults grow up to 30 in. long.

Only the fleshy wings are sold, and the monster-like remains are often washed ashore after being jettisoned from trawlers.

Rook see Crow
Rooting shank toadstool see Fungus

Rose

There are more than 1000 varieties of cultivated rose, but they bear little resemblance to the roses that flower wild in woods and hedges in the summer. Over 100 species of wild rose have been identified in the British Isles; the burnet rose, field rose, dog rose, downy rose and apple-scented rose are the most common and easily recognisable.

Britain's most common wild roses

More than 100 species of wild rose grow in the British Isles. The five most common are shown here, together with their fruits. The burnet rose, a low-growing shrub, may be as little as 6 in. high, but the most common of all our wild roses, the dog rose, can attain a height of 10 ft. This species provides a rootstock on to which garden roses can be grafted

Burnet rose *Rosa pimpinellifolia*

Apple-scented rose *Rosa rubiginosa*

Dog rose *Rosa canina*

Field rose *Rosa arvensis*

Downy rose *Rosa villosa*

Colourful occupants of the autumn hedgerow—the fruits, or hips, of the dog rose

The burnet rose has leaves like the salad burnet and small, solitary, creamy-white flowers. These blossom from May to July and develop into purple-black fruits or hips in the autumn. The burnet rose is a low-growing shrub, 6-18 in. high, and spreads by suckers forming large patches, especially in sand dunes by the sea.

Despite its name the field rose is usually seen in woods and deeply shaded places. It also grows over hedges, sometimes climbing to 6 ft where there is support for its flexible stems. Clusters of pure white flowers open in June and July and produce small bright red hips. The field rose is absent from Scotland.

The other three wild roses have pink flowers. The most common is the dog rose, a stout 3-10 ft bush with hairless leaves. It grows in woods and hedges and is abundant everywhere except in Scotland. Its delicate shell-pink flowers blossom in June and July, usually in small clusters. This rose is cultivated by nurserymen to provide strong rootstocks on to which the more delicate garden roses are grafted.

In contrast to the dog rose, the downy rose is a low shrub, 3-6 ft high, with leaves densely covered in soft hairs. The deep pink flowers blossom from June to August. The downy rose is rare in southern England but is the most common wild rose in Scotland.

The apple-scented rose or sweet-briar is usually smelt before it is seen, especially on a warm showery day. Its apple-like fragrance is given off by brownish glands covering the underside of the leaves. This branching shrub is common in the south, growing 3-6 ft high and bearing bright pink flowers in June and July.

The cultivated roses that are so popular in the gardens of England have all evolved over hundreds of years from wild originals, most of them foreign; among the most important are the French rose *Rosa gallica*, the Damask rose *R. damascena*, the Phoenician rose *R. phoenicia*, the musk rose *R. moschata* and the dog rose *R. canina*. The important hybrids known as Hybrid Perpetuals used in rose breeding came about originally through chance pollination by insects. Improved forms, mostly in shades of red, pink and white, have been developed from these natural crosses.

The fruits or hips of wild roses are rich in vitamin C, and during the Second World War a campaign to collect them each autumn produced 2½ million bottles of rose-hip syrup, which contained as much vitamin C as 25 million oranges.

Northern rose beetle
Cetonia cuprea

Rose beetle

The 1 in. long adult rose beetle or rose chafer is a metallic green colour flecked with white. One species, *Cetonia aurata*, has been reported in places throughout the British Isles, but is becoming rare, mainly appearing in the Midlands and the south in the summer.

The northern rose beetle *C. cuprea* is slightly duller in colour, and is found only in the north of England and Scotland.

Both beetles are most likely to be found among the petals of large flowers, especially roses, on which they feed. Their larvae are fat, white grubs that live in rotten wood or vegetation and—in the case of the northern species—in ants' nests. They take two years to reach the adult stage.

Rose-of-Sharon *Hypericum calycinum*

A low, trailing, evergreen shrub that is often planted in shrubberies and rock gardens. It rapidly covers large areas of ground, trailing up to 30 in., and bears handsome, solitary, yellow flowers from July to September. It was introduced into

The rose-of-Sharon may be the rose referred to in the biblical Song of Solomon

Britain from south-east Europe and has now become established in many parklands and on roadside banks throughout the British Isles.

Sharon is in Israel, and it is thought that this species is the rose referred to in the Song of Solomon—'I am the rose-of-Sharon and the lily of the valleys'.

Roseroot *Sedum rosea*

A succulent perennial that grows in the crevices of cliffs and mountain rocks that are almost 4000 ft high. Roseroot occurs on sea cliffs in north and west Scotland and Ireland and on mountain ledges in Wales and northern England. Its stems are unbranched, about 12 in. high, with leaves that are bluish, broad, thick and fleshy. Greenish-yellow flowers appear from May to August and are crowded at the top of the stem. Male and female flowers are on separate plants. They are followed by fruits which are orange when ripe.

Roseroot is so-called because it gives off a smell resembling that of a rose when its root is cut or bruised.

Rotation

Patterns of crop succession designed to prevent soil impoverishment or the build-up of pests and diseases are called rotations. The simplest was the medieval three-course system: wheat in the first year, barley or oats in the second, with the land lying fallow in the third.

In the 18th century, two new crops—turnips and artificial grasses (sown mixtures of grass and clover)—were introduced and this revolutionised the centuries-old open-field system of rotation.

The Norfolk four-course rotation proved most successful and set the subsequent pattern for much English farming. It is still followed in places. It runs: wheat, roots, barley, clover and grasses. Hoeing the turnips helped to keep the soil weed-free, and sheep on them enriched the soil with manure. Ploughing in the grasses and clover enriched it for the wheat crop.

Today there are many variations in rotation patterns and, since the Second World War, a new type of rotation—arable with grass—has been developed. After following an arable rotation—the Norfolk four-course —for a period of years, the farmer will sow the field with a grass mixture to provide grazing for three to six years. During this grass, or ley, period, the pasture is grazed by many animals whose manure brings the soil to a high state of fertility which ensures good crops when the field is ploughed again.

Roundhouse

Found on village greens or near market-places, this building was used as a temporary 'cage' for the drunks, beggars or vagrants who appeared at market centres, and was the lock-up of parish constables who kept the peace until the 1840's.

Most surviving roundhouses date from the 18th century, when older wooden designs were replaced by circular or octagonal buildings of stone; some, with no windows, were known as blindhouses. Gradually, they fell into disuse: the Lingfield 'cage' in Surrey was last used in 1882.

The Cornish village of Veryan, where there are thatched roundhouses, has given its name to the Veryan Round Houses—Regency cottages built around the old village perimeter. They are circular or hexagonal in shape, so that there are no corners where the Devil could hide. Each cottage has a conical roof surmounted by a cross.

The lock-up at Castle Cary, Somerset, built in 1779 in the traditional roundhouse style

Roundworm

Unlike earthworms, the often microscopic nematodes or roundworms are not divided into segments, and their bodies are covered by a tough skin or cuticle. They live in soil and water, or are parasites of animals and plants. Those which are either free-living or plant parasites are called eelworms. All are dependent on moisture except in their resting stages. The potato-root eelworm *Heterodera rostochiensis* is a pest which can be controlled effectively only by a long cycle of crop rotation so that large numbers die before a new crop of potatoes is grown. The larva penetrates the potato root, on which it feeds, then moults four times before maturing, when it leaves the plant. The female, about 1/20 in. long, produces a few hundred eggs before dying. Her dead body hardens to form a protective case or cyst around the eggs, which need to be stimulated by a chemical given off by potato roots in order to hatch. In some species the cyst can survive for 20 years before hatching. Other eelworms are parasitic on other plants but not all form cysts.

There are a large number of roundworms parasitic in animals, often causing illness. *Ascaris suum* causes digestive upsets in pigs. *Toxocara canis* produces 'worms' in dogs. *Parascarum equorum* affects horses and *Ascaris lumbricoides* is found in man. The different parasitic species have specific hosts but their life cycle is usually similar. For example, the many thousand eggs laid by the female *A. suum* escape from the pig in its droppings, and the larvae develop within the egg in the soil. If the animal eats one of these eggs with its food, the larva is released in the pig's intestine. Once liberated, the larva penetrates the gut wall and migrates by way of the liver, heart and lungs to re-enter the gut. By this time it has reached the adult stage.

Rove beetle

The biggest single group of British beetles, there are 945 different species, varying in length from $\frac{1}{32}$ in. to $1\frac{1}{3}$ in. Most are black and resemble earwigs without pincers but have large back wings which enable them to fly well.

An alternative name is 'cocktail beetles' which comes from their habit of cocking their tails over their backs to squirt a strong-smelling vapour at enemies. This movement also enables them to place their wings under the small wing cases.

Most are predators and, although many of them eat decaying matter, the majority of those seen near decaying material are preying on other insects and larvae. Rove beetles are found throughout Britain on paths, soil or under stones.

Among the larger and better-known beetles of this family are the devil's coach-horse *Staphylinus olens* and the burying beetles. Some rove beetles are found in ants' nests, being tolerated for their larvae, which have a secretion the ants relish.

The rove beetles' larvae resemble those of ground beetles but the pupae are rigid, red-brown and have a flattened upper side.

See also BURYING BEETLE and DEVIL'S COACH-HORSE

Rowan see Mountain ash
Rubbing post see Standing stone

Rudd *Scardinius erythrophthalmus*

Although often confused with the roach, the rudd differs from it in a number of ways. Its dorsal fin is well behind the pelvic fin base (in the roach it is directly above), its body has a sharp keel behind the pelvic fins and its eye has an orange iris. Also the rudd usually has much redder fins — the pectoral, pelvic and anal fins are blood red.

It is a member of the carp family and thrives in small ponds, lakes and slow-moving rivers in the English lowlands and Ireland; but anglers have introduced it to the waters of mountainous regions such as the Lake District.

Rudd feed in mid-water or at the surface and mainly eat insects and their larvae, but young fish will eat small crustaceans and large ones will often take small fish.

They spawn from April to June, depending on the temperature, among vegetation in the shallows. The fry stay attached to the plants for a while but quickly become active feeders on minute organisms. Being prolific breeders, rudd often become overcrowded and consequently stunted.

Feeding time for female ruffs. The sexes form separate flocks and meet only for breeding

Ruff *Philomachus pugnax*

Although the ruff is a dull brown bird for most of the year, the males are transformed in spring by the growth of a ruff of feathers around their heads. The ruff varies from white to chestnut and black.

The male is 11 in. long and the female, or reeve, 2 in. smaller. In summer, the female is generally brown with a boldly patterned back; in winter she resembles the male.

During the summer males form a group, known as a lek, and engage in a frenzied display to show off their ruffs in a ritualised combat that never leads to proper fighting. The object is to win a mating territory. A female will walk unconcernedly among the males and choose a mate by touching him

A male ruff displays his mane of feathers. Despite his aggressive stance, the ruff rarely fights

delicately on his ruff feathers with her bill.

Mating takes place on the spot or the ruffs may fly away together. They are promiscuous and the males in the centre of the lek secure the most mating. The males play no part in nesting or raising the young. The nest is usually hidden in a hollow and lined with dry grass. Four eggs are laid in May, varying from pale brown to pale blue with bold spots or blotches. The chicks hatch in three weeks and begin to walk almost immediately.

The natural home of ruffs is marshland, and they now breed only in East Anglia, mostly on the Norfolk-Cambridgeshire border, but others appear as passage migrants in autumn and spring.

Ruffs feed mainly on insects, molluscs, worms and plant seeds.

Ruffe *Gymnocephalus cernua*

This small fish is found only in eastern England in slow-flowing rivers and in large lakes and reservoirs. Within these habitats, however, its distribution is patchy; there may be none in a seemingly suitable place when not far away they are common.

The ruffe, or pope, is usually found in small shoals, feeding on insect larvae and crustaceans; the larger fish eat smaller fish. Ruffes grow to an average of 5-7 in. long.

It resembles its close relative, the perch, in that it has a spiny fin on the back. But it lacks the bold colours of that fish, being a pale green-brown with numerous dark flecks on the back and sides. The belly fins are flushed with pink.

Rush

A grass-like plant with long, narrow leaves and green or brown flowers whose parts are arranged in sixes. The flowers form either in a head at the top of the stem or in a cluster some distance below the top. There are nearly 30 wild species in the British Isles, and most grow in bogs, marshes and other wet places. The leaves are rigid and tough, and many species have been used for making baskets and seats of chairs and for strewing on the floor.

There are three widespread species with flowers at the top of the stem.

Heath rush is the rush most often seen in bogs, especially in the mountains of the north and west. Its leaves are often flattened on the ground, and it has a short, wiry flowering stem about 1 ft high. This first appears in June and persists for most of the following year.

Salt-marsh rush grows in grassland by the sea, and is occasionally covered by the tide. It has dark brown, even blackish, flowers and narrow, flexible leaves. Both heath rush and salt-marsh rush are perennials and often

grow in patches. The third species which has flowers at the stem top, toad rush, is an annual. It grows in open ground, especially cow-trodden ditches, pond margins and even in arable fields in the west.

Three species with flowers in a head below the top of the stem are also widespread, and all grow in marshy ground.

The most common is soft rush, which is found in great tussocks and dominates wet meadows, particularly in parts of Devon and Cornwall. It can be recognised by its smooth, shiny green unridged stems. The loose, branched head of greenish brown flowers can be 2-3 in. across. When split open, the stems are seen to have a continuous pith. This was used to make candlewicks or the wicks of rush-lights in the days before electricity.

Compact rush is similar, but the pith is not continuous and the stems are not shiny and have ridges.

Hard rush also has ridged stems, but they are greyish-green. It is not as common as the other two rushes, and is not found in areas with acid soils.

Rust

Parasitic fungi, often rust coloured, can live in the spaces between the cells of other plants, and especially in the leaves. These rusts, like the smuts which may sometimes be seen on the larger mushrooms and toadstools, belong to the group of fungi called Basidiomycetes.

Rusts can be seen in summer on brambles, meadowsweet, hollyhocks and on mint stems. Broad bean rust is caused by *Uromyces fabae*; wheat rust by *Puccinea graminis*, which in winter produces black spores and is therefore known as black rust.

A typical rust, such as wheat rust, has a complex life cycle which involves host plants of two different species. The cycle begins in early summer, when orange-yellow spots and streaks appear on the leaves of grasses, wheat and other cereals, where spores have settled. These germinate, spreading more spores which in turn infect more plants.

By the end of July, the spores of a new and darker type are produced. These will remain dormant through the winter, germinating in the spring to produce yet a third type of spore which can develop only on barberry leaves. From the barberry a new generation arises and moves on to wheat to start the cycle again.

As a result of rusting, the grain of the attacked wheat tends to remain small and shrunken, though some wheats are more resistant to infection. As a long-term solution to the problem, the removal of barberry bushes adjacent to wheat will interrupt the cycle and ultimately bring the disease to an end. Such measures have met with wide success in the USA, where extensive crops have been saved.

Rye

An old proverb says that when a farmer starts to grow rye, his creditors should send in their bills—meaning that the fertility of the farm must have sunk so low that only rye, which needs little nutriment from the soil, will grow.

Although there is some demand for this grain for making rye crispbreads or for livestock feeding, it is not usually used for breadmaking in Britain; however, in eastern Europe black bread is widely made from rye flour.

A recent survey showed that only 10,000 acres of rye were planted in the whole of Britain, despite a modest revival in its use as a fodder crop, for grazing by cattle and by sheep. When sown for cattle fodder in autumn and early spring, such a crop is often cut before ripening, and the straw, which is thin but extremely strong and up to 6 ft long, provides an excellent material for thatching.

In appearance, rye resembles barley, with long awns, or whiskers, but the grains are naked like those of wheat, though longer and thinner.

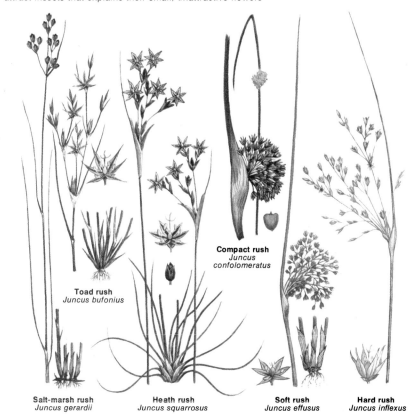

Six common rushes

There are nearly 30 species of rushes growing wild in the British Isles. This chart shows the most common six. Three produce flowers at the top of the stem, three below the top; all are widespread. Like grasses, rushes are pollinated by the wind; it is probably the fact that they do not need to attract insects that explains their small, unattractive flowers

Compact rush
Juncus confolomeratus

Toad rush
Juncus bufonius

Salt-marsh rush
Juncus gerardii

Heath rush
Juncus squarrosus

Soft rush
Juncus effusus

Hard rush
Juncus inflexus

S

Saffron, Meadow see Crocus
Sage see Clary

Sainfoin *Onobrychis vicifolia*
A plant that for centuries has been grown as a forage crop on lime-rich soils in southern and eastern England. It grows on roadside verges and waste places, where it has spread from cultivation, and also on chalk downs. Its deep roots make it drought-resistant and able to thrive on light, dry soils. The name is French and means wholesome hay. Sanfoin's 2 ft high spikes of red or bright pink flowers appear from June to August.

St Elmo's fire
This green or blue electrical discharge occurs round sharp, elevated objects like lightning conductors on buildings, the masts of ships, and occasionally mountaineers' axes. It caused much anxiety in the era of piston-engine aircraft, when the propellers appeared to become wheels of flame, although the amount of electricity involved is too small to cause a fire. The phenomenon is caused by an intense electrical field which builds up between earth and air when storm clouds are overhead. The field is strengthened near high, sharp points in the landscape where it may grow strong enough for a discharge. See also LIGHTNING

St George's mushroom see Fungus

St John's wort
The long, narrow, blunt leaves of the common St John's wort show glands which look like perforations when the leaves are picked and held up to the light. These were traditionally associated with wounds and were prescribed to stop bleeding. The word wort means plant or herb. St John's wort grows 1-3 ft high in open woodland, hedgerows and grassland throughout the British Isles except the north of Scotland, and is most abundant in lime-rich soils.

There are 14 British species of St John's wort—all have leaves which grow in pairs on opposite sides of the stalk and five-petalled yellow flowers which appear in mid-summer.

Another lime-loving species is hairy St John's wort which also grows 1-3 ft high. Its leaves and stems, which have no raised lines, are covered in hairs. It grows in woods and damp grassland throughout England, except the south-west, and in eastern Scotland; it is rare in Wales and Ireland.

In contrast, slender St John's wort and trailing St John's wort grow on acid heaths and grassland. The first, which is 1-2 ft high, has heart-shaped leaves and slender,

smooth stems and is found throughout the British Isles. Trailing St John's wort has slender stems that lie flat on the ground and are rarely more than 6 in. long. The flowers do not open in bad weather.

Square-stemmed St John's wort, 1-2 ft high, is common in marshes and wet meadows beside rivers and streams throughout the British Isles, except northern Scotland. Its square stems have wings at the angles.

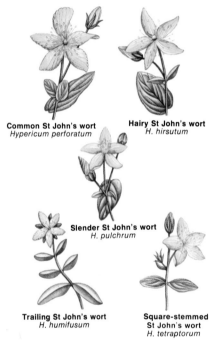

Common St John's wort
Hypericum perforatum

Hairy St John's wort
H. hirsutum

Slender St John's wort
H. pulchrum

Trailing St John's wort
H. humifusum

Square-stemmed St John's wort
H. tetraptorum

All species of St John's wort have five-petalled yellow flowers and opposite leaves

St Mark's fly *Bibio marci*
A stout, black and hairy insect common in grassy areas, so named because it makes its first appearance around St Mark's Day, April 25. The males form dancing swarms close to the ground over open country, their long legs dangling. Females spend most of their time on flowers, where they feed on the nectar.

Once on the wing, females are seized by the males for mating in the air. Large batches of eggs are then laid in underground chambers, and the larvae often live in groups of 100 or more. These feed at the roots of plants and can cause damage to cereal crops. By late summer they reach their full size of $\frac{3}{4}$ in. and spend winter in an underground chamber.

At $\frac{1}{2}$ in. long, the St Mark's fly is the largest

of the *Bibio* genus. There are 13 smaller British species in the genus, also sometimes called St Mark's flies even though they may not hatch in spring.

Saithe *Pollachius virens*
A fish which has been valued as a food for thousands of years. The remains of saithe have been found in the refuse heaps of prehistoric sites on Oronsay in the Inner Hebrides.

Today, the saithe is a valuable commercial fish to the trawler industry, although its rather dark flesh used to deter people from eating it. It is common in the north and is found all round the coasts of Britain, except the southern North Sea coast.

The young saithe, also called coalfish or coley, has a minute barbel or fleshy filament on the chin, which disappears with age. It is usually green-brown on the back and sides, shading to a dull silvery grey on the belly. Young fish are found close inshore, but larger ones—up to 4 ft long—keep to deep water.

Spawning takes place in the early spring in deep water. The eggs and young fish float near the surface and in time drift into inshore waters.

Salad burnet *Poterium sanguisorba*
The cucumber-like smell that sometimes pervades chalk grassland on a summer's day comes from the crushed leaves of salad burnet, a plant which can in fact be used in salads.

Between May and July salad burnet bears balls of green flowers on stalks less than 1 ft high. In each ball the flowers at the top are female, those in the middle hermaphrodite and those at the bottom male; they are pollinated by the wind.

Poterium comes from a Greek word meaning drinking cup—an allusion to the ancient practice of flavouring wine with the plant. Salad burnet grows on lime-rich soils throughout lowland England and Wales, but is rare in Scotland and Ireland.

Sallow see Willow

Salmon *Salmo salar*
One of the world's most valued food fishes, the salmon is the basis of a £7 million-a-year industry in Britain, which is now threatened by pollution and over-fishing. Although the salmon breeds in fresh water, much of its life is spent in the sea. No one knows how it returns thousands of miles to its native stream. Possibly it has an inbuilt sun compass, and can judge time, or it may detect by

smell the river from which it originally came.

Salmon begin breeding in late November, and egg laying continues until February. Each female digs a hollow or redd in silt-free gravel with powerful strokes of her body. When the redd is 6-12 in. deep, she is joined by a male for spawning. Up to 15,000 eggs are laid, covered with gravel excavated by other digging salmon. Fry or alevins hatch in March or early April, emerging from the gravel in about a month.

Year old fishes are called parr. They are marked with dark blotches along their sides and may remain in the stream up to four years. Eventually the marks are obscured by a dense silvery pigment and the silver fish, now called smolts, migrate to the sea for one to four years, feeding and growing while ranging along the coasts of Europe into the Norwegian sea and off Greenland.

A salmon returning to spawn in little more than a year is known as a grilse. In fresh water it loses its silvery blue-green sea colours, becoming greenish or brown, mottled with red or orange with large dark spots. Spawning salmon become deeply coloured, and the large males have hooked jaws known as the kype. After spawning, the adults, now called kelts, are very emaciated. Many die, but some recover in the sea to return, as mended kelts, to spawn again.

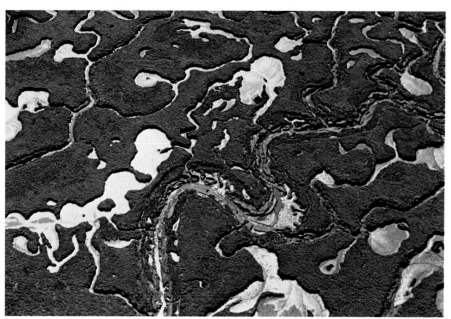

The typical snaking irregularity of salt marshes, seen from the air, near Walton-on-the-Naze, Essex

Salmon have leapt waterfalls up to 11 ft high, indicating a take-off speed of 20 mph

Salt marsh

Areas of silt and mud along some tidal estuaries and bays are periodically covered by the sea at high tide. Where the geographical features prevent any scouring action by waves, the silt accumulates and salt marshes form.

The types of plants which grow on such a marsh depend on its height above the sea. On low-lying marshes, which are regularly covered by salt water, only green algae, such as Enteromorpha, eel grass, sea blight and marsh samphire grow. Sea asters may be found if there is sand beneath the mud.

If such vegetation grows profusely, it slows the flow of the tides and allows silt to build up the height of the marsh. Then sea manna grass can grow and, spreading by means of creeping stems, form a turf. When it is used for grazing sheep, this turf is known as salting pasture, valued because it is free from the eggs of parasitic liver flukes. Ultimately, scurvy-grass and sea plantain establish themselves among the turf.

A salt marsh covered by the sea for fewer than 50 hours a year favours the growth of sea lavender, thrift, sea arrow grass, sea spurreys and shrubby sea purslane. In May and June the blooming thrift turns such marshes pink, and by late summer sea lavender flowers change the colour to purple.

Where the initial growth of sea manna grass is uneven, deep drainage channels cut through the turf. Shrubby sea purslane generally grows best along the edges of these channels. Low patches of salt marsh between the hummocks of turf stay bare of vegetation because the evaporation of water left by the ebbing tide makes the mud too salty for plants. These are salt pans.

On the highest parts of elevated marshes the plants include red fescue, buck's-thorn plantain, sea milkwort, sea rush and maritime rush. The type of vegetation at the edge of a salt marsh, where it merges with the neighbouring countryside, depends on the land. If it is pasture, barley grass, red and white clover and crested dog's tail grow on the intermediate area. Where a salt marsh blends into freshwater marsh, common reed and lesser spearwort grow.

Many salt marshes are changing due to the spread of rice grass *Spartina townsendii*, which grows vigorously and binds the silt together. Farmers use rice grass to cover land they want to reclaim from the sea.

Few animals live in salt marshes because of the tidal flooding, although small worms, snails and sandhoppers are abundant, especially in the drainage channels.

Saltwort *Salsola kali*

A common seashore plant around the coasts of the British Isles, which can thrive in salt soils, saltwort often grows partly buried in the sand. Its pale blue-green branched stems and narrow, cylindrical, spiny leaves form a bush 1-2 ft high. Tiny green flowers appear in late summer at the base of the leaves, each protected by a pair of sharp prickles.

It was once dried in heaps, like hay, and then burnt over a large hole into which flowed a semi-fluid alkaline matter from the plant; this was used as washing soda. *Kali* is Arabic for such semi-liquid ashes, and the word alkali derives from it.

Samphire, Marsh

Many species of marsh samphire grow on bare mud in salt marshes all round the coast and are periodically submerged by the sea. Often difficult to tell apart, they are succulent plants with jointed, much-branched stems, varying in height from 1 in. to 15 in. In late summer spikes appear, jointed like the stem. Three flowers are hidden on both sides at the base of each joint.

Great quantities of marsh samphire used to be gathered and burnt, like saltwort, to produce soda; this was used in the manufacture of soap and glass, and from this is derived the plant's other name—glasswort. The young stems can be eaten fresh or pickled.

Sand

Each grain of sand is a quartz fragment, worn away from an older sandstone or a rock such as granite. Sand can be moved quite easily by flowing water, so it is found in river beds and on the sea coast. The smaller grains can also be wind-blown, hence the coastal dunes. Sands and sandstone give sandy soils, as in the East Anglian Breckland or the New Forest. These soils are usually rather infertile because they let water drain through rapidly, washing out minerals and humus and leaving little for plants to feed on. Even so, dunes are often colonised by grass and scrub.

Sand grains—fragments of quartz—magnified to 20 times their normal size

Sand dune see Dune

Sand eel

Cod, mackerel, herring and saithe feed on sand eels, as do many seabirds. Sand eels are thus of great economic importance, since so many of the fish caught commercially depend on them. They are found in large numbers in the shallow seas around British shores, but are rarely seen as they are expert burrowers in sand.

The most common sand eel is the launce *Ammodytes tobianus*, a thin fish, up to 8 in. in length, with a pointed lower jaw enabling it to burrow. It is yellowish-green on the back with silvery sides and a white belly. Under water, sand eels always swim in shoals, moving with their heads pointing obliquely downwards. They feed on worms, small crustaceans and fish. They live for a maximum of four years.

Sanderling see Sandpiper

Sandhopper

If stones or decaying seaweed are moved on a seashore, sandhoppers usually emerge, leaping frantically in all directions. Sandhoppers are small relatives of shrimps and lobsters. Their curving bodies, up to 1 in. long, are flattened from side to side. They hop by using the abdomen and the last three pairs of legs as a spring. They also walk and 'swim' in the sand by wriggling along on their

sides, but they never go into the sea and would drown if submerged for long. They are able to navigate by using the angle of the sun as a compass. They feed at low tide on decaying weeds and carrion.

There are two common British species: *Talitrus saltator* which is green-buff or fawn and has a black line down the side; and the slightly smaller red to green-brown *Orchestia gammarella*, which is sometimes called a shorehopper.

Sandpiper

A large number of long-legged, long-billed shore birds and waders are grouped together under the name sandpiper. They are all brown in colour and difficult to tell apart except in flight, when wing and tail patterns can be seen. They feed on molluscs, fish and occasionally plants, or insects caught on the wing.

The most numerous and widespread sandpiper is the dunlin, which breeds on the moors in the north and west, in central Wales and western Ireland. The female lays four eggs in a nest on the ground in May. The eggs hatch after three weeks and the young fly three weeks later. The dunlin winters in estuaries and as a bird of passage is seen on marshes and reservoirs. It is a dumpy wader and is often to be seen feeding, stabbing its long beak into the sand, or asleep, often on one leg. Dunlins gather in large numbers and on some estuaries more than 100,000 have been counted.

The white wing bar and white tail patches show in flight. Its upper colouring is a mixture of browns, deeper in summer than in

The dunlin, Britain's most common sandpiper, as seen by the 18th-century engraver Thomas Bewick

winter, and underneath it is white. Smaller than the dunlin are the two stints—the little stint and Temminck's stint. Both breed in the Arctic and are usually seen in Britain only in the autumn. The little stint is more numerous and marked by two white stripes on the back which meet to form an inverted 'V'. It is often seen on estuaries, marshes and inland waters. The even smaller Temminck's stint is a grey bird, found only on freshwater marshes. It is rarely seen, but most often in autumn.

The 10 in. long knot is the largest common wader of the stout-bodied dunlin group, and can be confused with the dunlin. It breeds only in the high Arctic on the Siberian coast but winters in vast numbers on the Cheshire Dee, Morecambe Bay, Foulness and The Wash. It is seldom numerous elsewhere. Proposed reclamation in each of these areas is causing concern to conservationists as it may discourage knots from wintering in Britain.

Sanderlings are aptly named for they are

In flight the sanderling displays a boldly contrasted white stripe on a dark wing

most frequently seen following the waves up and down sandy beaches, feeding on minute organisms uncovered by the sea. Apart from a mottled grey back, they have an almost white plumage, broken by a black patch at the bend of the wing, which makes identification easy.

The purple sandpiper, a winter visitor from the Arctic, is a dark colour and difficult to detect among seaweed. It is found only along rocky shores, mostly on the west coast.

Curlew sandpipers, which are often mistaken for dunlin, are seen in large numbers only in autumn on passage to winter in Africa. The best field mark is the square white rump which is obvious in flight. Curlew sandpipers are seldom seen in large flocks and usually mix with dunlin on coastal marshes and sewage farms.

The green sandpiper and wood sandpiper are freshwater waders—the wood sandpiper on open marshes and the green most often on dykes or drainage ditches. Both birds have square white rumps in flight but the green sandpiper appears almost black at a distance and the wood sandpiper a dull brown. Since 1959, the wood sandpiper has bred in a secret area in Scotland and though the green did breed in Inverness that year, it has not yet become established. A few, however, do stay the winter in Britain.

The common sandpiper is a more widespread summer visitor to Britain, nesting along mountain streams. Its peculiar bobbing action, similar to that of a wagtail, makes it easy to identify. It also has a prominent patch of brown on each side of the breast, separated from its brown wings by a wedge of white. Like the green and wood sandpipers, it seldom forms large flocks.

Sand-smelt *Atherina presbyter*
Silversides or sand-smelts are small fish, rarely growing more than 6 in. long. They live in large shoals all round the coasts of the British Isles, but are less common in the north and north-east. In summer, their numbers are increased by northward migrations from the western Channel. Bass will eat them. But although the flesh is delicious, the sand-smelt is not fished commercially in Britain.

Sand-smelts swim in tight shoals. They have light olive-green backs with each scale outlined with small black points. A pronounced silvery stripe runs along each side, and the undersides are silvery-white.

Breeding takes place in shore pools in summer. The numerous eggs stick to the pool seaweeds by long threads and the young fish are often seen in high shore pools, both on rocky and muddy shores, in late summer.

Sand-spurrey
A small trailing herb with narrow, succulent leaves and five-petalled pink flowers produced throughout the summer. There are four species in Britain, only one of which, the common sand-spurrey, grows inland. It is 2-9 in. across and although widespread on sandy or gravelly heaths in the lowlands of Britain it is rare in Ireland.

One of three coastal species, rock sand-spurrey, which is 2-6 in. across, is confined to rocks, cliffs and walls. Common on the south and west coasts of Britain and all around Ireland, it is distinguished from other species by being covered in sticky glands and having large flowers.

The other two species grow in salt marshes all around the coast. They are very similar, but can be distinguished by their seeds when the pods are ripe: those of greater sand-spurrey have broad wings; those of lesser sand-spurrey have none.

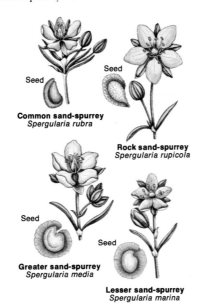

Common sand-spurrey
Spergularia rubra

Seed

Seed

Rock sand-spurrey
Spergularia rupicola

Seed

Seed

Greater sand-spurrey
Spergularia media

Lesser sand-spurrey
Spergularia marina

Rock, greater and lesser sand-spurrey grow on the coast; common sand-spurrey inland

Sandstone
A rock made of coarse or fine grains of sand compacted or cemented together, making it one of the easiest rocks to identify. Sandstones vary in colour as the result of the presence of iron oxides or other materials. They can be yellow, white, red or black.

Sandstones have been formed in several geological periods in a variety of ways. Basically they consist of material from ancient quartz rocks which was laid down as sediment on the sea-bed and compressed solid over vast periods of time. Some sandstones, in which there is considerable calcium carbonate, merge into limestones.

Sandwort
A small trailing plant with tiny, white, five-petalled flowers. Three-nerved sandwort grows throughout the British Isles. It is found in dry woods and copses, and is similar to chickweed but with undivided petals. It is 3-15 in. high and flowers in May and June. If a leaf is held up to the light, the three veins can be clearly seen.

Thyme-leaved sandwort, 1-9 in. high and much-branched, is more compact with smaller leaves. It grows in dry, open, sunny places, such as quarries, sand dunes and even on the tops of walls. It flowers throughout the summer.

Sea sandwort is one of Britain's most common seashore plants. Found all round the coastline, it grows in large patches in loose sand or shingle, its yellowish-green leaves crowded together on 2-10 in. stems that are often almost buried in the sand. From May onwards, tiny greenish-white flowers develop, hidden amongst the leaves. These ripen with large round green fruits.

Sanicle see Parsley
Sarsen see Standing stone

Saucer bug *Ilyocoris cimicoides*
Beware the aggressive saucer bug, which can inflict a painful bite. Found in still, muddy water, it has sharp, piercing mouthparts for preying on pond lice and shrimps. It is $\frac{1}{2}$ in. long, saucer-shaped and brown with a yellowish head. It cannot fly, and crawls overland to colonise new ponds.

The eggs are laid in spring in the stems of water plants, and hatch in about a month. The young bugs reach their full size in around eight weeks. It is not found in Scotland or northern England.

Savoy see Cabbage

Sawfly
The saw-edged egg-depositing organs of the females give sawflies their name. These are used to cut into plant tissue where the eggs are laid. The larvae resemble butterfly caterpillars, but have a greater number of false legs, at least seven pairs, in addition to their true legs.

Like caterpillars, they feed by boring into plant leaves. Adult sawflies lack the characteristic narrow waist of their relatives, the bees, wasps and ants.

Of several hundred British species, the hawthorn sawfly *Trichosoma tibiale* is among the most common. The pale green larvae have a whitish powdery coating and feed on hawthorn from July to September. They spend the winter in parchment-like, oblong cocoons, $\frac{3}{4}$ in. long, which they attach to hawthorn twigs. The adults cut their way out in May.

Wood-wasps are close relatives, the largest in Britain being the giant wood-wasp *Urocercus gigas*, $1\frac{1}{2}$ in. long. The females have long, sting-like organs with which eggs are inserted into the stumps of cut or dead pine trees. This organ gives rise to the alternative name, horntail. The larvae are wood borers and take up to three years to mature, often emerging from timber cut and put to use.

Saw-wort

Named after the saw-like edge of its leaves, this plant was once, because of its shape, supposed to heal cuts and other wounds. The leaves produce a greenish-yellow dye formerly used to colour woollens.

Saw-wort grows about 2 ft high in open woodland and damp, lime-rich grasslands throughout England and Wales, but is rarely seen in Scotland and Ireland. It bears red-purple flowers from July onwards.

Alpine saw-wort is a fairly common plant on cliffs in mountain areas. Smaller than saw-wort and with leaves only slightly serrated it bears a crowded tuft of large purple flowers from July to September.

Saw-wort
Serratula tinctoria

Alpine saw-wort
Saussurea alpina

Alpine saw-wort is smaller than the common species, but has more flowers

Saxifrage

The name means 'stone-breaker' and was given because most of these flowers live on rocks which their roots appear to split as they penetrate the cracks. An exception is the meadow saxifrage, an increasingly rare plant of old meadows and pastures, which is scattered throughout lowland Britain. It is about 1 ft high, has kidney-shaped leaves and produces clusters of pure white flowers in May. The only other lowland species— and the only annual—is the rue-leaved saxifrage, which grows on limestone rocks and walls. Rarely more than 6 in. high, its white flowers often appear in April when the plant is only 1 in. high. Rue-leaved saxifrage has three-fingered leaves, usually tinged with red.

The other 14 British saxifrages are mountain plants. The two most common have white flowers and grow beside streams and on wet rock ledges. Starry saxifrage, 3-6 in. high, is easily recognised by the rosette of oblong leaves at its base and the star-like flowers that appear in June. Mossy saxifrage, 3-9 in. high, has tufted, moss-like leaves that form extensive mats; for this reason it is often grown in rock gardens.

Yellow saxifrage, 2-8 in. high, is absent from the mountains of Wales and all except the north-west mountains of Ireland. It has narrow leaves and the upright stems bear yellow, orange-spotted flowers from June to September.

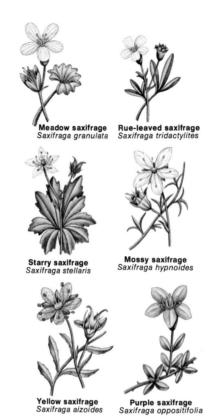

Meadow saxifrage
Saxifraga granulata

Rue-leaved saxifrage
Saxifraga tridactylites

Starry saxifrage
Saxifraga stellaris

Mossy saxifrage
Saxifraga hypnoides

Yellow saxifrage
Saxifraga aizoides

Purple saxifrage
Saxifraga oppositifolia

Most saxifrages are mountain plants, living on rocks where their roots take hold in cracks

The earliest species to flower is purple saxifrage, which produces its attractive purple flowers between March and May. Later in the year it has creeping, ribbon-like stems and four rows of small, overlapping leaves. Purple saxifrage grows in the mountains of Britain and north and west Ireland.

Scabious

The three British species of scabious have slender stems topped by button-like heads of flowers. Field scabious, which reaches a height of 3 ft, has divided, hairy leaves and lilac-blue flowers that appear in late summer. If touched by a lighted cigarette, they turn bright green. The plant grows in

Field scabious
Knautia arvensis

Devil's-bit scabious
Scabiosa succisa

Small scabious
Scabiosa columbaria

Slender stems and button-like heads of flowers characterise the three species of scabious

dry grassland and on banks throughout the British Isles, but is rare in northern Scotland and northern Ireland. Field scabious was once known as the scabies herb and its juice was used to cure sores of all kinds.

Devil's-bit scabious is a shorter plant with undivided leaves and deep blue flowers, which bloom from June to October. It grows in marshes and wet meadows everywhere. The root ends abruptly, and the plant was given its name as the result of an ancient belief that the Devil bit the end off because of the root's power to cure diseases.

Small scabious is restricted to lime-rich grassland in England, Wales and the extreme north of Scotland. Up to 2 ft tall, it has finely divided leaves and lilac-blue flowers which appear in July and August.

Scale insect

The female of this fat, yellow insect is covered with a scale which is always the same colour as the plant stem on which it lives. The female scale insect produces eggs in the summer—in most species, without mating—and dies. The eggs are hidden by the scale during winter and hatch in spring as nymphs. The female nymphs crawl a little way before producing a scale of their own; the males develop a pair of wings, but have no mouthparts and do not feed.

Scale insects are up to $\frac{1}{8}$ in. long and resemble flattened aphids; females and nymphs feed like aphids, with mouthparts buried in the plant stem to extract sap.

A common species is the oyster-scale insect *Quadraspidictus ostreaeformis*, which looks like a minute oyster. This lives on fruit trees, birch, horse chestnut and poplar.

Scale worm

A sea worm, $\frac{2}{5}$-8 in. long, with paired scales along the back. The scales usually number 24-36, but one species, *Sthenelais boa*, has 312. There are about 30 British species. Many live on the lower shore under stones and among seaweed. These include one of the most common species, the broad, stiff, 1 in. long, brownish-yellow *Lepidonotus squamatus*. One species, the colourless, $\frac{3}{4}$-1 in. long *Scalisetosus assimilis*, lives between the spines of edible sea urchins, and two others, the brown, red-headed $\frac{2}{5}$ in. long *Harmothoë lunulata* and the iridescent, 2-5 in. long *Polynoë scolopendrina*, often inhabit the tubes of burrowing bristle worms. All feed on algae. When scale worms of some species are disturbed, they shed their scales.

Scallop see Shell

Scarecrow

A traditional device for keeping birds away from crops—usually a standing stick with a cross-section for arms, dressed in old clothes. Today it is being displaced by other devices for scaring off birds, such as guns which go off automatically at intervals.

Dead crows or moles are sometimes hung

from boughs or fences by pest-exterminators. Although they frighten away birds, they are hung up primarily to show the landowner that the job has been properly done.

Scaup see Duck, Wild

Scavenger beetle

These beetles, related to the larger water scavenger beetles, feed on decomposing matter in damp places. There are 29 species which live in the British Isles. Many scavenger beetles eat rotting vegetation near the edge of ponds; three species feed on dung; and another eats rotting seaweed and can survive being covered by the sea.

The beetles are oval, $\frac{1}{8}$-$\frac{1}{3}$ in. long and usually glossy black with red legs. The legless grubs feed on the same material as the adults.

Scorpion fly

This harmless insect is so-called because the male's genitals curve over its back like a scorpion's sting. The wings of both sexes, which reach a span of $1\frac{1}{3}$ in., are a transparent brown with darker brown markings. The mouthparts are at the end of a downward-pointing, beak-like extension of the head.

Scorpion flies scavenge among hedgerows and trees for dead insects; they also eat plant sap. Eggs, which are laid in the soil, hatch into grey-brown caterpillar-like larvae. These burrow for dead animal matter, then spend the winter underground in a pupal, or resting, stage.

The most common of the three British species is *Panorpa communis*, which is on the wing from May to July. During daylight the scorpion fly takes many short, quick flights in search of food.

The vicious-looking scorpion fly is harmless to man. Its 'sting' is the male genitals

Scotch argus see Brown butterfly
Scoter see Duck

The rugged slope of scree below Bow Fell, in the wild region of the Lake District, Cumberland

Scree

When frost causes the water contained in rock faces to freeze and expand, the rock splits and boulders and stones fall away. This happens particularly at high altitudes, where frost is more severe. The rock fragments collect in piles called scree or talus; the slope of these is constantly a little over 30 degrees. Where the fragments are coarse few plants grow. An outstandingly large slope of scree falls into the south-east edge of Wastwater in the Lake District.

Screech beetle *Hygrobia hermanni*

This water beetle produces a squeaking noise by rubbing the tip of its body on the rough underside of its wing-cases—hence its name. It is black or brown and $\frac{1}{3}$-$\frac{2}{5}$ in. long. In spring and summer it lives in muddy-bottomed ponds mainly in south and east England; in winter it hibernates in the mud.

Although the adults eat a variety of worms and insects, the three-tailed larvae, which hatch from eggs laid on the pond bottom, eat only small red tubifex worms. Unlike most water beetle larvae, they have gills and do not need to surface to breathe. The full-grown larvae crawl on to pond-side mud before turning into pupae.

Scrub

Abandoned farmland or cleared woodland that has been colonised by bird-sown shrubs and saplings—most commonly hawthorn, blackthorn, wild rose and dogwood. If left alone, the saplings would eventually form forest, but most scrub is reclaimed for farming, controlled forestry or recreation before this can happen.

Where scrub survives, mainly in nature reserves, it provides a wealth of nesting and feeding haunts for small song-birds, and cover for foxes, badgers and rabbits.

Scurvy grass *Cochlearia officinalis*

Sailors suffering from scurvy sores found that they could be cured by eating the dried herb, or drinking a distillation made from it. The leaves contain ascorbic acid—vitamin C—which prevents scurvy.

Scurvy grass grows 2-18 in. high in salt marshes and on banks all round the coasts of the British Isles except in south-east England, and is also found inland in the north and west where an alpine form sometimes grows beside streams at over 3000 ft above sea level.

It has shiny round leaves and white, four-petalled flowers which bloom from May to August. Pea-sized seed pods follow the flowers and their semi-transparent, central division remains after the seeds are shed.

Scythe

An implement with a long, curved blade for cutting a crop of grass an inch or two above ground level. Before the invention of the reaping machine in the 19th century, all grass for hay-making was cut with a scythe or sickle. English scythes, as opposed to continental ones, have a sinuous double curve in their handle, or snead, from which two small side-handles, or doles, project. The scythes of northern England are less markedly curved.

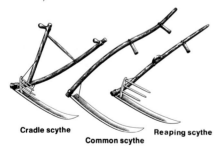

Cradle scythe **Reaping scythe**
Common scythe

Three examples of the scythes used to cut grass in the last century. Scythes are still used to cut small or awkward areas of grass

Sea adder see Pipefish

Sea anemone

A flower-like animal widespread around British shores wherever there are rocks, stones, shells or weeds to which it can attach itself by means of its suction disc. It consists of a hollow cylinder with a crown of

The deceptive beauty of the dahlia sea anemone—the petals are stinging tentacles

Beadlet anemone
Actinia equina

Plumose anemone
Metridium senile

The plumose anemone attaches itself to piers; the beadlet is seen at low tide

tentacles surrounding a mouth. These contain stinging cells which stun or kill prey—prawns, worms and other small sea animals. The anemones themselves are eaten by sea spiders.

The beadlet anemone, ½-1½ in. tall, is red, green or brown, with a ring of 24 blue spots at the top. When exposed at low tide it contracts into a stiff, flat-topped blob. The dahlia anemone, 2 in. tall, is, at 4 in. across, the largest British inter-tidal sea anemone. It has red and white banded tentacles but at

low tide retracts these into its warty column. The white, cream, orange or brown plumose anemone is 2-5 in. tall and has many feathery tentacles.

There are about 40 British species of sea anemones. Most are male or female, but a few are hermaphrodite. They reproduce by laying eggs or by producing small, bud-like anemones at the base of the column. These slowly detach themselves from the parent to become independent anemones.

HOW A SEA ANEMONE FEEDS

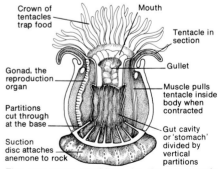

Crown of tentacles trap food

Mouth

Tentacle in section

Gullet

Gonad, the reproduction organ

Muscle pulls tentacle inside body when contracted

Partitions cut through at the base

Gut cavity or 'stomach' divided by vertical partitions

Suction disc attaches anemone to rock

The numerous partitions in the anemone's 'stomach' increase its digestive surface, allowing the anemone to swallow and digest large animals such as fish and crabs

Sea blite *Suaeda maritima*

A much-branched, low-growing annual plant found along all coastlines of the British Isles, usually below the high-water mark of spring tides. Its stem has a reddish tinge and the almost cylindrical leaves are pointed at the tip. Two or three flowers appear at the base of the leaves from July to October. They are green and have no petals. After flowering, the calyx remains as a seed case.

Shrubby sea blite *S. fruticosa*, a rare plant on salt marshes in south-east England, was one of the plants burnt in southern Europe to produce barilla, an impure alkali used in the manufacture of soda, soap and glass.

Close-up of flower

Sea blite
Suaeda maritima

Shrubby sea blite
Suaeda fruticosa

Sea buckthorn *Hippophae rhamnoides*

A rare native shrub on the east coast, but it has been widely planted to hold drifting sand in place. A spiny shrub with grey-brown twigs, it has scaly, slender, grey-green leaves adapted to retaining moist air and reflecting the sun's heat; it grows only on sand dunes. A meshwork of tough roots, gripping the sand, makes its thickets almost indestructible. Each bush is either male or female, but the flowers are inconspicuous. The orange berries, which ripen in October, have an exceptionally high vitamin C content and can be used in marmalade-making. It is also known as sallow-thorn.

When cultivated, sea buckthorn sometimes becomes a tree with a trunk up to 20 ft tall.

Sea cucumber

A worm-like animal related to the starfish and sea urchin. Most sea cucumbers have thick, leathery skin and move by means of suckers or feet, but some small species have thinner, sandpaper-like skin and burrow through sand. Tentacles surround the mouth.

The largest British species, the nigger or cotton spinner *Holothuria forskali*, 3-8 in. long, is dark brown above and pale beneath. It lives off the shore of south-west England and feeds on minute particles of dead animal matter. When disturbed it can confuse or entangle an attacker by ejecting cotton-like threads from its anus. The sea cucumber *Cucumaria saxicola* is white and grows up to 6 in. long. It lives beneath rocks on the lower shore.

In most species the males and females shed sperm and eggs into the water where fertilis-ation takes place. The eggs then develop into larvae and sink to the sea-bed before changing into adult sea cucumbers.

Sea fan *Eunicella verrucosa*

The branching growth of the sea fan looks like a miniature tree, as it sways in the water anchored by its base to a rock face. But a sea fan is a colony of many tiny animals, called polyps, living together. When there is a constant water current, they grow in a plane edge-on to the current; in still water, they branch in all directions.

The sea fan is supported by an internal black horny skeleton, which is covered by a thin layer of orange, pink or white living tissue, through which polyps extend to feed. Each polyp has tentacles, which it uses to seize small organisms. When a sea fan dies, the outer layer breaks to reveal the black skeleton.

Sea fir

Resembling fine seaweed, sea firs are animals that live in colonies attached to rocks, weeds and shells on the shore and in the sea. Each sea fir grows up from a creeping root-like network and carries one or more polyps—small anemone-like structures. The polyps have tentacles armed with stinging cells, which immobilise the plankton on which they feed.

The polyps produce bud-like jellyfish without mating. Some of these remain attached to the parent polyp. The females of those that move away discharge eggs into the water, where they are fertilised by the males. The eggs develop into larvae, which eventually become sea firs.

Oaten pipes sea firs, *Tubularia* species, grow on moorings on rocky shores. They are up to 6 in. tall, have yellow stalks and pink, flower-like polyps. These are preyed on by sea slugs.

Sea gooseberry

In late summer or early autumn, balls of colourless jelly the size of a gooseberry are washed up on shores all around the British Isles. These are sea gooseberries or comb jellies *Pleurobrachia pileus*, and if they are dropped into a rock pool or a jar of sea water, eight rows of iridescent plates and a pair of trailing tentacles become visible. The plates are used to propel the sea goose-berry in the water and the tentacles to capture plankton—often herring larvae—and draw it up to the mouth which is on the underside of the body.

Their chief enemy is a related species, *Beroë cucumis* (also known, with four other British species, under the general name of the sea gooseberries). It is pale pink, thimble-shaped and 2 in. across. Its diet is almost entirely sea gooseberries, and it is itself eaten by cod.

All sea gooseberries are hermaphrodites which cross-fertilise one another to produce larvae.

Sea hare *Aplysia punctata*

A red-brown to olive-green animal, 3-6 in. long, which resembles a crouching hare. It lives offshore among seaweed, crawling on its single foot like a snail but occasionally swimming by flapping the lobes of its foot. Its tentacles resemble hares' ears.

Sea hares feed on sea lettuce, a common seaweed. When disturbed they release a purple slime which stains, but is not a fast dye like the sepia of the cuttle fish. The animals are hermaphrodites which cross-fertilise one another. They often mate in chains. In summer they move up to the inter-tidal zone to spawn and lay strings of pink or yellow eggs on rocks or weeds, after which they die. The eggs hatch into larvae, which eventually become adults.

The slug-like sea hare has paired front and rear tentacles which resembles hares' ears

Sea heath *Frankenia laevis*

This creeping plant has numerous leaves like those of heath or heather but is in no way related. Its flowers, which appear in July and August, have five separate pink petals each with a long claw at its base. With wiry purple stems up to 12 in. long, sea heath grows on soil on the landward side of salt marshes on the south and east coasts from Hampshire to Norfolk.

Sea hen see Lumpsucker

Sea holly *Eryngium maritimum*

Once common on sand or shingle on shores all round the British Isles, sea holly is now rare in the north and east and is becoming rarer elsewhere as a result of human encroachment on sand dunes and beaches.

Dried specimens of its large, prickly, waxy leaves and thistle-like heads of blue flowers have been used in flower arrangements. Sea holly has an extensive system of cylindrical fleshy roots which were once candied with sugar and orange-flower water to produce sweets called eringoes. Colchester was famed for this product in the 17th century.

Seal

Britain's largest wild mammal, the grey seal, can grow to 9½ ft and weigh more than 600 lb. It is also called the Atlantic seal and is larger and far more numerous than the other species of seal seen around the British Isles which is called—misleadingly—the common, or harbour, seal.

Both species are fast, graceful swimmers and although they come ashore to bask or breed are primarily aquatic creatures. On land they are clumsy, wriggling along, aided by their front flippers.

The grey seal *Halichoerus grypus* establishes its breeding colonies, or 'rookeries', on rocky shores, mainly to the west of the British Isles. The common seal *Phoca vitulina* prefers estuaries and tidal sandbanks to the east.

Grey seal colonies are established in the Orkneys, Shetlands and Hebrides, on the Isle of Man, Ramsey Island, and along the Irish, Scottish, Welsh, north Cornish and Devon coasts, the Scilly Isles and—on the east coast—at Farne Island, off Northumberland, and Scroby Sands, off Great Yarmouth.

On the east of Britain, common seal colonies are found in the Orkneys and Shetlands, Dornoch and Moray Firths, The Wash and Scroby Sands; and also in the Bristol Channel and Northern Ireland, where Strangford and Carlingford Loughs are the main breeding centres.

The two species have quite different breeding patterns: grey seals produce their young between September and December and common seals in May and June. In both cases, the female seals mate again two or three weeks after giving birth and the development of their eggs is suspended for two or three months after fertilisation—a process known as delayed implantation—which ensures that pups are born at almost the same time each year. Usually each female produces one pup.

In the case of grey seals, about a month before the breeding season large numbers of pregnant females and bulls gather on the colony sites. The largest bulls fight or merely challenge one another to establish supremacy. After the females have given birth to

The grey seal, like all seals, is clumsy on land and comes ashore only to breed and bask

their pups, the bulls establish territories and form harems of the cows, usually three to seven in number.

Grey seal mothers feed their young on land for about three weeks and teach them to swim. After this period, pups are left to fend for themselves and then the adults mate.

After mating, all the seals disperse; the adults stay round British coasts, but the pups often travel considerable distances. A pup born on Ramsey Island, off Pembrokeshire, on October 5, was found 250 miles away, off the Brittany coast on November 12. Allowing three weeks for weaning, this pup had travelled 250 miles in 17 days. Young seals from Farne Island and the Orkneys are frequently found hundreds of miles away, off Norway.

Grey seals have spotted coats and vary in colour from dark grey, through silver, to brown. They are darker on their backs than

on their bellies. Males are normally bigger than females.

Female seals return to the breeding ground to moult in January; the males in March. Pups are born with a white, long-haired coat, and moult into adult coats about three weeks later, before taking to water.

Common seals have snub noses compared with the straight, or 'Roman', noses of grey seals. Common seals are also smaller—adult males are 5-6 ft long, weigh about 560 lb. and are bigger than cows. Their colouring is as variable as that of grey seals but they are usually more mottled. They spend far more time ashore than grey seals, most often 'hauling out' of the sea on the low tide at night.

They go through what is apparently a courtship display of aquabatics, near their colonies in the spring. Afterwards the females, which are pregnant from the previous year's mating, give birth to their young, usually on land or offshore sandbanks.

The pups are able to swim immediately. Their mothers suckle them, sometimes in the water, for three weeks. When the pups are weaned the adults moult and mate, almost invariably in the sea. It is thought that common seals are monogamous. Perhaps because they do not establish land territory or extensive nursery sites, common seals appear to be much less aggressive than grey seals.

Both species are well adapted for diving in search of almost any kind of fish or shellfish for food. A seal of either species can stay under water for more than half an hour. When submerged a seal's heartbeat drops from 150 to 10 beats per minute. Oxygen is

A common seal swimming under water. Seals can stay submerged for more than 30 minutes

carried in the bloodstream and a seal has an ample supply of oxygen because it has half as much blood again as a land animal of similar size. Its muscles contain a chemical compound which assists the storage of oxygen and it can tolerate more carbon dioxide in the blood than other creatures. Its thick layer of blubber protects it from cold seas.

Seals have always been hunted for their skins and the oil their blubber produces, and by the turn of this century grey seals were in danger of becoming extinct. But after laws protecting them were passed in 1914 and 1932, their numbers increased rapidly. The Farne Island colony, which has existed since at least the 12th century, grew from about 100 seals and today produces more than 1700 pups a year. Britain's present grey seal breeding population of more than 35,000 represents well over 60 per cent of the world's population.

As the seal population grew so did the complaints of salmon fishermen who claimed that seals were reducing the number of salmon and also damaging their nets. The close season — September 1 to December 31 — was lifted for killing seals in those areas where complaints were held to be justified.

Usually it was the pups that were killed, and to preserve their fur they were clubbed to death, which brought forth public protests; now they are usually shot. Culling, the legal killing of the surplus population, may be in the interests of the species to some extent in preventing the rookeries becoming overcrowded and insanitary.

Sea lace see Seaweed

Sea lavender

A seaside flower with rosettes of simple, bright green leaves and branched heads of blue flowers, sea lavender is valued by flower arrangers for winter decoration. Although it blooms only from July to October and the petals soon wither, its colour persists for many months.

Growing 3-12 in. high, it is found in muddy salt marshes all round the coasts of England, Wales and southern Scotland. In Irish salt marshes it is replaced by the lax-flowered sea lavender.

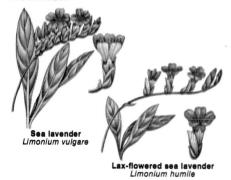

Sea lavender
Limonium vulgare

Lax-flowered sea lavender
Limonium humile

Lax-flowered sea lavender grows only in Ireland; the other species is confined to Britain

Sea lemon see Sea slug
Sea lettuce see Seaweed
Sea mat see Moss animals

Sea milkwort *Glaux maritima*

A plant of salt marshes and damp grassland near the sea all round the British Isles, sea milkwort is also found occasionally where salt occurs inland, as in certain parts of Cheshire.

Its flowers, which appear from June to August, have no petals. But the bell-shaped calyx is divided into five pink, petal-like segments. The creeping stems are densely covered with oblong fleshy leaves which are pale underneath and have a salty taste.

Sea mouse *Aphrodite aculeata*

A scaly backed worm which lives in muddy sand below the low-tide mark and is sometimes found washed up on the shore after a storm. It has 15 pairs of grey-brown, hair-covered scales, flanked with iridescent green and gold hairs and dark brown spines. It is 3-7 in. long and 1-2 in. wide and is vaguely mouse-like in appearance.

The sea mouse feeds on minute particles of animal matter in the sand. In autumn the female lays eggs which the male fertilises in the surrounding sea water. These later hatch into planktonic larvae.

Sea mouse
Aphrodite aculeata

The sea mouse is in fact a worm, named after its plump, hair-fringed body

Sea purslane *Halimione portulacoides*

Halimione is Greek for 'daughter of the sea' — an apt name, for this salt-marsh species is covered by most high tides. Sea purslane is much-branched and usually about 1-2 ft high. It occurs in great abundance, especially along the edges of muddy creeks. Its creeping stems root in mud and the whole plant is covered in a grey meal or flour.

Sea purslane is common around the coasts of England and Wales and on the south and east coasts of Ireland, but reaches only the south-west of Scotland. Its minute green flowers appear in clusters at the end of branches from July to September.

Sea scorpion *Taurulus bubalis*

An abundant fish in shore pools and inshore waters around the British Isles, except the southern North Sea. It lives chiefly among

seaweed where it is camouflaged by its colouring. It is up to 7 in. long. Young, red-brown fish, about 1 in. long, find cover among the red seaweed common in higher shore pools; older, green and brown fish live among seaweed of their colour. The dangerous-looking spines on the head and gill covers are harmless.

The sea scorpion feeds on a wide variety of crustaceans and fish, darting out at them from its seaweed cover. It breeds in early spring, and eggs are laid in small clumps offshore, in rock crevices and under rocks. The young sea scorpions swim to shore in late summer.

The sea scorpion is harmless in spite of the vicious-looking spines to which it owes its name

Seashore

Britain and her off-shore islands (not including Ireland) have 6000 miles of coastline — much of it providing a haven for wildlife.

The seashore is a harsh world, more subject to extremes than any other natural environment. The plants and animals that live there are dependent on sea water for survival, but at varying intervals the sea retreats and leaves them exposed to the drying heat of the summer sun or to the freezing temperatures of mid-winter.

This rugged environment varies greatly from one part of the country to another. The coastline itself ranges from sheer cliffs to gently sloping sands or mudflats. Tides vary enormously in height, from 30 ft and more in the Bristol Channel to only a few feet in almost land-bound Scottish lochs. And at low tide the shoreline in different parts of Britain is exposed to a multitude of different conditions — the east coast is swept by icy winter winds; the west coast is pounded by the Atlantic rollers; while the river valleys of Cornwall and Milford Haven offer warm shelter.

This turbulent and constantly changing world has, nevertheless, an abundant supply of all the basic requirements of life — light, water, oxygen and minerals — and supports a large number of plant and animal species. The pulse of their lives beats to a tidal rhythm.

The tide ebbs and flows twice every day, and once a fortnight there are high-ranging spring tides whose high and low points dictate the boundaries of the shore line. In alternate fortnights there are the neap tides which have the smallest range between high and low-water marks.

Britain's coasts, varied as they are, can be divided into two main types — rocky shores and sandy beaches. Both types support great quantities of wildlife, ranged in horizontal bands, according to the length of time the land is left exposed by the ebb tide.

On rocky shores, the uppermost layer is the splash zone—actually beyond the reach of the highest spring tides but kept damp by salt spray. In this zone live lichens and some insects more usually found inland. A few marine animals such as sea slaters and sandhoppers live in deep crevices by day and emerge at night to forage for food.

At the highest water mark begin the rock pools, which can be found right down the shore. Rock pools provide a more constant environment for both plants and animals.

In the highest strip of shore is the small winkle, and slightly lower down it is followed by the rough winkle. Both feed on minute algae on the rocks. Lower down the shore, near the level of average high tides, acorn barnacles cling to rough-textured rocks.

All plants and animals below high water of neap tides are covered by the sea twice every day. At this level, the seaweed bladder wrack begins to grow. The first limpets are found in this zone.

The rock pools of these lower zones contain such animals as prawns and snakelocks anemones which cannot survive long out of the sea.

Several predators are to be found in shady crevices, where they are kept moist during low tide. These animals include beadlet anemones, shore crabs, and those which prey on barnacles such as the shanny and dog

An apparently lifeless beach at Shipload Bay, north Devon—but a variety of shore animals may be under

whelk. Grazers, such as the topshells, and filter-feeders, such as the common mussel, may also be found.

Below the lowest neap-tide mark, many different species live, including large acorn barnacles, calcareous tube worms, honeycomb worms and a variety of snails and shellfish. There is a broad zone of serrated wrack and the first of the red algae begin to grow.

Lower down and exposed only at the lowest spring tides are the brown oarweeds.

The other main type of coast, the shingle and sandy beaches, are hostile environments to plants and animals because wave action constantly grinds the pebbles and sand together. But where the mud and organic content of the sand builds up, many creatures live beneath the surface.

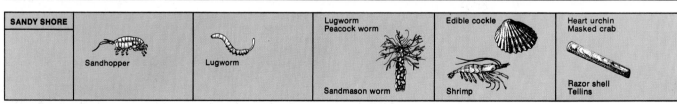

ROCKY SHORE	Splash zone	Upper shore	Mid shore	Lower shore	Sub-littoral zone
Animals on seaweeds	Sea slater		Flat-topped winkle Hydroid Sea mat	Flat-topped winkle Sea mat Snail Star sea squirt Tubeworm	Blue-rayed limpet Edible sea urchin
Seaweeds and lichens	Black lichen Orange lichen	Channelled wrack	Bladderwrack Knotted wrack	Irish moss Serrated wrack	Furbelows Oar weed
Animals on rocks	Small winkle	Barnacle Limpet Rough winkle Shore crab	Beadlet sea anemone Dog whelk Green sea urchin Keel worm Mussel	Blenny Breadcrumb sponge Dahlia sea anemone Edible winkle Painted-top shell Star sea squirt	Ballan wrasse Edible crab Lobster Octopus Ormer shell Plumose sea anemone Starfish

SANDY SHORE					
	Sandhopper	Lugworm	Lugworm Peacock worm Sandmason worm	Edible cockle Shrimp	Heart urchin Masked crab Razor shell Tellins

The variety of life on the seashore depends on the structure of the shore—whether sandy or rocky—and the amount of water present. Plants and animals in the splash zone spend most of the time out of water, while those of the sub-littoral zone are rarely exposed to the air. Animals are easily seen on rocky shores, where they cling to rock surfaces, but those on sandy shores are usually burrowers and live beneath the surface

stones, and worms and shellfish under the sand

They are zoned just like the creatures of rocky shores, but less conspicuously, as they live in the sand. At the top of the beach as the tide comes in, air bubbles mark the burrows of various types of sandhopper which scavenge for their food. A little lower on the beach, the surface is covered with the casts and hollows of lugworm burrows. Ragworms and catworms also inhabit this zone.

Below the level of neap tides, the variety of animals increases. Razor-shell burrows are marked by keyhole depressions. Cockles, clams, parchment worms, masked crabs, peacock worms, each with their individual methods of feeding, inhabit this belt. Other creatures which may be found are sea cucumbers, bootlace worms, tellin shells and heart urchins.

The struggle for survival goes on even under the sand. The carnivorous necklace shell preys on shellfish, especially banded wedge shells, by producing an acid to eat into their shells. Other predators include burrowing anemones, shore crabs, sand eels, sand gobies, dabs and flounders.

When the tide is high, shoals of large fish visit the shore over all types of coast and, as it ebbs, their place is taken by gulls, waders and herons. Many of these birds nest close to the shore; gulls on cliffs and waders on shingle or sand dunes. Birds which feed at high tide include cormorants and terns. See also ROCK POOL

Sea slater *Ligia oceanica*
Sometimes known as quarry-lice, sea slaters are related to woodlice, which they resemble. They are grey-green with pale markings, but can change colour to blend with their surroundings. At night they become paler as their pigment cells contract. They have two antennae and black eyes and are about 1 in. long. They live high on the shore, all

around the British Isles, in seaweed and under stones, and they scavenge for minute particles of animal matter. By day, they usually hide, from the gulls and crabs which prey on them. Sea slaters are active animals and can run at about 1 mph. After mating, the female carries her eggs in a pouch.

The sea slater can run very fast—about 1 mph— and is particularly active during the night

Sea slug
The sea lemon and the common grey sea slugs are the two most common around Britain. They live under stones on rocky shores and, like all sea slugs, they are molluscs without any trace of shell.

The 2-3 in. long sea lemon *Archidoris pseudoargus* has a pair of tentacles at its head end and nine gills at the end of its body. It is usually yellow with green, pink or brown blotches. The adults feed on the sponge *Halichondria panicea*. In spring, these bisexual animals pair and each lays a coiled white egg ribbon, an inch wide and several inches long. The eggs hatch into tiny larvae which, after a few weeks, settle and change into the adult form.

The common grey sea slug *Aeolidia papillosa* feeds on sea anemones, browsing on the

The sea slug *Eubranchus farrani* feeding on a sea fir of the genus *Obelia*

tentacles without triggering off the anemone's stinging cells.

Sea slugs are difficult to find as they are often camouflaged. *Rostanga·rufescens*, which is about ½ in. long, is bright red with black spots and feeds on red sponges, while the orange *Tritonia plebia* crawls over orange sea fans.

Sea snail
A soft, plump, jelly-like fish, up to 2 in. long, sometimes pink, sometimes drably coloured. The fin rays are enveloped in a thick skin and are barely distinguishable.

The sea snail is difficult to find, for it conceals itself in the crevices or on the undersides of rocks, to which it firmly attaches itself with a sucker situated on the belly, just behind the head. It feeds on a wide variety of small crustaceans. Breeding takes place in early summer. Eggs are laid in clumps among weeds.

Only Montagu's sea snail *Liparis montagui* —named after the naturalist, George Montagu—is usually found on British shores.

Seasons see p. 406

Sea spider
A sea animal so named because of its eight legs. It is found all around the coastline. There is no room in the small body—no more than ⅛ in. long in most of the 18 British species—for the gut, which extends into the upper part of the legs. Sea spiders feed chiefly on sea firs and sea anemones, to which they attach themselves, with apparent immunity to their stinging cells. They themselves are eaten by a variety of fish.

The largest British species is *Pycnogonum littorale*, a knobbly, dirty yellow-grey animal, up to ¾ in. long, with stubby legs. It clamps itself on to the column of a dahlia sea anemone or under a stone.

The female emits eggs from her legs; the male then fertilises these and attaches them with a cement to a pair of smaller legs he possesses in addition to the normal eight. He then broods them until they hatch.

The sea spider may be found under stones, on sea anemones or among flotsam

Sea squirt
A sedentary bag-like animal with two siphons. It generally lives on shells, seaweed and boulders on the lower shore. Water is drawn in through one siphon and pumped through a delicate sieve-like structure which

extracts food – plankton – and oxygen from it. The water is then pumped out of the other siphon. There are about 60 British species, distributed all around the coastline.

Sea squirts are hermaphrodites, which cross-fertilise one another. Eggs and sperm are deposited in the sea and the fertilised eggs hatch into tadpole-shaped larvae, which later develop into small sea squirts.

A common British sea squirt is *Ciona intestinalis*, a soft, transparent animal up to 7 in. long with yellow-fringed siphons. It lives on floating buoys, harbour installations and boulders.

Star sea squirt *Botryllus schlosseri* is a colonial species – several individual animals, $\frac{1}{8}$ in. long, clustered together in a star pattern beneath a jelly-like covering and sharing a common exhaling siphon. The whole colony, containing several clusters of individuals, forms an orange, yellow, blue or white patch, about 6 in. or more across, on wracks and seaweeds on or below the shore. The individual species are preyed on by starfish and fish, the colonial species by cowries.

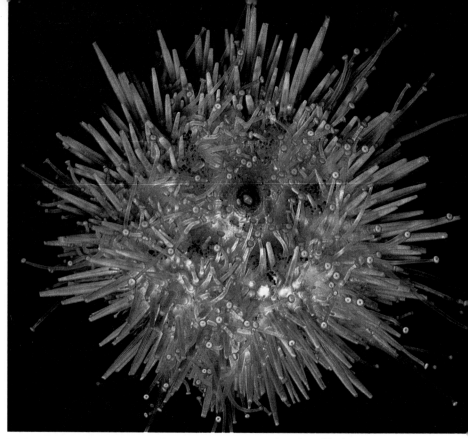

The spiny undersurface and mouth of a sea urchin, enlarged to three times life size

Star sea squirts live in colonies, spreading over rock surfaces in a jelly-like mass

Sea urchin

A group of sea animals in the same group as the echinoderms, starfish, brittle stars, feather stars and sea cucumbers. Like these animals, sea urchins have a beautiful, five-rayed symmetry.

Sea urchins are globular animals with a brittle chalky skeleton (or test) covered with movable spines attached by ball-and-socket joints. On the inside of the test is the gut, which spirals up from the mouth on the underside to the anus on top, and the five pairs of gonads (sex glands).

The gonads of the common sea urchin *Echinus esculentus* are edible, and the cleaned tests are sold as ornaments. Sea urchins are up to 4 in. high and 6 in. across, and are tinted purple and red. Urchins usually live below low-water mark.

They are vegetarians, feeding on seaweed, which they eat by using the five teeth projecting through the centre of the underside. The teeth are manipulated by an elaborate skeletal structure called Aristotle's lantern.

Urchins move slowly on their spines and on their suckered feet. These feet enable them to walk up vertical rock faces, and are linked to the main body tissues through small holes in the shell.

A greenish sea urchin *Psammechinus militaris*, which is up to 2 in. across, lives under stones on the lower shore. Its purple-tipped spines are often camouflaged with pieces of seaweed or shell.

The longer-spined, dark purple *Paracentrotus lividus* is 2 in. across, and is familiar in the Mediterranean. It is also common in Ireland and is found in Devon and Cornwall. The test is greenish and the spines purple. Large numbers of this species are often found below low-water mark, and also on the lower shore.

In sea urchins the sexes are separate and the eggs, which are fertilised externally, develop into a planktonic larval stage called *Echinopluteus*. The small urchin settles, when half-formed, upon the sea bottom. See also HEART URCHIN

Seaweed

All seaweeds are algae. They grow along shores that are sheltered and rocky, and round the coasts of Britain they can be found to a depth of 100 ft in clear water. They are not found below that depth or in unclear water because light is essential for their growth.

Valuable as a manure and a foodstuff, seaweed is collected from beaches for use on coastal farms. It is spread on the ground and ploughed in to enrich the soil with potash and nitrogen.

Seaweeds are divided into four main groups, based on colour. These are the blue-greens, greens, browns and the reds. This division is not always obvious, as some reds take on a brownish hue and some browns appear as olive-green. Moreover, decaying seaweed, or that which has been torn by storms, often turns orange. All seaweeds, whatever their colour when alive, eventually fade and bleach white when dead.

The blue-greens, which are believed to have existed in their present form more than 600 million years ago, are rare compared with the other groups.

Two of the most common green seaweeds are *Enteromorpha*, which has paper-thin green straps and is often seen in pools high on the shore, and sea lettuce, which has flat, blade-like fronds about 12 in. long. Both

Common seaweeds of British shores

A selection from the 800 species of seaweeds to be found in Britain. The simplest guide to identifying them is colour, which forms four groups: the blue-greens, greens, browns and reds. Generally speaking, most seaweeds will be found growing on other seaweeds, rocks or shells — the smallest on sandy beaches or shingle where the waves inhibit growth.

Small fronds may be collected and mounted, although they must be cut with care to avoid disturbing surrounding plants and animals. Samples can be carried in water in polythene bags, and then floated on to cartridge paper in a tray. To mount them, put them between sheets of muslin and blotting paper, and dry under a light weight

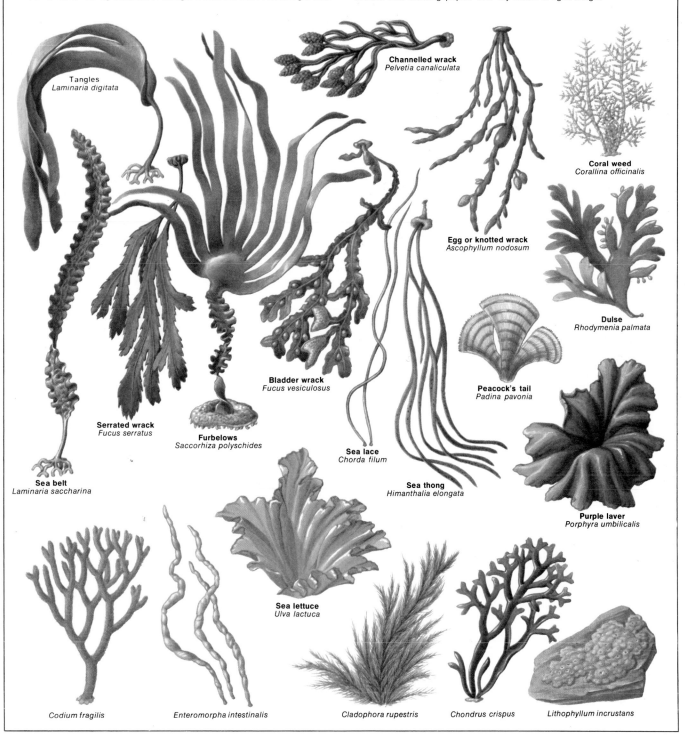

Tangles
Laminaria digitata

Channelled wrack
Pelvetia canaliculata

Coral weed
Corallina officinalis

Egg or knotted wrack
Ascophyllum nodosum

Dulse
Rhodymenia palmata

Serrated wrack
Fucus serratus

Bladder wrack
Fucus vesiculosus

Furbelows
Saccorhiza polyschides

Sea lace
Chorda filum

Peacock's tail
Padina pavonia

Sea belt
Laminaria saccharina

Sea thong
Himanthalia elongata

Purple laver
Porphyra umbilicalis

Sea lettuce
Ulva lactuca

Codium fragilis

Enteromorpha intestinalis

Cladophora rupestris

Chondrus crispus

Lithophyllum incrustans

thrive in areas washed by freshwater outflows and form slippery carpets. The dark green, velvety, finely tufted *Cladophora* grows under larger brown seaweeds on rocks close to the shore.

The most conspicuous seaweeds on rocky shores are the browns. Channelled wrack may be found at the top of the shore. It turns black and becomes brittle when not washed by the tide for several days. Egg or knotted wrack grows lower down the shore. This is the longest-lived British brown seaweed and continues to grow for up to 13 years. Its approximate age may be calculated by counting the large single air bladders—one for each year—which lift the weed clear of rocks when the tide comes in. Further down the shore is bladder wrack, which has smaller, paired bladders—although it may grow higher on exposed shores.

Other brown seaweeds are revealed at low water during spring tides, particularly giant kelps. These are more commonly known as oarweeds, and form dense underwater forests. The four common species of oarweeds can be identified by examining the shape of the blade, the stalk and the holdfast which attaches the weed to the rock. Tangles has a smooth, slightly flattened stalk and a strap-like blade slit into several sections. Cuvie has a stalk that is often covered with sponges, sea squirts and small red algae. Sea belt has a long single blade with wavy margins. Furbelows, an annual which grows in deep water, has a large, hollow holdfast which often gets washed on to the shore.

Some animals gain protection inside the branching base of oarweed holdfast. These include various small crabs, scale worms, brittle stars and young mussels. Sedentary animals encrust the outside of the holdfast and sometimes the stalk. Among them are hydroids, sea mats, sponges, sea squirts and tube worms.

In gulleys which retain sea water at low tide there can be found two other brown seaweeds. These are sea thong, which has 2 ft long olive-brown fronds and, in the summer only, mermaid's tresses or sea lace, which has olive-brown cord-like fronds 10-20 ft long. Another small brown seaweed is the spherical oyster thief, which grows to the size of a tennis ball and, when filled with air at low tide, acts as a small buoyancy tank capable of lifting any small object to which it is attached, including oysters, off the sea bottom.

Red seaweeds are generally smaller than the browns. Carragheen or Irish moss grows on rocks and in pools, and when under water it has a bluish iridescence. It contains a gelatinous substance which can be used to set jellies. Purple laver grows in thin sheets in winter, and in parts of South Wales and Ireland is made into laver bread by boiling until tender.

Some seaweeds, including sea lettuce, reproduce vegetatively through bits breaking off and developing into new plants. Others, such as dulse, produce new plants by putting out runners. Most seaweeds also reproduce sexually by the fusion of male and female cells. The cells are produced by male and female organs, which may occur on a single plant, or on separate plants. See also ALGAE

Serrated wrack, which has toothed fronds, is a brown seaweed of the lower shore

Sedges

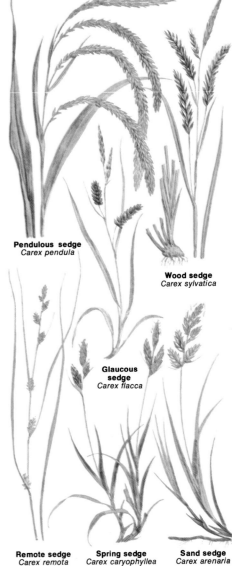

Pendulous sedge
Carex pendula

Wood sedge
Carex sylvatica

Glaucous sedge
Carex flacca

Remote sedge
Carex remota

Spring sedge
Carex caryophyllea

Sand sedge
Carex arenaria

Sedges are grass-like plants, most of which grow in bogs and marshland. About 80 species occur in the British Isles

Sedge

About 80 species of this grass-like plant grow in the British Isles. With narrow leaves and triangular stems, they range in height from a few inches to 5 ft. Their spikes of greenish flowers are like those of grass, although they have separate male and female flowers which, with one exception, are both on one plant.

Most species grow in bogs and marshes but several types are widespread in other locations. Sand sedge, for example, is common on most coastal sand dunes and is sometimes found on loose sand inland. It has long underground stems which help it to maintain a firm footing in sand. These stems often grow in straight lines, putting up tufts of leaves a few inches apart.

Two species are common on chalk downs and limestone hills. Spring sedge, which has dark green leaves, produces spikes of male flowers with yellow anthers in April; and glaucous sedge, which has blue waxy leaves and flowers in May and June.

In woodlands there are three common species. Largest is the pendulous sedge, with leaves almost 1 in. wide, tall stems 3-5 ft high and long drooping female spikes. It is often grown in gardens. Smallest is the remote sedge, which has tiny, well-separated spikes almost hidden at the base of its narrow, bright green leaves. The most common species is wood sedge, which also has bright green but wider leaves, and conspicuous pendulous spikes. It flowers during May and June and is common in deciduous woodlands, except in the north of Scotland.

In most British species, the upper spike and perhaps a few below it are male and the rest female. A few species have male and female flowers on the same spike. Each flower is protected by a small leaf-like sheath. Male flowers consist of only two or three stamens but the female stigma is surrounded by a small, often inflated, sac, crowned by a beak from which the stigma projects. The sac later encloses ripe seed.

Sedgefly see Caddisfly

Seed

Flowering plants produce seeds as a result of sexual union between male and female elements, which may be present in the same plant or in separate plants. The female organ, or ovary, which lies at the heart of the flower, contains one or more ovules. These ovules develop into seeds when they are fertilised by the male element—pollen—which is produced in the flower by organs called stamens. Once fertilised, the ovules cause the ovary to swell, forming a fruit, inside which the seed or seeds ripen.

Every seed contains within itself a set of genetic instructions—a 'blueprint' for a new plant which, in turn, will produce seeds of its own. To ensure the growth of the plant each seed contains a supply of food—largely starch and protein. The hard dry coat of the seed helps to protect it during the winter months, until the warm weather initiates growth.

Ripe seeds vary in size from the powder-like seeds of orchids to the conkers of horse-chestnut trees. All plants produce more seeds than survive. In some cases, thousands of seeds are lost for every one that takes root under the right conditions in the right kind of soil. But while the survival of an individual seed is largely a matter of blind chance, plants have evolved methods of seed-dispersal which, combined with the vast numbers of seeds involved, make the laws of chance work in favour of the survival of the species.

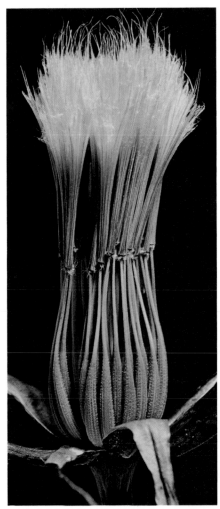

The long, silky 'parachute' hairs of goatsbeard help the wind to spread its seeds

Small seeds, such as those of the orchid, can be carried several hundred miles by the wind. Some larger seeds, such as those of the poppy, are produced in capsules at the top of long stalks and spread for several yards when the stalks are shaken in the wind.

Many seeds, such as those of willows and willow-herbs, can travel for miles because they are carried on a tuft of hairs which forms a kind of parachute. Dandelion and goatsbeard have similar dispersal devices. Seeds with parachutes can be carried 100 miles or more.

Broad-leaved trees produce the largest seeds, but the seedlings which develop from them will not grow to maturity in the shade of their parents, and many types are winged to ensure that they land some distance from the parent tree. Examples are ash, sycamore and elm seeds. Other trees, such as the oak and the chestnut, produce nuts which animals carry away to store or eat. Many of these are either dropped or forgotten, and so the seed is dispersed.

Seeds inside berries and edible fruits such as cherries and blackberries are also spread by animals which eat the fruit and pass the seeds in their droppings. Hooked seeds, or burrs—such as those of cleavers, wild carrot, avens, agrimony and burdock—spread by catching on the fur or feathers of animals or birds and later dropping off.

Other plants have developed explosive pods which shoot the seeds away from the plant when the ripe pod is touched. The most spectacular is Himalayan balsam, which shoots its seed several feet. The pods of vetch and gorse and other members of the pea family split explosively into two parts and also shoot their seeds some distance. Herb Robert and the cranesbills produce five one-seeded lobes around a long, central beak. When the seeds are ripe the outside of each lobe springs up, along with a strip from the beak, and the seeds are flung out.

Seeds of some water plants are carried long distances by streams or currents in the sea. The seeds of white water lily have a spongy covering and float until saturated, then sink to the bottom. Sea rocket has a floating seed capsule which can withstand up to six weeks in sea water.

SEED DISPERSAL MECHANISMS

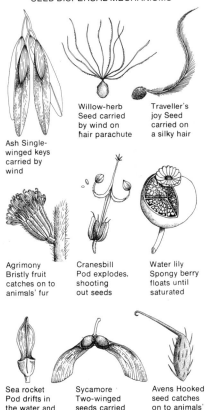

Ash Single-winged keys carried by wind

Willow-herb Seed carried by wind on hair parachute

Traveller's joy Seed carried on a silky hair

Agrimony Bristly fruit catches on to animals' fur

Cranesbill Pod explodes, shooting out seeds

Water lily Spongy berry floats until saturated

Sea rocket Pod drifts in the water and breaks in two

Sycamore Two-winged seeds carried by the wind

Avens Hooked seed catches on to animals' fur

The end result of these varied methods of seed distribution is that the young plants do not grow in the shade of the adults or become overcrowded, but colonise new ground

The seasons, a rhythm created by the sun

As the earth makes its annual orbit of the sun, it spins on an axis that is tilted in relation to the sun. It is to this tilt that we owe the miracle of the changing seasons, for at different times of the year different parts of the earth are tilted towards the sun so that it appears to be directly overhead. At such times, these areas take the sun's rays with full force, at right angles; but other parts of the earth and of its protecting atmosphere curve away from the sun, so that the rays are first of all weakened by having to pass for a greater distance through the atmosphere, and then further weakened by being spread over a greater area of the earth.

In June, when the sun is 'overhead' at the Tropic of Cancer, Britain is tilted as close to the sun as it ever gets. In December, when the sun is above the Tropic of Capricorn, these islands tilt furthest away from the sun; the sun is low on the horizon, the days are short and such sunshine as we get is weak and diffused. The effect of these seasonal changes is tempered by the proximity of the Atlantic Ocean, from which blow the warm westerly and south-westerly winds that make our winters so mild and the sea winds that cool the land in summer.

Traditionally, there are four seasons, but modern climatologists divide Britain's year into five. The dates given are approximate only.

High summer lasts from June 18 until September 9. The

January – beyond the hedge winter wheat springs up

February – spring barley sown in foreground field

March – snow covers the tender young crops

July – haymaking in the meadows

August – wheat and barley are golden ripe

September – the harvest is just in

weather is generally warm, with bright and rainy days alternating; this helps to keep the countryside green.

Autumn extends from September 10 until November 19. Long spells of warm and mainly calm weather, often accompanied by mist, characterise this season in southern England. The end of October and early November are sometimes stormy, with heavy rains which saturate the soil. Occasionally there are spells of particularly fine weather around October 18 (St Luke's summer) and November 11 (St Martin's summer).

Early winter is reckoned from November 20 until January 19. It is characterised by strong, westerly winds and later by night frosts. Snow sometimes falls as early as late November.

Late winter and early spring extend from January 20 until March 31. Severe conditions, including icy easterly winds, are common, but there are also periods of warmer, westerly weather. In recent years bad weather has tended to last until late March or early April, bringing cold Easters. Nevertheless, there is less rainfall than in the previous period and this, with the increasing evaporation, causes soils to begin drying out.

Spring and early summer last from April 1 until June 17. The early part of this period is changeable. Cold nights alternate with warm, sunny days that bear the promise of high summer. May and early June are among the driest periods of the year in southern England but are often wet in Scotland.

In the British countryside the changing face of the farmland indicates the passing of the months just as surely as the changes in animal and plant life. This series of pictures of Park Farm, Great Brickhill, Buckinghamshire, shows the ever-changing pattern of arable fields throughout the year, as crops push through the ground, ripen, reach maturity and are eventually harvested to be replaced by others. The pattern is modified in some years by very mild winters, which bring forward sowing, and bad summers, which delay harvesting

April — growth gets well under way

May — the far meadows are lush with new grass

June — ears of corn begin to appear, trees are in full leaf

October — foreground field ploughed for a new crop

November — beneath the fine tilth newly sown winter wheat

December — in the damp and cold new wheat emerges

The yearly miracle of life renewed

All life responds to the changing rhythm of the seasons. Summer, following the prelude of spring, brings growth and regeneration to plants and animals alike. Autumn is a time when the living world prepares to endure the grip of winter

Plants and animals of the temperate zones have evolved many complicated mechanisms which adjust their lives to the changing seasons—from the short and frequently frozen days when the Northern Hemisphere is tilted away from the sun, to the warm, 17-hour days of summer. The human impression of seasonal change comes not only from awareness of the length and warmth of the day, but also from the way in which plants show evidence of the time of year.

Until man began clearing the forests 5000 years ago the natural vegetation of much of the British Isles was a blanket of broad-leaved deciduous trees—mostly oak, but with beech in some southern areas. Today, large tracts of the countryside have been reafforested by the Government and by private landowners. Conifers are usually planted because of their rapid growth potential, but they are not the type of vegetation that our seasonal climate would naturally produce.

The broad, thin leaves of a deciduous tree give a large surface area over which the sun's rays can be brought in contact with carbon dioxide and water for the efficient synthesis of food. But the broad leaf also allows a lot of water to be lost by evaporation. This does not matter when water is freely available in the soil, but evaporation on a clear winter's day when the ground is frozen would mean that the plant was losing water faster than it could be replaced. And, on particularly cold days, the leaves would be liable to direct damage from frost. Many trees and shrubs overcome this problem by shedding all their foliage in winter. Smaller, non-woody plants may lose all their above-ground growth and survive the winter as subterranean bulbs or tubers. Some plants leave no vegetative structure at all, and persist through the cold months only as seeds. Evergreen conifers, with their thick-skinned needle-shaped leaves which last throughout the year, are less efficient at using the sun's energy to manufacture food but are better at conserving moisture. Although conifers virtually cease growth in mid-winter, their leaves allow them a longer growing season than would otherwise be possible.

In spring, as the earth's orbit brings the Northern Hemisphere closer to the sun again, the days increase in length and warmth, and conditions become more favourable for plant growth. Seeds that have remained dormant germinate, and thrust fresh, green shoots above the ground. Bulbs and tubers sprout, and buds break open on the broad-leaved trees. Some plants steal a march on their fellows by flowering before winter is fully spent. By adapting to the colder conditions of early spring they avoid the fierce competition for space, light and insect pollinators that increases as the year progresses. Coltsfoot and lesser celandine are typical examples. In early spring, plants must exploit their winter store of food to pro-duce fresh growth. By summer their growth is based on their current production and they are also building reserves for the great activities of flowering and fruiting.

As the days shorten and cool into autumn, plant growth slows. Most leaves and shoots are mature and dark green. Flowering is coming to an end, but there is an abundance of fruits, the seeds of which will germinate the following spring. As autumn progresses, the green leaves of deciduous plants turn to gold, brown and red. This is because chlorophyll is being broken down, and the resultant products are being carried away to the storage areas. The loss of green chlorophyll reveals previously masked yellow pigments. Red colours are sugars resulting from the breakdown of leaf starches. With much of its useful material removed the leaf dies, turns brown and falls from the plant. The fall of the leaf is brought about by the production of a layer of soft-walled cells at the base of the stalk, so that it is readily detached from the plant by the wind. At the end of the fall, trees are bare to face the winter cold. The cycle is complete.

Experiments have shown that plants detect changes in day length, and that this triggers the various phases of the annual cycle—budding, flowering, fruiting and leaf-fall. Temperature changes also play a part in modifying the cycle in different plants.

Animals, too, are profoundly influenced by the changing seasons. Protective structures or behaviour may be needed to survive the cold, but winter adaptations such as a thicker coat may be a grave disadvantage in the height of summer. But it is the changes in vegetation that have the most fundamental impact on the animal world, because all animal food comes ultimately from plants. Seasonal vegetation changes mean differences in food supply, and in the shelter afforded by plants. Animals also detect changes in day length, and their bodies adjust to the yearly cycle.

Summer vegetation can support a great number and diversity of animals. They feed on buds and leaves, flowers, fruit, sap, wood, roots, dead plants—and on one another. The barn owl catches the shrew, that ate the spider, that caught the moth, whose caterpillar ate the leaves of the oak tree. Abundant food supplies favour breeding, many species producing more than one brood in the course of the summer. The most favourable time for young animals to appear is in spring or early summer. Then they will be growing through a time of abundant food supplies, in the form of plants, insects and other animals.

In animals, changing day length brings the reproductive organs of both sexes to a state of readiness. As a secondary effect of their reproductive condition there is a seasonal change in the physical appearance of many animals. Male deer have an annual cycle of antler growth; many male birds exhibit colourful plumage; while male newts and sticklebacks assume gaudy hues.

Summer is the season when the living community functions at its fullest pitch. Spring and autumn are transition periods, while in winter the life of the countryside is at its lowest ebb.

Many birds—especially those which rely on flying insects for their food—escape this period by migration, while those that remain often shift their habitat. For other species—those that breed in the Arctic or Siberia—Britain's winters are mild compared with those they leave behind, and they become winter visitors to these islands. The insects that form the diet of birds in summer pass the winter as pupae—like many moths and butterflies—or as larvae, underground or in water. Aphids survive the winter as eggs: annual plants as seeds. Many adult insects assume a state of suspended animation, or at least reduced activity. Bees stay in the nest and consume honey stores. Snails seek shelter, often with their fellows, and seal their shells with mucus until spring. Frogs and newts rest in the soft mud on the bottom of ponds, while toads, lizards and snakes burrow into the soil. Bats, which also eat flying insects, hibernate through the winter, their pulse rate and temperature dropping sharply as they hang in the shelter of caves or buildings. Dormice and hedgehogs hibernate in self-built nests. Squirrels become less active and subsidise their foraging

with food stored during the rest of the year. Winter is a time of widespread animal death. The primary cause is shortage of food, without which disease and low temperatures are difficult to resist. Most small mammals—mice, voles and shrews—live only a year, but their young survive to breed the following spring.

Many mammals moult at the end of the summer and grow a thicker, warmer coat for the winter. In the northern part of their range, where snow may lie for long periods, stoats, weasels and blue hares have evolved a form of winter camouflage—they moult to a winter coat of white. Similarly, the ptarmigan moults to a white plumage.

THE CHANGING PATTERN OF LIFE THROUGHOUT THE YEAR

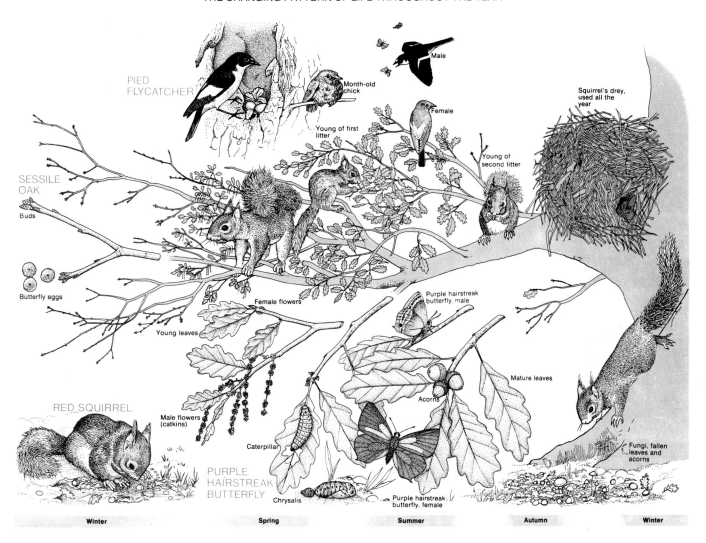

PIED FLYCATCHER · Month-old chick · Male · Female · Young of first litter · Young of second litter · Squirrel's drey, used all the year · SESSILE OAK · Buds · Butterfly eggs · Female flowers · Young leaves · Purple hairstreak butterfly, male · Mature leaves · Acorns · RED SQUIRREL · Male flowers (catkins) · Caterpillar · PURPLE HAIRSTREAK BUTTERFLY · Chrysalis · Purple hairstreak butterfly, female · Fungi, fallen leaves and acorns

Winter · Spring · Summer · Autumn · Winter

The varying seasons govern all plant life and subsequently animal life. The animals living among the branches of the sessile oak have active and inactive times that are in tune with the growth and rest periods of the tree. Most young animals are born during the spring when the days are getting warmer and food more plentiful, so that by the autumn they are strong enough to endure the harsher months ahead. The purple hairstreak butterfly passes the winter in the egg stage, the caterpillars hatching out in the spring when there are young oak leaves for them to eat. In April the pied flycatcher, a migratory bird, arrives from the African savanna to rear a family. It feeds on the many

insects in the air, including the hairstreak butterfly, but when the insect population dwindles in the autumn the flycatcher migrates back to Africa. The warm-blooded red squirrel is one animal that is active all the year round, eating whatever is available. Oak catkins, young leaves and caterpillars, such as those of the hairstreak, are food for the first, spring litter. Ripening acorns are eaten by the second, summer litter. In the autumn the squirrel stores acorns to supplement its winter diet of fungi now growing among the fallen oak leaves. Winter is the least active time for the squirrel, and its conspicuous drey in the bare oak branches is a warm retreat

Selfheal *Prunella vulgaris*

Early botanists believed this herb provided a cure for sore throats and named it Prunella, the old medical term for that infection. However, this property has never been proved.

One of the most common grassland plants throughout the British Isles, it grows up to 12 in. high and spreads by short underground shoots. It is recognised easily by its square, upright stems which appear in June, bearing a dense spiked head of deep purple flowers, with a pair of stalked leaves at the base.

Sewage

Originally disposed of in cesspits and waterways, and even directly on to the land as fertiliser, sewage was the cause of so many epidemics of cholera and typhoid that Tudor monarchs tried to introduce regulations for its disposal. The Public Health Act of 1875 introduced modern sewer construction.

There are sewage plants outside most large towns. In these the sewage is first screened to remove the grosser solids, then filtered to remove further impurities. The solids removed by the first process are either emptied into the sea or further treated to provide fertiliser.

Shad

An estuary fish which enters fresh water only to spawn in spring. A close relative of the herring, it is the same colour—silver, with a green-blue back—but the head and mouth are proportionately larger. It is up to 2 ft long. Two species live in British waters. The twaite shad *Alosa fallax* is the more common and is distinguished by a line of dark blotches along its sides. The allis shad *A. alosa* has only a single dusky spot on the gill covers. Both are edible.

Shads have suffered badly from pollution and obstructions like weirs, which hinder their progress upstream. The Thames, once famous for its shad fishing, is now almost empty of them. Some of Britain's cleaner rivers, such as the Severn and Shannon, still have shad runs—upstream migrations of adults in May to spawn; hence their local name, may-fish. After spawning, the adults return to the estuary.

Lake Killarney in Ireland is inhabited by a land-locked race of twaite shad, which, at 9 in. long, is smaller than the migratory form. It is known locally as the goureen, or lake herring.

Shag see Cormorant
Shaggy cap fungus see Lawyer's wig

Shamrock

A plant having leaves consisting of three leaflets and thought to have been used by St Patrick to illustrate the Trinity. The lesser yellow trefoil is often used as the shamrock—the national emblem of Ireland.

A spotted redshank in its winter plumage. It thrives in fresh, brackish or salt-water habitats

Shank

These birds are closely related to sandpipers, though distinguished from them by long colourful legs. They are medium-sized waders, found on salt or fresh marshes, and are noisy when disturbed. The redshank *Tringa totanus* has been called 'watch-dog of the marshes' because of its alertness and shrill 'tu-tu-tu, tuey-tuey' alarm call. It is the most numerous of the three British species, especially on coastal marshes, breeding in most counties in Britain. It lays four eggs, well hidden in a tussock of grass; its young merge perfectly with their surroundings.

Outside the April to July breeding season, redshanks gather on estuaries and sandbanks, often forming quite large flocks. Some of Britain's redshanks move south to the French coast but others from further north, including Iceland, stay in the British Isles, mixing freely with other estuarine waders and feeding on small shellfish, crustaceans, worms and insects.

The redshank is less than 11 in. long, and its upper parts are darker in summer. The broad, white bar on each wing is the chief identification mark. The legs of the young are yellower in colour than the mature bird. The rarer spotted redshank *T. erythropus*—a passage migrant—is distinguishable by its lack of a wing-bar. The spotted redshank, a black bird spotted with white in its Arctic breeding plumage, is usually a pale grey by the time it arrives in Britain.

Its long legs trail behind the tail in flight and a prominent V of white extends up the back from the rump. The spotted redshank passes through Britain on its way to Africa from Scandinavia, mainly in autumn, though it is not unknown at other seasons, including late winter.

The greenshank *T. nebularia* with its long green legs and melodious 'tu-tu-tu' call-note is the most elegant of waders. It is about 12 in. long, slightly larger than the redshank, and favours all types of fresh marshes and occasionally tidal creeks, though seldom open flats.

It breeds sparingly in Scotland from April to July, mainly in the Highlands and Hebrides. Four eggs are usually laid. Though invariably it places its nest near a prominent landmark, such as a dead tree or large stone, it remains among the most difficult nests to find. The parents regularly feed at a loch some distance away and fly in and out only a few times each day to feed. Though most greenshanks leave Europe in winter, a few sometimes remain in the south-west of England and Ireland. Their heads, necks and breasts then appear almost white.

Shanny *Blennius pholis*

The most abundant of the blennies—a family of small shore and inshore fish—along Britain's coasts; it is especially prevalent in rocky areas. It lives chiefly in the inter-tidal zone, in pools; less often under stones. It is rarely seen further out because it lives in rocky crevices. It is usually a dull green-brown, with a dark spot on the first fin rays, and sometimes faintly barred. Like other blennies, it has two long rays in the belly fin but, unlike them, lacks fleshy flaps on the top of the head. It grows up to 6 in. long.

The shanny feeds on a wide variety of smaller animals, chiefly crustaceans.

Spawning takes place in summer. The eggs are laid on the underside of a rock, usually by several females at one site. The male guards the eggs from intruders for the four to six weeks they take to hatch. The young, whose disproportionately large pectoral fins make them look like moths, float at the surface before moving inshore.

Shark

Although some of the sharks around Britain's coast are large and potentially dangerous, they do not enter shallow waters and are therefore no threat to bathers.

The blue shark *Prionace glauca*, which is up to 13 ft long and migrates from the Atlantic to Britain's south-west coast, and the porbeagle *Lamna nasus*, up to 10 ft, which lives all around the coast, are the most common of the large sharks. Both are sought by anglers fishing from boats.

The largest shark in British waters, the 35 ft long basking shark *Cetorhinus maximus* may be seen off western coasts in calm weather, lying on the surface—hence its name. It is quite harmless.

Shaw

A small wood or copse—more especially a long strip of woodland. In the Weald of Kent and Sussex the shaw, rather than the hedgerow, is the field boundary. Often a right of way runs beside the shaw towards common land. The name is derived from the Scandinavian *skog*, meaning woodland.

Shearwater

For most of their life, shearwaters feed at sea, ranging across the world's oceans and surviving the worst storms. The distances these birds travel can only be guessed at, but British-bred Manx shearwaters *Puffinus puffinus* regularly winter in the south Atlantic off the coast of Argentina. During the breeding season—May to October—'off-duty' birds have flown from Wales to the Bay of Biscay to feed. Some, released in New York as part of a homing experiment, found their way home in little over a week across 3000 miles of ocean.

Only the Manx shearwaters breed in Britain and they are now absent from the Isle of Man, but some have returned to the Calf of Man in recent years. Otherwise, they breed only on remote and usually uninhabited islands round Britain's western and northern coasts, although they are seen all round our coasts in summer.

Because the shearwater is so helpless on land—being adapted to an oceanic life with its feet set well back on its body, the best design for propulsion through the water—it arrives at the breeding sites only after dark. Its shrill, wailing cries, particularly when there is no moon, take on an eerie quality as each bird lands with a thump and scuffles into its nesting hole.

By flying at night, shearwaters avoid predators, principally the big gulls and, on the Isle of Rum in the Inner Hebrides, golden eagles.

At shearwater colonies, the ground is soft, often giving way easily underfoot because of the burrowing activity of generations of these birds. They have also been known to take over rabbit warrens for nesting. The shearwaters' single white eggs are incubated by both parents taking turns of two to three days for about seven weeks.

The young chicks grow strongly and, even before fully feathered, they are deserted by both parents. When six weeks old they fly down to the sea, where they learn to feed themselves on squid or small fish such as sprats, pilchards and herrings.

The trademark of the black and white shearwater is the way it glides for long periods, tipping from side to side on stiffly held wings, so low over the water they sometimes shear the tops of waves.

Other species of shearwaters occur in British waters but are rarely seen from land; they are the Cory's shearwater *P. diomedea*, the great shearwater *P. gravis*, and the sooty shearwater *P. grisea* from New Zealand and South America.

Leading breeds of British sheep

Dorset Horn
Breeds at any season and can produce three crops of fast-growing lambs in two years. Fleece 5-7 lb. in ewes, 10-14 lb. in rams

Swaledale
A hardy mountain breed with long legs and curly fleece. Kept for producing lambs for fattening in lowlands. Fleece 4-5 lb. in ewes, 10 lb. in rams

Clun Forest
Hardy, prolific, adaptable. Long body with small head held erect, giving alert appearance. Lambs mature rapidly. Fleece about 6-7 lb.

South Down
Barrel-like body, smaller than most lowland sheep. Good meat producer. Fine wool; fleece 4-7 lb. in ewes, 7-12 lb. in rams

Wensleydale
Large with long, curly wool; fleeces average 14 lb. Prolific. Rams generally used for crossing with other breeds

Welsh Mountain
Common in Welsh mountains. Small, hardy and agile. Produces lean meat. Rams horned; ewes hornless. Fleece 2-4 lb.

Blackface
Once a Scottish breed, but now widespread. Kept mainly for meat, but has long, flowing wool. Fleece 4-7 lb.

Romney Marsh
Numerous in south Kent. Large, heavy; short legs. Produces excellent lamb. Wool on forehead forms topknot. Fleece 10 lb. in ewes, 17-18 lb. in rams

Shropshire
Large, heavy body. Bred chiefly for producing rams for crossing with other breeds. Dense, good-quality wool; fleeces averaging 8-10 lb.

Suffolk
Broad, long and heavy body, used for meat production. Rams crossed with many other breeds. Good-quality fleece, averaging 6-8 lb.

Cheviot
Short-legged and hardy. Produces good lamb from either pure-bred flocks or crosses. Some rams horned. Fleece 4-5 lb.

Border Leicester
Very prolific. Rams usually crossed with other breeds for early lambs. Fleece 10 lb. in ewes, 15 lb. in rams

Kerry Hill
Large, broad-bodied sheep, originally from the Kerry Hills, in Montgomeryshire. Fleece 7 lb. in ewes, 10-12 lb. in rams

Hampshire Down
Compact, medium-sized body. Rams crossed with other breeds to produce fat lambs. Fleece 10 lb. in ewes, 15 lb. in rams

Sheep *Ovis aries*

Except for New Zealand, the British Isles has the highest density of sheep in the world—about 200 to the square mile. There are 26 million of them, belonging to more than 40 different breeds. In addition there are many cross-breeds. All are classified into three main types: longwools, shortwools and hill breeds.

The longwools, which include Lincoln, Border Leicester and Romney Marsh, are white-faced—except for Wensleydale—and hornless. Their long, shiny fleeces are used in the manufacture of smooth worsted cloth. The meat from them is not up to the quality of that from specialist meat-producing breeds of sheep.

The shortwools have dark faces and legs, and their short-haired fleeces are used to make the woollen yarns favoured for knitwear. They include the Down breeds, Shropshire and Suffolk, and produce good-quality meat.

The hill breeds are by far the most numerous and include Cheviot, Welsh Mountain and Blackface. They are small and hardy, and develop into good mutton, and their fleeces are used for a variety of purposes. The coarsest goes into carpets, the intermediate quality is generally used for the making of tweeds, and the finest for flannel and knitwear.

The type of sheep varies with the terrain. Small, active sheep are found on hilly, exposed land with thin grass. In the rich pastures of the lowlands the sheep are big and have heavy coats. They can endure great cold, but damp ground induces diseases. Like cows they chew the cud. Farmers will sometimes give them hay, oats and rootcrops to supplement the natural pasture.

Sheep have been domesticated since prehistoric times, but Britain probably never had wild sheep. Domesticated ones were introduced from Europe before the Roman invasion. Apart from providing food and wool, their milk, which is rich in fats and solids, was made into cheese.

By the Middle Ages the sale of wool to the Continent was one of Britain's main sources of wealth, but in the 18th century the emphasis began to switch to sheep bred for their meat. This was to feed the increasing number of people living in towns as a result of the Industrial Revolution.

Today Britain's sheep produce more than 220,000 tons of meat a year—42 per cent of the nation's requirements—and more than 100 million lb. of wool.

Males (rams or tups) are bigger than females (ewes). Castrated males (wethers) fatten faster than rams, and as one ram can serve a flock of up to 100 ewes most males are castrated when they are two or three weeks old.

Although the birth of five lambs has been recorded, most ewes produce one or two lambs at a time, most being bred to produce twins. Usually they lamb for the first time at the age of two, but some do so at 12 months. The gestation period is about 21 weeks. Mating therefore takes place in November for spring lambs, which are born in the fields, woolly and open-eyed, when the grass starts growing. They then have the summer in which to fatten for market.

Lamb prices are higher earlier in the year, and many lowland farmers arrange for their flocks to lamb in February to take advantage of this, providing shelter for the ewes in farmyards. Lambing is a month earlier than this for pedigree flocks, so that the rams will be mature enough for mating in the following autumn.

Some lambs are taken to the slaughterhouse at ten weeks, but most are killed when they are between 3 and 15 months. Hill lambs weigh about 25 lb. and others 35-40 lb. Mutton is a word used by butchers, not farmers, and is usually applied to the meat of sheep at least a year old. These are often animals from which the farmer does not wish to continue breeding.

Years ago many abattoirs kept a 'Judas-sheep' which would trot willingly into the building, leading the lambs to their slaughter. The 'Judas' was let out by another door ready for its next mission. The natural life of a sheep is about 12 years.

Sheep are subject to a number of skin parasites, and to destroy these they are put through a trough of disinfectant—sheep-dip—in the summer and winter.

Some primitive breeds of sheep, such as the soay, shed their wool in summer; it can in fact be plucked off. Most sheep, however, have to be shorn, and an expert using a mechanical clipping machine—in the past hand shears were used—can remove an entire fleece without breaking it.

The shearing of fleeces usually takes place between the start of May in the south and the middle of July in the north. Fleeces weigh from 4 lb. to 20 lb., depending on the breed, but a South Devon ram has produced one weighing 45 lb. The finest wool, 1/660 in. thick, comes from Southdowns, and the coarsest, 1/500 in. thick, from Leicesters.

As most sheep spend their lives in the fields, the work of their shepherds demands physical toughness, especially in hill country, across which they may have to walk many miles in bad weather.

Shepherds have a work vocabulary which mixes Latin with the language of pre-Roman Britain and has been passed down the centuries. For instance, many count to ten in this way: 'Yan, tan, tethera, pethera, pimp, sethera, lethera, hovera, covera, dik.' Fifteen is 'bumfit' and 20 'figgit'.

Sheep are usually silent, except for bleating at lambing time, and those on pastures far from the farm often have bells hung round their necks. These bells serve as a double warning to the shepherd. A gentle tinkling of bells indicates that all is well, but a rapid jangling may mean that the sheep are running from trouble. The bells are usually fastened to the necks of old ewes, the natural leaders of flocks, but sometimes they are put on a young ram, known as the bell-wether.

The bells are often home-made—merely a tin with a bolt for a clapper. A century ago shepherds would combine with blacksmiths to make bells that were works of art, and many of these are now used as ornaments.

The shepherd's crook—made of iron and mounted on a straight shaft about 4 ft long—is used for catching a sheep by hooking it round a hind leg. Scottish crooks, usually made of horn, are put round the sheep's neck.

Dogs have been used to control sheep since Roman times. Old English bob-tails or collies, they take about six months to train.

Never barking and never touching his charges, a sheepdog herds a flock of Clun Forest sheep exactly where the shepherd wants them

Sheep creep

Separate feeding of lambs apart from the adult sheep can be arranged by making an enclosure of special hurdles which have holes in them just large enough to let lambs through, but not sheep. These holes are called lamb, or sheep, creeps. They can be adjusted to the size of the lambs and have wooden rollers on the top and sides to let the animals through easily. In this way feeding can be rationed, giving the lambs the best grazing land a day ahead of the sheep.

Sheepsbit *Jasione montana*

Despite its appearance and its alternative name of sheep's scabious, sheepsbit is not a scabious. It differs in having almost untoothed florets and leaves. The plant has rosettes of long, narrow leaves from which almost leafless flowering stems grow up to 12 in. high between May and August. The flowers are deep blue, clustered together in button-like heads.

Sheepsbit is found all along the coast on exposed cliff tops, and inland on dry banks and rough grassland where grazing sheep may feed on it. On poor open soils it spreads, growing low and bushlike. Although found throughout the British Isles, it is more abundant in the acid soils of the west. Soils with a lime content do not suit the plant.

Shelduck see Duck

Shell

Most of the shells found on beaches round the British Isles are produced by a large group of animals called molluscs. They are of varying shapes, but all have a head, soft body, and tough muscular foot. There are 800 species in Britain, most of which are aquatic, and 650 of them live in the sea. Molluscs include such widely different types as the oyster, garden snail, and the octopus—one species that does not possess a shell.

When the animals die, their shells, which are often of great beauty, are washed up on the shore. Especially rich beaches, such as that on Herm in the Channel Islands, are known as shell beaches.

Shells are made of lime-based materials produced by glands contained in a fleshy part of the mollusc known as the mantle. The shells are built up in three layers: a horny outer layer, then a chalky one beneath, and finally a glossy inner one.

Most molluscs have either a single shell, when they are known as univalves, or a pair of shells, when they are called bivalves.

Univalve shells are usually spirally coiled. Many belong to creatures that live on the shore, such as cowries, winkles, top shells, needle shells (relatives of the winkles which feed on debris), edible ormers, common whelks and oyster drills, so-called because they drill through oyster shells and barnacles to feed on the creatures within. Small spire shells are found in crevices or in old barn-

The actaeon, crawling on the broad white foot with which it ploughs through the sand. When alarmed, it is able to withdraw completely into its shell, sealing the opening with slime

acles high up on the shore. Well down sandy shores or just offshore live the actaeon, the auger or tower shell, and the pelican's foot shell, which resembles a bird's foot. Actaeon ploughs through the sand on a broad white foot. Also low on the shore are velvet shells, which have soft outer covers to their shells and live under boulders.

Offshore live the beautiful wendletraps, which are whorled, ridged and dark-banded or mottled, and the spindle shells, which are related to whelks. On the surface of the sea, buoyed up by air bubbles, floats the violet sea snail, whose shell is sometimes washed up on western beaches.

The two shells of bivalves may be the same size, as in mussels, of unequal size, as in scallops, or extremely small in relation to the body, as in shipworms. Many have a thick mother-of-pearl lining.

The largest British bivalve is the fan mussel, a deep-water animal up to 14 in. long and half as broad; the smallest is *Neolepton skyesi*, less than $\frac{1}{16}$ in. long, which is found only off Guernsey.

Some bivalves do not close their shells. The orange tentacles of the gaping file shell, which lives on the sea-bed, always project between the open valves, and the oval valves of gapers, which burrow deep into the sand, cannot close because of the animals' large projecting siphons.

Many bivalves live on sandy beaches. Razor shells are so-called because their long rectangular valves resemble a cut-throat razor. Pandora shells, found only at Wey-

mouth and Studland, Dorset, and in the Channel Islands, have one flat and one convex shell. The rose-pink valves of the thin tellin open out like butterfly wings when the animal dies. The larger Baltic tellin lives in estuaries. The banded wedge shell, brown outside, violet within, is often found with a neat hole near the top—the work of the necklace shell, a univalve which erodes the shell with acid and eats the animal within. Carpet shells are so-called because of their varicoloured patterns. Closely related to them are the smaller venus shells, of which there are three common species: the banded venus, the striped venus, and the oval venus, which resembles the cockle. The boat-shaped Noah's ark shell attaches itself by threads to the interior of rock crevices and empty shells.

Shipworms and piddocks are bivalves which bore into soft rock, such as chalk.

The edible great scallop, or escallop, which has ribbed valves, lives offshore on sandy or gravelly sea-beds. It is dredged commercially off Brixham, the Isle of Man, the Clyde and in Galway Bay. Several species of small scallops live on the lower shore.

In addition to univalves and bivalves, there are other small groups of shelled sea molluscs, among them coat-of-mail shells or chitons, which have eight shell plates on the back, cling to rocks with a broad foot and feed on seaweed; and tusk or elephant-tooth shells, which live offshore on sandy sea-beds and whose shells are sometimes washed up on beaches.

Common shells on British beaches — 1

The shells found along the shore are the hard outer skeletons of soft-bodied animals known as molluscs. There are 650 species of molluscs living around Britain's coasts, but every beach, whether sandy or rocky, sheltered or exposed, has its own characteristic inhabitants. The best time to collect shells is at low spring tide which occurs for a few days every fortnight, coinciding with the full moon and new moon.

The shells shown below belong to univalve molluscs, animals with a single, spirally coiled shell or a bowl-shaped shell. They are all life-size, and in each case the type of beach where they are most likely to be collected is indicated. Many of these univalve shells, such as winkles, limpets and whelks, belong to animals living among seaweeds and on rocks, and can usually be found with the occupants inside them.

Oyster drill or sting winkle
Ocenebra erinacea
Rocks, muddy gravel
South-west and Wales

Wendletrap
Clathrus clathrus
Sand and mud
Common

Rough winkle
Littorina saxatilis
Rocks and in crevices
Common

Slipper limpet
Crepidula fornicata
On mussel and oyster beds
South-east, south and
west coasts to Scotland

Common necklace shell
Natica alderi
Sand, common

Thick top shell
Monodonta lineata
Rocks
Between Dorset and Anglesey

Pelican's foot shell
Apporhais pes-pelecani
Sand and muddy gravel
Common

Common limpet
Patella vulgaris
Rocks, common

Thick-lipped dog whelk
Nassarius incrassatus
Rocks and stony shores
Common

Flat winkle
Littorina littoralis
On wracks
Common

Tusk shell
Dentalium entalis
Sand offshore
Common, especially in north

Blue-rayed limpet
Patina pellucida
On kelps, common

Common whelk
Buccinum undatum
Muddy gravel, sand and
rocky shores
Common

Violet sea snail
Ianthina janthina
Floats upside down at
water's surface; shells
sometimes driven on to shore

Dog whelk
Nucella lapillus
Rocks, barnacle zone
Common

Keyhole limpet
Diodora apertura
Stones, under rocks
South and west

Cowrie
Trivia arctica
Rocks, common

Actaeon
Actaeon tornatilis
Sand
Widely distributed, but local

Smooth buckie or spindle shell
Neptunea antiqua
Sand and mud
North

Common or edible winkle
Littorina littorea
Rocks and beneath seaweeds
Common

Ormer
Haliotis tuberculata
On and under stones
Channel Isles

Painted top shell
Calliostoma zizyphinum
Rocks, common

Needle shell
Bittium reticulatum
Rocks and seaweeds
Common

Tower or auger shell
Turritella communis
Sand, mud and muddy gravel
Common

Tortoiseshell limpet
Acmaea tessulata
Among kelp holdfasts, under stones
North

Netted dog whelk
Nassarius reticulatus
Muddy sand, on eel grass
and under rocks
Common

European cowrie
Trivia monacha
Rocks, common

Slender spindle shell
Colus gracilis
Muddy sand
Offshore in north, rare in south

Large necklace shell
Natica catena
Sand
Widely distributed, but local

415

Common shells on British beaches—2

The south-western beaches of Britain are especially rich in sea shells, and low tide—when the maximum amount of shore is uncovered—will yield the largest collection. The shells illustrated below, four-fifths life-size, are all bivalves. They have two valves, or shells, hinged together, enclosing the mollusc's body. Many bivalves, for example the edible cockle and curved razor, burrow into the sand and are hidden from view. Their empty shells, brought to the surface by the waves, are usually broken apart. To find the live animals a spade is needed. The cockle does not burrow very deeply into the sandy mud, but the razor can move rapidly down deeper into the sand to escape detection. The common mussel is one of the few bivalves that does not burrow but lives in clusters on rocks, held firmly by its byssus threads or guy ropes.

Horse mussel
Modiolus modiolus
Among kelp holdfasts
Common, especially north

Pullet carpet shell
Venerupis pullastra
Sand and muddy gravel
Common

Common or native oyster
Ostrea edulis
Creeks, estuaries in dense beds
Common, especially south-east
and south-west

Cross-cut carpet shell
Venerupis decussata
Mud, sand and muddy gravel
South and west coasts

Banded wedge shell
Donax vittatus
Sand, common

Baltic tellin
Macoma balthica
Muddy gravel and estuaries
Common

Banded carpet shell
Venerupis rhomboides
Coarse sand and shell gravel
Very common

Pandora shell
Pandora albida
Sand and muddy sand
South and Channel Isles

Nut shell
Nucula turalda
Sand, sandy mud and silt
Common offshore

Great scallop or escallop
Pecten maximus
Coarse sand
Common offshore

Queen scallop
Chlamys opercularis
Coarse sand and gravel
Common

Thin tellin
Tellina tenuis
Fine, clean sand
Common

SHELL

Prickly cockle
Cardium echinata
Sand and muddy sand
Common

Edible cockle
Cardium edule
Sand and sandy mud
Common

Curved razor
Ensis ensis
Sand, common

Grooved razor
Solen marginatus
Sandy mud
South and west coast

Common otter shell
Lutraria lutraria
Sand and sandy mud
Common

Rayed trough shell
Mactra corallina
Clean sand
Common

Elliptical trough shell
Spisula elliptica
Sand and shell gravel
Common

Warty venus shell
Venus verrucosa
Shell gravel
South and west coast

Sand gaper or old maid
Mya arenaria
Clay, sand and sandy mud
Common

Banded carpet shell
Venerupis saxatilis
Coarse sand and shell gravel
Very common

Striped venus shell
Venus striatula
Sand, common

Common piddock
Pholas dactylus
Shale, chalk and red sandstone
South-west

Blunt gaper
Mya truncata
Sand, clay and muddy gravel
Common

417

Shelterbelt see Windbreak

Shepherd's needle *Scandix pecten-veneris*
Once a common weed of arable fields in southern and eastern England, shepherd's needle has become rare since the introduction of herbicides. But some still grow and flower in cornfields from April until July.

It is 6-18 in. high and has groups of about five tiny white flowers which develop into erect 'needles' up to 3 in. in length. They are so regularly arranged and equal in length that they are responsible for the plant's other name—Venus's comb. Shepherd's needle is extremely rare outside southern and eastern England. See also PARSLEY

Shepherd's purse *Capsella bursa-pastoris*
The heart-shaped seed pods of this annual resemble the type of purse carried by shepherds in the Middle Ages.

It grows 1-15 in. high in waste places and arable fields in almost every country in the world, and its white flowers can be found in every month of the year. Before the plant flowers it can be recognised by its rosette of leaves, with the outer ones pressed close to the ground.

Shepherd's purse was once widely used as a herb to relieve inflammation. A cloth steeped in its juice used to be put up the nose to stop bleeding.

Sherd
A broken fragment of pottery, a sherd or potsherd is a valuable and durable indicator to the archaeologist of the age of a site and as evidence of human activity. Sherds belong to any age, whether the Bronze or Iron Age, Norman, Tudor or Early Victorian. They may be dug up in the garden, picked up from a ploughed field or found on the site of a dig. The reconstruction of the original piece of pottery by painstakingly assembling sherds, enables accurate dating to be made. See also POTTERY

Shield bug
The broad, flattened bodies of these bugs are shaped like heraldic shields. There are two British families, most species of which are $\frac{1}{3}$-$\frac{1}{2}$ in. long. They vary in colour but many have a black and white margin to the body. They give off a distinctive, not unpleasant smell. Like beetles, they fly with their hindwings, which, at rest, they cover with the forewings.

Most shield bugs live among plants and feed on seeds and fruits which they pierce with their beak-like mouthparts.

A common species, except in Scotland, is the hawthorn shield bug which feeds on haws and, when these are not available, oak leaves. The gorse shield bug lives wherever gorse grows. Since gorse flowers throughout the year, the bugs are continuously supplied with seeds.

There are two families of smaller bugs which, because of their shape, are also

sometimes called shield bugs. One species of these is the mottled black and cream pied shield bug which feeds on the fruits of white dead-nettle. Unlike most insects, the female looks after her eggs, which she lays in a hole in the ground, and sits on them for several weeks until they hatch.

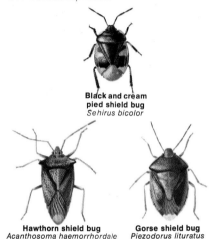

Black and cream pied shield bug
Sehirus bicolor

Hawthorn shield bug
Acanthosoma haemorrhordale

Gorse shield bug
Piezodorus lituratus

Shield bugs are named after their flat, broad bodies, which are shaped like heraldic shields

Shiel or shieling
A roughly constructed hut of timber or stone built on or near summer grazing areas—often hill pastures—as a temporary home for the herdsman and his family. Shielings existed in Scotland and northern England until the last century. Foundations surviving in Scotland and the fells of Cumberland and Northumberland show that the huts consisted of two or three rooms and had outbuildings.

The word shiel survives in many farm names, because the huts often became the sites of permanent farms.

Shingle see Gravel

Shipworm
Borings in fossilised wood found in London clay deposits are proof that shipworms were active around the British Isles 50 million years ago. Today, three species live in our waters. The largest, *Teredo norvagicus*, is also the most common and, like the smaller *T. navalis*, bores into pier piles and wooden boats. The remaining British species, *T. megotara*, lives only in floating timber.

Despite their common name, shipworms are really bivalve molluscs, relatives of the oyster and mussel, in which the shells are reduced to small but highly specialised boring instruments at the end of a long worm-like body. Shipworms bore circular $\frac{1}{4}$ in. burrows, usually along the grain of the wood. In heavy infestations, however, the burrows run in any direction, turning aside only to avoid knots or the burrows of other shipworms. They line their burrows with a layer of lime.

Shipworms are attached to the entrances to their burrows, and their bodies elongate as they bore through wood. A pair of siphons extend through the entrance of a burrow—one draws in water and the other expels it. If the wood is removed from sea water, the burrow is sealed with two limy plates which trap sea water inside, so that the worm can stay alive even if the wood is out of water for several weeks.

Plankton, drawn in with water, and wood fragments produced during boring, provide the shipworms' food. Shipworms are among the few animals capable of digesting cellulose; they convert it into sugar by producing a special enzyme called cellulase.

There are male and female shipworms, and eggs and sperm are shed into the sea. Fertilised eggs hatch into larvae which produce a pair of valves at one end and a pair of siphons at the other. They do not develop further until they come into contact with wood, when they develop plates and begin to bore into it.

Although shipworms live for less than a year, they can cause serious damage to wooden ships and pier piles, which become riddled with their burrows unless protected by metal sheeting.

Shire
The word shire is derived from the Old English *scir*, meaning a division, and the first shires were the main sub-divisions of the Anglo-Saxon kingdoms for local-government purposes. Wessex is known to have been divided into units such as Berkshire and Wiltshire by the 9th century. The other Anglo-Saxon kingdoms adopted the system, often basing shires on fortress towns such as Stafford and Leicester. The process of dividing England into shires was completed by the Normans in the 11th century, who called the shires 'counties'. The chief officer of a shire was at first the ealdorman, later the sheriff or shire-reeve, who was directly responsible to the Crown—a system that was not replaced until county councils were established in 1888.

Shore see Seashore

Shoreweed *Littorella uniflora*
A submerged plant, 1-6 in. high, found along the shores of lakes and ponds, mostly in the north and west where the water is lacking in lime.

A member of the plantain family, it has long and narrow grass-like leaves and produces runners which root in soft mud or gravel and form a sort of turf. Two kinds of flowers may be found from June to August when the water level is low and the plants are exposed. Those on slender stalks up to 4 in. high are male. The female flowers are without stalks and are hidden among the bases of the leaves.

Shoveler see Duck

Earthworms are among the wide range of small animals that are caught by the shrew for food

Shrew

A restless, insect-eating mammal, distinguished from the mouse by its needle-like teeth and long, twitching snout. It is active day and night, and does not hibernate. It is the animal's quarrelsome, noisy behaviour which has given the word shrew its secondary meaning of a scolding woman.

There are five species in the British Isles. The smallest and most widespread is the pygmy shrew *Sorex minutus*, which is the only species found in Ireland; it is absent, however, from the Channel Islands, Scillies and Shetland. Just over 2 in. long, it has, like the other shrews, a tail two-thirds as long again.

It is grey-brown above, white below. The pygmy shrew lives in woods, grassland and anywhere with plenty of ground cover. Unlike other shrews, which generally make their own tunnels in undergrowth and leaf litter, it always uses the old holes of other animals, such as moles and mice.

The common shrew *S. araneus* also lives in thick ground cover but is more common in woodland than the pygmy shrew. It is found in most parts of the British Isles, except for Ireland, the Scillies, Lundy, the Isle of Man and certain Scottish islands. The body is up to 3 in. long, and the fur is dark brown above, pale brown on the flanks and dirty white beneath.

The teeth of both these species have orange-red tips, in contrast to the wholly white teeth of the other three.

The greater white-toothed shrew, or musk shrew *Crocidura russula*, lives only on the three Channel Islands of Alderney, Guernsey and Herm, where it inhabits woods, gardens and farmland. The body is up to 3½ in. long, grey-brown above and grey below. Almost identical, but slightly smaller, is the lesser white-toothed shrew *C. suaveolens* which lives on the Channel Islands of Jersey and Sark and the Scillies. In both these species the young often follow the mother in crocodile fashion, each holding the rump of the one in front.

The water shrew *Neomys fodiens* is found only on the British mainland, Anglesey and a few small Scottish islands. It lives near water, especially clear, slow-moving streams.

It is about 3½ in. long, with a slaty black back and white belly.

Shrews' tunnels are narrow. The tight fit squeezes dry the wet fur of the water shrew (without this, the animal might die of cold) and keeps the fur of other shrews clean and polished as they wriggle through.

A shrew's saliva is toxic, like that of some snakes, and when the animal bites a human's hand it causes a burning sensation. Injected into a mouse, shrew saliva can cause death in a few minutes. Shrews feed on a wide range of small animals, such as earthworms, beetles, caterpillars, spiders, flies and woodlice. The water shrew also eats fish, frogs, water snails, crustaceans and water insects, which it sometimes leaps from the water to catch. This shrew enters the water for short periods only; it swims gracefully, using its tail as a rudder, and sometimes walks on the river bottom. Whenever it leaves the water, the water shrew grooms its fur in order to keep it waterproof.

Shrews possess scent glands with which they leave trails to locate each other and mark out territories. The glands make them distasteful to eat and, although several mammals kill them, including cats, the only animals which regularly eat them are owls and foxes; water shrews, however, often fall victim to large pike, salmon and eels.

Mating takes place between early spring and late summer, and up to five litters of seven or eight young may be born during that period. The breeding nest is a ball of woven grass. The mother suckles the young for their first three or four weeks, after which they fend for themselves. Shrews live for only a year.

Shrews are solitary, aggressive animals, guarding their territories jealously and screaming shrilly at intruders. At other times they whimper or chatter. They move swiftly and occasionally rear up on hind legs, apparently sniffing the air.

A study made of the common shrew showed the population varying between about 8 and 25 per acre, according to the time of year. In Scotland the common shrew is known as the thraw mouse, the pygmy shrew as the wee thraw, and the water shrew as the water rannie. See also MOUSE

Shrike

Like hawks, shrikes have strong, hooked bills for tearing at their prey. Though largely dependent on insects, they often catch small birds and are particularly fond of nestlings. The habit of impaling their catches on thorns, where they build up a larder, has earned them the name of butcher-birds. They hunt from a prominent perch, such as an overhead wire or a bush, on the open heaths and commons where they breed.

Once numerous and widespread in Britain, the red-backed shrike is now confined to southern England, particularly the New Forest. Only 150 pairs now breed. The male is red-backed, with a grey hood and rump and a black tail and eye stripe; the female is a dull, mottled brown. The bird arrives from Africa in May. The male builds a nest of stalks and moss in a thorn bush, in which the female lays four to six pale pink to creamy green eggs, mottled with pale brown. The female incubates the eggs, which hatch after 14 days. The young birds leave the nest 14 days later.

The great grey shrike is an autumn and winter visitor to the east coast of Britain. Some birds return to the same small area year after year. About 9½ in. long, the great grey shrike is half as big again as the red-backed shrike. It is black, white and grey and is distinguished from the rare lesser grey shrike by its larger size and the absence of black on its forehead. It often lives on those parts of the heathland occupied by red-backed shrikes in summer.

The red-backed shrike has earned the name butcher-bird, because it hangs its prey on thorns

SHRIMP

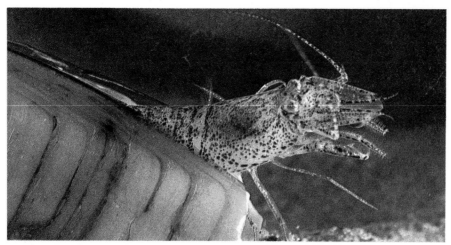

Shrimps burrow into sand or shelter in empty shells during the day, emerging at night to feed

Shrimp *Crangon vulgaris*
A sea animal up to 3 in. long, with a flat body which can change colour from yellow to almost black to match the colour of the sand over which it lives; like many other crustaceans, it turns red when boiled. The first pair of legs end in pincers which are used to pick up food including small molluscs, worms, crustaceans, and dead animal and plant material. The remaining four pairs of legs are used for walking, but shrimps can also swim using the paired paddle-like limbs, or swimmerets, which are situated beneath the tail.

In summer, shrimps migrate from the sea into estuaries and return in late autumn. Shrimps start mating when they are one year old. The fertilised eggs, several batches of which may be produced each year, are carried cemented to the swimmerets beneath the female. The eggs take about a month to hatch in summer, three months in winter. The larvae which emerge moult five times before settling on the bottom.

Shrimps are caught commercially off the Kent and Essex coasts and in Morecambe Bay, Lancashire. Inshore boats with trawls are used. In Somerset, nets attached to stakes are used to trap shrimps as the tide ebbs. See also PRAWN

Shrub
A shrub or bush is a woody plant which branches repeatedly and shows no tendency to send up a leading shoot to make a main trunk. Shrubs never attain a great height, 10 ft being about the usual limit. Their ability to produce side branches, or root sucker shoots, after damage by browsing animals, clipping or even fire, gives them great powers of survival.

Many shrubs, such as hawthorn hedge bushes, are trees restrained by cutting, or freak strains of trees, such as bushy garden cypresses. Others, like gorse, have no tree counterpart. Shrubs form an important component of scrub. See also WOODLAND

Sickener, The
A scarlet-capped poisonous fungus found in coniferous woods—sometimes in large numbers in autumn. There are slight grooves around the margin of the cap, which is 2½-3 in. across. The gills, spores and stem are all white.

The outer skin of the sickener *Russula emetica* peels easily—disproving the belief that 'if its cap peels easily, a fungus is edible'. If the sickener is eaten raw it causes vomiting, and even though proper cooking renders it harmless, it is best avoided as it has a peppery taste. A related species, *R. mairei*, is similar, having a red cap and white stalk, but is confined to beechwoods.

Signpost
A sign, at crossroads or road junctions, indicating the direction to towns or villages. Signposts were introduced in the late 17th century and became compulsory at turnpike crossroads under the Turnpike Acts of 1766 and 1773. Few of the earliest timber ones remain, but many elegant 18th-century cast-iron ones survive in Derbyshire, some mounted on pedestals to keep them clear of drifting snow.

Sika see Deer

Silica
Made up of silicon and oxygen, silica is the earth's most common mineral, the main component of more than 95 per cent of all rocks, which are thus known as silicates. As small grains, it forms sand; as pebbles, it takes various forms, such as flint, quartzite and chalcedony; and as crystals, it forms quartz, which occurs as white, glass-like fragments in granite and as coloured veins in old rocks in upland areas. Silica is also an important constituent of clay. See also CLAY, FLINT, QUARTZITE

Sill see Dyke

Silo
A building, or part of a building, for storing silage—grass, lucerne or other plants whose moisture has been conserved by excluding air from it. The silo may be a concrete vacuum tower, in which the air in the silage is pumped out; or simply a section of a barn partitioned off, where the silage is compressed as tightly as possible and clamped down.

Grass silage has two advantages over hay. The grass can be cut when it is young, tender and more nutritious than that used for hay; and damp weather does not interfere with its making.

Silt
Particles of material finer than sand and coarser than clay. They provide no nutrition for plants and are small enough to block up pore spaces in soil and cause poor drainage. Silty soils are therefore difficult to cultivate. Most silt occurs in estuaries, where it is partly brought in by tides and partly carried down by rivers. The biggest area of silt in England is the Fens.

Silverfish see Bristletail
Silverhorn see Caddis fly
Silvermoth see Plusia moth
Silverside see Sandsmelt

Silverweed *Potentilla anserina*
A low-growing perennial with large, yellow flowers and much-divided silvery leaves. The silvery effect is produced by long, silky hairs. There are three kinds of silverweed. Most have leaves which are silvery on both sides, some have silver on the underside only, and a few have no silver at all.

The plant flowers from June to August everywhere in the British Isles, except in the higher mountains, and is common in waste places, on roadsides, and in damp meadows that are flooded in winter. It spreads by overground runners like a strawberry, and often occurs in large patches.

Silverweed roots are edible, and the plant was cultivated in west Scotland before the introduction of the potato. The roots were boiled and dried and then ground into a mealy flour for bread or porridge. The leaves were often placed in boots to keep the feet comfortable. The plant's Latin name—from *anser* (goose)—may be an allusion to the fact that it grows freely on grassland where geese feed.

Simmental see Cattle

Singing sand
Sand grains blown against each other by wind become fine, smooth and rounded. When beaches consisting of such sand are

420

trodden on in very dry, warm weather, the grains, rubbing against each other, emit a squeaky, singing sound. An outstanding British example is the beach of Porth Oer in North Wales, known as Whistling Sands.

Siskin see Finch
Skelly see Whitefish

Skep
An old-fashioned beehive made of plaited straw. Until the start of this century skeps were often kept on benches under the eaves of cottages. Bees were usually killed off when their honey was gathered.

Skipper butterfly
Their fast wing-beat and darting, hard-to-follow flight gave skipper butterflies their name. Skippers look rather like moths, and at rest they often fold their wings, moth-fashion, by the side of the body. None of the eight species living in the British Isles has a wingspan of more than 1½ in.

The first three species of skippers to appear are on the wing from April to June. Most widespread of these is the dingy skipper which can be seen in most parts of southern England and Wales, in a few parts of Scotland, and even in western Ireland, where it is the only member of the family to be found. The grizzled skipper, another early flyer, is confined chiefly to southern England and Wales.

Although both these butterflies live in open, grassy areas, they are the only skippers whose caterpillars do not feed on grass. Those of the dingy skipper eat birdsfoot-trefoil, and those of the grizzled skipper eat wild strawberry leaves. All skipper caterpillars live in shelters which they make by sewing leaves together with silk and from which they emerge to feed.

Rarest of the spring skippers is the chequered skipper which lives only in a few woodland clearings in Rockingham Forest, Northamptonshire, and in other parts of the East Midlands, and around Fort William in Scotland. It is on the wing during the first two weeks in June only.

The later skippers can be seen from June to August in open grassy places or scrubland. The most common is the small skipper which lives in many parts of England and Wales. It has two close relatives. The Essex skipper is named after the county where it was first identified, but can be seen in the company of the small skipper in many areas of south and east England. Unlike the small skipper it has black instead of yellow tips to the undersides of its antennae. The Lulworth skipper is exclusive to the Dorset and Devonshire hillsides near the sea.

The large skipper has a pretty pattern of light and dark brown on the upper parts of its wings. It makes its home in much the same areas as the small skipper but extends slightly further north, just reaching Scotland. It spends nearly 11 months as a caterpillar and changes its skin six times.

Much rarer is the silver-spotted skipper. This is found only on the Chilterns and the North and South Downs. It is the same size and colour as the large skipper, but the undersides of its hindwings are beautifully marked in green and white.

Skua
These ocean birds live by piracy. They feed on fish caught by other birds, particularly terns. A skua waits for a tern to catch a fish or sand eel, then chases it and forces it, in its twistings and turnings to escape, to vomit its catch. So dependent are skuas on harrying other birds for food that they travel with terns to the southern oceans in autumn and winter.

Though skuas often breed in spring and summer in colonies on moors many miles from the sea, at other times they approach land only by accident. All four species are brown birds with white flashes on the wings. Their hawk-like character is heightened by a hooked bill and sickle-like wings.

The great skua, or bonxie, *Stercorarius skua* is the largest—about 23 in. long, the size of a large gull. The central tail feathers project only as two indistinct notches. It was once confined to the Shetland Islands, but since the Second World War has spread to the Orkneys, St Kilda, the Outer Hebrides and northern Scotland. Two olive-green eggs, blotched with dark brown, are laid on the ground and incubated by both parents for nearly a month. The chicks fly after about 45 days. After breeding, great skuas move down the west coast of Ireland and out into the Atlantic.

The Arctic skua *S. parasiticus* breeds in the same places but is more widespread and numerous. At 18 in., it is smaller than the great skua and has a swifter, more menacing flight. Some birds are brown all over but others are pale cream below and have a dark cap. The two types interbreed. The central tail feathers, which account for up to 3½ in. of its length, are often broken off by the end of the breeding season, as are those of the long-tailed skua and the pomarine skua. Two

Skipper butterflies

Essex skipper
Thymelicus lineola
underwings

Lulworth skipper
Thymelicus acteon
underwings

Grizzled skipper
Pyrgus malvae
underwings

Small skipper
Thymelicus sylvestris
underwings

Large skipper
Ochlodes venatus
underwings

Chequered skipper
Carterocephalus palaemon
underwings

Silver-spotted skipper
Hesperia comma
underwings

Dingy skipper
Erynnis tages
underwings

Skippers are small, dull-coloured butterflies which look rather like moths. About 30 species occur in Europe, of which eight live in the British Isles. None of the British species has a wingspan greater than 1½ in. Skippers are most common in southern Britain, and only one, the dingy skipper, occurs in Ireland. Their quick, darting flight makes skippers hard to observe.

eggs, similar in colour to those of the great skua, are laid on the ground, often on a slight rise, from which the birds can spot danger from an intruder. During incubation, which lasts nearly a month, the off-duty bird often stands guard next to its sitting mate and will be boldly aggressive towards intruders. The young birds leave the nest soon after hatching.

Most of the Arctic skuas which breed in Britain winter off the coast of West Africa and in the southern oceans.

The long-tailed skua is rare in Britain. The majority, on leaving their breeding grounds in the far north, pass out into the Atlantic between Iceland and Shetland, but a few visit the east coast of Britain in autumn. This skua is the most graceful species and has the longest central tail feathers; they account for up to 8 in. of its 22 in. length. It has creamy underparts and a dark cap.

The pomarine skua is another autumn visitor to Britain, regularly to the east coast, occasionally to the south coast. It may be pale, with a dark chest band, or dark, and is about 20 in. long. The 2 in. long central tail feathers are twisted, giving the bird a broad-tailed appearance which is easy to recognise at a distance.

An aggressive great skua rises in defence of its nest, hidden in a scrape in the ground

Skullcap

This 6-18 in. high perennial takes its name from the calyx, which resembles a *galerum* — the leather skull-helmet worn by the Romans. It has a square stem, like all members of the Labiatae family, but is unusual because the flowers, which are deep blue, are arranged in pairs facing the same way and growing from the base of the dark green leaves.

Skullcap is not abundant, but may be found flowering from June to September throughout England and Wales, except in the far

north, and in isolated parts of Ireland. It is usually seen in damp places, such as river banks, around ponds, or in damp, overgrown meadows and shady bogs and marshes.

Lesser skullcap is often not more than 6 in. high and less hairy. It flowers from June to October and its flowers are half as long as those of skullcap.

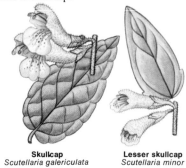

Skullcap
Scutellaria galericulata

Lesser skullcap
Scutellaria minor

The calyx, or flower sheath, of the skullcaps resembles a Roman soldier's helmet

Sky

The seven rainbow colours which combine to form the white light of the sun have different wavelengths. Red and yellow waves are the longest; blue, indigo and violet are the shortest. Anyone looking at the sky is seeing sunlight scattered by air molecules and further deflected by dust particles. The sky appears blue since the shorter wavelengths are scattered rather than the longer waves, and the human eye is less sensitive to violet light.

The intensity of the blue depends on the quantity and size of the dust particles. Most are large enough to scatter all the wavelengths of sunlight so that the colour of the sky is lightened. This is why skies appear to be darker blue when seen from places relatively free of dust, such as a mountain top, or when the wind is blowing from the Atlantic rather than the Continent.

Skylark see Lark

Slag

Heaps of unwanted material from furnaces, mostly fused mixtures of silica and lime, have presented a disposal problem since the Iron Age began, about 1100 BC. However, slag produced as a by-product of the steel industry provides a valuable phosphate fertiliser for farmland.

The bulk of British iron ore contains considerable quantities of phosphorus which passes into the pig iron when the ore is smelted. To make steel, oxygen is blown through a mixture of molten iron and lime. The phosphorus present combines with the lime to form a scum on top of the metal. When poured off, this solidifies into basic slag, which is ground for use as a fertiliser.

Much modern slag is re-smelted or used to make bricks, paving blocks and slag wool

for lagging boilers. Slag heaps of the past, many now levelled out, can be found all down the coast of the Lake District from Whitehaven to Barrow-in-Furness. In the Wigan district of Lancashire, among others, shale heaps have been sown with cocksfoot and other grasses, and trees such as sycamore and silver birch encouraged in an effort to disguise the heaps.

Bloomeries (forges) for producing slag-free bars (blooms) of iron date from the Iron Age to the medieval period. Knobbly bits of iron-cinder or slag can be found in the soil of most of the old iron-producing forest areas where bloomeries flourished. These include Grizedale Forest, Lancashire, the Forest of Dean, Gloucestershire, the Weald of Kent, Surrey and Sussex and parts of Worcestershire.

Slag heaps from the old Wealden iron industry are often found near hammer ponds, where water-wheels drove hammers and bellows. Large lumps of imperfectly fused ore, known as bears, were used by the Romans for road-surfacing.

Some of the earliest traces of smelting in old iron-working areas, such as Shropshire, are the bale or bole-hills. These are small heaps about a yard or more in diameter composed of slag and charcoal. Often covered in vegetation, they are difficult to identify.

Sleet

A mixture of raindrops and snowflakes. It is formed when snowflakes, falling from the cold upper air, pass through warm air nearer the ground and start to melt. This usually happens when the air temperature is 2-3°C (about 36°F). Sleet is often followed by snow, because as it falls it cools the air sufficiently to take it below 1°C (33°F), the temperature at which snowflakes can reach the ground without melting.

Sloe see Blackthorn
Slow-worm see Lizard

Sludge worm

Masses of the red sludge worms belonging to the *Tubifex* species are sold in pet shops as live food for aquarium fish. They are extracted from river mud by suspending the mud in hessian over a tub of clean water. The worms drop through the hessian and collect in masses at the bottom of the tub.

Other species of these aquatic worms, which are related to the earthworm, are able to live in water polluted by sewage. There are vast numbers of both *Tubifex tubifex* and *Limnodrilus hoffmeisteri* in the filter beds of sewage farms. Sludge worms survive because their blood is rich in the red pigment haemoglobin which enables them to exploit to the full the minute quantities of oxygen in polluted water.

Normally the worms live head down in a chimney-like tube which projects from the mud. The tail end of the worm extends out of the top of the tube, and by thrashing the water creates a current towards the head where decayed organic matter is extracted from the mud. At the slightest disturbance, the tail contracts into the tube.

The $\frac{1}{2}$-2 in. long worms contain reproductive organs of both sexes, but pairing does occur. Between four and nine eggs are laid in $\frac{1}{16}$ in. long oval cocoons, and $\frac{1}{4}$ in. young worms hatch in 8-56 days, according to temperature and species.

In the British Isles, 66 species of the two closely related families of sludge worms have been found, some of which reproduce asexually by fragmentation.

The worms filter out organic matter from mud and help to purify water by eating the bacteria and fungi in it.

Slug

A familiar and unwelcome animal in the garden and field because of its voracious appetite. The slug rasps its way through carrion, fungi and plant tissues including cereals, clover, root and potato crops.

The 23 species of slugs living in the British Isles are basically snails without shells, though a few, such as the earthworm-eating *Testacella,* have tiny shells. The remaining slugs belong to two groups—the roundbacks and the keeled slugs.

The roundbacks, such as the 1 in. long garden slug, have dome-shaped bodies. The keeled slugs, such as the great grey slug, which grows up to 8 in. long, have a ridge or keel along the back.

As water is quickly lost from the slug's soft, moist and unprotected body it lives in damp places in the soil and among debris. It emerges only at night or on wet days. A slug's organs of smell are in its tentacles and enable it to detect food several feet away.

Although a hermaphrodite, the slug rarely fertilises itself and usually mates with another animal. Mating is preceded by a long courtship ritual, particularly elaborate in the

Courting slugs. Great grey slugs, like other slugs, circle and lick one another before mating

great grey slug. At first the two animals climb a wall or tree. They circle around licking each other and eating their slime for as long as $2\frac{1}{2}$ hours. Eventually they become tightly twisted together and lower themselves on a thick cord of slime which may be up to 18 in. long. While suspended in mid-air each slug unrolls its 2 in. long penis and entwining them together exchanges sperm. The slugs

then fall to the ground or climb up the slime cord, eating it as they go. Soon after mating they lay soft amber eggs in several clusters under stones or any other suitable damp place. If the eggs are laid in late autumn they do not hatch until the following spring. Otherwise tiny slugs emerge in a month. They may live for three years.

Smelt *Osmerus eperlanus*
A relative of the salmon, the 18 in. smelt or sparling is a light olive-brown fish with silvery sides and belly and a general transparent appearance. When fresh it has a strong smell of cucumbers, although its flesh has an excellent fishy flavour.

It is a migratory estuarine fish entering a river mouth in winter and moving upstream to spawning sites by March and April. The eggs are adhesive but frequently break loose from their mooring. Then the outer skin of the egg ruptures to form a parachute-like float which keeps it off the river bottom where it might be damaged.

The smelt is not common today as so many estuaries have been severely affected by pollution. The fish is still found fairly frequently on the east coast and, to a lesser extent, in the north-east Irish Sea and the Shannon area.

Smew see Duck
Smithy see Blacksmith

Common British slugs

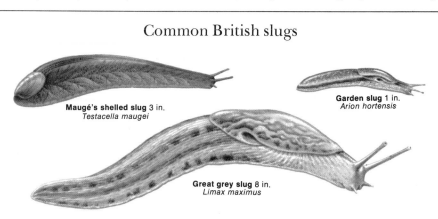

Maugé's shelled slug 3 in.
Testacella maugei

Garden slug 1 in.
Arion hortensis

Great grey slug 8 in.
Limax maximus

The 23 species of slugs that live in the British Isles are classified into three groups, each of which is represented here. Most slugs lack shells, as for example the great grey slug (a keeled slug) and the garden slug (a roundback). A few species are shelled, such as the Maugé's shelled slug which has a tiny ear-shaped shell at the end of its body

Smog

A mixture of smoke and fog produced by the water droplets of fog forming around microscopic particles of carbon or smoke. In the most heavily polluted areas these smoke particles exist in concentrations of tens of thousands per cubic centimetre. They stain the droplets, giving them a yellowish appearance in the weak sunlight. Until the improvements following the Clean Air Act of 1956, London and most of the industrial cities of central and northern England and Scotland were plagued by smogs or 'pea-soupers' each winter. With the reduced burning of coal, smogs have become rare.

Smolt see Salmon

Smooth snake *Coronella austriaca*

Although it may bite when picked up, the smooth snake—so-called because its silky scales lack the ridge on those of the adder and grass snake—is not poisonous. Like the grass snake, it may discharge an evil-smelling fluid.

It is widespread over western Europe, but rare in the British Isles. It is sighted only a few times each year, always in the same group of counties: Hampshire, Dorset, Wiltshire, Surrey and Sussex. These appear to be the western limit of its European range. The smooth snake favours dry and sandy places, on heaths, among rocks and in open woodland, with water near by. In Dorset, where it is probably most common, its typical home is open heath with heather, rough grass, bog myrtle in the wet places and a border of willow or thorn bush. It spends much of its time basking in the sun or lying in the water.

The average length of both sexes is 18-20 in. Colour varies from grey to red or mahogany brown, with dark spots along the back and a dark patch on each side of, and on top of, the head. The marks along the back sometimes cause the smooth snake to be mistaken for, and killed as, an adder. The snake's small mouth often means a large meal may take several hours to swallow.

The snake once fed chiefly on sand lizards. These are now rare and it preys on other young lizards and slow-worms, supplementing these with small mammals, nestlings and insects. It grips its prey in its mouth, then coils round it, not to crush it but to subdue its struggles.

Smooth snakes hibernate in late September or October. They bury themselves in loose soil or use a disused rabbit burrow or mouse tunnel. They usually emerge at the end of March and about two weeks later begin mating. This takes place several times, often with different partners, until about mid-May. In mid-summer nine or ten young snakes, 7 in. long, hatch out of eggs which until then have been retained in the female. They shed their skins a week later, and this is repeated about twice a year. Young smooth snakes eat only a few insects before hibernating, as they can live through the winter on the reserves of fat with which they are born.

Smut

A group of fungi with black spores which attacks the leaves, stems, fruit or stamens of cereals, grasses and some other plants. The spores are scattered by the wind and germinate in the spring. Plants become infected during the seedling stage and by the time they flower the ovaries are filled with spores. On grasses and cereals the smut replace the grain with fungal spores.

In covered smut of barley and stinking smut of wheat the spores are covered by the skin of the destroyed grain and become visible only when the crop is threshed. Healthy grain which becomes contaminated with spores during threshing can be treated with fungicides. In loose smut of barley and wheat the spores are blown away by the wind, leaving a bare stalk instead of an intact ear of grain.

Anemones, onions, leeks and violets which have been attacked by smut appear to be covered in grey dust.

Snail

Snails belong to the group of animals known as molluscs, which also includes octopuses, squids, oysters and limpets. All are descended from the same ancestor, a mollusc which once crawled over rocks in shallow water.

There are few places in the countryside where a snail of one kind or another will not be found. Apart from the whelks,

The courtship of snails begins with the two animals pressing their bodies together

periwinkles and other marine kinds, there are 80 land and 40 freshwater species. The common or garden land snail with its brown-banded shell is typical of this group of molluscs.

Characteristic of all snails is the 'home' or whorled shell that they carry on their backs. Made mainly of chalk, it is a hollow cone coiled around a central hollow column. Most snails have right-handed shells—that is, if the snail is held upright, the opening facing one is on the right of the shell. The freshwater ram's-horn species, however, have left-handed shells. The snail's body is in a bag-like structure coiled up within the shell; only the head and bottom part, known as the foot, are ever visible. The laborious movement is the result of the passage of muscular waves along the foot, which secretes a trail of slime as it goes. The head is merely a

The body of the whirlpool ram's-horn snail, coiled inside its transparent shell

Common snails of the British Isles

There are 120 species of snails in the British Isles. Eighty of these live on land and the rest in fresh water. Fifteen of the more common species are shown here. The measurements given are the height of the shell and the number of whorls in the shell. Both measurements, which are useful aids to identification, apply to full-grown snails. Between one to three years are required for snails to mature and they may live for up to 10 years

Land snails

Grove snail or Dark-lipped banded snail $\frac{1}{2}''$-$\frac{3}{4}''$ 5½
Cepaea nemoralis

White-lipped banded snail $\frac{1}{2}''$ 5
Cepaea hortensis

White or Sandhill snail $\frac{1}{2}''$ 5½-6
Euparypha pisana

Heath snail $\frac{1}{4}''$-$\frac{1}{2}''$ 6
Helicella itala

Plated door snail $\frac{1}{2}''$-$\frac{3}{4}''$ 12
Marpessa laminata

Roman or edible snail 1½''-1¾'' 5
Helix pomatia

Common or garden snail 1½'' 4½-5
Helix aspersa

Water snails

River snail 1-1½'' 6-7
Viviparus viviparus

Freshwater nerite $\frac{1}{4}''$ 3
Theodoxus fluviatilis

White ram's-horn $\frac{1}{16}''$ 4-5
Planorbis albus

Great ram's-horn $\frac{1}{2}''$ 5-6
Planorbarius corneus

Ear pond snail 1-1½'' 4-5
Lymnaea auricularia

Great pond snail 1¾''-2½'' 7-8
Lymnaea stagnalis

Dwarf pond snail $\frac{1}{4}''$-$\frac{1}{2}''$ 5-6
Lymnaea truncatula

Moss bladder snail $\frac{1}{2}''$ 6-7
Aplexa hypnorum

continuation of this foot, distinguishable by two pairs of tentacles, the longer of which bear eyes at their tips. Freshwater snails have only one pair of tentacles, with eyes at the base.

Snails, being slow-moving, cannot capture nimble prey. The diet of land snails varies according to the species, ranging from plants, fruits, even dead earthworms and slugs in the case of the garden snail to decaying matter, mosses and fungi. Most freshwater snails browse on the algae growing on submerged objects. But a few, such as the great pond snail, will also eat dead beetle larvae, small newts and sticklebacks.

Food passes from the mouth into a large area in the intestine, the crop, so that the animal can feed in haste but digest at leisure in the safety of its hideout. Some can go without food for long periods. Snails are eaten by birds—chiefly thrushes—foxes and the snail beetle.

Land snails are nocturnal creatures. They are very susceptible to water-loss from their moist bodies, but at night the humidity is always greater. In hot weather they retreat into their shells and plug the aperture. In the autumn they go into hibernation in crevices, under logs and stones or among leaf litter, then emerge in spring and start their courtship display. Snails are hermaphrodite (bisexual). This is of definite advantage to these slow-moving animals as it increases their chances of meeting a suitable partner. Court-

ship begins with the two animals pressing their bodies together, rocking to and fro and touching each other with their tentacles. Then each snail pushes a harpoon-like calcareous dart, about $\frac{1}{3}$ in. long, into the foot of its partner. The shooting of these 'love darts' triggers off the exchange of sperm. After mating the snails part and each lays several batches of round, whitish eggs in the soil or under stones or logs. Freshwater species lay eggs in long strings of jelly attached to stones and water plants. Most snails die after they have spawned; eggs hatch into miniature snails in three to four weeks.

Snails can live for several years, but most die before they are two years old.

Snail beetle

A carrion-eating beetle that also feeds on snails, found in the chalky areas of the British Isles. The snail beetle *Phosphuga atrata* is about ½ in. long and has a shiny, rough, black body. It hides under stones during the day, emerging to feed at night. It bites the foot of the snail which retreats into its shell, attempting to seal the entrance with slime. Despite this slime the beetle crawls into the shell continuing to bite its victim and squirting fluid from the tip of its abdomen. This secretion helps to dissolve the slime and kill the snail. In Ireland the larger reddish-brown *P. subrotundata* is more common.

Snake

There are about 2500 species of snakes in the world, ranging in length from a few inches to 30 ft. Most are confined to the Tropics, and Britain has only three—the adder (or northern viper), the grass snake and the rarer smooth snake. There are no snakes in Ireland—for which its inhabitants thank St Patrick—and the adder is the only common snake in Scotland.

Of all groups of animals, snakes are perhaps the most maligned, persecuted and misunderstood. Many who handle one for the first time discover how false the popular beliefs can be. The body is clean and soft to the touch, not slimy. The flickering tongue is not a sting, but a harmless organ of smell—particles of scent caught in the air or picked up from the ground are transferred to a sense organ in the roof of the mouth.

Venomous snakes, such as vipers, cobras, mambas and rattlesnakes, form a minority of the world population. The adder is Britain's only venomous snake.

Most snakes are egg-laying, and the young are equipped with a special egg-tooth to cut through their shell. Adult snakes manage to swallow animals several times larger than their heads by separating their loosely linked jaw-bones and stretching their mouths. Snakes have no external ears and cannot hear airborne sounds, so snake-charming is not the result of the charmer's music, but is possibly caused by the swaying of his body and the vibration of his tapping foot. As the inner ear is still present in snakes, they can detect vibrations through the bones of the skull.

In venomous snakes the hollow teeth in the upper jaw, called fangs, are connected with ducts leading to the venom sacs. In cobras and mambas the fangs are fixed, but in

A grass snake swallows a frog alive by separating its jaw-bones and stretching its mouth wide

vipers they rotate into position when the snake is about to strike. This is nature's version of the hypodermic needle.

In Britain snakes help to keep the rodent population in check and should not be killed needlessly—the chances of being

MOVEMENT WITHOUT LEGS

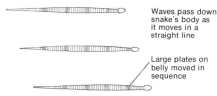

Peg represents stone against which snake pushes

Snake moves in a series of curves

Serpentine movement A snake usually moves by hitching and pushing its body against stones and plants. Its head, neck and tail follow exactly the same winding path

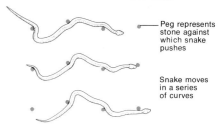

Waves pass down snake's body as it moves in a straight line

Large plates on belly moved in sequence

Caterpillar movement The snake uses the large plates on its belly as 'feet', lifting them, moving them forwards and setting them down again

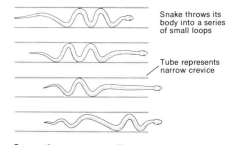

Snake throws its body into a series of small loops

Tube represents narrow crevice

Concertina movement The snake moves through a narrow crevice by bracing its looped body against the passage walls and extending the head forwards

---

Snakes and the slow-worm

Britain has three species of snakes, the adder, the grass snake and the rarer smooth snake. The slow-worm, which is a limbless lizard, is often mistaken for a snake and needlessly killed. Snakes are perhaps the most persecuted of animals. They are inoffensive and help to keep rodents in check. Even the venomous adder will not attack man unless provoked

Smooth snake
Coronella austriaca

Grass snake
Natrix natrix helvetica

Adder
Vipera berus

Slow-worm
Anguis fragilis

struck dead by lightning are greater than dying from the bite of an adder.

In spite of the absence of limbs, snakes of different species are capable of crawling, swimming, climbing, burrowing, leaping and even gliding through the air. As snakes are cold-blooded they control their temperature by moving from sun to shade and back again. In Britain they normally hibernate. See also ADDER, GRASS SNAKE and SMOOTH SNAKE

Snakefly

This fierce-looking but harmless dark brown insect, found throughout the British Isles, has wings like those of the lacewing, with a 1 in. span, an upraised head and, in the female, a sting-like tube for laying eggs. There are four British species, each of which lives on the leaves or trunk of a different type of tree. The most common is *Raphidia maculicollis*, found on conifers from May to July. The females lay eggs in the burrows made by wood-boring beetles, and the larvae which hatch eat the beetle larvae; adult snakeflies feed on aphids. The full-grown larvae emerge from the burrows and bury themselves in the ground at the foot of the tree, where they spend the winter in their pupal, or resting, stage. In May they emerge as adults.

Snakeshead see Fritillary

Snapdragon *Antirrhinum majus*

Familiar as a garden plant, snapdragon has become well established on old walls throughout England and occasionally elsewhere, particularly in ruined abbeys and castles.

It flowers from July to September. Wild forms are mostly reddish-purple and yellow. Flowers of other colours are usually garden varieties. The mouth of the flower is closed by a large, bearded projection resembling the face of an animal or a mask. The name antirrhinum means snout-like.

At one time the plant was supposed to possess supernatural powers and to be able to destroy spells. A garland of snapdragons was regarded as a protection against witches —and possibly dragons.

Sneezewort *Achillea ptarmica*

The white flowers of this 1-2 ft perennial can cause it to be mistaken for yarrow, to which it is related, but the leaves of sneezewort are quite different: long, narrow and undivided with a saw-like edge. Sneezewort flowers in July and August in wet meadows, marshes and beside streams throughout the British Isles, especially in hilly areas.

The plant is said to make one sneeze if it is dried and powdered, but so would many other plants. Its root has a sharp taste and causes a flow of saliva and was once used to relieve toothache.

Forms with double flowers, known as bachelors' buttons, are a cultivated variety often grown in gardens.

Snipe *Gallinago gallinago*

The long, straight bill and striped head of the snipe make it an easy bird to identify. It is 10½ in. long, the bill making up a quarter of its total length. Its plumage is brown, streaked and patterned with white, and the sexes look alike.

Snipe are present all year throughout the British Isles and breed in almost every county, but are more common in winter when migrants arrive from northern Europe. Their territory is usually in the vicinity of marshy pools and overgrown and flooded grassland.

The long bill, which has a flexible tip, is used for probing into mud for worms. The bird also eats water-beetles, insect larvae, snails, woodlice and the seeds of some marsh plants.

It usually nests in hollows lined with grass, or in rushes or tussocks of grass near water. Between April and August four pear-shaped, olive-brown or olive-grey eggs are laid. The chicks emerge about 20 days later and fly in three weeks.

Snipe take to the air with surprising speed. There is usually a nasal 'scarp' sound as the bird leaps into the air and begins its zigzag flight. It seldom feeds far from cover and, when faced with danger, tends not to move until the last possible moment.

A snipe marks out its territory with a peculiar display flight. It rises high in the sky and suddenly dives, the wind vibrating its stiff outer tail feathers and producing a bleating noise that serves instead of a song. Then it rises and dives again until it has circled its territory. The sound made by a diving snipe has earned it the country name of heather bleater.

The jack snipe *Lymnocryptes minimus*— so-called because it is smaller than the snipe —is a winter visitor only and lives in the same sort of country. It has a shorter bill and no white on the tail.

Snout moth see Noctuid moth

Snow

Water droplets can remain unfrozen in clouds until the temperature falls as low as −40°C (−40°F), when they freeze spontaneously. Above this temperature, tiny particles of dust and other material, known as freezing nuclei, must be present before the super-cooled droplets change into ice crystals. Once freezing starts, it gathers momentum and hundreds of crystals interlock to form snowflakes. At very low temperatures, the flakes tend to be small and simple in shape. At just below freezing point, the crystals are star-shaped and link with others to form snowflakes up to several inches across. Three main factors influence the number of days on which snow falls in different parts of the British Isles: latitude, longitude and altitude. Southern Cornwall averages fewer than five days' snow a year, compared to 35 days in north-east Scotland.

Altitude results in even larger increases. At 2000 ft there are likely to be 52 more days with snow than in an otherwise similar location near sea level. At 3000 ft the figure is 90 extra days with snow. Britain's greatest recorded snowfalls were of 60 in. during 1947 in Upper Teesdale and Denbighshire.

The number of days with snow lying is more variable, averaging fewer than five days in south and west coastal districts; more than 50 in parts of Wales and the Pennines; and more than 100 in the Scottish Highlands. The average number of days with snow on the ground has doubled since 1940, compared with the previous 30 years.

In the British Isles, most snowfalls occur between December and March but in the Scottish Highlands only mid-summer is free from the chance of snow. In some shaded spots, a few patches of snow survive many summers—the only examples of 'permanent' snow in the British Isles.

Snowberry *Symphoricarpos rivularis*

A hardy deciduous shrub which grows to 10 ft. It was introduced from North America in 1817 and is now found in hedges and thickets throughout the British Isles. It thrives in a variety of soils and situations, and has been planted to provide pheasant cover.

Snowberry has clusters of small, pink flowers from June to September. These develop into large, white berries which persist through the winter. Few contain ripe seeds, and the shrub spreads mainly by long, underground stems.

The white berries of the snowberry persist through the winter. Few contain fertile seeds

Snowdrop

In sheltered places in south-west England, the snowdrop begins to flower at Christmas, and in other parts it is welcomed as one of the first signs of spring, flowering from January to March.

The drooping, bell-shaped flowers have six segments—three white ones outside the flower and three tipped with a bright green spot inside it.

It is doubtful whether the snowdrop *Galanthus nivalis* is a native of Britain. It was probably introduced in medieval times from central Europe and is rare in Ireland. The large-flowered forms grown in gardens belong to another species *G. elwesii*.

Snow-in-summer see Dusty miller

Soapwort *Saponaria officinalis*

Closely resembling the garden plant sweet william, it has taller and stouter flowering stems, growing 1-3 ft, and fragrant, rose-pink flowers which appear in hedgebanks and waste places from July to September.

The leaves of soapwort produce a lathery liquid when crushed and boiled, and this was once used for washing cloth. The plant was probably introduced from Europe for this purpose and was cultivated near woollen mills. It grows throughout the British Isles, except in the far north and west.

Soil see p. 430

Soldier beetle

These beetles, which vary in length from $\frac{1}{3}$ to $\frac{3}{4}$ in., probably get their name from the 'uniform' they wear—brown or black wingcases and red or black heads. Their bright colours act as a warning to birds that they are unpalatable—young birds which taste one will avoid others in the future.

Forty species are found throughout Britain. Most of these can be found on umbelliferous flowers, especially hogweeds, in late summer.

The adults and larvae of these beetles are mainly carnivorous, living off small insects; they are sometimes cannibalistic. Their jaws are not strong enough to bite humans. In some localities they are known as sailor beetles.

Soldier fly

Most of the 53 British species of soldier flies have bright, metallic markings and it may be this, or the spines arming the thorax of some species, which gave them their popular name. They vary from $\frac{1}{8}$ to $\frac{1}{2}$ in. long. One of the largest species is *Stratiomys potamida*. It has a black and yellow wasp-like pattern and is seen in the south and east of England from June to August.

The adults feed on flowers of marsh plants, and the larvae are aquatic. At the rear of the larvae, the spiracles (breathing openings) are surrounded by hairs which hold a bubble of air when submerged and spread out to bring the spiracles into contact with air

as soon as the body tip touches the water.

The larvae feed on small water animals. Some members of this family have soil-living larvae which eat decomposing organic matter. The bright colours of many soldier flies are thought to be important for recognition purposes during courtship.

Solomon's-seal *Polygonatum multiflorum*

The name is derived from the belief that the plant's white knotted roots are formed in the star design approved by King Solomon for putting evil spirits to flight. The seal of Solomon was the Star of David, made of two interwoven triangles.

The plant's stem is about 2 ft long. Its lower half is bare and the upper half, which curves horizontally, has broad, stalkless leaves. In May and June clusters of green-white drooping flowers appear beneath the leaves and develop into bluish-black berries.

Solomon's-seal grows in woods throughout Britain, but is common only in the south.

Sorrel

One of the most common grassland plants in the British Isles, common sorrel *Rumex acetosa* grows about 2 ft high and has easily recognised arrow-shaped leaves and tall spikes of dock-like flowers, which turn brilliant crimson when in fruit.

Sheep's sorrel *R. acetosella* is similar but rarely exceeds 1 ft in height. Its leaves are also arrow-shaped but have two outward-pointing lobes at the base. It is most often seen on acid heaths and rough grassland.

Common sorrel
Rumex acetosa

Sheep's sorrel
Rumex acetosella

The crimson flowers and fruits of sorrel often redden the countryside from May to July

Sow thistle

Tall herbs up to 5 ft high with yellow flowers and prickly, thistle-like leaves which produce a milky white latex when the stems are broken. The three common British species, which occur throughout the lowlands and flower from June onwards, are all weeds of arable fields and waste places.

Perennial sow thistle has large, dandelion-shaped flowers which, like its stems, are thickly covered in glandular hairs. It spreads rapidly by underground stems. The other two species are annuals with smaller flowers: prickly sow thistle has shining, spiny dark

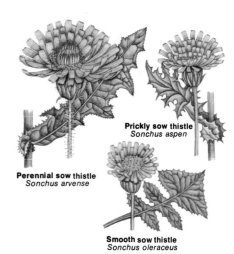

Prickly sow thistle
Sonchus aspen

Perennial sow thistle
Sonchus arvense

Smooth sow thistle
Sonchus oleraceus

The three species of sow thistle, tall dandelion-like plants, are best told apart by their leaves

green leaves which are rounded at the base, whereas smooth sow thistle has dull and spineless pale green leaves which are pointed at the base.

Sparrow

Though probably the most often seen of British birds, sparrows are not the most numerous; they are outnumbered by chaffinches and blackbirds. Sparrows appear numerous because they live in close association with man, building untidy nests in holes, in thatch and walls and in hedges.

Only two species of sparrows are found in the British Isles: the house sparrow and the tree sparrow. The bird commonly known as the hedge sparrow is not a sparrow at all —although rather similar in appearance. It is the dunnock *Prunella modularis*.

House sparrows throughout Britain breed from May to August and may rear two or three broods of from three to five young. The eggs are grey or white, speckled with black and brown markings. Hens incubate them for 12-14 days and both parents feed the young which can fly at 15 days.

Depending largely on man for food and for nesting sites, sparrows occur in great numbers in urban areas. Because of the practice of feeding birds, most survive the winter to cause damage in gardens, allotments, farms and market gardens. In the autumn, flocks of sparrows feed on ripening split corn.

Besides damaging grain, sparrows disbud plum trees, currants and gooseberries and tear at crocuses, primroses, polyanthus, chrysanthemums and lettuces.

In cereal-growing areas, the house sparrow is considered a serious pest and under the Protection of Birds Act 1954, may be taken or killed by the owner or occupier of the land or someone authorised by them.

The cock house sparrow is an attractive, rusty-backed bird $5\frac{3}{4}$ in. long, with a black bib and grey crown. In spring he is exceptionally aggressive. He adopts a variety of postures when courting a hen which sometimes attracts other cocks who then join in a noisy 'sparrow party'.

The tree sparrow is much the same size and shape as the house sparrow. It is widespread in England and southern Scotland, more local in Wales and confined to the coastal counties in Ireland.

They can be distinguished from the house sparrows in having two white wing bars, a chocolate-coloured crown and a black patch on their white cheeks. Whereas hen house sparrows are dull brown, hen tree sparrows have the same colouring as the males.

Tree sparrows have similar breeding habits to house sparrows. Feeding mainly on weed seeds, however, tree sparrows cause little damage to crops.

Spawn

The egg mass laid in water by various creatures: fish, amphibians, molluscs such as snails, crustaceans such as crabs, and aquatic worms.

The number of eggs produced can be immense. Common frogs may produce up to 4000, and a toad lays up to 7000 eggs. A 30 lb. pike may lay up to 300,000 eggs, and a 10 lb. carp up to 700,000.

Such a prodigal production of eggs compensates for heavy losses among the young, as they provide food for other creatures, such as fish and birds.

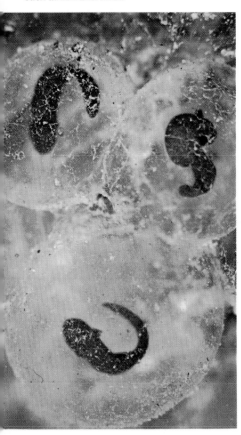

Tadpoles developing inside frog spawn. As many as 4000 eggs may be laid during each year by the common frog

Greater spearwort
Ranunculus linqua

Lesser spearwort
Ranunculus flammula

Spearworts, which belong to the buttercup family, are named for their long, pointed leaves

Spearwort

Members of the buttercup family with long, narrow, undivided leaves, spearworts grow in wet places such as marshes and fens and flower throughout the summer. One of the most handsome is greater spearwort which produces flowers up to 2 in. across on stems 2-4 ft high. Though never common it is scattered throughout Britain apart from the far north. Lesser spearwort is common everywhere. It has smaller flowers, up to 1 in. in diameter, narrower leaves and a hollow stem which rarely exceeds 2 ft in height. Both species have poisonous sap, which has been known to kill livestock.

Speckled wood see Brown butterfly

Speedwell

The gay blue or white flowers of speedwell grow wild on roadside verges throughout the British Isles. Speedwells are herbs with opposite leaves and four-petalled flowers.

Several speedwells are creeping plants up to 1 ft high, with spikes of blue flowers. The most common is germander speedwell, which grows in grassland and hedgebanks everywhere and flowers from March to July. Its flowers have a white centre and there are two lines of hairs on opposite sides of its stems. Wood speedwell is similar but the hairs are all round the stems. It grows in damp woods everywhere except in central and eastern England and the north of Scotland. It flowers between April and July. A third hairy species is common speedwell, which grows on dry soil. Its lilac flowers appear on very short stalks from May onwards.

In contrast, thyme-leaved speedwell is hairless, and grows only in damp grassland. It flowers from March to October.

Two speedwells with long narrow leaves grow in wet places. Marsh speedwell, which grows in meadows, bogs and beside ponds, most frequently in the north and west, has flower spikes which develop from only one of a pair of opposite leaves. Water speedwell, which grows in ponds and streams, has flower spikes from both leaves.

The annual speedwells are abundant in arable fields, gardens and waste places. Buxbaum's speedwell has shining green leaves and bright blue flowers all the year round. Ivy-leaved speedwell has greyish leaves and small, sometimes almost white, flowers. It is common in the south and east. Wall speedwell is smaller and more upright than the other two. It blossoms in summer on heaths, walls and grassland.

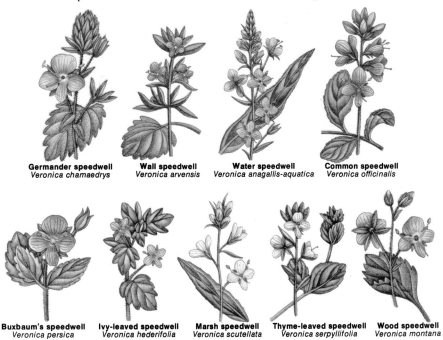

Germander speedwell
Veronica chamaedrys

Wall speedwell
Veronica arvensis

Water speedwell
Veronica anagallis-aquatica

Common speedwell
Veronica officinalis

Buxbaum's speedwell
Veronica persica

Ivy-leaved speedwell
Veronica hederifolia

Marsh speedwell
Veronica scutellata

Thyme-leaved speedwell
Veronica serpyllifolia

Wood speedwell
Veronica montana

Nine of the most common of the 18 species of speedwells that grow throughout the British Isles. One or another of the species is in bloom from March until October

Soil—the hidden jungle under foot

Hidden in the soil structure is a complex living world of animals and plants. Beneath a square foot of earth there may be as many as 20,000 small animals, the majority of which are impossible to see with the naked eye

Creatures invisible to the naked eye assume fearsome proportions when the jungle in a speck of soil 1/10 in. square is magnified 84 times. Picking their way

The study of the soil is a relatively new science. It is only in the last century that soil scientists, or pedologists, have come to realise that soil is not a dull, inert substance, but that it is teeming with life. One ounce of soil may contain 4000 million tiny organisms—more separate living things than there are people in the world.

The simplest definition of soil is that it is the material in which plants grow. As such it is essential to all life. Its chemical foods support plants which, in turn, sustain animals.

Just as peel covers an orange, so over most of the world's land surface soil covers the solid rocks of the earth's crust. Its depth varies from more than 20 ft to less than an inch. No two soils are ever identical; even within the area of a single farm, quite different soils may occur.

Soil is formed by the disintegration of rock, chiefly by gradual weathering. Temperature changes cause the surface layers to expand and contract more than the layers beneath and this daily cycle of stresses, repeated over many years, begins the break-up. Cracks form to let in water which, when it freezes and expands, sets up further strains and creates further disintegration. Minerals are an important content of all soil. The two most valuable to plant life are potassium and phosphorus, although other elements are needed in minute quantities for plants to grow well. These include iron, aluminium and calcium.

Lichens and a few hardy plants may begin to grow on the rocks, their filaments and roots probing any crevices. The breakdown is also aided by chemical action. Carbon dioxide, for instance, dissolves in the soil water to form carbonic acid which attacks many of the minerals in rocks. At the same time, rain washes out any soluble minerals, weakening the rock further.

Although most soil was formed in prehistoric times, assisted by the movement of glaciers in the Ice Ages, the process continues today.

Thus the skeleton of the soil is created—mineral particles, ranging in diameter from 1/200 to 1/12 of an inch, stacked upon one another like a microscopic pile of coal. At first sight soil appears to be a dense, solid mass, but only half its bulk is solid matter while the other half consists of pores, cracks and crevices, the smaller of which are filled with water and the larger with air.

This skeleton is far from lifeless. Just as a town is a collection of buildings filled with people, so the soil is a complex structure filled with life. One acre of soil contains up to 4 tons of living organisms.

Infinitesimally small viruses, bacteria, complex protozoa, slime moulds and fungi are all active in breaking down organic matter such as decaying plants. Fungi are especially energetic in breaking down matter like decaying wood. As different fungi attack at different stages of decay, there is usually a predictable sequence in which fungi occur. Toadstools and mushrooms are the most conspicuous species of soil fungi.

There is a vigorous animal life too. An acre of soil may well contain 100 million small animals. Among them are likely to be thread-like eelworms, mites, springtails, millipedes, centi-

tinually migrating up and down in the soil in response to changes in temperature and moisture and the availability of food. One thing that most soil animals have in common is their dependence on moisture. If it is not available, many die. On the other hand, if the soil becomes flooded, many animals are killed while others manage to survive for a time by keeping in the little pockets of air.

The amount of life in the soil varies with the season. Many organisms most active in the spring and autumn are dormant in the extreme temperatures of winter and summer. In severe weather their numbers fall dramatically, as generally they live in the top few inches of the soil, close to supplies of moisture and food. Soil organisms are not evenly distributed, but congregate in colonies that are probably related to their breeding or feeding.

As each organism dies, its body decays and is used as food by other organisms which, in their turn, are also devoured. In each case, the organic matter is broken down a little further until it finally becomes mixed into the soil structure, either by rain or through the activities of the animals themselves. The compounds may be carried about by the animals as they make their burrows or nests, or be deposited as droppings. Without this continual mixing of the organic matter with the minerals there would be no soil structure and plants would be unable to grow.

Looking like something from outer space, the beetle mite *Punctoribates* creeps through the soil in search of food — 86 times life size

An abundant species, the springtail *Sminthurinus* sits with its forked springing mechanism tucked under its body — 50 times life size

When the beetle mite *Liebstadia* is disturbed it draws in its legs and looks like an egg — 76 times life size

Long hairs on the body of the beetle mite *Platynothrus* pick up soil, camouflaging the mite from predators — 55 times life size

through a tangle of fungus threads are three mites: the plant-eating *Hypochthomius* (top right) and two predators called *Mesostigmatid* mites

pedes, woodlice, hordes of fly larvae, beetles, caterpillars, ants, earthworms, slugs and snails. Some feed on decaying plant and animal material, some on the roots of living plants, and many prey upon each other. Many spend their lives in restless movement, seeking food or mates, or searching for more favourable living conditions. The smaller animals, such as the mites, are much more numerous than the larger animals, and decompose much more soil matter. Some animals are con-

431

Newly hatched spiders of the species *Pisaura listeri* swarm in their nest before dispersing

Spider

Britain has more than 600 species of spiders, all of them harmless to man. They prey on other creatures, have eight legs and a body divided into only two parts: a combined head and thorax and a large abdomen. Most have eight eyes, arranged in two rows of four.

Spiders produce silk strands which, thickness for thickness, have a breaking strain greater than that of iron. Spider silk is only about 1/200 of a millimetre in diameter and is so light that if a spider could spin a single strand of silk the whole way round the world it would weigh less than 6 oz. The silk usually emerges from six spinnerets at the rear of the body. Different qualities such as sticky or dry can be given to the silk; those spiders which make sticky webs to catch insects spin dry radial threads to approach their prey. The thread which spiders use is extremely fine and has been used in telescopic gunsights.

Not all species produce webs. Some capture their prey by leaping upon them, while the spitting spider projects two streams of gummy thread at insects ¼-½ in. away. This species, which has a body length of ¼ in., is found only in southern England, where it hunts by night. It may be seen on walls and ceilings in homes or out-buildings.

However caught, the victims are stabbed by the fangs of the spiders which inject poison. Often the spiders then wrap their prey in silk and carry them to their nests.

The purseweb spider spins a tube, closed at both ends. Most of it is buried vertically in the ground, but the top lies on the surface.

Insects alighting on it are stabbed through the mesh by the spider and taken down the vertical section to be eaten, once the trap has been repaired.

Some species make a horizontal 'hammock' web on to which insects are tripped by a haphazard maze of threads. The web which is most often seen is that spun by the common spider. One radial of this web can be spun in about a second.

About 250 British spiders belong to the money spider family, most of which are only 1/10 in. long and black. Popular superstitions, which associate these spiders with wealth, may account for the fact that they are more widely tolerated than many larger spiders. Adult money spiders are widespread and common throughout the British Isles in late summer and autumn.

A common species of money spider spins hammock-like webs which are often seen close to ground level on garden plants, long grass, gorse, bramble or other vegetation. Money spiders are responsible for the clouds of gossamer which fall on fields, or even ships at sea, on fine days in autumn and early winter. The spiders spin their webs on warm mornings following a cool night and are carried aloft by the rising air currents. Cooler air brings them back to earth, sometimes over 100 miles from their starting point.

The cobweb spider is common in southern areas of the British Isles, where it lives in the corners of rooms at ceiling level, hanging motionless from a flimsy but extensive web. If disturbed, the spider rapidly vibrates its web, making itself almost invisible. About ⅓ in. long with long legs, it has a yellow and brown back with a grey abdomen.

There are three species of house spider— *Tegenaria domestica*, *T. atrica* and *T. parietina*. The last two are the biggest, with very long legs and a body length of up to ¾ in. *T. domestica* is smaller—about ⅖ in.—and lighter in colour. *T. parietina*, often called the Cardinal spider from the legend that members of this species used to frighten Cardinal Wolsey at Hampton Court, has legs that are longer and more furry. Not all of them live permanently in houses, but those from the open country often crawl up bathroom waste

COMMON TYPES OF SPIDER WEBS

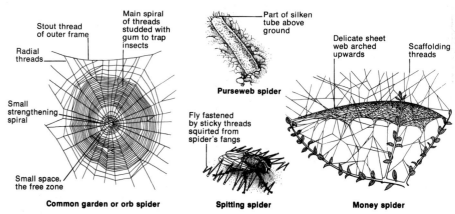

Most spiders spin characteristic silken webs; illustrated above are some typical examples. The common garden spider sits in the centre of its orb web, waiting for an insect to get caught in the sticky drops on the spiral thread. The money spider hangs beneath its hammock web, ready to dart at any small insect that gets trapped by the scaffolding and falls on to the sheet. The spider then bites the prey and pulls it down through the web to eat. The purseweb spider lives inside a sealed silken tube, 10-12 in. long, 2-3 in. of which is above ground. It strikes out with its two curved fangs at any insect crawling over this exposed part, wounds the prey and pulls it into the tube. The slow-moving spitting spider does not build a web, but spits streams of gummy threads at its victims to secure them to the ground

pipes as the cooler weather of autumn approaches.

The only spider in the world which lives permanently under water, the water spider, is found throughout the British Isles. It spins itself a 'diving bell' in which it lives and which it fills with air transported from the surface trapped in its body hairs. The water spider leaves the bell to prey on small aquatic animals, mainly water lice. The water spider is brown, but under water it appears silver, because of the air trapped in its body hairs.

The largest spider found in the British Isles is the raft spider, the female of which can have a body of ¾ in. or longer. It lives in swamps and dykes, where the water is usually still, and sits on leaves from which it darts over the water to capture passing insects.

The courtship of spiders is an elaborate affair, but few females devour their mates like the notorious black widow of North America. Males that die soon after mating generally do so from starvation or exhaustion, rather from any attack by the female. Male spiders have palpal organs at the end of their leading legs for mating. Most of them deposit sperm on a small sperm web, then absorb it into these organs, which act like a fountain pen filler, and go in search of a mate.

Courtship consists of visual displays, touching the female, or vibrating the female's web in a special way—spiders have receptors on their legs which are hypersensitive to vibrations.

The males then insert the palpal organs into sperm-storing organs of receptive females who receive sufficient sperm from one mating to fertilise eggs of several layings.

The number of eggs varies from just two laid by the *Oonops* to up to a thousand by *Araneus quadratus*. They are usually cocooned or guarded by the female until they hatch. Some females carry the cocoon of eggs around with them.

Young spiderlings hatch in the cocoon. A few days after emerging they moult into spiders, acquiring eyes, spinnerets and claws on the ends of their legs. They then disperse; each spider climbs to the top of a blade of grass or a plant, and produces a single strand of silk which eventually catches the wind and carries the young spider away.

To reach full adult size, young spiders moult three to ten times, depending on the species. Most species live for a year. Those that live longer moult annually to renew their external skeletons, which become damaged during the year.

The Arachnid class, to which spiders belong, is one of the oldest on earth, with a history stretching back 350 million years. It is named after the mythological maiden Arachne, who challenged the goddess Athena to a weaving contest and was changed into a spider. Hence the belief that it is unlucky to kill a spider.

The belief that spiders are fond of music is mere superstition. It is true that when the vibrations produced by a musical instrument set a spider's web trembling it becomes excited, but any vibration will do this; the spider believes that the movement is caused by the struggles to escape of newly trapped prey.

Camouflaged killer. The crab spider *Misumena vatia* matches the colour of the white or yellow flowers in which it lies in wait for insect prey

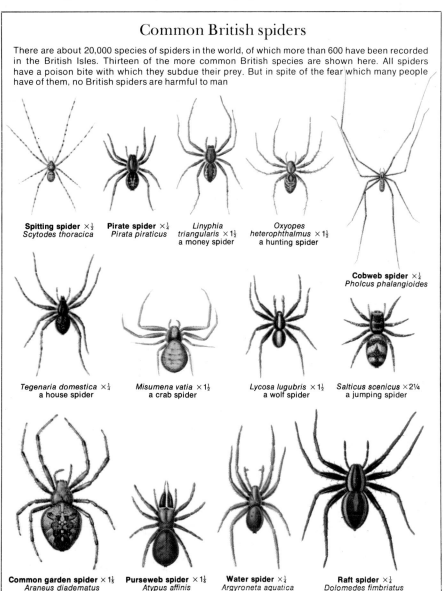

Common British spiders

There are about 20,000 species of spiders in the world, of which more than 600 have been recorded in the British Isles. Thirteen of the more common British species are shown here. All spiders have a poison bite with which they subdue their prey. But in spite of the fear which many people have of them, no British spiders are harmful to man

Spitting spider ×½
Scytodes thoracica

Pirate spider ×⅓
Pirata piraticus

Linyphia triangularis ×1½
a money spider

Oxyopes heterophthalmus ×1½
a hunting spider

Cobweb spider ×⅓
Pholcus phalangioides

Tegenaria domestica ×¼
a house spider

Misumena vatia ×1½
a crab spider

Lycosa lugubris ×1½
a wolf spider

Salticus scenicus ×2¼
a jumping spider

Common garden spider ×1½
Araneus diadematus

Purseweb spider ×1½
Atypus affinis

Water spider ×⅓
Argyroneta aquatica

Raft spider ×⅓
Dolomedes fimbriatus

Spindle shank fungus see Fungus

Spindle tree *Euonymus europaeus*

For thousands of years before the invention of the spinning wheel all the thread used for woollen cloth was spun by women twirling a stick called a spindle between their fingers. The spindle tree got its name because its thin stems came to be used for this purpose. They had the advantage of being very hard, smooth and firm, and of not splintering. Hand-spinners fed wool towards the spindle from a hank, twisting it as it went; the spindle's rotary motion gave the tension needed to draw loose fibres into tight thread. To maintain the spindle's momentum, a circular stone weight with a hole in it was fixed on one end. Such 'spindle whorls' have been found on prehistoric sites. The wood was also used by gipsies to make pegs, knitting needles and skewers, hence its country name of skewer-wood.

The tree is never more than 15 ft tall, and grows mainly on lime-rich soils in southern counties of England. Young twigs are greyish-green and square in cross-section; older stems are rounded with thin, grey bark. The grey-green leaves, in opposite pairs, are small and oval. Small greenish flowers, which may be male, female, or a combination of the two, open in May. A complete flower holds four sepals, four petals, four stamens and a central pistil.

After pollination by insects this pistil ripens to the beautiful autumn fruit. This is a bright pink, four-lobed capsule, which splits to reveal the bright orange flesh surrounding each hard yellow seed. This gay colour contrast attracts birds, which spread the seeds. People also gather the branches as decorations. Seedlings, which bear two small seed-leaves, spring up along the hedgerows. At Norbury Park, near Dorking in Surrey, there is a spindle tree thicket – the only one in Britain.

Spiny-headed worm

This name applies to a group of worms which are parasites in the intestines of birds, fish and mammals including, rarely, man. Most spiny-headed worms are less than 1 in. long. The adults have elongated bodies consisting of a tube-like trunk with a neck and short retractable head covered in backward-curving spines. The worms attach themselves to the walls of their hosts' intestines by their spines. They have no digestive system, and absorb food through their own body walls.

After fertilisation the eggs develop within the female, and when they reach the larval stage each is encased in a shell and laid. In this form, the larva passes out of the host. If the larva is eaten by certain insects or aquatic crustaceans, it emerges from its shell and bores into the intestine walls of the new, intermediate host. There it grows until nearly adult, when development ceases. Then, if the host is eaten by a fish, bird or mammal, the worm attaches itself to the host's intestine wall where development is completed.

A typical spiny-headed worm, *Polymorphus boschadis* is ⅓ in. long and lives in the intestines of birds such as ducks and swans. Its intermediate host is the freshwater shrimp.

Spit

Waves and currents deposit sand and shingle along the coastline, and where the coastline is broken by estuaries and similar inlets these deposits may continue part of the way across them to form spits. Waves and currents further modify these deposits, giving them hooked ends. Well-known British examples are Hurst Castle spit at the entrance to The Solent, and Spurn Head across the Humber. See also COAST

Spleenwort see Fern

Sponge

Large, pliant bath sponges come from the Mediterranean, but about 250, mostly small species, are found in British waters. Sponges are animals – the most primitive multi-celled animals in the world. They live both in the sea and in fresh water. They draw in water through fine holes in their body walls, extract minute food particles and oxygen from it, and discharge it through a larger opening. The body shape and colour of the British species is so variable that microscopic examination is necessary to identify many of them.

Spicules – small, splinter-like granules – stiffen the sponges' bodies and their chemical composition helps identification. In some sponges the spicules are made of silica, as in the encrusting sponges on rocks and boulders found low down on rocky shores. They include the green, yellow or brown bread-crumb sponge *Halichondria* and the red or orange *Hymeniacidon*.

Two common freshwater sponges are *Spongilla fluviatilis*, found on tree roots and posts in lakes, and *S. lacustris*, found in deep water in quiet stretches of rivers and on the sides of locks; both have spicules of silica. Purse sponges – such as the 1-2 in. long *Grantia*, which is common on rocky shores, *Leucosolenia* which looks like a bunch of tiny white bananas, and the white cylinders of *Sycon* – all have spicules which are calcareous or chalky.

The boring sponge *Cliona* attacks oysters. It drills holes 1/10-1/5 in. across in oyster shells, weakening them, and making them unfit to sell.

Sponges reproduce in various ways. Some marine sponges grow buds, which break off, each one becoming the nucleus of a new sponge.

Freshwater sponges reproduce sexually. They produce drought-resistant capsules, containing male and female organs; the male organs release sperm which fertilises eggs in the female organs, and these eggs then develop within the sponge's body wall into larvae. The larvae have a short free-swimming existence.

Pieces of sponge are used by spider crabs and hermit crabs to camouflage the tops of their shells.

This spiny-headed worm is a common parasite of many fish, including trout, perch and roach

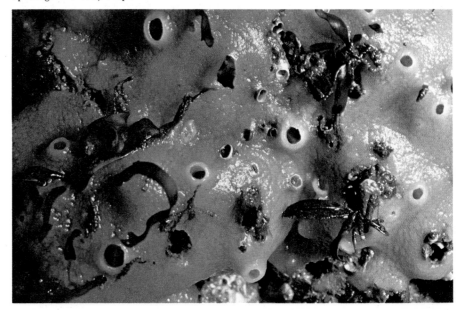

The bread-crumb sponge, which can be green, yellow or brown, is usually found on rocks and boulders

Spoonbill see Heron

Springtail

There are more than 300 British species of springtails, tiny insects which live in huge numbers in soil or litter. They are also common in grass or foliage. One study of the top 6 in. of an acre of pasture revealed 174 million of them and when the top 12 in. was sampled, the total reached 248 million.

Springtails owe their name to a special forked spring at the end of their abdomens. The spring is usually bent forwards and held on the underside of the body by a knob which passes between the two prongs; when this knob is contracted, the spring is released, propelling the insect forwards, sometimes as much as 12 in.

Species which live on the surface are brightly patterned and have well-developed eyes and springing mechanisms. Others, which live in the soil and never come to the surface, are white and have no springing organs or eyes. One species *Podura aquatica*, which is black or slaty-grey, lives on the water of ponds and streams. Most springtails have elongated bodies up to $\frac{1}{4}$ in. long, but some have grotesque, globular bodies.

The only springtail without a springing mechanism is the black *Anurida maritima*.

JUMPING WITHOUT LEGS

At rest

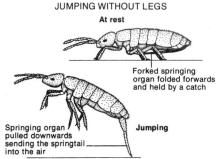

Forked springing organ folded forwards and held by a catch

Springing organ pulled downwards sending the springtail into the air

Jumping

When disturbed the ⅜ in. springtail can spring a distance of a foot or more, the equivalent of a man jumping 250-300 yds

Spring usher moth see Winter moth

Spruce

An evergreen, symmetrically cone-shaped conifer of which two species, the Norway spruce and the Sitka spruce, both members of the pine family, are widely grown in British forests. In May, yellow male flowers open. The wind carries pollen from these to the crimson female flowers; by autumn these have ripened to brown downward-pointing cones. Each cone scale carries two small winged seeds, which the wind blows to the forest floor where they sprout the following spring.

Spruce is unique among the conifers: if one of its slender needles is pulled off, the peg to which it is attached comes off too. However, if a needle drops naturally it leaves its peg behind.

Norway spruce *Picea abies* is familiar to

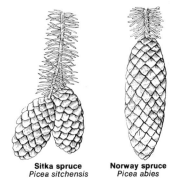

Sitka spruce
Picea sitchensis

Norway spruce
Picea abies

Sitka spruce cones have wavy-ended scales; those of Norway spruce have rounded ends

everyone as the Christmas tree. The custom of decorating it at Christmas was introduced from Germany in 1844 by Prince Albert, Queen Victoria's Consort. The tree is also planted extensively for timber. The needles are dark green and the cones have leathery, rounded scales.

More widespread as a timber tree, because it grows much faster, is Sitka spruce *P. sitchensis*, which was introduced from Alaska in 1831. Its needles are flat, silvery underneath and sharper than those of Norway spruce, and its cones have wavy scales. The bark, unlike that of Norway spruce, flakes off.

Spruce timber, also called whitewood, is pale brown, soft and easily worked.

The natural life-span of the spruce is 150 years and it can reach a great height. British records are—Sitka spruce: 164 ft at Murthly Castle near Perth; Norway spruce: 138 ft at Strathallan, Perthshire. See also CONIFER

Spurge

There are three widespread species of spurge in the British Isles, all of them annual herbs yellowish-green in colour. The stems, which rarely exceed 1 ft in height, exude a milky juice when broken. The flowers are borne in separate male and female clusters. Each flower consists of a single stamen or a single ovary surrounded by a cup of bracts—modi-

Dwarf spurge
Euphorbia exigua

Sun spurge
Euphorbia helioscopia

Petty spurge
Euphorbia peplus

fied leaves around the flower head. They blossom throughout the summer.

Sun spurge is a common weed of arable fields and waste places in south and east England. It has broad blunt leaves, and the bracts are arranged in a regular pattern. Petty spurge has similar leaves but the whole plant is much smaller than the sun spurge, and the glands on the bracts are crescent shaped. Dwarf spurge, least common of the three and usually confined to lime-rich soils, has narrow, pointed leaves.

Spurge-laurel *Daphne laureola*

A shrub 2-4 ft high, with bright green evergreen leaves clustered at the top of the stems, hiding the sweet-scented, greenish flowers. These appear between February and April and later develop into black oval fruits. All parts of the plant, especially the berries and bark, are acrid and poisonous, though the bark was once used to treat cancer.

Spurge-laurel grows in woods throughout the lowlands of England and Wales.

The sweet-scented flowers of spurge-laurel, a poisonous plant of lowland woods

Spurrey, Corn *Spergula arvensis*

A common and troublesome weed of cornfields and bare ground, especially where the soil is light and sandy. It is sometimes called pick purse because of the damage it causes. However, in some parts of Europe corn spurrey is grown as a crop. Sheep are fond of it and it gives a fine flavour to mutton. Cows fed on it are said to give rich milk.

Corn spurrey is a scrambling plant about 1 ft high with long, narrow leaves arranged in whorl-like clusters at the swollen joints of the downy stems. The white flowers appear from June to August and when the fruits are ripe the flower stalks turn downwards.

Squash bug

The name, which covers 18 species of British bugs, comes from America where the bug damages gourd (squash) plants. Like their American relatives, British squash bugs feed on the ripening seeds of plants but, since they do not damage commercially important seeds, they are not often brought to notice.

Squash bugs are usually dull brown or green, ¼-½ in. long, and have long antennae. One of the most common species is the dock squash bug *Coreus marginatus* which lays its eggs on dock leaves or the leaves of related plants such as sorrel. Young bugs feed on the stems and leaves but, as they grow, concentrate on ripening seeds. Adults hibernate in the winter and mate in May or June.

Squat lobster

A mini version of the lobster. It has a flattened body, a pair of long pincers and a tail flap, which is usually kept tucked underneath the body. The two largest of the five British species are common on rocky shores. *Galathea squamifera* has a greenish-brown body 2-3 in. long. It lives in pools and beneath boulders. Sometimes several dozen may be found underneath one boulder. The 3-6 in. long *G. strigosa* has a red body with blue lines along it, and can give a painful nip with its pincers.

Squat lobsters have five pairs of legs. The

The 2-3 in. long squat lobster *Galathea squamifera* is the most common British species

first pair form pincers. The next three pairs are used for crawling on the sea-bed. The fifth pair is small and weak. When startled in the water squat lobsters can swim backwards by straightening the tail flap and then flicking it under the body. They are scavengers, drawing in pieces of animal remains with the bristles on their mouth.

The three other species may sometimes move on to the lower shore in spring and early summer, but they are small and difficult to find: *G. nexa* and *G. dispersa* are only 1½ in. long, and *G. intermedia* is less than 1 in. long.

Squill, Vernal

The bright blue, star-like flowers of this 3-9 in. high plant stud the grassy cliffs of the western coasts of Britain and the eastern coasts of Ireland in spring and early summer. The long, narrow, dark green leaves appear before the flowers and remain, twisted, in the grass long after the petals have fallen. Flowers found in August and September on the coasts of Devon and Cornwall will be of the autumn squill.

The squill formerly used to treat certain forms of dropsy came from the Mediterranean species *Urginea maritima*.

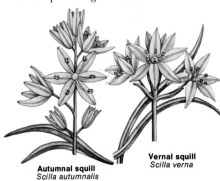

Autumnal squill
Scilla autumnalis

Vernal squill
Scilla verna

Squinancy wort *Asperula cynanchica*

A small trailing plant related to the bedstraws, with very narrow leaves arranged in fours round the slender stem, which produces white, waxy four-petalled flowers tinged with pink in June and July. It grows in grassland on chalk and limestone and is scattered throughout England, South Wales and western Ireland. It also sometimes occurs on sea cliffs.

Squinancy is another word for quinsy, and a gargle made from this plant was once believed to cure a sore throat.

Squire

The principal landowner of a country locality is often customarily known as 'the squire'. Although he does not have an official status, he usually exercises considerable influence as a substantial landlord and employer.

He may also often have the right to nominate the parson of the local Anglican church whenever there is a vacancy.

In the 18th and 19th centuries, before everyone had the vote and before voting became secret, the squire had immense political power as most people were dependent on him for their living.

The word 'squire' has come down from feudal times, when people rendered military service in exchange for being allowed to hold land. Under this system a squire was ranked next to a knight. The word was possibly derived from 'esquire'—a man who attended a knight in battle.

Squirrel

Despite a widespread belief, Britain's native red squirrel was not ousted by the larger and stronger grey squirrel, although individuals of the two species have been observed fighting. An epidemic disease is thought to have decimated the reds, whereupon the more adaptable greys, introduced from America in the 1870's, invaded their feeding territories.

Both rodents are active climbers with long bushy tails. They sit upright to nibble a nut or acorn between their forepaws. Red squirrels *Sciurus vulgaris leucourus* have lived

The squat lobster *Galathea strigosa* swims backwards by using its tail flap as a paddle

The grey squirrel, slightly larger than the red, can be tame enough to feed by hand

The red squirrel usually eats sitting on a tree stump, but is shy and difficult to spot

in Britain since prehistoric times. They prefer conifers, and their numbers appear to be increasing with the spread of conifer plantations. Red squirrels are most common in Wales, Ireland, the West Country, the East Anglian Breckland, the northern counties and much of Scotland.

They are about 8 in. long, with 7 in. long, pale tan tails which bleach almost white in summer. They have ear tufts, which grey squirrels do not possess. Their reddish-brown coats turn more grey-brown in winter. Introduced continental squirrels *S. v. vulgaris* are much darker, almost black.

Red squirrels build a nest or drey of leafless twigs and strips of bark lined with moss and grass, usually in a fork of a conifer. They produce two litters of three or four kittens a year, in spring and autumn. If disturbed, the mother will carry them away in her mouth. Red squirrels are very shy and difficult to spot amongst the dense cover of conifer needles, but pine cones littering the ground and their 'breakfast table' tree stumps signal their presence. These squirrels will populate a pine forest at the rate of one pair an acre.

The grey *S. carolinensis* is bigger than the red squirrel, being 10 in. long with a less bushy, 8 in. long tail. In winter the coat is pale grey with longer fur than in summer. Occasional black individuals turn up. Greys began appearing in the countryside between 1876 and 1929, having been released deliberately or accidentally from a number of centres, especially London Zoo and Woburn

Park, Bedfordshire. They have now invaded almost every county of England, except for much of East Anglia and Cornwall, and are established in central Scotland and central Ireland. So far, greys have not reached the Isle of Wight.

Grey squirrels have survived repeated Government-sanctioned attempts at extermination by shooting, trapping and poison. Greys do considerable damage to trees when present in large numbers. They attack trees in early summer gnawing at the main stem, seeking the sweet, sappy layers immediately beneath the bark. Sometimes the tree is

THE DISTRIBUTION OF SQUIRRELS

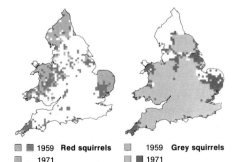

1959 **Red squirrels**　1959 **Grey squirrels**
1971　　　　　　　　1971

Grey squirrels, introduced from America about 100 years ago, have spread throughout most of England and Wales, except for Cornwall and parts of East Anglia. In the same period, red squirrels have lost territory, probably because of disease, and not 'defeat' by the grey invaders

completely ringed and dies. It is usually checked and spoilt. It is now illegal to import a grey squirrel or keep one as a pet. They will adapt to any area covered by trees, whether broad-leaved or conifer, with an average density of about five per acre. Greys will live in suburban parks and gardens, becoming tame enough to feed from the hand. The drey is a ball of twigs, often with leaves attached, lined with grass, moss and fur. Summer dreys are attached to branches, but breeding and winter nests may be inside a hollow tree. There are two breeding seasons, in early spring and early summer, each of which produces a litter of three or four kittens.

Both reds and greys keep to well-defined runways along tree branches in their territory. They feed on a variety of nuts, seeds, buds, bark, berries, fungi and occasional eggs, young birds and insects. Pine seeds are important to red squirrels and beech mast to greys. Surplus food is buried at all times when plentiful, making squirrels useful agents in seed dispersal and tree planting.

Stable

The mechanisation of agriculture has resulted in many farm stables being used for purposes other than housing horses, such as storing equipment and fodder. Coaching inns and country houses have also adapted their stables to modern use.

When used for horses, a stable has a stall for each horse, a manger and a hay-rick. There is also usually a loft for storing hay and an annexe with bins for chaff and oats. A harness room is often attached.

Stable is also sometimes used to describe a building in which cattle and goats are kept. See also FARM

Stable fly *Stomoxys calcitrans*

Although this ¼ in. long fly is usually found in farmyards or fields, it occasionally enters houses in the country and is usually mistaken for a housefly—until it bites.

It resembles the housefly in colouring—grey with indistinct darker stripes—and is sometimes known as the 'biting housefly'. The bite is inflicted by the stable fly's rigid tubular proboscis or mouth through which it sucks blood. The stable fly feeds on the blood of horses, cattle and other mammals—including humans.

The female can lay up to 600 eggs in batches of 60-70 among stable refuse. The larvae hatch in two or three days, need dark conditions for their development, and feed on stable rubbish. When fully grown they resemble housefly maggots. The larvae live for two or three weeks before spending 9-13 days in the pupa stage.

There is about one generation of flies a month during the summer, and adult flies can be seen in any month from May to October. The adult females can often be seen on the bellies of cattle, which appear to be a favourite feeding place.

Stack

One of several words—such as stack, mow, cock—for a pile of unthreshed corn. The words are generally interchangeable, as in 'haystack' and 'hayrick', although 'rick' is sometimes used for a long pile and 'stack' for a round pile. A cock is a small heap of newly mown hay built to a height of about 3 ft to dry.

The mechanisation of harvesting has resulted in the development of a standard rectangular bundle of hay, and this has eliminated regional variations in haystacks.

Round stacks with conical tops to prevent rainwater penetrating are still found, although many have plastic covers on top.

Stack see Coast
Staddle stones see Granary

Stag beetle *Lucanus cervus*

Male stag beetles can grow to more than 2½ in. and are the longest beetles found in Britain. They are dull black and usually live only in south-east England.

Males have large, antler-like jaws which give them a fierce appearance. The purpose of the antlers is obscure. They cannot be used for feeding as they would hold the food too far from the mouth—and adults do not usually eat. The jaws cannot inflict a painful bite because the muscles are too weak, but their intimidating appearance is a good deterrent against enemies, and the mouth is possibly of some importance in courtship.

Females burrow into rotting tree stumps to lay their eggs, and the fat, white larvae live on the wood, taking about three years to reach full size.

Stag beetles mating; the female will burrow into a rotting tree stump to lay her eggs

Stalactite and stalagmite see Underground Britain
Standing stone see p. 442

438

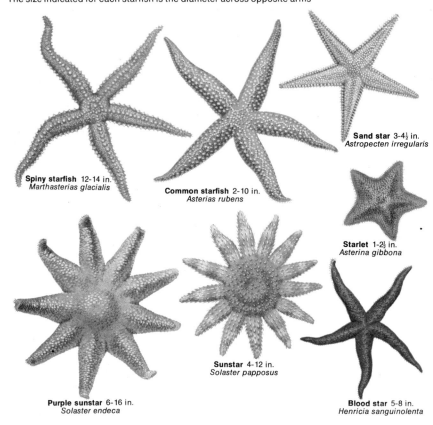

Common starfish of the British seashore

There are 2000 species of starfish in the world, most of them living in shallow seas. Seven species live inshore around the coasts of the British Isles where they are often serious pests on oyster and mussel beds. A number of other species live offshore and are occasionally washed up on beaches. The size indicated for each starfish is the diameter across opposite arms

Spiny starfish 12-14 in. *Marthasterias glacialis*
Common starfish 2-10 in. *Asterias rubens*
Sand star 3-4½ in. *Astropecten irregularis*
Starlet 1-2½ in. *Asterina gibbona*
Purple sunstar 6-16 in. *Solaster endeca*
Sunstar 4-12 in. *Solaster papposus*
Blood star 5-8 in. *Henricia sanguinolenta*

Starfish

A typical starfish has five arms, although the number varies. A starfish may abandon an arm if in danger or handled roughly, growing another to replace it.

Seven species live round the shores of the British Isles. The reddish-brown common starfish grows up to 10 in. across. It usually lives on rocky shores, feeding mostly on bivalve molluscs such as mussels which cling to the rocks. The starfish grips a mussel's shell with many tiny tube feet ending in suction discs, which extend from the underside of the starfish arms. These slowly pull the valves apart, and then the starfish can insert its stomach—which it extrudes through its elastic mouth—into the mussel and digest it. The tube feet are also used for walking over rocks, including vertical surfaces. Common starfish can be serious predators on oyster beds, and so are often collected and dumped on shore to die. The old practice of tearing them in two and throwing them back into the sea merely doubled their numbers since, provided at least one-fifth of the central disc is attached to an arm, a completely new starfish will develop from it.

Also found on rocky shores is the grey-green spiny starfish and the short-armed starlet. Starlets grow to about 2½ in. across and lie well camouflaged amongst sponges beneath boulders.

The sand star lives on the sea-bed in clean, sandy areas. Its flattened arms and pointed tube feet are adaptations for burrowing into sand. Sand stars feed by swallowing worms and small molluscs whole.

Other species live below the low-water mark and only occasionally get washed ashore. They include the sunstar and the purple sunstar. Both have more than the usual five arms; the sunstar has 8-13 and is a predator on the common starfish. On the east coast, the red, orange or purple-coloured blood star may also be seen.

In the spring, the female starfish sheds 2-3 million eggs into the sea where they are fertilised when the male sheds his sperm. The eggs develop into larvae, which two months later become small starfish. The female blood starfish is an exception: she broods over her eggs until they hatch.

Starling *Sturnus vulgaris*

A bird which can adapt to most conditions, from those of the remote Shetlands to central London. The starling is about 8½ in. long with a short tail. It has a glossy, blue-black plumage with a purple and green sheen, and the beak is yellow. In winter the bird is speckled with white and buff and the beak is a darker hue.

There is little difference in appearance between the sexes, but the female is more speckled than the male in winter, and less shiny than the male in summer. Young birds are grey-brown.

Starlings run about with a curious waddling movement looking for insects and grubs to eat. A favourite food is leather-jackets, the larvae of the cranefly. They also eat click-beetles and their larvae (wireworms) and other pests.

The birds can often be seen among cattle, feeding on the insects disturbed by the grazing animals. They also pick parasites off the backs of sheep.

When natural food is scarce they clamour for bread, fruit and other kitchen scraps, often bullying other birds to ensure that they get more than their fair share. They also damage crops by eating soft fruit, apples and pears, and sprouting cereals.

Starlings breed in holes in buildings and trees, and often take over the nest holes of woodpeckers. The nests are usually of straw, lined with feathers, moss or wool. About six pale blue eggs are laid in April or May and hatch in 12-13 days. The young become independent in three weeks. Usually there is only a single brood in a season.

The song of the starling is a mixture of twitters and clicks with occasional high whistles. It also mimics the calls of other birds.

Most starlings are resident, but large numbers of migrants arrive from the Continent in late autumn, boosting the winter population of starlings in the British Isles to many millions. At this time in particular the birds seek the greater warmth of the cities, where their droppings foul buildings and pavements. Many methods of keeping them at bay have been tried, including broadcasting distress calls and painting their roosting ledges with sticky jelly.

Starlings feed on apples and other fruit when their normal diet of insects and insect larvae runs out

Star of Bethlehem
Ornithogalum umbellatum

A bulbous plant with long narrow leaves and a conspicuous branched flowering stem which appears in the spring and reaches 12 in. high. It is called Star of Bethlehem because of its white star-like flowers, made up of six petals, and because it is abundant in Palestine. Each petal has a green stripe on the back which can be clearly seen until the flower opens in the middle of the morning — hence the plant's other name, ten o'clock lady. The flowers close again in dull weather. Their normal season is from April until June. The flowers develop into small, heart-shaped capsules each of which contains a few round, black seeds.

Star of Bethlehem is possibly a native of sandy grassland in the Breckland of East Anglia, but elsewhere it has almost certainly spread from gardens. It is found on roadsides and waste places, spreading by bulbs and seeds throughout lowland Britain, but is absent from Ireland.

Named after its white, star-like flowers, the Star of Bethlehem grows up to 12 in. high

Stick-dressing

A traditional activity in many villages connected with sheep-farming, especially those in the Scottish borders. A horn from an old ram is joined to a shaft of hazel or holly and is decorated either with nail-heads or carvings.

Usually the horn alone is decorated, but some craftsmen carve the shaft as well, often with representations of country scenes and animals.

The craft is still carried on and the finest stick-dressers live in the North Tyne Valley and in Rennington, Northumberland.

Stickleback *Gasterosteus aculeatus*

Probably the most familiar freshwater fish in the British Isles, the stickleback is found in rivers, lakes and ponds everywhere, except for mountainous regions. It is also seen in salt water—in estuaries, rock pools and brackish dykes.

A stickleback can grow to 4 in. long, but most measure less than 2½ in. They have three dorsal spines in front of the dorsal fin, and the upper parts are blue-black or green, with paler colours below.

In the breeding season—March to July—the female's colours take on a yellow tinge. The male's throat and belly become a brilliant orange-red, his back a clear green, and his eyes electric-blue.

With these attractive colours and an elaborate courtship ritual, he entices the female into a nest he has prepared in the vegetation at the water's edge. The nest is made from vegetable fibres bound with sticky threads ejected from the male's kidneys. The eggs and newly born fry are guarded in the nest by the male for about a week after hatching.

Sticklebacks eat worms, insects and crustaceans, and are in turn eaten by pike, perch, otters and kingfishers. Sticklebacks mature after about a year, and though some may live for three-and-a-half years, few survive for more than 18 months. See also TEN-SPINED STICKLEBACK

Stile

The word comes from the Old English *stigel,* meaning to climb.

Stiles give people access to a footpath through or over a fence or hedge, while barring the way to sheep and cattle. They are usually made of wood in the form of steps, though some are of metal. Many have deteriorated in this century with the decline in the use of country footpaths.

In the Lake District the word refers directly to footpaths leading to high ground, as in High Stile.

Stilt-legged fly

This fly gets its name because of its long second and third pairs of legs. It walks rather awkwardly on its 'stilts' as it searches for small insects to eat — mainly gnats, midges and aphids.

Stilt-legged flies are ¼ in. long and are found

during the summer in marshy areas, usually among the vegetation at the waterside. They are mostly black, but some species have reddish faces and legs. A common British species is *Calobata petronella*. There are four similar species and three smaller, rarer relatives. The eggs are laid on rotten wood; the larvae are thought to burrow into it.

Stinkhorn

A common fungus which appears in late summer and autumn in rich soils of gardens and woods. A whitish ball about the size of a hen's egg first appears above the ground. When the 'egg' is ripe, the outer skin becomes ruptured, the inner tissue elongates and grows within a few hours into a white spongy tube 4-5 in. high and 1 in. thick, with a conical cap covered with a dark green sticky spore mass.

Substances in the spore mass of the stinkhorn *Phallus impudicus* rapidly break down on exposure to air to produce an unpleasant smell. This attracts flies, which feed on the spore mass and thus distribute the spores.

The characteristic smell usually means this fungus is smelt before it is seen. Needless worries about bad drains are often caused by stinkhorns growing near houses. Once the spore mass has been removed by flies a stinkhorn no longer smells. The egg stage is edible, but the smell of the ripe stage usually deters people from eating it. The fungus spreads through leaves and soil by means of white, cord-like strands.

The smaller dog stinkhorn *Mutinus caninus* has a faint smell, which is quite mild by comparison with the stinkhorn. It grows among dead leaves and old stumps in woodlands. The slender, 3-4 in. stalk is orange with a dark green spore mass on top.

Both fungi appear from July to November. See also FUNGUS

Stint see Sandpiper

Stitchwort

The name stitchwort was given to these straggling plants because they were once thought to cure the stitch—a pain in the side —when drunk in wine with the powder of acorns. Stitchworts have white star-like flowers with five petals divided half way to their base, or more, and narrow-pointed leaves arranged in pairs.

Three species are commonly found throughout the British Isles, their stems growing up to 2 ft long. Greater stitchwort has flowers up to 1 in. across which appear in April in woods and hedgebanks.

The flowers of the lesser stitchwort are smaller, only about ½ in. across, and the whole plant is very slender with grass-green coloured leaves. It begins to flower in May on heaths and dry grassland. The flowers of bog stitchwort are even smaller, rarely more than ¼ in. in diameter and with the petals shorter than the sepals. It

Greater stitchwort
Stellaria holostea

Bog stitchwort
Stellaria alsine

Lesser stitchwort
Stellaria graminea

grows in wet places, by streams, in marshes and in wet woods, flowering from May to July.

Stoat

With the possible exception of weasels, stoats are the most common carnivorous mammals in the British Isles. Because of the damage they cause to game and poultry, they are often killed by farmers and gamekeepers. Many stoats perished in the gin traps (steel net traps, now illegal) set for rabbits, and in south-west Wales they were exterminated.

With more intensive modern farming methods and the growth of forests in Britain, stoats are now more valued because they keep down vermin such as mice, rats and voles. Until the spread of myxomatosis in the 1950's, rabbits formed the stoats' main diet, augmented by smaller mammals, such as mice, voles and shrews, and some birds and reptiles. With their bounding gait, stoats pursue their prey relentlessly, using their excellent hearing and sense of smell; their eyesight is poor.

Rabbits and hares appear to be petrified by stoats and lie down and scream just before the kill, which the stoat administers with a bite behind the neck. Stoats are good at climbing and swimming, and usually track down their victim to the finish. When cornered, a stoat will make a spitting 'bark'.

Male stoats are slender, about 17 in. long, including their 4½ in. tails, and nearly half as heavy again as the females. They are bigger than weasels and they always have black tips to their tails. In summer their coats are red-brown on top and white underneath and they moult in spring and autumn.

Stoat, weasel and polecat

These three animals, all relentless hunters, are shown together because their body shapes are similar and they are sometimes confused by the inexpert. The stoat is shown in both its winter and summer coats. The sizes given are for length, including tail

Winter coat

Summer coat

Stoat 17 in.
Mustela erminea

Weasel 10 in.
Mustela nivalis

Polecat 22 in.
Putorius putorius

In northern parts, they turn completely white after the autumn moult, when their fur is called ermine—used traditionally to trim the gowns of royalty and the peerage in Britain. The black spot at the end of the tail, which remains even in winter, is used for decorative effect. The change in colouring is determined by temperature and length of daylight. Stoats in the south also produce a winter pelt. It is similar to the summer coat, but thicker.

Stoats make their dens in or near wooded areas, where they settle in hollow trees, old rabbit burrows or crevices. The females produce one litter a year in the spring, which is the result of mating the previous summer; this apparently long gestation period is due to a process called 'delayed implantation', in which embryos remain in a suspended state for about 280 days until spring temperatures set off their development. The embryos reach full term in 21-28 days.

Young stoats, usually about six in number, remain with their mother after weaning and hunt in family parties. Family groups can sometimes be seen apparently at play, chasing, boxing and turning somersaults. Stoats sometimes use this display to lure rabbits or water fowl within reach.

Man is the stoat's enemy, but it is also preyed on by owls and hawks.

Smaller types of stoats are found in Ireland, where they are called weasels—there are no true weasels in Ireland—and on the isles of Jura and Islay off western Scotland. See also POLECAT, WEASEL

Stock

Two kinds of stock grow wild along the coasts of Britain. Both are sweet-scented with purple or white flowers and are rare.

Hoary stock or gilliflower may have originally spread from gardens but now thrives on sea cliffs in a few places in southern England. It has a woody stem up to 30 in. high and flowers from May to July.

Sea stock is shorter, 9-24 in., without a woody stem, and flowers later—from July to August. It is mainly a plant of sand dunes in the south-west and can be recognised by its lower leaves, which are divided into narrow lobes.

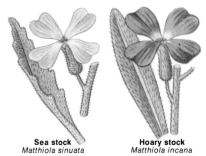

Sea stock
Matthiola sinuata

Hoary stock
Matthiola incana

Hoary stock is the parent plant from which the many varieties of the garden stock arose

Stock dove see Pigeon

Two Puritans suffer ridicule in the stocks in this engraving by William Hogarth (1697-1764)

Stocks

Villages were once required by law to maintain stocks for the punishment of offenders. Their legs or hands were held in apertures cut in two planks which were padlocked together and held by stone or wooden vertical supports. Stocks were usually erected in public places such as village greens or market squares so that passers-by could add to the severity of the sentence according to their reactions to the crime, details of which were often displayed on a noticeboard.

Many still remain, especially near churchyards, as at South Harting, Sussex. Others are found at the market cross in Ripley, Yorkshire, and at Little Budworth, Cheshire. Stocks by Scots Gate, Berwick-upon-Tweed, were last used in the 1840's.

Stone see p. 444
Stonechat see Chat

Stonecrop

Creeping plants which colour rocks, cliffs and walls with patches of white or yellow during summer. They have succulent leaves which store water and enable them to grow for several weeks during a dry spell.

Four species are commonly found growing wild in the British Isles, two of them yellow and two white. The most common throughout the British Isles is the yellow biting stonecrop or wall-pepper, named from the acrid taste of its blunt yellow-green leaves. It grows 1-4 in. high, not only on walls, but on sand hills near the sea.

The other yellow species is the 6-12 in. reflexed stonecrop, introduced from southern Europe and now widely naturalised on old walls in England and Wales. The pointed, dark green leaves were once eaten as a salad.

The most widespread white-flowered species is white stonecrop with leaves almost $\frac{1}{2}$ in. long and much-branched flowering stems, 3-9 in. high. English stonecrop is found only in the west of Britain where it is often abundant on rocks; it has tiny leaves and the flowering stem has only two main branches. It grows 1-3 in. high.

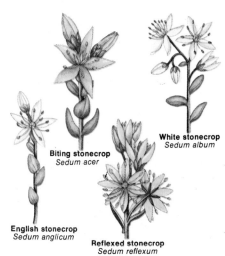

Biting stonecrop
Sedum acer

White stonecrop
Sedum album

English stonecrop
Sedum anglicum

Reflexed stonecrop
Sedum reflexum

All four species of stonecrops have fleshy leaves which enable them to store water

Stones erected by man or shaped by nature

Massive stones or boulders, standing in isolation or clustered together in groups, may represent the aspirations of man or the freak effects of nature — shaped by the elements throughout centuries of time and exposure

Stones erected by man to symbolise a belief or commemorate an event, place or person are known as standing stones, but many other large upright stones created by the forces of nature also look as if they are the work of man.

Natural standing stones vary considerably in shape and size and some, called erratics, bear no apparent relationship to the area in which they are found. Erratics are stones which were carried by Ice Age glaciers from one part of the country to another, sometimes deposited miles away from their original source

A rocking stone or logan — where one boulder is perched upon another and can be rocked back and forth without overturning — may be an erratic that came to rest in this way by chance. Rocking stones in the extreme south of England beyond the reach of glaciers are the freak results of weathering, wind-blown sand, frost and rainwater having eroded the soil or rock face underneath.

The best-known rocking stone is the Logan Rock near Land's End, estimated to weigh over 70 tons. There is also a good example on the Pass of Llanberis in Wales and there are at least seven others near Warton Crag in Lancashire and numerous examples throughout Yorkshire, Derbyshire, Scotland and Ireland.

Sarsens — blocks of sandstone roughly rectangular in shape — are found chiefly on the chalk downs of southern England. Although sarsens appear to have been brought to the soil on which they stand, they may be residual boulders from a bed

One of the massive rocking stones formed by erosion among the Brimham Rocks — an outcrop of millstone grit in Yorkshire

of sandstone which once covered the chalk, the soft, surrounding layers of the stone having been eroded by centuries of weathering, leaving only the harder, isolated boulders. It is more likely, however, that sarsens, like erratics, were deposited by Ice Age glaciers.

The name sarsen is derived from the 17th-century use of the word Saracen to denote something foreign and unusual. Sarsens — also known as grey-wethers because of their resemblance to sheep — were often used by prehistoric men, who stood them on end in formal arrangements for religious purposes.

One of the best-known examples is the Avebury Stone Circle in Wiltshire, consisting of nearly 100 sarsens set up by Bronze Age man about 3000 years ago. Sarsens also occur in Berkshire, Kent and Somerset.

Another type of natural stone formation is pudding-stone, consisting of pebbles stuck together by a natural limestone cement that has washed between them and hardened into solid rock. Pudding-stones — their resemblance to plum puddings accounts for their popular name — are usually found near old river beds or shores. Geologists have plotted the outline of lakes and seas some millions of years old by studying the position of such stones.

The Devil's Chimney on Leckhampton Hill in Gloucestershire is an inland stack, left as a result of surrounding quarrying. According to local superstition the 50 ft high pinnacle of natural oolitic limestone arose from Hell.

Other unusual forms of standing stones that occur inland are tors — outcrops of volcanic rock that have been isolated from their surroundings by centuries of weathering. Saddle Tor at Dartmouth is a typical example of the many tors to be seen in Devon and Cornwall.

In addition to the standing stones created by nature, there are those erected by man, chiefly during the Stone Age and Bronze Age, for ritualistic purposes, as monuments, or as part of a burial chamber.

The great majority of these are menhirs (single standing stones) also known as monoliths. They were usually erected as monuments and stood in isolated positions, often in the middle of fields, on mounds, near villages or at crossroads.

Some of these stones carried an ogham, or ogam — an inscription in the Ancient British and Irish alphabet, consisting of characters formed by groups of short, parallel lines cut into one or more surfaces of a stone.

A single standing stone, column or menhir taken from a ruined building, adapted as a monument and carved with a sculptured panel or inscribed is known as a stele.

Menhirs were often erected on high points to be seen from afar, such as the Brethren Stones on the skyline to the east of Dryburgh in Berwickshire; others, like the stone row at Hownam in Roxburghshire, are small boulders barely visible on the ground. Legend interprets the Hownam stones as a line of women who went out to reap on the Sabbath and were turned to stone.

Other single standing stones erected for commemorative purposes were medieval crosses, either carved as crosses or incised into the surface of standing stones that had been erected centuries beforehand by pagan cultures.

Often a very large single standing stone, or megalith, may be the only visible survivor of a more complex construction involving many other stones, such as an avenue or row or a circular monument. When two megaliths were used to support

Natural stones

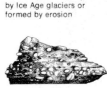

Inland stack
Rock column created by
quarrying or subsidence

Tor
Granite outcrop weathered to
resemble huge pile of rocks

Sarsen
Massive boulders deposited
by Ice Age glaciers or
formed by erosion

Pudding-stone
Pebbles stuck together
by natural cement

Erratic
Stone deposited during Ice Age,
miles from original source

Rocking stone or logan
An Ice Age erratic or the
freak result of weathering

Stones used by man

Rubbing stone
Erected by farmers
for their cattle
to scratch against

Menhir or monolith
Single stone used
for religious or
ritualistic rites

Cross or ogham
Commemorative stone
carved or incised

Cairn
Pyramidal heap of
stones as marker

Henge
One or several concentric circles of
stones creating primitive monument for
religious rites or solar observation

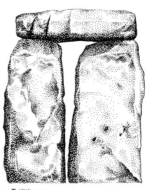

Dolmen
Burial chamber formed with
upright slabs and a capstone

Trilithon
Stones used in groups of three in
the formation of neolithic henges

Part of Castlerigg Stone Circle, also known as the Druids' Circle, at Keswick, Cumberland. The 100 ft diameter henge has 38 standing stones

a third—a horizontal capping stone—the construction is called a trilithon, and when a group of megaliths or trilithons were arranged in one or several concentric circles they formed a henge, creating some of the most spectacular of Stone Age and Bronze Age monuments. The Ring of Brodgar in the Orkneys and the monument at Stonehenge in Wiltshire are two examples.

Other standing stones are dolmens—tombs consisting of three to five huge stone slabs, set on end, topped by a capstone. Dolmens were originally covered with soil, which was later removed by grave robbers or weathering.

Perhaps the most practical of standing stones in present-day use are the cairn and the rubbing post.

A cairn is a heap of stones—sometimes shaped like a pyramid—erected on the peak or summit of a ridge as a parish boundary marker or as a guide to walkers on long-distance paths in moorland country, for example on the Pennine Way and on Exmoor. Some cairns date from the Iron and Bronze Ages and mark prehistoric burial sites.

A rubbing post is a stone erected by a farmer for grazing cattle to scratch their hides against. Many old standing stones have been left for this purpose. See also BRECCIA, CAIRN, CROSS, HENGE, TOR

Stonefly

Most of a stonefly's life is spent as an aquatic nymph, usually in a stream or river. Adults live for only two or three weeks and do not move far from the water's edge; they can fly but spend much of their time hiding under stones or among vegetation. Adults of the larger species, such as *Dinocras cephalotes* do not feed at all but only drink. Many of the smaller species feed on algae and lichens on stones and trees.

Fishermen, who use many of the species for bait, invented their common names. The yellow sally has a yellow and brown body and is common near stony streams and rivers from April to August. The yellow sally's body is only ½ in. long, but it has long antennae and two tails, giving it an overall length of about 1 in.

The early browns begin to emerge in February around moss-covered stones in streams. Needleflies also appear in February. Like the larger willow fly, which appears in summer, needleflies roll their wings tightly round their bodies when resting, giving them a needle-like appearance.

Though nymphs of the large stoneflies take up to three years to reach full size, most species have an annual life cycle. Nymphs crawl about under stones and in gravel at the bottom of streams, rivers and lakes throughout Britain. Like adult stoneflies they have two tails. Most of the nymphs are vegetarian but some will prey upon other nymphs.

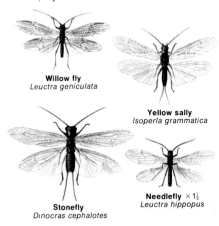

Willow fly
Leuctra geniculata

Yellow sally
Isoperla grammatica

Stonefly
Dinocras cephalotes

Needlefly × 1½
Leuctra hippopus

Stoneflies seldom use their wings, resting with them folded or tightly rolled

Storksbill *Erodium cicutarium*

A sand-loving plant which grows throughout the British Isles on dunes by the sea and in sand and gravel pits inland. Like cranesbill, to which it is related, it has beaked fruits. Its hairy stems range in height from 3 in. to 3 ft. The flowers appear in June and vary from rose-purple to white. The petals, which often have a black spot at the base, fall quickly: flowers opening early in the morning are self-pollinated and lose their petals by mid-day.

Storm-driven waves pound a rocky shore near Hartland Quay, north Devon

Storm

Any violent disturbance of the atmosphere, usually accompanied by high winds, is called a storm. But it can also mean a deep depression, which is a centre of low pressure around which the winds rotate in an anti-clockwise direction in the Northern Hemisphere. Their speed depends on the intensity of the low-pressure systems which usually move from west to east.

Storm cones are hoisted at ports and coast-guard stations when strong or damaging winds are expected. The cones are black, 3 ft high and 3 ft wide at the base. Their points indicate from which quarter the wind is expected: up for northerly, down for southerly.

One of the worst storms in Britain was in November 1703, when 8000 died and the first Eddystone lighthouse was destroyed.

A storm is Force 10 (55-63 mph) according to the Beaufort Scale—a grading of wind speeds from 0-12 laid down by Admiral Beaufort when he was hydrographer to the Navy from 1829 to 1855. A violent storm is Force 11 (64-72 mph). Force 12 (75 mph) is a hurricane. See also HAIL, RAIN, SNOW, THUNDER and WIND

Stone

The earth's crust, a shell only 25 miles thick, is composed mainly of a mineral called silica, or quartz. Combined with different forms of aluminium it makes up granite, the rock that forms the foundation of the continents. Combined with different forms of magnesium it makes plates of basalt, which support both the continents and the oceans of the world. Like all minerals, silica has its molecules arranged in a crystal-like pattern; this is why a stone or rock will split or flake when given a sudden blow.

Granite forms 40 per cent of the earth's crust, and is known as an igneous rock—one created by fire—because it originated in magma, the mass of molten rock within the earth. The other two types of rocks in Britain are sedimentary rocks—formed from the sediment of now-vanished seas; and metamorphic rocks, which were once either igneous or sedimentary, but have been altered by heat or intense pressure.

There are two kinds of igneous rocks—

volcanic ones which cooled quickly, like the lava which poured out on to the earth's surface to form basalt, and slow-cooling ones, like granite, which solidified from magma deep in the earth. These are known as plutonic or crystalline rocks, because they had ample time to crystallise naturally. The naked eye can see the minerals in Dartmoor or Cornish granite: glass-like quartz, the large white crystals of feldspar and the shiny black flakes of mica.

If a glass of water containing sand is allowed to stand for a while, the sand will settle to the bottom as a sediment. This, on a massive scale, is exactly what happened with sedimentary rocks. Particles eroded from older igneous rocks, by the action of rain, winds, rivers and ice, settled in layers at the bottom of prehistoric seas, gradually becoming denser and more solid under the pressure of their own weights and that of the water above them.

These layers can be readily seen in shale, which is compressed mud. It splits into thin sheets. Sandstone layers are formed by sand carried into the sea by wind or river currents. Limestone is the remains of shell-fish and corals which settled on the sea-bed. A feature of sedimentary rocks is the presence of fossils.

When the sedimentary rocks are metamorphosed by heat and pressure they become harder and more compact: sandstone is turned into quartzite, shale becomes slate, and the grains of calcite in limestone are converted into the crystals of marble.

Over most of the British Isles the rich vegetation produced by the fertile soil and mild climate covers the rock which forms the skeleton of the land. Even so, the many different kinds of stone are conspicuous in quarries, cliffs, river beds and beaches and also by roadsides and in fields.

Man began making use of stone more than a million years ago, and from about 4000 BC was shaping and polishing it to make tools and weapons. It is still used today.

Limestone marbles, particularly those with interesting patterning such as 'landscape' marble from Bristol and 'shelly' marble from Purbeck, Dorset, are quarried for decorative use. Granite patterned with feldspar crystals is quarried in Cornwall and Westmorland as an ornamental building stone. Alabaster, soft-grained and crystalline, was once popular for sculpture and ornamental carving that did not have to stand up to rough treatment or weathering. Derbyshire is renowned for its alabaster and also for the blue-and-yellow variety of fluorite called Blue John, mined at Castleton, probably since Roman times.

The number of attractive minerals varies from place to place in Britain. The comparatively recent sedimentary rocks of the southeast, from Lincolnshire to Dorset, possess few. An exception occurs in the pebble beaches of the east coast and parts of the south coast, which have crystal-quartz varieties, amber (fossil resin) and jet (a form of coal). Throughout the chalk country of the south-east, fine nodules of flint, which is chemically the same as quartz, are abundant and give a characteristic look to the buildings there. Also in the chalk are nodules of pyrite known locally, because of their odd shapes, as cannonballs, thunderbolts or burnt sausages.

Some minerals always present the same colour and appearance, but others vary. Galena, the chief ore in which lead is found, shows as bright silvery-grey when freshly exposed but gradually turns to a dull grey, as does lead itself.

The West Country, Wales and the Pennines from Derbyshire to Northumberland are rich in minerals. Almost every rock type occurs: granite, volcanic rock, serpentine, shales and limestones exist side by side. The older limestones of Somerset, Derbyshire and the North Pennines contain calcite or dolomite and lead and zinc ores.

Occasionally, because of its beauty, rarity and strength, a mineral is prized as a gemstone. In Britain these are most likely to be found as semi-precious stones in the form of pebbles, which are rock fragments worn smooth by the action of water or glacier ice or by being ground against one another by waves. Pebbles are most common on the seashore but often occur far from the sea in gravel beds—the remains of ancient beaches or debris left behind by Ice Age glaciers.

The semi-precious stones most common as pebbles are jasper, agate, amethyst, citrine and chalcedony (all forms of quartz tinted by different impurities), amber, jet and the decorative serpentines. The granite of Scotland contains many gem-stones, such as beryl, topaz and zircon, usually too small and rough to be valuable. Good quality amethyst and cairngorm (another variety of quartz) sometimes line fissures in the granite. Cavities in basaltic lavas contain agates or white, yellow or red crystals of zeolites.

Metamorphic rocks give up many characteristic minerals. The gneiss and schist rocks of the Highlands yield garnet and the blue-green to colourless kyanite. Talc, soapstone, copper and calcite are associated with serpentine rock, while slate may contain crystals of quartz, calcite, wavellite and pyrite.

WHERE TO FIND ROCKS AND MINERALS

Igneous–intrusive	Metamorphic	Sedimentary	Chalk	Limestone	Coast
Amethyst	Quartz	Fluorite	Flint	Fluorite	Jet
Quartz	Garnet	Barite	Pyrite nodules	Barite	Amber
Smoky quartz	Serpentine	Selenite		Calcite	Flint
(Cairngorm)	Connemara marble	Jasper		Blue John	Quartz
Porphyry	Marble	Flint			Agate
Granite	Slate	Red sandstone	Sand/Clay		Jasper
Pegmatite	Schist	Limestone	Barite	Ore mining areas	Garnet
Luxullianite	Pyrite	Breccia	Selenite	Chalcopyrite	Smoky quartz (Cairngorm)
	Gneiss			Pyrite	
Igneous–lava	Quartzite			Sphalerite	
Agate				Haematite	
Basalt				Galena	

A distribution map to show the main rock structure of the British Isles together with the associated minerals. The rocks and minerals are illustrated and described overleaf

445

British stones — minerals

All stones and rocks are made up of minerals, naturally occurring chemical compounds. When molten minerals solidify they form crystals — angular, but perfectly regular, smooth-faced structures. Many crystals are microscopic; others, such as those illustrated below, can be seen with the naked eye. They are not only attractive — some, for example amethyst and garnet, are semi-precious. Most semi-precious and ornamental stones are found in the form of pebbles, usually along the seashore. The true beauty of these stones comes to light when they are cut and polished. Minerals that are mined for the valuable metals they contain are called ores. Haematite is the richest iron-containing mineral.

Crystals

Calcite
Calcium carbonate formed in veins. Raw material for quicklime and cement

Barite
Barium sulphate 'cockscomb' formation from limestone. Somerset

Fluorite
Large cubic crystals of calcium fluoride. Mined and used in iron smelting. Crinch, Derbyshire

Barite
Spray of small crystals lining a fissure in a clay nodule. Isle of Sheppey, Kent

Quartz
Extremely hard crystallised silica. Used in the form of sand for building, glass-making and abrasive

Amethyst
Violet-coloured translucent crystals of quartz. Ornamental value

Smoky quartz (cairngorm)
Brownish-grey to black translucent crystals of quartz. Ornamental value

Garnet
Red crystals embedded in mica schist. Some semi-precious

Fluorite
Small cubic crystals of calcium fluoride. Scordale lead mines, Westmorland

Selenite
Crystalline gypsum. In sand and clay beds of north Kent coast and Midlands. Raw material of plaster of Paris

Ornamental stones

Jasper
Dark red, opaque, microscopically grained quartz

Jet
A hard coal which polishes to a glossy lustre. Found chiefly near Whitby, Yorkshire

Serpentine
Serpentine mineral which may be mixed in lesser amounts with other minerals such as tremolite, bastite or chromite

Agate
Smooth, translucent, chalcedony, a microscopically crystallised quartz

Connemara marble
Bands of green serpentine alternate with calcite. Quarried for ornamental use

Amber
Fossilised pine resin. Fragments washed up on beaches in Norfolk and Lincolnshire

Blue John
Blue-banded variety of fluorite. Quarried at Castleton, Derbyshire

Ores

Chalcopyrite
Copper-iron sulphide. Most important copper ore

Pyrite nodules
Iron sulphide, 'Fools' Gold'. Used in manufacturing sulphuric acid. Nodules found in many rocks

Sphalerite
Zinc sulphide. Principal ore of zinc

Haematite
Iron oxide. Richest ore of iron

Galena
Lead sulphide. Principal ore of lead

447

British stones—rocks

The rocks of the earth's crust are divided into three groups, according to the way in which they were formed. Igneous rocks were formed from intensely heated material that later cooled and solidified into crystals. Intrusive igneous rocks formed from material that solidified below the earth's surface, for example granite, whereas igneous lavas are solidified material that spilled out on to the earth's surface, for example basalt. Sedimentary rocks formed from the accumulation of layers of sediment washed down and deposited on the sea-bed and at the bottom of rivers and lakes. The sediment came from the breakdown, by the sun, rain, wind and frost, of exposed rocks. Metamorphic rocks were once sedimentary or igneous rocks that have been changed by being subjected to intense heat or pressure.

Igneous rocks

Pegmatite
A very coarse granite with large quartz and feldspar crystals. Cornwall

Porphyry
A granite, or any other rock, in which large detached crystals, usually feldspar, are embedded

Granite
Contains about 30 per cent quartz, 60 per cent feldspar and 10 per cent mica

Luxullianite
A variety of granite with red feldspar against black tourmaline. Quarried at Luxulyan, Cornwall

Granite
Jumbled mass of pink feldspar, mica and quartz crystals. Used in road-making and as a building material. Shap, Westmorland

Pegmatite
A coarse granite with large pink feldspar crystals. Shap, Westmorland

Basalt
Solidified lava, fine-grained black rock of feldspar, olivine, pyroxene

Sedimentary rocks

Flint
Non-crystalline silica.
Found in most chalk pits.
Used for road-making and
as a building material

Carboniferous limestone
Carboniferous era 345-280
million years ago.
Builds the Peak and Fells,
the Mendip Hills and
helps form the Pennines

Red sandstone
Triassic era 225-199
million years ago.
Wind-blown quartz grains
coloured by red iron oxide.
Used as a building stone.
Penrith, Cumberland

Limestone with great scallop fossil
Jurassic era 195-136
million years ago.
Very finely textured calcite.
Used as a building stone
and source of lime

Breccia
Angular fragments of
quartzite broken up by volcanic
action or pressure then bonded
together by natural cement

Metamorphic rocks

Slate
Formed from clay under
great pressure, cleaves
easily into flat, thin
sheets.
Used as roofing material

Marble
Carboniferous limestone
in which the calcite
is re-crystallised by
heat.
Used in sculpture and
ornamental building work

Slate
With broken crystals
of pyrites

Gneiss
Quartz, feldspar and mica
arranged in irregular bandings
of crystalline grains

Schist
Minerals such as mica,
quartz, hornblende or
garnet grouped in
flaky layers

Quartzite
Sandstone which has
been fused by heat

449

Strawberry

The wild strawberry *Fragaria vesca* is smaller but sweeter than garden varieties, which are descended from two American species. The wild plant is up to 1 ft high and grows in scrub, open woods and hedges throughout the British Isles, especially on lime-rich soils. It bears white flowers from April until July.

Barren strawberry *Potentilla sterilis* does not produce fruits worth eating. It also bears white flowers, sometimes as early as February, but is distinguishable from wild strawberry by its leaves, which have a blue tinge and spreading hairs beneath. It grows everywhere except the north of Scotland.

The name strawberry was given because straw is laid around the plants to prevent the fruits becoming dirty in wet weather.

Wild strawberry | **Barren strawberry**
Fragaria vesca | *Potentilla sterilis*

Both the sweet-flavoured wild strawberry and the barren strawberry produce white flowers

Strawberry tree *Arbutus unedo*

A bushy evergreen tree, also known as arbutus, with fruits which, though sweet, lack the flavour of the true strawberry and are chiefly used for making jam. A member of the heather family, the tree needs an average January temperature of at least 4°C (40°F) and will not grow in shaded or waterlogged conditions. The oval, tooth-edged leaves are deep, glossy green above, paler below. The bark is rust-red and flakes away from the many branches, which begin a short distance above ground. The hard, strong, red-brown wood is used in Ireland for making walking sticks and ornaments for tourists. The tree grows to a height of 30 ft. Its cultivation in England was first recorded in 1640.

Between September and December white, waxy, bell-shaped flowers, which look and smell like lilies of the valley, open in clusters near the tips of the branches. From each flower a round, greenish-white berry forms, which takes a year to ripen, turning through white, yellow and orange to red. Often a single tree displays these berries in various stages of development, which gives the strawberry tree a colourful appearance. Each berry is covered with small warts, and the soft yellow flesh contains many tiny brown, gritty seeds. Birds eat the fruit and thus spread the seeds.

The Irish call the tree by its Gaelic names, *caithne* and *suglair*.

Stream

Flowing water which has been channelled into a well-defined course due to irregularities in the ground. The scouring action of the current will gradually shape the land into a pattern of river valleys. It is hard to believe that a small stream can have cut the valley in which it flows, but this is possible because of the enormous period of time it has had to accomplish the task. A stream is also known as a beck, gill or burn in different regions of Britain. See also RIVER

Stubble

After a cereal crop has been cut, the growth which remains, attached to the roots, is called stubble. Ploughed in, it contributes a little to the fertility of the soil.

Harvesting often leaves loose grains and ears of corn lying amid the stubble and in days of severe poverty, village women used to gather them for their own use – a process known as gleaning. Free-range hens are often turned out on stubble fields, where they find sufficient grain to feed for several weeks. This reduces the number of stray plants in subsequent crops.

Sturgeon *Acipenser sturio*

Eggs from the female sturgeon form the famous dish caviar. The sturgeon also has edible flesh. Two centuries ago it was caught in our larger rivers, especially the Severn, Avon, Thames, Ouse and some of the Scottish rivers. Today, presumably because of pollution and over-fishing, it is unknown as a river fish in Britain and rarely more than half a dozen a year are caught by fishing vessels in British waters. It is a royal fish, and the Queen has a claim on any caught in our waters or washed up on a British beach. The last time one was eaten at Buckingham Palace was in 1969. In the same year the Queen gave a live one to an aquarium and in 1970 a dead one to an orphanage.

A fully grown sturgeon can weigh 700 lb. and measure 11 ft. It is immediately recognisable by its size, the flat, bony scutes along its sides and its lop-sided tail, with the upper lobe much longer than the lower. It has a small mouth which can extend to suck in food, composed of bottom-living organisms, snails, small crustaceans, worms and some fish.

Like other migratory fish, sturgeons make their way up rivers to spawn, the adults returning to the sea after spawning is complete.

Sucker see Clingfish

Sugar beet

More than one-third of the sugar used in Britain comes from sugar beet – a plant derived from sea beet *Beta vulgaris*, which grows wild round the shores of the British Isles. Sugar beet develops a white, pointed root, weighing up to 2 lb. and containing about 17 per cent sugar. An acre of sugar beet yields about 15 tons, from which more than 2 tons of sugar can be extracted. In

SUGAR BEET HARVESTER

The latest harvesters cut off the tops of the beet and lift the roots before conveying them by elevator to a waiting trailer

1973, 468,000 acres of sugar beet were planted in Britain – mostly in the east.

The crop is harvested by a self-propelled mechanical digger, which first cuts off the green tops for use as animal fodder, then lifts the roots. Root pulp left after the sugar has been extracted is also used as animal feed.

Sugar was first commercially produced from beet in France during the Napoleonic wars, when a British naval blockade cut off sugar from the West Indies. Experiments in commercial extraction began in Britain in 1830, and large-scale production began in 1912. See also BEET, CROPS

Sulphur tuft see Fungus

Sundew *Drosera rotundifolia*

The spoon-shaped leaves of this plant are covered with glands which trap and digest any insects which land on them. The insects supply the sundew with essential minerals and enable it to grow in acid, peaty soils which are deficient in minerals. Sundew grows throughout the British Isles but drainage has made it rare in the lowlands. The leaves grow in a rosette, and the stem, which is 2-10 in. high, carries white flowers from June to August.

The dew from its glands was once thought to cure warts, corns, freckles and sunburn, and a liqueur was made from its leaves.

Swallow

With its red chin and long forked tail, the swallow is fairly easy to distinguish in flight from its relatives, the house martins, and from the swift. All of them catch insects in flight, and all of them designed for speed, with long, curved wings. Some experts assert that swallows can reach up to 100 mph in flight, but they normally seldom exceed 30 mph.

Swallows, martins and swifts depend mainly on man for nesting sites: the swallow breeds in barns and sheds; the house martin under the eaves of houses; the sand martin increasingly in the man-made sand cliffs of quarries and pits; and the swift under eaves or in thatch. Swallows often return to the

A swallow with its young. Swallows often breed in barns, returning to the same nest each year

Sometimes the streams reappear as springs. Geologists have traced their routes by putting strong dye into the water at the point where the streams disappear into the ground, and watching for its emergence.

A splendid example is Gaping Gill, on the slopes of Ingleborough Hill in Yorkshire. Here a stream drops 365 ft into a cave and reappears more than a mile away in Ingleborough cave. Most swallowholes are less dramatic, the water usually disappearing underground through a mass of boulders.

A VANISHING RIVER

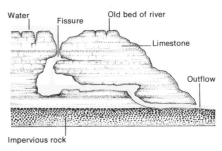

Water dissolves limestone. So, when a river reaches a crack in limestone this is widened. The dissolving process continues underground until a new outflow is created, and the river disappears at the surface

same nest year after year. A reported decline in the numbers of swallows may be attributable to greater farm hygiene which not only has reduced potential nesting sites but, with greater use of insecticides, has limited food supplies.

Like martins and swifts, swallows have evolved a particularly large mouth behind a tiny bill, ideal for snapping up insects in the air, and their large wings and tails enable them to change direction rapidly. They are adept at drinking from the water's surface in flight.

Swallows stay in Britain from late March to October, house martins from April to October and sand martins from March to September. All three species are found throughout Britain, except for north-west Scotland, Orkney and Shetland. They winter in Africa south of the Sahara.

The swallow is a blue-black bird, 7½ in. long, with pinkish underparts and a red and blue face pattern. The outer feathers of its deeply forked tail form streamers, longer in males than females. Its nest is a carefully made cup of grass and dried mud, lined with feathers and hair and often found on beams. The three to six eggs are white, speckled with rust, and the birds usually produce two broods.

The house martin is a bold black and white bird, easily identified by its square white rump patch. It is about 5 in. long and its tail is less deeply forked than the swallow. It builds its nest of mud, allowing one layer to dry before adding another and leaving only

a small entrance hole. Martins originally nested in cliffs and caves, and some colonies still do. They also nest under bridges and although one famous colony under the Clifton Hampden bridge on the Thames at Oxford has been abandoned—probably because of traffic vibration—a large one still exists at Atcham bridge, over the Severn, near Shrewsbury. Started in the 1930's, it now has more than 400 nests.

House martins produce two, or sometimes three, broods of four or five white eggs. Cleaner air encouraged them to nest in inner London in 1966 for the first time since 1889.

The smallest of the three birds, the sand martin is plain brown above and white below with a brown band across its chest. Its tail is least forked of the three.

Nesting in large colonies, sand martins breed in sand cliffs, steep river banks and even railway cuttings. Both sexes dig a tunnel 2-3 ft long before excavating a small chamber, which they line for a nest. They produce two broods of four or five eggs. Sand martins roost communally in reed beds with swallows, usually feeding on insects they catch over water.

Swallowhole
A pothole into which a surface stream pours, eventually emerging some distance away after making its way through underground channels. Swallowholes, also known as sinkholes and swallets, are common in the limestone areas of Derbyshire and Yorkshire.

Swallowtail butterfly *Papilio machaon*
One of the most beautiful and rare British butterflies. It has a 3 in. wingspan and is yellow and black with blue and red markings. The swallowtail is usually seen only in the Norfolk Broads, where it is native. Those found in other parts are wanderers either from East Anglia or from the Continent.

The swallowtail hatches in May on the Broads from pupae which overwinter on reed stalks. The caterpillars feed only on milk parsley, which grows among the reeds. Usually there is only one brood a year, but sometimes a few chrysalids hatch before winter and give a second, August brood.

The young caterpillars are black and white and resemble bird droppings. As they grow they turn green with black and red markings. If disturbed, the bigger caterpillars protrude an orange, Y-shaped organ from just behind the head. This emits a smell of rotting fruit, presumably to repel attackers.

The swallowtail has a strong, flapping flight and is on the wing during May and June.

The swallowtail is one of the rarest and most beautiful British butterflies

451

Swallowtail moth *Ourapteryx sambucaria*

The light colouring of this moth gives it a ghostly outline as it flies in the moonlight. It has a wingspan of 2¼ in. and is greenish-yellow. There is a projection on each hind-wing, from which it gets its name.

Swallowtail moths may be seen from July until the autumn, in most parts of the British Isles except the north of Scotland. The eggs are usually laid on ivy, privet and hawthorn, and the caterpillars resemble twigs. They hibernate and complete their

The swallowtail moth is on the wing from July until autumn

growth by the following June. The pupal stage, which lasts only a few weeks, is spent in a thin cocoon attached to the food-plant.

Swamp

A swamp is a low-lying area of land in which the soil is always covered with water, even in summer. Reeds are usually the only plants that grow in these conditions, though rushes sometimes occur. The only extensive area of swamp in the British Isles is the Norfolk Broads, where it gives way to marsh as decaying vegetation brings the soil above water level. Elsewhere swamp is confined to the edges of lakes, rivers and ponds. See also BOG, BROAD, MARSH

Swan

Mute swans were known for centuries as 'birds royal' because only the king, or those licensed by the Royal Swanherd, could keep them. Mutes are Britain's only resident species of swan and one of the world's heaviest flying birds, weighing up to 40 lb.

Two other swans, the whooper *Cygnus cygnus* and Bewick's swan *C. bewickii*, named after the bird illustrator, Thomas Bewick (1753-1828), are regular winter visitors and frequently are referred to jointly as 'wild' swans to distinguish them from the hyper-tame mute *C. olor*.

White swans are a familiar sight throughout Britain but to determine their species in winter requires a close view of the bill. The mute's bill is orange and the 'wild' swan's is yellow, but whereas the whooper's colour takes the form of a triangular yellow wedge, the Bewick has a rounded yellow patch. Both 'wild' swans hold their necks straighter than does the gracefully curved mute and their wings lie flatter on their backs. The whoopers,

like the mutes, are 60 in. long; Bewick's swans are only 48 in.

Though mute swans will occupy even the tiniest village pond and successfully rear young within yards of busy roads, they also form quite large swanneries, as at Abbotsbury in Dorset. Here the Swanherd, the last remaining link with the Middle Ages, when swans were served at banquets, keeps the swannery down to 800 pairs—probably the second largest herd in Europe.

Mute swans build a huge platform of twigs and vegetation on which their five to seven greenish eggs are laid. Incubation, which is shared, lasts about 35 days, and cygnets fly about four months later, though they remain in family parties through the winter.

All mute swans on the River Thames belong to one of two London livery companies or to the Queen. A swan-upping ceremony is carried out every July or August to establish ownership: cygnets owned by either the Dyers' Company or the Vintners' Company are nicked in the bill with the company

mark, and those that remain unmarked belong to the Queen. This is a survival from the days of Elizabeth I, when there were 900 different swan marks establishing private ownership.

Whooper swans visit north and west Britain in large numbers every winter, stopping over on large lakes. Only a few—perhaps injured birds—remain in summer, and occasionally breed in northern Scotland.

Bewick's swans occupy southern and eastern England and are seldom seen in mixed flocks with whoopers. They come from Siberia, and are concentrated usually in three major groups: on the Derwent Floods in Yorkshire, the Ouse Washes of East Anglia and at Slimbridge in Gloucestershire. The birds at Slimbridge have been encouraged to make their home within the confines of the Wildfowl Trust where they become quite tame alongside the captive waterfowl collection.

When arriving in October or departing in April, the 'wild' swans fly high in V formation.

A winter visitor to Britain, the whooper swan stretches its great wings as it starts to take off from the water

Swan mussel see Freshwater mussel

Sweat house
An early medieval form of the modern sauna bath. Several may be seen in Ireland, usually by streams or loughs, as at Killelagh Lough in Co. Londonderry. They are small, dry-stone structures, shaped like beehives, which were heated by peat fires.

People would build up extreme perspiration in the sweat house, then plunge into the cold water of the stream or lough. The process was claimed to be beneficial to health in general, and to be especially good for rheumatism.

Swede
A root crop introduced from Sweden and at first known as 'Swedish turnip'. It has a closer texture than the turnip and, apart from being bigger, has a greater food value for humans and animals. The interior of the swede is a rich yellow or orange colour.

It flourishes in cool areas, and large crops are grown in the north of England and in Scotland as winter food for cattle and sheep. Swedes, usually stored in clamps or barns, are sometimes left in the fields where they grow, and sheep are allowed to forage for them. The fields are divided by movable fences for systematic feeding.

Sweet cicely see Parsley

Sweet-flag *Acorus calamus*
This plant was introduced into England from Asia in the 17th century for its fragrant, tangerine-like odour; it was strewn on floors to disguise unpleasant smells. The second part of its name is derived from its leaves, which are like those of the flag.

Sweet-flag grows up to 3 ft high on riverbanks, canals and ponds throughout lowland England but is rare elsewhere. It spreads slowly by means of stout, underground stems. Spikes of tightly packed yellow-green flowers appear from May to July.

Sweet gale see Bog myrtle

Swift *Apus apus*
No bird spends more time in the air than the swift—it feeds, sometimes mates and even sleeps on the wing. Some experts believe that it cat-naps as it glides on currents of air between spells of flapping to maintain height. It used to be thought that after soaring out of sight at dusk swifts returned to their nests after dark, but it is now known that those that are not incubating eggs or brooding young stay aloft until sunrise.

Because they are rarely used, their legs have become so weak that swifts are almost helpless on the ground and alight only by accident.

Swifts, which are about 6½ in. long, have black-brown plumage, except for a white chin patch. Their long wings are scythe-shaped and their tail forked. They are found throughout Britain and Ireland, apart from the extreme north of Scotland.

After arriving in early May, they nest in buildings, entering through holes under the eaves, or, occasionally, in rock crevices. Usually two or three white eggs are laid and the young can fly and feed themselves as soon as they leave the nest. By the middle of August, most swifts have set off to winter in Africa south of the Equator.

Swifts, which have been timed at 60 mph in courtship flights, can usually outfly most predators. Devil birds was a country name given to them through their habit of screaming while flying round houses in late spring and early summer evenings.

Swift moth
From June to August swift moths can often be seen flying over long grass at twilight. There are two common species: the common, or garden, swift *Hepialus lupulina* and the ghost swift *H. humili*.

The common swift has a drab, brown colour with white patterns on the wings, which span 1-1½ in. The ghost swift is much larger, with a wingspan of 2-2¾ in. Males have white wings and females have yellow-orange ones with red markings.

Most female moths release a scent which attracts males, but the reverse is the case with ghost swifts. The male releases a scent as he flies and this, with his easily visible wings, attracts the female. After mating, the female lays 200-300 eggs, dropping them as she flies over grass. The eggs hatch 10-18 days later into long, white caterpillars with brown heads, which burrow into the soil. Moles and birds prey on the caterpillars which stay in the soil over winter before entering the pupal, or resting, stage in spring.

A summer twilight is the best time to see a common, or garden, swift moth

Swine-cress
This waste-ground weed is particularly common on trampled areas. The finely divided leaves lie flat on the ground. Minute white flowers appear in a central cluster from June to September. Each flower develops a fruit consisting of two round pods.

There are two British species. Swine-cress *Coronopus squamatus* is abundant in south and east England but mainly coastal elsewhere. The fruits are covered with warts. The leaves have been used for salads. On the other hand, the leaves of lesser swine-cress *C. didymus* exude an unpleasant smell when crushed.

Flowers

The sycamore, one of Britain's hardiest trees, can seed itself in any wood or garden

Sycamore *Acer pseudoplatanus*
This tree, introduced from France in the Middle Ages, is a member of the maple family. It now grows naturally throughout the British Isles and is the most successful tree invader of waste ground. It was named sycamore because it was thought to be a fig-mulberry *Sycomorus* mentioned in the Bible. In Scotland it was thought to be the plane tree, hence its botanical name, and some Scots still refer to it as plane.

The sycamore's mid-green leaves, each with five rounded lobes, are always set in opposite pairs. The hard green winter buds are also paired, and so the branches spread out evenly.

The greenish-yellow flowers open in hanging clusters in June. Only those halfway down each bunch prove fertile. They are pollinated by bees.

By October the fruits ripen to a pair of hard brown seeds, each with a brown, papery, oval wing. When they fall, they twirl through the air like the blades of a helicopter. The seeds spend winter on the ground and germinate in spring, opening out two long seed leaves which, surprisingly, are already green even in the husk. The smooth, pinkish-grey bark of the sycamore often breaks away in flakes.

The wood is pale cream and strong, though not durable in the open. It is used indoors for furniture, flooring, textile rollers and carved woodware. The back, sides and stock of every violin and fiddle are made of sycamore (the resonant soundboard is always spruce).

The sycamore is a particularly hardy tree, able to survive conditions detrimental to most other trees. It can resist high winds and thrives in coastal districts as well as the smoky atmosphere of towns. It also thrives on a wide range of soils.

Sycamores are grown in woods for timber, around farmsteads in exposed northern uplands for shelter, and as ornamental trees in parklands everywhere. They form magnificent rounded foliage crowns, but Britain's tallest, at Cobham Hall in Kent, is only 110 ft high.

TU

Tabby moth see Pyralid moth
Tadpole see Frog
Tall fescue see Grass

Tamarisk *Tamarix anglica*
An evergreen shrub, 3-10 ft high, with slender purple-green branches and tiny scale-like leaves. From July to September it bears spikes of pale pink or white flowers. Introduced in Tudor times from the Mediterranean to the coasts of England and Wales, it grows well on dunes, where its roots help to bind the sand. It is widely grown in coastal areas as a windbreak. Tamarisk grows from cuttings as readily as willow and, like willow, was used for making lobster pots.

Tansy *Chrysanthemum vulgare*
An erect, perennial herb, up to 3 ft high, with fern-like leaves and golden-yellow flower heads which often form a flat-topped mass. The plant, which grows throughout the British Isles, has a strong, spicy scent and a very bitter flavour.

Tansy was once used in medicine to staunch wounds and prevent miscarriages. In the kitchen it was valued as a flavouring, and in some country districts it was customary to eat tansy pudding at Easter in remembrance of the 'bitter herbs' eaten by the Jews at the Passover. It was also used as an insect repellent.

Tapestry moth see Clothes moth

Tapeworm
A parasite in the intestines of various animals. Some species can live as long as 20 years, producing up to a million eggs a day throughout their adult lives. Except for a few found in fish, tapeworms are very long creatures with a head-like region, the scolex, armed with suckers and sometimes hooks. Behind this is the body or tape, composed of segments called proglottids. There may be up to 40,000 segments to a tape 21 yds long. Each has its own set of sex organs. Tapeworms have no separate digestive system; their food is absorbed over the whole of the body surface.

The life cycle of a tapeworm involves the transfer of the eggs through intermediate hosts. The common dog tapeworm *Dipylidium caninum*, measures only 20 in. and has up to 150 segments. From time to time segments full of eggs break off from the end of the worm and are voided in the droppings of the dog. These are eaten by the larvae of certain fleas and of the dog louse. Inside the insect the egg hatches into a larva which is fully grown by the time the insect

is an adult. If the infected insect is then swallowed by a dog, usually when it is cleaning itself, the larval tapeworm grows to an adult in the dog's intestine. Dog tapeworms sometimes infect humans, especially children.

In Britain, properly cooked meat and good sanitation have made the human tapeworm a rarity. It occurs when eggs in untreated human effluent are swallowed by small freshwater crustaceans which are in turn eaten by fish, or when pigs, cattle or sheep take the eggs in with their food.

The most common tapeworms to affect man in Britain are *Taenia solium* from pork, and *T. saginata* from beef.

Tare
A slender annual with weak stems up to 2 ft high, which grows in long grass and low bushes and flowers from May to August. Smooth tare has pale blue flowers and smooth, four-seeded pods. It grows mainly in clay soils in lowland England and on the Welsh coast. Hairy tare has dirty white flowers and hairy, two-seeded pods. It grows on all kinds of soils throughout lowland Britain and is particularly abundant on old railway lines. Both are members of the pea family. See also VETCH

Teal see Duck

Teasel-gatherers of Yorkshire in 1814. The plant is still grown commercially in Somerset

Teasel
A prickly biennial up to 6 ft high with compact heads of flowers surrounded by small narrow leaves. These persist throughout the winter, providing food for goldfinches and decoration in the house. The saw-edged leaves have stout spines on the underside.

Dipsacus sylvestris sylvestris is the most common teasel in the British Isles. It grows on stream banks and in rough grassland as far north as Fife and round the coast of Ireland. The hooked bracts of fullers' teasel *D. s. fullonum* are used in the woollen industry to raise the nap on newly woven cloth. It is still cultivated for this purpose in Somerset. Both these plants bear rose-purple flowers in July and August.

The small teasel *D. pilosus* is rarely higher

than 3 ft, and bears white flowers in August. It grows only in southern England, in damp woods and along shady ditches.

Teasel
Dipsacus sylvestris

Small teasel
Dipsacus pilosus

There is nothing better than spiky teasel for raising the nap on velour or cashmere

Tedder

To ted hay is to turn it, toss it and generally aerate it to get it dry. When labour was cheap and plentiful, this was done by men with rakes. Horse-drawn machinery included the horse rake, which raked the fields clean, and the side rake, which turned the swathes of drying hay.

A typical modern tractor-drawn rotary tedder has a series of angled tines fitted to discs. These roll and fluff up the hay, allowing air to penetrate, and scatter it over the surface of the field.

Tench *Tinca tinca*

An old legend credits the slime-coated tench with acting as 'doctor' to other fish. It was said that a sick or wounded fish would seek out a tench and rub itself against the mucus, after which it would recover. For this reason, the pike supposedly never ate a tench. In fact it sometimes does.

A wild tench is always dark coloured, varying from dull brown to green, sometimes with a golden sheen on the belly. There is also a cultivated golden variety. The wild tench lives mainly in ponds and shallow lowland lakes, but a few may be found in slow-flowing rivers. It inhabits weed beds and will often lie buried in mud at the bottom of a pond. It can live in oxygen-deficient water and spend severe winters lying dormant in the mud.

The male tench matures at around three years and may grow up to 12 in. long. Spawning takes place in shoals in late spring and early summer. The small, sticky green eggs adhere to water plants and hatch in six to eight days. A young tench eats considerable quantities of algae. An adult feeds intensively during the summer on a wide range of bottom-living insects, crustaceans, pond snails and plants.

Ten-spined stickleback

Pungitius pungitius

Named after the row of nine or ten short spines along its back, the ten-spined stickleback is rarely more than 2 in. long. A slim fish, it is usually dark olive on the back and light yellow on the sides and belly. The male acquires brighter colours in the breeding season when the pelvic spines under its belly turn white or blue.

The ten-spined stickleback inhabits densely weeded areas and marshy swamps and is sometimes found in the same pond or stream as its relative, the common stickleback. It is found in England and eastern Ireland and is abundant in some areas.

Breeding takes place in spring and early summer. A male builds a nest of plant fibres inches above the bottom among dense weeds; the fibres are glued together by a secretion from the kidneys. He then attracts several females to the nest, which lay up to 700 eggs between them. These are guarded by the male, which drives off intruders and fans the eggs, keeping them clean of fungus and well-oxygenated. They hatch in ten days. The young stay in the nest for a short time but later scatter into the surrounding vegetation. They do not come into open water until autumn or early winter.

When living in brackish water, the ten-spined stickleback feeds mainly on small crustaceans and sometimes fish eggs. In fresh water, its diet is more varied and includes insect larvae, adult midges and aquatic worms.

Tern

Graceful flight, long swept-back wings and deeply forked tails have earned terns the nickname of sea swallows. The lightness and grace of their flight is the best way of telling them from their larger relatives, the gulls. Six species of terns breed regularly in the British Isles. All are summer visitors and long-distance migrants. Except for the rare black tern, a fen and marsh bird, they live along the coast.

The five marine species are light grey above and white below and have a prominent black cap. At close quarters or through binoculars, bill colour and leg size help accurate identification. They feed by diving into the water for small fish, especially sand-eels. The black tern hovers over the water, dipping now and then to pick up an insect or small fish.

The breeding habits of the five marine terns are similar. The nest is a hollow scraped in the ground. Incubation, by both parents, lasts about 23 days, and the chicks fly after about four weeks. The black tern builds a floating nest of grass and rushes, and incubation, by both sexes, is shorter—about 14 days; the chicks fly after three weeks.

The common tern, which is 14 in. long, is both widespread and numerous. It sometimes breeds inland, along rivers and in gravel pits. In May or June it lays two or three heavily speckled buff, green or blue-white eggs. Colonies often consist of several hundred pairs, which react aggressively to intruders: they rise in a mass and, with cries of 'keeyah', dive-bomb them, sometimes hitting them and drawing blood.

The Arctic tern acts in the same way and has been known to attack man. This is a slightly larger bird than the common tern but has shorter legs; also the red bill lacks the black tip of the common tern. There are many mixed colonies of Arctic and common terns, but the Arctic is outnumbered by the common everywhere in the British Isles except the north of Scotland and a few isolated places, such as the Farne Islands; no large colonies exist south of a line from Northumberland to Anglesey. Unlike common terns, Arctic terns breed only by the coast. They undertake amazing journeys each autumn: after breeding as far north as the Arctic, they fly 10,000 miles to winter in Antarctic seas, making them the greatest long-distance travellers of the bird world. Their eggs are similar in colour and pattern to those of the common tern.

The roseate tern, which is the same size as the Arctic tern, is named after the pink flush that marks its breast in the breeding season. The bill is black but turns red at the base in mid-summer. The forked tail is longer than that of the other marine terns. The cry is a drawn-out 'aach-aach' with a softer 'tchu-ick' or 'chik-ik'. The roseate tern lays one or two chestnut-marked cream or buff eggs in June or July. The birds are confined to only 20 or so colonies, most of which border the Irish Sea, on both sides; other large colonies

The graceful flight of the Arctic tern, the long-distance traveller of the bird world

include those on the Farne Islands and the Scilly Isles.

The sandwich tern is named after the Kentish town where it once used to breed. It is now confined to about 40 colonies, most of which are along the east coast of Britain. At 16 in., it is the largest British tern. Its black bill is tipped with yellow and it has a ragged crest. The call is a harsh 'kirrick'. Sandwich terns nest in dense colonies, where in May or June one or two eggs in one of a wide range of colours are laid. They sometimes set up colonies on the same sites as more aggressive birds, relying on them to drive off intruders.

The little tern is, at 9 in., much smaller than the other terns; it is also the rarest breeder among Britain's seabirds. It nests on beaches, where over the years it has been so disturbed by holidaymakers that there are now only about 800 breeding pairs left. However, at Minsmere, in Suffolk, the little tern has been successfully lured inland so that it can be protected. The bird has a yellow, black-tipped bill and bright orange feet. Its cry is a 'kik-kik' or 'pee-e-eer'. The two or three speckled buff eggs are laid in May.

The black tern bred commonly in the Fens until the mid-19th century, but then became a spring and autumn migrant. It has now started breeding again, irregularly, in East Anglia. In spring it is easily recognised by its black and dark grey plumage; in autumn it is grey and white like other terns. It is only slightly bigger than the little tern. The black tern is a silent bird, only occasionally emitting a 'kik-kik'. The two to four eggs, laid in May or June, are speckled buff to brown.

Terrace

Most of Britain's larger rivers flow in valleys floored by gravel. Steps in the gravel higher up the valley sides, which show the river's earlier levels, are known as terraces; in many places they contain bones, shells, plant remains and stone implements dating from different stages of the Ice Age. Terraces are also formed near sea and lake shores. Because they are flat and usually well drained, they are often sites that have been extensively settled and developed.

Clapham Common, Wimbledon Common and Trafalgar Square all lie on terraces of the Thames.

Territory see Animal behaviour

Thale-cress *Arabidopsis thaliana*

An annual weed which grows throughout the British Isles on walls, rocks and bare places in dry, often sandy soils. At the base there is a rosette of toothed, hairy leaves from which slender stems, usually up to 1 ft high and bearing tiny white flowers, develop in April and May. The flowers are followed by ¾ in. long pods on sprawling stalks. The plant persists as a skeleton long after it has died. The plant is named after Johannes Thal, a 16th-century German herbalist.

Thatching

A traditional method of roofing cottages, barns and other country buildings, widely used throughout Britain until tiles and slates became popular in the 18th and 19th centuries.

Thatching is most common south of the Humber-Mersey line but many examples exist in the north, including Scotland. The craft of thatching has changed little since the Middle Ages, and was probably in use before the Norman Conquest.

Thatching materials include straw, reed, heather, gorse and broom. Before the introduction of the combine-harvester the most common thatching material was wheat straw, and the best was reed. Norfolk reed thatching lasts from 50 to 60 years and is the finest of all; it consists of reeds cut in low-lying areas of Norfolk, Hampshire and other counties. Straw thatch lasts 10-20 years; combed wheat straw about 30-40 years.

Bundles of thatching material are secured to the roof timbers with sways—hazel sticks and iron hooks—and bramble that has been

A cottage near Salisbury in Wiltshire which has been

skinned to make a strong, flexible cord. At the ridge, where a roof is weakest, thatching is usually doubled and strengthened with

THE THATCHER'S CRAFT AND HIS TOOLS

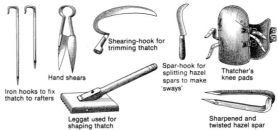

Iron hooks to fix thatch to rafters

Hand shears

Shearing-hook for trimming thatch

Spar-hook for splitting hazel spars to make 'sways'

Thatcher's knee pads

Leggat used for shaping thatch

Sharpened and twisted hazel spar

Some of the thatcher's essential tools. The leggat's design varies from county to county, according to the thatching materials used. The most common material is reed, but straw, heather, gorse and broom are also used.

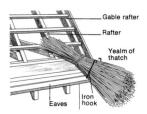

Gable rafter / Rafter / Yealm of thatch / Eaves / Iron hook

A yealm—a tight bunch of thatch—is fixed temporarily to the roof with two iron hooks

Hazel sway

Additional yealms are added and secured to roof timbers with spars, hooks and a hazel sway

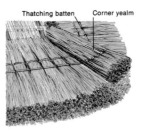

Thatching batten / Corner yealm

An extra yealm is fixed at the corners to provide added strength and thickness and weatherproofing qualities

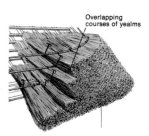

Overlapping courses of yealms

Further courses are laid, each overlapping the one below and rising up to the top of the roof

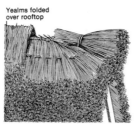

Yealms folded over rooftop

Bunches of thatch, or yealms, are fixed along the top of the roof and at each end of the gables

Hazel sways

Further yealms are folded and fixed on the top of the roof for extra thickness and strength

Spar-hook

Hazel sways may be used to decorate as well as to strengthen the weakest parts of the roof

newly thatched with a traditional design

rows of hazel pegs driven into the thatch.

Every thatcher has his individual style of work which he adapts to the varying architectural styles of different areas. Thatched roofs in East Anglia, for instance, are usually high-pitched and have gable-ends, whereas those in Devon are often low-pitched, chunky and with rounded ends.

The great advantages of thatching are that it is easily fitted to any shaped roof and that it is warmer in winter and cooler in summer than most other coverings. Once the cheapest form of roofing, thatching is now expensive and there is a shortage of thatchers.

Thistle

A biennial or perennial weed that flourishes on grassland, by roadsides and in waste places. It can be recognised at all seasons by its prickly leaves, in summer by its heads of red-purple or white florets and in autumn by its thistledown, which may fill the air and carry the seed for miles. Some species also spread by underground stems. Their spikes serve as a defence against grazing animals, but donkeys and goats eat the young leaves before the spikes have hardened. Some insects lay their eggs in the axils of leaves whose spikes protect them against predators.

There are 11 wild species which commonly occur in the British Isles. Although superficially alike, they are easily distinguished. Two are much shorter than the rest. One, carline thistle, which is rarely higher than 1 ft, has white flowers surrounded by straw-coloured bracts, which open when dry to look like petals. It is found on dry grassland in most parts of Britain. The other, stemless thistle, bears flowers at ground level. The leaves lie flat on the downland turf of south and east England, where the plant commonly grows.

Four of the other species have a prickle-free area of stem below the flower heads. Meadow thistle, which is rarely more than 30 in. high, grows in fens and bogs in south and east England, South Wales and Ireland. Melan-

Eleven common thistles

The 11 wild species of thistles which are commonly seen in the British Isles are superficially alike, but they can easily be distinguished and named by reference to this chart and the accompanying text, which details their height and describes their flowers

Welted thistle
Carduus acanthoides

Spear thistle
Cirsium vulgare

Melancholy thistle
Cirsium heterophyllum

Marsh thistle
Cirsium palustre

Musk thistle
Carduus nutans

Stemless thistle
Cirsium acaule

Carline thistle
Carlina vulgaris

Woolly thistle
Cirsium eriophorum

Cotton thistle
Onopordon acanthium

Creeping thistle
Cirsium arvense

Meadow thistle
Cirsium dissectum

choly thistle reaches a height of 5 ft, and grows in damp woods and by the side of streams and roads in Scotland, northern England and North Wales. Both these species have 1 ft or more of prickle-free stem, and a white cottony growth on the underside of their leaves. Musk thistle reaches a height of 3 ft, and grows in dis-

turbed ground, particularly dry, lime-rich soil in England and Wales. The flower heads are solitary and drooping. Welted thistle, 1-4 ft high, bears clusters of upright flowers, and grows beside ditches and streams in England, Wales, southern Scotland and eastern Ireland.

Four other species have completely prickly

457

stems. Creeping thistle, up to 2 ft high, springs up in overgrazed or unmown meadows. Marsh thistle often reaches 6 ft. It grows in wet woods and by ditches and streams. Both these species have flower heads less than ¾ in. across and grow throughout the British Isles. Spear thistle, which also reaches 6 ft, grows on grassland, waste ground and seashores throughout the British Isles. This is the thistle that is shown on Scottish emblems. Much rarer is the woolly thistle, 2-6 ft high, which grows on grassland, open scrub and roadsides, on lime-rich, clay soils. These two species have large flower heads. Those of the woolly thistle are covered with a white, cotton-like growth and, at 3 in. across, are the largest of any British thistle.

The tallest thistle, often over 6 ft, is the cotton thistle, so-called because it is covered with white hairs. It is scattered throughout lowland England by roadsides and in waste places. Although it is rare in Scotland, it is sometimes known as the Scots thistle.

Thong weed see Seaweed

Thorn-apple *Datura stramonium*
Introduced in the 17th century from America, where it is a common, troublesome weed, this poisonous annual, 1-3 ft high, was grown here for its medicinal properties. A 'tea' made from its leaves was used to relieve asthma, and tinctures and extracts of stramonium are still used in contemporary medicine. The leaves are glossy and spiky-toothed and the trumpet-shaped flowers, which appear in late summer, are purple or white. They develop into green thorn-apples, prickly fruits about the size of a horse-chestnut case. When ripe, these split into four from the top, releasing dark, kidney-shaped seeds. These contain atropine, hyoscyamine and hyoscine which act on the nervous system, causing hallucinations and dilating the pupils of the eyes.

Thorn-apple grows sporadically on waste ground throughout England.

Thorn insect
The horned treehopper *Centrotus cornutus* is often called the thorn insect because there are spine-like growths behind its head. At rest on a twig it resembles a spiny outgrowth of the plant. It is ½ in. long, and brown.

Treehoppers live mainly in oak foliage, and feed by probing their sharp mouth-parts into stems and sucking the plant sap. The adults can be seen in spring and summer in most parts of the country.

This bug belongs to a mainly tropical family, and only one other member, the smaller *C. genistae*, is found in Britain, usually on dyer's greenweed.

Thorn moth
The caterpillars of thorn moths have long bodies, with fewer than the usual number of legs. They have six true legs on the thorax

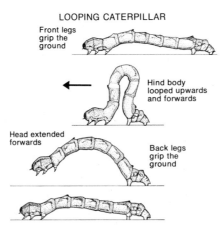

LOOPING CATERPILLAR

Front legs grip the ground

Hind body looped upwards and forwards

Head extended forwards

Back legs grip the ground

The thorn moth caterpillar inches forward by moving its fore-legs and rear legs in turn, while the legless part of the body loops upward

and two pairs of claspers at the end of the body; in between is a long legless section.

The section without legs loops upwards as the caterpillar inches forward, measuring its length, and it is this action which has resulted in the family name, the geometers, which means earth-measurer, and its American name—inch-worm.

The moths have wingspans of up to 2 in. and live on trees. When the caterpillars are not feeding they rest on a twig, holding on by their claspers and standing out straight so that they look like side twigs.

A common species throughout the British Isles is the peppered moth *Biston betularia*, which feeds on oak and many other species of trees. Near cities and over the polluted eastern half of the country they are black, but in the cleaner west most are white, peppered with black, which provides camouflage when they rest on lichen-covered trees.

In southern England the September thorn *Deuteronomos erosaria* is common. It feeds only on oak. See also EVOLUTION

Thorow-wax *Bupleurum rotundifolium*
An annual weed found mainly in cornfields, growing 6-12 in. high, with round leaves through which the stems appear to grow, hence the name thorow-wax, given by the 16th-century botanist William Turner,

Close-up of flower

Thorow-wax is now almost extinct, due to the use of selective weedkillers and clean seed

because 'the stalks waxeth throw the leaves'. Another name, which is equally appropriate, is hare's ear. The umbels of small yellow flowers, surrounded by yellow leafy bracts, appear in June and July. Once common in south and east England, thorow-wax is now almost extinct because of the use of clean corn seed and selective weedkillers.

A similar plant, *B. lancifolium*, is often confused with thorow-wax. It grows in gardens where people put out bird food containing seed from southern Europe. See also PARSLEY

Threshing
All cereal crops have to be threshed, or beaten, to separate the grain from the husks in which it grows. The earliest method of threshing was with a hand-operated flail or drashel. After threshing the chaff was blown away by means of a winnowing machine. These processes are now combined and done by one machine.

A flail consisted of a handle, about 4 ft long and usually made of ash attached to a swingle, or beater rod, the part which threshed the corn. This was often made of crab apple or holly wood and was about 3 ft long. The hinge was traditionally made of a thong of eelskin, though leather was often used.

Flail threshing, usually carried out on a barn floor, was a skilful job, since the swingle was whirled around the head to be brought down flat on the corn, and inexpert handlers could crack themselves on the skull.

The flail was doomed by the invention in 1788 by Andrew Meikle, a Scotsman, of the first threshing machine, an improved version of which came into popular use in the 1830's, when farm labourers throughout the country rioted through fear that the machines would deprive them of winter work with the flail. Gangs of men went round smashing the new machines. In the first machines cereal crops were passed through rapidly revolving drums, which beat out the grain, separating it from the straw. Some of the machines were portable and they were a familiar sight in the rural lanes until well into the first half of this century. They moved in a convoy consisting of a steam engine, thresher, straw elevator and wooden hut in which the men slept.

During the 1940's threshing machines began to be replaced by combine harvesters, powered by tractors, which cut and threshed corn in one operation.

Some threshing machines survive. They are still used in hilly areas and other places where cereals are grown in small fields and combine harvesters cannot operate. Others are kept for threshing wheat from straw which is required for thatching, to prevent the straw being battered by the drum of a combine harvester. This type of thresher has a 'reed comber', a device which holds the straw fast while the grain is knocked out of it. See also FARM

Thrift *Armeria maritima*

Salt marshes and sea cliffs are often covered with the delicate pink or white buttons of thrift, or sea pink, rising on leafless stalks, 2-12 in. high, from a cushion of narrow, grass-like leaves. It flowers throughout the summer and is common all round the coasts of the British Isles and on mountain tops in Scotland, northern England and western Ireland.

Thrips

These black or brown insects are normally inconspicuous: they are only 1/50-1/8 in. long and live mainly on wild plants, especially inside flowers. But on humid days in late summer they swarm, and settle on people's skin. This association with sultry weather has led to their other common name, thunder-flies.

Thrips have feather-like wings, which are almost invisible against their dark bodies; their function is merely to enable the insects to take off; once airborne they are at the mercy of air currents. Thrips feed on plant sap or on insects even smaller than themselves. They lay their eggs in or on the surface of plant stems; the eggs hatch in 2-21 days. A pupal, or resting, stage follows before the thrips become fully adult.

There are 168 species in the British Isles. A few, such as the onion thrip *Thrips tabaci*, attack garden plants. The grain thrip *Limothrips cerealium* attacks cereal crops.

Thrush

Although the buff-brown speckled song thrush is the bird which leaps to mind immediately, there are five other members of the thrush family in the British Isles, including perhaps the most common and certainly one of the most familiar of our birds, the blackbird. Four of the six species are widespread breeders here, the other two are mainly winter visitors in large numbers but have started to breed in the north of Scotland in recent years.

All thrushes are medium-sized birds that find most of their food on the ground. Those that feed in parks and gardens are often seen hopping on lawns and making sudden pounces on worms and insects.

The blackbird is as common in woodland and on agricultural land as in town squares and suburban gardens. There may be as many as 10 million blackbirds in the British Isles. The male is all black with a yellow eye ring and beak. Females are duller and browner. Young birds are a rather redder brown with pale spots.

Blackbirds nest on a variety of sites from ground level to 40 ft high. They build solid nests of grasses reinforced with mud and often manage to rear four broods in a season. The female incubates three to five blue-green eggs with brown spots, which hatch in about 13 days.

In addition to the resident blackbirds, there are substantial numbers of immigrants

During the breeding season the mistle thrush may dive on any intruder approaching its nest

from the Continent which overwinter in Britain. The mellow song of the blackbird stands out in the dawn chorus, but when disturbed it flies off with a series of loud, chattering cries.

The song thrush also has a beautiful song which can be distinguished because each loud, clear phrase is repeated. This bird can be heard in most months of the year and is often seen in gardens, head cocked to one side – a habit which has been described as 'listening for worms'.

In addition to earthworms, snails are a major part of the diet of song thrushes, one of the few species to use this source of food. They locate a suitable stone which they use to break the snails' shells. Berries and insects augment their diet.

Their nests are similar to the blackbird's except that the lining is of dried mud, whereas the blackbird lines its nest with dead grasses over a layer of mud. The eggs are light blue with black spots.

The song thrush is smaller than the mistle thrush and in most areas considerably

THE THRUSH'S ANVIL

The song thrush feeds on snails and uses a stone as an anvil to break open their shells

more common. While the song thrush eats mainly animal food, the mistle thrush is predominantly vegetarian and takes its name from the fact that it is one of the few birds which feed on mistletoe berries. It is also known as the storm cock because it sings even in bad weather. Its song is not as mellow as the blackbird's and the phrases are not repeated as in the song thrush.

The largest of British thrushes, the mistle thrush is grey-brown with distinctive white tips to the outer tail feathers. Its pale blue to buff eggs, with red-brown spots, are laid in bulky cup nests of grass, twigs and moss, often high in a tree and as early as the end of February. During the breeding season mistle thrushes may dive on man, birds or even cats which approach their nests.

The ring ouzel is a summer visitor to Britain which breeds in the hills and moorlands of the north and west. It is superficially similar to the blackbird but, because of its remote habitat, far less familiar. Its most useful distinguishing mark is the white bib, more pronounced in the male, and it has a silvery sheen to its wings. Arriving in April and staying until September, ring ouzels eat insects, small snails and worms in spring and summer and gather berries in the autumn, before leaving with their young to winter in the Atlas mountains or the Mediterranean.

Both the redwing and the fieldfare are winter visitors, principally from Scandinavia. The redwing is the smallest of the thrushes and resembles a diminutive song thrush. It has red flanks and a pronounced eye stripe which gives it a severe look. It has bred regularly in Scotland since 1953 and about 25 pairs are now breeding.

The fieldfare is boldly marked and has a grey head and rump. It nested in Orkney in 1967 and Shetland in 1968. Its diet is similar to the other thrushes. Both winter visitors roam the fields in mixed flocks.

Thuja *Thuja plicata*

A tree often called by its American name of western red cedar. Thuja is frequently planted in woodlands as well as for hedges and garden ornament. It is a cypress-like evergreen that can be recognised by its frond-like foliage, reddish lower twigs and thin fibrous bark.

The yellow male flowers and green female ones, which both open in spring, are small and bud-shaped. In autumn they produce small, slender brown cones with long scales. Tiny brown seeds, edged with papery wings, become wind-borne. The seedlings bear two early seed-leaves and later narrow needles develop. Crushed foliage is aromatic.

The sapwood is pale, the heartwood red-brown, light but exceptionally durable.

Thuja comes from British Columbia where it was widely used by Haida Indians for building houses, war canoes and totem poles. In Britain it is used for fencing, building and ladder poles, thanks to its straightness, strength and lightness. The tallest thuja in Britain, 125 ft high, is at Bicton Arboretum near Exeter.

Thunder

The heat of a lightning flash expands the air around it so rapidly that it sets up sound waves known as thunder. These sounds reach the listener from several parts of the lightning flash and are also reflected from hills and clouds—hence the typical drawn-out rumble of thunder. As light travels about 1 million times faster than sound, a lightning flash is seen much earlier than the accompanying thunder is heard.

The distance of lightning can be gauged by allowing 1 mile for every five seconds that elapse between flash and thunder. The greatest distance at which thunder can be heard is about 10 miles.

Thunder is often accompanied by pressure waves of too low a frequency to be heard; it is these which make windows rattle during a storm. See also LIGHTNING

Thunderstorm

A disturbance in the air caused by electrical charges in a large cumulo-nimbus cloud, sometimes called thunderhead. This electricity is discharged in the form of lightning —either between clouds, or between cloud and earth—which is accompanied by thunder.

A thunderstorm is usually heralded by a downdraught of cold air shortly after the onset of heavy rain. This lowers the temperature by as much as 10°C and spreads outwards as a gusty wind.

In the British Isles thunderstorms are most frequent—about 20 a year—in inland areas of south-east and midland England.

Thyme *Thymus drucei*

A creeping, much-branched perennial which often forms a dense carpet to the exclusion of all other plants. It grows on dry grassland, heaths, sand dunes and rock ledges throughout the British Isles. The tiny, two-lipped, rose-purple flowers appear from May onwards and attract honey bees.

Once applied externally as a cure for headaches and giddiness, the plant was called Mother Thyme to distinguish it from the garden variety.

Thyme forms a dense carpet on heaths and dry ground. It was once thought to be a cure for headaches

Tick

Oval, brown, eight-legged animals, up to ⅝ in. long, ticks are a specialised group of mites that suck the blood of man and other animals. Each species keeps to a particular animal. Only 22 species live in the British Isles, compared with many thousands in tropical countries. Many ticks carry disease.

When seeking a host animal on which to feed, a tick climbs from ground level on to foliage. Special heat-sensitive organs enable the tick to locate passing animals, to which it clings. Scent enables it to determine if the animal is a suitable host. If it is not, the tick drops off to resume its search; but if it is, the tick begins sucking its blood. When fully fed it becomes swollen and falls off the host.

One of the most common British ticks is the castor bean or common sheep tick *Ixodes ricinus*, which feeds on sheep and cattle and is often found on dogs that have been taken for a walk in a field. The castor bean tick infects cattle with red water fever.

There are two types of ticks: hard ticks, which have sculptured plates on their backs, and soft ticks, which do not. Ticks have a life cycle with four distinct forms: egg, larva, nymph, adult. The female hard tick, over a period of one or two weeks, sucks up 80 to 100 times her own weight of blood. She then lays a batch of between 1000 and 10,000 eggs on the ground, some of which hatch after a few weeks into a six-legged larva. This feeds for two to four days on the blood of an animal and then drops from its host to moult into an eight-legged nymph. This feeds on another animal for four to five days before moulting into an eight-legged adult.

The female soft tick has several feeds, each lasting several minutes or hours, and after each lays a batch of 50-150 eggs. There are two to four nymphal stages in the development of the soft tick, which otherwise matures in the same way as the hard tick.

The cleaning activities of host animals and failure to find suitable hosts keep the tick population in check.

The hedgehog tick *Ixodes hexagonus* clinging to its host. When fully fed it swells and falls off

Tiddler see Stickleback

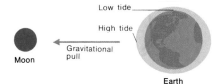

THE TIDAL FORCE OF THE MOON

Where the gravitational pull of the moon is greatest, high tides occur. The sun, 390 times further away than the moon, has a similar but weaker effect on the tides than the moon

Tide

Julius Caesar first learnt of tides when he came to Britain, where the tide may make a difference of 40 ft to the depth of water, compared with the Mediterranean's tide of at most 6 in.

The gravitational forces of the moon, sun and earth combine to give two high and two low tides a day to most parts of the coast of the British Isles. Though smaller than the sun, the moon has a greater gravitational pull on the oceans because it is nearer to earth. The water of the oceans forms a bulge directly below the moon as it circles the earth. Complex gravitational forces produce a corresponding bulge on the opposite side of the world. Midway between these points water is at its lowest, giving the low tides.

When the sun is in line with the moon on the same side of earth, their joint gravity causes extra high tides, known as spring tides. Very low, or neap, tides result when the pull of the sun acts at right angles to that of the moon. Spring and neap tides occur every 14¾ days.

Because the moon takes 24 hours and 50 minutes to circle the earth, high tides occur about 12½ hours apart and are 50 minutes later each day.

The depth of the ocean and coastal configuration affects tides—for example, when it is high tide at Dover it is low tide at Falmouth. Local, quite unusual tide patterns may occur. Both at Southampton and on the other side of the English Channel near Cherbourg, a prolonged or double high tide occurs with four, or even six, high tides a day. Poole and Weymouth have four.

Tides are a vital factor to shipping entering ports or tidal estuaries which often exaggerate the tide's effect. To enable ships to load and unload whatever the state of the tide at Liverpool, the ½ mile long Pier Head landing stage, the world's largest floating structure, was built.

The size of tides is reckoned from the mean sea level at Newlyn, Cornwall, chosen as Ordnance datum because it has a stable horizontal level, hard, granite rocks, and because the tides are not distorted by shallow water. The highest and lowest tides in the British Isles occur at Avonmouth on the River Severn. The highest and lowest tides there since records were kept were: 47·9 ft on January 9, 1936, and minus 1·9 ft on February 6, 1935. See also SEASHORE and BORE

Tiger beetle

Brightly coloured, patterned beetles, about ¾ in. long, with large eyes and large, powerful scissor-like mandibles, or jaws, living throughout the British Isles on sandy heaths, beaches and moorland. During the spring and summer months they can be seen running and flying about in search of the insects on which they feed.

The tiger beetle larva digs a burrow in an open patch of ground up to 1 ft deep and wedges itself in the entrance, so that its head and jaws fill the hole—its hook-like spines gripping the sides of the burrow. When a small insect comes within reach the larva uses its jaws to seize the prey and carry it to the bottom of the burrow, where it can be eaten at leisure.

There are five British species. The most common is the green tiger beetle *Cicindela campestris*, which is green with yellow spots. Three of the other species are brown with yellow stripes. The remaining tiger beetle *C. germanica* varies in colour from green to black with yellow marks. It is restricted to southern and eastern England.

Tiger moth

The brilliant colours of these moths sometimes cause them to be mistaken for butterflies. The hindwings of all six British species are bright red or orange, marked with black. In all except the small ruby tiger the forewings, too, are a boldly patterned white and black or white and brown. The colouring of tiger moths probably protects the insects in two ways: the forewing markings break up their outline and therefore camouflage them, and if they are disturbed by birds the gaudy hindwings warn them off, for all tiger moths appear to be distasteful to birds, and the garden tiger is poisonous to them. The moths are stout-bodied and have a wingspan of 1¼-2¾ in.

The garden tiger, which flies mainly at night but makes little effort to hide by day, is both widespread and common. The ruby tiger, which is chiefly active by night, is also found throughout the British Isles. The other four species, however, are local or rare. The scarlet tiger, also active by day, lives only in southern England, chiefly Kent. The cream-spot tiger, which flies at night, is restricted to southern England and East Anglia. The Jersey tiger, a day and night flyer, is known only in south Devon and the Channel Islands. The widespread but rare wood tiger is, despite its name, most often found in open, heathery places.

The caterpillars of all six species are hairy and are often called woolly bears. Their hairs contain an irritant which prevents all birds except the cuckoo family from eating them. No one has established so far what element in the cuckoo's gullet enables it to eat the hairy species which other birds cannot tolerate. The caterpillars, which hatch from August onwards, feed on a wide variety of low-growing plants; the garden tiger likes stinging nettles. They all hibernate and resume feeding the following spring. Adult tiger moths have no tongue and do not feed—they live on the reserves built up in the caterpillar stage.

Tiger moth caterpillars wander a great deal. In May or June they spin a cocoon of silk mixed with their hairs. The adult moths emerge in July or August.

The bright red and brown cinnabar moth is related to the tiger moths. It flies by day and night and is common throughout the British Isles, except the extreme north of Scotland. Its orange and black-banded caterpillars feed on the poisonous ragwort.

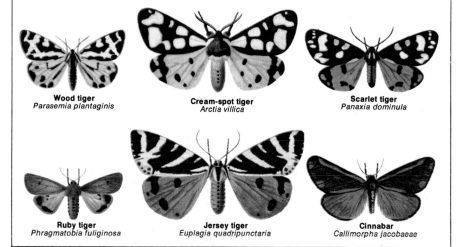

Tiger moths and the cinnabar moth

The six British species of tiger moths and their relative the cinnabar moth are brightly coloured and sometimes mistaken for butterflies. The garden tiger is illustrated under the entry Moth.

Wood tiger *Parasemia plantaginis*

Cream-spot tiger *Arctia villica*

Scarlet tiger *Panaxia dominula*

Ruby tiger *Phragmatobia fuliginosa*

Jersey tiger *Euplagia quadripunctaria*

Cinnabar *Callimorpha jacobaeae*

Tile-hanging

Introduced into south-east England from the Low Countries during the 17th century, tile-hanging is one of the most efficient methods of weather-proofing an outside wall. The tiles, made from clay, are hung on wooden laths and fixed with nails—two to a tile—in such a way that each tile overlaps two others, keeping out the rain and the snow. Decorative effects are created by using alternating rows of plain and shaped tiles. In some early forms of tiling the tiles were fixed with wooden pegs or bones. In northern England and parts of Scotland slates were often used in place of tiles.

During the 18th and 19th centuries, when tile-cladding of walls was widespread, the mathematical tile (so-called because of the precision with which it was made) was introduced. This was a tile made to imitate brickwork exactly and was widely used to avoid the Brick Tax imposed in 1784. Good examples have survived in Lewes, Sussex.

Tile-hanging has been revived in recent years as a convenient way of cladding modern industrialised housing. See also COTTAGES

Tillage see Farm

Timber line

This is the upper limit of altitude at which trees will grow. The main factor limiting tree growth is temperature—trees need a continuous period of at least two months each year in which the average temperature does not fall below 10°C (50°F). In the British Isles the temperature falls by about 1°C for every 300 ft increase in altitude, and this gives a line varying in general from 1200 to 2000 ft above which trees will not grow. The lower limits are usually found in the exposed areas of the north and west, and the limit moves upwards in the south and east. There are other limiting factors, such as strong winds, heavy rain and saturated soil, so that in certain exposed areas, especially in western Scotland, the timber line may be as low as 600 ft. The nearer trees are to the timber line, the smaller they grow. A species that grows 50 ft tall at sea level will only grow to 30 ft at an altitude of 1500 ft.

Timothy see Grass

Tinder *Fomes fomentarius*

As the name suggests, this perennial woody fungus was used as tinder to catch sparks generated by striking steel on flint. It was first beaten and soaked in saltpetre. Tinder was also used for staunching wounds. The fungus grows on living trees, causing the wood to rot. It is most often found on birch in the Scottish Highlands, but also occurs on birch in Lincolnshire and on beech at Knole Park in Kent.

The upper surface of young tinders is pale brown and velvety; the older ones turn grey, with light and dark zones, and are hoof-shaped. See also FUNGUS

This Welsh tip heap is typical of many which disfigure the landscape of industrial Britain

Tip heap

Dumps of waste material from coal mines and other underground workings, common in northern England, southern Scotland and Wales. Sometimes they can be dangerous. During the 1960's one slipped and engulfed the Welsh village of Aberfan, killing nearly all the children in the local school.

Besides being unsightly and potentially dangerous, many tips used to pollute the air as they often smouldered and sometimes burst into flames. But since the 1950's vast numbers have been reshaped, covered with soil and planted with a variety of vegetation and even made into small parks.

This work of restoring the countryside cannot be started, however, until the tips have been left to settle. They are also known as spoil heaps and dirt tips, and a group in Lancashire is called ironically the Wigan Alps. See also SLAG HEAP

Tithe

From the 9th century until 1936 a tax called a tithe was levied on the produce of all land in England. Originally, tithes were the income from church property held in trust for the poor. One-tenth of the wood, corn, milk and eggs, and one-tenth of the increase in the number of farm animals, was handed to the owner of the tithe rights until 1836, when the equivalent value in money became payable.

In many places the produce was stored in specially erected tithe barns. Some of these remain today: a particularly good example is the 14th-century barn at Bredon in Worcestershire.

In the early Christian era the tithe system was widespread in Europe. King Offa of Mercia made it compulsory in his kingdom in 794, and it spread throughout England in the following century. No one could escape paying. If a farmer did not till his fields, an estimate was made of what the crop would have been if he had cultivated the land, and he had to pay one-tenth of the value in money.

The tithe went to the rector of the parish for his maintenance and the upkeep of the church. In some cases the rector was an individual, but in others the post was vested in a monastery.

On the Dissolution of the Monasteries in the reign of Henry VIII, many rectories passed into royal hands and were granted to laymen, who became entitled to the tithes.

The rules for the payment of tithes varied from parish to parish. It was originally payable only in kind, but sometimes arrangements were made to pay in money or to give a bigger proportion of one crop in lieu of others. At Drayton Bassett in Staffordshire, for example, a tithe-payer was permitted to deliver nine cartloads of wood in place of all other tithes.

Generally, the substances of the earth, such as slate, gravel and coal, were not subject to tithe, but in some areas the fish in local ponds were tithed, and in some fishing villages one-tenth of the catch had to be paid to the rector. In many places an annual tithe was paid on the value of houses.

The Tithe Act of 1836 abolished the payment of tithe in kind and substituted a financial levy on the land related to the average price of wheat, barley and oats. In 1925 the levy was stabilised, and it was abolished by Parliament in 1936. There had been widespread objections to paying the money, especially from farmers who were not members of the Church of England and who resented having to contribute to its funds.

The owners of tithe rights were compensated by the issue of tithe redemption stock, on which interest of 3 per cent a year is paid. This is less than the amount of tithe formerly received, but it is guaranteed by the Government and the stock is redeemable in 1996. In place of the levy, the former tithe-payer contributes to tithe redemption annuities collected by the Inland Revenue. These cease in 1996. The last vestige of the tithe system will then be extinguished, except for the tithe barns dotted about the countryside.

Tits

Typical tits are blue and yellow or buff and brown, but all have pronounced caps. They are agile feeders, being as much at home

The reed-dwelling bearded tit is misnamed: its 'beard' is merely a moustache-like facial stripe

feeding upside-down as on a flat bird table. They are intelligent birds and have learnt to pierce milk-bottle tops with their beaks to steal the cream. They are also adaptable and several species take readily to man-made nest boxes hung in gardens.

Eight species breed regularly in Britain and Ireland; five of them are regular visitors to the garden, three of them are not.

The long-tailed tit feeds mostly on insects,

Tail outspread and wings fluttering, a male coal tit pays court to a female

and though seen in gardens is not a common visitor. Crested tits are confined to the old Caledonian forests and the nearby new plantations in the Scottish Highlands. The bearded tit is never found away from large reed beds; it is confined to East Anglia and a few isolated areas in the southern half of England and Wales.

The great tit, resplendent in yellow and green with a black cap and line down its chest, is the easiest to recognise and most widespread of the tits. It is also the noisiest. Ornithologists have described no fewer than 57 distinct calls, most of which are piercingly repetitive to the human ear. It nests in natural holes in trees and will take readily to nest boxes. A pair will rear up to ten young, feeding them caterpillars at what seems a non-stop rate: it has been estimated that the young eat 7000-8000 in the 20 days that they spend in the nest.

Blue tits are not as noisy, but may often gather at bird tables in larger numbers and are usually the dominant members of the loose winter tit flocks which spend their time roaming Britain's woodlands. They have a bold yellow breast and blue crown and wings.

Coal tits, though really birds of coniferous forests, are frequently found in gardens and woods miles from the nearest fir trees. Their high-pitched 'tsee' call note can be heard in many of the dense plantations, but the birds themselves can be difficult to spot as they flit through the trees. They are best identified by the pronounced white spot on the nape of their necks. They nest in natural

tree holes but will readily take to nest boxes. Marsh and willow tits are extremely difficult to tell apart except by their calls and songs. The marsh calls a 'pitcheeoo' note whereas the willow tit's call consists of nasal 'chay-chay-chay' notes. Voice apart, the marsh tit has a glossy crown and the willow tit a light patch on the edges of its wings.

Despite their names the willow tit is not associated with willows, nor the marsh tit with marshes. In fact the willow tit is more likely to be found in damp surroundings. While the marsh tit uses natural nesting holes the willow tit only nests in holes in rotten trees and stumps which it has excavated itself. Recently, one ornithologist persuaded this species to breed in a nest box for the first time by filling a box with expanded polystyrene which the bird could then excavate.

The long-tailed tit is one of Britain's master builders. The beautifully camouflaged domed nest is covered with lichens and cobwebs and lined with hundreds of feathers. Up to a dozen eggs are laid inside the tiny nest and there is just room for the adult to incubate them if it folds its tail over its back. Outside the breeding season family parties and loose flocks can be seen flitting along hedges and woodland edges.

The crested tit and bearded tit are confined to Scottish conifers and mainly East Anglian reed beds and so are almost unknown to the public. Both are quite unmistakable when seen close to, though anyone seeking a bearded tit for the first time may identify it as a miniature pheasant as it flies a few inches above the reed beds, its long tail streaming out behind. In contrast the crested tit, so named because of its pronounced crest, is much more like the other tits searching the trees for insects.

Toad

These amphibious animals are distinguishable from frogs, to which they are related, by their squatter appearance, shorter limbs and drier, wart-covered skin. Although able to swim, the two British species spend most of their lives on land, returning to ponds only to breed.

The common toad lives throughout England and Scotland and in parts of Wales and Ireland. Its muddy brown, olive or grey colours merge well against the soil; some specimens have dark red patches. The female is up to 4 in. long, the male only $2\frac{1}{2}$ in.

Much less common is the natterjack which is not found in the West Country, Wales or Ireland, apart from County Kerry. Its colour ranges from yellow-green to olive-grey, with a yellow line down the middle of the back. The warts are larger and flatter than those of the common toad and have brown or red marks on them. It is smaller than the common toad—both sexes are about $2\frac{1}{2}$ in. long—and has shorter hind legs.

By day toads live in holes—either natural ones beneath tree roots or in a hedge, or

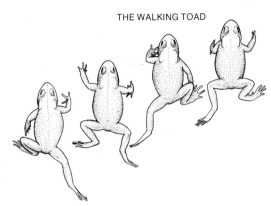

THE WALKING TOAD

Unlike frogs, the toad has a feeble hop and moves in a clumsy walk. However, it swims well with its hindlegs, its forelegs kept by its sides

ones which they have scraped in the earth. At dusk, toads leave their holes and search for worms, snails and ants, beetles, caterpillars, woodlice and other moving insects; motionless prey is not taken. The toad feeds voraciously, eating hundreds of insects at a single meal. Prey is studied for several seconds before the toad darts out its tongue and captures it; the whole operation lasts only one-tenth of a second.

On land, natterjacks are more nimble than toads and move faster, but they are poorer swimmers. Several times during the summer both species shed their skins to reveal new, wet ones, which soon dry. They swallow the old skins.

Toads and natterjacks hibernate in October and November. Common toads choose disused animal burrows, particularly those protected by trees, and abandoned sand-martin holes in clay pits. To reach these they often have to climb considerable heights.

Both animals emerge from hibernation in late March or April and make for their breeding pond. The common toad is particular in its choice. It passes several apparently suitable ponds and ditches and makes for a particular one, which may be up to a mile away and probably, like migratory fish, it returns to the spot where it was born year after year. The migration lasts one to ten days, and travelling is by day as well as by night. The toad then becomes an easy prey to birds and mammals, and many are run over as they cross roads. Natterjacks, however, are indiscriminate in their choice of ponds, and travel much shorter distances.

Common toads prefer deep water for spawning. They often pair on their way to the pond, the male riding on the female's back, and grasping her firmly with his limbs. Others pair in the water; the male supports himself on a branch or plant and repeatedly utters a short, high-pitched croak until he has attracted a female, whom he then mounts. The toads swim around until the female reaches a water plant. She then lays a 7-10 ft long jelly-like string of as many as 7000 black eggs, which become entangled in

the plant. As she lays them the male fertilises them. At night the female leaves the pond but the male stays, sometimes to fertilise the eggs of other females.

Natterjacks, like frogs, choose shallow water for spawning, sometimes small puddles. They tolerate brackish water and some breeding sites are near the sea, among sand dunes. The male's call is much louder than the common toad's. The egg string is 5-6 ft long and contains up to 4000 eggs.

A week after fertilisation the round egg of the common toad has become oval-shaped; a few days later the first faint traces of the tadpole's head, body and tail appear. After a further two weeks the black tadpole frees itself from the jelly surrounding it, and mouth and gills begin to develop. It feeds on algae, later progressing to animal food. The time taken for the egg to develop into a toad varies with the weather. It may be only nine weeks, but in a cold summer as much as 15 weeks.

The natterjack's progress from egg to adult is similar but faster. It frees itself from the spawn in five to ten days, and development is complete after six to eight weeks. The young toads and natterjacks soon leave the pond and disperse into the surrounding countryside.

Both animals secrete a poisonous substance in their skin, which protects them against many would-be predators. However, birds such as herons and crows disembowel them, and other mammals, such as the brown rat, skin them.

Many common toads become host to the greenbottle fly and die a singularly unpleasant death. The fly lays its eggs on the toad's body and the larvae crawl into the toad's nasal cavity, blocking it up so that the animal can hardly breathe. They then penetrate the rest of the head. The toad dies after two or three days and the larvae eat it, leaving only skin and skeleton. The normal life span of a common toad is up to ten years, that of a natterjack unknown.

Toadflax *Linaria vulgaris*
The narrow leaves and upright stems growing 12-30 in. high among flax, and looking like flax, gave toadflax its name. But it is

more often found as a weed on roadsides and railway banks, where its spikes of yellow and orange snapdragon-like flowers can be found in late summer and autumn. Its spurred flowers contain nectar which can be obtained only by long-tongued bees.

A curious form in which each flower has five spurs is found occasionally. Toadflax is found throughout England, Wales and southern Scotland, but is rare elsewhere.

Small toadflax is a tiny annual, only 3-9 in. high, with purple flowers. It grows in abundance on the cinders of railway tracks and has spread along the railways to all parts of the British Isles, except northern Scotland, where conditions are unsuitable for its growth. It is also found occasionally as a weed in arable fields and gardens, especially on lime-rich soils. It flowers from May until October.

Toadstool see Fungus

Toothwort *Lathraea squamaria*
A perennial herb which grows in damp woods or shady hedgerows as a parasite on the roots of various trees, mainly hazel and elm. Its white, pink-tinged, leafless stems, about 1 ft high, are crowned in April and May with two rows of drooping white or pale pink flowers.

The plant's branched root is covered with fleshy, tooth-like scales. For this reason herbalists recommended preparations of it as a cure for toothache. Scattered throughout the British Isles, it is absent from northern Scotland. See also HERB

Tor
Masses of rocks or boulders crowning a hill are known as tors. The most famous are those which stud the skyline of Dartmoor in Devon. Another well-known group is Brimham Rocks, west of Harrogate in Yorkshire. The northern tors were probably formed in the Ice Age. Water trickled into cracks and as it froze, expanded, splitting the rocks.

The tors of Devon and Cornwall, and some others, particularly those with large, rounded boulders, are probably even older, as they are tough volcanic blocks produced beneath a layer of weathered rock during tropical or sub-tropical conditions. They have been revealed as the weaker weathered rock has gradually been eroded.

Tormentil *Potentilla erecta*
A trailing herb similar to creeping cinquefoil but with the upper leaves divided into threes, not fives, and with many of the yellow flowers having four rather than five petals. It is a common perennial on poor grasslands, heaths, bogs and marshes everywhere in the British Isles. It flowers in summer.

The woody roots were once boiled in milk and the liquid was given to cure the torment of stomach ache, hence the English name. The roots were also used in the Shet-

Toadflax
Linaria vulgaris

Small toadflax
Chaenorhinum minus

Only long-tongued bees can sip nectar from the spurred flowers of the yellow toadflax

Tormentil roots have had a variety of uses from curing stomach ache to tanning leather

lands for tanning leather, and in the Outer Hebrides fishermen used them to preserve their nets.

Tornado
During extremely violent, thundery weather there will occasionally be a tremendous disturbance in the form of tube-shaped black clouds in which the air is rotating at possibly 200 knots.

They move across the country with a loud, shrieking sound at up to 40 mph, usually from south-west to north-east, and can create havoc for up to a dozen miles along a path a few hundred yards wide.

The exact cause of tornadoes is uncertain, but it is known that some result from a sudden decrease in atmospheric pressure and that a mass of warm, moist air must meet a mass of cold, dry air before one can form. These conditions occur about every two years in southern England. The resulting tornadoes rarely reach devastating intensity, but some tear the tops of trees from their trunks, flatten crops and wreck buildings.

In July 1965, a tornado roared through the gardens of the Royal Horticultural Society at Wisley, Surrey, uprooting trees and damaging fruit plantations. Three years later a tornado destroyed buildings and cars in the village of Barnacle, near Coventry.

Tortoiseshell butterfly
There are two species of tortoiseshell butterflies: the small, with a wingspan of 2 in., and the large, with a 2½ in. wingspan. The small tortoiseshell *Aglais urticae* is by far the more common and is found throughout the British Isles. It is orange, with brown, black, yellow and blue marks, and is one of the first butterflies to be seen in early summer. The buddleia is one of its favourite plants, but it is often to be seen resting on other garden flowers.

The caterpillar is dark grey or black with yellow stripes and is covered with tufts of short spines. It feeds on the leaves of stinging nettles, often on large patches in farmyards. There are two broods in the year, one in June and the second in August or September. The butterflies feed on nectar from autumn flowers before hibernating.

The large tortoiseshell *Nymphalis polychloros* is similar in appearance but different in habits and is usually seen only in Suffolk and north Essex. Its caterpillar feeds high in elm trees, and there is only one brood a year. Many of the caterpillars are killed by parasitic flies. For illustration see VANESSID

Tortrix moth
Although these pea-green or brown moths normally fly only at night, they are often flushed out from the foliage of the oak trees in which they live during the day. Tortrix moths have wingspans of ¾-1 in. and small, thin bodies.

In some years, oaks are stripped almost bare of leaves. This is the work of a variety of oak-feeding caterpillars, among which the tortrix caterpillars are the most active. They roll up the leaves and live inside them, having hatched from overwintered eggs at the beginning of May. By the beginning of June they are ready to pupate. The moths hatch in June or July. The most common species is the green oak roller *Tortrix viridana*. There are 11 brown species, marked in varying shades of black and brown.

Touch-me-not see Balsam
Townhall clock see Moschatel
Town wildlife see p. 466
Tracks see p. 468
Tractor see Farm
Trailer see Farm

The hairy seeds of traveller's joy, often called old man's beard, cast a white mantle over autumn hedges

Traveller's joy *Clematis vitalba*
A quaintly named woody climber, so-called from the beauty of its massed fruits along wayside hedgerows. It is also called virgin's bower, after its interlaced stems, old man's beard, after its white seed hairs, and wild clematis.

It belongs to the buttercup family and is common on chalk downs and limestone hills but rare elsewhere. It starts life as a two-leaved seedling, then develops a slender shoot bearing deeply lobed, pale green leaves on long stalks. If a leaf stalk touches a hedgerow stem it quickly becomes a tendril, twisting round to grasp it.

Supported in this way, the main stem, though weak, climbs high into tree crowns, eventually becoming thick and woody with pale brown fibrous bark. It can reach a height of 50 ft and live for 60 years.

In May, traveller's joy opens green-white clematis-shaped flowers, with five petals, many stamens and a cluster of separate carpels which ripen by October to small brown seeds, bearing shaggy, divided, white hairs that eventually carry them away on the wind.

Nurserymen use traveller's joy seedlings as stock for choice varieties of clematis; but foresters dislike them, as they smother young timber trees. Gipsies used to smoke lengths of the dry stems.

Where wildlife hides in the heart of a town

For the town dweller, the world of nature begins before he reaches his front door. Up to 50 species of plants and animals may live in and around his house, and beyond the door there is an even greater wealth of wildlife

A tangle of bindweed, ragwort, grasses and other plants spreads over a city dump. In the country, farmers would soon eradicate these plants

Over the centuries roads, buildings and industry have gradually submerged large areas of Britain's natural landscape. Nevertheless, wildlife has not been exterminated in towns — it exists even in the heart of great conurbations; and while it can be argued that London's starling flocks and the Trafalgar Square pigeons, not to mention the pelicans of St James's Park, are merely grace-and-favour residents fed by man, many species of insects, invertebrates, mammals, birds and plants have displayed nature's ability to overcome even the most unpromising of man-made habitats.

Most towns have parks, commons or other open spaces which provide 'mini-countrysides' especially attractive to birds: more than 100 different species have been recorded in London's Regent's Park in one year. But even if migrant birds settle and are able to breed in such areas, they do not become part of the town's natural history in the strict sense for, without the artificial habitat created by man, they would not survive.

True town wildlife exists because of its ability to adapt and live in close proximity to man. Wild flowers in towns have to overcome the following handicaps: reduced light caused by the screening effect of smoke, dust and fog; choked pores from oily deposits; sour soil and reduced soil bacteria; the corrosive effects of sulphates absorbed through the leaves; and limited water. In spite of all this, some thrive.

Within a space of seven years a bombed site in the City of London turned from barren rubble to a teeming haven of wildlife. A study carried out between 1946 and 1953 showed that the first plants to arrive were those which reproduce by airborne spores: algae, mosses and ferns. Then came the plants with light seeds borne by 'parachutes' — dandelion and sycamores, fruiting thistles, rosebays and Oxford ragwort.

Grasses followed: seaside species came from the contents of sandbags and fodder plants from food for horses stabled in London. Apple, tomato, plum, date and cherry plants developed from food remnants. Plants with hooked fruits were carried in by man. Pellitory-of-the-wall and ivy grew in the dry cracks of walls, and Canadian fleabane, brambles and buddleia also appeared. Before the blitz, only pellitory-of-the-wall was firmly established in the City, but by 1952 there were 269 species of wild flowers, grasses and ferns on record.

Where previously few wild animals were seen in the City, apart from pigeons, starlings and rats, by the end of the seven-year study, four mammals, 31 birds, 56 insects and 30 other invertebrates had been noted. They included snails, slugs, woodlice, centipedes, aphids, spiders, caterpillars, moths and butterflies. The cat, mouse and rat population was augmented by hedgehogs, lizards, snakes and tortoises, and other lost pets.

Ornithological history was made when the black redstart, formerly a rare summer migrant, bred in the ruins. It now nests regularly in factory yards, sidings and power stations.

Railways and canal embankments reach into the centres of most cities bringing wildlife with them. Embankments, covered with grass, flowers, shrubs and a variety of trees, harbour insects, birds, mice, voles, shrews and rabbits and provide foraging ground for hedgehogs, foxes, badgers and squirrels.

The fish in canals attract a variety of birds, including herons, and many aquatic plants thrive in disused waterways.

Sewage farms and rubbish tips are an important source of food for birds and animals on the fringe of towns. It has been estimated that 40 million flies feed on each acre of filter beds. This attracts wagtails, flycatchers, warblers and starlings.

Reservoirs contain bacteria, algae, small crustaceans and insect larvae. Pike, perch, roach and trout are often introduced for sport, and herons, grebes and cormorants appear, together with visiting waders, ducks, geese and swans. Common, herring and blackheaded gulls roost on the water after spending the winter days scavenging on rubbish tips.

Open rubbish dumps also provide a ready supply of food for insects, invertebrates, birds and even rats, foxes, hedgehogs, rabbits and badgers.

Away from town centres, suburban gardens form an ideal habitat for birds, particularly where man stocks bird tables and provides nest boxes. In addition to the ubiquitous house sparrow and starling, robins, blue and great tits, greenfinches, chaffinches, dunnocks, wood pigeons, blackbirds, song and mistle thrushes are common suburbanites. Swifts and house martins are numerous, feeding on flying insects.

While squirrels and hedgehogs have long been known as visitors to the garden, in recent years, possibly because of the decline in rabbits since 1953, foxes have become a nuisance in some areas, tearing open modern paper-bag type dustbins. Most gardens contain a large number of insects and, if neglected, soon display a variety of weeds. In return, many attractive 'wild' flowers, such as the michaelmas daisy and lupin, have spread from gardens to grow wild.

In many places, old churchyards survive and are often neglected. Colonies of lichen grow on tombstones, the older ones carrying more species since aerial pollution, particularly sulphur dioxide, has killed off less hardy forms. Owls and weasels may sometimes be found, preying on rats and mice.

Dockland is an area where wildlife can flourish, with foreign plants growing among the native wild flowers. The food produced by spillage attracts insects, rats, mice, hedgehogs, weasels and rabbits, which are preyed on by owls, kestrels and even foxes. In addition, linnets, goldfinches, wrens, blackbirds, song thrushes and gulls live and breed in the area.

The average householder would be surprised if it were possible for him to count the number of wild creatures which shelter under his roof; there are at least 50 species which are often found indoors. Rats, mice or bats are usually eradicated as soon as discovered, and common toads hibernating in basements and cellars are usually removed promptly. But a whole range of insects, including houseflies, silverfish, furniture beetles, clothes moths, house ants, earwigs, spiders and scavenging beetles are not so conspicuous. Minute spores can produce mould on neglected food, clothing or walls, and

dry rot fungi can germinate in suitable places. Open windows let in moths and other night-flying insects, and garden insects are often brought into the house on clothes or flowers.

Some animals show a remarkable ability to adapt to specialised urban environments: brown rats and mice living and breeding in sub-zero temperatures at a refrigerated store developed thicker fur and a protective layer of fat. Moths have developed darker colours to merge with sooty backgrounds — a process known as industrial melanism.

As man changes the environment, some species of plants and animals are driven out, while others thrive. In this process man's waste products have come to form an important link or supplement to the natural food chain in urban areas.

In watching for changes in urban wildlife, it is important not to be misled by oddities mentioned from time to time in the Press, such as peregrines hunting over Big Ben, a stone curlew resting in a child's sandpit or field mice appearing in an uncompleted office block. While no doubt interesting additions to town wildlife, they are merely freak occurrences.

LIVING WILD IN TOWNS

Pellitory-of-the-wall
Parietaria diffusa

Heron
Ardea cinerea

Black redstart
Phoenicurus ochruros

Fox
Vulpes vulpes

Hedgehog
Erinaceus europaeus

These and many other wild plants and animals manage to survive even in the most crowded and bustling modern towns

A barn owl carries a rat back to its nest in a church tower. Churches and churchyards often provide quiet nesting places for many birds

467

Tracks—clues to animals' secret lives

The footprints of land animals in mud, sand, dust and snow are important pointers to their whereabouts, habits and homes. They also provide evidence of rare, elusive or nocturnal animals, otherwise undetectable

Animal tracks sometimes provide the first evidence of an unwelcome visitor, such as a fox on a poultry farm, or the presence of a rare animal. They also provide clues to the existence of shy, elusive, neutrally coloured and often silent and nocturnal animals, which would otherwise live undetected by man.

No backboned animal ever has more than five digits in hand or foot. Usually there are fewer, with adaptations as varied as the cat's four toes with claws to the horse's single toe with hoof. These modifications are the result of an evolutionary process which began during the Carboniferous or coal forest period when amphibians began to develop limbs for walking in place of fins for swimming. Fossilised tracks of the first known land animals have been dated at over 250 million years old.

British mammals illustrate a range of foot plan. A badger is adapted for walking and digging, a cat for running and climbing, a rabbit for hopping and a deer and horse for running and jumping. As a general rule, powerful claws on short, stocky limbs indicate a digging animal like a badger or mole, while delicate sharp claws on slender limbs belong to climbers and predators, like squirrels and cats.

Among hunting animals, movement is more on the toes, so that a four-toed track is formed. The 'heel' is clear of the ground and so is the 'thumb' or 'big toe', called the dew-claw. It is often very much reduced and can even be missing, as in the fox and the cat.

Deer tracks in the mud. The spreading of the digit marks indicates galloping, while the cracked earth shows that the tracks are old

In hopping animals, such as rabbits and hares, the hind feet are usually longer than the forefeet, with a stronger kick and longer reach. In these two, the hind limbs are four-toed and the forelimbs five-toed with claws. In both, the tracks are usually blurred due to hair between the pads.

Tracks may be identified by their size and shape, the areas where they are found and an interpretation of the condition of the animal which made them. For example, a fox's prints are about the same size as a fox terrier's. But a dog following its master will mingle its prints with those of the human. Otherwise, its trail will be erratic, with leaps and bounds. The fox normally keeps to cover or low ground, leaving tracks beneath hedgerows or in ditches and hollows. It hunts largely by scent, ending in a careful stalk. Its normal gait is a trot, although it also walks and bounds. The tracks are neat and four-toed.

Domestic animals, deer, badgers and rabbits tend to follow existing pathways. Badger setts are sometimes centuries old, with ancient paths leading to their latrines and drinking places. Man is the badger's only real enemy, and it has no need for speed to catch its food, which includes insects and plants, or to escape capture. It is therefore a relatively slow-moving animal and walks on its soles, making a five-toed, five-clawed imprint. Deer tracks often show traces of buck-jumping, sitting, lying, turning and creeping.

Mud or snow will obviously carry the clearest tracks. Squirrel prints show up on a muddy woodland path; rabbits will leave snow trails near their warren; and otters will make any snow-covered bank into a slide, detouring from their path to do so.

From tracks can be deduced the faster gait and more direct trail of an alarmed animal, or the shorter steps, drag of feet and erratic path of an exhausted animal.

Arrow-like footprints—the large web-footed tracks of a swan show distinctly in the mud of an estuary

Tracks of British mammals

Spotting wildlife in the countryside is not always easy — most animals run or hide at the approach of man. But many creatures, especially mammals, leave tracks which provide clues to their whereabouts. This chart shows the tracks of 28 common British mammals. They are fresh adult tracks impressed in a soft surface. Actual tracks, however, are seldom perfect and other signs may have to be looked for, such as droppings or damage to vegetation. On hard surfaces, tracks are usually shallow. On very soft surfaces, the tracks may splay out.

l left
r right
f fore
h hind

Horse and donkey
The unshod hoof print is almost circular, with a notch in the back

Cattle
Heavy, broad, rounded toe marks, with only a narrow gap between their inner concave walls

Sheep
Toe marks rounded at both ends. Inner walls concave at the front. Usually different-sized toes

Fallow deer
Long, narrow hoof prints, about 2½ in. long. Inner walls of toes are concave. Marks of dew-claws are rare

Muntjac
Pointed, narrow track, up to 1⅜ in. long. The two toe marks are of unequal size

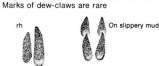

Red deer
Footprints 3-3½ in. long; more rounded than in fallow deer and tending to splay out in heavy animals

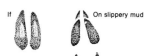

Roe deer
The two toe marks converge and narrow at the front; 1½-2 in. long. Dew-claw marks show on soft ground

Badger
A bar-like pad mark, five toe prints, long claw marks, especially on the front feet

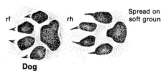

Dog
The ball print is triangular and larger than the toe prints. Claw marks blunter than fox's

Fox
Track similar to the dog, but trail is straighter. The two central toes point inwards

Domestic cat
Four-toed track without claw prints, but claw marks show after landing from great height

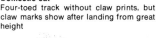

Wild cat
Track identical to that of domestic cat but larger. Tracks of male larger than female's

Otter
Large twisted pad mark with five pointed toe marks turned inwards. Drag mark of tail may show

Polecat
Five toe marks, though only four seen sometimes. Divided pad mark. Claw marks long and distinct

Weasel
Five toe prints, with inner toe lying behind others, sharp claw marks, pad indistinct

Stoat
Five-toed tracks with sharp claw marks. Rather pointed, with inner toe print behind others

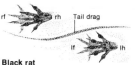

Shrew
Five-toed tracks in bunches of four when bounding. Usually found only in soft mud, or clay

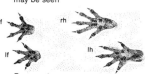

Hedgehog
Hind tracks longer than fore. Toe prints short and slightly out-turned

Mole
Fore tracks show only curved claw marks; hind tracks show as normal five-toed prints

Rabbit
Hind tracks, which have four toes, are longer than the five-toed fore tracks

Hare
Tracks larger than rabbit's with different claw marks. Often blurred because of hairy pads

Coypu
Front tracks four-toed, hind tracks five-toed with web marks

Red squirrel / Grey squirrel

Squirrels
Red and grey squirrels' tracks similar, but red's hind print is not so distinct

Black rat
Front footprints four-toed, hind ones five-toed. Short claw marks. Drag mark of tail may be seen

Brown rat
Track similar to that of black rat but larger. The stride is also shorter

Bank vole
Four-toed front tracks, five-toed hind tracks. Show up most clearly in soft mud

Field vole
Tracks similar to bank vole's but larger. The claws, unlike the bank vole's, usually show

House mouse
Front tracks four-toed, hind tracks five-toed, elongated and with outside toes set back

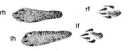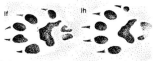

469

Autumn tints in a mixed woodland at Hewood, Dorset, where natives, such as oak and willow, grow alongside introduced species such as larch and spruce

Tree

Britain's trees disappeared during the Ice Age, 10,000 years ago, but by the time the country had separated from the Continent 2000 years later, 35 species had returned by natural means—brought in by the wind and birds—as the climate grew warmer. These trees are regarded as native species. Among them are many of today's more common British trees, such as willow, oak, beech, ash, birch, elm and alder, and two conifers, the Scots pine and yew.

After the Roman invasion, trees such as sweet chestnut and walnut were imported to grow in villa gardens. Later, monks, often returning from pilgrimages, brought other continental trees to produce fruit in monastery gardens. Sycamores, first brought in during the Middle Ages as decorative trees, soon became firmly established.

Explorers of the 17th and 18th centuries and the Victorian empire-builders, traders and botanists, sent home many specimens of

trees, and during this era many country estates had collections of unusual trees from such countries as China and India. About 1300 species of trees can be found in Britain today.

Most species are used ornamentally or for landscaping and shelter; only some two dozen are used commercially, largely for pulp. Almost 80 per cent of the commercial timber is coniferous; of the remaining broad-leaved trees, two-thirds are oak and beech.

Man has always respected trees. They grow larger and live longer than himself and have provided wood for his houses, boats, tools and weapons, and fuel for his fire.

They even became objects of worship. The ancient Greeks dedicated the oak to Zeus, their greatest god, and the Norsemen associated the ash, which they used for weapons, with Thor, their god of war. In Britain the Celtic druids worshipped in oak groves and their rituals featured the parasitic evergreen mistletoe.

Trees renew most tissues annually and can thus live for hundreds of years. One tissue —wood—is the substance that distinguishes trees and shrubs from soft-stemmed plants. It consists of close-packed, stiff-walled cells, visible only under a microscope, which carry sap, store food and support the stem, and is formed as a living tissue by the cambium, a cell layer below the bark.

Cambium, which arises after the seedling tree's first year of growth, forms all the wood inside it. In spring, when the tree needs water to help the growth of its shoots and leaves, cambium makes open wood with thin walls and much space, creating pale spring-wood, or early-wood. In summer, when the need for water is less great, it makes denser wood, with thicker walls and less space, so creating dark summer-wood, or late-wood.

These two layers taken together form one annual ring. The rings can be counted by looking at a clean cross-cut log or tree stump, and show how many years the tree took to grow. If the rings are wide, the timber is fast-grown and coarse-grained; if narrow, the timber is the opposite. As growth rates vary from time to time, both types may be seen on one cross-cut surface. Carpenters prefer fine-grained timber for precise work.

Wood serves to support the tree's crown of foliage and also to carry root sap upwards. All wood starts life as sapwood; the main volume of sap goes up through the younger, outer rings, and as a trunk or branch grows larger its inner zone changes character, becoming heartwood. This still holds moisture, but ceases to transport it and becomes stronger, helping to support the tree.

The oldest British trees are yews, a few of which are probably almost 2000 years old. This is less than half the age of the oldest trees in the world—some small, gnarled, bristle-cone pine trees growing in the Colorado desert in the United States. A good lifetime for an oak is 500 years, and Scots pines at Ballochbuie Forest in Aberdeenshire are known to have stood for three centuries.

Britain's tallest trees are two Douglas firs. They are both 181 ft high. One is at Welshpool in Montgomeryshire and the other at Dunkeld in the Scottish Highlands. England's tallest tree is a 162 ft high wellingtonia, growing near Tavistock in Devon. The country's stoutest trees are veteran oaks; the largest, standing near Chirk in North Wales, is more than 43 ft in girth.

The shape and size of trees is affected by the ground in which they grow. Oak trees, for example, grow in a number of different habitats. The noblest trees are found in the rich soils of sheltered lowlands while a few miles away they may occur as stunted bushes on a hillside. Wistman's Wood, near Two Bridges on Dartmoor, is a good example. There, about 500 oaks are growing on a scree. Exposed and undernourished, these 300-year-old trees have grown to little more than 15 ft in height.

Trees are very vulnerable to attacks and accidents, especially during their young seedling and sapling stages. They are threatened by diseases, insects and animals, and above all by man. Cultivation, timber harvesting and the careless lighting of fires all take their toll. In Britain, laws to protect trees, or promote their planting, have only come into force since 1920.

The value of trees to the environment was recognised in the 1947 Town and Country Planning Acts. These established Tree Preservation Orders to protect notable trees and woodland from felling. Twenty years later the Civic Amenities Act required tree planting and preservation to be considered in all plans for future development, and insisted that protected trees are replaced when they die. In the same year a new Forestry Act confirmed the powers of the Forestry Commission to encourage the orderly management of private woodlands and to ensure replanting when long-established woods

SECTION THROUGH A TREE TRUNK

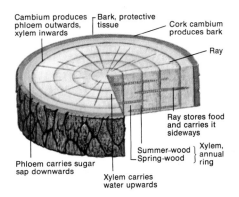

Cambium produces phloem outwards, xylem inwards

Bark, protective tissue

Cork cambium produces bark

Ray

Ray stores food and carries it sideways

Summer-wood
Spring-wood
Xylem, annual ring

Phloem carries sugar sap downwards

Xylem carries water upwards

Each year the cambium produces a layer of spring-wood and summer-wood which together make one annual ring. The tree rests in autumn and winter

were felled for timber. There are more than 1,500,000 acres of private woodland growing timber for industry.

These moves, allied to growing public interest in trees and the benefits they bring, are starting to reverse the centuries-old process of forest clearance. In prehistoric times, woods covered about 70 per cent of Britain's land surface, only the exposed higher hills and the waterlogged valley marshes being treeless. Today woodland occupies only 8 per cent of the land.

The skills of tree-tending, mainly for fruit production, date back to biblical times. To cope with the growing demand for softwoods, foresters have introduced many new, fast-growing trees which thrive in the British climate. These include Douglas firs and western red cedars from the west coast of America, Japanese and European larch, and spruce from Norway and Alaska. Nowadays, strains of cultivated trees, like plants and animals, can also be improved by scientific breeding.

A typical programme starts with the selection of suitable parent trees in a well-grown plantation. These will have grown fast, shown disease-resistance, maintained straight trunks with light branches and have been found, on examination under a microscope, to have good timber characteristics.

Shoots of these trees are obtained by firing a shot-gun into their crowns, which takes less time than climbing the trees to cut them. The shoots are then skilfully grafted on to rootstocks of a similar tree growing in a research nursery.

Because these shoots, called scions, came from a mature tree, they will flower within a few years. Female flowers are enclosed, well before they open, in polythene bags so they cannot receive wind-borne pollen from unknown male parents. Pollen from the male flowers of selected trees is collected by hand and put into the bags. The pedigree seedlings, which are grown from the seeds produced, are sown in trial beds. Next, scions of the pedigree trees are grafted on rootstocks on a large scale. Since all have selected parentage, pollination can be left to the wind.

THE WAY A TREE FEEDS

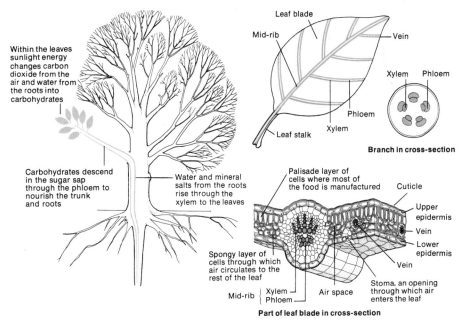

Within the leaves sunlight energy changes carbon dioxide from the air and water from the roots into carbohydrates

Carbohydrates descend in the sugar sap through the phloem to nourish the trunk and roots

Water and mineral salts from the roots rise through the xylem to the leaves

Leaf blade

Mid-rib

Vein

Xylem   Phloem

Phloem

Xylem

Leaf stalk

Branch in cross-section

Palisade layer of cells where most of the food is manufactured

Cuticle

Upper epidermis

Vein

Lower epidermis

Vein

Spongy layer of cells through which air circulates to the rest of the leaf

Mid-rib

Xylem
Phloem

Air space

Stoma, an opening through which air enters the leaf

Part of leaf blade in cross-section

A tree is nourished by carbohydrates manufactured in the leaves by a process called photosynthesis. The necessary ingredients are water conveyed from the roots to the leaves by the xylem, carbon dioxide which is absorbed from the air through openings in the leaves called stomata, and sunlight to provide energy. The food is then carried to all parts of the tree by the phloem.

Trees of the British countryside

Trees cover about 5 million acres of the land of Britain, apart from those in parks, gardens and hedgerows. Here, ranged in order from the largest to the smallest, are 32 common broad-leaved trees. They are shown in summer and winter forms, together with leaf, fruit or twig—all important identification features. Density of summer foliage is often a clue to tree identification. Some trees, such as the horse chestnut, usually hide their structure completely, while others, such as the poplars, often let the skeleton show through the leaves. Flowers and bark patterns are further useful guides when identifying a tree. Each tree illustrated is the subject of a separate entry in the book.

Oak, Common
Quercus robur

Oak, Evergreen
Quercus ilex

Ash
Praxinus excelsior

Poplar, Lombardy
Populus nigra
variety italica

Poplar, Black
Populus nigra

Poplar, Aspen
Populus tremula

Plane
Platanus × acerifolia

Beech
Fagus sylvatica

Chestnut, Sweet
Castanea sativa

Horse chestnut
Aesculus hippocastanum

Elm, Field
Ulmus procera

Elm, Wych
Ulmus glabra

Lime
Tilia europaea

Sycamore
Acer pseudoplatanus

Maple, Field
Acer campestre

Walnut
Juglans regia

Acacia
Robinia pseudoacacia

Alder
Alnus glutinosa

Hornbeam
Carpinus betulus

Mountain ash
Sorbus aucuparia

Whitebeam
Sorbus aria

Strawberry tree
Arbutus unedo

Wild service tree
Sorbus torminalis

Holly
Ilex aquifolium

473

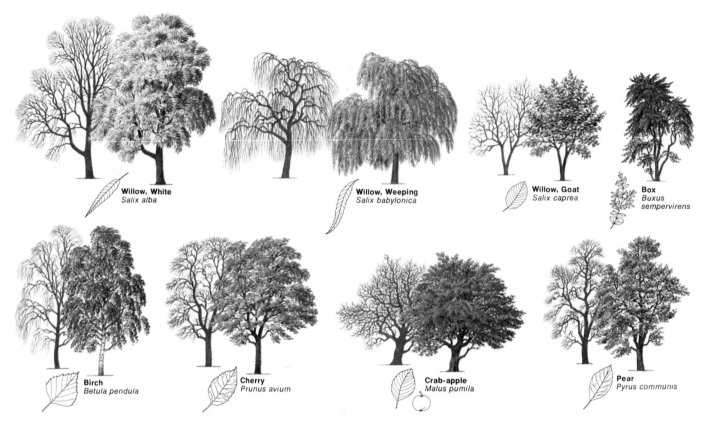

Willow, White
Salix alba

Willow, Weeping
Salix babylonica

Willow, Goat
Salix caprea

Box
Buxus sempervirens

Birch
Betula pendula

Cherry
Prunus avium

Crab-apple
Malus pumila

Pear
Pyrus communis

Common British shrubs

Shrubs are woody plants which branch repeatedly without forming a trunk. This irregular pattern of growth means that they do not form distinctive outlines in the manner of trees. Moreover, shrubs rarely grow in isolation—they are usually massed together in hedgerows. For this reason they are identified here by their leaves, flowers and fruits.

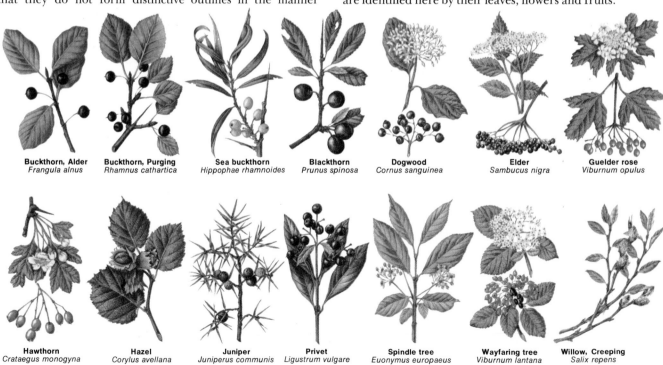

Buckthorn, Alder
Frangula alnus

Buckthorn, Purging
Rhamnus cathartica

Sea buckthorn
Hippophae rhamnoides

Blackthorn
Prunus spinosa

Dogwood
Cornus sanguinea

Elder
Sambucus nigra

Guelder rose
Viburnum opulus

Hawthorn
Crataegus monogyna

Hazel
Corylus avellana

Juniper
Juniperus communis

Privet
Ligustrum vulgare

Spindle tree
Euonymus europaeus

Wayfaring tree
Viburnum lantana

Willow, Creeping
Salix repens

Coniferous trees in Britain

Britain has only three native conifers—Scots pine, yew and juniper. But over the last 300 years many others have been introduced, either for ornamental purposes or for their timber. Those shown here are the most widely planted species.

Thuja
Thuja plicata

Cypress, Lawson
Chamaecyparis lawsoniana

Spruce, Norway
Picea abies

Wellingtonia
Sequoiadendron giganteum

Fir, Douglas
Pseudotsuga menziesii

Fir, Silver
Abies alba

Pine, Corsican
Pinus nigra
variety *maritima*

Pine, Scots
Pinus sylvestris

Yew
Taxus baccata

Cedar, Lebanon
Cedrus libani

Larch
Larix decidua

Ginkgo
Ginkgo biloba

Cypress, Swamp
Taxodium distichum

The treecreeper nests behind loose bark and picks insects from crevices with its long beak

Treecreeper

The name exactly describes the life of this bird. It is easy to overlook, as its dull, buff-streaked plumage matches the bark of the trees where it spends its life climbing in search of insects and their larvae. The long, curved bill picks prey from crevices that the stouter-beaked woodpeckers would have to smash their way to.

The treecreeper nests behind a piece of loose bark where the six rust-spotted white eggs are laid between April and June. They are incubated for about 15 days, mainly by the hen. The young spend a similar period in the nest before fledging.

The treecreeper's thin 'tsee-tsee-tissi-tsee' notes can be heard in woodlands throughout the year. In winter it often joins flocks of tits as it flies from the top of one tree to the bottom of the next before working its way skywards once more. It may be found wherever there are trees, and so is rare in north-western Scotland, and absent from Orkney and Shetland, where few trees grow.

In the early 1970's there were sightings of the short-toed treecreeper—from the Continent—which differs from the common treecreeper by having buff flanks and a distinctive call, 'teet-teet-teetrotit'. This bird is probably more widespread than the number of sightings would suggest and may even be breeding in Britain.

Tree mallow *Lavatera arborea*

A tall plant as high as a hollyhock with rose-purple flowers. It is often found on rocks, among boulders and in waste places on the shores of south-west England, Wales, the Isle of Man and round most of Ireland. It does not grow inland in the wild.

Tree mallow may be seen in cottage gardens, where it used to be grown for the mucilage in the stems from which were made ointments and poultices. In the wild it is usually 3-4 ft high, but when cultivated may reach 10 ft with stems 3-4 in. thick. It flowers from July to September.

Trefoil

Clovers with creeping stems and heads of pale yellow flowers which spread by seed and are found in grassland, by roadsides and waste places.

Hop trefoil is the larger of the two common species, with 40 flowers in the heads. These resemble, in miniature, the cones of the hop, especially when they are withered and brown. Hop trefoil grows 3-15 in. high and is found most often on lime-rich soils. It is widespread but not common in the north and west.

Lesser trefoil has only about 20 flowers in each head and grows to about 9 in. high, in all kinds of soil. It is found throughout the British Isles, except in the Highlands. Lesser trefoil is often confused with black medick, but it does not have the central nerve of the leaves protruding beyond the margin. Both plants are sold as shamrock. See also SHAMROCK

Hop trefoil
Trifolium campestre

Lesser trefoil
Trifolium dubium

The pale yellow flowers of trefoil are to be found in grassland and waste places

Trout *Salmo trutta*

Although trout vary considerably in colour, size and shape, there is only one native species. The typical trout of smaller rivers and lakes ranges from light olive to black, with white, golden or silvery bellies. There are always dark spots on the back, often with a light halo. In larger rivers and lakes the fish tend to be more silvery. Sea trout, which are migratory and spend some time in the sea before spawning in fresh water, are also silvery.

Trout from small, swift streams can be less than 10 in. long and weigh 6-8 oz., but fish up to 3 ft long and weighing several pounds may be found in large lakes and rivers. The smaller fish have a diet mainly of insects, snails and crustaceans. Larger ones eat other fish.

Spawning takes place during winter, usually on gravel banks washed by running water. The eggs sink into the gravel. The time they take to hatch varies with the temperature of the water. Eggs will hatch in about 77 days at 6°C (43°F).

Young trout have dark blotches along their sides and are known as parr. See also RAINBOW TROUT

Truffle

A rough-textured, edible fungus which forms underground from the late summer onwards. In Britain it usually grows in chalky soils near the roots of trees, especially beech. *Tuber aestivum,* which has a warty surface, is the best-flavoured British truffle. Brown-black when fresh, it turns black when dry.

Ripe truffles give off a strong smell. This attracts truffle flies, which lay their eggs on the truffles when they break through the ground. The flies' larvae then feed on the fungi. Many animals can detect the presence of truffles. At Winterslow, Wiltshire, which used to be the chief truffle-hunting area in Britain, dogs were used; these could sometimes scent truffles 100 yds away. In France, where truffles are used to make *pâté de foie gras*, pigs are used to hunt them. See also FUNGUS

Tubeworm
A worm of the seashore which lives in a protective tube built from sand grains, chalky material and mucus. Tiny white coiled tubes are commonly seen on seaweed, shells and stones on the shore. These are the homes of tubeworms of the Spirobis genus, which withdraw into their tubes at low tide but push out a crown of green-white tentacles as soon as they are covered by the sea. The tentacles filter food particles from the water.

The twisting 2-4 in. long tubes of the keelworm *Pomatoceros triqueter,* also known as German writing, are found on flat stones and shells. These tubes are triangular in cross-section. The 2 in. long feather duster worm *Serpula vermicularis* lives in tubes 3-5 in. long, circular in cross-section, usually attached to scallop shells. Under water, it feeds by means of a fan of scarlet, feathery tentacles.

The sand mason worm *Lanice conchilega* is much bigger—usually up to 6 in. but sometimes a foot long. It uses sand grains to make a tube 12 in. long and $\frac{1}{3}$ in. across.

The parchment tube worm *Chaetopterus variopedatus* makes flexible U-shaped tubes up to 15 in. long from a slime secretion and sand. The tubes may be attached beneath boulders or sunk in the sand. See also FAN WORM, HONEYCOMB WORM, LUGWORM

Tulip *Tulipa sylvestris*
Garden tulips were introduced to England from Turkey by way of Vienna in the 16th century. In 1830 new varieties were in such demand that £100-170 was being paid for a single bulb.

Only one of these has become naturalised—the wild tulip which may be found occasionally in meadows or orchards in lowland England or southern Scotland where it blooms in April and May. It has fragrant yellow flowers on stems 1-2 ft high and can be distinguished from any of the cultivated varieties by its much narrower leaves. It spreads by bulbs and seeds.

Tulipa is from a Persian word for a turban, to which the flowers were originally likened.

Turkey *Meleagris gallopavo*
The Pueblo Indians of North America first domesticated the turkey, which was brought to Britain in 1521, where it soon displaced the peacock as a table bird for the rich. In the 18th century turkeys were established as part of the Christmas festivities.

Until 1947 the turkey population had been static at 600,000-800,000 for several decades, but intensive methods of rearing began to be practised and in the early 1970's the population was about 5 million. The largest turkey farm, at Great Witchingham, Norfolk, processes 3 million birds a year. Turkeys are

reared exclusively for the table. The broad-breasted bronze is the biggest British breed. Males, called stags, weigh 25-30 lb. and hens up to 15 lb. The hens lay about 25 eggs, which are edible.

Turkey breeds

Beltsville white Small, quick maturing 10-15 lb.

Broad-breasted bronze Heaviest British breed 25-30 lb.

Norfolk black Small, high-quality bird 10-15 lb.

Turkeys, once bred exclusively for the Christmas market, are now intensively reared in huge numbers for all-year-round sale

Turnip *Brassica rapa*
A root crop of Asiatic origin thought to have been first cultivated in Britain by the Romans. In the 18th century, farmers began growing it for their livestock. Today, sheep farmers use turnips to feed their flocks in winter. Often the sheep are allowed into the turnip field, controlled by hurdle pens, to forage. Turnips are also a popular vegetable for human consumption, particularly in the north. In spring, the tops of the plant are eaten when other green vegetables are scarce.

The roots are oval, round or globe-shaped, depending on the variety.

Turnstone *Arenaria interpres*
In winter, small feeding parties of turnstones, short-legged dumpy birds about 9 in. long with a bold, broken face pattern and rusty back, can be seen on the beaches, turning over stones and seaweed in search of insects and shellfish. They are often in the company of purple sandpipers and other waders, blending well with their background because of their mottled brown-black plumage.

Turnstones are common winter visitors to all British coasts, flying in from the Arctic regions of Scandinavia and Siberia where they breed. Some come from Canada. In summer, the upper parts appear tortoise-shell and the head is more white. A few non-breeders stay in Britain during summer.

Tussock moths
The caterpillars of these moths have brilliant colours and tufts of hair which usually contrast with the rest of their colouring. They are best admired from a distance, for the hairs are part of the defensive system and can inflame sensitive skins. When eaten by birds the sharp, brittle points of the hairs cause intense irritation in the throat. The cuckoo, by some adaptation of the gullet, can tolerate the bristles and feeds on tussocks.

The moth's body, too, has a coating of irritant hairs, and in some of the nine species in the British Isles the eggs are covered with a mat of hairs from the female's body. The moths have a wingspan varying from $1\frac{1}{4}$ to 2 in., and most species are brown or white. In some species the females do not have wings.

One of the most common tussock moths is the vapourer *Orgyia antiqua* whose caterpillars can be found from April to June on hawthorn and other trees and shrubs. The moths emerge from July to September.

Male vapourers, like most male tussocks, have large, feathery antennae with which they can detect the scent of a female more than a mile away. The female cannot fly, and as a mature adult lives off food consumed as a caterpillar. She waits for a mate and then lays her pale brown eggs on the cocoon from which she emerged at the end of the pupa stage. The eggs survive the winter and the caterpillars hatch in the spring.

Almost as common as the vapourer, except in Scotland, is the yellow-tail *Euproctis similis.* Males and females have white wings and bodies with a tuft of yellow irritant hairs at the tip of the abdomen. The eggs are laid in June and July, usually on hawthorn, with a protective covering of hairs from the female's tail tuft. They soon hatch but the young caterpillars hibernate in individual cocoons until the spring.

The similar browntail *E. chrysorrhoea* becomes a nuisance in the coastal regions of south-east England in some years, when the caterpillars are so numerous that bushes are stripped of foliage and people develop a skin irritation and swelling from coming into contact with the caterpillars' hairs.

There are five other fairly common species of tussock moth in Britain and one great rarity—the Black V moth *Arctornis l-nigrum* which is most probably a stray migrant. See also COLOUR AND CAMOUFLAGE

Tutsan *Hypericum androsaemum*
A shrubby herb, up to 3 ft high, that is common in damp woods and hedges in southern England, western Britain up to the Isle of Skye, and in Ireland. The stems have two raised lines and the large oval leaves give off a resinous smell. Yellow flowers appear in June and develop into elliptical fruits which turn from green to red to black.

Tutsan leaves were once wrapped round fresh wounds to heal them. In Normandy the plant was called *toute-saine,* meaning all-heal, from which the English name is derived.

The silent, colourful world of caves

Beneath Britain's countryside lies a world of bizarre beauty — the world of caves, with their intricately eroded galleries, their hanging limestone curtains and their pillars of joined stalactites and stalagmites, all emitting a milky sheen

The world of caves is one of silence — broken only by the drip of water — and colour, where the walls have been stained by minerals. This world provided the earliest known dwellings in Britain. Men of the Neanderthal race began occupying them a little before the last Ice Age, about 130,000 years ago — as evidenced by the depth of flint and other implements that have been found — and man carried on using them, on an ever-decreasing scale, until about 2000 years ago.

When man lived in caves, he chose sites which were easily defended and which overlooked his domain. To the caves he brought his cooking utensils and implements, which became buried over the years, to be unearthed by archaeologists

ANIMAL AND PLANT LIFE IN CAVES

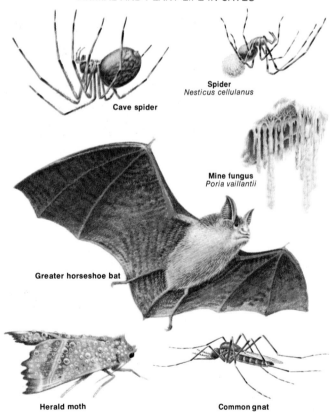

Cave spider

Spider
Nesticus cellulanus

Mine fungus
Poria vaillantii

Greater horseshoe bat

Herald moth

Common gnat

During the winter months the two spiders (top) live at cave entrances, while the common gnat, greater horseshoe bat and herald moth hibernate underground. The mine fungus that hangs in stalactite-like growths makes timber decay and can be very destructive, especially to pit-props

centuries later. The caves of Attermire and Victoria Scars, above Settle, Yorkshire, have revealed a wealth of such artefacts, which are now housed in a museum in the town. Kent's Cavern, near Torquay, Devon, contained implements which have dated it as the oldest inhabited British cave. Animals were even earlier inhabitants of caves than men, and in Kent's Cavern remains of the sabre-tooth tiger, the beaver and a tailless hare were discovered. Practically all of Britain's inland caves are found in limestone rocks. Others were formed in volcanic regions or were created by wave action or by the bridging of huge boulders.

Limestones are basically the solidified calcium carbonate shells of prehistoric sea animals. When earth movements caused vast mountains to rise from the seas millions of years ago, the sedimentary limestones carried with them were tilted, folded or thrust on end; in some cases they were even overturned, so that older rocks lay over them. Further earth movements have cracked the limestones, producing horizontal fissures, or bedding planes, and vertical fissures, or joints. These bedding planes and joints are penetrated by rainwater and their sides are dissolved. This is because rainwater is weak carbonic acid: it absorbs carbon dioxide from the atmosphere and the soil through which it passes. The water carries with it grit and other debris, which further erode the bedding planes and joints, enlarging them into passages and galleries. Where these cross each other, large chambers or caves may appear. Eventually, through such undermining, many passages collapse, causing further enlargement of caves. The forceful flow of underground waterfalls gouges deep, narrow canyons, or sometimes potholes.

In caves at upper levels, long deserted by the streams that once formed them, water continues to seep through small bedding planes and joints. Where it drips from the ceiling of the cave it forms stalactites; heavily loaded with lime, each successive drip deposits its own layer of calcite in the form of a ring. These rings develop into a tubular stalactite, which slowly fills up to form a solid one.

Excess solution on the end of a stalactite may fall to the floor of the cave and, because it splashes, leave a larger deposit there than those deposits forming the stalactite above; the resultant stalagmite which is built up is therefore thicker but takes longer to reach any appreciable size. Sometimes a stalactite and stalagmite join to form a stalagmitic pillar or column. For an unknown reason, some stalactites are hook-shaped; these are called helic-tites or helic-mites. The rate of growth of stalactites and stalagmites varies greatly; in one cave in Yorkshire the stalagmites grow 1 cu. in. every thousand years, whereas on recently abandoned mining machinery in Swaledale, Yorkshire, 6 ft long stalactites have formed.

Where a solution of lime trickles from a small fissure in a cave roof, a thin hanging curtain forms; and where lime-saturated water flows over a wide area of rock, it deposits flowstone. In a cave where the air is saturated with moisture the walls may become covered with soft calcium crystals known as moonmilk. At the edge of rock basins, a rim of calcite, known as a rimstone pool or gour, sometimes forms. Grit or small grains of other material may become coated and form 'cave pearls'. All these calcite formations may be coloured by the minerals in the rock through which the water forming them has filtered. For example, iron colours calcite red, copper green and manganese black. Peat, sometimes carried down by floodwaters, colours cave walls brown or black.

Magic underground—the red, orange and white stalactites and stalagmites of the Ladye Chapel, a small chamber in Cox's Cave, Cheddar. The warm colouring is produced by iron and lead, the white by carbonate of lime. Cox's Cave is open to the public

Caves support a wide variety of life. Spiders often live at cave entrances, most commonly the cave spider. Cave entrances also contain hibernating moths. Flatworms, springtails and ground beetles, often blind and colourless, live in cave passages, where they are preyed on by bats. Small pools support crustaceans. Trout are the most common vertebrates, but most have come into caves from outside and cannot be classed as true cave dwellers. Other temporary residents include flies and animals such as frogs that develop from spawn or larvae which have accidentally entered the cave. These may develop at the cave mouth, and after death their remains may help other cave dwellers to survive.

Most cave entrances and pothole shafts provide suitable conditions for a wide variety of shade and moisture-loving flowering plants, liverworts, ferns and algae, while in caves themselves many species of fungi have been found on decaying animal and plant matter brought in by floods or cavers.

The longest cave system in the British Isles is Ogof-Ffynnon-Ddu, meaning 'cave of the black spring', a 21 mile long series of passages under the Tawe Valley in South Wales; about 760 ft below ground, it is also Britain's deepest cave system.

The second deepest is the 700 ft deep Giant's Hole, near Castleton, Derbyshire. The second longest are Ogof Agen Allwedd, near Ogof-Ffynnon-Ddu, and the cave system linking the entrance to three caves—Lancaster Hole, Bull Pot of the Witches and Easegill—in the fells of Lancashire and Westmorland; both are between 12 and 13 miles long.

Although few British cave systems have the grandeur of continental ones, the varied topography of most British caves is of more interest to speleologists, or cave explorers.

British caves that are open to the public and are electrically lit include Yorkshire's White Scar Cave, near Ingleton, Clapham Cave, near Clapham, and Stump Cross Caverns, near Pateley Bridge; Derbyshire's Peak Cavern, Blue John Caverns and the Caverns of Treak Cliff, all near Castleton; Somerset's Wookey Hole, near Wells, and the Cheddar Gorge caves; and Devon's Kent's Cavern.

Caving is becoming increasingly popular and increasingly sophisticated in the equipment it uses. Lightweight alloy wire-rope ladders have replaced hemp and wood ones, ropes are now made of synthetic fibres, and skin divers' neoprene wet suits have taken the place of old woollens as cave wear.

479

V

Valerian

A fragrant herb of which there are three species growing wild in the British Isles. Common valerian is the most widespread. Up to 5 ft high, it grows in rough grassland and hedges and beside streams throughout the British Isles. It bears pale pink flowers throughout the summer. The dried roots smell like new leather.

Marsh valerian is less than 1 ft high, and has separate male and female plants. The flowers, which are pink, appear in May and June; the male flowers are twice as big as those on female plants. It is common in marshy meadows and bogs throughout England, Wales and southern Scotland.

Red valerian, 1-3 ft high, was introduced from southern Europe in the 16th century and has become established on old walls, cliffs and quarries, to which its downy seeds are easily spread by the wind. Red or white flowers are borne from June to August. The leaves are bitter but, if cut young, can be used in salad. Red valerian grows throughout England and Wales, in eastern Scotland and south and east Ireland.

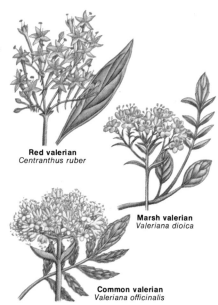

Red valerian
Centranthus ruber

Marsh valerian
Valeriana dioica

Common valerian
Valeriana officinalis

Red valerian spread from gardens to become well established throughout the countryside

Valley

The shape of a valley gives a clue to how it was formed. Steep-sided, U-shaped valleys like those in Snowdonia and the Lake District were cut by glaciers in the last Ice Age, which ended 10,000 years ago; gentle,

Nant Ffrancon glen in Snowdonia, a U-shaped valley produced by a glacier during the Ice Age

sloping V-shaped valleys, like many in southern England, were cut by rivers.

Rivers deepen their valleys by carrying away clay, sand and gravel towards the sea. Widening is caused as soil is washed down the sloping valley sides and carried away. Most large rivers swing from side to side within their valleys, cutting into the walls in places to form steep bluffs or cliffs called meander scars. As they swing across the valley floor, they create gravel and sand flats which the river covers when it floods.

Glaciated valleys are usually smoother and straighter, since the ice has worn away any projecting spurs. They quite often contain lakes, because the ice has scooped out deep hollows in the valley floor. In lopping off spurs, the glaciers also cut off the lower parts of the valleys of tributary streams. After the ice receded, these side-valley streams became waterfalls, dropping straight

into the main valley. These side valleys are called hanging valleys.

Where rivers cross bands of hard rock, they cut deep notches, or gorges, usually finding some line of weakness such as a fault where the rocks have been crushed. The material dislodged is swept away by the water. Examples are the Avon Gorge and the Pass of Aberglaslyn, North Wales.

Dry valleys in chalkland areas were apparently formed in the Ice Age, when the ground was frozen solid and rainwater, unable to penetrate the surface, flowed away as a river. Today, rainwater soaks straight through the chalk. Such valleys are often deep and steep-sided, especially where the river, in addition to its normal erosive action, has dislodged limestone rock along its course. Some dry valleys occur in limestone country where a river cuts through impervious rock to reach a limestone layer or joint; over the years the water dissolves the limestone and disappears underground at what is termed a swallowhole.

Various local names for a valley include: clough (Lancashire and Cheshire), cleugh (Scotland), dene (Yorkshire and south-east England) and ghyll (Cumberland and Lake District). See also ICE, RIVER

Vanessid butterflies

Vanessids are a genus of beautiful and fairly large butterflies, with wingspans of 2-2¾ in. They include all the common brightly coloured species which frequent gardens, such as the red admiral, painted lady, the tortoiseshells, peacock and comma. Some migrate to southern Europe in the autumn, while other species hibernate successfully in Britain. The red admiral and painted lady may sometimes try to hibernate here, but rarely survive. They usually spend the winter in southern Europe and North Africa, returning to Britain in the spring or early summer to produce a new generation of migrants.

All the vanessids pass the winter in the adult stage. The undersides of their wings

The comma, which has tattered-looking wings, is named from the white commas under the wings

are dull in comparison with the upper sides, and this disguise enables them to hibernate safely. When the butterfly rests with its wings folded together, and the forewings tucked between the hindwings, only the camouflage shows; it looks like a dead leaf.

The bright colours of all these butterflies probably help them to recognise others of their own species. Since the males and females of each species are nearly identical it is believed to be differences of scent and behaviour that enable courtship to proceed. The eye-like marks on the peacock help to protect the butterfly from birds by making it look like the face of a large animal.

The caterpillars of the vanessids are black or brown, with white or yellow marks. All are covered in spiky outgrowths and most feed on nettles. The exceptions are the large tortoiseshell which feeds on elm, the painted lady which eats thistles, and the comma which will eat either nettles or hops. In all species the caterpillars spin leaves together with threads which they can produce from their silk glands. The spun leaves make tents in which the caterpillars feed. The female peacocks and tortoiseshells lay eggs in batches and the caterpillars live together in a large group tent. The other species lay single eggs spaced well apart, and the caterpillars lead solitary lives.

Vanessid chrysalids hang down, attached only by hooks at their tail ends to a silk pad sewn by the full-grown caterpillar. The chrysalids have metallic markings and it was probably chrysalids of this type which first earned the name 'chrysalis', which means golden.

Two colourful butterflies similar in shape and appearance to the vanessids are the white admiral and the rare purple emperor. They are grouped as two separate tribes closely related to the vanessids, but are strictly woodland species and differ from the vanessids in many points of their life cycles. Both species hibernate as small caterpillars, so the undersides of the adults do not need to resemble dead leaves. Their caterpillars are unlike those of the vanessids. The white admiral caterpillar is spiky, but green, and it feeds on honeysuckle; while that of the purple emperor is green, not spiky, and

Britain's most colourful butterflies

Large tortoiseshell
Nymphalis polychloros   underwings

Small tortoiseshell
Aglais urticae   underwings

Peacock
Nymphalis io   underwings

Purple emperor
Apatura iris   underwings

Painted lady
Vanessa cardui   underwings

Comma
Polygonia c-album   underwings

White admiral
Limenitis camilla   underwings

Red admiral
Vanessa atalanta   underwings

The uncertain British climate is not very suitable for butterflies, and we have fewer brightly coloured species than the rest of Europe. The Nymphalid family, to which the vanessids and the white admiral and purple emperor belong, is the most spectacular

feeds on goat willow and sallow. Only the purple emperor has any difference of colour between the sexes, the males being iridescent purple and the females a dull, dark brown with no trace of purple.

Vapourer moth see Tussock moth

Vapour trail

High-flying aircraft often leave behind them streaks of white cloud criss-crossing the sky. These are popularly called vapour trails. The correct meteorological description is condensation trail or contrail. They are caused by aircraft releasing water vapour from their engines in sufficient quantities to saturate a narrow band of air and produce condensation.

In the British Isles such trails are usually at heights of about 28,000 ft in summer and 20,000 ft in winter. At these heights temperatures are often so low that the droplets freeze almost as soon as they leave the engine. The vapour is then composed of tiny, slowly falling ice crystals. The crystals evaporate more slowly than water droplets, making vapour trails fairly persistent and allowing time for the bands of vapour to broaden and sometimes combine.

Velvet ant see Wasp
Vendace see Whitefish

Venus's looking-glass *Legousia hybrida*

A cornfield weed found only on chalk or limestone soils in south and east England. It is erect, rarely taller than 6 in., and has narrow leaves. From May until harvest-time it produces small, purple to lilac, five-petalled flowers at the top of a narrow, three-sided capsule; these open in the morning and close in the evening.

When the capsule is ripe, the oval pale brown seeds escape through three holes at the top. The seeds shine brightly, like tiny mirrors—hence the plant's name.

Vervain *Verbena officinalis*

A herb believed by the Anglo-Saxons to be holy and able to frighten away the Devil. In the Middle Ages, people used to carry it to bring them luck, and to ward off the skin disease of scrofula, or the King's Evil.

It stands 1-2 ft tall, has toothed leaves and bears lilac, five-petalled flowers from July to September. Nectar is secreted below the ovary, and white hairs at the mouth of the corolla-tube prevent entry of unwelcome insects. Either cross-pollination or self-pollination may take place.

Vervain grows by roadsides and in waste places throughout the lowlands of England and Wales and in the southern half of Ireland.

Vetch

A scrambling plant with compound leaves and tendrils which twine around neighbouring plants. At the base of each leaf is a leaf-

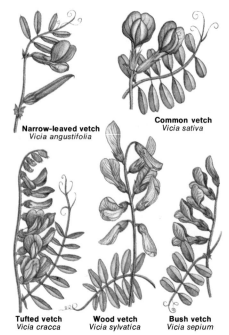

Narrow-leaved vetch
Vicia angustifolia

Common vetch
Vicia sativa

Tufted vetch
Vicia cracca

Wood vetch
Vicia sylvatica

Bush vetch
Vicia sepium

All five common species of vetch are scrambling plants with pea-like flowers

like structure called a stipule. Vetch bears purple or blue flowers continuously throughout the summer.

Five species grow wild in the British Isles. The common vetch, or tare, grown by farmers for fodder, is 1-3 ft high and bears 1 in. long purple flowers singly or in pairs; at the end of the summer these develop into 2-3 in. long seed-containing pods. The plant grows on roadsides and in waste places, where it has spread from cultivation.

Narrow-leaved vetch is similar but smaller: it is 6-18 in. high; the flowers are only ½ in. long and the pods are less than 2 in. It grows in grassland and on roadside verges.

Both common and narrow-leaved vetch are annuals which can be distinguished from the other vetches by a black spot on the underside of the stipule.

The other three species are perennials. Two of them, bush vetch and tufted vetch, are common by roadsides and in rough grassland and bushy places. Bush vetch, which is up to 3 ft high, carries purple flowers in groups of two to six. Tufted vetch bears spikes of up to 40 attractive blue flowers on longer stalks. When it climbs up hedges to a height of about 6 ft, cattle often browse on it as it emerges from the top.

Wood vetch, 2-5 ft high, is thinly scattered throughout the British Isles in a great variety of places—from woods and rocky places inland to cliffs and shingle by the sea. On shingle it grows in flat patches, but in woods it climbs up to 8 ft over bushes. The flowers are white or pink with blue or purple veins. There are often nectaries beneath the stipules which secrete nectar in sunny weather. These attract ants, which protect the plant from caterpillars. See also TARE

Vetchling

A plant which differs from the vetch in having leaves with only one or two leaflets, instead of several pairs, or in having no leaves at all. Like the vetch it has at the base of each leaf a stipule, or leaf-like structure which is often enlarged and takes over the functions of the leaves. The stems are winged or angled.

The most common of the ten British species is meadow vetchling which grows throughout the British Isles along roadsides and in hedgerows and rough, grassy places. It climbs to 4 ft and bears yellow flowers from May until August.

Bitter vetchling, 6-18 in. high, is most common in the mountains and hills of north and west Britain, where it grows in woods, thickets and hedge banks. From April to July its crimson flowers add a splash of bold colour to the countryside. Its thick underground stems were once eaten in the Hebrides, and are said to taste like chestnuts.

Grass vetchling, or grass-leaved pea, is a rare plant confined to dry places in south and east England. Up to 3 ft high, it grows in long grass, where it is completely camouflaged until May when it produces crimson flowers which last until July. It has no true leaves, but its long, narrow stipules resemble enormous leaves of grass.

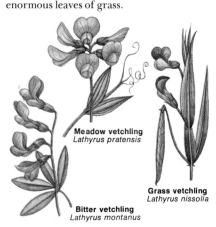

Meadow vetchling
Lathyrus pratensis

Grass vetchling
Lathyrus nissolia

Bitter vetchling
Lathyrus montanus

The vetchlings are wild relatives of the fragrant, garden sweet pea

Village see p. 484

Vineyard

Vines were introduced to Britain by the Romans, but faded away in the later Middle Ages. Now there are signs of a renewed interest in commercial vine-growing, and more than 20 vineyards exist in southern and eastern England and in South Wales. Most of them produce a clean, dry, white wine of the Riesling or Sylvaner type, one exception being Beaulieu Abbey in Hampshire which markets a rosé.

The most northerly commercial vineyard in Europe is at Stragglethorpe Old Hall, near Lincoln, which grows a hybrid French grape, Seyve-Villard, an early ripening and disease-resistant variety. On the South Downs at Hambledon, Sir Guy Salisbury-Jones, one of the first people to start producing wine in England in modern times, produces 12,000 bottles a year from 4½ acres of Seyve-Villard and Chardonnay vines.

The heyday of English wine was after the Norman Conquest, and there were 38 references to vineyards in the Domesday Survey. The extensive monastic vineyards lost their importance after 1152 when Henry II married Eleanor of Aquitaine and gained access to the superb vineyards of Bordeaux.

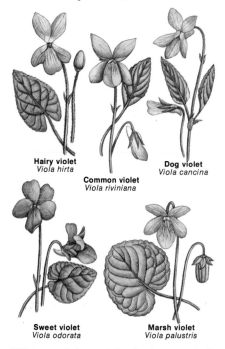

Hairy violet
Viola hirta

Common violet
Viola riviniana

Dog violet
Viola cancina

Sweet violet
Viola odorata

Marsh violet
Viola palustris

Violets owe their reputation for fragrance to the sweet violet. Most common species are scentless

Violet

A spring-flowering plant which sometimes flowers again in the autumn. Ten species grow wild in Britain. All have more or less heart-shaped leaves and blue or violet flowers. In addition, there are white forms of the normally deeply coloured sweet violet. This is up to 9 in. high and flowers early—from February to April. It is common in hedgerows and planted woodland in England, but is rare elsewhere and does not grow in the north of Scotland.

Common violet, which is up to 6 in. high, grows everywhere in woods, hedgerows and dry grassland, and among mountain rocks. It bears dark blue-violet flowers, with the lowest petal paler than the rest.

Dog violet, up to 12 in. high, has clear blue flowers and much narrower leaves than other species. It grows on heaths and in sand dunes and fens throughout the British Isles, but is not common. The prefix dog is often used to describe an inferior type of plant, and dog violet is so-called because

it lacks the distinctive odour of sweet violet.

The easiest species to recognise is the hairy violet, which has hairy leaves and stalks. Up to 9 in. high, with scentless flowers, it grows in grassland, hedges and open woods on dry lime-rich soils in England.

Marsh violet, which grows to a height of only 3 in. and has lilac flowers, is common in wet, lime-poor soils. It is scentless, with almost round leaves. Abundant in the north and west of Britain, it is rare elsewhere.

Viper see Adder

Viper's bugloss *Echium vulgare*

A tall plant, up to 3 ft high, with spikes of vivid blue flowers which colour cliffs and dunes by the sea, and waste places on sandy soil inland. It has rough, hairy stems and long, narrow leaves, and is biennial, flowering from June to September.

Its bell-shaped flowers are attractive to bees, butterflies and moths. After pollination each flower produces four nutlets which resemble a viper's head. For this reason it was once prescribed as an antidote for snake-bite. It was also recommended as a cure for melancholy.

Vole

A close relative of the rat and mouse, the vole can be distinguished from either of them by its blunt snout, tiny ears and short tail. The short-tailed vole or field vole is probably the most numerous British mammal and is found in all parts of Britain except for Ireland. Voles spread to England from the Continent after the end of the Ice Age when Ireland was separated from the mainland, which accounts for their almost total absence there.

The short-tailed vole *Microtus agrestis* is 4 in. long and its colour varies from ochre to deep brown, with grey below. It lives in hedgerows, rough grassland, the borders of woodland, marshland, dunes and on moorland. In young forestry plantations the population can grow to plague proportions of up to 500 an acre, with the voles causing considerable damage by eating young shoots and seed. However, voles feed mainly on grass,

often biting off long stems at ground level. Nests are built under grass tufts or fallen trees, and breeding is from March to September, when litters of three to six young are born.

The bank vole *Clethrionomys glareolus* is about the same size as the short-tailed vole and has chestnut-coloured fur above with creamy-grey below. It is found everywhere and in 1964 was discovered in Ireland. These voles live in deciduous woods and scrub, especially along banks and hedgerows, where they feed on green plants and fruits such as hips and haws and, occasionally, insects. The bank vole builds its nest of grass under roots and in tree stumps. Four or five litters, with an average of four young, are reared in succession from April to September.

There are two other voles of similar appearance found locally on islands, but not in Ireland. These are both races of the common vole *Microtus arvalis* of western Europe. The 4 in. long Guernsey vole *M. a. sarnius* lives in rough grassland on the island of Guernsey. The 5 in. long Orkney vole *M. a. orcadensis* lives among heather or on pasture land on the Orkneys.

Living along the banks of canals, slow-moving rivers and lakes, and in marshes, is the large 8 in. long water vole *Arvicola amphibius*. It is sometimes incorrectly called the water rat, a confusion with the brown rat which also swims well. The water vole is usually seen as it dives into the water to swim. Its normal tendency is to submerge, whereas a rat keeps to the surface.

After swimming, the water vole often sits upright on the bankside, feeding on a water plant or washing its face. One sign of its whereabouts is a patch of the bank where the plants have been bitten off. There may also be tracks in the mud near by. The water vole has a home territory based on a burrow, the entrance to which is sometimes just below the surface of the water. A nest of rushes or grass is made inside the burrow. Two to four litters of usually less than six young in each are produced a year.

Voles have many enemies, including weasels, cats, foxes, pike, owls and other birds of prey, and adders. See also MOUSE

The water vole, sometimes wrongly called the water rat, is a good diver and underwater swimmer

The village—hub of country life

Surrounding a green, lining a street or just sprawling, the village is an essential part of the British countryside; in the midst of our highly industrialised nation, it survives as a witness of more peaceful and leisurely times

Most of Britain's villages were already ancient by the time of the Norman Conquest in 1066, and those as far north as Yorkshire were listed in the Domesday Book of 1086, which was compiled on the orders of William the Conqueror. Their past is the nation's past in microcosm, with its periods of poverty and prosperity reflected in the buildings; their future in a country as highly urbanised and industrialised as Britain is uncertain. But for the present, they remain havens of peace in a bustling world, nostalgic reminders of how most of the inhabitants of these islands used to live.

Prehistoric man is known to have lived in village-like settlements more than 4000 years ago, and the remains of one built in 2500 BC may be seen at Skara Brae in the Orkney Islands. The houses and their contents, even the beds, are made of stone because of the lack of timber on the island. It was this lack which preserved Skara Brae, for many early villages built of wood, mud and similar materials have perished. Remains of an early British village are preserved at Chysauster, near Penzance, where tin was smelted in the 2nd century BC.

The Celts sometimes lived in villages and there is evidence of their presence at Ashmore in Dorset and Buttermere in Wiltshire; but generally they lived in very small communities and have mostly left their mark in the hamlets of Wales and Cornwall. Generally the Celts lived in hill country, because they found the fens and forests of the lowlands too difficult

The fishing village of Clovelly, Devonshire, has only one street—steep, cobbled, a quarter of a mile long and barred to all vehicles

to clear. Then successive waves of invaders—Anglo-Saxons, Jutes, Danes and Norsemen—brought with them axes which cleared the forests, and massive ploughs which could turn the heavy soils. They stamped their characteristics and their names on many of the existing communities, as well as establishing new ones and giving the villages their basic shape.

Villages grew in conjunction with the open-field system of agriculture and developed as almost self-sufficient communities. Each village was surrounded by large, unfenced fields which were divided into strips, yielding different crops in rotation. Common grazing land for sheep and cattle lay beyond the arable fields, and beyond the grazing were often wasteland and forest.

New—and often ugly—types of village came with the Industrial Revolution. Cottages were built in strict rows, often in terraces, near swift streams needed for textile factories in Lancashire and Yorkshire.

In most pre-18th-century villages, the oldest building is the church, often surviving from the Middle Ages, containing in its records and memorial plaques a social history of the area.

Most villages fall into one of three categories—green villages, street villages and sprawling villages.

Green villages are grouped round an open space—the village green. The grouping of buildings varies considerably, for instance the triangle of Matfield in Kent, the rectangle of Stamfordham in Northumberland, or the open-spaced style of Finchingfield in Essex. In some cases, greens have disappeared or been reduced by public or municipal buildings such as churches or schools.

Street villages are built along both sides of a main road, often on stretches running east to west, giving each inhabitant an equal share of the sun on his cottage and land and access to the main road. Some follow the course of an ancient road, such as Staplehurst in Kent, which is on a Roman route—an early example of ribbon development.

A settlement of the remote past—the remains of a pre-Roman village at Chysauster, near Penzance. Cornwall. Each house had its own courtyard

The third group has no clearly defined pattern, having grown spasmodically over the years.

Fishing villages usually have cottages built near the harbour in narrow lanes.

The sites most favoured by early settlers had a gravel base. This gave a well-drained area and often water from springs. Many of these villages are found by the main rivers, especially the Thames, the Trent and the Severn. Also highly regarded were places at the foot of escarpments, such as those in the Chilterns, the South Downs and the Cotswolds, where there was plenty of spring water.

Medieval lords and monasteries encouraged further settlement in forest clearings and established villages as a means of increasing their tenantry and revenue. The Abbot of St Albans, for instance, was active in establishing villages at Cassio and Bushey in Hertfordshire.

The charm of a village lies in the manner in which it fits into the landscape. This has usually been achieved by the use of local materials and timber for the buildings, and some of the best examples are the villages of the Cotswolds, built of the yellow-grey stone which underlies much of Gloucestershire and Somerset.

In some cases villages were built by landowners for their workers, especially in the north during the late 17th and 18th centuries. Examples are Lowther in Westmorland, Inverary in Argyllshire, Gavinton in Berwickshire, and Blanchland on the Northumberland-Durham border. Often, as in these cases, existing villages were destroyed and houses of better quality built in accordance with a plan.

Some industrialists built model villages for their workers in this century, as at Port Sunlight near Liverpool and Bourneville near Birmingham, and attempts have been made to create modern planned 'villages' as at New Ash Green in Kent. See also LOST VILLAGES and PLACE NAMES

Windsor, Berkshire, in the early 17th century, as shown in a plan by the map-maker John Norden. Although created a borough in 1277, its population in Norden's time was only 1000 and it conformed to the lay-out of a typical street village. In most villages the pre-eminent building was the church, the repository of the village records, but Windsor has been dominated by its castle since it was founded by William the Conqueror. The surrounding countryside, divided into hedged arable fields, is not characteristic of the 17th-century village: hedges became widespread only with the enclosure acts of the 18th and 19th centuries

Mirrored calm—the picturesque village of Finchingfield in Essex reflected in its pond. The village, consisting predominantly of whitewashed cottages, is built around a triangular green

W

Waggon

Horse-drawn waggons were the farmer's heavy-duty vehicles before the days of tractor-drawn trailers. The occasional one may still be in use in remoter hill districts where tractors are less practical. Built almost entirely of wood, they consisted of a four-wheeled flat bed with sides only a foot or so high, although in some types the front and rear ends rose up like the prow and stern of a boat. The shafts were detachable and could be fixed singly or side by side. A one-horse or two-horse team could be doubled or even trebled by attaching trace-horses in front by means of chains.

Waggons were used frequently for hauling sacks of corn. When light, but bulky, materials such as sheaves or loose straw or hay were being carried, retaining ladders were fitted front and rear so that bigger loads could be carried. The brake was a primitive sheath of iron over the rim of the rear offside wheel. This allowed the driver to skid the waggon safely downhill.

The period from the late 18th to the early 19th century was the great age of waggon building. A well-made waggon had scores of parts, each with its own name and fashioned from a particular kind of wood. The shafts and frame were made of ash. Wheel spokes were oak and the hubs elm.

Various districts developed their own types of waggon: Midland waggons tended to be plain and rectangular, whereas those in Somerset, Wiltshire and Gloucestershire were shallow but had arched mudguards over the large rear wheels. In East Anglia, waggons were deeper in the body, curving up fore and aft and often possessing slatted retaining ladders at the sides. A northern Lincolnshire type with a very deep body is thought to have been developed from waggons used in Holland.

Tradition also governed the use of colours. West Country waggons were usually painted Prussian blue, whereas Midland farmers preferred yellow. The head-board, at the front of the waggon, was almost always a different colour and usually bore the owner's name. See also CART

ENGLISH FARM WAGGONS

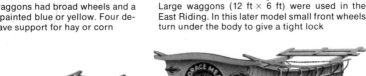

WEST MIDLANDS — Hereford
West Midlands waggons had broad wheels and a fairly deep body painted blue or yellow. Four detachable poles gave support for hay or corn

YORKSHIRE — East Riding
Large waggons (12 ft × 6 ft) were used in the East Riding. In this later model small front wheels turn under the body to give a tight lock

SOUTH-WEST — Devon
The waggons of the south-west of England, particularly Devon, had fairly small wheels, making the floor lower and so easier to load

EAST MIDLANDS — Rutland
Waggons in the East Midlands had deep bodies and an almost horizontal profile. In Rutland, axles were made of wood until the 20th century

Wagtail

This slim, elegant, long-tailed bird does not 'wag' so much as 'bob' its tail. The three species of wagtail which breed in Britain usually live near water. The most familiar is the 7 in. pied wagtail which is largely resident all year, breeding throughout the British Isles except Shetland. Its plumage is black above and white below with a prominent black bib which extends to the chest and round to meet the black of the back. It is expert at snapping up large flying insects and like the other wagtails its flight is deeply undulating. Most of the time it patrols the water's edge, picking small insects from the wash. The wagtail usually nests in a hole in a wall or bank. The five or six eggs take 14 days to incubate and the young a further 14 days to fledge. Outside the breeding season pied wagtails often gather in communal roosts, and have recently developed the habit of spending the night in greenhouses — presumably in search of warmth and protection.

The 8 in. grey wagtail has the longest tail — 4 in. long — of the three species. It has a grey back and bright yellow underparts, and in summer the male has a bold black bib and bright yellow chest. It lives along swift-flowing streams in the hill districts of the north and west. In winter many birds move to lowland streams and to southern England.

The 6½ in. yellow wagtail is a true migrant, leaving the country to winter south of the Sahara. British yellow wagtails belong to the sub-species *Motacilla flava flavissima* which is completely yellow and green, but many different races have spread right across Eurasia indicating that this species is in a state of evolutionary flux. The yellow wagtail is a bird of damp meadows, grassy marshes and arable land. It often feeds on insects disturbed by the feet of cattle and horses. It tends to breed in small colonies of 10-20 pairs, each pair laying five or six eggs in a hollow in the ground.

Wallaby, Red-necked

Macropus rufogriseus
A native of eastern Australia and Tasmania, the red-necked wallaby is a popular zoo animal, breeding readily in captivity. As a result of escapes from private zoos or parks 30 years ago, there are now at least two small colonies of wild wallabies in this country — in the Ashdown Forest and in the north of England.

This wallaby is a medium-sized kangaroo. The males average about 29 lb. and females 22 lb., about the same weights as badgers. It has a dark grey back, a rusty patch over the shoulders and a white belly, while the tail is rather silvery, but has a black tip. The hands, toes, ear tips and muzzle are also black, and there is a pale line along the upper lips and on the eyebrows.

Being rather timid in the wild, the wallaby crouches down like a hare and is easily overlooked. Though its eyesight and sense of smell are poor, its hearing is very good and the mobile ears swing back and forth like radar scanners. The northern colony lives mainly on grouse moors, and the food is largely heather, supplemented by grass, bracken, bilberry and, particularly in cold weather, pine shoots.

Not much is known about the breeding of wild populations, but in zoos the single young is usually born in February or March. Pregnancy lasts 30 days, so presumably mating occurs in January or February. The young wallaby spends over nine months in the pouch. It is unlikely that a female in England has more than one young a year.

Wall butterfly see Brown butterfly

Wallflower *Cheiranthus cheiri*
Although the flowers of garden varieties vary in colour from white through orange to the deepest reds, the wild wallflower is always bright yellow. It was introduced as a garden plant in the Middle Ages from southern Europe, where it grows on cliffs, and soon became established on old walls and in quarries. Troubadours wore a bouquet of wallflowers as an emblem of love, because they grew so constantly. The wallflower reaches 6-24 in. high, spreads from seed, and flowers from April to June.

Wall pepper see Biting stonecrop

Wall-rocket
A plant of the wallflower family which has seeds in two rows in long, flattened pods. Two species grow wild, both having been introduced from central and southern Europe. They have yellow flowers from May or June to September and reach 12-30 in.

Annual wall-rocket or stinkweed has a disagreeable smell when the leaves are rubbed; perennial wall-rocket does not. Both grow throughout lowland England and Wales, and may be found near the coast in Scotland; but the annual is the only one likely to be found in Ireland.

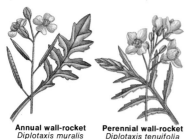

Annual wall-rocket *Diplotaxis muralis*   **Perennial wall-rocket** *Diplotaxis tenuifolia*

Annual wall-rocket is smaller than the perennial species and its leaves smell foul when crushed

The walnut develops inside a green plum-like husk, which rots away when the nut is ripe

Walnut *Juglans regia*
The Romans probably brought the walnut tree to Britain. It is a native of Turkey and has been grown as an orchard tree since the days of the Ancient Greeks. The Saxons knew it as the welsh (meaning strange or foreign) nut—a name still used in Somerset. Its botanical name means the royal nut of the god Jove. The walnut grows best in the southern half of England.

Walnut develops a stout trunk with boldly ribbed, ash-grey bark with a silvery sheen. The stout twigs bear large, brown, rounded buds, set singly. When a twig is broken at an angle the large core of pith shows narrow bands of thin tissue, broken by gaps.

The leaves, which open in May, each consist of about seven rounded leaflets. When they are crushed they release a strong aroma and brown juice which stains the fingers.

In May, a mature tree bears drooping green male catkins and, separately, groups of two or three bottle-shaped female catkins. After fertilisation by wind-borne pollen, these ripen rapidly and by September look like large, green plums.

At this stage, while the inner shell is still soft, many are steeped in vinegar to make pickled walnuts. Those left to ripen rapidly lose their fleshy outer coating and expose the wrinkled shell of the nut.

The custom of beating a walnut tree was carried out firstly to bring down the fruits and also to break the long shoots, so encouraging short fruiting spurs to grow. Walnut stems have a thin pale layer of sapwood and chocolate-brown heartwood zoned with paler and darker shades. The timber is valuable and is used for decorative veneers, fine furniture, carving and gun stocks. It is strong, firm, stable and naturally durable. Records for height and girth are 87 ft tall and 21 ft round. The tree lives for 200 years.

Warble fly *Hypoderma bovis*
The larvae of the warble fly are serious parasites on cattle. The adults do not eat and are concerned solely with mating and egg-laying. About ½ in. long, the fly is hairy and bee-like in shape and colour. It is found throughout the British Isles, except in northern Scotland.

Females deposit groups of 4-12 eggs on the hair around the lower part of the fore-

legs of cattle in early summer, and the larvae hatch out in three or four days. They crawl to the base of the hair and burrow under the animal's skin until they reach the gullet in late summer. In the winter they move through the body again to the skin on the animal's back. Each larva then makes a small hole in the skin to breathe though. A large swelling called a warble develops below the hole and the larva lives in this, feeding on pus and tissues. When fully grown, the larva crawls out through the hole in the skin and falls to the ground, where it pupates. A month later, in late May or early June, the adults emerge and restart the annual cycle.

As well as causing distress to cattle, warble flies leave holes in the skin which reduce the value of the leather. Holes in vellum manuscripts in the British Museum show that the warble fly was a problem even in AD 760.

Warblers
A large group of lively little birds that are a familiar part of the British summer scene. All except the Dartford warbler, an all-year resident, are summer visitors that winter in warmer countries. Many fly 2000 miles across the Sahara to reach tropical Africa, and it is one of the wonders of bird migration that the little willow warbler, only 4½ in. long, can make this taxing flight at a never-faltering 25 mph.

The different species are not easy to tell apart. They can be divided into three main groupings. The first group are the leaf warblers, which spend most of their time in the canopy of woodlands and forests. They include the willow warbler, which, with a population of over a million, is the most common British warbler. It is a green, yellow and buff bird that restlessly flits among the branches of trees. It is very difficult to distinguish from its close relative, the chiffchaff. However, the songs of the two birds are quite distinct. The willow warbler utters a sweet series of notes on a descending scale, while the chiffchaff endlessly repeats 'chiff-chaff-chiff-chaff'. The female of both species builds a well-hidden domed nest on or near the ground, and incubates the six or seven eggs. Although the willow warbler arrives in Britain in mid-April, a month later than the chiffchaff, it often produces two broods in the summer against the chiffchaff's one. Both birds can be found throughout the British Isles.

A third leaf warbler, the wood warbler, is larger than the other two. It is also more brightly coloured: a purer yellow on the throat and white below, not buff. It confines itself to woodlands even more than the other two species. It is most common in northern and western Britain but likes beech-woods on chalkland in the south. Its song is a distinctive rattling trill, preceded by a plaintive 'peu-peu', as the bird flies from one tree to another below the canopy with an almost butterfly-like display flight. The

The whitethroat, most familiar of the scrub warblers, is found in undergrowth and hedges

nest is built on the ground, and the five to seven white, brown-spotted eggs are incubated by the female.

The second main group are the scrub warblers, which live in undergrowth and hedges. The most familiar is the whitethroat, which lives throughout Britain. Like other scrub warblers, it generally stays well hidden. It is brown above and buff below, with prominent rusty wings. The male has a grey head, the female a brown one. As the bird flits along hedgerows and from bush to bush over heathland, it shows only its white outer tail feathers. Its song is a chattering warble, often given during a fluttering flight display; but it also calls 'tac' when hidden in the undergrowth. Four or five grey-marked pale green or pale buff eggs are laid in a delicate cup of grasses built near the ground.

The lesser whitethroat is a similar bird, but has grey, not rusty, wings. The grey head has dark marks behind the eyes, giving the bird a bespectacled look. This species is quite common in scrubland, and on farmland wherever there are thick hedges. It is almost restricted to England and Wales. It lays four to six sepia and grey-marked pale cream eggs in a nest built by the male from stalks, roots and hair.

The blackcap is an overall grey except for a black cap in the male and a ginger brown one in the female. Though grouped with the scrub warblers, it lives chiefly in woodland, where its superb song—a succession of varied, mellow tunes—advertises its presence. The blackcap is common throughout England and Wales, scarce elsewhere. It

builds a nest in brambles or low bushes, attaching it to the vegetation with 'handles'. In this are laid four or five white eggs, marked with green and brown.

The garden warbler, which lives mainly in woods, like the leaf warblers, is an olive-brown bird. Its song can easily be confused with that of the blackcap but it lacks the blackcap's loud fluty notes. The garden warbler breeds in England and Wales. Both sexes build a nest from dried grass, lined with hair and rootlets, usually low to the ground. Four or five olive-freckled white or pale green eggs are laid.

The Dartford warbler, a heathland species, named after the town in Kent where it formerly bred, is one of the most rarely seen of British birds. In spring it sings, but only briefly and seldom in the open. As it flits through gorse, it cocks its elongated tail and utters a harsh 'chack'. It is dark grey above and maroon below; young birds are dark grey all over. The species is confined to large areas of heathland which have gorse—the New Forest, the Dorset heathlands and one or two smaller areas.

The barred warbler is a regular autumn visitor to the east coast. It is a large grey bird with a white-tipped tail. It receives its name from the bars on its chest, but these are lacking in autumn birds.

The third main group are 'marsh' warblers, which skulk among reeds and other water plants. These can be divided into two subgroups: those with striped black and brown backs and those with plain brown backs.

The sedge warbler is a striped bird with a prominent cream eye-stripe. Common

throughout the British Isles, it lives chiefly in large reed beds, where it emits harsh croaks.

The grasshopper warbler remains hidden most of the time. The only indication of its presence is its song, a sound like a cricket chirping or a fishing reel being wound in. Predominantly a waterside bird, it is also found on heaths and has spread into young conifer plantations. It breeds throughout Britain and Ireland, but is scarce in the north and absent from the Scottish Highlands. The nest, built by both sexes low among ground vegetation and approached by the birds along a tunnel, is always difficult to find.

The reed warbler is confined to large reed beds and thus to southern England. It is a uniformly brown bird with no distinguishing marks. Its song is a variety of harsh notes. The female attaches her cup-shaped nest to the upright stems of reeds or similar plants. Four or five grey-marked green-white eggs are laid.

The marsh warbler, which is virtually confined to the lower Severn Valley, is almost identical to the reed warbler.

Savi's warbler was extinct as a British breeding bird for nearly a century before recently returning to reed beds in Kent and Suffolk.

Warping

A method, now seldom used, for reclaiming marshland from a tidal estuary. A wall of earth was built along the seaward edge of the marshland to be reclaimed, with one entrance guarded by a sluice gate. When the tide rose the gate was opened, allowing the silt-laden water to spread over the land. As the water drained away it left a deposit of rich silt, and within a few years the land inside the wall was raised by a foot or two. The new land was extremely fertile and did not require additional fertiliser for many years. Warping stopped chiefly because it made heavy demands on manpower. Examples of warping can be seen by the River Humber.

In some areas warping is a natural process: the silt from the estuary water is trapped by plants growing on the marsh.

Warren see Rabbit

Wasp

The name wasp embraces a large group of insects in Britain which with the related bees, ants and sawflies form the order Hymenoptera, with 6200 known species, and new species being discovered every year. This wide variety includes many species which do not have the distinctive black and yellow stripes of the common wasp and other species which have females that cannot fly.

In all cases, it is only the females that sting. They inject a complex poison by an adaptation of their egg-laying organ, the ovipositor. They do not die once they have stung. Normally, antihistamine creams cure the irritation, but in very rare cases a person who has suffered repeated stings in the past, or in some other way has become hypersensitive to wasp stings, may need urgent treatment for allergic shock. Death from wasp stings is extremely rare.

Wasps can be classified into three groups: social, solitary and parasitic.

The common wasp is one of the few British social species. Like bees, it builds nests and produces queens, workers (females) and drones (males). The queen, which hibernates after mating in the autumn, is the only common wasp to survive the winter. She emerges in spring and seeks a suitable nesting hole such as a disused mouse burrow. Then she finds a source of dry wood—often a fence paling—and scrapes off small pieces of wood which she chews into a pulp. With this she builds a nest of a few cells suspended from the roof of the nesting chamber, where the pulp soon hardens into wasp paper. In each cell the queen lays an egg. These eggs hatch into grubs which she feeds with chewed-up remains of captured insects. The grubs pupate, to emerge after

a week or so as worker wasps—infertile females, smaller than the queen.

The workers take over the task of enlarging the nest and catching food for the next generation of grubs while the queen concentrates on egg-laying. By August the colony may number 2000. Until this period, wasps are entirely beneficial to man, as the workers destroy large numbers of insect pests to feed the grubs. In return the workers feed on a sweet saliva which the grubs produce. Then, towards the end of August, larger cells are made and eggs which develop into new queens are laid. Males are produced at the same time and the new queens leave the nest and mate with them, before seeking food and suitable hibernation sites.

The males die off and the old colony begins to disintegrate. The queen stops laying and, deprived of the sweet saliva of the grubs, the redundant workers go in search of other sources of sweetness. It is at this stage that they become a nuisance to man by feeding on fruit and foods containing sugar.

There are five species of the social vespula

The common wasp lives in colonies of up to 2000; it becomes a pest only in late summer when the colony breaks up and it needs to find new sources of food

wasp and all are very similar. One species, the tree wasp, nests in trees. Large wasps seen in spring and often wrongly called hornets are common wasp queens.

Solitary wasps, which do not form large colonies, are longer and much thinner than the social species. Many are black and red rather than black and yellow.

The sand wasp lives on sandy heathland. The female digs her own nest, then uses her sting to paralyse a hairless caterpillar which she drags to the nest hole. Then she lays an egg on the caterpillar and seals up the entrance. After hatching, the wasp grub eats the living but paralysed caterpillar.

Spider-hunting wasps of the Pompilidae family have a similar life cycle but prey on spiders, and build their burrows after catching the prey. Potter wasps make little clay pots which are fixed to heather twigs and stocked with tiny caterpillars. One egg is suspended from the top of each cell which is then sealed.

Parasitic wasps build no home for their offspring but lay their eggs inside suitable living hosts. One large red ichneumon wasp, about $\frac{3}{4}$ in. long, *Ophion luteus* is a parasite on caterpillars of the noctuid moths. The female seeks out the caterpillars, and injects an egg into each. The egg hatches into a grub which eats its living host from within, leaving the vital organs until last. When fully grown, the grub eats its way out of the body and pupates in a cocoon. The many species of ichneumon wasps are an important natural check on the caterpillar population. Some of the smaller ones lay several eggs in a single caterpillar, which becomes host to a number of grubs.

Many species of wasps are parasites on plants and cause galls. Oak apples are produced by the tree as a result of the presence of eggs of the oak apple gall wasp laid under buds. Grubs, which live and feed inside the gall, emerge in July—all wasps from one 'apple' are of the same sex. After mating,

---

Common British wasps

Nearly 300 species of wasps live in the British Isles. Ten of the most common are shown here. Common wasps, tree wasps and hornets live in colonies; most other species are solitary. Only female wasps sting and, unless otherwise stated, only the female is illustrated.

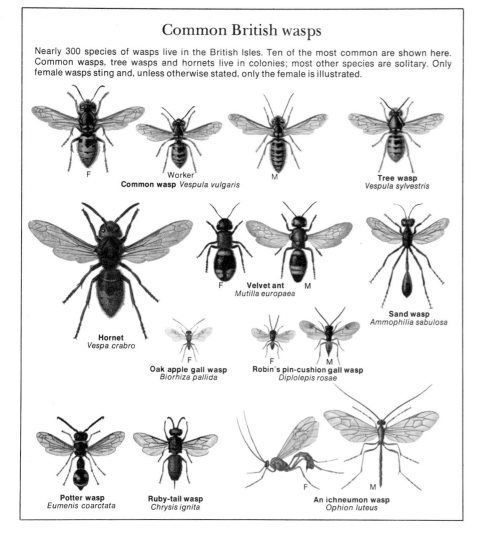

Common wasp *Vespula vulgaris*
F
Worker
M

Tree wasp *Vespula sylvestris*

Hornet *Vespa crabro*

F
Velvet ant *Mutilla europaea*
M

Sand wasp *Ammophilia sabulosa*

Oak apple gall wasp *Biorhiza pallida*
F

Robin's pin-cushion gall wasp *Diplolepis rosae*
F
M

Potter wasp *Eumenis coarctata*

Ruby-tail wasp *Chrysis ignita*

An ichneumon wasp *Ophion luteus*
F
M

the females lay eggs on oak roots, forming root galls. The eggs hatch into grubs which 16 months later emerge from the galls as wingless females. These do not need to mate. They crawl up the tree and lay eggs under the buds. This double cycle is a common feature of many gall wasps.

A few wasps are parasitic on the social insects. The velvet ant wasp, so-called because the furry females are wingless, eats the stored food in bumble-bee nests. Their eggs are laid in the bee grubs, where they hatch to feed on the host. The ruby-tail wasp is a parasite on solitary bees and wasps. Several related species of parasitic wasps occur in bright shades of blue or green. See also GALL, HORNET

Water boatman

The slightest movement in the water of a pond is detected by the brown and yellow water boatman, and few small creatures escape its attack. Although only ⅔ in. long, this aggressive bug can spear a small fish or a tadpole with its piercing mouthparts and inject a poisonous saliva. Its bite can also be painful to man. In its turn the water boatman falls prey to waterfowl, frogs, toads and sometimes fish.

There are four very similar species which hunt in different types of pond. The most common is *Notonecta glauca*. The body of the water boatman resembles a tiny boat. The hull is formed by the wings and the oars are the large third pair of legs. Its habit of swimming upside-down has given the boatman its other name of back-swimmer. When diving, the boatman carries down a store of air held by a coat of bristles on its body. This trapped bubble of air gives the bug a silvery appearance.

In early spring the female lays about 60-70 cigar-shaped eggs individually in slits made in water plants. The female *N. maculata* glues her eggs to stones. The eggs hatch out after two months into larvae that resemble the adult but are wingless. However, by late summer young boatmen are flying from pond to pond on warm evenings.

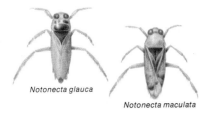

Notonecta glauca

Notonecta maculata

As it swims upside-down, the water boatman resembles a boat, its hull formed by wings

Watercress

The familiar watercress of the salad bowl is a wild native plant which is found growing throughout the British Isles in fast-flowing streams or around springs, especially where the water is rich in lime. A member of the wallflower family, it produces clusters of

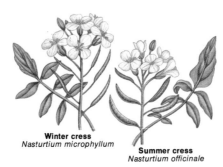

Winter cress
Nasturtium microphyllum

Summer cress
Nasturtium officinale

A year-round supply of watercress is ensured by the cultivation of these two varieties

white, four-petalled flowers at the tips of its branches from May to October. After fertilisation they develop into long, sausage-shaped pods. Watercress varies in height from 6 in. to 24 in.

Watercress for the table is grown in large beds, especially along chalk streams in the southern half of England. Two forms are cultivated: one known as green or summer cress, and a hybrid between this and another wild species, brown or winter cress. They are distinguished by colour and time of harvesting, as their names suggest. In cultivation they are propagated from cuttings, but in the wild they spread by creeping stems or seed. Watercress is rich in vitamin C, and used to be prescribed for the treatment of scurvy.

Water divining

The art of locating underground water by means of a forked hazel twig or other flexible material held in the hands. The water diviner, or dowser, holds one arm of the fork in each hand and forces the two arms apart so that they are at extreme tension. When the twig passes over water it sometimes twists violently. How this happens has never been satisfactorily explained, but water diviners are frequently successful. One theory is that the water gives off some form of radiation which has an effect on the dowser's muscles. Water divining used to be common in the countryside before the advent of piped water. Some diviners work with pendulums, others use copper rods or flexible sticks held by the tip at arm's length. Some diviners claim to be able to locate buried metals as well as water.

Water dropwort   see Parsley

Waterfall

Many waterfalls are formed where a river, after running over hard rock, reaches softer material. This is worn away and the water pouring from the hard rock excavates a pool at the lower level. Constant widening of the pool undercuts the upper rock so that the waterfall gradually moves upstream. High Force waterfall, which pours over Whin Sill on the River Tees in Co. Durham, was formed in this way.

High Force, a waterfall on the River Tees, Co. Durham, pours 70 ft over a bed of hard rock

Other waterfalls occur where Ice Age glaciers cut deep valleys leaving tributary valleys 'hanging' along their sides. Lodore Falls, which feeds into Derwent Water in the Lake District, is an example of a waterfall left by a glacier.

The highest waterfall in the British Isles is Eas-Coul-Aulin, in Sutherland, which has a drop of 658 ft. Other notable waterfalls are Powerscourt Falls, 350 ft, in Co. Wicklow; Pistyll Rhaiadr, 240 ft, in Denbigh; and Caldron Snout, 200 ft, on the borders of Co. Durham, Yorkshire and Westmorland. In general, the best waterfalls in Britain are to be found in the Lake District, North Wales and the north-west dales of Yorkshire.

In the northern part of Britain a waterfall

HOW A WATERFALL IS FORMED

Hard rock
Soft rock

Turbulent water wears away the soft rock undercutting the hard rock

When a river flows down a steep slope from hard to soft rock the soft rock becomes slowly worn away. Eventually a vertical drop is formed over which the river plunges

is known as a 'force'; the word comes from the Icelandic *foss*.

Water lily
The two common wild water lilies are easily identified when in flower: *Nymphaea alba* bears white flowers in July and August and has rounded leaves, while *Nuphar lutea,* from June to August, bears yellow flowers which are much smaller, and has oval leaves. Both have massive underground stems or rhizomes by which they are anchored to the bottom of the lakes, ponds or slow-moving rivers in which they grow. Leaves and flowers grow up from the bottom and float on the surface, because their stems are spongy and full of air spaces. Although the leaves are large, they do not shut out enough sunlight to harm other pond life.

The white water lily is most common in the north and west of the British Isles, where a form with small flowers also grows. At night the petals collapse and the flower may sink below the surface of the water to emerge again next morning. The rooting stems are sometimes eaten in northern Europe, and in the past were used as a cure for baldness.

The yellow water lily, which grows mostly in the south and east, is sometimes called brandy bottle because its flowers smell like stale brandy and the seed-head which develops after the petals fall is like a green-glazed carafe.

Yellow water lily *Nuphar lutea*   **White water lily** *Nymphaea alba*

The two species of water lilies bloom on the surface of still or slow-moving waters

Water-meadow
Riverside grazing fields which are deliberately flooded are called water-meadows. The flooding is carried out in December and the water is usually kept running over the land until March as a precaution against frost. Since only the hardest frosts will freeze the moving water, the meadows remain green even in the coldest winters and the grass continues to grow. It is therefore available for sheep several weeks before grass from unflooded pasture.

A typical water-meadow is laid out on a grid-iron pattern with parallel ditches 4-5 yds apart on two levels, one several feet lower than the other. River water is channelled into the upper ditches, spilling over the rims and trickling over the grass to the lower ditches, keeping the whole surface of the meadow covered with water.

Nowadays, water-meadows are uneconomical to maintain, though a few still survive in Wiltshire, Dorset and Hampshire.

Water measurer
This fragile-looking insect, which walks slowly on the surface of the water at the edges of ponds and lakes, is a fierce predator on water fleas. When it detects vibrations made by a flea just below the surface, the water measurer creeps up on it and spears it with its sharp barbed mouthparts. The water flea is not strong enough to pull the water measurer under the water.

These black insects, $\frac{1}{3}$-$\frac{1}{2}$ in. long, also live at the edges of weedy, slow-flowing streams. The common water measurer *Hydrometra stagnorum* is found throughout the British Isles, and a rare, smaller species *H. gracilenta* lives in a few places in England.

Adult measurers overwinter on the bank under stones and mate in the spring. The eggs are laid on stones or plant stems above the water. The young bugs take about a month to reach full size in June and July.

Water-milfoil
Flowers are the only living parts of this plant to appear above the surface of the water in the lakes, streams and ditches in which it grows throughout the British Isles. The plant roots in the mud and develops long, flexible stems on which grow finely divided feather-like leaves arranged in whorls of four or more. The stems break off and float to the water's edge, but they collapse as soon as they are taken out of the water.

The flowers, which appear from June to August, are inconspicuous and arranged in spikes with males on the top and females below; the plant is pollinated by the wind. Spiked water-milfoil has whorls of leaves about 2 in. across, and crimson male flowers. It is more common in lime-rich water in south and east England. Alternate-flowered water-milfoil has whorls about 1 in. across, and male flowers with yellow petals streaked with red. It is more often seen in acid water in the north and west.

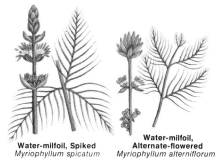

Water-milfoil, Spiked *Myriophyllum spicatum*   **Water-milfoil, Alternate-flowered** *Myriophyllum alterniflorum*

The two water-milfoils can be told apart by the arrangement of flowers on their stems

Water parsnip   see Parsley

Water pepper   *Polygonum hydropiper*
A slender, yellow-green annual, 9-30 in. high, that is often found in wet places—in shallow water at the edge of streams and ponds, and in ditches. It is closely related to

redshank and develops a spike of green flowers from July to September. The leaves of water pepper have a peppery taste and contain an acrid juice which makes the skin itch, especially between the fingers and on the back of the hand. The plant used to be put into beds to repel fleas.

Water pepper is found throughout the British Isles, but is rare in north-east Scotland. It spreads by seed.

Water plantain   *Alisma plantago-aquatica*
The roots of water plantain are edible after the bitter taste has been removed by drying; its leaves were once applied to the skins of sufferers from dropsy because it was believed that they 'drew out the water'.

It grows in shallow water at the edge of rivers, canals, ditches and ponds throughout the lowlands of the British Isles, and has large, long-stalked oval leaves which stand erect above the water. The leafless stem grows up to 3 ft and produces many three-petalled white flowers from June to August. They open only in the afternoon.

Water plantain spreads by seed and corm-like underground tubers. These are dormant during the winter and develop into new plants the following spring.

Water purslane   *Peplis portula*
An inconspicuous creeping herb found at the edge of pools or in marshes throughout the lowlands of the British Isles, especially on gravelly soil. It has branching stems up to 9 in. long, rooted to the soil at intervals. The green flowers are difficult to spot. They are at the base of the spoon-shaped leaves near the tip of the stem and appear from June to October. If there is a summer flood and the flowers are submerged, they do not open and are self-pollinated.

Water scorpion   *Nepa cinerea*
This 1 in. brown pond bug is not related to the true scorpion at all, but resembles it in some ways. At the tip of its flat, oval body is a sting-like spine which it uses as a breathing tube, pushing it above the surface of the water. Special organs warn it when it is going too deep for its 'snorkel' to work.

Although the water scorpion cannot sting, its bite is quite painful. Its pincers are front legs modified for catching and holding pond animals. The bug lies in wait until a small fish or insect swims close by and then grabs out with its jackknife-like front legs and pierces the prey with its sharp mouthparts.

Water scorpions live in shallow weedy water throughout the British Isles, and do not move about much, being rather poor swimmers. In fact, instead of swimming they tend to walk about on submerged plants.

The female lays her eggs in late spring, embedding them in plant stems below the water surface. Young bugs take about two months to reach full size. The adults overwinter in the water but live for only a year.

Water singer *Micronecta poweri*

This water insect is a minute member of the plant-eating water boatman family. It looks like a small water boatman with a pale ground colour and dark markings. Like most of this group the males can make a singing noise by rubbing the hairs on the inside of the front legs against their mouthparts. For such a small bug, 1/12 in. long, the water singer's song is very loud.

Water singers live only in non-polluted waters of lakes and rivers. Some of the best localities are clean northern lakes such as Malham Tarn and Windermere. They feed by scraping particles of plant or dead animal material from the bottom of the lake.

Water soldier *Stratiotes aloides*

A floating plant, resembling the leaves at the top of a pineapple or an American aloe — hence its Latin name. The leaves are long and narrow, with sharp, saw-like edges.

Water soldier grows in lime-rich water in ponds, ditches and canals in northern and eastern England, and can be seen at flowering time from June until August, when it floats to the surface. The rest of the year is spent on the bottom. The plant floats when the amount of lime in the leaves decreases, and sinks when it increases.

The flowers are white with three petals. Separate male and female flowers are known, but only the female occurs in the British Isles. Therefore seeds are not produced and the plant spreads by the production of offsets which break off and float away. It is possibly for this reason that water soldier is a rare and declining species, but in a few spots such as canals it can become locally very abundant.

Water starwort *Callitriche stagnalis*

A widespread plant found in ponds, ditches and streams or on wet mud at their edges. It grows to 2 ft in water and 6 in. on land. Its leaves are broad and spoon-shaped when floating in star-like rosettes on the surface or scrambling over the mud, but they are much longer and narrower when under water. Separate male and female flowers appear on the same plant from May to September, but both are inconspicuous and hard to find.

Often stems grow together, forming a dense patch. Great differences may be noticed between one patch and another, especially in leaf-shape. There are half-a-dozen species of water starwort, but they are hard to tell apart.

Water stick insect *Ranatra linearis*

Closely related to the water scorpion, the water stick insect has a thin body, 1½ in. long, which is well camouflaged in a forest of reed stems in shallow water. Like the water scorpion it has a long projection from the rear of its body which keeps it in contact with the air while it lies hidden. Any small water creature is suitable food for this carnivore.

In spring the female lays her eggs embedded in reed stems. Each egg has a long, fine tube which reaches the water surface and supplies the egg with air. The young take two months to mature, and the adults can live for up to 18 months. Water stick insects are not as common as water scorpions and are found only in the southern half of England and Wales.

With a quick movement of its first pair of legs, a water skater seizes a bluebottle for its meal

Water skater

This insect, from ⅓ in. to ¾ in. long, can walk on water—a feat made possible by the surface tension of water, which resists rupturing. The surface acts as if it were covered with a thin skin, and the water skater's feather-light body is able to skim across this propelled by its slender legs. The tips of its second and third pairs of legs dimple but do not pierce the surface, and a rowing or leaping movement pushes the insect across the pond. It can drown, but when submerged usually floats to the surface.

The water skater, which is also known as the pond skater, is a carnivorous bug and will eat any small insect. It holds the prey with its first pair of legs and pushes its mouthpiece into the insect and sucks out the juices.

There are eight species in the British Isles. The most common, *Gerris lacustris*, is found on ponds during the spring and summer.

Adults spend the winter hidden in vegetation away from the pond. In the spring they return, and the females lay eggs in the water. The young water skaters live and feed on the surface from the day they hatch.

WALKING ON WATER

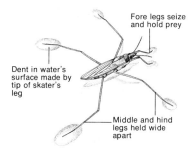

Fore legs seize and hold prey

Dent in water's surface made by tip of skater's leg

Middle and hind legs held wide apart

The water skater skims over the water's surface making rowing movements with its middle legs and steering with its hind legs

Water tower

A reservoir into which water is pumped, to be drawn off as needed, under the force of gravity. Probably the earliest example in the British Isles is the tower built in Canterbury in 1160 by Friar Wybett to supply water through lead pipes to his Benedictine monastery. The superstructure was rebuilt during the 14th century, but the Norman vaults and lower half of the friar's building still exist.

Many towers were built by the Victorians to store water for people living on high ground, and several may be seen on the rim of hills surrounding London—for instance, at Enfield and Shooter's Hill. Some of these are ornate brick structures, but later water towers are generally of concrete, as at Rothwick and Roade in Northamptonshire.

Towers usually stand 60-100 ft above the ground and some, such as Chatterton Tower at Spalding in Lincolnshire, contain offices within their structures.

Water violet *Hottonia palustris*
The long, silvery roots of water violet are suspended in the water or attached to the muddy bottoms of some ditches and small ponds in lowland England. The leaves, which are submerged, are feather-like and arranged in a tuft. A long, solitary stalk up to 15 in. high rises out of the water from the middle of the leaves in May and June bearing a pyramid of primrose-like lilac flowers with yellow throats.

As with primroses, there are flowers of two kinds—some with long styles (female organs) and short anthers (male organs) concealed in the throat, and others with short styles and long, exposed anthers. This arrangement ensures cross-pollination. Pollen from the exposed anthers is transferred to the long styles and pollen from concealed anthers to the short styles.

Waxwing *Bombycilla garrulus*
Unlike most rare migrant birds, the waxwing penetrates inland and may be seen in gardens, even though it does not breed in Britain. It nests in the forests of northern Europe, where it feeds on berries, particularly those of rowan. If a good breeding season is followed by a poor crop of rowan berries, the birds migrate to Britain and southern Europe. Generally only a few birds reach Britain, although in 1965-6 more than 10,000 waxwings were seen. They roam the countryside in flocks, and descend on berry-bearing hedges which they strip rapidly. The waxwing is a pale buff-pink and its tail and

The waxwing appears in Britain in winters when food is short in its north European haunts.

wings are boldly marked with yellow and white. It is 7½ in. long, and its head bears a prominent crest. The bird gets its name from the wax-like red appendages on the tips of its secondary wing feathers. See also MIGRATION

Wayfaring tree *Viburnum lantana*
The 16th-century botanist Gerard gave the wayfaring tree its poetic name. He came across it along the hedgerows bordering the old drove roads over the chalk downs from Winchester to Epsom and London. It still grows there and can be found on similar chalk and limestone soils throughout southern Britain, although not elsewhere.

Its earlier English name was 'hoarwithy', which expresses the white hairiness of its twigs, buds and leaves, and the willow-like suppleness of its twigs. These are fibrous, easily twisted and so hard to break that countrymen still use them for tying bundles. It is a member of the honeysuckle family.

The wayfaring tree seldom grows taller than 15 ft and is bush-like. It has a long life-span, shooting up repeatedly after a hedge is cut and laid.

Winter buds, set in opposite pairs except at the shoot-tips, need no scales to protect them, for their thick down prevents water loss. In mid-winter, the outline of leaf and flower can be seen already formed. The oval, paired leaves also have a hairy coating which limits water loss on dry soils.

In May, the wayfaring tree opens gay clusters of white flowers. By August, bunches of berries are ripening through green and white, to red and finally black. The berries hold single, flat, ribbed, buff-coloured seeds, which birds scatter along hedgerows.

Weald
An Old English word meaning wooded country, generally applied today only to the area between the North and South Downs in Kent, Surrey, Sussex and Hampshire. This is a district of farms, woods and villages once covered by forest, of which all that remains are Tilgate, Ashdown and St Leonard's forests.

From the 16th century to the 19th century vast numbers of trees were used for charcoal, which was burnt as fuel in Sussex ironworks. The word is found in several place names, such as Sevenoaks Weald, in Kent.

Weasel *Mustela nivalis*
Britain's smallest flesh-eating mammal, though attractive-looking, is a savage killer, dispatching its prey with a powerful bite in the neck. It grows to about 10 in. long including a 2 in. tail; its narrow body has chestnut-coloured fur above and white below. Among its close relatives are the stoat and the polecat.

The weasel is found all over the British Isles, except Ireland. It hunts mainly at night—when it usually patrols a hedge-

row or stone wall, investigating every hollow in search of a victim—but is sometimes seen in daylight. It has a habit of standing on its hind legs to investigate its surroundings. If cornered, it will hiss and spit. Voles, frogs, rats and mice are among its prey, but it will also climb bushes in search of eggs and nestlings and raid chicken runs. It will also sometimes kill a rabbit. Gamekeepers kill weasels as vermin, although they keep down voles and mice. Their other main enemies are hawks and owls.

There are normally two litters a year of about six kittens, which are born six weeks after mating. The nest is of grass or leaves in a shallow hole, tree stump or haystack. See also STOAT

Weather see p. 494

Weed
To the farmer, as to the gardener, the standard definition of a weed is a plant growing in the wrong place. For instance, white clover in a lawn is a weed, but the same plant in a pasture is a valuable crop.

Millions of people over the centuries spent the greater part of their working lives chopping away at weeds. When Jethro Tull invented the seed-drill and horse-hoe in 1701 he made the task easier. Tull's drill planted seeds in rows, between which the horse-hoe could operate without ruining the crop. Tractors now pull multiple hoes through the fields.

Another way of dealing with soils heavily infested with weeds is to give the field a year's rest from cropping, and to spend the summer ploughing and harrowing again and again so that the weed seeds do not get a chance to germinate.

Weeds growing in a fallow period can be eliminated by chemicals. One of the most effective is paraquat. This kills all the vegetation it touches but becomes inactive immediately it enters the soil. There are also selective weed-killers which will poison or scorch certain weeds without damaging the crops among which they are growing.

Weeds reduce the yield by competing for water and food in the soil, or by being parasitic on the crop plant. Like other flowers, they fall into two main categories—annual and perennial. Annual ones are a problem because of their abundant growth, and perennials because most of them have stubborn, creeping roots.

Under the Weeds Act 1959 the Ministry of Agriculture, Fisheries and Food can order the occupier of any land to prevent certain weeds from spreading.

Common perennials include bindweed, couch-grass, bent-grass, creeping thistle, creeping buttercup, dock, nettle, ragwort, rush and bracken. Common annual weeds of arable land are charlock, shepherd's purse, goose-foot, knotgrass, mayweed, groundsel, chickweed, shepherd's needle, fumitory, sow-thistle, wild oat and meadow-grass.

Britain's weather – free from harsh extremes

Over millions of years the weather has carved out valleys and fashioned plains with wind, water and ice; over the centuries it has controlled the distribution of peoples and of plant and animal life; and from day to day it sets the scenic mood

A satellite photograph of western Europe. The warm ground causes rising air and cloud, while the cool sea makes air sink and produces less cloud

ANNUAL AVERAGE RAINFALL

Inches
- under 25
- 25 – 30
- 30 – 40
- 40 – 60
- 60 – 100
- over 100

ANNUAL ACCUMULATED TEMPERATURE

Day degrees per annum
- 3500 – 3000
- 3000 – 2500
- 2500 – 2000
- 2000 – 1500
- 1500 – 1000
- 1000 – 500
- under 500

Rainfall in Britain generally increases with height and distance from the east coast. Average temperatures decrease from south to north and with height. Most of southern England has an annual accumulated temperature of 2500-3000°F. Such a temperature is arrived at by expressing average daily temperatures in terms of degrees over 43°F – the rough threshold for vegetation growth – and totalling these over a year

For all its endless interest as a talking point, the most remarkable thing about the British weather is its moderation. Since British weather records began, in the late 17th century, the coldest it has ever been is −27·2°C (−17°F), recorded at Braemar, Aberdeenshire, Scotland in 1895; and the highest temperature on official record is 38°C (100·5°F), at Tonbridge, Kent in 1868. There are many places on earth which are both hotter in summer and more piercingly cold in winter. As with temperature, so with rainfall: the wettest place in Britain is Sprinkling Tarn, Cumberland which received 257 in. of rain in 1954; and the longest drought, at Mile End, London, in 1893 lasted only 73 days.

This moderation is mainly the result of geography. To the west of the British Isles lie some 3000 miles of the Atlantic, and water both gains and loses its heat more slowly than land; it acts, via the air, as a moderating influence on neighbouring areas of land. Most features of our climate are generated over the Atlantic. Cold, dry air, moving down from the Arctic, and warm, moisture-laden air moving up from the Azores, are drawn into the depressions which commonly move east towards Britain, often bringing rain. Most of the rain falls in the north and west, because of the barrier of mountains that force the moisture-laden air to rise and cool, so that its water vapour condenses into the clouds that frequently shroud the peaks.

The tiny water droplets that make up the clouds then combine in their thousands to produce each of the raindrops that fall on more than 200 days a year in the uplands of Wales and Scotland. The annual rainfall amounts to 50-200 in. a year – two to eight times as much as falls in the drier, sunnier parts of eastern England.

In the lee of the mountains, known as the rainshadow area, the air sinks and warms, the skies are clearer and the rainfall is less. During long, clear nights in upland valleys, air cooled by contact with the ground moves downslope. This cold air accumulates in low-lying parts, whitening the grass with dew or even hoar frost. Thick hedges and railway embankments built across slopes dam the cold air and in the same way act as traps for dew or frost. Frost hollows are widespread, not limited to upland areas. At the bottom of many valleys in the Cotswolds, the Chilterns and the Downs, ground frost occurs throughout the year, even in mid-summer, on as many as three nights in five.

In upland Britain the opposing sides of east-west valleys sometimes have contrasting plant life and land use. North-facing slopes receive less direct sunshine than south-facing ones, and in western Britain the north-facing sides of some deep valleys are covered in rough grass or trees, while the south-facing ones are farmed. But this contrast is much less pronounced than that in the Alpine areas of Europe because, at the relatively low altitudes of upland Britain, a great deal of the sunlight is scattered by particles of dust in the atmosphere and reaches the ground from all angles.

One feature of the climate in upland Britain is the rapid fall in temperature with increasing height. The line marking the maximum upper limit of tree growth is reached at little more than 2000 ft in Britain, well below the levels in central Europe.

In lowland Britain, cloud, drizzle and rain are less dominant than in the uplands, and days of sunshine, with the shadows of clouds drifting slowly across the landscape, are common in summer. Such days often begin bright and clear but, as the ground warms—especially dark-coloured areas which rapidly absorb heat, such as ploughed fields and coniferous forest—so parcels of warm air, known as thermals, lift and rise through the cooler air around them.

Above a certain height, the thermals become saturated with moisture and are visible as rising, expanding masses of white cloud, sometimes alone and sometimes as individual turrets in a larger cloud system. Many clouds boil up so high that their tops are frozen into a crystalline froth which is blown ahead of the main cloud mass in what is known as an anvil. Near the ground, visibility will be good. As the day progresses, these clouds, known as cumulo-nimbus, become deeper and more numerous and cast wider and darker shadows across the landscape. Heralded by a cold, gusty breeze, a curtain of heavy rain, or even hail, will often fall from the dark base of the cloud, and thunder and lightning will follow.

When an airstream from the south blows day after day in summer, air temperatures may rise to more than 25°C (77°F) and surface temperatures even higher, reaching perhaps 55°C (131°F) above tarmac roads and 40°C (104°F) in the first few inches above lawns. The air will be dry and rather dusty, often containing thousands of tons of red dust that it has picked up from North Africa and Spain. Visibility is reduced and views are blurred, though conditions may improve after rain has washed the dust from the air. Along the coast on such days, temperatures may be lowered by a breeze blowing off the sea; at night a weaker breeze blows off the land.

In winter and early spring, easterly or south-easterly airstreams often blow from northern and eastern Europe, where temperatures may be 20°C below zero. As they cross the North Sea they pick up water vapour which, across eastern and south-eastern England, is deposited as a blanket of snow.

Among the more recent changes in the world's climate has been the so-called 'Little Ice Age', which lasted from the mid-16th to the mid-19th century. Over the 100 years after 1850 temperatures generally increased, but since 1950 they have fallen again—quite sharply.

As a deep layer of ragged grey cloud blots out the sky and decreases visibility, snow falls over the Derbyshire moors. At very low temperatures the small flakes drift easily, but at higher temperatures the larger, star-shaped flakes cling together and drifting rarely occurs

Weever *Trachinus vipera*

A bather at the seaside who feels a sharp jab in the foot, followed by a searing pain in the leg, has probably trodden on a weever, the only venomous fish in British seas. The fish, about 6 in. long, lies buried in the sand with only its first dorsal fin and eyes above the surface, looking for shrimps and other small crustaceans and fish which are its main food source. The spines supporting its back fin have venom glands, and there are other venom-filled spines on each gill cover. Anyone stung by a weever fish should seek medical treatment.

Weevil

A plant-eating beetle which can be a serious pest. There are over 500 British species, ranging from 1/16 in. to ½ in. long. Weevils differ from other beetles in that their heads are elongated to form snouts, at the end of which are the mouthparts. The antennae, attached halfway down the snout, have 'elbow' joints. Snout lengths vary between species, some being only as long again as the rest of the head, while others are longer than the rest of the body.

Many weevils damage cultivated plants. Grain weevils *Sitophilus granarius* attack all kinds of whole grain and some cereal products, such as macaroni. The females can lay more than 6000 eggs during their nine-month life span.

With their snouts they bore into the grain particles, laying an egg in each. The larvae produce powdery, whitish excreta which, in quantity, taint grain and make it unpala-

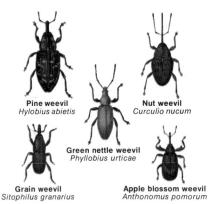

Pine weevil
Hylobius abietis

Nut weevil
Curculio nucum

Green nettle weevil
Phyllobius urticae

Grain weevil
Sitophilus granarius

Apple blossom weevil
Anthonomus pomorum

Five typical weevils. There are more than 500 British species, many of which are pests of crops

table. Clover weevils, of the genus Apion, lay eggs in clover seed pods and the larvae eat the seeds. Apple blossom weevils *Anthonomus pomorum* lay eggs in apple buds and the larvae destroy the flowers before they open.

The pine weevil *Hylobius abietis* does more damage as an adult than as a larva. When a pine wood is felled the weevils lay eggs in the old stumps. The larvae eat the rotting wood and do little harm. But if the land is replanted with pines, large numbers of adult weevils can damage the saplings by eating the bark and so stopping the sap-flow.

The nut weevil *Curculio nucum* has a remarkably long snout. This is used to nibble deep into a green hazel nut. An egg is laid in the hole, which usually closes up as the nut matures. The larva hatches and feeds inside until the nut falls to the ground. It then bores its way out and into the soil, where it enters its pupal, or resting, stage.

The green nettle weevil *Phyllobius urticae* is very common on stinging nettles. It has a short snout and its body is covered with green scales.

Weir

A type of dam built across a river or stream to raise the level of water above it or regulate its flow. Weirs have been known since the 9th century and get their name from the Old English *wearen,* to dam up. They provided water power for corn, cloth and other mills and were also used as fish traps. A clause in Magna Carta calls for the removal of all fish weirs from the Thames, the Medway and 'throughout all England' except along the sea coast.

The Countess Weir on the River Exe is one of the earliest still in existence. It was built in 1282 and, because it obstructed the river, a canal, completed in 1566, was dug to carry river traffic. Today, weirs in use are mainly found on canals and navigable waterways, where it is necessary to maintain a sufficient depth of water for boats.

Early weirs had flash locks or movable sections to allow traffic to pass on a 'flash' or flood of water. Weir gates, which allow the passage of excess water, are known on the Thames as 'lashers'.

Weld *Reseda luteola*

This plant, also known as dyers' weed, is one of the oldest and best dye plants, producing a brilliant and fast yellow. Weld, together with madder and woad, was one of the three most important dyes used in medieval times for cotton and wool. A paint made from it was called Dutch-pink.

Weld is common on waste ground, arable fields and walls throughout most of the lowlands in the British Isles, but it does not grow in north and west Scotland. It has a single, often unbranched, stem up to 5 ft high with many glossy, narrow leaves, and has a spike of yellowish-green flowers nodding at the top from June to August.

Well

Before water pipes were invented, every village or community had a well or pump. Here a shaft had been sunk through the earth to reach an underground water supply which supplemented or took the place of surface supplies. The importance of the well is reflected in place names. Elwell in Dorset is named after its ancient wishing well, from Old English *hael*, an omen, and *well*, a spring or stream.

The 'miracle' of underground water, which sometimes rose spontaneously to the surface, led to wells gaining many supernatural associations. The Celts frequently raised altars and made sacrifices at wells. This custom may be the origin of the Derbyshire well-dressing ceremonies, in which large trays of smoothed clay are decorated with fluorspar, cones, petals, bark and grasses to form elaborate and usually reli-

The nut weevil uses its long snout to burrow a hole into a green hazel nut, in which it lays an egg. When the larva hatches, it feeds on the kernel, and escapes by boring its way out when the nut falls

gious pictures. These are displayed by the well on Ascension Day.

Holy wells abound. They are often of pagan origin, adapted to Christian beliefs. St Winifred's Well at Woolston in Shropshire, still a place of pilgrimage, is said to have appeared in 1138 when St Winifred's body rested there during the night.

Some wells are dry for part of the year. To provide a permanent water supply, a well must be deep enough to reach the water-table at all seasons.

Artesian wells, where the water springs spontaneously to the surface, occur only where the water-bearing bed is sandwiched between two beds of impervious rock. The water is forced up the well-shaft by pressure to reach the surface.

So many have been sunk in the London area, the Chilterns and North Devon that pumps are now needed to force the water up.

Well-water is not always clean. Snails, insect larvae and algae are often drawn up from shallower wells; moss and lichen sometimes grow on the walls of the shaft as far as light reaches; and ferns and moss grow round the well-head. See also SPRING

Wellingtonia *Sequoiadendron giganteum*

An enormous, stately conifer found only in large parks, wellingtonia was discovered in 1841 by John Bidwell when exploring the Sierra Nevada mountain range in California. A member of the pine family, it is a relic of a

The thick, soft bark of wellingtonia, the world's biggest tree, protects the wood from fire

prehistoric age. In 1853, when the first seeds arrived in Britain, it was named after the Duke of Wellington, who had died the previous year.

A 272 ft tall wellingtonia in Sequoia National Park, California, is the world's biggest tree. It is 75 ft round, probably 4000 years old. The tallest British wellingtonia is a 165 ft tree at Endsleigh, Devon, which was planted more than 100 years ago, and has a girth of over 22 ft.

Wellingtonia has a tapering trunk, thick, pink-grey, deeply furrowed, soft bark and long, drooping branches. Its twigs are completely hidden by short, spiky, grey-green evergreen needles.

In spring it opens small, yellow male flowers, which scatter wind-borne pollen. Its bud-shaped female flowers ripen, by October, to curious knobbly oblong brown cones that hold, under their scales, tiny seeds edged with papery wings. Although many prove infertile, some sprout in the following spring.

Wels see Catfish
Welsh black see Cattle
Welshman's button see Caddis fly

Wet-rot fungus

This fungus grows and feeds only on wet wood, reducing it to crumbling decay. Unlike the dry-rot fungus, it cannot produce water and will die rapidly in dry conditions.

The fungus causes decay by digesting and absorbing the substance of the wood. It spreads by producing spores.

The cellar fungus *Coniophora cerebella* attacks any damp buildings, gate-posts, dog kennels, garden sheds and wooden garages. It can also attack damp floors which have been covered over. Even though infected wood becomes discoloured, the fungus is difficult to detect.

Wet-rot fungus also grows on dead wood in forests, where it more frequently forms a fruiting body. At first flat and yellow, it develops a warty surface and turns olive green. The whole fruiting body, which may be 1 in. to 2 ft in diameter, is much thinner than that of the dry-rot fungus, and is often bordered by a mass of fine white threads. Larger hyphal threads, which darken with age, creep over the wood surface in a repeatedly branching pattern.

The mine fungus *Poria vaillantii* attacks pit props in damp mines. It forms white sheets over the wood and may hang down in long, stalactite-like growths.

Wheat

Farmers in the British Isles grow about 3 million acres of wheat each year. Most is used for bread, the rest for cakes, biscuits and feeding livestock. Bread is usually made from a mixture of home-grown and Canadian and American wheat. The harder wheats that ripen in the hot American summers are said to be better for bread-

making than the soft ones resulting from Britain's cool, moist climate.

The wheat plant has an erect stem which carries the seed-head upright until just before harvest, when it tends to bend over. In the seed-head the grains are protected by a stiff, spiked sheath. After threshing, this is known as chaff. Each seed-head is 3-6 in. long, and the grain is about $\frac{1}{4}$ in. long and oval with a cleft down one side. The colour varies from reddish-gold to pale fawn or brown.

Wheat is grown on soil of the highest fertility. Most is sown in autumn and will survive all but the hardest winters. There are special varieties for spring sowing. After a mild winter the young wheat plants may be grazed by sheep in spring, and often yield a better harvest as a result.

There are many varieties of wheat, and work on producing new strains that will give bigger yields and resist disease is constantly in progress. In consequence the life of the majority of varieties is short. Before 1939 a yield of 20 cwt an acre was considered to be good, but in the 1970's yields of 40 cwt an acre are common. A record 71·4 cwt an acre was produced near Doncaster, Yorkshire in 1962.

Wheat-bulb fly *Leptohylemia coarctata*

From June to August the wheat-bulb fly can be found on the ears of wheat, especially when the crop is in flower. It is probably the most serious insect pest of winter wheat in the British Isles, and it also attacks rye and barley. It is similar in appearance to the house fly, but slightly smaller, being $\frac{1}{4}$-$\frac{3}{8}$ in. long and grey-black.

Females lay their eggs in July and August on bare ground or under root crops. The larvae—small, white maggots—hatch out in January and February and die unless wheat, barley or rye have been sown or wild grasses are present. They burrow into the stem of the crop and feed from it, causing the plant to wither or become stunted. In the late spring the larvae leave the plant, burrow into the soil and pupate. The adult flies emerge in early June.

Wheatear see Chat

Whelk

A flesh-eating sea snail with a distinct groove at the bottom of the shell. From the shell the siphon, a tube, extends to detect food and take in clean water. Often dozens of whelks converge on the body of a dead crab or fish.

The common whelk or buckie, up to 6 in. long, is the largest snail on British shores, but offshore whelks are even larger.

The buckie has a brown felt-like covering and lives on the lower part of the shore, especially on muddy sand or gravel. It lays its eggs in a pale yellow, sponge-like mass of capsules. As with all whelks, there are several hundred eggs in each capsule; but only 10-20 emerge as young whelks. Those which survive to this early stage do so at the expense of their fellows, for the first to emerge will eat the rest of the eggs.

Other whelks may be edible, but the buckie is the only one that is collected commercially for food.

The 1½ in. long common dog whelk is common on rocky shores where it feeds mainly on acorn barnacles by boring a hole through them or forcing their plates apart. It is usually off-white but may be brown, yellow or pink. It lays masses of vase-shaped yellow eggs on rocks in the inter-tidal zone; huge bands of these can sometimes be seen when the tide recedes.

The 1 in. long brown shell of the netted dog whelk has a network of ridges and grooves. It feeds on carrion and lives below low-tide mark on sandy shores, where it often buries itself with its siphon protruding like a periscope.

Water is drawn in through this and as soon as food is detected in it, the whelk surfaces and crawls forward with outstretched siphon. This whelk lays egg capsules in neat rows along blades of eel-grass. See also SHELL

Common whelk or Buckie
up to 6 in. *Buccinun undatum*

Netted dog whelk 1 in.   **Common dog whelk**
Nassarius reticulatus   1½ in. *Nucella lapillus*

Dog whelks are much smaller than the common whelk, the species which is gathered for food

Whey

When milk goes sour the solid part is called curd and the liquid is known as whey. Cheese-makers allow the sour milk to stand in vats and use rennet—a milk-curdling enzyme—to solidify the curd, which is then processed into cheese. The whey is drained off and fed to pigs or calves. One gallon of whey has the feeding value of 1 lb. of barley.

Whimbrel see Curlew
Whin see Gorse
Whinchat see Chat

Whirligig beetle

This oval, flattened beetle, ⅕-⅜ in. long, spends its life half in and half out of the water, its whole structure specialised for this peculiar life. Its shiny black back repels the water, enabling the beetle to float with its underside and legs submerged, but its back quite dry. The second and third pairs of

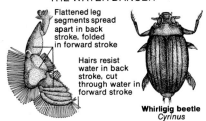

THE WATER DANCER

Flattened leg segments spread apart in back stroke, folded in forward stroke

Hairs resist water in back stroke, cut through water in forward stroke

Whirligig beetle
Cyrinus

Hind leg detail

Making breaststroke movements with its flattened, oar-like legs, the whirligig beetle whirls through the water with its body half submerged

legs are oar-like and fringed with hairs that help in swimming. Each compound eye is divided into two parts. One part is on the lower surface of the head and can see under water. The other half looks upwards and can see best out of the water, through air.

Several common kinds of whirligig beetle *Gyrinus* congregate on the surface of ponds and canals in the summer and swim erratically—like whirligigs. They are not restricted to the surface but can dive down carrying a bubble of air with them. They feed on insects that fall into the water and sometimes on dead animals that float to the surface.

In spring the females lay their eggs on submerged water plants. The larvae have gills and spend all their time on the bottom of the pond. At about the end of July they climb up the stems of water plants to pupate in cocoons made of mud and other materials which are attached to plants by the water's edge. The adults emerge in late summer.

The hairy whirligig *Orectochilus villosus*, a more slender species, is also common but not often seen, because it is active only at night on the surface of running water from June to September.

White admiral *Limenitis camilla*

Britain's climate does not suit this beautiful woodland butterfly and it is usually seen only south of a line from Birmingham to The Wash. After several years of fine weather it can be quite common within this area, but a long period without sunshine can kill all but a few.

The white admiral has a 2¼ in. wingspan and is a powerful flyer. The upper sides of its wings are black with a white band, the undersides ornamented in brown and white. It prefers fairly open woods with plenty of bramble and honeysuckle. Nectar from bramble flowers is a favourite food in July and August, and it is probably injuries caused by bramble thorns that often give the butterfly a tattered appearance.

The eggs are laid in July and hatch out in one or two weeks. The green caterpillar feeds on honeysuckle leaves and camouflages itself by fixing droppings and bits of dry leaves on its back. During the winter it rests inside a leaf tied securely to a twig with silk. After hibernation, the caterpillar feeds

The pupa of the white admiral butterfly hangs from a silk pad spun on a honeysuckle leaf

again and is ready to pupate in June. The name white admiral is a corruption of 'white admirable', a tribute to the insect's beauty.

Whitebeam *Sorbus aria*

A tree whose name derives from the Saxon word *beam*, meaning tree, and the white underside of its leaves. This whiteness is caused by the felted hairs that check water loss on the dry chalk or limestone soils where the tree thrives.

The toothed, oval leaves, set singly on the twigs, open from large, pale green buds in April. They then form goblet-shaped groups, clear white below, resembling blossoms. As they expand, the whiteness is hidden, to be revealed in autumn as the fading leaves drift to the forest floor.

Clusters of white flowers appear in May, and are followed in October by yellow-brown berries, too sour to be eaten raw, though they make a tasty jelly. Birds scatter the small, hard brown seeds.

The tree is a member of the rose family

The whitebeam is named for the dense white fur which covers the undersides of its leaves and is related to the mountain ash. A vigorous hybrid between them, the Swedish whitebeam, is often grown in streets and gardens.

Whitebeam bark is green-grey and remains smooth. The mid-brown timber, with paler sapwood, is occasionally used for wood turnery. The trees live for about 80 years, but rarely exceed 50 ft in height.

Whitebeam is also called the whiteleaf tree, and a notable specimen gave this name to a field near Caterham on the Surrey Downs. When a wealthy Victorian built a mansion there he created the fanciful spelling of 'Whyteleafe' for its name. This was eventually adopted by a hamlet, a post office and two railway stations.

White butterfly

Contrary to popular opinion, not all white butterflies are cabbage whites. There are five species of which the two that cause damage to garden crops are the small white and the large white. Both can be found throughout the British Isles, and each produces two broods a year. The indigenous population is sometimes increased by migration from the Continent.

Caterpillars of both species feed on plants of the cabbage family, although usually on wild plants such as hedge mustard and garlic mustard. The small white will lay eggs on cultivated cabbage. The caterpillars of both species are green and well camouflaged against the leaves of their food plant.

The green-veined white, which takes its name from the markings on the underside of the wings, is common throughout the British Isles. It is one of the few butterflies that will fly on cloudy days. Both caterpillar and pupa match their surroundings exactly.

The large white is mostly a migrant from the Continent and varies in number from

The green-veined white butterfly is one of the few butterflies to be found on the wing on a cloudy day

year to year. It prefers to live among cultivated cabbage, and the female lays its eggs in large batches. Unlike the smaller species, the caterpillars of the large white are easy to see: they are yellow and black and live in large groups. Birds find them distasteful, but they are attacked by parasitic wasps and bacteria.

In May and June the orange tip butterfly can be seen over most of the British Isles, flying along country roadsides or across damp pastures. Only the male has orange wingtips: the female has the appearance of a small green-veined white.

The undersides of both sexes appear to be dappled with green and white, and when the butterfly is at rest among the white flowers and green stalks of garlic mustard it is well hidden. The green dappling effect is produced by a mixture of yellow and black spots. Since none of the white butterflies can make a green pigment, the insect substitutes this fake green as a camouflage.

Eggs are laid among the flowers of jack-by-the-hedge, wild mustard and other wild plants of the cabbage family. They are laid singly and are well spaced out, so that the caterpillars do not often meet. If they do, the stronger oftens eats the weaker.

The wood white is rare and found only in a few woods in eastern Wales, southern England and Ireland. It is not related to the other whites and is a poor flyer. It occupies the shady parts of woodlands in May and June, and there is a second brood in July. Unlike the other whites, the caterpillars feed on vetches and trefoils.

All white butterflies winter as pupae.

Whitefish

Related to the salmon and the trout, and with a superficial resemblance to the herring, the whitefish has silvery sides and a small, rayless fin on the back just in front of the tail. It is found in deep lakes in the mountain areas of Scotland, the Lake District, North Wales and Ireland. Breeding populations have been isolated in these lakes since shortly after the last Ice Age. During the several thousand years since this isolation the whitefish of different lakes have changed slightly in shape and other features so that no two populations are exactly the same. However,

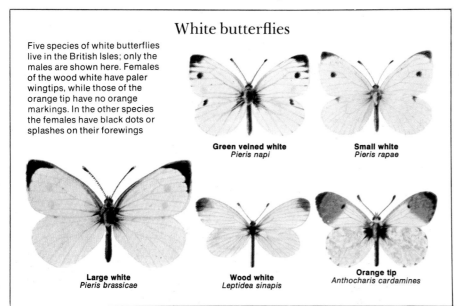

White butterflies

Five species of white butterflies live in the British Isles; only the males are shown here. Females of the wood white have paler wingtips, while those of the orange tip have no orange markings. In the other species the females have black dots or splashes on their forewings

Green veined white
Pieris napi

Small white
Pieris rapae

Large white
Pieris brassicae

Wood white
Leptidea sinapis

Orange tip
Anthocharis cardamines

two main types are recognisable: the vendace and the powan.

The vendace type *Coregonus albula* lives in Loch Maben, Scotland; Derwentwater and Bassenthwaite, in the Lake District; and Loughs Neagh, Erne, Derg and Ree in Ireland, where it is known as pollan. The powan type *C. lavaretus* is found in Lochs Lomond and Eck in Scotland; Haweswater, Red Tarn and Ullswater in the Lake District; and Bala Lake in Wales, where it is known as the gwyniad. In both groups spawning takes place in winter, usually in inshore waters over gravelly banks. Most whitefish feed on minute planktonic crustaceans, taken near the surface of the lake or in mid-water. At some times of the year they also feed on animals at the bottom of the lake.

A marine species, the pouting *C. oxyrinchus*, used to be found in the coastal waters of the North Sea and in the estuaries of eastern England, but none has been reported for 50 years.

Whitefly

The 27 species of whiteflies in the British Isles resemble their close relatives, the aphids. They may also be mistaken for very small moths, as their bodies and wings are covered in a fine, white, powdery wax. The winged, white adults are no more than $\frac{1}{8}$ in. long. They breed throughout the summer, laying eggs on the undersides of leaves. The young are yellowish and remain fixed to the leaves of the host plant. They feed by sucking the plant sap and excrete a sugary honeydew.

A common species is the cabbage whitefly which feeds on wild plants of the cabbage family. It also sometimes infests cultivated cabbages, causing considerable damage. The greenhouse whitefly attacks anything growing under glass and is particularly fond of tomatoes. It is an immigrant and cannot survive the winter out of doors.

Both species can be controlled by the introduction of a species of chalcid wasp, whose grubs feed on young whiteflies.

Cabbage whitefly
Aleyrodes brassicae

Greenhouse whitefly
Trialeurodes vaporariorum

Whitethroat see Warbler

White weed

A sea animal which grows offshore attached to stones, shells or crabs. It is off-white or pale pink, 8-10 in. high, and looks like a miniature tree. Polyps—minute buds, each with its crown of tentacles—are the feeding mechanisms of the animal. The polyps are arranged in two rows along the smaller branches; each can withdraw into a protective cup if it is disturbed. There are several species of white weeds, each of which bears urn-shaped reproductive parts, inside which small, jellyfish-like organisms develop. These produce eggs and sperm. The fertilised eggs develop into larvae, which swim off to form new white weed.

Tufts of white weed are often washed up on the beach after stormy weather. They are also collected by dredging and, after they have dried, are dyed various colours to be sold as 'sea fern'. See also SEA FIR

Whiting *Merlangus merlangus*

Adult whiting are usually found close to the sea-bed in shoals but young fish, up to $1\frac{1}{4}$ in. long, live close to large, floating jellyfish at the sea's surface. If larger fish threaten they hide among the tentacles of the jellyfish where most predators will not follow for fear of the stinging cells in the tentacle threads. The young whiting do not seem to be affected by the venom in these cells.

The whiting is one of the most abundant members of the codfish family in inshore waters and is valuable commercially as well as being caught in large numbers by sea anglers. It has the usual codfish features of three fins on the back and two anal fins, but lacks the large chin barbel. It gets its name from its distinctive white belly and sides. The colour of the back varies from one fish to another but is often dark blue or green, sometimes sandy. At the base of each pectoral fin is a conspicuous black spot. A predatory fish, the whiting feeds on sand eels, sprats, shrimps and crabs. A seven-year-old female may reach a length of 20 in.

Whitlow-grass *Erophila verna*

Sometimes barely an inch in height, this annual is common on old walls, in gravel paths and other dry places such as rocks and sand dunes. Each plant consists of a rosette of oval leaves and one or more leafless flowering stems which bear white, four-petalled flowers from March to June. The tallest plants do not exceed 6 in. The fruit is a short, round pod divided by a thin partition which persists long after the minute seeds have been shed. Whitlow-grass was once supposed to contain a cure for the painful lumps known as whitlows—hence the name of the plant.

Whortleberry see Bilberry
Wigeon see Duck

Wildcat *Felis sylvestris grampia*

Although it has lived in Britain since prehistoric times, the wildcat is not the ancestor of the domestic tabby cat, which it closely resembles. The domestic cat is descended from races of *Felis sylvestris* found in North Africa and Asia. The British wildcat is about 2 ft long, excluding the tail, and weighs 7-13 lb. Apart from its size and more robust appearance, it has bigger feet than the domestic cat and a bushy, bottle-shaped,

The wildcat is larger than the domestic cat and has a much more bushy tail

black-ringed tail about 1 ft long with a black tip. The fur is yellow-grey, with pronounced black stripes.

Although wildcats formerly lived all over Britain, by the 19th century they were restricted to the Scottish Highlands. They were regarded as vermin and hunted because they preyed on game birds, rabbits, hares and other sporting animals. Today landowners and particularly the Forestry Commission recognise the usefulness of wildcats in keeping down voles, woodmice and other small animals which can do considerable damage to young trees. Their numbers appear to be increasing and their range to be extending southwards. Numbers are almost impossible to calculate because of their solitary habits and the problem of distinguishing a pure-bred wildcat from a wild tabby or a cross-breed.

Occasionally a pair of wildcats will hunt together, but most hunt alone in a well-established territory where there are regular routes and resting places. The wildcat hunts its prey at night, by stalking or waiting in ambush; prey sometimes includes baby lambs or roe deer fawns.

Although the wildcat climbs and swims well, it keeps mainly to the ground where it lives in woodland and among rocks on exposed mountainsides. In suitable weather much time is spent in resting and sunning itself in the open and, during wet periods, lying up in shelter. The wildcat's den is usually in some inaccessible hideout between rocks or under fallen trees or in a large deserted bird's nest.

The pure-bred wildcat breeding season starts in March and the female bears a single litter of two to four kittens in May; but there is evidence that many Scottish wildcats have a second season in late summer, probably because of interbreeding with domestic cats. The kittens are light-coloured with grey-brown tabby markings which deepen with age. Although very playful when young, they rarely become hand-tame when reared in captivity.

The female is extremely fierce when she has young to protect and usually rears them away from the tom, which is liable to kill and eat his own kittens. These hunt with their mother when 10-12 weeks old and are not fully weaned until four months old. They leave her at about five months.

A wildcat growls in anger, purrs when pleased and at other times meows, screams or caterwauls. Like the domestic cat, it buries its scat, or droppings. See also CAT

Wild service tree

A rare tree found only in a few ancient woods, usually on rough slopes along the sides of streams in southern England and Wales. The wild service tree *Sorbus torminalis* is seldom planted and is often unrecognised. It is a small tree with grey bark, broken into squares like the hawthorn – hence the old Kentish name of chequers tree, since it resembles a draughts board.

The tree's unusual name derives from the Latin for beer, *cerevisia*. The Romans used the fruits of a related tree, the true service *S. domestica*, to flavour their beer.

The leaf of the wild service tree is lobed like that of a sycamore or maple. The white flowers, which open in clusters in May, resemble those of the mountain ash. The fruits, which ripen in October, are bunches of apple-shaped, greenish-brown berries. They are said to have a pleasantly acid flavour but are not commonly eaten nowadays. Birds devour them eagerly, scattering the small, red-brown seeds which have to lie on the ground for 18 months before sprouting as two-leaved seedlings.

The service tree, which rarely exceeds 40 ft in height, may live for 50 years. Its timber is strong and tough, with red-brown heartwood and pale brown sapwood.

The Devon service tree, or French hales tree, *S. devoniensis*, lies botanically midway between wild service and whitebeam. It is rare, but can be found in Devon, eastern Cornwall and in the Irish counties of Kilkenny, Wexford and Carlow. Its egg-shaped leaves are partly lobed, with serrated edges. It bears cream blossoms followed by round, orange-brown berries with prominent breathing pores.

Wild service tree
Sorbus torminalis

Devon service tree
Sorbus devoniensis

The wild service tree has more deeply lobed leaves than the Devon service tree. Both are rare

Crack willow, the tallest of the willows, is named for its brittle twigs which break with a cracking sound

Willow

The willows that grow in Britain range from tall, stately trees to ground-hugging shrubs. They are trees with many different names, including osier, withy, palm, sallow or, in Scotland, saugh.

A good life span for a willow is 50 years. Each tree is usually wholly male or female, and can be easily reproduced by cuttings, which repeat the same sex. Its buds are always enclosed within a single leaf scale, which aids identification. Leaves vary from rounded ovals to long, narrow blades, but are never lobed or divided.

Willow flowers are borne in oval, fluffy catkins – hence pussy-willow – which open in March before the leaves break. Male and female catkins are similar and both produce nectar to attract insects for pollination, although some pollen is wind-borne. Female catkins, holding many seed pods, ripen by mid-summer. These split to release many tiny winged seeds, which are short-lived and only sprout on damp earth. Most willows grow beside water and their seedlings thrive on wet mud. Stranded broken branches may also take root and spring up into bushes, which can also arise from drooping branches that have touched the ground and rooted.

Willow wood is pale yellow or brown throughout, and although not particularly durable is tough, pliant and exceptionally light. Cricket bats are made from a variety of white willow *Salix alba* called *coerulea*. It is raised from cuttings in Essex and neighbouring counties on fertile riverside land, and felled for bat making when only 12-15 years old. Each bat length is cleft – not sawn – from the trunk, then seasoned and shaped to form the blade of the bat. The method of construction ensures it will not warp and will withstand repeated hard battering without splitting.

This linking of lightness with strength leads to other specialised uses of willows, such as in artificial limbs. Baskets are commonly made from willow wands, which are easily interwoven when moist, becoming harder and firmer but remaining resilient when dry. Pieces of cleft willow are used in Sussex for making garden trugs.

Crack willow *S. fragilis* is the tallest kind, growing up to 90 ft. It has long, slender, silver-green leaves and is often found beside lowland rivers. It is named because its small yellow-barked twigs readily break away from the joints with a sharp crack. The weeping willow *S. babylonica* originated in China, but the first specimens were imported from the Euphrates region in 1730. Many of those seen in Britain are hybrids. Their main branches always droop gracefully earth-wards, or to water from which they gain reflected sunlight. Bay willow *S. pentandra* has fragrant, glossy, dark green foliage and conspicuous male catkins. The goat willow

S. caprea has oval leaves and springs up on muddy patches everywhere. Both its English and Latin names refer to the fondness of goats for its early spring foliage. Its flowers are sometimes used to provide 'palms' for Palm Sunday. Its grey-green bark yields tannin, used for tanning leather, and salicin from which salicylic acid – used in aspirin – is made.

The reddish, wiry stems of creeping willow

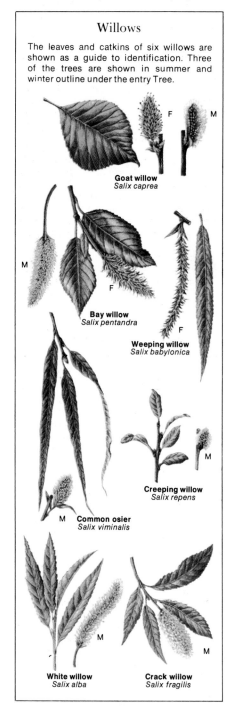

Willows

The leaves and catkins of six willows are shown as a guide to identification. Three of the trees are shown in summer and winter outline under the entry Tree.

Goat willow
Salix caprea

Bay willow
Salix pentandra

Weeping willow
Salix babylonica

Creeping willow
Salix repens

Common osier
Salix viminalis

White willow
Salix alba

Crack willow
Salix fragilis

S. repens crawl through low turf and bear catkins at ground level on heaths and sand dunes. The osiers, or basketry willows, which include the green-stemmed *S. viminalis* and the purple-stemmed *S. purpurea*, are still grown in some districts, particularly on Sedgemoor in Somerset. Rooted cuttings are planted in fertile, well-watered and well-drained farmland. The first growth is cut back, and each stump then sends up a clump of young shoots, which rise to 6 ft in one summer. These are harvested annually to obtain pliant lengths, which may be barked to give white willow or first boiled with their bark attached to dye them bright buff.

Few trees are more liable to attack by insect pests, including aphids, beetles, moths, weevils and the larvae of the purple emperor butterfly. Watermark disease in cricket bat willows is caused by bacteria.

In folklore, the willow is said to taste bitter because the Christchild was once whipped with one; and, because willows decay early, to beat a child with a willow rod was believed to stunt his growth.

Willow-herb

Named after its long, narrow, willow-like leaves, the willow-herb grows as an upright spike covered with pink or crimson flowers.

Its ability to spread and colonise is demonstrated by three species common in Britain only in the last 100 years. Rosebay willow-herb, or fireweed, was a rare native species which suddenly began to spread about 1860, perhaps as a result of genetic change; it is now everywhere, except the far west of Ireland, and is abundant on waste land round towns, and in cleared woodland. It grows to 4 ft in height, with purplish flowers, and tapering leaves up to 6 in. long. Each flower appears to be on a long stalk, but this is really an undeveloped capsule which later develops into a seed pod. This has four flaps which open from the top, releasing numerous cottony seeds which spread on the wind. The plant also spreads by means of stems, either above or beneath the ground.

New Zealand willow-herb is a creeping plant with small round leaves and flowers on 2 in. stalks. First recorded in Edinburgh in 1904 it is now widespread throughout Ireland and the north and west of Britain. It grows on damp rocks, in stream beds and even on stones by the roadside. The third species, American willow-herb, was recorded in Leicester in 1891; it is now one of the most common species on old railway lines and waste places. It has reddish stems, covered in stalked glandular hairs, and small flowers with deeply notched petals.

Short-fruited willow-herb is a native species similar to American willow-herb but with fewer glandular hairs and lacking the reddish tinge. It is common in hedgerows, and on stream and ditch banks. Marsh willow-herb is smaller than most other species, growing up to 2 ft, with an un-branched stem and pairs of narrow opposite

Eight species of willow-herbs

Rosebay willow-herb
Epilobium angustifolium

Great willow-herb
Epilobium hirsutum

New Zealand willow-herb
Epilobium nerterioides

Short-fruited willow-herb
Epilobium obscurum

Marsh willow-herb
Epilobium palustre

Hoary willow-herb
Epilobium parviflorum

American willow-herb
Epilobium adenocaulon

Broad-leaved willow-herb
Epilobium montanum

New Zealand willow-herb is a round-leaved creeping plant. The other species are upright, with willow-like leaves

leaves held upright at an angle of about 45 degrees to the stem. Broad-leaved willow-herb is also easily recognised by its opposite leaves, but these are broad and not erect.

Great willow-herb grows up to 6 ft high and, as its Latin name *Epilobium hirsutum* suggests, it is hairy. It is also called codlins-and-cream. Codlins are red-blossomed cooking apples, which used to be boiled and eaten with cream; and the willow-herb's deep rose flowers, up to 1 in. across with a creamy white stigma in the centre, resemble the apple blossom. Hoary willow-herb is similar but smaller, rarely growing over 3 ft in height. Its flowers are less than ½ in. across.

All willow-herbs flower during the summer from June until August.

Wind

The air is never completely still—even on those days in summer described as being without a breath of air. There may be no wind, but there are still gentle eddies of air and movements of individual air molecules.

In the first 2000 ft or so of air above the ground, friction between wind and earth produces eddies or rotations of air, on a variety of scales; these are responsible for the gustiness of winds near the ground. The swaying of branches and the ripples which appear to move over the surface of growing grain both indicate eddies.

A smoke plume issuing from a tall chimney can reveal the presence of a range of eddies. The plume is driven in one direction by the prevailing wind but its shape may be distorted by the largest of the local eddies. At the same time, the plume broadens downwind under the influence of smaller eddies, so that its shape resembles a distorted cone.

The strength of winds generally increases rapidly with height, as the frictional drag of the earth's surface in the first 2000-3000 ft of the atmosphere gradually lessens. Winds are therefore much stronger on the tops of hills; moreover, the wind speeds up as it moves over the hill barrier. On hill tops winds are generally stronger by night; at low altitudes they are stronger by day.

Strictly speaking, it is inaccurate to think of wind as *blowing* in a certain direction; rather it is *sucked* from an area of high pressure into an area of low pressure. The strength of the wind depends on the difference in pressure.

Areas of high pressure are known as anticyclones or highs, areas of low pressure as depressions or lows, and winds move around these areas. In the Northern Hemisphere they rotate outwards in a clockwise direction around anticyclones and inwards in an anticlockwise direction around depressions. Near the centre of anticyclones winds are light and variable in direction, but near the centre of depressions they are strong, sometimes reaching gale force—39-46 mph.

The speed and direction of the wind near the earth is affected by the landscape. Valleys running in the same direction as the wind channel it, those running at right angles to the wind turn it into large eddies, and gaps in high ground concentrate it. Frictional drag with the ground also affects wind direction.

The strength of a wind is far from steady. As it moves across country, eddies cause rapidly changing gusts and lulls. The strongest gusts usually experienced in Britain are of about 115 mph, but they last only a few seconds.

The highest recorded surface wind speed in the British Isles was 144 mph at Cairngorm, Inverness-shire in March 1967. A gust of 177 mph in the Shetlands in February 1962 was not recorded on standard equipment. See also LEE WAVE

Windbreak

Trees have been planted not only to glorify the English countryside but also to protect it. A screen of hardy trees can check the force of the wind and benefit crops and livestock. Yields are improved, and sheep and cattle can survive much higher up the hills if there are trees to shield them.

Solid barriers cause strong eddies, but branches and foliage allow the wind to filter slowly through and direct the stronger currents away from the ground. On level land, a windbreak can provide shelter over a distance along the ground of roughly 20 times its height; this means that a line of 70 ft high trees will protect a quarter-mile wide strip of land.

On rich farmland, such as in Kent, a single row of hawthorns, elms or poplars is enough to protect hop fields and orchards. Conifers provide a denser barrier, and conifer belts 60 ft wide are used on the bleak uplands of Scotland and northern England.

THE PROTECTIVE WINDBREAK

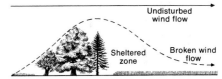

Closely planted trees form a barrier against wind flow and so shelter animals and crops

Windmill see Mill

Window fly *Scenopinus fenestralis*

At one time the window fly was called the carpet fly because it was thought that its larvae damaged carpets. Later research has shown that they are beneficial—although the larvae do live in carpets or among the litter on the floors of outbuildings, they feed on the larvae of clothes moths, fleas and other insects which cause damage.

The fly is usually seen during the summer, walking sluggishly on the windows of old buildings or resting with its wings folded. It is $\frac{1}{4}$ in. long, has an elongated, tapering, yellowish head and a dull black body with reddish-brown legs. It lives mainly in southern England.

Wind pump see Mill

HOW WIND FORCE IS DEFINED

The Beaufort Scale, which is used to define wind force, was devised in 1808 by Admiral Sir Francis Beaufort, Hydrographer to the Navy, 1829-55. Force 12 is a hurricane, with wind speeds of 73-82 mph, but the scale now goes up to Force 17 (126-136 mph). Wind speed can be roughly estimated from fairly simple observations, as the following table shows:

Land observations	Sea observations	Wind speed (mph)	Force	Description
Smoke rises vertically	Sea like a mirror	Less than 1	0	Calm
Light drift of smoke	Light ripples	1-3	1	Light air
Wind felt on face; leaves rustle	Small wavelets. No foam on crests	4-7	2	Slight breeze
Leaves in motion. Wind extends light flag	Large wavelets. Crests begin to break	8-12	3	Gentle breeze
Wind raises dust and small pieces of paper. Small branches of trees move	Small waves; frequent white horses	13-18	4	Moderate breeze
Small trees in leaf begin to sway; crested wavelets on inland waters	Moderate waves; chance of some spray	19-24	5	Fresh breeze
Large branches in motion. Whistling in telegraph wires	Large waves and spray	25-31	6	Strong breeze
Whole trees in motion. Difficulty in walking against the wind	Heavy sea with foam from breaking waves blown in the direction of the wind	32-38	7	High wind
Twigs break off trees	High waves and foam blown in streaks	39-46	8	Gale
Chimney pots and slates blown off some houses	Sea begins to 'roll'. Spray may affect visibility	47-54	9	Strong gale
Trees uprooted and severe structural damage. Seldom experienced inland	High waves covered in foam, and poor visibility because of spray	55-63	10	Whole gale
Widespread structural damage. Rarely experienced	Exceptionally high waves. Sea covered in long white patches of foam	64-72	11	Storm

The white campion, a hedgerow plant and a weed of arable land, has fragrant flowers which open in the evening and attract night-flying moths

Wild flower

There are more than 400,000 species of plants in the world, of which about 250,000 reproduce by means of seeds. These are the plants that produce flowers. The other plants, which include algae, bacteria, fungi, lichens, mosses and liverworts, reproduce by cell division or spores.

Flowers are the parts of a seed-bearing plant which contain the organs of reproduction. Just as with animals, most plants reproduce sexually; that is, by the fusion of male and female elements.

The male element, or sperm, is carried inside grains of pollen produced by organs called anthers. The female element, the ovule or egg, is contained in an ovary. This has a short beak—the style—surmounted by a sticky organ, called the stigma, which catches the pollen. The pollen can be brought in contact with the stigma in a number of different ways—it can be carried by wind or water; or it can be carried by insects.

After the transfer of pollen to the stigma, the pollen grain, containing the male sperm, develops a tube which penetrates the stigma and grows until it reaches the female egg. When the sperm and the egg meet they fuse and a seed develops.

The simplest flowers consist of little more than male and female organs, but most have a number of parts, of which the most conspicuous are usually the petals. In simple flowers, pollination—the transfer of pollen to the stigma—usually depends on wind or water. Colourful flowers usually rely on insects for pollination.

In these plants the petals serve to make the flower conspicuous to insects which come to feed on the nectar they produce. Flowers secrete their nectar in sacs deep inside the petals. In order to reach the nectar, an insect has to enter the flower. As it does so, pollen from the anthers brushes off on its body. Sometimes the pollen rubs off on the stigma inside the same flower—this is self-pollination; but more often the insect transfers the pollen to other flowers, as it continues its hunt for nectar. This is cross-pollination. Self-pollination results in seeds which produce plants that cannot vary much from the parent. Cross-pollination brings together elements from different parents. This allows the development of variation within a species. Those individuals with variations that fit their environment will thrive, while those with less suitable variations will tend to die out.

Most flowers depend on cross-pollination, but if this fails to take place, some fall back on self-pollination.

In the case of the rosebay willow-herb, if the early-opening flowers, low on the plant, are not cross-pollinated, flowers high on the stem—which open later—become self-pollinated.

504

Flowers have a number of devices to ensure that self-pollination does not take place. Though most flowers are hermaphrodite—containing both male and female organs—these organs mature at different times. This ensures that the pollen is shed either before or after the stigma ripens. Some plants, such as dog's mercury, bear male and female flowers on separate plants. Others, such as the dog violet, are self-sterile—even if pollen is transferred within the flower, nothing will happen.

The primrose produces flowers that are made up of five joined petals at the mouth of a tube. These flowers are of two kinds: one called thrum-eyed has anthers near the top of the tube while the stigma is halfway down; the other is called pin-eyed in which the anthers are halfway down and the stigma occupies the mouth. There is nectar at the base of the tube which is attractive to bees. When a bee alights on the petals and puts its long tongue into a thrum plant, pollen is dusted near the insect's head. If it then visits a pin plant the pollen is transferred to the stigma, while it collects further pollen lower down its tongue, at the right level for pollinating the next thrum flower.

Bees, butterflies, moths and flies are the chief insect pollinators and many flowers have devices adapted to ensure pollination by particular insects. Night-flowering plants, for example honeysuckle and evening primrose, are often strongly scented and pale-coloured, making them conspicuous to night-flying moths. Members of the deadnettle family have flowers in which the petals are fused together in a tube. The upper petals form a hood over the stamens and stigma, while the lower one forms a lip,

THE PARTS OF A FLOWER

Ripe fruit consisting of many achenes. Each achene contains a single seed

Sepals enclosing bud

Anthers

Petals

Place where petals and sepals were attached

Stamen, male part of the flower, consists of a filament supporting an anther

Meadow buttercup

Stigma, receives pollen from another flower

Carpel containing ovule, female part of the flower, forms an achene when fertilised

Receptacle, swollen part of the flower stalk

Petal, coloured, attracts insects

Nectary produces nectar, a sugary solution, drunk by insects

Sepal, encloses and protects flower in bud

Flower stalk

Half flower of a buttercup

Stamen { Anther, Filament }

Pollen sacs containing the pollen grains that fertilise the carpel

Anther close-up and cross-section

The flower is the reproductive part of a plant. The colourful, often sweetly scented, petals not only protect the male stamens and female carpels but attract insect pollinators

which provides a convenient landing stage for insects.

When a bee alights on the lower lip in search of the nectar at the base of the tube, it fills the mouth of the flower completely with its body, and its back comes up against the anthers and stigmas. The bee rubs on

to the stigma any pollen that has adhered to it from the last flower it visited—and removes pollen from the anthers to fertilise the next flower it visits.

The most complex of all flowers belong to the Compositae, the thistle family, for here what appears to be a single flower is in fact a collection of many small flowers, called florets, surrounded and protected by modified leaves called bracts. The florets are of two kinds: those which are reduced to narrow tubes and those with one tongue-shaped petal. Thistles have only tubular flowers, dandelions only tongue-shaped ones, but the common daisy has both—tubular ones in the centre and tongue-shaped ones at the margin: each of the petals in a daisy represents one flower. Members of the Compositae family are insect-pollinated.

Seeds are not the only means by which flowers reproduce. Creeping plants, such as creeping jenny, often put out roots from nodes on their stems; if these pieces of stem break off, new plants are formed. Underground stems may give rise to new plants, as with the bindweeds, nettles and ground elder. Other flowers, including the daffodil, grow from a bulb—a mass of fleshy leaves forming a food store for the plant. New bulbs start as buds between the leaves of an old bulb. Corms, which superficially resemble bulbs, are food storage swellings on the underground stem of plants such as the crocus. New corms develop from buds on the old ones.

ROOT SYSTEMS AND STORAGE ORGANS

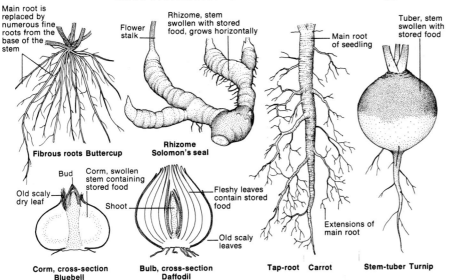

Main root is replaced by numerous fine roots from the base of the stem

Flower stalk

Rhizome, stem swollen with stored food, grows horizontally

Main root of seedling

Tuber, stem swollen with stored food

Fibrous roots Buttercup

Rhizome Solomon's seal

Bud

Old scaly dry leaf

Corm, swollen stem containing stored food

Shoot

Fleshy leaves contain stored food

Old scaly leaves

Extensions of main root

Corm, cross-section Bluebell

Bulb, cross-section Daffodil

Tap-root Carrot

Stem-tuber Turnip

Roots anchor a plant in the soil, absorbing and transporting water and mineral salts to the stem. There are two basic root patterns. The tap-root system has a recognisable main root. Bulbs, corms, tubers and rhizomes, roots modified to store food, are tap-roots. Where there is no distinguishable main root the arrangement is called a fibrous system

505

Common British wild flowers

About 1300 different species of flowers grow wild in the British Isles, of which 370 are shown on the following pages. Each flower shown here has a separate entry in the book, where related species are also described and illustrated. Altogether, nearly 600 flowers are described. Those shown in the chart have been grouped firstly according to their colours and secondly according to their apparent number of petals. The bluebell, for example, really has six petals, but these are joined together in a single bell, so it is placed in the 'up to 4 petal' section of the blue flower group. Flowers that have more than one colour form, such as the rose, which may be red or white, are shown in all the appropriate colour

groupings. Members of the parsley family, orchids, and rare flowers have separate entries and separate charts. Many of the flowers shown in this chart are common and may be picked in moderation, provided that they are growing abundantly in the places where they are found. Flowers which may be picked are marked with the symbol ✳. Pick cleanly, using scissors or a sharp knife, taking care not to wrench a plant up by its roots or even to loosen them. Flowers not marked for picking on this chart should be left alone, as should flowers on private land, Nature Reserves, Nature Trails and National Trust property. If there is any doubt about the identity of a flower, it should not be picked.

White flowers: up to 4 petals

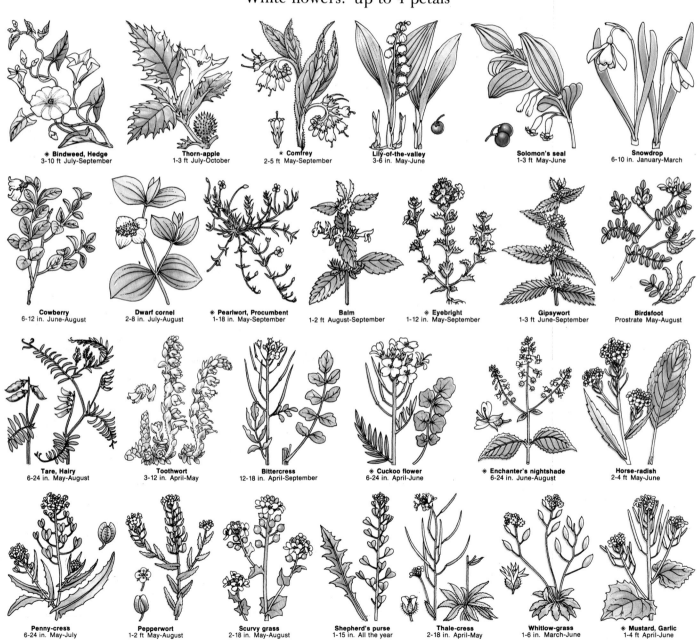

✳ Bindweed, Hedge
3-10 ft July-September

Thorn-apple
1-3 ft July-October

✳ Comfrey
2-5 ft May-September

Lily-of-the-valley
3-6 in. May-June

Solomon's seal
1-3 ft May-June

Snowdrop
6-10 in. January-March

Cowberry
6-12 in. June-August

Dwarf cornel
2-8 in. July-August

✳ Pearlwort, Procumbent
1-18 in. May-September

Balm
1-2 ft August-September

✳ Eyebright
1-12 in. May-September

Gipsywort
1-3 ft June-September

Birdsfoot
Prostrate May-August

Tare, Hairy
6-24 in. May-August

Toothwort
3-12 in. April-May

Bittercress
12-18 in. April-September

✳ Cuckoo flower
6-24 in. April-June

✳ Enchanter's nightshade
6-24 in. June-August

Horse-radish
2-4 ft May-June

Penny-cress
6-24 in. May-July

Pepperwort
1-2 ft May-August

Scurvy grass
2-18 in. May-August

Shepherd's purse
1-15 in. All the year

Thale-cress
2-18 in. April-May

Whitlow-grass
1-6 in. March-June

✳ Mustard, Garlic
1-4 ft April-June

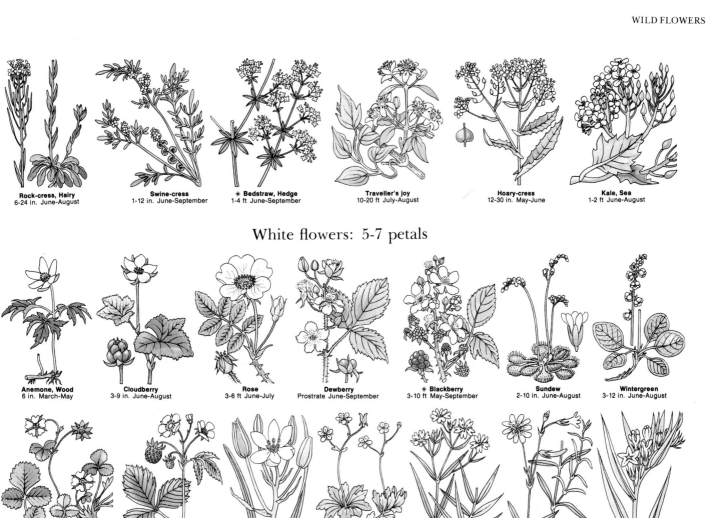

Rock-cress, Hairy
6-24 in. June-August

Swine-cress
1-12 in. June-September

✽ **Bedstraw, Hedge**
1-4 ft June-September

Traveller's joy
10-20 ft July-August

Hoary-cress
12-30 in. May-June

Kale, Sea
1-2 ft June-August

White flowers: 5-7 petals

Anemone, Wood
6 in. March-May

Cloudberry
3-9 in. June-August

Rose
3-6 ft June-July

Dewberry
Prostrate June-September

✽ **Blackberry**
3-10 ft May-September

Sundew
2-10 in. June-August

Wintergreen
3-12 in. June-August

Strawberry, Barren
3-6 in. February-May

Strawberry, Wild
3-12 in. April-July

Star of Bethlehem
6-12 in. April-June

Saxifrage, Starry
3-6 in. June-August

Stitchwort, Greater
6-24 in. April-June

Dusty miller
6-12 in. May-August

Gromwell, Corn
6-18 in. May-July

Campion, Bladder
1-2 ft June-August

✽ **Campion, White**
1-3 ft May-July

Chickweed, Water
1-2 ft July-August

✽ **Chickweed, Common**
3-18 in. All the year

Mouse-ear, Common
1-12 in. April-September

Brookweed
6-11 in. June-August

Sandwort
3-15 in. May-June

✽ **Spurrey, Corn**
3-15 in. June-August

✽ **Pearlwort, Knotted**
2-6 in. July-September

Raspberry
3-5 ft June-August

Nightshade, Black
6-24 in. July-September

✽ **Knotweed**
3-6 ft July-October

507

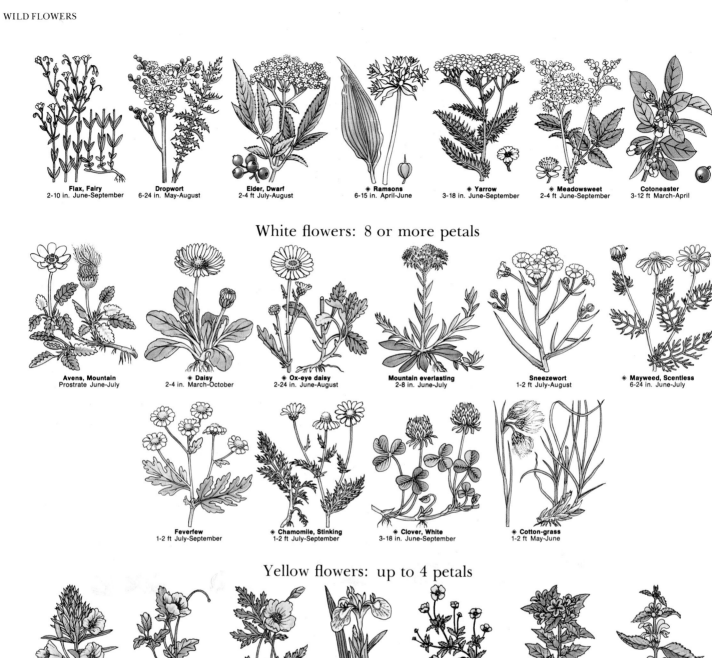

Flax, Fairy
2-10 in. June-September

Dropwort
6-24 in. May-August

Elder, Dwarf
2-4 ft July-August

✽ **Ramsons**
6-15 in. April-June

✽ **Yarrow**
3-18 in. June-September

✽ **Meadowsweet**
2-4 ft June-September

Cotoneaster
3-12 ft March-April

White flowers: 8 or more petals

Avens, Mountain
Prostrate June-July

✽ **Daisy**
2-4 in. March-October

✽ **Ox-eye daisy**
2-24 in. June-August

Mountain everlasting
2-8 in. June-July

Sneezewort
1-2 ft July-August

✽ **Mayweed, Scentless**
6-24 in. June-July

Feverfew
1-2 ft July-September

✽ **Chamomile, Stinking**
1-2 ft July-September

✽ **Clover, White**
3-18 in. June-September

✽ **Cotton-grass**
1-2 ft May-June

Yellow flowers: up to 4 petals

Evening primrose
2-3 ft June-September

Horned poppy
1-3 ft June-September

Poppy, Welsh
1-2 ft June-August

Iris, Yellow
1-5 ft May-July

Tormentil
Creeping June-September

Henbane
1-3 ft June-August

Archangel
1-2 ft May-June

Cow-wheat
6-24 in. May-October

Fluellen
Prostrate July-October

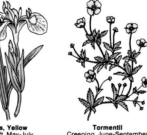

✽ **Gorse**
2-6 ft March-June

Melilot
2-4 ft July-September

Cabbage, Wild
2-3 ft May-August

✽ **Yellow-rattle**
6-18 in. May-August

✽ **Charlock**
12-30 in. May-July

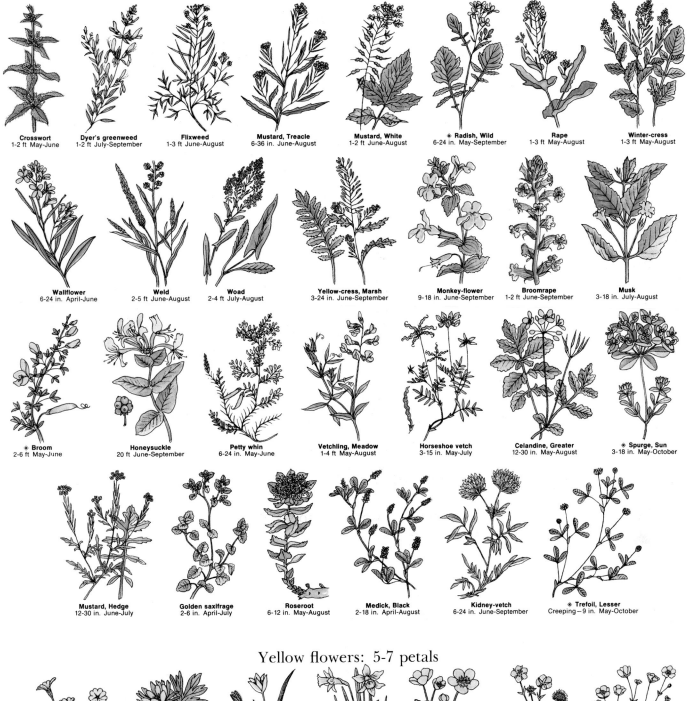

Crosswort
1-2 ft May-June

Dyer's greenweed
1-2 ft July-September

Flixweed
1-3 ft June-August

Mustard, Treacle
6-36 in. June-August

Mustard, White
1-2 ft June-August

✽ **Radish, Wild**
6-24 in. May-September

Rape
1-3 ft May-August

Winter-cress
1-3 ft May-August

Wallflower
6-24 in. April-June

Weld
2-5 ft June-August

Woad
2-4 ft July-August

Yellow-cress, Marsh
3-24 in. June-September

Monkey-flower
9-18 in. June-September

Broomrape
1-2 ft June-September

Musk
3-18 in. July-August

✽ **Broom**
2-6 ft May-June

Honeysuckle
20 ft June-September

Petty whin
6-24 in. May-June

Vetchling, Meadow
1-4 ft May-August

Horseshoe vetch
3-15 in. May-July

Celandine, Greater
12-30 in. May-August

✽ **Spurge, Sun**
3-18 in. May-October

Mustard, Hedge
12-30 in. June-July

Golden saxifrage
2-6 in. April-July

Roseroot
6-12 in. May-August

Medick, Black
2-18 in. April-August

Kidney-vetch
6-24 in. June-September

✽ **Trefoil, Lesser**
Creeping—9 in. May-October

Yellow flowers: 5-7 petals

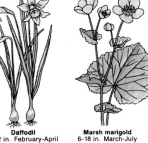

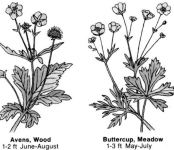

Primrose
2-8 in. January-May

Aconite, Winter
2-6 in. January-March

Tulip
1-2 ft April-May

Daffodil
6-12 in. February-April

Marsh marigold
6-18 in. March-July

Avens, Wood
1-2 ft June-August

Buttercup, Meadow
1-3 ft May-July

509

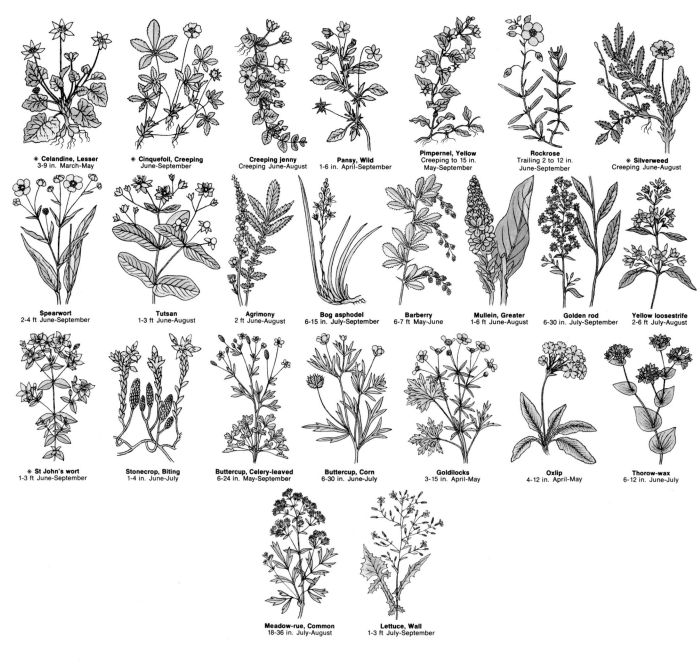

Celandine, Lesser
3-9 in. March-May

Cinquefoil, Creeping
June-September

Creeping jenny
Creeping June-August

Pansy, Wild
1-6 in. April-September

Pimpernel, Yellow
Creeping to 15 in.
May-September

Rockrose
Trailing 2 to 12 in.
June-September

Silverweed
Creeping June-August

Spearwort
2-4 ft June-September

Tutsan
1-3 ft June-August

Agrimony
2 ft June-August

Bog asphodel
6-15 in. July-September

Barberry
6-7 ft May-June

Mullein, Greater
1-6 ft June-August

Golden rod
6-30 in. July-September

Yellow loosestrife
2-6 ft July-August

St John's wort
1-3 ft June-September

Stonecrop, Biting
1-4 in. June-July

Buttercup, Celery-leaved
6-24 in. May-September

Buttercup, Corn
6-30 in. June-July

Goldilocks
3-15 in. April-May

Oxlip
4-12 in. April-May

Thorow-wax
6-12 in. June-July

Meadow-rue, Common
18-36 in. July-August

Lettuce, Wall
1-3 ft July-September

Yellow flowers: 8 or more petals

Hottentot fig
Trailing May-July

Bur-marigold
1-2 ft July-September

Catsear
1-2 ft June-September

Coltsfoot
3-9 in. March-April

Dandelion
2-12 in. March-October

Elecampane
2-5 ft July-August

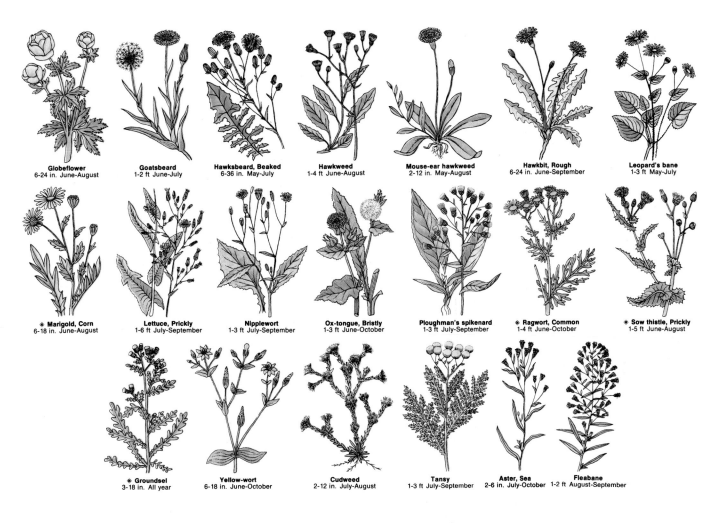

Globeflower
6-24 in. June-August

Goatsbeard
1-2 ft June-July

Hawksbeard, Beaked
6-36 in. May-July

Hawkweed
1-4 ft June-August

Mouse-ear hawkweed
2-12 in. May-August

Hawkbit, Rough
6-24 in. June-September

Leopard's bane
1-3 ft May-July

✽ **Marigold, Corn**
6-18 in. June-August

Lettuce, Prickly
1-6 ft July-September

Nipplewort
1-3 ft July-September

Ox-tongue, Bristly
1-3 ft June-October

Ploughman's spikenard
1-3 ft July-September

✽ **Ragwort, Common**
1-4 ft June-October

✽ **Sow thistle, Prickly**
1-5 ft June-August

✽ **Groundsel**
3-18 in. All year

Yellow-wort
6-18 in. June-October

Cudweed
2-12 in. July-August

Tansy
1-3 ft July-September

Aster, Sea
2-6 in. July-October

Fleabane
1-2 ft August-September

Blue flowers: up to 4 petals

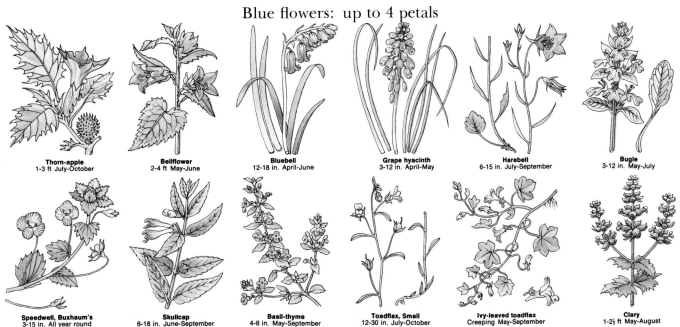

Thorn-apple
1-3 ft July-October

Bellflower
2-4 ft May-June

Bluebell
12-18 in. April-June

Grape hyacinth
3-12 in. April-May

Harebell
6-15 in. July-September

Bugle
3-12 in. May-July

Speedwell, Buxhaum's
3-15 in. All year round

Skullcap
6-18 in. June-September

Basil-thyme
4-8 in. May-September

Toadflax, Small
12-30 in. July-October

Ivy-leaved toadflax
Creeping May-September

Clary
1-2½ ft May-August

511

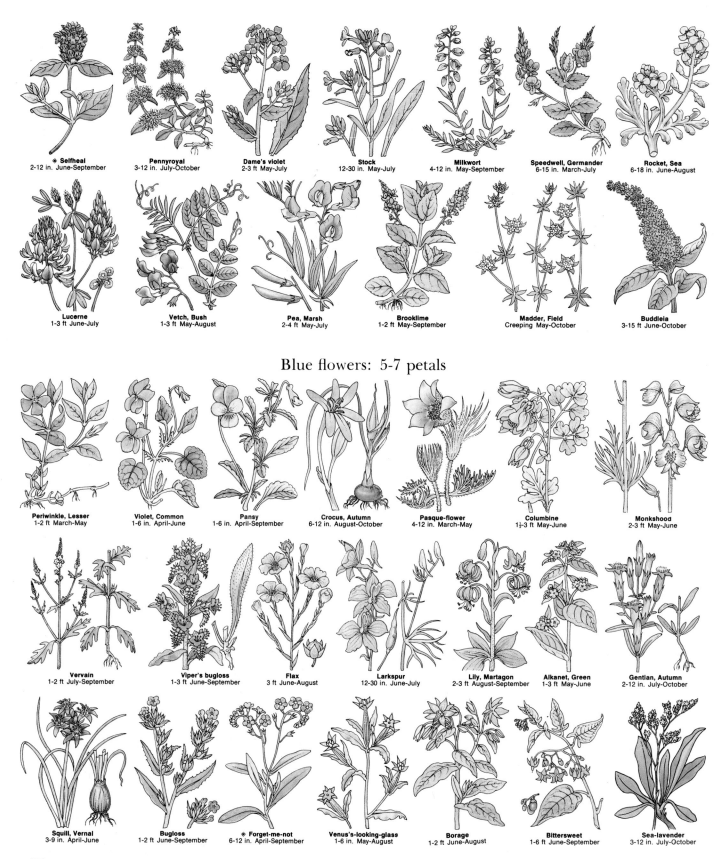

✻ Selfheal
2-12 in. June-September

Pennyroyal
3-12 in. July-October

Dame's violet
2-3 ft May-July

Stock
12-30 in. May-July

Milkwort
4-12 in. May-September

Speedwell, Germander
6-15 in. March-July

Rocket, Sea
6-18 in. June-August

Lucerne
1-3 ft June-July

Vetch, Bush
1-3 ft May-August

Pea, Marsh
2-4 ft May-July

Brooklime
1-2 ft May-September

Madder, Field
Creeping May-October

Buddleia
3-15 ft June-October

Blue flowers: 5-7 petals

Periwinkle, Lesser
1-2 ft March-May

Violet, Common
1-6 in. April-June

Pansy
1-6 in. April-September

Crocus, Autumn
6-12 in. August-October

Pasque-flower
4-12 in. March-May

Columbine
1½-3 ft May-June

Monkshood
2-3 ft May-June

Vervain
1-2 ft July-September

Viper's bugloss
1-3 ft June-September

Flax
3 ft June-August

Larkspur
12-30 in. June-July

Lily, Martagon
2-3 ft August-September

Alkanet, Green
1-3 ft May-June

Gentian, Autumn
2-12 in. July-October

Squill, Vernal
3-9 in. April-June

Bugloss
1-2 ft June-September

✻ Forget-me-not
6-12 in. April-September

Venus's-looking-glass
1-6 in. May-August

Borage
1-2 ft June-August

Bittersweet
1-6 ft June-September

Sea-lavender
3-12 in. July-October

512

Blue flowers: 8 or more petals

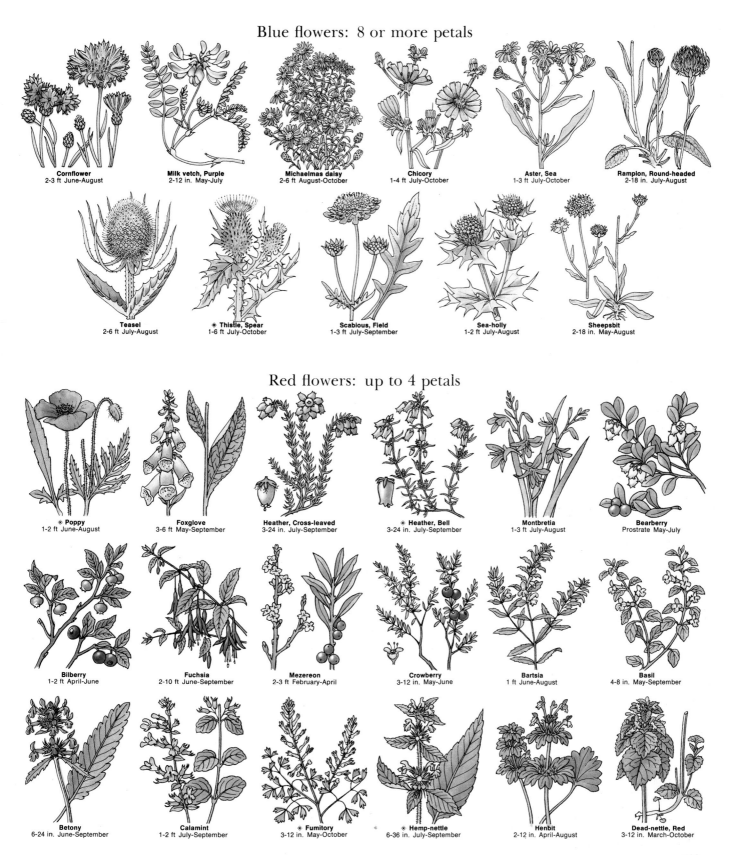

Cornflower
2-3 ft June-August

Milk vetch, Purple
2-12 in. May-July

Michaelmas daisy
2-6 ft August-October

Chicory
1-4 ft July-October

Aster, Sea
1-3 ft July-October

Rampion, Round-headed
2-18 in. July-August

Teasel
2-6 ft July-August

❋ **Thistle, Spear**
1-6 ft July-October

Scabious, Field
1-3 ft July-September

Sea-holly
1-2 ft July-August

Sheepsbit
2-18 in. May-August

Red flowers: up to 4 petals

❋ **Poppy**
1-2 ft June-August

Foxglove
3-6 ft May-September

Heather, Cross-leaved
3-24 in. July-September

❋ **Heather, Bell**
3-24 in. July-September

Montbretia
1-3 ft July-August

Bearberry
Prostrate May-July

Bilberry
1-2 ft April-June

Fuchsia
2-10 ft June-September

Mezereon
2-3 ft February-April

Crowberry
3-12 in. May-June

Bartsia
1 ft June-August

Basil
4-8 in. May-September

Betony
6-24 in. June-September

Calamint
1-2 ft July-September

❋ **Fumitory**
3-12 in. May-October

❋ **Hemp-nettle**
6-36 in. July-September

Henbit
2-12 in. April-August

Dead-nettle, Red
3-12 in. March-October

513

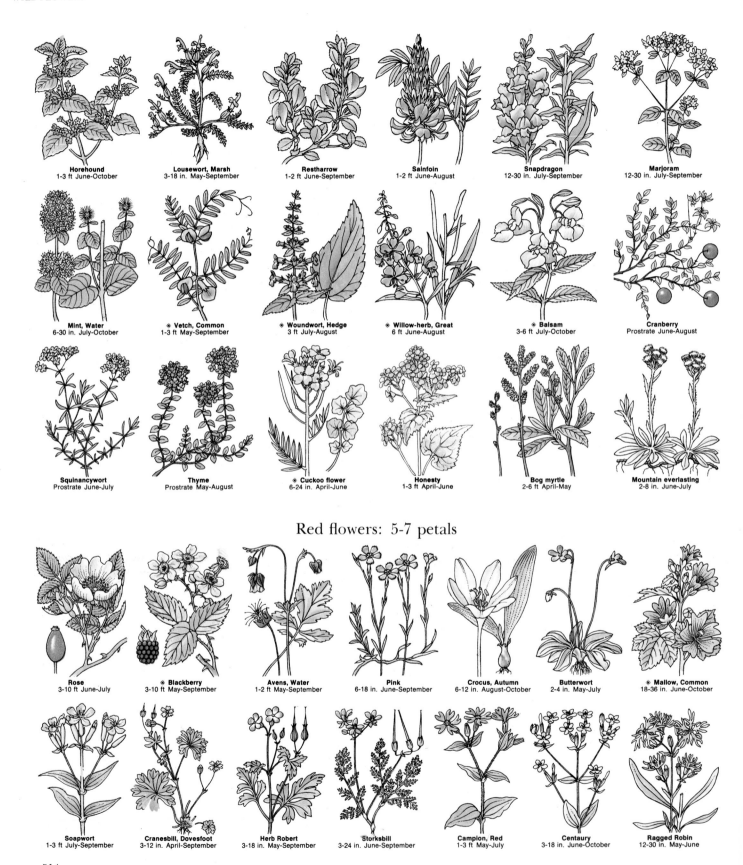

Horehound
1-3 ft June-October

Lousewort, Marsh
3-18 in. May-September

Restharrow
1-2 ft June-September

Sainfoin
1-2 ft June-August

Snapdragon
12-30 in. July-September

Marjoram
12-30 in. July-September

Mint, Water
6-30 in. July-October

❋ Vetch, Common
1-3 ft May-September

❋ Woundwort, Hedge
3 ft July-August

❋ Willow-herb, Great
6 ft June-August

❋ Balsam
3-6 ft July-October

Cranberry
Prostrate June-August

Squinancywort
Prostrate June-July

Thyme
Prostrate May-August

❋ Cuckoo flower
6-24 in. April-June

Honesty
1-3 ft April-June

Bog myrtle
2-6 ft April-May

Mountain everlasting
2-8 in. June-July

Red flowers: 5-7 petals

Rose
3-10 ft June-July

❋ Blackberry
3-10 ft May-September

Avens, Water
1-2 ft May-September

Pink
6-18 in. June-September

Crocus, Autumn
6-12 in. August-October

Butterwort
2-4 in. May-July

❋ Mallow, Common
18-36 in. June-October

Soapwort
1-3 ft July-September

Cranesbill, Dovesfoot
3-12 in. April-September

Herb Robert
3-18 in. May-September

Storksbill
3-24 in. June-September

Campion, Red
1-3 ft May-July

Centaury
3-18 in. June-October

Ragged Robin
12-30 in. May-June

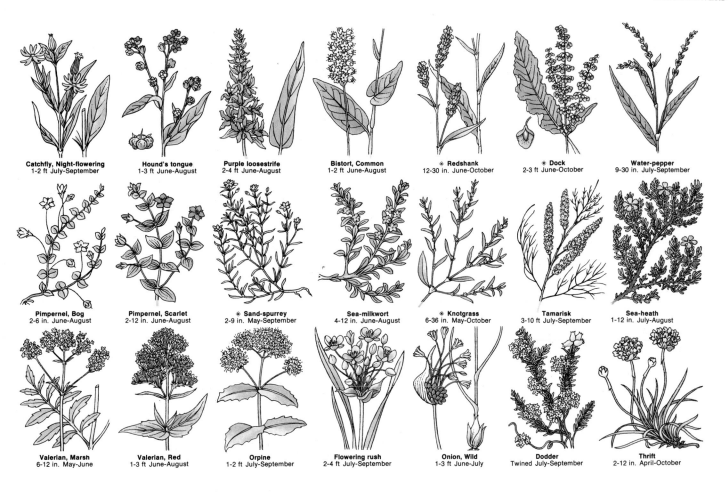

Catchfly, Night-flowering
1-2 ft July-September

Hound's tongue
1-3 ft June-August

Purple loosestrife
2-4 ft June-August

Bistort, Common
1-2 ft June-August

* **Redshank**
12-30 in. June-October

* **Dock**
2-3 ft June-October

Water-pepper
9-30 in. July-September

Pimpernel, Bog
2-6 in. June-August

Pimpernel, Scarlet
2-12 in. June-August

* **Sand-spurrey**
2-9 in. May-September

Sea-milkwort
4-12 in. June-August

* **Knotgrass**
6-36 in. May-October

Tamarisk
3-10 ft July-September

Sea-heath
1-12 in. July-August

Valerian, Marsh
6-12 in. May-June

Valerian, Red
1-3 ft June-August

Orpine
1-2 ft July-September

Flowering rush
2-4 ft July-September

Onion, Wild
1-3 ft June-July

Dodder
Twined July-September

Thrift
2-12 in. April-October

Red flowers: 8 or more petals

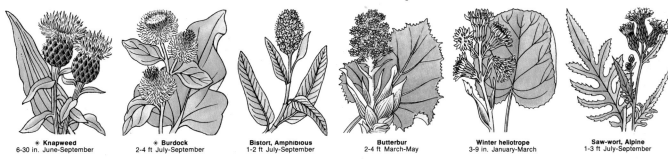

* **Knapweed**
6-30 in. June-September

* **Burdock**
2-4 ft July-September

Bistort, Amphibious
1-2 ft July-September

Butterbur
2-4 ft March-May

Winter heliotrope
3-9 in. January-March

Saw-wort, Alpine
1-3 ft July-September

Green and inconspicuous flowers: up to 4 petals

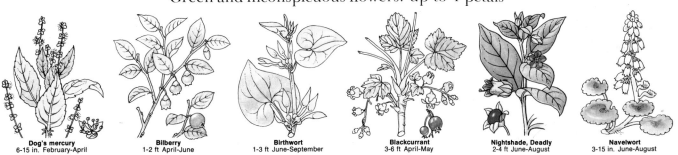

Dog's mercury
6-15 in. February-April

Bilberry
1-2 ft April-June

Birthwort
1-3 ft June-September

Blackcurrant
3-6 ft April-May

Nightshade, Deadly
2-4 ft June-August

Navelwort
3-15 in. June-August

515

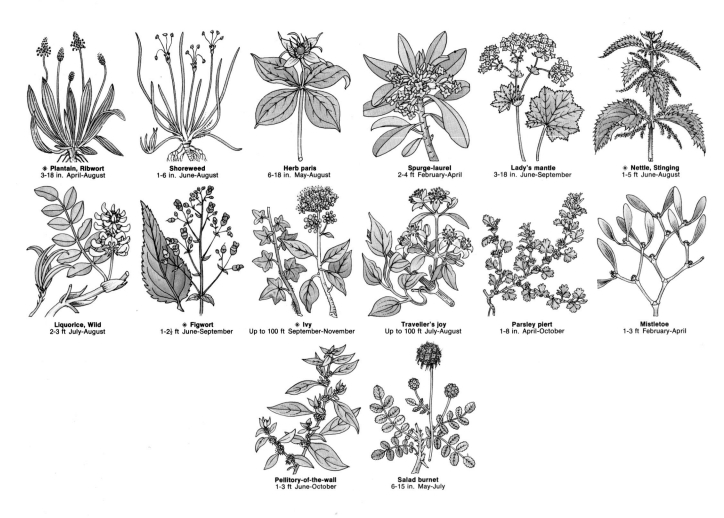

Plantain, Ribwort
3-18 in. April-August

Shoreweed
1-6 in. June-August

Herb paris
6-18 in. May-August

Spurge-laurel
2-4 ft February-April

Lady's mantle
3-18 in. June-September

Nettle, Stinging
1-5 ft June-August

Liquorice, Wild
2-3 ft July-August

Figwort
1-2½ ft June-September

Ivy
Up to 100 ft September-November

Traveller's joy
Up to 100 ft July-August

Parsley piert
1-8 in. April-October

Mistletoe
1-3 ft February-April

Pellitory-of-the-wall
1-3 ft June-October

Salad burnet
6-15 in. May-July

Green and inconspicuous flowers: 5 or more petals

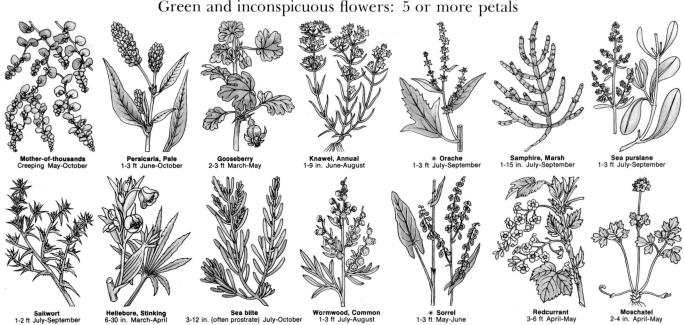

Mother-of-thousands
Creeping May-October

Persicaria, Pale
1-3 ft June-October

Gooseberry
2-3 ft March-May

Knawel, Annual
1-9 in. June-August

Orache
1-3 ft July-September

Samphire, Marsh
1-15 in. July-September

Sea purslane
1-3 ft July-September

Saltwort
1-2 ft July-September

Hellebore, Stinking
6-30 in. March-April

Sea blite
3-12 in. (often prostrate) July-October

Wormwood, Common
1-3 ft July-August

Sorrel
1-3 ft May-June

Redcurrant
3-6 ft April-May

Moschatel
2-4 in. April-May

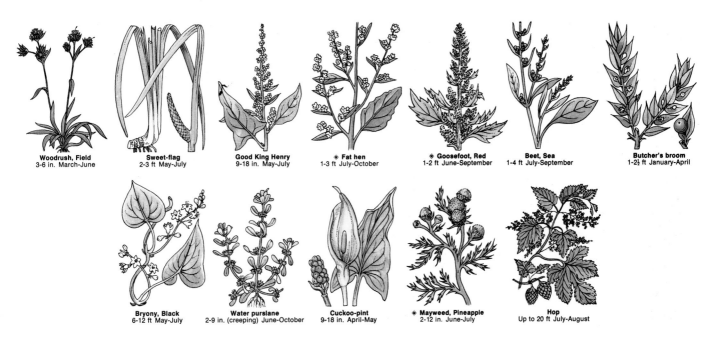

Woodrush, Field
3-6 in. March-June

Sweet-flag
2-3 ft May-July

Good King Henry
9-18 in. May-July

❋ **Fat hen**
1-3 ft July-October

❋ **Goosefoot, Red**
1-2 ft June-September

Beet, Sea
1-4 ft July-September

Butcher's broom
1-2½ ft January-April

Bryony, Black
6-12 ft May-July

Water purslane
2-9 in. (creeping) June-October

Cuckoo-pint
9-18 in. April-May

❋ **Mayweed, Pineapple**
2-12 in. June-July

Hop
Up to 20 ft July-August

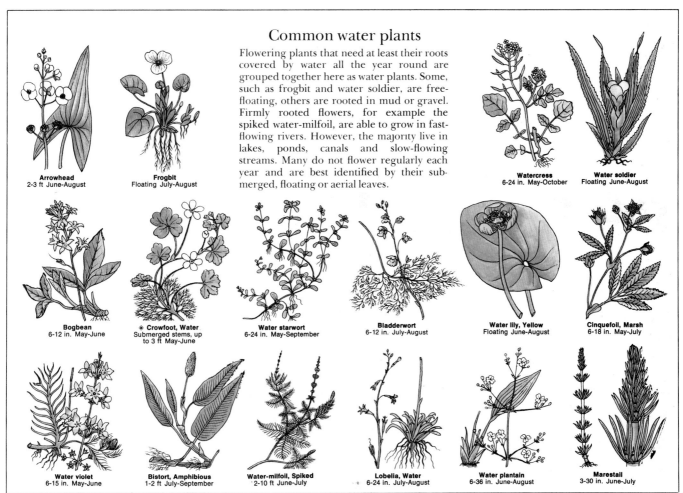

Common water plants

Flowering plants that need at least their roots covered by water all the year round are grouped together here as water plants. Some, such as frogbit and water soldier, are free-floating, others are rooted in mud or gravel. Firmly rooted flowers, for example the spiked water-milfoil, are able to grow in fast-flowing rivers. However, the majority live in lakes, ponds, canals and slow-flowing streams. Many do not flower regularly each year and are best identified by their submerged, floating or aerial leaves.

Arrowhead
2-3 ft June-August

Frogbit
Floating July-August

Watercress
6-24 in. May-October

Water soldier
Floating June-August

Bogbean
6-12 in. May-June

❋ **Crowfoot, Water**
Submerged stems, up to 3 ft May-June

Water starwort
6-24 in. May-September

Bladderwort
6-12 in. July-August

Water lily, Yellow
Floating June-August

Cinquefoil, Marsh
6-18 in. May-July

Water violet
6-15 in. May-June

Bistort, Amphibious
1-2 ft July-September

Water-milfoil, Spiked
2-10 ft June-July

Lobelia, Water
6-24 in. July-August

Water plantain
6-36 in. June-August

Marestail
3-30 in. June-July

Flat winkles are about the same size as the bladders of the wrack on which they lay eggs

Winkle
Also known as a periwinkle, this snail is common on rocky shores. There are four British species.

The brown or blue-black small winkle *Littorina neritoides*, which is ¼ in. high, lives in crevices in the splash zone at the top of the shore where the sea reaches it only during the high water of spring tides or in rough weather.

The rough winkle *L. saxatilis*, ¼-½ in. high, lives lower down the shore, between the splash zone and mid-tide level. Its yellow, orange, white or brown shell is ribbed.

The flat winkle *L. littoralis*, which is up to ½ in. high, lives on the middle and lower shore. It is misleadingly named, as its shell is rounded. It may be yellow, orange, green, brown or black and is about the same size as a bladder of the bladder wrack on to which it crawls to feed and lay its egg capsules. The flat winkle also crawls beneath the wrack to prevent itself being dried out at low tide.

The brown-black common or edible winkle *L. littorea*, ½-1 in. high, is the largest and most common species. It lives on the middle shore. Large numbers of this winkle cluster beneath seaweeds or in crevices when the tide recedes. Edible winkles are eaten by gulls, oystercatchers, plovers and redshanks, as well as man.

The small winkle lays eggs once a fortnight from September to April, when it is covered by the high water of spring tides. The larvae which hatch from the eggs swim about in the water until they become miniature adults, when they settle in the barnacle zone. From this they crawl laboriously up to the splash zone.

The rough winkle does not lay eggs. The young develop inside the female and are born as miniature adults complete with tiny shells in a matter of weeks. The flat winkle lays white eggs between March and October in a layer of jelly on bladder wrack and serrated wrack. There is no larval stage, and the eggs develop directly into small winkles.

The common winkle spawns from February to April, producing many egg capsules which each contain three eggs. The free-swimming larvae have only a short planktonic life and settle on the shore during May and June.

The small winkle feeds on lichens, the other three species on seaweeds and on detritus on rocks. All can seal the opening to the shell with a horny plate known as the operculum. See also SHELL

Winter-cress *Barbarea vulgaris*
A tall plant, growing to over 3 ft, winter-cress has dark divided leaves, each with a large round terminal lobe, which remain green throughout winter. Yellow, wall-flower-like blooms begin to appear in May, forming a dense cluster, which later develops into a long spike of stalked four-angled pods.

Winter-cress is common throughout the lowlands of Britain on stream banks, in ditches and other damp waste places. It was once valued as a salad, but disappeared from the table when finer-flavoured vegetables appeared.

A double-flowered variety named yellow rocket grows in gardens.

Winter fungus see Fungus

Wintergreen *Pyrola minor*
In the depth of winter, when most woodland herbs have withered, the leaves of wintergreen remain. Nearly round and over an inch in diameter, they closely resemble the leaves of pear trees in size and shape, and the scientific name stems from the Latin for pear.

Between June and August, pinkish-white flowers develop in short spikes up to 12 in. long. The plant spreads readily by underground stems and often grows in large patches. It also has very light seeds which carry long distances on the wind. It is widely but thinly scattered throughout the British Isles, though rare in the south and west. It is chiefly a plant of woodlands, especially pine woods, but also grows on open moorland and on sand dunes.

Winter heliotrope *Petasites fragrans*
In mild winters the lilac heads of winter heliotrope appear just after Christmas, growing 3-9 in. high. The flowers, which appear before the leaves, are sweet and vanilla-scented and so attract early flies and honey bees.

A native of the western Mediterranean, winter heliotrope was introduced to Britain as a garden plant; it is now common in the south and south-west, where it is often the dominant plant by streams or on roadside banks. It spreads through strong underground stems.

Winter moth
One of the most common moths in the British Isles, the winter moth is on the wing in early winter when other species are hibernating. Its green looper caterpillars—so called because of the way they move—can be found in May and June on almost any deciduous tree, especially oak and fruit trees. They are sometimes so numerous that they strip a tree of leaves. The number of caterpillars depends on how well the hatching out of the eggs coincides with the appearance of young leaves. Caterpillars which hatch very early cannot find leaves on which to feed, while those which hatch late find the leaves are too tough.

In years when there is a big population of caterpillars, there is a higher death rate in the chrysalis stage, probably because ground beetles concentrate on eating the easily obtainable chrysalids.

When fully grown, the caterpillars descend from the trees on silk threads and burrow into the soil to pupate. The moths hatch out in October or November and crawl back on to the tree trunks. The females are wingless and look like spiders. The males are thin-bodied, brownish-grey and have a 1 in. wingspan.

The moths hide during the day but the males are easy to see at night. They settle on tree trunks or fly lazily until they find a female. The females are well camouflaged and difficult to see. The best way to find one is to look for a male that is facing head

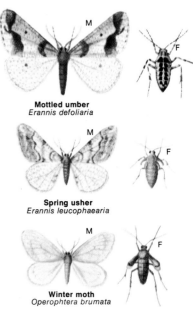
Mottled umber
Erannis defoliaria

Spring usher
Erannis leucophaearia

Winter moth
Operophtera brumata

These three moths, which are active in winter, all have spider-like, wingless females

downwards on a tree trunk. It will almost certainly be mating, and closer observation will reveal the female. After mating the female walks up to a branch of the tree to lay her eggs. Many females are trapped on the sticky bands growers put around the trunks of fruit trees.

Several other moths which appear in the winter months also have wingless females. Two common examples are the mottled umber, which can be seen from October to January, and the spring usher, which appears in February or March. In both species the males fly at night.

Wireworm see Click beetle

Witches' broom

Freak outgrowths of bunched twigs, resembling brooms, which appear on the branches of trees, particularly birches. All tree branches carry minute buds which do not normally develop. In a witches' broom some abnormal stimulus—an insect attack, a fungus, or a virus—causes a whole cluster of such buds to grow out together. Only minor harm is done to the tree's growth, and its timber is unaffected.

If twigs from witches' brooms are grafted on to normal rootstocks, freak trees result, showing that the attacking organism has changed the inherited growth pattern of the twigs.

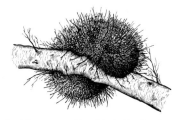

Witches' broom on silver birch. The freak growth is caused by insect attack, a fungus or a virus

Witches' butter see Fungus
Withy see Willow

Woad *Isatis tinctoria*

A plant whose leaves, when crushed and boiled, yield a deep and fast blue dye. Contrary to the widely held belief, woad was probably not used as a kind of war paint by the ancient Britons; the evidence suggests that it was introduced to Britain from southern Europe in Anglo-Saxon times. But woad *was* used by later Britons. Before the introduction of chemical dyes, in 1855, it was one of the most important dye plants in Britain. (The others were madder, which gave a deep rose or brown-pink, and weld, which produced yellow.) As late as the 1930's, woad cultivated in the Lincolnshire fens was used as a dye for policemen's uniforms. The dye is obtained by fermenting the leaves.

Today, woad grows as a wild plant only on a few inland cliffs in the south of England. It reaches a height of 4 ft, and a spike of four-petalled, honey-scented yellow flowers appears in July and August. The flowers develop into winged seed capsules.

Wolf *Canis lupus*

The wolf has been extinct in the British Isles for more than 200 years, but its memory lives on in many place names, such as Wolford, in Warwickshire, and Woolmer Forest, in Hampshire—names which show that the animal was once common and widespread. As late as the 10th century there is a record of the Anglo-Saxon King Edgar imposing a tribute of 300 dead wolves a year on a subject prince in Wales. That was in 962, at a time when much of the country was covered in forest. Gradually, as the land was cleared for agriculture, the wolf retreated to the more remote areas. In England, the last wolf was probably killed early in the 16th century, but a few lingered on in Scotland, Wales and Ireland. There is a tradition that the last wolf in Scotland was killed in Sutherland in 1743. There are no later records for Ireland and Wales. See also DOG

Wood-boring beetle

Britain has five wood-boring beetles, the most numerous and widespread of which is the furniture beetle *Anobium punctatum*. This tiny $\frac{1}{8}-\frac{1}{5}$ in. brown insect, also known as 'woodworm', can reduce pieces of woodwork to mere powder. It lays its eggs on dead wood in external cracks and crevices. The larvae hatch out in about a month and burrow into the wood, feeding on it for one to three years. Then they burrow to a point just below the surface before pupating. The adults hatch in June and burrow the short distance to freedom, making circular exit-holes, the familiar 'woodworm' holes. The adults live for one or two months.

The furniture beetle is closely related to the death-watch beetle, and there are many unrelated species which are sometimes given the general name of wood-boring beetles. These include the powder-post, stag, longhorn, cardinal, bark and ambrosia beetles.

Woodcock *Scolopax rusticola*

A shore bird that has taken to the woods. There, its russet plumage provides camouflage as it sits quietly among the leaves and grasses of the woodland floor. At dusk it flies to nearby marshy spots to probe in the ground for earthworms and insects.

In spring the male woodcock defines and defends its territory with a 'roding' flight. With its bill pointed downwards, it flies round and round its territory, uttering a thin 'tsiwick' and a low-pitched croaking call.

The only way to find a woodcock's nest is to tramp backwards and forwards through likely areas in the hope of flushing the sitting bird; even then it will sit tight on its four blotched grey-white to brown eggs until the last minute. The eyes, set on the sides of

EYES IN THE BACK OF ITS HEAD

Eyes set high and well to the sides of the woodcock's head giving it a 360° field of vision

The position of the woodcock's eyes gives it all-round vision, enabling it to see approaching enemies even when probing the mud for insects

the head, give it all-round vision, even when its long bill is probing the ground.

Chicks leave the nest a few hours after they are hatched. Fully grown birds are $13\frac{1}{2}$ in. long.

Woodland see p. 522

Woodlouse

This is the only land-living relative of the aquatic crabs, shrimps and lobsters. The woodlouse or sowbug most likely to be seen is about $\frac{1}{2}$ in. long, oval in shape, with a slightly domed back, and is slate-grey in colour with irregular lighter markings. It lives under logs, stones and leaves. Another fairly common species is the pill-bug which rolls up into a ball when disturbed.

Woodlice do not have a fully waterproof body covering and will die of desiccation in just a few hours if they become too dry. They avoid the light and emerge from their hiding places only at night, when it is cool and damp, to feed. They will eat anything within reach, and many are scavengers. Their favourite foods are dead wood and leaves, but some eat soft, living materials such as ripe fruit.

Several broods of between seven and 200 eggs are produced each year. The female carries her eggs in a pouch beneath the front part of her body. They hatch out within the pouch in three to five weeks and the young woodlice emerge after a few days. A woodlouse has a normal life-span of just over a year, during which time it passes through nine or ten moults.

A common woodlouse
Oniscus asellus

Pill-bug
Armadillidium vulgare

The pill-bug curls into a ball when danger threatens, but *Oniscus asellus* cannot roll up tightly and usually runs away when disturbed

Green woodpecker and its nest—a hole bored in a tree with its tough beak

THE WOODPECKER'S TONGUE

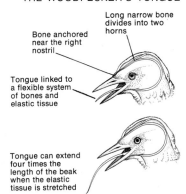

Long narrow bone divides into two horns

Bone anchored near the right nostril

Tongue linked to a flexible system of bones and elastic tissue

Tongue can extend four times the length of the beak when the elastic tissue is stretched

The green woodpecker can stretch its tongue up to 6 in. beyond the end of its beak to winkle out insects hidden behind the bark of a tree.

Woodpecker

There are three species of woodpeckers in Britain, but none in Ireland. Only the greater spotted is numerous in Scotland, although the population of green woodpeckers there is increasing.

A woodpecker makes its nest by pecking a hole in a tree or telegraph pole. The hen bird lays four to seven white eggs on wood chippings in the hole. Woodpeckers get most of their food by digging into bark or rotten wood for grubs and insects. They also tattoo on resonant dead branches to produce a territorial 'song', a warning to other woodpeckers to keep out of their territory.

The green woodpecker is, at 12½ in. long, the largest and most destructive. Its loud laughing call, which is one of the most characteristic woodland sounds, gives the bird its country name of yaffle. As well as eating tree insects, it often feeds on ants on the ground. It has also learnt to take scraps from bird-tables. The female lays her eggs in April or May. They hatch after

19 days and the nestlings fly three weeks later.

The two other species of woodpeckers are black and white. The greater spotted, 9 in. long, has two prominent white ovals on its back, and the lesser spotted, 5¾ in. long, has a barred back. Both have a touch of red on the head. The greater spotted woodpecker is common, especially in woods, whereas the lesser spotted is much rarer. The lesser spotted is also less of a woodland bird than its larger relative and spends much of its time searching for food in hedgerow timber and smaller trees that are ignored by the greater spotted.

The greater spotted woodpecker raids the nests of other birds, and in its quest for chicks has learnt to break open nest boxes, even ones made from concrete. It has no song, but instead makes a loud drumming by hammering with its beak on dead wood. The eggs, laid in May, hatch after 16 days and the nestlings fly three weeks later.

The greater spotted woodpecker was extinct in northern Britain in the early 19th century when Thomas Bewick made this engraving. It has since re-established itself and is now widespread

Woodrush

Woodrush is distinguished from the true rushes, to which it is related, by flattened grass-like leaves with long hairs on their margins. The plant usually grows in tufts,

spreading by short horizontal stems; the six-petalled flowers are chestnut-brown and develop into a shiny capsule containing three seeds.

Ten species occur in Britain. The most common, field woodrush, is also known as cuckoo-grass because it looks like a grass and flowers between April and June, when the cuckoo is present. It grows in grassland everywhere and rarely exceeds 6 in. in height.

In contrast, great woodrush grows up to 3 ft, usually in the acid soil of oak woods and on the rocky slopes of moors, where perhaps oak once grew. It flowers everywhere in the British Isles from May to June, but is more common in the north and west.

Hairy woodrush is also a common woodland plant, but grows to only 1 ft high. It also occurs in hedgebanks, and flowers from April until June throughout Britain: in Ireland it grows mainly in the east. Each flower is on a long stalk which turns downwards as the fruits ripen.

Wood woolly foot fungus see Fungus
Woolly bear see Tiger moth

Wormwood

Common wormwood *Artemisia absinthium* is a bushy plant up to 3 ft tall with silvery leaves and yellow flowers. It grows in waste places throughout England, Wales and southern Scotland, flowering between July and August. It is an exceedingly bitter herb and, infused in alcohol, is used to make the French liqueur absinthe or to flavour vermouths. As an infusion in water it was once taken by country people as a tonic and as a method of expelling intestinal worms. It was also used as an insecticide.

Sea wormwood *A. maritima* is a smaller plant, 6-18 in. tall, with very finely divided leaves which are woolly on both sides. It grows in the drier parts of salt-marshes and on sea walls, except in the far north.

Woundwort

The soft hairy leaves of woundwort were once used in dressing wounds—hence its name. The stems are square and the two-lipped flowers are arranged in a spike which gives its name to the genus Stachys, from the Greek for spike.

Three species are widespread in Britain, all with purplish flowers. Field woundwort is low-growing, with small flowers only ¼ in. long which appear from June until October. The stems, branching from the base, may reach 9 in. Once a common arable weed on soils poor in lime, it has declined following the introduction of stubble burning and earlier ploughing.

Hedge woundwort is one of the most common plants of hedgebanks in lowland Britain, easily recognised by its ½ in. long claret-coloured flowers and heart-shaped hairy leaves which smell rank when crushed. It grows up to 3 ft tall, flowers in July

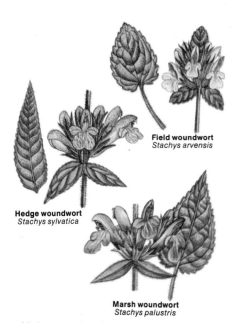

Hedge woundwort
Stachys sylvatica

Field woundwort
Stachys arvensis

Marsh woundwort
Stachys palustris

All three species of woundworts have soft, hairy leaves which were once used to dress wounds

and August and may also be found in woods and shaded waste places. Marsh woundwort is similar, but has much narrower leaves and usually grows in wetter conditions. Where these last two species grow together they hybridise, and plants with intermediate leaf shapes may be found.

Wrasse

The most colourful fish in the seas round the British Isles are the three wrasses. They have stout bodies with well-developed spiny fins and large scales, and strong teeth with which they eat heavy-shelled molluscs and crustaceans. In addition to the teeth in their jaws there are flat grinding teeth in the back of the throat, behind the gills, which can crush the hardest of shells into powder.

The ballan wrasse *Labrus bergylta* is the largest of the three, growing to about 20 in. It is also the most widespread, being common along the western coast and occasionally seen elsewhere. It is usually green or greeny-brown, sometimes reddish. The scales on its sides have white centres.

The cuckoo wrasse *L. mixtus* is more strikingly coloured. The male has a vivid blue head, orange sides and belly. The female and immature male are a uniform orange or red with three black blotches along the back near the tail. The cuckoo wrasse is less common than the ballan, but is found in the same areas.

A more common species is the corkwing *Crenilabrus melops*, which grows to 6 in. It is usually a green colour, but sometimes brown, and has a dark spot just in front of the tail fin. It is most abundant near rocky shores, and young fish are often caught in tide pools.

Wren *Troglodytes troglodytes*

At 3¾ in. long, the wren is one of the smallest and best known of British birds (only the goldcrest is smaller). It is easily recognised by its short turned-up tail and a song which seems penetratingly loud for so small a bird. In folklore, anyone who harmed a wren was sure to meet a terrible fate soon after.

Wrens are found throughout Britain, even on remote uninhabited islands, where they sometimes form a separate sub-species, as at St Kilda in the Outer Hebrides. They are present all year.

On the mainland, wrens hunt in woods, copses and gardens, looking for insects in the bark of trees and among ground plants. They are sensitive to bad weather and their numbers fell severely in the exceptionally cold winter of 1962-3. They often huddle together on winter nights to keep warm, and as many as 40 have been found roosting in a single nest box.

The cock bird builds several domed nests of moss, leaves and grass in low bushes, creepers, stacks of wood or hollows in walls, and the hen chooses one of these and lines it with feathers. She lays 5-12 white eggs with fine red-brown spots from late April onwards. Incubation, by the female only, lasts about 14 days. The nestlings, which are fed by both parents, fly after about 15 days. Two broods are generally raised each year.

In areas where there is a plentiful food supply, males have several mates.

The wren often chooses a hole in a wall in which to build its nest of moss, leaves and grass

Wryneck *Jynx torquilla*

A bird named for its ability to turn its head completely round on its neck. It is a relative of the woodpeckers but lacks their bold patterning and colouring. The browns and greys and the barring and mottling of its plumage enable it to merge with trees, bark and lichens.

The wryneck, 8½ in. long, is a summer visitor to Britain, and favours old orchards. It picks insects, mainly ants, from the bark and from the ground. It was once common in southern and eastern England but has declined in numbers drastically over the past 20 years, possibly through insecticide poisoning. By the late 1960's only a few pairs remained in Kent and Surrey. However, birds which are probably of Scandinavian descent have started to breed in Scotland.

The wryneck does not bore into trees with its bill for food or to make a nest, like woodpeckers, but uses a ready-made hole in a tree or wall, or a nest box, in which to lay its seven to ten white eggs.

The 'quee-quee-quee' which it emits for a fortnight or so in May is the best means of locating the bird on its territory. It is likely to be seen in autumn on the east coast.

Woodland's hidden wealth of wildlife

The deceptive stillness of a wood conceals thousands of animals, from aphids to owls; feeding on the plant-eaters are predators, above these other predators and so on. Their inter-relationships form an intricate web

The autumn sun lights up the edge of a wood. Still and soundless, it seems to

A larger variety of plants and animals live in woodland than in any other part of the countryside. The casual visitor will see only about a dozen animals—most commonly birds and butterflies—but a detailed survey which was undertaken in a wood near Oxford has identified at least 4000 different species and has revealed the complex web of relationships by which they live together.

This wood, which is typical of deciduous woodland on calcareous soil in southern England, covers a 700 acre hill. The lower slopes are on clay and support oak, ash, sycamore and maple, often with dense bracken and bramble beneath. Then comes a thinner layer of sand, much used by burrowing animals, such as badgers, foxes and rabbits. On top is a limestone cap with poorer soil where patches of silver birch and planted beeches intrude and the undergrowth is much sparser.

In this wood a certain amount of forestry management has taken place, and substantial areas are covered with young trees—mainly oaks and beeches, interspersed with some conifers. The foresters have cleaned up some of the remaining woodland, thinning the younger trees and removing some of the older ones that were dead or dying. Nevertheless, there are still considerable areas which are reasonably close to the original state of the woodland.

The organisms in woodland fall into two broad categories: producers and consumers. The producers are the plants, which, in the presence of sunlight, synthesise substances from minerals, water and carbon dioxide. The consumers are, first, the plant-eating animals, ranging from aphids to deer; above them their predators; above these, their predators; and so on. There are also the parasites which live on animals of all levels. In addition to these green-plant food-relationships are the dead-plant ones involving the 'decomposers'. The most important of these are the fungi and bacteria, whose role is to break down dead animal and plant material and return the nutrients to the soil for further plant growth.

As most animals eat many kinds of food, the food-relationships in woodland take the form of an intricate web rather than independent chains.

The living space in a wood can be divided into layers. Some animals move between layers—for example the grey squirrel, which forages for food on the ground but takes to the treetops for sleeping, breeding, travelling and escaping from predators. Others live their whole life cycle at one level—for example shrews keep mainly to the ground zone and the spotted flycatcher nests in the shrub layer and catches insects on the wing at this level.

By specialisation of the last kind many more animal species

can be fitted into the woodland environment, since competition for space is not as great as in less complex habitats, such as fields, marshes and moorland, which do not provide as many 'places to live' as woodland.

The lowest layer is the subsoil derived from bedrock. It is biologically inactive and the only forms of life there are burrowing animals such as rabbits and badgers and, occasionally, earthworms, which take refuge there during drought.

The next layer, the topsoil, is the lowest organic layer and, together with the layer above—which consists of dead leaves

the casual onlooker devoid of life, but in fact every part—canopy, tree trunks, plants, fallen leaves and soil—is teeming with animal activity

and plants up to 6 in. high—is rich in decomposing organisms which live on dead and dying plant material and dead animals. Fungi and bacteria are the primary decomposing agents of dead plants but a community of specialised animals follows them. These include earthworms, moth caterpillars, the larvae of flies, beetles and other insects, centipedes, millipedes and woodlice; the smaller springtails and mites; and species of minute worms.

Without all these 'decomposers', dead leaves, wood and animals would accumulate year after year without releasing materials to contribute to the growth of new plants.

The actual surface of the ground and its vegetation of mosses, lichens, liverworts and low-growing flowering plants contain a great variety of animals that are more mobile than those of the soil and litter—grasshoppers, flies, beetles, spiders, harvestmen, ants, voles, mice and shrews, some living on plants and some on other animals. Some have their shelters or hibernation sites in the underlying soil and emerge on to the ground or move up to higher levels of the woodland environment with various rhythms, daily or seasonal.

Of the bird species, the chiffchaff and willow warbler, for example, nest on the ground but ascend to the canopy to live and feed; others, such as the robin and pheasant, feed and nest on the ground but roost higher up; and the tawny owl catches its main prey, mice and voles, on the ground but stays aloft the rest of the time.

Again, the winter moth emerges from its pupal stage in the ground during November and December, but the wingless females climb the tree trunks to lay their eggs around the leaf buds in the canopy. These eggs hatch in the spring and the larvae grow by feeding on the tender young leaves as they unfold; in some years the larvae are so abundant that the trees are completely defoliated and grow a second set of leaves. At this stage the larvae become apparent even to the casual observer; on a still day the rain-like pattering of masses of their droppings falling can be heard, and in the open spaces beneath the canopy larvae letting themselves down to the ground on silken threads can be seen; they pupate in the ground where they remain out of sight until the following winter, when they emerge as moths.

The layer up to about 6 ft above the ground is known as the field layer. It is composed mainly of herbaceous and low woody plants, including tree saplings and bracken. In places where there is more light—in glades, along the edges of woodland or on clay soils under an interrupted canopy—the field layer may be an impenetrable tangle. This is the layer where flowering plants flourish, and its animals include insects that eat plant tissues and those that visit flowers for nectar, pollen or, later, fruits.

The visitors include hoverflies, beetles, wasps and bees, gnats, tabanid flies and mosquitoes, the last three of which suck blood from mammals and birds. The most striking are butterflies, such as the speckled wood and brimstone and, at night, a multitude of moths. Here spiders trap hosts of flying prey in their webs, and wasps pounce on others.

Dead wood of fallen trees and branches provides some of the most densely populated woodland habitats. A single dead tree may contain hundreds of animal species as well as supporting mosses, fungi and other plants

Many species of birds feed, shelter and nest in the field layer. They include most of the warblers, the hedge sparrow, the wren and some hole-nesting species such as the coal tit. Small mammals, such as the dormouse, live mostly at this level (though not in the wood near Oxford), while others—woodmice and bank voles—occasionally climb up to this level from the ground. The leafy growth of young tree saplings also provides forage for fallow and roe deer.

Above the field layer is the shrub layer, or lower canopy, which extends between 6 ft and 15 ft above the ground. This contains such attractive flowering shrubs as hawthorn, blackthorn, dogwood, elder, guelder rose, dog rose, spindle and buckthorn. As in the field layer, many insects feed on the leaves, flowers and fruits of these shrubs. Titmice, redstarts and pied flycatchers nest in holes here, as do grey squirrels. This is also about the lowest level to which the climbing birds—woodpeckers, nuthatch and tree creepers—descend to seek food on the trunks and large branches of trees. These carry out the rest of their searching for insects in the highest layer of all, the canopy.

In Britain the canopy usually extends up to about 60 ft. Animal life is poorer at these higher levels, but in the canopy of oak woods there is a rich and varied community of insects for the short period when the leaves are opening. In the wood near Oxford 1600 insect species have been recorded, closely associated with oak.

The canopy of the sycamore, on the other hand, is remarkable not for the range of its insects but for the numbers. Sometimes every leaf has a score or more aphids sucking at it and excreting honeydew which, in summer, makes the upper sides of the leaves glisten. This dense aphid population attracts such predators as spiders and the larvae of lacewings, ladybirds and hoverflies, while the honeydew attracts parasitic wasps, soldier beetles, hoverflies and bibionid flies. In other woods, wood ants often take charge of the aphids and 'farm' them for honeydew.

The high canopy is a relatively safe place, and most of the larger birds nest there: predators such as the sparrowhawk, tawny owl and hobby, plant-eaters such as the wood-pigeon, and omnivorous species such as the carrion crow, magpie, jackdaw and jay.

In addition to these layers there are other small, short-lived habitats scattered throughout woodland. The most abundant and long-lived is dead wood: in one part of the Oxford wood about 30 per cent of the hawthorn and of the oak wood above ground was dead. Samples of dead wood contained nearly 200 species of animals. In managed woodland, where foresters remove rotting wood, much of this rich life is lost. Dung is widespread and provides another scattered habitat, inhabited by more than 300 animal species—chiefly beetles and flies—which rapidly break it down. Carrion is also widespread and is colonised by burying-beetles, blowflies and, later, many other beetles and flies.

Many fungi are transitory, like dung and carrion, and as quickly broken down, mainly by fungus flies. Others are comparatively long-lived, such as those that infect dead and dying wood and produce bracket-like fruiting bodies. An example is the birch bracket fungus, which grows in late summer and early autumn, produces spores through the winter and dies the following spring, after which it may remain on the tree for up to three years. In this time, a succession of animals, mainly beetles and flies, inhabit and finally destroy it.

Tawny owl Roosts by day in the canopy, nestling against ivy in the crook of the oak

Mobbing birds Songthrush, chaffinch, great tit, blue tit and jay. The roosting owl can often be located by the noise made by these smaller birds as they mob their predator in an attempt to dislodge him.

The Complexity of Woodland Life

In its living and feeding habits —even in death—the tawny owl affects the lives of countless of its neighbours. In life, the owl preys on many small animals, and at the same time supports a community of fleas, lice and other parasites among its feathers. In death, the owl's body feeds carrion beetles and other scavengers. The owl is just one of thousands of woodland species, each of which is the centre of a similar network, in the complex, interconnected world of a woodland community

Wood mouse A favourite food of the owl. Most of its prey is caught from the ground layer of the woodland

Mole Large numbers of moles are hunted by young tawny owls that have just left their nest

Tawny owl Perches on its hunting station at night, waiting for small birds and mammals to move below it.

Young tawny owls The 2-4 eggs are laid in a hole in the tree. The young birds are fed mainly by the male

Robin and blackbird Birds of the shrub layer. The owl gets a small part of its food from the animals of this layer

Rabbit The tawny owl often snatches small mammals, such as young rabbits, from the ground layer. It detects them by sound rather than sight

Dung beetles Minotaur beetles on rabbit dung

Earthworms When mice and moles are scarce the owl will eat earthworms

Carrion beetles The owl eats the beetles that feed on a dead tawny owl

Owl pellets Bones, fur and feathers are regurgitated by the owl as large pellets

Y Z

Yarrow *Achillea millefolium*

One of the most common wild flowers, found in grassland all over the British Isles. It is a perennial which blooms throughout summer, especially by roadsides.

Growing up to 18 in. tall, with rough angular stems, yarrow bears flat heads of white, pink and occasionally deep purple flowers, which at first sight appear to be one large flower.

Yarrow was once prized as a herb to heal wounds. It was called *Achillea* because, in Homer's *Iliad*, Achilles is said to have cured his soldiers' wounds with yarrow.

Millefolium means literally thousand leaf and refers to the feathery leaves.

The flat flower heads of yarrow bloom all summer in grassland throughout Britain

Yeast

A microscopic single-celled fungus which occurs naturally on the surface of fruits. There are several different species. In the presence of oxygen, yeast cells convert sugar to carbon dioxide and water. On the other hand, if they are starved of oxygen, they convert sugar to equal parts of carbon dioxide and alcohol by fermentation.

In baking, yeast is added to the raw dough which is kept in a warm place so that the carbon dioxide bubbles given off will make it rise. In brewing, yeast feeds on a sugar called maltose extracted from germinating barley grain. Both carbon dioxide and alcohol are produced. Hops are then added to give the beer its characteristic bitter flavour. Spirits, such as whisky, are obtained by distilling a fermented liquor. Wine is fermented by natural yeasts on the skin of the fruit—the bloom on a grape. Under favourable conditions the spherical yeast cells reproduce rapidly by budding—each cell giving rise to two. If budding takes place quickly, a chain of cells becomes formed, as new cells start to bud off cells before they separate. Sometimes two cells become fused together. They then divide into four and a thick wall is formed around the group. This spore can survive unfavourable conditions, such as drying.

Yellow butterfly

The name butterfly was probably first coined to describe the bright butter-yellow male brimstone. This species is the first to be seen in Britain each year, since it hibernates as an adult, emerging in February or March to mate. The green-yellow female lays green eggs singly on buckthorn leaves on which the caterpillars feed after hatching. The old butterflies die in May or June, after up to 11 months in the adult stage. In July the caterpillars pupate, emerging as adults after about 14 days. They spend the rest of the summer flying and feeding on flowers. When the first frosts kill the autumn flowers, sometimes as late as October, the brimstone hibernates, usually among ivy leaves.

Brimstones are common throughout most of England, Wales and southern Ireland, but are rare in Scotland.

Three species of Clouded Yellow butter-

The yellow butterflies

Pale clouded yellow
Colias hyale

Common clouded yellow
Colias crocea

Brimstone
Gonepteryx rhamni

Berger's clouded yellow
Colias australis

The three species of Clouded Yellow butterflies are migrants from southern Europe; the brimstone is a native

The brimstone emerges in February—the first butterfly to be seen in Britain each year

flies are seen in Britain; all are migrants from the warmer parts of Europe. The most common species is the deep orange-yellow Common Clouded Yellow; the others are the Pale Clouded Yellow and Berger's Clouded Yellow, both much paler.

In most years only a few Clouded Yellows reach southern England. But sometimes large numbers migrate to Britain and breed here, making the butterfly common in late summer. Only rarely is the Common Clouded Yellow found as far north as Scotland.

The green caterpillars of all three species feed on clover and lucerne. The butterflies emerge in autumn, and sometimes produce a new generation of caterpillars, but these rarely survive the British winter.

Yellow cress

Three species of yellow cress grow in the British Isles. The most widespread is the annual marsh yellow cress. It germinates on bare mud in places that are wet in winter and dry in summer—such as the margins of ponds and lakes—and may reach a height of 2 ft. Like other yellow cresses, it bears four-petalled yellow flowers from June to September, with petals barely as long as the sepals—the leaf-like scales which enclose the flower. It has short seed pods. Marsh yellow cress grows throughout the British Isles, except the far north.

Creeping yellow cress grows to about the same height, but has creeping stems and petals twice as long as its sepals. The flowers develop into long seed pods. The plant grows in wet areas by streams and occasionally persists as a weed by roadsides and in gardens.

Greater yellow cress grows up to 5 ft tall and often lines streams and ditch banks in central and southern England, and Ireland. It also has creeping stems and petals twice as long as its sepals, but is most remarkable for the variety of its leaves. Those under water develop first and are deeply cut into narrow segments; those out of water develop later and are much less feathery.

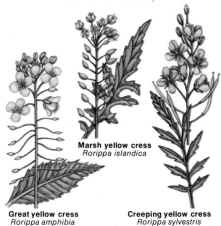

Marsh yellow cress
Rorippa islandica

Great yellow cress
Rorippa amphibia

Creeping yellow cress
Rorippa sylvestris

The three species of yellow cress can be found on wet ground near streams

Yellow flag see Iris
Yellowhammer see Bunting

Yellow loosestrife *Lysimachia vulgaris*

A giant member of the primrose family. It may grow as high as 6 ft and has five-petalled yellow flowers. It can easily be recognised by its willow-like leaves arranged in whorls of three or four.

Yellow loosestrife has strong underground stems and spreads widely in marshes or along the banks of streams and rivers. It flowers in July and August and is found throughout the British Isles, except in northern Scotland.

It was once believed that the plant pacified unruly horses and oxen—hence the botanical name *Lysimachia* meaning 'ending strife'.

Yellow rattle *Rhinanthus minor*

A common annual weed found in grassland throughout the British Isles, often growing in its thousands in old meadows. Yellow rattle is a semi-parasite—its roots make contact with the roots of grasses and herbs, drawing food from them. It is recognisable by its narrow, coarsely toothed leaves and straight, spotted stems, up to 18 in. tall, terminating in a spike of yellow flowers. The flowers appear from May until August. Each flower has an upper hood and a lower

lip tinged with violet, and develops into a swollen capsule containing numerous large kidney-shaped seeds. If, when the capsule is dry, the stem is knocked or shaken, the loose seeds inside make a rattling sound, hence the flower's name.

Yellow sally see Stonefly

Yellow underwing moth *Noctua pronuba*

This large, night-flying moth is named after its hindwings, which are yellow with a dark band at the margin. When the moth is at rest only the forewings show. These are mottled brown with patterns that vary considerably between individuals.

If, during the day, a yellow underwing is disturbed by a predator—usually a bird—it will suddenly take flight, displaying its bright hindwings as it twists and turns. When the moth settles without warning, the disappearance of the yellow confuses the bird, which often fails to find its prey.

The yellow underwing flies from June to October in gardens and grassy places throughout the British Isles. Its white eggs are laid in batches on grass or low-growing plants which will provide food for the brown caterpillars. These usually hibernate, but a few may give rise to a second brood of moths late in the year. There are four other species of yellow underwings, which differ in size and in the width of the dark hindwing margin.

Yellow-wort *Blackstonia perfoliata*

A slender erect plant, rarely over 1 ft high, with an eight-petalled flower. Yellow-wort has leaves in pairs, opposite each other and without stalks, which are joined at the base so that the stems appear to grow through them, hence the Latin name *perfoliata*. The stems branch at regular intervals with a flower in the angle of each pair of branches. The whole plant is smooth and covered with a dusty bloom, like a grape.

Yellow-wort grows in sunny places on lime-rich soils, chalk downs and among sand hills by the sea in the southern half of Britain. The flowers open only in sunlight. The plant is bitter to the taste.

Yew *Taxus baccata*

The ancient tradition that this evergreen sheltered the first Christian missionaries to Britain before their churches were built, is one of the many explanations put forward to account for the large numbers of yews found in country churchyards. The yew is also a life symbol, and was sometimes scattered on graves. The longbows of medieval archers came from straight, knot-free lengths cut from tall, selected trees. But these were unlikely to be churchyard yews—the best bow staves were imported from Spain. The foliage is poisonous. Hundreds of yews grow in the New Forest and on the South Downs at Kingley Vale in Hampshire, but cattle, ponies and sheep graze round them and suffer no ill effects. However, farm stock have often been poisoned by eating yew clippings. It may be that animals recognise the growing tree as poisonous, but will eat its foliage if they meet it in an unaccustomed situation. The thin, red-brown, flaking bark is also poisonous, and so is the seed, though the scarlet flesh covering it is harmless, with an insipid taste. Thrushes and other birds pass the seeds unharmed.

Every yew is either male or female. Male trees open yellow, catkin-like flower clusters in February, whose pollen is wind-borne to green bud-shaped flowers along the branches of female trees. By October each flower has become a berry, with a collar of scarlet pulp surrounding a single hard seed. This sprouts after lying dormant for about 18 months, putting forth two thin deciduous seed-leaves. The normal dark green needles follow, forming flat fronds.

Yew trunks have pale thin sapwood and rust-red heartwood, which is strong and extremely durable. Because of its irregular shape, most of it is used for wood-carving, fine furniture and turned bowls and platters, although it may be used locally for cleft fence stakes or gate posts. Old yews become extremely stout, but their age is often difficult to determine because their central heartwood usually decays. The Fortingall churchyard yew in Perthshire, Scotland, now a relic, once measured 50 ft round and may

A tradesman delivering goods with a yoke near Broadway, Worcestershire, at the turn of the century

Yoke

A frame of wood that fits over the shoulders, with a chain at each end for carrying buckets or baskets on farms or by tradesmen delivering goods. A yoke transfers the weight of a burden from the arms to the shoulders and makes the containers easier to carry than by hand, as it keeps them clear of the legs. It is now extremely rare, having passed out of common use early this century.

Yokes were generally made of willow because of the strength and lightness of the wood.

A CARRYING YOKE

The lightweight willow yoke frame was once an indispensable piece of farm equipment. Fitting across a man's or woman's shoulders, it transferred the weight of loaded baskets or full milk pails from the arms to the shoulders

The fruit of the yew is poisonous, but the scarlet flesh covering is harmless

well be nearly 2000 years old. These large yews are favoured as nesting sites by many birds, including thrushes, robins, finches, dunnocks, wrens and spotted flycatchers. Goldcrests sometimes hang their cup-shaped nests at the branch tips.

Britain has the tallest yew hedge in the world—in Lord Bathurst's Park, Cirencester, Gloucestershire. Planted in 1720, it is 35 ft high and extends for 130 yds.

Yorkshire fog see Grass
Young animals see Nest

Zander *Stizostedion lucioperca*

A member of the perch family from eastern Europe, introduced into the lakes at Woburn Park, Bedfordshire. Zanders taken from these lakes have been put into other waters including some Fenland drains. From these

the zander has spread widely through the Great Ouse river system with which the drains connect and it seems likely that it will eventually spread through England.

It is a predatory fish, feeding almost entirely on smaller fish from the first year of its life, although earlier it eats insect larvae and crustaceans. Growth is rapid in waters where food is abundant, and the zander can be 16 in. long at the age of two. It matures at three to four years when the average weight is about 6 lb. It is prized as a food fish in eastern Europe.

The fish has two separate dorsal fins, the first of which is spiny. It is green-brown with lighter sides, and young fish have a series of vertical dark bars along the sides. This pike-like appearance is the reason for the zander sometimes being called pike-perch. It is not a hybrid of these fish.

THE COUNTRY CODE

Guard against all risk of fire Almost every public holiday weekend is marked by countless fires throughout the countryside. The result of a careless action may cost hundreds of thousands of pounds and disrupt the natural life of a large area.

Do not throw away matches and cigarettes while they are alight. Do not knock out a pipe against a tree; do not leave bottles or jars where they can catch the sun's rays.

Fasten all gates Any farm animal that is left to wander on to a road may cause a serious accident or, if it gets into the wrong field, gorge itself to death. Always close gates—even if you find one standing open. Remember that every cow is worth more than £200 to the farmer.

Keep dogs under proper control The friendly household pet may prove a killer in the open countryside. It may spread disease or it may worry sheep to death. Almost 4000 sheep—worth £30,000 —are killed by visiting dogs each year.

Remember that every farmer is legally entitled to shoot a dog found worrying his animals.

Keep to the paths across farm land The law obliges all walkers in the countryside to keep to public footpaths. If there is some obstruction, walk round it—but keep to the edge of the field and cause as little damage as possible. Even grass is a valuable crop. Remember that what seems to be grass may be more costly wheat, oats or barley. When walking along a narrow track, keep in single file.

Avoid damaging fences, hedges and walls Fencing can cost £1 a yard, and drystone walls may be as expensive as £8 a yard. Keep to the public footpaths and there should be no obstructions. If there are, go carefully and cause no damage.

Leave no litter Take home any litter after a picnic. It is unsightly and it can kill farm animals. Remember that it is more expensive to organise litter collection in the countryside than in the towns.

Safeguard water supplies Most of the water used in Britain comes from country streams. Do not pollute them with empty cans and waste food. Remember that a river by a camping site may provide a water supply for the local population.

Water is important for livestock. Do not interfere with cattle troughs.

Protect wild life, wild plants and trees The countryside is a closely knit community of animals, plants and trees—all of them depending on the others for survival. Do not be tempted to pick the pretty clump of flowers or break off the branch of an attractive tree.

The Countryside Commission's advice is 'drive delicately, tread softly and walk warily'.

Go carefully on country roads Narrow winding country lanes are attractive and dangerous. The unsuspected tractor trundling around a hidden corner, or a flock of sheep meandering up the entire width of the road, can cause a serious and expensive accident.

When walking, keep to the right, facing oncoming traffic, if there is no footpath.

Do not drive into fields or on to verges to park. Find a suitable parking place where no damage will be caused. Do not park in narrow lanes.

Respect the life of the countryside Country people are often suspicious of the summer visitors from the towns. Help to overcome this distrust.

Do not harm animals, farm machinery or property. Keep to the Country Code.

Open countryside

Many areas of open countryside are specially protected to preserve them for public enjoyment. They are mainly open moorland, mountains and woodland, but they may also include whole towns or villages.

National Parks

Ten areas of wild, attractive scenery in England and Wales are designated as National Parks. They are the Brecon Beacons (519 sq. miles), Dartmoor (365), Exmoor (256), the Lake District (866), the Northumberland National Park (398), the North Yorkshire Moors (553), the Peak District (542), the Pembrokeshire Coast (225), Snowdonia (845) and the Yorkshire Dales (680).

An eleventh area—the Cambrian Mountains (467 sq. miles) in Wales—was proposed as a National Park by the Countryside Commission in 1972.

The public have no special rights in these National Park areas: most of the land is still privately owned. The main importance of their designation is to place the land included under special protection against development which would destroy the character of the landscape.

The parks are not entirely areas of conservation, however. Nearly one-sixth of the Dartmoor Park is used by the Ministry of Defence. Snowdonia has a nuclear power station, and there is a potash mine on the North Yorkshire Moors. The Pembrokeshire Coast houses sprawling caravan sites.

The Brecon Beacons This extends from the Black Mountain in the west to the Black Mountains in the east. It includes pleasant valley farms and is ideal for pony-trekking.
Dartmoor On the moor are granite tors weirdly carved by rain and wind, and ancient stone circles built by man. Wild ponies roam all over the moor.
Exmoor Less wild than Dartmoor, but the Doone Valley has an eerie emptiness. Red stags are hunted in the park.
Lake District The biggest park, with England's highest mountain (Scafell Pike, 3210 ft) and largest lake (Windermere, 10½ miles long).
Northumberland A stretch of lonely hill and moorland including the Cheviots in the north, and Hadrian's Wall in the south.
North Yorkshire Moors Combines densely heathered moorland with a towering coast interspersed with excellent beaches. A 5-mile belt of wild daffodils blooms at Easter in lonely Farndale.
Peak District A few of the mountains—for example Thorpe Cloud and Losehill—are peak-shaped, but most of the area is faintly undulating highlands.
Pembrokeshire Coast Almost the whole coastline is accessible by means of a long-distance footpath. Sailing and bird-watching are encouraged in the park.

Yorkshire Dales Stone villages, stone bridges, stone castles and abbeys and strange stone formations, such as Kilnsey Crag. An area of wild uplands and gentle dales.
Snowdonia Includes Snowdon (3560 ft), and the lovely Mawddach Estuary. The largest natural lake in Wales (Llyn Tegid) and 15 nature reserves are within the park boundaries.

Areas of Outstanding Natural Beauty

Several areas have a lesser degree of protection than the National Parks, but they are regions nevertheless where obtrusive industrial development is discouraged by local and central government. They include part of the Anglesey coast, Cannock Chase in Staffordshire, Chichester Harbour, the Chilterns, Cornwall, North, South and East Devon, much of Dorset, the Forest of Bowland in Lancashire and the West Riding of Yorkshire, Gower in South Wales, South and East Hampshire, part of the Isle of Wight, Lleyn in North Wales, the Malvern Hills, the Norfolk Coast, the Northumberland Coast, the Quantock Hills, the Shropshire Hills, the Solway Coast, the Surrey Hills and the Sussex Downs.

The public have no special rights of access to land in these areas.

Long-distance paths

Several long-distance footpath routes have been approved by the government. They include the Pennine Way, from Derbyshire to the Scottish Border; the Cleveland Way, round the North York Moors; Offa's Dyke (Welsh border); the South West Peninsula Coast path from Minehead in Somerset, round Devon and Cornwall into Dorset; the Pembroke Coast path; the North Downs Way; and a bridleway along the South Downs in Sussex.

Although these routes have been designated, there are still considerable stretches over which the public have no right of way. Until negotiations with all the landowners involved are complete, walkers should find out from the local council offices or from the Countryside Commission, 1 Cambridge Gate, Regent's Park, London NW1 4JY, whether the path they intend to take is entirely open to the public.

Nature reserves

More than 250 areas have been established as nature reserves by Act of Parliament. Some are run by the Nature Conservancy, others by local authorities. There are also many reserves owned and managed by private, voluntary bodies.

Those reserves set up by Act of Parliament are chosen for their wildlife or geological interest. In many, the public have complete freedom to walk; but in some access is allowed only to people who have applied for a special permit.

Forest parks

Scotland has neither National Parks nor Areas of Outstanding Natural Beauty. When these classifications were devised it was felt that if they were applied to Scotland half the country would have to be included.

But Scotland does have four Forest Parks, publicly owned through the Forestry Commission. They are the Glen More (Inverness-shire), Argyll, Queen Elizabeth (Trossachs and Loch Lomond) and Glen Trool (borders of Ayr and Kirkcudbright) parks. The Border Forest Park is partly in Scotland and partly in England. Also in England are the Dean and New Forest Parks. Wales has the Snowdonia Forest Park, completely within the National Park.

The Forestry Commission is a commercial organisation whose main business is to plant quick-growing conifers, but it also encourages public use of the Forest Parks for recreation by providing picnic and camping sites and laying out forest trails.

National Trust land

More than 480,000 acres of land are owned by the National Trust and the National Trust for Scotland. The Trusts, incorporated by Act of Parliament, are independent of the government and rely on voluntary contributions. Much of their land and property throughout Britain is open to the public, but some is leased to farmers. In these cases, public access is limited to footpaths and bridleways.

Trust land that is open to the public is shown on 1 in. Ordnance maps with red letters NT. Other National Trust property is marked in blue.

Local authority land

Local authorities often own estates or country parks where the public can walk, subject to 'good behaviour' byelaws. In some cases the authority may pay a private owner compensation to allow public access.

Many councils publish guides showing land to which there is access in their areas.

Water board land

Many water boards allow the public to sail boats on their large reservoirs.

Most Acts of Parliament that enable reservoirs to be built include provisions for public access to any open moorland taken over by the water board.

Private estates

Many private landowners open their country homes and estates to the public. There is usually an entrance charge and access is allowed only to certain parts of the land.

Areas protected for the public's enjoyment

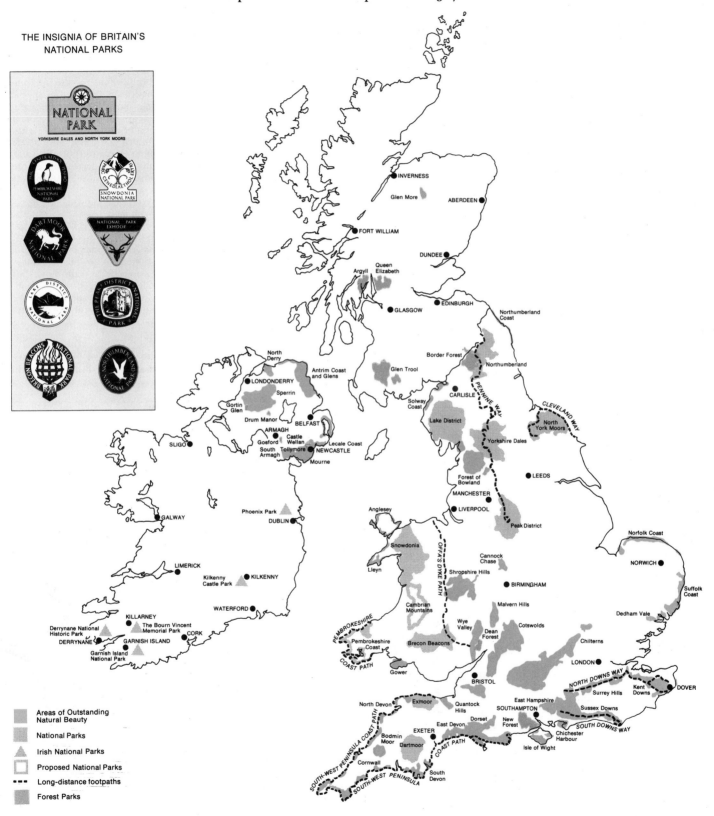

THE INSIGNIA OF BRITAIN'S
NATIONAL PARKS

NATIONAL PARK
YORKSHIRE DALES AND NORTH YORK MOORS

Areas of Outstanding Natural Beauty

National Parks

Irish National Parks

Proposed National Parks

Long-distance footpaths

Forest Parks

Countryside law

All land in Britain, even commons and the part of the beach between high and low water, is owned by someone: a private landowner, a company, a public authority or the Crown. Unless an owner permits access or the law allows it—on a right of way, for example—anyone going on to another person's land without permission is a trespasser.

Even when land is publicly owned it may not be open to the public. For example, the Ministry of Defence owns hundreds of thousands of acres; and many local authorities own extensive playing fields. Anyone who goes on such land without permission is as much a trespasser as if it were owned by a private person.

Occasional visitors to the countryside should be familiar with the restrictions that exist in law if they are to avoid unnecessary conflict with country dwellers.

Animals

A person who is looking after a dog—that is, its keeper, not necessarily its owner—is liable for any damage it does to livestock, except when the livestock have strayed on to land where the dog is authorised to be by the landowner.

The occupier of land is entitled to kill a dog that is worrying his livestock if that is the only way to protect them.

Keepers of other animals are also liable for any damage done by these animals if they knew, or ought to have known, that the animals were dangerous. Generally, this does not apply if an animal injures a trespasser, but the keeper must show that it was reasonable for him to have a guard animal.

Camping and caravanning

Anyone who pitches a tent or parks a caravan on somebody else's land without permission is a trespasser and can be ordered to leave. See TRESPASS

Details of authorised camping sites can be obtained from motoring organisations or from the Camping Club of Great Britain and Ireland, 11 Lower Grosvenor Place, London SW1W 0EY and the Caravan Club, 65 South Molton Street, London W1Y 2AB.

Commons

A common is land where certain people—but not necessarily the general public—have or had the right to take a share of the natural produce.

The rights of common include pasture (grazing of animals), pannage (pigs foraging for acorns and beech mast), estovers (collecting wood or bracken), turbary (lifting peat for fuel), piscary (fishing in inland waters), or common in the soil (taking sand or gravel for use on the commoner's land).

These rights can be enjoyed only by a local person living near the common, and his right can exist only if he registered it with the county council under the Commons Registration Act 1965.

All common land is shown on special maps kept by county councils. A register shows the names and addresses of the commoners and indicates whether there is a public right of access.

In towns, common rights have mostly lapsed and commons are now owned by local authorities, which usually maintain them for public use. In rural areas, commons are usually owned by a private person, a company (gravel companies, for example, own a number of commons) or the Crown.

Although the public have no general right to use common land, several Acts of Parliament allow public access to particular commons. These include:

1 All commons within a borough or urban district. 'Urban district' is a local government term that describes areas not normally regarded as 'urban'—for example, Helvellyn Mountain in Westmorland and Ilkley Moor, in Yorkshire.
2 Commons managed by a rural district council.
3 National Trust commons.
4 Commons where the owner has made a deed granting access.
5 Some large important commons that were opened to the public by a special Act of Parliament—for example the Malvern Hills Act 1884 and Ashdown Forest Act 1887.

When the public have the right to use commons their behaviour is governed by special byelaws. Driving motor vehicles, camping and lighting fires are usually prohibited, and the public may not have commoners' rights.

Commons to which the public have access account for about a quarter of the total. On other commons the permission of the owner is required. In fact most owners tolerate public access, although the public are technically trespassers and can be ordered to leave the common.

Cycling

Cyclists may use any ordinary road except a motorway. In some areas special cycle tracks are provided alongside a main road, but cyclists are not legally obliged to use them.

Although cyclists are also allowed to use bridleways, the local highway authority is not obliged to keep these fit for cycling.

Fishing

The public have a right to fish in the sea and in tidal waters, but fishing rights in inland lakes and rivers are private. If a

---

CLOSE SEASONS FOR HUNTING AND FISHING

The law has established 'close seasons' when certain birds, animals and fish must not be killed.

Wild birds There is a general close season from February 1 to August 31 inclusive, but there are exceptions:

CLOSE SEASON

Capercaillie	February 1 to September 30
Woodcock not in Scotland	February 1 to September 30
Snipe	February 1 to August 11
Wild duck and wild goose (over water areas)	February 21 to August 31

Game birds It is unlawful to kill or take game birds during the following periods:

Black grouse	December 11 to August 11 (August 31 in Somerset, Devon and New Forest)
Red grouse	December 11 to August 11
Partridge	February 2 to August 31
Pheasant	February 2 to September 30
Ptarmigan Scotland only	December 11 to August 11

Grouse, partridge, pheasant and ptarmigan must not be killed on Sundays or on Christmas Day.

Foxes There is no legal close season for the killing of foxes, but the fox-hunting season is regarded as November 1 to mid-April.

Rabbits Rabbits may be killed at any time of the year, but not at night.

Hares Hares may be killed at any time except on moorland and unfenced, cultivated land. In these cases there are close seasons in England and Wales from April 1 to December 10, in Scotland from April 1 to June 30 and in Northern Ireland from February 1 to August 11. Hares must not be killed at night.

It is illegal to sell hares between March 1 and July 31.

Deer The periods when deer must not be killed are:

Red and Sika deer	
Stags	May 1 to July 31
Hinds	March 1 to October 31
Fallow and Roe deer	
Bucks	May 1 to July 31
Does	March 1 to October 31

It is illegal to kill or take any deer from one hour after sunset to one hour before sunrise on any day.

Fish There is no restriction on sea fishing but there are close seasons for freshwater fish:

Salmon	October 31 to February 1
Trout	September 30 to March 1
Coarse fish	March 14 to June 16

These standard close seasons may be varied by local river authorities.

trespassing fisherman takes fish away, he also commits an offence under the Theft Act 1968. Many owners allow clubs or individuals to fish in their rivers. But the law does not allow certain fishing during certain months. See CLOSE SEASONS

Footpaths and bridleways
Footpaths on which the public have a right to walk are shown on maps published by county councils and on Ordnance Survey maps. They are normally marked with red dots (footpaths) or red dashes (bridleways).

On a footpath the public have a right only to walk; on a bridleway they may walk, ride or lead a horse, and ride a pedal cycle.

Even though there may be a right of way on a footpath, the fact that it passes over somebody's land means that the legal rights of people using the footpath are restricted. They are entitled to use the path only to make a genuine journey—to go from one place to another. They may rest for a short while, but are not entitled to sit down and picnic, or wander, if the landowner objects, from the route of the path or pick plants or flowers. Anybody who does becomes a trespasser. See TRESPASS

Each county council has a duty to maintain footpaths in its area. If it fails to do so, and a user suffers injury as a result, he can sue. He is unlikely to recover damages, however, if the council can show that it took reasonable care to inspect the path.

Obstructions It is an offence to obstruct a public footpath. Any landowner who does so may be prosecuted and the obstruction can be forcibly removed by the local council.

Any person using a public path has the right to remove as much of an obstruction as will allow him to pass. If he goes too far he may commit a criminal offence—wilful damage to property.

If an obstruction cannot be moved, the walker is entitled to leave the path to walk round it. He must cause no more damage than is necessary.

Ploughing A farmer may have a common law right to plough over a public path, but usually only when he has regularly ploughed it for many years. The public right of way still exists, but the path must be trodden out afresh after each ploughing.

When a farmer has no common law right he can apply for permission to plough to the local highway authority. He must restore the surface of the path within six weeks after ploughing.

Stiles and gates It is the duty of all landowners to repair stiles and gates across any public paths on their land. They can claim a highway grant to do this, but if they fail to maintain gates and stiles the authority can undertake the work and charge the full cost to landowners.

Signposts Every highway authority must erect direction posts wherever a footpath or bridleway leaves a metalled road. The only exceptions are when the local parish council agrees that a sign is unnecessary.

Hunting
No licence is needed to hunt foxes or deer with hounds, but the consent of all the occupiers of the land a Hunt crosses is necessary. An occupier may give his consent by implication—for example by habitual acquiescence. If a Hunt goes on to any land without consent, it is trespassing and is liable for any damage. See CLOSE SEASON

Parking
It is an offence to park a car so that it obstructs the highway. In many narrow country roads this rules out all parking.

To drive a motor vehicle on to land adjacent to a road without the owner's consent is trespass. He can remove parked cars and sue for damages. See TRESPASS

In particular cases, parking may be an offence under special laws. For example, under the Law of Property Act 1925 it is an offence to park *anywhere* on a common in a borough or urban district. In many areas, council byelaws prohibit parking.

The only safe rule is to park in places authorised by local authorities.

Seaside
At the seaside, the public have the right to sail and the right to fish. Their right of navigation covers not only the open sea, but applies also to the foreshore when it is covered with water, to estuaries and to tidal rivers. Local authorities may make byelaws to control navigation out to 1000 ft beyond the low-water mark.

On the beach There is no general public right to walk on the foreshore—the land between low and high-water marks. Most of the foreshore around Britain (except Cornwall) belongs to the Crown Estate Commissioners, however, and it is their policy to allow public access in most places—but not in areas leased to the Ministry of Defence.

The beach—land above the high-water mark—can be privately owned and may be fenced. An owner may not extend his fences below the high-water mark, however, since this could interfere with navigation.

Where a beach or coastal land is in private hands, there is no legal right to cross it to reach the foreshore and the sea. The public may reach the sea only by public highway or right of way.

Shooting
The use of firearms is strictly controlled. A person wishing to use a gun must apply to the police for a certificate every three years.

If the police refuse a certificate, the applicant can appeal to the Crown Court.

A person who has a shotgun certificate may, if he is the occupier of land, permit other responsible people to use the gun in his presence.

Anyone who wants to shoot game also needs a game licence. This is obtained from the local authority or post office and may be for a year, the three-month 'shooting season' (August-October) or 14 days. See CLOSE SEASON. Only the holder of a year's licence can sell game.

There is no public right to shoot. Shooting rights are enjoyed only by a landowner, including the owner of common land. Commoners have no shooting rights.

It is an offence to enter property without the owner's permission to pursue game. A poacher, therefore, can be prosecuted even before he has shot, or has tried to shoot, anything. A poacher with a gun is guilty of the offence of armed trespass. See TRESPASS

Trespass
Trespassers cannot usually be prosecuted in a criminal court, but they may always be sued for civil damages by a landowner—even when they have done no obvious harm to the land or to any property on it. The compensation awarded would be in relation to the actual damage done.

The only occasions on which a trespasser lays himself open to criminal action are when he has broken a specific law. For example, under the Firearms Act 1968 it is illegal to trespass carrying a firearm. Under special byelaws approved by Parliament, it is illegal to enter British Railways' land. Military land is similarly protected.

When a trespasser damages crops, trees, property or animals he may be prosecuted under the Malicious Damage Act 1861. He is guilty of an offence under the Theft Act 1968 if he removes fruit or cultivated plants. Picking wild flowers is not theft unless he has taken them to sell. It is, however, an act of trespass, for which the trespasser may be sued.

A landowner is allowed to remove a trespasser physically, provided that he uses only the minimum amount of force needed.

Village greens
A village green is land on which villagers have been granted a right to play games by a local Enclosure Act or on which they have played games for centuries. Many greens are cared for by the parish council, but in some cases they may still be owned by the lord of the manor, who must allow the villagers their traditional rights to play games.

Public behaviour on greens owned or managed by a council is usually governed by special byelaws.

USEFUL ORGANISATIONS

Association for the Preservation of Rural Scotland
1 Thistle Court, Edinburgh EH2 1DE
Protects rural scenery

Automobile Association
Fanum House, Leicester Square, London WC2H 7LY

British Caravanners' Club
11 Lower Grosvenor Place, London SW1 0EY

British Cycling Federation
26 Park Crescent, London W1N 4BL

British Deer Society
Hay Bridge Deer Museum & Sanctuary, Bouth by Ulverston, Lancashire
Conserves deer

British Ecological Society
Monks Wood Experimental Station, Abbots Ripton, Huntingdon PE17 2LS
Encourages the study of living organisms in relation to their surroundings

British Field Sports Society
26 Caxton Street, London SW1H 0RG

British Mountaineering Council
Room 314, 26 Park Crescent, London W1N 4BE

British Naturalists' Association
Willowfield, Boyneswood Road, Four Marks, Alton, Hants
Supports schemes for the improvement of wildlife, preservation of natural beauty, promotion and maintenance of national parks, nature reserves, conservation areas and sanctuaries

British Ornithologists' Union
Zoological Society of London, Regent's Park, London NW1 4RY
Encourages the study of birds

British Speleological Association
4 Kingston Avenue, Acklam, Middlesbrough, Yorkshire TS5 7RS
Furthers all aspects of caving

British Tourist Authority
64 St James's Street, London SW1A 1NF

British Waterways Board
Melbury House, Melbury Terrace, London NW1 6JX
Responsible for 2000 miles of waterways

Camping Club of Great Britain & Ireland Ltd
11 Lower Grosvenor Place, London SW1 0EY

Caravan Club
65 South Molton Street, London W1Y 2AB

Central Council of Physical Recreation
26 Park Crescent, London W1N 4AJ
Supplies information on all sports

Civic Trust
17 Carlton House Terrace, London SW1Y 5AW
Aims to improve the appearance of town and country

Commons, Open Spaces and Footpaths Preservation Society
166 Shaftesbury Avenue, London WC2H 8JH
Aims to preserve commons and village greens for public use

Council for British Archaeology
8 St Andrew's Place, Regent's Park, London NW1 4LB
Provides information on facilities for those wishing to assist at excavations

Council for the Protection of Rural England
4 Hobart Place, London SW1W 0HY

Council for the Protection of Rural Wales
Meifod, Montgomeryshire SY22 6DA

Countryside Commission
1 Cambridge Gate, Regent's Park, London NW1 4JY
Responsible for national parks and other matters concerning the provision of facilities for enjoyment of the countryside

Countryside Commission for Scotland
Battleby, Redgorton, Perth PH1 3EW
Responsible for the development of facilities in the Scottish countryside.

Department for the Environment
2 Marsham Street, London SW1P 3EB
Government department dealing with all environmental issues

Forestry Commission
Priestley Road, Basingstoke RG24 9NS

National Trust for Places of Historic Interest or Beauty
42 Queen Anne's Gate, London SW1H 9AS
Preserves land and buildings of historic interest or natural beauty

National Trust for Scotland
5 Charlotte Square, Edinburgh EH2 4DU
Preserves places of historic or architectural interest or natural beauty

Nature Conservancy
19 Belgrave Square, London SW1X 8PY
Maintains nature reserves

Ramblers' Association
1/4 Crawford Mews, London W1H 1PT
Fosters knowledge and care of the countryside, and public access to open country

Royal Society for the Protection of Birds
The Lodge, Sandy, Bedfordshire
Protects wild birds

Scottish Tourist Board
2 Rutland Place, Edinburgh EH1 1YU

NOUNS OF CONGREGATION

Collective names for groups of animals which live in societies, or come together during the breeding season, at feeding places or migration, are old and numerous. Many are of Anglo-Saxon origin or have been imported by continental invaders such as the Danes and Normans.

Animals	Menagerie; tribe; cluster
Ants	Colony
Asses	Pace
Badgers	Colony; cete
Bees	Swarm; cluster; hive; erst
Boars	Sounder; herd; singular
Cats	Clowder; clutter
Cattle	Drove; herd
Colts	Rake
Conies	Bury; warren
Deer	Herd; leash (set of three)
Dogs	Kennel
Elks	Gang
Ferrets	Business
Flies	Business
Foxes	Skulk; leash (set of three)
Frogs	Colony
Gnats	Horde; cloud
Goats	Tribe; trip
Greyhounds	Leash (set of three)
Hares	Drove; down; husk; kindle; trip; leash (set of three)
Horses	Harass (wild); string (racing); field (hunting); team (carriage or polo); stud (breeding)
Hounds	Stable; pack (hunting); couple (a pair); cry; mute; leash (set of three)
Kittens	Kindle; litter; brood
Mares	Stud
Moles	Labour; company
Mules	Pack; span
Otters	Bevy
Oxen	Team; yoke
Pigs	Drove; flock; litter
Porpoises	School; pod; gam
Rabbits	Colony; kindle
Roe deer	Bevy
Seals	Herd; pod
Sheep	Flock; drove; trip; down
Snakes	Den
Spiders	Clutter; cluster
Stoats	Pack
Toads	Knot
Vipers	Nest

Weasels	Pack
Whales	School; pod; gam
Wild pigs	Sounder; drift; singular
Wolves	Pack; route
Birds	Flight; volery; dissimulation
Bitterns	Sedge; siege
Chicks	Brood; clutch
Choughs	Chattering
Coots	Covert
Cranes	Sedge; siege
Crows	Hover; murder
Curlews	Head
Doves	Flight
Ducks	Team (in flight); brace (a pair); flush; brood
Eagles	Convocation
Falcons	Cast
Finches	Charm
Game	Brood
Geese	Gaggle; skein (in flight); flock
Goldfinches	Charm
Grouse	Covey (single family); pack (larger group)
Gulls	Colony
Hawks	Cast
Hens	Brood
Herons	Sedge; siege
Lapwings	Deceit
Larks	Exaltation; bevy
Magpies	Tiding
Mallard	Flush
Nightingales	Watch
Partridges	Covey
Peacocks	Muster
Pheasants	Nye; nest; nide; brood; flock
Pigeons	Flight; flock
Plovers	Congregation; wing
Poultry	Run
Quails	Bevy; covey
Ravens	Unkindness
Rooks	Building
Sea fowl	Cloud
Snipe	Wisp; walk
Sparrows	Host
Starlings	Murmuration
Swans	Herd; game; bevy; drift; sounder
Teals	Spring
Turkeys	Rafter
Widgeon	Company
Wildfowl	Trip; plump
Woodcock	Fall; covey; flight
Wrens	Herd
Fish	School; draft; shoal
Clams	Bed
Cockles	Bed
Dogfish	Troop
Herrings	Shoal
Jellyfish	Stuck
Mussels	Bed
Oysters	Bed; hive

GLOSSARY OF NATURAL HISTORY TERMS

Amphibian Gk. *amphi*, both; *bios*, life. Vertebrate that has to return to the water to breed because its young go through a gill-breathing tadpole stage.
Examples: frogs, toads, newts

Amphipod An order of small shrimp-like CRUSTACEANS mostly living in water. Usually laterally flattened, with curved bodies. They move forwards by jumping.
Examples: freshwater shrimp, sand shrimp, skeleton shrimp, sand hopper

Annual A plant completing its life cycle within one year. It grows from seed, produces flowers, fruits and then dies.
Examples: birdsfoot, cleavers

Biennial A plant that completes its life cycle in two years. In the first year the plant forms only leaves, and stores surplus food manufactured in roots, stems or specially modified leaves. In the second year the reserve is wholly used in producing flowers and seeds before the plant dies.
Examples: cabbage, wallflower

Biology The scientific study of the physical life of animals and plants.

Bioluminescence The production of light by living plants and animals. A chemical reaction, promoted by an enzyme, creates small amounts of heat (sometimes incorrectly called phosphorescence).
Examples: the jellyfish *Pelagia noctiluca*, the bristle-worm *Chaetopterus variopedatus*, the glow-worm, the honey fungus and some bacteria

Biome Gk. *bios*, life. A community of living organisms belonging to a particular environment.

Biosphere That part of the earth that is inhabited by living organisms.

Bivalve A large class of aquatic MOLLUSCS that have twin valves in their shell.
Examples: mussels, cockles, oysters

Chlorophyll Gk. *chloros*, grass-green; *phyllon*, leaf. Colouring that is concentrated within the cell-bodies (chloroplasts) of plants. Essential to the plants' food-building process. See PHOTOSYNTHESIS

Cold-blooded animals Animals that cannot sustain a constant body temperature. During winter they hibernate or die.
Examples: insects, amphibians, reptiles

Corm The swollen underground storage stem of a plant, covered by protective scales with buds at the top.
Example: bluebell

Crustacean Animal with a body divided into head, thorax and abdomen, and two pairs of antennae. Crustaceans are mostly aquatic and breathe through gills.
Examples: barnacles, lobsters, crabs, prawns, shrimps and woodlice

Echinoderm Gk. *echinos*, hedgehog; *derma*, skin. Marine INVERTEBRATES which move by means of tube feet operated by a system of water-filled canals running through the body.
Examples: brittle stars, feather stars, starfish, sea cucumbers and sea urchins

Ecology Scientific study of plants and animals in relation to one another and to their surroundings.

Ephemeral A plant with more than one life cycle in a year, producing more than one crop.
Example: groundsel

Fauna L. *faunus*, god of the woods. A collection of animals belonging to a particular country, HABITAT or period.

Field studies Studies based on observation and experiments on location rather than in the laboratory.

Flora The plants of a particular area or HABITAT.

Habitat L. *habitare*, to inhabit. A distinctive piece of countryside or living quarter that has its own physical and chemical features, to which certain species of animals and plants are adapted.
Because of its varied geology, Great Britain is rich in different kinds of habitat, probably more so for its size than anywhere on earth.

Herbivores Animals that eat only plants.
Examples: deer, horses, cattle, sheep and goats

Herpetology The study of REPTILES and AMPHIBIANS.

Hybrid Normally two different species of animal or plant cannot inter-breed. If this does occur the offspring—a hybrid—is infertile.
Example: mule (horse and donkey)

Indigenous Animals and plants that are native to a country.
Examples: red deer, badger and fox; Scots pine, yew and juniper, are all indigenous to Britain

Insectivores Primitive, small mammals that feed on insects.
Examples: hedgehog, mole and shrew

Mammals L. *mamma*, a breast. Backboned, warm-blooded, air-breathing animals whose young, with few exceptions, are born alive and suckled on mother's milk.

Mollusc Animal with a hard shell and a tough muscular foot. There is no standard mollusc shape.
Molluscs are found everywhere—in the sea, in fresh water and on the land.
Examples: octopus, razor shell and garden snail

Oviparous L. *ovum*, egg; *parere*, to bring forth. Egg-laying.
Example: birds

Ovo-viviparous L. *ovum*, egg; *vivus*, living; and *parere*, to bring forth. A reproductive process in which the embryo in its shell is retained inside the mother's body up to the point of hatching, when it is produced alive.
Example: common lizard

Perennial A plant that continues to grow from year to year. A herbaceous perennial is one in which the leaves and stems (the parts above the ground) die down each autumn, the new shoots come up from the roots each spring and the plant increases in size each year.
Examples: trees, shrubs, many flowers

Photosynthesis Gk. *phos*, light; *synthesis*, putting together. The green leaves of plants—with the energy of sunlight and CHLOROPHYLL as a catalyst—combine carbon dioxide with water to produce sugar and starch.

Reproduction Means of producing further members of a species.
ASEXUAL REPRODUCTION The plant or animal divides itself into separate units, or it buds off part of its body. The hereditary makeup of the 'offspring' is unchanged: they resemble the 'parent' in every detail.
Examples: amoeba divides into two; some plants reproduce by sending out runners (strawberries) or underground suckers (wild roses).
SEXUAL REPRODUCTION Two parents are involved. Hereditary characteristics from each parent produce variation. Some plants and animals carry both male and female cells and are hermaphrodites.

Examples: earthworms and most flowering plants.
Symbols are commonly used—♂ (male), ♀ (female), ⚥ (hermaphrodite)

Reptiles L. *repere*, to creep. Air-breathing, cold-blooded vertebrates whose bodies are covered by some form of protective scaling. Most lay eggs, but a few species produce living young.
Examples: snakes and lizards. Only six are native to Britain—adder, grass snake and smooth snake, viviparous and sand lizards, and the slow-worm

Rodent L. *rodere*, to gnaw. Mammal that is characterised by incisor teeth which are curved, chisel-shaped and rootless.
Examples: mice, rats, voles, dormice, squirrels and coypus

Ruminant L. *rumen*, a stomach. Mammal whose stomach has four chambers. It regurgitates and chews food already swallowed.
Examples: cattle, deer and sheep

Species L. *species*, a particular kind. A unit of plants or animals which interbreed and normally cannot cross with other species. When this happens, the HYBRID offspring are usually infertile.
In some species there are many varieties grading from one to the next. This is called a cline. Where the two extremes of the cline are so far removed from the ancestral form, they may no longer be able to interbreed. In this way two new species are evolving from the one original. A species is always identified scientifically by the use of two Latin names.
Examples: common oak *Quercus robur*, hedgehog *Erinaceus europaeus*, robin *Erithacus rubecula*, salmon *Salmo salar*

Symbiosis Gk. *symbion*, living together. A close-knit association of two organisms that normally cannot exist apart.

Vertebrate L. *vertebratus*, jointed. An animal with a backbone. The vertebrates are the fish, amphibians, reptiles, birds and mammals.

Viviparous L. *vivus*, living; *parere*, to bring forth. Giving birth to living young.
Example: mammals

Warm-blooded Maintaining a temperature constantly higher than the surroundings, as opposed to COLD-BLOODED.
Examples: birds, mammals

Acknowledgments

The photographs which appear in this book are the work of the following photographers:

READING FROM LEFT TO RIGHT ACROSS THE PAGE AND FROM TOP TO BOTTOM: **10-11** Copyright Reserved **12-13** Marcus/Uniphoto **14-15** Copyright Reserved **17** British Crown Copyright reproduced with the permission of the Controller of Her Britannic Majesty's Stationery Office **18** G. Kinns/AFA **19** Gerald Wilkinson **20** Neal Martin, Heather Angel **24** W. Harstrick/Bruce Coleman A. E. McR. Pearce/Bruce Coleman **25** S. Dalton/NHPA **26** Reproduced by kind permission of the Royal Horticultural Society **26-27** Tessa Traeger **28** Mansell Collection **29** G. Matthews/Natural Science Photos **30** Ray Kennedy **31** D. & K. Urry/Bruce Coleman, G. V. Black/University of Edinburgh **32** Royal Institute of British Architects, London, A. J. Deane/Bruce Coleman **33** G. Kinns/AFA **34** Jill Gardiner **35** Neal Martin **36** Michael St Maur Sheil **38** Eric Hosking, Neal Martin **39** N. A. Callow/NHPA **40** J. B. Free **41** J. Pope/Natural Science Photos, M. Tweedie/NHPA **43** Gerald Wilkinson **44** J. Burton/Bruce Coleman **46** Heather Angel **47** Ray Kennedy **48** Tessa Traeger **49** G. Matthews/Natural Science Photos, John Markham, Tessa Traeger, Heather Angel, Gerald Wilkinson, Pharmaceutical Society of Gt Britain, Albert Barber, A. Eddy/Natural Science Photos, G. Matthews/Natural Science Photos, Tessa Traeger, George E. Hyde (2) **50** Rave/Jacana **61** J. Bulmer/Uniphoto **62** Heather Angel **63** N. A. Callow/NHPA **64** N. A. Callow/NHPA **65** W. J. C. Murray/NHPA **67** Christine Pearcey **68** Gerald Wilkinson **68-69** John Vigurs **70** Peter Wrigley **70-71** Malcolm Aird **71** Heather Angel (2) **72** Anthony Howarth/Susan Griggs **74** Robin Fletcher **75** C. Foord/NHPA **76** D. Middleton/Bruce Coleman **77** G. Matthews/Natural Science Photos, John Vigurs **78** J. Burton/Bruce Coleman **78-79** John Markham **79** H. Barnfather/Bruce Coleman **81** I. & L. Beames/Ardea **82** Robin Fletcher/Natural Science Photos **83** C. Foord/NHPA **84-85** Albert Barber **86** Robin Fletcher **88-89** Malcolm Aird **90** N. A. Callow/NHPA **91** John Vigurs, Toni Angermayer **94** Gerald Wilkinson **96** R. Smith/Ardea **97** Neville Fox-Davies **98** Picturepoint **99** Robin Fletcher **100-1** Aerofilms **102-3** Maurice Nimmo **103** Prof. Richard Scorer (2), Maurice Nimmo, H. Frawley/Natural Science Photos, Prof. Richard Scorer (2) **104** Alan McG. Stirling **106-7** Neville Fox-Davies **108** Copyright Reserved **109** Aerofilms **110** Alfred Leutscher **110-11** C. K. Mylne/Ardea **111** W. Curth/Ardea **112** Robin Fletcher, reproduced with the sanction of the Controller of Her Majesty's Stationery Office, Crown Copyright Reserved and with the permission of the Verderers of the New Forest; S. C. Bisserot/Bruce Coleman **114** Neville Fox-Davies **116** D. Corke/Photo Aquatics, B. Hawkes/NHPA **117** Copyright Reserved **120** S. C. Porter/Bruce Coleman, P. Morris **121** P. Green/Ardea **122** G. Matthews/Natural Science Photos **123** John Markham **124** Robin Fletcher, J. Bulmer/Uniphoto **125** Spectrum Colour Library **126** Albert Barber **127** Peter Wrigley **128** S. Dalton/NHPA **129** W. Harstrick/Bruce Coleman, S. C. Bisserot/Bruce Coleman **130** J. Good/NHPA, Oxford Scientific Films/Bruce Coleman **131** G. Waters/Uniphoto, Pic-on-Tour, J. Grant/Natural Science Photos (3) **132** Neville Fox-Davies (2) **133** George E. Hyde **134-5** B. Hawkes/NHPA **135** Roy A. Harris & K. R. Duff **136** Oxford Scientific Films/Bruce Coleman, Heather Angel **138** Roy A. Harris & K. R. Duff, C. Morris/Uniphoto **139** Neville Fox-Davies **140** Kenneth Scowen **142** Neal Martin **143** Tessa Traeger **144** R. Kinne/Bruce Coleman **144-5** S. Roberts/Ardea **145** Dennis Green **146** P. H. Ward/Natural Science Photos, N. A. Callow/NHPA **147** Julian Plowright **148** A. Visage/Jacana **149** Heather Angel **150** J. Bradley/Natural Science Photos **151** Gerald Wilkinson **152** Frank Thompson, P. H. Ward/Natural Science Photos **153** P. H. Ward/Natural Science Photos **154-5** Copyright Reserved **156** R. K. Murton/Bruce Coleman **157** P. H. Ward/Natural Science Photos **158** Heather Angel, S. C. Porter/Bruce Coleman **159** Heather Angel **160** Bodleian Library, Tessa Traeger **161** Gerald Wilkinson **162** By courtesy of the Trustees of the British Museum, Mansell Collection **163** University of Reading Museum of English Rural Life **166-7** Malcolm Aird **168** Tessa Traeger **169** Tessa Traeger **170** Spectrum Colour Library **171** Tessa Traeger **172** Maurice Nimmo **173** S. Gooders/Ardea **175** Penny Tweedie **176** John Vigurs **178** F. Blackburn/NHPA **178-9** G. Langsbury/Bruce Coleman **179** Heather Angel, Maurice Nimmo **180** Roy A. Harris & K. R. Duff **181** J. Grant/Natural Science Photos **187** J. Burton/Bruce Coleman **188** J. Grant/Natural Science Photos **189** Aerofilms **190** Drive Publications **191** Reproduced with the sanction of the Controller of Her Majesty's Stationery Office, Crown Copyright Reserved **193** J. Blossom/NHPA, Daily Telegraph Colour Library **194** By courtesy of the Trustees of the British Museum **195** Tom Wright **196** Robin Fletcher **197** S. Dalton/NHPA **198** Neville Fox-Davies **199** F. Greenaway/Natural Science Photos, John Markham **200** L. Dawson/Bruce Coleman **201** Neville Fox-Davies **204** P. H. Ward/Natural Science Photos **205** Anthony & Elizabeth Bomford (3) **206** M. Allman, from *Fossils in Colour*, courtesy Blandford Press **207** Gerald Wilkinson, A. W. Cundall/Natural Science Photos **208** P. H. Ward/Natural Science Photos **209** Heather Angel, Eric Hosking **210** B. Hawkes/NHPA **211** Bodleian Library, J. S. Wightman/Ardea **212** Popperfoto **213** Neville Fox-Davies, Spectrum Colour Library, P. Morris **215** C. M. Dixon **216** Heather Angel **217** Heather Angel, W. J. C. Murray/NHPA **218** Eric Hosking **219** Julian Plowright **220-1** Eric Hosking **221** George E. Hyde **222** P. Germain/Ardea **223** Rebouleau/Jacana **225** Gerald Wilkinson, W. Schraml/Jacana **226** John Vigurs, Eric Hosking **228** Neville Fox-Davies, Gerald Wilkinson **229** Heather Angel **230-1** Robin Fletcher **232** G. Kinns/AFA **233** T. Graham/Uniphoto **236** The Masters & Fellows of Trinity College, Cambridge, G. Matthews, S. Gooders/Ardea (2) **237** C. Foord/NHPA, G. Matthews **238** S. C. Porter/Bruce Coleman, Popperfoto **240** Robin Fletcher, Peter Wrigley **241** Robin Fletcher, John Vigurs **242** Gerald Wilkinson **243** Robin Fletcher, Heather Angel **244** University of Reading Museum of English Rural Life **245** F. Dalgety **246** Gerald Wilkinson **247** J. Grant/Natural Science Photos, George E. Hyde **248** North of Scotland Hydro-Electricity Board **250** Heather Angel **251** John Vigurs **252** Neville Fox-Davies **255** Heather Angel **256** Dennis Green **257** H. Reinhard/Bruce Coleman, Gerald Wilkinson **258** John Vigurs, S. Dalton/NHPA **259** Robin Fletcher **260-1** Gerald Wilkinson **261** Eric Hosking **263** C. K. Mylne **264** J. Burton/Bruce Coleman **265** Peter Wrigley, Robin Fletcher **266** S. C. Bisserot/Bruce Coleman **267** R. K. Pilsbury **268** Neville Fox-Davies, Gerald Wilkinson, Heather Angel **269** D. Holyoak/Natural Science Photos **271** Gerald Wilkinson **272** C. Foord/NHPA **273** T. D. Bonsall/Natural Science Photos **274** Heather Angel **275** Daily Telegraph Colour Library **276** Robin Fletcher **277** Prudence Grice **278** N. A. Callow/NHPA **279** Heather Angel **280** Heather Angel **280-1** C. K. Mylne **281** P. H. Ward/Natural Science Photos **282** John Vigurs, George E. Hyde **282-3** J. Pope/Natural Science Photos **283** Heather Angel **284-5** J. Burton/Bruce Coleman **287** P. Morris **288-9** J. Grant/Natural Science Photos **290** Maurice Nimmo **291** J. Burton/Bruce Coleman **292** Gerald Wilkinson, A. Pearce/Bruce Coleman **295** Christine Pearcey **297** Julian Plowright, G. Matthews/Natural Science Photos **298** Robin Fletcher **300** Tom Wright **302** Spectrum Colour Library, G. Kinns/AFA, Roy A. Harris & K. R. Duff **305** Heather Angel **306** C. Morris **307** B. Hawkes/NHPA, J. Grant/Natural Science Photos **308** R. K. Murton/Bruce Coleman **309** E. Breeze-Jones/Bruce Coleman **310** Michael St Maur Sheil **313** H. Reinhard/Bruce Coleman **314** Robin Fletcher **316** John Vigurs **317** Gerald Wilkinson **318-19** Robin Fletcher **320** Julian Plowright, P. Morris/Ardea **322** N. A. Callow/NHPA **324** J. V. Wormer/Bruce Coleman **324-5** Eric Hosking **326** H. Reinhard/Bruce Coleman, D. Holyoak/Natural Science Photos **327** W. Curth/Ardea, G. Langsbury/Bruce Coleman **328** Heather Angel **329** N. F. Davies/Bruce Coleman **332-3** The Tate Gallery, London; The Victoria and Albert Museum, Crown Copyright; by Courtesy of The Medici Society Ltd, London; Frederick Warne and Co Ltd; from *The Concise British Flora in Colour* by W. Keble Martin, copyright George Rainbird Ltd **334** M. Peters/Uniphoto **335** Bodleian Library **336** Chevalier/Jacana, N. F. Davies/Bruce Coleman **337** Daily Telegraph Colour Library, S. Dalton/NHPA **338** Gerald Wilkinson **339** Peter Wrigley **341** Eric Hosking **342** Eric Hosking **342-3** J Burton/Bruce Coleman **344** Roy A. Harris & K. R. Duff, R. Foord/NHPA **345** Robin Fletcher **346** W. Curth/Ardea, W. J. C. Murray/NHPA **347** Heather Angel **348** D. Corke/Photo Aquatics, John Vigurs **349** J. Good/NHPA **351** R. J. Johns/Bruce Coleman, Heather Angel **352** Roger Worsley **353** Picturepoint **354** Peter Corkhill/Wildlife Photos **355** Roger Worsley **357** Angie Downing **358-9** Daily Telegraph Colour Library **359** Gerald Wilkinson **360** John Vigurs **361** Spectrum Colour Library **362** Picturepoint **363** Heather Angel, R. C. Revels/Natural Science Photos **364** G. Temple/NHPA, P. Morris **365** C. M. Dixon **366** Roger Worsley **367** Choussy/Jacana **368** Heather Angel **369** W. J. C. Murray/NHPA, W. H. D. Wince/Bruce Coleman **370** Mansell Collection **371** Maurice Nimmo **374** J. Burton/Bruce Coleman **375** P. H. Ward/Natural Science Photos (2) **377** P. H. Ward/Natural Science Photos **379** Tessa Traeger **382-3** Neal Martin **383** Radio Times Hulton Picture Library **384** Neville Fox-Davies **386** John Vigurs **387** G. Matthews/Natural Science Photos **388** A. J. Deane/Bruce Coleman, Akë Lindau/Ardea **391** Picturepoint, P. Morris **392** Picturepoint, Eric Hosking **395** L. Beames/Ardea, Michael St Maur Sheil **396** Heather Angel **397** J. Burton/Bruce Coleman **398** Anthony & Elizabeth Bomford, J. Cranham/Uniphoto **400-1** Neville Fox-Davies **401** Heather Angel **402** Heather Angel (2) **404** Peter Wrigley **405** John Vigurs **406-7** David Sheppard (12) **410** Eric Hosking **412** Malcolm Aird **413** Heather Angel **414-17** Robert Dowling **419** F. Greenaway/NHPA, W. Puchalski/Bruce Coleman **420** Heather Angel **422** J. Gooders/Ardea **423** S. C. Bisserot/Bruce Coleman **424** Heather Angel **426-7** K. Hoy/Ardea **427** John Vigurs **428-9** L. Beames/Ardea **430-1** Roger Turner **431** Clive Edwards (2), Roger Turner (2) **432** S. Dalton/NHPA **433** Robin Fletcher **434** D. W. Greenslade/Ardea **435** C. Foord/NHPA **436** J. S. Wightman/Ardea, Su Gooders/Ardea **437** S. C. Bisserot/Bruce Coleman **438** Eric Hosking **439** R. Vaughan/Ardea **441** Mansell Collection **442** Spectrum Colour Library **443** Spectrum Colour Library **444** Neville Fox-Davies **446-9** Robert Dowling **451** R. K. Murton/Bruce Coleman **452** Varin/Jacana **454** Su Gooders/Ardea **455** T. Marshall/Ardea **456-7** Christine Pearcey **459** R. Blewitt/Ardea **460** M. Chinery/Natural Science Photos, J. Grant/Natural Science Photos **462** J. Walmsley/Uniphoto **463** Ardea, Bruce Coleman **465** M. Savonius/NHPA **466** Picturepoint **467** S. Dalton/NHPA **468** Heather Angel, Bruce Coleman **470** Peter Wrigley **476** S. Dalton/NHPA **479** Picturepoint **480** Heather Angel **481** Robin Fletcher **482** C. M. Dixon, Popperfoto **483** Radio Times Hulton Picture Library, Spectrum Colour Library **485** J. Burton/Bruce Coleman **488** Bruce Coleman **489** P. H. Ward/Natural Science Photos **490** Maurice Nimmo **492** Heather Angel **493** Ardea **494** Crown Copyright, by permission of the Controller of Her Majesty's Stationery Office **495** Neal Martin **496** L. Beames/Ardea **497** G. Matthews/Natural Science Photos **498** Robin Fletcher **499** N. F. Davies/Bruce Coleman **501** Gerald Wilkinson **504** John Vigurs **518** Heather Angel **520** R. Blewitt/Ardea **521** Eric Hosking **522-3** Gerald Wilkinson **524** Peter Wrigley **526** Heather Angel **527** Neville Fox-Davies **528** John Vigurs, University of Reading Museum of English Rural Life

The drawings and diagrams throughout the book are the work of the following artists:

Robin Armstrong S. R. Badmin Norman Barber Peter Barratt David Baxter Leonora Box David Carl-Forbes Pat Casey David Cook Roy Coombes Patrick Cox Brian Delf Barry Driscoll Helen Fisher Ian Garrard Robert Gillmor Vana Haggerty Herman Heinzel Gary Hinks Roger Hughes Joanna Langhome Richard Lewington Peter McGinn David Nash John Norris-Wood Richard Orr Denys Ovenden Patrick Oxenham Josephine Rankin John Rignall Colin Rose Kathleen Smith Les Smith Peter Stebbing Reece Toothill Norman Weaver Michael Woods Sidney Woods Elsie Wrigley

The publishers also acknowledge their indebtedness to the following books and journals which were consulted for reference or as sources of illustrations:

Abbot's Hall Museum, Suffolk Aberdeen Angus Cattle Society Agricultural Research Council An Taisce (Irish National Trust) Apple & Pear Development Council Eric Ashby Association of County Naturalists' Trusts Ayrshire Cattle Society Belted Galloway Cattle Society Blackface Sheep Breeders' Association Blandford Press Ltd BBC Natural History Unit British Charolais Cattle Society British Deer Society British Friesian Cattle Society British Goat Society British Horse Society British Landrace Pig Society British Percheron Horse Society British Railways Board British Simmental Cattle Society British Waterways Board John Cator Central Electricity Generating Board L. Christie City of London Corporation Civil Aviation Authority Cleveland Bay Horse Society Conchological Society of Great Britain and Ireland Connemara Pony Breeders' Society Council for Small Industries in Rural Areas Court of the Verderers of the New Forest Dartmoor Pony Society Department of Agriculture and Fisheries, Dublin Department of Agriculture and Fisheries, Scotland Department of Lands (Forest and Wildlife Service), Dublin Department of the Environment Derwent Valley Water Board Devon Cattle Breeders' Society English Guernsey Cattle Society Fell Pony Society Forestry Commission Galloway Cattle Society James Grant Hereford Herd Book Society Highland Cattle Society Hydrographer of the Navy Institute of Geological Sciences Irish Tourist Board Jersey Cattle Society Shelagh Jones John Lavender Lincoln Red Cattle Society Professor Arthur Ling M.SC., N.D.A. Long Ashton Research Station, University of Bristol David McClintock Massey-Ferguson (United Kingdom) Ltd Master and Fellows of Trinity College, Cambridge George Matthews Dr A. Melderis Meteorological Office Ministry of Agriculture and Fisheries and Food Ministry of Agriculture for Northern Ireland National Botanic Gardens, Dublin National Coal Board National Environmental Council National Farmers Union National Institute of Agricultural Botany National Pig Breeders' Association National Trust Nature Conservancy New Forest Pony Breeding & Cattle Society North of Scotland Hydro-Electric Board Office of Public Works, Dublin Hugh Pasmore Pharmaceutical Society of Great Britain Poultry Club Arthur Qvist Mrs E. Beryl Rands Red House Museum, Christchurch Red Poll Cattle Society Rentokil Ltd Dr A. L. Rice Graham Rose Royal Archaeological Society Royal Botanic Gardens, Kew Royal Dublin Society Royal Geographical Society Royal Horticultural Society Royal Institute of British Architects Royal Society for the Protection of Birds St Albans City Museum Scottish Nature Conservancy Scottish Tourist Board Shire Horse Society Shorthorn Society of the U.K. of Great Britain and Ireland Dr D. W. Snow Society for the Border Leicester Sheep Breeders Society for the Promotion of Nature Reserves Society for Protection of Ancient Buildings South Devon Flock Book Association South Devon Herd Book Society Suffolk Horse Society Suffolk Sheep Society Trustees of the British Museum (Natural History) University of Reading Museum of English Rural Life Wakefield and District Water Board Welsh Black Cattle Society Welsh Mountain Sheep Society Welsh Pony and Cob Society Wensleydale Longwool Sheep Breeders' Association Westminster City Libraries Yorkshire Archaeological Society

Drawings and diagrams are based on many sources. The publishers acknowledge the following in particular:

18 The Adder's poison bite *The British Amphibians and Reptiles* Malcolm Smith COLLINS **21 Ambrosia beetle: Elm tree killer** THE FORESTRY COMMISSION **23 Animal behaviour: Grasshopper's song** *The Life of Insects* Sir Vincent B. Wigglesworth WEIDENFELD & NICOLSON **25 Aphid: The yearly cycle of the black bean aphid** *Introduction to Biology* D. G. Mackean JOHN MURRAY **29 Arrow worm** *The Invertebrates* Hyman—used with permission of McGRAW HILL BOOK COMPANY **36 Barrow** by kind permission of *Chambers's Encyclopaedia* published by INTERNATIONAL LEARNING SYSTEMS CORPORATION LIMITED *Ancient Burial Mounds of England* L. V. Grinsell METHUEN **39 Bees: The bee's sting** *The Anatomy and Dissection of the Honey bee* H. A. Dade THE BEE RESEARCH ASSOCIATION **40 Bees: How bees speak to each other** *The Dancing Bees* Karl von Frisch METHUEN **41 Mining Bee: Underground nest** EDUCATIONAL PRODUCTIONS LTD in collaboration with THE BEE RESEARCH ASSOCIATION **48 Berries and fruits: How berries are constructed** *Agricultural Botany* Gill and Vear GERALD DUCKWORTH & CO. LTD **51 Bird: How a bird flies** *The Life of Vertebrates* J. Z. Young CLARENDON PRESS **121 Crab: New legs for old** *Physiology of Crustacea* T. H. Waterman ACADEMIC PRESS **163 Farming: How a modern Combine Harvester works** MASSEY FERGUSON **164-5 Farming: The smooth routine of a modern dairy farm** Bulbourne Farm, Tring, run by FARMERS WEEKLY **168-9 Farming: Agricultural machinery** MASSEY FERGUSON **216 Grasshopper: The mole cricket's loudspeaker** Dr H. C. Bennet-Clark, Zoology Department UNIVERSITY OF EDINBURGH **244 Horse brasses: Charms against evil** *Discovering Horse Brasses* John Vince SHIRE PUBLICATIONS **245 Horse: Collar harness of a draught horse/Modern saddle and double bridle** *Discovering Harness and Saddlery/Discovering Horse Brasses* SHIRE PUBLICATIONS **246 Horse-fly: How a horse-fly bites** *The Life of Insects* Sir Vincent B. Wigglesworth WEIDENFELD & NICOLSON **252 Insect: How an insect sees** *The Life of Insects* Sir Vincent B. Wigglesworth WEIDENFELD & NICOLSON **255 Jellyfish: How the sting-ing cell stings** *Zoology* Chapman and Barker LONGMANS **262 Lake: Lakes formed by glaciers** *Physical Geography* Arthur N. Strahler JOHN WILEY & SONS **268 Lichen: How lichens reproduce** *The Fungi of Lichens* Vernon Ahmadjian—by permission of W. H. FREEMAN & CO. SCIENTIFIC AMERICAN **271 Limestone: Plants that grow over limestone** *Warne's Natural History Atlas of Great Britain* Arnold Darlington FREDERICK WARNE & CO. LTD **275 Lock** *The Canals Book* LINK HOUSE PUBLICATIONS **287 Mill** *Windmills and Watermills* John Reynold HUGH EVELYN **291 Mole's fortress** *The Living World* David Stanbury MACMILLAN **298 Moth: Flight spiral of a moth** *The Life of Insects* Sir Vincent B. Wigglesworth WEIDENFELD & NICOLSON **298 Moth's interlocked wings** *The Oxford Book of Insects* John Burton OXFORD UNIVERSITY PRESS **342 Phantom gnat: The buoyant phantom larva** *The Life of Insects* Sir Vincent B. Wigglesworth WEIDENFELD & NICOLSON **343 Pigeon: Pigeon in flight** *The Life of Vertebrates* J. Z. Young CLARENDON PRESS **345 Pine Marten: Scattered locations of the pine marten** based on results of the MAMMAL SOCIETY'S distribution scheme 1964/70 **369 Rain: Rain cycle** *Children's Encyclopaedia* ENCYCLOPAEDIA BRITANNICA INTERNATIONAL LTD **396 Sea anemone** *Zoology* Chapman and Barker LONGMANS **421 Snake: Movement without legs** *Animal Locomotion* Sir James Gray WEIDENFELD & NICOLSON **435 Squirrel distribution** *Ministry of Agriculture Fisheries and Food* **459 Thorn moth** *The Life of Insects* Sir Vincent B. Wigglesworth WEIDENFELD & NICOLSON **470 Tree: Section of a tree trunk** *Introduction to Biology* D. G. Mackean JOHN MURRAY **471 Tree: How a tree feeds** *Introduction to Biology* D. G. Mackean JOHN MURRAY **486 Waterskater: Walking on water** *The Life of Insects* Sir Vincent B. Wigglesworth WEIDENFELD & NICOLSON **490 Waterfall** *The Living Landscape of Britain* Walter Shepherd FABER & FABER **498 Whirligig beetle: Water dancer** *The Life of Insects* Sir Vincent B. Wigglesworth WEIDENFELD & NICOLSON **503 Windbreak** *Ministry of Agriculture Fisheries and Food*

Many people and organisations assisted in the preparation of this book. The publishers wish to thank all of them, particularly:

Agricultural Botany N. T. Gill and K. C. Vear DUCKWORTH *Agriculture* James A. S. Watson and James A. More OLIVER & BOYD *Animal Behaviour* J. D. Carthy ALDUS BOOKS *Animal Life* *Animal Locomotion* Sir James Gray WEIDENFELD & NICOLSON *Animals in the night* J. H. Prince ANGUS & ROBERTSON *Animals without Backbones* Ralph Buchsbaum PENGUIN *The Arachnids* Keith R. Snow ROUTLEDGE & KEGAN PAUL *Atlas of the British Flora* F. H. Perring and S. M. Walters NELSON *Birds of our Countryside* David Seith-Smith HUTCHINSON *Birds of the World* *Britain's Changing Countryside* Mary C. Morris OUP *Britain's Structure and Scenery* L. Dudley Stamp COLLINS *The British Amphibians and Reptiles* Malcolm Smith COLLINS *British Caenozoic Fossils* TRUSTEES OF THE BRITISH MUSEUM *British Castles, Follies and Monuments* E. M. Hatt and Paul Sharp THE REPRINT SOCIETY *British Caving* C. H. D. Cullingford ROUTLEDGE & KEGAN PAUL *British Ferns and Mosses* P. G. Taylor EYRE & SPOTTISWOODE *The British Isles* G. H. Dury HEINEMANN *The British Isles: A Systematic Geography* J. W. Watson with J. B. Sissons NELSON *British Mammals* L. Harrison Matthews COLLINS *British Mesozoic Fossils* TRUSTEES OF THE BRITISH MUSEUM *British Palaeozoic Fossils* TRUSTEES OF THE BRITISH MUSEUM *British Plant Life* W. B. Turrill COLLINS *British Poultry Standards* C. F. May ILIFFE *British Trees* M. Hadfield DENT *British Trees and Shrubs* R. D. Meikle EYRE & SPOTTISWOODE *British Watermills* Leslie Syson BATSFORD *British Wild Flowers* John Hutchinson PENGUIN *Butterfly Book for the pocket* Edmund Sandras OUP *Butterfly Miracles and Mysteries* Bernard Ackworth EYRE & SPOTTISWOODE *The Canal Age* Charles Hadfield PAN *The Canals of England* Eric de Maré ARCHITECTURAL PRESS *Castles* B. H. St J. O'Neil HMSO *Castles, Houses and Gardens of Scotland* N. Pattullo BLACKWOOD *Chambers's Encyclopaedia, New Revised edition* International Learning Systems Corporation Limited PERGAMON *Cloud Types for Observers* Meteorological Office HMSO *Coasts and Beaches* J. A. Steers OLIVER & BOYD *Collins Field Guide to Archaeology* Eric S. Wood COLLINS *Collins Guide to Mushrooms and Toadstools* Morten Lange and F. Bayard Hora COLLINS *Collins Guide to the Freshwater Fishes of Britain and Europe* Bent J. Muus and P. Dahlstrom COLLINS *Collins Pocket Guide to the Seashore* John H. Barrett and C. M. Yonge COLLINS *The Complete British Butterflies* L. Hugh Newman EBURY PRESS & MICHAEL JOSEPH *The Concise British Flora in Colour* W. Keble Martin EBURY PRESS & MICHAEL JOSEPH *A Concise History of English Painting* William Gaunt THAMES & HUDSON *Country Life* *Countryman* *Countryside* *A Course in Elementary Meteorology* Meteorological Office HMSO *The Dancing Bees* Karl von Frisch METHUEN *Derelict Britain* John Barr PENGUIN *A Dictionary of Archaeology* Warwick Bray and David Trump ALLEN LANE, THE PENGUIN PRESS *'Discovering' Series* Leon Metcalfe and John Vince SHIRE PUBLICATIONS *Drawings of British Plants* Stella Ross-Craig G. BELL & SONS LTD *The Earth* Carl O. Dunbar WEIDENFELD & NICOLSON *The Ecology of Water Life* Alfred Leutscher FRANKLIN WATTS *The English Abbey* F. H. Crossley BATSFORD *English Castles* R. Allen BATSFORD *The English Farm Wagon* J. Geraint Jenkins OAKWOOD PRESS *The Englishman's Flora* Geoffrey Grigson PHOENIX HOUSE *English Village Homes* Sydney R. Jones BATSFORD *The English Windmill* Rex Wailes ROUTLEDGE & KEGAN PAUL *Epping Forest* Alfred Qvist CORPORATION OF LONDON *Farms and Farming* Rowland W. Purton ROUTLEDGE & KEGAN PAUL *Field and Meadow Life* Leif Lyndeborg BLANDFORD PRESS *Field Guide to British Deer* F. J. Taylor Page BLACKWELL *A Field Guide to the Birds of Britain and Europe* Roger Peterson, Guy Mountfort and P. A. D. Hollom COLLINS *A Field Guide to the Butterflies of Britain and Europe* Lionel F. Higgins and Norman D. Riley COLLINS *A Field Guide to the Mammals of Britain and Europe* F. H. van der Brink COLLINS *Field Natural History* Alfred Leutscher G. BELL & SONS LTD *Fleas, Flukes and Cuckoos* Miriam Rothschild and Theresa Clay COLLINS *Flies of the British Isles* Charles Colyer and Cyril Hammond WARNE *Flint Implements* TRUSTEES OF THE BRITISH MUSEUM *Flowers of the Field* Rev. C. A. Johns ROUTLEDGE & KEGAN PAUL *Food Facts No. 29* Ministry of Agriculture Fisheries and Food HMSO *Forestry Commission Leaflets Booklets and Bulletins* HMSO *The Forestry Commission Report Census of Woodland 1965/7* HMSO *The Freshwater Life of the British Isles* John Clegg WARNE *Gazetteer of the British Isles* BARTHOLOMEW *Geography and Regional Administration England and Wales 1830-1968* T. W. Freeman HUTCHINSON UNIVERSITY LIBRARY *Geology and Scenery in England and Wales* A. E. Trueman PENGUIN *The Glory of the Tree* Dr B. K. Boom and H. Kleijn HARRAP *Grasses* C. E. Hubbard PENGUIN *The Guinness Book of Animal Facts and Feats* Gerald L. Word GUINNESS SUPERLATIVES *The Guinness Book of Records* Norris & Ross McWhirter GUINNESS SUPERLATIVES *A Handbook for Naturalists* Winwood Reade and R. M. Stuttard EVANS BROTHERS *The Handbook of British Mammals* H. N. Southern BLACKWELL *Handbook of Coniferae* W. Dallimore and Jackson A. Bruce EDWARD ARNOLD *Hedges* Ministry of Agriculture Fisheries and Food HMSO *A History of English Architecture* Peter Kidson and Peter Murray HARRAP *A History of Fishes* J. R. Norman BENN *Household Insect Pests* Norman E. Hickin HUTCHINSON *The Identification of British Mammals* G. B. Corbet TRUSTEES OF THE BRITISH MUSEUM *Illustrated Glossary of Architecture* John Harris and J. M. Lever FABER *An Illustrated History of Civil Engineering* J. P. M. Pannell THAMES & HUDSON *Illustrated Social History* G. M. Trevelyan PENGUIN *Inns and Villages of England* Garry Hogg NEWNES *Insect Natural History* A. D. Imms COLLINS *Insects and their World* Harold Oldroyd TRUSTEES OF THE BRITISH MUSEUM *Instant Weather Forecasting* Alan Watts ADLARD COLES *Introducing Geology* D. V. Ager FABER *Introduction to Biology* D. G. Mackean MURRAY *Invertebrate Zoology* Robert D. Barnes W. B. SAUNDERS & CO. *Ireland* T. W. Freeman METHUEN *Know your Broadleaves* Herbert L. Edlin and Christine Darter HMSO *The Land and People of Britain* R. A. Beddis UNIVERSITY OF LONDON PRESS *The Land of Britain* Dudley L. Stamp LONGMANS GREEN *Life and Work of the People of England* D. Hartley and Margaret Elliot BATSFORD *Life in Lakes and Rivers* T. T. Macan and E. B. Worthington COLLINS *The Life of Fishes* N. B. Marshall WEIDENFELD & NICOLSON *The Life of Insects* Sir Vincent B. Wigglesworth WEIDENFELD & NICOLSON *The Life of Mammals* L. Harrison Matthews WEIDENFELD & NICOLSON *The Life of Plants* E. J. H. Corner WEIDENFELD & NICOLSON *The Life of Vertebrates* J. Z. Young CLARENDON PRESS *Living Amphibians of the World* Doris M. Cochran HAMISH HAMILTON *Living Invertebrates of the World* Ralph Buchsbaum and Lorus J. Milne HAMISH HAMILTON *Living Trees of the World* Thomas H. Everett THAMES & HUDSON *The Living World* David Stanbury MACMILLAN *Lords and Ladies* Cecil T. Prime COLLINS *The Magic of the Senses* Vitus B. Dröscher W. H. ALLEN *The Making of the English Landscape* W. G. Hoskins PENGUIN *Mammals of Britain* M. J. Lawrence and R. W. Brown BLANDFORD *Man the Toolmaker* Kenneth P. Oakley TRUSTEES OF THE BRITISH MUSEUM *Meteorological Glossary* Meteorological Office HMSO *Mimicry in Plants and Animals* Wolfgang Wickler WEIDENFELD & NICOLSON *A Modern Biology* John Clegg WARNE *Modern Meteorology and Climatology* T. J. Chandler NELSON *Monograph and Iconograph of Native British Orchidaceae* Colonel M. J. Godfery CUP *The Moths of the British Isles* Richard South WARNE *Mountains and Moorlands* W. H. Pearsall COLLINS *Name this Insect* Daglish DENT *The Naming of Wild Flowers* Gareth H. Browning WILLIAMS & NORGATE *The Neolithic Revolution* Sonia Cole TRUSTEES OF THE BRITISH MUSEUM *A New Dictionary of British History* S. H. Steinberg EDWARD ARNOLD *The Observer's Book of Wild Animals* WARNE *Odd Aspects of Britain* Garry Hogg DAVID & CHARLES *Old English Houses* Hugh Braun FABER *The Oxford Book of British Birds* Bruce Campbell and Donald Watson OUP *The Oxford Book of Flowering Plants* B. E. Nicholson and Frank H. Brightman OUP *The Oxford Book of Insects* John Burton OUP *The Oxford Book of Vertebrates* Marion Nixon OUP *The Oxford Book of Wild Flowers* S. Ary and M. Gregory OUP *Oxford Junior Encyclopaedia* OUP *Parish Churches* J. C. Cox and C. B. Ford BATSFORD *The Pattern of Animal Communities* Charles S. Elton METHUEN *The Pattern of English Building* Alec Clifton-Taylor BATSFORD *A Penguin Dictionary of Architecture* John Fleming, Hugh Honour and Nikolaus Pevsner PENGUIN *The Penguin Dictionary of British Natural History* Richard and Maisie Fitter PENGUIN *Physical Geography* M. A. Cain LONGMANS *Physical Geography* Thomas Pickles DENT *The Plant World* Prof. Jean Vallin STERLING PUBLISHING CO. *The Pocket Guide to Wild Flowers* David McClintock and R. S. R. Fitter COLLINS *Poisonous Plants and Fungi* Pamela North BLANDFORD PRESS *Rabbits and their History* John Sheail DAVID & CHARLES *Rural Crafts of England* K. S. Woods HARRAP *Seals of the World* Judith E. King TRUSTEES OF THE BRITISH MUSEUM *The Seas* Sir Frederick S. Russell and C. M. Yonge WARNE *The Sea Shore* C. M. Yonge COLLINS *Secrets of Plant Life* Marcel Sire COLLINS *The Severn Bore* Fred Rowbotham DAVID & CHARLES *Shell and BP Guide to Britain* Geoffrey Boumphrey EBURY PRESS *The Shell Country Alphabet* Geoffrey Grigson MICHAEL JOSEPH *The Shell Country Book* Geoffrey Grigson PHOENIX HOUSE *The Shell Guide to England* John Hadfield MICHAEL JOSEPH *Shell Life on the Seashore* Philip Street FABER *Shell Treasure of the Countryside* John Baker PHOENIX HOUSE *A Short History of Farming* Ralph Whitlock JOHN BAKER *Signals in the Animal World* Dietrich Burkhardt, Wolfgang Schleidt and Helmut Altner GEORGE ALLEN & UNWIN *The Status of Birds in Britain* D. W. Snow BLACKWELLS for the BRITISH ORNITHOLOGISTS' UNION *Study of Plants* F. E. Fritsch and Sir Edward Salisbury G. BELL & SONS *The Styles of English Architecture* Arthur Stratton BATSFORD *Textbook of Botany* Transeau HARPER BROS *A Textbook of Entomology* Herbert H. Ross JOHN WILEY & SONS *The Thatcher's Craft* RURAL INDUSTRIES BUREAU *Through the Microscope* M. D. Anderson ALDUS BOOKS *Ticks and Disease* Don R. Arthur PERGAMON *Tomorrow's Countryside* Garth Christian MURRAY *Tracks and Signs of British Animals* A. Leutscher CLEAVER HUME PRESS *Tree Planting and Cultivation* H. L. Edlin COLLINS *Trees and Bushes* Helge Vedel and Johan Lange METHUEN *Trees, Woods and Man* Herbert L. Edlin COLLINS *The Vanishing Wild Life of Britain* Brian Vesey-Fitzgerald MAYFLOWER *Vernacular Architecture* R. W. Brunskill FABER *Victoria County History of the Counties of England* OUP *Wayside and Woodland Fungi* W. P. K. Findlay WARNE *Weather* Paul E. Lehr GOLDEN PRESS *Weather* R. S. Scorer PHOENIX HOUSE *The Weather Guide* A. G. Forsdyke HAMLYN *What Wood is that?* Herbert L. Edlin THAMES & HUDSON *Wild Flowers* John Gilmour and Max Walters COLLINS *Wild Mushrooms* Linus Zeitlmayer FREDERICK MULLER *The World of Spiders* W. S. Bristowe COLLINS *The World of the Soil* Sir E. John Russell COLLINS *Yorkshire Journal of Archaeology*

Typesetting by PURNELL & SONS LTD, PAULTON (SOMERSET) AND LONDON: Separations by SCHWITTER LTD, ZURICH: REPROCOLOR LLOVET, BARCELONA:
LITRA MACHINE PLATES LTD, EDENBRIDGE: Printing by SMEETS LITHOGRAPHERS, WEERT: TAYLOWE LTD, MAIDENHEAD:
Paper and bookbinding material by KONINKLIJKE NEDERLANDSCHE PAPIERFABRIEK N.V., MAASTRICHT: BOWATER SALES CO LTD, LONDON:
WINTERBOTTOM PRODUCTS LTD, SALFORD: Bookbinding by ANDRÉ BRUN, MALESHERBES